DATE DUE

DEMCO 128-5046

SOMETHING ABOUT THE AUTHOR®

Something about
the Author *was named
an "Outstanding
Reference Source,"
the highest honor given
by the American
Library Association
Reference and Adult
Services Division.*

ISSN 0276-816X

SOMETHING ABOUT THE AUTHOR®

**Facts and Pictures about Authors
and Illustrators of Books for Young People**

EDITED BY
ALAN HEDBLAD

VOLUME 99

GALE

DETROIT · LONDON

STAFF

Editor: Alan Hedblad

rs: Sheryl Ciccarelli, Melissa Hill, Thomas F. McMahon
Assistant Editor: Sara L. Constantakis

Sketchwriters/Copyeditors: Joanna Brod, Ronie Garcia-Johnson, Mary Gillis, Motoko Fujishiro Huthwaite,
Arlene M. Johnson, J. Sydney Jones, Judson Knight, Gerard J. Senick, Pamela L. Shelton,
Crystal A. Towns, Arlene True, Stephen Thor Tschirhart, and Kathleen Witman

Managing Editor: Joyce Nakamura
Publisher: Hal May

Research Manager: Victoria B. Cariappa
Project Coordinator: Cheryl L. Warnock
Research Specialists: Michele P. LaMeau, Andrew Guy Malonis, Gary J. Oudersluys
Research Associates: Jeffrey D. Daniels, Tracie A. Richardson, Norma Sawaya, Robert Whaley
Research Assistants: Phyllis Blackman, Corrine A. Stocker

Permissions Manager: Susan M. Trosky
Permissions Specialist: Maria L. Franklin
Permissions Associates: Sarah Chesney, Edna M. Hedblad, Michele Lonoconus

Production Director: Mary Beth Trimper
Production Assistant: Deborah Milliken

Graphic Artist: Gary Leach
Image Database Supervisor: Randy Bassett
Imaging Specialists: Robert Duncan, Michael Logusz
Imaging Coordinator: Pamela A. Reed

Library of Congress Catalog Card Number 72-27107
ISBN 0-7876-1981-7
ISSN 0276-816X

Printed in the United States of America

10 9 8 7 6 5 4 3 2 1

Contents

Authors in Forthcoming Volumes vii
Introduction ix
Acknowledgments xi
Illustrations Index 229
Author Index 253

A

Agell, Charlotte 1959- 1

Aldrich, Ann
    See Meaker, Marijane (Agnes) 157

Armitage, David 1943- 2

Armitage, Ronda (Jacqueline) 1943- 3

B

Bell, Clare (Louise) 1952- 7

Bell, David Owen 1949- 10

Bellingham, Brenda 1931- 11

Berton, Pierre (Francis Demarigny) 1920- 13

Biale, Rachel 1952- 20

Bilson, Geoffrey 1938-1987 21

Bisson, Terry (Ballantine) 1942- 22

Bjoerk, Christina 1938- 26

Brown, Laurene Krasny
    See Brown, Laurie Krasny 28

Brown, Laurie Krasny 1945- 28

Bull, Emma 1954- 32

C

Calhoun, T. B.
    See Bisson, Terry (Ballantine) 22

Campbell, Peter A. 1948- 35

Carter, Nick
    See Crider, (Allen) Bill(y) 54

Catalano, Grace (A.) 1961- 36

Cazet, Denys 1938- 37

Cheney, Glenn (Alan) 1951- 41

Cherry, Lynne 1952- 45

Christopher, Matt(hew Frederick) 1917-1997
    Obituary Notice 49

Coleman, Clare
    See Bell, Clare (Louise) 7

Collington, Peter 1948- 49

Cooper, Elisha 1971- 51

Crary, Elizabeth (Ann) 1942- 52

Crider, (Allen) Bill(y) 1941- 54

Crutcher, Chris(topher C.) 1946- 58

Cuyler, Margery (Stuyvesant) 1948- 68

D-E

Dabcovich, Lydia 73

Davies, Nicola 1958- 77

Edmonds, Walter D(umaux) 1903-1998
    Obituary Notice 78

Elmer, Robert 1958- 78

G

Gardner, Craig Shaw 1949- 81

Gehr, Mary 1910(?)-1997
    Obituary Notice 84

Gerrard, Roy 1935-1997
    Obituary Notice 84

Golenbock, Peter 1946- 85

Griffin, Peni R(ae Robinson) 1961- 88

H

Hauth, Katherine B. 1940- 92

Henry, Marguerite 1902-1997
    Obituary Notice 93

Herman, Charlotte 1937- 93

Holub, Joan 1956- 96

Howard, Ellen 1943- 97

I-J

Inkpen, Mick 1952- 102

James, Mary
    See Meaker, Marijane (Agnes) 157

Jones, Rebecca C(astaldi) 1947- 107

K

Kerr, M. E.
    See Meaker, Marijane (Agnes) 157

Klass, Sheila Solomon 1927- 110

Kline, Suzy 1943- 114

Kogawa, Joy (Nozomi) 1935- 118

Koscielniak, Bruce 1947- 121

Kroniuk, Lisa
   See Berton, Pierre (Francis Demarigny) 13

L

Le Guin, Ursula K(roeber) 1929- 124

Leroe, Ellen W(hitney) 1949- 138

Levinson, Riki 140

Lynn, Elizabeth A(nne) 1946- 144

M

Maclane, Jack
   See Crider, (Allen) Bill(y) 54

Manes, Stephen 1949- 147

Manuel, Lynn 1948- 151

Martel, Suzanne 1924- 152

Martin, Fredric
   See Christopher, Matt(hew Frederick) 49

McDonald, Megan 1959- 154

Meaker, M. J.
   See Meaker, Marijane (Agnes) 157

Meaker, Marijane (Agnes) 1927- 157

Meringoff, Laurene Krasny
   See Brown, Laurie Krasny 28

Morgan, Stevie
   See Davies, Nicola 77

Murch, Mel
   See Manes, Stephen 147

O-P

O'Keeffe, Frank 1938- 168

Oppel, Kenneth 1967- 170

Packer, Vin
   See Meaker, Marijane (Agnes) 157

Pemsteen, Hans
   See Manes, Stephen 147

Pollack, Rachel (Grace) 1945- 173

Q-R

Quentin, Brad
   See Bisson, Terry (Ballantine) 22

Quirk, Anne (E.) 1956- 176

Rattigan, Jama Kim 1951- 177

Reaves, J. Michael
   See Reaves, (James) Michael 180

Reaves, (James) Michael 1950- 180

Reed, Neil 1961- 182

Roche, Denis (Mary) 1967- 183

Rosenfeld, Dina 1962- 185

S

St. George, Judith 1931- 187

Starr, Ward
   See Manes, Stephen 147

Starr Taylor, Bridget 1959- 191

Stephensen, A. M.
   See Manes, Stephen 147

Stott, Dorothy (M.) 1958- 192

Stott, Dot
   See Stott, Dorothy (M.) 192

Sunderlin, Sylvia (S.) 1911-1997
   Obituary Notice 194

Szasz, Suzanne (Shorr) 1915-1997
   Obituary Notice 194

T

Talbert, Marc 1953- 195

Teague, Mark (Christopher) 1963- 198

Thompson, Julian F(rancis) 1927- 200

Toten, Teresa 1955- 204

V-W

Van Hook, Beverly H. 1941- 207

Wallace, Daisy
   See Cuyler, Margery (Stuyvesant) 68

Walsh, Ellen Stoll 1942- 208

Walters, Eric (Robert) 1957- 211

Waterton, Betty (Marie) 1923- 213

Wegen, Ronald 1946-1985 216

Weir, Joan S(herman) 1928- 217

Wellington, Monica 1957- 221

Williams, Karen Lynn 1952- 224

Authors in Forthcoming Volumes

To commemorate the publication of one hundred volumes of *Something about the Author,* our next issue will include entries on the most notable and best-loved creators of books for children from 1850-1950. Below are a few of the authors and illustrators who will be featured.

Louisa May Alcott: Nineteenth-century American author Alcott is considered a pioneer in the creation of realistic fiction for children. Her novels—*Little Women* prominent among them—are noted for their perceptive and highly entertaining depictions of childhood.

Hans Christian Andersen: Danish author Andersen is recognized as one of the masters of the fairy-tale genre. Such simple-seeming but many-leveled masterpieces as "The Little Mermaid" and "The Red Shoes" have enchanted children around the world, making Andersen one of the best-loved authors of all time.

Margaret Wise Brown: An imaginative innovator who helped to shape the modern concept book for preschoolers, Brown is the author of scores of highly regarded books for children. Many of her works, including *Noisy Book, The Runaway Bunny,* and *Goodnight Moon,* are considered classics of the picture-book genre.

Frances Hodgson Burnett: Burnett was a prolific writer who won lasting acclaim for such popular children's books as *Little Lord Fauntleroy, A Little Princess,* and *The Secret Garden,* a highly esteemed story that is generally considered her greatest work.

Randolph Caldecott: Caldecott is known as the father of the modern picture book. A gold medal bearing his name has been awarded annually since 1938 to the illustrator of what is considered the most distinguished American picture book for children published in the U.S. during the preceding year.

Lewis Carroll: The creator of *Alice's Adventure's in Wonderland* and *Through the Looking Glass,* Carroll is widely acclaimed as a master of "nonsense" verse and fairy tales. For more than two decades beginning in 1958, The Lewis Carroll Shelf Award was presented annually by the University of Wisconsin to those children's books presenting enough of the qualities of "Alice in Wonderland" to enable them to sit on the same shelf.

Kate Greenaway: Among the first authors to look at childhood from the child's viewpoint, influential illustrator and author Greenaway is considered with Walter Crane and Randolph Caldecott one of the great triumvirate of English picture book illustrators. She achieved lasting recognition when the Library Association of Great Britain began granting the Kate Greenaway Medal in 1955 to illustrators of distinguished picture books for children.

Rudyard Kipling: Nobel Prize-winning author Kipling is one of the best-known late Victorian poets and storytellers. His tales of Mowgli in *The Jungle Books* and his *Just So Stories* for children about how things came to be, are perhaps Kipling's best-remembered and most enduring works.

A. A. Milne: Playwright, critic and novelist Milne achieved his greatest fame for his books of stories and poems for children about the adventures of Christopher Robin, "Winnie-the-Pooh," and their friends in the Hundred Acre Wood.

L. M. Montgomery: Canadian writer Montgomery is recognized worldwide as the creator of "Anne," the sprightly, imaginative orphan first introduced in the author's classic tale *Anne of Green Gables.* Published in 1908, the book became an immediate success and was followed by several popular sequels.

Beatrix Potter: One of the most beloved creators of books for children, Potter is credited with bringing a new realism to the genre. In a striking departure from the animal fables common in her time, Potter, in such celebrated works as *The Tale of Peter Rabbit,* invented an original world filled with characters who were clearly faithful to their animal natures yet human in their thoughts and actions.

E. B. White: Regarded as one of the finest essayists of the twentieth century, White is perhaps best-known for his award-winning children's books *Charlotte's Web, Stuart Little,* and *The Trumpet of the Swan,* which embody the timeless themes of classic literature.

Introduction

Something about the Author (*SATA*) is an ongoing reference series that examines the lives and works of authors and illustrators of books for children. *SATA* includes not only well-known writers and artists but also less prominent individuals whose works are just coming to be recognized. This series is often the only readily available information source on emerging authors and illustrators. You'll find *SATA* informative and entertaining, whether you are a student, a librarian, an English teacher, a parent, or simply an adult who enjoys children's literature.

What's Inside SATA

SATA provides detailed information about authors and illustrators who span the full time range of children's literature, from early figures like John Newbery and L. Frank Baum to contemporary figures like Judy Blume and Richard Peck. Authors in the series represent primarily English-speaking countries, particularly the United States, Canada, and the United Kingdom. Also included, however, are authors from around the world whose works are available in English translation. The writings represented in *SATA* include those created intentionally for children and young adults as well as those written for a general audience and known to interest younger readers. These writings cover the entire spectrum of children's literature, including picture books, humor, folk and fairy tales, animal stories, mystery and adventure, science fiction and fantasy, historical fiction, poetry and nonsense verse, drama, biography, and nonfiction.

Obituaries are also included in *SATA* and are intended not only as death notices but also as concise overviews of people's lives and work. Additionally, each edition features newly revised and updated entries for a selection of *SATA* listees who remain of interest to today's readers and who have been active enough to require extensive revisions of their earlier biographies.

Two Convenient Indexes

In response to suggestions from librarians, *SATA* indexes no longer appear in every volume but are included in alternate (odd-numbered) volumes of the series, beginning with Volume 57.

SATA continues to include two indexes that cumulate with each alternate volume: the Illustrations Index, arranged by the name of the illustrator, gives the number of the volume and page where the illustrator's work appears in the current volume as well as all preceding volumes in the series; the Author Index gives the number of the volume in which a person's Biographical Sketch or Obituary appears in the current volume as well as all preceding volumes in the series.

These indexes also include references to authors and illustrators who appear in Gale's *Yesterday's Authors of Books for Children, Children's Literature Review,* and *Something about the Author Autobiography Series.*

Easy-to-Use Entry Format

Whether you're already familiar with the *SATA* series or just getting acquainted, you will want to be aware of the kind of information that an entry provides. In every *SATA* entry the editors attempt to give as complete a picture of the person's life and work as possible. A typical entry in *SATA* includes the following clearly labeled information sections:

- *PERSONAL:* date and place of birth and death, parents' names and occupations, name of spouse, date of marriage, names of children, educational institutions attended, degrees received, religious and political affiliations, hobbies and other interests.

- *ADDRESSES:* complete home, office, electronic mail, and agent addresses, whenever available.

- *CAREER:* name of employer, position, and dates for each career post; art exhibitions; military service; memberships and offices held in professional and civic organizations.

- *AWARDS, HONORS:* literary and professional awards received.

- *WRITINGS:* title-by-title chronological bibliography of books written and/or illustrated, listed by genre when known; lists of other notable publications, such as plays, screenplays, and periodical contributions.

- *ADAPTATIONS:* a list of films, television programs, plays, CD-ROMs, recordings, and other media presentations that have been adapted from the author's work.

- *WORK IN PROGRESS:* description of projects in progress.

- *SIDELIGHTS:* a biographical portrait of the author or illustrator's development, either directly from the biographee—and often written specifically for the *SATA* entry—or gathered from diaries, letters, interviews, or other published sources.

- *FOR MORE INFORMATION SEE:* references for further reading.

- *EXTENSIVE ILLUSTRATIONS:* photographs, movie stills, book illustrations, and other interesting visual materials supplement the text.

How a SATA Entry Is Compiled

A *SATA* entry progresses through a series of steps. If the biographee is living, the *SATA* editors try to secure information directly from him or her through a questionnaire. From the information that the biographee supplies, the editors prepare an entry, filling in any essential missing details with research and/or telephone interviews. If possible, the author or illustrator is sent a copy of the entry to check for accuracy and completeness.

If the biographee is deceased or cannot be reached by questionnaire, the *SATA* editors examine a wide variety of published sources to gather information for an entry. Biographical and bibliographic sources are consulted, as are book reviews, feature articles, published interviews, and material sometimes obtained from the biographee's family, publishers, agent, or other associates.

Entries that have not been verified by the biographees or their representatives are marked with an asterisk (*).

Contact the Editor

We encourage our readers to examine the entire *SATA* series. Please write and tell us if we can make *SATA* even more helpful to you. Give your comments and suggestions to the editor:

BY MAIL: Editor, *Something about the Author,* Gale Research, 27500 Drake Rd., Farmington Hills, MI 48331-3535.

BY TELEPHONE: (800) 347-GALE

BY FAX: (313) 961-6599

Acknowledgments

Grateful acknowledgment is made to the following publishers, authors, and artists whose works appear in this volume.

AGELL, CHARLOTTE. Photograph of Charlotte Agell by Peter J. Simmons. Reproduced by permission.

ARMITAGE, RONDA. Illustration from *The Lighthouse Keeper's Lunch,* by Ronda and David Armitage. Andre Deutsch, 1977. Copyright © 1977 by Ronda and David Armitage. All Rights Reserved. Reproduced by permission of Scholastic UK. / Illustration from *Harry Hates Shopping!* by Ronda and David Armitage. Scholastic Inc., 1992. Illustrations copyright © 1992 by David Armitage. All Rights Reserved. Reproduced by permission of Scholastic UK.

BELL, CLARE. Harrington, Glenn, illustrator. From a cover of *Ratha's Challenge* by Clare Bell. Margaret K. McElderry Books, 1994. Copyright © 1994 by Clare Bell.

BELL, DAVID OWEN. Photograph of David Owen Bell. Reproduced by permission.

BELLINGHAM, BRENDA. Photograph of Brenda Bellingham, 1989. Scholastic Canada, Ltd. Reproduced by permission.

BERTON, PIERRE. Berton, Patsy, illustrator. From a cover of *The Secret World of Og* by Pierre Berton. McClelland & Stewart Inc., 1984. Illustrations copyright © 1974 by Patsy Berton. All rights reserved. Reproduced by permission. / Illustration by Henry Van Der Linde from *Bonanza Gold: The Great Klondike Gold Rush* by Pierre Berton. McClelland & Stewart Inc., 1991. Copyright © 1991 by Pierre Berton Enterprises Ltd. Reproduced by permission of the illustrator. / Cameron, Scott, illustrator. From a cover of *The Death of Isaac Brock* by Pierre Berton. McClelland & Stewart Inc., 1991. Copyright © 1991 by Pierre Berton Enterprises Ltd. Reproduced by permission. / Illustration by Paul McCusker from *The Men in Sheepskin Coats: Canada Moves West* by Pierre Berton. McClelland & Stewart Inc., 1992. Copyright © 1992 by Pierre Berton Enterprises Ltd. Reproduced by permission. / Berton, Pierre, photograph by Jack Dobson. The Globe and Mail, Toronto. Reproduced by permission.

BIALE, RACHEL. Photograph of Rachel Biale. Reproduced by permission.

BISSON, TERRY. Santos, Jesse J., illustrator. From a cover of *Nat Turner: Prophet and Slave Revolt Leader* by Terry Bisson. Melrose Square Publishing Company, 1989. © 1989 by Holloway House Books. Reproduced by permission of Melrose Square Publishing Company, a division of Holloway House Publishing Company. / Jainschigg, Nick, illustrator. From a cover of *Bears Discover Fire and Other Stories* by Terry Bisson. Tom Doherty Associates, Inc., 1993. Copyright © 1993 by Terry Bisson. All rights reserved. Reproduced by permission. / Bisson, Terry, photograph by Larry Laszlo. Reproduced by permission.

BJÖRK, CHRISTINA. Illustration by Lena Anderson from *Linnea in Monet's Garden* by Christina Björk. Rabén & Sjögren, Publishers, 1985. Illustrations © 1985 by Lena Anderson. Reproduced by permission of the author. / Peterson, Nisse, photographer. From a cover of *Big Bear's Book: By Himself* by Christina Björk. Rabén & Sjögren, Publishers, 1988. Copyright © 1988 by Christina Björk. Reproduced by permission of the author.

BROWN, LAURIE KRASNY. Illustrations by Marc Brown from *Dinosaurs Divorce: A Guide for Changing Families* by Laurie Krasny Brown. Little, Brown and Company, 1986. Illustrations copyright © 1986 by Marc Brown and Laurie Krasny Brown. Reproduced by permission. / Illustration from *The Vegetable Show* by Laurie Krasny Brown. Little, Brown and Company, 1995. Copyright © 1995 by Laurene Krasny Brown. Reproduced by permission of Warner Books, Inc. / Brown, Laurie Krasny, photograph. Reproduced by permission.

BULL, EMMA. Illustration by Susan Gaber from *The Princess and the Lord of Night* by Emma Bull. Harcourt Brace & Company, 1994. Illustrations copyright © 1994 by Susan Gaber. Reproduced by permission. / Bull, Emma, photograph by Will Shetterly. Reproduced by permission.

CAMPBELL, PETER A. Photograph of Peter A. Campbell. Reproduced by permission.

CATALANO, GRACE. From a cover of *LeAnn Rimes: Teen Country Queen* by Grace Catalano. Bantam Doubleday Dell,

something about the author®

AGELL, Charlotte 1959-

■ Personal

Born September 7, 1959, in Norsjo, Sweden; daughter of L. Christer Agell (a businessman) and Margareta Segerborg McDonald (an artist and teacher); married Peter J. Simmons (an arts administrator and master gardener), May 15, 1981; children: Anna, Jon. *Education:* Bowdoin College, B.A., 1981; Harvard Graduate School of Education, Ed.M., 1986.

■ Addresses

Agent—Edite Kroll Literary Agency, 12 Grayhurst Park, Portland, ME 04101.

■ Career

Author and illustrator. Conducts workshops for youths and adults. Has worked previously as a teacher and education consultant. *Member:* Maine Writers and Publishers Alliance (board member).

■ Writings

SELF-ILLUSTRATED

The Sailor's Book, Firefly Books (Buffalo, NY), 1991.
Mud Makes Me Dance in the Spring, Tilbury House (Gardiner, Maine), 1994.
I Wear Long Green Hair in the Summer, Tilbury House, 1994.
Wind Spins Me Around in the Fall, Tilbury House, 1994.
I Slide into the White of Winter, Tilbury House, 1994.

Dancing Feet, Harcourt Brace, 1994.
I Swam with a Seal, Harcourt Brace, 1995.
To the Island, DK Ink, 1998.

Some of Agell's works have been published in France.

■ Work in Progress

Several sequels to *To the Island.*

■ Sidelights

Charlotte Agell told *SATA:* "I have always written and illustrated little books. When I speak to school children, one of my favorite 'show and tell' items is *Tommy Pickle,* an illustrated story about an elf and the girls who spy on him, 'written by Charlotte Agell, age 8 3/4. Pictures by C. Agell also.' A testimony to dreams, or stubbornness, perhaps.

"I grew up in Sweden, Canada, and Hong Kong. When I was a child in Montreal, I wrote a story about a boy in Maine. Vacationing friends had told me that Maine was a wonderful place. I called his town Halibut and imagined myself to *be* him. I would fish for my dinner and have ruddy cheeks. It was a snippet of a story, really, but years later, I ended up coming to Maine for college for quite flimsy reasons. I wonder if that early piece of fantasy had not, in part, directed me. Life imitates art. I have been living happily ever after in Maine since 1977.

"I love to read, bake, and to be outside—in the woods, on a mountain, or by the water—all three at once,

CHARLOTTE AGELL

sometimes, preferably on cross-country skis on new snow."

Agell's love of water and the outdoors translated into her first work, *The Sailor's Book,* about a boy and girl who sail on a sea they imagine to be a dragon. Irene Aubrey, a reviewer in *Canadian Materials,* praised the book's "lyrical tone," adding: "The great appeal of this picture-book fantasy lies in its simplicity and naivete."

Dancing Feet, another lyrical picture book offering from Agell, poetically celebrates the function of a variety of human body parts. *Booklist* reviewer Ilene Cooper called attention to the book's "jaunty rhyme," maintaining that *Dancing Feet* would be "especially good for story hours where kids will clap along to the catchy rhythm." Lesley McKinstry, writing in *School Library Journal,* called Agell's book "delightful," noting that it "shows individuals from a variety of cultures engaging in activities, making this a good choice to introduce similarities and differences among people." The *New York Times Book Review* called *Dancing Feet* "ebullient" and "celebratory."

■ Works Cited

Aubrey, Irene, review of *The Sailor's Book, Canadian Materials,* January, 1992, p. 18.
Cooper, Ilene, review of *Dancing Feet, Booklist,* July, 1994, p. 1952.
Review of *Dancing Feet, New York Times Book Review,* September 25, 1994, p. 32.
McKinstry, Lesley, review of *Dancing Feet, School Library Journal,* May, 1994, p. 84.

■ For More Information See

PERIODICALS

Publishers Weekly, March 28, 1994, p. 95.

*   *   *

ALDRICH, Ann
See MEAKER, Marijane (Agnes)

*   *   *

ARMITAGE, David 1943-

■ Personal

Born in 1943, in New Zealand; moved to England, 1974; married Ronda Minnitt (an author), 1966; children: Joss, Kate.

■ Addresses

Home—Old Tiles Cottage, Church Lane, Hellingly, East Sussex BN27 4HA, England.

■ Career

Author and illustrator. *Exhibitions:* Dunedin Public Arts Gallery, 1974.

■ Awards, Honors

Esther Glen Award (with wife, Ronda Armitage), New Zealand Library Association, 1978, for *The Lighthouse Keeper's Lunch.*

■ Writings

WITH WIFE, RONDA ARMITAGE; AND ILLUSTRATOR

The Lighthouse Keeper's Lunch, Deutsch (London), 1977.
The Trouble with Mr. Harris, Deutsch, 1978.
Don't Forget Matilda!, Deutsch, 1979.
The Bossing of Josie, Deutsch, 1980, published as *The Birthday Spell,* Scholastic, Inc. (New York City), 1981.
Ice Creams for Rosie, Deutsch, 1981.
One Moonlit Night, Deutsch, 1983.
Grandma Goes Shopping, Deutsch, 1984.
The Lighthouse Keeper's Catastrophe, Deutsch, 1986.
The Lighthouse Keeper's Rescue, Deutsch, 1989.

Watch the Baby, Daisy, Deutsch, 1991.
When Dad Did the Washing, Puffin, 1992.
Looking after Chocolates, Deutsch, 1992.
A Quarrel of Koalas, Deutsch, 1992, published as *Harry Hates Shopping!,* Scholastic, 1992.
The Lighthouse Keeper's Picnic, Deutsch, 1993.
The Lighthouse Keeper's Cat, Deutsch, 1995.

FOR CHILDREN; AND ILLUSTRATOR

Portland Bill's Treasure Trove (activity book), Deutsch, 1987.
Giant Stories, illustrated by Carol Watson, Carnival, 1988.
Jasper Who Jumps, Collins (London), 1990.

ILLUSTRATOR

(With Sandra Biggs) Lorna Hinds, *Beds,* F. Watts (New York City), 1975.
(With Sandra Biggs) Jonathan P. Rutland, *Chairs,* F. Watts, 1975.
Freda Linde, *The Singing Grass,* Oxford University Press, 1975.
John C. Siddons, *Fun with Electricity,* Kaye & Ward, 1976.
Miriam Smith, *Kimi and the Watermelon,* Penguin (Auckland, New Zealand), 1983.
Phillippa Pearce, *Freddy,* Deutsch, 1988.
Judy Corbalis, *The Cuckoo Bird,* Deutsch, 1988, HarperCollins (New York City), 1991.
Stephen Berry, *Dad and Beth Clean Up,* Collins (London), 1990.
Stephen Berry, *Shopping,* Collins, 1990.
Stephen Berry, *A Day Out with Granny Magee,* Collins, 1990.

OTHER

(Contributor) International Institute for Conservation of Historic and Artistic Works, *Conservation in Museums and Galleries: A Survey of Facilities in the United Kindgom,* I. I. C. United Kingdom Group (London), 1974.
(Illustrator) Penny Visman, *Kent: A Visitor's Sketchbook,* Pekoe (London), 1987.
(Illustrator) P. Visman, *Sussex: A Visitor's Sketchbook,* Pekoe, 1987.

■ Sidelights

For *Sidelights* information on David Armitage, please see the entry on Ronda Armitage in this volume.

■ For More Information See

PERIODICALS

Booklist, July 15, 1979, p. 1623; October 1, 1979, p. 234; February 1, 1989, p. 935.
Books for Keeps, September 1988, p. 8; November 1991, p. 7; November 1992, p. 15.
Books for Your Children, autumn-winter 1993, p. 9.
Bulletin of the Center for Children's Books, December 1981, p. 62.
Growing Point, July 1980, p. 3733; November 1984, p. 4345.

Junior Bookshelf, October 1977, pp. 272-73; December 1978, p. 292; December 1980, p. 279; February 1982, p. 13; June 1990, p. 125; April 1992, p. 53; October 1992, p. 187; April 1995, p. 64; April 1996, p. 56.
Magpies, May 1991, p. 29.
New York Times Book Review, September 2, 1984, p. 12.
Publishers Weekly, April 9, 1979, p. 110; December 26, 1986, p. 56.
School Librarian, December 1986, p. 331; May 1993, p. 53.
School Library Journal, October 1979, p. 132; February 1982, pp. 63-64; May 1984, pp. 61-62; February 1989, p. 83; January 1981, p. 46; August 1991, p. 144.

*   *   *

ARMITAGE, Ronda (Jacqueline) 1943-

■ Personal

Born March 11, 1943 in Kaikoura, New Zealand; moved to England in 1974; daughter of Jack (a farmer) and Beatrix (Shand) Minnitt; married David Armitage (a painter and illustrator), 1966; children: Joss, Kate. *Education:* Attended University of Auckland, 1963, 1969, and Massey University, 1965; Hamilton Teacher's College, certificate of teaching, 1963, diploma of teaching, 1969.

■ Addresses

Home—Old Tiles Cottage, Church Lane, Hellingly, East Sussex BN27 4HA, England.

■ Career

School teacher in Duvauchelles, New Zealand, 1964-66, London, England, 1966, and Auckland, New Zealand, 1968-69; Dorothy Butler, Ltd., Auckland, advisor on children's books, 1970-71; Lewes Priory Comprehensive School, Sussex, England, assistant librarian, 1976-77; East Sussex County Council, East Sussex, England, member of teaching staff, 1978—. Family therapist at local family center.

■ Awards, Honors

Esther Glen Award, New Zealand Library Association, 1978, for *The Lighthouse Keeper's Lunch.*

■ Writings

FOR CHILDREN; WITH HUSBAND, ILLUSTRATOR DAVID ARMITAGE

The Lighthouse Keeper's Lunch, Deutsch (London), 1977.
The Trouble with Mr. Harris, Deutsch, 1978.
Don't Forget Matilda!, Deutsch, 1979.

The Bossing of Josie, Deutsch, 1980, published as *The Birthday Spell,* Scholastic, Inc. (New York City), 1981.
Ice Creams for Rosie, Deutsch, 1981.
One Moonlit Night, Deutsch, 1983.
Grandma Goes Shopping, Deutsch, 1984.
The Lighthouse Keeper's Catastrophe, Deutsch, 1986.
The Lighthouse Keeper's Rescue, Deutsch, 1989.
Watch the Baby, Daisy, Deutsch, 1991.
When Dad Did the Washing, Puffin, 1992.
Looking after Chocolates, Deutsch, 1992.
A Quarrel of Koalas, Deutsch, 1992, published as *Harry Hates Shopping!,* Scholastic, Inc., 1992.
The Lighthouse Keeper's Picnic, Deutsch, 1993.
The Lighthouse Keeper's Cat, Deutsch, 1995.

OTHER

Let's Talk about Drinking, Deutsch, 1982.
New Zealand, photographs by Chris Fairclough, Deutsch, 1983, Bookwright Press (New York City), 1988.

■ **Sidelights**

Comprising one half of the husband-and-wife team of David and Ronda Armitage, Ronda Armitage uses her talent for language to help spin the stories that her husband brings to life with his illustrations. "In an age when so much in this genre seems calculated to impress sophisticated adults," commented Water McVitty of the couple's work in *Twentieth-Century Children's Writers,* "it is refreshing to encounter books that are so clearly intended for young children and that keep this focus always in mind." Noting that Ronda Armitage uses a "simple" prose style, McVitty added that such simplicity should not be confused with lack of substance. "Her style is distinguished by fluid, literate sentences that, rather than condescend, happily include words like 'brusque' or 'irascible' when these are ones that best suit their context. While being entertaining and child-centered," the critic added, "her stories still manage to enrich and delight."

The Armitages' picture-book partnership got its start in New Zealand, where both Ronda and David were born and raised. Married in 1966, the couple moved to England eight years later, Ronda working as a school teacher and David as an illustrator. Their first picture book collaboration, *The Lighthouse Keeper's Lunch,* was published in 1977 to much critical praise. Despite the fact that they had left their native country, New Zealand also honored the Armitages' accomplishments; *The Lighthouse Keeper's Lunch* earned the New Zealand Library Association's Esther Glen award for the most distinguished contribution to that country's children's literature.

The Lighthouse Keeper's Lunch finds lighthouse keeper Mr. Grinling and his cat, Hamish, in a quandary. A series of delicious lunches packed by Mrs. Grinling and cabled over the sea separating the Grinling cottage from the lighthouse have found their way into the stomachs of a group of wily seagulls rather than to the hungry inhabitants of the lighthouse. With growling tummies and growing frustration at not being able to outsmart the clever birds—who have now set up a permanent roost at the lighthouse due to the daily supply of delicious food—Mr. Grinling and his long-tailed companion are eventually saved by Mrs. Grinling, who packs a series of meals so awful that the gulls quickly lose interest in the lighthouse-bound lunch basket and depart in search of more tasty fare.

In Ronda Armitage's award-winning picture book, illustrated by her husband, David, seagulls confiscate a lighthouse keeper's delicious lunch until his wife prepares a series of noxious meals which deter the gluttonous birds. (From *The Lighthouse Keeper's Lunch.*)

The Lighthouse Keeper's Lunch, which "boasts Ronda's light touch in the telling," according to a *Publishers Weekly* reviewer, was followed by several more stories featuring Mr. Grinling and his feline companion. In *The Lighthouse Keeper's Catastrophe,* Hamish decides to handle lunch for himself when Mr. Grinling's catch from a morning spent fishing is left in easy reach. Unfortunately, keeping the cat from the fish results in the lighthouse keeper locking himself out of the lighthouse, an event that starts a chain of humorous mishaps. Graham Nutbrown had praise for the work in *School Librarian,* particularly noting "the unusual viewpoints" used by illustrator David Armitage. David's illustrations were also praised by a *Publishers Weekly* critic, who cited "the sun-filled watercolors of beaches and atmospheric depictions of storm-tossed seas" as adding to *The Lighthouse Keeper's Catastrophe*'s appeal. Other tales featuring the irascible Hamish and his ocean-dwelling owner include *The Lighthouse Keeper's Picnic, The Lighthouse Keeper's Rescue,* and *The Lighthouse Keeper's Cat.*

The Armitages' sense of fun has extended to numerous other picture books for young children. In *The Bossing of Josie,* a young girl who is always told what to do by older members of her family imagines that a witch costume she receives for her birthday will give her special powers. She casts a practice spell on her stubborn little brother and he winds up missing for part of the day, resulting in a frantic search and Josie's growing tolerance for being bossed by her elders. "There is a splendid relish and humour in this entirely satisfying glimpse of family life," according to Margery Fisher of *Growing Point,* while Mary B. Nickerson opined in *School Library Journal* that David Armitage's "deep drenched watercolors" in *The Bossing of Josie* "give a mild sense of mysteriousness to a story in which only the young heroine thinks there is magic."

The warm humor of family life is the thread running throughout the Armitages' work for young children. In *When Dad Did the Washing,* events unfold in a way that many young children can relate to: Dad manhandles the housework and ends up causing more mess than he cleans up. And a young toddler is lucky enough to have more lives than a cat in *Watch the Baby, Daisy,* as Dad takes Mom's directive to "watch the baby" literally—he watches disasters in the making but does nothing to prevent them. Noting that the story serves as an excellent way to alert readers to the dangers to young children that lurk around the house, a *Junior Bookshelf* critic also praised the illustrations in *Watch the Baby, Daisy* as "striking" and "full of color and movement." Illustrations are also central to *Grandma Goes Shopping,* as a young-at-heart grandma indulges in a wild shopping spree "rendered in bold wash and ink with ... a plentiful allowance of humour," according to *Growing Point* critic Fisher. The flip-side of shopping served as the focus of the Armitages' *A Quarrel of Koalas* (published in the United States as *Harry Hates Shopping!*), as a mother koala turns the tables on her bored and unruly youngsters during an arduous but necessary excursion to

Koala bear Harry learns to behave after his mother punishes his quarrelsome behavior by embarrassing him. (From *Harry Hates Shopping!,* written by Ronda Armitage and illustrated by David Armitage.)

the mall by finding ways to embarrass them into obedience.

The Armitage partnership continues to be an effective one due to each partner's common goal. "To me the fascination of creating a picture book lies in making something that will work in several different ways," Ronda Armitage once told *SATA.* "I need to enjoy writing it, but, equally, the story needs to work in terms of the young child's experience. Unlike books for older children, picture books are for reading aloud, so the story must flow smoothly and each sentence needs to be rhythmic. This form of writing is perhaps more akin to poetry than to prose in the sense that each word has to play its part—after all, there aren't very many of them. And then there is that other vital ingredient—that other half—the illustrations. Ideally these should complement the text, filling it out, adding those essential details that, if included in the text, would make the story too unwieldy for the young."

■ Works Cited

Fisher, Margery, review of *The Bossing of Josie, Growing Point,* July, 1980, p. 3733.

Fisher, Margery, review of *Grandma Goes Shopping, Growing Point,* November, 1984, p. 4345.

Review of *The Lighthouse Keeper's Catastrophe, Publishers Weekly,* December 26, 1986, p. 56.

Review of *The Lighthouse Keeper's Lunch, Publishers Weekly,* April 9, 1979, p. 110.

McVitty, Walter, "Ronda Armitage," *Twentieth-Century Children's Writers,* Fourth edition, St. James Press, 1995, pp. 32-33.

Nickerson, Mary B., review of *The Bossing of Josie, School Library Journal,* January, 1981, p. 46.

Nutbrown, Graham, review of *The Lighthouse Keeper's Catastrophe, School Librarian,* December, 1986, p. 331.

Review of *Watch the Baby, Daisy, Junior Bookshelf,* April, 1992, p. 53.

■ For More Information See

PERIODICALS

Booklist, July 15, 1979, p. 1623; October 1, 1979, p. 234; February 1, 1989, p. 935.

Books for Keeps, September, 1988, p. 8; November, 1991, p. 7; November, 1992, p. 15.

Books for Your Children, autumn-winter, 1993, p. 9.

Bulletin of the Center for Children's Books, December, 1981, p. 62.

Junior Bookshelf, October, 1977, pp. 272-73; December, 1978, p. 292; December, 1980, p. 279; February, 1982, p. 13; June, 1990, p. 125; October, 1992, p. 187; April, 1995, p. 64; April, 1996, p. 56.

Magpies, May, 1991, p. 29.

New York Times Book Review, September 2, 1984, p. 12.

School Librarian, May, 1993, p. 53.

School Library Journal, October, 1979, p. 132; February, 1982, pp. 63-64; May, 1984, pp. 61-62; February, 1989, p. 83.

B

BELL, Clare (Louise) 1952-
(Clare Coleman, a joint pseudonym)

■ Personal

Born June 19, 1952, in Hitchin, Hertfordshire, England; immigrated to the United States, 1957; daughter of Ronald Lancelot Bell and Edna Kathleen (Wheldon) Steward; lives with M. Coleman Easton. *Education:* University of California, Santa Cruz, B.A., 1975; postgraduate studies at University of California, Davis, c. 1978; Stanford University, M.S.M.E., 1983. *Politics:* Green Party. *Hobbies and other interests:* Electric cars, music, hiking, cycling, swimming.

■ Addresses

Home and office—5680 Judith St., San Jose, CA 95123-2033. *Agent*—c/o Margaret K. McElderry Books, 866 3rd Ave., New York, NY 10022. *Electronic mail*—Ce96ed@aol.com.

■ Career

Writer and editor. U.S. Geological Survey, Menlo Park, CA, field assistant, 1976-78; International Business Machines (IBM), San Jose, CA, test equipment engineer, 1978-89; freelance writer, c. 1983—. *Current Events* (newsletter of Electric Auto Association), San Jose, CA, managing editor, c. 1995—. *Member:* American Civil Liberties Union, National Writers Union, Science Fiction Writers of America, Electric Vehicle Association, San Jose Peace Center.

■ Awards, Honors

PEN Center USA West Award, 1983, and Children's Book Award, International Reading Association, 1984, both for *Ratha's Creature;* Best Books, American Library Association (ALA), 1983, for *Ratha's Creature,* 1984, for *Clan Ground,* and 1990, for *Ratha and Thistle-chaser.*

■ Writings

FANTASY NOVELS FOR YOUNG ADULTS; "RATHA" SERIES

Ratha's Creature, Atheneum / M. K. McElderry Books, 1983.
Clan Ground, Atheneum, 1984, Gollancz (London), 1987.
Ratha and Thistle-chaser, McElderry, 1990.
Ratha's Challenge, Macmillan / McElderry, 1994.

FOR YOUNG ADULTS

Tomorrow's Sphinx, Macmillan / McElderry, 1986.

NOVELS

People of the Sky, Tor / St. Martin's, 1989.
(As Clare Coleman; with M. Coleman Easton) *Daughter of the Reef,* Jove, 1992.
The Jaguar Princess, Tor / St. Martin's, 1993.
(As Clare Coleman; with Easton) *Sister of the Sun,* Jove, 1993.
(As Clare Coleman; with Easton) *Child of the Dawn,* Jove, 1994.

■ Sidelights

A respected fantasist and science fiction writer for young people and adults, Bell—who also writes with her companion M. Coleman Easton as Clare Coleman—is praised as an original and talented author whose fantasies are particularly evocative and compelling. She is best known for the "Ratha" series of fantasies for young adults about a society of anthropomorphic cats who lived twenty-five million years ago in an alternate universe. Bell sets her works in historical and futuristic periods and underscores her books, which feature both humans and animals as main characters, with sophisticated themes such as mother/daughter relationships, the nature of leadership, and the need for spiritual expression. She is often credited as an exceptional literary stylist who fires the imaginations of young readers with her works, which, although considered demanding and complex, are noted for their compelling plots, well-realized characters, and depiction of powerful emotions.

Born in England, Bell came to the United States when she was about five years old. After attending the University of California at Santa Barbara, she did postgraduate work at UC-Davis and later received her master's degree in engineering from Stanford University. Bell began writing fantasy novels for young adults while working as a test engineer for International Business Machines (IBM). Her first novel in the award-winning "Ratha" series about prehistoric sentient cats, *Ratha's Creature,* was published in 1983. By 1989, Bell's fiction was successful enough for her to leave engineering and become a freelance writer. Since 1995, she has also served as the editor of a newsletter on electric automobiles, a subject that is one of her main interests.

In *Ratha's Creature,* Bell describes two groups of cats, both descendants of the sabre tooth tiger: the Named, a community that follows an organized set of laws, are herders and farmers who can speak; their traditional enemies, the Un-Named, are clanless animals—considered mute and witless by their rivals—who exist by coming together to raid the herds of the Named. Ratha, a Named yearling, is due to become a herder, but her discovery of fire and how to harness it threatens the leader of her clan; when she tries to initiate the Named, she is exiled. She lives for a time with the Un-Named, and breeds with one of them, Bonechewer, whom she finds can speak. When Ratha realizes that their resulting kittens are unintelligent, she reacts so strongly that Bonechewer sends her back into exile. When a war breaks out between the clans, Ratha is caught in the middle until her knowledge of fire—Ratha's "creature", called Red Tongue—helps her in a successful battle against the Un-Named. She eventually persuades the Named to accept her gift of fire, fights and defeats the leader of the clan, and becomes their new leader. *Booklist* reviewer Sally Estes hailed *Ratha's Creature* as a "powerful, moving, and memorable story that will draw readers right in and hold them to the final page." Trev Jones of *School Library Journal* also praised the book, noting that "the characters will come vividly alive to readers" and adding that for "special readers who enjoy a challenge, this is a rewarding experience." Mary Ellen Baker of *Voice of Youth Advocates* said, "Fans of Richard Adams's *Watership Down* will enjoy this moving tale of survival" and gave the novel that periodical's highest rating for quality. Reviewers also noted how Bell skillfully parallels the early stages of the human race with her cat clans while depicting Ratha's growth from adolescent to mature adult.

In the next "Ratha" book, *Clan Ground,* Ratha's leadership of the Named is challenged by Shongshar, a male cat who turns the clan's use of fire into a religious cult. Exploiting the power of fire as well as the Named's spiritual needs, Shongshar convinces the clan to worship Red Tongue as a god and to use it as a weapon. He turns the Named against Ratha and drives her out; with a few loyal followers, she learns to tame water and to regain control of the clan. In addition, she realizes the impor-

In Clare Bell's fantasy novel, set in an alternate, prehistoric world, wildcat leader Ratha reconciles with her ostracized daughter when the two clash with the tyrannical leader of a rival clan.

tance of spiritual well-being to the members of her community. Considered a more introspective novel than its predecessor, *Clan Ground* was also praised by critics. *School Library Journal* contributor Hazel Rochman observed that "as before, Bell creates characters that are authentically wild and feline and also sensitive, intelligent and complicated. Young people will be fascinated by the parallels with human society's painful evolution; the needs and power struggles that threaten to bring back savagery, in prehistoric times and now." Eileen Colwell of *Junior Bookshelf* called the book an "exciting story of drama and characterization" and added that *Clan Ground* "could well have been a moving story of *people* in a primitive world." A reviewer in *Bulletin of the Center for Children's Books* noted that, as in the first book, "the strength is in the convincing personalities and culture of Ratha and her fellow felines."

In *Ratha and Thistle-chaser,* Ratha is reunited with the daughter that she tried to kill due to her mistaken belief that she was a throwback to a more mindless race of cats. Instead, it turns out that Thistle-chaser and others like her are the next evolutionary step in sentient cats—

kittens who take longer to come to maturity. In this volume, the clan searches for new grazing lands for the herd beasts that provide their survival; they head for the coast, where they encounter Newt, a young wild cat lamed as a kitten who has been rejected by the Un-Named and has formed a symbiotic relationship with a group of sea mammals. Thakur, a Named cat who is the herding teacher, discovers Newt and teaches her to speak; in return, she teaches him the successful herding methods that she has developed. Thakur brings Newt to Ratha, who recognizes the daughter that she accidentally maimed when she thought her to be genetically inferior. Newt, who has dreamed of taking revenge on the cat who disabled her, fights with Ratha, who learns that misguided judgements regarding intelligence are capable of destroying her clan. Catherine D. Moorhead, writing in *Voice of Youth Advocates,* called *Ratha and Thistle-chaser* an "incredible fantasy.... As good an anthropomorphic fantasy as I have read in a long time." Writing in *School Library Journal,* Carolyn Polese noted, "Skilled readers of fantasy who demand excellent craftsmanship, complex characters, a compelling plot, and fresh insights into family and society will be more than satisfied with this powerful novel."

In the next volume in the series, *Ratha's Challenge,* mother and daughter are still creeping towards reconciliation, but they come together to deal with and understand another clan of intelligent cats controlled by a communal song. This song, which is sung by the leader of the clan, True-of-Voice, and projected telepathically, is comforting but inhibits individuality. Disturbed by the song's effects, the Named are wary of accepting the new group as allies. When an accident leaves True-of-Voice near death, Ratha must choose between destroying or saving his group. Drawing upon her own experience as an outcast, Thistle-chaser acts as an interpreter to the new tribe. Through Thistle's work, the Named initiates a truce with the new clan, and Ratha realizes that much of the violence that she has fostered as protection for her community has actually been prompted by fear and lack of understanding. Leslie A. Acevedo of *Voice of Youth Advocates* concluded that the themes that Bell addresses in *Ratha's Challenge* "are pressing ... in any youth's life and are presented in a well-paced and thought provoking manner...." Writing in *Booklist,* Jeanne Triner praised the "subtle but effective message concerning tolerance" and declared that "overall, readers will find enough suspense, adventure, and even romance to satisfy them." Carolyn Polese of *School Library Journal* noted that in this volume Bell continues to explore "themes of culture, politics, individuation, and family relations, all through the eyes of a riveting set of characters." She added that those readers "who like fantasy or cats will fall under the spell of the vivid descriptions of ... life on the veldt."

Bell continues her fascination with cats in *Tomorrow's Sphinx,* a novel for young adults that blends fantasy and science fiction. In this book, she depicts the lives of two black cheetahs—one in Egypt during the reign of the pharaoh Tutankhamen, the other in a future devastated by environmental waste—and describes their telepathic links, both with each other and with humans. Kichebo, the female cheetah who lives on an earth destroyed by holocaust and devoid of humans, possesses unusual gold markings that cause her to develop special hunting techniques as well as ways of avoiding the hunters who have returned to Earth from outer space to see what has happened to the animals left behind by their ancestors. She communicates with Kheknemt, a male cheetah who shares his experiences with the young pharaoh, Tut, through ESP. When Kichebo pulls a boy, Menk, from a burning wreck, she becomes his companion. Through the power of Kheknemt's mind, Kichebo travels back to ancient Egypt, where she discovers her heritage as one of a rare race of animals who can bond with humans to create an amazing strength; Kichebo realizes that she and Menk are meant to forge their bond together. *Kirkus Reviews* called *Tomorrow's Sphinx* "one of the year's most original fantasies.... Older readers with a strong appreciation for fantasy will enjoy a memorable experience." Sally Estes of *Booklist* said that Bell "has woven another mesmerizing tale of realistically depicted felines.... Sure to be relished by all fantasy fans." Writing in *Bulletin of the Center for Children's Books,* Betsy Hearne noted that what "carries the overextended plot is the power Bell has always brought to portraying her anthropomorphized cats." Connie C. Epstein of the *Horn Book Magazine* concluded that *Tomorrow's Sphinx* is a "strikingly original fantasy.... Animal lore, Egyptian history, and the geography of the Nile Valley fuse into a novel that stretches the reader's imagination."

In addition to the works she has written specifically for young adults, Bell is the creator of several books that are directed to an adult audience but are also enjoyed by young people. In *People of the Sky,* the author features Kesbe Temiya, a young woman of the twenty-third century who is of Puerto Rican descent. Several hundred years before the story begins, most of Kesbe's ancestors left Earth in order to preserve their traditions. While flying an old airplane to its new owner, Kesbe goes down in a storm and is rescued by Imiya, a young boy who is a member of a tribe called the People of the Sky, a lost interstellar colony made up of the descendants of Hopi Indians. Kesbe realizes that Imiya, who is trying to escape from his coming-of-age rituals, is a descendant of her own long-lost tribe; in addition, she learns about the tribe's symbiotic relationship with insect-like creatures called aronans. When Kesbe unwittingly creates a cultural crisis by helping Imiya avoid his rites of passage, she resolves the problem by joining the society and connecting symbiotically with her own aronan. A reviewer in *Publishers Weekly* stated, "This futuristic novel is an intriguing blend of adult material and YA tone.... Bell creates a believable cultural blend of Indian and alien." *Kirkus Reviews* described *People of the Sky* as a "well-crafted, medium-future, cultural science-fiction tale," and added that the work is "carefully detailed and often evocative." Writing in *Booklist,* Roland Green concluded, "Generally, the author seems to be working the anthropological sf territory of Le Guin and Cherryh with a skill that promises a bright future."

Another of Bell's adult novels that appeals to young adults is *The Jaguar Princess,* a historical fantasy set during the time of the Aztecs. This book concerns Mixcatl, a slave girl who turns out to be descended from a royal race of shape-changers. Mixcatl, who was stolen from her village and bound into slavery at six, is apprenticing as a scribe when Wise Coyote, the Speaker King of the client state Texcoc, learns that she is a member of a magical clan from a distant time called the Jaguar's Children. While Wise Coyote tries to use Mixcatl's gifts as a shape-shifter in his struggle for independence against the bloodthirsty king of the Aztecs, the girl explores her powers while developing her love for Wise Coyote's son, the artist Huetzin. A reviewer in *Publishers Weekly* called *The Jaguar Princess* a "vivid tale of a seldom-plumbed time and place.... Bell brings a vanished civilization to life in this unusual fantasy." A critic in *Kirkus Reviews* called the book "rather ponderous historical fantasy" but added that it was "reasonably rewarding as regards Aztec culture and environment" and that it was "worth a try for historical-fantasy regulars."

Daughter of the Reef, Bell's first collaboration with M. Coleman Easton under the joint pseudonym Clare Coleman, is the first volume of a series of historical fantasies set in long-ago times on an island of the South Pacific. Tepua, the heroine, is the daughter of her island's chief; washed away from the celebration of her own wedding by a tropical storm, she lands in Tahiti, where she must learn to fit in with a new society. Her dancing skills help her to be accepted by her adopted tribe and allow her entrance in the Arioi, a group of women dancer/warriors. In addition, Tepua's dancing brings her a new love interest—Matopahu, the brother of the tribe's high chief. Matopahu has the gift of prophecy, which tells him that famine may be imminent. A reviewer in *Publishers Weekly* stated that "the challenges [the characters] face and the exotic society in which they move give the work a dynamism that keeps it afloat." As Clare Coleman, Bell and Easton continue the series with *Sister of the Sun* and *Child of the Dawn.*

■ Works Cited

Acevedo, Leslie A., review of *Ratha's Challenge, Voice of Youth Advocates,* June, 1995, p. 101.

Baker, Mary Ellen, review of *Ratha's Creature, Voice of Youth Advocates,* October, 1983, pp. 196-97.

Review of *Clan Ground, Bulletin of the Center for Children's Books,* January, 1985, p. 80.

Colwell, Eileen, review of *Clan Ground, Junior Bookshelf,* February, 1987, p. 52.

Review of *Daughter of the Reef, Publishers Weekly,* November 9, 1993, p. 78.

Epstein, Connie C., review of *Tomorrow's Sphinx, Horn Book,* November, 1987, pp. 776-77.

Estes, Sally, review of *Ratha's Creature, Booklist,* March 15, 1983, pp. 956-57.

Estes, Sally, review of *Tomorrow's Sphinx, Booklist,* October 15, 1986, p. 344.

Green, Roland, review of *People of the Sky, Booklist,* December 15, 1989, p. 815.

Hearne, Betsy, review of *Tomorrow's Sphinx, Bulletin of the Center for Children's Books,* November, 1986, p. 42.

Review of *The Jaguar Princess, Kirkus Reviews,* August 15, 1993, p. 1034.

Review of *The Jaguar Princess, Publishers Weekly,* October 4, 1993, p. 68.

Jones, Trev, review of *Ratha's Creature, School Library Journal,* September, 1983, p. 130.

Moorhead, Catherine D., review of *Ratha and Thistle-chaser, Voice of Youth Advocates,* June, 1990, p. 112.

Review of *People of the Sky, Kirkus Reviews,* November 1, 1989, p. 1567.

Review of *People of the Sky, Publishers Weekly,* October 27, 1989, p. 60.

Polese, Carolyn, review of *Ratha and Thistle-chaser, School Library Journal,* June, 1990, pp. 136-37.

Polese, Carolyn, review of *Ratha's Challenge, School Library Journal,* January, 1995, p. 134.

Rochman, Hazel, review of *Clan Ground, School Library Journal,* October, 1984, p. 164.

Review of *Tomorrow's Sphinx, Kirkus Reviews,* September 1, 1986, p. 1372.

Triner, Jeanne, review of *Ratha's Challenge, Booklist,* January 1, 1995, pp. 815-16.

■ For More Information See

BOOKS

Clute, John and Peter Nicholls, *The Encyclopedia of Science Fiction,* St. Martin's Press, 1993.

Helbig, Althea K. and Agnes Regan Perkins, *Dictionary of American Children's Fiction,* Greenwood Press, 1988.

Pringle, David, editor, *St. James Guide to Fantasy Writers,* St. James Press, 1996.

PERIODICALS

Booklist, January 1, 1995, pp. 814-16.

Bulletin of the Center for Children's Books, July, 1983, pp. 202-03; May, 1990, p 208.

Locus, September, 1993, pp. 31, 71-72.

Voice of Youth Advocates, June, 1995, p. 101.

—*Sketch by Gerard J. Senick*

*   *   *

BELL, David Owen 1949-

■ Personal

Born August 8, 1949, in New York, NY; son of Shephard and Rhea Bell; children: one daughter. *Education:* San Francisco Art Institute, B.F.A., 1972; M.F.A. (filmmaking), 1974. *Religion:* Jewish.

■ Addresses

c/o Tidewater Publishers, Box 456, Centreville, MD 21617.

DAVID OWEN BELL

■ Career

Writer and photographer, 1977—; Master Mariner, captain, and mate, 1981—. President, Environmental Fund for Maryland, 1996—. *Member:* Maryland Association of Science Teachers, Maryland Congress of Parents and Teachers.

■ Writings

The Celestial Navigation Mystery: Solved, Oceanic Society, 1977.

Dockmanship, Cornell Maritime Press (Centreville, MD), 1992.

Awesome Chesapeake: A Kid's Guide to the Bay, illustrated by Marcy Dunn Ramsey, Tidewater Publishers (Centreville, MD), 1994.

(Editor) *Hands On! Feet Wet!,* Echo Hill Outdoor School, 1997.

If Dads Can Eat, Dads Can Cook!, Bell Books, 1997.

Chesapeake Bay Walk, Tidewater Publishers, 1998.

■ Sidelights

David Owen Bell told *SATA:* "I was born and raised in New York City. While attending the San Francisco Art Institute, I started sailing. Upon graduating with a master's degree in filmmaking, I went to sea to make a movie.

"I've been sailing and exploring estuaries and oceans ever since. This interest has led me to undertake conservation projects on San Francisco Bay, water quality monitoring of Long Island Sound, and teaching ecology to children on Long Island Sound and the Chesapeake Bay.

"Oceanic research and sail training expeditions have taken me from Canada to South America and as far as the Galapagos Islands and the Aegean Sea. A U.S. Coast Guard licensed Master Mariner, I have captained tug boats, sailing ships, excursion boats, and research vessels.

"My lively and varied career has also included teaching undergraduate and graduate motion picture production courses, managing a ski lodge, directing a boating education program, raising money for education and environmental protection, and leading the environmental fund for Maryland. Through it all, I have kept writing and taking photos. I have done this professionally since 1977.

"In 1987, I settled in Maryland to manage a sailboat charter fleet. In this and other maritime work, I became increasingly angry and dismayed at the way both commercial and recreational interests were mistreating our natural heritage. I felt that by being a part of the industry I was partly responsible, so I decided to put together my writing, teaching, and nautical skills and experience and do something positive.

"Currently, I take school groups out on the Chesapeake Bay, visit schools to do book talks and assemblies, conduct workshops and write for teachers about hands-on learning activities, and write for children. I'm a single parent raising a school-aged daughter."

*   *   *

BELLINGHAM, Brenda 1931-

■ Personal

Born August 14, 1931, in Liverpool, England; immigrated to Canada, 1958; daughter of Thomas (a feed mill foreman) and Beatrice (Morris) Brown; married Ramsay Stephen Bellingham, February 20, 1959; children: Sheena, Kevin. *Education:* Received Certificate in Social Science and Diploma in Industrial Sociology from University of Liverpool; University of Alberta, Teacher's Diploma, 1970.

■ Addresses

Home—266-52249 Range Rd. 233, Sherwood Park, Alberta, Canada T8B 1C7.

■ Career

Provincial Government of Alberta, Calgary, social worker, 1958-62; schoolteacher in Strathcona County, Alberta, 1971-77; writer. *Member:* Canadian Authors Association (president of Edmonton branch, 1974-75); Canadian Society of Children's Authors, Illustrators, and Performers; Writers Guild of Alberta.

■ Writings

Joanie's Magic Boots, Tree Frog Press (Edmonton, Alberta), 1979.
Two Parents Too Many, Scholastic Canada (Richmond Hill, Ontario), 1985.
Storm Child, Lorimer (Toronto, Ontario), 1985.
The Curse of the Silver Box (sequel to *Two Parents Too Many*), Scholastic Canada, 1989.
Like a TV Hero, General (Toronto, Ontario), 1991.
Princesses Don't Wear Jeans, illustrated by Carol Wakefield, Scholastic Canada, 1991.
Dragons Don't Read Books (sequel to *Princesses Don't Wear Jeans*), illustrated by Carol Wakefield, Scholastic Canada, 1992.
Lilly to the Rescue, illustrated by Kathy Kaulbach, Formac (Halifax, Nova Scotia), 1997.
Drowning in Secrets, Scholastic Canada, 1998.

Some of Bellingham's works have been published in braille and translated into German and French. *Storm Child, The Curse of the Silver Box,* and *Like a TV Hero* were recorded on audio cassette and released by CNIB, 1991, 1992, 1993, respectively.

■ Sidelights

Brenda Bellingham writes books for young adults as well as easy-to-read chapter books for newly independent readers. Critics often praise the author for her dialogue, fast-paced action, and realistic characters. Often, these characters are children from broken homes who, through experiences presented in Bellingham's tales, manage to grow to a better understanding both of themselves and of the people around them.

Born and raised in Liverpool, England, Bellingham immigrated to Canada in 1958. As a child, the author enjoyed reading and writing stories. She once commented, "I used to bore my family with my efforts while we sat in the candlelight in our Anderson shelter in the backyard of our home during World War II." After she became a schoolteacher and had two children of her own, Bellingham began to fashion her stories into books. When her first work, *Joanie's Magic Boots,* was published, Bellingham decided to stop teaching and instead pursue writing full-time.

It was not until 1985, however, that young adult audiences were treated to more of Bellingham's work. In that year *Storm Child* and *Two Parents Too Many* were published. Both of these books feature girls of separated or divorced parents. Set in the 1830s, *Storm Child* portrays twelve-year-old Isobel MacPherson, a girl who is half Scottish and half Peigan Indian. After her father deserts his family by moving back to Scotland, her mother quickly remarries another white man. Instead of living with her new family, Isobel decides to stay with her Peigan grandparents. While adapting to her new life, she faces challenging situations arising from her mixed heritage. Sarah Ellis, writing in *Canadian Children's Literature,* concluded that "the story of Isobel's growth from rage to understanding is the emotional heart of the

BRENDA BELLINGHAM

book." In *Two Parents Too Many,* twelve-year-old Katy and her fourteen-year-old sister Jenny devise ways to prevent their divorced mother from remarrying, as their father had the previous year. *Canadian Children's Literature* contributor Leonore Loft noted: "Though there are some hilarious moments ... [the girls'] slow realization of adult needs is seriously and touchingly presented."

Katy and her sister Jenny return in *The Curse of the Silver Box,* in which mysterious happenings occur after Katy's stepmother purchases a silver box at an antique auction. As Katy tries to solve the mystery, she learns much about herself and her step- and biological parents. In a review for *Canadian Materials,* Theo Hersh maintained that "one of the appealing aspects of the novel is the family relationships. Katy's divorced parents ... are still caring friends. The caring extends to Katy and her sister Jenny and to the new spouses, too." Frieda Wishinsky, writing in *Quill & Quire,* concluded that "lots of dialogue, quick and surprising action, and sympathetic characters make this an enjoyable book."

Bellingham's next work, *Like a TV Hero,* features a boy named Kris Higgins, who must play the role of brother and parent to his younger sister, Lisa. The children are often left alone while their parents work long hours and then socialize well into the night. Kris constantly wishes his life could be more like the happy lives of his favorite

TV heroes. He seizes the opportunity, however, to become a real-life hero, when he outwits some neighborhood bullies. "Children ... would enjoy the story and possibly discover a new kind of hero in the process," claimed *Canadian Materials* contributor Donna Doyle.

Bellingham introduces two other popular characters in the easy-to-read chapter book *Princesses Don't Wear Jeans.* Eight-year-old Jeff, who wants to be like everyone in his class, befriends Tilly, a new girl in school who isn't concerned about what other people think of her. Jeff enjoys Tilly and her outrageous stories, until the class labels Tilly a liar. Jeff eventually gains confidence in his own opinions rather than his classmates' and remains Tilly's friend. *Canadian Materials* contributor Carol Carver appreciated Bellingham's "believable characters" in this work, while Barbara Powell, writing in *Canadian Children's Literature,* enjoyed both the "verbal and visual" features. Bellingham wrote a sequel to this work, *Dragons Don't Read Books,* featuring Tilly and a library book-eating dragon. This time, Tilly must convince her classmates that the school's mascot is eating all of the missing library books.

The author once explained to *SATA,* "I've learned that [writing children's books] is not as easy as it looks. I've had a few minor successes and my share of failures. What keeps me writing? The challenge! I'm sure writing is an activity I'll never totally master. There's always a new problem to work out, some skill I haven't properly developed. Besides, there's nothing else I know that allows me to live in my imagination for hours on end and call it work."

■ Works Cited

Carver, Carol, review of *Princesses Don't Wear Jeans, Canadian Materials,* September, 1991, p. 218.

Doyle, Donna, review of *Like a TV Hero, Canadian Materials,* March, 1992, p. 64.

Ellis, Sarah, review of *Storm Child, Canadian Children's Literature,* Number 46, 1987, pp. 87-89.

Hersh, Theo, review of *The Curse of the Silver Box, Canadian Materials,* July, 1990, p. 184.

Loft, Leonore, review of *Two Parents Too Many, Canadian Children's Literature,* Number 53, 1989, pp. 61-62.

Powell, Barbara, review of *Princesses Don't Wear Jeans, Canadian Children's Literature,* Number 66, 1992, pp. 77-78.

Wishinsky, Frieda, review of *The Curse of the Silver Box, Quill & Quire,* July, 1990, pp. 35, 39.

■ For More Information See

PERIODICALS

Canadian Children's Literature, Number 62, 1991, pp. 76-78.

Canadian Materials, May, 1991, p. 156.

Quill & Quire, October, 1985, p. 15; December, 1985, p. 30; April, 1991, p. 20; November, 1992, p. 35.

BERTON, Pierre (Francis DeMarigny) 1920- (Lisa Kroniuk)

■ Personal

Born July 12, 1920, in Whitehorse, Yukon Territory, Canada; son of Francis George (a mining recorder) and Laura Beatrice (Thompson) Berton; married Janet Walker, 1946; children: Penny, Pamela, Patricia, Peter, Paul, Peggy Anne, Perri, Eric. *Education:* University of British Columbia, B.A., 1941. *Politics:* New Democrat.

■ Addresses

Home—R.R. 1, Kleinburg, Ontario L0J 1C0 Canada. *Agent*—Elsa Franklin, 21 Sackville Street, Toronto, Ontario, M5A 3E1, Canada.

■ Career

Vancouver News Herald, Vancouver, British Columbia, city editor, 1941-42; *Vancouver Sun,* Vancouver, feature writer, 1946-47; *Maclean's* magazine, Toronto, Ontario, 1947-58, began as assistant editor, became managing editor; host of *The Pierre Berton Show,* CBC-TV, 1957-73; television commentator and panelist, *Front Page Challenge,* beginning 1957, and *Close-Up; Toronto Star,*

PIERRE BERTON

Toronto, associate editor and author of daily column "By Pierre Berton," 1958-62; host of weekly television programs *Heritage Theatre*, 1947-58, *The Pierre Berton Show*, 1962-73, and *My Country, Under Attack*, and *The Great Debate*; *Maclean's Magazine*, managing and contributing editor, 1963-64; editor-in-chief, Canadian Centennial Library, beginning 1963; Yukon College, chancellor, 1988-93. Member of board of directors, McClelland & Stewart Ltd.; past chair, Heritage Canada; former chair, Canadian Civil Liberties Union; editorial director, Natural Science of Canada Ltd. *Military service:* Canadian Army, 1942-45; became captain/instructor at Royal Military College in Kingston. *Member:* Association of Canadian Radio and Television Artists, Writers' Union of Canada, American Federation of Radio and Television Artists, Authors League of America.

■ Awards, Honors

Governor General's Awards for creative nonfiction, 1956, for *The Mysterious North*, 1958, for *The Klondike Fever*, and 1971, for *The Last Spike, 1881-1885;* J. B. McAree Award for columnist of the year, 1959; Film of the Year Award in Canada and Grand Prix at Cannes for *City of Gold*, 1959; National Newspaper Awards for feature writing and staff corresponding, 1960; Stephen Leacock Medal for Humor, 1960, for *Just Add Water and Stir;* Nellie Award, Association of Canadian Television and Radio Artists (ACTRA), for integrity in broadcasting, 1972; Officer of Order of Canada, 1975; Nellie Award, ACTRA, for public affairs radio broadcasting, 1978; Canadian Author's Association Literary Award for nonfiction, 1981, for *The Invasion of Canada, 1812-1813;* Canadian Booksellers' Award and Ohassto Perspective Award, both 1982; Companion of Order of Canada, 1986; inducted into the Canadian News Hall of Fame; recipient of numerous honorary degrees.

■ Writings

FOR YOUNG PEOPLE; FICTION

The Golden Trail: The Story of the Klondike Rush, Macmillan (Toronto), 1955, published in the U.S. as *Stampede for Gold*, Knopf, 1955.

The Secret World of Og, illustrated by daughter, Patsy Berton, McClelland & Stewart, 1961, Little, Brown (Boston, MA), 1962, published with new illustrations by Patsy Berton, McClelland & Stewart, 1974, republished with new cover art and new color plates, McClelland & Stewart, 1991.

NONFICTION FOR CHILDREN AND YOUNG ADULTS; "ADVENTURES IN CANADIAN HISTORY" SERIES

The Death of Isaac Brock, McClelland & Stewart, 1991.
The Capture of Detroit, McClelland & Stewart, 1991.
Canada under Siege, McClelland & Stewart, 1991.
Revenge of the Tribes, McClelland & Stewart, 1991.
Bonanza Gold, illustrated by Henry van der Linde, McClelland & Stewart, 1991.
The Klondike Stampede, illustrated by Henry van der Linde, McClelland & Stewart, 1991.

Parry of the Arctic, illustrated by Paul McCusker, McClelland & Stewart, 1992.
Jane Franklin's Obsession, illustrated by Paul McCusker, McClelland & Stewart, 1992.
A Prairie Nightmare, illustrated by Paul McCusker, McClelland & Stewart, 1992.
The Men in Sheepskin Coats, illustrated by Paul McCusker, McClelland & Stewart, 1992.
The Railway Pathfinders, illustrated by Paul McCusker, McClelland & Stewart, 1992.
Steel across the Plains, illustrated by Paul McCusker, McClelland & Stewart, 1992.
Dr. Kane of the Arctic Seas, illustrated by Paul McCusker, McClelland & Stewart, 1993.
Trapped in the Arctic, illustrated by Paul McCusker, McClelland & Stewart, 1993.
Before the Gold Rush, illustrated by Paul McCusker, McClelland & Stewart, 1993.
Kings of the Klondike, illustrated by Paul McCusker, McClelland & Stewart Books, 1993.
Attack on Montreal, illustrated by Paul McCusker, McClelland & Stewart, 1994.
The Battle of Lake Erie, illustrated by Paul McCusker, McClelland & Stewart, 1994.
The Death of Tecumseh, illustrated by Paul McCusker, McClelland & Stewart, 1994.
Steel Across the Shields, illustrated by Paul McCusker, McClelland & Stewart, 1994.
City of Gold, McClelland & Stewart, in press.
Trails of '98, McClelland & Stewart, in press.

ADULT WRITINGS; NONFICTION, EXCEPT AS NOTED

The Royal Family: The Story of the British Monarchy from Victoria to Elizabeth, Knopf (New York City), 1954, McClelland & Stewart (Toronto), 1954.
The Mysterious North, McClelland & Stewart, 1956, Knopf, 1956.
Klondike: The Life and Death of the Last Great Gold Rush, McClelland & Stewart, 1958, republished as *The Klondike Fever: The Life and Death of the Last Great Gold Rush*, Knopf, 1958, revised edition published in Canada as *Klondike: The Last Great Gold Rush, 1896-1899*, McClelland & Stewart, 1972.
Just Add Water and Stir (also see below), McClelland & Stewart, 1959.
Adventures of a Columnist (also see below), McClelland & Stewart, 1960.
(With Henri Rossier) *The New City: A Prejudicial View of Toronto*, Macmillan (Toronto), 1961.
Fast, Fast, Fast Relief (also see below), McClelland & Stewart, 1962.
The Big Sell: An Introduction to the Black Arts of Door-to-Door Salesmanship and Other Techniques (also see below), Knopf, 1963, McClelland & Stewart, 1963.
The Comfortable Pew: A Critical Look at Christianity and the Religious Establishment in the New Age, Lippincott (Philadelphia, PA), McClelland & Stewart, 1965.
My War with the Twentieth Century, Doubleday (New York City), 1965.

Remember Yesterday, Canadian Centennial Library (Toronto), 1966.

(With wife, Janet Berton) *The Centennial Food Guide,* Canadian Centennial Library, 1966, published as *Pierre and Janet Berton's Canadian Food Guide,* McClelland & Stewart, 1974.

The Cool, Crazy, Committed World of the Sixties, McClelland & Stewart, 1966, enlarged version published as *Voices from the Sixties,* Doubleday, 1967.

(Editor) *Great Canadians,* McClelland & Stewart, 1967.

(Editor) *Historic Headlines: A Century of Canadian News Dramas,* McClelland & Stewart, 1967.

The Smug Minority, McClelland & Stewart, 1968, Doubleday, 1969.

Pierre Berton Omnibus (boxed set; contains *Just Add Water and Stir, Adventures of a Columnist, Fast, Fast, Fast Relief,* and *The Big Sell*), McClelland & Stewart, 1969.

The Great Railway, McClelland & Stewart, Volume I: *The National Dream: 1871-1881,* 1970, Volume II: *The Last Spike: 1881-1885,* 1971, published in one volume as *The Impossible Railway: The Building of the Canadian Pacific,* Knopf, 1972, abridged edition published in one volume as *The National Dream/The Last Spike,* with color photographs from the CBC-TV production, McClelland & Stewart, 1974.

Drifting Home (autobiographical journal), McClelland & Stewart, 1973, Knopf, 1974.

Hollywood's Canada: The Americanization of the National Image, McClelland & Stewart, 1975.

My Country: The Remarkable Past (also see below), McClelland & Stewart, 1976.

The Dionne Years: A Thirties Melodrama, McClelland & Stewart, 1977, Norton (New York City), 1978.

The Invasion of Canada, 1812-1813, McClelland & Stewart, 1977, Little, Brown, 1980.

The Wild Frontier: More Tales from the Remarkable Past (also see below), McClelland & Stewart, 1978.

Flames across the Border: The Canadian-American Tragedy, 1813-1814, Little, Brown, 1981, McClelland & Stewart, 1981.

Why We Act Like Canadians: A Personal Exploration of Our National Character, McClelland & Stewart, 1982, Penguin (Markham, Ont.), 1987.

The Klondike Quest: A Photographic Essay, 1897-1899, Little, Brown, 1983, McClelland & Stewart, 1983.

The Promised Land: Settling the West, 1896-1914, McClelland & Stewart, 1984.

(Under pseudonym Lisa Kroniuk) *Masquerade: 15 Variations on a Theme of Sexual Fantasy* (fiction), McClelland & Stewart, 1985.

The Berton Family Cookbook, McClelland & Stewart, 1985.

Vimy, McClelland & Stewart, 1986.

Starting Out, 1920-1947 (autobiography), McClelland & Stewart, 1987.

The Arctic Grail: The Quest for the North West Passage and the North Pole, 1818-1909, Viking (New York City), 1988, McClelland & Stewart, 1988.

The Great Depression, 1929-1939, McClelland & Stewart, 1990.

The Mysterious North: Encounters with the Canadian Frontier, 1947-1954, St. Martin's Press, 1991.

Niagara: A History of the Falls, McClelland & Stewart, 1992, Kodansha International (New York), 1997.

A Picture Book of Niagara Falls, McClelland & Stewart, 1993, as *Niagara Falls: A Picture Book,* St. Martin's Press, 1993.

Winter, Stoddart (Toronto), 1994.

The Remarkable Past: Tales from 'My Country' and 'The Wild Frontier,' McClelland & Stewart, 1995.

My Times: Living with History, 1947-1995 (autobiography), Doubleday Canada, 1995.

Farewell to the Twentieth Century (anthology), Doubleday Canada, 1996.

The Great Lakes, Stoddart, 1996.

Also author of screenplay and narrator for the National Film Board of Canada's documentary *City of Gold.* Author of plays, skits, songs, and lyrics for musical reviews. Author of book for musical *Paradise Hill,* first performed in 1967. Host of and participant in many Canadian television programs, such as *The Pierre Berton Show, Front Page Challenge,* and *The Great Debate.*

Contributor of numerous articles to magazines. Contributor of text to *Canada: Pictures of a Great Land,* produced by Jourgen F. Boden and Hans Scherz, Gage, 1976. Contributor of forewords to *The Pierre Berton Papers in McMaster University Library,* compiled by Susan Bellingham, University Library Press, 1974, and *Hell No, We Won't Go: Vietnam Draft Resisters in Canada* by Alan Haig-Brown, Raincoast Books, 1996. Contributor to *Bruce Lee: The Lost Interview,* Little-Wolff, 1994. Subject of interviews in Suzanne Levert's *Ontario* and *Quebec,* both Chelsea House, 1991, and *To Mark Our Place: A History of Canadian War Memorials* by Robert Shipley, University of Toronto Press, 1987. Two books by Janice Patton—*The Exodus of the Japanese* and *How the Depression Hit the West,* both McClelland & Stewart, 1973—are based on Berton's interviews from his television program *The Pierre Berton Show.* A collection of Berton's papers has been placed in McMaster University Library, Hamilton, Ont.

■ Adaptations

The National Dream: 1871-1881 and *The Last Spike: 1881-1885* were adapted into an eight-part television miniseries produced by the Canadian Broadcasting Corporation (CBC-TV) in 1974; *The Dionne Years: A Thirties Melodrama* was adapted for CBC-TV; *The Secret World of Og* was animated by Hanna Barbera, 1983.

■ Work in Progress

Worth Repeating, an anthology of out-of-print works; *Seacoasts; Farewell to the 20th Century, Volume II; Pierre Berton's Canada;* A picture book for children about the true adventures of a cat, illustrated by daughter Patsy Berton.

■ Sidelights

Often considered Canada's most popular writer as well as one of its best-known celebrities, Pierre Berton has become recognized among the most prominent Canadian voices of the late twentieth century. A journalist and editor; social commentator and satirist; scriptwriter for radio, television, and films; songwriter and librettist; and media personality as well as a writer of fiction and nonfiction for adults and young people, Berton is perhaps most highly regarded as a popular historian, an author whose well-researched, compelling studies of Canadian history are credited with informing Canadians about their rich heritage while helping to instill pride in the values and accomplishments of the Canadian people. Concerned with the establishment of a truly Canadian identity, Berton attempts in his writings to portray the past in an enlightening and entertaining manner. His narrative histories of the events that helped to shape Canada are praised for informing a large section of the Canadian public about their roots in an accessible and highly effective manner; several of these works are best-sellers that are considered definitive volumes on their subjects. Writing history for adults, Berton has created books on such subjects as the Klondike Gold Rush; the making of the Canadian Pacific Railway; the quest for the North West Passage and the North Pole; the War of 1812; the English Royal Family; the Great Depression; the cultural effects of the birth of the Dionne quintuplets; the history of the Great Lakes and Niagara Falls; the history of Western Canada, including frontier and pioneer life; and Canada's participation in World War I. He has also compiled collections of his newspaper columns, an introduction to salesmanship techniques, an assessment of contemporary Christianity, food guides, coffee-table books on Canada, an erotic novel, and two volumes of autobiography. As a writer for children and young adults, Berton is perhaps best known as the author of *The Secret World of Og,* a fantasy for primary graders about a group of children based on his own family who enter a strange underground world, and the "Adventures in Canadian History" series, a multivolume collection that addresses significant events and individuals in the development of Canada. As a literary stylist, Berton favors colorful, lively prose, and he is often lauded for the readability of his books. Many of his histories include first-person narrations, a feature that is appreciated for its immediacy by general readers and often disparaged by serious historians; the author has also been criticized for his prolificacy and for recycling some of his subjects. However, Berton is most often considered a Canadian national treasure, a writer whose body of work has greatly influenced the development of an authentic Canadian consciousness.

In her entry on Berton in the *Dictionary of Literary Biography,* Linda Shohet predicted, "It is likely that he will be judged by posterity as Canada's first genuine media man, a man who knew how to manipulate every medium to transmit his message. The journalism will be of scant interest and the books of the 1960s will gather dust, but the volumes of history will be read as long as

Canadians want to know about their roots and be entertained as they learn. Pierre Berton has altered Canadians' perceptions of themselves...." A contributor to *Current Biography* called Berton "the doyen of the Canadian media [who] has pursued with boundless energy what lesser mortals would consider to be the careers of half a dozen individuals.... [Even] his severest critics had to concede that, amidst the reams of film footage, newsprint, and other published material bearing his name, there lay a body of work of considerable literary value." *Maclean's* reviewer John Bemrose wrote that Berton has "championed the notion that Canadian history is as exciting as that of any other country. And more than any other writer, he has proven the truth of his own dictum by entertaining Canadians with expansive tales of their pasts." Writing in *Canadian Children's Literature,* Douglas Leighton called Berton "probably Canada's best-known writer" and claimed that his books "have brought the passion and drama of Canadian history to a wide popular audience, including younger readers." The critic concluded, "No one has done more to make Canadians aware of their pasts and of their collective selves than Pierre Berton.

In *The Secret World of Og,* Berton's highly successful book illustrated by his daughter, characters resembling the Berton children take a fantastic trip to a strange underground world and eventually befriend its inhabitants. (Illustrated by Patsy Berton.)

He is still an enthusiastic and articulate national voice as the twentieth century nears its end."

Born in Whitehorse in the Yukon Territory, Berton gained a love of knowledge and adventure from his father Frank and a talent for writing from his mother Laura, a journalist from a literary family. Frank Berton, a civil engineer, had been offered a teaching post at Queen's University in 1898 but instead went to the Klondike Valley to search for gold; he held a variety of jobs upon his return, including mountie, school principal, cabinetmaker, and self-taught dentist. Laura Berton was the daughter of Philips Thompson, a well-known Canadian journalist and socialist, and was herself a reporter for local newspapers as well as an aspiring novelist; an early member of the Canadian Authors Association, she published a memoir of her life in the Canadian Northwest, *I Married the Klondike,* in 1954.

Berton's childhood and youth on the frontier is credited with helping to spark his interest in his country's pioneer history. His mother remembers him as a small boy writing stories and telling tales to his younger sister Lucy. From the age of eleven, Berton wrote, illustrated, and published his own newspapers, which he would sell for a nickel or rent for a penny. At about the same time, Berton and his family went to visit relatives in Toronto, an experience that transformed him: he later noted in an interview in *Maclean's,* "I discovered the world at a much later date than most children. That initial sense of wonder and excitement has never quite left me. That's important, since part of writing is to make people see things." After graduating from high school, Berton entered Victoria College in Victoria, British Columbia, where his family had moved. He transferred to the University of British Columbia at Vancouver in 1939, and received a job after school as a reporter for the Vancouver *News-Herald.* At the end of the school year, Berton was selected to remain on the staff for the summer. After receiving his bachelor's degree in 1941, he stayed on at the *News-Herald* and became the youngest city editor on any Canadian daily newspaper of the time.

After joining the army for four years and attaining officer status, Berton returned to Vancouver, where he became a feature writer for the Vancouver *Sun.* In 1946, Berton married Janet Walker; the couple had eight children: five girls and three boys. He also became a freelancer for *Maclean's* and was offered the position of assistant editor at the magazine; in 1953, he was named managing editor. During the early 1950s, Berton began to supplement his income by writing books and appearing on radio and television programs. His first book, *The Royal Family: The English Monarchy from Victoria to Elizabeth,* became a best-seller in the United States; his second book, *The Mysterious North,* won the first Governor General's Award for nonfiction; his third book, *The Golden Trail: The Story of the Klondike Rush,* was his first book for children; his fourth book, *Klondike: The Life and Death of the Last Great Gold Rush,* won the author his second Governor General's Award and served as the basis for *City of Gold,* a documentary

Canadian historian Berton recounts the first discovery of gold in the Klondike and the wave of prospectors who came to the Yukon seeking fortune. (From *Bonanza Gold: The Great Klondike Gold Rush,* illustrated by Henry Van Der Linde.)

film that won the Grand Prix at the Cannes Film Festival. Convinced that public appearances would help sell his books, Berton left Maclean's in 1958 to join Canada's largest daily newspaper, the Toronto *Star.* As associate editor he wrote a daily column, "By Pierre Berton." For four years, Berton wrote twelve-hundred-word essays on a variety of topics, from his adventures in cooking to discussions of Aristotelian philosophy to exposes of government officials and shady business owners. In order to keep his columns available, Berton began publishing them in book form; his first collection, *Just Add Water and Stir,* won the Stephen Leacock Medal for Humor in 1959. In 1962, Berton became the first Canadian journalist to win two National Newspaper Awards in the same year. Shortly thereafter, he left the Toronto *Star* to concentrate on his writing and also launched *The Pierre Berton Show,* a television program that ran for eleven years.

After the Centennial Celebration of Confederation in 1967, an event that inspired a new interest in Canadian history, Berton began to concentrate on writing informational books on Canada's past. *The Great Railway,* a two-volume documentation of the building of the Canadian Pacific Railway, incorporates *The National Dream, 1871-1881* and *The Last Spike, 1881-1885.* Both volumes were best-sellers; the former set a sales record in Canadian publishing while the latter won Berton his third Governor General's Award for nonfiction. "The C.P.R. books," as they were known, became the basis for a well-received television miniseries produced by CBC; their popularity, wrote Linda Shohet in *Dictionary of Literary Biography,* caused Berton to be "hailed as creator of a new Canadian mythology." Throughout the 1970s, Berton continued to write books about both historical and contemporary Canada. At the beginning of the 1980s, he produced two volumes of history on the War of 1812—*The Invasion of Canada, 1812-1813* and *Flames across the Border: The Canadian-American Tragedy, 1813-1814*—which, Shohet noted, "fired the public imagination as much as his railway books did." In 1984, Berton completed his four-part saga of the opening of the Canadian West with *The Promised Land: Settling the West, 1886-1914.* Next, the author turned to World War I for subject matter. *Vimy,* his book about the Canadian assault on Vimy Ridge in 1917, was generally well received. However, the work also attract-

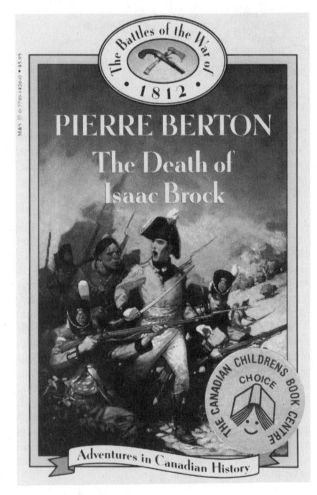

Part of a series of books on the important battles of the War of 1812, Berton's title recounts the details of the Battle of Queenston Heights, in which the renowned general Isaac Brock lost his life. (Cover illustration by Scott Cameron.)

ed some criticism, as have many of his books, especially from the academic community, which has sometimes faulted the author for his popular style. However, Berton is not usually bothered by his detractors. "History is history. Good history is good history," he told Linda Shohet in the *Dictionary of Literary Biography.* "I don't make any distinctions. If it's popular, it's something large numbers of people read. I would say my history is also scholarly. It's narrative history which is easier to read than expository history.... History books should read as much like novels as possible."

In 1987, Berton published the first volume of his autobiography, *Starting Out, 1920-1947,* which was praised for its candor; he completed his personal chronicle in *My Times: Living with History, 1947-1955,* a volume published in 1995. Berton received major critical attention for his epic *The Arctic Grail: The Quest for the North West Passage and the North Pole, 1818-1909,* which was published in 1988. During the 1990s, Berton continued to expand his oeuvre by addressing the natural wonders of Canada such as the Great Lakes and Niagara Falls as well as the beauty of Canadian winters; he was especially lauded for *The Great Depression, 1929-1939,* a passionate, searing account of Canada's lean years that is often considered among the author's finest works.

Several of the books that Berton directed to adults have also become popular with—and are recommended for—young people. Although he had written for children in the 1950s and 1960s, Berton began addressing his works to younger audiences most consistently in the 1990s. Due to the popularity of his fantasy story *The Secret World of Og,* the author was already respected as a children's writer when he began publishing his "Adventures in Canadian History" series. Berton based the protagonists of *Og* on five of his own children: Penny, Pamela, Patsy, Peter, and Paul, nicknamed the Pollywog. The children are playing in their playhouse on a summer afternoon when their cat, Earless Osdick, is carried off by a little green man; the youngest child, the Pollywog, follows. When they open a trapdoor sewn through their playhouse floor, the other children, accompanied by their faithful dog Yukon King, discover a secret tunnel and find themselves in a mushroom land filled with tiny green inhabitants who can only say the word "Og." Threatened by the children, whom they see as giants, the residents of Og try to capture the invaders. However, the two groups find a common bond when the siblings discover that the Og people are the keepers of the story books, comic books, toys, and other belongings lost by the children. Illustrated with color and black-and-white line drawings by Berton's daughter Patsy, *The Secret World of Og* was an immediate success in Canada when it was first published in 1961; the book was published in the United States in 1962, reissued in Canada with new illustrations by Patsy Berton in 1974, and republished with additional color plates in a Canadian edition in 1991. Writing in *Canadian Children's Literature,* Douglas Leighton said that "this delightful book ... may be [Berton's] most popular work." Evaluating the most recent edition in *Quill and Quire,*

Berton studies the industrious Slavic immigrants who, despite ridicule and prejudice, achieved prosperity in the Canadian West during the late nineteenth century. (From *The Men in Sheepskin Coats,* illustrated by Paul McCusker.)

Joan McGrath called *Og* "one of the most successful of Canadian children's fantasies." The critic noted, "Some of Berton's language will certainly demand a stretch on the part of young readers ... but for three generations now, child readers who seem to know what they like have been willing to make that stretch." She concluded, "This is a story for any 5-to-9 year-old who would love to visit a world of childlike (and childsize) little green people, just scary enough.... A classic of Let's Pretend." Writing in *Canadian Materials,* Ila D. Scott predicted, "[Future] young readers will no doubt enjoy visiting Og every bit as much as their counterparts have done in the past." In an interview with J. R. Moehringer in the *New York Times Book Review,* Berton called *The Secret World of Og* his favorite among his own works. The author said, "I get 30 letters a week from children who liked it. I got one that said, 'I'm six years old and this is the best book I ever read in my whole life.'"

In the late 1950s, Macmillan of Canada asked Berton to write a book about the Yukon gold rush for young readers to be part of their "Great Stories of Canada" series. Berton complied with *The Golden Trail,* which,

he told Douglas Leighton, "acted as kind of a pilot project" for his major adult work *Klondike.* "I got started in history," Berton said, "because I wrote my book on the Klondike Gold Rush." Berton's more recent histories for adults have also led to his current concentration on literature for older children and young adults. At his suggestion, McClelland & Stewart began publishing "Adventures in Canadian History," a series that began with four books on the War of 1812. In a review of the first volume in the series, *The Death of Isaac Brock,* Michele F. Kallio of *Canadian Materials* commented that in this new series Berton "brings the War of 1812 to life. His exciting retelling of the battle for Queenston Heights and the resulting death of General Isaac Brock is written with today's junior high school students in mind .... [The] reader feels part of the action. We are there in the thick of the battle." Writing in *Canadian Children's Literature* about two of the books covering the war, *Canada under Siege* and *Revenge of the Tribes,* Anna Chiota claimed that Berton addresses his material "in a manner both vivid and engaging. As adults have been drawn to his popularized histories, so too should a younger readership.... Pierre Berton, the storyteller, excels in weaving the facts, events and people of the period into compelling stories." In his next section of books within the series, Berton describes the Canadian gold rush from the first discovery of gold in the Klondike through the resulting influx of prospectors eager to make their fortunes. Reviewing two of these volumes, *Bonanza Gold* and *The Klondike Stampede,* in *Canadian Materials,* Jo Anna M. Patton claimed, "With the desperate need for readable Canadian history at the middle school level, these titles fill a real void." Berton also wrote several volumes in the subset "Exploring the Frozen North" that center on individuals such as Edward Parry, one of the Arctic's earliest explorers, and John Franklin, a British captain who searched for the elusive Northwest Passage. In her review of *Trapped in the Arctic,* an account of Robert John McClure's successful discovery of the route from the Atlantic to the Pacific, Anne Kelly said that as a lover of historical fiction, "I felt that the drama and suspense of the story would be lost in a simple retelling of the facts. I quickly realized this was not true. Pierre Berton has written an exciting, easy-to-read, well-researched tale." In the subset "Canada Moves West," Berton introduces young readers to the Canadian pioneers who helped to settle the West and to "The C.P.R.," the first Canadian transcontinental railway. Writing in *Canadian Children's Literature* about several volumes in the "Adventures in Canadian History" series, Eric Henderson noted, "Berton likes stories of the Promised Land, stories of ambitious mavericks doomed to disillusionment who engage in wild, idealistic quests for honour, fame or wealth.... Berton's interest here, as in his popular adult histories, is in the role personal ambition played in Canada's development." However, Douglas Leighton of *Canadian Children's Literature* countered that for "younger and mature readers alike, Berton's descriptions and insights have opened doorways that lead to enthusiastic rediscoveries of the Canadian past." Berton told Leighton, "I write the kind of book that I would read if I saw it in the windows of a bookstore.... I figured if it interests me, then maybe it would interest a lot of other people." Speaking on writing for the young, Berton concluded, "Young people are not interested in revisionist history.... What they are interested in is a recitation of events as interesting as we can make it. For young readers, I say what seems to have happened...."

■ Works Cited

Bemrose, John, comments in *Maclean's,* September 3, 1984.

Chiota, Anna, "Berton's Canadian History," *Canadian Children's Literature,* no. 67, 1992, pp. 75-77.

Current Biography Yearbook, Wilson, 1991.

Henderson, Eric, "Footnotes in Canadian History," *Canadian Children's Literature,* winter, 1993, pp. 78-80.

Kallio, Michele F., review of *The Death of Isaac Brock, Canadian Materials,* September, 1991, pp. 241-42.

Katz, Sidney, interview in *Maclean's,* October 20, 1962.

Kelly, Anne, review of *Trapped in the Arctic, Canadian Materials,* November, 1993, p. 221.

Leighton, Douglas, "*Profile:* Talking with Pierre Berton," *Canadian Children's Literature,* no. 83, 1996, pp. 43-49.

McGrath, Joan, review of *The Secret World of Og, Quill & Quire,* January, 1992, pp. 33-34.

Moehringer, J. R., "By Stagecoach in the Klondike," *New York Times Book Review,* November 20, 1988, p. 1.

Patton, Jo Anna M., review of *Bonanza Gold* and *The Klondike Stampede, Canadian Materials,* September, 1992, p. 218.

Scott, Ila D., review of *The Secret World of Og, Canadian Materials,* March, 1992, pp. 64-65.

Shohet, Linda, "Pierre Berton," *Dictionary of Literary Biography, Volume 68: Canadian Writers, 1920-1959,* Gale, 1988.

■ For More Information See

BOOKS

Hamilton, K. A., editor, *Canada Writes!,* Writers' Union of Canada, 1977.

PERIODICALS

Atlantic, November, 1988, p. 99.

Book World, April 4, 1982, p. 3.

Canadian Children's Literature, no. 15, 1980, p. 29; spring, 1993, pp. 40-42; no. 83, 1996, pp. 101-04.

Canadian Materials, October, 1992, pp. 273-74; January, 1993, p. 28; October, 1993, pp. 191-92.

Emergency Librarian, March, 1992, p. 58; March, 1994, p. 45.

Globe and Mail (Toronto), September 8, 1984; September 6, 1986; September 12, 1987; September 17, 1988; September 8, 1990.

Kirkus Reviews, August 1, 1988, p. 1111.

Los Angeles Times Book Review, May 30, 1982, p. 16; November 6, 1983, p. 4.

Maclean's, September 10, 1990, p. 79.

Newsweek, October 31, 1988, p. 73.

New York Times Book Review, November 12, 1972; December 10, 1978; February 22, 1981, p. 18; November 20, 1988, p. 1.

Publishers Weekly, August 9, 1985, p. 22.

Quill & Quire, December, 1991, p. 26; April, 1992, p. 34.

Village Voice Literary Supplement, May, 1989, p. 15.

Washington Post Book World, November 13, 1988, p. 5.

—Sketch by Gerard J. Senick

* * *

BIALE, Rachel 1952-

■ Personal

Born August 13, 1952, in Israel; daughter of Chaim (a teacher) and Anina (a therapist) Korati; married David Biale (a professor), 1973; children: Noam, Tali. *Education:* University of California, Los Angeles, B.A., 1976, M.A., 1978; Yeshiva University, Wurzweiler School of Social Work, M.S.W., 1981. *Religion:* Jewish.

■ Addresses

c/o—Jewish Family and Children's Services, 2484 Shattuck Ave, #210, Berkeley, CA 94704. *Electronic mail*—biale@socrates.berkeley.edu.

RACHEL BIALE

■ Career

Jewish Family and Children's Services of the East Bay, Berkeley, CA, clinical social worker and psychotherapy senior clinician, 1990-97. Jewish studies lecturer.

■ Awards, Honors

Smilen Award, 1985, for *Women in Jewish Law.*

■ Writings

FOR CHILDREN; "LET'S MAKE A BOOK ABOUT IT" SERIES

(And illustrator) *We Are Moving,* Tricycle Press (Berkeley, CA), 1996.
(And illustrator) *My Pet Died,* Tricycle Press, 1997.

OTHER

Women in Jewish Law, Schocken (New York, NY), 1984.

■ Work in Progress

Co-editing *Feminist Readings of Jewish Texts* for UC Press.

■ Sidelights

Rachel Biale told *SATA:* "My book series for parents and children, "Let's Make a Book About It," came out of my clinical work with children. Over and over, I found in my practice that making a book about a painful or challenging experience helps children cope with their experience, feel good about their abilities, and bring parents and kids closer."

*   *   *

BILSON, Geoffrey 1938-1987

■ Personal

Born January 27, 1938, in Cardiff, Wales; died of a brain tumor, July 25, 1987, in Saskatoon, Saskatchewan, Canada; married; wife's name, Beth; children: Max, Kate. *Education:* University College of Wales, Aberystwyth, B.A. (history); University of Omaha, M.A. (history and political science); Stanford University, Ph.D. (history). *Religion:* Anglican. *Hobbies and other interests:* Reading, travel, hiking in the mountains, movies, theatre, music.

■ Career

Writer. University of Saskatchewan, professor of history. *Member:* Saskatchewan Writers Guild, Open Door Society.

■ Awards, Honors

The Canadian Children's Book Centre established the Geoffrey Bilson Award for Historical Fiction in Bilson's memory.

■ Writings

FOR YOUNG PEOPLE

Goodbye Sarah (Kids Canada Series), illustrated by Ron Berg, Kids Can Press, 1981.
Death over Montreal (Kids Canada Series), Kids Can Press, 1982.
Hockeybat Harris, Kids Can Press, 1984.

NONFICTION; FOR ADULTS

The Boston Massacre, University of Saskatchewan, 1977.
A Darkened House: Cholera in Nineteenth-Century Canada, University of Toronto Press, 1980.
The Guest Children: The Story of the British Child Evacuees Sent to Canada during World War II, Fifth House Publishers, 1988.

Also author of articles on historical subjects for academic journals such as *Acadiensis.*

■ Adaptations

Goodbye Sarah was adapted for the stage and performed by Persephone Theatre, Saskatoon.

■ Sidelights

In a writing career cut short by his untimely death in 1987, Geoffrey Bilson published three novels for children that were inspired by his research as a historian and his experiences as a father. He was especially concerned to show the effects of historical events on children like his own. "I ask myself," he explained to the Canadian Children's Book Centre, "what it would be like to be a child in a particular time."

The son of a ship's radio officer, Bilson got his first sense of a world beyond his home from the postcards his father sent to the family from various ports of call. He displayed an appetite for writing at an early age: he and his brother produced a family magazine; at school, he won a class story competition. Later, as a professor of history, he researched and wrote about issues in his field. But as a father Bilson turned to fiction. He told the Canadian Children's Book Centre that while he was writing *A Darkened House,* his study of cholera in nineteenth-century Canada, he found that he "was making an interesting story dull." Bilson re-addressed the cholera epidemic in a work of fiction intended for his son Max, then age twelve. He began to write *Death over Montreal* one summer while his family was away on holiday. In this work, Bilson imagined Canada as it was in the 1830s and attempted to convey the devastation wrought by the cholera epidemic upon newly immigrated Scottish families.

Goodbye Sarah, Bilson's next novel for children and the first of these works to be published, was written with his daughter Kate in mind. In this story, the Winnipeg General Strike of 1919 poses a dilemma for friends whose parents have chosen different sides. Yet another academic project, a history of the children evacuated to Canada from Britain during World War II, culminated not only in the planned volume—*The Guest Children,* which was published posthumously—but also in *Hockeybat Harris,* a re-creation of the evacuees' experience from the point of view of one child, David Harris. This character, Bilson told the Canadian Children's Book Centre, "appeared one morning as a name and a face and a personality all quite vividly alive for me."

For Bilson, the process of developing a plot and characters was usually gradual, taking two years or more. He told the Canadian Children's Book Centre that he began his books lying in bed and thinking about the characters. Calling his methods "old-fashioned," he said he wrote the first draft in longhand—*Death over Montreal,* for example, was written at the kitchen table—and then transferred the story to the computer.

Bilson's works for children were praised for their seamless research. Writing about *Death over Montreal* in the Toronto *Globe and Mail,* Sandra Martin commented that the novel ended "rather abruptly," noting that Bilson had already proved that he had "the historical background and the creative juices ... to spin a few more chapters." Reviewing *Hockeybat Harris,* Martin concluded it "an excellent example of weaving period flags and signposts into a narrative." At the same time however, she suggested that, for Bilson, the story seemed to take second place to "the business of explaining times past and the currency of particular attitudes." Other commentators note, however, that Bilson clearly understood the importance of the story and purposely took liberties with some of his research material. "In *Death over Montreal,* for instance, Bilson takes the name of an actual doctor from his *Darkened House* and has him do and say things he probably never did or said," wrote Eric O. Burt in the *Saskatoon Star-Phoenix.* "Bilson is sure it doesn't cause any distortion of history and it does make the children's book more interesting."

Bilson's later career took on a more public character. The play he wrote based on *Goodbye Sarah* enjoyed considerable success when Saskatoon's Persephone Theatre staged it and took it on a tour of Saskatchewan schools. At the same time, Bilson was an active member of Writers in the Classroom, a joint program of the Saskatchewan Writers Guild and the Arts Board that brought together published authors and children wishing to cultivate their writing skills. Nor was his sensitivity to the immigrant experience confined to the printed page: as a member of the Open Door Society, he offered help and encouragement to many who were newly arrived in Canada.

In an obituary after Bilson's sudden death, his publisher, Valerie Hussey of Kids Can Press, described him as a "truly gentle man, so without guile." Indicating Bilson's stature among his colleagues, the Canadian Children's Book Centre established the Geoffrey Bilson Award for Historical Fiction in his memory.

■ Works Cited

Burt, Eric O., "Historian Furthers Children's Knowledge of Canada," *Saskatoon Star-Phoenix.*

"Introducing Geoffrey Bilson," Canadian Children's Book Centre, 1986.

"Geoffrey Bilson Dies Suddenly," *Children's Book News,* 1987, p. 6.

Martin, Sandra, "Pre-Adolescent Market Proves a Thorny One," *Globe and Mail* (Toronto), April 9, 1983, p. P4.

Martin, Sandra, "Tough Writing and Views about a Rough Childhood," *Globe and Mail* (Toronto), January 5, 1985, p. E14.

■ For More Information See

PERIODICALS

Booklist, March 15, 1985, p. 1055.

Canadian Children's Literature, No. 29, 1983, p. 45; No. 43, 1986, p. 60; No. 57, 1990, p. 82.

Quill & Quire, February, 1981, p. 45; November, 1982, p. 26; December, 1988, p. 25.*

* * *

BISSON, Terry (Ballantine) 1942-
(T. B. Calhoun; Brad Quentin)

■ Personal

Born February 12, 1942, in Hopkins County, KY; son of Max and Martha (Ballantine) Bisson; married Deirdre Holst, 1962 (divorced 1966); married Judy Jensen; children: (first marriage) Nathaniel, Peter, Zoe; (second marriage) Kristen, Gabriel, Welcome. *Education:* Attended Grinnell College, 1960-62; University of Louisville, B.A., 1964.

■ Addresses

Home—Brooklyn, NY. *Agent*—Susan Ann Protter, 110 West 40th St., New York, NY 10018.

■ Career

Writer. Magazine comic writer/editor, 1964-72; automotive mechanic, 1972-77; editor and copywriter with Berkley Books, New York City, and Avon Books, New York City, 1976-85; consultant to HarperCollins, 1994-98. *Member:* Science Fiction Writers of America, Authors Guild.

■ Awards, Honors

World Fantasy Award nomination, 1987, for *Talking Man;* Nebula Award, Science Fiction Writers of America, Hugo Award, World Science Fiction Convention, and Theodore Sturgeon Award, Center for the Study of

TERRY BISSON

Science Fiction, all 1991, all for story "Bears Discover Fire"; Phoenix Award, 1993.

■ Writings

FOR YOUNG ADULTS; NONFICTION

Nat Turner: Slave Revolt Leader, Chelsea, 1988.

"THE REAL ADVENTURES OF JONNY QUEST" SERIES; UNDER PSEUDONYM BRAD QUENTIN

Peril in the Peaks, HarperPrism, 1996.
The Demon of the Deep, HarperPrism, 1996.
Attack of the Evil Cyber-God, HarperPrism, 1997.

"NASCAR POLE POSITION ADVENTURES" SERIES; UNDER PSEUDONYM T. B. CALHOUN

Rolling Thunder, HarperPrism, 1998.
In the Groove, HarperPrism, 1998.
Race Ready, HarperPrism, 1998.

SCIENCE FICTION

Wyrldmaker, Pocket Books, 1980.
Talking Man, Arbor House (New York City), 1986.
Fire on the Mountain, Arbor House, 1988.
Voyage to the Red Planet, Morrow, 1990.
Bears Discover Fire and Other Stories, Tor Books (New York City), 1993.

Pirates of the Universe, Tor Books, 1996.

NOVELIZATIONS

Johnny Mnemonic: A Novel (from the screenplay by William Gibson), Pocket Books, 1995.
Virtuosity, Pocket Books, 1995.
Alien Resurrection, HarperCollins, 1997.
Fifth Element, HarperCollins, 1997.

OTHER

(With Tom and Ray Magliozzi) *Car Talk with Click and Clack, the Tappet Brothers* (adult nonfiction), Dell, 1991.
(With Elizabeth Ballantine Johnson) *A Green River Girlhood,* Green River (Owensboro, KY), 1991.
(Adaptor) *Roger Zelazny's Amber: The Guns of Avalon,* illustrated by Christopher Schenck and Andrew Pepoy, DC Comics, 1996.
(Adaptor) *Roger Zelazny's Nine Princes in Amber,* illustrated by Tom Roberts, DC Comics, 1996.
(With Walter M. Miller, Jr.) *Saint Leibowitz and the Wild Horse Woman: A Novel,* Bantam, 1997.

Contributor to *Washington Post, Omni, Playboy, Magazine of Fantasy and Science Fiction* and *Harper's.*

■ Adaptations

The stories "Two Guys from the Future," "They're Made out of Meat," "Next," "Are There Any Questions?," "Partial People," and "The Toxic Donut," were all adapted for the stage and produced at the West Bank Theatre, New York, 1992-93.

■ Sidelights

Terry Bisson is the author of several science fiction novels and short stories, including the critically acclaimed *Talking Man* and *Fire on the Mountain* novels and the Hugo and Nebula award-winning short story "Bears Discover Fire." Critics often compliment Bisson on his well-written prose, dry wit, and unique imagination. According to a *Publishers Weekly* commentator, Bisson "is one of science fiction's most promising short story practitioners." In addition to writing science fiction, Bisson has also written a young adult biography on antislavery leader Nat Turner and has collaborated

ISBN 0-87067-551-6 $3.95   *Illustrated Edition*

BLACK AMERICAN SERIES * BLACK AMERICAN SERIES * BLACK AMERICAN S

Nat Turner
PROPHET AND SLAVE REVOLT LEADER

By Terry Bisson

In his first work of nonfiction, Bisson writes of Turner's early life as a slave in Virginia, his mission as a preacher, and the infamous slave revolt he led in 1831. (Cover illustration by Jesse J. Santos.)

with other authors—including funnymen Tom and Ray Magliozzi, known for their popular "Car Talk" series on National Public Radio—to produce both fiction and nonfiction works.

Bisson's first science fiction novel, *Wyrldmaker,* features romance, action, and adventure. In the story, warrior and king Kemen receives a sword from a magical woman, Noese, who is also his lover. When Noese disappears, Kemen travels to faraway lands, meeting the most unusual people and creatures. He eventually finds Noese, only to discover that she is an extra-human creature. "Although flawed," wrote a *Publishers Weekly* reviewer, "this is an ambitious, action-filled first novel."

Bisson's next novel, *Talking Man,* was embraced by both readers and critics alike. In this work, a rural eccentric ironically nicknamed Talking Man (he never speaks) sets out on a cross-country journey. As the trip unfolds, Talking Man finds that the farther he travels from home, the more drastically the nation changes. By the time he returns home to rural Kentucky, society has undergone a radical alteration into a near-utopia. Jesus Salvador Trevino in the *Los Angeles Times Book Review* called *Talking Man* "an action-filled romp through a surreal landscape of ever-changing America." Roland Green, writing in *Booklist,* described it as an "intelligent, literate book ... filled with original ideas, well-chosen details, and finely polished characterizations."

Turning his attention to non-fiction, Bisson wrote *Nat Turner: Slave Revolt Leader* for young adult readers. In this work the author describes Turner's early life as a slave in Southampton County, Virginia, his mission as a preacher, and the infamous slave revolt of 1831. He also includes details about pre-Civil War Virginia and an overview of the history of slavery. *School Library Journal* contributor Elizabeth M. Reardon called Bisson's *Nat Turner* "a well-written, sympathetic biography of the leader of our nations' bloodiest slave revolt."

Again addressing the topic of slavery, Bisson's science fiction novel *Fire on the Mountain* posits an alternate history in which John Brown's raid on Harper's Ferry in 1859 was successful. The result is a national slave revolt and the establishment of an independent black country in the Southern United States. A *Publishers Weekly* reviewer claimed that the novel displays Bisson's "talent for evoking the joyful, vertiginous experiences of a world at fundamental turning points." In *Kirkus Reviews,* a critic noted that the author's "approach is original, fleshed with vivid detail and peopled with utterly convincing characters and incidents."

Bisson turned to satire in *Voyage to the Red Planet,* creating a future world where, following a great depression, government services have been sold to private corporations. In this privatized society, a movie producer named Markson sends a crew to Mars to make a film. During the long voyage, the corporation running mission control back on Earth has cash flow problems. They must focus their efforts on more lucrative activities.

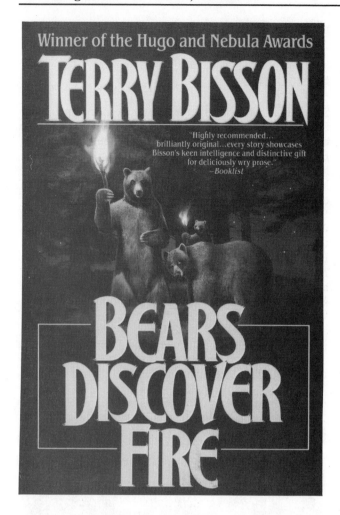

Including Bisson's award-winning title story, this collection contains nineteen of his acclaimed science fiction tales. (Cover illustration by Nick Jainschigg.)

Paul Kincaid, writing in the *St. James Guide to Science Fiction Writers,* called the novel "a comedy of ram-shackled adventure, and there are the predictable disasters and problems along the way, most of them casting a satirical light on the Earth left behind." In his "Science Fiction" column in the *New York Times Book Review,* Gerald Jonas stated that Bisson shows a "genuine affection for his characters" and has an "ability to remind us of the excitement and wonder of space travel even while poking fun at the conventions of space fiction."

In 1991, Bisson won three major literary awards—the Nebula, the Hugo, and the Theodore Sturgeon—for his short story "Bears Discover Fire," a story that manages to combine the nonsensical with the ordinary to remarkable effect. Martha Soukup in the *Washington Post Book World* describes "Bears Discover Fire" as "a gentle, wise tale of a man whose mother is dying, whose nephew wants to learn how to mount tires, and of bears who discover fire and now sit around campfires instead of hibernating." Two years later, this work was bound with a collection of other short stories in *Bears Discover Fire and Other Stories.* Commenting on the entire collection, Soukup noted that there is "a sharpness and wit that is

quite Bisson's own." Similarly, a *Kirkus Reviews* critic declared: "Bisson's distinctive style and priceless imagination lift his work to an altogether more exalted plane."

More recently, Bisson penned *Pirates of the Universe.* In this novel, Space Ranger Gunther Ryder is close to winning his coveted place in the retirement theme park Pirates of the Universe. But when he returns from his latest mission, Gunther "finds himself entangled in a Kafkaesque conundrum," as a critic for *Publishers Weekly* explained. When Gunther's anticipated paycheck never reaches him, he fears that he may not reach his beloved retirement home. Unable to e-mail anyone or use computer systems because of a bureaucratic snafu, Gunther is thus also unable to contact the proper bureaucracy to fix the problem. Eventually, after returning to the family home in rural America, Gunther discovers why he hasn't been paid and learns how he can get his money back. *New York Times Book Review* critic Jonas admired Bisson's "knack for capturing a reality that is never as simple as we would like to believe." Tom Easton, in his *Analog* review, asks, "Will anyone try to imitate ... *Pirates of the Universe?* I'm not at all sure Bisson is imitable, for he has a quite idiosyncratically cockamamie way of satirizing the world he sees." The reviewer added, however, that the story "does keep my disbelief in suspension well enough to let me marvel at the virtuosity of his imagination."

■ Works Cited

Review of *Bears Discover Fire and Other Stories, Kirkus Reviews,* September 1, 1993, p. 1105.

Review of *Bears Discover Fire and Other Stories, Publishers Weekly,* November 1, 1993, p. 70.

Easton, Tom, review of *Pirates of the Universe, Analog,* September, 1996, p. 145-52.

Review of *Fire on the Mountain, Kirkus Reviews,* June 1, 1988, p. 797.

Review of *Fire on the Mountain, Publishers Weekly,* June 3, 1988, p. 73.

Green, Roland, review of *Talking Man, Booklist,* October 1, 1986, p. 191.

Jonas, Gerald, review of *Voyage to the Red Planet, New York Times Book Review,* September 2, 1990, p. 18.

Jonas, Gerald, review of *Pirates of the Universe, New York Times Book Review,* May 12, 1996, p. 27.

Kincaid, Paul, "Terry Bisson," *St. James Guide to Fantasy Writers,* St. James Press, 1996.

Review of *Pirates of the Universe, Publishers Weekly,* March 25, 1996, p. 67.

Reardon, Elizabeth M., review of *Nat Turner: Slave Revolt Leader, School Library Journal,* February, 1989, p. 104.

Soukup, Martha, review of *Bears Discover Fire and Other Stories, Washington Post Book World,* November 28, 1993, p. 8.

Trevino, Jesus Salvador, review of *Talking Man, Los Angeles Times Book Review,* November 9, 1986, p. 13.

Review of *Wyrldmaker, Publishers Weekly,* May 29, 1981, p. 39.

For More Information See

BOOKS

St. James Guide to Science Fiction Writers, 4th edition, St. James Press, 1996.

PERIODICALS

Booklist, July, 1988, p. 1786; October 1, 1993, p. 258.
Kirkus Reviews, September 1, 1986, p. 1325; June 15, 1988, p. 896; February 1, 1996, p. 181.
Locus, April, 1990, p. 35; February, 1994, pp. 39, 42, 74.
Magazine of Fantasy and Science Fiction, April, 1989, p. 38; February, 1994, p. 39.
New York Times Book Review, November 13, 1988, p. 26; May 4, 1997, p. 32.
School Library Journal, December, 1990, p. 134; October, 1996, p. 162.
Voice of Youth Advocates, December, 1981, p. 38; February, 1987, p. 290; February, 1989, p. 298; August, 1996, pp. 165-66.
Washington Post Book World, November 27, 1988, p. 8; March 31, 1996, p. 8.

*   *   *

BJOERK, Christina 1938-

Personal

Born July 27, 1938, in Stockholm, Sweden.

Addresses

Home—Folkungagatan 78, 116 22 Stockholm, Sweden.

Career

Author, journalist, educator. *Member:* Swedish Authors Union, Swedish Journalists Union, Swedish Publicists Club.

Writings

How to Build and Fly Kites, Bonniers, 1974.
Inning Instead of Outing, Bonniers, 1975.
Stop Spraying, Bonniers, 1975.
You Are in Love, Aren't You?, Bonniers, 1976.
Are You Crazy?, Bonniers, 1976.
Mimmi's Book, Prisma, 1976.
Fiffi and Birger and Left and Right, Prisma, 1976.
Linnea in Monet's Garden, translated by Joan Sandin, illustrated by Lena Anderson, Farrar, Straus (New York City), 1987.
Linnea's Windowsill Garden, translated by Sandin, illustrated by Anderson, Farrar, Straus, 1988.
Linnea's Almanac, translated by Sandin, illustrated by Anderson, Farrar, Straus, 1990.
Elliot's Extraordinary Cookbook, translated by Sandin, illustrated by Anderson, Farrar, Straus, 1991.
The Story of Alice in Her Oxford Wonderland, illustrated by Inga-Karin Eriksson, R & S, 1994.

Big Bear's Book: By Himself, translated by Joan Sandin, R & S, 1995.

Sidelights

Swedish author Christina Bjoerk is best known for her books about a little girl named Linnea. In each of these books, which have been translated by Joan Sandin into English from the author's original Swedish, Linnea's love of flowers and gardening and her natural curiosity lead her to people like Mr. Bloom, from whom she can learn about plants and animals, and even the seasons of the year. In the book *Linnea in Monet's Garden,* which was published in English translation in 1987, Linnea travels with Mr. Bloom to Giverny and learns about French Impressionist painter Claude Monet, while in *Linnea's Almanac* she and Mr. Bloom study the animal and plant worlds as they change with the passage of the seasons. A. R. Williams in *Junior Bookshelf* calls Linnea "a city girl who brings the countryside into her home and heart. There is no plodding ... but some fresh interest or excitement at every turn." Among Bjoerk's other books for young readers are *Elliot's Extraordinary Cookbook, The Story of Alice in Her Oxford Wonder-*

In Christina Bjoerk's spirited *Linnea in Monet's Garden,* a young girl travels to Giverny to visit the home of the famous painter, learning about his life, his work, and nature through the instruction of her gardener friend, Mr. Bloom. (Illustrated by Lena Anderson.)

CHRISTINA BJÖRK

Big Bear's Book

BY HIMSELF

R&S BOOKS

Through the viewpoint of one of her treasured teddy bears, Bjoerk relates the story of her childhood, complemented by well-loved tales from her favorite children's books. (Cover photo by Nisse Peterson.)

land, and *Big Bear's Book: By Himself,* a history of the teddy bear.

The name that Bjoerk gives to her young protagonist is derived from that of Carolus Linnaeus, a Swedish botanist of the eighteenth century who created the system of plant and animal classification we now call the science of botany. The Linnea books are designed to give the young reader a knowledge of plants and animals. The popular success of *Linnea in Monet's Garden* has made the book almost a childhood classic, providing young readers with both a look at the restored home of the famous French painter and a colorful glimpse of life in Paris, where Linnea and Mr. Bloom spend several afternoons touring art museums in search of Monet's waterlily paintings and taking in the city sites. *Linnea's Windowsill Garden* provides an "informative, accurate, comprehensive, clear and well-organized" introduction for the beginning gardener, according to Zena Sutherland in the *Bulletin of the Center for Children's Books.* Frances E. Millhouser also praised the book in *School Library Journal,* writing that "Bjoerk offers a lively, chatty romp through indoor gardening, with a grinning Linnea as guide." Similarly, *Linnea's Almanac* gives recipes, craft projects, and nature lore suitable for each season of the year. The book is, according to Amy Adler in *School Library Journal,* "simultaneously instructive and entertaining."

In addition to the Linnea books, Bjoerk has written several other works for young readers. In *Elliot's Extraordinary Cookbook,* illustrated by Lena Anderson, a young boy spends the day with Stella Delight, a neighbor who teaches him how to cook the Swedish way and who, as the former cook to a ship, can make even the simplest potato dish seem dramatic. The entertaining conversation between Stella and Elliot provides the framework for a large collection of recipes, cooking tips, and cooking-related lore. Calling *Elliot's Extraordinary Cookbook* "pleasantly idiosyncratic," Deborah Stevenson noted in the *Bulletin of the Center for Children's Books* that Bjoerk's nonfiction shows "how many things a book with a well-executed single focus can embrace." In addition to instructions for preparing everything from hamburgers to fried eggs, the book touches upon such topics as world hunger, anatomy, nutrition, and the treatment of animals. Linnea even shows up at one point to help sample one of Elliot's concoctions, in a book that "works wonderfully because of [his] enthusiasm and sense of adventure," in the opinion of *School Library Journal* contributor Carolyn Jenks.

Bjoerk has always loved stuffed bears, and, in *Big Bear's Book: By Himself,* she lets her teddy bears speak for themselves. In photographs and text, Big Bear, the largest teddy in Bjoerk's collection, tells about his life experiences, which mostly revolve around the telling of bedtime stories. Recalling the years when Bjoerk was a child, Big Bear remembers the stories told to the author by her parents, tales taken from books like *The Wind in the Willows, Winnie the Pooh,* and *Heidi.* Although Big Bear and his furry friends were packed in boxes and stored in a dark attic for what seemed like an eternity when Bjoerk got too old to play with such things or listen to bedtime stories, the boxes came back down and the collection of stuffed bears was once more displayed when the writer moved out on her own as an adult. Comparing *Big Bear's Book* to a family photograph album, *School Library Journal* commentator Marilyn Taniguchi called the book "a whimsical reminiscence of childhood ... filled with intimate details."

In *The Story of Alice in Her Oxford Wonderland,* Bjoerk writes about the classic story of Alice and her trip to Wonderland, as well as about Alice's creator, nineteenth-century British author and mathematician Charles Ludwig Dodgson, alias Lewis Carroll. Containing drawings by both Dodgson and Inga-Karin Eriksson, early black and white photographs, and copies of some of Dodgson's own letters and mathematical puzzles, the book is, according to *School Librarian* contributor Elspeth S. Scott, an unusual but nonetheless enjoyable mixture of fact and fiction that "could stimulate all sorts of discussion, especially with children who have read *Alice.*" Calling the book "enchanting" and praising Eriksson's illustrations for their ability to "reveal most convincingly the spirit of Victorian Oxford," *Junior Bookshelf* reviewer Marcus Crouch agreed with Scott, commenting that Bjoerk "gives a lively account of the known facts.... Mostly she is amusing, sincere and accessible."

■ Works Cited

Adler, Amy, review of *Linnea's Almanac, School Library Journal,* April, 1990, p. 102.

Crouch, Marcus, review of *The Story of Alice in her Oxford Wonderland, Junior Bookshelf,* February, 1995, pp. 31-32.

Jenks, Carolyn, review of *Elliot's Extraordinary Cookbook, School Library Journal,* May, 1991, p. 100.

Millhouser, Frances E., review of *Linnea's Windowsill Garden, School Library Journal,* November, 1988, p. 100.

Scott, Elspeth S., review of *The Story of Alice and Her Oxford Wonderland, School Librarian,* May, 1995, p. 68.

Stevenson, Deborah, review of *Elliot's Extraordinary Cookbook, Bulletin of the Center for Children's Books,* May, 1991, pp. 210-11.

Sutherland, Zena, review of *Linnea's Windowsill Garden, Bulletin of the Center for Children's Books,* December, 1988, p. 92.

Taniguchi, Marilyn, review of *Big Bear's Book: By Himself, School Library Journal,* April, 1995, p. 130.

Williams, A. R., review of *Linnea's Almanac, Junior Bookshelf,* February, 1990, pp. 21-22.

■ For More Information See

BOOKS

Children's Literature Review, Volume 22, Gale (Detroit), 1991.

PERIODICALS

Bulletin of the Center for Children's Books, February, 1988, p. 111.

Children's Literature in Education, June, 1989, pp. 91-101.

Junior Bookshelf, December, 1987, p. 272.

Kirkus Reviews, October 1, 1988, p. 1464.

Publishers Weekly, September 30, 1988, p. 64.

School Library Journal, January, 1993, p. 35.*

*   *   *

BROWN, Laurene Krasny
See BROWN, Laurie Krasny

*   *   *

BROWN, Laurie Krasny 1945-
(Laurene Krasny Brown, Laurene Krasny Meringoff)

■ Personal

Born December 16, 1945, in New York, NY; daughter of Morris Krasny (an accountant) and Helen Brauner (a former teacher; maiden name, Meyer); married Stephen Meringoff, August 27, 1967 (divorced September, 1974); married Marc Brown (an author and illustrator), September 11, 1983; children: Eliza Morgan; (stepchil-

dren) Tucker Eliot, Tolon Adam. *Education:* Cornell University, B.S., 1966; Columbia University, M.A., 1967; Harvard University, Ed.D., 1978. *Religion:* Jewish. *Hobbies and other interests:* Letter writing, photography, paper-making and marbling, and gardening.

■ Addresses

Home and office—562 Main St., Hingham, MA 02043. *Agent*—Phyllis Wender, 3 East 48th St., New York, NY 10017.

■ Career

Freelance author, children's books and magazines, 1984—. Harvard University, Cambridge, MA, research associate and co-director of Project Zero (program of media research with children), 1978-83; consultant to academic researchers, children's advocacy organizations, and to Federal Trade Commission on effects of TV advertising on children, 1974-80. Has also taught in Head Start, sold educational toys, and been active in local schools and synagogue. *Member:* American Film Institute, Society for Research in Child Development, Massachusetts Horticultural Society.

Laurie Krasny Brown with daughter, Eliza Morgan

What About You?
When your parents divorce, it's natural to feel

sad | angry | ashamed | guilty

afraid | confused | relieved | worried about who will take care of you.

The bad feelings won't last forever, and there is plenty you can do to help yourself feel better.

Through the experiences of a family of dinosaurs, the author and her husband, illustrator Marc Brown, relate a child's concerns about divorce and the formation of blended families. (From *Dinosaurs Divorce: A Guide for Changing Families.*)

■ Awards, Honors

Grants from the National Association of Broadcasters, 1976-77, and John and Mary R. Markle Foundation, 1977-83; Notable Children's Book, Association for Library Services to Children of the American Library Association, runner-up for Best Children's Book of the Year, *Redbook,* and Best Books, *School Library Journal,* all 1984, all for *The Bionic Bunny Show; Reading Rainbow* title, PBS-TV, 1989, for *Visiting the Art Museum;* Notable Book designation, *New York Times,* 1986, for *Dinosaurs Divorce: A Guide for Changing Families.*

■ Writings

FOR CHILDREN; ILLUSTRATED BY MARC BROWN

The Bionic Bunny Show, Atlantic/Little, Brown (Boston), 1984.
Visiting the Art Museum, Dutton, 1986.
Dinosaurs Divorce: A Guide for Changing Families, Atlantic/Little Brown, 1986.
Dinosaurs Travel: A Guide for Families on the Go, Joy Street (Boston), 1988.
Yellow Fish, Blue Fish, Heath, 1989.
Dinosaurs Alive and Well: A Guide to Good Health, Little, Brown, 1990.
Dinosaurs to the Rescue! A Guide to Protecting Our Planet, Joy Street, 1992.
Rex and Lilly Family Time, Little, Brown, 1995.
Rex and Lilly Play Time, Little, Brown, 1995.
(And illustrator) *The Vegetable Show,* Little, Brown, 1995.
When Dinosaurs Die: A Guide to Understanding Death, Little, Brown, 1996.
Rex and Lilly School Time, Little, Brown, 1997.
What's the Big Secret? Talking about Sex with Girls and Boys, Little, Brown, 1997.

How to Be a Friend: A Guide to Making Friends and Keeping Them, Little, Brown, 1998.

OTHER

(Contributor, as Laurene Krasny Meringoff) R. Adler, editor, *Effects of TV Advertising on Children,* Lexington Books, 1980.
(Editor, as Laurene Krasny Meringoff) *Children and Television: Annotated Bibliography,* Council of Better Business Bureaus, 1980.
(Contributor, as Laurene Krasny Meringoff) J. Bryant and D. R. Anderson, editors, *Children's Understanding of TV,* Academic Press, 1983.
Taking Advantage of Media: A Manual for Parents and Teachers, Routledge (Boston), 1986.
Baby Time: A Grownup's Handbook to Use with Baby, Knopf, 1989.
Toddler Time: A Book to Share with Your Toddler, Joy Street, 1990.

Contributor to periodicals, including *School Library Journal, Journal of Aesthetic Education, Language Arts,* and *Journal of Educational Psychology.*

■ Sidelights

Laurie Krasny Brown is a picture book author fortunate enough to be married to an illustrator. Beginning her writing career working alongside author/illustrator Marc Brown, she has amused and entertained both children and their parents while educating her readers as well. The experiences of Brown's Dinosaur family, whom readers first meet in *Dinosaurs Divorce: A Guide for Changing Families,* are presented in a way that appeals to a wide readership; their adventures while on vacation, their concerns about the environment and nutrition, and their efforts to understand and cope with death are all recounted in sensitive prose that doesn't talk down to children. In addition to her books for young people, Brown has also authored several book for their parents, including *Toddler Time: A Book to Share with Your Toddler,* and *Baby Time: A Grownup's Handbook to Use with Baby,* a new-parent survival guide to the stages of infancy that offers encouragement and perspective on those first, trying years together.

Brown was born and raised in New York City, which she recalls as "a wonderfully exciting place to explore, always changing, always surprising you with something new." Accepted at New York's High School of Music and Art, she studied piano and played violin in a

student orchestra. While she tinkered with the idea of becoming a concert pianist, Brown eventually decided that spending more than three hours of each day at practice wasn't a sacrifice she was willing to make. Instead, she enrolled at Cornell University, where she received a B.S. in child development, psychology, and education, before going on to graduate school at both Columbia and Harvard Universities. After graduating with advanced degrees in the education field, it's not surprising that Brown would find herself working closely with children. "I've sold toys, done counseling and intelligence testing, taught preschool, testified in Washington, D.C. about the effects on children of television

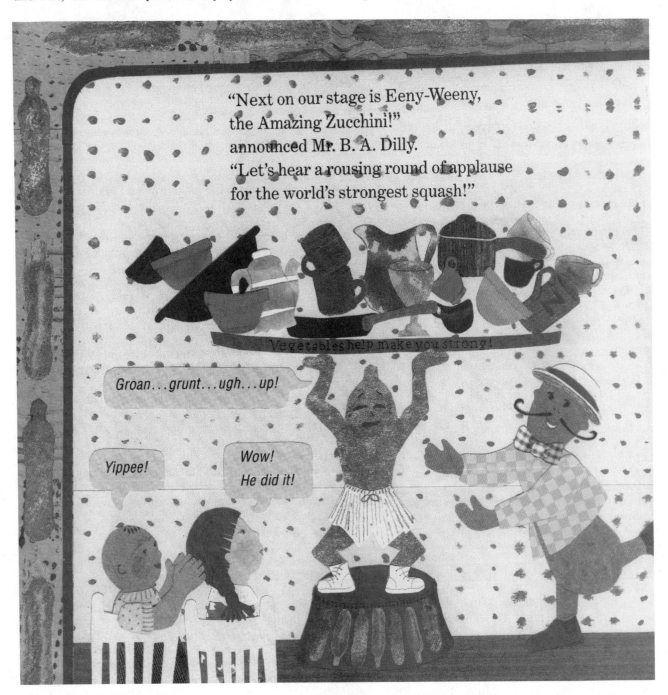

Brown employs mixed-media cut-paper artwork in her humorous portrayal of a circus show featuring vegetable characters. (From *The Vegetable Show.*)

advertising, investigated what children learn from radio, film, television and picture books, and evaluated commercials for toys, breakfast cereals, and other products promoted to children," Brown once explained to *Something about the Author* (*SATA*). "I still give producers advice about the various videos, films or other media projects they hire me to look at."

Despite her varied jobs in a field she loved, which kept her around children and their books, Brown soon realized that *she* wanted to be the person writing the books or producing the videos—"that is, I wanted to do the creating myself. Rather than finding out what children as audience members liked or disliked, I wanted to try making the materials for them to enjoy." It would be a quick step from idea to reality, especially because she knew one of the best illustrators of children's books in the business—her husband, Marc Brown, author and illustrator of the popular *Arthur* books. "It was simply too tempting to resist," Brown recalled. Beginning with *The Bionic Bunny Show,* the team of Brown and Brown have entertained children and parents alike with stories of dinosaurs, bears, and children exploring their world.

Dinosaurs Divorce, a joint effort of the Browns, is written in comic-book format. Looking at parents' marriage problems from a child dinosaur's perspective, the book offers sage advice ("If parents want you to carry messages back and forth, ask them to do it themselves") that help young people cope with the emotional upheaval of divorce, while also trying to understand their parents' side of things. Finding a new place to live, where to go on the holidays, getting along with step-brothers, step-sisters, and step-parents, dealing with family counselors while parents try to hash out their problems, and not having as much money as before are all things that readers can share with these green-faced young dinos. Calling the book an "upbeat treatment" of the impact of divorce, *School Library Journal* contributor Mary Lou Budd predicted that *Dinosaurs Divorce* would become a "'security blanket' for those young readers in need."

Other books featuring the dinosaur family include *Dinosaurs Travel: A Guide for Families on the Go,* which finds the reptile bunch on everything from skateboards to bikes to boats as they undertake a family vacation. In *Dinosaurs Alive and Well,* the Browns teach young readers how to care for their own bodies. "Taking care of yourself means treating yourself well every single day—looking out for your body, your mind, and your spirit" is the message of this book, which covers such topics as diet, exercise, first aid, stress, and self-esteem through the antics of the carefree dino twins, whose shenanigans provide "the levity necessary to raise this book from the didactic to the delightful," according to *Horn Book* reviewer Ellen Fader.

Who would be more concerned about environmental problems than a family of supposedly extinct dinosaurs? In *Dinosaurs to the Rescue: A Guide to Protecting Our Planet,* the dino family lays it on the line for young readers: If we don't conserve our planet's gifts, the Earth's natural resources, they won't be around long, and neither will we. Showing the antics of the ecologically unaware Slobosaurus, children are shown what *not* to do in a humorous fashion that keeps their interest. Conservation, recycling, and combating pollution in all its forms are covered, making *Dinosaurs to the Rescue* "a forceful environmental guide for the youngest readers—and listeners," according to a *Publishers Weekly* critic. Containing several do-at-home projects that allow readers to actively participate in making a positive impact on the planet, the book is also printed on recycled paper.

The most serious message of Brown's dinosaur books comes in *When Dinosaurs Die: A Guide to Understanding Death.* Even young children sometimes have to cope with death—the loss of an elderly great-grandparent or other family relative, or friends and family members who die under more tragic circumstances. In *When Dinosaurs Die,* death is depicted as a part of living, different from sleep, but inevitable to us all. Feelings of sadness and how different people mourn are discussed in a manner characterized by *Bulletin of the Center for Children's Books* reviewer Deborah Stevenson as "quiet, respectful, and unthreatening." However, other critics felt that the comic-book format and dinosaur characters that served to communicate with children in previous dinosaur books was out of place here; "somehow, bright and cheerful dinosaurs with cartoon dialogue balloons are not suited to the subject," was the opinion of Melissa Hudak in *School Library Journal.* However, a *Publishers Weekly* critic disagreed, praising the Browns for "a commendable service for grieving children and the adults in their lives."

In addition to her dinosaur books, Brown has collaborated with her husband on other volumes, also in the lighthearted comic-book format that engages young readers. In *Visiting the Art Museum,* published in 1986, they provide a humorous view of how children really behave at an art museum. Including reproductions of major works of art, the book provides suggestions to parents as to how to make these family trips more enjoyable for all parties concerned, and attempts to present a basic introduction to different styles of art—from the Masters to Jackson Pollock. Ethel L. Heins of *Horn Book* characterized the work as "lighthearted but not facetious," noting that *Visiting the Art Museum* "should quicken the interest of children without trivializing the subject matter." And in *What's the Big Secret? Talking about Sex with Girls and Boys,* Brown grapples with that most difficult of topics with what *Horn Book* commentator Nancy Vasilakis called "a healthy mix of sensitivity and humor."

"Picture books are especially fun, because words and pictures can work together so well," Brown once explained. "You get to be involved in designing the whole book—with the publisher's help—and figuring out things like just how much to say in the text on each page and how much to show in the illustration." The birth of Brown's daughter, Eliza, inspired the author with even more ideas, "because I read to her so much and see what kinds of things interest her." Eventually, Brown even decided to try her hand at the picture part of the picture book, publishing her self-illustrated *The Vegetable Show* in 1995. Featuring such characters as Eeny-Weeny, the Amazing Zucchini, the agile Tip-Tip Tomato Twins, and the dancing Veggettes all cavorting beneath the big top, the book is sure to capture a child's interest with its bright colors and silly humor. "Even the vegetably challenged will be won over by the pixiness of Brown's whimsical collages," maintained a *Publishers Weekly* reviewer.

"I love writing for children," Brown told *SATA*. "Every book is a great challenge, a mystery to be solved."

■ **Works Cited**

Brown, Laurene Krasny, *Dinosaurs Alive and Well: A Guide to Good Health,* Little, Brown, 1990.

Brown, Laurene Krasny, *Dinosaurs to the Rescue! A Guide to Protecting Our Planet,* Joy Street, 1992.

Budd, Mary Lou, review of *Dinosaurs Divorce: A Guide for Changing Families, School Library Journal,* October, 1986, pp. 156-57.

Review of *Dinosaurs to the Rescue! A Guide to Protecting Our Planet, Publishers Weekly,* January 27, 1992, p. 95.

Fader, Ellen, review of *Dinosaurs Alive and Well: A Guide to Good Health, Horn Book,* May-June, 1990, pp. 345-46.

Heins, Ethel L., review of *Visiting the Art Museum, Horn Book,* November, 1986, p. 754.

Hudak, Melissa, review of *When Dinosaurs Die: A Guide to Understanding Death, School Library Journal,* April, 1996, p. 122.

Stevenson, Deborah, review of *When Dinosaurs Die: A Guide to Understanding Death, Bulletin of the Center for Children's Books,* March, 1996, p. 220.

Vasilakis, Nancy, review of *What's the Big Secret? Talking about Sex with Girls and Boys, Horn Book,* January-February, 1998, pp. 89-90.

Review of *The Vegetable Show, Publishers Weekly,* April 10, 1995, p. 61.

Review of *When Dinosaurs Die: A Guide to Understanding Death, Publishers Weekly,* April 1, 1996, p. 75.

■ **For More Information See**

PERIODICALS

Booklist, April 15, 1992, p. 1533; April 15, 1995, p. 1509; June 1 & 15, 1995, p. 1774; October 1, 1997, p. 326.

Bulletin of the Center for Children's Books, November, 1986, p. 43; February, 1987, p. 102; May, 1990, p. 209.

Horn Book, January, 1987, p. 42; March-April, 1990, p. 223; January, 1991, pp. 92-93; July, 1992, pp. 464-65.

Kirkus Reviews, July 15, 1986, p. 1125; October 15, 1986, p. 1586; July 15, 1988, p. 1056; March 15, 1992, p. 403.

Publishers Weekly, November 10, 1989, p. 59; July 7, 1997, p. 67.

School Librarian, May, 1991, p. 64.

School Library Journal, March, 1990, pp. 205-06; January, 1991, pp. 85-86; August, 1995, p. 115; March, 1998, p. 193.

*   *   *

BULL, Emma 1954-

■ **Personal**

Born December 13, 1954, in Torrance, CA; daughter of Volney R. and Dorothy (Harris) Bull; married Will Shetterly (a writer and editor), October 17, 1981. *Education:* Beloit College, B.A., 1976.

■ **Addresses**

Home—Studio City, CA. *Agent*—Valerie Smith, 1746 Route 44/55, Modena, NY 12548.

■ **Career**

Writer. Performer with Cats Laughing, a Minneapolis psychedelic jazz/folk band, and with the Flash Girls, a Celto-Goth acoustic duo; co-owner of SteelDragon Press, specializing in hardcover fantasy and comic books. Worked variously as an editor of corporate publications, a rubber stamp maker, a car parker at a summer resort, a security guard, a folksinger, and a car salesman. *Member:* Minnesota Science Fiction Society,

EMMA BULL

Minneapolis Scribblies, Writers Guild of America, West.

■ Awards, Honors

Selection, three hundred best books for young adults, New York Public Library, 1987, and Best First Novel, *Locus* magazine poll, 1987, both for *War for the Oaks;* Nebula Award nomination, Hugo nomination, both for *Bone Dance.*

■ Writings

War for the Oaks, Ace/Berkley, 1987.
Falcon, Ace, 1989.
"A Bird that Whistles," *Hidden Turnings: A Collection of Stories Through Time and Space,* edited by Diana Wynne Jones, Greenwillow, 1990.
Bone Dance, Ace, 1991.
"Silver or Gold," *After the King: Stories in Honor of J. R. R. Tolkien,* edited by Martin H. Greenberg, Tor, 1992.
(With Will Shetterly) *Double Feature,* NESFA Press, 1994.
The Princess and the Lord of Night (picture book), illustrated by Susan Gaber, Harcourt Brace, 1994.
Finder: A Novel of the Borderlands, Tor, 1994.
(With Steven Brust) *Freedom and Necessity,* Tor, 1997.

Contributor to anthologies, including *Sword and Sorceress,* DAW, 1984; *Liavek,* Ace/Berkley, 1985; *Liavek: The Players of Luck,* Ace/Berkley, 1986; *Bordertown,* New American Library, 1986; *Life on the Border,* Tor, 1991; *The Armless Maiden and Other Tales for Childhood's Survivors,* Tor, 1995.

■ Work in Progress

Territory, a historical fantasy set in Tombstone, Arizona in the early 1880s; with Will Shetterly, "Virtual Meltdown," a feature-length animated science fiction movie, in development with Perfect World Entertainment.

■ Sidelights

Since the publication of her first book, *War for the Oaks,* Emma Bull has won attention from critics for her engaging, imaginative fantasies featuring tough, non-traditional characters. In the words of *Booklist* critic Carl Hays, Bull has "forged a stellar reputation for sharply original storytelling." While most of Bull's fantasy works, short stories, and novels are written for adult and young adult audiences, she has also contributed an original fairy tale, *The Princess and the Lord of Night,* to children's literature.

Bull, who has performed in rock and folk bands in Minneapolis, set her first novel in that city. Although *War for the Oaks* takes place in contemporary Minneapolis, it involves characters seemingly invisible to almost everyone but the book's fictional heroine, Eddi McCandry. The war for the oaks is being fought by fairies, some of whom want Eddi to help them out. Meanwhile, Eddi,

Cursed at birth to receive everything she wants or else see her kingdom be destroyed, a young princess sets out on a quest for true contentment. (From *The Princess and the Lord of the Night,* written by Bull and illustrated by Susan Gaber.)

a guitarist, forms a band, which takes part in the story's final duel of magic. *Booklist*'s Roland Green appreciated the novel's female protagonist, and Barbara Evans of *Voice of Youth Advocates* found that the book provides "exciting reading."

A member of a royal family on the fictional planet Cymru is the subject of *Falcon.* The title hero, Falcon, defies his family to pursue justice for his people. Then, despite attempted assassinations and a coup that destroys his family, Falcon survives to become an exile. As a space pilot, Falcon experiences adventure, romance, and intrigue while discovering more about his family's past. Gerald Jonas of *New York Times Book Review* noted Bull's "love of language" and "well-formed descriptive sentences." Roland Green of *Booklist* lauded Bull's "world building."

Bone Dance, set in Minnesota years after a nuclear holocaust, features a teenaged video and CD dealer named Sparrow. Sparrow, an androgynous character who has suffered from blackouts for years, enjoys his own secret stock of video and audio equipment and works at a nightclub when he is not dealing. Yet, gradually, two warring members of the esoteric Horsemen group appear and change his life. The Horsemen, who have the power to take over the minds of others, worked for the United States government before the war. Clones, created as hosts for Horsemen, were stored then, but the nuclear war caused by the Horsemen leads to their neglect. Sparrow is one such clone, and despite his moderate success building a human self, he becomes an integral part of the Horsemen's feud. A *Publishers Weekly* critic found that "eventually the off-beat characters draw the reader in." A *School Library Journal* critic called the book "another winner." Writing in *Analog,* Tom Easton commented that the book is "worthy of applause."

Bull's fourth novel is a contribution to the Borderland series created by Terri Windling, which includes anthologies as well as two novels written by Bull's husband, Will Shetterly. *Finder: A Novel of the Borderlands,* a detective, science fiction, and fantasy novel, is set in the fictional city of Bordertown. In this magical city where young elves and humans mingle, a new drug called Passport is rumored to allow humans to turn into elves and cross into the land of the elves. Instead, the drug kills its users. Sunny Rico, a female police officer, enlists Orient in her attempt to find the Passport drug dealer. Orient, a "finder" who is pulled to anything or anyone one wants to find, helps Rico only because she threatens to reveal his criminal past if he does not. Together, Sunny and Orient work to stop the dissemination of Passport and the new virus that is affecting elves—including Orient's best friend, a female elf motorcycle mechanic.

A *Kirkus Reviews* critic described *Finder* as "refreshing" and "ingenious," and noted its "splendid ideas and beguilingly life-like characters." *Voice of Youth Advocates* contributor Paula Lewis remarked that the book is an "excellent choice for sophisticated YA readers." *School Library Journal* contributor Cathy Chauvette praised Bull's "genre crossover": "one finds the tears on one's cheek with a shock." Faren Miller of *Locus* commented that Bull's work "brings new maturity" to the Borderlands series.

Freedom and Necessity, a novel which Bull wrote with fantasy writer Steven Brust, is set in Victorian England. It opens as a young Englishman appears to die in an accident while out boating. Then, when the man's cousin receives a letter from him, the story, according to Roland Green in *Booklist,* "becomes an exceptional page-turner." Referring to the book as a "romantic mystery-adventure," a *Publishers Weekly* critic lauded its "engaging characters and surprises."

A curse threatens an entire kingdom in *The Princess and the Lord of Night,* Bull's first picture book. When the Lord of Night deems that a newborn princess must be given everything she wants, or else the king and queen will die and the kingdom will be ruined, the princess tries to live a life devoid of greed. She takes great pleasure in what she already has: beloved pets and a magical cloak. Yet, on her thirteenth birthday, the princess feels that she wants something and goes out in search of it. On her journey, the generous princess gives away her possessions. The story concludes when the girl's good deeds and good motives—along with a magical ring she has been given—release her from the curse. A *Publishers Weekly* critic described the heroine of this "enchanting" and "lyrical fairy tale" to be "spunky and intelligent." Lauralyn Persson of *School Library Journal* found the book's "formal language" to be "elegant and vivid."

■ Works Cited

Review of *Bone Dance, Publishers Weekly,* April 12, 1991, p. 54.

Review of *Bone Dance, School Library Journal,* December, 1991, p. 152.

Chauvette, Cathy, review of *Finder, School Library Journal,* June, 1995, p. 143.

Easton, Tom, review of *Bone Dance, Analog,* November, 1991, p. 164.

Evans, Barbara, review of *War for the Oaks, Voice of Youth Advocates,* February, 1988, p. 286.

Review of *Finder, Kirkus Reviews,* December 15, 1993, p. 1555.

Review of *Freedom and Necessity, Publishers Weekly,* January 27, 1997, p. 77.

Green, Roland, review of *Falcon, Booklist,* October 1, 1989, p. 265.

Green, Roland, review of *Freedom and Necessity, Booklist,* March 15, 1997, p. 1231.

Green, Roland, review of *War for the Oaks, Booklist,* September 15, 1987, p. 112.

Hays, Carl, review of *Finder, Booklist,* February 15, 1994, p. 1064.

Jonas, Gerald, review of *Falcon, New York Times Book Review,* October 1, 1989, p. 40.

Lewis, Paula, review of *Finder, Voice of Youth Advocates,* June, 1994, pp. 96-98.

Miller, Faren, review of *Finder, Locus,* February, 1994, p. 19.

Persson, Lauralyn, review of *The Princess and the Lord of Night, School Library Journal,* May, 1994, p. 89.

Review of *The Princess and the Lord of Night, Publishers Weekly,* February 28, 1994, p. 87.

■ For More Information See

PERIODICALS

Horn Book Guide, Fall, 1994, p. 299.
Kirkus Reviews, March 1, 1994, p. 300.
Kliatt, September, 1995, p. 18.
Science Fiction Chronicle, June, 1994, p. 42.
Voice of Youth Advocates, December, 1990, p. 269.

C

CALHOUN, T. B.
See BISSON, Terry (Ballantine)

*   *   *

CAMPBELL, Peter A. 1948-

■ Personal

Born January 14, 1948, in Providence, RI; son of
Roland (a grocer) and Irene (Laliberte) Campbell;
married Karen (a director of office operations), April
22, 1978; children: Seth, Jeremy, Brendan. *Education:*
Vesper George School of Art, 1970. *Religion:* Catholic.

■ Addresses

Home—42 Holiday Dr., Lincoln, RI 02865.
Agent—Stauch-Vetromile & Mitchell, 55 South Brow
St., East Providence, RI 02914. *Electronic
mail*—svmpcampbl@aol.com.

■ Career

Artist. Has also worked as an art director and creative
director for several Rhode Island advertising agencies.
Member: National Society of Painters in Casein and
Acrylic.

■ Writings

(And illustrator) *Launch Day,* Millbrook Press (Brookfield, CT), 1995.

■ Work in Progress

Alien Encounters, a self-illustrated book for Millbrook
Press.

■ Sidelights

Peter A. Campbell told *SATA:* "The completion of my
first children's book, *Launch Day,* was the culmination
of a wonderful journey. It began in 1989 when I was

PETER A. CAMPBELL

accepted as a member of the NASA Space Art Program.
Through this program I saw first-hand all the preparations and excitement that surround a space shuttle
launch at the Cape Kennedy Space Center in Florida. I
also witnessed a day launch and a spectacular night
launch of the space shuttle Atlantis.

"How fortunate I was to be able to record with pencil,
paper, and paint space history in the making. Very
much in the spirit of artists like George Catlin, Winslow
Homer, and Frederic Remington, who documented
important events in their lifetimes.

"From these experiences came the idea for a book, *Launch Day.* A book that would show young children this great adventure through the words and paintings of a NASA space artist."

According to *Booklist* reviewer Carolyn Phelan, Campbell's paintings distinguish *Launch Day* from other books taking a close look at a space shuttle as it prepares for take-off. "[U]nusual, given the almost universal use of NASA photos (often the same ones) in books on the space program, are the attractive paintings that illustrate this volume," Phelan wrote.

Campbell said, "I owe much to Millbrook Press in Connecticut who shared my vision and gave an unpublished author the opportunity to design, write, and illustrate his first book. *Launch Day* was released to bookstores, libraries, and schools in September of 1995. The book has also given me the opportunity to speak to school children about the importance of NASA, space exploration, and what writing and illustrating a children's book is all about.

"In my lifetime, I have witnessed one of the greatest adventures in the history of mankind: man's first steps into space. I believe through my words and paintings I can help keep the dream of space exploration alive for future generations. So onward to the red sands of Mars and the moons of Jupiter, where wonder and mysteries await!"

■ Works Cited

Phelan, Carolyn, review of *Launch Day, Booklist,* December 1, 1995, p. 630.

■ For More Information See

PERIODICALS

School Library Journal, March, 1996, p. 202.
Science Books and Films, April, 1996, pp. 86-87.

* * *

CARTER, Nick
See CRIDER, (Allen) Bill(y)

* * *

CATALANO, Grace (A.) 1961-

■ Personal

Born September 5, 1961, in Jamaica, NY; daughter of Salvatore (a postal worker) and Rosemarie (a fashion designer; maiden name, Miele) Catalano; married Gregory Marlowe (a doctor), June 4, 1992. *Education:* Attended Hofstra University, Columbia University, and Art Students League, 1980-84; fourteen months of private study in England. *Hobbies and other interests:* Photography, painting, directing stage productions, teaching writing to children.

■ Career

Writer. Worked as an advertising copywriter, 1980-81.

■ Writings

Kirk Cameron: Dream Guy, Bantam, 1987.
Teen Star Yearbook, Paperjacks, 1987.
Elvis: A Tenth Anniversary Tribute, Ultra, 1987.
River Phoenix: Hero and Heartthrob, Bantam, 1988.
Elvis and Priscilla, Ultra, 1988.
Alyssa Milano: She's the Boss, Bantam, 1989.
New Kids on the Block, Bantam, 1989.
New Kids on the Block Scrapbook, Signet/New American Library, 1990.
Richard Grieco: Hot 'n' Cool, Bantam, 1990.
Paula Abdul: Forever Yours, Signet/New American Library, 1990.
Fred Savage: Totally Awesome, Bantam, 1991.
Gloria Estefan, St. Martin's, 1991.
Just Jason, Bantam, 1991.

Grace Catalano documents the life of young country western singing star LeAnn Rimes, who worked toward her music career for most of her childhood. (Cover photo by Zuma.)

Joey Forever: A Biography of Joey Lawrence, Bantam, 1993.
Brad Pitt: Hot and Sexy, Bantam, 1995.
LeAnn Rimes: Teen Country Queen, Bantam, 1997.
Leonardo DiCaprio: Modern Day Romeo, Bantam, 1997.
Meet the Stars of Dawson's Creek, Bantam, 1998.

OTHER

Author of column in *Maileader,* 1977-79. Contributor to periodicals, including *Afternoon TV, Movie Digest,* and *Teen Life.* Editor in chief of *Dream Guys,* 1986-92, *Rock Legend,* 1989-90, *Rock Focus,* 1992—, and *Country Beat,* 1993—.

Author's work has been published in Spanish, French, German, Italian, and Swedish.

■ Sidelights

Grace Catalano has produced many writings on celebrities, particularly youthful singers and television performers. Among her works, many of which are targeted to teenage readers, are biographies of Kirk Cameron, Alyssa Milano, Paula Abdul, Fred Savage, Brad Pitt, LeAnn Rimes, and Leonardo DiCaprio. "I try to work about seven hours every day," Catalano once commented, "but when I am on a deadline I usually work seventeen hours." She added that she typically begins writing after conducting research and discussing specifics with her editor. "I just take a group of clippings and interviews and start to write the chapter," she related. "After rewriting a chapter about three times in long hand, I type it and store it in my computer. It is then ready to be sent to my editor."

In 1989 and 1990, Catalano released works on the musical group New Kids on the Block which were noteworthy for several reasons. Her biography *New Kids on the Block* became Bantam's first instant paperback for young readers. With over one and a half million copies sold, the book was Bantam's fastest, best-selling young readers title ever and the second best-selling instant paperback in Bantam's history. It spent twenty-two weeks on the *New York Times* best seller list. Also on the list at the time was Catalano's *New Kids on the Block Scrapbook,* which sold over three-quarters of a million copies and spent nine weeks on the chart. At age twenty-eight, Catalano thus enjoyed the distinction of being the youngest author ever to have two books simultaneously on the *New York Times* best-seller list.

■ For More Information See

PERIODICALS

Booklist, February 15, 1989, p. 1008; July, 1989, p. 1908; March 15, 1990, p. 1467.
School Library Journal, November, 1989, p. 130; December, 1990, p. 12; December, 1991, p. 18; July, 1991, p. 14.
Voice of Youth Advocates, April, 1988, p. 45; October, 1989, p. 231; June, 1990, p. 123; August, 1991, p. 186.*

CAZET, Denys 1938-

■ Personal

Born March 22, 1938, in Oakland, CA; son of Alex Denys (in finance and banking) and Yvonne (Aye) Cazet; married Carol Hesselschwerdt, August 8, 1958 (divorced), married Donna Maurer, 1982; children: Craig, Robert, Scott, Michelle. *Education:* St. Mary's College, Moraga, CA, B.A., 1960; attended Fresno State College (now California State University, Fresno), 1960-61; San Francisco State College (now San Francisco State University), Teaching Credential, 1961; attended University of California, Berkeley, 1962; Sonoma State College (now California State College, Sonoma), M.A., 1971; Pacific Union College, Librarian Credential, 1974.

■ Addresses

Home and office—1300 Ink Grade Rd., Pope Valley, CA 94567.

■ Career

Worked as a gardener, writer, mail carrier, warehouse worker, cable line worker, cook, stock clerk, and process server, 1955-60; taught school in Corcoran, CA, and in St. Helena, CA, 1960-75; writer, 1973—; Elementary School, St. Helena, librarian and media specialist, 1975-

DENYS CAZET

85; University of California, Davis, extension classes, member of faculty, 1976-78; St. Helena School District Media Centers, St. Helena, director, 1979-81; California College of Arts and Crafts, instructor, 1985-86. Founder of Parhelion & Co. (printers and designers of educational materials), 1972-73.

■ Awards, Honors

California Young Reader award, 1992, for *Never Spit on Your Shoes.*

■ Writings

FOR CHILDREN; SELF-ILLUSTRATED

Requiem for a Frog, Sonoma State College, 1971.
The Non-Coloring Book: A Drawing Book for Mind Stretching and Fantasy Building, Chandler & Sharp, 1973.
The Duck with Squeaky Feet, Bradbury, 1980.
Mud Baths for Everyone, Bradbury, 1981.
You Make the Angels Cry, Bradbury, 1983.
Lucky Me, Bradbury, 1983.
Big Shoe, Little Shoe, Bradbury, 1984.
Christmas Moon, Bradbury, 1984.
Saturday, Bradbury, 1985.
December 24th, Bradbury, 1986.
Frosted Glass, Bradbury, 1987.
A Fish in His Pocket, Orchard, 1987.
Mother Night, Bradbury, 1987.
Sunday, Bradbury, 1988.
Great-Uncle Felix, Orchard, 1988.
Good Morning, Maxine!, Bradbury, 1989.
Daydreams, Orchard, 1990.
Never Spit on Your Shoes, Orchard, 1990.
I'm Not Sleepy, Orchard, 1992.
Are There Any Questions?, Orchard, 1992.
Born in the Gravy, Orchard, 1993.
Nothing at All!, Orchard, 1994.
Dancing, music by Craig Bond, Orchard, 1995.
Night Lights: Twenty-four Poems to Sleep On, Orchard, 1997.
Minnie and Moo Go to the Moon, Dorling Kindersley, 1998.
Minnie and Moo Go Dancing, Dorling Kindersley, 1998.

ILLUSTRATOR

Dan Elish, *The Great Squirrel Uprising,* Orchard, 1992.
Donna Maurer, *Annie, Bea, and Chi Chi Dolores: A School Day Alphabet,* Orchard, 1993.
Leah Komaiko, *Where Can Daniel Be?,* Orchard, 1994.

■ Sidelights

"Every moment in a writer's life exerts some influence on his work," author and illustrator Denys Cazet once commented to *Something about the Author* (*SATA*). With such whimsical works as *The Duck with Squeaky Feet* and *A Fish in His Pocket* to his credit, Cazet had become well known in the world of children's picture books. A prolific author and illustrator, he has more than twenty-five self-illustrated storybooks to his credit, and is known for his ability to depict "a significant

emotional moment and [give] dignity to a child's need to feel special," according to *School Library Journal* contributor Leda Schubert.

Born in Oakland, California, in 1938, Cazet was raised in what he has described as a "traditional 'first American' French family [with] ... a strange mix of features—European with a touch of American." Each member of his large family was an individualist, which, Cazet recalled, "made for impossible personality situations.... They were a lively and noisy cast of characters." The most lively times were those spent around the table, during meals that were followed by card playing and discussions that evolved into arguments ranging from "current political conflicts to how many layers of custard in a proper Napoleon." No sooner had one meal been completed, but the table was being set for another. "Family functions were like participating in a Renaissance fair held in the middle of a Barnum and Bailey freak show," the author/illustrator added. "Everyone had a position to maintain and a point to get across. The intellectuals got theirs across by dismissing everyone else's arguments as so much rubbish, and those less endowed, by not knowing the difference. Stories were told with great gusto, laughter, and animation. Each version became more elaborate than the last. Children walked and talked with adults. They were treated with care, respect, and above all, were listened to. For a child, it was like being at the bottom of the funnel of love."

Many of Cazet's picture books reflect these close relationships between the generations, especially between children and grandparents or other elderly relatives. *December 24th* is a holiday story with a difference, as Grandpa Rabbit's doting grandchildren, Emily and Louise, stump him the day before Christmas by having him guess what holiday it is (it turns out that Grandpa was born on Christmas Eve, so it is his birthday). Leslie Chamberlin of *School Library Journal* observes that there's "more than enough love to go around in this warm, vibrant and charming family story." In *Great-Uncle Felix,* a young rhino named Sam eagerly awaits the arrival of the dapper Great-Uncle Felix. While Sam worries that his small social blunders will make his uncle think less of him, Felix quickly reassures the youngster that Sam holds a special place in his heart precisely *because* he is who he is. A *Publishers Weekly* critic called *Great-Uncle Felix* "a quiet and satisfying evocation of intergenerational love and mutual respect." *Sunday,* with its pen-and-ink drawings and text simplified for more inexperienced readers, recounts Barney's Sundays with his grandparents. Grandpa Spanielson (yes, the family is a dog family), a war veteran, proudly wears his medals to church; later the group participates in the church pancake breakfast and a game of Bingo. When Grandpa attempts to help fix a neighbor's clothes dryer, chaos ensues before everyone goes home to a quiet dinner and stories. While maintaining that the plot of *Sunday* is subdued, *Booklist* reviewer Denise Wilms added that "there is a strong sense of family warmth" in the story. A *Kirkus Reviews* critic called the book "a friendly look at the comedy in some familiar activities."

Second-grader Arnie amuses his mother with an account of his class field trip to the aquarium. (From *Are There Any Questions?*, written and illustrated by Cazet.)

If a human baby has a babysitter, then Louie, a young rabbit, has bunnysitters, and in *Big Shoe, Little Shoe,* his most favorite of all bunnysitters are his grandma and grandpa. While the three usually spend quiet, relaxing days together playing checkers, this day is different: Grandpa has to make an important delivery at 4:00 and must watch the clock. Louie isn't allowed to go but must stay and clean his room; Grandpa tells the disappointed bunny that only those who wear the big shoes are allowed on this trip. Louie, who would rather his grandfather stayed at home, hatches on a clever plan—to hide the older man's big shoes so he can't leave the house either. A *Publishers Weekly* commentator called *Big Shoe, Little Shoe* "a merry story, spiced by fun, colorful art." "Nicely told," commended Diane S. Rogoff in *School Library Journal,* "without becoming cloying."

In *Frosted Glass,* Cazet uses pencil and watercolor to help paint a portrait of a budding artist who is unaware that there is more to talent than being able to draw shapes exactly the same way the teacher does. Young Gregory, a pup struggling through art lessons at school, tries hard to concentrate on his lessons, but his vivid imagination turns flower vases into rocket ships soaring into space. Fortunately, his wise and supportive teacher recognizes the youngster's talent, in a story useful for "[sparking] a discussion on creativity and imagination," according to *Booklist* reviewer Denise M. Wilms. A *Publishers Weekly* critic also praised *Frosted Glass,* calling it "an affirmation of friendship and childhood creativity." Writing in *Bulletin of the Center for Children's Books,* Betsy Hearne dubbed the book "insightful and entertaining," and added: "The art keeps the quiet story perking along in perfect harmony with its leading character."

Childhood is full of new experiences, and children are sometimes faced with strange situations that cause more than a little anxiety or confusion. Cazet addresses several of these situations in such books as *A Fish in His Pocket, Are There Any Questions?,* and *You Make the Angels Cry.* In *A Fish in His Pocket,* illustrated in brown-toned watercolor and pencil, Russell the bear cub drops his math book into a pond on the way to school; when he fishes it out, he discovers that a small fish became caught within its pages and died. Feeling responsible for the fish's death and confused about what to do, he ponders on it all day, even discussing the matter with his teacher before finally deciding to make a paper boat in which the ex-fish can fittingly sail into the sunset. David Gale, in an appraisal for *School Library Journal,* praised the volume as "a respectful and amusing book that celebrates the renewal of life," while in the *Bulletin of the Center for Children's Books,* Betsy Hearne commented that Russell's "childlike behavior will strike sympathetic chords" with youngsters concerned about the results of their own mishaps. A *Kirkus Reviews* critic pronounced *A Fish in His Pocket* a "fine exploration of a sensitive subject."

Are There Any Questions? is the title of Cazet's story about school field trips, events that can strike both excitement and terror into young scholars—sometimes simultaneously. In his humorous story, readers meet Arnie, who goes with his class to the local aquarium to see everything from snakes and turtles to piranhas, squid, and alligators. There is a lot of confusion about permission slips, who sits with whom on the bus, and who brought what for lunch, and "children will enjoy recognizing themselves and their friends in Arnie's class," in the opinion of *School Library Journal* contributor Nancy Seiner. "Cazet accurately portrays a primary-grade field trip," notes *Booklist*'s Karen Hutt, while his "homey illustrations hilariously fill in details

"THERE'S A MOUSE IN MY PANTS!"

Cazet's self-illustrated verse story echoes the sounds of various farm animals as they awaken, culminating in a quiet scarecrow's uncharacteristic outburst. (From *Nothing at All.*)

Arnie leaves out," according to a *Kirkus Reviews* critic. Cazet's comic-book style complements his text, with Arnie's recounting of the day to his parents balanced against what really went on. "I'm glad you had a good day," Arnie's mom tells him at the end of his story. "I think the teacher did too," Arnie answers innocently. "She went home early."

While most of Cazet's books feature anthropomorphized animal characters—animals given the mental and physical characteristics of civilized human beings—his more recent work has also featured human characters. Fans of Cazet's books meet young Alex and his dad in a series of two books, beginning with *I'm Not Sleepy.* The title tells the story—Alex will try any trick to keep from going to sleep, despite his dad's efforts to tire him out with tales of high adventure and derring-do, all starring his young son. Both language and illustrations alternate between Alex's realistic bedroom and the dreamlike tropical jungles and mysterious shadows of the storyteller's world. "This is Cazet at his best," hailed Luann Toth in her *School Library Journal* review; "he has taken an age-old theme and given it fresh, humorous enchantment." A *Publishers Weekly* critic predicted that "families will embrace this warm, wry and reassuring celebration of father and son in a familiar ritual." Alex and his dad appear again in *Dancing,* as the arrival of a new baby breaks the quiet of their evening hours together. Although frustrated at first and afraid that he has lost his father's devotion, Alex is eventually reassured that his dad will always be there for him; a dance in the moonlight cements their strong relationship. "Luminous watercolors," as a *Kirkus Reviews* commentator attested, illustrate a story with a musical score that "works both as a lesson about sibling rivalry and as a lullaby."

The nighttime setting of *I'm Not Sleepy* and *Dancing* is repeated by Cazet in the poetry collection *Night Lights: Twenty-four Poems to Sleep On* and the lyrical story *Mother Night. School Library Journal* contributor Angela J. Reynolds appraised the former work as a collection "[deserving] a place in the plethora of bedtime books, where it will spice up those sleepy poems and give children a fun place to dream." In *Mother Night,* Cazet gently depicts a variety of bedtime rituals, undertaken by bears, foxes, birds, and field mice. As the new day approaches, the animals rise to greet the sun, reminding young listeners that a new day can only be reached after good nights are said. "Cazet succeeds best with his impressionistic watercolor renditions of the night sky and nighttime landscapes," wrote *School Library Journal* contributor Ruth K. MacDonald, who described the result as "solemn and elegant."

A prolific author whose career has spanned three decades, Cazet's books continue to range in theme from such gentle, reassuring stories to tales comprised of total nonsense, complete with appropriately silly illustrations. In *The Duck with Squeaky Feet,* "especially for the whimsically minded," as Barbara Elleman remarked in *Booklist,* foolishness reigns among the animal kingdom, as a stagestruck duck with new shoes brings down the house amid a menagerie of other whimsical animals. And in *Nothing at All,* what *Bulletin of the Center for Children's Books* reviewer Betsy Hearne characterized as "upbeat barnyard buffoonery" follows the announcement, via megaphone, "Cock-a-doodle-dooooo! Good morning to you!," by a farm's resident rooster M.C. Pairs of animals greet the day in a swinging verse story that features animal sounds and that "rewards [youngsters] with a colorful cast, a lively scarecrow rap, and a surprise ending," according to *Booklist* critic Kathryn Broderick.

In addition to the books he writes himself, Cazet has also contributed illustrations to the works of other authors, including Donna Maurer and Leah Komaiko. While most of the characters in Cazet's illustrations are animals, he admits: "the truth is, they are all based on the wonderful people who influenced my life. They gave me much, and I try not to forget them. By putting them in my books, I hope to make them live forever."

■ Works Cited

Review of *Are There Any Questions?*, *Kirkus Reviews*, July 1, 1992, p. 847.

Review of *Big Shoe, Little Shoe*, *Publishers Weekly*, February 10, 1984, p. 194.

Broderick, Kathryn, review of *Nothing at All*, *Booklist*, March 1, 1994, p. 1268.

Cazet, Denys, *Are There Any Questions?*, Orchard, 1992.

Cazet, Denys, *Nothing at All*, Orchard, 1994.

Chamberlin, Leslie, review of *December 24th*, *School Library Journal*, December, 1986, p. 82.

Review of *Dancing*, *Kirkus Reviews*, July 15, 1995, p. 1021.

Elleman, Barbara, review of *The Duck with the Squeaky Feet*, *Booklist*, February 1, 1981, p. 751.

Review of *A Fish in His Pocket*, *Kirkus Reviews*, July 1, 1987, p. 988.

Review of *Frosted Glass*, *Publishers Weekly*, March 13, 1987, p. 82.

Gale, David, review of *A Fish in His Pocket*, *School Library Journal*, December, 1987, p. 72.

Review of *Great-Uncle Felix*, *Publishers Weekly*, December 25, 1987, p. 73.

Hearne, Betsy, review of *Frosted Glass*, *Bulletin of the Center for Children's Books*, May, 1987, p. 163.

Hearne, Betsy, review of *A Fish in His Pocket*, *Bulletin of the Center for Children's Books*, January, 1988, p. 84.

Hearne, Betsy, review of *Nothing at All*, *Bulletin of the Center for Children's Books*, July-August, 1994, pp. 351-52.

Hutt, Karen, review of *Are There Any Questions?*, *Booklist*, August, 1992, pp. 2016-17.

Review of *I'm Not Sleepy*, *Publishers Weekly*, March 9, 1992, p. 55.

MacDonald, Ruth K., review of *Mother Night*, *School Library Journal*, January, 1990, p. 78.

Reynolds, Angela J., review of *Night Lights: Twenty-four Poems to Sleep On*, *School Library Journal*, May, 1997, p. 99.

Rogoff, Diane S., review of *Big Shoe, Little Shoe*, *School Library Journal*, August, 1984, pp. 57-58.

Schubert, Leda, review of *Great-Uncle Felix*, *School Library Journal*, March, 1988, p. 160.

Seiner, Nancy, review of *Are There Any Questions*, *School Library Journal*, September, 1992, p. 200.

Review of *Sunday*, *Kirkus Reviews*, March 1, 1988, p. 360.

Toth, Luann, review of *I'm Not Sleepy*, *School Library Journal*, February, 1992, p. 72.

Wilms, Denise M., review of *Frosted Glass*, *Booklist*, April 15, 1987, pp. 1283-84.

Wilms, Denise M., review of *Sunday*, *Booklist*, April 15, 1988, pp. 1426-28.

■ For More Information See

PERIODICALS

Booklist, February 15, 1982, p. 755; February 15, 1990, p. 1160; March 15, 1992, p. 1387; February 15, 1993, pp. 1063-64.

Bulletin of the Center for Children's Books, October, 1984, pp. 19-20; November, 1986, pp. 44-45; December 1993, p. 117.

Horn Book, July-August 1993, p. 447.

Kirkus Reviews, November 1, 1984, p. 87; March 15, 1989, p. 460; August 1, 1989, pp. 1154-55; February 15, 1997, p. 297.

Publishers Weekly, December 12, 1980, p. 47; September 26, 1986, p. 74; June 29, 1990, p. 100; July 26, 1993, p. 69.

School Library Journal, May, 1983, p. 58; November 1985, p. 67; November, 1994, pp. 83-84.*

*   *   *

CHENEY, Glenn (Alan) 1951-

■ Personal

Born September 6, 1951, in Melrose, MA; son of Theodore Albert Rees (a writer and educator) and Dorothy (Bates) Cheney; married Solange Aurora Cavalcante (an exporter), May 26, 1978; children: Ian. *Education:* Fairfield University, B.A. (philosophy), 1974, post-graduate certificate (professional writing), 1982, M.A. (human communication), 1982; Universidade Federal de Minas Gerais (Brazil), M.A. (English-language literature), 1990; Vermont College, M.F.A. (writing), 1991. *Politics:* Green Party.

■ Addresses

Home—P.O. Box 284, Hanover, CT 06350. *Electronic mail*—cheney@compuserve.com.

■ Career

Grey Advertising, Inc., New York City, public relations account executive, 1982-85; Cheney & Associates, Hanover, CT, and Belo Horizonte, MG, Brazil, partner, 1985—. Institute for Children's Literature, Redding Ridge, CT, instructor; Norwalk Community College, Norwalk, CT, adjunct professor, 1988; Fairfield University, Fairfield, CT, adjunct professor, 1988-94; Albertus Magnus College, adjunct professor, 1989; Connecticut College, visiting instructor, 1994—. Correspondent for *Tax Notes* and *Accounting Today* magazines.

■ Awards, Honors

Books for the Teen Age citation, New York Public Library, 1994, for *Drugs, Teens and Recovery: Seven Real-Life Stories*, and 1997, for *They Never Knew: The Victims of Nuclear Testing*; Quick Picks for Reluctant

Young Adult Readers citation, American Library Association, 1996, for *Teens with Physical Disabilities: Real Life Stories of Meeting the Challenges;* Notable Trade Book citation, National Council for Social Studies, for *Television in American Society.*

■ Writings

El Salvador, Country in Crisis, Franklin Watts, 1982, revised edition, 1990.
Television in American Society, Franklin Watts, 1983.
Mohandas Gandhi, Franklin Watts, 1983.
The Amazon, Franklin Watts, 1984.
Mineral Resources, Franklin Watts, 1984.
Revolution in Central America, Franklin Watts, 1985.
Responsibility, Franklin Watts, 1985.
The Mariana Scouts in the Valley of the Spirits, McGraw-Hill (Sao Paulo, Brazil), 1986.
The Mariana Scouts in Amazonia, McGraw-Hill (Sao Paulo), 1987.
Drugs, Teens and Recovery: Seven Real-Life Stories, Enslow Publishers, 1993.
Chernobyl: The Ongoing Story of the World's Deadliest Nuclear Disaster, Macmillan, 1993.
Life in Caves (novel), Royal Fireworks Printing Co., 1994.
Teens with Physical Disabilities: Real Life Stories of Meeting the Challenges, Enslow Publishers, 1995.
Acts of Ineffable Love: Short Stories by Glenn Cheney, Shetucket Press, 1995.
Journey to Chernobyl: Encounters in a Radioactive Zone, Academy Chicago Publishers, 1995.
Why I Didn't Go, Dark Valley Press, 1995.
They Never Knew: The Victims of Nuclear Testing, Franklin Watts, 1996.
Nuclear Proliferation, Franklin Watts, 1998.

Also contributor of poems and short stories to periodicals, including *Verve, Anathema Review, Bottomfish,* and *Maple Twig.* Contributor of articles to business journals, including *Accounting Today* and *Journal of Accountancy.*

■ Sidelights

Glenn Alan Cheney told *SATA:* "I've been writing since I was a child. I could not stop any more than I could stop thinking. In fact, writing has become my mode of thought. By a mysterious process I do not understand, language leads me to thoughts, conclusions, ideas, stories, and discoveries. It all starts with words.

"I write all kinds of things: long and short fiction, creative nonfiction, traditional journalism, essays, lots of letters to editors, the occasional poem. I wish these projects more often led to publication and a paycheck. I wish I had more time to focus on a worthwhile project that someone is willing to pay for.

"But I can't complain. This is a great profession, a noble craft, a sacred art. It satisfies my curiosity. It leaves me independent. I work at home or wherever I happen to

GLENN CHENEY

be. I like to think that the product of my effort leaves the world a little better than it used to be.

"My profession also gives me license to pursue any studies or travels that pique my interest. For the sake of a solid career, I suppose I should have pursued a Ph.D. As a writer, however, I wanted an education that was wide rather than deep. I've ended up with a B.A. in philosophy, an M.A. in communication, an M.A. in English (from a university in Brazil), and an M.F.A. in writing.

"I've done quite a bit of traveling, usually on a budget that required me to sleep outdoors or beg for space in someone's house. In 1974, I hitch-hiked to Brazil. In 1977, I traveled around northern Africa. In 1978, I moved to Brazil and got married. In 1980, I moved back to the States, but by 1985, I was ready to live on a banana farm in Brazil, so off I went. I came back in 1987. Since then, I've been to Russia and Ukraine, El Salvador, Amazonia, and Europe."

Several of Cheney's books reflect his well-traveled background, with titles on peoples and events in El Salvador, Central America, and the Amazon. *El Salvador, Country in Crisis* deals with the civil war that gripped that nation and the conditions that contributed to the bloodshed. *Booklist* critic Sally Estes described *El Salvador* as a "solid" introduction to the crisis in that land. In a *School Library Journal* review, Isabel Schon found that "the value of this book lies in its perceptive analysis of the many issues which prevail in El Salvador today." *Voice of Youth Advocates* reviewer Sherry Hoy noted that the revised edition was "aesthetically improved," with new typeface and photos, adding that the book "succinctly explains all the fuss about El Salvador."

Revolution in Central America focuses not only on El Salvador, but neighboring Nicaragua, Honduras, and Guatemala, as well. "An objective, concise, and readable description of the many serious issues involving the people" within Central America, according to Schon in *School Library Journal.* Karen Stang Hanley, writing in *Booklist,* praised the book's "timely and well-rounded survey of the turmoil that characterizes most of Central America."

Maintaining focus on that region is Cheney's *The Amazon,* about the ecosystem and its human inhabitants. In his review for *School Library Journal,* William G. Piekarski deemed the book "worthwhile," and *Booklist* reviewer Denise M. Wilms called it "thorough." Wilms added, "Readers learn why the rain forest is important, not only to the Amazon region but to all the world ... and that the area's future lies in careful, ecologically sound management."

Cheney continued to *SATA,* "My career as a writer began just as I finished graduate studies in human communication with a concentration in professional writing. Through a contact at a publishing house, I started writing books for young adults. Over the next decade, I'd write a dozen of them. Some I wrote after a hard and unsatisfying day at a public relations agency. Sometimes I worked on two or three books at a time.

"The book that satisfied me most was *Journey to Chernobyl: Encounters in a Radioactive Zone.* I did the research during a very intense and challenging month in Russia and Ukraine during the very weeks when the Soviet Union fell apart. I arrived in Kiev with the name of one contact, but for the first few days I couldn't find her. Yet within hours of my arrival I was talking with people who had witnessed the Chernobyl disaster and its aftermath. I ended up writing not only the young adult book I'd been asked to write but also an odd travelogue. Unlike any other book about Chernobyl, it looked at how the disaster affected people. The story alternated between horrific human drama and a humorous account of myself stumbling around the shambles of the Evil Empire."

The young adult book Cheney had been asked to write was *Chernobyl: The Ongoing Story of the World's Deadliest Nuclear Disaster.* A *Booklist* review by Chris Sherman called *Chernobyl* "a truly frightening book ... of the worst man-made disaster of all time." Regarding *Journey to Chernobyl,* a *Publishers Weekly* commentator wrote, "In this brief, informal report, this self-appointed investigator describes his travel adventures (with an expired visa) and his encounters with officials and victims of the Chernobyl catastrophe." The reviewer

added, "[Cheney's] poignant account humanizes the events of April 26, 1986, at Chernobyl."

"*Journey* is a good example of a new genre known as creative nonfiction or literary journalism," Cheney told *SATA.* "It uses the devices of fiction—characters, tension, scenes, voice, drama, plot—to portray the real world. The product is nonfiction that grips the reader, generates emotion and shows a truth beyond the reach of traditional journalism. Until my father wrote a book about this new genre (*Writing Creative Nonfiction,* Theodore A. Rees Cheney, Ten-Speed Press), I always assumed that the novel was the genre of great art. As it turns out, the novel may be close to passe."

Indeed, Cheney's nonfiction efforts have proven most successful for him, starting with a Notable Trade Book citation from the National Council for Social Studies for *Television in American Society,* a look at the current problems of and future potential for television. Ruth Horowitz, writing for *School Library Journal,* praised the book's "straightforward and ... lively style." Ilene Cooper, writing in *Booklist,* said *Television* "raise[s]

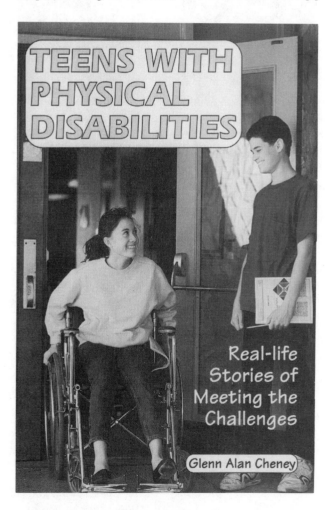

Cheney offers readers insight into the lives of eight disabled teenagers as well as general information about living with a physical disability. (Cover photo by Dale Wittner, PhotoSeattle.)

Cheney documents the effects of radiation from nuclear testing in the United States during the twenty years following World War II, and also outlines the government's deception and victims' attempts to obtain compensation.

some thought-provoking issues and will serve as a good jumping-off point for discussion."

Drugs, Teens, and Recovery: Real Life Stories of Trying to Stay Clean—a collection of first-person accounts of drug addiction and the problems it creates—netted Cheney a Books for the Teen Age citation from the New York Public Library. *Voice of Youth Advocates* reviewer Connie Allerton wrote, "Even the most jaded of readers ... will be sobered by the self-destruction, self-loathing, and utter waste of young lives in these personal accounts."

The American Library Association named *Teens with Physical Disabilities: Real Life Stories of Meeting the Challenges* a Quick Pick for Reluctant Young Adult Readers. Like *Drugs, Teens* deals with specific teens and their day-to-day concerns. *Booklist* reviewer Mary Harris Veeder called the book a "gritty, tough collection of stories." Writing in *Voice of Youth Advocates*, Dorie Freebury said, "This commendable book will appeal to both boys and girls and is a tremendously valuable source of information for learning about the experiences of teens with physical disabilities."

The following year, Cheney's *They Never Knew: The Victims of Nuclear Testing* was published. "A disturbing look at the effect of nuclear test fallout, particularly in the western United States," Shannon VanHemert wrote in *School Library Journal*, adding: "An important book on a neglected subject." *Booklist* reviewer Debbie Carlton wrote, "Cheney's straightforward presentation, attention to research (he makes good use of available records), and extensive footnotes give his book credibility." For *They Never Knew,* Cheney received his second Books for the Teen Age citation from the New York Public Library.

Despite his success with nonfiction, Cheney concedes interest in writing fiction. "I'm working on a novel," he told *SATA*. "I'm also tinkering with a history of the Pilgrims. I'm also working on my bi-weekly article about the exciting world of accounting. Yesterday, I wrote a letter to a newspaper editor, and today, if I get time, I'll write another. I don't know if I'll take out my poem about my bees—I'm a beekeeper—and work on it, but I might. In the next few weeks I have to update a manuscript of a book about nuclear proliferation. I also owe a few people some letters.

"Such is my life as a writer. It's good."

■ Works Cited

Allerton, Connie, review of *Drugs, Teens, and Recovery: Real Life Stories of Trying to Stay Clean, Voice of Youth Advocates,* December, 1993, p. 318.

Carlton, Debbie, review of *They Never Knew: The Victims of Nuclear Testing, Booklist,* January 1-15, 1997, pp. 832-33.

Cooper, Ilene, review of *Television in American Society, Booklist,* November 15, 1983, p. 494.

Estes, Sally, review of *El Salvador, Country in Crisis, Booklist,* July, 1982, p. 1432.

Freebury, Dorie, review of *Teens with Physical Disabilities: Real Life Stories of Meeting the Challenges, Voice of Youth Advocates,* August, 1995, pp. 179-80.

Hanley, Karen Stang, review of *Revolution in Central America, Booklist,* May 15, 1984, p. 1341.

Horowitz, Ruth, review of *Television in American Society, School Library Journal,* December, 1983, p. 72.

Hoy, Sherry, review of *El Salvador, Country in Crisis, Voice of Youth Advocates,* August, 1990, p. 172.

Review of *Journey to Chernobyl: Encounters in a Radioactive Zone, Publishers Weekly,* September 11, 1995, p. 70.

Piekarski, William G., review of *The Amazon, School Library Journal,* December, 1984, p. 79.

Schon, Isabel, review of *El Salvador, Country in Crisis, School Library Journal,* August, 1982, p. 124.

Schon, Isabel, review of *Revolution in Central America, School Library Journal,* December, 1985, pp. 36-37.

Sherman, Chris, review of *Chernobyl: The Ongoing Story of the World's Deadliest Nuclear Disaster, Booklist,* January 15, 1994, p. 908.

VanHemert, Shannon, review of *They Never Knew: The Victims of Nuclear Testing, School Library Journal,* April, 1997, p. 146.

Veeder, Mary Harris, review of *Teens with Physical Disabilities: Real Life Stories of Meeting the Challenges, Booklist,* August, 1995, p. 1937.

Wilms, Denise M., review of *The Amazon, Booklist,* December 15, 1984, p. 587.

■ For More Information See

PERIODICALS

Booklist, June 1, 1983, p. 1266; April 15, 1985, pp. 1188-89; February 15, 1986, pp. 864-65.

Bulletin of the Center for Children's Books, July-August, 1983, p. 205.

Kirkus Reviews, July 1, 1993, p. 857.

School Library Journal, August, 1984, p. 82; December, 1985, p. 87; February, 1986, p. 82; November, 1993, p. 129; March, 1994, p. 240; August, 1995, pp. 159-60.

Science Books and Films, January-February, 1994, p. 12; March, 1997, p. 37.

*   *   *

CHERRY, Lynne 1952-

■ Personal

Born January 5, 1952, in Philadelphia, PA; daughter of Herbert B. (a pharmacist) and Helen (an illustrator; maiden name, Cogan) Cherry. *Education:* Tyler School of Art, Philadelphia, PA., B.A., 1973.

■ Career

Author and illustrator. Platt & Munk, Bronx, NY, paste-up artist and designer, 1973; Harcourt Brace Jovanovich, Inc., New York City, designer, 1974; Xerox Education Publications, Middletown, CT, illustrator, 1974-75; freelance illustrator, 1975—. *Member:* Bicycle Coalition (Philadelphia), Folk Dance Society, Sierra Club, Friends of the Earth, People's Action for Clean Energy, Society of Illustrators Club (NY).

■ Awards, Honors

Educational Press Award for editorial art, 1975, for *My Weekly Reader,* and 1977, for *Scholastic* magazine; New York Society of Illustrators Show Award, 1979, for Illustrators Annual; Connecticut Art Directors Club Annual Show Awards, 1976-80; National Science Teachers Award, 1981, for *Hidden Messages;* New York Academy of Science Annual Children's Book Award, 1983, for *The Snail's Spell* by Joanne Ryder; Alumni Association award, New Jersey Institute of Technology, 1983, for outstanding children's book illustrations; Please Touch award, 1989, for *Who's Sick Today?;* Charlotte Book award, 1992, for *The Great Kapok Tree: A Tale of the Amazon Rain Forest.*

■ Writings

FOR CHILDREN; ALL SELF-ILLUSTRATED

Who's Sick Today?, Dutton, 1988.
Archie, Follow Me, Dutton, 1990.
The Great Kapok Tree: A Tale of the Amazon Rain Forest, Harcourt, 1990.
A River Ran Wild, Harcourt, 1992.
The Armadillo from Amarillo, Harcourt, 1994.
The Dragon and the Unicorn, Harcourt 1995.
Flute's Journey: The Life of a Wood Thrush, Harcourt, 1997.
(With Mark Plotkin) *The Shaman's Apprentice: A Tale of the Amazon Rain Forest,* Harcourt, 1998.

ILLUSTRATOR; FOR CHILDREN

Carolyn Meyer, *Coconut: The Tree of Life,* Morrow, 1976.
Solveig Paulson Russell, *What's the Time, Starling? A First Look at Nature's Clocks,* McKay, 1977.
Dorothy Van Woerkom, *Hidden Messages,* Crown, 1979.
Jan Roberts, *Emir's Education in the Proper Use of Magical Powers,* Delacorte, 1979.
Ranger Rick's Holiday Book, National Wildlife Federation, 1980.
Judith Viorst, *If I Were in Charge of the World, and Other Worries: Poems for Children and Their Parents,* Atheneum, 1981.
Joanne Ryder, *The Snail's Spell,* Warne, 1982.
Ron Roy, *What Has Ten Legs and Eats Cornflakes? A Pet Book,* Clarion, 1982.
Houghton-Mifflin English Book, Grade Two, Houghton, 1982.
John McCormack, *Rabbit Travels,* Dutton, 1983.
Ranger Rick's Story Book, National Wildlife Federation, 1983.
Valerie Scho Carey, *Harriet and William and the Terrible Creature,* Dutton, 1985.
Jane Howard, *When I'm Sleepy,* Dutton, 1985.
Ron Roy, *Big and Small, Short and Tall,* Clarion, 1986.
Joanne Ryder, *Chipmunk Song,* Dutton, 1987.
Ryder, *Where Butterflies Grow,* Dutton, 1989.

ILLUSTRATOR; "HELP SAVE US" SERIES; ALL WRITTEN BY LUCIA MONFRIED

Grizzly Bear, Dutton, 1987.
Orangutan, Dutton, 1987.
Seal, Dutton, 1987.
Snow Leopard, Dutton, 1987.

ILLUSTRATOR; FOR ADULTS

Sheilah Kaufman, *Sheilah's Easy Ways to Elegant Cooking,* Delacorte, 1979.
Guide to Marine Fisheries, Conservation Law Foundation (Boston), 1980.
Kaufman, *Sheilah's Fearless, Fussless Cookbook,* Delacorte, 1982.
New Directions in Energy, Massachusetts Public Interest Research Group, 1982.

Contributor of illustrations to magazines and newspapers, including *New York Times, Hartford Courant, Connecticut Magazine,* and *National Wildlife.*

■ Sidelights

Beginning her career in children's literature as an illustrator in 1976, Lynne Cherry has expanded her expertise into the art of writing, becoming a well-respected author of juvenile fiction. Noted for books that feature her respect and concern for the natural world, Cherry has been hailed as "a leading author of environmental stories" by *Booklist* critic Lauren Peterson. Books by Cherry include *The Great Kapok Tree: A Tale of the Amazon Rain Forest,* the mythic *The Dragon and the Unicorn,* and *Flute's Journey: The Life of a Wood Thrush.*

Graduating from Philadelphia's Tyler School of Art in 1973, Cherry moved north to New York City, where jobs with publishing companies were plentiful. She was quickly hired by Platt & Munk, Bronx, where she worked as a paste-up artist and designer until moving to Harcourt Brace Jovanovich in 1974 to work as a book designer. Doing illustration work for Xerox Education Publications in Connecticut convinced Cherry to make the break and become her own boss; in 1975, at the age of twenty-three, she began devoting her time to illustration.

A wood thrush migrates thousands of miles and faces many obstacles in Cherry's naturalistic rendition of a bird's struggle for survival. (From *Flute's Journey: The Life of a Wood Thrush,* written and illustrated by Cherry.)

Cherry's first illustration project was *Coconut: The Tree of Life,* a book for children by author Carolyn Meyer. Other writers for whom Cherry has provided artwork include Judith Viorst, John McCormack, Joanne Ryder, and Ron Roy. Her favorite projects, which have drawn on her longstanding love of nature, have been for such organizations as the National Wildlife Federation, for which Cherry illustrated *Ranger Rick's Holiday Book* and *Ranger Rick's Story Book.* Throughout her childhood, Cherry spent countless hours in the woods, observing in detail the natural world around her. She has brought this understanding of plants, animals, and the effect of the elements on natural habitats to her work, educating observant young readers while entertaining them with her lighthearted illustrations as well.

Eventually, Cherry decided to try her hand at writing as well as illustrating; her first published effort, *Who's Sick Today?,* offers a lighthearted look at childhood ailments. Beginning in an empty classroom during roll call, Cherry switches from sickbed to doctor's office; as each name is called by the teacher, the illustration shows a young animal tended by caring parents as they rebound from fevers, flus, sore throats, sore muscles, and a myriad other minor illnesses or injuries. Finally the teacher receives one "Here!"—a "porcupine who's feeling fine." Cherry's "encouraging message and the witty joining of everyday aches and pains with exotic creatures will make [*Who's Sick Today?*] a popular choice," according to *School Library Journal* contributor Nancy Seiner. Ellen Fader of *Horn Book* maintained, "Just what the doctor would prescribe for children, bedridden or well."

Other humorous stories have issued from Cherry's vivid imagination and adept pen- and brush-strokes, among them *The Armadillo from Amarillo,* a book that *School Library Journal* contributor Claudia Cooper hailed as an "ecological jewel." Describing the work as "an excellent map-skills book for beginners," Cooper praised Cherry's humorous story of Sasparillo Armadillo, who tries to travel around the vast state of Texas without a map. Unable to get his bearings on the ground, the baffled armadillo hitches a ride with an eagle for a better view, then jumps a space shuttle for a long-distance look at the Lone Star State. Despite Sasparillo's happy-go-lucky attitude, Cherry's illustrations—featuring desert plants and animals, and several endangered species of wildlife—are the real star of the book, according to a *Kirkus Reviews* critic, who called her detailed landscapes "enchanting" due to her "contagious enthusiasm."

The Dragon and the Unicorn presents nature of another sort, as Cherry delves into a mythic fantasy kingdom she calls the Ardet Forest. In a world inhabited by princes and princesses, armor-clad knights, and mysterious, ancient forests, the young princess Arianna is introduced to the forest's fragile ecology by the dragon, Valerio, and Allegra, a beautiful, magical unicorn. Ultimately, Arianna is able to convince her father, the powerful King Orlando, to constrain the behavior of his knights who have been ransacking the forest and chop-

In her original fairy tale, Cherry recounts the plight of a dragon and a unicorn whose forest home is endangered by a powerful king. (From *The Dragon and the Unicorn,* written and illustrated by Cherry.)

ping down six-hundred-year-old trees in their efforts to search for elusive Allegra, in this parable of the similar plight facing many of Earth's wild places. Calling the book "another Lynne Cherry tour-de-force," Stephen Fraser noted in *Five Owls* that "a child's love of dragons may get him or her to [*The Dragon and the Unicorn*], but a message about protecting the environment is what the child will absorb." Cherry's watercolor renderings, done in tones of rich green and gold, were called "breathtaking" by *Booklist* contributor Lauren Peterson for their ability to "draw readers deep into the hushed and secret world."

The most significant of Cherry's works for children have been her books dealing with nature. In *The Great Kapok Tree,* readers watch as a woodsman naps under a giant tree that he has hiked into the rain forest to fell. As he slumbers, animals of the forest come to his side, imploring him to change his mind and save the tree—and their threatened forest home. Cherry traveled to Brazil to provide her audience with an accurate view of rain forest ecology, with its myriad species of plants, animals, and insects, all protected by a dense canopy of foliage that preserves the humid climate needed by these species in order to survive. Offering a favorable assessment of *The Great Kapok Tree, School Library Journal* contributor Luanne Toth maintained that Cherry "totally engages readers' attention and senses through vivid detail, dramatic perspective, and lifelike accuracy." *Horn Book* reviewer Carolyn K. Jenks described the book as "a modern fable with [an] urgent message," concluding that "the timely ecological subject makes the book an important one." In *Flute's Journey: The Life of a Wood Thrush*, described by Lauren Peterson of *Booklist* as "a nice addition to Cherry's impressive body of environmental literature for children," the author-illustrator follows the migration of a young wood thrush from a Maryland forest preserve to Costa Rica and back again. A *Kirkus Reviews* critic lauded the "canny understatement that gives the story its power," and also commented favorably on the author's presentation of "crucial, copiously researched natural information."

In *A River Ran Wild,* Cherry again turns to the world of nature, on this occasion a bit closer to home, as she tells the story of the Nashua River that runs through New Hampshire and Massachusetts. Paralleling the rise of industry in New England, she begins her story before the arrival of colonists from Europe, and shows the rise of smokestacks and the increase in pollution after the once-clear waters of the Nashua become, first, the power behind textile mills during the late 1800s and then the dumping ground for heavy industry during the early twentieth century. Praising the book's design and intent, *Booklist* critic Chris Sherman maintained that *A River Ran Wild* will prompt readers to "be moved to consider their personal impact on the environment and what they can do to make a difference." Carolyn K. Jenks of *Horn Book* described the tale as "inspiring" and observed that the text was "straightforward and readable" with a "pleasing and informative" layout she likens to Holling C. Holling's classic *Paddle to the Sea.*

"When I was a small child," Cherry once told *Something about the Author* (*SATA*), "my mother used to buy me dolls. She tells me that I used to undress them and draw all over their bodies. I remember liking the feel of the ball-point pen against the rubber dolly. Now I have moved up to Rapidograph pens, and for all my work this is what I use. For full-color art I add magic marker, inks, dyes, water colors and colored pencil to the black line." Her illustration style has been strongly influenced by her study of such classic illustrators as Aubrey Beardsley, Carl Larsson, Edmund Dulac, and Maurice Sendak, as well as by her teacher, Stanislaw Zagorski. In addition to book illustration, Cherry has contributed many drawings to magazine and newspaper editorials and retail advertising. She has also designed calendars, notecards, and letter stationery.

"My philosophy of life is that I must compensate for my existence by trying to make the world a better place," Cherry once explained to *SATA*. "I do this in many ways, including artwork for Massachusetts Public Interest Research Group, the Conservation Law Foundation, and the Connecticut Citizen Action Group. I lobby for anti-smoking legislation (in public places) and Solar Energy Research and Development. I also do work to stop the proliferation of nuclear weapons and to limit the use of nuclear power."

■ Works Cited

Review of *The Armadillo from Amarillo, Kirkus Reviews,* March 1, 1994, p. 300.

Cooper, Claudia, review of *The Armadillo from Amarillo, School Library Journal,* April, 1994, p. 101.

Fader, Ellen, review of *Who's Sick Today?, Horn Book,* May-June, 1988, p. 339.

Review of *Flute's Journey: The Life of a Wood Thrush, Kirkus Reviews,* April 1, 1997, pp. 551-52.

Fraser, Stephen, review of *The Dragon and the Unicorn, Five Owls,* March-April, 1996, pp. 92-93.

Jenks, Carolyn K., review of *The Great Kapok Tree: A Tale of the Amazon Rain Forest, Horn Book,* May-June, 1990, p. 321.

Jenks, Carolyn K., review of *A River Ran Wild, Horn Book,* May-June, 1992, p. 355.

Peterson, Lauren, review of *The Dragon and the Unicorn, Booklist,* January 1 & 15, 1996, pp. 842-43.

Seiner, Nancy, review of *Who's Sick Today?, School Library Journal,* June-July, 1988, p. 89.

Sherman, Chris, review of *A River Ran Wild, Booklist,* March 15, 1992, p. 1382.

Toth, Luann, review of *The Great Kapok Tree: A Tale of the Amazon Rain Forest, School Library Journal,* May, 1990, p. 82.

■ For More Information See

PERIODICALS

Bulletin of the Center for Children's Books, May, 1997, p. 316.

Booklist, March 1, 1994, p. 1268.

Children's Literature Association Quarterly, Winter, 1994-1995, p. 166.

Five Owls, May-June, 1995, pp. 93-96.
Horn Book, September-October, 1990, p. 589.
Publishers Weekly, February 26, 1988, p. 196.
School Library Journal, November, 1990, p. 90; February, 1996, p. 82.*

*   *   *

CHRISTOPHER, Matt(hew Frederick) 1917-1997 (Fredric Martin)

OBITUARY NOTICE—See index for *SATA* sketch: Born August 16, 1917, in Bath, PA; died of complications following an operation for a brain tumor, September 20, 1997, in Charlotte, NC (one source says Rock Hill, SC). Laborer, editor, athlete, and author. Christopher is remembered for his books for children and young adults that often center around sports. Characterized by simple plots and language, his stories emphasize sportsmanship and team effort by demonstrating how their young protagonists, including minority and disabled children, learn to overcome personal fears through discipline and self-acceptance. Before becoming a full-time writer in 1963, Christopher held a series of jobs. He worked as a laborer for Cayuga Rock Salt, an assembler for Allen-Wales Adding Machines, a group leader and assembler for General Electric, and a member of the production staff at National Cash Register. He also worked as a technical editor at General Electric Electronics Center. As a writer, Christopher often borrowed from his experiences as a minor-league baseball player. He developed an interest in writing as a youth, despite the fact that his immigrant parents were unable to read or write in English. After winning an award in a *Writer's Digest* short story contest, he spent his free time penning articles, stories, and other fiction. His first book was an adult mystery, published in 1952, entitled *Look for the Body.* His first children's book was *The Lucky Baseball Bat,* a story that remains one of his most popular. Among his other books for children are: *Baseball Pals, Basketball Sparkplug, Touchdown for Tommy, The Catcher with a Glass Arm, Wingman on Ice, Shortstop from Tokyo, The Pigeon with a Tennis Elbow, The Hockey Machine, Pressure Play, Man out at First, Beloved St. Anne, Zero's Slider, Top Wing, The Winning Stroke, The Dog that Pitched a No-Hitter,* and *The Dog that Stole Home.* He also wrote novels for young adults under the pseudonym Fredric Martin. Among these works are *Mystery on Crabapple Hill, Mystery at Monkey Run,* and *Mystery under Fugitive House.*

OBITUARIES AND OTHER SOURCES:

PERIODICALS

New York Times, September 24, 1997, p. D23.
Publishers Weekly, October 13, 1997, p. 27.
Washington Post, September 26, 1997, p. B4.

COLEMAN, Clare See BELL, Clare (Louise)

*   *   *

COLLINGTON, Peter 1948-

■ Personal

Born April 2, 1948, in Northcotes, England; son of Nick Edward (a draftsman) and Barbara (Pope) Collington; married Bonnie Winfield, February 17, 1979; children: Sasha. *Education:* Attended Bournemouth College of Art, 1964-67.

■ Addresses

Agent—Gina Pollinger, 4 Garrick St., London WC2E 9BH, England.

■ Career

Writer and illustrator, 1984—. Worked as an elevator operator, child minder, and cleaner while writing and drawing, 1967-84.

■ Awards, Honors

Mother Goose Award runner-up, British Book Club Books for Children, 1987, for *Little Pickle;* Smarties Prize, 1988, for *The Angel and the Soldier Boy.*

■ Writings

SELF-ILLUSTRATED PICTURE BOOKS

Little Pickle, Dutton, 1986.
The Angel and the Soldier Boy, Knopf, 1987.
My Darling Kitten, Knopf, 1988.
On Christmas Eve, Knopf, 1990.
The Midnight Circus, Knopf, 1992.
The Tooth Fairy, Random House, 1995.
A Small Miracle, Random House, 1997.

PICTURE BOOKS FOR OLDER READERS

The Coming of the Surfman, Jonathan Cape (London), 1993, Knopf, 1994.

■ Sidelights

English author and illustrator Peter Collington is noted for creating picture books that rely on their detailed illustrations, rather than text, to relate a story. Creating images that a *Kirkus Reviews* critic characterizes as "distinguished by plenty of interesting, funny details and by the artist's elegant design," Collington has published such books as *Little Pickle, The Midnight Circus,* and *A Small Miracle* for young listeners. He has also turned his talents as a storyteller to older primary readers in *The Coming of the Surfman,* an unusual allegory set in the ganglands of the inner city about a quirky and rather mysterious businessman who starts a surf shop in an abandoned storefront far away from the beach. The man's actions seem odd until he transforms a vacant factory building into a giant wave machine, to the delight of bored area teens, whose violent behavior ceases as they become entranced by the Surfman's activities. Gang warfare stops for a time, but ultimately swells back up again, destroying the Surfman's efforts to bring the young people together.

Collington knew from an early age that he wanted to be an artist. In 1964, at age sixteen, he enrolled at Bournemouth College of Art, graduating three years later. From there, he found work to support his artistic habit: jobs as an elevator operator, child minder, and cleaner each helped to keep the bills paid while Collington worked at developing his drawing technique. In 1979 he married, and two years later he and his wife had their first child, a girl they named Sasha.

Sasha's birth changed Collington's career, although he didn't know it at the time. Suddenly, instead of devoting much of his time to art, the new father found his hours at home revolving around diaper changing, bottle warmings, and playtime. "I would draw little pictures for her," Collington once told *Something about the Author* (*SATA*), "of mum and dad, granny and grandpa, and anyone else she was interested in." In fact, the author/artist credits his daughter with the inspiration for his first book, *Little Pickle.* "When Sasha was nearly two she loved to push about her own stroller," he explained. "One day I did a drawing of a little girl pushing along her sleeping mummy. My daughter was delighted. This was how I got the idea for *Little Pickle.*"

Although he had the idea for the book, Collington spent some nine months preparing all of the illustrations for the story, which has no words. "Every day I would bring to Sasha the latest installment of the book and hold her up to view it. She would have a look and then we would have to act it out. She would be Little Pickle (not too far from the truth), and I would be the sea captain and rescue her from a makeshift boat of cardboard."

Little Pickle uses only pictures in telling the story of a small girl who seems to have a knack for finding trouble. After a busy morning, she goes out in her stroller for an afternoon walk; tired, she soon falls asleep. Little Pickle's dreams take Collington's audience into a topsy-turvy world, where mothers ride in strollers pushed by toddlers and adventures at sea include card-playing, floating rubber rafts, fishing, and near-disaster, all before going home to safety. With its comic-book-frame format, the story flows clearly, with illustrations "soft in style and quite encompassing in the world they create," according to *Bulletin of the Center for Children's Books* reviewer Betsy Hearne.

"The idea of the rescue at sea has parallels within my own family," Collington explained about the story line in *Little Pickle.* "My grandfather was a sea captain who took part in the evacuation of Russian refugees from Odessa in 1919. My grandmother was a passenger aboard my grandfather's ship. She had been a private secretary to the commander of the navy base in Odessa

and was escaping the Bolsheviks. They met, fell in love, and married. I feel that my grandmother was rescued from impending disaster in the same way as Little Pickle is in my book."

After the success of *Little Pickle,* Collington decided to devote himself to writing and illustrating books for children. His next effort, *The Angel and the Soldier Boy,* is also told with watercolor instead of words. Lulled into sleep on the wings of a bedtime story about pirates, the young girl in Collington's story dreams that miniature pirates enter her room and engage in all sorts of piratical doings, including stealing money from her piggy bank. The girl's wooden soldier comes to life and attempts to stop the thievery, but is caught and dragged aboard the pirate ship; a toy angel—another beloved toy—must then save him, not only from the pirates but from the curious family cat as well. *School Library Journal* contributor Barbara S. McGinn maintained that Collington has lavished as much attention on the background details as on the focal points of each drawing. "Carpet design and wallpaper patterns, curtain and bedclothing texture add interest and liveliness ... as does the artist's use of light and shadow," noted the critic. Praising the book in the *New York Times Book Review,* Jim Trelease asserted that *The Angel and the Soldier Boy* "succeeds because it is the stuff of children's dreams—heroes and heroines, villains and treasure, danger and narrow escapes, toys and make-believe."

Other wordless picture books by Collington include *The Tooth Fairy,* an imaginative story of how a young tooth fairy repays children for their baby teeth (and where the teeth go when they are taken away!); *Midnight Circus,* about a small boy whose sadness over the disappearance of an old mechanical horse from his neighborhood is allayed when he dreams that he rides with the horse to a land that hosts the Midnight Circus; and *A Small Miracle,* a story about a poor, elderly woman who is repaid for her bravery and kindness in rescuing the church charity box and the Nativity scene from a local thief. After attempting to restore the Nativity figures to their proper places, the old woman faints from hunger, so Mary, Joseph, and company head to the supermarket to fill the woman's cupboards with nourishing food as a Christmas gift. A *Publishers Weekly* reviewer described *The Tooth Fairy* as a "splendid work" with an "inventive, heartwarming conclusion." Lauren Peterson wrote in *Booklist* that the story "unfolds through an intricately detailed series of clear, amazingly realistic pictures" that "[draw] us into a magical world." Reviewing *Midnight Circus, Horn Book* critic Margaret A. Bush praised Collington's "pencil sketches, mutely shaded ... judicious in detail and sometimes marvelous in perspective" in what she concluded is a "beautifully developed, satisfying visit to the land of midnight." *Booklist*'s Stephanie Zvirin averred that this "elaborate and dramatic story" is "a wonderful excursion into a realm where fantasy and reality collide," while Shirley Wilton of *School Library Journal* offered further tribute, calling the fantasy "a gentle wordless tale of loss, adventure and triumph." "Collington is a master of the wordless form," noted Deborah Stevenson in reviewing *A Small*

Miracle for the *Bulletin of the Center for Children's Books,* "and his narrative, which flows from panel to panel with clarity and rhythm, is effective and understandable."

In his departure from wordless picture books for the very young to what Hazel Rochman of *Booklist* described as "a sophisticated, illustrated story for older readers," Collington's "paintings are haunting" in *The Coming of the Surfman,* and, though the truce between gangs breaks down and the destructive forces appear to have won, Rochman observed that the narrator "dreams that the Surfman will come back."

■ Works Cited

Bush, Margaret A., review of *Midnight Circus, Horn Book,* September-October, 1993, pp. 582-83.

Hearne, Betsy, review of *Little Pickle, Bulletin of the Center for Children's Books,* September, 1986, p. 4.

Review of *Little Pickle, Kirkus Reviews,* May 15, 1986, p. 785.

McGinn, Barbara, review of *The Angel and the Soldier Boy, School Library Journal,* August, 1987, p. 66.

Peterson, Lauren, review of *The Tooth Fairy, Booklist,* October 1, 1995, p. 325.

Rochman, Hazel, review of *The Coming of the Surfman, Booklist,* December 15, 1993, p. 754.

Review of *A Small Miracle, Publishers Weekly,* October 6, 1997, p. 53.

Stevenson, Deborah, review of *A Small Miracle, Bulletin of the Center for Children's Books,* January, 1998, p. 157.

Review of *The Tooth Fairy, Publishers Weekly,* July 24, 1995, p. 64.

Trelease, Jim, review of *The Angel and the Soldier Boy, New York Times Book Review,* May 17, 1987, p. 32.

Wilton, Shirley, review of *Midnight Circus, School Library Journal,* August 1993, p. 140.

Zvirin, Stephanie, review of *Midnight Circus, Booklist,* December 15, 1993, p. 763.

■ For More Information See

PERIODICALS

Booklist, September 15, 1990, p. 168.

Bulletin of the Center for Children's Books, June 1987, p. 185; October 1990, p. 25.

Horn Book, November, 1990, p. 718.

Junior Bookshelf, February, 1991, p. 13.

Kirkus Reviews, May 1, 1987, p. 716; December 15, 1993, p. 1588.

New York Times Book Review, December 16, 1990, p. 27.

School Library Journal, October, 1997, p. 41.*

COOPER, Elisha 1971-

■ Personal

Born February 22, 1971, in New Haven, CT; son of Peter (a lawyer and farmer) and Diana (a writer and farmer) Cooper. *Education:* Yale College, B.A., 1993.

■ Addresses

Home—77a Tamalpais Rd., Berkeley, CA 94708. *Agent*—Darhansoff & Verrill Literary Agency, 179 Franklin St., 4th fl., New York, NY. *Electronic mail*—elicooper@aol.com.

■ Career

New Yorker magazine, messenger, 1993-95; writer and artist, 1995—.

■ Writings

FOR CHILDREN

Country Fair, Greenwillow, 1997.
Ballpark, Greenwillow, 1998.

OTHER

A Year in New York, City and Company (New York, NY), 1995.

ELISHA COOPER

Off the Road: An American Sketchbook, Villard (New York, NY), 1997.

A Day at Yale, The Yale Bookstore (New Haven, CT), 1998.

■ Sidelights

Elisha Cooper told *SATA:* "I grew up drawing cows. In the fields below our house there was a herd of Jerseys, and when I was three or four I sat on our porch with pencils and paper and tried to sketch them. The results were pretty lousy, or so I thought at the time, and I remember having tantrums and ripping up the drawings when they didn't look exactly right.

"When I got older, my best friend and I started a lawn-mowing business; we took the money we made and went on trips. I disliked cameras—more accurately, I disliked the loud splashy tourists who used them—so I kept notebooks and wrote down things we saw, what we ate, smells. My mother gave me a tin of watercolors (the same one I use now) and I took that on my trips, too. At home I read a lot, especially *Tintin* and *Asterix.* I took books and newspapers on walks with my goats.

"When I was at Yale and playing football, I brought sketchbooks with me on road trips. I also wrote for the *New Journal,* a magazine, usually about things I had done—like bottling beer at a factory or playing in a game. I spent the summer before my senior year in Idaho working for the Forest Service (inspired by Norman Maclean's short stories) and wrote in a notebook and missed my friends. When I graduated and came to New York, I took a sketchbook along on the subway when I made deliveries as a messenger for the *New Yorker* magazine. That became my first book, *A Year in New York.* I think at this time I fell in love with books, and with New York. They both have a richness to them. Then I quit my job and drove around the country, sleeping in the front seat, showering in rivers, and seeing what I could find. That book was called *Off the Road: An American Sketchbook.*

"I think most kids' books are stories. I like reading stories, but can't write them. I write what I see. For my first two kids' books, I spent a fall hanging out at country fairs and ballparks. I like nosing around and looking for the weird, something that hits me, a goofy gesture."

Nosing around paid off for Cooper's book *Country Fair,* an illustrated look at one day in the life of the popular rural event, from corn-shucking to award-winning cows. *Booklist* reviewer Susan Dove Lempke called the work "as removed from big, splashy preschool books as it can be. It is brimming with tiny, precisely described moments." Lolly Robinson wrote in *Horn Book:* "The small size of this book and the quiet honesty of text and art indicate a book that will be shared one-on-one and frequently revisited by children who enjoy an amiable ramble." A *Kirkus Reviews* critic called Cooper's work "a quirky, engaging look at the sights, sounds, and scents of a country fair."

Cooper next turned his gaze to baseball, for his book *Ballpark.* A *Kirkus Reviews* critic noted Cooper's attention to detail and his ability to evoke the baseball experience and share it with everyone: "Sports fan or not, spectators or athletes, children will be engaged for the full nine innings." Elizabeth Bush, in *Bulletin of the Center for Children's Books,* noted Cooper's "tidy phrasing ... and restrained humor" in recommending *Ballpark* as "an elegant visual presentation."

Cooper acknowledges his penchant for reporting on a particular event—be it a fair or a ballgame—but only up to a point. "I think of myself as a lazy journalist," he told *SATA.* "If I were more serious, I'd write long pieces with lots of facts. I read too much, the *New York Times* and *Calvin and Hobbes.*

"In some way, I've never evolved. I'm most happy when I'm about to set off on a trip with a sketchbook in my back pocket. There's a lot of cool stuff out there. For me, books are a way of looking. I still have tantrums when I can't draw cows."

■ Works Cited

Review of *Ballpark, Kirkus Reviews,* February 15, 1998, p. 265.

Review of *Country Fair, Kirkus Reviews,* June 15, 1997, pp. 947-48.

Bush, Elizabeth, review of *Ballpark, Bulletin of the Center for Children's Books,* March, 1998, p. 239.

Lempke, Susan Dove, review of *Country Fair, Booklist,* September 15, 1997, p. 240.

Robinson, Holly, review of *Country Fair, Horn Book,* September-October, 1997, p. 554.

■ For More Information See

PERIODICALS

Five Owls, March-April, 1998, p. 79-80.

New York Times Book Review, February 25, 1996, p. 20.

Publishers Weekly, January 8, 1996, p. 22; May 26, 1997, p. 85.

School Library Journal, September, 1997, p. 179; March, 1998, p. 194.

*   *   *

CRARY, Elizabeth (Ann) 1942-

■ Personal

Born May 18, 1942, in New Orleans, LA; daughter of Charles Harold and Lora Anne (Briggs) Deinken; married Fred Dailey Crary, August 14, 1966; children: Karl, Karen. *Education:* Louisiana State University, B.S., 1964, M.S., 1966. *Religion:* Methodist. *Hobbies and other interests:* Active in Girl Scouts, U.S.A.

■ Addresses

Office—7750 31st Ave. N.E., Seattle, WA 98115.

■ Career

Educator, author, publisher, and parenting consultant. Food Research Institute, University of Wisconsin, Madison, research assistant, 1966-70, food science department, 1971-77; Parenthood Education Programs, Madison, WI, founder and director, 1974-77; North Seattle Community College, instructor in parent education, 1977; Parenting Press, publisher, 1978; Parent Education Associates, codirector, 1980. *Member:* National Association for the Education of Young Children.

■ Writings

NONFICTION

Without Spanking or Spoiling: A Practical Approach to Toddler and Preschool Guidance, illustrated by Ellen B. Ochs, Parenting Press (Seattle), 1979.
Kids Can Cooperate, Parenting Press, 1984.
Pick Up Your Socks—and Other Skills Growing Children Need, illustrated by Pati Casebolt, Parenting Press, 1990.
Historical Activity Guide, Parenting Press, 1993.
365 Wacky, Wonderful Ways to Get Your Children to Do What You Want, illustrated by Dave Carbot, Parenting Press, 1994.
Love and Limits: Guidance Tools for Creative Parenting, Parenting Press, 1994.
Magic Tools for Raising Kids, illustrated by Rebekah Strecker, Parenting Press, 1994.
Help! The Kids Are at It Again: Using Kids' Quarrels to Teach "People" Skills, illustrated by Mits Katayama, Parenting Press, 1997.

"CHILDREN'S PROBLEM SOLVING" SERIES

I Can't Wait, illustrated by Marina Megale Horosko, Parenting Press, 1982.
I Want It, illustrated by Marina Megale Horosko, Parenting Press, 1982.
I Want to Play, illustrated by Marina Megale Horosko, Parenting Press, 1982.
My Name Is Not Dummy, illustrated by Marina Megale, Parenting Press, 1983.
I'm Lost, illustrated by Marina Megale, Parenting Press, 1985.
Mommy Don't Go, illustrated by Marina Megale, Parenting Press, 1986.
Finders, Keepers?, illustrated by Rebekah Strecker, Parenting Press, 1987.

"DEALING WITH FEELINGS" SERIES

I'm Proud, illustrated by Jean Whitney, Parenting Press, 1991.
I'm Frustrated, illustrated by Whitney, Parenting Press, 1992.
I'm Mad, illustrated by Whitney, Parenting Press, 1992.
I'm Excited, illustrated by Whitney, Parenting Press, 1994.
I'm Furious, illustrated by Whitney, Parenting Press, 1994.
I'm Scared, illustrated by Whitney, Parenting Press, 1994.

Twins Annie and Jessie are so wound-up about their impending birthday party, they find it hard to stay out of trouble until their mother and grandfather teach them how to control their feelings. (From *I'm Excited,* written by Elizabeth Crary and illustrated by Jean Whitney.)

"FEELINGS FOR LITTLE CHILDREN" SERIES

When You're Happy, illustrated by Mits Katayama, Parenting Press, 1997.
When You're Mad, illustrated by Katayama, Parenting Press, 1997.
When You're Shy, illustrated by Katayama, Parenting Press, 1997.
When You're Silly, illustrated by Katayama, Parenting Press, 1997.

■ Sidelights

Elizabeth Crary is a publisher, educator, author, and consultant who specializes in parent education. In the mid-1970s, she and her husband founded Parenting Press, a publishing firm located in Seattle, Washington, that focuses on subjects of child development, child guidance, and parenting. In addition to her role as publisher, Crary is also the author of numerous works issued by the small press, including the parenting guidebooks *Without Spanking or Spoiling: A Practical Approach to Toddler and Preschool Guidance* and *Magic Tools for Raising Kids.* Crary has also written a series of problem-solving books for children and two series of juvenile works that explore ways to handle emotions.

Crary's "Children's Problem Solving" series, which includes such titles as *I Can't Wait* and *Finders,*

Keepers?, is intended for preschoolers and primary graders. The books present such problematic situations as conflicts over toys, taking turns, joining a group already at play, and name-calling, providing examples of both effective and ineffective behaviors that are intended to serve as a basis for discussion between adults and children reading the story. Elaine Knight, reviewing *Finders, Keepers?* for *School Library Journal,* noted that the message of the book is clear and the outcome of decisions made by the book's characters are "logical and natural." Other volumes in the series include *My Name Is Not Dummy, I'm Lost,* and *Mommy Don't Go.*

Crary is also the author of the series "Dealing with Feelings," comprised of six works examining pride, frustration, excitement, fear, and anger. As in her problem-solving series, each volume describes a problem and then explores responses to the situation. According to Janice Glover in *Small Press,* "This innovative series ... has as much to say to parents as it does to their offspring." Celia A. Huffman, in a review of the books *I'm Frustrated, I'm Proud* and *I'm Mad* in *School Library Journal,* described Crary's works as "practical vehicles to help children work through feelings."

■ Works Cited

Glover, Janice, review of the "Dealing with Feelings" series, *Small Press,* summer, 1992, p. 59.
Huffman, Celia A., review of *I'm Frustrated, I'm Mad,* and *I'm Proud, School Library Journal,* June, 1992, pp. 90-91.
Knight, Elaine, review of *Finders, Keepers?, School Library Journal,* January, 1988, p. 96.

■ For More Information See

PERIODICALS

Bloomsbury Review, September, 1995, p. 20.
Children's Bookwatch, February, 1994, p. 1; October, 1996, p. 12.
Publishers Weekly, September 14, 1990, p. 102.
School Library Journal, January, 1983, p. 58; February, 1984, p. 57; April, 1984, p. 100.*

* * *

CRIDER, (Allen) Bill(y) 1941-
(Jack MacLane; Nick Carter, a house pseudonym)

■ Personal

Born July 28, 1941, in Mexia, TX; son of Billy (a freight agent) and Frances (Brodnax) Crider; married Judy Stutts, June 4, 1965; children: Angela, Allen. *Education:* University of Texas at Austin, B.A., 1963, Ph.D., 1971; North Texas State University, M.A., 1966.

■ Addresses

Home—1606 South Hill St., Alvin, TX 77511-4356. *Office*—Department of English, Alvin Community College, Alvin, TX 77511. *Electronic mail*—abc@wt.net.

■ Career

High school English teacher in Corsicana, TX, 1963-65; Howard Payne University, Brownwood, TX, associate professor, 1971-74, professor of English, 1974-85, chair of department, 1977-83; Alvin Community College, Alvin, TX, professor of English and chair of department, 1984—. *Member:* Mystery Writers of America, Private Eye Writers of America, Sisters in Crime, American Crime Writers League, Western Writers of America.

■ Awards, Honors

Anthony Award for best first novel, for *Too Late to Die;* Shamus Award nominee for best first private-eye novel, for *Dead on the Island.*

■ Writings

FOR YOUNG PEOPLE

A Vampire Named Fred (young adult novel), Maggie Books, 1990.
Mike Gonzo and the Sewer Monster (young adult novel), Minstrel, 1996.
Mike Gonzo and the Almost Invisible Man (young adult novel), Minstrel, 1996.

BILL CRIDER

Mike Gonzo and the UFO Terror (young adult novel),
   Minstrel, 1997.
Muttketeer ("The Adventures of Wishbone" series;
   children's fiction), Lyrick, 1997.

MYSTERIES; "SHERIFF DAN RHODES" SERIES

Too Late to Die, Walker & Co. (New York City), 1986.
Shotgun Saturday Night, Walker & Co., 1987.
Cursed to Death, Walker & Co., 1988.
Death on the Move, Walker & Co., 1989.
Evil at the Root, St. Martin's, 1990.
Booked for a Hanging, St. Martin's, 1992.
Murder Most Fowl, St. Martin's, 1994.
Winning Can Be Murder, St. Martin's, 1996.
Death by Accident, St. Martin's, 1998.

MYSTERIES; "PROFESSOR CARL BURNS" SERIES

One Dead Dean, Walker & Co., 1988.
Dying Voices, St. Martin's, 1989.
. . . A Dangerous Thing, Walker & Co., 1994.

MYSTERIES; "TRUMAN SMITH" SERIES

Dead on the Island, Walker & Co., 1991.
Gator Kill, Walker & Co., 1992.
When Old Men Die, Walker & Co., 1994.
The Prairie Chicken Kill, Walker & Co., 1996.
Murder Takes a Break, Walker & Co., 1997.

WESTERNS

Ryan Rides Back, M. Evans (New York City), 1988.
Galveston, M. Evans, 1988.
A Time for Hanging, M. Evans, 1989.
Medicine Show, M. Evans, 1990.

HORROR NOVELS; UNDER PSEUDONYM JACK MacLANE

Keepers of the Beast, Zebra Books (New York City),
   1988.
Goodnight Moom, Zebra Books, 1989.
Blood Dreams, Zebra Books, 1989.
Rest in Peace, Zebra Books, 1990.
Just Before Dark, Zebra Books, 1990.

OTHER

(With Jack N. Davis, under house pseudonym Nick
   Carter) *The Coyote Connection* (espionage novel),
   Charter Books, 1981.
Blood Marks, St. Martin's, 1991.
The Texas Capitol Murders (mystery), St. Martin's,
   1992.
(With Willard Scott) *Murder Under Blue Skies* (mys-
   tery), Dutton, 1997.

OTHER

(Editor; as Allen Billy Crider) *Mass Market American
   Publishing,* G. K. Hall (Boston), 1982.

Also contributor to *Murder for Mother,* a collection of
mystery stories published by NAL/Dutton in 1994.
Contributor to *Dictionary of Literary Biography* and
Twentieth-Century Western Writers, both published by
Gale Research. Contributor to *Dimensions of Detective
Fiction,* Popular Press, 1976, and *Twentieth-Century
Crime and Mystery Writers,* St. Martin's, 1980. Contrib-

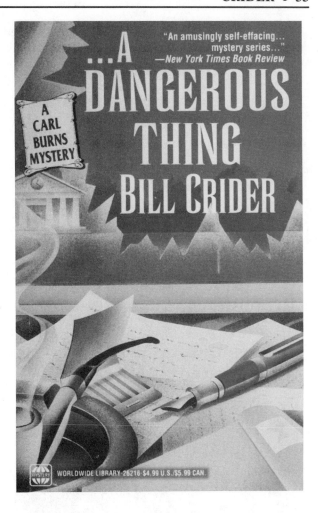

College professor sleuth Carl Burns tries to unravel the
mystery of his colleague's murder.

uting editor of *Paperback Quarterly.* Founder and
publisher of *Macavity,* a fanzine of mystery fiction.

■ **Adaptations**

Dead on the Island was released on audio cassette by
Ingram in 1995, while *Gator Kill* and *When Old Men
Die* were released by the same company in 1996.

■ **Sidelights**

Bill Crider is a writer of genre novels—mysteries,
westerns, and horror stories that are directed to adults
but are appreciated by young people—who also writes
fiction for children and teenagers. Publishing his works
both pseudonymously and under his own name, Crider
is perhaps best known for the three series of mystery
novels he has written as Bill Crider that each feature
personable, easygoing sleuths—a small-town sheriff, a
college professor, and a private detective—as protagonists. The author, who often sets his books in his home
state of Texas, is praised for creating folksy, unpretentious works with colorful, idiosyncratic characters and
lots of Texas-style wit. Recognized for his astute observations of human nature, Crider is also acknowledged
for bringing a fresh approach to the genres he addresses

and for writing novels that are both understated and entertaining.

Crider was born in Mexia, Texas, and educated at the University of Texas at Austin and North Texas State University; he received his Ph.D. in English in 1971. He worked as a high school English teacher in Corsicana, Texas, and as a professor of English at Howard Payne University in Brownsville; currently, he chairs the English department at Alvin Community College in Alvin, Texas. Crider began his literary career as part of the team that contributed to a popular series of spy novels under the name Nick Carter; he also contributed biographical and critical material to reference books on the writers of detective fiction and edited a mystery fanzine. In 1986, Crider published his first self-penned mystery, *Too Late to Die,* which introduced one of his most popular creations, Sheriff Dan Rhodes. Residing in Blacklin County, Texas, Rhodes is a nonviolent, laid-back investigator who bears, according to Wes Lukowsky of *Booklist,* "more than a passing resemblance to Andy Taylor of television's Mayberry" and is, according to the critic, "a genuinely likable character." Rhodes finds himself involved with murders, disappearances, and other incidents that test his powers of detection and

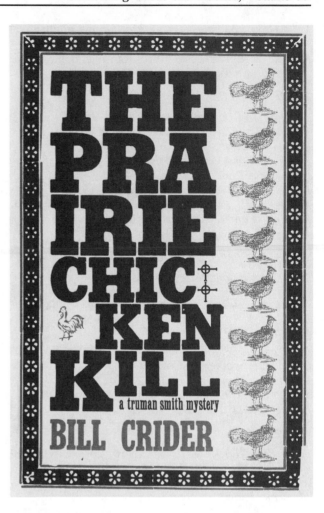

The murder of a bird on federally protected land leads to escalating violence in Crider's book featuring unorthodox private investigator Truman Smith.

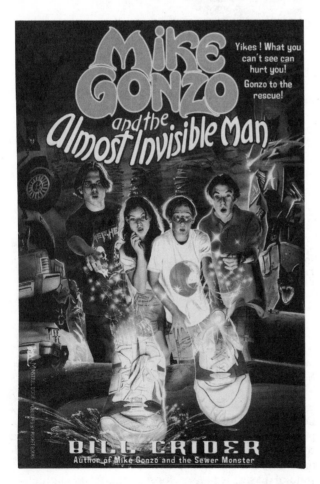

Mike Gonzo and his friends get involved with an invisible man in this installment of Crider's series of books featuring the fearless Gonzo. (Cover illustration by Broeck Steadman.)

reveal the vagaries of human nature in his area of jurisdiction, which *Booklist* reviewer Emily Melton described as "a dusty, dying Texas county in which emu rustling, beer drinking, and cockfighting are the major recreational activities." Crider received the Anthony Award for best first novel for *Too Late to Die,* his first contribution to the Rhodes series. Described by *Kirkus Reviews* as a "respectable debut," the story outlines how Rhodes—recently widowed and running for reelection—investigates three murders: the first of a beautiful young housewife who entertained male guests while her husband worked the night shift; the second of the older woman who screams insults at her funeral; and the third staged by the killer as a suicide. The *Kirkus* critic concluded that "the small-town atmosphere is completely pervasive" and that Rhodes is a "likably strong-and-silent hero"; a reviewer in *Publishers Weekly* agreed, noting that the scenes of "small-town politics and police work are nicely done" and calling the sheriff a "diffident, commensensical, delightful character." In *Shotgun Saturday Night,* Rhodes confronts a neighborhood motorcycle gang of drug dealers while investigating the murder of a local handyman who had discovered two boxes filled with severed limbs. "Red herrings, colorful characters, and an agreeable sense of humor redeem this

Crider's retelling of *The Three Musketeers* is based on the celebrated *Wishbone* television series in which a small dog places himself as a character in the classics of literature. (From *Muttketeer!*, written by Crider and illustrated by Don Punchatz.)

unambitious mystery," noted Benjamin Segedin in *Booklist*. In *Cursed to Death*, Rhodes tries to find a local dentist and landlord who has disappeared after one of his tenants places a curse on him; in addition, he attempts to solve the subsequent murder of the man's wife. Lukowsky of *Booklist* called the novel "very enjoyable," while *Kirkus Reviews* noted its "agreeably folksy blend of pokey detection, lean action, and small-town Texas drollery." *Evil at the Root* finds Rhodes investigating another murder and disappearance: when a nursing home resident is found dead, the prime suspect—a man who had been implicated for a murder that occurred sixty years before—is nowhere to be found. *Publishers Weekly* claimed that Crider "packs his small-town procedural with telling details and clear-eyed observations of human nature." In *Murder Most Fowl*, Rhodes encounters emu rustling as well as two murders. Melton of *Booklist* called the novel "a breath of fresh air" and named it "fun, clever, humorous, well written, and highly entertaining." *Kirkus Reviews* opined, "Blacklin County's getting to be such a sink of iniquity it's a wonder unflappable Rhodes doesn't pack it in for the more peaceful climes of Dallas or L.A."

With the "Professor Carl Burns" books, a series that blends detection and humor, Crider draws on—and subtly pokes fun at—his academic background. In *One Dead Dean*, the author introduces Burns, an English professor at Hartley Gorman College, a fundamentalist Baptist school in West Texas. In this novel, Burns is drawn into an investigation of the murder of the school's unpopular dean when he discovers the man's body. "The sendup of low-level academia is occasionally tart and specific," wrote a critic in *Kirkus Reviews*, who concluded that the book is "harmless foolishness, with a few smile-worthy moments, for a Charlotte MacLeod-ish readership." Writing in *Booklist*, Wes Lukowsky noted that Crider "has a firm grasp of small-town academia and its inhabitants" and called the novel "a witty, stylish effort." In *Dying Voices*, Burns—an "outwardly wimpy hero" whose "quirky personality retains an offbeat charm," according to *Kirkus Reviews*—again tries to solve a murder at Hartly Gorman, this time of a celebrated poet, a former instructor at the college who is killed after a campus appearance. While he stays fairly true to the academic mystery formula, claimed Peter Robertson in *Booklist*, "Crider manages that often-difficult alliance of good sleuthing and smart-ass verbal patter. His detective is pretty smart some of the time and pretty funny most of the time." In ... *A Dangerous Thing*, a professor falls to his death from a window; the murder is investigated by Burns and his assistant, attractive librarian Elaine Tanner. One of the book's main subplots involves the feminist dean Gwendolyn Partridge, who tries to foist political correctness on the conservative backwater campus. Writing in *School Library Journal*, Hugh McAloon said, "Sharp personalities, realistic dialogue, humor, and an uncomplicated plot with an easy vocabulary combine for a readable book that teens will enjoy." *Kirkus Reviews* also noted Crider's "witty, well-aimed barbs for the pompous edicts of the politically correct...."

Kirkus Reviews called Truman Smith, a semiretired private investigator who lives on the Texas Gulf Coast and is featured in several of Crider's novels, "the slowest-moving of Crider's three series detectives...." Smith, a sleuth who likes to stay home, drink Big Red, listen to Elvis records, and read novels such as *Tobacco Road* and *Look Homeward, Angel*, is considered one of Crider's most fully-realized characters. The first volume of the series, *Dead on the Island*, received a Shamus Award nomination for best private eye novel. The story outlines how Smith, who has returned to his hometown of Galveston to find his missing sister, tries to locate a missing girl whose mother was a prostitute; in his search, Tru encounters murder and must look to his own past to solve the mystery. A reviewer in *Publishers Weekly* called *Dead on the Island* "a promising start of a series" and said that Crider created "another well-drawn protagonist, this one a moody, introspective PI in the finest tradition...." In *When Old Men Die*, the detective, whose feelings of inadequacy mask a sharp mind, searches for a well-known homeless man on Galveston Island and tries to solve the murder of a second homeless person. In *The Prairie Chicken Kill*, Smith is hired by an old high-school classmate to find the killer of a grouse—or "prairie chicken"—on the man's federally protected land; a murder takes place after a local birdwatcher is charged with the grouse's death. A reviewer in *Publishers Weekly* noted that when Smith "gets on a case, he's methodical. So's Crider, who fashions a tight plot filled with laconic charm and idiosyncratic characters." *Kirkus Reviews* called *The Prairie Chicken Kill* "lazily understated, with a surprisingly energetic windup—even if that inconsequential grouse is no Maltese Falcon." In *Murder Takes a Break,* a friend asks Tru to look for a missing college boy, a situation that leads to the murder of a girl at the young man's school. Writing in *Voice of Youth Advocates,* Jane Van Wiemokly wrote that Smith's quick wit and smart-aleck attitude "hold the reader.... Tru impels the reading, not the urge to find out who done it."

In addition to his mysteries and the horror novels he has written as Jack MacLane, Crider has written several well-received westerns. In *A Time for Hanging,* a novel set in Texas during the 1880s, the author describes how sheriff Ward Vincent tries to prove the innocence of a young Mexican man accused of the brutal murder of a preacher's daughter. *Booklist* reviewer Wes Lukowsky claimed, "This excellent mystery in a western setting should delight fans of both genres." In *Medicine Show,* gunman Ray Storey struggles with his desire to revenge the death of his younger brother as he travels with a medicine show; again writing in *Booklist,* Lukowsky called the book a "wonderfully written novel that will be at or near the top of the list of 1990's best westerns."

Bill Crider comments, "I've been reading mystery novels almost since the time I learned to read, beginning with Nancy Drew and the Hardy Boys and moving on to practically everything else in the field. When I wrote my doctoral dissertation, it seemed only natural for me to write on private-eye fiction, and even before I received my degree I became a genuine mystery fan, writing articles and reviews for most of the fanzines in the field. I've published my own mystery fanzine, *Macavity,* for an amateur press association for nearly twenty years without missing a mailing. In 1980, when a friend suggested that we collaborate on a Nick Carter novel, it seemed like a logical progression, and to my amazement the novel was published. After that I moved on to writing several mystery series under my own name and then branched out into western and horror fiction. Currently I'm doing a few humorous adventure novels for young readers. I love reading, and I love writing. My hope is that my stories will give someone a small portion of the pleasure that I've derived from reading the work of others over the years."

■ **Works Cited**

Review of ... *A Dangerous Thing, Kirkus Reviews,* May 15, 1994, p. 964.
Review of *Cursed to Death, Kirkus Reviews,* March 15, 1988, pp. 411-12.
Review of *Dead on the Island, Publishers Weekly,* April, 14, 1991, p. 46.

Review of *Dying Voices, Kirkus Reviews,* November 1, 1989, p. 1564.
Review of *Evil at the Root, Publishers Weekly,* May 4, 1990, p. 57.
Lukowsky, Wes, review of *A Time for Hanging, Booklist,* December 15, 1989, p. 811.
Lukowsky, Wes, review of *Cursed to Death, Booklist,* March 1, 1988, p. 1097.
Lukowsky, Wes, review of *Medicine Show, Booklist,* August, 1990, p. 2158.
Lukowsky, Wes, review of *One Dead Dean, Booklist,* August, 1988, p. 1892.
McAloon, Hugh, review of ... *A Dangerous Thing, School Library Journal,* December, 1994, p. 142.
Melton, Emily, review of *Murder Most Fowl, Booklist,* September 1, 1994, p. 26.
Review of *Murder Most Fowl, Kirkus Reviews,* August 1, 1994, p. 1024.
Review of *One Dead Dean, Kirkus Reviews,* July 15, 1988, p. 1015.
Review of *The Prairie Chicken Kill, Kirkus Reviews,* July 15, 1995, p. 1009.
Review of *The Prairie Chicken Kill, Publishers Weekly,* June 24, 1996, p. 48.
Robertson, Peter, review of *Dying Voices, Booklist,* December 1, 1989, p. 725.
Segedin, Benjamin, review of *Shotgun Saturday Night, Booklist,* November 1, 1987, p. 434.
Review of *Too Late to Die, Kirkus Reviews,* June 15, 1986, p. 896.
Review of *Too Late to Die, Publishers Weekly,* May 23, 1986, p. 92.
Van Wiemokly, Jane, review of *Murder Takes a Break, Voice of Youth Advocates,* December, 1997, p. 316.

■ **For More Information See**

BOOKS

Henderson, Lesley, editor, *Twentieth-Century Crime and Mystery Writers,* St. James Press, 1991.

PERIODICALS

Detroit News, January 24, 1998, p. 26D.
Kirkus Reviews, September 15, 1987, p. 1351; May 1, 1991, p. 565.
Locus, February, 1989, p. 49; September, 1990, p. 60; December, 1990, p. 53.
New York Times Book Review, August 21, 1994, p. 16.
Publishers Weekly, June 6, 1994, p. 59; December 24, 1994, p. 53.

—Sketch by Gerard J. Senick

*   *   *

CRUTCHER, Chris(topher C.) 1946-

■ **Personal**

Born July 17, 1946, in Dayton, OH; son of John William (a county clerk) and Jewell (Morris) Crutcher. *Education:* Eastern Washington State College (now University), B.A., 1968. *Hobbies and other interests:*

Running, basketball, swimming, biking, competing in triathlons.

■ Addresses

Home—Spokane, WA. *Agent*—Liz Darhansoff, 1220 Park Ave., New York, NY 10128.

■ Career

Writer, therapist, teacher, and child advocacy worker. Received teaching certificate, 1970; teacher, Kennewick Dropout School, Kennewick, WA, 1970-73; Lakeside School, Oakland, CA, teacher, 1973-76, director, 1976-80; Community Mental Health Center, Spokane, WA, child protection team specialist, 1980-82, child and family mental health professional, 1982-95; full-time writer, 1995—.

■ Awards, Honors

Best Book for Young Adults, American Library Association, for *Running Loose, Stotan!, The Crazy Horse Electric Game, Chinese Handcuffs,* and *Athletic Shorts;* Best Books, *School Library Journal,* for *The Crazy Horse Electric Game;* ALAN Award for significant contributions to young adult literature.

■ Writings

FICTION; FOR YOUNG ADULTS

Running Loose, Greenwillow, 1983.
Stotan!, Greenwillow, 1986.
The Crazy Horse Electric Game, Greenwillow, 1987.
Chinese Handcuffs, Greenwillow, 1989.
Athletic Shorts (short stories), Greenwillow, 1991.
Staying Fat for Sarah Byrnes, Greenwillow, 1993.
Ironman: A Novel, Greenwillow, 1995.

CHRIS CRUTCHER

OTHER

Deep End: A Novel of Suspense (psychological fiction), Morrow, 1992.

Contributor of short stories to anthologies and of articles to periodicals, including *Spokane.*

■ Adaptations

Crutcher created screenplays from his novels *Running Loose* and *The Crazy Horse Electric Game. The Deep End* has been optioned by Interscope Pictures; *Staying Fat for Sarah Burns* by Columbia Pictures; and "A Brief Moment in the Life of Angus Bethune," a short story from the collection *Athletic Shorts,* by Disney Pictures.

■ Sidelights

Considered among the most respected American authors of young adult literature, Crutcher is regarded as a dynamic and insightful writer whose works are both exciting sports stories and authentic reflections of the inner lives of his protagonists. Praised for the tough yet thoughtful nature and evocative quality of his novels and short stories as well as for the believability of both his characters and the sports background he favors, Crutcher, who has worked as a mental health professional in child and family services as well as for child advocacy, is consistently celebrated for the honesty and appeal of his books as well as for his understanding of teenagers.

Crutcher profiles young male high school students who are involved in such sports as baseball, basketball, football, swimming, wrestling, and track. While preparing for and participating in their games or meets, these characters—sensitive young people noted for being far removed from the "jock" stereotype—are faced with problems, moral dilemmas, and tough choices with which they struggle. Crutcher uses high school athletics as the proving ground for personal achievement; by testing their own limits, the boys in his books emerge from their crises as stronger and more mature individuals. Throughout his works, Crutcher addresses challenging topics; his protagonists encounter sickness and death, divorce, rape and sexual abuse, disability, discrimination, AIDS, abortion, and other issues as well as pimps, prostitutes, and motorcycle and youth gangs; in addition, his characters must cope with the attitudes and actions of their parents, coaches, teammates, and friends. Despite the seriousness of his themes, Crutcher underscores his books with positive messages that stress integrity, dignity, honor, courage, tenacity, survival, and hope. In addition, he stresses the joys of competitive sports and often includes positive friendships—between boys and between both sexes—and romantic relationships in his works. The author also invests his books with humor, which ranges from subtle wit to raw, locker-room style banter. Due to their subject matter and use of rough language, some of Crutcher's books have been censored; the author is also criticized for the complexity of his books and for his concentration on male protagonists, though he is also credited with

Crutcher's collection of six short stories features characters from his previous works of fiction, as well as a few fresh faces. (Cover illustration by Bryce Lee.)

creating well-realized female characters in supporting roles. As a stylist, Crutcher writes spirited, fast-paced works that incorporate both first- and third-person narrations; he often uses the formats of the diary or personal letter to structure his books. Writing in *Twentieth-Century Children's Writers,* Bonnie O. Ericson said, "Many authors have used sports as a metaphor for the ups and downs of life, but very few with the combined humor and poignancy of Chris Crutcher.... [In the goal of] writing books that will hook young male readers, Crutcher is entirely successful. At the same time, he's created rich and complex works for all readers." In her essay in *Horn Book,* Christine McDonnell claimed that Crutcher "gives readers the inside story on young men, sports, and growing up," while Anita Silvey, writing in the same periodical, commented that whether Crutcher is writing "about the baseball field or the basketball court, he makes sports and the young boys who play them come alive and in the process presents the issues and problems of adolescence." *Booklist* reviewer Stephanie Zvirin called Crutcher "one of the most successful novelists writing for young adults today.... Chris Crutcher knows the right moves on and off the court."

Crutcher has devoted his career to helping troubled young people deal with their situations. "I'm forever being astonished at the heroism of kids who've made it," he once said in an interview with *Authors and Artists for Young Adults* (*AAYA*). "You look at their lives, and you look at what happened, and you don't understand why they're still standing—but they are, and they have enough strength to keep powering them on." Crutcher's experiences with young people have helped to inspire his books, and he often interweaves his own background into his novels and stories. Born in Dayton, Ohio, Crutcher grew up in Cascade, a remote logging town in central Idaho: "My dad was in the Air Force, and my parents were just passing through," he told Dave Jenkinson of *Emergency Librarian,* adding that his parents "were in Cascade before I got dry." Crutcher told *AAYA,* "It was eighty miles from the nearest movie—and I don't mean eighty miles over freeway, I mean over two-lane highway. One street in the whole town was paved." For entertainment the town turned to high school sports, especially football, which was followed with a fierce devotion. "On a Friday afternoon you couldn't buy a tank of gas until the game was over," Crutcher recalled. The people of Cascade were typically the rugged, active kind—loggers, ranchers, and hunters. Crutcher came away with mixed feelings about these latter-day frontiersmen: he didn't always like their politics, and he didn't like hunting, either, but he admired their willingness to take care of one another. In Cascade, he observed, "there are no street people, there are no homeless people, because you can always find a place to put somebody. It's real hard to let people freeze to death if you know who they are."

Crutcher got along so well with his parents John and Jewell that he dedicated his first book, *Running Loose,* to them and included them as characters. "They've been a real influence on me," he told the *Idaho Statesman.* "They let me go. It's real important to have been allowed not to carry around your parents' garbage. I knew I could take off and go hitchhiking around the country and I wouldn't lose my mom and dad." As he explained to *AAYA,* "My mother gave me a sense of passion, of doing things that weren't necessarily rational, of going with my feelings. And my dad was the balance point to that. He was a tremendously rational man, the problem solver. He gave me an ability to make things simple ... and get to what the problem really is." As an adult counseling people about their issues, Crutcher said, "I draw far more on my dad's voice for making simple sense of things than I do for any class I ever took."

Crutcher found school "a good place to be a stand-up comic." As he told *AAYA,* "My brother was the valedictorian of his class, and it seemed like an awful lot of pressure to put on yourself, so I coasted through school." His goal was to be a "perfect C student," he explained. "If I could have done it exactly right I would never have gotten any other grade than a C, but I would screw up and get a D and then I'd need a B to counterbalance." In any case, "there were always ways to get through without doing any work"—his brother's old book reports, for instance, were a goldmine. "I was rebellious, really, and I didn't want to do anything anybody told me to do. Also, I could charm my way out of trouble." Crutcher's introduction to writing came through punishment themes: as he told Dave Jenkinson, "Teachers used to like to give me 500-word themes, and I gave them lots of reasons to do it. I would get real creative doing these because there was no school structure to them." When he was in junior high, Crutcher's journalism teacher, impressed by one of his themes, invited him to write for the school paper. Until his senior year, Crutcher recalled, "I had this column where I took pot shots at everybody." He told *AAYA,* "It was kind of a smartass thing—I would take shots at people—and I really liked it. I liked being able to say things and not have anybody have the chance to get even with me." Crutcher claimed that the only book that he read all the way through as a high school student was Harper Lee's *To Kill a Mockingbird,* which he began in preparation for a test. He recalls scanning the jacket copy to see if he could actually get out of reading the book, but once he read the first page, he was, as he told Heather Vogel Frederick of *Publishers Weekly,* "swept away"; Crutcher finished the book, he noted, "about three weeks after the test."

Instead of academics, Crutcher was drawn to sports. "I really liked the sense of belonging," he told *AAYA.* In Cascade, he told Frederick of *Publishers Weekly,* "It didn't matter if you were a good athlete or not. You tried out for the football team with a stethoscope—if you could breathe you could play. And if you didn't show up, they'd come get you." Crutcher told *AAYA,* "My characters are always much better athletes than I was. I really didn't become proficient in basketball until after the twelfth grade—I was a bench sitter of gross proportion. In track I was somewhere in the middle. Football was probably my best sport, just because it required less athleticism." The camaraderie that Crutcher found in athletics allowed him to apply himself to team play. "Finding out how far you can push yourself if you have the support of your friends—that's very important to me about sports."

By the mid-1960s Crutcher was out of high school and studying at Eastern Washington State College. "I knew I was going to college but I didn't have any idea why," he told *AAYA.* "I was rebellious as hell—I mean rebellious with ideas—and really enjoyed it." He remained involved with sports, joining the swim team and reaching the small-college nationals, but he was not a conventional athlete. "I couldn't have been happier than when Tommie Smith and John Carlos raised their black fists at the 1968 Olympics," Crutcher noted, referring to the famous gesture of black pride made by the runners when they received their Olympic medals. "I was one of three or four lettermen at Eastern Washington who stood up for that stuff and got a lot of hate mail," Crutcher recalled. Meanwhile, he finally found something to like about school. "I took my first sociology class," he said, "and I realized that institutions were in the world for some purpose other than what I had been told they were there for—religion as a social control or education as

somebody else's idea of a social control. Things weren't exactly how I'd been told. My rebellion had a purpose."

At the beginning of his senior year, Crutcher got a phone call from the administration—he still hadn't declared a major. "I got my transcript and tried to find out what I had the most credits in," he said, "and it was psychology and sociology so I chose that, with no idea what to do with it." Next, Crutcher said, "I spent a year running around playing *Route 66* with a friend of mine"—the guys hopped in a car and flipped coins at major intersections, ending up in places like Texas and Hawaii—"and then I went back to school for a teaching credential, mostly because people said that was a saleable skill." When a new, experimental school in Washington State—Kennewick Dropout School—finally made Crutcher an offer, he took it. "I got the job because I had the psych background and I wouldn't cost them much money because I didn't have any experience," he admitted. "They had a building, they put me in it, and in two years I never saw another adult in the

Crutcher's controversial novel concerns the friendship between two emotionally traumatized young people, one scarred by his brother's suicide, the other by sexual abuse. (Cover illustration by Hiroko.)

place. It was like, 'Do what you do,' and I learned by fire." The goal was to convince the kids, usually juniors and seniors, to stay with the program long enough to get a high school diploma. "I learned a lot about what turned kids off," Crutcher said. "I did a lot of 'free-school' things. I tried a tremendous amount that *didn't work*. And the key was that I recognized that early and would just say 'This isn't working—let's stop it, it's driving me nuts.'"

When Crutcher switched to teaching in a regular high school after the money for the experimental school ran out, he felt that his situation was boring by comparison, so he headed for California. Crutcher got a job with an alternative school in Oakland, a poor city with a high crime rate. The school, Lakeside, taught students from kindergarten through twelfth grade, often on a contract from the Oakland public schools. Many were kids who'd been expelled—and "if you get thrown out of the Oakland public schools," Crutcher observed, "you've gone a ways." At first he taught the younger students, but the older ones made themselves impossible to ignore. "It was that time in the early Seventies when the learn-when-you-want-to attitude was prevalent," he recalled, "so the high school would hold classes that nobody came to. The older kids were basically out throwing water balloons at the elementary kids and terrorizing them and smoking dope and getting drunk." After about three years, he took his concerns to Lakeside's executive director. "I said, 'You know, in a lot of schools people *go*.' And he asked me if I wanted to be the director and I asked him if that paid more and he said 'no,' so I took it." Crutcher recalled, "Those were twelve- and fifteen-hour days, and I just ate it up."

Crutcher has observed that the most remarkable thing about his Lakeside experience was the "incredible togetherness" that helped to sustain the school. For his part, Crutcher said, "It was always a great challenge to make sure people knew I was fair and that the school stood for everybody." Crutcher had many chances to practice his fairness because, as director, he was also the school disciplinarian. "A lot of the high school kids would come in and just *try* to get themselves thrown out," he told *AAYA*. So he developed a novel strategy. "I said, 'You just can't *get* thrown out of here. This is it. If you're hurting people I'll send you home, but you can't get thrown out.' That really screwed people up," he admitted. "We were on equal ground then and we had to learn together." And the kids had plenty to teach Crutcher. One time he tried discussing the rules of Lakeside with a group of kids, and they pointed out, relentlessly, that he didn't really do what he had written down. Take the rule, the students said, about sending people home for bad behavior, including drug use. "That's not the rule at all," kids told him—"the rule is that if you think we're going to get hurt if we go home you won't send us there, you'll do something else." "And every one of my rules was like that," Crutcher admitted. "I started looking at what reality was, and that was tremendous for me. From then on, that was how I dealt with kids. I had a bunch of keys hanging from my belt—you could hear me coming—and I'd

walk into a room and they'd say 'Crutcher is narking on us, he's looking for somebody doing drugs.' They'd expect me to say 'No I'm not,' but I'd say 'You're damn right I'm looking for drugs. Because I'm the cop and you guys are the robbers, and it's my job. I'm here to bust your butt—and I'm also here to try and find some way for you to get interested in *something*.'"

More often than not, the program worked. "I think we did some really good things," Crutcher said. "Teachers worked really hard at individualizing things for kids. We had small classrooms and kids could go as fast as they could go—you could be a good math student and a horrible English student and still stay in the same grade." The teachers at Lakeside, he declared, included some authentic heroes. "They were getting zero—I mean nothing—for money, and we all knew that they probably weren't going to stay very long. I had a teacher say to me one time, 'There's a lot of crazy things about this school, but if you can teach here you can teach anyplace. You'll never be intimidated. Ever.'"

Crutcher left Lakeside in 1980. "It was just a ripping away to leave that place," he told *AAYA*, but "I really don't like crowds and I think that growing up in the mountains really got to me. I could feel myself becoming physically agitated as it got more crowded." He went back to the Northwest, to Spokane, Washington, where he became a therapist at the Spokane Community Mental Health Center, which specialized in dealing with both family violence and the problems of young people; in addition, Crutcher became the head of Spokane's Child Protection team. Many of Crutcher's clients were referred to him from the school system, sent because they were struggling with problems beyond the scope of a guidance counselor. "As an adolescent," Crutcher recalled, "what I remember most is that I was *told* things. I was told how they worked and how I was supposed to feel and what my values were. To me therapy is allowing kids to come in, close the door, and talk about what life's really like for them. Let them know that I understand that things aren't working right. Sometimes it's just a place to come bitch—to talk about what doesn't feel good, fears that they may not be able to talk about anyplace else. It's a place for all those crazy questions about drugs, about sex, about love, and what's the difference between lust and love and need and want and all those things—because kids find themselves doing things that scare them, and they can't tell anybody they're scared. Therapy can provide a place to talk about that and not have somebody tell you what you're supposed to feel." Crutcher concluded, "Therapy is a place to come and be safe, to talk about what you don't understand and not feel silly, and know that there's somebody here who went through this, too. I didn't know the answers then either, and there are a lot of answers I don't know now, but we might—if we put our heads together—we might be able to find one."

At about the same time that Crutcher became a therapist, he also became a writer. "I recognized the need for a creative outlet in my life," he said in *Horn Book Magazine*. "In my work, the daily crisis of people's lives is so immediate. Time moves so fast. But books are so permanent. They have their own life in time." As Crutcher told *AAYA,* he wasn't the usual budding author. "As a teenager I was a famous non-reader," he said, "so I didn't engage in books, particularly fiction, until I was out of college. But I did like stories. I was told stories as a little kid a lot and I was read to a lot. Television came to Cascade when I was in the fifth grade, and I remember being really curious about why one show was funny and another wasn't when both were meant to be. I used to take stories apart; I paid close attention to how things worked among my friends—I was a real student of behavior."

In 1970, Crutcher went to stay with Terry Davis, a college friend and aspiring novelist who was a Stegner Fellow at Stanford. Davis was at work on his first novel, *Vision Quest,* which describes the coming of age of a high school athlete in Spokane. The book became a best-seller when it was published in 1979 and was eventually turned into a movie; in 1997, Davis published a biography of his friend, *Presenting Chris Crutcher.* "We had a lot of the same background," Crutcher recalled, "so I got to read some of the chapters for believability.

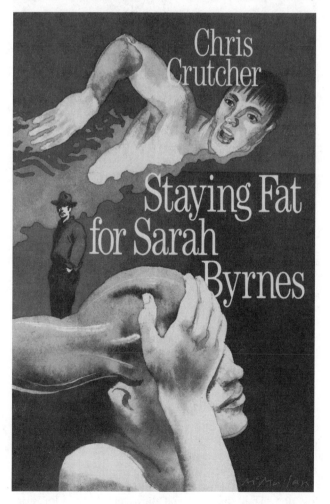

Two ostracized and emotionally withdrawn teenagers, one disfigured and one obese, help each other with unselfish loyalty in Crutcher's powerful young adult novel. (Cover illustration by James McMullan.)

We would talk about his story and what he was trying to get across. I got to watch the raw material turn into something that's really smooth and does the job. Terry's a wonderful writer, and there was magic in that process." But it was a magic, Crutcher realized, that mere mortals could attain. "Here's a guy that I could beat one-on-one in basketball. He wasn't from outer space— he was a guy who rolled up his sleeves and did his storytelling, and I realized that writing was a human thing to do." Finally, after Crutcher left Lakeside School in 1980, he had four months free before his new job started; he had an idea, and he couldn't get *To Kill a Mockingbird* out of his head, so he dared himself to write a book. "I just sat down and wrote *Running Loose*—long-hand!" Crutcher told *AAYA.* He sent a typed copy to Davis, who recommended it to his own agent, Liz Darhansoff, in New York. Within a week Darhansoff agreed to represent Crutcher. By the time that the book was published, Crutcher remembered, "I was addicted. I just never wanted to stop." When he was writing *Running Loose,* Crutcher did not realize that he was creating a YA novel. He told Dave Jenkinson of *Emergency Librarian,* "I didn't know there was such a thing. I'd just spent ten years in the toughest school in Oakland, and so I just wrote it in that language."

In his works for teenagers, Crutcher surveys the struggle of young people to grow up and take charge of their own lives. "People always want us to *be* adults rather than *become* adults," he told *AAYA.* "Everybody wants the finished product, and nobody wants to look at how it's made." Louie Banks, the hero of *Running Loose,* knows better. "The thing I hate about life, so far, is that nothing's ever clear," he declares. "Every time you get things all figured out, somebody throws in another kink." Inspired by a conversation Crutcher overheard in a locker room fifteen years before in which a racist coach directed his players to eliminate an African American player, the novel is set in Trout, Idaho—a small town much like Crutcher's hometown of Cascade. As his senior year begins, Louie thinks his life is set. He's at peace with his parents, a good-natured, insightful couple modeled on Crutcher's own mother and father; he's a starter on the school's eight-man football team, where he's surrounded by his buddies; and he has Becky, a wonderful girlfriend. But his perfect life soon begins to unravel. The trouble begins after a game with a rival school with a challenging team anchored by Washington, a talented black quarterback. In a bigoted harangue, Louie's coach orders the Trout team to sideline Washington with crippling tackles, and one of Louie's teammates complies. Louie denounces the play and storms off the field, ending his football career. His football buddies won't join the walkout, even if they agree with him. The coach lies his way out of the situation, and the townspeople are left to assume that Louie just lost control. Washington turns out not to be hurt very badly. Even though Louie is sure he did the right thing, he doesn't have the chance to feel very heroic. Becky dies in a pointless traffic accident, trying to drive around some rowdy kids on the only bridge in town. At the funeral, Louie hears Becky fondly eulogized by an out-of-town minister who never met her, and he rages again. However, a young track coach, who recognizes Louie's potential and respects the stand he took on the football play, recruits him for the team, and he wins the two-mile event. When the principal dedicates a memorial plaque to Becky—emblazoned with his own signature—Louie stays calm and takes care of it: he sneaks onto the school grounds and smashes up the memorial with a sledgehammer.

The solution to pain such as Louie's, Crutcher believes, lies in "letting go"—letting go of the search for a satisfying answer that doesn't exist; letting yourself admit that you're just a human being in pain. "If I keep asking why and keep not coming up with an answer," Crutcher observed, "I'm either going to get so frustrated I want to scream, or I'm just going to say 'There's no answer—hooray!' You know—'Hooray that there's no answer because I don't *have* one.'" As for sorrow, he declared, "you're not really hurt—injured—by your sadness or your grief, you're hurt by resisting it." "There's a case to be made for life being a series of losses, from the time that you lose your mother's womb, and all the times that you have to change schools, or your friends go away, or people die. If you live from zero to sixty you're going to have suffered a lot of losses. And what you can do for yourself is learn to hold yourself and grieve and allow that grief to be the focus. Just say, 'I don't need to fight this, I don't need to do anything but just feel bad. Why? Because I *do* feel bad.'" So Louie lets go: "The tears came. And man, they came. I must have lost five pounds."

Writing in *Voice of Youth Advocates,* Mary K. Chelton noted of *Running Loose,* "Best of all, ... you love [Louie] and grieve with him when Becky dies because she is presented as a really neat person." Chelton also wrote that *Running Loose* is a "good stepping stone up from Hinton and toward titles like *Vision Quest* and *Stop Time.* Good 'bridge books' are rare and first novelists this good even rarer." *Kirkus Reviews* claimed that Louie tells his story with "strong feeling and no crap, as he might say," and added that as a "dramatic, head-first confrontation with mendacity, fate's punches, and learning to cope, it's a zinger." Zena Sutherland of *Bulletin of the Center for Children's Books* called *Running Loose* an "unusually fine first novel," while Trev Jones in *School Library Journal* said that Louie tells his story with "sensitivity, humor, and outrage" and that the book "raises important issues for adolescents to consider."

For his second novel, *Stotan!,* Crutcher returned to the arena of high school sports. "One of the things I like about sports is that the rules are clear," he told *AAYA.* "I use sports in young adult fiction to talk about rules, usually back-to-back with information about the rules of life. Sports provides an arena for an athlete, or a character, to test himself or herself and learn about tenacity or about putting things in perspective." In *Stotan!,* the focus is on self-discipline. The story begins when four high-school swimmers—Walker, the team captain; Lion; Nortie; and Jeff—volunteer for "Stotan Week," an endurance test given by their coach, a

Perpetually angry teenager Bo Brewster, who has vowed to use his physical prowess to become a triathlete, becomes enamored with a girl who rivals his strength in Crutcher's novel about challenge and persistence. (Cover illustration by James McMullan.)

Korean-American named Max II Song. When the boys sign up, they learn that a "Stotan" is a cross between a Stoic and a Spartan, and Max makes them live up to the billing with harsh exercises, exhausting laps in the pool, and a "Torture Lane" for swimmers who try to slack off. "I took Stotan Week out of real life," Crutcher confessed. "Actually I calmed it down to put in the book. My college coach was a madman, an absolute madman." Feats of physical courage, like falling off the diving board backward, were mandatory on Crutcher's team. "If you didn't do it you were doing push-ups until you couldn't walk. And then you'd have to run outside over the snowbank, wet, and bear-walk [hands and feet only]—we did all that. The Torture Lane was there, it was all there. It was *bizarre.*"

Amazingly, Walker and his teammates start to like Stotan Week. Sharing the challenge brings them closer together. They discover that they can endure a lot more than they thought. They realize that the less they struggle against the pain, and the more they accept and push beyond it, the easier things get. They feel energetic and confident. When the week is over, Max tosses aside his authoritarian props—bullhorn, firehose, Airborne cap—and shares some human insights, inspired by his study of Asian philosophy. "There are lessons in this week that can serve you for the rest of your lives," he says. "Remember the times when you gave up the fight [against Max and his discipline] and just went with Stotan Week—saw which way the river was flowing and went that way too. Most times the depth of your well isn't measured in how hard you fight—how tough you are—but in your ability to see what is and go with that." The team expects their toughest challenge to be the statewide swimming meet, but they must face a far greater challenge when Jeff develops a withering case of leukemia; their Stotan wisdom helps the friends through their crisis. At Jeff's urging the team goes on to the state meet without him, where they excel—for his sake—and swim an illegal three-man relay at the finals. At the end of the book, as Walker looks back over his experiences, it's clear that he hasn't soured on life; instead, he's come to an understanding of how precious it is. "I think my job in this life is to be an observer," he writes in his diary, and concludes, "I'll be a *Stotan* observer: look for the ways to get from one to the other of those glorious moments when all the emotional stops are pulled, when you're just so ... glad to be breathing air." *Voice of Youth Advocates* reviewer Mary K. Chelton noted that *Stotan!* depicts "beautifully the joy, pain, and emotional strength of a male adolescent friendship" and called it a "lovely story and a model of the realistic adolescent novel." Writing in *School Library Journal*, Jerry Flack called *Stotan!* "a fine coming-of-age novel," while Anita Silvey of *Horn Book* compared it to the books of John R. Tunis and Bruce Brooks's *The Moves Make the Man*, works "that use a sports setting and competition to discuss the greater issues of being young and alive."

The Crazy Horse Electric Game takes a much different look at sports: it concerns a high school student who knows the thrill of having athletic talent, then loses it all and has to rebuild his life. As the novel begins, Willie Weaver is a sixteen-year-old amateur baseball player in small-town Coho, Montana, pitching for a team sponsored by the Samson Floral Shop. In the greatest moment of his career, Willie throws a winning game against a championship team sponsored by Crazy Hose Electric. By the standards of Coho, he's a living legend. Then a water-skiing accident leaves Willie brain-damaged; he's crippled and must struggle even to talk. His father, who was a winning college athlete, can scarcely stand the sight of him; friends feel awkward around him; and, most important of all, Willie hates his own life. Finally, he runs away from home and, in reality, from human contact. Willie never expected life to be so flawed—he expected it to be as perfect as the Crazy Horse Electric game. "There's a lot to hate yourself for if you listen to those expectations," Crutcher told *AAYA*, "because no one ever meets them."

Crutcher learned a different—and healthier—way of looking at life from Dr. Gil Milner, a supervising therapist in Spokane. Milner is steeped in the East Asian philosophy that appears from time to time in Crutcher's books. "He is one of the most amazing men I've ever

been around," Crutcher recalled. "He's a Buddhist monk, he's been all over the world, he's an internationally renowned child psychologist, a smart and insightful guy and an absolutely *allowing* man. He does not judge people. I remember hearing him say: 'Root out self-hate.' It was one of those situations where you hear this little thing and it just spreads inside you." It made Crutcher want "to help someone else understand that—understand that what looks bad in you is just self-hate, and that you need to care for yourself more. If you care for yourself then you can care for others—that's the core to being healthy."

In the second half of *The Crazy Horse Electric Game*, Willie makes the long journey back from self-hatred to self-respect. After traveling as far as he can by bus, he finds himself in Oakland, California, at a fictionalized version of Lakeside called the One More Last Chance High School. The OMLC instructors encourage him to use physical therapy, and even basketball, to reclaim control of his body; with his pride restored, Willie becomes a valuable part of the school's community and earns his diploma. He then has the strength to return to Coho and face his family and friends, even though the reunion is a difficult one. A reviewer in *Publishers Weekly* said that *The Crazy Horse Electric Game* "resound[s] with compassion for people tripped up by their own weaknesses" and praised its "poetic sensibility and gritty realism." *Kirkus Reviews* predicted that "readers will find themselves cheered by the courageous way Willie battles back, and by the way nearly everyone gets what they deserve or work for." Writing in *Voice of Youth Advocates*, Pam Spencer noted that, as in his previous novels, Crutcher writes about a young man being forced "to dig deep for the stabilization offered in reaching one's inner strength"; the critic concluded, "Crutcher writes powerfully and movingly of Willie's attempts to 'become whole' again. . . . It's authors like Chris Crutcher who make our job of 'selling books' that much easier." *Horn Book* reviewer Anita Silvey claimed that *The Crazy Horse Electric Game* "magnificently portrays the thoughts and feelings of a crippled athlete and is a testimony to the indomitability of the human spirit."

Perhaps the grittiest of Crutcher's YA novels is his fourth, *Chinese Handcuffs*, which describes the friendship between two emotionally traumatized young people. Dillon Hemmingway grew up watching his older brother Preston destroy himself, first through drugs and then through suicide; Preston, in fact, made a point of killing himself in Dillon's presence. Dillon is close friends with Jennifer Lawless, who has been sexually abused most of her life, by her father when she was a small child, and by her stepfather in the years since. Dillon thinks he is in love with Jennifer, but she has been too deeply wounded to fully reciprocate; her emotional lifeline is sports, because the basketball court is the only place where she feels she can control her own fate. The title of the book refers to the efforts of Dillon and Jennifer to confront their pain. "Chinese handcuffs" are a classic basket-weaver's toy: they only loosen their grip when you stop pulling against them.

Dillon is so preoccupied with his brother's death that he writes long letters to him, letters that make up much of the narrative. Jennifer has similarly strong memories of her abuse. In particular, readers see a vivid portrait of her stepfather, T. B. Himself brutalized as a child, T. B. survived through cold cunning, and now he uses it to intimidate both Jennifer and her mother. Finally Jennifer tries to kill herself, but Dillon stops her. Moved to desperate action, he gathers videotaped evidence against T. B. and uses it to drive him out of Jennifer's life; Jennifer turns T. B. in to the police. Having confronted the painful truths of his world, Dillon finds that he is no longer haunted by his brother. "I've got better things to do with my life than spend it with a pen in my hand, writing to a man who never reads his mail," he says in his last letter. "My struggle with you is finished. I'm going to let you go, push my finger in and release us from these crazy Chinese handcuffs. I wish you'd stayed, though. God, how I wish you'd stayed."

Chinese Handcuffs received some favorable response from critics. Writing in *Horn Book*, Margaret A. Bush claimed that Crutcher "constructs his painful web with intelligent insight, creating a painful, powerful story.... In the end the story is a compelling, well-paced, and even humorous one of human failing, survival, and hope." Writing in *Voice of Youth Advocates*, Randy Brough called *Chinese Handcuffs* a "rewarding novel, tough, topical, compelling, and well written." The strong subject matter, however, was also a cause for controversy. A notable example was the reaction of the American Library Association: its own *Booklist* magazine refused to review the book and offered a column questioning its merit. Conceding that Crutcher was "a strong writer" capable of making a "powerful moral point," *Booklist*'s Stephanie Zvirin went on to suggest that parts of the work, including Preston's suicide, were unduly graphic. She concluded that *Chinese Handcuffs* is "an unsuccessful book—and a disappointment—because the overloaded plot strains the novel's structure and diminishes the vital message Crutcher is trying to covey." In addition, *Kirkus Reviews* commented that his teenage characters "have been knocked around in Crutcher's other stories, but not to this extent.... Crutcher probes so many tender areas here that readers may end by feeling exhausted and emotionally bruised." However, Crutcher thinks that the amount of fan mail the book generated may have worked in the book's favor; although *Chinese Handcuffs* was almost not named an ALA Best Book for Young Adults, it did eventually receive that honor.

In response Crutcher points to the reality of his experience—and the experiences of kids. "I think there's a case to be made for being careful with language, but I want a kid to read it and believe it," he said. "I don't want some kid to say, 'God, kids don't talk like this,' because that negates everything else there. It would be nice to be able to blame things on language, because that would sure be simple—we could change the language and things would be better. Language ain't the problem. I had just come out of seven years in Oakland, for cryin' out loud, when I wrote *Running Loose*." He has a

similar reaction to critics of *Chinese Handcuffs:* "My line is, Look, I *got* that stuff from kids. I *toned that down*." Crutcher knows that many of his readers are people in pain, and he suggests that he may have helped some of them through some difficult times. "Hard times are magnetic to hard times," he observed. "If I'm a kid who has had awful things happen to me, I'm going to look for other kids that have had that same experience because I want to be validated in the world. You get three or four of us together and we've got some pretty hard stories to tell. I'm not going to be running around with the quarterback on the football team or the head cheerleader." Not long after the controversy over *Chinese Handcuffs*, Crutcher was in Houston speaking to a group of students. "A girl came up after everyone was gone and said, 'I read that book and I thought you knew me.'" At such a moment, the complaints of a few critics didn't seem to matter. "I thought, To hell with that—this is what it's really about."

In 1991, Crutcher published his first collection of short stories, *Athletic Shorts;* the volume, which includes six stories, features some of the characters from the author's novels as well as some new characters. The first story, which outlines how a fat, clumsy boy raised by two sets of homosexual parents finds dignity when he is chosen as a joke to be the king of the senior ball, and the final entry, in which Louie Banks, the title character of *Running Loose,* accepts a boy dying from AIDS as a friend even though his decision threatens his relationship with a fellow athlete, have been singled out as especially effective. Writing in *School Library Journal,* Todd Morning said, "These *Athletic Shorts* will appeal to YAs, touch them deeply, and introduce them to characters they'll want to know better." *Horn Book* reviewer Nancy Vasilakis noted, "One need not to have read Crutcher's novels to appreciate the young men within these pages. They stand proudly on their own," while *Voice of Youth Advocates* contributor Sue Krumbein concluded that all six stories "live up to the high expectations we've come to expect of Crutcher." In 1992, the author published his first book for adults, the suspense novel *The Deep End.* Called an "outstanding, yet wrenching, look into child abuse" by *School Library Journal* contributor Mike Printz, the novel was directed to adults but is considered appropriate for teenage readers. The story outlines how child therapist Wilson Corder investigates the disappearance—and eventual murder—of a young girl as well as the possible abuse of a three-year-old boy by his father, an expert in domestic violence. Printz concludes that "Crutcher's superb, sensitive style coupled with the prudent use of his unique humor makes this a first-rate, 'can't-put-it-down' novel" while *Kirkus Reviews* observed that the author's "needle-sharp focus on hurting kids makes this memorably harrowing from the starting gun."

In his next novel for young adults, *Staying Fat for Sarah Byrnes,* Crutcher features Eric Calhoune, a senior nicknamed "Moby" for his swimming ability and size; his best friend, Sarah Byrnes, suffered terrible facial burns as a small girl and has recently retreated into silence. After Sarah escapes from the psychiatric unit of a local hospital, her psychotic father Virgil—whom readers discover was the cause of his daughter's disfigurement and who refused to let her have reconstructive surgery—stabs Eric and hijacks his car when he refuses to reveal Sarah's hiding place. Eric brings in his sympathetic coach as his ally; at the end of the novel, Eric gets a new stepfather, Sarah a new set of parents, and Virgil a beating and a jail sentence. "This is a book that punches you in the stomach and never gives you a moment to breathe," wrote Susan R. Farber in *Voice of Youth Advocates,* who concluded that the novel is Crutcher's "darkest and most riveting work to date." Writing in *Horn Book,* Nancy Vasilakis called Sarah Byrnes "one of [Crutcher's] strongest female characters to date." *Kirkus Reviews* praised the novel as "pulse-pounding, on both visceral and emotional levels—a wild, brutal ride," and Janice Del Negro of *Booklist* considered it "strong on relationships, long on plot" and with "enough humor and suspense to make it an easy booktalk with appeal across gender lines."

With *Ironman,* Crutcher chronicles the senior year of Bo Brewster, who has been assigned to an anger management group after quitting the football team and calling the coach a rude name. The group's instructor, Mr. Nak, a Japanese American from Texas, gives Bo the tools to come to realizations about himself and his relationship with his vicious father; at the same time, Bo trains rigorously for an upcoming triathlon event, a race added to in intensity by the fact that Bo's father is trying to fix the event by bribing his son's main competitor. At the end of the novel, Bo competes in the triathlon with the support of the anger management group and discovers his personal strength and self-respect. Crutcher presents the story as both a third-person narrative and in the form of letters from Bo to talk-show host Larry King, the only adult the boy feels will listen to him. Writing in *School Library Journal,* Tom S. Hurlburt said, "Crutcher has consistently penned exceptional reads for YAs, and *Ironman* is one of his strongest works yet." Roger Sutton of *Bulletin of the Center for Children's Books* claimed, "If you like Crutcher, this is vintage stuff ... [If] you haven't succumbed before, you aren't likely to now, but fans will welcome the winning formula." Writing in the *New York Times Book Review,* James Gorman noted, "The heart of the story is small and painful, and rings thoroughly true," while *Horn Book* reviewer Peter D. Sieruta concluded that *Ironman* is a novel that "doesn't strive for easy answers, but does ask many intriguing questions of both its characters and its readers."

In 1995, Crutcher became a full-time writer, although he still works on the Child Protection Team in Spokane, Washington. He told Heather Vogel Frederick of *Publishers Weekly,* "When it came down to it, I could not give up writing.... What's known can't be unknown. As a writer and a human being, ... I have to keep myself in a position where I can scream and yell and be just obnoxious about getting something done." Crutcher once told *Something about the Author,* "It is a joy to write a tale that is believable, that is real. Writing is also a way to express humor and to present human perspec-

tives. I like to explore the different ways in which people make sense of what goes on around them...." In an interview with Christine McDonnell in *Horn Book,* Crutcher remarked, "I want to be remembered as a storyteller, and I want to tell stories that seem real so that people will recognize something in their own lives and see the connections. We are all connected. That's what I like to explore and put into stories." Quoted in *Twentieth-Century Children's Writers,* Crutcher concluded, "My mission is to write truths as I see them, reflect the world as it appears to me, rather than as others would have it. I would like to tell stories so 'right on' that they punch a hole in the wall between young adult and adult literature." In his collection *Athletic Shorts,* Crutcher wrote, "There are a significant amount of people who ... think kids should not be exposed in print to what they are exposed to in their lives. But I believe what I believe, and so I write my stories."

Crutcher has found that some of the most gratifying comments that he gets about his works come in the mail. "I get a lot of responses from kids who don't read very much," he told *AAYA,* "and that's great because I didn't read—it's like me writing to me." He described a recent batch of letters: "One said, 'My mom's dying of cancer and this book helped me come out of my shell. I've just been saying that what's happening isn't true, but it is true. And the things that Louie Banks went through tell me a way that I can let it be true, and then go on. Things *will* go on.' There were letters from kids who had just lost people, whether it was a death or not, and they learned that there is another way to look at a loss. I was astonished at these letters—that's the feedback I like."

■ Works Cited

Brough, Randy, review of *Chinese Handcuffs, Voice of Youth Advocates,* June, 1989, p. 98.

Bush, Margaret A., review of *Chinese Handcuffs, Horn Book Magazine,* July-August, 1989, p. 487.

Chelton, Mary K., review of *Running Loose, Voice of Youth Advocates,* April, 1983, p. 36.

Chelton, Mary K., review of *Stotan!, Voice of Youth Advocates,* April, 1986, p. 29.

Review of *Chinese Handcuffs, Kirkus Reviews,* February 15, 1989, p. 290.

Review of *The Crazy Horse Electric Game, Publishers Weekly,* May 29, 1987, p. 79.

Crutcher, Chris, *Athletic Shorts: Six Short Stories,* Greenwillow, 1991.

Crutcher, *Chinese Handcuffs,* Dell, 1991.

Crutcher, *Running Loose,* Greenwillow, 1983.

Crutcher, *Stotan!,* Dell, 1988.

Crutcher, telephone interview with Thomas Kozikowski for *Authors and Artists for Young Adults,* March 11, 1992, published by Gale, Volume 9, 1992, pp. 85-95.

Review of *The Deep End, Kirkus Reviews,* November 15, 1991, p. 1436.

Del Negro, Janice, review of *Staying Fat for Sarah Byrnes, Booklist,* March 15, 1993, p. 1313.

Frederick, Heather Vogel, "Chris Crutcher: 'What's Known Can't Be Unknown'," *Publishers Weekly*, February 20, 1995, pp. 183-84.

Gorman, James, review of *Ironman, New York Times Book Review*, July 2, 1995, p. 13.

Hurlburt, Tom S., review of *Ironman, School Library Journal*, March, 1995, p. 222.

Jenkinson, Dave, "Portraits: Chris Crutcher," in *Emergency Librarian*, January-February, 1991, pp. 67-71.

Farber, Susan R., review of *Staying Fat for Sarah Byrnes, Voice of Youth Advocates*, August, 1993, p. 150.

Fleck, Jerry, review of *Stotan!, School Library Journal*, May, 1986, p. 100.

Jones, Trev, review of *Running Loose, School Library Journal*, May, 1983, p. 80.

Krumbein, Sue, review of *Athletic Shorts, Voice of Youth Advocates*, April, 1992, p. 26.

McDonnell, Christine, "New Voices, New Visions: Chris Crutcher," *Horn Book*, May, 1988, p. 332.

Montgomery, Lori, "Idaho Novelist: First Book Wins Raves," *Idaho Statesman* (Boise, ID), July 28, 1983.

Morning, Todd, review of *Athletic Shorts, School Library Journal*, September, 1991, p. 278.

Printz, Mike, review of *The Deep End: A Novel of Suspense, School Library Journal*, September, 1992, p. 189.

Review of *Running Loose, Kirkus Reviews*, April 15, 1983, p. 461.

Sieruta, Peter D., review of *Ironman, Horn Book*, October, 1995, p. 606.

Silvey, Anita, review of *The Crazy Horse Electric Game, Horn Book*, November-December, 1987, p. 741.

Silvey, Anita, review of *Stotan!, Horn Book*, September-October, 1986, p. 596.

Spencer, Pam, review of *The Crazy Horse Electric Game, Voice of Youth Advocates*, June, 1987, p. 76.

Review of *Staying Fat for Sarah Byrnes, Kirkus Reviews*, March 15, 1993, p. 369.

Sutherland, Zena, review of *Running Loose, Bulletin of the Center for Children's Books*, May, 1983, p. 165.

Sutton, Roger, review of *Ironman, Bulletin of the Center for Children's Books*, April, 1995, p. 269.

Vasilakis, Nancy, review of *Athletic Shorts, Horn Book*, September-October, 1991, pp. 602-03.

Vasilakis, Nancy, review of *Staying Fat for Sarah Byrnes, Horn Book Magazine*, May-June, 1993, p. 337.

Zvirin, Stephanie, "The YA Connection: *Chinese Handcuffs*," *Booklist*, August, 1989, p. 1966.

■ For More Information See

BOOKS

Children's Literature Review, Gale, Volume 28, 1992, pp. 98-108.

Davis, Terry, *Presenting Chris Crutcher*, Twayne/Prentice-Hall, 1997.

Gallo, Donald R., editor, *Speaking for Ourselves: Autobiographical Sketches by Notable Authors of Books for Young Adults*, National Council of Teachers of English, 1990, p. 59.

Silvey, Anita, editor, *Children's Books and Their Creators*, Houghton Mifflin, 1995, pp. 181-82.*

—Sketch by Gerard J. Senick

* * *

CUYLER, Margery (Stuyvesant) 1948-
(Daisy Wallace)

■ Personal

Born December 31, 1948, in Princeton, NJ; daughter of Lewis Baker and Margery Pepperell (Merrill) Cuyler; married John Newman Hewson Perkins (a psychoanalyst), August 23, 1979. *Education:* Sarah Lawrence College, B.A., 1970.

■ Addresses

Home—32 Edgehill St., Princeton, NJ 08540. *Office*—Golden Books Family Entertainment, 888 Seventh Ave., New York, NY 10106.

■ Career

Atlantic Monthly Press, Boston, assistant to editor of children's books, 1970-71; Walker & Co., New York City, editor of children's books, 1972-74; Holiday House, New York City, vice president and editor-in-chief of children's books, 1974-95; Henry Holt and Co., New York City, Vice President and Associate Publisher, Books for Young Readers, 1996-97; Golden Books Family Entertainment, Vice President, Director of Trade Publishing, 1997—. Lecturer on children's book editing, Rutgers University, 1974, New School for Social Research, 1975, Vassar College, 1984. Board member, Women's National Book Association Children's Book Council, 1980-82. Library trustee and member of alumnae board, Sarah Lawrence College.

■ Awards, Honors

Children's Choice Books, International Reading Association and Children's Book Council, for *The Trouble with Soap* and *Witch Poems;* New Jersey Institute of Technology Author's Award, 1988, for *Fat Santa*.

■ Writings

PICTURE BOOKS

Jewish Holidays, illustrated by Lisa C. Wesson, Holt, 1978.

The All-Around Pumpkin Book, illustrated by Corbett Jones, Holt, 1980.

The All-Around Christmas Book, illustrated by Corbett Jones, Holt, 1982.

Sir William and the Pumpkin Monster, illustrated by Marsha Winborn, Holt, 1984.

Freckles and Willie, illustrated by Marsha Winborn, Holt, 1986.

MARGERY CUYLER

Fat Santa, illustrated by Marsha Winborn, Holt, 1987.

Freckles and Jane, illustrated by Leslie Holt Morrill, Holt, 1989.

Shadow's Baby, illustrated by Ellen Weiss, Clarion, 1989.

Baby Dot, illustrated by Ellen Weiss, Clarion, 1990.

Daisy's Crazy Thanksgiving, illustrated by Robin Kramer, Holt, 1990.

That's Good! That's Bad!, illustrated by David Catrow, Holt, 1991.

The Christmas Snowman, illustrated by Johanna Westerman, Arcade, 1992.

Buddy Bear and the Bad Guys, illustrated by Janet Stevens, Clarion, 1993.

The Biggest, Best Snowman, illustrated by Will Hillenbrand, Scholastic, 1998.

From Here to There, illustrated by Yu Cha Pak, Henry Holt, in press.

FOR YOUNG READERS

The Trouble with Soap, Dutton, 1982.

Weird Wolf, illustrated by Dirk Zimmer, Holt, 1989.

Invisible in the Third Grade, illustrated by Mirko Gabler, Holt, 1995.

EDITOR; UNDER PSEUDONYM DAISY WALLACE; ALL FOR CHILDREN

Monster Poems, illustrated by Kay Chorao, Holiday House, 1976.

Witch Poems, illustrated by Trina Schart Hyman, Holiday House, 1976.

Giant Poems, illustrated by Margot Tomes, Holiday House, 1978.

Ghost Poems, illustrated by Tomie De Paola, Holiday House, 1979.

Fairy Poems, illustrated by Trina Schart Hyman, Holiday House, 1980.

■ **Sidelights**

Margery Cuyler was already an experienced editor of children's books for the publishing firm of Holiday House when she decided to try her hand at writing. While she once admitted to *Something about the Author* (*SATA*) that her passion has been for editing children's books, she has come to love writing as well, "since it exercises my imagination in a more personal and introspective fashion." In addition to authoring a wide range of both nonfiction and fiction picture books, including *Freckles and Willie, Fat Santa,* and *Daisy's Crazy Thanksgiving,* Cuyler has written several chapter books for readers with more experience. She has also published under the pseudonym Daisy Wallace, editing several collections of poetry grouped under a variety of themes designed to catch the interest of young readers. *Witch Poems, Ghost Poems,* and *Fairy Poems* are just a few of these verse collections, which were published between 1976 and 1980.

Born in Princeton, New Jersey, Cuyler was raised in a large family. Competing with four siblings and an equal number of cousins who had joined Cuyler's family after their own mother died, she learned early how to fend for herself, as she once told *SATA.* After graduating from high school, she attended Sarah Lawrence College, earning her bachelor's degree in 1970. From there, it was a quick move to Boston to work for Atlantic Monthly Press before Cuyler returned to New York City and found a job with Holiday House. "I'm a great supporter of the type of small institution that allows the creative spirit to flourish," the author/editor once told *SATA.* "For example, both Sarah Lawrence and Holiday House value independent thinking, and provide the kind of nourishing environment where new ideas can take seed and ripen naturally." Cuyler found Holiday House to be the perfect fit with her own career aspirations; beginning there in 1974, she served as its editor-in-chief for children's fiction for many years before moving to Henry Holt and then Golden Books Family Entertainment, where she continues to push quality.

Cuyler's first attempt at a self-penned work was *Jewish Holidays,* published in 1978. It was a book she admits she should never have written because, not being Jewish, she was not completely familiar with her subject matter and had to rely on the generous assistance of Jewish friends to get her facts straight. Still, it was a first step that would lead to greater successes. *School Library Journal* contributor Joan C. Feldman praised this first work as "a clear, factual, and useful book for teaching the significance of the Jewish holidays." Zena Sutherland of the *Bulletin of the Center for Children's Books* noted that following each section is a craft project, "always a simple and inexpensive one," with a useful glossary and index appended as well.

Cuyler's second picture book, *The All-Around Pumpkin Book,* was written in three days, and was inspired by a dream. "I woke up ... at two in the morning and I started writing," she told interviewer Jim Roginski in *Behind the Covers: Interviews with Authors and Illustrators of Books for Children and Young Adults.* Visualizing all the illustrations in her mind, she quickly made a dummy of the book, sketched out the pictures as she imagined them, and then added the text. Following the entire life span of the typical Halloween jack-o'-lantern, from seed to garden to its ultimate destiny as either scary goblin or pumpkin pie, the book that Ethel L. Heins of *Horn Book* called "a compendium of fascinating and practical facts" also contains nontraditional uses for the fall squash. Pumpkin hamburgers anyone? "Here's a way to stretch Halloween all around the year," commented Barbara Elleman in her *Booklist* appraisal of *The All-Around Pumpkin Book.*

Cuyler followed her pumpkin book with *The All-Around Christmas Book,* using much the same format: the story of the Nativity is followed by a discussion of folklore, crafts, recipes, games, and other information about the holiday, both in its Christian and secular manifestations. The wide variety of celebrations undertaken by many different cultures around the world is explored, with answers to such questions as where the tradition of decorating trees came from and an explanation of the history of advent wreaths. Praising the information presented, a *Publishers Weekly* reviewer termed the work "a treasure of holiday lore."

Although her early books were nonfiction, Cuyler has more recently turned to fiction, penning a number of entertaining picture books for preschoolers and children in the early grades. In *Shadow's Baby,* a little dog is determined to take care of the new baby in his house, but when the baby grows older and wants to play with other things, the attentive Shadow gets in the way. Fortunately, the dog's owner realizes that Shadow feels useless with nothing to care for; the introduction of a new puppy into the home provides a ready solution. Ann A. Flowers of *Horn Book* called *Shadow's Baby* "as warm and affectionate as a puppy," while a *Publishers Weekly* critic commended Cuyler's "sensitivity to the feelings of all involved" in this warmhearted story.

Dogs and their human companions also figure prominently in Cuyler's stories about Freckles the dog and Willie, the teenage boy. In *Freckles and Willie,* Freckles feels forlorn when Willie starts to spend most of his time with a girl named Jane; the girl, for her part, is obviously not a person of character—she dislikes dogs and makes Willie keep Freckles away from her when she's around, which is most of the time. Ultimately, Willie realizes where his true loyalty lies, and boy and dog are once again the best of friends—"a nice lesson in relationships and loyalty," according to a *Publishers Weekly* critic. However, despite her faux pas in bringing a jar of flea powder to Freckles's birthday party, Jane redeems herself in *Freckles and Jane,* as Freckles gets the stuck-up teen out of a tight situation involving a German shepherd on the loose and finally gains her affection. A *Kirkus Reviews* commentator dubbed *Freckles and Jane* "a satisfying 'here and now' story."

With *Fat Santa,* Cuyler returned to the subject she had covered in *The All-Around Christmas Book,* although this time in fictional form. Molly is determined to wait up for Santa's arrival; she settles into a comfortable chair and listens to Christmas carols on her headphones while she waits. Awakened out of a semi-sleep in the wee hours of the morning by a cloud of ash, Molly hears a voice coming from inside her fireplace—Santa has gotten stuck in the chimney! One experience of being stuck in the chimney is enough for the old fellow; he

A few lights were beginning to go on in some houses, and Molly knew she had to hurry. She looked down and saw Santa in the distance, waving at her from her front yard.
The reindeer flew to Molly's house and swirled down to the ground as softly as snowflakes.

In Margery Cuyler's award-winning picture book, young Molly waits up to meet Santa and winds up assisting him when he finds himself wedged in her chimney. (From *Fat Santa,* **illustrated by Marsha Winborn.)**

Discovering that a certain brand of bubble gum makes him invisible, Alex decides to use his new power to pull off a series of practical jokes that quickly get out of hand. (From *Invisible in the Third Grade,* written by Cuyler and illustrated by Mirko Gabler.)

convinces Molly to don his red jacket and make the rest of his gift-giving rounds, which she does. Praising the book's energy, *Bulletin of the Center for Children's Books* contributor Betsy Hearne cited *Fat Santa* as "a holiday picture book that will be easy for children to listen to, look at, and like." Phillis Wilson of *Booklist* pointed out that "the open end works in this well-constructed plot," while a *Publishers Weekly* critic praised Cuyler for "amiably captur[ing]" the spirit of Christmas Eve.

Another holiday story written by Cuyler is *Daisy's Crazy Thanksgiving.* Daisy begs to be excused from her parents' busy restaurant to join her grandparents, only to discover pandemonium in a house full of eccentric relatives, a menagerie of pet animals, and an absent-minded Granny who has again forgotten to turn on the oven for the turkey. "No getting around the success of the story's wacky humor," observed *Booklist*'s Denise Wilms. "Offbeat and, intermittently, very funny."

That's Good! That's Bad!—Cuyler's story of a little boy traveling by balloon in a wild trip over a zoo—success-fully combines sound effects, a large format, and plenty of opportunity for audience participation where "kids will enjoy the push-me-pull-me tension," according to Roger Sutton of *Bulletin of the Center for Children's Books.* Deborah Abbott pointed out in *Booklist* that the author "uses the familiar ... refrain adroitly."

Cuyler's first novel, *The Trouble with Soap,* was written after she attended a writer's conference in her capacity as editor. "I sat around for two weeks listening to people read their stuff," she told interviewer Roginski. "Then I started writing." *The Trouble with Soap* is based on its author's own experiences as a not-so-model child. In the novel, thirteen-year-old Lucinda Sokoloff (a.k.a. Soap) is suspended for her excessive zeal in playing practical jokes. After an incident involving Saran Wrap and the toilets in the boys' lavatory cause her to be shipped off to Miss Pringle's Private School for Girls along with partner-in-crime and narrator Laurie Endersby, Soap rejects the snobbish students in favor of her own company. Laurie, on the other hand, desperately wants to be accepted by the in-crowd at her new school. She ultimately tells a painful secret about her friend's father as a way of gaining that acceptance. A *Publishers Weekly* writer observed that the novel is completely unlike any of Cuyler's former works and "displays impressive versatility."

"I wanted to write about what it is that makes twelve- and thirteen-year-old kids so sensitive to peer pressure," Cuyler explained to Roginski. "Why do they care so much about what other kids think of them? They're really imprisoned by collective values—how they think, how they dress, how they look at the world. It's a very conformist way of living. It's hard to be outside the collective spirit at that age and yet my character Soap is. That fascinates me because the whole key of life is to break through the walls that parents and society build around you, to be an individual, to express yourself."

The Trouble with Soap was followed by several more novels for young people, including *Invisible in the Third Grade* and *Weird Wolf,* the latter a story whose protago-nist also has trouble fitting in with his friends. It's not so much that nine-year-old Harry Walpole is unpopular, but he has a terribly embarrassing problem—he turns into a wolf when the moon is full. As inconvenient as this is—it gets increasingly difficult to come up with excuses for being caught running around naked outside at sunrise—Harry is fortunate that his blood-lust only extends to hamburgers. A research trip to the library results in several possible cures for his problem, and one of them actually works, in a book that critics praised as appropriately seductive for even the most reluctant of readers. "Destined for greatness in the opinion of werewolf-crazy eight-year-olds," predicted Kathryn Pi-erson of *Bulletin of the Center for Children's Books.*

■ Works Cited

Abbott, Deborah, review of *That's Good! That's Bad!, Booklist,* December 1, 1991, pp. 702-03.
Review of *The All-Around Christmas Book, Publishers Weekly,* September 17, 1982, p. 115.
Cuyler, Margery, interview with Jim Roginski in *Behind the Covers: Interviews with Authors and Illustrators of Books for Children and Young Adults,* Libraries Unlimited (Littleton, CO), 1985, pp. 51-58.
Elleman, Barbara, review of *The All-Around Pumpkin Book, Booklist,* July 15, 1980, p. 1674.

Review of *Fat Santa, Publishers Weekly,* October 30, 1987, p. 70.

Feldman, Joan C., review of *Jewish Holidays, School Library Journal,* January, 1979, p. 41.

Flowers, Ann A., review of *Shadow's Baby, Horn Book,* January, 1990, p. 50.

Review of *Freckles and Jane, Kirkus Reviews,* November 1, 1989, p. 1602.

Review of *Freckles and Willie, Publishers Weekly,* April 25, 1986, p. 78.

Hearne, Betsy, review of *Fat Santa, Bulletin of the Center for Children's Books,* November, 1987, p. 46.

Heins, Ethel L., review of *The All-Around Pumpkin Book, Horn Book,* October, 1980, p. 534.

Pierson, Kathryn, review of *Weird Wolf, Bulletin of the Center for Children's Books,* January, 1990, pp. 107-08.

Review of *Shadow's Baby, Publishers Weekly,* October 13, 1989, p. 51.

Sutherland, Zena, review of *Jewish Holidays, Bulletin of the Center for Children's Books,* January, 1979, p. 77.

Sutton, Roger, review of *That's Good! That's Bad!, Bulletin of the Center for Children's Books,* December, 1991, p. 87.

Review of *The Trouble with Soap, Publishers Weekly,* May 28, 1982, p. 72.

Wilms, Denise, review of *Daisy's Crazy Thanksgiving, Booklist,* October 1, 1990, p. 338.

Wilson, Phillis, review of *Fat Santa, Booklist,* November 1, 1987, p. 474.

■ For More Information See

BOOKS

Seventh Book of Junior Authors and Illustrators, H. W. Wilson, 1996, pp. 73-74.

PERIODICALS

Bulletin of the Center for Children's Books, November, 1982, p. 45; October, 1984, p. 22; February, 1986, pp. 105-06; November, 1990, p. 57.

Horn Book, April, 1982, pp. 162-63; November, 1990, p. 718.

New York Times Book Review, October 26, 1980, p. 27.

School Library Journal, December, 1984, p. 69; April, 1986, p. 69; April, 1990, p. 116; February, 1990, p. 72; November, 1991, p. 92.

D–E

DABCOVICH, Lydia

■ Personal

Born in Bulgaria; immigrated to Palestine (now Israel), then to the United States in 1957; married a naval architect in 1957; children: two daughters. *Education:* Attended night classes in Israel; attended Central School of Arts and Crafts (London), 1956-57; Boston Museum of Fine Arts School, B.F.A. (highest honors), 1960.

■ Addresses

Home—29 Sargent-Beechwood, Brookline, MA 02146. *Office*—Art Institute of Boston, 700 Beacon St., Boston, MA 02159.

■ Career

Freelance author and illustrator; teacher of illustration at Art Institute of Boston, 1983-88, 1998—. *Military service:* Compulsive service in Israeli Army. *Member:* Graphic Artists' Guild.

■ Awards, Honors

One of Best Illustrated Children's Books of the Year, *New York Times,* 1978, for *There Once Was a Woman Who Married a Man;* one of Best Science Trade Books, 1980, for *Follow the River;* Books of the Year, Library of Congress, 1985, for *Sleepy Bear; Reading Rainbow* selection, 1985, and Children's Choice designation, International Reading Association/Children's Book Council, 1986, both for *Mrs. Huggins and Her Hen Hannah;* Parents' Choice awards, 1984, for *Mrs. Huggins and Her Hen Hannah,* 1989, for *William and Grandpa,* 1990, for *Ducks Fly,* and 1991, for *The Night Ones;* Christopher Award, 1989, for *William and Grandpa;* Pick of the List, American Booksellers, 1991, for *The Night Ones.*

■ Writings

FOR CHILDREN; SELF-ILLUSTRATED

Follow the River, Dutton, 1980.
Sleepy Bear, Dutton, 1982.
Mrs. Huggins and Her Hen Hannah, Dutton, 1985.
Busy Beavers, Dutton, 1988.
Ducks Fly, Dutton, 1990.
The Keys to My Kingdom: A Poem in Three Languages, Lothrop, 1992.
(Reteller) *The Polar Bear Son: An Inuit Tale,* Clarion, 1997.

ILLUSTRATOR

Barbara Corcoran, *A Trick of Light,* Atheneum, 1972.
Marjorie Stover, *Trail Boss in Pigtails,* Atheneum, 1972.
Jack London, *White Fang,* Limited Editions Club, 1973, Heritage Press, 1973.
Adrienne Richard, *The Accomplice,* Little, Brown, 1973.
Frank Emerson Andrews, *Nobody Comes to Dinner,* Little, Brown, 1976.
(With Tomie dePaola, Trina Schart Hyman, Charles Mikolaycak, Hilary Knight, Friso Henstra) Norma Farber, *Six Impossible Things Before Breakfast,* Addison-Wesley, 1976.
Norma Farber, *There Once Was a Woman Who Married a Man,* Addison-Wesley, 1978.
(With Charles Mikolaycak and Jim Arnosky) Richard Kennedy, *Delta Baby and Two Sea Songs,* Addison-Wesley, 1979.
Marjorie Lewis, *The Boy Who Would Be a Hero,* Coward, 1982.
Paul Fleischman, *The Animal Hedge,* Dutton, 1983.
Arielle North Olson, *Hurry Home, Grandma!,* Dutton, 1984.
Deborah Hartley, *Up North in Winter,* Dutton, 1986.
Alice Schertle, *William and Grandpa,* Lothrop, 1989.
Patricia Grossman, *The Night Ones,* Harcourt, 1991.
Ruth Gordon, *Feathers,* Macmillan, 1993.
Alice Schertle, *Maisie,* Lothrop, 1995.
Edith Tarbescu, *Annushka's Voyage,* Clarion, 1998.

LYDIA DABCOVICH

■ Adaptations

Follow the River was adapted for Canadian television, 1985.

■ Sidelights

Author and illustrator Lydia Dabcovich has produced a number of striking picture books for pre-readers. In an illustration style that some critics have compared favorably with that of Robert McCloskey and James Stevenson for its ability to give animals personality without adding human characteristics, Dabcovich uses mediums like crayon and watercolor as background for her heavily inked figures. "Dabcovich's stories could serve as models for preschool picture books," noted a *Publishers Weekly* reviewer, praising the simple, happy texts and boldly outlined illustrations that the author/illustrator uses in such picture books as *Mrs. Huggins and Her Hen Hannah, Ducks Fly,* and *Up North in Winter,* as well as in *The Keys to My Kingdom,* a Mother Goose rhyme that Dabcovich translates into English, French, and Spanish for her young audience.

Born in Bulgaria, Dabcovich and her family moved to Palestine when she was a child. During her years in that country, war plagued the region; Palestine became the Jewish state of Israel, and suffered from the Arab-Israeli War in 1948 as a result. Despite the fighting, Dabcovich recalls many pleasant memories of her childhood, mostly centering on family members, the beautiful Mediterranean climate, and the books she grew to know and love. She attended high school in the city of Tel Aviv, where her greatest joy was dancing. After graduation, Dabcovich attended mandatory military training, worked at headquarters, and spent her nights taking art classes.

In 1956, Dabcovich enrolled at London's Central School of Arts and Crafts, intending to graduate, but a trip to Turkey would change all that. There she met her future husband, a Turkish citizen of Yugoslav background and a naval architecture student at the Massachusetts Institute of Technology (M.I.T.). Dabcovich came to the United States on a student visa and enrolled at the Boston Museum School; she and her fiance from M.I.T. were married in 1957. Later, both became U.S. citizens. The couple had two daughters together, keeping Dabcovich busy for the next decade. By the late 1960s, she began her career as an illustrator with contributions to two books published in Israel in 1969 and 1970. Her first illustration project in America was for Barbara Corcoran's *A Trick of Light,* published in 1972. Besides her own subsequent writing and illustrating, Dabcovich has taught classes in her craft at the Boston Art Institute.

After her first book for Corcoran, Dabcovich completed several other illustration projects for various American publishers, including a popular version of Jack London's *White Fang,* first brought out by Limited Editions Club and later republished by Heritage Press. In 1979 Dabcovich's editor suggested that she write some of her own texts as well. Dabcovich took the suggestion to heart, and, with *Follow the River,* a children's author was born. A simple book describing the life of a river, from mountain top to the sea, as its course is followed by a pair of hikers, *Follow the River* features brightly colored ink and crayon illustrations that a *Kirkus Reviews* critic characterized as "set, exotically, in a very Mittel European landscape" containing castles. "A pleasant book," observed Zena Sutherland of the *Bulletin of the Center for Children's Books,* "that can help develop children's concepts of space and geographical differences." A television adaptation of *Follow the River* appeared frequently on Canadian television between 1985 and 1990.

Dabcovich's bold use of line, which characterizes *Follow the River,* has been a trademark of her illustration style. She uses it to good effect again in *Sleepy Bear,* as the life

Dabcovich's crayon-and-ink illustrations capture the warm affection of Alice Schertle's narrative about an old woman recounting her ninety years. (From *Maisie.*)

of a brown bear is traced through the passing seasons. Although the book contains minimal text, "boldly stroked and colored cartoon drawings ... fill in personality and detail," according to Nancy Palmer in her *School Library Journal* appraisal of the book. A *Bulletin of the Center for Children's Books* critic maintained that the large type, large-scale drawings, and upbeat tone "make this an exemplary book for very young children." Another story about animals, *Busy Beavers,* uses much the same techniques, with heavily outlined figures in watercolor, while *Ducks Fly* uses the same medium in shades of green and blue to tell the story of an independent young duckling. Of the former work, Ellen Mandel of *Booklist* commented: "Dabcovich engagingly takes children into the realm of the beaver world"; Ellen Fader of *Horn Book* asserted of the latter, "Nature at its most elemental and adventurous."

In *Mrs. Huggins and Her Hen Hannah,* Dabcovich creates perhaps her most ambitious story—a depiction of the friendship between an elderly woman and her feathered companion, a hen named Hannah, that ends sadly when Hannah dies (no, she does not end up as Sunday dinner). Fortunately, Hannah left behind a small chick who grows up to take her mother's place in Mrs. Huggins' life. "The simple text celebrates friendship's joys and recognizes death's sorrow," noted *School Library Journal* contributor Kathy Piehl. Dabcovich explained to *SATA:* "I got the idea for [*Mrs. Huggins and Her Hen Hannah*] when I visited the real Mrs. Huggins' house and garden. I do not remember her real name, but she was an old lady who lived there with her pet hens over a hundred years ago. When the hens died, she buried them in her garden, put up headstones for them, and sold little poems about them to tourists. There was a ready-made story there. All it needed was a conclusion."

A similar story is told in *The Polar Bear Son: An Inuit Tale,* as Dabcovich illustrates a traditional Eskimo story about an old woman who adopts a polar bear cub; in return for her care, the cub helps gather food for the pair during the harshest months of the year until the woman is forced to send the bear away to save it from being hunted by the men of her village. "The story gives a picture of motherly love toward an 'adopted child,'" noted Mollie Bynum in her appraisal of the book for *School Library Journal,* "one the woman will love always." Dabcovich, describing the creative process behind the book, told *SATA:* "For *The Polar Bear Son,* the strength and power of Inuit sculpture inspired me to try to convey weight and volume in my figures, and dramatic interaction between them, by using big, simple shapes with a minimum of line and shading." She added, "Whenever possible, I like to start the research for a book by sketching my characters from life. I had a wonderful time sketching polar bears at the Rhode Island zoo."

A Mother Goose rhyme provided the inspiration for another of Dabcovich's well-received titles. "*The Keys to My Kingdom,*" Dabcovich told *SATA,* "represents some aspects of making picture books that I like best:

Spring, summer, and long dark winter passed. Kunikdjuaq grew quickly. When spring came again, he was big and strong enough to go hunting and fishing for the old woman.

An old woman adopts an orphaned polar bear cub and unselfishly sends him away when the bear's life is endangered. (From *The Polar Bear Son: An Inuit Tale,* retold and illustrated by Dabcovich.)

visually interpreting a story's rhythm and pace, 'directing' the picture book 'movie,' 'choreographing' its dance.

"'The Keys to *the* Kingdom, a Mother Goose poem or chant, was the starting point for a sort of pictorial autobiography, told with the aid of metaphor,' Dabcovich continued. "*The Keys to MY Kingdom,* and to that of the little girl in the story, are paints and brushes. Brushes and paint take her and her little dog on a journey through the kingdom. They pass through various places, which are listed one after the other, each place contained within the next: The city is in the kingdom, the town in the city, the street is in the town, and so on. Finally, they arrive at 'the room in the house'—the little girl's room up in the attic, where an easel, paints, and brushes are waiting for her to recreate impressions and flowers she has collected on her way.'"

A *Publishers Weekly* reviewer, commenting on *The Keys to My Kingdom: A Poem in Three Languages,* asserted: "the simultaneous simplicity and complexity of this singular work prove most uncommon—and most noteworthy." Ann Welton, writing in *School Library Journal,* noted that the artist's "colored pencil and crayon illustrations have a sense of volume and life, as well as an endearingly childlike character." She adds that the literal translation into Spanish and French offers further use for ESL and language classes. Favorably comparing *The Keys to My Kingdom* with Diane Worfolk Allison's version of the tale, *This Is the Key to the Kingdom,* Paul Zelinsky concluded in his *New York Times Book Review* piece that "Lydia Dabcovich found some meat in the structure of the poem; her pictures illustrate that with vigor, and make a stronger book." Dabcovich continued to *SATA,* "*The Keys to My Kingdom* is in some ways quite personal, but it also contains elements important to me in all my books: to play a game with words and

pictures, to explore my 'kingdom,' and to encourage my readers to explore their own."

In addition to creating artwork to accompany her own texts, Dabcovich has contributed illustrations to the works of several other authors for young people. In Deborah Hartley's *Up North in Winter,* Dabcovich's drawings of winter landscapes were praised by *Horn Book* reviewer Ethel L. Heins as her best work ever. And of the award-winning *William and Grandpa,* Alice Schertle's story of a boy and his grandfather, a *Publishers Weekly* critic noted that Dabcovich's "bright pictures reinforce and extend the text." In Schertle's affectionate *Maisie,* the story of a woman's life from birth to old age, *Publishers Weekly* again praised Dabcovich's artwork, writing that her softly focused crayon and ink pictures reflect the title character's "spunk and warmth, and perceptively convey both those things that changed and those that remained constant during this woman's lifetime."

Asked which writers and illustrators have influenced her work, Dabcovich told *SATA:* "I very much admire a group of British illustrators, ranging from the eighteenth century to the present, and including Rowlandson, Cruikshank, Edward Ardizzone, Quentin Blake and John Burningham. All have in common a fluid, witty line, economical and effective use of tone, color and wash, lively, expressive characters, a great sense of humor, and the ability to convey charm without getting sweet or cloying. . . .

"I have to mention a few more favorites of mine," Dabcovich continued: "I admire Leo Lionni for his sense of design and color, his inventive use of collage and printmaking, and for the wonderful fables he tells. I think *Little Blue and Little Yellow* is a masterpiece, and a great introduction to abstract art. I like Roger Duvoisin for his sense of humor, energetic line and composition, and expressive animals and humans.... I am sure that looking at these artists' work has energized me and many others to go on with our own. But I mustn't forget Margot Zemach, Boutet de Monvel, Edward Gorey, Sempe, James Marshall, Hugh Lofting, ... stop me or I'll go on for weeks!"

■ Works Cited

Bynum, Mollie, review of *The Polar Bear Son: An Inuit Tale, School Library Journal,* June, 1997, p. 106.
Review of *Ducks Fly, Publishers Weekly,* May 18, 1990, p. 82.
Fader, Ellen, review of *Ducks Fly, Horn Book,* September-October, 1990, pp. 589-90.
Flowers, Ann A., review of *Follow the River, Horn Book,* February, 1981, p. 40.
Review of *Follow the River, Kirkus Reviews,* January 1, 1981, p. 1.
Heins, Ethel L., review of *Up North in Winter, Horn Book,* January, 1987, p. 45.
Review of *Maisie, Publishers Weekly,* January 30, 1995, p. 101.
Mandel, Ellen, review of *Busy Beavers, Booklist,* May 15, 1988, p. 1607.
Palmer, Nancy, review of *Sleepy Bear, School Library Journal,* March, 1982, p. 130.
Piehl, Kathy, review of *Mrs. Huggins and Her Hen Hannah, School Library Journal,* January, 1986, p. 56.
Sutherland, Zena, review of *Follow the River, Bulletin of the Center for Children's Books,* April, 1981, p. 149.
Sutherland, Zena, review of *Sleepy Bear, Bulletin of the Center for Children's Books,* July-August, 1982, p. 204.
Review of *William and Grandpa, Publishers Weekly,* May 19, 1989, p. 82.
Welton, Ann, review of *The Keys to My Kingdom, School Library Journal,* April, 1992, p. 106.
Zelinsky, Paul, review of *The Keys to My Kingdom, New York Times Book Review,* May 17, 1992, p. 33.

■ For More Information See

PERIODICALS

Booklist, October 1, 1985, p. 219; April 1, 1992, p. 1452; October 15, 1993, pp. 446-47; April 15, 1995, p. 1508.
Horn Book, June, 1982, p. 278; November-December, 1985, p. 725.
Kirkus Reviews, February 1, 1988, p. 199; April 15, 1992, p. 547.
Publishers Weekly, April 23, 1982, p. 93; September 20, 1993, p. 72.
School Library Journal, July, 1990, p. 58; November, 1993, p. 98; April, 1995, p. 116.

*   *   *

DAVIES, Nicola 1958-
(Stevie Morgan)

■ Personal

Born May 3, 1958, in Birmingham, UK; daughter of William Howard Davies and Beryl Rona Morgan; married Mark Harrison, July 21, 1984 (divorced December 19, 1997); children: Joseph, Gabriel. *Education:* Kings College, Cambridge, UK, honours degree (zoology).

■ Addresses

Home—Luckleigh Cottage, Hockworthy, Wellington Somerset, UK TA210NN. *Agent*—Celia Catchpole, 56

Nicola Davies' informational picture book includes facts and anecdotes ranging from the texture of the blue whale's skin to what food whales like to eat. (From *Big Blue Whale,* illustrated by Nick Maland.)

Gilpin Ave., East Sheen, London. *Electronic mail*—nicola.davies@btinternet.com.

■ Career

Freelance broadcaster and writer. Writes newspaper column for *The Independent* under the pseudonym Stevie Morgan.

■ Writings

Big Blue Whale, illustrated by Nick Maland, Candlewick (Cambridge, MA), 1997.

■ Work in Progress

Delphineum Blues, a novel for Hodder and Stoughton.

■ Sidelights

Nicola Davies told *SATA:* "I am interested in communication—communication about zoology, about science and about how we as humans experience and interpret our existence. I'm convinced that art and science are all part of the same picture and can contribute enormously to each other. It's the crossovers and combinations of fields of interest that motivate me in life and work."

Such a multiplicity of interests is evident in *Big Blue Whale*, Davies' highly regarded look at one of earth's most majestic animals. The book is filled with facts and anecdotes ranging from the texture of the blue whale's skin to its diet. "Conversational text and soft, cross-hatched pen-and-ink illustrations ebb and flow in a fluid look at the largest mammal ever to inhabit the earth," noted a *Kirkus Reviews* critic, who added: "This unassuming book is teeming with new discoveries upon each rereading." Ellen Fader, writing in *Horn Book*, maintained that *Big Blue Whale* "offers young readers exactly what they want to know about this magnificent animal." Fader continued, "The narrative maintains a brisk pace and something of an informal storytelling quality, without veering into sentimentality." *Booklist* reviewer Ellen Mandel concluded that *Big Blue Whale* "will definitely satisfy youngsters' curiosity."

■ Works Cited

Review of *Big Blue Whale, Kirkus Reviews*, June 1, 1997, pp. 871-72.
Fader, Ellen, review of *Big Blue Whale, Horn Book*, May-June, 1997, pp. 338-39.
Mandel, Ellen, review of *Big Blue Whale, Booklist*, September 1, 1997, p. 128.

■ For More Information See

PERIODICALS

School Library Journal, July, 1997, pp. 81-82.

EDMONDS, Walter D(umaux) 1903-1998

OBITUARY NOTICE—See index for *SATA* sketch: Born July 15, 1903, in Boonville, NY; died January 28, 1998, in Utica, NY. Author. Among Edmonds's several titles for adults and children were three historical novels, the best-known of which is *Drums Along the Mohawk,* a 1936 book that was on the bestseller list for two years and was made into a film starring Henry Fonda and Claudette Colbert in 1939. Edmonds received the Newbery Medal in 1942 for his children's work *The Matchlock Gun.* Most of his books are part history, part fiction and were set in Mohawk Valley in the Adirondack region of upstate New York, where he grew up. His first book, also made into a movie starring Fonda, was *Rome Haul*, published in 1929. Edmonds's other books for adults include *The Big Barn* (1930), *Erie Water* (1933), *Mostly Canallers* (1934), *Moses* (1939), *The Wedding Journey* (1939), *Chad Hanna* (1940), *Young Ames* (1942), *In the Hands of the Senecas* (1947), *The First Hundred Years* (1948), *They Fought with What They Had* (1951), *The Boyds of Black River* (1953), *The Erie Canal* (1960), *The Musket and the Cross* (1968), *The South African Quirt* (1985) and *Tales My Father Never Told* (1995). In addition to his Newbery-winning *Matchlock Gun,* Edmonds also wrote the children's books *Tom Whipple* (1942), *Two Logs Crossing* (1943), *Wilderness Clearing* (1944), *Cadmus Henry* (1949), *Mr. Benedict's Lion* (1950), *Corporal Bess* (1952), *Hound Dog Moses and the Promised Land* (1954), *Uncle Ben's Whale* (1955), *They Had a Horse* (1962), *The Time to Go House* (1969), *Seven American Stories* (1970), *Wolf Hunt* (1970), *Beaver Valley* (1971), *The Story of Richard Storm* (1973), *Bert Breen's Barn* (1975), and *The Night Raider* (1980). *Bert Breen's Barn* won the National Book Award in 1976.

OBITUARIES AND OTHER SOURCES:

PERIODICALS

Chicago Tribune, January 29, 1998, sec. 3, p. 12.
Los Angeles Times, January 28, 1998, p. A18.
New York Times, January 28, 1998, p. D23.
Publishers Weekly, February 23, 1998, p. 24.
Washington Post, January 28, 1998, p. B6.

* * *

ELMER, Robert 1958-

■ Personal

Born January 17, 1958, in Berkeley, CA; son of Knud and Evy Elmer; married Ronda D. (a homemaker), August 9, 1980; children: Kai, Danica, Stefan. *Education:* Attended University of California at Berkeley, 1979-80; Simpson College (San Francisco, CA), B.A. (communication), 1980; St. Mary's College (Moraga, CA), post-graduate teaching certificate, 1987. *Religion:* Baptist.

■ Addresses

Office—c/o Bethany House Publishers, 11300 Hampshire Ave. South, Minneapolis, MN 55438. *Electronic mail*—relmer@compuserve.com.

■ Career

Assistant pastor in Olympia, WA, 1983-85; director of admissions, Simpson College, San Francisco, CA, 1981-83; newspaper editor and reporter, 1980-81, 1985-87; advertising copywriter, Baron & Co., Bellingham, WA, 1988—. Speaker, Young Writers' Institute, Hershey, PA. *Member:* American Christian Writers.

■ Writings

FOR CHILDREN; "THE YOUNG UNDERGROUND" SERIES

A Way Through the Sea, Bethany House (Minneapolis, MN), 1994.
Beyond the River, Bethany House, 1995.
Into the Flames, Bethany House, 1995.
Far From the Storm, Bethany House, 1995.
Chasing the Wind, Bethany House, 1996.
A Light in the Castle, Bethany House, 1996.
Follow the Star, Bethany House, 1997.
Touch the Sky, Bethany House, 1997.

"ADVENTURES DOWN UNDER" SERIES

Escape to Murray River, Bethany House, 1997.
Captive at Kangaroo Springs, Bethany House, 1997.
Rescue at Boomerang Bend, Bethany House, 1998.
Dingo Creek Challenge, Bethany House, 1998.
Race to Wallaby Bay, Bethany House, 1998.

■ Work in Progress

Books 6-8 in the "Adventures Down Under" series, for Bethany House Publishers.

■ Sidelights

Robert Elmer told *SATA:* "I think I started getting serious about writing in the second grade. Actually, serious isn't the right word. Writing has always been fun for me. I wrote a family newspaper. I wrote about things in the neighborhood. Lots of people encouraged me, which was good, and I eventually became a newspaper and advertising writer. But one thing I especially remember was my eighth-grade English teacher, Mr. Little. He wrote in my yearbook that he expected to teach his future students from a book I had written. I never forgot that. For twenty years, what he had said was ringing in my ears. I knew I wanted to write books, I just never knew I had anything to say until my own three kids started growing up.

"Now, when I get letters from kids in Michigan or Mississippi or California, I understand a lot better why I write: to open a window into a world where kids may never have been before. When that's historical fiction, the idea is to understand the past, to know that people

ROBERT ELMER

back then were kids, too. I want to keep writing exciting books that help plug kids into history and help them understand that historical people were real and that their faith mattered.

"In my first series ('The Young Underground'), each book is based on a real historical event or character. They're set in World War II Denmark. It was a natural, because my family is Danish; both my parents grew up during that time. I would look into history books for exciting things that happened, then ask them questions to find out how it really happened. A Danish man—I used to clean his yard and he was a friend of my parents—would tell me stories about being in the Danish Underground movement, and one of the stories he told me inspired book number three, *Into the Flames.* My uncle was in the Underground, too, although I never met him.

"Ideas in general? I get them from history books, mostly, and from my family. Australian friends over the Internet are helping me with research for our "Adventures Down Under" series, set in pioneer Australia. My wife and kids are my writing team. They help me sift out the good ideas from the dumb ones, and they read through a lot of the early manuscripts. I watch them when they're reading. If they get to a part and say,

'Huh?' I know I'd better go back and do some rewriting. But even if it's hard work, I can't think of anything else that's more fun or exciting!"

■ For More Information See

PERIODICALS

Booklist, May 15, 1995, p. 1645; February 15, 1996, p. 1020; May 1, 1996, p. 1506.
School Library Journal, August, 1995, p. 140; August, 1997, p. 157; February, 1998, p. 106.

G

GARDNER, Craig Shaw 1949-

■ Personal

Born July 2, 1949, in Rochester, NY. *Education:* Attended Boston University.

■ Addresses

Home and office—P.O. Box 1281, E. Arlington, MA 02174. *Agent*—Merrilee Heifetz, Writers House, 21 W. 26th St., New York, NY 10010.

■ Career

Science fiction and fantasy novelist and short story writer. *Member:* Horror Writers of America (president, 1990-92).

■ Writings

"EBENEZUM" SERIES

A Malady of Magicks, Ace, 1986.
A Multitude of Monsters, Ace, 1986.
A Night in the Netherhells, Ace, 1987, Headline (London), 1989.
The Exploits of Ebenezum (includes all three novels), Nelson Doubleday, 1987.

"BALLAD OF WUNTVOR" SERIES

A Difficulty with Dwarves, Ace, 1987, Headline, 1989.
An Excess of Enchantment, Ace, 1988, Headline, 1989.
A Disagreement with Death, Ace, 1989, Headline, 1989.
The Wanderings of Wuntvor (includes all three novels), Nelson Doubleday, 1989.

"CINEVERSE" SERIES

Slaves of the Volcano God, Ace, 1989, Headline, 1989.
Bride of the Slime Monster, Ace, 1990.
Revenge of the Fluffy Bunnies, Ace, 1990.
Cineverse Cycle (includes all three novels), Guild America (New York), 1990.

"ARABIAN NIGHTS" SERIES

The Other Sinbad, Ace, 1991.
A Bad Day for Ali Baba, Ace, 1992.
The Last Arabian Night, Ace, 1993.

"DRAGON CIRCLE" SERIES

The Dragon Circle: Dragon Sleeping, Ace, 1994.
The Dragon Circle: Dragon Waking, Ace, 1995.
The Dragon Circle: Dragon Burning, Ace, 1996.

NOVELIZATIONS

The Lost Boys: A Novel, Berkley, 1987.
Wishbringer (novelization of a computer game), Avon (New York), 1988.
Back to the Future, Part II: A Novel, Berkley, 1989, Headline, 1989.
Batman, Warner, 1989.
The Batman Murders, Warner, 1990.
Back to the Future, Part III: A Novel, Berkley, 1990, Firecrest (London), 1992.
Batman Returns, Warner, 1992.

OTHER

(With Matthew J. Costello) *The 7th Guest,* Prima Publications, 1995.

Several chapters of Gardner's books originally appeared as short stories.

■ Adaptations

Batman Returns was released on audio cassette in 1992.

■ Sidelights

Craig Shaw Gardner is a popular writer of fantasy and science fiction who characteristically blends humor and adventure to create works noted for their imagination, wit, and enjoyable qualities. Gardner is best known for writing several series that feature both human characters and figures from myth and legend such as wizards, witches, dwarves, and demons. Although his works include traditional plot elements like the hero's quest and the battle between good and evil, Gardner, who is favorably compared to such fantasy writers as Piers Anthony and Terry Pratchett, is credited for giving his books an original personality through his spoofing of the conventions of the fantasy genre and his use of cultural references and irreverent, even slapstick humor. As a stylist, Gardner favors lively narratives filled with wordplay and, in the words of critic Don D'Ammassa, "literary sight gags"; although he is most often recognized for his wildly exaggerated situations, Gardner is also acknowledged for his humorous understating and for his sharp commentary on human nature. Although Gardner's works are published for an adult audience, they have great appeal for young people; the author often includes teenage characters in prominent roles. In addition to his original fantasy novels, Gardner is the author of novelizations of screenplays for films with a fantasy basis such as *Batman,* which was a best-seller in novel form; *Back to the Future;* and *The Lost Boys;* he is also the author of a fantasy novel based on an interactive computer game. Writing in *Twentieth-Century Science Fiction Writers,* Don D'Ammassa says of Gardner that he "has acquired an enviable reputation based almost entirely on two series of amusing fantasy and science fiction novels .... Gardner's humor is genuinely funny, and his writing skills are sufficient to put him in good stead no matter what direction his future takes."

Gardner's first cycle of books, the "Ebenezum" series, depicts the exploits of a luckless wizard who becomes allergic to magic through a spell placed on him by the demon Guxx. In the first volume of the series, *A Malady of Magicks,* Ebenezum and his bumbling apprentice Wuntvor encounter dragons, trolls, assassins, and even Death himself in their quest for the cure to the wizard's malady. In the second volume, *A Multitude of Monsters,* Ebenezum faces more attacks from Guxx as well as problems from a group of creatures that want to control the world; the third volume, *A Night in the Netherhells,* describes Ebenezum's journey to Hell in order to rescue the city that holds the cure for his allergy. The Ebenezum tales were collected in *The Exploits of Ebenezum,* a volume published in 1987.

Gardner followed his "Ebenezum" cycle with a second, related series that focuses on Ebenezum's apprentice Wuntvor. In these works, the wizard's allergy to magic has spread throughout his community, thanks to the demon Guxx; throughout the trilogy, which includes the titles *A Difficulty with Dwarves, An Excess of Enchantments,* and *A Disagreement with Death,* Wuntvor travels to the far lands, outwits an evil witch, and successfully plays games against Death. Accompanied by his lady love, the witch Norei, and a variety of human and mythic companions, Wuntvor battles to rescue his master's powers and save their land. In a review of the third volume in *Voice of Youth Advocates,* Jo Holtz concluded, "Gardner has successfully combined buffoonery and fantasy to create a series that even an adult will enjoy. It truly made a believer out of me." The trilogy was collected into a single volume and published as *The Wanderings of Wuntvor* in 1989.

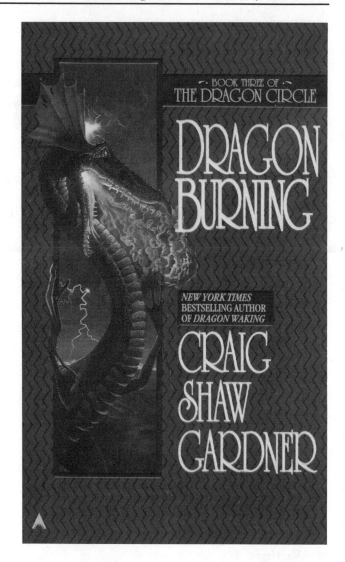

In the concluding volume of Craig Shaw Gardner's "Dragon Circle" trilogy, a formidable dragon awakens and seventeen-year-old Nick Blake must fight to keep the beast from falling into the wrong hands. (Cover illustration by Glenn Kim.)

In the "Cineverse" series, which includes *Slaves of the Volcano God, Bride of the Slime Monster,* and *Revenge of the Fluffy Bunnies,* Gardner broadly parodies the "Grade B" movies and serials of the 1930s, 40s, and 50s. The series focuses on the exploits of public relations man and movie aficionado Roger Gordon, who finds a Captain Crusader decoder ring that enables him to cross over into the Cineverse, an alternate dimension filled with the characters and characteristics of old movies, and become one of the superheroes of the universe. Gordon visits a variety of shlock film scenarios where beach-party fruggers evolve into the disco age and biker gangs run amok; in each volume, Gordon must rescue his girlfriend Dolores after she is kidnapped and held captive by dastardly villains. Don D'Ammassa of *Science Fiction Chronicle* called the first volume of the series "wildly funny, even more entertaining than the string of humorous fantasies Gardner has already presented us with." Writing in *Voice of Youth Advocates* about the second volume of the series, Debbie Earl said, "Teens enjoying the uproarious changes of pace evident in the *Back to the Future* movie series will love this book; more serious readers may find it a bit too frantic." *Locus* reviewer Scott Winnett claimed, "This is funny stuff, sharper and faster paced than last year's *Slaves of the Volcano God* but just as silly." Winnett of *Locus* said of the last volume in the series, "This is enjoyable, simple-minded fun," while D'Ammassa of *Science Fiction Chronicle* called it "absurdist fluff at its best." All three works were published as a single volume, *Cineverse Cycle*, in 1990.

In the early 1990s, Gardner reworked the legendary Arabian Nights tales into nontraditional retellings filled with action and humor; the new versions of the old tales are meant to show the "reality" behind the myths. *The Other Sinbad* introduces a second Sinbad—not the legendary sailor, but a porter who narrates the epic tale revolving around an eighth journey that takes place after the original seven voyages. A peripheral character in the traditional tale, Sinbad the Porter encounters monsters, demons, and other villains as he and Sinbad the Sailor journey together; during their voyage, the porter learns about the strengths and weaknesses of his traveling companion. Writing in *Kliatt*, Hugh M. Flick, Jr. noted, "Those familiar with Gardner's other works ... will love this new series," while *Voice of Youth Advocates* reviewer Kim Carter Sands called the volume a "delightful romp" and added, "Readers who live for Piers Anthony's style of humor will devour Gardner's book as well. Highly recommended." In *A Bad Day for Ali Baba*, Gardner features another familiar character, the poor woodcutter Ali Baba, in a tongue-in-cheek version of the Arabian Nights tale. Ali Baba's bad day begins when he meets forty thieves, who take him along on an adventure that leads him into encounters with djinni, magicians, malevolent eunuchs, and fair maidens in need of rescuing. Ali Baba's brother, who has been sliced into six pieces but—in Gardner's tale—survives, accompanies the hero and the thieves on their escapades. A reviewer in *Science Fiction Chronicle* commented, "This is even funnier than its predecessor ... a carousel tale through the Arabian Nights and a sure cure for the blues." Kim Sands noted in *Voice of Youth Advocates* that the book is a "good read for all who enjoy linguistical acrobatics, human foibles, and unpredictable plots." The third installment of the series, *The Last Arabian Night,* features another character from the original Middle Eastern legends, the storyteller Scheherazade. Her wondrous tales, which cannot be finished in a single session, are designed to keep her husband, a king enchanted by a curse that directs him to murder his wife, from killing her on their wedding night. At the conclusion of the book, readers realize that Scheherazade is actually telling her tales to the characters in the first two books in Gardner's Arabian Nights series. Writing in *Science Fiction Chronicles*, Don D'Ammassa said, "This must have been great fun to write, but it's even more fun to read."

In his fifth series—the "Dragon Circle," which includes *Dragon Sleeping, Dragon Waking,* and *Dragon Burn-* *ing*—Gardner skewers middle-class suburbia of the late 1960s by launching the residents of the neighborhood Chestnut Circle into a magic realm after a particularly bad storm. The mysterious land is ruled by a sleeping, malevolent dragon, who awakens periodically to wreak some havoc; the novels revolve around quests for jewels with magic powers called "dragon's eyes." After their arrival, the parents and children of Chestnut Circle are separated; the strongest individuals work to be reunited with their families while the weaker ones fall away. The teenagers of the transplanted society learn new skills to do battle with the soldiers, wizards, and monsters who serve as the local governors of their new home. One young man, Nick, emerges as a hero; a teenage girl, Mary Lou, is the only one of the Chestnut Circle residents who suspects the truth about the dragon, that it has enlisted the humans to fight in an upcoming battle. Gardner also addresses teen psychology, as the young people wrestle with their sexuality and rebel against their parents. Both deaths and resurrections punctuate the novels, which are filled with witty banter. In her review of *Dragon Sleeping* in *Voice of Youth Advocates,* Carrie Eldridge noted, "Gardner is an imaginative writer. He has no trouble creating the most fantastic of realms." Although the critic had difficulty with the episodic chapters and the amount of characters in the book, she concluded, "Gardner fans and dedicated fantasy fans may enjoy, and even look forward to further adventures...." *Science Fiction Chronicle* reviewer Don D'Ammassa commented, "The story has the feeling of the better Young Adult SF novels despite its fantasy elements, but without the condescension and simplification that would dissuade adults from reading it." A reviewer for *Publishers Weekly* claimed that although Gardner "is not a consistently adept stylist, his clear enjoyment of the proceedings should be infectious." Another *Publishers Weekly* critic called *Dragon Waking* "Gardner's delightful, if not wholly fulfilling, follow-up" and praised his "infectiously enthusiastic storytelling," while reviewer Sue Krumbein recommended in *Voice of Youth Advocates,* "A library that has *The Dragon Circle: Dragon Sleeping* should add this second title to its collection." A critic in *Publishers Weekly* concluded that although *Dragon Burning* "is the conclusion to the trilogy, new readers need not fear: Gardner provides enough background and writes clearly enough to make them feel right at home."

In addition to his series books, Gardner is the author of screenplay novelizations that are also well-received by critics. Writing in *Twentieth-Century Science Fiction Writers,* Don D'Ammassa noted of two of the books, "*Batman*'s darker humor was something of a departure, but *The Lost Boys* was a serious tale of horror unlike anything Gardner had written at novel length." Gardner is also the creator of *Wishbringer,* a novel from the Infocom series of popular fantasy role-playing computer games. In this book, con artist Simon is arrested on Festeron, a small island that is nice during the day but turns into scary Witchville at night. Simon, who encounters ghosts, goblins, and other creatures, is the only person who can remember the town in its previous incarnation; he has until midnight to retrieve a magical stone, the Wishbringer, from the Evil One, a figure who plans on turning Festeron into Witchville permanently. A reviewer in *Publishers Weekly* noted that although the origin of *Wishbringer* is "evident in its myriad traps, goal-oriented plot and gimmicky ending, Gardner's light, cartoony approach defuses all threat and keeps one reading in anticipation of humorous imbroglios." A critic in *Science Fiction Chronicle* agreed, claiming that Gardner "captures much of the spirit of the game in this offbeat little fantasy."

■ Works Cited

Review of *A Bad Day for Ali Baba, Science Fiction Chronicle,* October, 1992, p. 34.
D'Ammassa, Don, review of *Dragon Waking, Science Fiction Chronicle,* July, 1994, p. 37.
D'Ammassa, Don, review of *The Last Arabian Night, Science Fiction Chronicle,* June, 1993, pp. 32-33.
D'Ammassa, Don, review of *Revenge of the Fluffy Bunnies, Science Fiction Chronicle,* February, 1991, pp. 44-45.
D'Ammassa, Don, review of *Slaves of the Volcano God, Science Fiction Chronicle,* January, 1990, p. 34.
Review of *A Disagreement with Death, Publishers Weekly,* January 4, 1989, pp. 98-99.
Review of *Dragon Burning, Publishers Weekly,* September 30, 1996, p. 66.
Review of *Dragon Sleeping, Publishers Weekly,* April 4, 1994, p. 62.
Review of *Dragon Waking, Publishers Weekly,* September 25, 1995, pp. 48-49.
Earl, Debbie, review of *Bride of the Slime Monster, Voice of Youth Advocates,* December, 1990, p. 296.
Eldridge, Carrie, review of *Dragon Sleeping, Voice of Youth Advocates,* August, 1994, p. 156.
Flick, Hugh M., Jr., review of *The Other Sinbad, Kliatt,* April, 1992, p. 14.
Holtz, Jo, review of *A Disagreement with Death, Voice of Youth Advocates,* October, 1989, pp. 222-23.
Krumbein, Sue, review of *Dragon Waking, Voice of Youth Advocates,* February, 1996, p. 382.
Sands, Kim Carter, review of *A Bad Day for Ali Baba, Voice of Youth Advocates,* December, 1992, p. 292.
Sands, Kim Carter, review of *The Other Sinbad, Voice of Youth Advocates,* February, 1992, p. 182.
Winnett, Scott, review of *Bride of the Slime Monster, Locus,* March, 1990, p. 23.
Winnett, Scott, review of *Revenge of the Fluffy Bunnies, Locus,* August, 1990, p. 29.
Review of *Wishbringer, Publishers Weekly,* July 8, 1988, p. 49.
Review of *Wishbringer, Science Fiction Chronicle,* May, 1989, p. 40.

■ For More Information See

BOOKS

Nicholls, Peter, editor, *Encyclopedia of Science Fiction: An Illustrated A to Z,* Granada Publishing (London), 1979, p. 448.

Watson, Noelle and Paul E. Schellinger, editors, *Twentieth-Century Science-Fiction Writers,* 3rd edition, St. James Press, 1991, p. 920.

PERIODICALS

Fantasy Review, November, 1986, p. 28.
Kirkus Reviews, March 15, 1994, pp. 348-49; September 1, 1995, p. 1232.
Kliatt, January, 1993, pp. 16-17; July, 1993, p. 16.
Locus, October, 1989, p. 29.
Voice of Youth Advocates, June, 1986, p. 86; August, 1993, pp. 163-64.
Washington Post Book World, February 23, 1986, p. 12.

—Sketch by Gerard J. Senick

*　　*　　*

GEHR, Mary 1910(?)-1997

OBITUARY NOTICE—See index for *SATA* sketch: Born c. 1910 in Chicago, IL; died November 19, 1997, in Chicago, IL. Dancer, artist, educator, author. Gehr is remembered for her work as the author and illustrator of children's books. Early in her career, she worked as a dancer, first with the Chicago Opera Company for four seasons before joining the Ruth Page-Stone Ballet, where she enjoyed a major role in the production *Frankie and Johnnie.* She also pursued an interest in art and eventually developed skills in batik and intaglio. Her work was featured in various exhibitions in cities such as Chicago, San Francisco, New York, Washington, D.C., Boston, Athens (Greece), and Vienna (Austria). In addition, her art is part of permanent collections in institutions such as the Philadelphia Museum of Fine Art, the Art Institute of Chicago, and the Library of Congress. Her work as a book illustrator and designer began in 1954. She wrote and illustrated several books, including *The Littlest Circus Seal* and *Leaves from South Pacific and Asian Sketchbooks.* Gehr also provided pictures for the works of author authors, among them Caroline H. Mallon, Betty Russell, Carla Greene, Benjamin Elkin, and Margaret Friskey. In addition, she lectured at the Art Institute of Chicago from 1979 to 1982.

OBITUARIES AND OTHER SOURCES:

PERIODICALS

Chicago Tribune, November 21, 1997, section 2, p. 14.

*　　*　　*

GERRARD, Roy 1935-1997

OBITUARY NOTICE—See index for *SATA* sketch: Born January 25, 1935, in Atherton, Lancashire, England; died of a heart attack, August 5, 1997, in England. Educator, artist, illustrator, and author. Gerrard, who devoted much of his career to education, embarked on a second career later in life as the author and illustrator of picture books in verse for children. After attending the Salford School of Art, he found work as an art teacher at Egerton Park County Secondary School in Denton, England, beginning in 1956. He also served as department head until 1966. Gerrard then spent the next fourteen years at Hyde Grammar School in the same capacity. In 1980 he left teaching to paint and began illustrating books for children. His illustrations consist of detailed, highly decorative watercolors that he described as "remorselessly whimsical." He first illustrated a book by his wife, Jean, entitled *Matilda Jane.* The book was a Mother Goose Award runnerup. Gerrard followed with a work of his own, *The Favershams,* which earned him critical recognition as well as awards from *Choice* magazine and the *New York Times.* Gerrard gave his books period settings, such as Ancient Egypt, the American West, and Victorian England. Among his later works are *Sir Cedric, Sir Cedric Rides Again, Sir Francis Drake: His Daring Deeds, Rosie and the Rustlers, Croco'nile,* and *Wagons West!* One of his final efforts, *The Roman Twins,* is in press.

OBITUARIES AND OTHER SOURCES:

PERIODICALS

Books for Keeps, November, 1997, p. 15.
New York Times, August 13, 1997, p. A21.
Publishers Weekly, August 18, 1997, p. 26.

* * *

GOLENBOCK, Peter 1946-

■ Personal

Born July 19, 1946; son of Jerome and Annette (Sklarin) Golenbock; married Rhonda Sonnenberg; children: Charles. *Education:* Dartmouth College, B.A., 1967; New York University School of Law, J.D., 1970.

■ Addresses

Agent—Frank Weimann, 270 Lafayette St., New York, NY 10012.

■ Career

Writer, 1975—. Prentice-Hall, Inc., Englewood Cliffs, NJ, worked in legal department, summer, 1972; *Bergen Record,* Hackensack, NJ, reporter and editor, 1977-1980. Sports talk show host, WOR, New York, 1980; color broadcaster for St. Petersburg Pelicans, Senior Professional Baseball League, 1989-90; frequent guest on television and radio talk shows, including "Good Morning America," "Larry King Live," and "Geraldo."

■ Awards, Honors

Ten Best Children's Books list, *Redbook,* 1990, for *Teammates.* Many of Golenbock's books have been on the *New York Times* best-seller list.

■ Writings

Dynasty: The New York Yankees, 1949-1964, Prentice-Hall, 1975.
(With Sparky Lyle) *The Bronx Zoo,* Crown, 1979.
(With Billy Martin) *Number 1,* Delacorte, 1980.
(With Ron Guidry) *Guidry,* Prentice-Hall, 1980.
(With Graig Nettles) *Balls,* Putnam, 1984.
Bums: An Oral History of the Brooklyn Dodgers, Putnam, 1984.
(With Pete Rose) *Pete Rose on Hitting: How to Hit Better Than Anybody,* Perigee Books, 1985.
(With Davey Johnson) *Bats,* Putnam, 1986.
How to Win at Rotisserie Baseball: The Strategic Guide to America's New National (Armchair) Pastime, introduction by Bryant Gumbel, additional material by Alex Patton, Vintage Books, 1987, featuring the Rotistics of Les Leopold, Taylor Publishing, 1996.
Personal Fouls, Carroll and Graf, 1989.
Teammates (for children), illustrated by Paul Bacon, Harcourt Brace, 1990.
The Forever Boys: The Bittersweet World of Major League Baseball As Seen though the Eyes of the Men Who Played One More Time, Carol Publishing, 1991.
Fenway: An Unexpurgated History of the Boston Red Sox, Putnam, 1992.
American Zoom: Stock Car Racing—From the Dirt Tracks to Daytona, Macmillan, 1993.
Wild, High and Tight: The Life and Death of Billy Martin, St. Martin's Press, 1994.
Wrigleyville: A Magical History Tour of the Chicago Cubs, St. Martin's Press, 1996.
Cowboys Have Always Been My Heroes: The Definitive Oral History of America's Team, Warner Books, 1997.

PETER GOLENBOCK

(With Bernardo Leonard) *The Superstar Hitter's Bible: Featuring the 20 Commandments of Hitting,* Contemporary Books, 1998.
The Last Lap, Macmillan, 1998.

■ Work in Progress

Spirit of St. Louis, a history of baseball in St. Louis, focusing on the Cardinals and Browns, for Avon.

■ Sidelights

Peter Golenbock is the best-selling author of sports books including *The Bronx Zoo, Bums, Personal Fouls, American Zoom, Wild, High and Tight,* and *Balls.* Many of his works deal with the world of major league baseball, and paint incisive portraits of teams, managers, and individual players. Golenbock has also turned his hand to stock car racing, professional football, and corruption in collegiate basketball. He writes for a general audience, but he also finds numerous fans among younger readers. His 1990 title, *Teammates,* describing the trials of major league baseball's first black player, Jackie Robinson, was written specifically for a younger audience. "I have always believed that the people in sports—the players, coaches, managers, and owners—are what make sports special," Golenbock told *Something about the Author* (*SATA*). "Who won or who lost is quickly forgotten, but the players involved rarely are, and never should be."

Trained as a lawyer, Golenbock accepted a position with the legal department of Prentice-Hall publishers in 1972. Six weeks after taking the job, however, he had an idea for a book. He went to the head of the trade division, negotiated a contract, and subsequently produced his first best-seller, *Dynasty.* Golenbock described the book to *SATA* as the "definitive history of the Casey Stengel-Ralph Houk-Yogi Berra era of Yankee greatness." He interviewed former stars Mickey Mantle, Roger Maris, Whitey Ford, Berra, and Tony Kubek, among dozens of others. "Their stories and recollections are what made *Dynasty* the best-seller it became," Golenbock explained. A *Publishers Weekly* commentator called *Dynasty* a "walloping book that goes out of the park like a Mantle home run," and added that "this is surely *the* book of the Yankees of the 1949-1964 era." Golenbock's inside stories about the players were a hit with readers as well, and set him on a course for future sports books.

"Since [that book] I have made it my personal quest to rescue as many stories and memories of baseball's former players as possible," Golenbock told *SATA*. With subsequent titles, he kept to his winning formula, writing a string of best-sellers over the next several years. These included *The Bronx Zoo,* written with Yankee pitcher Sparky Lyle; *Number 1,* the Billy Martin story; *Guidry,* with Yankee pitcher Ron Guidry; and *Balls,* with Yankee third baseman Graig Nettles. "The publication of *Balls,*" Golenbock told *SATA,* "which in part outlined the disastrous nature of the ownership of George Steinbrenner, prompted Nettles to be traded

from the Yankees to the San Diego Padres." *The Bronx Zoo* was on the *New York Times* best-seller list for 29 weeks; *Balls* was on that same list for 14 weeks.

With *Bums: An Oral History of the Brooklyn Dodgers,* Golenbock researched a new ball club, and the book did for the Dodgers what *Dynasty* had for the Yankees. In-depth interviews with Carl Furillo, Roy Campanella, Pee Wee Reese, Duke Snider, and Jackie Robinson's widow, Rachel, among others, combined to create a book "crammed with so many memories that no Brooklyn Dodger fan could resist it," according to a *Kirkus Reviews* critic. "It's a grand modern saga," the same reviewer wrote, "messily but vigorously told . . ." *Booklist*'s Wes Lukowsky noted that Golenbock "has amassed interviews with players, coaches, journalists, and fans, which are arranged to create a sense of time and place that transcends on-field heroics." Lukowsky concluded that the author "carves out his own niche [in baseball books] by focusing on the reaction to the team rather than the team itself." *Publishers Weekly* noted that "probably no book has ever captured the spirit of the Brooklyn baseball team and its influence on the borough better than this one," and wrapped up its favorable review by calling *Bums* "a top-drawer effort."

Golenbock wrote another popular baseball book, *Bats,* a diary of the 1985 baseball season, with New York Mets manager Davey Johnson. He then moved on to new fields, or in this case, gymnasiums. *Personal Fouls* was an investigation of what Golenbock described for *SATA* as "the corrupt basketball program at North Carolina State University as it was run by coach Jim Valvano." Golenbock went on to explain that "I discovered, quite by accident, that one of the most highly acclaimed college basketball coaches, Jim Valvano, was a really bad actor, a money-grubbing conniver whose greed prompted his players to either shave points or fix games at two of his colleges, Iona and North Carolina State. . . . The book was controversial in that it resulted in the resignation of both the chancellor of the university and Mr. Valvano. Despite a threat by the state of North Carolina to sue for $50 million, the book was published by Carroll and Graf and became an immediate *New York Times* best-seller. Its publication helped spark a revolution in college athletics with educators and administrators passing legislation to insure that college athletes leave school with an education and not just a pile of press clippings." Lukowsky of *Booklist* noted that "this highly publicized expose . . . offers a locker-room ambience and sometimes funny, sometimes vicious repartee between players and coaches, all of which ring true." Tim Whitaker in the *New York Times Book Review* called it a "sports book . . . on the fast break." Golenbock's career was not made easier by the release of *Personal Fouls.* "Upon the book's publication," Golenbock told *SATA,* "I was pretty much shunned by the collegiate sports world for my reporting, and the controversy has not been pleasant, but I felt that the youngsters playing collegiate sports across America deserved better treatment from the adults entrusted with their welfare, and my hope was that by writing the truth about college basketball, there would be some

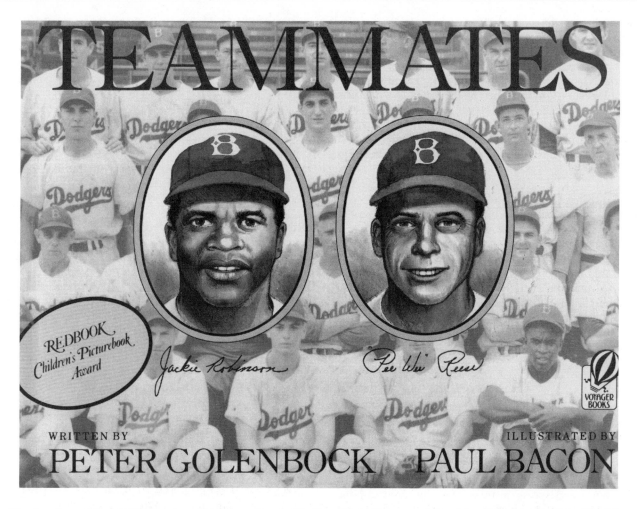

TEAMMATES

REDBOOK
Children's Picturebook
Award

Jackie Robinson   *"Pee Wee" Reese*

VOYAGER
BOOKS

WRITTEN BY   ILLUSTRATED BY
PETER GOLENBOCK   PAUL BACON

The heroism of Jackie Robinson, major league baseball's first black player, and Brooklyn Dodgers shortstop Pee Wee Reese, who offered him a public display of support while playing before a hostile crowd, is the focus of Golenbock's heartwarming book.

meaningful change. I have heard hurrahs from professors from all over the country. To them I am a hero. To the coaching fraternity, I am Judas, alas. But colleges must now print their graduation rates, and the rules have been tightened for college athletes. The worst coaches have been targeted by the NCAA, and I like to think *Personal Fouls* has had something to do with that." Turning to more uplifting topics, though still focusing on sports, Golenbock wrote a book for young readers, *Teammates,* dealing with an incident during Jackie Robinson's first season as a major league baseball player. Robinson, the first black player in the majors, was the center of racist abuse when he took the field with the Dodgers. Golenbock's book recounts the time when Pee Wee Reese, the famous Dodger shortstop and a white southerner, left his position and went over to Robinson, who was being booed by the fans. Reese put his arm around Robinson's shoulder, talked with him for a few moments, and then returned to his position. The act "stunned [the crowd] into silence," according to Elaine Fort Weischedel writing in *School Library Journal.* "This is a wonderful and important story, beautifully presented," concluded Weischedel. A *Publishers Weekly* commentator echoed those remarks, calling the book "an unusual story, beautifully rendered." *Horn*

Book reviewer Anita Silvey observed: "Baseball history is brought vividly to life.... Since far too few sports books of any quality are ever published for children, the attention and care given to this portrayal of an important period in baseball and civil rights history is indeed welcome."

A baseball book with a different slant is *The Forever Boys,* about former major league players who were taking part in the Senior Professional Baseball League. Golenbock took an intimate look at the St. Petersburg Pelicans, where he "rode the buses and was welcomed into the clubhouse and dugout," as he told *SATA.* He also compiled a team history of the Boston Red Sox in his *Fenway,* employing the same interviewing technique—talking with over fifty former players—that he used for his books on the Yankees and Dodgers. A *Kirkus Reviews* critic called that book "fine fare for baseball buffs, regardless of their allegiances," and Margaret E. Guthrie in the *New York Times Book Review* commented that "this is one of those books the baseball fan enters and gets happily lost in for several hours." Guthrie concluded that "Golenbock ... uses these voices to great effect," while Lukowsky of *Booklist* dubbed *Fenway* "extraordinarily enjoyable." The Chicago Cubs got the same treatment in another popular Golenbock title, *Wrigleyville*, which Lukowsky called "a winner all the way" in another *Booklist* review. "For me," Golenbock told *SATA*, "the highlight of that experience was interviewing Woody English, at the time the oldest surviving member of the Cubs.... He was there the day Babe Ruth did *not* call his shot, and he explained to me that Ruth had in fact pointed, but that he was pointing at the Cubs bench and at pitcher Charlie Root as part of the bantering that was going on between the teams."

Having earlier teamed up with former Yankee's manager Billy Martin on *Number 1*, Golenbock in 1994 published a biography of Martin in *Wild, High and Tight*. A warts-and-all biography, the book "looks into Martin's womanizing, his prodigious drinking and his death in a car accident," according to *Publishers Weekly*. The reviewer went on to conclude that it "is an extremely thorough and comprehensive biography of one of baseball's most controversial figures." Compared to a Russian novel by other reviewers, the book explores the darker side of professional athletics and of American manhood.

Golenbock has made other departures from his usual beat of major league baseball, including his 1993 look at stock car racing, *American Zoom*, and his history of the Dallas Cowboys football team, *Cowboys Have Always Been My Heroes*. In a starred review of *American Zoom*, Lukowsky wrote: "This fine book will enthrall existing fans and may even generate a few new ones. A valuable contribution to sports history." For his book on the Dallas Cowboys, Golenbock interviewed players and coaches dating to the team's inception in 1960, including Roger Staubach, Tom Landry, Drew Pearson, and Bob Lilly. "This book looks at the team," Golenbock told *SATA*, "but also at the change in society from the turbulent sixties [to] the present through the eyes of these players." *Publishers Weekly* found this football book "absorbing and revealing," while *Kirkus Reviews* concluded that it "should not be missed."

Golenbock is hard at work on further sports titles, including a history of baseball in St. Louis. In Golenbock's books, sports becomes a metaphor for life in general. "Beauty and truth, truth and beauty," he concluded for *SATA*. "Plus a hell of a lot of fun and games. That's how I see the world of sports."

■ Works Cited

Review of *Bums, Publishers Weekly*, August 3, 1984, p. 61.

Review of *Bums, Kirkus Reviews*, August 15, 1984, p. 789.

Review of *Cowboys Have Always Been My Heroes, Publishers Weekly*, May 26, 1997, p. 72.

Review of *Cowboys Have Always Been My Heroes, Kirkus Reviews*, June 1, 1997, p. 850.

Review of *Dynasty, Publishers Weekly*, April 21, 1975, p. 43.

Review of *Fenway, Kirkus Reviews*, December 15, 1991, p. 1573.

Guthrie, Margaret E., review of *Fenway, New York Times Book Review*, April 15, 1992, p. 18.

Lukowsky, Wes, review of *Bums, Booklist*, September 15, 1984, p. 102.

Lukowsky, Wes, review of *Personal Fouls, Booklist*, September 1, 1989, p. 4.

Lukowsky, Wes, review of *Fenway, Booklist*, February 15, 1992, p. 1081.

Lukowsky, Wes, review of *American Zoom, Booklist*, September 15, 1993, p. 117.

Lukowsky, Wes, review of *Wrigleyville, Booklist*, February 1, 1996, p. 912.

Review of *Teammates, Publishers Weekly*, April 13, 1990, p. 68.

Review of *Teammates, Horn Book*, May-June, 1990, p. 349.

Weischedel, Elaine Fort, review of *Teammates, School Library Journal*, June, 1990. p. 112.

Whitaker, Tim, "Coach on the Line," *New York Times Book Review*, August 27, 1989, p. 12.

Review of *Wild, High and Tight, Publishers Weekly*, May 30, 1994, p. 44.

■ For More Information See

BOOKS

The Ballplayers, Morrow, 1990.

PERIODICALS

Esquire, August, 1997, p. 22.

Kirkus Reviews, July 1, 1993, p. 834; April 15, 1994, pp. 522-23; January 1, 1996, p. 40.

Library Journal, April 15, 1975, p. 778; September 15, 1984, p. 1768; August, 1989, p. 137; December, 1990, p. 130; February 1, 1992, p. 96; July, 1993, p. 87; May 15, 1994, p. 78; January, 1995, p. 163; February 1, 1996, p. 78; July, 1997, p. 91.

Los Angeles Times Book Review, October 7, 1984, p. 5; August 26, 1990, p. 8; October 7, 1990, p. 14; July 10, 1994, p. 2.

New York Times Book Review, November 9, 1975, p. 53; April 14, 1991, p. 14; April 7, 1996, p. 16.

Sports Illustrated, June 11, 1990, pp. 8-9.

Voice of Youth Advocates, February, 1993, pp. 368-69.

—*Sketch by J. Sydney Jones*

* * *

GRIFFIN, Peni R(ae Robinson) 1961-

■ Personal

Born July 11, 1961, in Harlingin, TX; daughter of William Jay (retired Air Force) and Sandra Sue (a Methodist lay pastor; maiden name, Roberts) Robinson; married Michael David Griffin (a programmer for Bexar county), July 13, 1987; stepchildren: Morgan Leigh. *Education:* Attended Trinity University, 1979-80, and University of Texas at San Antonio, 1982-84. *Politics:* "All systems fail eventually, and ours is going."

Religion: Agnostic. *Hobbies and other interests:* "Exploring the Net with a 'Computer Gothic' in view; always reading history, archaeology, mysteries; gardening."

■ Addresses

Home—1123 West Magnolia Ave., San Antonio, TX 78201.

■ Career

Writer. City Public Service, San Antonio, TX, clerk, 1985-89; Manpower Temporary Services, San Antonio, temporary worker, 1990; MASCO, production assistant, 1991-95; Eckmann, Groll, Runyan and Waters, Inc., word processor, 1996—. *Member:* Society of Children's Book Writers and Illustrators, Science Fiction Writers of America.

■ Awards, Honors

Third place, *Twilight Zone* magazine writing contest, 1986, for "Nereid"; second place, National Society for Arts and Letters (San Antonio branch) short story contest, 1988, for "The Truth in the Case of Eliza Mary Muller, by Herself"; Edgar Award nominee, 1993, for *The Treasure Bird;* Best Western Juvenile Fiction, Golden Spur Awards finalist, 1993, for *The Switching Well.*

■ Writings

FOR YOUNG PEOPLE

Otto from Otherwhere (fantasy), McElderry/Macmillan, 1990.
A Dig in Time (fantasy), McElderry/Macmillan, 1991.
Hobkin (fantasy), McElderry/Macmillan, 1992.
The Treasure Bird (mystery), McElderry/Macmillan, 1992.
The Switching Well (fantasy), McElderry/Macmillan, 1993.
The Brick House Burglars (mystery), McElderry/Macmillan, 1994.
The Maze (fantasy), McElderry/Simon & Schuster, 1994.
Vikki Vanishes (mystery), McElderry/Simon & Schuster, 1995.
Margo's House (fantasy), Margaret K. McElderry, 1996.

The Switching Well has been translated into Italian.

OTHER

Contributor to magazines including *Dragon, Fantasy Macabre, Figment, Isaac Asimov's Science Fiction Magazine, Leading Edge, Magazine of Fantasy and Science Fiction, Pandora, Pulphouse, Space and Time,* and *Twilight Zone.* Also contributor of "The Truth in the Case of Eliza Mary Muller, by Herself," to *Stay True: Short Stories for Strong Girls,* edited by Marilyn Singer, Scholastic, 1998.

PENI R. GRIFFIN

■ Sidelights

Peni R. Griffin, who writes fantasy and mystery novels for young people, had developed a reputation for her work by the time she had published her fourth book. "Communication—singing and speaking—is important in Griffin's novels," wrote a *Kirkus Reviews* critic in a review of *The Treasure Bird.* In another review of the same book, Deborah Stevenson wrote in *Bulletin of the Center for Children's Books,* "Griffin's Texas settings are always atmospheric." The following year, Carolyn Cushman of *Locus* wrote that Griffin "has a knack" for "giving ... [an] otherworldly twist" to the concerns of pre-teens.

Griffin told *SATA* that writing comes naturally to her. "I have been absorbing stories through my skin since the hour I was born, and an untold story is only half a story. Being an Air Force brat helped. Crossing the broad, apparently empty landscape of Mid-America, my brain had plenty of leisure to absorb and get to work on the implied stories of the houses, the landmark names, and the historical markers we passed. Arriving at a new town, it was easier to infiltrate the world of a new library than of a new school. Books don't reject you, don't let you down, and they make the world so much broader than the scope of one little life. Louisa May Alcott never lied to me. Anne Frank died, but the diary preserved her alive. Words were Helen Keller's road out of lonely, silent darkness."

Griffin attended college in Texas and began to write, working day jobs only when necessary. She once told *SATA* that she came up with the idea for her first book,

Otto from Otherwhere, when her husband told her about a lake covered with fog, that "looked as if you could walk out across it into another world. I knew at once what people in that other world looked like." *Otto from Otherwhere* begins as Ahto, ten years old, is leading the family sheep home. He gets lost in a bank of mist and steps into the world we know. There, Paula and her brother, riding to school, are also encountering fog. The children run into, and then befriend Ahto, whom they call Otto, and he very quickly learns to speak English (with a southern accent). Claiming that Otto is a cousin from Brazil, Paula takes him to school. Because he looks different, with holes for his nose and ears, and has no hair or pinkies, the children avoid him. Meanwhile, Otto grows lonely for his old world, replete with music. After the school's music teacher discovers Otto's beautiful voice, the children begin to change their minds about him.

The "E.T.-style plot is likely to ensnare readers," wrote Barbara Elleman of *Booklist.* While many critics noted the theme of accepting others for who they are, not what they look like, Annette Curtis Klause of *School Library Journal* commented that "readers are not beaten over the head with the theme." Deborah Stevenson of the *Bulletin of the Center for Children's Books* described the book as "a cozy and wish-fulfilling venture into science fantasy."

Griffin told *SATA* that her second book "came bursting out of my head in about six months.... The idea of two children having an archaeological dig in their back yard and literally digging up the past took hold of me and made me write it." The result, wrote Gene LaFaille in *Wilson Library Bulletin,* is "a superb example of young adult fiction in general" which "blends genre fiction with a realistically and warmly drawn family life." The story is set in contemporary time, where twelve-year-old Nan and her brother Tim are living with their grandmother in San Antonio while their parents are out of the country on an archaeological dig. The children decide to work on their own dig in the backyard and they find their grandfather's pipe. Tim's poem about the pipe magically transports them through time to the moment of their grandfather's death.

After this discovery, Nan and Tim then travel to other important and meaningful moments in their family's history, including their parents' wedding. The children get into trouble in one trip, when a flood threatens their lives and the life of their grandmother (still a baby). After they save her and return home, they find their grandmother dead. Nan and Tim explain their activities to their parents upon their return for the funeral, and, with their mother, take one last trip through time. A *Kirkus Reviews* critic described Griffin as a "powerful storyteller" and asserted that "few illustrate the continuity of place and family so well" in stories about time travel. Roger Sutton of the *Bulletin of the Center for Children's Books* concluded, "this would be a good introduction for those readers put off by the more arcane reaches of the genre."

Hobkin begins as two girls—bearing names changed to Kay and Liza—are running away from their abusive stepfather. (Although the younger sister, Liza, does not know it, the abuse Kay has suffered has been sexual, and Kay wants to protect Liza.) The girls find an abandoned house and, telling those they meet that it belongs to a relative, they make it home. Kay finds a job in the West Texas town, and Liza stays home to cook and clean (a difficult task in a place without running water or heat). It is not long until a brownie, Hobkin, makes himself known to Liza; he helps her as she works in different ways. Readers find that Hobkin followed a woman from England years ago to the house. By the end of the story, he is finally released to make his own way in the world, and the girls' mother comes to live with them.

"Kay and Liza are fully realized, by turns resourceful or frightened," wrote a *Kirkus Reviews* critic. According to Zena Sutherland of the *Bulletin of the Center for Children's Books,* the fantasy of Hobkin and the story of the girls' lives works: "It's the seamless blending that is impressive." "This mixture of stark realism with fantasy may remind some people of some of the books of Madeleine L'Engle," observed Edith S. Tyson in *Voice of Youth Advocates.* Deborah Abbott of *Booklist* commented that the work "offers an interesting variation on the survival theme."

Vikki Vanishes is another of Griffin's books that treats serious young adult issues, but this one adds mystery. Vikki (sixteen) and her half-sister Nikki (nine) have lived their lives without their respective fathers; when Vikki's father reappears and takes her for a ride, Nikki is jealous. Yet the father attempts to abuse Vikki, who disappears. Nikki is the only one who has some idea what has happened to Vikki, but the adults ignore her. According to a *Kirkus Reviews* critic, the novel is "tightly written" and builds "dramatic tension until the girls are reunited."

Fantasy works to the advantage of another girl with a serious problem in *Margo's House.* The father in this novel is near death when, magically, his spirit and his daughter Margo's make their way into the dolls he has made for Margo (Sis and Butch). Margo and her father, as Sis and Butch, move in creaky doll bodies from the handmade doll house and through the large family house (despite the scary pet cat) to save Margo's father.

Maintaining a beloved home is difficult in Griffin's mystery, *The Treasure Bird.* When Jessy and her family move to a house in Texas, they are uncertain that they will be able to pay the taxes on the house. Jessy and her stepbrother, along with a parrot, search for a hidden treasure by piecing together a message found in some inherited samplers. This story, according to Renee Steinberg in *School Library Journal,* "deals with loyalty, trust, love, and family" as well as treasure.

The Brick House Burglars, another of Griffin's mysteries, is "full of excitement," according to *School Library Journal* contributor Suzanne Hawley. Four adolescent girls set up a club, and, in the process of protecting their meeting place in San Antonio, foil the plans of criminals. A *Kirkus Reviews* critic found that Griffin provided "some realities of urban living" in the novel, and Hazel Rochman of *Booklist* noted Griffin's "lively voice that captures the immediacy of the community in all its rich diversity."

One of Griffin's books treats historical San Antonio as well as the contemporary city. *Switching Well* is the story of two girls, one living in 1891 and one living in 1991, who wish themselves into the past and future. As a *Kirkus Reviews* critic noted, the girls' stories unfold in "alternating chapters, using parallel experiences." The characters, confused and lost, are eventually taken in by each other's families. According to Bruce Anne Shook of *School Library Journal,* this work of fantasy and historical fiction features "plucky, intelligent characters who are believable and easy to like."

Griffin, who told *SATA* that her work is as essential to her as breathing, finds that writing fiction is important for another reason. She explained, "You don't reach people by talking to them straight. You reach them by telling stories, and letting them work out the truth for themselves, the same way you're doing as you write. It's simple."

■ Works Cited

Abbott, Deborah, review of *Hobkin, Booklist,* March 15, 1992, p. 1378.

Review of *The Brick House Burglars, Kirkus Reviews,* February 1, 1994, pp. 143-44.

Cushman, Carolyn, review of *Switching Well, Locus,* May, 1993, p. 58.

Review of *A Dig in Time, Kirkus Reviews,* April 1, 1991, p. 471.

Elleman, Barbara, review of *Otto from Otherwhere, Booklist,* May 1, 1990, pp. 1702-04.

Hawley, Suzanne, review of *The Brick House Burglars, School Library Journal,* June, 1994, p. 128.

Review of *Hobkin, Kirkus Reviews,* April 15, 1992, p. 537.

Klause, Annette Curtis, review of *Otto from Otherwhere, School Library Journal,* August, 1990, pp. 146-48.

LaFaille, Gene, "Science Fiction Universe," *Wilson Library Bulletin,* March, 1992, p. 102.

Rochman, Hazel, review of *The Brick House Burglars, Booklist,* March 1, 1994, p. 1259.

Shook, Bruce Anne, review of *Switching Well, School Library Journal,* June, 1993, p. 106.

Steinberg, Renee, review of *The Treasure Bird, School Library Journal,* November, 1992, p. 91.

Stevenson, Deborah, review of *Otto from Otherwhere, Bulletin of the Center for Children's Books,* July-August, 1990, pp. 264-65.

Stevenson, Deborah, review of *The Treasure Bird, Bulletin of the Center for Children's Books,* February, 1993, p. 177.

Sutherland, Zena, review of *Hobkin, Bulletin of the Center for Children's Books,* June, 1992, p. 261.

Sutton, Roger, review of *A Dig in Time, Bulletin of the Center for Children's Books,* October, 1991, p. 38.

Review of *Switching Well, Kirkus Reviews,* April 15, 1993, p. 529.

Review of *The Treasure Bird, Kirkus Reviews,* November 1, 1992, p. 1375.

Tyson, Edith S., review of *Hobkin, Voice of Youth Advocates,* June, 1992, pp. 94-95.

Review of *Vikki Vanishes, Kirkus Reviews,* May 1, 1995, p. 634.

■ For More Information See

PERIODICALS

Booklist, June 1, 1993, p. 1812; September 1, 1996, p. 130.

Bulletin of the Center for Children's Books, July-August, 1993, p. 345; November, 1996, p. 97.

Locus, April, 1992, p. 33.

Publishers Weekly, November 9, 1992, p. 86.

School Library Journal, June, 1991, p. 104; January, 1995, p. 108; September, 1995, p. 218; October, 1996, p. 122.

Voice of Youth Advocates, August, 1991, p. 180.

H

HAUTH, Katherine B. 1940-

■ Personal

Born November 13, 1940, in Flint, MI; married George Hauth. *Education:* Marquette University, B.A. (English), 1962; University of Washington, M.A. (educational psychology), 1973. *Politics:* Independent. *Hobbies and other interests:* Photography, hiking, skiing, swimming, travel, archaeology, anthropology, and geology.

KATHERINE B. HAUTH

■ Addresses

Office—c/o Roberts Rinehart, 6309 Monarch Pk. Pl., Suite 101, Niwot, CO 80503.

■ Career

South Milwaukee High School, Milwaukee, WI, teacher, 1962-65; University of Washington and King County, Seattle, WA, personnel analyst, 1966-76; writer, Rio Rancho, NM, 1976—. Mentor, counselor, sponsor, and facilitator for New Mexico mentorship program Celebrate Youth! Conducts neighborhood reading program. *Member:* Bernalillo County Chapter of International Reading Association, Society of Children's Book Writers and Illustrators, Nature Conservancy, Audubon Society.

■ Writings

Night Life of the Yucca, illustrated by Kay Sather, Harbinger House (Boulder, CO), 1996.

■ Work in Progress

The Spider's Christmas, a Christmas picture-book fantasy from the spider's point of view, for North-South Books.

■ Sidelights

Katherine B. Hauth told *SATA:* "I'm a late bloomer. During English 101, during college, and teaching with roommates who took creative writing and children's literature courses, I had no clue that I'd ever write, especially write for children.

"Some of my fondest childhood memories are of the vacant lots where things grew wild and had their own set of rules. I climbed trees, collected butterflies, and took a taxidermy course by mail before fitting myself into the predictable roles of teacher and wife.

"In 1976, when my husband George and I realized that the quality of our material lives was managing the quality of our personal lives, we decided to 'drop out.' We left gray skies in Seattle and settled under blue skies in rural New Mexico where we lived up-close-and-personal with nature.

"Watching the life cycle of a black widow spider and raising a raven to return to the wild, I was a child again, suspending judgment and entering awe. My fascination needed an outlet, which was writing. I first wrote about the raven's intelligence and the black widow spider for *Cricket* magazine.

"The stories that don't leave me are the ones I write to share with children. I also enjoy visiting schools and talking and teaching about writing and nature with young people."

■ For More Information See

PERIODICALS

Horn Book Guide, Spring, 1997, p. 118.

* * *

HENRY, Marguerite 1902-1997

OBITUARY NOTICE—See index for *SATA* sketch: Born April 13, 1902, in Milwaukee, WI; died November 26, 1997, in Rancho Santa Fe, CA. Writer. Best known for her many books about horses, Henry delighted young readers with stories about animals, people, and places during a lengthy writing career that spanned more than four decades. She received the Newbery Medal in 1949 for *King of the Wind* (1948), and Newbery honors for other books, including *Misty of Chincoteague* (1947), which is perhaps her best-known work. *Misty of Chincoteague* sold more than one million copies, spawned several sequels, and was made into a movie. Though almost all of her books feature a rugged, outdoors setting, Henry grew up a city girl and didn't live an outdoor lifestyle until she and her husband moved to an Illinois farm in 1939. Henry graduated from Milwaukee State Teacher's College and attended the University of Wisconsin-Milwaukee. Her first paid article as a professional writer was for *Delineator* magazine and her byline also appeared in *The Saturday Evening Post, Reader's Digest* and several trade and business publications. She published her first children's book, *Auno and Tauno: A Story of Finland,* in 1940. She also wrote *Dilly Dally Sally* (1940), *Birds at Home* (1942), *Geraldine Belinda* (1942), *Their First Igloo on Baffin Island* (1943), *A Boy and a Dog* (1944) *The Little Fellow* (1945), *Robert Fulton: Boy Craftsman* (1945), and *Justin Morgan Had a Horse* (published in 1945 and winner of the 1948 Junior Scholastic Gold Seal Award). Other works featuring the horse "Misty" include *Misty, the Wonder Pony by Misty, Herself* (1956), *Stormy, Misty's Foal* (1963) and *Misty's Twilight* (1992). The real Misty died in 1972. Another of Henry's popular horse stories, her 1953 book *Brighty of the Grand Canyon,* was a Junior Library Guild selection and was

made into a feature film in 1967. Walt Disney Productions made *Justin Morgan Had a Horse* into a movie in 1972 and *Peter Lundy and the Medicine Hat Stallion* (1976) was made into a television movie by NBC in 1977. In addition to novels for children, Henry also worked on "Pictured Geographies," a nonfiction series illustrated by Kurt Weise.

OBITUARIES AND OTHER SOURCES:

PERIODICALS

Chicago Tribune, November 28, 1997, sec. 3, p. 6.
Los Angeles Times, November 28, 1997, p. A58.
New York Times, November 29, 1997, p. A13.
Publishers Weekly, December 15, 1997, p. 27.
Washington Post, November 27, 1997, p. C6.

* * *

HERMAN, Charlotte 1937-

■ Personal

Born June 10, 1937, in Chicago, IL; daughter of Harry (a mattress manufacturer) and Leah (Kossof) Baran; married Melvin Herman (an attorney), January 27, 1957; children: Sharon, Michael, Deborah, Karen. *Education:* Attended University of Illinois, 1955-57; Roosevelt University, B.A., 1960. *Hobbies and other interests:* "I enjoy antiquing for old toys, bicycling along Lake Michigan, and playing with my grandchildren."

■ Addresses

Home—6623 North Monticello, Lincolnwood, IL 60645.

■ Career

Writer of children's books. Teacher in the public schools of Chicago, IL, 1960-63. Instructor and lecturer in writers workshops and author-in-residence programs. *Member:* Society of Children's Book Writers and Illustrators, Children's Reading Round Table, Society of Midland Authors.

■ Awards, Honors

Children's book award, Society of Midland Authors, 1978, for *Our Snowman Had Olive Eyes;* IRA-CBC Children's Choice selection, for *My Mother Didn't Kiss Me Good-Night;* Best Books, *Christian Science Monitor,* 1985, and Editor's Choice, *Booklist,* both for *Millie Cooper, 3B;* Carl Sandburg award, 1990, for *The House on Walenska Street;* Children's Book of the Year selection, Bank Street Child Study Children's Book Committee, 1996, for *Millie Cooper and Friends.*

■ Writings

String Bean, illustrated by Tom Funk, J. Philip O'Hara, 1972.

CHARLOTTE HERMAN

The Three of Us, illustrated by Mia Carpenter, J. P. O'Hara, 1973.

You've Come a Long Way Sybil Macintosh: A Book of Manners and Grooming for Girls, illustrated by Trina Schart Hyman, J. P. O'Hara, 1974.

The Difference of Ari Stein, illustrated by Ben Shecter, Harper, 1976.

Our Snowman Had Olive Eyes, Dutton, 1977.

(Adapter with D. Francis) Ulises Wensell, *Come to Our House,* illustrated by Ulises Wensell, Rand McNally, 1978.

On the Way to the Movies, illustrated by Diane Dawson, Dutton, 1980.

My Mother Didn't Kiss Me Good-Night, illustrated by Bruce Degen, Dutton, 1980.

What Happened to Heather Hopkowitz?, Dutton, 1981.

Millie Cooper, 3B, illustrated by Helen Cogancherry, Dutton, 1985.

Millie Cooper, Take a Chance, illustrated by Cogancherry, Dutton, 1988.

The House on Walenska Street, illustrated by Susan Avishai, Dutton, 1990.

Max Malone and the Great Cereal Rip-Off, illustrated by Catherine Smith, Holt, 1990.

A Summer on Thirteenth Street, Dutton, 1991.

Max Malone Makes a Million, illustrated by Cat Bowman Smith, Holt, 1991.

Max Malone, Superstar, illustrated by Cat Bowman Smith, Holt, 1991.

Max Malone the Magnificent, illustrated by Cat Bowman Smith, Holt, 1993.

Millie Cooper and Friends, illustrated by Helen Cogancherry, Viking, 1995.

How Yussel Caught the Gefilte Fish: A Shabbos Story, illustrated by Katya Krenina, Dutton, in press.

Our Snowman Had Olive Eyes has been translated into French, German, Danish, and Dutch; *Millie Cooper, 3B* has been translated into Chinese and Dutch; *Millie Cooper, Take a Chance* has been translated into Chinese, and *The House on Walenska Street* into Dutch.

■ Sidelights

Charlotte Herman began to write for children as a public school teacher in Chicago. Thirty years later, she has some twenty picture books, chapter books, and longer novels to her credit. Notable among her works are books that bring the varied lifestyles, perspectives, and problems of Jewish children to middle-grade readers. Others focus on such universal childhood concerns as strict teachers and younger brothers. Many of Herman's books are set in the 1940s; the author has been praised for her realistic evocation of that period, and for demonstrating that the troubles of her protagonists then are very similar to those of children today. Herman once told *SATA* that her goal is to "write *good books,* books of value.... Young readers are the best people around, and I want to give them my best."

One of Herman's first books, *The Difference of Ari Stein,* features eleven-year-old Ari, who has been brought up in a religious immigrant family. Ari eats kosher foods and is careful in his observance of holidays. Yet, in 1944 Brooklyn, Ari's Jewish lifestyle differs from those of the other boys he'd like to play with. Despite the attempts of these boys to sway him from his training, Ari demonstrates that he can maintain his faith and various friendships. *Bulletin of the Center for Children's Books* critic Zena Sutherland asserted that in *The Difference of Ari Stein,* the "writing style is deft, the details of locale and period convincing."

Written for the same age group, *Our Snowman Had Olive Eyes* tells how Sheila, ten years old, accepts her grandmother in her home and shares her room with her. The grandmother (referred to as Bubbie, the Yiddish word for grandmother) is happiest when she can do things with Sheila, like making cookies and even a snowman. Still, Sheila's mother insists that seventy-nine-year-old Bubbie relax and rest. In part due to Sheila's discussion of her grandmother's relationship with an elderly man, Bubbie decides to move away and live with her son. The story, in the words of a *Publishers Weekly* reviewer, is "warm, comic and touching." A *Horn Book* critic described the book as an "unpretentious, haunting novel which handles a difficult topic with delicacy and humor."

What Happened to Heather Hopkowitz is the story of Heather, who, at fourteen-years-old, has not had much immediate exposure to Orthodox Judaism. Her own family is Jewish, but Heather eats bacon and does not strictly observe the Sabbath. When her parents go on a cruise, Heather stays with an Orthodox family and discovers that she enjoys the Orthodox lifestyle. She decides to live an Orthodox life in secret, so that she does not alienate her family. Nevertheless, by the end of the story, Heather has explained her decision, and her parents have accepted it. "Heather is a resolute heroine and an appealing narrator," wrote Karen Jameyson in *Horn Book.*

Millie Cooper, 3B is set in Chicago in the mid-1940s. Third-grader Millie must come up with an essay about why she is special as an assignment for a strict teacher. The plot, according to Sally T. Margolis in *School Library Journal,* "unfolds in a time and place so specific that readers are immediately involved." Ilene Cooper of *Booklist* maintained that the story is "full of contemporary appeal." *Millie Cooper, Take a Chance* finds Millie in 1947, working to get a bicycle and dealing with Valentine's Day. She needs courage to sell newspaper subscriptions and to recite a poem at school. As a *Kirkus Reviews* critic observed, Millie "realizes that risk-taking can make life worthwhile." "Millie is definitely a child of her times, though her pleasures and concerns are universal," remarked *Horn Book* reviewer Nancy Vasilakis. *Millie Cooper and Friends* features fourth grader Millie suffering with the notion that her best friend has found a new favorite. "The best so far in this engaging and uncomplicated series," wrote Connie Parker in *School Library Journal.*

According to *School Library Journal* contributor Louise L. Sherman, fans of Herman's Millie Cooper books may be interested as well in *A Summer on Thirteenth Street.* This novel, also set in the 1940s, focuses on one eleven-year-old girl's activities in wartime. Shirley Cohen tends a victory garden, nurtures a crush on a teenager who eventually enlists in the armed forces, and even watches a janitor she suspects is a German spy. Herman presents a setting further back in time, and in a different country, in *The House on Walenska Street,* another book about the adventures of a spirited girl. A Carl Sandburg award winner, *The House on Walenska Street* features tales of an eight-year-old Jewish girl living with her mother and sisters in a Russian village in the early 1900s.

Herman's series of "Max Malone" books begin with *Max Malone and the Great Cereal Rip-Off.* In this story, Max gets a box of cereal promising a prize inside, but when he opens the box the prize is missing. He sends a letter to complain, even as he tries to take advantage of Austin Healy, a younger child and the new kid on his block, in the swapping of baseball cards. "Herman's story adeptly fashions familiar experiences into a humorous story with a message about integrity," maintained *Booklist* reviewer Denise Wilms, who added that the story is "just right for kids easing into chapter books." *Max Malone Makes a Million* again pairs Max and Austin Healy; when Max attempts to make money and refuses Austin's help, the younger boy outdoes him with his own efforts. *Max Malone, Superstar,* finds Max auditioning for a spot on a peanut butter commercial. A

Kirkus Reviews critic described the work as "a funny, engaging story for newly independent readers."

My Mother Didn't Kiss Me Good-Night, one of Herman's picture books, finds young Leon ready for bed and wondering why his mother did not give him the usual good-night. Leon's imagination runs wild until he learns that his mother did not kiss him because she had a cold. *On the Way to the Movies* features two brothers, the younger one demanding to see a scary movie with the older. When a friend passes by and describes the movie, Simon, the eldest, is the more reluctant to go into the theater. As Barbara Elleman of *Booklist* commented, "Herman humorously turns the tables on condescending big brothers."

■ Works Cited

Burns, Mary M., review of *Our Snowman Had Olive Eyes, Horn Book,* April, 1978, p. 166.

Cooper, Ilene, review of *Millie Cooper, 3B, Booklist,* April 1, 1985, p. 1120.

Elleman, Barbara, review of *On the Way to the Movies, Booklist,* May 15, 1980, p. 1365.

Jameyson, Karen, review of *What Happened to Heather Hopkowitz? Horn Book,* February, 1982, pp. 52-53.

Margolis, Sally T., review of *Millie Cooper, 3B, School Library Journal,* August, 1985, pp. 64-65.

Review of *Max Malone, Superstar, Kirkus Reviews,* March 15, 1992, p. 394.

Review of *Millie Cooper, Take a Chance, Kirkus Reviews,* December 1, 1988, p. 1739.

Review of *Our Snowman Had Olive Eyes, Publishers Weekly,* October 10, 1977, p. 70.

Parker, Connie, review of *Millie Cooper and Friends, School Library Journal,* September, 1995, p. 200.

Sherman, Louise L., review of *A Summer on Thirteenth Street, School Library Journal,* January, 1992, p. 109.

Sutherland, Zena, review of *The Difference of Ari Stein, Bulletin of the Center for Children's Books,* October, 1976, p. 25.

Vasilakis, Nancy, review of *Millie Cooper, Take a Chance, Horn Book,* January-February, 1989, pp. 69-70.

Wilms, Denise, review of *Max Malone and the Great Cereal Rip-Off, Booklist,* July, 1990, pp. 2089-90.

■ For More Information See

PERIODICALS

Bulletin of the Center for Children's Books, February, 1975, p. 94; September, 1980. pp. 11-12; June, 1991, p. 238.

Horn Book, July-August, 1985, p. 449.

Kirkus Reviews, October 15, 1991, p. 1343.

Publishers Weekly, December 2, 1974, p. 63; January 8, 1982, p. 83.

School Library Journal, January, 1975, p. 45; November, 1977, p. 57; June, 1991, p. 79.

HOLUB, Joan 1956-

■ Personal

Born in Texas in 1956; daughter of an engineer and an attorney; married George, an architect. *Education:* University of Texas, B.F.A. *Hobbies and other interests:* Swimming, aerobics, hiking, gardening, reading, traveling, eating.

■ Addresses

Electronic mail—joanholub@aol.com.

■ Career

Communications Plus, Texas, art director, 1980-89; Scholastic, New York City, associate art director, children's trade books, 1989-91; author and illustrator, 1991—. Librarian for America Online Children's Book Writers Chat; contributing editor to *Children's Book Insider* newsletter. *Member:* Society of Children's Book Writers and Illustrators (state board), Authors Guild, International Reading Association.

■ Awards, Honors

SCBWI Magazine Illustration Merit Honor Award, 1993.

■ Writings

(Self-illustrated) *Pen Pals,* Grosset & Dunlap, 1997.
(Self-illustrated) *Boo Who? A Spooky Lift-the-Flap Book,* Scholastic, 1997.
(Self-illustrated) *Ivy Green, Cootie Queen,* Troll, 1998.
(Self-illustrated) *Red, Yellow, Green: What Do Signs Mean?,* Scholastic, 1998.
Pajama Party, illustrated by Julie Durrell, Grosset & Dunlap, 1998.
Space Dogs from Planet K-9, Troll, 1998.

ILLUSTRATOR

Elizabeth Levy, *If You Were There When They Signed the Constitution,* Scholastic, 1992.
Judy Gire, *A Boy and His Baseball,* Zondervan, 1993.
Kirsten Hall, *I'm Not Scared,* Children's Press, 1994.
Mary Winston, editor, *The American Heart Association Kids' Cookbook,* Times Books, 1994.
Kirsten Hall, *My Brother, the Brat,* Scholastic, 1995.
My First Book of Sign Language, Troll, 1996.
Wendy Lewison, *Ten Little Ballerinas,* Grosset & Dunlap, 1996.
Angela Medearis, *The 100th Day of School,* Scholastic, 1996.
Caren Holtzman, *No Fair!,* Scholastic, 1997.
Iris Hiskey Arno, *I Love You, Mom,* Troll, 1997.
Iris Hiskey Arno, *I Love You, Dad,* Troll, 1998.
Josephine Nobisso, *Hot Cha-Cha!,* Winslow Press, 1998.

JOAN HOLUB

Contributor to periodicals, including *Instructor, Lady-Bug, Let's Find Out, Pre-K Today, Spider,* and *Children's Book Insider.*

■ Sidelights

Joan Holub told *SATA:* "I left a perfectly good job I'd had for nine years, my home, and family behind and moved to New York because I wanted to work in the children's book field. When I look back on it, I can hardly believe I had the guts to make the move. I had been happy working at my job as an art director at a graphic design firm in Texas, but after the move I was ecstatic to be working with children's books in New York. Both the city and the work were exciting.

"Before long, I began illustrating full time. At the same time, I was writing manuscripts. Bad manuscripts. My writing began to improve when I began reading lots of children's books. Previously, I'd primarily been interested in the art in children's books. But now I began reading them, too. This sounds basic, but it helped me tremendously. I found out what kids are reading today. And I found out what subjects and age groups interested me. In general, I like funny books about kids interacting in school or at play; funny, weird outer space books; and softly scary stories. So far, I've sold seven books: easy readers, novelty books, and chapter books. I have about a dozen other manuscripts circulating. Many people dream of writing and illustrating children's books, so there's a lot of talent and competition in this field. I think that the reason I've gotten published is because I have lots of determination and energy. And I don't have trouble making myself sit down and work.

"I sometimes begin a book with a title. That may be a result of having worked in design/advertising where I watched the copywriters come up with catchy product names or ad headlines. If I think of a phrase that seems funny, I write it down. I keep thinking about it until a story begins to form. Then I sit down and write. I usually have several stories in progress at once. That way, if one story stumps me momentarily, I can move on to another one for a while. Once I really get a clear vision of the storyline, though, I'm reluctant to stop working on it. Some of my books that began with a title are *Boo Who?, Ivy Green, Cootie Queen,* and *Red, Yellow, Green: What Do Signs Mean?*

"I've developed three illustration styles in response to specific books that I've worked on. I call them my 100th Day (pencil and watercolor), Sign language (ink and watercolor), and Sleepover (gouache) styles, based on the first or more well-known books I've illustrated in each style. My illustrations can be seen at my website (http://www.joanholub.com)."

Describing her early years and how she eventually fell in love with books, Holub continued to *SATA:* "I loved elementary school and made good grades. I did especially well in English and math. I was not a class clown. I was shy. My family moved every few years because of my father's job with an oil company. Sometimes it took a while to make new friends. I stayed inside a lot, sat at my desk and drew. My Mom took me to the public library regularly. I saw her read and followed her example. That's how my love of books began."

■ For More Information See

BOOKS

Children's Writer's & Illustrator's Market, Writer's Digest, 1996, pp. 188-89.

PERIODICALS

Bulletin of the Center for Children's Books, December, 1997.
Publishers Weekly, October 6, 1997, p. 50.
School Library Journal, December, 1988, pp. 102-03; February, 1989, p. 82; August, 1990, p. 145; June, 1993, pp. 117-18; October, 1997, p. 98; February, 1998.

*   *   *

HOWARD, Ellen 1943-

■ Personal

Born May 8, 1943, in New Bern, NC; daughter of Gerald Willis Phillips (a salesman) and Betty Jeane Chord (a banker; maiden name, Slate); married Kermit W. Jensen, June 15, 1963 (divorced June 15, 1969); married Charles F. Howard, Jr. (a research administrator), June 29, 1975; children: (first marriage) Anna Elizabeth; stepchildren: Cynthia, Laurie, Shaley. *Education:* Attended University of Oregon, 1961-63; Portland State University, B.A. (with honors), 1979. *Politics:* Liberal Democrat. *Religion:* Unitarian-Universalist.

■ Addresses

Home—Greeley, CO. *Agent*—Emilie Jacobson, Curtis Brown, Ltd., 10 Astor Pl., New York, NY 10003.

■ Career

Writer. Worked in various libraries and offices, 1963-1977; Secretary, the Collins Foundation, Portland, OR, 1980-88; volunteer for various social causes. *Member:* Authors Guild, Society of Children's Book Writers and Illustrators (regional advisor, 1985-88).

■ Awards, Honors

Golden Kite Honor Book, Society of Children's Book Writers and Illustrators, 1984, for *Circle of Giving;* Notable Children's Trade Book in the Field of Social Studies, National Council for Social Studies-Children's Book Council, 1985, for *When Daylight Comes,* 1986, for *Gillyflower,* and 1988, for *Her Own Song;* Best Books, *School Library Journal,* 1987, for *Edith Herself:*

ELLEN HOWARD

Children's Middle Grade Award, International PEN USA Center West, 1989, for *Her Own Song;* Notable Children's Book selection, American Library Association, 1990, for *Sister.*

■ Writings

Circle of Giving, Atheneum, 1984.
When Daylight Comes, Atheneum, 1985.
Gillyflower, Atheneum, 1986, reissued as *Gilly's Secret,* Aladdin, 1993.
Edith Herself, illustrated by Ronald Himler, Atheneum, 1987.
Her Own Song, Atheneum, 1988.
Sister, Atheneum, 1990.
The Chickenhouse House, illustrated by Nancy Oleksa, Atheneum, 1991.
The Cellar, illustrated by Patricia Mulvihill, Atheneum, 1992.
The Big Seed, illustrated by Lillian Hoban, Simon & Schuster, 1993.
The Tower Room, Atheneum, 1993.
Murphy and Kate, illustrated by Mark Graham, Simon & Schuster, 1995.
A Different Kind of Courage (also published as *The Children's War*), Atheneum, 1996.
The Log Cabin Quilt, illustrated by Ronald Himler, Holiday House, 1996.

Contributor to periodicals, including *The Lion and the Unicorn.*

■ Sidelights

As a child growing up in Portland, Oregon, Ellen Howard dreamed of being a writer. Encouraged by her family to think in more practical terms, she abandoned the notion. She attended college for a few years without earning a degree, and then married and began a family. Some years later, Howard returned to college and earned her bachelor's degree (with honors). She also took up writing. The publication of one of her stories in a magazine encouraged her and, after much hard work and many submissions, her first book, *Circle of Giving,* was published in 1984. Since the publication of *Circle of Giving,* Howard has produced a variety of works for young people, including historical novels, stories based on her own family experiences, and problem novels. Howard has been praised for presenting lively stories in well-researched settings and for her sensitive portrayal of characters facing difficult issues.

Circle of Giving is the story of two young girls who move to Los Angeles in the 1920s. Marguerite, once popular in Oregon, has the most difficulty making friends and adjusting to her new surroundings. She begins to develop a friendship with Francie, a neighbor with cerebral palsy. Marguerite takes the time to discover that Francie has the potential to read and write, so Marguerite and Francie work to surprise Francie's mother at a neighborhood Christmas party. According to Karen Stang Hanley in *Booklist, Circle of Giving* is a "tender, moving story" based on an actual occurrence related to Howard "by her mother and grandmother."

Howard's second book, *When Daylight Comes,* is historical fiction set in 1733 on one of the U.S. Virgin Islands. In the story, slaves revolt and the ruling Danish government is killed along with all of the white people, except the doctor and the daughter of the magistrate, who is held captive. Helena, the captive girl, narrates the story as she deals with her grief. Noting that the author added just three fictional characters to the story, Tom S. Hurlburt wrote in *School Library Journal:* "Howard strives to be historically accurate.... *When Daylight Comes* is good reading, has a solemn and realistic ending and deals with a significant occurrence in the quest for freedom by enslaved blacks."

Her Own Song is a story based on actual events and set in early twentieth-century Portland, Oregon. Mellie, the eleven-year-old protagonist, hesitantly joins her friends as they mock the Chinese man at the laundry, but when her adoptive father has an accident, and her aunt is away on vacation, the Chinese man (Geem-Wah) helps her. Gradually, from Geem-Wah and her own recovered memories, Mellie learns that she was once a part of the Chinese family's household. Her mother, desperate for money, had sold her to a Chinese couple—Geem Wah's brother and his wife. Mellie was once "Mei-Li" and much loved. It was only later that authorities took her away from them and settled her with her adoptive parents. Despite the prejudice that separates the Chinese community from the white community, Mellie attempts to maintain her new friendship. According to *Horn Book* critic Margaret A. Bush, Howard's "use of timeless themes to illuminate a particular historical situation are well conceived and executed." *Junior Bookshelf* commentator Marcus Crouch described *Her Own Song* as "a remarkable piece of writing," and added: "the intricate details which eventually fit into a kind of jig-saw are cleverly traced, and the feelings of Mellie—Mei-Li—are most sensitively described."

World War II is the setting for *A Different Kind of Courage,* which is based on efforts to save children during the war. In the story, two French children must escape from Hitler's armies. Bertrand leaves Paris with his mother, and Zina stays at a camp until her family is forced to move on. The children end up on the same bus, bound to the coast and then to the United States. They do not understand, however, why they have been sent away, and feel abandoned as well as frightened. The work, according to Mary M. Burns in *Horn Book,* "evokes time and place, and the unusual subject is treated with the sensitivity and insight characteristic of Howard's writing." *School Library Journal* contributor Ann W. Moore maintained that the novel "gives an interesting and unusual look at World War II."

In the late 1980s, Howard began to publish stories based on her grandmother's experiences. The first, *Edith, Herself,* is set in the 1890s. Edith is going through a difficult period in her life. Her mother has died, and she must live with her older sister Alena, her sister's strict

Elvirey tries to make her family's new cabin more like home when they move north after her mother's death. (From *The Log Cabin Quilt,* written by Howard and illustrated by Ronald Himler.)

Christian husband John, their son Vernon, who is close in age to Edith, and John's mother. Adjusting to her new home is made even more difficult when the others discover that Edith has "fits," or epileptic seizures. Epilepsy was not well understood in the 1890s, and Edith's family must decide whether she can attend school given her condition. Roger Sutton of *Bulletin of the Center for Children's Books* appreciated Howard's "complex characterizations," her "lyrical prose," as well as her "infusion of great drama into the quietest scenes." After noting Edith's "inner toughness," Marcus Crouch of *Junior Bookshelf* remarked, "I think that many small girls will respect and warm to the strength of this heroine."

Sister, published after *Edith, Herself,* is set in an earlier period, before Edith is born, when Alena is still living at home in Illinois in 1886. Since the father of the family is away, and Alena's mother has many children to care for, twelve-year-old Alena has a great deal of responsibility. There are meals to prepare and laundry to finish, in addition to caring for the children. Alena is also a good student and dreams of going to Normal School. When her mother gives birth, Alena, who knows nothing about her body or babies, must assist; although terrified by much of the process, she marvels at the result, and grieves when the baby dies days later. Depressed by the death of the child, Alena's mother cannot work, and Alena must give up school to run the household. "This is a slow paced, thoughtful treatment of a year of growth and change in one young woman's life," wrote Christine Prevetti in *Voice of Youth Advocates.* Ethel R. Twichell of *Horn Book* remarked that Howard provided "a convincing portrayal of a sturdy and appealing heroine." "Howard manages to instill excitement and momentum into the drama of everyday life," concluded Zena Sutherland of *Bulletin of the Center for Children's Books. Gillyflower* takes up the sensitive issue of sexual abuse. Gilly's life is difficult now that her father is out of work and her mother must work evenings at the hospital. Gilly must keep the house clean and care for her sister Honey, and also deal with the sexual abuse of her father, which she does not completely understand. To help her cope, she imagines the existence of a beautiful, good princess named Juliana. When another family moves in next door, Gilly develops a friendship with new neighbor Marie Rose, and comes to realize that what her father is doing to her is wrong. When she perceives a threat to her sister Honey, she brings herself to tell her mother what has happened. She does not need Juliana any more. "Gilly's story is developed sensitively and crafted capably," commented Betsy Hearne in *Bulletin of the Center for Children's Books*. A *Publishers Weekly* critic asserted that the strength of the book is that it "is no sugar-coated parable."

Another of Howard's books deals with grief and recovery, and touches on the subject of abortion. *The Tower Room* features fifth-grader Mary, whose mother has died. The year is 1953, and Mary is living with her Aunt Olive in a Michigan town. Without the overt love of her aunt, or of her classmates at school, Mary takes solace in the tower room, a sealed-off room to which she has found another entrance. One day, a girl tells Mary that her mother died from an abortion; Mary runs from school and hides in the tower room. When she hears her aunt crying, Mary reveals herself and, as Donna Houser of *Voice of Youth Advocates* noted, Aunt Olive realizes that "both of them have some ghosts in their past that should be discussed." Mary learns the truth about her mother, and also discovers why the tower room was sealed. According to a *Kirkus Reviews* critic, the story is "unusually engaging" and has "a real heartwarmer of a conclusion."

Howard has also written picture books and chapter books for younger children. Two of these involve characters she introduces in *Edith, Herself* and *Sister*. *The Chickenhouse House*, a chapter book for readers in grades two to four, features Alena as a young child. Alena's family leaves her grandfather's house for a new farm an hour away. As their house is not ready, the family must live in a small building which they intend to make into a chicken house. Although Alena is initially disturbed by these developments, by the time the new home is ready it too seems odd. According to *Horn Book*'s Burns, the "narrative ... provides a sense of family solidarity" and "the joys of simple pleasures." *School Library Journal* contributor Virginia Golodetz similarly maintained: "This warm family story about a universal experience is sure to please young and beginning readers."

The Cellar is also based on the childhood of Howard's grandmother. In this story, Faith (another of Alena and Edith's sisters) is teased by her brothers as she attempts to do what they do. She proves her bravery and competence by making her way into the dark root cellar to bring her family apples for a treat. Praising the portrayal of nineteenth-century farm life, a *Kirkus Reviews* critic described the story as "beautifully crafted." Similarly, a *Publishers Weekly* critic noted that Howard "evokes the simple pleasures of rural life of a century ago."

Murphy and Kate is another book for younger children that follows the growth of Kate—a baby girl—and her puppy companion, Murphy. The two play together, and learn together, until Kate begins school. Even then, they remain the best of friends. One day, returning home from school, fourteen-year-old Kate finds that Murphy is not around, waiting for her as he usually does. Kate finds Murphy just in time to say good-bye. "A sensitive, honest focus on coping with the loss of a beloved pet," concluded Ellen Mandel in *Booklist*. *School Library Journal* contributor Marianne Saccardi recommended *Murphy and Kate* as "a comforting story for children experiencing a similar loss."

Howard, who makes her home in Colorado, continues to write for children. She once wrote in a speech she shared with *SATA* that the joy of writing a book "goes on and on, as we watch our book go out into the world in the same way we watch our children grow up. Sometimes we doubt that we have done as well as we could have. Sometimes we feel so proud! But always we know that we have done something important. That is the thing about writing. It is an important thing to do."

■ Works Cited

Burns, Mary M., review of *The Chickenhouse House, Horn Book,* July-August 1991, p. 453.

Burns, Mary M., review of *A Different Kind of Courage, Horn Book,* November-December, 1996, p. 736.

Bush, Margaret A., review of *Her Own Song, Horn Book,* November-December, 1988, p. 783.

Review of *The Cellar, Kirkus Reviews,* April 15, 1992, p. 538.

Review of *The Cellar, Publishers Weekly,* April 6, 1992, p. 65.

Crouch, Marcus, review of *Edith, Herself, Junior Bookshelf,* February, 1989, p. 29.

Review of *Gillyflower, Publishers Weekly,* August 22, 1986, pp. 99-100.

Golodetz, Virginia, review of *The Chickenhouse House, School Library Journal,* July, 1991, p. 58.

Hanley, Karen Stang, review of *Circle of Giving, Booklist,* May 15, 1984, pp. 1343-44.

Hearne, Betsy, review of *Gillyflower, Bulletin of the Center for Children's Books,* November, 1986, p. 51.

Review of *Her Own Song, Junior Bookshelf,* December, 1989, p. 296.

Houser, Donna, review of *The Tower Room, Voice of Youth Advocates,* December, 1993, p. 293.

Hurlburt, Tom S., review of *When Daylight Comes, School Library Journal,* November, 1985, p. 86.

Mandel, Ellen, review of *Murphy and Kate, Booklist,* May 1, 1995, p. 1580.

Moore, Ann W., review of *A Different Kind of Courage, School Library Journal,* November, 1996, pp. 106-07.

Prevetti, Christine, review of *Sister, Voice of Youth Advocates,* December, 1990, p. 284.

Saccardi, Marianne, review of *Murphy and Kate, School Library Journal,* June, 1995, p. 87.

Sutherland, Zena, review of *Sister, Bulletin of the Center for Children's Books,* December, 1990, p. 87.

Sutton, Roger, review of *Edith, Herself, Bulletin of the Center for Children's Books,* May, 1987, p. 169.

Review of *The Tower Room, Kirkus Reviews,* September 1, 1993, p. 1146.

Twichell, Ethel R., review of *Sister, Horn Book,* November-December, 1990, pp. 749-50.

■ For More Information See

PERIODICALS

Booklist, December 15, 1996, p. 731.

Bulletin of the Center for Children's Books, November, 1993, p. 85.

Horn Book, November, 1987, p. 737.

Kirkus Reviews, November 1, 1987, p. 57; November 1, 1990, p. 140; September 15, 1996, p. 1402.

Publishers Weekly, September 28, 1990, p. 103.

School Library Journal, June, 1992, p. 115.*

I–J

INKPEN, Mick 1952-

■ Personal

Born December 22, 1952, in Romford, England; married Deborah, 1973; children: Simon, Chloe.

■ Addresses

Office—c/o Hodder and Stoughton Ltd., 338 Euston Road, London NW13BH.

■ Career

Graphic designer, 1970-86. Greeting card designer; TV AM (England), writer for "Rub-a-Dub-Tub." Freelance writer and illustrator of children's books, 1986—.

■ Awards, Honors

Acorn Award, Nottinghamshire Libraries (England), and Children's Book Award, Federation of Children's Book Groups (England), both 1991, both for *Threadbear;* Acorn Award, Nottinghamshire Libraries, 1992, for *Kipper;* runner-up, Illustrated Children's Book of the Year, British Book Awards, 1992, for *Penguin Small.*

■ Writings

ILLUSTRATOR; WITH NICK BUTTERWORTH

Malcolm and Meryl Doney, *Who Made Me?,* Marshall Pickering (London, England), 1987, Zondervan, 1992.

ILLUSTRATOR; WITH NICK BUTTERWORTH; WRITTEN BY ELIZABETH LAWRENCE AND NOREEN WETTON

Can You Do This?, Nelson, 1986.
Come Up and Play, Nelson, 1986.
Do You Like My Hat? Nelson, 1986.
Do You Like My House, Nelson, 1986.
I Am Going to Hide, Nelson, 1986.
It Is Too Big, Nelson, 1986.
Look What I Can Do, Nelson, 1986.
May I Come In, Nelson, 1986.

May I Play with You, Nelson, 1986.
Where Is Monster, Nelson, 1986.
Where Is the Mouse, Nelson, 1986.
Mrs. Rabbit Gets Locked Out, Nelson, 1987.
Lolli and Pop in Trouble, Nelson, 1987.

WRITTEN AND ILLUSTRATED WITH NICK BUTTERWORTH

The Nativity Play, Hodder and Stoughton (London, England), 1985, Little, Brown, 1985.
The House on the Rock, Marshall, Morgan & Scott (Basingstoke, England), 1986, Multnomah Press, 1986.
The Precious Pearl, Marshall, Morgan & Scott, 1986, Multnomah Press, 1986.
The Lost Sheep, Marshall, Morgan & Scott, 1986, Multnomah Press, 1986.
The Two Sons, Marshall, Morgan & Scott, 1986, Multnomah Press, 1986.
Nice and Nasty: A Book of Opposites, Hodder and Stoughton, 1987, published in the United States as *Nice or Nasty: A Book of Opposites,* Little, Brown, 1987.
I Wonder at the Zoo, Marshall Pickering, 1987, Zondervan, 1987.
I Wonder in the Garden, Marshall Pickering, 1987, Zondervan, 1987.
I Wonder in the Country, Marshall Pickering, 1987, Chariot Victor, 1994.
I Wonder at the Farm, Marshall Pickering, 1987, published in the United States as *I Wonder on the Farm,* Chariot Victor, 1994.
Who Made . . . In the Country, HarperCollins, 1987.
Who Made . . . On the Farm, HarperCollins, 1987.
Who Made . . . At the Zoo, HarperCollins, 1987.
Who Made . . . In the Garden, HarperCollins, 1987.
Sports Day, Hodder and Stoughton, 1988.
The Magpie's Story: Jesus and Bacchaeus, Marshall Pickering, 1988.
The Mouse's Story: Jesus and the Storm, Marshall Pickering, 1988.
The Cat's Story: Jesus at the Wedding, Marshall Pickering, 1988.

The Fox's Story: Jesus Is Born, Marshall Pickering, 1988.

The Good Stranger, Marshall Pickering, 1989.

Just Like Jasper!, Hodder and Stoughton, 1989, Little, Brown, 1989.

The Little Gate, Marshall Pickering, 1989, HarperCollins, 1992.

The Rich Farmer, Marshall Pickering, 1989, HarperCollins, 1992.

Ten Silver Coins, Marshall Pickering, 1989.

The School Trip, Hodder and Stoughton, 1990, Delacorte, 1990.

The Wonderful Earth, Hunt & Thorpe (Alresford, England), 1990.

Field Day, Delacorte, 1991.

Jasper's Beanstalk, Hodder and Stoughton, 1992, Bradbury Press, 1993.

Opposites, Hodder and Stoughton, 1997.

SELF-ILLUSTRATED

One Bear at Bedtime: A Counting Book, Hodder and Stoughton, 1987, Little, Brown, 1987.

If I Had a Pig, Macmillan (London, England), 1988, Little, Brown, 1988.

If I Had a Sheep, Macmillan, 1988, Little, Brown, 1988.

Jojo's Revenge, Walker, 1989.

The Blue Balloon, Hodder and Stoughton, 1989, Little, Brown, 1990.

Gumboot's Chocolatey Day, Macmillan, 1989, Doubleday, 1991.

Threadbear, Hodder and Stoughton, 1990, Little, Brown, 1991.

Billy's Beetle, Hodder and Stoughton, 1991, Harcourt Brace, 1992.

Penguin Small, Hodder and Stoughton, 1992, Harcourt Brace, 1993.

Anything Cuddly Will Do!, Orchard (London, England), 1993.

Crocodile!, Orchard, 1993.

The Very Good Dinosaur, Orchard, 1993.

This Troll, That Troll, Orchard, 1993.

Lullabyhullaballoo!, Hodder and Stoughton, 1993, Artists and Writers Guild Books, 1994.

Nothing, Hodder and Stoughton, 1995, Artists and Writers Guild Books, 1996.

Don't Do That, Hodder and Stoughton, 1996, Intervisual Books, 1997.

Bear, Hodder and Stoughton, 1997, Talman, 1997.

Little Spotty Thing, Intervisual Books, 1997.

Say "Aaah"!, Intervisual Books, 1997.

Silly Billies, Intervisual Books, 1997.

Arnold, Hodder and Stoughton, 1998.

Honk, Hodder and Stoughton, 1998.

Sandcastle, Hodder and Stoughton, 1998.

Splosh!, Hodder and Stoughton, 1998.

"KIPPER" SERIES

Kipper, Hodder and Stoughton, 1991, Little, Brown, 1992.

Kipper's Toybox, Hodder and Stoughton, 1992, Harcourt Brace, 1992.

Kipper's Birthday, Hodder and Stoughton, 1993, Harcourt Brace, 1993.

Kipper's Book of Colours, Hodder and Stoughton, 1994, published in the United States as *Kipper's Book of Colors,* Harcourt Brace, 1995.

Kipper's Book of Counting, Hodder and Stoughton, 1994, published in the United States as *Kipper's Book of Numbers,* Harcourt Brace, 1995.

Kipper's Book of Opposites, Hodder and Stoughton, 1994, Harcourt Brace, 1995.

Kipper's Book of Weather, Hodder and Stoughton, 1994, Harcourt Brace, 1995.

Where, Oh Where, Is Kipper's Bear: A Pop-Up Book with Light!, Hodder and Stoughton, 1994, Red Wagon Books, 1995.

Kipper's Snowy Day, Hodder and Stoughton, 1996, Harcourt Brace, 1996.

"WIBBLY PIG" SERIES

Wibbly Pig Is Upset, Hodder and Stoughton, 1995, Golden Books, 1995.

Wibbly Pig Can Dance!, Hodder and Stoughton, 1995, Golden Books, 1995.

Wibbly Pig Can Make a Tent, Hodder and Stoughton, 1995, Golden Books, 1995.

Wibbly Pig Likes Bananas, Hodder and Stoughton, 1995, Golden Books, 1995.

Wibbly Pig Makes Pictures, Hodder and Stoughton, 1995, Golden Books, 1995.

Wibbly Pig Opens His Presents, Hodder and Stoughton, 1995, Golden Books, 1995.

Everyone Hide from Wibbly Pig, Hodder and Stoughton, 1997, Viking, 1997.

■ Adaptations

Kipper has been adapted for a British television series, 1997, on Anglia Television's ITV.

■ Sidelights

Mick Inkpen is a British graphic artist-turned children's book writer and illustrator best known for such award-winning titles as *Kipper, Threadbear,* and *Penguin Small.* His picture book characters include charming pigs, raucous mice, sleepy bears, and of course the playful puppy called Kipper. "I entered the world of children's books relatively late," Inkpen told *Something about the Author (SATA),* "after twelve years in graphic design." Quickly making up for lost time, Inkpen created several children's books with his long-time graphics partner, Nick Butterworth. He began publishing projects of his own in 1987. Inkpen has since developed a distinctive style marked by his unique humor and expressive characters in the dozens of children's books that he has both written and illustrated.

Born in Romford, England, on December 22, 1952, Inkpen grew up in a "very suburban estate with white concrete roads all named after Scottish rivers," as the writer-illustrator told Stephanie Nettell in a *Books for Keeps* article. Inkpen's father was a store manager and later a warehouse manager, and Inkpen grew up with a brother two years older and a sister three years younger. As Nettell noted in her article, "English and Art

Kipper rollicks in the snow with his best friend, Tiger, in this installment of Inkpen's popular series about the playful puppy. (From *Kipper's Snowy Day,* written and illustrated by Inkpen.)

marched side by side in Mick's affections throughout the Royal Liberty School, an old-fashioned grammar school that assumed most of its pupils would go to university." Such were Inkpen's plans, as well, but a job taken while he was waiting to study English at Cambridge became a turning point in his life. An older friend from Romford, Nick Butterworth, had set up a graphic design studio, and Inkpen was offered a temporary job there. "After twelve months the temporary job became permanent," Inkpen told *SATA.* "It was an excellent grounding—a kind of informal apprenticeship where I learned as much about dealing with stroppy printers and difficult clients as about the finer points of typography." Inkpen told Nettell that those years at the design studio were "marvelous for learning all the stuff that usually takes so long: Nick was an extremely good teacher—I'd choose that informal teaching over a college course every time—and I think I'm a good learner."

Initially, times were tough, for the firm was still building a client base and the partners were anything but good businessmen. Soon, however, things began to pick up. At age twenty-one, Inkpen married a school friend of his sister's, and continued working at design, illustrating everything from bra packages to banking cartoons. Soon Butterworth and he were turning their hands to children's books, creating a series based on a *Sunday Express* cartoon strip about a gang of mice that live in a deserted railway station called Upney Junction. There was also a brief excursion into television, with Inkpen

writing "thirty or so stories about a pink haired punk character called Steve which Nick [Butterworth] narrated and illustrated live on camera," Inkpen recalled for *SATA.*

"The move into children's books happened after my wife Deborah gave birth to our children," Inkpen told *SATA.* "Although it is true for me that without children I don't think I would produce a good children's book, I am also aware that when I am working I am really only trying to please myself." He expounded on the same theme to Nettell: "There's such a fine line between cute and sentimental, that meal ticket of big eyes with a knee-jerk, Pavlov-dog response .... It was essential for me to have been grounded by being a parent, experiencing the blood and guts of real life that disabuses you of any romanticising of children." In addition to the Upney Junction mice books, Inkpen created a number of popular children's titles with Butterworth, including *Just Like Jasper, Jasper's Beanstalk,* and *Nice and Nasty.* By 1986, however, he was ready to have a go at writing and illustrating his own books.

One of Inkpen's early titles was *One Bear at Bedtime,* a counting book in which, according to *Booklist*'s Barbara Elleman, "a young boy's imagination takes flight as he readies for bed." Three kangaroos bounce on his bed, four giraffes take a bath with him, six snakes decorate the toilet paper, and eight crocodiles share his toothpaste. Elleman noted that the "subtly shaded illustrations come alive through the expressive faces and situations," and concluded that this was a counting book "that will have youngsters making up their own verses as they nod off to dreamland." A critic in *Kirkus Reviews* observed that the illustrations "are lighthearted and clearly arranged on plenty of white space." In the end, the boy's teddy bear—which started the counting, literally, in the first place—helps put the young boy to sleep.

A pair of "what-if" books followed: *If I Had a Pig* and *If I Had a Sheep.* A boy and girl imagine they have been sent a pig and a sheep respectively and then wonder about all the things they would do with their new friend. The little girl's sheep would chase leaves and join her in a rock band, while the boy and his pig would bake a cake and paint a picture. Patricia Pearl, writing in *School Library Journal,* noted the watercolor illustrations of "round-faced, dot-eyed, pink-cheeked children" that were enhanced by "warm color tones and a gentle sense of humor," and concluded that these two books "are sure to have appeal to young children." A *Publishers Weekly* reviewer observed that "comic watercolors depict the wish-filled antics" of the children, while Moira Small wrote in *Books for Keeps* that the pair of books were "truly delightful."

In *The Blue Balloon,* Inkpen indulged his own affection for balloons as "wonderful graphic objects with an endless list of properties," according to Nettell, by telling the story of a dog who brings home a soggy blue balloon. In this fold-out book, the balloon turns out to have wonderful form-changing powers that delight the dog's young owner. "Both boy and dog have wonderfully expressive faces as they react to the balloon's extraordinary feats," noted a critic in a *Publishers Weekly* review. "Inkpen has created an imaginative, beautifully produced book." A congenial pig is the star of *Gumboot's Chocolatey Day,* wherein the pig in question gets the last centimeter of delight from the chocolate bar his aunt has given him. A *Publishers Weekly* reviewer concluded that "Inkpen's droll illustrations do not disappoint." A critic writing in *Kirkus Reviews* found both story and illustrations effective: "Like his sympathetically humorous, deftly phrased text, Inkpen's watercolor illustrations are guilelessly engaging."

Inkpen's first award-winning title was *Threadbear,* an appropriate name for the patched-up old teddy bear protagonist of the story. Threadbear decides to find Santa Claus in hopes of getting the squeaker in his stomach repaired. Even though young Ben loves his bear, squeaker or no, the bear sets off on his journey to the North Pole. Readers discover on the last page if the journey has been successful or not: Pressing the picture of Threadbear on the final page sets off a plaintive squeak. A *Publishers Weekly* contributor decided that "the book is a real charmer throughout," while in a *Junior Bookshelf* review, Marcus Crouch noted that Inkpen "has given his tubby hero a pleasing image supported by some suitably chilly night colours."

Inkpen went on to explain his illustrating and writing techniques in his interview with Nettell. "I find it fairly

With the help of a tabby cat, an abandoned stuffed animal gains an identity and a loving family. (From *Nothing,* **written and illustrated by Inkpen.)**

easy to visually create characters that people find sympathetically real," he said. Such characters tend to be more impressionistic than photographically precise, created by round lines and soft colors. Surprisingly for this draughtsman-turned children's writer, he also told Nettell that he enjoys writing more than illustrating his books, "because there's less craft between you and the idea. You put the words down and there's the reality on the page." Inkpen also mentioned the danger in children's literature of people mistaking simplicity for lack of substance. "It's not easy to be simple," he noted.

Perhaps Inkpen's most popular creation to date has been the young dog, Kipper, in his many incarnations. The initial title, *Kipper,* told the story of a puppy who has grown tired of his old blanket and basket and decides to search among the animals outdoors for a new place to sleep. Finally, after looking unsuccessfully, he figures that his old basket and blanket were best after all. George Delalis, in *School Library Journal,* noted particularly Inkpen's "deceptively simple" watercolor illustrations, both "playful and humorous," and concluded that "children will adore [Kipper]." Marcus Crouch, writing in *Junior Bookshelf,* observed that this "delightful picture-book ... should find favour with play-groups and story-tellers," while *School Librarian* contributor Richard Brown decided that "Mick Inkpen has created an engaging little character, Kipper, a large-faced, toylike dog—a type from which series are made." Brown's comments were indeed prophetic.

Inkpen has followed the original Kipper title with a batch of sequels, and his playful pup has even inspired a TV series in England. In *Kipper's Toybox,* the little dog's life changes when he discovers why there is a hole in his toybox. Dumping out the toys, he counts one too many; putting them back in the box there are two too many noses. Inkpen uses the clever device of a pair of mice to develop a subtle counting book. A *Kirkus Reviews* critic called the puppy a "charmingly fubsy dog," and concluded that *Kipper's Toybox* is "an elegantly simple, satisfying story with a lot of opportunities for counting." *School Librarian* contributor Elizabeth Hormann wrote that "Inkpen has created a gentle tale to delight preschoolers, tickle their funnybones and charm the adults who read it to them." The fun continues in *Kipper's Birthday,* in which a delay in sending out invitations causes Kipper's friends to come to his birthday party on the wrong day. "Just right for small people intrigued by the concepts of 'yesterday' and 'tomorrow'," concluded a *Kirkus Reviews* critic.

In *Kipper's Snowy Day,* the puppy spends the day enjoying the snow with his best friend, Tiger, leaving paw prints and shapes all over the garden. Fiona Waters in *Books for Keeps* wrote that Kipper was "one of the most famous puppies of them all," and that with *Kipper's Snowy Day* Inkpen "captures perfectly the real magic and excitement of snow for very young children." *School Library Journal* contributor Martha Topol declared that this book "is fun, pleasurable, and pleasant .... Perfect for group sharing, this title is sure to be a wintertime favorite." Kipper has also made an appearance in a pop-up book, *Where, Oh Where, Is Kipper's Bear?*, as well as four concept books, *Kipper's Book of Numbers*, *Kipper's Book of Colors*, *Kipper's Book of Opposites*, and *Kipper's Book of Weather*. Reviewing the four titles in *School Library Journal*, Helen Rosenberg concluded that while "concept books abound, Inkpen's engaging character and clear, clean presentations make these charming offerings stand above the crowd."

Another popular Inkpen series features Wibbly Pig, "a naked little pig with a round tummy who runs around with his big ears flopping," according to a *Kirkus Reviews* contributor in a review of *Wibbly Pig Makes Pictures*. In these simple stories, the gleeful pig explores single activities, painting or dancing or putting up a tent. A critic for *Kirkus Reviews* concluded that "Each volume is short and sweet." A further award-winning title from Inkpen is *Penguin Small*, the story of a little penguin who, with the help of a snowman and a whale, makes a miraculous journey to join his friends at the South Pole. In Inkpen's version, penguins actually hailed from the North Pole, but, tired of being eaten by polar bears, they swam south. All but Penguin Small, who is afraid of water. In a *Junior Bookshelf* review, Marcus Crouch thought the book was a "neat story … enriched with the author's deadpan pictures and helped a little by some bibliographical tricks—folding pages which open to a four-page whale or a panoramic tropical island." *School Librarian* contributor Sarah Reed maintained that "this is a book that will be enjoyed by children of all ages. It's worth every penny."

In *Nothing*, Inkpen explores the themes of loneliness and loss. Toby, an old stuffed cat, forgets his name and who he is because he has been separated from his owners for so many years. Thinking his name is Nothing, he is finally reunited with his family and restored to his old glory by Grandpa. "Inkpen's familiar, unadorned watercolors animate this simple and fetching story," noted a *Publishers Weekly* reviewer. Liz Waterland, writing in *Books for Keeps*, was enthusiastic about the work, asserting "I don't think Mick Inkpen has written anything I like better than this lovely book," while a *Kirkus Reviews* critic concluded that readers "searching for deep meanings will find plenty to ponder, especially in the perfect balance between the profoundness of Nothing's mission and the humor of the text."

Inkpen, whose training was of a practical sort, enjoys the rigors and discipline of the commercial world. As he told Nettell in *Books for Keeps*, "It's like a limited palate—you can get a good effect with a few colours—and after all there's no point producing books no one's going to read." For Inkpen, "childhood is a rich seam," and his readers hope he continues mining it.

■ Works Cited

Review of *The Blue Balloon*, *Publishers Weekly*, December 22, 1989, p. 56.

Brown, Richard, review of *Kipper*, *School Librarian*, August, 1991, p. 101.

Crouch, Marcus, review of *Kipper*, *Junior Bookshelf*, October, 1991, pp. 202-03.

Crouch, Marcus, review of *Penguin Small*, *Junior Bookshelf*, April, 1993, p. 60.

Delalis, George, review of *Kipper*, *School Library Journal*, May, 1992, p. 90.

Elleman, Barbara, review of *One Bear at Bedtime*, *Booklist*, March 15, 1988, p. 1259.

Review of *Gumboot's Chocolatey Day*, *Kirkus Reviews*, March 1, 1991, p. 326.

Review of *Gumboot's Chocolatey Day*, *Publishers Weekly*, January 18, 1991, p. 58.

Hormann, Elizabeth, review of *Kipper's Toybox*, *School Librarian*, November, 1992, p. 142.

Review of *If I Had a Pig* and *If I Had a Sheep*, *Publishers Weekly*, August 26, 1988, p. 85.

Review of *Kipper's Birthday*, *Kirkus Reviews*, April 1, 1993, p. 457.

Review of *Kipper's Toybox*, *Kirkus Reviews*, September 1, 1992, p. 1130.

Nettell, Stephanie, "Authorgraph No. 107," *Books for Keeps*, November, 1997, pp. 12-13.

Review of *Nothing*, *Kirkus Reviews*, January 15, 1998, p. 112.

Review of *Nothing*, *Publishers Weekly*, January 19, 1998, pp. 376-77.

Review of *One Bear at Bedtime*, *Kirkus Reviews*, April 1, 1988, p. 539.

Pearl, Patricia, review of *If I Had a Pig* and *If I Had a Sheep*, *School Library Journal*, December, 1988, p. 88.

Reed, Sarah, review of *Penguin Small*, *School Librarian*, February, 1993, p. 16.

Rosenberg, Helen, review of *Kipper's Book of Counting* and others, *School Library Journal*, August, 1995, p. 124.

Small, Moira, review of *If I Had a Pig* and *If I Had a Sheep*, *Books for Keeps*, March, 1992, p. 6.

Review of *Threadbear*, *Junior Bookshelf*, February, 1991, pp. 12-13.

Review of *Threadbear*, *Publishers Weekly*, June 29, 1991, p. 101.

Topol, Martha, review of *Kipper's Snowy Day*, *School Library Journal*, December, 1996, p. 94.

Waterland, Liz, review of *Nothing*, *Books for Keeps*, November, 1996, p. 6.

Waters, Fiona, "A Christmas Round-Up," *Books for Keeps*, November, 1996, p. 21.

Review of *Wibbly Pig Makes Pictures*, *Kirkus Reviews*, September 1, 1995, p. 1282.

■ For More Information See

PERIODICALS

Booklist, January 1, 1989, p. 788; April 15, 1992, p. 1537.

Books for Your Children, spring, 1993, p. 19; autumn-winter, 1993, p. 8.

Bulletin of the Center for Children's Books, March, 1998, p. 247.

Junior Bookshelf, April, 1988, p. 84; October, 1992, p. 191; October, 1996, pp. 184-85.

Kirkus Reviews, February 15, 1992, p. 256; March 15, 1992, p. 395; April 1, 1995, p. 470.
Magpies, March, 1998, p. 27; May, 1998, pp. 16-19.
New York Times Book Review, July 1, 1990, p. 19.
Publishers Weekly, September 26, 1995, p. 55.
Reading Time, November, 1997, pp. 19-20.
School Librarian, February, 1991, p. 19; February, 1992, p. 16; November, 1997, p. 186.
School Library Journal, July, 1990, p. 60; June, 1993, p. 78; January, 1994, p. 91; December, 1997, pp. 93-94.*

—Sketch by J. Sydney Jones

* * *

JAMES, Mary
See MEAKER, Marijane (Agnes)

* * *

JONES, Rebecca C(astaldi) 1947-

■ Personal

Born September 10, 1947, in Evergreen Park, IL; daughter of Lawrence J. (an accountant) and Ruth (Speitel) Castaldi; married Christopher Jones (a research manager), August 8, 1970; children: Amanda, David. *Education:* Northwestern University, B.S., 1969, M.S., 1970. *Religion:* Roman Catholic.

■ Addresses

Home—130 Pinecrest Dr., Annapolis, MD 21403. *Office*—American School Board Journal, 1680 Duke St., Alexandria, VA 22314.

■ Career

Warsaw Times-Union, Warsaw, IN, reporter, 1965-66; Illinois Children's Home and Aide Society, Chicago, public relations aide, 1967; *Cue,* New York City, staff intern, 1968; *Ingenue,* New York City, staff intern, 1968; *Newark Advocate,* Newark, OH, reporter, 1970-71; WBNS-TV, Columbus, OH, assignment editor and reporter, 1971-72; Ohio State University, Columbus, instructor of journalism, 1972-75; University of Maryland, University College, College Park, MD, professor of journalism, 1975-93; Anne Arundel Community College, Arnold, MD, English instructor, 1977, 1984-86; *American School Board Journal,* senior editor, 1993-98.

■ Awards, Honors

Excellence in Teaching Award, University of Maryland, University College, 1992; Outstanding Faculty Award, National Universities Continuing Education Association, 1993; Children's Choice, International Reading Association, 1983, 1990; Best Children's Books, New York Public Library, 1987; Notable Books, National Council for Social Studies, 1990, 1992; Pick of the List, American Booksellers Association, 1992; Bronze Medal

for Feature Writing, Society of National Association Publications, 1995, Gold Medal, 1997; Honorable Mention, Benjamin Fine Award, 1997; Distinguished Achievement, Educational Press Association, 1997.

■ Writings

Angie and Me, Macmillan, 1981.
The Biggest, Meanest, Ugliest Dog in the Whole Wide World, illustrated by Wendy Watson, Macmillan, 1982.
Madeline and the Great (Old) Escape Artist, Dutton, 1983.
I Am Not Afraid, illustrated by Patricia Mattozzi, Concordia (St. Louis, MO), 1986.
The Biggest (and Best) Flag That Ever Flew, illustrated by Charles Geer, Tidewater (Centreville, MD), 1988.
The Believers, Arcade (New York City), 1989.
Down at the Bottom of the Deep Dark Sea, illustrated by Virginia Wright-Frierson, Bradbury, (Scarsdale, NY), 1991.
Matthew and Tilly, illustrated by Beth Peck, Dutton, 1991.
Great-Aunt Martha, illustrated by Shelley Jackson, Dutton, 1994.
The President Has Been Shot: True Stories of the Attacks on Ten U.S. Presidents, Dutton, 1996.

"JEREMY BLUETT" SERIES

Germy Blew It, Dutton, 1987.
Germy Blew It—Again!, Holt, 1988.
Germy Blew the Bugle, Arcade, 1990.

REBECCA C. JONES

Germy in Charge, Dutton, 1993.

■ Sidelights

Author Rebecca C. Jones writes for a variety of juvenile audiences, including middle graders, beginning readers, and pre-schoolers. Often her stories address problems children face growing up, such as a young boy overcoming his fear of dogs or a twelve-year-old girl coping with her parents' divorce. On a more humorous note, Jones penned the "Jeremy Bluett" series, in which readers laugh at and learn from the protagonist's often comic mistakes at school. In addition to fiction, Jones has also penned a nonfiction work about the assassinations or attempted assassinations of several American presidents.

In Jones's first published work, *Angie and Me,* the author introduces twelve-year-old Jenna Matthews, who is hospitalized for treatment of rheumatoid arthritis. While there, Jenna meets Angie, a girl terminally ill with a rare blood disorder. From Angie, Jenna learns about acceptance, friendship, and courage. Although Angie eventually dies, Jenna finds a strong will to live and

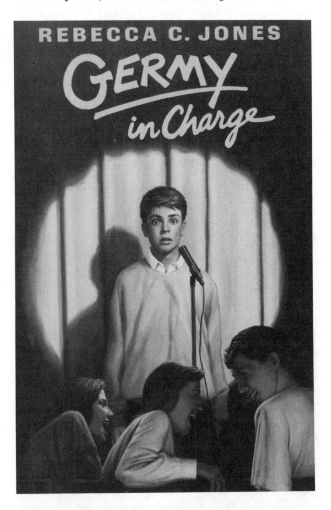

Sixth-grader Jeremy Bluett finds it difficult to live up to his campaign promises when he is elected to a seat on the school board. (Cover illustration by Scott Gladden.)

recovers from her illness. "Jenna's recovery and her growth as a person are convincingly portrayed," according to Ethel R. Twichell in a *Horn Book* review. A critic for the *Bulletin of the Center for Children's Books* similarly remarked that Jones's "first-person approach is convincingly that of a pre-teenager."

Jones's next work for middle schoolers also features a twelve-year-old girl who winds up in the hospital and befriends another patient. In *Madeline and the Great (Old) Escape Artist,* published in 1983, Madeline is sent to the hospital after she has a seizure in school. While there she meets and forms a bond with ninety-four-year-old Mary Gibson. Mary is eventually sent to a nursing home, and Madeline is released after she is diagnosed with and treated for epilepsy. However, the two remain friends, even after their plan to run away together fails and Mary has a stroke. *Booklist* contributor Denise M. Wilms concluded that "Madeline's problems are effectively portrayed and her attitude change, not only toward herself but toward her disliked surroundings, is absorbing and believable."

In *The Believers,* published in 1989, Jones introduces Tibby, a girl who longs for more time with her career-minded adoptive mother. While spending much of her time with her mother's Aunt Evelyn, Tibby meets Verl and Esther Milner—two children from a strict religious sect. After Tibby secretly attends their prayer meetings, one of the Milner children falls very ill. Tibby must choose whether to take the child to the hospital—against the Milners' religious beliefs—or to get her own mother involved. A critic from *Kirkus Reviews* complimented Jones on "the turns of her plot which raise and explore genuine moral issues without oversimplifying them."

Also for middle schoolers are the humorous "Jeremy Bluett" (a.k.a. Germy Blew It) books, which *Booklist* contributor Ilene Cooper called "an always amusing series." Appearing in 1987, *Germy Blew It* features a fifth-grade boy seeking his fifteen-minutes of fame by holding a bubble-gum-chewing contest. Like many of his other schemes showcased in later stories, the contest blows up in his face. Not a problem for long, as Jeremy immediately starts a new project. Jones elaborates on this project in the sequel *Germy Blew It—Again!,* in which Jeremy tries to raise gerbils in an effort to return the money he misused for his bubble-gum contest. Claudia Mills, writing about books that "culminate in failure" in *Children's Literature in Education,* noted that readers enjoy comic failures such as *Germy Blew It—Again!* "because the hero's failure has been far more entertaining to read about than any success would have been."

For pre-schoolers and beginning readers, Jones has penned some appealing picture books, including *The Biggest, Meanest, Ugliest Dog in the Whole World* and *Great-Aunt Martha.* The former work features Jonathan—a young boy afraid of the large dog named Pirate living next door. Face to face with Pirate one day, a frightened Jonathan throws a ball at the dog to scare

In Jones's intergenerational story, a young girl dreads her great-aunt's visit, but instead is in for quite a pleasant surprise. (From *Great-Aunt Martha,* illustrated by Shelley Jackson.)

him off. Pirate, however, fetches the ball and returns it to Jonathan. After a game of ball tossing, Jonathan no longer fears his new friend. *Horn Book* contributor Ann A. Flowers called the story "predictable but satisfying." In *Great-Aunt Martha,* the young narrator laments about changes at home for Aunt Martha's arrival: The family has to eat healthier food instead of pizza and pretzels, and the narrator has to clean her room and take a bath. When Aunt Martha arrives, everyone has to keep quiet—that is until they hear the elderly woman dancing, tapping her cane, and complaining that the house is too quiet! "While shattering an undeserved stereotype, Jones's pithy tale also offers a heartening glimpse of three-generational *joie de vivre,*" declared a *Publishers Weekly* reviewer. Jody McCoy, writing in *School Library Journal,* exclaimed: "*Great Aunt Martha* really is great!"

In her first nonfiction work for middle schoolers, Jones offers accounts of several assassinations and assassination attempts on American presidents. She not only describes the attacks in detail, but also offers intriguing bits of information on the assailants before and after the attacks. Quotes from the dying presidents, surviving victims, and presidential families and friends are included as well. "Jones's detailed accounts ... benefit

from her insightful, accessible presentation," noted a *Publishers Weekly* reviewer.

Jones commented: "I was sick a great deal as a child, and our parish priest used to warn me of the dangers of 'playing with yourself' when alone in bed. I wasn't sure what that meant but interpreted it to be the same as 'playing *by* yourself.' I avoided the evil by creating great imaginary characters to keep me company in the sickroom. Today many of those imaginary characters stand by my computer and wait for me to tell their stories."

■ Works Cited

Review of *Angie and Me, Bulletin of the Center for Children's Books,* December, 1991, p. 70.

Review of *The Believers, Kirkus Reviews,* September 1, 1989, p. 1328.

Cooper, Ilene, review of *Germy in Charge, Booklist,* October 1, 1993, p. 344.

Flowers, Ann A., review of *The Biggest, Meanest, Ugliest Dog in the Whole Wide World, Horn Book,* April, 1983, p. 161.

Review of *Great-Aunt Martha, Publishers Weekly,* June 26, 1995, p. 106.

McCoy, Jody, review of *Great-Aunt Martha, School Library Journal,* July, 1995, p. 64.

Mills, Claudia, review of *Germy Blew It—Again!, Children's Literature in Education,* September, 1990, pp. 192-93.

Review of *The President Has Been Shot! True Stories of the Attacks on Ten U.S. Presidents, Publishers Weekly,* July 8, 1996, p. 85.

Twichell, Ethel R., review of *Angie and Me, Horn Book,* April, 1982, p. 164.

Wilms, Denise M., review of *Madeline and the Great (Old) Escape Artist, Booklist,* February 1, 1984, p. 814.

■ For More Information See

PERIODICALS

Booklist, December 1, 1982, pp. 499-500; July, 1987, p. 1680; August, 1990, p. 2176.

Bulletin of the Center for Children's Books, February, 1983, p. 110; December, 1983, p. 70; September, 1989, p. 8; September, 1996, p. 18.

Five Owls, January, 1990, p. 43.

Junior Bookshelf, October, 1988, p. 250; October, 1989, p. 228.

Kirkus Review, April 1, 1987, p. 554; February 15, 1991, p. 255; July 1, 1993, p. 861.

Publishers Weekly, October 8, 1982, p. 62; December 14, 1990, p. 65.

School Library Journal, November, 1981, pp. 92-93; January, 1984, p. 78; August, 1987, p. 86; December, 1988, p. 104; March, 1991, p. 174; September, 1993, p. 233.

K

KERR, M. E.
See MEAKER, Marijane (Agnes)

* * *

KLASS, Sheila Solomon 1927-

■ Personal

Born November 6, 1927, in Brooklyn, NY; daughter of Abraham Louis (a presser) and Virginia (Glatter) Solomon; married Morton Klass (a professor of anthropology), May 2, 1953; children: Perri Elizabeth, David Arnold, Judith Alexandra. *Education:* Brooklyn College (now Brooklyn College of the City University of New York), B.A., 1949; University of Iowa, M.A., 1951, M.F.A., 1953. *Religion:* Jewish.

■ Addresses

Home—900 West 190th St., Apt. 2-0, New York, NY 10040. *Office*—Department of English, Manhattan Community College of the City University of New York, 199 Chambers St., New York, NY 10007. *Agent*—Ruth Cohen, P.O. Box 7626, Menlo Park, CA 94025.

■ Career

Writer, 1960—. Worked as an aide in a psychopathic hospital in Iowa City, IA, 1949-51; Julia Ward Howe Junior High School, New York City, English teacher, 1951-57; Manhattan Community College of the City University of New York, began as an assistant professor, currently professor of English, 1965—. Guest at Yaddo colony, 1974. *Member:* International PEN.

■ Awards, Honors

Bicentennial Prize, Leonia Drama Guild, 1976, for one-act play, *Otherwise It Only Makes One Hundred Ninety-Nine;* New Jersey Institute of Technology children's literature award, 1983, for *Alive and Starting Over,* and 1988, for *The Bennington Stitch.*

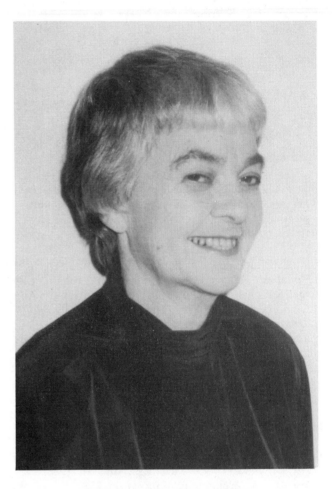

SHEILA SOLOMON KLASS

■ Writings

FOR MIDDLE GRADE READERS

Nobody Knows Me in Miami, Scribner, 1981.
Kool Ada, Scholastic, 1991.
A Shooting Star, Holiday House, 1996.
The Uncivil War, Holiday House, 1997.

FOR YOUNG ADULTS

To See My Mother Dance, Scribner, 1981.
Alive and Starting Over, Scribner, 1983.
The Bennington Stitch, Scribner, 1985.
Page Four, Scribner, 1986.
Credit-Card Carole, Scribner, 1987.
Rhino, Scholastic, 1993.
Next Stop: Nowhere, Scholastic, 1995.

FOR ADULTS

Come Back on Monday, Abelard-Schuman, 1960.
Everyone in This House Makes Babies, Doubleday, 1964.
Bahadur Means Hero, Gambit, 1969.
A Perpetual Surprise, Apple-Wood, 1991.
In a Cold Open Field, Black Heron, 1997.

Also author of one-act play, *Otherwise It Only Makes One Hundred Ninety-Nine.* Contributor of short stories and humorous articles to *Ms., Hadassah, Bergen Record, New York Times, Manhattan Mind,* and other publications.

■ Work in Progress

Louey in Paradise, a young adult novel about "one strange summer" in the life of author Louisa May Alcott.

■ Sidelights

Sheila Solomon Klass writes novels for middle readers and young adults that are largely character-driven, and which are often told in the first person. Usually domestic in setting, Klass's books speak of family relations—of learning to cope with inflated parental expectations, or of dealing with a new stepmother or a distant, noncustodial parent. Loosely labeled 'problem novels', such books as *To See My Mother Dance, The Bennington Stitch, Alive and Starting Over,* and *Next Stop: Nowhere* often feature youthful female narrators whose distinctive voices Klass manages to capture on paper. Klass writes of issues central to adolescents: self-image and self-worth, abandonment, death of a parent, friendship values, and the moral costs of materialism. A more recent departure in her fiction has been historical novels about Annie Oakley and Louisa May Alcott. In these books, as in her other works, Klass manages to reproduce the unique voice of her female protagonist, and it is this voice and the development of character that are at the heart of a Klass novel.

As Klass once told *SATA,* "My life and what happens around me, what I hear about and read about—these are the sources that initiate the act of writing. But almost immediately, imagination takes over and the story acquires its own energy and direction. What *really* happened is not pertinent. It's forgotten. Fiction is not autobiography. It is experience transmuted by the imagination in inexplicable ways. It has its own truth and its own life." It is this transmutation that makes Klass's novels come to life, and her years of experience of not only writing but also teaching writing come to play in all her books.

Klass was an early writer. As she told *SATA,* "I've been a writer since adolescence. I write because writing is a supreme pleasure." She started her career as an author with adult novels and plays, juggling her commitment to words with her other roles of being a wife, mother, and a college professor. Her first novel, *Nobody Knows Me in Miami,* appeared in 1981. With this initial title, Klass established the basic formula she would continue to work with throughout her writing career: a young female protagonist learns basic values about family and friendships by making difficult decisions. Set in Brooklyn in 1937, *Nobody Knows Me in Miami* features ten-year-old Miriam, who is faced with a choice between staying with her poor family and assuming a richer material life with relatives in Miami. Uncle Mac and Aunt Lili (they were once simply Max and Lily) want to take Miriam—whom they call Mimi as "it's more American"—back with them to Florida as their adopted daughter. At first this looks pretty good to Miriam, whose family is poor and who is tormented in her school. Eventually, however, Miriam sees her aunt for the snob she is, and opts to stay with her close-knit Jewish family which is not ashamed of its ethnic roots. As a critic in *Bulletin of the Center for Children's Books* stated, "Miriam decides to stay in Brooklyn, a rich little poor girl .... [The novel] has a convincing first-person style and some flavorful dialogue." A contributor in *Kirkus Reviews,* while noting the obvious snobbishness of Aunt Lili, also concluded that "this is a full enough story so that children who are inclined toward such ethnic nostalgia and old-timey values will take to Miriam, her loving family, and her clearly projected Brooklyn neighbors."

Klass wrote companion volumes in her next two novels, both featuring Jessica Van Norden. In the first of these, *To See My Mother Dance,* Klass deals with issues of abandonment by a parent and the acceptance of a stepparent. Jess is thirteen years old and resents her new stepmother, Martha. She dreams of seeing her mother again—the woman who abandoned her when she was one year old to pursue her own dreams of becoming a professional dancer. Martha, however, is not to be put off by her stepdaughter and locates Karen, the absent mother, in a religious commune in San Francisco. The subsequent visit with the burnt-out, abstracted Karen is enough to make Jess lose any illusions she may have had about her mother and ultimately brings her closer to Martha who wants the new family to work. A *Publishers Weekly* critic felt that "Klass captures the flippant, disdainful levity typical of wounded young adolescents" in Jess's speech, while *Booklist*'s Ilene Cooper concluded that "the book is well crafted and has sufficient character and plot appeal for a junior high audience." A reviewer in the *Bulletin of the Center for Children's Books* felt that the book was "sad" rather than tragic, and "the story [is] strong in its characters, relationships, and dialogue." The award-winning *Alive and Starting Over* picks up Jess's story a couple of years later when a mysterious new boy at school, an illness in her family, and the loss of a friend bring both unsettling and challenging changes into her life. Diane Gersoni Edelman, writing in the *New York Times Book Review,* noted that the premise of the book was "that it's ... never too late to take your life in hand, to make constructive changes, to come to terms with circumstances not likely to change.... What readers will like best about this book is its message of realistic hope. It's palatably inspirational and upbeat without being saccharine."

Another award-winning Klass title is *The Bennington Stitch,* a novel cleverly named after the college which Amy's mother wants her to attend and the handicraft for which Amy seems better suited than an academic career. Low SAT scores make it virtually impossible for Amy to attend Bennington, and she does not want to anyway. Instead, she apprentices with a skilled quilt-maker while her mother achieves the dream of Bennington herself. Amy's situation is echoed in a subplot involving her boyfriend Rob, who wants to go to art school instead of medical school as his doctor father wishes. "This is ably written," commented a reviewer in the *Bulletin of the Center for Children's Books,* "has believable characters, and should appeal to readers who are facing the terrors of PSAT and SAT." Writing in the *New York Times*

Klass's historical novel dwells on the early life of Annie Oakley, the best sharpshooter in the world at the end of the nineteenth century. (Cover illustration by Ronald Himler.)

Book Review, Meg Wolitzer observed that in spite of some flaws in the work, "it is still rewarding to read a novel about young adults who have minds and ambitions of their own, and whose lives extend beyond the parameters of their families."

Another novel with a subtext of college application is *Page Four,* which takes its title from the fourth page of college application forms in which the applicant writes a personal essay. The novel also deals with a recurring theme in Klass' novels of an absent parent, in this case Dave's father who has run off to Alaska with a new wife, leaving behind a mother "paralyzed by her husband's sudden desertion," according to Roger Sutton in the *Bulletin of the Center for Children's Books.* Sutton went on to note that the "first-person, present-tense narrative ... is nicely balanced between Dave's hurt at what his father has done and his attempts to move on. . . ." In *Credit-Card Carole,* a father once again initiates changes in a child's life; in this case not by running away but by making a career move from successful dentist to aspiring actor. The subsequent loss of income makes the daughter, Carole, change her shopping ways and learn "about real values through the experiences of good friends and her parents' struggle to realize a dream," according to a *Publishers Weekly* contributor. That same reviewer concluded that the book was a "meaty story about likable people" and that it was "fun to applaud [the parents'] small victory and Carole as she grows from a mall groupie into a person." Bonnie L. Raasch, writing in *School Library Journal,* noted that dialogue in the book was "realistic, and so are the characters." Betsy Hearne concluded in *Bulletin of the Center for Children's Books* that "this is a light-hearted book despite the weighty theme."

Troubles in suburbia are left behind with Klass's next work, *Kool Ada,* about the difficulties of adjustment after the loss of one's family. Eleven-year-old Ada adjusts initially by becoming silent. As Ada says to herself in the book: "I took shelter in the cave of my mind where it is warm and safe. I just sat and sucked my thumb and bit my cuticles until they bled. I stopped talking and I lived back inside my head where I was a little bit protected." Sent to live with an aunt in Chicago after the death of her entire family, her one means of communication with new schoolmates is her feisty nature and ready fists. Ada, however, slowly comes out of her self-imposed shell through the intervention of an understanding teacher, neighbors, and her aunt. Katherine Bruner in *School Library Journal* thought the book was "Simple, but effective," and Frances Bradburn in the *Wilson Library Bulletin* observed that the "portrait Klass paints of Ada is a classic one.... Ada is a lovable, gutsy kid, one worthy of the special attention she receives. . . ."

With *Rhino,* Klass tackled a seemingly much less vital theme, that of self-image and cosmetic surgery. Yet Klass imbued this story with more than skin-deep detail. "This could be a shallow book, but it's not," noted Deborah Stevenson in the *Bulletin of the Center for Children's Books.* "Klass takes on images of self-worth

The UNCIVIL WAR
Sheila Solomon Klass

Asa Andersen fights against her doting mother and a contentious classmate in Klass's book about the dynamic sixth grader. (Cover illustration by Tony Meers.)

and cosmetic adjustments honestly," Stevenson went on to observe, making Annie's quest for a nose job, or rhinoplasty, represent a process of growth and acceptance of change. In *Next Stop: Nowhere*, Klass returned to the theme of an absent parent, when fourteen-year-old Beth is sent by her wealthy mother to live with her divorced father in Vermont. The theme of materialism versus deeper values comes to play when Beth slowly learns to respect her ceramist father's less lavish style of life. A *Publishers Weekly* reviewer commented that "Beth's first-person narration contains insightful gems," while *Booklist*'s Jeanne Triner noted that this "is a light, humorous story with a sweet romantic subplot." Susan Ackler in *Voice of Youth Advocates* concluded that "The warm cast of characters longs for another appearance, so I hope there is a sequel where we find out how Beth grows up."

Instead of a sequel, however, Klass made an abrupt departure with her next novel, *A Shooting Star*. "Recently," Klass told SATA, "I have become interested in writing novels based on the lives of real people—historical novels. I wrote *A Shooting Star* about the childhood of Annie Oakley, the best sharpshooter in the

world at the end of the nineteenth century, and I had such a good time doing that research that I went on to do a book about one strange summer in the life of Louisa May Alcott, the author of *Little Women*. That book, *Louey in Paradise*, is still in manuscript, but will be published soon." Reviewers responded warmly to Klass's story of Annie Oakley. A *Kirkus Reviews* critic dubbed it a "fast-moving first-person narration" with an "inventive plot . . . and a great happy ending." A contributor in *Publishers Weekly* noted that "Klass's portrayal of Oakley's courageous individualism makes this tale hit the mark," and Roger Sutton, writing in *Horn Book*, observed that "Annie Oakley shoots straight from the page in this fictionalized biography," and that "the real triumph of the book is its sure assumption of Annie Oakley's narrative voice. . . ."

Sandwiched between *A Shooting Star* and *Louey in Paradise*, Klass's *The Uncivil War* brings twelve-year-old Asa to do battle with her overprotective mother. The conflict rises when Asa's mother keeps trying to over-feed Asa, who is overweight and wants to lose some pounds. A cute new boy in class compounds her frustration when he calls her "Fatso." A writer in *Publishers Weekly* called the novel a "down-to-earth narrative" but noted that eating "smart" is more difficult for young people than the story suggests. Yet the critic goes on to claim Asa as a "worthy role model" because of her "self-determination" and "honesty." Deborah Stevenson, critiquing the work in *Bulletin of the Center for Children's Books*, stated that "several strands of the story don't always fit together as well as they might" but added, "the charm and credibility of the characters pull things together." After writing novels for over three decades, Klass—whose three children are also successful writers—still finds enjoyment in the craft. "Creating a story on paper is a peculiar joy unlike any other," she told SATA. "Just the writing itself is the first reward. . . . Writing books for young people is a particular pleasure; I regularly go into the New York City public schools to talk to students about writing and to hear their opinions on my books. Often they are very honest and outspoken, and I learn much." In her capacity as an English professor, she also teaches writing, "the most pleasurable of jobs," according to Klass. "What I do in my classrooms is introduce my students to the highest high in the whole world—the high that is achieved by creating marvelous original works from their own imaginations."

■ **Works Cited**

Ackler, Susan, review of *Next Stop: Nowhere*, *Voice of Youth Advocates*, February, 1995, pp. 339-40.
Review of *The Bennington Stitch*, *Bulletin of the Center for Children's Books*, January, 1986, p. 89.
Bradburn, Frances, review of *Kool Ada*, *Wilson Library Bulletin*, June, 1992, p. 122.
Bruner, Katherine, review of *Kool Ada*, *School Library Journal*, August, 1991, p. 168.
Cooper, Ilene, review of *To See My Mother Dance*, *Booklist*, December 1, 1981, p. 499.

Review of *Credit-Card Carole, Publishers Weekly,* July 10, 1987, p. 72.

Edelman, Diane Gersoni, review of *Alive and Starting Over, New York Times Book Review,* December 11, 1983, p. 44.

Hearne, Betsy, review of *Credit-Card Carole, Bulletin of the Center for Children's Books,* October, 1987, pp. 32-33.

Klass, Sheila Solomon, *Nobody Knows Me in Miami,* Scribner, 1981.

Klass, Sheila Solomon, *Kool Ada,* Scholastic, 1991.

Review of *Next Stop: Nowhere, Publishers Weekly,* December 19, 1994, p. 55.

Review of *Nobody Knows Me in Miami, Bulletin of the Center for Children's Books,* November, 1981, pp. 47-48.

Review of *Nobody Knows Me in Miami, Kirkus Reviews,* August 1, 1981, p. 935.

Raasch, Bonnie L., review of *Credit-Card Carole, School Library Journal,* October, 1987, p. 140.

Review of *A Shooting Star, Kirkus Reviews,* November 15, 1996, p. 1671.

Review of *A Shooting Star, Publishers Weekly,* December 2, 1996, p. 61.

Stevenson, Deborah, review of *Rhino, Bulletin of the Center for Children's Books,* November, 1993, p. 87.

Stevenson, Deborah, review of *The Uncivil War, Bulletin of the Center for Children's Books,* February, 1998, pp. 209-10.

Sutton, Roger, review of *Page Four, Bulletin of the Center for Children's Books,* March, 1987, p. 128.

Sutton, Roger, review of *A Shooting Star, Horn Book,* May-June, 1997, p. 323.

Review of *To See My Mother Dance, Bulletin of the Center for Children's Books,* May, 1982, pp. 173-74.

Review of *To See My Mother Dance, Publishers Weekly,* December 18, 1981, p. 71.

Triner, Jeanne, review of *Next Stop: Nowhere, Booklist,* January 15, 1995, p. 912.

Review of *The Uncivil War, Publishers Weekly,* December 22, 1997, p. 60.

Wolitzer, Meg, review of *The Bennington Stitch, New York Times Book Review,* October 27, 1985, p. 37.

■ **For More Information See**

PERIODICALS

Booklist, September 15, 1985, p. 125.

Bulletin of the Center for Children's Books, February, 1984, p. 110; February, 1995, p. 203.

Horn Book, January-February, 1994, p. 74.

Kirkus Reviews, July 15, 1991, p. 932; December 1, 1993, p. 1525; April 1, 1998, p. 497.

School Library Journal, January, 1982, p. 88; April, 1982, p. 71; December, 1983, p. 75; October, 1985, pp. 182-83; February, 1987, p. 91; November, 1993, p. 125; April, 1995, p. 134.*

—*Sketch by J. Sydney Jones*

KLINE, Suzy 1943-

■ **Personal**

Born August 27, 1943, in Berkeley, CA; daughter of Harry C. (in real estate) and Martha S. (a substitute school teacher) Weaver; married Rufus O. Kline (a college teacher, newspaper correspondent, and children's author), October 12, 1968; children: Jennifer, Emily. *Education:* Attended Columbia University; University of California, Berkeley, B.A., 1966; California State College (now University), Hayward, Standard Elementary Credential, 1967. *Politics:* Democrat. *Religion:* Presbyterian. *Hobbies and other interests:* Writing, walking, dancing, sports, reading, movies and plays.

■ **Addresses**

Home—124 Hoffman St., Torrington, CT 06790. *Office*—Southwest School, Torrington, CT.

■ **Career**

Elementary schoolteacher in Richmond, CA, 1968-71; Southwest School, Torrington, CT, elementary teacher, 1976—. Makes author visits to schools and conducts workshops for teachers. *Member:* Society of Children's Book Writers and Illustrators, PEN, New England Reading Association, Connecticut Education Association, Torrington Education Association.

SUZY KLINE

■ Awards, Honors

Best books, *Christian Science Monitor*, 1985, and West Virginia Children's Book Award, 1987-1988, for *Herbie Jones;* Editor's Choice, *Booklist*, 1986, for *What's the Matter with Herbie Jones;* International Reading Association Children's Choice Awards, 1986, for *Herbie Jones,* 1987, for *What's the Matter with Herbie Jones?,* 1989, for *Horrible Harry in Room 2-B,* 1990, for *Orp,* and 1991, for *Orp and the Chop Suey Burgers;* School District Teacher of the Year Award from State of Connecticut, 1987; Probus Educator of the Year Award, 1988.

■ Writings

FOR CHILDREN

Shhhh!, illustrations by Dora Leder, Albert Whitman, 1984.

Don't Touch!, illustrations by Leder, Albert Whitman, 1985.

Ooops!, illustrations by Leder, Albert Whitman, 1987.

The Hole Book, illustrations by Laurie Newton, Putnam, 1989.

"HERBIE JONES" SERIES

Herbie Jones, illustrations by Richard Williams, Putnam, 1985.

What's the Matter with Herbie Jones?, illustrations by Williams, Putnam, 1986.

Herbie Jones and the Class Gift, illustrations by Williams, Putnam, 1987.

Herbie Jones and the Monster Ball, illustrations by Williams, Putnam, 1988.

Herbie Jones and Hamburger Head, illustrations by Williams, Putnam, 1989.

The Herbie Jones Reader's Theater, illustrations by Williams, Putnam, 1992.

Herbie Jones and the Dark Attic, illustrations by Williams, Putnam, 1992.

Herbie Jones and the Birthday Showdown, illustrations by Carl Cassler, Putnam, 1993.

"ROOM 2-B" SERIES

Horrible Harry in Room 2-B, illustrations by Frank Remkiewicz, Viking, 1988.

Horrible Harry and the Green Slime, illustrations by Remkiewicz, Viking, 1989.

Horrible Harry and the Ant Invasion, illustrations by Remkiewicz, Viking, 1989.

Horrible Harry's Secret, illustrations by Remkiewicz, Viking, 1990.

Horrible Harry and the Christmas Surprise, illustrations by Remkiewicz, Viking, 1991.

Horrible Harry and the Kickball Wedding, illustrations by Remkiewicz, Viking, 1992.

Song Lee in Room 2-B, illustrations by Remkiewicz, Viking, 1993.

Song Lee and the Hamster Hunt, illustrations by Remkiewicz, Viking, 1994.

Song Lee and Leech Man, illustrations by Remkiewicz, Viking, 1995.

Horrible Harry and the Dungeon, illustrations by Remkiewicz, Viking, 1996.

Horrible Harry and the Purple People, illustrations by Remkiewicz, Viking, 1997.

Horrible Harry and the Drop of Doom, illustrations by Remkiewicz, Viking, 1998.

Horrible Harry Moves up to Third Grade, illustrations by Remkiewicz, Viking, 1998.

Song Lee and the "I Hate You" Notes, illustrations by Remkiewicz, Viking, in press.

"ORP" SERIES

Orp, Putnam, 1989.

Orp and the Chop Suey Burgers, Putnam, 1990.

Orp Goes to the Hoop, Putnam, 1991.

Who's Orp's Girlfriend?, Putnam, 1992.

Orp and the FBI, Putnam, 1995.

"MARY MARONY" SERIES

Mary Marony and the Snake, illustrations by Blanche Sims, Putnam, 1992.

Mary Marony Hides Out, illustrations by Sims, Putnam, 1993.

Mary Marony Mummy Girl, illustrations by Sims, Putnam, 1994.

Mary Marony and the Chocolate Surprise, illustrations by Sims, Putnam, 1995.

Marvin and the Mean Words, illustrations by Sims, Putnam, 1997.

OTHER

Also author of plays for local elementary school. Contributor to *Instructor.*

■ Work in Progress

Molly Zander and the Deadly Hook Shot, the beginning of a new series.

■ Sidelights

Suzy Kline should know a lot about kids; she has devoted much of her adult life to working as a second-grade teacher and more recently a third-grade teacher, inspiring young children with a love of reading that she hopes will remain with them throughout their lives. The author of several series of award-winning books featuring realistic characters like third grader Herbie Jones, second-grade stutterer Mary Marony, a basketball-crazy middle schooler who goes by the nickname "Orp," and Horrible Harry, the rambunctious nemesis of room 2-B, Kline has a sure-fire ability to create true-to-life plots, which she relates in a humorous way that includes plenty of down-to-earth humor. Her "characters are all well defined, with their own unique personalities finely drawn," noted Cheryl Cufari in an appraisal of one of Kline's books for *School Library Journal.*

Kline was born in Berkeley, California, in 1943. Her first foray into writing occurred when she was eight years old. "I wrote letters to my grandfather in Indiana, telling him what was happening at our house. It seemed to me that he missed his son—my dad—very much, and he would be interested in hearing about him. Our home in California was three thousand miles away. My aunt told me that my letters helped him live a little longer, which made me feel really good about writing."

After high school Kline attended Columbia University for a year before transferring to the University of California, Berkeley, where she received her bachelor's degree in 1966; she would earn her teaching credentials the following year. In 1968 Kline got a job teaching in an elementary school in Richmond, California, where she remained for three years. She also married Rufus O. Kline, a local college teacher and writer; the couple would eventually have two daughters. In 1976 the Kline family moved to New England, and have made their home in Connecticut ever since.

Kline's first books for children were picture books. In 1984's *Shhhh!*, an energetic, chatty youngster lists all the people who tell her to pipe down during the day, until she tiptoes out of doors to make all the noise she possibly can before she settles down to being quiet again. "Delightful," lauds *School Library Journal* contributor Lisa Redd, "a situation common to all children." *Don't Touch!* finds young Dan similarly reprimanded: sharp edges, hot pans, wet paint, and the like are barriers to his curiosity. Finally, he gets hold of some modelling clay, which he can touch to his heart's content in this picture book that Joan McGrath noted in *School Library Journal* should be "satisfying to kids who are constantly admonished to keep hands off."

Kline introduced the first of her popular elementary-school characters in *Herbie Jones*. A reluctant reader, Herbie tries to get out of the "slow" class while finding that causing trouble seems to impress his peers. Finally, he sets his mind on his schoolwork, and his grades start to climb. *Booklist*'s Ilene Cooper offered a favorable assessment of Kline's "shrewd depictions of childhood concerns," and added: "a fine supporting cast of characters." *What's the Matter with Herbie Jones?* finds our young hero in a romantic muddle as he falls head over heels for Annabelle Louisa Hodgekiss. When his friends catch him reading poetry and being seen with a GIRL in public, they take swift—and humorous—action to save their comrade, in a book that Cooper of *Booklist* called "a fun read." Other books featuring the popular third-grader include *Herbie Jones and the Monster Ball*, called "another sure winner" by a *Publishers Weekly* reviewer, in which Herbie tries out for the local baseball team coached by his favorite uncle, and *Herbie Jones and the Dark Attic*, as Herbie, now a fourth grader, is bumped up to an attic bedroom—much to his dismay—when Grandpa comes for a long-term visit.

In *Horrible Harry in Room 2-B*, readers meet the impish Harry as seen through the eyes of his best friend, Doug. Dubbed "horrible" in a lighthearted way, Harry loves to play practical jokes, especially when they prompt screams of terror from second-grade girls. Kline illustrates each of Harry's antics in short chapters; in *Horrible Harry and the Green Slime*, he not only concocts some nasty green slime, but drapes the school

with spider webs and gets involved in other mischief, "[fitting] comfortably into the genre of light classroom realism" according to Betsy Hearne of *Bulletin of the Center for Children's Books*. *Horrible Harry's Secret* teams Harry with fellow classmate Song Lee, a Korean girl who has a water frog that eats liver—a sure-fire magnet for second-grade boys. But Harry is attracted to more than the frog; falling for Song Lee sends him into a tizzy. "Harry's appeal is that he's both 'gross' and vulnerable," according to *Booklist* contributor Hazel Rochman, who found Kline's classroom tales full of kid appeal. The antics in Room 2-B further unfold in *Song Lee and the Hamster Hunt*, as Song Lee brings yet another pet to school and someone leaves the cage open. "Amusing characterizations, snappy dialogue, and a happy ending" distinguish this book, according to a *Kirkus Reviews* critic. Commenting on *Horrible Harry and the Kickball Wedding*, Rochman states: "Grade-school teacher Kline evokes the farce of the classroom, and just a glimpse of the hurt, too." Although Song Lee is shy, her sensitivity to animals and troubled classmates in *Song Lee in Room 2B* prompts Maggie McEwen to remark in *School Library Journal* that "Kline has an exceptional talent for capturing the language, humor, and group dynamics of a primary-grade classroom."

Orville Rudemeyer Pygenski Jr. survives elementary school only with the use of a nickname, Orp. When he starts an "I hate my name" club during the summer vacation after sixth grade class, he realizes that he is not alone in wishing his parents had been a little less creative when he was born. In *Orp Goes to the Hoop*, the young teen decides that a good way to avoid chores is to join the middle school basketball team. Ultimately, he becomes one of the team's star players, balancing his new sport with a long-distance romance with a girl named Jenny Lee. "Something for older Matt Christopher fans," recommends a *Bulletin of the Center for Children's Books* contributor, "who have noticed girls." Orp's social life gets complicated in *Who's Orp's Girlfriend?* when two different girls at school catch his eye, while longtime pen-pal Jenny Lee announces that she is coming for a visit. "Kline's gentle humor, well-paced plot, and likeable characters" are "just right" for middle school readers, in the opinion of *Booklist* contributor Chris Sherman. *Orp and the FBI* tells of Orp and his private detective agency, Famous Bathtub Investigators (FBI), and his rival, sister Chloe's CIA (Chloe's Investigation Agency). "The plot develops smoothly ... the level of suspense is maintained," commented *School Library Journal* contributor Carol Torrance, who added: "A fun addition."

In addition to her series featuring school-aged boys, Kline has also delved into girls' experiences through the adventures of Mary Marony, a new second-grader at school. In *Mary Marony and the Snake*, Mary fears being teased because of her speech impediment—she stutters. Her fears are realized in at least one student—the mean Marvin Higgins, who makes her school day miserable. Fortunately, with the help of a speech teacher, Mary gets her stutter under control, and when she is the only one in her class brave enough to pick up a snake that has gotten loose in the classroom, Marvin's taunts can do little to tarnish her reputation among her classmates. "Any child who's been teased (that is, any child) will enjoy Mary's triumph," Roger Sutton asserted, while *School Library Journal* contributor Gale W. Sherman suggested: "Make room on the shelves for this one—young readers will love it." In the entertaining *Mary Marony Mummy Girl,* Halloween is around the corner and Mary wants to be a mummy—but where to find a costume? Without permission, she rips up her bedsheet, which works fine as a costume but makes her mom more than a little upset. Kline's spunky protagonist is "resourceful," dealing with both her stutter and "other challenges in a positive manner," maintained Elaine Lesh Morgan, describing the book in *School Library Journal. Mary Marony and the Chocolate Surprise,* hailed by Stephanie Zvirin of *Booklist* as "one of Kline's best," raises the moral question of whether cheating is always wrong.

In addition to her busy writing schedule and her teaching duties, Kline served between 1983-88 as the drama director at the elementary school where she teaches. "Each year we present a special, original play," she once told *Something about the Author (SATA).* "I write the script and lyrics, and a fellow teacher composes the music." She is also frequently invited to other teachers' schools, to talk about her books with young fans. "When I ... talk to students about writing, I always bring my bag of rejections (or No Thank You's as I tell primary children). I also bring my box of flops, the stories no one wanted. But I tell the students how I still save them and how some ideas can be reworked—even my third grade poem! The children know that the first book I got published was *not* the first story I wrote."

"Being a teacher is the most difficult job in the world," Kline recently told *SATA.* "At least twice a week I feel like going to an island and not returning to the classroom. But the truth is I wouldn't do anything else. I still love it. I know how hard my fellow teachers work, and how much they care about each student.

"Most of my stories have been inspired by the classroom, my family and my childhood. When I visit other schools, I try to encourage the students to carry a notebook, keep a diary and a scrapbook. Everyday life is full of stories if we just take the time to write them.

"I think I could go on forever writing about Herbie Jones and Horrible Harry and Song Lee. To me, these series are about family, friendships, and the classroom, three things that are so close to my heart. Most of all, I am blessed with a strong Christian faith, and that has made all the difference in my life." In addition to teaching and writing, the popular author conducts workshops for both teachers, students, and adults interested in writing for children.

■ Works Cited

Cooper, Ilene, review of *Herbie Jones, Booklist,* August, 1985, p. 1666.

Cooper, Ilene, review of *What's the Matter with Herbie Jones?, Booklist,* December 1, 1986, p. 579.

Cufari, Cheryl, review of *Herbie Jones and the Dark Attic, School Library Journal,* December, 1992, p. 85.

Hearne, Betsy, review of *Horrible Harry and the Green Slime, Bulletin of the Center for Children's Books,* May, 1989, p. 227.

Review of *Herbie Jones and the Monster Ball, Publishers Weekly,* September 9, 1988, p. 135.

McEwen, Maggie, review of *Song Lee in Room 2B, School Library Journal,* September, 1993, pp. 209-10.

McGrath, Joan, review of *Don't Touch!, School Library Journal,* February, 1986, p. 76.

Morgan, Elaine Lesh, review of *Mary Marony Mummy Girl, School Library Journal,* December, 1994, p. 77.

Review of *Orp Goes to the Hoop, Bulletin of the Center for Children's Books,* July-August, 1991, pp. 266-67.

Redd, Lisa, review of *Shhhh!, School Library Journal,* February, 1985, p. 66.

Rochman, Hazel, review of *Horrible Harry and the Kickball Wedding, Booklist,* October 1, 1992, p. 327.

Rochman, Hazel, review of *Horrible Harry's Secret, Booklist,* December 1, 1990, p. 751.

Sherman, Chris, review of *Who's Orp's Girlfriend?, Booklist,* August, 1993, p. 2062.

Sherman, Gale W., review of *Mary Marony and the Snake, School Library Journal,* April, 1993, p. 98.

Review of *Song Lee and the Hamster Hunt, Kirkus Reviews,* July 15, 1994, p. 987.

Sutton, Roger, review of *Mary Marony and the Snake, Bulletin of the Center for Children's Books,* June, 1992, pp. 266-67.

Torrance, Carol, review of *Orp and the FBI, School Library Journal,* May, 1995, p. 108.

Zvirin, Stephanie, review of *Mary Marony and the Chocolate Surprise, Booklist,* December 1, 1995, p. 636.

■ For More Information See

PERIODICALS

Booklist, October 15, 1988, p. 410; November 1, 1988, p. 484; November 1, 1989, p. 553; July, 1991, p. 2048; July, 1992, p. 1941; November 15, 1994, pp. 601-02; April 15, 1995, p. 1500; April 1, 1997, p. 1334.

Bulletin of the Center for Children's Books, October, 1984, p. 29; December, 1985, pp. 70-71; December, 1986, pp. 70-71.

Kirkus Reviews, February 15, 1989, p. 295.

Publishers Weekly, October 30, 1987, p. 72; March 3, 1997, p. 76.

School Library Journal, March, 1988, p. 192; April, 1989, pp. 102-03; July, 1992, pp. 69-70; December, 1992, p. 85; July, 1993, p. 86; November, 1993, p. 85; September, 1994, p. 187; May, 1995, p. 108; December, 1995, p. 83.

KOGAWA, Joy (Nozomi) 1935-

■ Personal

Born June 6, 1935, in Vancouver, British Columbia, Canada; daughter of Gordon Goichi (a minister) and Lois (a kindergarten teacher; maiden name, Yao) Nakayama; married David Kogawa, May 2, 1957 (divorced, 1968); children: Gordon, Deidre. *Education:* Attended University of Alberta, 1954, Anglican Women's Training College, 1956, Conservatory of Music, 1956, and University of Saskatchewan, 1968.

■ Addresses

Home—845 Semlin Dr., Vancouver, British Columbia V5L 4J6, Canada.

■ Career

Office of the Prime Minister, Ottawa, Ontario, Canada, staff writer, 1974-76; freelance writer, 1976-78; University of Ottawa, writer in residence, 1978; freelance writer, 1978—. *Member:* League of Canadian Poets, Writers' Union of Canada, Order of Canada.

■ Awards, Honors

Books in Canada First Novel Award, 1981, Canadian Authors' Association Book of the Year Award, 1982, Before Columbus Foundation American Book Award, 1982, and American Library Association notable book citation, 1982, all for *Obasan;* Periodical Distributors Best Paperback Fiction Award, 1983.

■ Writings

FICTION

Obasan, Lester and Orpen Dennys (Toronto, ON, Canada), 1981, David Godine (Boston, MA), 1982.
Naomi's Road (for children), illustrated by Matt Gould, Oxford University Press (Toronto), 1986.
Itsuka (sequel to *Obasan*), Viking Canada (Toronto), 1992, Anchor Books, 1994.
The Rain Ascends, Knopf Canada (Toronto), 1995.

POETRY

The Splintered Moon, University of New Brunswick (St. John), 1967.
A Choice of Dreams, McClelland & Stewart (Toronto), 1974.
Jericho Road, McClelland & Stewart, 1977.
Woman in the Woods, Mosaic Press (Oakville, Ontario), 1985.

OTHER

Author of introduction, *Special Treatment: The Untold Story of the Survival of Thousands of Jews in Hitler's Third Reich,* by Alan Abrams, Carol Publishing Group, 1985. Contributor of poems to magazines in the United States and Canada, including *Canadian Forum, West Coast Review, Queen's Quarterly, Quarry, Prism Inter-*

JOY KOGAWA

national, and *Chicago Review.* Kogawa's works have been translated into Japanese, French, and German.

■ Adaptations

Obasan was adapted as a sound recording by Crane Library (Vancouver), 1983, and by CNIB (Toronto), 1987, and was published in a large print edition by Albert Education (Calgary), 1991. *Naomi's Road* was adapted as a sound recording by CNIB, 1987, and by Crane Library, 1988; as a Braille edition by CNIB, 1987; and as a stage play by the Toronto Young People's Theatre. *Itsuka* was adapted as a sound recording by Library Services Branch (Vancouver), 1992.

■ Sidelights

Joy Kogawa is best known for the novel *Obasan,* a fictionalization of her own experiences as a Japanese-Canadian during World War II. She has adapted *Obasan* for children under the title *Naomi's Road.* Like *Obasan*'s narrator, Kogawa was torn from her family by government officials and exiled into a detention camp in the Canadian wilderness. Having received national acclaim for *Obasan,* she followed it up with the sequel, *Itsuka.* Kogawa is also a poet, having published her first book of poetry, *The Splintered Moon,* in 1967.

Obasan, Itsuka, and *Naomi's Road* are all based on the author's personal experience. Like the character of Naomi, Kogawa was exposed to both Eastern and Western folk tales at home. At school, however, she tried to deny her Japanese heritage as a means of dealing with the prejudice she encountered. She was an avid reader until World War II, when her family was forcibly removed from their comfortable home in Vancouver. They ended up living in a small shack in Slocan, British Columbia. There was no library in Slocan, and the only reading material available to Kogawa were the books she used in school. However, when Kogawa was ten the family relocated to Coaldale, Alberta, where the school had a small library of its own.

Before turning to fiction, Kogawa was a "seasoned poet," wrote Gurleen Grewal in *Feminist Writers*. Gary Willis wrote in *Studies in Canadian Literature* that Kogawa's first three volumes of poetry are filled with "lyric verse" and poems "expressing feelings that emerge from a narrative context that is only partly defined." Kogawa explained to Janice Williamson in *Sounding Differences: Conversations with 17 Canadian Women Writers* that her poems often arise out of her dreams: "The practice of poetry...," she says, "is the sweeping out of debris between the conscious and the unconscious."

Obasan was the first Canadian novel to deal with the internment of Canadian citizens of Japanese heritage. The novel focuses on 36-year-old Naomi. She and brother Stephen were separated from their loving parents during World War II. Their mother, visiting relatives in Japan, was not allowed to return to Canada, and their father was shipped to a labor camp. Naomi and Stephen were sent to a frontier town along with their Uncle Isamu and Aunt Obasan. When their parents never returned, the children were raised by their aunt and uncle in a house filled with silence. One of the mysteries of Naomi's childhood was the yearly pilgrimage to the Canadian prairie. As a child, Naomi continually asked, "Why do we come here every year?" As an adult, Naomi has lost the ability to communicate; as Kogawa writes, she is a victim of "the silence that will not speak."

Obasan explores Naomi's search for the answer to her childhood question and shows her long-awaited acknowledgment of, wrote Grewal, "life's imperative to heal." Urged by her Aunt Emily, an activist seeking justice for internment victims, Naomi relives her past, thus enabling her to learn about the secrets long held by her family. Naomi reviews documents about the Japanese internment to understand what happened to her and her family. At the end of the novel, she learns the truth that has been kept from her, that her mother suffered and died in Nagasaki, a victim of the "other holocaust," as Grewal calls it. Naomi, through her examination of the past and of the truth, at last is free and learns to speak again.

In 1986, five years after the initial publication of *Obasan*, Kogawa adapted the story for children as *Naomi's Road*. The author explains in an introductory note that the story takes place during World War II, when widespread fear of the Japanese resulted in North Americans of Japanese descent being sent to internment camps. She also reveals that Naomi's mother does not return because she is being detained in Japan.

The main text is in the first-person present, told by Naomi between the ages of five and nine. Thus the reader sees Naomi's life through her eyes. Her parents both leave home, and she cannot understand why they do not return. Then she and her brother are taken by their aunt from their home in Vancouver to an internment camp, and then to a farm in Alberta. Along the way, Naomi has a number of experiences, including befriending a Caucasian girl. Naomi is too young to know what an internment camp is, or why she is there. She is deeply hurt by the loss of her parents and by all her unanswered questions. However, because she does not grasp the concept of racism, she is never angry or bitter. She speaks to the reader from a place of sadness, confusion, and hope.

Reviewers appreciated the way *Naomi's Road* works as a children's book, while also noting an effect similar to that of *Obasan*. *Canadian Children's Literature* contributor Sandra Odegard praised the "changes in language and perspective as the child matures," which "will probably bind the young reader into a closer identification with Naomi." Judith Saltman commented in *Cana-*

JOY KOGAWA

OBASAN

"A tour de force, a deeply felt novel, brilliantly poetic in its sensibility."
— New York Times Book Review

In this award-winning novel, Kogawa fictionalizes her experiences as a Japanese-Canadian during World War II, when she was torn from her family by government officials and exiled to a detention camp in the Canadian wilderness.

dian Materials, "there is also a poet's instinct in the imagistic use of small objects and incidents that loom large in a child's life and symbolize significant emotions and perceptions." However, Roger Sutton maintained in *Bulletin of the Center for Children's Books* that he found the book's intended audience unclear—"the ironic overlays are too sophisticated for young children, and older ones will want more context and narrative structure."

Kogawa told *Canadian Children's Literature* interviewer Kathleen Donohue about the process of adapting *Obasan* for children. "It came out very fast," Kogawa said, "a chapter a day almost. It's the easiest thing I've ever written, just like walking down the street for me or getting on a bike. It's a very easy thing to think about little stories for children, because when I was a child I did that all the time. I was always telling stories to kids."

However, the actual planning of the book required more effort, as Kogawa described to Donohue. "In *Obasan,* Naomi's mother dies. I didn't think that would do for a children's book. There had to be a problem and a resolution. As I thought about that, I remembered the little blond girl in Slocan who is referred to in *Obasan.* It seemed to be a good idea to make friendship the main issue."

Itsuka is generally thought of as the sequel to *Obasan,* but Sandra Martin wrote in *Quill & Quire* that Kogawa is not so much writing a sequel as reclaiming themes and characters from *Obasan.* In *Itsuka,* Naomi goes to Toronto where she works on a multicultural journal and takes her first lover, Father Cedric, a French Canadian priest. With his help, Naomi turns to activism in her desire to win redress for the victims of Canada's internment policies. In *Itsuka,* the political and erotic plots become intertwined. The book, using a technique similar to that used in *Obasan,* closes with an apology from the Canadian government, in which it admits to instituting policies "influenced by discriminatory attitudes" toward Japanese Canadians and also to its own "unjust" actions.

Grewal maintained that *Itsuka* allows "the reader to witness Naomi's growth and personal fulfillment" and that it "openly bears the message of hope and trust implicit in *Obasan.*" Yet, Martin compared *Itsuka* unfavorably to the first novel, finding that "Kogawa seems too close to the partisan squabbling that accompanies any such [political] movement. She hasn't yet absorbed the facts and translated them into fiction." Janice Kulyk Keefer, writing in *Books in Canada,* admitted to "a certain disappointment" with the book, focusing on "the absence in *Itsuka* of the kind of poetically charged language and intensity of perception that give *Obasan* its extraordinary power and beauty." However, Keefer also realized that "it would be wrong to fault *Itsuka* for not being *Obasan Revisited.*" She wrote, "What Kogawa has done in her new novel is to move into a different kind of imaginative territory, exposing the politics of multiculturalism that has in many ways abetted rather than eradicated the racism

that she presents as an institutionalized aspect of Canadian life."

Kogawa turned back to poetry after the publication of her novels. The "insight found [in *Woman in the Woods*] is enlightening" wrote Frank Manley in *Books in Canada.* He also lauded its "passion for life" along with "its ability to say volumes with only a few words." These attributes are apparent in all of Kogawa's work. Martin wrote, "Through her poetry, her sublime novel *Obasan,* her children's story *Naomi's Road,* and now *Itsuka,* Kogawa has written poignantly about how innocent and loyal Japanese Canadians were stripped of their home and their possessions, interned, and dispersed." Grewal saw a more universal message in Kogawa's work: an emphasis on "compassion and arduous work of healing."

■ Works Cited

Grewal, Gurleen, *Feminist Writers,* St. James Press, 1996.

Keefer, Janice Kulyk, "A Celebration of Difference," *Books in Canada,* April 1992, p. 35.

Kogawa, Joy, *Obasan,* Lester and Orpen Dennys (Toronto), 1981.

Kogawa, Joy, *Itsuka,* Viking Canada (Toronto), 1992.

Kogawa, Joy, interview with Janice Williamson, *Sounding Differences: Conversations with 17 Canadian Women Writers,* University of Toronto Press, 1993.

Kogawa, Joy, interview with Kathleen Donohue, *Canadian Children's Literature,* No. 84, 1996, p. 35.

Manley, Frank, review of *Woman in the Woods, Books in Canada,* May, 1986, pp. 43-44.

Martin, Sandra, "Staking Out Literary Turf," *Quill & Quire,* March, 1992, p. 57.

Odegard, Sandra, review of *Naomi's Road, Canadian Children's Literature,* No. 49, 1988, pp. 51-53.

Saltman, Judith, review of *Naomi's Road, Canadian Materials,* March, 1988, p. 34.

Sutton, Roger, review of *Naomi's Road, Bulletin of the Center for Children's Books,* July-August, 1988, p. 232.

Willis, Gary, "Speaking the Silence: Joy Kogawa's *Obasan,*" *Studies in Canadian Literature,* Volume 12, number 2, 1987, pp. 239-249.

■ For More Information See

BOOKS

Cheung, King-Kok, *Articulate Silences: Hisaye Yamamoto, Maxine Hong Kingston, Joy Kogawa,* Cornell University Press (Ithaca, NY), 1993.

Contemporary Literary Criticism, Volume 78, Gale (Detroit), 1994.

Ling, Amy, and others, editors, *Reading the Literatures of Asian America,* Temple University Press (Philadelphia), 1992.

Pearlman, Mickey, editor, *Canadian Women Writing Fiction,* University Press of Mississippi (Jackson), 1993.

PERIODICALS

Booklist, January 1, 1994, p. 806.
Canadian Forum, February, 1982, pp. 39-40; December, 1992, p. 38.
Canadian Literature, summer, 1986, pp. 34-53; spring, 1988, pp. 58-66, 68-82; winter, 1990, pp. 41-57.
Feminist Studies, summer, 1990, pp. 288-312.
Los Angeles Times Book Review, July 11, 1982, p. 3.
Melus, fall, 1985, pp. 33-42.
New York Times Book Review, September 5, 1982; March 13, 1994, p. 18.
School Library Journal, May, 1988, p. 98.

*   *   *

KOSCIELNIAK, Bruce 1947-

■ Personal

Born July 9, 1947, in Adams, MA; son of Edwin and Irene Koscielniak. *Education:* Vesper George School of Art, Boston, MA, degree in commercial art, 1969; Williams College, B.A., 1975.

■ Addresses

Home—36 Summer St., Adams, MA 01220.

■ Career

Writer and illustrator. Former clerk, U.S. Postal Service, Adams, MA. *Military service:* U.S. Army, 1969-71.

■ Writings

FOR CHILDREN; SELF-ILLUSTRATED

Hector and Prudence, Knopf, 1990.
Hector and Prudence—All Aboard!, Knopf, 1990.
Euclid Bunny Delivers the Mail, Knopf, 1991.
Bear and Bunny Grow Tomatoes, Knopf, 1993.
Geoffrey Groundhog Predicts the Weather, Houghton, 1995.
Hear, Hear, Mr. Shakespeare: Story, Illustrations, & Selections from Shakespeare's Plays, Houghton, 1998.

ILLUSTRATOR

David Fair, *The Fabulous Four Skunks,* Houghton, 1996.

■ Sidelights

Writer and illustrator Bruce Koscielniak has produced a number of books, mostly for preschoolers and readers in the early grades. His characters are usually animals, and include the pigs Hector and Prudence, the mailman Euclid Bunny, the farmers Bear and Bunny, and the self-styled weatherman Geoffrey Groundhog.

Koscielniak's own experience is probably most akin to that of Euclid Bunny. For years until he became a full-time author and illustrator, Koscielniak worked for the United States Postal Service, and before that he served a two-year stint in the U.S. Army during the Vietnam War. By the late 1990s, however, his writing had given him a degree of freedom which made it possible to spend part of each year in Las Vegas and part of it in his native Adams, Massachusetts.

Hence Koscielniak was reliving elements of his own experience when he wrote *Euclid Bunny Delivers the Mail.* In the story, written for preschoolers and first-graders, all of the chickens who normally deliver the barnyard mail are sick with the flu. Bernie Bear, the postmaster, needs a replacement, so he calls the Euclid Bunny Speedy Delivery Service. Unfortunately, Euclid Bunny's service turns out to be a little too speedy. It takes him just 20 minutes to deliver all the mail, but he gets all the addresses wrong, and takes every single letter and package to the wrong animal. The story is filled with amusing mishaps, until Euclid is asked to take the place of the most famous bunny of all: the Easter Bunny.

Hector and Prudence centers on pigs rather than bunnies. The story is written for a slightly older group of readers than *Euclid Bunny,* and the subject matter is a bit more mature. Hector and Prudence are a married couple, and at the beginning of the story, Hector thinks Prudence is acting strangely because she no longer wants to wallow in the mud, but desires a proper house for the two of them. The reason behind her sudden determination soon becomes apparent when Hector realizes that Prudence is pregnant. After their six little piglets arrive,

BRUCE KOSCIELNIAK

Koscielniak provides the humorous illustrations for David Fair's tale of four smelly skunks who find they must provide clothespins for their audience in order to succeed as a rock band. (From *The Fabulous Four Skunks.*)

the couple's life changes dramatically, and at the end of each day, they are worn out from caring for their new family. One scene noted by reviewers in *Publishers Weekly* and *School Library Journal* finds Harold and Prudence, exhausted after a long day, resting in a pair of lawn chairs under the night sky; unknown to them, their children are sneaking out of their upstairs bedroom by means of a rope-ladder made from bedsheets. The *Publishers Weekly* commentator praised Koscielniak's "rambunctious, jolly illustrations," adding that "children and parents alike will find his understated wit hard to resist."

Koscielniak followed his first Hector and Prudence book with *Hector and Prudence—All Aboard!* This time it's Christmas, and Hector and Prudence present their children with a special present: a magical toy train which takes them on a mysterious journey. *Booklist* reviewer Ilene Cooper commented: "There's a lot going on in [Koscielniak's] ink-and-watercolor art as the train travels through forests, tunnels, and over bridges, often with near disastrous results."

Animal characters appear once again in *Bear and Bunny Grow Tomatoes,* written for preschoolers and primary graders. As a reviewer in *Publishers Weekly* pointed out, the story is related to that of "The Ant and the Grasshopper." In the original fable, the ant labors to provide for the future, while the grasshopper never thinks about tomorrow. Bear is the equivalent of the ant, planting and tending his field with care; and Bunny is more like the grasshopper, recklessly throwing his seeds onto the ground and running off to play when it's time to weed and water the crop. Naturally, when harvest time comes, Bear has plenty to show for his efforts, whereas Bunny can't even find his tomatoes. In the end, of course, Bear shares some of his abundant crop with Bunny. "Far from being a tiresome exercise in

preparedness," the *Publishers Weekly* critic commented, "Koscielniak imbues his story with touches of gentle humor that make the characters and their goofy antics quite irresistible."

Like the first Hector and Prudence book, *Geoffrey Groundhog Predicts the Weather* involves a grown-up theme. The title character's mother has taught him how to predict the weather as groundhogs do, and one February 2 he burrows out of his hole and makes a forecast that turns out to be accurate. This attracts the attention of the local paper, and Geoffrey Groundhog becomes something of a celebrity. Hence on the next February 2, his burrow is surrounded by well-wishers— and by reporters. In fact, the lights of the TV cameras are so strong that Geoffrey can't see whether or not he has a shadow. Finally he seeks assistance from his mother, who helps him make the right prediction.

Several reviewers observed that while children would enjoy the story of Geoffrey Groundhog's triumph, grownups are more apt to appreciate the portrayal of the media feeding frenzy that surrounds the celebrity groundhog. A *Publishers Weekly* commentator re-marked favorably on Koscielniak's "subdued palette of olive greens, browns, and other wintry hues," while *School Library Journal* contributor Tana Elias men-tioned his "energetic watercolor and pen drawings." Elizabeth Bush of the *Bulletin of the Center for Chil-dren's Books* noted that "Koscielniak's snappy line-and-watercolor cartoons cleverly spoof the annual hoopla at Punxsutawney, PA."

Koscielniak's skill as an illustrator also attracted notice in reviews of *The Fabulous Four Skunks,* a story written by David Fair. For young children, the book depicts a group of skunks who form a rock band: when their manager tells them "You stink," he means it literally.

Booklist reviewer Ilene Cooper observed that Koscielniak, with his illustrations, "highlights every bit of humor in the text and adds some of his own." In the words of *School Library Journal* contributor Lisa S. Murphy, "Koscielniak's humorous, cartoon-style illustrations invite individual browsing."

■ Works Cited

Review of *Bear and Bunny Grow Tomatoes, Publishers Weekly,* May 10, 1993, p. 71.

Cooper, Ilene, review of *Hector and Prudence—All Aboard!, Booklist,* November 1, 1990, p. 527.

Cooper, Ilene, review of *The Fabulous Four Skunks, Booklist,* February 1, 1996, p. 937.

Elias, Tana, review of *Geoffrey Groundhog Predicts the Weather, School Library Journal,* October, 1995, p. 105.

Review of *The Fabulous Four Skunks, Publishers Weekly,* January 15, 1996, p. 461.

Fader, Ellen, review of *Hector and Prudence, School Library Journal,* August, 1990, p. 132.

Review of *Geoffrey Groundhog Predicts the Weather, Bulletin of the Center for Children's Books,* November, 1995, pp. 95-96.

Review of *Geoffrey Groundhog Predicts the Weather, Publishers Weekly,* August 21, 1995, p. 65.

Review of *Hector and Prudence, Publishers Weekly,* April 13, 1990, p. 62.

Murphy, Lisa S., review of *The Fabulous Four Skunks, School Library Journal,* April, 1996, p. 108.

■ For More Information See

PERIODICALS

Booklist, October 15, 1995, p. 411-12.

Kirkus Reviews, September 1, 1990, p. 1258; January 1, 1991, p. 53; March 15, 1998, p. 406.

Publishers Weekly, January 11, 1991, p. 100; May 10, 1993, p. 71; April 6, 1998, p. 77.

School Library Journal, October, 1990, p. 37; May, 1991, p. 80; May, 1998, p. 118.

—Sketch by Judson Knight

*   *   *

KRONIUK, Lisa
See BERTON, Pierre (Francis DeMarigny)

L

Le GUIN, Ursula K(roeber) 1929-

■ Personal

Surname pronounced "luh-gwin"; born October 21, 1929, in Berkeley, CA; daughter of Alfred L. (an anthropologist) and Theodora Covel Brown (a writer; maiden name, Kracaw) Kroeber; married Charles Alfred Le Guin (a historian), December 22, 1953; children: Elisabeth, Caroline, Theodore. *Education:* Radcliffe College, A.B., 1951; Columbia University, A.M., 1952.

■ Addresses

Home—Portland, OR. *Agent*—Virginia Kidd, 538 East Harford St., Milford, PA 18337. *Dramatic Agent*—Matthew Bialer, William Morris Agency, Inc., 1325 Avenue of the Americas, New York, NY 10019. *Speakers Bureau*—Quest, 9 Meriam St., Lexington, MA 02173.

■ Career

Writer and educator. Part-time instructor in French at Mercer University, 1954-55, and University of Idaho, 1956; Emory University, department secretary, 1955; visiting lecturer and writer in residence at various locations, including Clarion West, Pacific University, Portland State University, University of California, San Diego, University of Reading, Kenyon College, Tulane University, Indiana University Writers Conference, Bennington Writing Program, Beloit, Flight of the Mind, Stanford, and First Australian Workshop in Speculative Fiction; guest of honor at science fiction conventions, including World Science Fiction Convention, 1975. Creative consultant for Public Broadcasting Service for television production of *The Lathe of Heaven,* 1979. *Member:* Authors League of America, Writers Guild, PEN, Science Fiction Research Association, Science Fiction and Fantasy Writers of America, Science Fiction Poetry Association, Writers Guild West, Amnesty International of the USA, National Abortion Rights Action League, National Organization for Women, Nature Conservancy, Planned Parenthood Federa-

tion of America, Women's International League for Peace and Freedom, Phi Beta Kappa.

■ Awards, Honors

Fulbright fellowship, 1953; *Boston Globe-Horn Book Award,* 1968, Lewis Carroll Shelf Award, 1979, *Horn Book* honor list citation, and American Library Association Notable Book citation, all for *A Wizard of Earthsea;* Nebula Award nomination for best novelette, Science Fiction Writers of America (now Science Fiction and Fantasy Writers of America), 1969, for "Nine Lives"; Nebula Award and Hugo Award, International Science Fiction Association, both for best novel, 1970, for *The Left Hand of Darkness;* Nebula Award nomination, 1971, and Hugo Award nomination and *Locus* Award, both 1973, all for best novel, for *The Lathe of Heaven;* Newbery Silver Medal Award and finalist for National Book Award for Children's Literature, both 1972, and American Library Association Notable Book citation, all for *The Tombs of Atuan;* Child Study Association of America's Children's Books of the Year citation, Junior Library Guild selection, 1972, and National Book Award for Children's Books, 1973, all for *The Farthest Shore;* Nebula Award nomination, 1972, and Hugo Award, 1973, both for best novella, for *The Word for World Is Forest;* Hugo Award for best short story, 1974, for "The Ones Who Walk Away from Omelas"; American Library Association's Best Young Adult Books citation, 1974, Hugo Award, Nebula Award, and Jupiter Award, all for best novel, 1975, and Jules Verne Award, 1975, all for *The Dispossessed: An Ambiguous Utopia;* Nebula Award and Jupiter Award, both for best short story, 1975, for "The Day before the Revolution"; Nebula Award nomination for best novelette, 1975, for "The New Atlantis"; Nebula Award nomination for best novelette and Jupiter Award, both 1976, both for "The Diary of the Rose"; National Book Award finalist, American Library Association's Best Young Adult Books citation, Child Study Association of America's Children's Books of the Year citation, and *Horn Book* honor list citation, all 1976, and Prix Lectures-Jeunesse, 1987, all for *Very Far Away from Anywhere Else;*

Gandalf Award (Grand Master of Fantasy) nomination, 1978; D.Litt., Bucknell University, 1978, and Lawrence University, 1979; Gandalf Award, 1979; Balrog Award nomination for best poet, 1979; Nebula Award nomination for best novelette, 1979, for "The Pathways of Desire"; D.H.L., Lewis and Clark College, 1983, and Occidental College, 1985; *Locus* Award, 1984, for *The Compass Rose;* American Book Award nomination, 1985, and Janet Heidinger Kafka Prize for Fiction, University of Rochester English Department and Writer's Workshop, 1986, both for *Always Coming Home;* Nebula Award nomination, 1987, and Hugo Award 1988, for *Buffalo Gals, Won't You Come Out Tonight;* Nebula Award nomination, 1990, for "The Shobies' Story"; Nebula Award for best novel, 1991, for *Tehanu: The Last Book of Earthsea;* Pushcart Prize, 1991, for "Bill Weisler"; Harold Vursell Award, American Academy and Institute of Arts & Letters, 1991; H. L. Davis Award, Oregon Institute of Literary Arts, 1992, for *Searoad; Hubbab* Annual Poetry Award, 1995, for "Semen"; Nebula Award nomination for best novelette, 1994, and James Tiptree Award, 1995, for "The Matter of Seggri"; Nebula Award nomination for best novella, 1994, *Locus* Readers Award, Asimov Readers Award, and Sturgeon Award, 1995, all for "Forgiveness Day"; Nebula Award, 1996, for "Solitude"; Tiptree Retrospective Award, 1996, for *The Left Hand of Darkness;*

Readers Award, *Locus* Magazine, 1996, for *Four Ways to Forgiveness;* Pulitzer Prize nomination, 1997, for *Unlocking the Air;* Tiptree Award, 1997, for "Mountain Ways."

■ Writings

"EARTHSEA" BOOKS; FANTASY NOVELS; FOR YOUNG ADULTS

A Wizard of Earthsea, illustrated by Ruth Robbins, Parnassus Press (Berkeley, CA), 1968.

The Tombs of Atuan, illustrated by Gail Garraty, Atheneum (New York City), 1971.

The Farthest Shore, illustrated by Garraty, Atheneum, 1972.

Earthsea (omnibus; contains *A Wizard of Earthsea, The Tombs of Atuan,* and *The Farthest Shore*), Gollancz, 1977, published as *The Earthsea Trilogy,* Penguin (London), 1979.

Tehanu: The Last Book of Earthsea, Atheneum, 1990, Bantam (New York), 1991.

REALISTIC FICTION AND FANTASY NOVELS

Very Far Away from Anywhere Else, Atheneum, 1976, published in England as *A Very Long Way from Anywhere Else,* Gollancz (London), 1976.

The Beginning Place, Harper, 1980, published in England as *Threshold,* Gollancz, 1980.

FOR CHILDREN

"CATWINGS" SERIES; FANTASIES

Catwings, illustrated by S. D. Schindler, Orchard Books (New York City), 1988.

Catwings Return, illustrated by Schindler, Orchard Books, 1989.

Wonderful Alexander and the Catwings, illustrated by Schindler, Orchard Books, 1994.

STORIES AND PICTURE BOOKS

Solomon Leviathan's Nine Hundred and Thirty-First Trip around the World (picture book; originally published in collection *Puffin's Pleasures*), illustrated by Alicia Austin, Puffin, 1976, Cheap Street (New Castle, VA), 1983.

Leese Webster, illustrated by James Brunsman, Atheneum, 1979, Gollancz (London), 1981.

The Adventures of Cobbler's Rune, illustrated by Alicia Austin, Cheap Street, 1982.

Adventures in Kroy, Cheap Street, 1982.

A Visit from Dr. Katz (picture book), illustrated by Ann Barrow, Atheneum, 1988, published as *Dr. Katz,* Collins (London), 1988.

Fire and Stone (picture book), illustrated by Laura Marshall, Atheneum, 1989.

Fish Soup (picture book), illustrated by Patrick Wynne, Atheneum, 1992.

A Ride on the Red Mare's Back (picture book), illustrated with paintings by Julie Downing, Orchard Books, 1992.

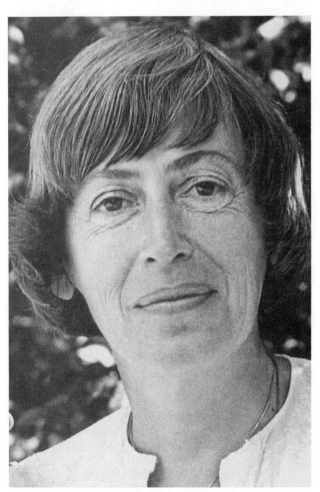

URSULA K. Le GUIN

NOVELS; FOR ADULTS

Rocannon's World (bound with *The Kar-Chee Reign* by Avram Davidson; also see below), Ace Books (New York City), 1966.

Planet of Exile (bound with *Mankind under the Leash* by Thomas M. Disch; also see below), Ace Books, 1966.

City of Illusions (also see below), Ace Books, 1967.

Three Hainish Novels (contains *Rocannon's World, Planet of Exile,* and *City of Illusions*), Doubleday (New York City), 1967.

The Left Hand of Darkness, Walker (New York City), 1969, with new afterword and appendixes by author, 1994.

The Lathe of Heaven, Scribner (New York City), 1971.

The Dispossessed: An Ambiguous Utopia, Harper (New York City), 1974.

Malafrena, Putnam (New York City), 1979.

The Eye of the Heron, and Other Stories (includes a novella originally published in collection *Millennial Women;* also see below), Panther, 1980, Harper, 1983.

The Visionary: The Life Story of Flicker of the Serpentine (bound with *Wonders Hidden: Audubon's Early Years,* by Scott Russell Sanders), Capra (Santa Barbara, CA), 1984.

Always Coming Home (includes audiocassette of "Music and Poetry of the Kesh," with music by Todd Barton; also see below), illustrated by Margaret Chodos, diagrams by George Hersh, Harper, 1985, published without audiocassette, Bantam (New York City), 1986, Gollancz (London), 1986.

World of Exile and Illusion, St. Martin's Press, 1996.

POETRY

Wild Angels (collection of early works), Capra, 1975.

(With mother, Theodora K. Quinn) *Tillai and Tylissos,* Red Bull, 1979.

Torrey Pines Reserve (broadsheet), Lord John (Northridge, CA), 1980.

Hard Words, and Other Poems, Harper, 1981.

Gwilan's Harp, Lord John, 1981.

(With artist Henk Pander) *In the Red Zone,* Lord John, 1983.

Wild Oats and Fireweed, Harper, 1988.

Buffalo Gals, Won't You Come Out Tonight, illustrated by Susan Seddon Boulet, Pomegranate Artbooks (San Francisco, CA), 1994.

Going Out with Peacocks and Other Poems, HarperPerennial (New York City), 1994.

(With Diana Bellessi) *The Twins, The Dream: Two Voices / Las Gemelas, El Sueno: Dos Voces,* Arte Publico (Houston, TX), 1996.

OTHER

The Word for World Is Forest (novella; originally published in collection *Again, Dangerous Visions;* also see below), Berkley (New York City), 1972.

From Elfland to Poughkeepsie (lecture), introduction by Vonda N. McIntyre, Pendragon Press (Portland, OR), 1973.

The Wind's Twelve Quarters: Short Stories, Harper, 1975.

Dreams Must Explain Themselves (critical essays), Algol Press (New York City), 1975.

(With Gene Wolfe and James Tiptree, Jr.) *The New Atlantis and Other Novellas of Science Fiction,* edited by Robert Silverberg, Hawthorn Books (New York City), 1975.

Orsinian Tales (short stories), Harper, 1976, Gollancz (London), 1977.

The Water Is Wide (short story), Pendragon Press, 1976.

(With others) *The Altered I: An Encounter with Science Fiction* (includes Le Guin's play *No Use to Talk to Me*), edited by Lee Harding, Norstrilia Press (Melbourne, Australia), 1976.

(Editor) *Nebula Award Stories 11,* Gollancz, 1976, Harper, 1977.

The Language of the Night: Essays on Fantasy and Science Fiction (critical essays), edited by Susan Wood, Putnam, 1979, revised edition, edited by Le Guin, Women's Press, 1989.

(Editor with Virginia Kidd) *Interfaces: An Anthology of Speculative Fiction,* Ace Books, 1980.

(Editor with Kidd) *Edges: Thirteen New Tales from the Borderlands of the Imagination,* Pocket Books (New York City), 1980.

The Compass Rose (short stories), Harper, 1982, Gollancz (London), 1983.

King Dog: A Screenplay (bound with *Dostoevsky: The Screenplay,* by Raymond Carver and Tess Gallagher), Capra, 1985.

(With Barton) *Music and Poetry of the Kesh* (audiocassette), Valley Productions, 1985.

(With David Bedford) *Rigel Nine: An Audio Opera* (recording), Charisma, 1985.

(With composer Elinor Armer) *Uses of Music in Uttermost Parts* (music and text), first performed in part in San Francisco, CA, and Seattle, WA, 1986, 1987, and 1988.

Buffalo Gals and Other Animal Presences (short stories and poems), Capra, 1987, published as *Buffalo Gals,* Gollancz, 1990.

Dancing at the Edge of the World: Thoughts on Words, Women, Places (essays), Grove (New York City), 1989, Gollancz (London), 1989.

The Way of the Waters Going: Images of the Northern California Coastal Range, photographs by Ernest Waugh and Alan Nicolson, Harper, 1989.

Searoad: Chronicles of Klatsand (short stories), HarperCollins (New York City), 1991, Gollancz (London), 1992.

Myth and Archetype in Science Fiction, Pulphouse, 1991.

Talk about Writing, Pulphouse, 1991.

Blue Moon over Thurman Street, photographs by Roger Dorband, NewSage Press (Portland, OR), 1993.

Earthsea Revisioned (lecture), Children's Literature New England (Cambridge, MA), 1993.

The Ones Who Walk Away from Omelas (short story), Creative Education (Mankato, MN), 1993.

(Editor with Brian Attebery) *The Norton Book of Science Fiction: North American Science Fiction, 1960-1990,* Norton (New York City), 1993.

A Fisherman of the Inland Sea: Science Fiction Stories, HarperPrism (New York City), 1994.

Four Ways to Forgiveness (contains "Betrayals," "Forgiveness Day," "A Man of the People," and "A Woman's Liberation"), HarperPrism, 1995.
Unlocking the Air: And Other Stories (includes "Standing Ground," "Poacher," "Half Past Four," and "Limberlost"), HarperCollins, 1996.
(With J. P. Seaton) *Lao Tzu: Tao Teh Ching: A Book about the Way and the Power of the Way,* Shambhala, 1997.

Author of postcard short story, *Post Card Partnership,* 1975, and *Sword & Sorcery Annual,* 1975. Contributor to anthologies, including *Orbit 5,* 1969, *World's Best Science Fiction,* 1970, *The Best Science Fiction of the Year #5,* 1976, and *The Norton Anthology of Short Fiction,* 1978. Contributor of introductions to *A Home-Concealed Woman: The Diaries of Magnolia Wynn Le Guin, 1901-1913,* edited by husband Charles A. Le Guin, 1990, and the Oxford University Press edition of Mark Twain's *The Diaries of Adam and Eve (1904, 1906),* 1997. Contributor of short stories, novellas, essays, and reviews to numerous science fiction, scholarly, and popular periodicals, including *Amazing Science Fiction, Science-Fiction Studies, New Yorker, Antaeus, Parabola, New Republic, Redbook, Playboy, Playgirl, New Yorker, Western Humanities Review, Yale Review,* and *Omni.* Le Guin has made recordings of several of her works, including *The Ones Who Walk Away from Omelas* (includes excerpt from *The Left Hand of Darkness*), Alternate World, 1976, *Gwilan's Harp and Intracom,* Caedmon, 1977, and *The Left Hand of Darkness* (abridged recording), Warner Audio, 1985; an abridged version of *The Earthsea Trilogy* was made into a sound recording by Colophone, 1981; *The Word for World Is Forest* was made into a sound recording by Book of the Road, 1986. Le Guin has also provided the texts for "Lockerbones/Airbones," music by Elinor Armer, 1985, and "Wild Angels of the Open Hills," music by Joseph Schwantner, 1983. Le Guin's papers are housed in a permanent collection at the University of Oregon Library, Eugene.

■ **Adaptations**

The Lathe of Heaven was televised by the Public Broadcasting Service in 1979; *The Tombs of Atuan* was adapted as a filmstrip with record or audiocassette by Newbery Award Records, 1980; "The Ones Who Walk Away from Omelas" was performed as a drama with dance and music at the Portland Civic Theatre in 1981. *A Wizard of Earthsea, The Tombs of Atuan, The Farthest Shore,* and *The Beginning Place* were made into sound recordings in 1992.

■ **Work in Progress**

Two books of short stories, *Love Stories* and *Science Fiction Stories,* for HarperCollins.

■ **Sidelights**

Considered one of the most significant authors of science fiction and fantasy to have emerged in the twentieth century, Le Guin is recognized as a gifted and original writer whose works address essential themes about the human condition in prose noted for its beauty and clarity.

A prolific author of great range and variety, she has written novels, novellas, short stories, poetry, plays, essays, reviews, and texts for musical compositions and has also edited collections of science fiction; she directs her books, which she categorizes as science fiction, fantasy, realism, and magical realism, to children and young adults as well as to adults. Le Guin is regarded as a groundbreaking writer who brought sophisticated themes and literary craftsmanship to the genre of science fiction; in addition, she is credited for being the first female writer to have made a major contribution to the genre. In her works, Le Guin characteristically explores issues important to humanity, such as relationships, communication, the uses of power, the search for identity, and the acceptance of death. Since the 1970s, her works have incorporated a marked feminist perspec-

Using a blending of fiction and fable, visual art and music, Le Guin has created the world of the Kesh, a futuristic race of people living on the Northern Pacific coast. (Cover illustration by Chris Hopkins.)

tive—she has addressed topics with special relevance to women, such as abortion—and have also reflected a strong environmental consciousness. Le Guin is often credited as an exceptional maker of worlds; her books, which take place on earth, on different planets, and in settings outside of our universe, are acknowledged for the author's invention and attention to detail in her depiction of landscapes and societies. Her works also reflect Le Guin's fascination with myths, archetypes, and dreams, especially in her use of language and symbols. Most critics regard Le Guin as the creator of provocative, profound books that insightfully articulate the concerns of humanity in the context of imaginative literature. In a jacket note to Le Guin's short story collection *Searoad: Chronicles of Klatsand,* Carolyn Kizer called Le Guin "our wise woman, our seeress, a writer of rage and power," while Frank Allen of *Library Journal* named her "our foremost woman of letters in fantasy and science fiction." Theodore Sturgeon, writing in the *Los Angeles Times,* noted that "above all, in almost unearthly terms, Ursula Le Guin examines, attacks, unbuttons, takes down and exposes our notion of reality." In her *Reading for the Love of It,* Michele Landsberg called Le Guin "the leading writer of fantasy in North America," while Derek de Solla Price of the *New Republic* wrote that no writer "inside the field of science fiction or outside of it [has] done more to create a modern conscience."

Since the first publications of her adult science fiction and fantasy, young people have been drawn to Le Guin's writings. She has directed several of her works specifically to young people and younger children; in several of these books, Le Guin outlines some of the same themes she addresses in her novels and stories for adults. Le Guin is perhaps best known for a series of fantasy novels that were published and marketed for readers in the upper elementary grades through high school: the Earthsea Quartet, which is composed of *A Wizard of Earthsea, The Tombs of Atuan, The Farthest Shore,* and *Tehanu: The Last Book of Earthsea.* The novels, which delineate the life of their main protagonist, the wizard Ged, from youth to old age, are set on various locations in Earthsea, a rural archipelago complete with its own anthropology, geology, and language. A world that is both like and unlike our own, Earthsea is a land of forests, islands, and bodies of water that incorporates many nations and customs. Although Earthsea is governed by secular rulers, its real laws are made by a hierarchy of wizards, men whose inborn affinity for magic is augmented by disciplined study that teaches them to know, and, importantly, to be able to name, the essence of each person or thing in the world. The basis of the magic in Earthsea is, therefore, in language: in knowing the true name of someone or something, one has power and control. Due to this fact, true names are given only to the trusted. The magi of Earthsea are also responsible for keeping the balance or equilibrium of the world: since order is not imposed by a deity, the wizards and other powerful humans act or refrain from acting based on their insights into both the world and themselves. Thus, individual responsibility and the

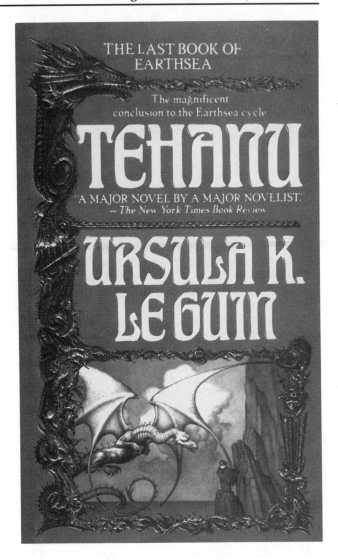

In the last volume of the "Earthsea" quartet, the priestess Tenar discovers that she is the one destined to succeed the noble mage Ged as savior of the kingdom. (Cover illustration by Ian Miller and John Jude Palencar.)

acceptance of oneself as both good and evil are pivotal qualities in maintaining the balance of Earthsea.

Le Guin depicts her wizards as artists, poets and shamans who devote themselves to retaining an integrated universe, a world in which light and darkness, life and death are equally acknowledged and revered. Throughout the quartet, Le Guin stresses the importance of self-knowledge through each stage of life, especially as it relates to the world. In the first three novels, Ged overcomes pride and fear and learns to accept himself and his own mortality as well as to love and trust others; as Archmage of Earthsea, he succeeds in laying the groundwork for a society based on justice and peace through his selfless and profoundly dangerous acts of will. In the fourth novel, Le Guin suggests that the responsibility for maintaining the equilibrium of the world, instead of belonging exclusively to male wizards such as Ged, whose final act as Archmage causes his loss of power, will henceforth be shared by women.

The Earthsea quartet is considered a major achievement as both fantasy literature and children's literature; in addition, the novels are often regarded as the best of Le Guin's oeuvre. Compared in stature to J. R. R. Tolkien's *The Lord of the Rings* and *The Chronicles of Narnia* by C. S. Lewis, the Earthsea books are generally considered works of genuine epic vision and depth that are good stories as well as moving, incisive examinations of basic human concerns such as achieving maturity, acknowledging individual responsibility and responsibility to others, learning to trust and love, and accepting death. The quartet also reflects Le Guin's integration of Eastern philosophy, especially Taoism; her use of Jungian archetypes; and her interest in cultures as diverse as medieval European and Native American. As a prose stylist, Le Guin invests the Earthsea books with rich, taut language that ranges from action-filled in the earlier titles to more meditative in the final volume; Michele Landsberg called Le Guin's prose in the series "vigorous, precise, clear, and sturdy enough to sustain a whole archipelago." The novels are often noted for their appeal to young readers: Le Guin provides her audience with a series of suspenseful adventures and magical events in an otherworldly setting while developing themes regarding coming of age and good versus evil, topics with which young people can identify; in addition, young adults are drawn to the characters, especially Ged, who faces crises successfully and finds the resources within himself to successfully complete his rite of passage.

Reviewers are generally captivated by the Earthsea Quartet, praising the novels for their intelligence, consistency, and sensitivity as well as for their emotional and psychological resonance. Writing in *Book World* about the first three volumes, Michael Dirda said, "Perhaps no modern work of fantasy has been more honored and loved than Ursula Le Guin's Earthsea trilogy. Though marketed as young-adult novels, [they] are as deeply imagined, as finely wrought, as grown-up, as any fiction of our time. They deserve the highest of all accolades: Everyone should read them"; in a later review in the same periodical, Dirda noted that the four Earthsea novels "are the finest juvenile fantasies of our time." Meredith Tax of the *Village Voice* claimed, "The *Earthsea* books are children's literature like the *Odyssey* and *Beowulf* are children's literature. Composed sparely and shaped by narratives so basic they must be inscribed upon our cells, they read as if they were not written but found, dug out like jewels from rock." Calling Le Guin "a prophet unhonored in her own country," Tax concluded, "Kid stuff? Sure, ... if children are the only ones who need stories that remind us of the firelight flickering on the walls of the cave." Writing in *English Journal* about the first three volumes, Richard Erlich commented that the highest art "is that which can entertain and instruct an entire culture. Le Guin's trilogy meets that criterion.... If it is 'kiddie lit,' well, 'The Tempest' is the world's greatest kid's show." In her essay on Le Guin in *Twentieth Century Children's Writers*, Jill Paton Walsh claimed, "No paraphrase of plot or setting can do justice to the profound originality of these books, which have been repeatedly imitated,

and always far exceed the imitation...."; the critic Fantastes of *Cambridge Review* noted, "Behind the brilliance of her books are some very subversive notions indeed." T. A. Shippey of the *Times Literary Supplement* concluded that the Earthsea books "challenge comparison with Virgil or Dante or James Frazer, exploring themes which can perhaps now only be treated outside realistic fiction, but doing so with the severity and power of modern rationalism.... [Le Guin] is an iconoclastic writer as much as a 'mythopoeic' one; but if ever myths were to come again, they would come from creations like her name-magery, her Shadowland."

"Mrs Le Guin," Shippey wrote, "is the daughter of famous anthropologists ... and the achievements of that science are embodied in her work." Le Guin herself noted, "My father studied real cultures and I make them up—in a way, it's the same thing." Born in Berkeley, California, to the noted anthropologist and educator Alfred Louis Kroeber and the writer Theodora Kroeber, Le Guin noted of her early life, "My father was a professor at the University of California at Berkeley, and our summer house ... was a gathering place for scientists, writers, students, and California Indians. Even though I didn't pay much attention, I heard a lot of interesting, grown-up conversation. What I did pay close attention to were tales. My father occasionally told

Using a magical wooden horse, a girl rescues her little brother after he is abducted by wicked trolls. (From *A Ride on the Red Mare's Back*, written by Le Guin and illustrated by Julie Downing.)

us stories around a fire; stories he had heard from Indians in their native language. He translated them into very impressive renditions of rolling skulls and other such horrifying things. My mother kept many collections of myths around the house. The ice and fire of Norse mythology were my special favorites and were much unlike the Greeks whose interests revolved around sex—so boring to me at the time.... The Norse, on the other hand, were always hitting each other with axes and so on—much more up a kid's alley, I would say." Le Guin began writing poetry at five and then graduated to stories, mostly fantasy and science fiction. "I wrote my first story at the age of nine," she noted, "about a man persecuted by invisible evil elves. Speculative fiction. My parents encouraged anything we did and took us seriously." She continued, "My closest brother and I used to save our quarters to buy *Astounding Stories*. We'd laugh a lot over the stories, because most of them were junk. At twelve I submitted one of my science fiction pieces to them only to have it promptly rejected. It was all right with me. It was junk. At least I had a real rejection slip to show for it."

As a child, Le Guin said, "I read everything I could—no holds barred." She was especially drawn to Celtic and Teutonic lore as well as to such authors as Hans Christian Andersen, Padraic Colum, and her main inspiration J. R. R. Tolkien, a writer to whom she is often compared. Le Guin was also inspired by the anthropological views of Sir James Frazer, whose study of the development of religion and folklore, *The Golden Bough,* first thrilled her as a child when she discovered a juvenile adaptation written by Frazer's wife and Bronislaw Malinowski. Another major influence was the Irish writer Lord Dunsany: "I was very impressed by the age of twelve," she commented, "with the 'Inner Lands' of Toldees, Mondath, and Arizim, bounded to the east by desert, to the south by magic, to the west by a mountain, and to the north by the polar wind in Lord Dunsany's *A Dreamer's Tale.* In spite of my familiarity with legends and myths, Dunsany came to me as a revelation." She continued, "What I hadn't realized, I guess, is that people were still making up myths. One made up stories oneself, of course; but here was a grownup doing it, for grownups, without a single apology to common sense, without an explanation, just dropping us straight into the Inner Lands. Whatever the reason, the moment was decisive. I had discovered my native country."

While they express definite humanistic values, the Earthsea books and several of Le Guin's other works have often been acknowledged for their independence from traditional Christian beliefs. Le Guin, who has described herself as an "unconsistent Taoist and a consistent unChristian," has been accused by fundamentalist groups of advocating foreign religions. She once commented about the influence of her background: "My father was a cultural relativist. He had been brought up in the Ethical Culture movement in New York in the late nineteenth century, which was a nonreligious but, as the title implies, highly moral system of thought. I was brought up in an unreligious household; there was no religious practice of any kind.

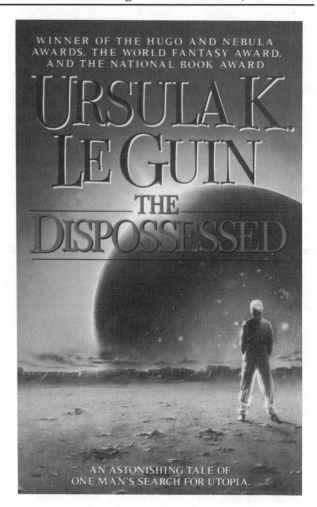

Shevek, a gifted physicist, risks everything to shatter the isolation of his planet from the rest of the universe in Le Guin's science fiction novel. (Cover illustration by Danilo Ducak.)

There was also no feeling that any religion was better than another, or worse; they just weren't part of our life.... Not having been brought up with a religion gives me a slightly different viewpoint, I realize, from a great many people. I look at Christianity not in any way as belonging to it, not in any way against it." As a child, Le Guin discovered the *Tao te ching* by Lao Tse. She remembered, "It was one of the books in my house when I was a kid. And it answered my need. It's a very quiet way of looking at the world which was developed at a time of great trouble and stress in China, rather like the twentieth century here.... Without being a religion, it has a lot of feeling in it, and it allows for being very much in tune with nature, which is very important to me. It seemed to fit my bill, and I love the poetry in it, too; it's paradoxical and ironic."

After graduating from high school, Le Guin attended Radcliffe College in Massachusetts, where, she said, "I received an excellent education.... Though Harvard and Radcliffe were far from coed at the time, women students were essentially attending Harvard classes." Although she claimed that she is "grateful to Harvard/ Radcliffe for a splendid education," Le Guin added that she has had "to *unlearn* a great deal of what I learned there. We were taught a sense of being *better* than other people. And yet, girls were taught to think that they were not as valuable as boys. I've had to fight against both these attitudes in myself—one is so easily influenced and malleable at eighteen." In 1951, Le Guin received her bachelor's degree in French from Radcliffe, graduating Phi Beta Kappa. "I never thought I wanted to be a writer," she noted, adding, "I always thought I was one. The big question was how could I earn a living at it? My father wisely suggested I get some training in a money-making skill so that I would not have to live off my writing.... With this in mind, I decided to work toward a higher degree in Romance languages and teach."

In 1953, Le Guin received her master's degree from Columbia University, again graduating Phi Beta Kappa. After starting on her Ph.D. in French and Italian Renaissance Literature, she received a Fulbright Fellowship to France. En route aboard the Queen Mary, she met Charles Le Guin and had a shipboard romance; the couple married six months later. After returning to the United States, Charles Le Guin finished his doctorate in history at Emory University in Atlanta while Ursula, deciding against getting her doctorate, taught French, worked at part-time jobs, and continued the serious writing she had begun two years earlier. Over the next eight years, she published poetry and wrote five unpublished novels, four of them about Orsinia, an imaginary country in central Europe. Then she discovered science fiction: "When I became aware of Philip K. Dick, Cordwainer Smith and other science fiction writers," she said, "I thought to myself, 'Hey, this stuff is just as crazy as what I'm doing.' I knew where my work might fit in." After selling a short story to the pulp magazine *Fantastic,* she was on her way.

After the publication of her first science fiction novel, *Rocannon's World,* a work that blends elements from both science fiction and fantasy, Le Guin determined to, as she wrote, keep "pushing at my own limitations and at the limits of science fiction. That is what the practice of art is, you keep looking for the outside edge. When you find it you make it a whole, solid, real, and beautiful thing; anything less is incomplete." With the publication of *A Wizard of Earthsea* in 1968 and her adult novel *The Left Hand of Darkness*—a work that explores the differences between the sexes in the context of science fiction—in 1969, Le Guin claimed that she "finally got my pure fantasy vein separated from my science fiction vein ... and the separation marked a large advance in both skill and content. Since then I have gone on writing, as it were, with both the left and right hands; and it has been a matter of keeping on pushing out towards the limits—my own and that of the medium."

In her book *Dreams Must Explain Themselves,* Le Guin explained, "I did not deliberately invent Earthsea. I am not an engineer, but an explorer. I discovered Earthsea." In 1964, Le Guin submitted a story to *Fantastic* magazine called "The Word of Unbinding," which had a wizard as its main character; soon after, *Fantastic*

published "The Rule of Names," a story in which the author developed the island setting and the rules of magic that she introduced in her first story. A few years later, Le Guin wrote a longer unpublished story about a prince who travels through the archipelago of the earlier stories in search of the Ultimate. In 1967, the publisher of Parnassus Press, Herman Schein, asked Le Guin to write a book directed to the young adult audience, a request that led the author to reconsider her ideas about wizards. In her essay in *Dreams Must Explain Themselves,* Le Guin remembered that she asked herself, "What were they before they had white beards? How did they learn what is obviously an erudite and dangerous art? Are there colleges for young wizards.... And so on." After drawing a map of Earthsea, she named her characters and islands. "People often ask me," she wrote, "how I think of names in fantasies, and again I have to answer that I find them, that I hear them. This is an important subject in this context." She added, "For me, as for the wizards, to know the name of an island or a character is to know the island or the person.... This implies a good deal about the 'meaning' of the trilogy, and about me. The trilogy is, in one aspect, about the artist. The artist as magician. The Trickster. Prospero. That is the only truly allegorical aspect it has of which I am conscious.... Wizardry is artistry. The trilogy is then, in this sense, about art, the creative experience, the creative process. There is always this circularity in fantasy. The snake devours its tail. Dreams must explain themselves."

The first volume of the quartet, *A Wizard of Earthsea,* is considered a classic story of coming of age as well as the most popular book of the series. In it, Le Guin describes how Sparrowhawk, a richly gifted but impetuous student of magic, unleashes an evil shadow through hubris; when the boy confronts the shadow, they call each other by the same name—Ged, Sparrowhawk's true name— and he and the shadow become one. Through this act, Ged is made whole, thus beginning his preparation to become Archmage of Earthsea; in addition, he has restored balance to the world. In her essay in *Dreams Must Explain Themselves,* Le Guin wrote that the "most childish thing about *A Wizard of Earthsea,* I expect, is its subject: coming of age. Coming of age is a process that took me many years; I finished it, so far as I ever will, at about age 31; and so I feel rather deeply about it. So do most adolescents. It's their main occupation, in fact." Reviewers were almost uniformly enthusiastic about *A Wizard of Earthsea.* In her review in *Horn Book,* Ruth Hill Viguers said that it "is wholly original, but has the conviction of a tale told by a writer whose roots are deep in great literature of many kinds, including traditional lore and fantasy.... Unusual allegory or exciting quest, it is an unforgettable and a distinguished book." A critic in the *Times Literary Supplement* noted that a survey of the outstanding books for the young of the last forty years "will reveal that almost all have drawn on the extra dimension of magic or fantasy—Tolkien, White, Lewis, Pearce, Garner, Hoban and the rest.... To find one novel a year to join the first group noted above is as much or more than one may expect, but there seems little doubt that *A*

Wizard of Earthsea is the likeliest candidate that we have had for some time; if a book as remarkable as this turns up in the next twelve months, we shall be fortunate indeed." Writing in *Crosscurrents of Criticism: Horn Book Essays 1968-1977*, Eleanor Cameron concluded that *A Wizard of Earthsea* "is a work which, though it is fantasy, continually returns us to the world about us, its forces and powers; returns us to ourselves, to our own struggles and aspirations, to the very core of human responsibility."

The next Earthsea book, *The Tombs of Atuan*, examines feminine coming of age as it describes the rite of passage of fifteen-year-old Arha, who has been hailed as the reincarnation of the Priestess of the Tombs of Atuan. At the age of five, Arha was taken away from her parents and placed in a desert environment where death is worshipped and no men are allowed. Arha, who is in her apprenticeship as priestess, encounters Ged in a lightless underground labyrinth, where he is seeking the lost half of an ancient ring that contains a lost rune of wholeness; once the two halves of the ring are joined, order can be restored to Earthsea. Since Ged has defiled a holy place, it is Arha's duty to have him put to death. However, the girl—who holds the other half of the silver ring—pities the wizard and saves his life; in return, Ged convinces Arha to renounce the darkness and choose freedom and liberation. He tells the girl her real name, Tenar, and entrusts her with the restored ring. After Tenar and Ged escape, an earthquake swallows the tombs and the labyrinth, which ends the worship of death and allows the kingdoms of the world to reunite. *The Tombs of Atuan* is regarded as both an account of religious experience and an exploration of adolescent sexuality; in addition, reviewers have noted the lesson that Ged receives—"the necessity of mutuality," in the words of Francis J. Molson in *Twentieth Century Children's Writers*. In her book *Dreams Must Explain Themselves*, Le Guin said, "The subject of *The Tombs of Atuan* is, if I had to put it in one word, sex.... [The] symbols can all be read as sexual. More exactly, you could call it a feminist coming of age. Birth, rebirth, destruction, freedom are the themes." Writing in *Horn Book*, Paul Heins noted that the storytelling in *The Tombs of Atuan* "is so good and the narrative pace so swift that a young reader may have to think twice before realizing that the adventures that befell Tenar were really the experiences that marked the growth of her personality.... Atuan, like Earthsea, is located in the mind of its maker, but was created out of the very stuff of mythology and reflects universal patterns that were once embodied in Stonehenge and in the Cretan labyrinth." Aidan Warlow of *School Librarian* called *The Tombs of Atuan* "a cold, colourless, humourless novel whose rather formal style and slowly unfolding plot make considerable demands on the young reader. But, for those who can manage it, this is very powerful stuff." Writing in *Book World*, Virginia Haviland concluded, "Children who love the strange will indeed revel in the drama of Ged's unlikely survival and the awesome aspects of the vast underworld—and will find them unforgettable."

Le Guin ends *The Tombs of Atuan* with the hope that Earthsea might be united under its true king; in the third volume of the quartet, *The Farthest Shore,* Ged guides teenage Arren, the future king of Earthsea, on a quest to discover the source of the evil that is demoralizing the archipelago. The wizard and the prince journey to an island peopled by the walking, silent dead, where a former classmate of Ged's has achieved a macabre immortality. In order to restore death to its rightful place in the universe, Ged heals the crack in the fabric of the world that has been caused by the crazed wizard; however, the difficulty of the task causes Ged to lose all of his mage power. Through his apprenticeship with Ged, Arren comes to understand his role in keeping the balance of the universe and accepts his position as Earthsea's governor, thus fulfilling the prophecy of the coming of a great king who restores peace to Earthsea. In her *Dreams Must Explain Themselves,* Le Guin wrote, "*The Farthest Shore* is about death. That's why it is a less well-built, less sound and complete book than the others. They were about things I had already lived through and survived.... It seemed an absolutely suitable subject to me for young readers, since in a way one can say that the hour when a child realizes, not that death exists—children are intensely aware of death— but that he/she, personally, is mortal, will die, is the hour when childhood ends, and new life begins. Coming of age again, but in a larger sense." The author concluded, "The book is still the most imperfect of the three, but it is the one I like best. It is the end of the trilogy, but it is the dream I have not stopped dreaming." A reviewer in the *Times Literary Supplement* noted, "Opinions may always differ on whether *A Wizard of Earthsea* or its current sequel, *The Farthest Shore,* is the greater book.... But few will dispute that both Le Guin books are cut from the same cloth, offer the same heady range of scene and plan, pose and meet no less audacious problems, in no less seductive style." Margery Fisher of *Growing Point* noted, "This book seems to me the most impressive of the three so far written.... In her imaginative embodying of the archipelago Ursula Le Guin has shown herself to be the only writer at present able to challenge Tolkien on his own ground."

Eighteen years after the publication of *The Farthest Shore,* Le Guin wrote *Tehanu: The Last Book of Earthsea,* a novel that begins twenty-five years after the end of its predecessor. In the process of raising her feminist consciousness, the author realized that she needed to tell another story about Earthsea, one about the power of womanhood; with this volume, then, Le Guin felt that she would provide a balance to the male-dominated trilogy. In an interview with Meredith Tax in the *Village Voice,* the author referred to the "long, purely male tradition of heroic adventure fantasy. My Earthsea trilogy is part of this male tradition—that is why I had to write this fourth volume. Because I changed, I had to show the other side." In *Tehanu,* Le Guin describes how Ged, who has entered a life of contemplation on his home island of Gont after the loss of his mage power, is joined once again with Tenar, the heroine of *The Tombs of Atuan.* Now a middle-aged widow, Tenar has chosen to forego her own powers and to live anonymously. Le Guin introduces a new and pivotal character, the abused child Therru, a six-year-old girl who is found by Tenar after she has been raped and beaten by her father and uncle and left to die in a fire. Therru begins to heal emotionally through her relationship with Tenar and Ged; when she discovers her power to call dragons, she saves her friends from the last of the wizards who have chosen to defy death. Receiving the name "Tehanu" from the eldest of the dragons, the child fulfills the prophecy that "a woman on Gont" will be Ged's successor. Thus, the power on Earthsea and the responsibility to keep its balance will be shared by men and women, and the patriarchal system is balanced by female power. Writing in *Locus* about the origins of *Tehanu*, Le Guin said that her novel "starts at the end of *The Farthest Shore*. There's no gap in time between the books, although there was a huge gap in my life. That in itself was a bit of an enchantment for me—like I was being carried around on dragons. It's strange to go back that way and yet be a different person, carrying the story on.... I was able to write it because I had changed, but of course a book changes you as you write it. That's why I write books. I was

Rescued by a magical winged cat, Alexander must now repay Jane by helping her overcome her biggest fear. (From *Wonderful Alexander and the Catwings,* written by Le Guin and illustrated by S. D. Schindler.)

tremendously free—the experience of writing it was really like flying." Writing in *Book World*, Michael Dirda said of *Tehanu*, "[Though] less sheerly exciting than the earlier books, it may be the most moving of them all." Robin McKinley of the *New York Times Book Review* called *Tehanu* "a major novel by a major novelist.... Ursula Le Guin shows courage in writing a sequel to an accomplished series that demonstrated the full but traditional intellectual and magical gifts of wizards who were always male. The astonishing clear-sightedness of *Tehanu* is in its recognition of the necessary and life-giving contributions of female magic—sometimes designated as domesticity." Writing in the *Times Literary Supplement,* John Clute claimed that after the trilogy, *Tehanu* comes "as kind of a shock. This is clearly deliberate. The first half of *Tehanu* is a forcible—and at times decidedly bad-tempered—deconstruction of its predecessors. It is a statement that the wholeness of the trilogy is an artefact and an imposition, because the order which expresses that wholeness is inherently male." The reviewer concluded, "[In] the end one resents the corrosiveness of *Tehanu,* for in telling this particular tale, Le Guin has chosen to punish her own readers for having loved books she herself wrote." Ann Welton of *Voice of Youth Advocates* noted that the strength of *Tehanu* lies in "the fact of its being a woman's book—about women, their lives, their concerns." Noting that the novel presents a yin view of Earthsea in order to balance the male-empowered yang of the trilogy, the critic claimed that Le Guin's "attempt to balance something already in harmony results in a serious weakening of both works.... Let us hope that in her concern for the rights of women, Ursula Le Guin has not lost sight of that human face." In a counter-argument in a later issue of the same periodical, Margaret Miles explained that for her, *Tehanu* "brought completion instead of disappointment." Calling the novel "by far the best book of the year but ... probably too good to win the Newbery," Miles concluded that with *Tehanu,* the shape of the series "is complete: what had been an uneasy, unbalanced triangle as a 'trilogy' now reveals itself as a completed cycle of interlinked smaller circles. The missing parts of the ring have been found and joined in *Tehanu,* and Tenar and Ged both can now be at peace together. Equilibrium has been restored."

Although the Earthsea books are the best known examples of Le Guin's juvenile literature, she has written several additional stories and picture books for children and novels for young adults. Her first contribution to the latter category is *Very Far Away from Anywhere Else,* published in England as *A Very Long Way from Anywhere Else.* The author's first purely realistic novel for young people, *Very Far Away* is a contemporary story about Owen Griffin and Natalie Field, talented high school seniors—Owen in science, Natalie in music—who become close friends. When Owen feels pressured to introduce sex into their relationship, Natalie gently but firmly rejects his advances; distraught, Owen flips his car over while driving recklessly. After his recovery, Owen and Natalie are reunited and realize that each of them has grown from their relationship; as the characters leave for separate colleges, it appears that they will remain friends. Writing in *Horn Book,* Ethel L. Heins called *Very Far Away* a "small jewel of a book.... For some readers the book may come as a revelation; for others it may provide welcome reassurance." A reviewer in *Junior Bookshelf* commented, "This for me, was the most sensitive book I read in 1976, in fact I could almost say for a long time." Margery Fisher of *Growing Point* acknowledged, "In this quiet, ironic, compressed story readers in their 'teens should find much to concern them," while Andrew Gordon, writing in the *Dictionary of Literary Biography,* noted, "Like all of Le Guin's fiction, *Very Far Away from Anywhere Else* concerns the painful effort in becoming a whole human being."

With *Leese Webster,* the story of a spider who is a talented artist, Le Guin wrote her first work specifically for younger children. Born inside a deserted palace, Leese spins webs based on the patterns in the tapestries, paintings, and carpets around her. Even though the other spiders dismiss her work, Leese keeps on spinning, and eventually begins creating beautiful original designs. When the palace is cleaned to be turned into a museum, Leese's designs are discovered, admired, and placed under glass. A cleaning lady drops her into the garden outside of the palace, where Leese discovers a new world of beauty, and she begins to spin wild webs that shine jewel-like from the light of the sun. Writing in the *Dictionary of Literary Biography,* Andrew Gordon commented that this "parable about the artist and her craft" shows Le Guin's style, "with its clarity and natural patterns of imagery, at its best." Kicki Moxon Browne of the *Times Literary Supplement* called *Leese Webster* "a perfect story," while a reviewer in *Publishers Weekly* described it as "a subtle allegory" and a "haunting tale." A critic in *Kirkus Reviews* noted, "Not the brilliant parable that might have been expected, but sound and expertly spun like any fine web."

The Beginning Place is a novel that, according to a reviewer in *Publishers Weekly,* brought Le Guin "back to the field in which she first gained fame (SF/fantasy) and simultaneously breaks new ground in her writing." Marketed as an adult book and reviewed as both an adult and young adult title, the novel, published in England as *Threshold,* features the adolescent characters Hugh Rogers and Irene Pannis. After running away from home to escape from his domineering mother and dead-end job, Hugh discovers a gateway to Tembreabrezi, a parallel world of eternal twilight. Irene, who has left home because of the sexual advances of her stepfather, had discovered Tembreabrezi years before and has made a home for herself there; in addition, she has become the lover of the master of the townspeople, who are reminiscent of figures from the Middle Ages. Hugh is hailed as a long-awaited savior of the town, which is under a dragon's curse. He agrees to slay the dragon, and he and Irene, who has left the town's master, go into the mountains. Although he kills the dragon, Hugh is wounded and has to be rescued by Irene. At the end of the novel, the protagonists go back to their suburban world; when Hugh's mother refuses to let him come

home, Hugh and Irene rent an apartment and begin their life together. "Read as a creation of a secondary world...." wrote Francis J. Molson in *Twentieth Century Children's Writers,* "the novel seems incomplete and, hence, teasing. Read as Hugh and Irene's struggle to trust in themselves and in each other, however, the novel satisfies and compares favorably with the best young adult fiction today." Writing in another edition of the same source, Jill Paton Walsh commented, "There are multiple resonances in this book, of Oedipus as well as of Sigurd among many others, and the position of the fantasy geography as a land of the inner world, of the mind, is clearer than in Earthsea, though less compellingly beautiful." Andrew Gordon noted, "The achievement of *The Beginning Place* is its vivid, detailed realism, which brings alive both the plastic suburb and the haunting twilight land and makes us believe in the possibility of crossing the threshold between the two." The critic also praised the author's "admirable new restraint in not spelling out her moral for the reader but allowing the story to speak for itself." In her review in *School Library Journal,* Amy Rolnick claimed that Le Guin's devoted fans "will recognize the artful melding of the real and the fantastic as the author at her best."

Solomon Leviathan's Nine Hundred and Thirty-First Trip Around the World is a picture book for early primary graders that includes text that Le Guin wrote at the age of twenty. The humorous tale concerns two philosophical friends, a giraffe and a boa constrictor, who go on a quest to find the horizon; while on their journey, they are swallowed by the title character, a whale—the same one who took in Jonah and Pinocchio—who becomes their friend. "[Only] special children are going to be amused by the wry, philosophical text," wrote a critic in *Kirkus Reviews,* who predicted that the book "will enchant a few sophisticates." Sally R. Dow of *School Library Journal* commented, "Language is rich and metaphorical, but a pompous tone and numerous literary allusions and historical references may lessen the story's appeal for children." Jill Paton Walsh called *Solomon Leviathan* a "youthful and exuberant blend of Kipling and Dr. Dolittle [that] clearly shows the seeds of her later achievement, the shaping intelligence that makes her fantasies always seem like paradigms of reality rather than escapes from it, and the power to evoke a sweep of lands and seas and weather and teeming life as a setting for even a simple story." Le Guin's second picture book, *A Visit from Dr. Katz,* is a story that, according to Ann A. Flowers of *Horn Book,* "has the feeling of a real incident recollected." When little Marianne is sick in bed, her mother offers to send in "Dr. Katz"— the family's two large marmalade cats, who cuddle with Marianne before all three fall asleep. Although the book begins like most picture books with a common experience, a reviewer in the *Junior Bookshelf* writes, "it develops into something slightly different as the book has a fantasy element." Cliff Moon of the *School Librarian* calls *Dr. Katz* a book "which will appeal to all cat-lovers and every child who has to spend a day in bed."

Le Guin continues her fascination with cats in her next series, the "Catwings" books, which feature flying kittens born with wings. The first of these stories, which are directed to readers in the early primary grades and are designed as small, slim volumes, is *Catwings,* which introduces the four kittens—Harriet, Thelma, James, and Roger—born to a single mother in a dumpster in a rough city neighborhood. Distrusted by winged, two- and four-footed creatures because of their appearance, the kittens are sent away from the city by their mother. After they settle in a wooded area, the kittens encounter danger before being discovered by Susan and Hank, two children from a neighboring farm who adopt them. Writing in the *New York Times Book Review,* Crescent Dragonwagon noted that Le Guin "rewards us richly for our acceptance" of the birth of winged kittens to an ordinary tabby cat, adding that "we easily believe every wing beat of the way. [Le Guin's] dialogue, humor, skill as a storyteller and emotional veracity combine near-flawlessly in a story that is both contemporary and timeless." The critic began her review with an allusion to E. B. White's *Stuart Little,* the story of a mouse born to human parents. "[So] gripping were his adventures," Dragonwagon wrote, "that 43 years after its publication children still laugh and weep over *Stuart Little*"; the critic concluded that children "will probably be reading *Catwings* to their children and grandchildren 43 years from now and more." Ruth S. Vose commented in *School Library Journal* that the story "barely skirts cuteness; the language has a self-conscious tone which works against the actions of the plot"; however, Carolyn Phelan in *Booklist* acknowledged, "Given its fanciful premise, this quiet tale is surprisingly convincing. Le Guin's language is devoid of precious sentimentality...." The second volume of the series, *Catwings Return,* begins where *Catwings* left off. The kittens, who are secretly cared for by Susan and Hank, are happy but miss their mother. Two of them, Harriet and James, embark on a journey back to the dumpster where they were born; when the kittens arrive, they learn that the slums are being demolished. Harriet and James find Jane, a lost, hungry, and traumatized kitten, and discover that, like themselves, she has wings. After a reunion with their mother, who is living among the flower pots on an apartment roof, James and Harriet return to the country with Jane, who is warmly accepted into the family. A reviewer in *Publishers Weekly* noted that although there is some repetition in this book, such as the single mother who, "somewhat curiously, sends the children away to a better life," it includes Le Guin's "graceful writing—especially of the new member of the family...." Writing in *Horn Book,* Ann A. Flowers called *Catwings Return* "a satisfying, delightful tale," and concluded, "Winged cats are an inspired invention, and the book is a gracious, loving tribute to the charm of cats." The third volume of the series, *Wonderful Alexander and the Catwings,* introduces a new character, the kitten Alexander, who is dubbed "wonderful" by his doting family. When Alexander sets out to explore the world, he becomes lost in a forest; Alexander is rescued by Jane, who herself was rescued in *Catwings Return,* and taken to her home. In return, Alexander helps Jane—who due to the terror of an earlier experience can

say only two words, "Me" and "Hate"—to overcome her fear of speaking, thus proving to everyone that he is truly "wonderful." A critic in *Kirkus Reviews* said of *Wonderful Alexander and the Catwings,* "Brief as it is, this is a deftly crafted bildungsroman." Writing in *Booklist,* Carolyn Phelan noted, "Although the writing is clear and fluid, the story is less satisfying," as, she conjectures, it's probably "easier to accept a cat who's part bird than a cat who's part psychoanalyst." Mary Jo Drungil of *School Library Journal* concluded that Alexander's appearance in "the charming series does more than tie up the loose threads of Jane's muteness: it also set the stage for further adventures." In an interview in *Contemporary Authors,* Le Guin noted that she had received a "lovely letter from a little boy, a fan letter for *Catwings.* He said, 'I keep looking at my cats and telling them, 'Fly! Fly!'"

In the picture book *Fire and Stone,* two children, Min and Podo, discover that the dragon who flies above their village breathing fire is really just hungry for rocks. When the children begin feeding the dragon, they are joined by the other villagers; as the dragon becomes satiated, it gets heavier and cooler until it turns into stone, thus becoming Dragon Hill. Betsy Hearne of the *Bulletin of the Center for Children's Books* called *Fire and Stone* "a beautifully written story," while a reviewer for *Publishers Weekly* said that it is an "intriguing myth." Writing in *School Library Journal,* Karen Litton claimed, "[This] works as a simple, well-shaped dragon tale ... of conquering fear with love [with] resonant mythic overtones." In the picture book *Fish Soup,* Le Guin describes the friends Thinking Man and Writing Woman, who magically conjure up their ideal children, a girl who flutters and twinkles and a boy who can catch fish to be put into soup. However, the boy grows too large while the girl is nothing more than a dress and shoes. "Part fantasy, part comic look at parents' unrealistic expectations," wrote a critic in *Publishers Weekly,* "this book may hold some vague appeal for children who like fantasy." Ruth Semrau of *School Library Journal* noted that Le Guin's "effort to avoid stereotype is almost a stereotype," but concluded that *Fish Soup* is a "good choice for those looking for easy fiction on gender discrimination." Writing in *Kirkus Reviews,* a critic claimed, "Though almost schematic in its simplicity, the tale engages with its imaginative touches of fantasy, elaborated with wry common sense.... A classic."

A Ride on the Red Mare's Back is considered one of Le Guin's most successful picture books. Written in language resembling epic poetry, the book is credited for successfully combining traditional folklore elements with a contemporary feminist undercurrent. The story describes how a nameless girl rescues her little brother after he is abducted by wicked trolls. When her parents are too upset to take action, the young heroine sets out on her quest with only a few provisions: some bread, a scarf, knitting needles, red yarn, and her only toy, a wooden horse that turns into a huge red mare to help the girl find her brother. By using each of the items she brought with her—for example, she tricks the guard at the entrance of the troll house by getting him involved in knitting—the girl is able to take her brother, who is enjoying living the life of a troll, back to their parents; when they return home, she is presented with a newly carved horse, which she decides is the colt of the red mare. A reviewer in *Publishers Weekly* claimed, "Text and artwork [the illustrations are by Julie Downing] of extraordinary beauty highlight this stirring tale." Kay E. Vandergrift of *School Library Journal* called *A Ride on the Red Mare's Back* "a real gem that demonstrates the value of determination and that one's sense of satisfaction in a task completed is reward enough. Bravo to such a creative work." Writing in *Book World*, Michael Dirda claimed that the story is "indisputably suspenseful, thought-provoking, and beautifully illustrated...." Ann A. Flowers of *Horn Book* compared the book to both Maurice Sendak's *Outside Over There* and Norse fairy tales and concluded that it is a "satisfying, rewarding tale."

In assessing Le Guin's oeuvre since the completion of the Earthsea quartet, Michael Dirda commented that the author has "had trouble with some of her books for younger kids, which have seemed a little inconsequential compared to the moral seriousness of *A Wizard of Earthsea* or *Tehanu*." Andrew Gordon of the *Dictionary of Literary Biography* added another perspective, noting that the Earthsea books are "her finest work thus far, but as her later works indicate, she is continuing to experiment with different modes of writing and to grow in artistic range." In her entry in *Twentieth Century Children's Writers*, Jill Paton Walsh concluded, "It is hard to see how Le Guin could exceed the merit of her existing work; but also hard to put any limit on what might be expected from a writer of such variety, such force, and such psychological depth."

■ Works Cited

Allen, Frank, review of *Going Out with Peacocks and Other Poems*, *Library Journal*, June 1, 1994, pp. 110-12.

Review of *The Beginning Place*, *Publishers Weekly*, December 3, 1979, p. 47.

Browne, Kicki Moxon, "To Amuse and Entertain," *Times Literary Supplement*, September 18, 1981, p. 108.

Cameron, Eleanor, "High Fantasy: 'A Wizard of Earthsea,'" *Crosscurrents of Criticism: Horn Book Essays 1968-77*, edited by Paul Heins, Horn Book, 1977, pp. 333-41.

Review of *Catwings Return*, *Publishers Weekly*, December 23, 1988, p. 82.

Clute, John, "Deconstructing Paradise," *Times Literary Supplement*, December 28, 1990, p. 1409.

Dirda, Michael, "The Twilight of an Age of Magic," *Book World—The Washington Post*, February 25, 1990, pp. 1, 9.

Dirda, Michael, review of *A Ride on the Red Mare's Back*, *Book World—The Washington Post*, August 9, 1992, p. 11.

Dow, Sally R., review of *Solomon Leviathan's Nine Hundred and Thirty-First Trip Around the World*, *School Library Journal*, December, 1988, pp. 88-89.

Dragonwagon, Crescent, "Upward Mobility in the Kitty Ghetto," *New York Times Book Review*, November 13, 1988, p. 40.

Drungil, Mary Jo, review of *Wonderful Alexander and the Catwings*, *School Library Journal*, September, 1994, p. 188.

Erlich, Richard, "Why I Like the Earthsea Trilogy," *English Journal*, October, 1977, pp. 90-93.

Fantastes, "Enchantress of Earthsea," *Cambridge Review: Fantasy in Literature*, November 23, 1973, pp. 43-45.

Review of *The Farthest Shore*, *Times Literary Supplement*, April 6, 1973, p. 379.

Review of *Fire and Stone*, *Publishers Weekly*, March 10, 1989, p. 88.

Fisher, Margery, review of *The Farthest Shore*, *Growing Point*, July, 1973, p. 2200.

Fisher, Margery, review of *A Very Long Way from Anywhere Else*, *Growing Point*, January, 1977, pp. 3041-42.

Review of *Fish Soup*, *Kirkus Reviews*, October 1, 1992, p. 1257.

Review of *Fish Soup*, *Publishers Weekly*, October 5, 1992, p. 71.

Flowers, Ann A., review of *A Visit from Dr. Katz*, *Horn Book*, May-June, 1988, p. 343.

Flowers, Ann A., review of *Catwings Return*, *Horn Book*, March-April, 1989, pp. 205-06.

Flowers, Ann A., review of *A Ride on the Red Mare's Back*, *Horn Book*, March-April, 1993, pp. 204-05.

Gordon, Andrew, essay in *Dictionary of Literary Biography, Volume 52: American Writers for Children Since 1960—Fiction*, Gale, 1986, pp. 233-41.

Haviland, Virginia, "A Magical Tour," *Book World—The Washington Post*, November 7, 1971, p. 4.

Hearne, Betsy, review of *Fire and Stone*, *Bulletin of the Center for Children's Books*, June, 1989, pp. 255-56.

Heins, Ethel L., review of *Very Far Away from Anywhere Else*, *Horn Book*, February, 1977, pp. 57-58.

Heins, Paul, review of *The Tombs of Atuan*, *Horn Book*, October, 1971, p. 490.

Kizer, Carolyn, jacket note for *Searoad: Chronicles of Klatsand*, HarperCollins, 1991.

Landsberg, Michele, "Fantasy," *Reading for the Love of It: Best Books for Young Readers*, Prentice Hall, 1987, pp. 157-82.

Review of *Leese Webster*, *Kirkus Reviews*, September 1, 1979, p. 998.

Review of *Leese Webster*, *Publishers Weekly*, July 30, 1979, p. 63.

Le Guin, Ursula K., "Dreams Must Explain Themselves," *Dreams Must Explain Themselves*, Algol Press, 1975, pp. 4-13.

Le Guin, interview with Rachel Koenig in *Something about the Author*, Gale, Volume 52, 1988, pp. 103-04.

Le Guin, interview with Jean W. Ross in *Contemporary Authors New Revision Series*, Gale, Volume 32, 1977, p. 253-54.

Le Guin, *The Language of the Night: Essays on Fantasy and Science Fiction,* edited by Susan Wood, Putnam, 1979.

Le Guin, essay on *Tehanu, Locus: The Newspaper of the Science Fiction Field,* January, 1990.

Litton, Karen, review of *Fire and Stone, School Library Journal,* April, 1989, p. 85.

McKinley, Robin, "The Woman Wizard's Triumph," *New York Times Book Review,* May 20, 1990, p. 38.

Miles, Margaret, "'Earthsea Revisited' Revisited," *Voice of Youth Advocates,* December, 1991, pp. 301-02.

Molson, Francis J., essay in *Twentieth Century Children's Writers,* 2nd edition, edited by D. L. Kirkpatrick, *St. Martin's Press,* 1983, pp. 466-67.

Moon, Cliff, review of *A Visit from Dr. Katz, School Librarian,* August, 1989, p. 100.

Phelan, Carolyn, review of *Catwings, Booklist,* August, 1988, p. 1928.

Phelan, Carolyn, review of *Wonderful Alexander and the Catwings, Booklist,* September 15, 1994, p. 136.

Price, Derek de Solla, commentary in *New Republic,* February 7, 1976.

Review of *A Ride on the Red Mare's Back, Publishers Weekly,* August 10, 1992, p. 70.

Rolnick, Amy, review of *The Beginning Place, School Library Journal,* April, 1980, p. 132.

Semrau, Ruth, review of *Fish Soup, School Library Journal,* January, 1993, p. 80.

Shippey, T. A., "Archmage and Antimage," *Times Literary Supplement,* July 15, 1977, p. 863.

Review of *Solomon Leviathan's Nine Hundred and Thirty-First Trip Around the World, Kirkus Reviews,* November 15, 1988, p. 1676.

Sturgeon, Theodore, commentary in *Los Angeles Times,* September 5, 1982.

Tax, Meredith, "Fantasy Island," *Village Voice,* October 30, 1990, p. 75.

Vandergrift, Kay E., review of *A Ride on the Red Mare's Back, School Library Journal,* September, 1992, p. 207.

Review of *Very Far Away from Anywhere Else, Junior Bookshelf,* April, 1977, pp. 116-17.

Viguers, Ruth Hill, review of *A Wizard of Earthsea, Horn Book,* February, 1969, pp. 59-60.

Review of *A Visit from Dr. Katz, Junior Bookshelf,* April, 1989, p. 71.

Vose, Ruth S., review of *Catwings, School Library Journal,* November, 1988, p. 91.

Walsh, Jill Paton, essay in *Twentieth Century Children's Writers,* 3rd edition, edited by Tracy Chevalier, St. James Press, 1989, pp. 569-71.

Warlow, Aidan, review of *The Tombs of Atuan, School Librarian,* September, 1972, p. 258.

Welton, Ann, "Earthsea Revisited: 'Tehanu' and Feminism," *Voice of Youth Advocates,* April, 1991, pp. 14-16, 18.

Review of *A Wizard of Earthsea, Times Literary Supplement,* April 2, 1971, p. 383.

Review of *Wonderful Alexander and the Catwings, Kirkus Reviews,* August 15, 1994, p. 1132.

■ **For More Information See**

BOOKS

Bittner, James, *Approaches to the Fiction of Ursula K. Le Guin,* UMI Research Press, 1984.

Bucknall, Barbara, *Ursula K. Le Guin,* Ungar, 1981.

Children's Literature Review, Gale, Volume 3, 1978, Volume 28, 1992.

Cogell, Elizabeth Cummins, *Ursula K. Le Guin: A Primary and Secondary Bibliography,* G. K. Hall, 1983.

Contemporary Literary Criticism, Gale, Volume 8, 1978, Volume 13, 1980, Volume 22, 1982, Volume 45, 1987, Volume 71, 1992.

Cummins, Elizabeth, *Understanding Ursula K. Le Guin,* University of South Carolina Press, 1990.

De Bolt, Joe, editor, *Ursula K. Le Guin: Voyager to Inner Lands and to Outer Space,* Kennikat Press, 1979.

De Montreville, Doris, and Elizabeth D. Crawford, *Fourth Book of Junior Authors and Illustrators,* Wilson, 1978.

Dictionary of Literary Biography, Volume 8: Twentieth-Century American Science Fiction Writers, Gale, 1981.

Haviland, Virginia, *The Openhearted Audience: Ten Authors Talk about Writing for Children,* Library of Congress, 1980.

Olander, Joseph D., and Martin Harry Greenberg, editors, *Ursula K. Le Guin,* Taplinger, 1979.

Reginald, Robert, and George Edgar Slusser, editors, *Zephyr and Boreas: Winds of Change in the Fiction of Ursula K. Le Guin,* Borgo Press, 1996.

Reid, Suzanne Elizabeth, *Presenting Ursula K. Le Guin,* Twayne's United States Authors Series, Simon Schuster (New York), 1997.

Silvey, Anita, editor, *Children's Books and Their Creators,* Houghton Mifflin, 1995.

Slusser, George Edgar, *The Farthest Shores of Ursula K. Le Guin,* Borgo, 1976.

Slusser, George Edgar, *Between Two Worlds: The Literary Dilemma of Ursula K. Le Guin,* Borgo Press, 1995.

St. James Guide to Science Fiction Writers, St. James Press, 1996.

Twentieth-Century Young Adult Writers, St. James Press, 1994.

PERIODICALS

Belle Lettres, spring, 1992, pp. 53-54.

Booklist, June 15, 1992, p. 1847; November 15, 1993, p. 598; February 1, 1997, p. 921.

Boston Globe, July 13, 1994, p. 65.

Children's Literature in Education, July, 1972, pp. 21-29; March, 1995, p. 90.

Extrapolation (Ursula K. Le Guin issue), fall, 1980.

Foundation, January, 1974, pp. 71-80.

Kirkus Reviews, July 1, 1995, p. 905.

Locus, October, 1994, pp. 17, 19.

Publishers Weekly, January 29, 1996, p. 86.

School Library Journal, April, 1996, p. 168.

Science-Fiction Studies (Ursula K. Le Guin issue), March, 1976.

—Sketch by Gerard J. Senick

*   *   *

LEROE, Ellen W(hitney) 1949-

■ Personal

Born April 26, 1949, in Newark, NJ; daughter of Bernard William (a mechanical engineer) and Iris (an educational secretary; maiden name, Brienza) Leroe. *Education:* Elmira College, B.A., 1971; University of Leicester, certificate, 1970. *Hobbies and other interests:* Reading (particularly British murder mysteries and biographies of movie stars), exercising, working as an extra on the local San Francisco television shows shot on location.

■ Addresses

Home and office—201 Harrison St., Ste. 920, San Francisco, CA 94105. *Agent*—The Authors Guild, 330 W. 42nd St., New York, NY 10036.

■ Career

Full-time writer, 1979—; freelance writer and illustrator, 1974-76. Hahne's (retail store), Newark, NJ, fashion buyer, 1971-74; International Engineering Co., San Francisco, CA, editorial assistant, 1976-77; San Francisco Junior Chamber of Commerce, San Francisco, administrative manager, 1977-79. *Member:* Society of Children's Book Writers and Illustrators, Authors Guild.

■ Awards, Honors

Authors Award, New Jersey Institute of Technology, 1983, for *Confessions of a Teenage TV Addict;* first prize, San Francisco Fair Poetry Competition, 1985.

■ Writings

YOUNG ADULT FICTION

Confessions of a Teenage TV Addict, Lodestar/Dutton, 1983.
Enter Laughing, Silhouette, 1983.
Give and Take, Silhouette, 1984.
Robot Romance, Harper, 1985.
The Plot Against the Pom-Pom Queen, Lodestar/Dutton, 1985.
Have a Heart, Cupid Delaney, Lodestar, 1986.
Robot Raiders, Harper, 1987.
Meet Your Match, Cupid Delaney, Lodestar, 1990.
Love's in Harmony (romance), Cora-Verlag (Germany), 1990.

FICTION FOR CHILDREN

Personal Business (novelization of ABC-TV "Afterschool Special"), Bantam, 1986.
The Peanut Butter Poltergeist, illustrated by Jacqueline Rogers, Dutton, 1987.
H.O.W.L. High, Pocket Books, 1991.

ELLEN W. LEROE

Leap Frog Friday, illustrated by Dee deRosa, Lodestar Books, 1992.
Heebie-Jeebies at H.O.W.L. High, Pocket Books, 1992.
H.O.W.L. High Goes Bats!, Pocket Books, 1993.
Ghost Dog, illustrated by Bill Basso, Hyperion, 1993.
Monkey Business (novelization of New Line Cinema film), Pocket Books, 1994.
Racetrack Robbery, illustrated by Bill Basso, Hyperion, 1996.

FIENDLY CORNERS SERIES

Monster Vision, #1, Hyperion, 1996.
Pizza Zombies, #2, Hyperion, 1996.
Revenge of the Hairy Horror, #3, Hyperion, 1996.
Nasty the Snowman, #4, Hyperion, 1996.

OTHER

Single Bed Blues and Other Poems (adult poetry), Tandem Press, 1981.
(Contributor) *A Night To Remember* (anthology), Avon, 1995.

Contributor of articles, short stories and poems to periodicals, including *California Living, Cosmopolitan, Frequent Flyer, Good Housekeeping, Ladies' Home Journal, National Business Woman, Total Fitness, Travel,* and *Women's Week.*

■ Work in Progress

Two middle-grade books for Hyperion: *Anna in the Middle,* a historical fiction set in 1898 Russia, and a collection of real-life stories of young survivors of disasters. A third book, *T-Rex and the Saur Losers,* is an action-thriller comedy, also for middle graders.

■ Sidelights

Ellen W. Leroe began her career as a writer with the publication of romance and fantasy novels for young adults, and has since produced fantasy, mystery, and supernatural tales for younger readers. Her works have been described by critics as humorous, light, and enjoyable. Leroe once told *SATA* that she writes to entertain her readers. "And, hopefully, in the entertaining I can give my readers a new perspective about their problems, which will enable them to form their own conclusions."

Confessions of a Teenage TV Addict is the story of Jennifer Warrens, who, at sixteen, is obsessed with soap operas. After she transfers from private school to a public high school, her best friend, Andra, forces her to get out and involved in high school social life. Andra, secretly concerned only with her own plans to date a cute boy, arranges a double date; her plans are foiled when the boy, Mike, falls for Jennifer instead. Andra then plants drugs in Jennifer's locker to get her in trouble, but Jennifer's mother and Mike defend her. *Enter Laughing,* published the same year, finds Blaney Wilder, class president, intent on a spot in the Little Theatre Group. Although she begins the novel as an outspoken class clown, by the end, her feelings for the play's director force her to become more sincere.

Robot Romance features Bixby Wyler, a sixteen-year-old transfer student at Silicon Computer High School, and Maximum Integrated Systems-III, the robot assistant to the principal. Bixby builds a humanoid, Ally, in part to impress fellow student Frani; Ally is so well-built she passes for one of the students. Finding the story "lots of fun," Sally Estes of *Booklist* concluded, "classify it as humor, not science fiction." *Robot Raiders,* the sequel to *Robot Romance,* takes Bixby, Ally, Max and Frani on a mission to M.I.T. to save a government project. Barbara Evans of *Voice of Youth Advocates* described the story as "humorous and suspenseful" as well as "fast-paced."

Have a Heart, Cupid Delaney, another of Leroe's young adult novels, was described by Janet Bryan of *School Library Journal* as a "delightful, off-beat romance/fantasy for younger teens." The Love Bureau expects a cupid (working in the form of a butterfly) to make four high school students fall in love, or else it will take away her wings. Cupid Delaney has a difficult time carrying out her assignment, and even falls in love with one of the students. *Meet Your Match, Cupid Delaney* continues Cupid's story, only this time she must work in the body of a teenager. Once again, she falls in love with a human teenager, and by the end of the novel, her wish to be

Artie and his supernatural canine, Ghost Dog, solve the mystery when an imposter tries to impersonate race driver Speed Bryant. (From *Racetrack Robbery,* written by Leroe and illustrated by Bill Basso.)

with him is fulfilled. According to Connie Tyrrell Burns of *School Library Journal,* the work "is fast-paced and written with wit and humor."

The Peanut Butter Poltergeist, for younger readers, begins as M. J. and his new stepsister begin a vacation together in an old house. Annoyed by his stepsister, M. J. tries to scare her with ghostly pranks (including floating flowers and strange peanut butter), but he soon finds himself scared instead. By the end of the story, the step-siblings become friends. Children "will enjoy the prankish devices that comprise the plot," remarked Betsy Hearne in *Bulletin of the Center for Children's Books. Leap Frog Friday,* another book for children, opens as Ollie explains that he did not intend to turn his brother into a frog. The rest of the book, narrated by Ollie, relates how a gift of stones Oliver receives for his ninth birthday works a subtle magic. The morning after Ollie casts a spell, his older brother Danny appears hopping, speaking with a frog-like voice, and unrolling a very long tongue to catch flies. According to Stephanie Zvirin of *Booklist,* "there's plenty of appealing silliness" in this work. A *Kirkus Reviews* critic described the book as "[e]njoyable light fare."

Leroe's *Ghost Dog* features another nine-year-old, Artie; he discovers a ghost dog which only he can see while on vacation at his grandfather's house. Although the ghost dog makes trouble for Artie, it later helps him save Grandpa's valuable baseball card from a thief. When Artie returns home, he takes the dog with him. *School Library Journal* critic Elizabeth Hamilton remarked that the book's "humorous scenes ... will delight readers." In *Racetrack Robbery,* the dog helps Artie get a promised photo of a superstitious race car superstar and solve a mystery.

Leroe has also created a series of horror books for preteens, the "Fiendly Corners" Series. Fiendly Corners is a town which was hit by a meteorite years ago; the ghosts of the people killed still inhabit the town and make it a strange place to live. *Monster Vision,* the first book in the series, tells the story of a twelve-year-old named Jamie who receives the wrong pair of contact lenses in the mail; when Jamie puts them on, the ghost of a dead magician comes to claim them. *Pizza Zombies* demonstrates what happens when toy robots give Fiendly Corners residents an insatiable taste for pizza. A monster from a werewolf movie appears in the town in *Revenge of the Hairy Horror.* In *Nasty the Snowman* a pair of twins find a snow creature lurking about when they visit their archaeologist uncle. The books in the series, commented Cheryl Cufari of *School Library Journal,* have "just the right amounts of suspense and fright culminating in satisfying endings."

Leroe once told *SATA* that she has reread her "old high school diaries" and talks and listens to teens as well. "Because I put so much of myself and my own experiences into my novels, I tend to focus on main characters confronting, and eventually successfully altering, their insecure and vulnerable self-images. I start with a crisis ... and then I mix in complications." Leroe also revealed, "I strive to make my dialogue as realistic and as natural as possible." As a full-time writer, Leroe has explained to *SATA* that her work is "the most rewarding, the most personally satisfying, and the most liberating.... Though I often become discouraged when checks are late or when publishers reject my material, an inner voice still urges me to keep going."

■ Works Cited

Bryan, Janet, review of *Have a Heart, Cupid Delaney, School Library Journal,* December, 1986, p. 120.

Burns, Connie Tyrrell, review of *Meet Your Match, Cupid Delaney, School Library Journal,* October, 1990, p. 143.

Cufari, Cheryl, review of "Fiendly Corners" Series books, *School Library Journal,* May, 1997, p. 136.

Estes, Sally, review of *Robot Romance, Booklist,* May 1, 1985, p. 1250.

Evans, Barbara, review of *Robot Raiders, Voice of Youth Advocates,* June, 1987, p. 90.

Hamilton, Elizabeth, review of *Ghost Dog, School Library Journal,* June, 1993, p. 78.

Hearne, Betsy, review of *The Peanut Butter Poltergeist, Bulletin of the Center for Children's Books,* December, 1987, p. 69.

Review of *Leap Frog Friday, Kirkus Reviews,* October 15, 1992, p. 1311.

Zvirin, Stephanie, review of *Leap Frog Friday, Booklist,* September 1, 1992, p. 60.

■ For More Information See

PERIODICALS

Booklist, February 1, 1984, p. 809; November 1, 1986, p. 403; September 15, 1987, p. 155; January 15, 1988, p. 864; April 1, 1993, pp. 1431, 1434.

Publishers Weekly, August 2, 1991, p. 73.

*   *   *

LEVINSON, Riki

■ Personal

Born in Brooklyn, NY; daughter of Samuel E. (a jewelry designer, then cantor) and Anna S. (an insurance broker; maiden name, Blau) Friedberg; married Morton Levinson (an attorney), March 7, 1944 (deceased); children: Gerry L. (daughter); grandchildren: Mark Robert, Anna Sarah. *Education:* Cooper Union School of Arts and Sciences, B.A., 1943. *Religion:* Jewish. *Hobbies and other interests:* Natural history, especially animal behav-

RIKI LEVINSON

to Grandma's.

A huge extended family gathers for a festive reunion in Levinson's charming picture book. (From *I Go with My Family to Grandma's,* illustrated by Diane Goode.)

ior; architecture, particularly old homes and ancient cultures; the sea.

■ **Addresses**

Home—230 East 50th St., Apt. 7A, New York, NY 10022.

■ **Career**

Freelance designer, 1945-70; Western Publishing Co., Inc., New York City, design and manufacturing manager of Education Division, 1970-72; E. P. Dutton, New York City, art director, 1972-86, assistant publisher and art director, 1986-87, associate publisher and art director of children's books, 1987-91. Consultant art director and editor, 1991—. *Member:* American Institute of Graphic Arts, Authors Guild, Authors League of America, Cooper Union Alumni Association, Society of Children's Book Writers and Illustrators.

■ **Awards, Honors**

Numerous graphic awards as a freelance designer and art director; Notable Book designation, American Library Association, Children's Editor's Choice, *Booklist,* *Redbook* Top Ten Picture Book honor, and Parents' Choice Award for literature, Parents' Choice Foundation, all 1985, and *Reading Rainbow* feature book on PBS-TV, 1986, all for *Watch the Stars Come Out;* Notable Children's Trade Book designation, National

Council for the Social Studies-Children's Book Council, 1985, for *Watch the Stars Come Out,* 1986, for *I Go with My Family to Grandma's,* 1987, for *DinnieAbbieSister-r-r!,* and 1988 for *Our Home Is the Sea;* Child Study Association Children's Books of the Year honors, 1986, and Jefferson Cup Award, Virginia Library Association, 1987, both for *I Go with My Family to Grandma's;* Georgia Children's Book Award nomination, University of Georgia-College of Education, for *DinnieAbbieSister-r-r!*

■ **Writings**

FOR CHILDREN; FICTION

Watch the Stars Come Out, illustrated by Diane Goode, Dutton, 1985.

I Go with My Family to Grandma's, illustrated by Goode, Dutton, 1986.

Touch! Touch!, illustrated by True Kelley, Dutton, 1987.

DinnieAbbieSister-r-r!, illustrated by Helen Cogancherry, Bradbury, 1987.

Our Home Is the Sea, illustrated by Dennis Luzak, Dutton, 1988.

(Reteller) *The Emperor's New Clothes,* illustrated by Robert Byrd, Dutton, 1991.

Me Baby!, illustrated by Marilyn Hafner, Dutton, 1991.

Country Dawn to Dusk, illustrated by Kay Chorao, Dutton, 1992.

Boys Here—Girls There, illustrated by Karen Ritz, Lodestar, 1993.

Soon, Annala, illustrated by Julie Downing, Orchard, 1993.
Grandpa's Hotel, illustrated by David Soman, Orchard, 1995.

Watch the Stars Come Out has been translated into Danish, French, German, Swedish, and Spanish; *I Go with My Family to Grandma's* has been translated into German and Spanish; *Our Home Is the Sea* has also been translated into Spanish.

■ Adaptations

Watch the Stars Come Out has been adapted as a filmstrip with audiocassette, Miller-Brody, 1986; *I Go with My Family to Grandma's,* has also been adapted as a filmstrip.

■ Sidelights

For author and artist Riki Levinson, family relationships are central. Raised in a close ethnic family, she draws not only on her own memories of parenting and childhood but on the recollections of family members to create books that present loving, supportive relationships between parents and children. Several of her books, including *Watch the Stars Come Out,* focus on immigrants learning to adapt to a new culture, while others, such as *Boys Here—Girls There,* have a more humorous, lighthearted appeal to young readers.

Growing up in a family with two older brothers and two younger brothers, it is not surprising that family relationships serve as one of Levinson's main themes. "Family is the most important part of my life," the author once told *Something about the Author* (*SATA*), "and I find it a warm and personal experience to write about it. It is reassuring, to me, that children don't change, no matter when they live." Born in Brooklyn, New York, Levinson discovered her own creativity at a young age. "Drawing was a natural thing for me," Levinson once told *SATA,* "but I did not think it interesting enough in high school—it was too easy." Instead of art classes, Levinson focused on math—geometry was her favorite class—and creative writing during her four years of high school. "[W]hen I wanted to go to college, and there was no money to pay for it, I tried for Cooper Union at the suggestion of my art teacher. Cooper Union was, in effect, a scholarship school. At Cooper Union I found a direction that suited me well, and since that time I have been in art."

The year after graduating from college, Levinson opened her own design studio in New York City. She married Morton Levinson, a soldier-engineering student who became an attorney after the war, with whom she would have a daughter, Gerry. Many years later, Levinson landed a position with a major publisher, E. P. Dutton, as art director. One day in the fall of 1983, she was struck with the idea for a story. But Levinson hadn't sat down and attempted a story since those high school years long ago. "One day I told my husband that I had

In Hong Kong, a young boy looks forward to joining his father and grandfather in the family profession of fishing. (From *Our Home Is the Sea,* written by Levinson and illustrated by Dennis Luzak.)

an idea for a story but that I didn't know how to write. And he said, 'Don't worry about writing, hon—just put it down.'" With her husband's encouragement, the story that Levinson thought she couldn't write was published in 1985 as *Watch the Stars Come Out.*

Watch the Stars Come Out is Levinson's impression of what it must have been like when her mother sailed to the United States as a young girl. Forming the first recounting of her family's history, the book takes place in 1910 and follows the travel of a brother and sister who make the journey from Europe to the United States to join their parents. The nighttime sky is lost to the children, who spend twenty-three nights below ship on their small bunks waiting their arrival in the New World. The process is described of going through Ellis Island, reuniting with family members, and moving into their new small home on Hester Street, from which the night sky again comes into view. "Levinson's first book is a literary event," maintained a *Publishers Weekly* critic, "written with a quiet understatement that magnifies its emotional effects."

The second volume of Levinson's family history, *I Go with My Family to Grandma's,* was inspired by trips made to her great-grandmother's house in Brooklyn. During these family get-togethers, being lonely was impossible due to the number of cousins, aunts, and uncles that converged on the spot to enjoy the good company and good food. The story is narrated from five different points of view: a Manhattan family arrives on (1) tandem bicycle; another comes by (2) trolley; a grocer and his wife and children drive their (3) horse-drawn produce wagon out to Brooklyn for the afternoon; while two other families arrive by a variety of mechanical means—via (4) El (elevated train), and (5) car and ferry. "The scene where they all settle down for a family portrait," notes a *Kirkus Reviews* writer, "makes a satisfying conclusion to a warm-hearted reminiscence."

Levinson's family history continues with *Soon, Annala,* published in 1993 with illustrations by Julie Downing. The year is now 1911, and young Anna Sarah has lived in America for over a year, where she has begun to learn to speak English, although Yiddish is still spoken at home. Now other relatives, including Anna Sarah's two younger brothers, are preparing to arrive from Eastern Europe, and preparations are being made. A wait on the wharf where passengers arrive from Ellis Island seems endless, but Anna and her extended family are finally reunited in their new home. *Horn Book* reviewer Hanna B. Zeiger called *Soon, Annala* "a touching portrait of immigrant life in the early 1900s." Stephanie Zvirin agreed in a *Booklist* appraisal, praising Levinson's book as "a loving portrait" that "will capture young listeners and whisk them back to an earlier time."

DinnieAbbieSister-r-r! gets its title from the way Levinson's mother used to call her children in at the end of playtime, stringing all three names together into one long word. As the middle child among five children, Levinson remembers what it was like to play "catch up"

to her older brothers, and recalls the warm feelings that all her siblings had for her mother, who remained energetic and optimistic even though the family often found itself in tight financial circumstances. In the book, five-year-old Jennie (nicknamed "Sister") lives in Brooklyn during the 1930s, where she and her family do such everyday things as go to the store, bake together, or spend the day at the beach. Then tragedy strikes: Jennie's older brother Abbie becomes paralyzed, and the family worries, watching his slow recovery. Commenting on *DinnieAbbieSister-r-r!,* *Horn Book* reviewer Nancy Vasilakis asserted that "warm family scenes, Jewish traditions lovingly evoked, and the sense of a simpler time characterize this quiet, richly-flavored story." In the follow-up story, *Boys Here—Girls There,* Jennie has grown another year and is starting school, but the Depression has made life in her family difficult due to her father's jewelry firm going out of business. Rita Soltan termed it "A winning book," in her *School Library Journal* appraisal.

In addition to writing books that recall her own New York City upbringing, Levinson has been inspired by other locations. *Our Home Is the Sea* was inspired by her visits to Hong Kong—she has gone there numerous times as part of her job as associate publisher and art director—and the love of family that she shares with that culture. In the story, a nameless young boy makes his way home from the last day of school in the bustling city of Hong Kong to the *sampan,* or houseboat, he and his family live in. His father and grandfather were both fishermen, and the boy aspires to be just like them when he grows up. Illustrating "the universality of children's interests and concerns," according to Zena Sutherland in *Bulletin of the Center for Children's Books, Our Home Is the Sea* "sings praise of the boy's love for the city and for his family's way of living," noted Mingshui Cai in *Children's Literature in Education.* Similarly, *Country Dawn to Dusk* also depicts a child who is happy in her environment—this time a rural farm rather than a bustling city. In Levinson's picture book, the young girl in the story spends her days in a one-room schoolhouse, while afternoons allow her to play with her dog and enjoy the out-of-doors.

In a departure from her usual realistic family stories, Levinson retells the familiar Hans Christian Andersen tale of *The Emperor's New Clothes* in what a *Publishers Weekly* critic commends as "fitting understatement," adding that Levinson's "dialogue and descriptions [are] imbued with grace."

While being an author remains a part-time occupation for Levinson, she continues to write stories for young readers and listeners, each filled with a sense of joy about close family ties. Levinson recently told *SATA,* "I will, I hope, always write about family. It's still what interests me most."

■ Works Cited

Cai, Mingshui, review of *Our Home Is the Sea, Children's Literature in Education,* September, 1994, p. 181.
Review of *The Emperor's New Clothes, Publishers Weekly,* July 12, 1991.
Review of *I Go with My Family to Grandma's, Kirkus Reviews,* July 15, 1985, p. 1119.
Soltan, Rita, review of *Boys Here—Girls There, School Library Journal,* February, 1993, p. 74.
Sutherland, Zena, review of *Our Home Is the Sea, Bulletin of the Center for Children's Books,* January, 1989, p. 127.
Vasilakis, Nancy, review of *DinnieAbbieSister-r-r!, Horn Book,* July-August, 1987, pp. 459-60.
Review of *Watch the Stars Come Out, Publishers Weekly,* August 16, 1985, p. 71.
Zeiger, Hanna B., review of *Soon, Annala, Horn Book,* November-December, 1993, pp. 735-36.
Zvirin, Stephanie, review of *Soon, Annala, Booklist,* November 1, 1993, p. 531.

■ For More Information See

PERIODICALS

Booklist, August, 1995, p. 1956.
Bulletin of the Center for Children's Books, December, 1985, p. 71.
Growing Point, January, 1987, p. 4743.
Horn Book, November, 1986, p. 738; January, 1989, p. 55.
Kirkus Reviews, March 15, 1987, pp. 474-75; May 1, 1991, p. 606; September, 1993, p. 1147.
Publishers Weekly, July 5, 1993, p. 70.
School Library Journal, December, 1985, p. 78; August, 1987, pp. 70-71; November, 1991, p. 89.

*　　*　　*

LYNN, Elizabeth A(nne) 1946-

■ Personal

Born June 8, 1946, in New York, NY; daughter of Richard Nathan (an accountant) and Winifred (an artist; maiden name, Null) Lynn. *Education:* Case Western Reserve University, B.A., 1967; University of Chicago, M.A., 1968. *Hobbies and other interests:* First kyu (brown belt) Aikido (registered with the World Aikido Federation, Tokyo, Japan).

■ Career

Teacher in public schools, Chicago, IL, 1968-70; St. Francis Hospital, Evanston, IL, unit manager, 1970-72; French Hospital, San Francisco, CA, unit manager, 1972-75. Medical secretary in San Francisco, 1974-75. San Francisco State University, teacher in women's studies program. *Member:* Mystery Writers of America, Science Fiction Writers of America, Feminist Writers Guild.

■ Awards, Honors

Woodrow Wilson fellowship, 1967-68; World Fantasy Awards, 1980 (best novel), for *Watchtower,* and 1981, for *The Woman Who Loved the Moon, and Other Stories.*

■ Writings

A Different Light (science fiction novel), Berkley, 1978.
The Sardonyx Net (science fiction novel), Berkley, 1981.
The Woman Who Loved the Moon, and Other Stories, Berkley, 1981.
The Red Hawk (stories), illustrated by Alicia Austin, Cheap Street (New Castle, VA), 1983.
The Silver Horse (children's fantasy novel), Bluejay (New York City), 1984.
Babe Didrikson Zaharias, Chelsea House, 1989.
Tales from a Vanished Country (stories), Pulphouse (Eugene, OR), 1990.
Dragon's Winter, Ace, 1998.

"CHRONICLES OF TORNOR" TRILOGY

Watchtower, Berkley, 1979.
The Dancers of Arun, Berkley, 1979.
The Northern Girl, Berkley, 1980.

OTHER

Work represented in anthologies, including *Tricks and Treats,* edited by Joe Gores and Bill Pronzini, Doubleday, 1976; *Dark Sins, Dark Dreams,* edited by Barry Malzberg and Bill Pronzini, Doubleday, 1978; and *Millennial Women,* edited by Virginia Kidd, Delacorte, 1978. Contributor of stories to science fiction magazines.

■ Sidelights

Elizabeth A. Lynn writes both science fiction and fantasy. Her novels and short stories have won her the respect of critics in both genres, while her nonfiction has won her further acclaim.

Lynn's science fiction novels are, on the surface, tales of interplanetary crime. One deals with the theft of valuable crystal masks from an unrecorded planet, another with the smuggling of an illegal drug used to control the behavior of convicts in a slave colony. Below the surface, both novels raise philosophical issues as well. *A Different Light* examines the process of dying through its protagonist Jimson Alleca, who faces death from cancer. A *Publishers Weekly* reviewer notes that Lynn's singular achievement is her ability to make the "bizarre setting and characters so vividly real that they are taken for granted." *The Sardonyx Net* explores the complex institution of slavery in a treatment that some reviewers found provocative and compelling. Roland Green in *Booklist* praised "good world building, brisk pacing, and excellent writing," while Gayle Keresey in *Voice of Youth Advocates* described *The Sardonyx Net* as "a thought-provoking examination of slavery," lauding it "the best of Lynn's outstanding novels."

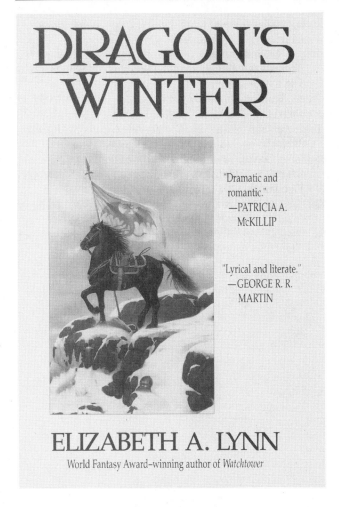

"Dramatic and romantic."
—PATRICIA A. McKILLIP

"Lyrical and literate."
—GEORGE R. R. MARTIN

ELIZABETH A. LYNN
World Fantasy Award-winning author of *Watchtower*

Karadun Atani battles his evil wizard twin to win back his birthright as dragon-king in Elizabeth A. Lynn's fantasy novel. (Cover illustration by Duane O. Myers.)

Lynn's fantasy novels, particularly the "Chronicles of Tornor" series, encompass a greater richness of scope, offering a wider selection of "equally weighted themes," as Liz Holliday maintained in *St. James Guide to Fantasy Writers.* In *Watchtower,* Prince Errel, the deposed heir to Tornor Keep, sets out for the Valley of Van, where he learns a dance form similar to some of the martial arts and becomes a *cheari* dancer. The *chearis,* who fight without weapons and will not kill, become important catalysts throughout the series. In this volume, Errel returns home after many years and raises an army to oust the usurper of Tornor Keep. He and his fellow *chearis* breach the security of the keep and open the gates to the advancing army. Though he himself will not kill, Errel's actions precipitate the ensuing slaughter, and Tornor is saved. Algis Budrys in *Booklist* praised the characterization of narrator Ryke, the captain of the guard, as "a full-fleshed, truly heroic figure, yet credible and likable."

The Dancers of Arun, set in Tornor many years later, explores the relationship of two brothers as the youngest grows to manhood. Kel, the elder, is a *cheari.* Kerris, who was orphaned young and disabled soon after, is a scribe's apprentice with a magical power of vision. The

two leave Tornor together, traveling with a *cheari* band. During the journey, the brothers strengthen the intimacy of their relationship, and Kerris struggles to understand his troubling visions and thus find inner peace. The siblings arrive at Elath, where Kel seems to believe there is help for his brother, only to experience a barbarian invasion. Elath provides no answers for Kerris. He resumes his travels, pursuing his quest for enlightenment. Budrys commented in *Booklist,* "Lynn is better at this sort of tale than most of its practitioners."

The Northern Girl completes a circle by returning the reader to Tornor Keep. Sorren is a servant to Arre Med, in the city of Kendra-on-the-Delta. Her magic visions reveal a place that she feels compelled to find. When she arrives at Tornor, she discovers the keep in a state of serious decline. Sorren proposes to save the keep through alliance with Arre Med, but achieving the alliance would involve the use of weapons banned by the *chearis.* Roland Green, writing in *Booklist,* pronounced this concluding volume as "thoroughly unconventional and quite outstanding." A *Publishers Weekly* reviewer praised the "convincing politics and sociology ... [plus the] more mature, thoughtful treatment of emotions, passions and relationships than is typical" for the genre, and predicted it would be one of the year's "top fantasies."

In these novels, according to Holliday, "the philosophy of the *chea*—the idea that the balance of the world must be maintained—is central." In keeping with that philosophy, what binds these novels together is the eternal ebb and flow of the fortunes of Tornor Keep and the stronghold's impact on the people who pass through. Holliday wrote: "Tornor starts out at the peak of its fortunes, falls and rises, then falls again, yet with the hope of a further rise to come. The characters ... struggle for survival and yet find survival is worth nothing without self-awareness and self-acceptance." She concluded, "Alone, each of these novels is a worthwhile read; taken together, they are much more than that."

Lynn also wrote a children's fantasy, *The Silver Horse,* and a biography of champion athlete Babe Didrikson Zaharias. The latter book, Lynn's contribution to the American Women of Achievement series, is "an interesting and thoughtful work," according to Ilene Cooper of *Booklist.* Cooper pointed out that the author "paints a vivid picture of what life was like for women athletes during the mid-twentieth century." Myrna Feldman in *Voice of Youth Advocates* highly recommended the book "both for the content and its likely appeal to low level readers."

Lynn's short fiction collections include *The Woman Who Loved the Moon, and Other Stories.* This offering of previously published work, ranging from the realistic to the fantastic, also includes an original introduction by the author for each of the sixteen stories. *Booklist's* Green praised her emotional power, mastery of language, and, despite a clearly feminist perspective, her "balanced" presentation "of both sexes." "The strength of Lynn's writing," concluded *Voice of Youth Advocates* contributor Gayle Keresey, "is her characterization and her ability to use understatement well."

■ Works Cited

Budrys, Algis, review of *Watchtower, Booklist,* April 1, 1979, p. 1203.

Budrys, Algis, review of *The Dancers of Arun, Booklist,* September, 1, 1979, p. 26.

Cooper, Ilene, review of *Babe Didrikson Zaharias, Booklist,* December 1, 1988, p. 652.

Review of *A Different Light, Publishers Weekly,* July 10, 1978, p. 132.

Feldman, Myrna, review of *Babe Didrikson Zaharias, Voice of Youth Advocates,* February, 1989, p. 303.

Green, Roland, review of *The Northern Girl, Booklist,* March 1, 1981, p. 917.

Green, Roland, review of *The Woman Who Loved the Moon, and Other Stories, Booklist,* November 15, 1981, p. 427.

Green, Roland, review of *The Sardonyx Net, Booklist,* February 15, 1982, p. 745.

Holliday, Liz, essay in *St. James Guide to Fantasy Writers,* St. James Press (Detroit), 1996.

Keresey, Gayle, review of *The Woman Who Loved the Moon, and Other Stories, Voice of Youth Advocates,* December, 1981, p. 39.

Keresey, Gayle, review of *The Sardonyx Net, Voice of Youth Advocates,* December, 1982, p. 38.

Review of *Northern Girl, Publishers Weekly,* November 21, 1980, p. 50.*

M

MacLANE, Jack
See CRIDER, (Allen) Bill(y)

* * *

MANES, Stephen 1949-
(Hans Pemsteen, A. M. Stephensen; joint double pseudonym: Mel Murch and Ward Starr)

■ Personal

Surname is pronounced MAN-ess; born January 8, 1949, in Pittsburgh, PA; son of Milton (a chemist) and Carol (Freeman) Manes; married Esther Selter, 1969; divorced, 1981; married Susan Kocik, 1989. *Education:* Attended University of Chicago, 1965-67; University of Southern California, A.B., 1973.

■ Addresses

Home—Seattle, WA.

■ Career

Writer, 1969—. American Film Institute, Beverly Hills, CA, assistant librarian, 1969-71; KCET-TV, Los Angeles, CA, co-producer, "The Curse of Los Feliz," 1971; National Telefilm Associates, Los Angeles, research director, 1972-73; Manhattan Cable Television, New York, NY, host of "PC TV," 1983; Hard/Soft Press, New York, NY, chairman, 1983-1988; American Program Service (Public Television), Boston, MA, co-host and co-executive editor of "Digital Duo," 1997-1998. *Member:* Authors Guild (member of National Council), Writers Guild, PEN American Center, Poets and Writers.

■ Awards, Honors

Children's Book of the Year, Child Study Children's Book Committee at Bank Street College, 1978, for *Mule in the Mail,* 1984, for *Be a Perfect Person in Just Three*

Days!, and 1991, for *Make Four Million Dollars by Next Thursday!;* Outstanding Science Trade Book for Children, National Science Teachers Association and Children's Book Council, 1982, for *Pictures of Motion and Pictures that Move: Eadweard Muybridge and the Photography of Motion;* Children's Choice, International Reading Association, 1986, for *Life is No Fair!,* and 1992, for *Make Four Million Dollars by Next Thursday!;* CRABbery (honor), 1983, Charlie May Simon award, 1984-85, Surrey School award, 1985, Nene award, 1986, Sunshine State award, 1986, Georgia Children's Book award, 1987, and California Young Reader (intermediate) award, 1988, all for *Be a Perfect Person in Just Three Days!*

■ Writings

FOR CHILDREN

Mule in the Mail, illustrated by Mary Chalmers, Coward, 1978.
The Boy Who Turned into a TV Set, illustrated by Michael Bass, Coward, 1979.
Slim Down Camp, Clarion, 1981.
(Under pseudonym Hans Pemsteen, adapter) *Clash of the Titans Storybook* (based on the screenplay by Beverly Cross), illustrated by Mike Eagle, Golden Books, 1981.
Socko! Every Riddle Your Feet Will Ever Need, illustrated by Nurit Karlin, Coward, 1982.
Be a Perfect Person in Just Three Days!, illustrated by Tom Huffman, Clarion, 1982.
Pictures of Motion and Pictures That Move: Eadweard Muybridge and the Photography of Motion (nonfiction), Coward, 1982.
(With Esther Manes) *The Bananas Move to the Ceiling,* illustrated by Barbara Samuels, F. Watts, 1983.
Life Is No Fair! illustrated by Warren Miller, Dutton, 1985.
The Great Gerbil Roundup, illustrated by John McKinley, Harcourt Brace Jovanovich, 1988.
It's New! It's Improved! It's Terrible!, Bantam Doubleday Dell, 1989.

Monstra vs. Irving, illustrated by Michael Sours, Holt, 1989.

Chocolate-Covered Ants, Scholastic, 1990.

Some of the Adventures of Rhode Island Red, illustrated by William Joyce, Lippincott, 1990.

Make Four Million Dollars by Next Thursday!, illustrated by George Ulrich, Bantam, 1991.

An Almost Perfect Game, Scholastic, 1995.

"HOOPLES" SERIES

Hooples on the Highway, illustrated by Merle Peek, Coward, 1978, Avon, 1985.

The Hooples' Haunted House, illustrated by Martha Weston, Delacorte, 1981.

The Hooples' Horrible Holiday, illustrated by Wally Neibart, Avon, 1986.

"OSCAR J. NOODLEMAN" SERIES

That Game from Outer Space: The First Strange Thing That Happened to Oscar Noodleman, illustrated by Tony Auth, Dutton, 1983.

The Oscar J. Noodleman Television Network: The Second Strange Thing That Happened to Oscar J. Noodleman, illustrated by Roy Schlemme, Dutton, 1983.

Chicken Trek: The Third Strange Thing That Happened to Oscar Noodleman, illustrated by Ron Barrett, Dutton, 1987.

"COMPUTER FUN" SERIES; WITH PAUL SOMERSON

Computer Monsters, Scholastic, 1984.
Computer Olympics, Scholastic, 1984.
Computer Craziness, Scholastic, 1984.
Computer Space Adventures, Scholastic, 1984.

FOR YOUNG ADULTS; FICTION

(As A. M. Stephensen) *Unbirthday,* Avon, 1982.
I'll Live, Avon, 1982.
Video War, Avon, 1983.
The Obnoxious Jerks, Bantam, 1988.
Comedy High, Scholastic, 1992.

FOR ADULTS; NONFICTION

(With Paul Somerson, under joint double pseudonym Ward Starr and Mel Murch) *Underground WordStar,* Hard/Soft Press, 1984.

(With Ron Barrett) *Encyclopedia Placematica,* Workman, 1985.

(With Paul Somerson) *StarFixer: The Ultimate WordStar Enhancement,* Bantam, 1987.

The Complete MCI Mail Handbook, Bantam, 1988.

(With Paul Andrews) *Gates: How Microsoft's Mogul Reinvented an Industry & Made Himself the Richest Man in America,* Doubleday, 1993.

Also author of screenplays, including "The Curse of Los Feliz," first broadcast by KCET-TV, 1971; "First Aid," 1973 (adaptation released as "Mother, Jugs, and Speed," Twentieth Century-Fox, 1976); "We Built the Bomb," 1974; "The Great Thaw," 1975; "The Red Room Riddle" (based on the book by Scott Corbett), ABC-TV, 1983; "The Littles" (based on a series of books by John Peterson), ABC-TV, 1983. Editor of

Focus!, 1967-69; contributor to *December* and *Gambit,* 1971; contributing editor, *PC Magazine, PC/Computing, PC Sources, PC jr, PC World,* and *InformationWeek;* monthly column, "Personal Curmudgeon," in *PC jr,* 1984; monthly column, "Parity Check," in *PC,* 1985; biweekly column, "Viewpoint: Stephen Manes," in *PC,* 1986-90; monthly column, "Stephen Manes," in *PC/Computing,* 1990-92; monthly column, "At Wit's End," in *PC Sources,* 1993; monthly column, "Desktop Agenda," in *InformationWeek,* 1994—; monthly column, "Full Disclosure," in *PC World,* 1995—; weekly column, "Personal Computers," in *The New York Times,* 1994—.

■ **Adaptations**

Be a Perfect Person in Just Three Days! was adapted as a motion picture and video recording entitled *How to be a Perfect Person in Just Three Days,* directed by Joan Micklin Silver, produced by Frank Doelger, and released by the Learning Corporation of America, 1984 and broadcast by PBS Television as part of the "Wonderworks" series. A portion of the book was also read as part of the "Books from Cover to Cover" series produced by WETA and aired on Public Television.

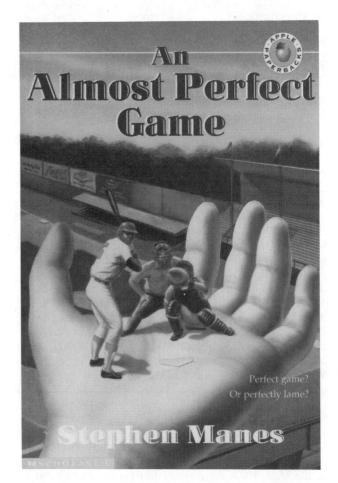

Baseball fan Jake finds out his magic scorecard can control the outcome of the minor-league games played by his favorite team in Stephen Manes's fantasy story.

Manes was a featured author in the Maryland Instructional Television programs "Read the Author," 1984, and "Writer's Realm," 1986.

■ Sidelights

Stephen Manes began his career as a writer in the third grade, when he toiled as a reporter for his school paper. Several years later, as a middle-grader, he won runner-up honors in a couple of statewide competitions to which he had submitted satire and humorous verse. He also developed a love of photography, and decided upon a career that would satisfy both of his primary interests: he would become a movie director. Manes attended college at the University of Chicago, and founded a film publication. He went on to Los Angeles, where he studied at the University of Southern California and wrote screenplays. Manes once told *SATA* that, disappointed with an adaptation of one of his scripts, he "began to realize that Hollywood and I were constitutionally incompatible." His first wife, Esther, a children's librarian, had been bringing home books that Manes enjoyed reading. He decided to move back East to try writing books for kids. It was not long before Manes developed a reputation for writing children's books with outrageous characters and situations that critics described as wacky, zany, and a great deal of fun. While Manes's novels for young adults are more serious in tone, these too are cited by some commentators for their unique humor.

One of Manes's first books for children, *The Boy Who Turned Into a TV Set,* is "good for a few giggles," according to a *Kirkus Reviews* critic. This story is about a boy who watches too much television despite the warnings of his mother. One day, when he tries to speak, he can only repeat television commercials (and inadvertently offend his listeners). Soon enough, a green glow from the boy's stomach becomes a television set which the television repair woman helps him adjust.

Another of Manes's early books, *Be a Perfect Person in Just Three Days!,* presents protagonist Milo Crinkley following the advice he finds in a book written by Dr. K. Pinkerton Silverfish. Dr. Silverfish recommends many outlandish activities to his readers, and Milo Crinkley does his best to perform them all (including doing nothing, fasting, and wearing broccoli around his neck). Milo's efforts do no more than teach him a lesson about accepting his imperfect self. The conclusion of the book, related a *Publishers Weekly* critic, "changes chuckles to belly laughs." *Booklist*'s Ilene Cooper found the book to be "not perfect but awfully funny." *Be a Perfect Person in Just Three Days!* won several awards and was adapted as a film, a drama in French and English, and an opera performed by children under the auspices of the Cincinnati Opera.

Make Four Million Dollars by Next Thursday! features another of Dr. K. Pinkerton Silverfish's books and another unsuspecting reader. Jason Nozzle pins homemade money to his clothes, concentrates on having millions of dollars, plants a dollar bill, and asks a rich

When Milo Crinkley tries to follow the goofy advice of Dr. K. Pinkerton Silverfish's book on how to be perfect, the boy learns instead that it's more important to accept imperfection. (Cover illustration by Chuck Pyle.)

family to take him in. Eventually, Jason learns that being rich is not as important as other things. Ruth Ann Smith of *Bulletin of the Center for Children's Books* wrote that readers "will enjoy seeing [Jason] make a fool of himself." According to *Booklist*'s Kay Weisman, "laughs abound."

Three of Manes's books feature the character Oscar Noodleman. In the first book, Noodleman plays with a video game that turns out to be a space ship, and in the second, he uses a video camera to broadcast his own shows on television. The third book, *Chicken Trek,* begins when Oscar goes to work for his cousin to pay him back for the camera he broke. Oscar soon learns that his job is to eat chicken for each meal, for his inventor cousin is trying to win a prize in a chicken-eating contest. "Raucous ridiculous fun," wrote Ilene Cooper in *Booklist.*

Chocolate-Covered Ants, featuring feuding brothers and a box of worms, was noted by critics for its presentation of disgusting pranks that may please some children. *Some of the Adventures of Rhode Island Red,* written in the punning style common to Manes's work, follows the

Dr. K. Pinkerton Silverfish alleges his book can make anyone rich, enticing Jason Nozzle until he finds there are things more significant than wealth. (From *Make Four Million Dollars by Next Thursday!*, written by Manes and illustrated by George Ulrich.)

feats of a tiny, red-haired protagonist. According to Ruth Ann Smith of *Bulletin of the Center for Children's Books,* this tale "squawks to be read aloud." *The Great Gerbil Roundup,* for upper-elementary readers, involves a plot to bring tourists to town. Celia A. Huffman of *School Library Journal* described the book as a "madcap and wacky adventure." Ilene Cooper of *Booklist* remarked that it "will elicit giggles and guffaws" from readers. *Monstra vs. Irving,* for younger readers, finds Irving annoyed by his younger sister. When Claire drinks a magic potion, she grows fangs and claws. "Manes' fans will welcome" the work, remarked Amy Adler, writing in *School Library Journal.*

One of Manes's more recent stories, *An Almost Perfect Game,* is a well-received baseball fantasy for middle graders. In this work, Jake and Randy accompany their baseball-loving grandparents to a crucial game for the minor-league Nottingham Shoppers. The four regularly attend Shoppers games together when the boys visit, but this particular contest is special: not only is this game an all-or-nothing climax to a heated pennant race, but Jake's favorite pitcher is on the hill, and Jake has

unwittingly purchased a magical scorecard which he quickly realizes will allow him to call the shots when his team's defense is on the field. "Manes captures the experience of a family sharing its love and knowledge of baseball and makes it easy for readers to follow the play-by-play action," asserted *Booklist* reviewer Karen Hutt. *School Library Journal* contributor Todd Morning also offered a favorable estimation of *An Almost Perfect Game,* maintaining: "Manes wonderfully evokes minor-league baseball at its most irrepressible, and the witty, first-person narration helps to carry the story along."

In addition to his books for children, Manes has produced novels for young adults. *I'll Live,* one of the first of these, focuses on the feelings of a young man whose father is dying of cancer. Dylan, who has fallen in love with his father's young volunteer nurse, must learn to cope not only with his father's determination to die with dignity and his own grief, but with a first real love. *Video War* relates what happens after the city council attempts to ban video games in Elmer's town. Elmer, an arcade regular, worries that he won't be able to break a record he has been working on, and struggles against the councilmen promoting the ban. Many critics noted the use of curse words in this book.

In *The Obnoxious Jerks,* Frank joins a club of teens intent on questioning conformity at their school. Yet Frank is troubled when the group refuses to let a young woman join. According to Stephanie Zvirin of *Booklist,* the work's "iconoclastic view of school" is "bound to appeal." Calling the book a "riotous read," Marian Rafal of *Voice of Youth Advocates* explained that the dialogue is "very, very funny." *Comedy High* is a story of a young man who has moved to Nevada; his high school is set up in an old hotel, and the students take courses to help them succeed in the entertainment business. *Booklist's* Zvirin noted the book's "intriguing Las Vegas send-up."

Manes also writes nonfiction books on computer and other subjects, including a well-received biography of Bill Gates, and has been a regular computer columnist for several magazines and for the *New York Times.* He continues, however, to pen fiction for children and young adults. He once explained to *SATA* that his influences range from Uncle Remus to Daffy Duck, and that writing for kids lets him "indulge and cultivate a sense of silliness and whimsy too many adults seem to lack." He continued, "Ultimately, 'Don't bore me' is the reader's first commandment to any writer. Much as we authors may hate to admit it, people don't *have* to read fiction. In the struggle to win a portion of people's precious leisure time, books are engaged in a fierce competition with everything from windsurfing to horticulture to video games. Unless writers offer something that's not available elsewhere—honesty, beauty, humor, intelligence, iconoclasm, ideas, personal vision—we can and should expect to find our potential readers hanging ten, hanging plants, or hanging out. But when we get 'em it's wonderful."

■ Works Cited

Adler, Amy, review of *Monstra vs. Irving, School Library Journal,* January, 1990, p. 106.

Review of *Be a Perfect Person in Just Three Days!, Publishers Weekly,* April 23, 1982, p. 93.

Review of *The Boy Who Turned into a TV Set, Kirkus Reviews,* September 15, 1979, p. 1068.

Cooper, Ilene, review of *Be a Perfect Person in Just Three Days!, Booklist,* July, 1982, p. 1446.

Cooper, Ilene, review of *Chicken Trek: The Third Strange Thing That Happened to Oscar Noodleman, Booklist,* August, 1987, p. 1750.

Cooper, Ilene, review of *The Great Gerbil Roundup, Booklist,* December 15, 1988, p. 712.

Huffman, Celia A., review of *The Great Gerbil Roundup, School Library Journal,* January, 1989, p. 78.

Hutt, Karen, review of *An Almost Perfect Game, Booklist,* June 1 & 15, 1995, pp. 1771-72.

Morning, Todd, review of *An Almost Perfect Game, School Library Journal,* June, 1995, p. 112.

Rafal, Marian, review of *The Obnoxious Jerks, Voice of Youth Advocates,* October, 1988, p. 183.

Smith, Ruth Ann, review of *Some of the Adventures of Rhode Island Red, Bulletin of the Center for Children's Books,* July-August, 1990, p. 272.

Smith, Ruth Ann, review of *Make Four Million Dollars by Next Thursday!, Bulletin of the Center for Children's Books,* February, 1991, p. 147.

Weisman, Kay, review of *Make Four Million Dollars by Next Thursday!, Booklist,* February 15, 1991, pp. 1193-94.

Zvirin, Stephanie, review of *The Obnoxious Jerks, Booklist,* August, 1988, p. 1915.

Zvirin, Stephanie, review of *Comedy High, Booklist,* December 1, 1992, p. 659.

■ For More Information See

BOOKS

Seventh Book of Junior Authors and Illustrators, H. W. Wilson, 1996, pp. 207-09.

PERIODICALS

Booklist, October 15, 1981, pp. 307-08; April 15, 1989, p. 1475; June 1 & 15, 1995, pp. 1171-72.

Bulletin of the Center for Children's Books, January, 1990, p. 115.

Horn Book, February, 1983, pp. 53-54; August, 1981, p. 425.

School Library Journal, April, 1983, p. 126; August, 1987, pp. 86-7; June, 1995, p. 112.

Voice of Youth Advocates, August, 1995, p. 161.

Wilson's Library Bulletin, June, 1995, pp. 120-21.

* * *

MANUEL, Lynn 1948-

■ Personal

Born January 21, 1948, in Hamilton, Ontario, Canada; daughter of Clarence Earl Maycock (a steelworker) and Verna Mary (Gorton) Maycock; children: Jennifer Vallee, David. *Education:* McMaster University, B.A. (history), 1969; Ontario Teacher Education College, B.Ed., 1975; University of British Columbia, M.F.A. (creative writing), 1993.

■ Addresses

Home—314-1280 Fir Street, White Rock, British Columbia, Canada V4B4B1.

■ Career

Writer and proofreader. *Member:* Writer's Union of Canada, Canadian Society of Children's Authors, Illustrators, and Performers.

■ Awards, Honors

"Our Choice" list, Canadian Children's Book Center, 1997-98, for *The Night the Moon Blew Kisses.*

■ Writings

Mystery at Cranberry Farm, illustrated by Sylvie Daigneault, Gage Educational Publishers (Scarborough, Ontario), 1981.

Mystery of the Ghostly Riders, illustrated by Sylvie Daigneault, Gage, 1985.

The Ghost Ships That Didn't Belong, illustrated by Paul McCusker, Gage, 1987.

Return to Cranberry Farm, illustrated by Rob Johannsen, Gage, 1990.

Lynn Manuel with granddaughter Emma.

The Princess Who Laughed in Colours, illustrated by J. O. Pennanen, Penumbra Press (Manotick, Ontario), 1995.

The Night the Moon Blew Kisses, illustrated by Robin Spowart, Houghton Mifflin, 1996.

Fifty-Five Grandmas and a Llama, illustrated by Carolyn Fisher, Gibbs Smith Publisher (Layton, UT), 1997.

Lucy Maud and the Cavendish Cat, illustrated by Janet Wilson, Tundra Books (Toronto, Ontario), 1997.

The Cherry Pit Princess, illustrated by Debbie Edlin, Coteau Books (Regina, Saskatchewan), 1997.

■ Sidelights

Lynn Manuel told *SATA:* "The books by Lucy Maud Montgomery were always very special to me when I was growing up. My two favourites were *The Story Girl* and *The Golden Road.* Years later, when I was reading *The Selected Journals of L. M. Montgomery,* I found it interesting that they were her own particular favourites. While I was reading these journals, I knew that I wanted to write a picture book for children about Maud's life, especially the period when she was working on *Anne of Green Gables.* My problem was how to write an interesting and accurate account of such a lonely time. Maud lived a very isolated life while she was caring for her elderly grandmother in Cavendish, on Prince Edward Island. She was often deeply depressed. But as I read volume 2 of the *Journals,* I came to see how much her gray cat Daffy meant to her, and how constant was her love for him. That was when I decided to write about this time of her life through the eyes of her cat. In that way, the loneliness could be kept in the background, and the focus of the story could be Maud and her cat Daffy. The result was the picture book *Lucy Maud and the Cavendish Cat.*"

Lynn Manuel's first picture book, *The Night the Moon Blew Kisses,* follows a little girl and her grandmother as they take a walk on a snowy, moonlit night. The child blows kisses to the moon and the moon responds with snowflake kisses—"Swirly kisses, twirly kisses, willowy-billowy wisps of kisses." "The text is fresh and gentle," noted Anne Louise Mahoney in *Quill & Quire.* In a review for *School Library Journal,* Ruth K. MacDonald called *The Night the Moon Blew Kisses* "a mystical, marvelous nighttime tour of a winter landscape."

In *Fifty-Five Grandmas and a Llama,* young Sam wishes desperately for a grandmother, finally placing an ad in the newspaper. He gets more than he bargained for when fifty-five grandmas show up, one even toting a llama. "The lesson that too much of a good thing is not a good thing packs a big comic wallop here when zany grandmas ... cavort in Waldo-esque scenes," asserted Pam McCuen in *The Bulletin of the Center for Children's Books.*

For older readers, *The Ghost Ships that Didn't Belong* offers a spine-tingling adventure based on a true incident from the Canadian Cariboo Gold Rush. Two ten-year-old cousins encounter a glowing sailing ship in a field near their grandparents' house, along with a spooky old woman who is the only other person able to see it. The children are in a race against time to solve a mystery as the ship bears down upon them. Gisela Sherman stated in *Canadian Children's Literature* that Manuel has created "an exciting modern ghost story, with vivid descriptions, some nice light spots and bits of history slipped in smoothly."

■ Works Cited

MacDonald, Ruth K., review of *The Night the Moon Blew Kisses, School Library Journal,* November, 1996, p. 88.

Mahoney, Anne Louise, review of *The Night the Moon Blew Kisses, Quill & Quire,* October, 1996, p. 46.

McCuen, Pam, review of *Fifty-Five Grandmas and a Llama, Bulletin of the Center for Children's Books,* July-August, 1997, pp. 402-03.

Sherman, Gisela, review of *The Ghost Ships that Didn't Belong, Canadian Children's Literature,* No. 53, 1989, pp. 71-73.

■ For More Information See

PERIODICALS

Kirkus Reviews, June 1, 1996, p. 827.
Publishers Weekly, July 15, 1996, p. 73.
School Library Journal, April, 1997, pp. 113-14.

*   *   *

MARTEL, Suzanne 1924-

■ Personal

Born October 8, 1924, in Quebec City, Quebec, Canada; married Maurice Martel (a corporate lawyer); children: six sons. *Education:* Monastery of the Ursulines, Quebec City, Quebec; University of Toronto. *Religion:* Roman Catholic. *Hobbies and other interests:* Traveling alone, which helps her think about and plan stories.

■ Addresses

Home—20258, rue Du Lakeshore, Baie d'Urfe, Quebec, Canada H9X 1P9.

■ Career

Writer. Has worked as a manager for Avon Canada, as an organizer of blood-donor clinics, and was in charge of a pavilion at Expo 67; published *Safari,* a weekly children's magazine, for three years.

■ Awards, Honors

Vicky Metcalf Award, Canadian Authors Association, 1976, for body of work; Ruth Schwartz Children's Book Award, Ontario Arts Council, 1981, for *The King's Daughter;* Canada Council Children's Literature Prize, 1982, for *Nos amis robots.* Martel has also won many French-language writing awards.

■ Writings

WORKS IN ENGLISH

The City under Ground, illustrated by Don Sibley, translated by Norah Smaridge, Viking Press, 1964.

The King's Daughter, translated by David Toby Homel and Margaret Rose, Douglas & McIntyre (Vancouver, BC, Canada), 1980, rev. ed., 1994.

Robot Alert, translated by Patricia Sillers, Kids Can Press, 1985.

Pee Wee, translated by John Fleming, Scholastic Canada, 1988.

Has written more than twenty-five books in French, both fiction and nonfiction, for children and adults. Also writes short stories.

■ Sidelights

Suzanne Martel's life-long love affair with writing began in early childhood. When she was seven, she and her four-year-old sister—the late Monique Corriveau, also a writer—created a family of imaginary characters who lived in the walls of their Quebec City home. "The family in the wall," which the two imaginative youngsters named the Montcorbiers, "became very important, more so than everyday life," Martel told the Canadian Children's Book Centre. "Even in our twenties, we didn't want to go out to meet friends."

The fictitious family, which included soldiers, aviators, mountain climbers, and even a woman admiral, absorbed the two girls completely. School vacations were spent locked in their room, writing. Evenings were often devoted to reading aloud what they had written. When their mother put her foot down and forbade them from writing more than eight hours a day, young Suzanne and Monique were unfazed. "We had to spend an hour walking, playing or swinging, but we spent it talking about our characters, so it was just the same," Martel told Dave Jenkinson of *Emergency Librarian.*

When they were teenagers, the sisters spent much of their time describing the appearance and personalities of the Montcorbiers, inspired by photographs of actors and actresses. Martel feels that she and her sister were feminists even at that early age, creating fascinating careers for both their male and female protagonists.

Martel met her future husband at a party when she was eighteen. She had accepted the invitation only at the urging of her mother, who was concerned that her daughter wasn't socializing enough and promised her five dollars if she would attend. "My mother said it was the best five dollars she'd ever invested," Martel told the Canadian Children's Book Centre.

After Martel and her sister each married, they set aside the Montcorbiers to concentrate on raising their own large families. Corriveau had ten children and Martel had six. For years, the only thing Martel wrote was an annual Christmas story, which she entered every year in a newspaper competition. She won the prize so often

In Suzanne Martel's award-winning historical novel, eighteen-year-old orphan Jeanne Chatel leaves France for North America to become the wife of a trapper. (Cover illustration by Harvey Chan.)

that the newspaper ended up appointing her to the jury that judged the stories.

The story that eventually became *Quatre Montrealais en l'an 3000,* which was translated into English as *The City Under Ground,* also had its beginnings in a writing contest. Martel found out about the contest just weeks before its submissions deadline. To meet the deadline, she hired a babysitter to look after the children during the day and her husband volunteered to look after them in the evenings. Martel not only won the contest, but also expanded the story into her first book, which was published in French when she was thirty-six.

The King's Daughter also began as a story submitted to a competition. This one, for historical fiction, was sponsored by *Chatelaine* magazine. The idea for the story arose out of a question Martel asked herself: What would I do if I were in the place of a girl who came to New France? Although the story won a prize and appeared in *Chatelaine,* Martel found that the main character, Jeanne, remained vividly in her imagination, and decided to write more about her. The result was *Jeanne, fille du roy,* which was translated into English as

The King's Daughter. Reviewing the translation in the Toronto *Globe and Mail,* Sandra Martin wrote that the main character, Jeanne Chatel, is "adventuresome, plucky, inventive, intelligent, loving, hardy, loyal and fun—as a role model, she is tough to beat."

Martel told the Canadian Children's Book Centre that the ideas for her stories come "from things I would like to have done when I was a child and still would enjoy— like riding a horse, even stealing one from the enemy, climbing mountains, sailing, being brave in the dark, or flying." Although her ideas are born in her imagination, Martel recognizes that facts and details are important, whether she's writing historical fiction such as *The King's Daughter,* or a contemporary novel about hockey, such as *Pee Wee.* When researching for *The King's Daughter,* Martel read widely about the orphans who were shipped to New France in the seventeenth century to become the wives of settlers. Such research proved useful to the tale, according to reviewer Joan McGrath. In *Books for Young People,* McGrath praised *The King's Daughter's* plot, maintaining that it utilizes "a good deal of interesting observation of the terrifying situation faced by newcomers to an utterly strange land." When writing *Pee Wee,* she talked to a nephew about his peewee hockey experiences, and attended the finals of a tournament in Quebec City. Although she confessed to Dave Jenkinson of *Emergency Librarian* that she knew nothing about hockey, she also said that *Pee Wee* is proof that "with research you can write about things that you don't know anything about."

Although they had set the Montcorbiers aside, neither Martel nor her sister forgot about the family in the wall. When their mother died, the two went through twenty boxes of material that had been stored away, a task that inspired them to begin writing the saga of the family they had created while growing up. The result was a series of manuscripts, seventeen by Corriveau, and ten by Martel. Two of Corriveau's have been published as books for adults, as have three of Martel's. When Corriveau died in 1976, Martel told the Canadian Children's Book Centre, "I died with her. She taught me how to die over two years. She asked me to finish the books."

For Martel, writing is a pleasure, something she would do whether she was published or not. She still enjoys it as much as she did when she was a child. "What is important to me while I'm writing is that I've had a wonderful time. Anything creative should be like that."

As she did in childhood, Martel often spends an entire day writing. She writes at home, often at night when everyone else is in bed. Sitting in a comfortable chair with a pillow on her knees, she uses a large children's book as a desk. Martel's husband and sons are the first to see her work, reading and commenting on her manuscripts. At the same time, her husband has typed her manuscripts for more than twenty years.

Although Martel speaks English fluently, she writes only in French. "I could write in English," she told Dave

Jenkinson of *Emergency Librarian,* "but I don't think my writing would be varied or rich enough. I know that because when I read the translations, I say, 'Isn't that well said.' I would never have thought of saying it that way."

Though she is now a grandmother, Martel still thinks that life is an adventure. An avid traveler, she has visited India, where she lived through some of the adventures of one of her adult characters, such as riding elephants and camels and stalking tigers, has trekked in the Himalayas, and loves nothing better than to hop a trans-continental train, hole up in a compartment, and write all the way to Vancouver. She hopes that young people recognize themselves in her stories, and that her stories help them step into another world. "This is why it is so exciting to be a writer," she told the Canadian Children's Book Centre. "You get to live hundreds of lives besides your own. The life in your head is just as important and real as the one outside."

■ Works Cited

Jenkinson, Dave, "Portraits: Suzanne Martel," *Emergency Librarian,* May-June, 1985, pp. 49-51.
Martel, Suzanne, comments in *Writing Stories, Making Pictures,* Canadian Children's Book Centre, 1994.
Martin, Sandra, review of *The King's Daughter, Globe and Mail* (Toronto), December 13, 1980, p. E15.
McGrath, Joan, review of *The King's Daughter, Books for Young People,* April, 1988, p. 6.

■ For More Information See

PERIODICALS

Canadian Materials, January, 1991, p. 16; May, 1991, p. 160.
Quill & Quire, October, 1995, p. 22.*

*   *   *

MARTIN, Fredric
See CHRISTOPHER, Matt(hew Frederick)

*   *   *

McDONALD, Megan 1959-

■ Personal

Born February 28, 1959, in Pittsburgh, PA; daughter of John (an ironworker) and Mary Louise (a social worker; maiden name, Ritzel) McDonald; married Richard Haynes. *Education:* Oberlin College, B.A., 1981; University of Pittsburgh, M.L.S., 1986.

■ Addresses

Home—Sebastopol, CA.

Career

Carnegie Library, Pittsburgh, PA, children's librarian, 1986-90; Minneapolis Public Library, Minneapolis, MN, children's librarian, 1990-91; Adams Memorial Library, Latrobe, PA, children's librarian, 1991-94; children's writer. *Member:* American Library Association, Society of Children's Book Writers and Illustrators.

Awards, Honors

Children's Choice Book, International Reading Association and Children's Book Council, 1991, and Reading Rainbow Book selection, both for *Is This a House for Hermit Crab?;* Notable Children's Trade Book in the Field of Social Studies, National Council for the Social Studies and Children's Book Council, for *The Potato Man;* Judy Blume Contemporary Fiction Award, Society of Children's Book Writers and Illustrators, for *The Bridge to Nowhere;* other honors received include the Keystone State Award, American Bookseller's Pick of the Lists and Best Books of the Year, *School Library Journal.*

Writings

FOR CHILDREN

Is This a House for Hermit Crab?, illustrated by S. D. Schindler, Orchard, 1990.

MEGAN McDONALD

The Potato Man, illustrated by Ted Lewin, Orchard, 1991.
Whoo-oo Is It?, illustrated by S. D. Schindler, Orchard, 1992.
The Great Pumpkin Switch, illustrated by Ted Lewin, Orchard, 1992.
Insects Are My Life, illustrated by Paul Brett Johnson, Orchard, 1995.
My House Has Stars, illustrated by Peter Catalanotto, Orchard, 1996.
Beezy, illustrated by Nancy Poydar, Orchard, 1997.
Tundra Mouse: A Storyknife Book, illustrated by S. D. Schindler, Orchard, 1997.
Beezy at Bat, illustrated by Nancy Poydar, Orchard, 1998.
Beezy Magic, illustrated by Poydar, Orchard, 1998.

FOR YOUNG ADULTS

The Bridge to Nowhere (novel), Orchard, 1993.

Work in Progress

The Bone Keeper, illustrated by G. Brian Karas, for DK Ink; *Judy Moody* (a novel), for Candlewick; *The Night Iguana Left Home,* illustrated by Ponder Goembel, for DK Ink; *Bedbugs,* illustrated by Paul Brett Johnson, for Orchard Books.

Sidelights

Megan McDonald brings her diverse experiences as a park ranger, bookseller, museum guide, librarian, and especially storyteller to her many picture books for young children. In books like *Whoo-oo Is It?* and *Insects Are My Life,* as well as her young adult novel, *The Bridge to Nowhere,* and her series of beginning readers featuring the lighthearted character Beezy, she combines an extensive knowledge of nature with a love of storytelling. "Connecting children with books has always been the centerpiece of my life's work," McDonald once told *Something about the Author* (*SATA*). In an effort to combat the statistics that show more and more children unable to read, McDonald has devoted much of her time to working in her local library, and views the books she writes as another step in the fight against illiteracy.

Illustrated by S. D. Schindler, *Is This a House for Hermit Crab?,* McDonald's first picture book, had its roots in a puppet show she hosted at her local library. "Its alliterative sounds, its rhythm and repetition worked so well with young children that I decided to write it as a picture book, in hopes that the story would find a wider audience," McDonald explained to *SATA.* In the story, a crab searches a rocky shoreline for a new home, finding the perfect abode in time to avoid becoming an afternoon snack for a crab-eating pricklepine fish. Praising both its rhythmic text and its pastel illustrations, *Five Owls* contributor Margaret Mary Kimmel lauded McDonald's debut work as "a beautiful book to look at again and again, to repeat over and over." "Best of all," Carolyn Phelan pointed out in *Booklist,* "the writer knows when to ask questions to involve the children and when to stop."

Best of all was the organ-grinder. He strolled down our hill playin' "Pop Goes the Weasel" on his hurdy-gurdy. When the music went POP! his lovebird, Rascal, would hand you a fortune in his beak:

YOU WILL HAVE THREE TIMES GOOD LUCK.

A young boy becomes friends with a vegetable vendor in McDonald's tale set in the days before the Great Depression. (From *The Potato Man,* illustrated by Ted Lewin.)

After the success of *Is This a House for Hermit Crab?,* McDonald decided to collaborate with illustrator Schindler on a second nonfiction picture book, titled *Whoo-oo Is It?* The story revolves around a mother barn owl's attempt to sit on her eggs in peace, while all of nature seems to be intent on being noisy. The noise—a strange sound that gradually gets louder—persists and is discovered to be the first young owlet pecking its way out of its shell. While the source of the noise, which begins at nightfall, is at first a mystery to listeners, "the final tender family scene will relieve any lingering concerns," according to *Horn Book* reviewer Elizabeth S. Watson. Praising the book, *Five Owls* critic Anne Lundin called *Whoo-oo Is It?* "a spirited book to read aloud, in a kind of celebration of life."

McDonald's *The Potato Man* and its sequel, *The Great Pumpkin Switch,* are based on her recollection of stories her father told about what it was like growing up in Pittsburgh before the Great Depression. The gruff, old Potato Man, with his one good eye, rode through the streets on a wagon, "calling out a strange cry that sounded like 'Abba-no-potata-man'," McDonald recalled. "When the children heard the cry, they became frightened and ran away. Because the story has its roots in the oral tradition of my own family, I tried to capture the feel, the setting, the language as I imagined it when the story was told to me as a young girl." In her book, a young boy (the author's father) tries to play tricks on Mr. Angelo, the Potato Man, but gets caught each time. When his hijinks cause him to have extra chores at home, he decides to make his peace with the old peddlar. Praising the story for its evocation of the past, *Horn Book* critic Mary M. Burns noted that the book's "text ... sets forth conflict and solution without moralizing." In *The Great Pumpkin Switch,* the same mischievous boy and his friend Otto smash his sister's prize pumpkin, by accident of course. Mr. Angelo comes

to their rescue, replacing the smashed pumpkin with another just as good, in a story that *School Library Journal* contributor Susan Scheps notes "will not seem the least old-fashioned to today's readers." The watercolor illustrations that Ted Lewin contributes to both books add greatly to the immediacy of McDonald's books. "Warm, beautifully cadenced storytelling," maintained a *Kirkus Reviews* critic, who also commented favorably on the book's "engaging period details."

Other fictional picture books by McDonald have included the humorous *Insects Are My Life.* In the intriguingly titled story, first-grader Amanda Frankenstein has a passion for bugs, much to the dismay of her friends and family. Not content merely to catch and collect dead bugs like most insect aficionados, Amanda thinks of her home as a bug sanctuary, and invites her flying and crawling friends *inside* the house rather than shooing them out. She remains terribly misunderstood until the arrival of Maggie, the new girl in school, who happens to feel equally as passionate about reptiles. "McDonald's single-minded, sometimes naughty heroine evokes chuckles with her feisty independence," according to Margaret A. Bush of *Horn Book,* while in *School Library Journal,* Virginia Opocensky dubbed "refreshing" McDonald's creation of "nonsqueamish female characters ... willing to take on all adversaries in defense of their causes." "A sturdy and endearing paean to kids in a topic-intensive phase," concluded *Bulletin of the Center for Children's Books* reviewer Deborah Stevenson.

McDonald leaves familiar surroundings in two books featuring unusual settings: the first, *My House Has Stars,* describes children from around the globe and the homes they live in from which they see the sky at night. "The concept of one earth, one sky," wrote Sally R. Dow in *School Library Journal,* "unfolds in poetic imagery, embracing the universality of people everywhere." In *Tundra Mouse,* McDonald, "sprinkling her tale generously with Eskimo terms" according to a *Publishers Weekly* critic, tells of Yup'ik Eskimo girls who scratch pictures in the ground with a knife's tip as they tell stories.

The Bridge to Nowhere, McDonald's semi-autobiographical novel for young adults, was a change of pace for its author. Readers meet seventh-grader Hallie O'Shea, who is frustrated over her now-out-of-work father's inability to cope with the loss of his job. Depressed and withdrawn from the rest of the family, Mr. O'Shea spends his time in the basement, building metal sculptures, or driving off to his former job site, a bridge over the Allegheny that he calls the "bridge to nowhere" because it was never finished. Hallie's mother, meanwhile, becomes absorbed with worry about her husband, and older sister Shelley escapes to college, leaving the young teen to fend for herself. Things improve after Hallie meets Crane Henderson, a ninth grader for whom she soon develops a crush, but when her father attempts to commit suicide by driving off the unfinished bridge, the young couple's relationship is tested. Praising the book as a fine first effort for former picture-book writer McDonald, a *Kirkus Reviews* critic called *The Bridge to Nowhere* "unusually well crafted: accessible, lyrical, with wonderful natural dialogue" between parent and teen. Deborah Abbott pointed out in *Booklist* that the novel provides "realistic characters, an attention-holding plot ... and an upbeat ending."

"Story can come from memory or experience," McDonald once explained to *SATA.* "It seems to come from everywhere, and out of nowhere. In everything there is story—a leaf falling, the smell of cinnamon, a dog that looks both ways before crossing the street. The idea, the seed of a story, is implicit—but requires paying attention, watching, seeing, listening, smelling, eavesdropping."

"To be a writer, I write. To be a writer for children, I continue to believe in the transformative power of story that connects children with books."

■ Works Cited

Abbott, Deborah, review of *The Bridge to Nowhere, Booklist,* April 1, 1993, pp. 1424-25.
Review of *The Bridge to Nowhere, Kirkus Reviews,* March 15, 1993, p. 374.
Burns, Mary M., review of *The Potato Man, Horn Book,* May, 1991, p. 318.
Bush, Margaret A., review of *Insects Are My Life, Horn Book,* March-April, 1995, p. 185.
Dow, Sally R., review of *My House Has Stars, School Library Journal,* October, 1996, pp. 102-03.
Review of *The Great Pumpkin Switch, Kirkus Reviews,* July 1, 1992, p. 851.
Kimmel, Margaret Mary, review of *Is This a House for Hermit Crab? Five Owls,* July-August, 1990, p. 105.
Lundin, Anne, review of *Whoo-oo Is It?, Five Owls,* May-June, 1992, p. 58.
Opocensky, Virginia, review of *Insects Are My Life, School Library Journal,* March, 1995, pp. 183-84.
Phelan, Carol, review of *Is This a House for Hermit Crab?, Booklist,* March 1, 1990, p. 1347.
Scheps, Susan, review of *The Great Pumpkin Switch, School Library Journal,* August, 1992, pp. 143-44.
Stevenson, Deborah, review of *Insects Are My Life, Bulletin of the Center for Children's Books,* April, 1995, p. 280.
Review of *Tundra Mouse, Publishers Weekly,* October 6, 1997, p. 55.
Watson, Elizabeth S., review of *Whoo-oo Is It?, Horn Book,* May-June, 1992, p. 332.

■ For More Information See

BOOKS

Seventh Book of Junior Authors and Illustrators, H. W. Wilson, 1996, pp. 223-25.

PERIODICALS

Booklist, March 1, 1995, p. 1249.
Horn Book, March-April, 1990, p. 222.
Kirkus Reviews, January, 1992, p. 117.
Publishers Weekly, December 14, 1990, p. 66; February 17, 1992, p. 62; September 29, 1997, p. 89.
School Library Journal, November, 1997, p. 92.

MEAKER, M. J.
See MEAKER, Marijane (Agnes)

*   *   *

MEAKER, Marijane (Agnes) 1927- (M. E. Kerr, Mary James, M. J. Meaker, Ann Aldrich, Vin Packer)

■ Personal

Born May 27, 1927, in Auburn, NY; daughter of Ellis R. (a mayonnaise manufacturer) and Ida T. Meaker. *Education:* University of Missouri, Columbia, B.A., 1949.

■ Addresses

Home—12 Deep Six Dr., East Hampton, NY 11937. *Agent*—Eugene Winick, McIntosh & Otis, Inc., 475 Fifth Ave., New York, NY 10017.

■ Career

Writer. Worked at several jobs, including assistant file clerk for E. P. Dutton (publisher), 1949-50; freelance writer, 1949—. Volunteer writing teacher at Commercial Manhattan Central High, 1968. Founding member of the Ashawagh Hall Writers' Workshop, Ashawagh, NY. *Member:* PEN, Authors League of America, Society of Children's Book Writers.

■ Awards, Honors

Media and Methods "Maxi" Award, *Media and Methods* magazine, 1974, for *Dinky Hocker Shoots Smack!* Children's Spring Book Festival honor book, *Book World—The Washington Post,* and Children's Book of the Year, Child Study Association, both 1973, both for *If I Love You, Am I Trapped Forever?;* Christopher Award, the Christophers, and Book of the Year Award, *School Library Journal,* both 1978, both for *Gentlehands,* which was also named one of the Best Books for the Teenage, New York Public Library, in 1980 and 1981; Golden Kite Award, Society of Children's Book Writers, 1981, for *Little Little;* Emphasis on Reading Award, 1985, for *Him She Loves?;* California Young Reader Medal, 1991, for *Night Kites;* Margaret A. Edwards Award, American Library Association, for body of work, 1993.

Several of Meaker's works written as M. E. Kerr have been named "Notable Books of the Year" and "Best Books for Young Adults" by the American Library Association, "Outstanding Books of the Year" by the New York *Times,* and "Best Books of the Year" by *School Library Journal* in their respective years of publication.

■ Writings

YOUNG ADULT FICTION AND NONFICTION; UNDER PSEUDONYM M. E. KERR, EXCEPT AS NOTED

Dinky Hocker Shoots Smack! Harper, 1972.
If I Love You, Am I Trapped Forever?, Harper, 1973.
The Son of Someone Famous, Harper, 1974.

MARIJANE MEAKER

Is That You, Miss Blue?, Harper, 1975.
Love Is a Missing Person, Harper, 1975.
I'll Love You When You're More Like Me, Harper, 1977.
Gentlehands, Harper, 1978.
Little Little, Harper, 1981.
What I Really Think of You, Harper, 1982.
Me, Me, Me, Me, Me: Not a Novel (autobiography), Harper, 1983.
Him She Loves?, Harper, 1984.
I Stay Near You: 1 Story in 3, Harper, 1985.
Night Kites, Harper, 1986.
Fell, Harper, 1987.
Fell Back, Harper, 1989.
(Under pseudonym Mary James) *Shoebag,* Scholastic, 1990.
Fell Down, HarperCollins, 1991.
Linger, HarperCollins, 1993.
Deliver Us from Evie, HarperCollins, 1994.
(Under pseudonym Mary James) *Frankenlouse,* Scholastic, 1994.
"Hello," I Lied, HarperCollins, 1997.
Blood on the Forehead: What I Know About Writing (nonfiction), HarperCollins, 1998.

ADULT FICTION

(Under name M. J. Meaker) *Hometown,* Doubleday, 1967.
(As Marijane Meaker) *Game of Survival,* New American Library, 1968.
(As Marijane Meaker) *Shockproof Sydney Skate,* Little, Brown, 1972.

ADULT FICTION; UNDER PSEUDONYM VIN PACKER

Dark Intruder, Gold Medal Books, 1952.
Spring Fire, Gold Medal Books, 1952.
Look Back to Love, Gold Medal Books, 1953.
Come Destroy Me, Gold Medal Books, 1954.
Whisper His Sin, Gold Medal Books, 1954.
The Thrill Kids, Gold Medal Books, 1955.
Dark Don't Catch Me, Gold Medal Books, 1956.
The Young and Violent, Gold Medal Books, 1956.
Three-Day Terror, Gold Medal Books, 1957.
The Evil Friendship, Gold Medal Books, 1958.
5:45 to Suburbia, Gold Medal Books, 1958.
The Twisted Ones, Gold Medal Books, 1959.
The Damnation of Adam Blessing, Gold Medal Books, 1961.
The Girl on the Best-Seller List, Gold Medal Books, 1961.
Something in the Shadows, Gold Medal Books, 1961.
Intimate Victims, Gold Medal Books, 1962.
Alone at Night, Gold Medal Books, 1963.
The Hare in March, New American Library, 1967.
Don't Rely on Gemini, Delacorte, 1969.

ADULT NONFICTION; UNDER PSEUDONYM ANN ALDRICH EXCEPT AS NOTED

We Walk Alone, Gold Medal Books, 1955.
We Too Must Love, Gold Medal Books, 1958.
Carol, in a Thousand Cities, Gold Medal Books, 1960.
We Two Won't Last, Gold Medal Books, 1963.

(Under name M. J. Meaker) *Sudden Endings,* Doubleday, 1964, paperback edition published under
pseudonym Vin Packer, Fawcett, 1964.
Take a Lesbian to Lunch, MacFadden-Bartell, 1972.

Contributor under pseudonym M. E. Kerr to *Sixteen,*
edited by Donald R. Gallo, Delacorte, 1984. A teacher's
guide for *Dinky Hocker Shoots Smack!* was published by
Learning Corporation of America in 1978. Meaker's
manuscripts as M. E. Kerr are housed at the Kerlan
Collection, University of Minnesota.

■ Adaptations

Dinky Hocker Shoots Smack! was broadcast as a television special by Learning Corporation of America, 1978;
it has also been optioned for film. *If I Love You Am I
Trapped Forever?* was released as an audio cassette by
Random House, 1979. *Fell* was made into a sound
recording in 1995 and *Gentlehands* in 1996.

■ Sidelights

Marijane Meaker, who writes for young adults almost
exclusively as M. E. Kerr, is regarded as one of the most
popular and highly respected authors in American
juvenile literature. Called "one of the grand masters of
young adult fiction," by Lois Metzger of the *New York
Times Book Review,* Meaker is generally considered a
brilliant and original writer whose novels, several of
which are acknowledged as landmarks of young adult
literature, address serious issues in a manner both
incisive and entertaining. She is perhaps best known for
creating coming-of-age stories and romances in which
her adolescent protagonists—male and female, straight
and gay—face change, deal with the difficulties of
relationships, and struggle to take charge of their own
lives. Her characters learn to define themselves as
individuals through their experiences with their parents,
their friends, and society; they ultimately learn, or at
least begin to realize, that successful relationships are
based on both acceptance and letting go. Often celebrated for her understanding of human nature in general
and young adults in particular, Meaker is lauded for the
color and variety of her characterizations, which often
feature offbeat or bizarre figures, as well as for her well-
rounded portrayals of adults, a quality considered
unusual in books for a teenage audience. Praised as a
keen social observer, she often uses a satiric, ironic tone
to describe contemporary American morals and mores,
which she sees as filled with hypocrisy and corruption.
Her books expose inhumanity and injustice in such
areas as small-town life and organized religion while
encouraging young readers to look beyond racial, cultural, and sexual stereotypes. While she addresses such
issues as mental illness, physical disability, substance
abuse, anti-Semitism, and AIDs as well as the pain of
adolescence, Meaker consistently includes wit and humor in her books and underscores them with a positive,
compassionate attitude toward the young. As a writer,
Meaker most often structures her stories as first-person
narratives told in a spare, direct prose style; the author
also regularly includes quotations from sources such as

the Bible, Shakespeare, and contemporary rock songs.
Although some of her books are considered controversial for their subjects and treatments while others are
criticized for facile dialogue and unsatisfying endings,
most observers acknowledge Meaker's works as both
funny and wise while recognizing the sincerity, integrity,
and perceptiveness of the author. Anita Silvey of *Horn
Book* claimed that Meaker "is one of the few young
adult writers who can take a subject that affects teenagers' lives, can say something important to young readers
about it, and can craft what is first and foremost a good
story, without preaching and without histrionics." Writing in another issue of *Horn Book,* Mary Kingsbury
noted that "the novels of M. E. Kerr can be judged as
among the most outstanding being published today." In
her *Presenting M. E. Kerr,* Alleen Pace Nilsen concluded, "M. E. Kerr is in a class by herself. Not often does
someone come along who is a true teacher and a good
writer. M. E. Kerr is both."

Much of Meaker's work as a writer of young adult
literature is drawn from her own experience; she wrote
in her autobiography *Me, Me, Me, Me, Me: Not a Novel*
that "whenever you find a little smart-mouth, tomboy
kid in any of my books, you have found me from long
ago . . . ." Born in Auburn, New York, a small town near
Rochester, she sets several of her books written as M. E.
Kerr in Cayuta, a town modeled after Auburn; in La
Belle, another small town in upstate New York; or in
Seaville, a resort town fashioned after the author's
current home of East Hampton, Long Island. "I grew up
always wanting to be a writer," Meaker related in her
essay in *Something about the Author Autobiography
Series;* she told Paul Janeczko of *English Journal,* "I was
always writing something, wanting to tell my own
story." Her father Ellis, a mayonnaise manufacturer for
Ivanhoe Foods, had a wide range of tastes in reading
that he passed on to his daughter; Meaker was also
influenced by the English teachers who encouraged her
as well as the librarians "who," she noted in *SAAS,* "had
to pull me out of the stacks at closing time . . . . And
there were my favorite writers like Thomas Wolfe,
Sherwood Anderson, the Brontes, and our hometown
hero, Samuel Hopkins Adams . . . . But in my heart, I
know who was responsible for this ambition of mine to
become a writer." It was her mother, Ida, whom Meaker
called "my lifelong abettor." Meaker recalled that her
mother, a terrific gossip, "would begin nearly every
conversation the same way: 'Wait till you hear this!'
Even today, when I'm finished with a book and sifting
through ideas for a new one, I ask myself: Is the idea a
'wait till you hear this'?" Ida Meaker, her daughter
noted, "taught me all a writer'd need to know about
socio/economic/ethnic differences, too . . . . The Reyer-
sons are very R-I-C-H, she'd say, and if she didn't spell
it out, she whispered it: *rich.*" Her mother, Meaker
wrote, taught her to "cut out all the labels from my coats
and jackets, anything I might remove in Second Presbyterian Church on a Sunday morning, so that no one
knew that we often bought out-of-town." When Meaker
was twelve, her younger brother Charles, nicknamed
Butchie, was born; Meaker also had an older brother,
Ellis, Jr. In her entry in *SAAS,* she said, "Twelve was the

M.E. KERR

Deliver Us From Evie

She has always known what she was . . .

Narrator Parr Burrman relates the varied reactions of the residents of his Missouri farm town to his sister's lesbian love affair in Meaker's young adult novel. (Cover illustration by Trevor Brown.)

age I was when my baby brother was born, and my older brother went off to military school. Thirteen was the year I became a hundred. Three things contributed to my rapid aging: the new baby in the house, the dramatic change in my older brother's personality, and my forced enrollment in Laura Bryan's ballroom dancing classes.... I was suddenly the nothing, sandwiched between two stars. Locked in my room, I wrote stories about murder and suicide, ... and listened to records like 'Blues in the Night' and 'Let's Get Away from It All.'" As an adolescent, Meaker realized that she was a lesbian. She was sent by her parents to ballet class to see if her homosexuality, she wrote in her foreword to *Hearing Us Out: Voices from the Gay and Lesbian Community,* "could be corrected." She was also sent to Stuart Hall, an Episcopal boarding school for girls in Staunton, Virginia. In her foreword to *Hearing Us Out,* Meaker remembered, "When my mother finally did come to terms with me and with terms ('I hate that word *lesbian* and I'll never call you one!'), she asked that there

be one promise: 'Never bring any of them to the house!... [Around] here I couldn't hold my head up if it ever got out.'" Meaker continued, "If only there had been literature to read.... If only she had some confirmation that this blight on our family was not as rare and terrible as she believed it was. My father could never even speak about it. So formed by what others thought, ... both my parents missed the chance to know my warm and loving friends—as well as to know me better." As a junior in high school, Meaker submitted romance stories with a wartime setting to popular women's magazines under the name Eric Ranthram McKay, a pseudonym chosen because her father's initials were E. R. M. Her stories, Meaker recalled in *Me, Me, Me, Me, Me,* "came back like boomerangs, with printed rejection slips attached. Sometimes these rejection slips had a 'sorry' penciled across them, or a 'try again.' These I cherished, and saved and used to buoy my spirits as I began new stories, and kept the old ones circulating." At Stuart Hall, Meaker became a rebel; in her senior year, she was expelled for throwing darts at pictures of faculty members before her mother arranged her reinstatement with a bishop. In *Me, Me, Me, Me, Me,* Meaker described herself during her Stuart Hall years as "the out-of-line black sheep," but in retrospect she realized the value of her experience; she wrote about Stuart Hall that "there was something stimulating and amusing, and very like life, as I came to know it, in its regulated, intense, dutiful and peculiar ambiance."

After graduation, Meaker went to Vermont Junior College, where she edited the school newspaper, the first publication to print one of her stories. In 1946, she transferred to the University of Missouri, where she initially majored in journalism; Meaker switched to the English program "partly because," she noted in *SAAS,* "I failed Economics, which one had to pass to get into J-School, and partly because I realized I didn't want anything to do with writing fact. I wanted to make up my own facts." After her graduation from college in 1949, she moved to New York City, began clerking at the E. P. Dutton publishing company, and continued to send out stories. "I wrote anything and everything in an effort to get published," Meaker wrote in *Me, Me, Me, Me, Me,* "I wrote confession stories, articles, 'slick' stories for the women's magazines, poetry, and fillers." After a variety of other day jobs, Meaker began working at Fawcett Publications, where she took long lunch breaks—leading to her quick dismissal—in order to visit editors and discuss the stories she had written under assumed names that were sent out as Marijane Meaker, Literary Agent. After publishing a story in *Ladies' Home Journal,* Meaker was interviewed on several radio shows about her dual identities. When the publicity reached an editor at her old employer Fawcett Publications, Meaker was offered the chance to write for the paperback series Gold Medal Books, and she began publishing mysteries and thrillers for adults under the names Vin Packer and Ann Aldrich. While writing adult novels and nonfiction titles, the author began taking classes in psychology, child psychology, sociology, and anthropology at the New School for Social Research in

New York City. Several of her novels as Vin Packer, which she called "whydunits instead of whodunits" in *SAAS,* are told from a teenager's viewpoint. In 1964, she published *Sudden Endings,* a nonfiction book on suicide, as M. J. Meaker; in 1972, she published a successful adult novel called *Shockproof Sydney Skate,* a story featuring an adolescent protagonist, as Marijane Meaker. At about this same time, her friend Louise Fitzhugh, a writer who had published the popular young adult novel *Harriet the Spy,* urged Meaker to write for the same audience. "I took a look at some of these young adult novels," Meaker wrote in *SAAS,* "and decided I could never write one ... *until* I picked up one called *The Pigman* by Paul Zindel." As she told Jim Roginksi in *Behind the Covers, Vol. II,* "I loved it and that really started me off."

In 1968, Meaker began volunteering as part of an experimental program in New York City where writers went into high schools one day a month in order to interest students in writing. In one of her classes, she met an overweight African American girl named Tiny who, Meaker wrote in *SAAS,* "wrote some really grotesque stories, about things like a woman going swimming and accidentally swallowing strange eggs in the water, and giving birth to red snakes.... One day her mother appeared, complaining that ... I was encouraging Tiny to write 'weird.'" In their discussion, Meaker learned that Tiny's mother was, the author claimed, "an ardent do-gooder" who left her daughter alone while she went out to do community service. "In other words," Meaker continued, "while Tiny's mom was putting out the fire in the house across the street, her own house was on fire. I was thinking a lot about this. A book was coming to me.... This was the birth of my first book for young adults. Tiny translated into 'Dinky'.... The result was *Dinky Hocker Shoots Smack!* Since I love pseudonyms, I decided to call myself M. E. Kerr, a play on my last name...." *Dinky Hocker* is the story of an obese teenager whose mother is so absorbed in her own work with drug addicts that she fails to notice her daughter; the novel also concerns Dinky's relationship with P. John, a sympathetic classmate who shares a weight problem, and P. John's relationship with his father, whose liberal values have caused the boy to adopt an ultra-conservative view. At the conclusion of the novel, Dinky grabs her mother's attention by inscribing the title legend on the wall of the building in which her mother is receiving the Good Samaritan Award, and P. John, who has been sent to a progressive school in Maine, grows thin and discovers labor organization. "M. E. Kerr's funny/sad first novel shoots straight from the hip," wrote Pamela D. Pollack in *School Library Journal,* who concluded, "the whole is a totally affecting literary experience." Writing in the *New York Times Book Review,* Dale Carlson claimed, "The pages rush by in this superb first novel ... This is a brilliantly funny book that will make you cry ... Few succeed so well as M. E. Kerr in this timely, compelling, and entertaining novel." Margery Fisher of *Growing Point* called *Dinky Hocker* "truly original," and Vivian J. Scheinmann claimed in *Twentieth Century Children's Writers* that the author is "matchless in this hilarious

but serious story...." After the success of *Dinky Hocker,* Meaker began to rethink the direction of her career. "I was in my forties, by then," she wrote in *SAAS,* "and not very interested any longer in murder and crime.... As I looked back on my life, things seemed funnier to me than they used to. *I* seemed funnier to me than I used to, and so did a lot of what I 'suffered.' Miraculously, as I sat down to make notes for possible future stories, things that happened to me long ago came back clear as a bell, and ringing, and making me smile and shake my head as I realized I had stories in me about *me...,* as the small-town kid I'd been, so typically American and middle-class and yes, vulnerable, but not as tragic and complicated as I used to imagine. So I had a new identity for myself in middle age: M. E. Kerr." Meaker continued, "I think the youngster in me remains vivid because I've never raised any children to compete with her, or compare with her, and I have not had to pace the floor nights worrying where they are or with whom, and what has happened to the family car."

An obese teenager resorts to deception when her mother becomes so absorbed in her own work with drug addicts that she fails to notice her daughter. (Cover illustration by Robert Sabin.)

After the publication of *Dinky Hocker Shoots Smack!,* Meaker continued to write young adult novels about adolescents who survive their situations while learning about the larger world. In *Is That You, Miss Blue?,* she tackles one of her most prominent subjects, religion, in the context of a boarding school story. The title character is a religious mystic who teaches science at an Episcopal boarding school in Virginia with strong similarities to the one Meaker attended as a teenager; Miss Blue, an inspired teacher, becomes an object of ridicule—and, eventually, a campaign for dismissal—because of her intense religious experiences, which are considered inappropriate by both school authorities and some of the students. The narrator, fifteen-year-old Flanders Brown, moves from mocking Miss Blue to respecting her former teacher, who suffers a mental breakdown as the result of the pressure. "This is a sophisticated book," wrote Zena Sutherland in *Bulletin of the Center for Children's Books,* "one that demands understanding from its readers and can, at the same time, lead them toward understanding." In her review in *Horn Book,* Mary M. Burns noted that in this "wryly funny, genuinely moving book, M. E. Kerr surpasses all of her previous achievements." Writing in *Best Sellers,* Mrs. John G. Gray said that Kerr "can dig deep and scurry around in the loneliest, saddest corners of a reader's soul and always come up with a perceptive thought for teenagers to mull over." Meaker's next book, *Love Is a Missing Person,* is the story of a rebellious white girl who runs off with a black sports hero from her high school. Inspired by an incident Kerr witnessed at a high school football game in East Hampton in which a white former cheerleader showed her biracial baby to her friends, the novel received a mixed reception: Alix Nelson of the *New York Times Book Review* noted that although Kerr's writing is "intelligent, warm, and witty in the way one has come to expect of the author, the book's questionable sociology is built on such slender stilts that it buckles and creaks with each new twist of the plot...." However, Zena Sutherland of *Bulletin of the Center for Children's Books* said that *Love Is a Missing Person* is "one of Kerr's best, honest and poignant and perceptive," while a critic in *Publishers Weekly* noted, "In time, M. E. Kerr may write something that's not real, touching, poignant, funny, and marvelous. And, in time, Gibraltar may crumble.... Her books get better; this is the finest yet." *I'll Love You When You're More Like Me* focuses on Sabra St. Amour, a teenage soap opera star, and Wally Witherspoon, the son of a mortician, who meet while Sabra is vacationing in Wally's hometown of Seaville, Long Island. The teens develop a common bond that is heightened by their shared experience: both are dealing with dominating parents. During the course of the story, Wally's friend Charlie comes out as a gay teen; at the end of the novel, he agrees to take Wally's place at the funeral home, and all three teenagers have learned to break free of the expectations of their parents. A critic in *Kirkus Reviews* noted that from "*Dinky Hocker* ... on, Kerr's projection of contemporary craziness and mixed-up kids has been about the sharpest in juvenile fiction, and her talent for combining the representative and the bizarre has never been so evident as in this inspired cast

which seems to write its own story." In her review in *School Library Journal,* Lillian M. Gerhardt praised the novel's "superb serio-comic writing ... [that] touches on nothing outside the ken or the conversation of young teens."

In 1978, Meaker, as M. E. Kerr, published *Gentlehands,* a novel often considered her best as well as her most controversial. The story describes the relationship between sixteen-year-old Buddy Boyle, a lower-middle-class boy, and Skye Pennington, a rich and beautiful girl; the larger story concerns Buddy's discovery that his grandfather, the cultured Frank Trenker, is actually Gentlehands, a Nazi officer who murdered Jewish prisoners at Auschwitz. By the end of the novel, Buddy has come to accept the double identity of his grandfather. Meaker includes pointed social commentary directed at the tiny Long Island village in which the story takes place as well as strong detail about Trenker's history as an SS officer; consequently, the novel provoked some negative reactions from both Jewish groups

Buddy Boyle discovers that his admired grandfather was a murderous Nazi officer at Auschwitz in Meaker's controversial young adult novel. (Cover illustration by Neal McPheeters.)

and critics of young adult literature. In an interview with Jim Roginski in *Behind the Covers, Vol. II*, Meaker noted that *Gentlehands* was "very much inspired by my older brother who was a World War Two pilot and never got over it. Then he became a mercenary and then he went to Vietnam with the C. I. A.'s Air America. They were provocateurs.... He's a charming guy with a great sense of humor. He seems so kind, so all-American. In the back of my head I think he was there somewhere when I wrote *Gentlehands.*" Meaker continued that "the Nazis ... were probably not a great deal different from some of us in Vietnam.... I got caught up in the idea of what is evil. I wanted to provoke the idea of what if you meet a nice guy, a really nice man, and what if you find out that in his past he wasn't such a nice man? How would you feel?" Writing in *Interracial Books for Children*, Ruth Charnes noted, "Whatever the author's intentions, I was infuriated by this book, which seems to give equal weight to the question of morality raised by the Holocaust and to an unrealistic teenage romance.... [It's] a great pity that her writings are so devoid of a moral heart." Geraldine DeLuca of *The Lion and the Unicorn* claimed that Kerr's achievement is that "she has illuminated a painful historical issue, sparing us no detail and yet avoiding sensationalism. The novel's weakness is that it depends so much on exaggeration and stereotype ... with little middle ground...." *Gentlehands* also received some unabashed praise. Writing in the *New York Times Book Review*, Richard Bradford called it a "remarkable novel" that is "important and useful as an introduction to the grotesque character of the Nazi period, as well as to the paradoxes that exist in the heart of man." A reviewer in *Publishers Weekly* commented that "Kerr's earlier novels, splendid as they are, seem like a prelude" to *Gentlehands;* the reviewer concluded, "It's a marvel of understatement, diamond insights, irony, and compassion." Despite the initial controversy surrounding it, *Gentlehands* is now generally considered an important title in the study of Holocaust literature as well as one of Meaker's signature works.

In *Little Little,* a novel published in 1981 that was inspired by the physically challenged child of an affluent young couple from the author's hometown, Meaker describes the developing relationship of teenagers Little Little La Belle, a sophisticated "little person" who is the daughter of her town's leading family, and Sydney Cinnamon, a hunchbacked dwarf abandoned at birth. Little Little's mother wants her to marry the famous but shallow midget evangelist Little Lion, but a party in honor of Little Little's eighteenth birthday exposes Little Lion's true nature as well as the growing romance between Little Little and Sydney. "This is a story about courage and tolerance and growing up without growing bigger," wrote Suzanne Freeman in *Book World—The Washington Post.* Freeman concluded, "M. E. Kerr doesn't stoop to tricks. Her dwarfs are real and sharp as nuggets." Writing in *The ALAN Review*, Norma Bagnall commented that *Little Little* "is an outrageously sad-funny book with humor and pathos consistently maintained throughout.... This one is hilariously funny in the tradition of black humor, and it is M. E. Kerr at her

very best." *School Library Journal* reviewer Jennifer FitzGerald called the novel a "brilliant comedy." In her essay in *SAAS,* Meaker called *Little Little* "the hardest book I ever wrote.... Maybe it is my favorite book, not because I think it's better than the rest, but because it was such a struggle. Maybe a parent, who's finally raised a particularly difficult child, feels this same affection and pride when the kid turns out okay." In her next book, *What I Really Think of You,* Meaker explores the world of fundamentalist preachers and its effect on the children of the ministers; the work also builds on the connection between organized religion and business that Meaker addressed with the character of Little Lion in *Little Little.* The story describes how Opal and Jesse, two teenage PKs, or preacher's kids, deal with the professions of their fathers—one a rich television star and the other a poor Pentecostal minister—and questions of faith while developing a tentative relationship. At the end of the novel, Opal receives the gift of tongues, even after some earlier ambivalence, and finds love with Jesse's religious older brother; her new gift also brings her celebrity status when she is filmed by a television crew in her father's church. After the publication of *What I Really Think of You,* Meaker was criticized for making fun of religion as well as for the inconsistency of Opal's character. However, Marilyn Kaye of the *New York Times Book Review* noted that the book "has integrity. It's hard to believe that a novelist could indulge in such concepts as being 'slain in the spirit,' waiting for 'The Rapture,' faith healing and speaking in tongues without either proselytizing or mocking them— but glory be, M. E. Kerr has done both.'"

Meaker's sole nonfiction title for young adults is her autobiography, *Me, Me, Me, Me, Me: Not a Novel,* a book written as M. E. Kerr in which she describes her life from the age of fifteen until the publication of her first story in 1951. The result of the many letters that the author has received from her readers, *Me, Me, Me, Me, Me* presents autobiographical vignettes as well as the author's explanations of the people and experiences that influenced her books. Paul A. Caron of *Best Sellers* stated, "She battles. She hurts. She grows. She matures. This *is* the story of Marijane and her friends and foes who influenced her formative years." Caron concluded that Meaker has written a "fascinating, yet timeless look at herself and others, which will not only delight her fans, but will no doubt increase their number." Writing in the *New York Times Book Review,* Joyce Milton noted, "Kerr unveils a deliciously wicked sense of humor, reminiscent in style, and occasionally in content, of Jessica Mitford's works.... [This] book offers a satisfying if brief encounter with a humorist whose delight in poking fun at the trappings of authority is unmarred by either self-hatred or pettiness toward others." In her review in *Horn Book,* Nancy C. Hammond explained that Meaker "confesses to being the 'smartmouth' tomboys populating many of her novels. And she is quite as entertaining as they are. Incisive, witty, and immediate, the book is vintage M. E. Kerr."

In 1986, Meaker published *Night Kites,* a novel in which she began trying, she told Jim Roginski, "to simplify my

While staying in the Hamptons one summer, Lang, seventeen years old and homosexual, meets a reclusive rock star and has a sweet, surprising love affair with a young woman. (Cover illustration by Mel Odom.)

style . . . . I decided to try writing more directly, without so many subplots, becoming more accessible." In this work, the author describes Erick Rudd's senior year, especially his betrayal of his best friend Jack with Nicki, Jack's girlfriend; his first sexual experience, with Nicki; and the discovery that his older brother Pete is gay and is ill with AIDS. Erick faces the imminent loss of his brother as well as the consequences of his illness on his family and friends. In addition, Erick deals with the consequences of his own actions and his breakup with Nicki, who drops Erick when she finds out that his brother has AIDS. Anita Silvey of *Horn Book* calls *Night Kites* "an important part of the Kerr canon and an important contribution to the literature for young adults," while Audrey B. Eaglen of the *New York Times Book Review* noted that Kerr "has managed to transcend [the problem novel], and has, with sensitivity and delicacy, described an issue that may face many more families if predictions about AIDS come true . . . . Kerr has simply never been better in her long and lauded

career; she too is a 'night kite,' unafraid to soar in the darkness of the human predicament."

With her "Fell" series of young adult novels—*Fell, Fell Back,* and *Fell Down*—Meaker combines her interest in detective fiction with some of her most prominent themes, including betrayal, class conflict, and the politics and prejudices that can be found in prep schools. The novels, which combine romance, mystery, and humor in what is generally considered a stylish and entertaining fashion, revolve around John Fell, a policeman's son from Seaville, New York. Fell, a sensitive, witty gourmet cook who possesses a talent for detection as well as a sharp eye for phoniness, is drawn into the world of privilege when he is asked to impersonate the son of a rich neighbor at the elite Gardner school. After he is asked to join a secret campus society called the Seven, Fell learns about the intrigue and tyranny underlying the school and discovers that his benefactor has been arrested for selling nuclear secrets. In her review of *Fell* in *Booklist*, Hazel Rochman claimed, "Not since *Gentlehands* has Kerr so poignantly combined a story of romance, mystery, and wit with serious implications of class conflict and personal betrayal." Christy Tyson of *Voice of Youth Advocates* noted that Kerr "manages an almost perfect balance of dry wit and suspense" and called the Gardner school one "that may well be the most darkly intriguing since Conroy's *The Lords of Discipline.*" In *Fell Back,* Fell searches for the cause of the suicide of one of his fellow members in the Sevens club and becomes involved in the drug scene and a love affair as well as with a murder. Reviewers gave the novel a mixed reception. A critic in *Publishers Weekly* noted that "the spark that ignited [Fell] seems to have fizzled out, and *Fell Back,* although entertaining, is just another mystery story starring a budding junior detective," while Marjorie Lewis of *School Library Journal* pointed out that "although this fell short in story, Fell's charm is considerable, and readers will like him and his insecurities." With *Fell Down,* Meaker was praised for a return to form. The novel describes how Fell, who has dropped out of Gardner, returns to the newly coed school to find April, the missing sister of his longtime girlfriend Delia; Fell becomes embroiled in a mystery that spans two generations and involves kidnapping and murder. *Fell Down* is unique among the volumes in the series in that it includes two narrators, Fell and "the Mouth," a ventriloquist who tells his story through the voice of his dummy. Writing in *Booklist,* Hazel Rochman called *Fell Down* "a brilliant mystery, one that will have genre fans fitting the pieces together for days," while Christy Tyson of *Voice of Youth Advocates* noted that Kerr's "mastery at character development is superb, and few can top her for style that can convey both wit and heartache."

Linger is a novel that takes place in the mythical small town of Berryville, Pennsylvania rather than in Meaker's usual Long Island or upstate New York settings. In this work, the author provides young readers with, in the words of Florence H. Munat of *Voice of Youth Advocates,* "a thoughtful treatment of patriotism and despotism as seen through the eyes of a teenager." The title refers to a popular restaurant that is owned by Ned Dunlinger, a powerful pillar of the community. The family of sixteen-year-old Gary Peel, like many of the Berryville residents, think that the Dunlingers are near royalty in status; Gary's father manages Linger, his mother does the books, and Gary and his older brother Bobby wait tables. After Bobby Peel has an argument with Ned Dunlinger over the latter's use of unethical tactics to close a competing Mexican restaurant, he quits Linger, joins the army, and is sent to Saudi Arabia as part of Desert Storm; several of the chapters in the novel are excerpts from Bobby's Gulf War journal. In his absence, the Dunlingers display his photo at Linger along with flags and yellow ribbons. Bobby, who has been wounded by friendly fire, returns to Berryville as a hero—a welcome that quickly fades—with his army buddy Sanchez, who has been disfigured and is openly treated with contempt by Dunlinger. For a while, Dunlinger's hypocrisy is acknowledged by the townspeople; however, at the end of the novel, the Berryville residents begin warming to Dunlinger and his new cause: the homeless. *Voice of Youth Advocates*'s Munat concluded that it is "great to have a sensitive and provocative book that reconstructs the emotional climate in the U. S. during the Gulf War." A critic in *Kirkus Reviews* wrote that *Linger* is "rich with varied characters and points of view.... It's an angry look at the US in microcosm, not on the cosmic scale of *Howards End* but with plenty of thought-provoking parallels." Writing in *Bulletin of the Center for Children's Books,* Roger Sutton noted, "As ever, Kerr has a sharp eye on the banalities that disguise hypocrisy and corruption, if not evil.... We've seen these characters before in Kerr's work, but they're looking at something new, and Dunlinger makes a bluff, extroverted intriguing companion to the more coolly sinister Gentlehands."

Although Meaker has included gay characters in her novels, with *Deliver Us from Evie* and *"Hello", I Lied* she makes them the focus of her stories. The former book features the Burrmans, a Missouri farm family whose eighteen-year-old daughter, Evie, a talented mechanic who looks like the young Elvis Presley, falls in love with Patsy Duff, the attractive daughter of the local banker. Evie's youngest brother, Parr, narrates the story and describes the varied reactions to Evie's coming out—mostly hostile and uncertain with some acceptance—as well as his own romance with Angel Kidder, a religious but hot-blooded girl. At the end of the novel, the Mississippi floods of 1993 provide both a symbolic representation to the town of God's warning about Evie and Patsy as well as an opportunity for the girls to escape to New York City. Writing in *Wilson Library Bulletin,* Cathi Dunn MacRae noted, "Kerr pioneers in tackling the female butch stereotype. Evie declares, 'I'm the way I am.'" Christine Jenkins of *Bulletin of the Center for Children's Books* called *Deliver Us from Evie* "a remarkable YA novel.... [This] is vintage Kerr...." Dorothy M. Broderick of *Voice of Youth Advocates* concurred: "Unquestionably, this is the best Kerr in years, if not ever." Writing in the *New York Times Book Review,* Lois Metzger concluded that *Deliv-*

er Us from Evie is "so original, fresh and fiery, you'd think that M. E. Kerr ... was just now getting started." In *"Hello", I Lied,* Meaker addresses the issues of homosexuality and identity. The novel is told by seventeen-year-old Lang Penner, a young man who has already come out to his mother but is concerned about how his friends will react. Lang and his mom are living in the Hamptons for the summer, where his mother is working as the housekeeper for the reclusive rock star Ben Nevada. Lang's lover, Alex, presses him to live openly as a gay man; however, Lang becomes attracted to Huguette, a young French woman who is visiting Nevada, a family friend. Lang and Huguette fall in— and make—love. However, at the end of the novel, Lang has learned about the complexities of relationships and the fluid nature of identity; in addition, he has acquired sweet memories of "the summer that I loved a girl." Writing in *Horn Book,* Roger Sutton commented, "[Gay] themes in young adult literature have been pressing beyond the standard coming-out story. And, as usual, M. E. Kerr is right out in front.... [Lang's] as gay at the end of the book as he was at the beginning, an unusual twist on the coming-of-age theme." A critic in *Publishers Weekly* claimed, "With its addictive combination of absorbing themes and glamorous setting, Kerr's newest stands up to the best of her oeuvre.... This book successfully challenges readers' assumptions, breaking them down to offer more hopeful, affirming ideas about love and truth."

In addition to her works as M. E. Kerr, Meaker has written for young people as Mary James. *Shoebag,* a parody of Kafka's *Metamorphosis* that satirizes both the human and roach worlds, describes a cockroach who turns into a boy. At school, Shoebag, who has been named for the site of his birth, makes friends with Gregor Samson, a boy who also used to be a cockroach. When Gregor decides to remain human, he grants Shoebag his ability to revert back to roach form, and Shoebag is happily reunited with his family. A critic in *Kirkus Reviews* called *Shoebag* "a highly original story crammed with clever detail, action, insight, and humor, all combined with impeccable logic and begging to be shared...." Robert Strang of the *Bulletin of the Center for Children's Books* guessed the identity of *Shoebag*'s author: "[Our] marker is on M. E. Kerr for this book is filled with *Little Little*-type repartee.... [For] all its cleverness, this has a Dale Carnegie stick-up-for-yourself theme that gives heart to the wit." Writing in *Junior Bookshelf,* Marcus Crouch concluded that *Shoebag* "will delight as much as it will fascinate." Another of Meaker's books written as Mary James is *Frankenlouse,* a young adult novel in which fourteen-year-old Nick, the son of a general who is also his commanding officer in military school, convinces his dad that he needs to be an artist. Throughout the story, Nick creates a cartoon strip featuring a book louse from Mary Shelley's *Frankenstein* who devours a whole collection of classic books—all except for those starting with the letter "m." Elizabeth S. Watson in *Horn Book* commented that the story "is, somehow, not as complicated as it sounds due to careful integration of the strip—just enough of this sub-story line to intrigue readers and maybe encourage some creative thinking along the same lines. Funny and thought-provoking."

"I love writing," Meaker wrote in *SAAS*, "and I particularly love writing for young adults. I know other young adult writers who claim that their books are just slotted into that category, and claim there's no difference between an adult novel and a young adult one ... I beg to disagree. When I write for young adults I know they're still wrestling with very important problems like winning and losing, not feeling accepted or accepting, prejudice, love—all the things adults ultimately get hardened to, and forgetful of. I know my audience hasn't yet made up their minds about everything, that they're still vulnerable and open to suggestion and able to change their minds.... Give me that kind of an audience any day!" Speaking to Jim Roginski, Meaker said, "I see myself as a storyteller. That's what I am. There are people who love words and know how to put them beautifully together, almost poetically, a writer like Alice Hoffman. I'm not that kind of writer.... I think I can tell a good story but I don't have her talent and the almost poetic love of words that she has. I think of her as an artist. I think I'm a writer. I do what I want to do. Joyce Carol Oates, in quoting James Joyce, said, 'Other people may have more talent perhaps, but I am willing to work.' That's being a writer. Say no more."

■ Works Cited

Bagnall, Norma, review of *Little Little, The ALAN Review,* fall, 1981, p. 21.

Bradford, Richard, "The Nazi Legacy: Understanding History," *New York Times Book Review,* April 30, 1978, p. 30.

Broderick, Dorothy M., review of *Deliver Us from Evie, Voice of Youth Advocates,* October, 1994, p. 208.

Burns, Mary M., review of *Is That You, Miss Blue?, Horn Book,* August, 1975. p. 365.

Carlson, Dale, review of *Dinky Hocker Shoots Smack!, New York Times Book Review,* February 11, 1973, p. 8.

Caron, Paul A., review of *Me, Me, Me, Me, Me: Not a Novel, Best Sellers,* June, 1983, p. 110.

Charnes, Ruth, review of *Gentlehands, Interracial Books for Children Bulletin,* Volume 9, number 8, 1978, p. 18.

Crouch, Marcus, review of *Shoebag, Junior Bookshelf,* June, 1991, p. 114.

DeLuca, Geraldine, "Taking True Risks: Controversial Issues in New Young Adult Novels," *The Lion and the Unicorn,* Winter, 1979-80, pp. 125-48.

Eaglen, Audrey B., review of *Night Kites, New York Times Book Review,* April 13, 1986, p. 30.

Review of *Fell Back, Publishers Weekly,* September 29, 1989, p. 70.

Fisher, Margery, review of *Dinky Hocker Shoots Smack!, Growing Point,* November, 1973, p. 2263.

FitzGerald, Jennifer, "Challenging the Pressure to Conform: Byars and Kerr," *School Library Journal,* September, 1986, pp. 46-47.

Freeman, Suzanne, "Growing Up in a Small World," *Book World—The Washington Post,* May 10, 1981, p. 15.

Review of *Gentlehands, Publishers Weekly,* January 9, 1978, p. 81.

Gerhardt, Lillian N., review of *I'll Love You When You're More Like Me, School Library Journal,* October, 1977, pp. 124-25.

Gray, Mrs. John G., review of *Is That You, Miss Blue?, Best Sellers,* May, 1975, p. 49.

Hammond, Nancy A., review of *Me, Me, Me, Me, Me: Not a Novel, Horn Book,* August, 1983, p. 462.

Review of *"Hello," I Lied, Publishers Weekly,* March 31, 1997, p. 75.

Review of *I'll Love You When You're More Like Me, Kirkus Reviews,* July 1, 1977, p. 673.

Janeczko, Paul, "An Interview with M. E. Kerr," *English Journal,* December, 1975.

Jenkins, Christine, review of *Deliver Us from Evie, Bulletin of the Center for Children's Books,* December, 1994, pp. 132-33.

Kaye, Marilyn, review of *What I Really Think of You, New York Times Book Review,* September 12, 1982, pp. 49-50.

Kingsbury, Mary, "The Why of People: The Novels of M. E. Kerr," *Horn Book,* June, 1977, pp. 288-95.

Lewis, Marjorie, review of *Fell Back, School Library Journal,* September, 1989, pp. 272-73.

Review of *Linger, Kirkus Reviews,* July 1, 1993, pp. 861-62.

Review of *Love Is a Missing Person, Publishers Weekly,* June 30, 1975, p. 58.

MacRae, Cathi Dunn, review of *Deliver Us from Evie, Wilson Library Bulletin,* September, 1994, pp. 116-17.

Meaker (under pseudonym M. E. Kerr), foreword to *Hearing Us Out: Voices from the Gay and Lesbian Community,* edited by Roger Sutton, Little, Brown, 1994, pp. viii-x.

Meaker (under pseudonym M. E. Kerr), *Me, Me, Me, Me, Me: Not a Novel,* Harper, 1983.

Meaker (under pseudonym M. E. Kerr), essay in *Something about the Author Autobiography Series,* Gale, Volume 1, 1986.

Meaker (under pseudonym M. E. Kerr) and Jim Roginski, interview in *Behind the Covers, Vol. II,* Libraries Unlimited, 1989, pp. 161-76.

Metzger, Lois, review of *Deliver Us from Evie, New York Times Book Review,* April 9, 1995, p. 25.

Milton, Joyce, review of *Me, Me, Me, Me, Me: Not a Novel, New York Times Book Review,* May 22, 1983, p. 39.

Munat, Florence H., review of *Linger, Voice of Youth Advocates,* August, 1993, p. 153.

Nelson, Alix, review of *Love Is a Missing Person, New York Times Book Review,* October 19, 1975, p. 10.

Nilsen, Alleen Pace, *Presenting M. E. Kerr,* Twayne, 1986.

Pollack, Pamela D., review of *Dinky Hocker Shoots Smack!, School Library Journal,* December, 1972, p. 67.

Rochman, Hazel, review of *Fell, Booklist,* June 1, 1987, pp. 1515-16.

Rochman, Hazel, review of *Fell Down, Booklist,* September 15, 1991, p. 135.

Scheinmann, Vivian J., essay in *Twentieth Century Children's Writers,* 2nd edition, edited by D. L. Kirkpatrick, St. Martin's Press, 1983, pp. 428-29.

Review of *Shoebag, Kirkus Reviews,* February 15, 1990, p. 264.

Silvey, Anita, review of *Night Kites, Horn Book,* September-October, 1986, p. 597.

Strang, Robert, review of *Shoebag, Bulletin of the Center for Children's Books,* March, 1990, p. 164.

Sutherland, Zena, review of *Is That You, Miss Blue?, Bulletin of the Center for Children's Books,* July-August, 1975, p. 179.

Sutherland, Zena, review of *Love Is a Missing Person, Bulletin of the Center for Children's Books,* November, 1975, p. 48.

Sutton, Roger, review of *Linger, Bulletin of the Center for Children's Books,* September, 1993, p. 14.

Sutton, Roger, review of *"Hello," I Lied, Horn Book,* July-August, 1997, pp. 457-58.

Tyson, Christy, review of *Fell, Voice of Youth Advocates,* October, 1987, p. 202.

Tyson, Christy, review of *Fell Down, Voice of Youth Advocates,* December, 1991, pp. 313-14.

Watson, Elizabeth S., review of *Frankenlouse, Horn Book,* January-February, 1995, pp. 62-3.

■ For More Information See

BOOKS

Chevalier, Tracy, editor, *Twentieth Century Children's Writers,* 3rd edition, St. James, 1989.

Children's Literature Review, Gale, Volume 29, 1993.

Contemporary Literary Criticism, Gale, Volume 12, 1980, Volume 35, 1985.

Crawford, Elizabeth D. and Doris de Montreville, *Fourth Book of Junior Authors and Illustrators,* Wilson, 1978.

Donelson, Kenneth L., and Alleen Pace Nilsen, *Literature for Today's Young Adults,* Scott, Foresman, 1980, 2nd edition, 1985.

Kirkpatrick, D. L., editor, *Twentieth Century Children's Writers,* 1st edition, St. Martin's Press, 1978.

Rees, David, *Painted Desert, Green Shade: Essays on Contemporary Writers of Fiction for Children and Young Adults,* Horn Book, 1984.

PERIODICALS

ALAN Review, fall, 1997.

Booklist, September 15, 1994, p. 125; April 15, 1997, p. 1423.

Book World—the Washington Post, June 10, 1990, p. 10.

Bulletin of the Center for Children's Books, June, 1998, p. 366.

Kirkus Reviews, November 15, 1994, p. 1533; March 15, 1998, p. 405.

Publishers Weekly, May 11, 1998, p. 69.

School Library Journal, June, 1997, p. 120; May, 1998, pp. 156-57.

—Sketch by Gerard J. Senick

*   *   *

MERINGOFF, Laurene Krasny
See BROWN, Laurie Krasny

*   *   *

MORGAN, Stevie
See DAVIES, Nicola

*   *   *

MURCH, Mel
See MANES, Stephen

O–P

O'KEEFFE, Frank 1938-

■ Personal

Born April 25, 1938, in Dublin, Ireland; immigrated to Calgary, Alberta, Canada, 1957; naturalized Canadian citizen, early 1960s; son of Charles (a manager in a wine merchant's) and Millie O'Keeffe; married Patricia (a school teacher), July 22, 1961; children: Kerry, Kevin, Michael. *Education:* University of Calgary, B.Ed., 1973. *Hobbies and other interests:* Reading, storytelling, walking in the woods, travel, people watching, avid Calgary Flames hockey fan.

FRANK O'KEEFFE

■ Addresses

Home—R.R. #1, Site 8, Compartment 20, Peachland, British Columbia, Canada V0H 1X0.

■ Career

Writer, 1985—. Worked as an insurance broker, Calgary, Alberta, 1957-1970; Yellowhead School Division, Edson, Alberta, teacher-librarian and teacher, 1973-1988, substitute teacher, 1988-1996. Has taught creative writing at Lakehead College and for the Edmonton Public School system in Alberta. Also worked briefly on a sheep station in Australia in the 1970s and owned a modest cattle farm before moving from Alberta to British Columbia in 1997. Conducts creative writing workshops for children. *Member:* Canadian Children's Book Centre, Canadian Society of Children's Authors, Illustrators and Performers (CANSCAIP), Writers' Union of Canada.

■ Awards, Honors

Canadian Library Association Notable Book, 1993, Our Choice selection, Canadian Children's Book Centre, 1993-94, and Manitoba Young Readers' Choice Award, 1996, for *Weekend at the Ritz;* Children's Literature Award finalist, Writers Guild of Alberta, 1995, and Our Choice selection, Canadian Children's Book Centre, 1995-96, for *Nancy Nylen—Ordinary Farm Girl / Explorer Extraordinaire;* Book of the Year for Children Medal finalist, Canadian Association of Children's Librarians, 1996, for *If It Rains Again Tomorrow, Can We Go Home?*

■ Writings

Guppy Love, or, The Day the Fish Tank Exploded, Kids Can Press, 1986, published in French as *Amour et petits poissons,* translated by Michelle Robinson, Editions Pierre Tisseyre (St. Laurent, Quebec, Canada), 1992.

School Stinks!, General Publishing, 1991.

(With Martyn Godfrey) *There's a Cow in My Swimming
  Pool,* Scholastic Canada, 1991.
It's Only a Game, Beach Holme Publishing (Victoria,
  BC, Canada), 1992, published in French as *Coup de
  theatre sur la glace,* translated by Martine Gagnon,
  Editions Pierre Tisseyre, 1993.
Weekend at the Ritz, Beach Holme Publishing, 1993,
  published in French as *Une fin de semaine au Ritz,*
  translated by Michelle Tisseyre, Editions Pierre
  Tisseyre, 1996.
*Nancy Nylen—Ordinary Farm Girl / Explorer Extraor-
  dinaire,* Beach Holme Publishing, 1994.
If It Rains Again Tomorrow, Can We Go Home?, Beach
  Holme Publishing, 1996.

■ Work in Progress

Mad about Marvin and *Harry Flammable* (working
titles), two novels for young people.

■ Sidelights

Frank O'Keeffe's books for young people recreate their
audience's world with an emphasis on its lighter side. As
a parent and a former teacher, he has had years of
experience working with children, observing them closely and sharing in the inevitable ups and downs associated with approaching and entering into the teenage
years. "O'Keeffe understands and sympathizes with the
thought processes of primary school children and the
perplexities they face," Celeste A. van Vloten commented in her *Canadian Children's Literature* review of the
author's first novel, *Guppy Love.* O'Keeffe also has a
knack for perceiving humor in the commonplace and
relating it effectively to the energy and resiliency of
youth. Fred Boer of *Quill & Quire* noted how "apparently effortlessly" O'Keeffe creates characters who are
"lively and familiar."

Although O'Keeffe's published writing has come on the
heels of a lively teaching career, there is evidence that he
has always been a man with a story tucked away for the
telling. He grew up in Ireland and, as early as grade four,
won the story prize a resourceful teacher offered when
called upon to do double duty with an absent colleague's
class of fifty boys. O'Keeffe's "best story" was about the
crash, in the South American jungle, of a plane carrying
a cargo of racehorses. His dramatic tale earned him
sixpence and represented his first income as a writer.

In 1957, when O'Keeffe was nineteen, he immigrated to
Canada and found work with an insurance company in
Calgary. The company's Christmas party provided an
annual opportunity to flex his creative writing muscles
and his humorous skits became traditional fare.
O'Keeffe married in 1961, continued to work in the
insurance industry throughout the 1960s and, by the end
of the decade, determined to return to school.

O'Keeffe applied for admission to the University of
Calgary and was accepted in 1970. Three years later,
with a Bachelor's degree in education, he accepted a
teaching position in Edson, Alberta, where, as a teacher-

librarian, children's literature and storytelling became
tools of his daily trade.

Over the years, O'Keeffe's interest in writing persisted.
He completed two adult novels but consigned them to a
cupboard at home. Finally, at the urging of Canadian
children's author Martyn Godfrey, O'Keeffe began to
seek publication for his stories. Godfrey, also a teacher
in Edson in the early 1980s, recognized O'Keeffe's
potential and encouraged him to write his stories and
pitch them to publishers. Godfrey's enthusiasm for
O'Keeffe's idea for a first children's book became a
powerful incentive for O'Keeffe.

Guppy Love, or, The Day the Fish Tank Exploded, the
author's debut work, introduced pre-teen readers to a
lively new storytelling voice with a good grasp of young
people and a strong sense of fun.

Guppy Love was well received and O'Keeffe began to
consider how he might arrange for more time to write.
In 1988, he decided to leave full-time teaching and,

**When a mill closing threatens the future of their school,
Robbie, Mona, and Spider fight to keep the company
open.** (Cover illustration by Christina Choma.)

instead, work occasionally as a substitute teacher. He has since added several more stories to his body of work, including *There's a Cow in My Swimming Pool,* co-written with Martyn Godfrey.

Fast pacing and authenticity are the key strengths O'Keeffe brings to his writing. Sheree Haughian, commenting on *If It Rains Again Tomorrow, Can We Go Home?* in *Quill & Quire,* noted the author's "convincing detail and authentic portrayal of rural life." O'Keeffe is adept, as well, at mining personal experiences and inside sources for material his readers will relate to and enjoy. The fish tank fiasco described in *Guppy Love,* for example, really happened at O'Keeffe's school. His son, a chef, worked in a hotel like the one in *Weekend at the Ritz.* His wife has even coached a hockey team, like Tony Dennison's mother does in *It's Only a Game.*

Early in 1997, O'Keeffe and his wife moved from their modest cattle farm in Alberta to a half acre property in British Columbia. Away from Alberta's Yellowhead School Division and its occasional demand for substitute teachers, O'Keeffe may find more time to write, tour and conduct creative writing workshops for children. As for new work, O'Keeffe already has two more books underway and indicates there are plenty more to follow. "There are lots of incidents in my mind," he comments. "The main thing is to work them into a story."

■ Works Cited

Boer, Fred, review of *Nancy Nylen—Ordinary Farm Girl / Explorer Extraordinaire, Quill & Quire,* December, 1994, p. 35.

Haughian, Sheree, review of *If It Rains Again Tomorrow, Can We Go Home?, Quill & Quire,* October, 1996, pp. 49, 51.

van Vloten, Celeste A., "Puppy Guppy Love," *Canadian Children's Literature,* Number 51, 1988, pp. 87-88.

■ For More Information See

PERIODICALS

Calgary Herald, December 31, 1994, p. H7.

Canadian Book Review Annual, 1992, pp. 327-328; 1993, p. 6174.

Children's Choices of Canadian Books, Volume 6, Number 1, 1988, p. 20.

Quill & Quire, June, 1991, p. 26; June, 1992, p. 36.

* * *

OPPEL, Kenneth 1967-

■ Personal

Born August 31, 1967, in Port Alberni, British Columbia, Canada; son of Wilfred (a lawyer) and Audrey (a visual artist; maiden name, Young) Oppel; married Philippa Sheppard (a university professor), September 8, 1990; children: Sophia Marie. *Education:* University of Toronto, B.A. (English and cinema), 1989. *Hobbies and other interests:* Photography, reading, cross-country skiing, watching movies, attending the theater.

■ Addresses

Home—19 Delaware Ave., Toronto, Ontario, Canada M6H 2S8.

■ Career

Freelance writer and book reviewer, 1989—; Scholastic Canada, Richmond Hill, Ontario, associate editor, 1989; *Quill & Quire,* Toronto, Ontario, Books for Young People editor, 1995-1996. *Member:* Canadian Society of Children's Authors, Illustrators and Performers (CAN-SCAIP), Writers' Union of Canada.

■ Awards, Honors

Canadian Library Association Notable Book, 1991, for *The Live-Forever Machine;* City of Toronto Book Awards finalist, 1992, and Our Choice selection, Canadian Children's Book Centre, 1992-93, both for *Cosimo Cat;* Canadian Library Association Notable Book, 1993, for *Dead Water Zone;* Our Choice recommendation, Canadian Children's Book Centre, 1995-96, for *Follow That Star;* Air Canada Award, Canadian Authors Association, 1995, for "outstanding promise" demonstrated by a young (under thirty years) Canadian writer; Pick of the List, American Booksellers Association, and Quick Pick for Reluctant Readers, American Library Association, both 1997, shortlist, Ruth Schwartz Award, shortlist, Silver Birch Award, Blue Heron Award, Mr Christ-

KENNETH OPPEL

ie's Book Award, and Book of the Year for Children, Canadian Library Association, all 1998, all for *Silverwing.*

■ Writings

Colin's Fantastic Video Adventure, illustrated by Kathleen C. Howell, Dutton, 1985.
The Live-Forever Machine, Kids Can Press, 1990.
Cosimo Cat, illustrated by Regolo Ricci, Scholastic Canada, 1990.
Dead Water Zone, Kids Can Press, 1992, Little, Brown, 1993.
Cosmic Snapshots, illustrated by Guy Parker-Reese, Penguin, 1993.
Galactic Snapshots, illustrated by Guy Parker-Reese, Penguin, 1993.
Follow That Star, illustrated by Kim LaFave, Kids Can Press, 1994.
Emma's Emu, illustrated by Carolyn Crossland, Penguin, 1995.
Silverwing, Simon & Schuster, 1997, HarperCollins Canada, 1997.

"BAD CASE" SERIES; ILLUSTRATED BY PETER UTTON

A Bad Case of Ghosts, Penguin, 1993.
A Bad Case of Magic, Penguin, 1993.
A Bad Case of Dinosaurs, Penguin, 1994.
A Bad Case of Robots, Penguin, 1994.
A Bad Case of Super-Goo, Penguin, 1996.

Some of Oppel's works have been translated into French, Danish, and Italian.

SCREENPLAYS

Several of Oppel's screenplays have been optioned for film, including *Live-Forever Machine,* 1990; *Dead Water Zone,* 1993; *Virtual Murder,* 1993; *Brothers Grim,* 1994; (with Michael McGowan) *Entitled,* 1996; *The Devil's Cure,* 1997; and *The Outlaw* (an adaptation of *The Outlaw of Megantic* by Bernard Epps), commissioned, 1997.

■ Work in Progress

Peg and the Whale, for Simon & Schuster and Harper-Collins Canada.

■ Sidelights

Kenneth Oppel has written several books for young people, ranging from picture books and first readers to young adult fiction, as well as authoring several screenplays. What is most impressive about Oppel's body of work is the amount he published before age twenty-nine. In recognition of this accomplishment, the Canadian Authors Association awarded him the 1995 Air Canada Award for promise demonstrated by a young Canadian writer.

As a young reader, Oppel was inspired by L. M. Montgomery's "Emily of New Moon" series. He related strongly to Emily's dream of becoming a published

writer and by grade seven determined that he, too, would write. He told the Canadian Children's Book Centre in *Writing Stories, Making Pictures,* "I remember making a vow to my father when I was thirteen, that I wanted to have something published before I'd turned fourteen." Although Oppel's first work, *Colin's Fantastic Video Adventure,* wasn't published until he was seventeen, he did, however, write the first draft at age fourteen. Oppel earned his lucky break when a family friend who knew British children's author Roald Dahl agreed to show him the young boy's story. Dahl was impressed enough to pass it on to his own literary agent. The agent agreed to represent the book and promptly sold it to publishers in London and New York.

Oppel's inspiration for *Colin's Fantastic Video Adventure* resulted from another of his passions—playing video games. In the story, eleven-year-old Colin wins video game contests with the help of two spacemen who escaped from the boy's favorite video game "Meteoroids." Colin eventually realizes that cheating isn't fair and goes on to play a third contest by himself. "Writing it was good therapy," Oppel told the Canadian Children's Book Centre of his work on the book, "a withdrawal technique if you will, enabling me to experience video games vicariously without spending huge amounts of money." As Susan Roman noted in *Booklist,* "the theme is very trendy and has appeal—especially to reluctant readers."

After his first book, Oppel had trouble getting a second one published. So he stopped writing and focused on his studies. While at the University of Toronto, he majored in English literature and cinema. Fascinated by his cinema studies, Oppel began making student films. When he returned to writing children's books in his final year of undergraduate study, *The Live-Forever Machine,* written for an independent studies course in creative writing, demonstrated the new cinematic influence. The story of fourteen-year-old Eric, who stumbles upon two men who discovered the secret of immortality in 391 A.D. and have been chasing each other through history ever since, reads as though a camera is mounted on Eric's shoulders. The reader sees a dank underworld where the Live-Forever machine is jealously guarded, a deceptively bland urban upper world melting under a ferocious sun, and a cool museum that offers refuge from the heat and a passageway into the past. The cinematic technique and themes introduced in this novel became a trademark of Oppel's later efforts.

Dead Water Zone, Oppel's next YA novel, details the relationship between two brothers possessing opposite characteristics. Paul, who is strong physically, travels to Watertown, in search of his missing brother Sam, who is the brainier half of the two. When he gets there, Paul suspects that his brother has discovered a secret hidden in the waters surrounding the eerie town. *Horn Book* contributor Elizabeth S. Watson, Lucinda Lockwood of *School Library Journal,* and Elizabeth MacCallum of the Toronto *Globe and Mail* all described *Dead Water Zone* as "Dickensian" in scope and flavor. *Voice of Youth Advocates* contributor Deborah Dubois wrote,

From Oppel's Christmas tale, *Follow That Star*, illustrated by Kim LaFave.

"Teens who like science fiction will find this a gripping novel that will leave them with much food for thought."

Geared for a younger audience, Oppel's "Bad Case" chapter books provide plenty of action and dialogue for newly independent readers, typically between the ages of six and nine. In *A Bad Case of Ghosts*, Giles discovers ghosts in an old house newly occupied by Giles and his family. With the help of two young ghost-hunters, Kevin and Tina, the harmless ghosts eventually leave the family alone. According to *School Librarian* contributor Cathy Sutton, "This is a well-written story with good character development." The trio's mystery-solving services are needed once again in *A Bad Case of Magic*, when books mysteriously float off the local library's shelves and right out the door. "The stories move along smartly, and they are full of fun, action, and the occasional deliciously scary bit," noted Fred Boer in *Quill & Quire*. Other titles within the series, including *A Bad Case of Robots*, were also received favorably.

Oppel returned to young adult fiction with the publication of *Silverwing*. In this book, dubbed a "mostly absorbing adventure story" by a *Publishers Weekly* critic, the author introduces his readers to the world of bats. After Shade, an irrepressibly curious young bat, becomes separated from the Silverwing colony during a storm, he experiences many challenges and adventures on his journey home. "Replete with appealing characters, scary adversaries, bat lore, natural history, unanswered questions, and conflicting theologies, the story takes on a promising epic sweep," proclaimed a *Kirkus Reviews* critic. Writing in *Voice of Youth Advocates*, reviewer Nancy Eaton urged: "Do not miss this rip-roaring adventure by a talented young writer."

In addition to his novels and short chapter books, Oppel has written a couple of picture books as well as a number of screenplays. The author's 1990 picture book *Cosimo Cat*, described as a "charming and magical" story by Terri L. Lyons in *Canadian Children's Literature*, features a young boy in search of an intriguing cat. Equally successful are the author's screenplays, several of which have been optioned for film. His screenplay for *The Live-Forever Machine* was optioned for film even before his book of the same title was published.

For Oppel, writing is more than a nine-to-five job. "I'm always thinking about it—during meals, in the evening, weekends, first thing when I wake up in the morning," he wrote for Kids Can Press's "Meet Kenneth Oppel." Since leaving a job at a children's book publisher in 1989, Oppel has devoted himself to writing full time.

■ Works Cited

Boer, Fred, review of *A Bad Case of Ghosts* and *A Bad Case of Magic, Quill & Quire,* April, 1995, p. 41.

Dubois, Deborah, review of *Dead Water Zone, Voice of Youth Advocates,* June, 1993, p. 104.

Eaton, Nancy, review of *Silverwing, Voice of Youth Advocates,* April, 1998, p. 58.

"Kenneth Oppel," *Writing Stories, Making Pictures: Biographies of 150 Canadian Children's Authors and Illustrators,* Canadian Children's Book Centre, 1995, pp. 245-247.

"Meet Kenneth Oppel" (booklet), Kids Can Press, 1994, (unpaged).

Lockwood, Lucinda, review of *Dead Water Zone, School Library Journal,* May, 1993, p. 127.

Lyons, Terri L., review of *Cosimo Cat, Canadian Children's Literature,* Number 71, 1993, pp. 87-88.

MacCallum, Elizabeth, "Journey through the Underworld Kindles a Glowing Novel," *Globe and Mail* (Toronto), September 19, 1992, p. C19.

Roman, Susan, review of *Colin's Fantastic Video, Booklist,* July, 1985, pp. 1558-59.

Review of *Silverwing, Kirkus Reviews,* September 1, 1997, p. 1394.

Review of *Silverwing, Publishers Weekly,* October 20, 1997, p. 76.

Sutton, Cathy, review of *A Bad Case of Ghosts, School Librarian,* August, 1993, p. 109.

Watson, Elizabeth S., review of *Dead Water Zone, Horn Book,* November-December, 1993, p. 747.

■ For More Information See

BOOKS

Egoff, Sheila, and Judith Saltman, *The New Republic of Childhood: A Critical Guide to Canadian Children's Literature in English,* Oxford University Press, 1990, p. 270.

PERIODICALS

Books for Keeps, January, 1996, p. 13.

Bulletin of the Center for Children's Books, October, 1985, p. 34; January, 1998, p. 170.

Canadian Children's Literature, Number 65, 1992, pp. 106-07; Number 86, 1997, pp. 52-54.
Canadian Materials, January, 1991, p. 35; May, 1991, p. 174; November, 1992, p. 312.
Horn Book, November-December, 1997, p. 684.
Junior Bookshelf, August, 1994, p. 138.
Publishers Weekly, May 24, 1993, p. 89.
Quill & Quire, November, 1990, p. 14; March, 1991, pp. 20-21; July, 1992, p. 48; August, 1994, p. 33; May, 1995, p. 48; April, 1997, p. 37.
School Library Journal, October, 1985, p. 175; October, 1997, p. 137.

*   *   *

PACKER, Vin
See MEAKER, Marijane (Agnes)

*   *   *

PEMSTEEN, Hans
See MANES, Stephen

*   *   *

POLLACK, Rachel (Grace) 1945-

■ Personal

Born in 1945.

■ Addresses

Agent—c/o HarperCollins Publishers, 8 Grafton St., London W1X 3LA, England.

■ Career

Writer.

■ Awards, Honors

Arthur C. Clarke Award for best British science fiction novel, 1988, for *Unquenchable Fire;* Nebula Award finalist, 1995, for *Temporary Agency.*

■ Writings

FOR YOUNG ADULTS

(With Cheryl Schwartz) *The Journey Out: A Guide for and about Lesbian, Gay, and Bisexual Teens,* Viking, 1995.

NOVELS

Golden Vanity, Berkley, 1980.
Alqua Dreams, Franklin Watts, 1987.
Unquenchable Fire, Century (London), 1988, Overlook (Woodstock, NY), 1992.
Temporary Agency, St. Martin's, 1994.
Godmother Night, St. Martin's, 1996.

NONFICTION

Seventy-Eight Degrees of Wisdom: A Book of Tarot (two volumes), Aquarian Press (Wellingborough, Northamptonshire, England), 1980-83, Borgo Press (San Bernardino, CA), 1986.
Salvador Dali's Tarot, Salem House (Salem, NH), 1985.
A Practical Guide to Fortune Telling: Palmistry, The Crystal Ball, Runes, Tea Leaves, The Tarot, Sphere/Rainbird (London), 1986, published as *Teach Yourself Fortune Telling,* Holt, 1986.
Tarot: The Open Labyrinth, Aquarian Press, 1986, Borgo Press, 1989.
The New Tarot: Modern Variations of Ancient Images, Aquarian Press, 1989, Overlook Press, 1990.
Tarot Readings and Meditations, Aquarian Press, 1990.
Haindl Tarot: The Major Arcana, Newcastle, 1990.
Shining Woman: Tarot Guide, Thorsons, 1991.
The Vertigo Tarot, 1995.
Burning Sky, Albatross, 1995.
The Body of the Goddess: Sacred Wisdom in Myths, Landscapes and Culture, Element, 1997.

EDITOR

(With Caitlin Matthews) *Tarot Tales,* Legend (London), 1989.
(With Mary K. Greer) *New Thoughts on Tarot: Transcripts from the First International Newcastle Tarot Symposium,* Newcastle Publishing (North Hollywood, CA), 1989.

OTHER

Author of short stories, including "Angel Baby," "The Protector," and "The Malignant One."

■ Sidelights

Rachel Pollack has used her interest in the occult to establish literary careers both as a Tarot expert and as a science fiction novelist, while also taking time to co-author a practical guide for teenagers dealing with questions of sexual identity. Pollack's first novel, *Golden Vanity,* was published in 1980, but it attracted little attention—David V. Barrett, in *Twentieth-Century Science-Fiction Writers,* called it "neglected." It would be another seven years before Pollack published her second entry in the genre, *Alqua Dreams.*

Golden Vanity, according to Barrett, is a traditional science-fiction yarn with New Age overtones: while describing first contact between earthlings and aliens, it also delves into the terrain of meditation and religious self-deception. Pollack's *Alqua Dreams* also establishes a traditional science-fiction premise, in this case an interstellar trader's attempt to establish trading links with a new planet in order to obtain an intelligent mineral used in spaceship drives. However, Pollack's second novel's ambitious underlying philosophical theme is, in Barrett's words, "the age-old debate between Platonic and Aristotelian life-views." *Analog* magazine reviewer Tom Easton termed this "a complex, difficult subtext of epistemological puzzling." In the framework of the plot, the space trader, Jaimi Cooper, visits Keela, a world whose inhabitants believe they are dead and that nothing is real—and who therefore believe that Cooper's desire to trade with them is also unreal. In order to trade successfully, Cooper must convince them to abandon their beliefs. A *Publishers Weekly* critic enjoyed the novel's premise but felt that it might have been explored more effectively as a short story. Barrett appreciated the "encyclopedic knowledge of religion and myth" which author Pollack brings to *Alqua Dreams,* and considered the book a worthy and intriguing study of its philosophical subject. Indeed, not since Philip José Farmer's *Night of Light,* a generation earlier, had Barrett found a more "disturbing and believable" exposition of an alien religion in a science fiction work.

Pollack's next novel, *Unquenchable Fire,* brought her the highest critical acclaim of any of her fiction to that point. Even so, the novel took several years to find a U.S. publisher, even after winning the Arthur C. Clarke Award for best British science-fiction novel of 1988. Reviewer Gregory Feeley, in the *Washington Post Book World,* speculated that the delay in acceptance by U.S. bookmakers resulted from Pollack's use of eclectic forms of magic as the basis for the book's fantasy, rather than the fairy tales and European folklore that underlie most novels in this genre. Aspects of the plot are familiar to fantasy and science fiction readers, however, as *Publishers Weekly* pointed out, for the book describes a future United States (Dutchess County, New York, to be specific) in which the laws of the universe have changed and magic reigns. The twist is that the original sense of wonder has fallen away, and magic now seems routine.

The main character of *Unquenchable Fire,* Jennifer Mazdan, finds herself pregnant with a child who, according to magical signs, may reawaken the lost sense of wonder at magic powers. This main plot is interwoven with tales of other aspects of life in the magical United States of America. Feeley found the novel's interpolations difficult and didactic, but thought the main story "witty, absorbing and frequently funny." John Clute, reviewing the novel for the *Observer,* went further and called it "dense, supple, and hilarious, by far her finest novel to date," and *Publishers Weekly* dubbed Pollack's third novel "compelling, surrealistic fantasy." Encyclopedist Barrett shared this critical consensus, but departed from Feeley by esteeming the interpolated tales more highly. "It's by no means an easy book," Barrett wrote, "but it is a very powerful and stimulating examination of the spiritual life"—one written with a depth, Barrett surmised, that might prevent its author from becoming widely popular.

Pollack's next novel, *Temporary Agency,* is actually two linked novellas, and acts as something of a sequel to *Unquenchable Fire* in that it assumes a knowledge of the magical beings who ran human affairs in the earlier book. In the title novella, the main characters, becoming involved with a being called a Malignant One, discover, according to *Publishers Weekly,* "what people will do in the name of pragmatism." In the second piece, "Benign Adjustments," two of the same characters, Ellen and

Alison, find out "how the most benign intentions can be adulterated by human frailties." The settings of the novellas include a Manhattan advertising agency, Westchester, and the floor of the New York Stock Exchange—a place where, in Pollack's alternate world, traders obtain assistance from magical robes and dolls. *Publishers Weekly* called *Temporary Agency* "a first-rate work" and commended it for combining rational speculation with an awareness that "the key to good fiction is people and what happens to them." Jackie Cassada of *Library Journal* hailed the book as a "brilliant extrapolation of a spiritually awakened society" that "bears witness to her [Pollack's] potent literary imagination." Science fiction novelist Maureen F. McHugh, assessing *Temporary Agency* for the *Washington Post Book World,* praised the novel for being unsentimental and "full of ambiguity and loss." Pollack, McHugh concluded, "has written a fantasy book for grown-ups." *Temporary Agency* was rewarded with finalist status in that year's Nebula Award competition.

Pollack's next novel, *Godmother Night,* explored a different fantasy world, one that exists on the back of a giant turtle as if in fulfillment of an ancient myth. The main characters in this 1996 work are two young women, Laurie and Jaqe, who are lovers. Meeting Mother Night, who is really Death, enable the couple to overcome social obstacles in their path, but at the price of the early death of one of the women soon after a child has been born to them. Mother Night then becomes a godmother figure to the child, easing its passage through life. *Publishers Weekly* noted the "resourceful and original" quality of this plot, and called the novel "another fine outing by one of the most gifted and sensitive fantasists working today."

In Pollack's simultaneous careers as occultist and nonfiction writer, she has also won acclaim. She has written a text for a Tarot deck illustrated by surrealist painter Salvador Dali, and has authored *The New Tarot,* which in "delightful and richly illustrated" fashion, according to Barrett, examines more than seventy commercial Tarot decks of the past generation. In 1986, Pollack published *A Practical Guide to Fortune Telling: Palmistry, the Crystal Ball, Runes, Tea Leaves, the Tarot,* which was issued in the United States as *Teach Yourself Fortune Telling.* Reviewing the work for the *Village Voice Literary Supplement,* Stacey D'Erasmo began by stating: "I've been waiting for this book my whole life." Pollack's wide-ranging introduction to divination deals with palmistry, tea-leaf reading, Tarot, and other methods of foretelling the future from the standpoint of character analysis rather than fortune telling in the strict sense. The author's thesis is that hidden patterns underlie the seemingly random events that occur in individuals' lives; examining the apparent randomness, whether in a shuffled deck of cards or in the arrangement of leaves or in other phenomena, will unveil these patterns. D'Erasmo called Pollack "a gentle and learned guide" and singled out the Tarot section, the book's longest, for praise, saying, "amidst the flood of Tarot decks and guides now on the market, Pollack's is remarkably clear and free of gooeyness."

The same qualities of clarity, informativeness, and lack of sentimentality that characterize Pollack's other work are found in a book of hers on a very different topic, 1995's *The Journey Out: A Guide for and about Lesbian, Gay, and Bisexual Teens,* co-written with Cheryl Schwartz. The authors combine advice, which *Publishers Weekly* called "frank, reassuring" and "authoritative," with quotes from gay or bisexual teens, "extensive" informational listings, and forthright, helpful discussion of sexually transmitted diseases. *School Library Journal* reviewer Claudia Morrow called the book a "gentle, informative, well-written guide.... An antidote to isolation for despairing kids," and a "hopeful, kind book" that encourages self-acceptance, understanding, and love.

■ Works Cited

Review of *Alqua Dreams, Publishers Weekly,* October 2, 1987, p. 87.

Barrett, David V., "Rachel Pollack," *Twentieth-Century Science-Fiction Writers,* third edition, edited by Noelle Watson and Paul E. Schellinger, St. James Press, 1991, pp. 631-32.

Cassada, Jackie, review of *Temporary Agency, Library Journal,* August, 1994, p. 139.

Clute, John, review of *Unquenchable Fire, Observer,* December 18, 1988, p. 43.

D'Erasmo, Stacey, review of *A Practical Guide to Fortune Telling: Palmistry, the Crystal Ball, Runes, Tea Leaves, the Tarot, Village Voice Literary Supplement,* July-August, 1993, p. 20.

Easton, Tom, review of *Alqua Dreams, Analog,* September, 1988, pp. 181-82.

Feeley, Gregory, review of *Unquenchable Fire, Washington Post Book World,* April 26, 1992, p. 6.

Review of *Godmother Night, Publishers Weekly,* August 26, 1996, p. 78.

Review of *The Journey Out: A Guide for and about Lesbian, Gay, and Bisexual Teens, Publishers Weekly,* November 27, 1995, p. 70.

McHugh, Maureen F., review of *Temporary Agency, Washington Post Book World,* September 25, 1994, p. 14.

Morrow, Claudia, review of *The Journey Out: A Guide for and about Lesbian, Gay, and Bisexual Teens, School Library Journal,* January, 1996, p. 136.

Review of *Temporary Agency, Publishers Weekly,* July 25, 1994, p. 38.

Review of *Unquenchable Fire, Publishers Weekly,* March 23, 1992, p. 64.

■ For More Information See

PERIODICALS

Booklist, December 15, 1986, p. 604; December 1, 1995, p. 616.

Bulletin of the Center for Children's Books, March, 1996, p. 239.*

Q–R

QUENTIN, Brad
   See BISSON, Terry (Ballantine)

*   *   *

QUIRK, Anne (E.) 1956-

■ Personal

Born January 11, 1956, in Springfield, MA; daughter of
John T. (a lawyer) and Mary E. (a lawyer; maiden name,
Hurley) Quirk; married Robert M. Carey (a physicist),
August 1, 1987; children: Isabel, Andrew. *Education:*
Dartmouth College, A.B., 1977; Tufts University, M.A.,
1986. *Politics:* Democrat. *Religion:* Roman Catholic.

■ Addresses

Home—124 Dudley St., Cambridge, MA 02140.

■ Career

Harper and Row, New York City, marketing, 1970-79,
1981-85; Philomel/Putnam, New York City, marketing,
1979-81; Little, Brown, Boston, MA, marketing, 1986-
93; freelance marketing and advertising consultant,
1993—.

■ Writings

Dancing with Great-Aunt Cornelia, HarperCollins, 1997.

■ Sidelights

Anne Quirk told *SATA:* "I grew up in a very large and
argumentative family. My parents are both lawyers, one
of my sisters is also an attorney, my grandfather was a
cop, and yet another sister now works for the prison
system. Crime and punishment is the family trade. I do
not come from a long line of writers.

"We were, however, readers, even though my father's
favorite book for dinnertime recitation, *Lives of the
Saints,* kept us from enjoying food until well into our
twenties. My mother leaned toward history and biogra-

Anne Quirk relates the adventures of thirteen-year-old
Connie on her annual trips to Manhattan to stay with
her eccentric, art-loving great-aunt. (Cover illustration
by Loren Long.)

phy. My oldest brother, a frustrated hipster, collected Kerouac and Ginsburg. My oldest sister claims to have read all of Dickens in grammar school, although some of us have our doubts. And on it went, through two parents and eight children and continuing ripples of grandchildren. My childhood house is still furnished with temporary bookshelves put up in the 1950s.

"My first and so far only novel for children, *Dancing with Great-Aunt Cornelia,* has absolutely nothing to do with my childhood. Except, maybe, that it was inspired by a respect for and delight in the messiness of families. I'm now nearly thirty years older than my heroine, Connie O'Malley, but like her I continue to discover how maddening my family is. And, like her, I wouldn't have it any other way."

Neither would critics, who found Quirk's tale of a thirteen-year-old's annual trip to Manhattan, her eccentric, art-loving great-aunt, and the family secrets she uncovers noteworthy. *School Library Journal* reviewer Julie Cummins described *Dancing* as a "'quirky' family farce with comedy, romance, intrigue, and self-realization that's ripe for a movie script." Janice M. Del Negro, writing in the *Bulletin of the Center for Children's Books,* continued the film motif: "The plot situations recall the movie hijinks of madcap heiresses . . . ." According to a *Kirkus Reviews* critic, Quirk "proves herself smart and funny as she establishes and then parodies Manhattan high life as experienced by a teenager from Queens."

■ Works Cited

Cummins, Julie, review of *Dancing with Great-Aunt Cornelia, School Library Journal,* May, 1997, p. 139.

Review of *Dancing with Great-Aunt Cornelia, Kirkus Reviews,* May 15, 1997, p. 806.

Del Negro, Janice M., review of *Dancing with Great-Aunt Cornelia, Bulletin of the Center for Children's Books,* June, 1997, p. 370.

*   *   *

RATTIGAN, Jama Kim 1951-

■ Personal

Name is pronounced *Jay*-mah; born November 20, 1951, in Honolulu, HI; daughter of James Young Nam (a carpenter) and Margaret (a secretary; maiden name Yang) Kim; married Leonard Rattigan (a civil engineer), September 2, 1978. *Education:* University of Hawaii, B.A., 1973, M.A., 1975. *Politics:* Independent. *Religion:* Christian. *Hobbies and other interests:* Travel, antiques, interior decorating, music, films, reading, bird watching, letter writing, collects teddy bears, character watches, stationery, and rubber stamps.

■ Addresses

Home—13609 White Barn Lane, Herndon, VA 20171-3341.

■ Career

Author. Has worked as a secretary and receptionist in several different settings, including college athletics, medical research, and environmental research. Leilehua High School, Wahiawa, HI, instructor, adult education, 1975-77; Leeward Community College, Aiea, HI, lecturer in English, 1975-77; University of Hawaii, Honolulu, HI, lecturer in English, 1975-77; American Community School, London, England, high school English teacher, 1977-79; tutor, Literacy Council of Northern Virginia, 1993—; writer-in-residence, Parklawn Elementary School, Alexandria, VA, 1995. *Member:* Society of Children's Book Writers and Illustrators, Author's Guild, Wolf Trap Associates, World Folk Music Association, International Wizard of Oz Club.

■ Awards, Honors

Smithsonian Notable Book, 1993, finalist, *Hungry Mind Review* Book of Distinction, 1994, Outstanding Trade Book in Social Studies, National Council for the Social Studies and Children's Book Council, 1994, and New Voices, New World Multicultural Fiction Contest winner, Little, Brown, all for *Dumpling Soup;* Book of the Year, *School Library Journal,* 1994, "Pick of the Lists" selection, American Booksellers Association, 1994, Smithsonian Notable Book, 1994, and Notable Trade Book in the Language Arts, National Council of Teach-

JAMA KIM RATTIGAN

ers of English, 1995, all for *Truman's Aunt Farm;* Aesop Accolade, American Folklore Society, 1996, for *The Woman in the Moon: A Story from Hawai'i.*

■ Writings

PICTURE BOOKS

Dumpling Soup, illustrated by Lillian Hsu-Flanders, Little, Brown, 1993.

Truman's Aunt Farm, illustrated by G. Brian Karas, Houghton Mifflin, 1994.

(Reteller) *The Woman in the Moon: A Story from Hawai'i,* illustrated by Carla Golembe, Little, Brown, 1996.

Contributor to periodicals, including *Cobblestone, Alive! for Young Teens, ALOHA: The Magazine of Hawaii, Country Living, Country Home, Children's Digest, Child Life, Hopscotch, Crayola,* and *Highlights for Children.*

■ Work in Progress

A biography of Mary Kawena Pukui, a short story collection, four picture books, and an easy reader; researching Hawaiian history and culture, and Asian Americans in Hawaii.

■ Sidelights

Jama Kim Rattigan, a children's picture book author, is noted for her works celebrating Hawaiian life. Most of her stories are in one way or another connected to her childhood and feature strong female characters. Clearly evident among her books, especially in *Dumpling Soup* and *The Woman in the Moon: A Story from Hawai'i,* are the importance of celebrating family, culture, tradition, and art. Critics often praise Rattigan for her detailed descriptions, rich language, and portrayal of a child's world. Deborah Stevenson, writing in *Bulletin of the Center for Children's Books,* concluded that "Rattigan has a gift for the kind of specifics that make a book come alive."

Rattigan explained to *SATA* the origin of her unique name. "'Jama' is short for 'James-Margaret.' My parents had to be creative since our surname, 'Kim,' was so common in Hawaii. When my kindergarten teacher mispronounced my name on the first day of school, I knew life was going to be tough. I have endured 'Hama,' 'Pajama,' 'Jamaica,' 'Jamer,' and 'Yama.' From the very beginning my life centered on words."

Rattigan's childhood days centered on reading and visiting her local library. "I grew up in the small rural town of Wahiawa, on the island of Oahu in Hawaii. Since both our parents worked, my older brother and I had to fend for ourselves much of the time. The library was safe, nearby, and offered answers to many of our questions. I was happy as long as I had a book to read.

"In school I always liked Language Arts. I felt most comfortable with anything that involved words—spelling, reading, grammar, composition. My first published story was a fourth grade field trip report included in the PTA newsletter. In high school I wrote poetry, and in college I took a lot of writing classes. Writing seemed to follow me around no matter what I did.

"I received a Masters degree in English from the University of Hawaii (1975). I had the rare privilege of working with several notable professors who profoundly shaped my thinking and still influence my writing today: Leon Edel, Asa Baber, and Phillip Damon. For four years I taught school in both Hawaii and England. My students came from all over the world, ranging in age from eight to sixty-five. I 'retired' from teaching in the mid '80s to pursue writing full time. Currently I visit schools, present writing workshops, and tutor on a voluntary basis for the Literary Council of Northern Virginia."

Rattigan's first award-winning story, *Dumpling Soup,* features Marisa, a seven-year old girl in Hawaii, and her family, who are a blend of Korean, Japanese, Chinese, Hawaiian, and Anglo ancestry. Each year Marisa's family celebrates the New Year by incorporating foods and festivities from many of these cultures. Much of the child-narrator's excitement comes from participating for the first time in making dumpling soup. Afterwards, Marisa becomes concerned that her odd-shaped dumplings won't taste as good as those made by her relatives. They do, of course, and Marisa is able to fully enjoy the rest of the New Year's festivities. "A lively celebration of setting, tradition, and the rich diversity of a loving family," concluded Hazel Rochman in *Booklist.* Similarly, *Horn Book* contributor Ellen Fader noted that the story is a "thoroughly enjoyable celebration of family warmth and diverse tradition."

Rattigan explained to *SATA* that she had been working on this New Year's celebration story for many years, revising it many times. It wasn't accepted for publication until she entered it in a contest for multicultural fiction—sponsored by the children's book publisher Little, Brown—and won. "I think part of the reason my story might have won," Rattigan told *SATA,* "is because there are so few stories for children set in contemporary Hawaii. When I was young I read about children from all over America, but I could never find a girl from Hawaii, just like me, in any of those books. I hope that by writing books like *Dumpling Soup,* children in Hawaii can see themselves, and children from the mainland USA can learn more about Hawaii."

Truman's Aunt Farm, Rattigan's second book for children, plays off the pun on "ant" throughout the story as a boy who sends away for an ant farm instead finds dozens of "aunts" arriving on his doorstep. The women fuss over Truman and he in turn trains them in such exercises as hugging, tickling, and the art of listening before sending each one off with another child. Rattigan, who grew up with many aunts, revealed to *SATA:* "This story was my husband's idea. He suggested I write about an ant farm since we were giving one to a nephew for his birthday. But when he said 'ant farm,' I thought 'aunt farm.'" "Kids will laugh at the wordplay," *Booklist* critic Rochman contended.

Instead of sending him an ant farm for his birthday, Truman's Aunt Fran presents the young boy with several aunts for him to raise and train. (From *Truman's Aunt Farm*, written by Rattigan and illustrated by G. Brian Karas.)

Rattigan returned to the setting of Hawaii for her third picture book, *The Woman in the Moon.* "I selected this particular Polynesian legend," Rattigan related, "because it featured a strong female role model." In this story, Hina leaves behind the demands of her work in the village making tapa cloth, and her husband who refuses to help her, in order to find a place where she will be free to enjoy the beauty of the world around her. Her search eventually leads her to the moon, where she continues to gaze down upon the earth every night, according to legend. "In retelling the tale," Rattigan explained to *SATA,* "I tried to emphasize the themes that I felt most strongly about: the power of the imagination to take us to a better place, the importance of the artistic sensibility to transcend reality, the artistic process as a journey in itself, art as a form of prayer, and

the inspiring spirit of adventure that has always characterized native Hawaiians." Judith Gloyer, writing in *School Library Journal,* appreciated Rattigan's "rich" and "concrete" language and noted that the story is "an interesting and striking addition to folklore collections."

"The Hawaii I grew up in was small," Rattigan continued, "but it contained people from almost every ethnic group in the world. People had no choice but to learn to get along with each other. Today, different languages, customs, foods, and traditions all blend together to make Hawaii a unique and fascinating place."

■ Works Cited

Fader, Ellen, review of *Dumpling Soup, Horn Book,* November-December, 1993, p. 727.

Gloyer, Judith, review of *The Woman in the Moon: A Story from Hawai'i, School Library Journal,* December, 1996, pp. 116-17.
Rochman, Hazel, review of *Dumpling Soup, Booklist,* September 15, 1993.
Rochman, Hazel, review of *Truman's Aunt Farm, Booklist,* February 15, 1994, p. 1093.
Stevenson, Deborah, review of *Dumpling Soup, Bulletin of the Center for Children's Books,* October, 1993, p. 56.

■ For More Information See

PERIODICALS

Booklist, November 1, 1996, pp. 497-98.
Kirkus Reviews, October 1, 1993, p. 1278; September 15, 1996, p. 1407.
Publishers Weekly, October 25, 1993, p. 60.
School Library Journal, December, 1993, p. 93.

*   *   *

REAVES, (James) Michael 1950-
(J. Michael Reaves)

■ Personal

Born 1950; married; children: three. *Education:* Attended California State University at San Bernadino; attended Clarion College Workshop in science fiction, 1972.

■ Addresses

Home—Los Angeles, CA. *Agent*—c/o Tor Books, 49 West 24th St., 9th Floor, New York, NY 10010.

■ Career

Novelist, television writer, and screenwriter. *Go-Bots,* Hanna-Barbera, performed development work, 1984; *Pole Position,* DiC Enterprises, development work, 1984; *Mighty Orbots,* TMS Entertainment and Intermedia Entertainment, story editor, developer, and writer, 1984; *Spinetinglers!,* Southern Star Productions, performed development work, 1985; *My Little Pony,* Sunbow Productions, story editor and writer, 1986; *The Ugly Dinosaur,* Southern Star, developer and writer, 1989; *Peter Pan and the Pirates,* Southern Star/TMS, story editor and writer, 1989-90; *Batman: The Animated Series,* Warner Bros., story editor and writer, 1991-93; *Conan and the Young Warriors,* Sunbow Productions, story editor, development work, and writer, 1993; *Gargoyles,* Buena Vista, story editor and writer; *Invasion America,* Dreamworks SKG, writer and producer, 1997—.

■ Awards, Honors

British Fantasy Award nomination for best novelette, 1978, for *The Big Spell;* Prometheus Award nomination for best novel, 1979, for *Dragonworld;* Writers Guild Award nomination for best teleplay, 1989, for *Street of Shadows;* Emmy award for best writing and story editing, 1991-92, for *Batman: The Animated Series;*

ASIFA Award nomination for best animation teleplay, 1995, for *Deadly Force.*

■ Writings

NOVELS; FOR YOUNG ADULTS

I-Alien, Ace, 1978.
(With Steve Perry) *Sword of the Samurai,* Bantam, 1984.
The Shattered World, Timescape, 1984.
(With Steve Perry) *Hellstar,* Berkley, 1984.
Street Magic, Tor, 1991.

NOVELS

(As J. Michael Reaves; with Byron Preiss) *Dragonworld,* Bantam, 1979.
(With Steve Perry) *Dome,* Berkley, 1987.
The Burning Realm, Baen, 1988.
(With Steve Perry) *The Omega Cage,* Ace, 1988.
Night Hunter, Tor, 1995.
Voodoo Child, Tor, 1997.

SHORT STORIES

(As J. Michael Reaves) *Darkworld Detective,* Bantam, 1982.

Many of Reaves's short stories have been featured in anthologies and periodicals, including *Fantasy & Science Fiction Magazine, Year's Best Horror, Gent, Fantasy Annual* and *Clarion III.*

SCREENPLAYS

Batman: Mask of the Phantasm, Warner Bros., 1993.
Full Eclipse, Citadel/HBO/Tapestry, 1993.
Gargoyles, Buena Vista, 1995.

MICHAEL REAVES

Also author of teleplays for live-action television series episodes, including *The Twilight Zone,* CBS, 1986-89; (with Diane Duane) "Where None Have Gone Before," *Star Trek: The Next Generation,* Paramount, 1987; *Pandora* (pilot), Laurel, 1987; *Captain Power and the Soldiers of the Future,* Landmark, 1987-88; *Star Runners* (pilot), Fallen Artists, 1988; *Monsters,* Villa Di Stefano, 1990; *The Flash,* Warner Bros., 1990; and *Father Dowling Mysteries,* Viacom, 1990-91. Author of teleplays for animated television series episodes, including *Space Sentinels,* Filmation, 1976; *Tarzan and the Super Seven,* Filmation, 1977-78; *The Shmoo,* Hanna-Barbera, 1979; *Tarzan, Lord of the Jungle,* Filmation, 1980; *Space Stars,* Hanna-Barbera, 1981; *Superfriends,* Hanna-Barbera, 1981; *Blackstar,* Filmation, 1981; *The Incredible Hulk,* Marvel, 1982; *U.S. 1* (promotional script), Marvel, 1982; *Flash Gordon,* Filmation, 1982; *Smurfs and Johan and Peewee,* Hanna-Barbera, 1981-83; *The Puppy's New Adventures,* Ruby-Spears Enterprises, 1983; *Biskitts,* Hanna-Barbera, 1983; *Spider-Man and His Amazing Friends,* Marvel, 1983; *He-Man and the Masters of the Universe,* Marvel, 1983; *Transformers,* Sunbow, 1984; *Pole Position,* DiC Enterprises, 1984; *Dungeons and Dragons,* Marvel, 1984-85; *CBS Storybreak,* CBS, 1984-85; *The Littles,* DiC, 1984-85; *Challenge of the Go-Bots,* Hanna-Barbera, 1985; *Droids,* Lucasfilm, 1985; *Centurions,* Ruby-Spears, 1986; *The Young Astronauts,* Marvel, 1986; *My Little Pony,* Sunbow, 1986; *Captain Eo* (development work), Disney, 1986; *Ewoks,* Lucasfilm, 1986; *The Real Ghostbusters,* DiC, 1986-87; *Starcom, the U.S. Space Force,* DiC, 1987; *Chuck Norris: Karate Kommandos,* Ruby-Spears, 1987; *Spiral Zone,* Kushner-Locke, 1987; *The Bionic Six,* TMS/Universal, 1987; *Teenage Mutant Ninja Turtles,* Murakami-Wolf-Swenson, 1988-90; *The Ugly Dinosaur,* Southern Star, 1989; *Dink, The Little Dinosaur,* Ruby-Spears, 1989-90; *The New Adventures of HE-MAN,* Jetlag, 1989; *Peter Pan and the Pirates,* Southern Star/TMS, 1989-90; *Tiny Toons Adventures,* Warner Bros./Amblin Entertainment, 1990; *Bobby's World,* Film Roman, 1990; *Young Robin Hood,* Hanna-Barbera/Crayon Animation, 1991; *Batman: The Animated Series,* Warner Bros., 1991-93; *Conan and the Young Warriors,* Sunbow, 1993; *Gargoyles,* Buena Vista, 1993-95. Author of issues for comic books, including *Teen Titans Spotlight,* DC Comics, 1988; *Fusion,* Eclipse Comics, 1988-89; and *The Batman Adventures,* DC Comics, 1993. Author of dialogue for a music video by Megadeth.

OTHER

Author of movie reviews for *Delap's F&SF Review.*

■ **Sidelights**

Michael Reaves sold his first short story in 1972, after attending the prestigious Clarion Workshop in science fiction at Clarion College, Pennsylvania. Since that time, he has established a reputation for combining genres in his work—for instance, science fiction and fantasy—and for writing for children and young adults as well as adult readers. Robert Reginald, assessing Reaves's career in *Twentieth-Century Science-Fiction Writers,* called the author a moralist whose protagonists

perceive some flaw, emptiness, or imbalance in themselves or in the universe, and who feel driven to correct it.

Reginald pointed to Reaves's first published short story, "The Breath of Dragons," as "uncannily" presaging the subjects and themes that would characterize Reaves's later work. The story, set on a planet where dragons are killed for their fire-producing bladders, sees its protagonist, Perrin, attempt to champion the dragons in the face of societal opposition, only to be destroyed by the fire-breathing creatures themselves. In Reaves's first novel, *Dragonworld,* co-written with Byron Preiss, a dragon quest is again the focus of the plot. Five years later, in the novel *The Shattered World,* Reaves produced what Reginald considered "the author's most popular work." Fantasy and science fiction themes intertwine, as magicians who have survived the fragmentation of their planet by a Necromancer travel from one world-fragment to another on ships made of dragon bone and skin in an effort to restore their planet before its fractured orbits decay. The action proceeds fast and furious, involving shapechangers, a land of demons, and a chase through flying castles. Tom Easton, in *Analog,* applauded Reaves's effects as "grand and glorious." *Library Journal* reviewer Janet Cameron, finding "intriguing" characters in this "impressive" novel, felt that at the core of *A Shattered World* was a "moving portrayal of a man's final reconciliation with the beast within." A sequel to *The Shattered World,* entitled *The Burning Realm,* appeared in 1988. Reginald commented that one of its characters, Beorn, was "as attractive a thief as one will find in modern fantasy literature."

While crafting novels about a fragmented world of wizards, Reaves was turning his hand to other kinds of fantasy as well. In 1984, with fellow writer Steve Perry, he created a do-it-yourself adventure book for readers in grades five through eight, in Bantam's "Time Machine" series. This volume, *Sword of the Samurai,* takes the reader to Japan in the year 1600 with the mission of retrieving the sword of a famous samurai. Also co-written with Perry was the 1984 novel *Hellstar,* which is primarily science fiction, although containing fantasy elements such as flight by its human characters. Perry also collaborated with Reaves on the 1987 novel *Dome,* which fellow science-fiction writer Algis Budrys, in reviewing the book for *Magazine of Fantasy and Science Fiction,* treated as a high-tech thriller rather than as science fiction. The story involves a mobile underwater city that survives a world war which destroys the rest of the human race.

A solo effort, Reaves's novel *Street Magic* is tailored for young adults. The sixteen-year-old protagonist, a runaway trying to survive on the streets of San Francisco, is recruited by a group of fairies who are looking for the door to their home world. *School Library Journal* reviewer Nora Jane Natke found the work "fast-paced" with an "explosive" ending. In Reaves's novel *Night Hunter,* the author brings his mixture of fantasy and teen concerns to Los Angeles for a tale about a vampire who kills teenagers. *Night Hunter* includes strong detective-story elements: Homicide Sergeant Jake Hull and

MURDER AND DARK MAGIC
PROWL THE NEW ORLEANS
STREETS

VOODOO CHILD
MICHAEL REAVES

At the service of evil forces, a drug lord searches New Orleans for an innocent young person to sacrifice and only a priest of vodun can save the child. (Cover illustration by Michael Koelsch.)

partner Dan Stratton are responsible for tracking down the bloodsucker. A *Publishers Weekly* reviewer credited Reaves for capturing "the tone and tenor of the seedy Hollywood scene."

Reaves's credits as a writer continue to grow, not only as the author of novels and short stories, but also as a prolific writer of screenplays and teleplays for film and television.

■ Works Cited

Budrys, Algis, review of *Dome, Magazine of Fantasy and Science Fiction,* July, 1987, pp. 23-24.
Cameron, Janet, review of *The Shattered World, Library Journal,* March 15, 1984, pp. 599-600.
Easton, Tom, review of *The Shattered World, Analog: Science Fiction/Science Fact,* December, 1984, p. 146.
Natke, Nora Jane, review of *Street Magic, School Library Journal,* April, 1992, p. 164.
Review of *Night Hunter, Publishers Weekly,* May 29, 1995, p. 68.
Reginald, Robert, essay on Michael Reaves, *Twentieth-Century Science-Fiction Writers,* third edition, St. James Press (Chicago), 1991, pp. 657-58.

■ For More Information See

PERIODICALS

Kirkus Reviews, June 15, 1995, p. 819; July 1, 1995, p. 938.
Library Journal, June 15, 1991, p. 109.
Publishers Weekly, February 3, 1984, p. 339; November 21, 1994, p. 74.
School Library Journal, September, 1984, p. 139.
Voice of Youth Advocates, December, 1984, p. 269.*

* * *

REAVES, J. Michael
See REAVES, (James) Michael

* * *

REED, Neil 1961-

■ Personal

Born October 10, 1961, in Romford, Essex; son of Martyn John and Jean Reed; married Abby (a health care assistant), July 26, 1997. *Education:* Falmouth College of Art and Design, H.N.D. in technical illustration, 1984. *Religion:* Church of England. *Hobbies and other interests:* Surfing, swimming.

■ Addresses

Home and office—Bumble Down Barn, Menagissey, Mt. Hawke, Cornwall, England TR4 8DQ. *Agent*—Gary Mills, Allied Artists, 31, Harcourt St., London, England.

■ Career

Self-employed illustrator, 1984—. Part-time lecturer in illustration at Falmouth School of Art and Design.

■ Illustrator

FOR CHILDREN

Coming Home, Simon & Schuster, 1991.
Something for James, Random House/Dial, 1995.
Treasure Island, Brimax (London), 1996.
Black Beauty, Brimax, 1997.
Unicorn City, Random House/Dial, 1997, published in the United States as *Unicorn Dreams,* 1997.
Storm Seal, Magi (London), 1998.

■ Work in Progress

When Lea Grows Up, for Scribner, and *Horse & Pony Stories,* for Dorling Kindersley.

■ Sidelights

Neil Reed told *SATA:* "Painting and drawing have always been a major part of my life. When at school, it's

NEIL REED

all I really wanted to do, but I couldn't see how to make it a career. Even after four years doing a technical illustration course—which I adapted to just practicing painting and drawing techniques, and with the support of two of England's top illustrators, Mike Heslop and John Raynes, who, luckily for me, were teaching at the college when I was there—I couldn't see that you could make a living doing something that you enjoy so much.

"But, luckily for me, I was pointed in the right direction by Mike and John, who recommended me to Gary Mills, an artistic agent who took me on and who I have been with ever since.

"The type of work varies a lot, but in the past few years I have been getting more and more involved in children's picture books, which is the area I am happiest working in.

"Illustrators who have influenced me include Robert Cunningham, Bernie Fuchs, Robert Heindel, and Mark English. All Americans, but all different styles which I can appreciate."

*   *   *

ROCHE, Denis (Mary) 1967-

■ Personal

Born January 5, 1967, in New Haven, CT; daughter of Kevin (an architect) and Jane (an artist) Roche. *Education:* St. Andrews University, Scotland, B.A., M.A. in art history.

■ Addresses

Home—Cambridge, MA. *Agent*—c/o Houghton Mifflin, 222 Berkeley St., Boston, MA.

■ Career

Author and illustrator; formerly an elementary school teacher.

■ Awards, Honors

Reading Magic Award, *Parenting* Magazine, 1997, for *Only One Ollie* and *Ollie All Over*; Best Books, *Child* Magazine, 1997, for *Brave Georgie Goat.*

■ Writings

FOR CHILDREN; SELF-ILLUSTRATED

Loo-Loo, Boo, and Art You Can Do, Houghton Mifflin, 1996.
Only One Ollie, Houghton Mifflin, 1997.
Ollie All Over, Houghton Mifflin, 1997.
Brave Georgie Goat: Three Little Stories About Growing Up, Crown, 1997.
Art Around the World!: Loo-Loo, Boo, and More Art You Can Do, Houghton Mifflin, 1998.

ILLUSTRATOR

Stephanie Calmenson, *The Teeny Tiny Teacher,* Scholastic, 1998.

■ Sidelights

Denis Roche told *SATA:* "I started writing and illustrating children's books after working as an elementary school teacher for a couple of years. I grew up in a household with no television so I read constantly. I still own all of the books I had as a child, and I re-read them all the time. My current favorite book is *Dominic* by William Steig."

Roche has written several books that center around animal characters, including Ollie, a puppy, and Brave Georgie Goat. But she is also known for her books on arts and crafts, which feature projects that children can do on their own. All of her books are self-illustrated, and she has illustrated the work of another author, Stephanie Calmenson, whose *Teeny Tiny Teacher* was published in 1998.

The daughter of an architect father and an artist mother, Roche was surrounded by tools of arts and crafts from an early age. Growing up in a household without television encouraged her to use her imagination, fostering her love of reading and creative endeavors. Her family lived in the United States, but Roche attended St. Andrews University in Scotland, where she studied art history.

Roche became an elementary-school art teacher, and out of that experience arose her career as an author and illustrator of books for children. With *Loo-Loo, Boo, and Art You Can Do,* targeted to primary graders, she offers eleven different art projects that young people can

Fictional television star Loo-Loo and her dog Boo narrate this book about eleven imaginative art projects for children. (From *Loo-Loo, Boo, and Art You Can Do,* written and illustrated by Roche.)

put together on their own, with a minimum of adult supervision. Narrated by the fictional TV star Loo-Loo and her dog Boo, the books are written in such a way as to speak to their readers directly. Loo-Loo and Boo begin by offering instructions and a few useful rules of thumb, such as "Water jars and paint almost always tip over, and it's easier to clean up if you've put down newspapers." They also encourage the use of plastic knives, rather than metal ones, for cutting cardboard. Then, having gotten the serious matters out of the way, the two narrators take their readers through a series of projects. One of the most popular of these is called "stinky clay"—clay mixed with pickle juice. Another unusual one is "bumpy paint"; but most of the projects in *Loo-Loo, Boo, and Art You Can Do,* such as potato prints and collage, will be familiar to anyone who has been involved in elementary-school arts and crafts projects. Several other features of the book make it particularly useful and attractive.

Among the first things readers notice when opening *Loo-Loo, Boo, and Art You Can Do* are the bright colors of the illustrations. These are created by using a technique called *gouache,* which is the use of opaque watercolor paints, as opposed to transparent (see-through) watercolors. A critic in *Kirkus Reviews* observed that the illustrations "are sure to entice readers," and a *Publishers Weekly* commentator noted that the bright colors create a "please-touch" effect to the book. The latter reviewer also pointed out the value of the book's layout: each project is on a single, open-page spread, meaning that "hands sticky from homemade paste don't have to touch these pages." Black lines between the steps of a project also make instructions easy to follow. Elizabeth Bush, in her review for *Bulletin of the Center for Children's Books,* maintained that young readers in search of "simple, sloppy entertainment" would come away satisfied.

Ollie, the star of *Ollie All Over* and *Only One Ollie,* is a puppy, but he might as well be a human toddler. Like the preschool audience for whom this book was written, Ollie often becomes restless and needs plenty of attention. To entertain himself, he turns first to hiding and later to counting. *Ollie All Over* begins: "Ollie was hiding. His mother wasn't finding him, so he hid some more." In these board books, Roche again offers the bright, rich colors that had made *Loo-Loo* pleasing. Several visual tricks help to hold the interest of a young audience. For instance, Ollie camouflages himself in front of a curtain with the same pattern as his shirt. The story is written in such a way that it may not be entirely clear whether Ollie's mother knows he is deliberately hiding from her, but when he "hides" on her lap, she has no trouble finding him. A *Kirkus Reviews* critic considered the book "terrific," and commented on its "healthy respect for the resourcefulness" of small children.

A *Publishers Weekly* commentator praised the "killer cute" illustrations in both *Ollie All Over* and its companion volume, *Only One Ollie.* In the latter story, Ollie cannot find anyone who will play with him, so he entertains himself by counting. He counts two blue sofas, three round carpets, and all manner of objects, and in the process becomes aware of the fact that there is "only one" Ollie. The story culminates with his counting of his ten siblings, who are finished with their work and ready to play with him. Janice Del Negro in *Bulletin of the Center for Children's Books* commented favorably on both books, concluding that they "do what board books are supposed to do—they introduce concepts easily and with toddler-appealing style."

The concepts Roche tackles in *Brave Georgie Goat: Three Little Stories About Growing Up* are not as easy as those presented in the Ollie books. A set of three stories united by the character of Georgie Goat (literally, a little kid), these tales help young readers confront deep and often unexpressed fears. In "Georgie Goat's Mommy Goes," Georgie is forced to address her fears that if she ever lets her mother leave the house, Mother Goat will never come back. She tries to leave with her mother, and expresses her fear of abandonment by asking, "But if you go without me, how do I know you'll come back?" Yet as Georgie looks around her, and sees that birds return to their nests and the sun comes back after hiding behind a cloud, she realizes that her mother will come back to her as well—and she does.

Georgie faces a closely related fear in "Georgie Goat's Best Friend Coat": as a growing little goat, she has become too big for her much-loved coat, and must give it up. Georgie worries, "I don't think I can be brave without Coat," but as *School Library Journal* contributor Anne Knickerbocker noted in her review, listeners will be thrilled to see the four items that Georgie's mother makes for her from the coat. Finally, in "Good Night, Georgie Goat," Georgie deals with a familiar fear, that of the dark. But this time she is in the position of reassuring someone else, her grandfather. She explains the causes of the sounds they hear in the house after the lights are out, showing that she has overcome some of her own fears. As usual, reviewers praised Roche's illustrations in this work, but they also had good things to say about the story itself. A *Publishers Weekly* reviewer noted that Georgie had "just the right mix of vulnerability and pluckiness," and *School Library Journal* contributor Knickerbocker concluded: "Simple but touching, the book won't sit on the shelf for long."

■ Works Cited

Review of *Brave Georgie Goat: Three Little Stories About Growing Up, Publishers Weekly,* October 27, 1997, p. 74.

Bush, Elizabeth, review of *Loo-Loo, Boo, and Art You Can Do, Bulletin of the Center for Children's Books,* September, 1996, p. 27.

Cooper, Ilene, review of *Ollie All Over, Booklist,* April 15, 1997, pp. 1436-37.

Del Negro, Janice M., review of *Ollie All Over* and *Only One Ollie, Bulletin of the Center for Children's Books,* June, 1997, p. 372.

Knickerbocker, Anne, review of *Brave Georgie Goat: Three Little Stories About Growing Up, School Library Journal,* January, 1998, pp. 91-92.

Review of *Loo-Loo, Boo, and Art You Can Do, Kirkus Reviews,* June 1, 1996, p. 828.

Review of *Loo-Loo, Boo, and Art You Can Do, Publishers Weekly,* July 1, 1996, p. 59.

Review of *Ollie All Over, Kirkus Reviews,* February 1, 1997, p. 227.

Review of *Only One Ollie* and *Ollie All Over, Publishers Weekly,* January 13, 1997, p. 77.

Peterson, Lauren, review of *Loo-Loo, Boo, and Art You Can Do, Booklist,* September 15, 1996, p. 244.

■ For More Information See

PERIODICALS

Bulletin of the Center for Children's Books, March, 1998, p. 257.

Horn Book Guide, spring, 1997, p. 135.

Kirkus Reviews, February 15, 1998, p. 274.

Los Angeles Times Book Review, October 27, 1996, p. 11.

School Library Journal, August, 1996, p. 140; August, 1997, p. 140.

—*Sketch by Judson Knight*

*   *   *

ROSENFELD, Dina 1962-

■ Personal

Born November 6, 1962, in Pittsburgh, PA; daughter of Emil W. (a lawyer) and Rita (a teacher; maiden name, Perelman) Herman; married Shimon Rosenfeld (a lawyer), March 13, 1983; children: Eliyohu, Frumi, Dovid, Malka, Yosef, Mendel, Zalman. *Education:* Beth Rivka Teachers' Seminary, 1979-81; Chatham College for Women, 1981-83. *Religion:* Jewish.

■ Addresses

Home—555 Crown St., #2a, Brooklyn, New York 11213.

■ Career

Yeshiva Achei Tmimim, Pittsburgh, PA, preschool teacher, 1981-83; Beth Rivka Academy, Brooklyn, NY, preschool teacher, 1983-84; freelance author and editor, 1984—.

■ Writings

The Very Best Place for a Penny, Merkos, 1984.
A Tree Full of Mitzvos, Merkos, 1985.
Tiny Treasures, Merkos, 1988.
A Chanukah Story for Night Number Three, Hachai (Brooklyn, NY), 1989.
All About Us, Hachai, 1989.
A Little Boy Named Avram, Hachai, 1989.
Labels for Laibel, Hachai, 1990.
Kind Little Rivka, Hachai, 1991.
Hot on the Trail, Hachai, 1991.
Why the Moon Only Glows, Hachai, 1992.
Peanut Butter and Jelly for Shabbos, Hachai, 1995.
David the Little Shepherd, Hachai, 1996.
The Very Best Book, Hachai, 1997.
On the Ball, Hachai, 1998.

■ Work in Progress

A Little Girl Named Miriam (working title), a "Little Greats" edition about Moses's sister; *Avi's List: A Journal of Discovery About Smoking,* a novel for middle school readers designed to educate them about the dangers of smoking.

DINA ROSENFELD

■ Sidelights

Dina Rosenfeld told *SATA:* "My books were born of necessity. As a preschool teacher in a Hebrew Day School, I simply could not find age-appropriate materials for my three- to four-year-old students. The children loved stories from the Torah (the five books of Moses), with details from Jewish commentaries. However, so many more aspects of Jewish life, moral values, and holiday and Shabbat celebrations needed to be addressed.

"In Jewish philosophy, there's an important concept of elevating all objects to a higher level by performing mitzvos, good deeds, with them. Translating this to the level of a three-year-old, I wrote a book about a little penny that couldn't find the right place to live until he finally found happiness inside a charity box (*The Very Best Place for a Penny*).

"Again, using preschool curriculum as my guide, I wrote a book about parts of the body called *All About Us.* The Jewish twist is that each body part can be used to perform a mitzvah; for example, hands can be used to light candles for Shabbat, feet can run to the synagogue, a mouth is for smiling at a friend. The lack of quality literature in the traditional Jewish market continued to be my main motivation for writing these books. Instead of producing each to look or sound similar, I tried to fill the need for variety by working with different artists, different sizes and formats, and working in both poetry and prose.

"In the rhyming adventure of *Labels for Laibel,* the all-important topic of sharing is addressed with humor. When two brothers decide not to share anything they learn that the world can only exist when people give freely to each other. In their next adventure, the two brothers go out of their way to do favors for a whole series of people they meet on a very hot, uncomfortable day (*Hot on the Trail*). Although the characters are Jewish, the values in these books are truly universal. The children in them are not perfect little people, but face the challenge of making moral choices.

"In a totally different series, "The Little Greats," I chose tales from Biblical times about great characters like Abraham, Rebecca, Miriam, and King David when they were small children. The intention was to enhance self-esteem in preschoolers, showing that they don't have to wait to grow up to make a difference. Even at a tender age, these great heroes and heroines of the Bible exhibited devotion, kindness, courage, and caring.

"When my oldest son was born thirteen years ago, I left teaching and wrote at home. When he got old enough, I used him as my test audience. Now, he helps me use our new computer. He and his younger brothers and sisters continue to be my toughest critics. None of this would have happened without the blessings of the Lubavitcher Rebbe and the constant encouragement of my parents and my husband—as well as the very insightful editing of my mother. She first introduced me to classic children's literature and delights in the opportunity to combine artistic and literary quality with important Jewish content.

"It is gratifying that my books have recently been translated into Russian, Portuguese, Italian, and even German for children around the world to benefit from and enjoy. After all, a trip to the synagogue is once a week. A holiday celebration is once a year. But with an engaging Jewish book, a young child can learn to love and live Judaism every day at story time."

S

ST. GEORGE, Judith 1931-

■ Personal

Born February 26, 1931, in Westfield, NJ; daughter of
John H. (a lawyer) and Edna (maiden name, Perkins)
Alexander; married David St. George (an Episcopal
minister), June 5, 1954; children: Peter, James, Philip,
Sarah. *Education:* Smith College, B.A., 1952. *Religion:*
Episcopalian.

JUDITH ST. GEORGE

■ Addresses

Home—8 Binney Rd., Old Lyme, CT 06371.

■ Career

Suburban Frontiers (re-locating service), Basking Ridge,
NJ, president, 1968-71; writer, 1970—. Instructor,
children's writing, Rutgers University; Commissioner,
Brooklyn Bridge Centennial Commission; York Correc-
tional Institution, Niantic, CT, instructor of creative
writing. *Member:* Authors Guild, Rutgers University
Advisory Council on Children's Literature, Mystery
Writers of America.

■ Awards, Honors

Best books for spring list, *Saturday Review,* 1976, for *By
George, Bloomers!;* runner-up, Edgar Allan Poe Award,
Mystery Writers of America, 1979, for *The Halloween
Pumpkin Smasher;* Children's Choice book, Children's
Book Council (CBC), International Reading Association, 1980, and *New York Times* Best Mystery of 1980,
for *Haunted;* American Library Association (ALA) Notable Book, American Book Award Honor Book, Gold-
en Kite Honor Book, *New York Times* notable book, all
1982, and New York Academy of Sciences award, 1983,
for *The Brooklyn Bridge: They Said It Couldn't Be Built;*
New Jersey Institute of Technology children's literature
award, 1983, for *Do You See What I See?,* 1988, for
Who's Scared? Not Me!, and 1989, for *Panama Canal:
Gateway to the World,* also Golden Kite Nonfiction
Award and ALA Notable for *Panama Canal: Gateway to
the World;* Notable Children's Trade Book in the Field
of Social Studies, National Council on the Social Studies
and CBC, ALA Notable Book, Golden Kite Honor
Book, all 1985, Christopher Award and Claremont
Graduate School Recognition of Merit Award, both
1986, for *The Mount Rushmore Story;* best juvenile
novel award, *Voice of Youth Advocates,* 1986, for *What's
Happening to My Junior Year?;* Recommended Books
for Teenagers, 1992, for *Mason and Dixon's Line of
Fire;* Young Hoosier Book Award, 1994-95, Notable

Book in the Field of Social Studies, and William Allen White Book Award, 1993-94 for *Dear Dr. Bell—Your Friend Helen Keller;* Young Adult's Choices, International Reading Association, Children's Book Council, 1998, for *To See with the Heart: The Life of Sitting Bull;* New York State Book Award, Sons of the American Revolution, 1998, for *Betsy Ross: Patriot of Philadelphia.* Nine of St. George's books have been Junior Literary Guild selections.

■ Writings

FOR YOUNG PEOPLE; FICTION

Turncoat Winter; Rebel Spring, Chilton, 1970.
The Girl with Spunk, Putnam, 1975.
By George, Bloomers!, Coward, 1976.
The Chinese Puzzle of Shag Island, Putnam, 1976.
The Shad Are Running, Putnam, 1977.
The Shadow of the Shaman, Putnam, 1977.
The Halloween Pumpkin Smasher, Putnam, 1978.
The Halo Wind, Putnam, 1978.
Mystery at St. Martin's, Putnam, 1979.
Haunted, Putnam, 1980.
Call Me Margo, Putnam, 1981.
The Mysterious Girl in the Garden, Putnam, 1981.
Do You See What I See?, Putnam, 1982.
In the Shadow of the Bear, Putnam, 1983.
What's Happening to My Junior Year?, Putnam, 1986.
Who's Scared? Not Me!, Putnam, 1987.

NONFICTION

The Amazing Voyage of the New Orleans, Putnam, 1980.
The Brooklyn Bridge: They Said It Couldn't Be Built, Putnam, 1982.
The Mount Rushmore Story, Putnam, 1985.
Panama Canal: Gateway to the World, Putnam, 1989.
The White House: Cornerstone of a Nation, Putnam, 1990.
Mason and Dixon's Line of Fire, Putnam, 1991.
Dear Dr. Bell—Your Friend, Helen Keller, Putnam, 1992.
Crazy Horse, Putnam, 1994.
To See with the Heart: The Life of Sitting Bull, Putnam, 1996.
Sacagawea, Putnam, 1997.
Betsy Ross: Patriot of Philadelphia, Holt, 1997.

■ Sidelights

Judith St. George writes both historical fiction and nonfiction, blending elements of mystery and exciting action along with closely detailed research to come up with such award-winning titles as *Haunted, The Halloween Pumpkin Smasher, In the Shadow of the Bear, The Brooklyn Bridge: They Said It Couldn't Be Built,* and *The Mount Rushmore Story.* Employing large elements of personal experience in both her fiction and nonfiction, St. George often writes of young girls confronting challenging situations, and of the importance of friendship and family history.

St. George has sufficient quantities of the latter to see her through any number of books. Born in Westfield,

New Jersey, in 1931, she was raised during the Depression and had close contact with grandparents on both sides. Her childhood was, as she typified it in *Something about the Author Autobiography Series (SAAS),* "idyllic." Raised in a close and loving family, St. George did not greatly feel the effects of the Depression years. Instead, her childhood memories are filled with the escapades of her four best friends on Maple Street in quiet Westfield, of hopscotch and roller skating in the summer, and of making snow angels and playing hockey on a frozen pond in winter. Her older brother, Jack, and younger sister, Anne, both influenced these early years as well, and later found their way into the pages of her fiction. In her *SAAS* entry, St. George recalled herself being "terribly shy" and a "worrier" as a child. Though she was a slight, rangy girl, she did excel at sports. "I have to admit that being selected as the only girl to play on the boys' sixth-grade baseball team still remains a high moment of my school career," she wrote in *SAAS.*

St. George's parents were also a strong influence in her life. High school sweethearts, her parents remained married for sixty-one years. Her father was an inveterate reader who "always had his nose in a book," and was the one who taught St. George the importance of ethics and integrity, the two words most often used to describe him. Her mother devoted her life to her family and provided a nurturing and secure environment. Another "powerful factor in the growing up years was having two sets of grandparents, who also lived in Westfield," St. George noted in *SAAS.* Her paternal grandfather, "rather foreboding," served as a stern father figure in later fiction, while her maternal grandparents were "another set of warm, loving, and caring parents." St. George spent a weekly overnight with these Perkins grandparents, listening to the tales of her mother's grandfather, who had been a sea captain for thirty-five years. These stories found their way into much of St. George's later fiction, as well.

"I have no recollection of when I learned to read," St. George wrote in *SAAS,* "probably in the first grade like everyone else." But once started, she coursed her way through everything from Nancy Drew to movie magazines and comics. "There was no question that reading became a permanent habit," St. George recalled in *SAAS,* "and to this day, if I'm not in the middle of a book, I feel a distinct void in my life." If she is vague about when she learned to read, St. George is very exact about when she first began writing: October 1941. This was the date she composed a play for her Woodrow Wilson School sixth-grade class, a reflective drama of four matrons sitting around a tea table reminiscing about their classmates of fifty years before. From a very early age, friendship formed a core to her life, and later took on great importance in the pages of her books.

If her years at elementary school were serene, those spent at "fortress-like" Roosevelt Junior High were less so. Placed in different classes from her old friends, she reverted to shyness, literally reduced to speechlessness one day when reciting in front of her classmates. The same year she began junior high, her paternal grandfather died, and her family moved into his large, imposing home in Westfield. Always afraid of the dark, St. George's fears were compounded in this draughty old house with its five exterior doors and several unused rooms on the second floor. She continued her reading and sports—adding tennis to her favorite competitions—and at age fifteen went off to boarding school. The next two years were, according to St. George in *SAAS,* "among my unhappiest." Not only did she have trouble making friends, but she also had an English teacher who made her feel "truly hopeless." All these experiences would provide grist for St. George's literary mill, however, and furnish her with scene, character, and incident for later fiction.

In 1948 St. George entered Smith College and the next four years "were the most wonderful and fulfilling . . . any college student could ask for," she noted in *SAAS.* She formed close friendships and was fortunate to study English in a department full of world-class instructors. She also wrote for and edited the college humor magazine, the *Campus Cat,* and continued her enjoyment of athletics. After graduation, she moved in with several friends in Cambridge, Massachusetts. Two years later she married David St. George, who was studying to become an Episcopal minister. St. George then "lapsed into the 50's syndrome of house-keeping with a capital H," as she once wrote in *Something about the Author.* Soon came the first child, and she and her husband went to Eastern Oregon for his ministry, serving a population of less than 6,000 in a county the size of New Jersey. It was St. George's first trip west of Ohio, but she soon found friends and settled into the new life. Another son was born, and then her husband received a ministry in New Jersey, where her next two children were born. "Those were baby years for me," St. George noted in *SAAS,* "filled with pregnancies, diapers, mumps, measles, chicken pox, colds, and little else." But she was close to her parents again, and to her grandparents, who all took an active role in helping with her children.

But by the time her youngest child was three, St. George began "to feel a definite itch," desiring to do more with herself than parenting. Another move, this time to Millington, New Jersey, near Morristown, set her researching the Revolutionary War, for it was there that George Washington and his troops once wintered. As a young reader, St. George had been hooked on historical fiction; now she began creating it herself, working on her old college typewriter. Soon she had a book, *Turncoat Winter; Rebel Spring,* the story of a fourteen-year-old patriot boy in the winter of 1779-80 who is torn between protecting a friend who saved him and turning him in as a British spy. After nine rejections, she finally sold the book. Now the typewriter came out of hiding. But the second book went unpublished, and it was not until her third, *The Girl with Spunk,* that she began publishing regularly.

Set in 1848 in a town in New York, *The Girl with Spunk* tells the story of fourteen-year-old Josie who loses her job due to gossip and finds help in the fledgling women's rights movement. In the end, she has hopes that maybe

St. George's biography traces the friendship between Helen Keller and Alexander Graham Bell, which began with Bell's recommendation to provide Helen with a special teacher. (Cover illustration by Troy Howell.)

she can eventually become a naturalist in a world controlled by men. Barbara Elleman, writing in *Booklist,* felt that the book was a "memorable recreation of a young girl's struggles against the attitudes of the times," while a *Kirkus Reviews* critic noted that there "is a sprinkling of ginger in Josie; her trials are realistic . . . and those who take their adventures on the tame side and their consciousness raising in small stages can share her growing imagination." Josie's habit of stuttering when faced with a threatening situation was a direct writing from life. The use of such real-life material became a hallmark for St. George's work.

St. George continued with historical fiction for her next title, *By George, Bloomers!,* set in the mid-nineteenth century and dealing with the disapproval that eight-year-old Hannah suffers when she wants to wear a pair of the new and daring lady's apparel, bloomers. She eventually wins the right to wear these pants after rescuing her brother from the roof in a story that "gives historical perspective" and that is both "pleasantly told and illustrated," according to a reviewer in *Bulletin of the Center for Children's Books.*

St. George employed both her maternal grandfather's reminiscences of a seafaring life and the domineering character of her paternal grandfather, as well as indulged in her love for mysteries and spooky ghosts in *The Chinese Puzzle of Shag Island.* Young Kim Laudall goes to the family ancestral home, Shag Island off the coast of Maine, to visit her supposedly senile ninety-three-year-old great-grandfather. He protests against selling his imposing mansion, and soon Kim is involved in a "Yankee gothic, with clues and curios," according to a critic in *Kirkus Reviews.* Some of these "curios" are the ghosts of Chinese pirates who may be haunting the house, though according to a reviewer for *Publishers Weekly,* "Everything is satisfactorily explained at the end of a fresh, entertaining mystery for young buffs of the genre." St. George's paternal grandfather also inspired the demanding father figure in *The Shad Are Running,* a historical novel that is partly based on the racing of Hudson River steamboats in the 1830s. Young Corny Van Loon overcomes his fear of water and of his stern fisherman father when he alerts his village to the collision of steamboats and participates in the subsequent rescue process. Patricia S. Butcher, writing in *School Library Journal,* noted that the "plot moves along at a good clip, climaxed by a well described rescue scene."

With her fiction, St. George has continued to explore her twin loves of history and mystery. In *The Halo Wind,* set on the Oregon Trail in 1845, St. George describes a mystery surrounding a young Chinook girl who joins a group of settlers and details the actual hardships such a journey involved in "a nicely balanced and well-written novel," according to Ann Flowers in *Horn Book.* Blending a contemporary setting with fantasy time-travel, St. George evoked nineteenth-century England in *The Mysterious Girl in the Garden* and the life of the naturalist painter, James Audubon, in *Who's Scared? Not Me!*

Other St. George fiction titles remain firmly planted in contemporary times and deal with adventure and suspense, as in the award-winning *Haunted,* the story of sixteen-year-old Alex who is hired to house-sit an estate which was recently the scene of a murder-suicide. Drew Stevenson, writing in *School Library Journal,* found the book to be "St. George's suspense at its best." Young male protagonists star in the mystery-adventures, *The Shadow of the Shaman,* set in Oregon, and *Do You See What I See?,* set on Cape Cod. The former involves mysterious Indian charms and a rickety old lodge with a "brisk" pace and "colorful" scenery, according to a *Kirkus Reviews* contributor, while the latter is, as Judith Geer noted in *Voice of Youth Advocates,* "an excellently written story with firm characterization and suspense enough to curl your toes." Church business and counterfeit money come into play in *Mystery at St. Martin's,* an opportunity for St. George to use material drawn from her husband's career, while adventures in Alaska involving a wilderness-trek and U.S.-Soviet relations form the core of the thriller, *In the Shadow of the Bear.* In two further fiction titles, *Call Me Margo* and *What's Happening to My Junior Year?,* St. George tackled material dealing with her own boarding-school years.

Increasingly however, St. George's fiction has given way to nonfiction. Starting with her first factual book, *The Amazing Voyage of the New Orleans,* she has created a number of award-winning titles dealing with everything from a history of the Brooklyn Bridge to biographies of Native Americans. Writing in *SAAS,* St. George noted that she began to realize that "nonfiction was a whole new field for me, a field in which I felt very much at ease." With *The Amazing Voyage of the New Orleans,* St. George told the story of the first steamboat to travel down the Ohio and Mississippi Rivers in 1811. *Booklist's* Elleman noted that the book "is recounted in an amiable, amusing narrative. . . ."

With *The Brooklyn Bridge: They Said It Couldn't Be Built,* St. George hit her stride with nonfiction, and much of her best creative effort has been devoted to that genre since 1982. Its publication coinciding with the centennial of the Brooklyn Bridge, St. George's book relates the seemingly impossible job of building a bridge over the East River in the nineteenth century, and focuses on the Roebling family, two of whose members were chief engineers on the project. "The author touches gently upon the personal trials and torments of this remarkable family, celebrating instead their public triumphs," Shirley Wilton stated in *School Library Journal.* Writing in *Horn Book,* Karen Jameyson called the book a "fascinating history."

Other famous man-made structures—both imaginary and real—are described in *The Mount Rushmore Story, Panama Canal: Gateway to the World, The White House: Cornerstone of a Nation, Mason and Dixon's Line of Fire* and *Dear Dr. Bell—Your Friend, Helen Keller.* For the award-winning book about Mount Rushmore, St. George climbed atop the Black Hills monument for her own personal up-close look, and blended stories of the sculptor Gutzon Borglum with those of the Sioux Indians for whom the Black Hills of South Dakota were a spiritual home. "*The Mount Rushmore Story* is a fine acquisition for basic general information and details," concluded George Gleason in a *School Library Journal* review of the work.

More recent nonfiction titles from St. George have examined the lives of notable Native Americans, including the Oglala warrior, Crazy Horse, the Hunkpapa Sioux chief, Sitting Bull, and Sacagawea of Lewis and Clark fame. Daniel Menaker, writing in the *New Yorker,* called St. George's *Crazy Horse* a "soundly written biography," while a *Publishers Weekly* critic noted that her *To See with the Heart: The Life of Sitting Bull* was "a biography of unusual depth."

It is this depth that St. George is striving for her in her work. While finding research to be "fun," as she noted in her *SAAS* entry, she concluded that "it's the writing that's hard. Writing *is* hard for me. Is that because I make more demands on myself with each new book? I hope that's the reason, but I'm not sure. All I know is that I want my readers to care as much about the outcome of historical events as if they were reading today's headlines."

■ Works Cited

Butcher, Patricia S., review of *The Shad Are Running, School Library Journal,* September, 1977, p. 137.

Review of *By George, Bloomers!, Bulletin of the Center for Children's Books,* September, 1976, p. 17.

Review of *The Chinese Puzzle of Shag Island, Kirkus Reviews,* May 15, 1976, p. 594.

Review of *The Chinese Puzzle of Shag Island, Publishers Weekly,* May 3, 1976, p. 64.

Elleman, Barbara, review of *The Girl With Spunk, Booklist,* February 15, 1976, p. 857.

Elleman, Barbara, review of *The Amazing Voyage of the New Orleans, Booklist,* May 1, 1980, pp. 1298-99.

Flowers, Ann, review of *The Halo Wind, Horn Book,* February, 1979, p. 66.

Geer, Judith, review of *Do You See What I See?, Voice of Youth Advocates,* December, 1982, pp. 35-36.

Review of *The Girl With Spunk, Kirkus Reviews,* December 1, 1975, p. 1336.

Gleason, George, review of *The Mount Rushmore Story, School Library Journal,* October, 1985, p. 188.

Jameyson, Karen, review of *The Brooklyn Bridge: They Said It Couldn't Be Built, Horn Book,* August, 1982, pp. 425-26.

Menaker, Daniel, review of *Crazy Horse, New Yorker,* December 12, 1994, p. 118.

Review of *The Shadow of the Shaman, Kirkus Reviews,* January 15, 1978, p. 47.

Stevenson, Drew, review of *Haunted, School Library Journal,* December, 1980, p. 74.

St. George, Judith, essay in *Something about the Author Autobiography Series,* Volume 12, Gale, 1991, pp. 267-81.

Review of *To See with the Heart: The Life of Sitting Bull, Publishers Weekly,* May 27, 1996, p. 80.

Wilton, Shirley, review of *The Brooklyn Bridge: They Said It Couldn't Be Built, School Library Journal,* February, 1983, p. 92.

■ For More Information See

BOOKS

Sixth Book of Junior Authors and Illustrators, H. W. Wilson, 1989, pp. 257-59.

PERIODICALS

Booklist, March 15, 1977, p. 1101; October 15, 1978, p. 386; January 1, 1980, p. 669; November 1, 1980, p. 401; January 1, 1982, p. 599; January 15, 1982, p. 668; December 15, 1986, p. 642; November 15, 1987, p. 555; March 1, 1996, p. 1174.

Bulletin of the Center for Children's Books, June, 1976, p. 163; October, 1976, pp. 30-31; December, 1977, p. 68; February, 1979, p. 105; February, 1980, p. 118; March, 1981, p. 138; September, 1981, p. 15; January, 1983, p. 96; January, 1987, p. 99; February, 1993, pp. 192-93; December, 1994, pp. 145-46; January, 1998, p. 178.

Horn Book, August, 1980, p. 430.

Kirkus Reviews, February 1, 1976, p. 132; May 1, 1982, pp. 557-58; November 1, 1983, p. 207.

Publishers Weekly, November 9, 1992, p. 88; June 30, 1997, p. 77.

School Library Journal, August, 1980, p. 70; December, 1981, p. 68; February, 1984, p. 85; February, 1987, p. 85; November, 1994, p. 117; July, 1996, pp. 96-97; February, 1998, p. 124; March, 1998, p. 242.

—*Sketch by J. Sydney Jones*

* * *

STARR, Ward
See MANES, Stephen

* * *

STARR TAYLOR, Bridget 1959-

■ Personal

Legal married name is Bridget Starr Taylor Coston; born April 8, 1959, in New Haven, CT; daughter of Henry H. (a manufacturer and farmer) and Herriet (a writer and garden lecturer; maiden name, Robinson) Taylor; married John R. Coston (an editor and systems director), 1985; children: Winnifred (stepdaughter), Reed, Elias. *Education:* Rhode Island School of Design, B.A., 1982.

■ Addresses

Home—675 Hudson St. #25, New York, NY 10014. *Agent*—(literary) Ginger Knowlton, Curtis Brown, 10 Astor Pl., New York, NY 10003; (art) The Artists Network, 9 Babbling Brook Lane, Suffern, NY 10901.

■ Career

Freelance illustrator, 1985—. Also does prop and set construction and painting for special events. *Member:* Graphic Artists Guild.

■ Illustrator

Louisa Campbell, *Gargoyles' Christmas,* Gibbs, Smith, 1994.

Louisa Campbell, *Phoebe's Fabulous Father,* Harcourt Brace, 1996.

Lois Grambling, *Happy Valentine's Day, Miss Hildy,* Random House, 1997.

Ann Alper, *Harry the Tooth Fairy,* Albert Whitman, 1998.

■ Work in Progress

The Roly Poly Pumpkin; Henry and the Circus.

■ Sidelights

Bridget Starr Taylor told *SATA:* "I grew up on a hillside farm in northwestern Connecticut with chickens, sheep, cows, and much solitude. There was plenty of time to draw. My father, when I asked, 'What should I draw?',

From *Phoebe's Fabulous Father*, written by Louisa Campbell and illustrated by Bridget Starr Taylor.

always responded with the same answer: 'Draw a man with a beard on a bicycle.'

"I love creating whole and detailed environments for the characters in each story to move about in. I have a particular interest in architecture and how it integrates with landscape. But I never lose sight of the best part of each story, which is, of course, the characters themselves. I love the form of the picture book because it allows you to show these things—setting and characters—from multiple angles and moving through time."

* * *

STEPHENSEN, A. M.
See MANES, Stephen

* * *

STOTT, Dorothy (M.) 1958-
(Dot Stott)

■ Personal

Born October 24, 1958, in Norwich, CT. *Education:* Graduated from Paier School of Art, 1981.

■ Addresses

Home—Mt. Antoine View, Rupert, VT 05768. *Agent*—Kirchoff/Wohlberg, 866 United Nations Plaza, New York, NY 10017.

■ Career

Author and illustrator. *Member:* Society of Children's Book Writers and Illustrators.

■ Writings

FOR CHILDREN; SELF-ILLUSTRATED

(As Dot Stott) *The Three Little Kittens,* Grosset & Dunlap, 1984.
Too Much, Dutton, 1990.
Little Duck's Bicycle Ride, Dutton, 1991.
A Christmas Book, Dutton, 1991.
Kitty and Me, Dutton, 1993.
Puppy and Me, Dutton, 1993.
Up, Up in a Plane!, Putnam, 1995.
Make It a Merry Christmas, Readers Digest Young Families, 1997.
The Big Book of Games, Dutton, 1998.

ILLUSTRATOR

Linda Apolzon Neilson, *Max Helps Out*, Golden Books, 1984.
(As Dot Stott) Cary Timm, *My Little Pony Learns to Count*, Random House, 1985.
Anne Miranda, *Baby Talk*, Dutton, 1987.
Anne Miranda, *Baby Walk*, Dutton, 1988.
Anne Miranda, *Baby-Sit*, Little, Brown, 1990.
Stephanie Calmenson, *Zip, Whiz, Zoom!*, Little, Brown, 1991.
Ann Kenny, *Night Walk*, R. C. Owen, 1996.
Doris Tomaselli, *My Special Valentine Kit: Creative Cards & Gifts to Make for People You Love*, Joshua Morris, 1997.

Contributor of illustrations to textbooks.

■ **Work in Progress**

Who Is My Mother?, Countdown to Bedtime, Countup to Nursery School, all for Dutton, expected 1999.

■ **Sidelights**

Dorothy Stott, who sometimes publishes under the name Dot Stott, has been writing and illustrating books for children since 1984. She has published almost twenty volumes, counting books she has illustrated for others, along with those she has written and illustrated herself. The first book Stott illustrated for another writer was *Max Helps Out* by Linda Apolzon Neilson. It marked the beginning of a number of illustrator-writer collaborations. Among these associations, the most notable has been Stott's alliance with Anne Miranda. Miranda wrote the text for, and Stott illustrated, three "Baby" lift-the-flap books, starting with *Baby Talk* in 1987.

Miranda and Stott followed up *Baby Talk* with *Baby Walk*, which a *Publishers Weekly* reviewer called "appealing." Written for the very young, the book is built around twelve scenes which show a day in the life of a toddler. During the course of that day, the little protagonist of *Baby Walk* experiences such key elements of a baby's daily routine as getting dressed and being taken to the park. The book is presented in a flap format, which enhances the simple phrases of Miranda's text. A *Publishers Weekly* reviewer noted Stott's "captivating" method of illustration, which helps listeners and viewers move effortlessly from scene to scene.

With *Baby-Sit* in 1990, Stott and Miranda brought the "Baby" series to a close. The story takes place over the course of an evening, when two toddlers' parents leave them at home with the baby-sitter and the dog. A *Publishers Weekly* critic commented favorably on Stott's "amusing" illustrations for this book.

Stott has worked as an illustrator with several other authors, and has also illustrated a number of textbooks. At the same time, however, she has penned a number of her own stories. *Too Much*, written for preschoolers, is the tale of Little Duck's search for a good swimming place. Nothing he tries seems to work: a bucket of paint is "too messy," a sink filled with dishes is "too soapy," and a wet upside-down umbrella "too tipsy." It is all "too, too much," in fact, until Little Duck discovers where he belongs—a pond. A *Publishers Weekly* critic observed that Stott's illustrations convey "her hero's many dismayed expressions and the absurdity of each moment." The actual story is very short, but in it, according to *School Library Journal* contributor Pearl Herscovitch, Stott has "created an endearing character." Herscovitch concluded that *Too Much* was "just right for toddler story hours." *Booklist* reviewer Barbara Elleman added that Stott's tale might aid in a young reader's first cautious steps: "the brief text, placed in large type, may well beckon those beginning to read on their own."

Stott followed *Too Much* with *Little Duck's Bicycle Ride*. Once again the hapless Little Duck is confronted with a tricky situation, though this time he's not looking for something; he's just trying to stay on his bike. The story ends in much the same way as its predecessor: bounced off of the bike and into the air, Little Duck gives up his wheeled transportation entirely and returns to the water where he belongs. Again, Stott keeps the words to a minimum, relying instead on wordless spreads in which youngsters would be apt to fill in commentary of their own. The most common phrase at story time, according to a *Publishers Weekly* reviewer, would be "Oh no!"—a most apt expression for the accident-prone Little Duck. *Booklist* reviewer Leone McDermott noted that "young children will empathize" with the challenges Little Duck faces as he attempts to find his way through a grown-up world.

Stott's *Kitty and Me* and *Puppy and Me* are books that complement one another. They are also the author's first flap books, although she had previously illustrated flap books for others, including *Baby-Sit*. Stott's stories and pictures center around a brother and sister and their two pets. Once again, the text in these books for toddlers is very short. A *Publishers Weekly* critic described a typical moment in *Kitty and Me*: with the words "hungry kitty," the cat enjoys a bowl of milk—but the lifted flap reveals that the frisky little creature has overturned the bowl. *Puppy and Me*, on the other hand, is "a little less whimsical," according to the same *Publishers Weekly* commentator, partly for the simple reason that puppies are expected to obey commands. A *Kirkus Reviews* critic commented favorably on both books, calling them "well-designed and appealing."

■ **Works Cited**

Review of *Baby Sit, Publishers Weekly*, September 28, 1990, p. 99.
Review of *Baby Walk, Publishers Weekly*, December 9, 1988, p. 61.
Elleman, Barbara, review of *Too Much, Booklist*, May 1, 1990, p. 1711.
Herscovitch, Pearl, review of *Too Much, School Library Journal*, April, 1990, p. 99.

Review of *Kitty and Me, Kirkus Reviews,* June 1, 1993,
p. 728.
Review of *Little Duck's Bicycle Ride, Publishers Weekly,*
May 10, 1991, p. 281.
McDermott, Leone, review of *Little Duck's Bicycle
Ride, Booklist,* June 1, 1991, p. 1881.
Review of *Puppy and Me* and *Kitty and Me, Publishers
Weekly,* May 3, 1993, p. 304.
Review of *Too Much, Publishers Weekly,* December 22,
1989, p. 56.

■ For More Information See

PERIODICALS

Booklist, January 1, 1994, p. 837.
Horn Book Guide, January, 1990, p. 207; Fall, 1991, p.
222.
Kirkus Reviews, June 1, 1993, p. 728.
Publishers Weekly, July 27, 1992, p. 61.
School Library Journal, January, 1988, p. 67; February,
1989, p. 74; April, 1990, p. 99; September, 1991, p.
243; January, 1993, pp. 90-91; October, 1993, p.
112.

—*Sketch by Judson Knight*

*   *   *

STOTT, Dot
See STOTT, Dorothy (M.)

*   *   *

SUNDERLIN, Sylvia (S.) 1911-1997

OBITUARY NOTICE—See index for *SATA* sketch:
Born September 22, 1911, in Lakeside, MT; died of
liver cancer, November 17, 1997, in Cambridge, NY.
Editor and author. Sunderlin is remembered for her
work with children as an editor and author. She served
with the Association for Childhood Education International in Washington, D.C. as an assistant editor from
1964 to 1966, rising to the rank of consulting associate
editor by 1970. In 1973 she joined the American
Association for Gifted Children in New York City as an
editor and staff associate. She began writing a monthly
column called "Address Book" about antiques for
House Beautiful magazine in 1976. She also worked as
an antiques appraiser in Washington's Christ Child
Shop. Sunderlin was the author of the children's book
Antrim's Orange and contributed to other magazines
such as *Modern Maturity* and *Country Home.* The
Educational Press Association of America honored her
with its All-American Award for editing.

OBITUARIES AND OTHER SOURCES:

PERIODICALS

Washington Post, November 19, 1997, p. B6.

*   *   *

SZASZ, Suzanne (Shorr) 1915-1997

OBITUARY NOTICE—See index for *SATA* sketch:
Born October 20, 1915, in Budapest, Hungary; came to
the United States; died in 1997 in Budapest, Hungary,
while visiting relatives. Photographer and author. Szasz
was a popular photographer of children, often capturing
their images in unsentimental ways. Born in Budapest,
she relocated to the United States following World War
II. Her career as a photographer began in New York
when she borrowed a camera and began taking pictures.
Szasz, who worked as a camp counselor, submitted a
photograph to a *Ladies' Home Journal* competition and
won, prompting her to pursue a career behind the
camera. Later, she became a founding member of the
Pinewoods Folk Music Club (now the Folk Music
Society of New York) and the American Society of
Magazine Photographers. Her work was featured in
magazines, including *Look, Good Housekeeping, Life,*
and many others. Szasz also had her work exhibited in
solo shows with the New York City Camera Club,
Donnell Library, Nassau Community College, and the
Hungarian National Gallery, among others. Her work
was also featured in *Family of Man* by Edward Steichen,
Helping Your Child's Emotional Growth by Anna W.
Wolf, *The Silent Miaow* by Paul Gallico, and *Now I
Have a Daddy Haircut* by Morey and Clara Appell.
Szasz studied women in Puerto Rico who used birth
control pills and presented a photographic report of the
results in 1962. She is credited with a number of
photographic books, including *Young Folks' New York*
(with Susan E. Lyman), *Child Photography Simplified,
Modern Wedding Photography, The Body Language of
Children, Sisters, Brothers and Others* (with Elizabeth
Taleporos), and *We Are Six: The Story of a Family* (with
Morey and Clara Appell). Szasz was named one of the
ten best women photographers in the United States in
1959.

OBITUARIES AND OTHER SOURCES:

BOOKS

Authors of Books for Young People, third edition,
Scarecrow Press, 1990.

PERIODICALS

New York Times, July 10, 1997, p. B12.

T

TALBERT, Marc 1953-

■ Personal

Born July 21, 1953, in Boulder, CO; son of Willard L. (a physicist) and Mary A. Talbert; married Moo Thorpe (a real estate broker and contractor); children: Molly, Jessie. *Education:* Attended Grinnell College, 1971-73; Iowa State University, B.S., 1976. *Politics:* Democrat. *Hobbies and other interests:* Running, reading, gardening, traveling, cooking.

■ Addresses

Home—PO Box 847, Santa Fe, NM 87504.

■ Career

Writer. Marshalltown Public Schools, Marshalltown, IA, teacher of fifth and sixth grade, 1976-77; Ames Public Schools, Ames, IA, teacher of fifth grade, 1977-81; Los Alamos National Laboratory, Los Alamos, NM, writer and editor, 1981-86; speech writer for National Science Foundation, 1984-85; University of New Mexico, instructor in children's literature, 1989-90. Youth Voice (board chair). *Member:* PEN, Society of Children's Book Writers and Illustrators, Authors Guild, Children's Literature Assembly.

■ Awards, Honors

Best Books for Young Adults Award, American Library Association, 1985, shortlist selection, British Children's Book Group Award, 1986, and West Australian Young Readers' Book Award, Library Association of Australia, 1988, all for *Dead Birds Singing;* Notable Children's Book in the Field of Social Studies, National Council for the Social Studies/Children's Book Council, 1987, for *Toby;* Owl of the Month Prize, *The Bulletin of Youth and Literature,* 1989, for *The Paper Knife.*

■ Writings

Dead Birds Singing, Little, Brown, 1985.
Thin Ice, Little, Brown, 1986.
Toby, Dial, 1987.
The Paper Knife, Dial, 1988.
Rabbit in the Rock, Dial, 1989.
Double or Nothing, illustrated by Toby Gowing, Dial, 1990.
Pillow of Clouds, Dial, 1991.
The Purple Heart, HarperCollins, 1992.
Heart of a Jaguar, Simon & Schuster, 1995.
A Sunburned Prayer, Simon & Schuster, 1995.

Also columnist, *Daily Tribune,* Ames, IA, *Cedar Valley Times,* Vinton, IA, and *Iowa State Daily.*

■ Work in Progress

Star of Luis, for Clarion, spring of 1999.

MARC TALBERT

■ Sidelights

Since the publication of his first book, *Dead Birds Singing,* Marc Talbert has won a reputation as a thoughtful author of young adult problem novels. Whether his books deal with abuse, death, or divorce, Talbert portrays the feelings of his characters with respect and empathy. "Few YA authors scrutinize the often painful process of growing up as intently" as Talbert, wrote a *Publishers Weekly* critic in 1995. Many of Talbert's books are notable as well for their New Mexico settings. In the mid-1990s, Talbert published two novels featuring characters of Mayan heritage which have elicited praise from critics, *A Sunburned Prayer* and *Heart of a Jaguar.*

Talbert grew up in Iowa, where he worked as a newspaper columnist and fifth and sixth grade teacher. He moved to New Mexico, he explained in a speech published in the *ALAN Review,* "ready to woo and marry" the woman who became his wife "or die trying." In New Mexico, Talbert lived with his wife and dogs and worked as a writer; he published his first novel for young adults in 1985.

In New Mexico, eleven-year-old Eloy makes a long pilgrimage to the Santuario de Chimayo shrine in hopes of keeping his grandmother from dying of cancer. (Cover illustration by Peter Fiore.)

Dead Birds Singing, Talbert's first novel, begins as Matt, a seventh grader, is riding home from a swim meet with his mother and sister. A drunk driver smashes into their car and, although Matt survives, his mother is killed and his sister is gravely injured. Matt, whose father died years before, is now an orphan; he is taken in by his best friend's family. For the remainder of the novel, he deals not only with his grief (his sister eventually dies) but also with the physical concerns of adolescent boys. In the words of *Horn Book* critic Karen Jameyson, Talbert's "insight into Matt's feelings is extraordinary." "Mr. Talbert . . . has done a very good job in tackling a difficult and potentially explosive subject," commented Marcus Crouch in *Junior Bookshelf.*

Talbert's second novel, *Thin Ice,* features a ten-year-old boy, Martin, who is troubled by his parents' separation. Martin's father has departed for Alaska, leaving his mother to care for Martin and his diabetic sister. Martin abandons his responsibilities at school and quarrels with his best friend. To make matters worse, after his mother meets Martin's teacher for a conference, they begin a relationship. Martin eventually runs away, and his sister grows very ill. Martin spends some time in the woods, and returns to his family with a new attitude. The story, explained a *Kirkus Reviews* critic, "is lightened by touches of humor." According to *Junior Bookshelf*'s Marcus Crouch, "there is much to admire and even more to think deeply about" in the book. *Thin Ice,* commented a *Publishers Weekly* critic, is "beautifully written."

Toby, the protagonist in the book of the same title, is the ten-year-old child of a mentally disabled father and a brain-damaged mother. While his illiterate parents are frequently incapable of helping Toby with his problems, they provide food, shelter, and an abundance of love. The local minister, however, insists that they cannot properly care for Toby, whom he thinks is a wild boy, and he tries to send Toby to a foster home. The minister's son, a delinquent himself, taunts Toby and insults his parents. When Toby is blamed for a break-in at a neighbor's house, the little family seems on the verge of dispersal. Toby reverts to bedwetting, but he finally stands up for himself and his problems are resolved. "Talbert has woven a story filled with unforgettable characters," wrote Nancy P. Reeder in *School Library Journal.* A *Publishers Weekly* critic remarked, "readers have a work of rare power."

In *The Paper Knife,* ten-year-old Jeremy and his mother flee from her boyfriend George to live with George's parents. Jeremy has mixed feelings about this move; George was kind, except when he was physically abusing Jeremy's mother, or sexually abusing Jeremy. As he struggles with his secret about George, and worries that George will come and get him, Jeremy has difficulty adjusting to his new school. Although his teacher, Mr. Williams, is helpful, the other boys in school taunt him. For protection, Jeremy writes down his secret and calls it his "paper knife." When Jeremy's paper knife is found by the bullies, Jeremy's mother believes that the letter is about Mr. Williams. To save Mr. Williams, who is asked to leave the school, Jeremy must finally report George's

Balam, on the threshold of his manhood, tests his strength and courage in feats intended to bring rain to his drought-plagued village. (Cover illustration by Felipe Davalos.)

abuse. A *Publishers Weekly* critic appreciated Talbert's "matter-of-fact gaze at the problems of childhood." "Jeremy's plight and its resolution will hold readers while conveying a valuable message," concluded a *Kirkus Reviews* critic.

Rabbit in the Rock, set in New Mexico, begins as a sixteen-year-old girl riding her horse meets a rock star in hiding. Runaway Sean is tired of the career his father has forced on him, and he shares his complaints with Bernie. Bernie does what she can to assist him and even helps him stage a kidnapping. When the FBI appears on the scene, matters get out of control and Bernie's brother breaks his leg. By the end of the novel, Bernie and her brother are safe, and Sean goes back to his father and work. Sean writes a song about Bernie, and sends her a letter with the hope of seeing her again.

Sam, nine years old, grieves for his magician uncle in *Double or Nothing.* Sam, left with his uncle's props, wants to become a magician himself. Uncle Frank,

readers learn through flashbacks, did more than show Sam some of the tricks of his trade: he taught him lessons about life. On the first birthday of his uncle since his death, Sam leaves home. He travels to a park to put on his own magic show as a tribute to his uncle. Kathryn LaBarbera of *Booklist* commented that the book is "a story about keeping love alive."

Chester, a young poet, is the child of divorced parents. The arrival of his thirteenth birthday forces Chester to make a difficult decision in *Pillow of Clouds:* should he live with his mother, a rich alcoholic in Iowa, or with his father and his artist wife in New Mexico? Chester goes to visit his mother, who tells him how much she needs him, but he realizes that he will be happiest with his father. After Chester's departure for New Mexico, Chester's mother attempts suicide. "More than a coming-of-age story," wrote Susan Oliver in *School Library Journal,* the novel is "about realizations and relationships." According to James E. Cook of *Voice of Youth Advocates,* "The writing in this novel is first-rate."

The Purple Heart is the story of Luke, whose father has been named a war hero and is returning from Vietnam. When Luke's father arrives, he is not the strong, proud man Luke expected. Instead, his father is wounded, tired, and reluctant to talk about the war. Confused, Luke takes his father's purple heart to show a friend and uses it to trick a neighbor. He loses the medal and is sent by his parents to help the neighbor, an elderly woman. Through the woman, whose husband also served in a war, he begins to understand that his father's time in Vietnam could not have been glorious. Then, when a tornado threatens the neighborhood, Luke's selfless bravery prompts his father to give him the medal, which he has recovered. Gerry Larson of *School Library Journal* observed that "Talbert delivers a positive statement on the healing power of family love." According to Karen Hutt of *Booklist,* Talbert's work is "perceptive and poignant."

By the mid-1990s, Talbert and his wife had two little girls and lived with them and their dogs in a diverse northern New Mexican community: "a sometimes uneasy mix of Native American, and Hispanic and Mexican mestizo, and Anglo," as he described it in the *ALAN Review.* Around that time, Talbert wrote two books that feature characters different from his others; these characters share a Mayan heritage and deep spirituality. "I have chosen to learn about my heritage and myself—as reflected back to me from the contrasting heritage and cultures of those around me," explained Talbert in the *ALAN Review.*

According to Talbert, he "noticed, on Good Friday, thousands of people walking along the highways north of Santa Fe." Curious, he learned that these people were making a pilgrimage to visit a Mayan statue and to taste the sacred dirt around it. Talbert himself made that journey. "It was a walk that changed my life," he revealed in the *ALAN Review.* "I began to write *A Sunburned Prayer,* much as I had started the pilgrimage, on faith, not knowing what would happen along the way.... I wrote to discover."

Set in New Mexico, and peppered with Spanish words, *A Sunburned Prayer* features eleven-year-old Eloy, who is determined to save his *abuela* (grandmother) from the cancer that is killing her. Although his parents have forbidden it, Eloy makes a grueling pilgrimage of seventeen miles on Good Friday to the Santuario de Chimayo shrine in order to taste sacred dirt and pray for his grandmother's health. As he walks, hungry from his fast as well as thirsty, a stray dog follows him and encourages him to continue. When Eloy finally reaches the church, he finds his brother Benito and his *abuela,* who assures him that he must accept her death. Later, she explains that her death is a part of God's work. Jack Forman of *School Library Journal* asserted that *A Sunburned Prayer,* which includes a glossary, is "one of Talbert's most moving and meaningful novels to date."

In a departure from his stories set in contemporary North America, Talbert takes readers back seven hundred years to the Yucatan of Mexico in *Heart of a Jaguar.* Balam, fourteen-years-old, has some very serious concerns and responsibilities. He works his way towards manhood and a beautiful young wife already selected for him as he toils alongside his father and develops his skill as a hunter. When drought comes, Balam's life is changed: raiders take what supplies his village has along with Balam's promised wife, who is later sacrificed. When the village warriors are captured in a raiding attempt of their own, the elders are forced to send the captors the very best among the village youth as a sacrifice. As Delia A. Culberson of *Voice of Youth Advocates* noted, "Talbert's careful research gives a fascinating look at . . . the ancient Mayas." Culberson called the book, which also includes a glossary, "one of the most stirring, sensitive YA books I have read in a very long time."

Talbert explained in the *ALAN Review,* "Any honest reader might look into the mirror that is *Heart of a Jaguar* and see reflected back struggles between life and death, love and hope. Certainly I wanted to portray the Maya view of life and death, love and hope as accurately as possible. And I also wanted their view to serve as a useful mirror for the reader, a mirror that could help the reader see more clearly his or her attitudes toward life and death, love and hope."

■ Works Cited

Cook, James E., review of *Pillow of Clouds, Voice of Youth Advocates,* April, 1991, p. 37.

Crouch, Marcus, review of *Dead Birds Singing, Junior Bookshelf,* April, 1986, p. 81.

Crouch, Marcus, review of *Thin Ice, Junior Bookshelf,* December, 1987, pp. 289-90.

Culberson, Delia A., review of *Heart of a Jaguar, Voice of Youth Advocates,* December, 1995, p. 310.

Forman, Jack, review of *A Sunburned Prayer, School Library Journal,* July, 1995, p. 82.

Hutt, Karen, review of *The Purple Heart, Booklist,* December 15, 1991, p. 760.

Jameyson, Karen, review of *Dead Birds Singing, Horn Book,* July-August, 1985, p. 459.

LaBarbera, Kathryn, review of *Double or Nothing, Booklist,* October 1, 1990, p. 333.

Larson, Gerry, review of *The Purple Heart, School Library Journal,* February, 1992, pp. 89-90.

Oliver, Susan, review of *Pillow of Clouds, School Library Journal,* March, 1991, p. 218.

Review of *The Paper Knife, Kirkus Reviews,* October 15, 1988, p. 1534.

Review of *The Paper Knife, Publishers Weekly,* September 9, 1988, p. 138.

Reeder, Nancy P., review of *Toby, School Library Journal,* January, 1988, p. 77.

Review of *A Sunburned Prayer, Publishers Weekly,* April 17, 1995, p. 61.

Talbert, Marc, "What Is a Mirror to Do?" *ALAN Review,* Fall, 1990, pp. 2-6.

Review of *Thin Ice, Kirkus Reviews,* October 1, 1986, p. 1512.

Review of *Thin Ice, Publishers Weekly,* December 12, 1986, p. 54.

Review of *Toby, Publishers Weekly,* November 27, 1987, pp. 82-3.

■ For More Information See

PERIODICALS

Booklist, August, 1995, p. 1950.

Bulletin of the Center for Children's Books, January, 1989, p. 137; December, 1990, p. 104; April, 1991, p. 206; March, 1992, pp. 194-95; July-August, 1995, pp. 398-99.

Horn Book, January-February, 1991, pp. 71-72; January-February, 1996, p. 110.

Kirkus Reviews, November 15, 1987, pp. 1633-34; March 1, 1991, pp. 323-34.

Voice of Youth Advocates, December, 1988, p. 243.

* * *

TEAGUE, Mark (Christopher) 1963-

■ Personal

Born February 10, 1963, in La Mesa, CA; son of John Wesley (an insurance agent) and Joan (Clay) Teague; married Laura Quinlan (an insurance claims examiner), June 18, 1988. *Education:* University of California, Santa Cruz, B.A., 1985. *Politics:* Democrat. *Religion:* Christian.

■ Addresses

Home—Coxsackie, NY. *Office*—c/o Scholastic, Inc., 555 Broadway, New York, NY 10012.

■ Career

Freelance illustrator and writer, 1989—. *Member:* Authors Guild, Authors League of America.

■ Writings

SELF-ILLUSTRATED

The Trouble with the Johnsons, Scholastic, Inc., 1989.

Moog-Moog, Space Barber, Scholastic, Inc., 1990.
Frog Medicine, Scholastic, Inc., 1991.
The Field beyond the Outfield, Scholastic, Inc., 1991.
Pigsty, Scholastic, Inc., 1994.
How I Spent My Summer Vacation, Crown, 1995.
The Secret Shortcut, Scholastic, Inc., 1996.
Baby Tamer, Scholastic, Inc., 1997.
Lost and Found, Scholastic, Inc., 1998.

ILLUSTRATOR

What Are Scientists, What Do They Do?, Scholastic, Inc., 1991.
Adventures in Lego Land, Scholastic, Inc., 1991.
Chris Babcock, *No Moon, No Milk!,* Crown, 1993.
Dick King-Smith, *Three Terrible Trins,* Crown, 1994.
Tony Johnston, *The Iguana Brothers, A Perfect Day,* Blue Sky Press, 1995.
Audrey Wood, *The Flying Dragon Room,* Blue Sky Press, 1996.
Dick King-Smith, *Mr. Potter's Pet,* Hyperion, 1996.
Cynthia Rylant, *Poppleton,* Blue Sky Press, 1997.
Cynthia Rylant, *Poppleton and Friends: Book Two,* Blue Sky Press, 1997.
Cynthia Rylant, *Poppleton Forever,* Blue Sky Press, 1998.
Audrey Wood, *Sweet Dream Pie,* Blue Sky Press, 1998.
Cynthia Rylant, *Poppleton Everyday,* Blue Sky Press, 1998.

■ Sidelights

Mark Teague has a quirky sense of humor; just how quirky can easily be discovered by reading any of his books for children. Peopled with characters with names

MARK TEAGUE

like Elmo Freem and Wallace Bleff, Teague's books poke fun at things that kids dread—homework, cleaning one's room, ritual first-day-of-school haircuts, and the like—while his illustrations bring to life his quasi-realistic settings. Comparing Teague to author and illustrator William Joyce due to the nostalgic quality of his acrylic paintings, a *Publishers Weekly* contributor remarked that Teague's "combination of deadpan text and unbridled art is a sure-fire recipe for a crowd-pleaser."

"I managed to graduate from college without having any idea what I was going to do with my life," Teague once admitted to *SATA*. "My degree was in U.S. history but I wasn't interested in teaching. I enjoyed art but had no formal training. I liked to write but was unsure how to make it pay." The solution? Pack up the auto and head East to New York City. By the spring of 1986 Teague had arrived and was living with his brother, who helped the author-to-be get a job in the display department at the giant Barnes & Noble bookstore at Rockefeller Center in Manhattan. "The job provided a sort of crash course in design and graphic arts techniques," Teague explained, "and exposed me to a lot of new books. Looking at children's books in the store reminded me of how much I had enjoyed picture books as a child and how much fun it had been to write and illustrate my own stories at that age."

Remembering the fun of being an author sparked *The Trouble with the Johnsons,* Teague's first picture book for children. Published in 1989, the book tells the story of Elmo Freem, who longs to return to the country after his family moves to the big city. Together with his equally homesick cat, Elmo returns to the old house for a visit, where he meets the new owners, the Johnsons. While they seem nice enough, the Johnsons are a bit odd; for one thing, they're a family of dinosaurs, and Elmo goes back to the city with the knowledge that home is really where your family is. "The book came out of my experience living in Brooklyn," Teague recalled to *SATA*. "The theme was somewhat melancholy, but I tried to offset this with humor and a plot which was energetic and bizarre." A *Publishers Weekly* commentator stated that "Teague's unique perspective is utilized magnificently both in words and pictures to produce a noteworthy first book." The same year as *The Trouble with the Johnsons* was accepted by its eventual publisher, Scholastic, Inc., Teague was able to escape the city, moving with his wife to upstate New York, where he continues to make his home.

Elmo would re-emerge in Teague's next book, *Moog-Moog, Space Barber.* Taking as its premise "the apparently universal horror inspired by a bad haircut," according to Teague, *Moog-Moog* is much more a fantasy than *The Trouble with the Johnsons,* incorporating elements of science fiction as well. The amazingly calm Elmo awakes one morning to find several rotund space aliens, suitably green in color, hanging around the refrigerator in his kitchen. What has Elmo more concerned than close encounters of the alien kind is the razzing he expects to take from fellow schoolmates as a result of his perfectly horrid back-to-school haircut. Fortunately, aliens are the ones to turn to when looking for a competent stylist; they fly Elmo off to Moog-Moog, barber to the extraterrestrials, and his problems are solved. Stephanie Zvirin praised the book as "sure-footed silliness, sometimes amusingly sly, with just the right touch of irony," in her *Booklist* review.

Fans of Elmo get another glimpse at his off-kilter world in 1991's *Frog Medicine,* which involves "that dreaded subject: homework—as well as giant frogs, and things of that sort," according to its author. Unfortunately for Elmo, fear of an impending book report causes him to sprout frog feet, and only a consultation with noted frog medicine practitioner Dr. Frank Galoof gives him hope of de-amphibianizing anytime soon. Once more, Teague reveals his "knack for dealing with the kinds of predicaments that loom large on children's horizons in a fresh and funny way," according to a *Publishers Weekly* contributor. The book was also praised for its acrylic illustrations, with an attention to detail that reflected its hero's gradual transformation. "Every scene is bathed in curiously pure light," noted a *Kirkus Reviews* critic, "with plenty of clever, funny details to discover."

Equally bizarre is the world casually inhabited by one Wendell Fultz, who, in the book *Pigsty,* is not surprised to find a large hog dozing on his bed. In fact, the abominable condition of Wendell's room makes the pig the cleanest thing in it, but instead of cleaning up the mess like his mother requested, the sly Wendell just pushes a few things out of sight and settles in to play with his new porcine companion. Problems arise, however, after the rest of the curly-tailed gang shows up, and their antics cause a commotion. Finally, Wendell himself is forced to lay down the law; the pigs grudgingly help clean up the room and then leave for messier parts. "... especially evident in [Teague's] artwork, there's enough fun to carry the story," in the opinion of *Booklist* reviewer Ilene Cooper. A *Publishers Weekly* critic lauded Teague's "gleefully inventive imagination" and stated that "much of the tale's fun resides in [his] quirky acrylic art."

Books by Teague continue to defy traditional classification. In *The Field beyond the Outfield,* a story about summer baseball camp becomes a full-scale fantasy involving a major-league playoff between teams of giant insects. Commented *School Library Journal*'s Dorothy Houlihan, "Teague's window to childhood is wide open, allowing him to address the realities of youthful fantasies without trivializing them." Readers opening the innocent-sounding *How I Spent My Summer Vacation* are drawn into the classroom of one Wallace Bleff and then immediately carried away to the Wild West, amid cowpokes, lariats, and stampeding cattle. "One rootin' tootin' tall tale," applauded a *Publishers Weekly* reviewer, pointing out "some laugh-out-loud funny expressions on animal faces." And *Baby Tamer,* Teague's 1997 contribution to the annals of quirky children's literature, depicts a face-off between incredibly competent, fully certified baby-sitter Amanda Smeedy and the Egmont children. When making a lot of noise doesn't cause even a raised eyebrow from the stoic Amanda, the twins grow desperate, finally resorting to producing a full-blown circus complete with fireworks before admitting defeat. Teague's "bright, sassy acrylics careen across the pages at near-warp speed," according to a *Publishers Weekly* critic.

Teague has also illustrated the work of other authors such as Dick King-Smith, Audrey Wood, and Cynthia Rylant. A *Publishers Weekly* contributor, appraising Wood's *The Flying Dragon Room,* asserted that the plot "gets a vital boost from Teague's buoyant whimsical art," while Ilene Cooper, reviewing *No Moon, No Milk!* in *Booklist,* noted that "Teague's ebullient artwork captures a very determined cow in ... uncowlike settings ... with humor and panache."

■ Works Cited

Review of *Baby Tamer, Publishers Weekly,* August 11, 1997, p. 401.
Cooper, Ilene, review of *No Moon, No Milk!, Booklist,* September 1, 1993, pp. 66-67.
Cooper, Ilene, review of *Pigsty, Booklist,* September 15, 1994, p. 145.
Review of *The Flying Dragon Room, Publishers Weekly,* January 22, 1996, p. 73.
Review of *Frog Medicine, Kirkus Reviews,* August 15, 1991, pp. 1094-95.
Review of *Frog Medicine, Publishers Weekly,* October 4, 1991, p. 88.
Houlihan, Dorothy, review of *The Field beyond the Outfield, School Library Journal,* June, 1992, pp. 103-4.
Review of *How I Spent My Summer Vacation, Publishers Weekly,* July 10, 1995, p. 56.
Review of *Pigsty, Publishers Weekly,* July 11, 1994, p. 78.
Review of *The Secret Shortcut, Publishers Weekly,* August 26, 1996, p. 98.
Review of *The Trouble with the Johnsons, Publishers Weekly,* September 8, 1989, p. 69.
Zvirin, Stephanie, review of *Moog-Moog, Space Barber, Booklist,* November 1, 1990, p. 531.

■ For More Information See

PERIODICALS

Booklist, September 1, 1991, p. 64; September 15, 1996, p. 251.
Five Owls, March-April, 1998, pp. 80-81.
Kirkus Reviews, March 15, 1992, p. 399; August 1, 1995, p. 1117; July 1, 1996, p. 975; August 15, 1997, p. 1313.
New York Times Book Review, July 12, 1992, p. 23.
School Library Journal, April, 1995, p. 103; March, 1996, p. 184.
Time, December 11, 1995, p. 77.

*   *   *

THOMPSON, Julian F(rancis) 1927-

■ Personal

Born November 16, 1927, in New York, NY; son of Julian Francis (a playwright and businessman) and

Amalita (maiden name, Stagg) Thompson; married Polly Nichy (an artist), August 11, 1978. *Education:* Princeton University, A.B., 1949; Columbia University, M.A., 1955. *Hobbies and other interests:* Sculpture, gardening, cooking, sports, reading, movies, dance.

■ Addresses

Home—P.O. Box 138, West Rupert, VT 05776. *Agent*—Curtis Brown Ltd., 575 Madison Ave., New York, NY 10022.

■ Career

Lawrenceville School, Lawrenceville, NJ, history teacher, athletic coach, and director of lower school, 1949-62 and 1965-67; CHANGES, Inc. (alternative high school), East Orange, NJ, director and teacher, 1971-77; writer, 1979—. *Member:* PEN American Center, Authors Guild, League of Vermont Writers.

■ Awards, Honors

Best Book for Young Adults selection, American Library Association (ALA), 1986, for *A Band of Angels;* Editor's Choice, *Booklist,* 1987, for *Simon Pure.*

■ Writings

YOUNG ADULT NOVELS

Facing It, Avon, 1983.
The Grounding of Group 6, Avon, 1983.
A Question of Survival, Avon, 1984.
Discontinued, Scholastic, Inc., 1985.
A Band of Angels, Scholastic, Inc., 1986.
Simon Pure, Scholastic, Inc., 1987.
The Taking of Mariasburg, Scholastic, Inc., 1988.
Goofbang Value Daze, Scholastic, Inc., 1989.
Herb Seasoning, Scholastic, Inc., 1990.
Gypsyworld, Holt, 1992.
Shepherd, Holt, 1993.
The Fling, Holt, 1994.
The Trials of Molly Sheldon, Holt, 1995.
Philo Fortune's Awesome Journey to His Comfort Zone, Hyperion, 1995.
Ghost Story, Holt, 1997.
Brothers, Knopf, 1998.

■ Sidelights

Often dubbed a controversial author, Julian F. Thompson writes novels for young adults which sometimes pit well-intentioned and intelligent teenagers against adults who are generally neither of the above. Thompson's lengthy and sophisticated books portray responsible kids challenging irresponsible situations, and in the writing he employs humor, elements of the thriller, and dollops of sex. Though Thompson himself eschews the label "controversial," books such as *The Grounding of Group 6* and *The Taking of Mariasburg* portray adults as ridiculous, uncaring, and even murderous. Thompson explores big issues in his works: nuclear threat, environmental problems, and national politics to name but a few, topics that leave a writer open to criticism by those who disagree with a book's viewpoint. Thompson once told *SATA* that he takes kids seriously. "I want them to know that a lot of the 'answers' grown-ups give to many questions should not be swallowed whole. I want them to hold onto their hopefulness and wonder and to their own real selves." And in an essay for *Something about the Author Autobiography Series* (*SAAS*), Thompson further clarified his position vis-a-vis his primary readership: "I'm forever interested in kids' efforts to become functioning, independent human beings and good decision makers. As a rule, the teenagers in my books sound like the kids I've known, and a lot of my fictional characters are modeled, in part, on real people." Thompson's many years spent teaching and coaching have supplied him with enough material for a score more books.

Publication came late for Thompson, whose first book appeared when he was fifty-two. Yet in many ways it was as if he were preparing his entire life for writing. Born in New York City in 1927, Thompson experienced a happy, carefree childhood until the death of his successful father in 1939. His father had been, in addition to treasurer for a large pharmaceutical company, a playwright whose play, *The Warrior's Husband,* was Katharine Hepburn's first starring role on Broadway. That play was later adapted for a Rodgers and Hart musical. But after the death of his father, Thompson's world was turned on its head: gone were the servants and weekend farm, and soon gone, too, was the swanky Park Avenue family address. Young Thompson remained in his private school, but now through dint of scholarships. His mother, originally from Ecuador, was "beautiful and bright, and a marvelous tennis player," according to Thompson in his *SAAS* sketch. The great-great-granddaughter of a general who had served under Simon Bolivar, she was resilient, as well, and held the family together despite their loss.

For the next five years, Thompson led a disoriented life, not really believing that his former world had disappeared forever. A further scholarship won him a place at the Lawrenceville School in New Jersey, where by his junior year he had begun to find a place for himself. His love of sports played no small part in this recovery, specifically coaching at summer camps and for intramural teams. Among his schoolmates at Lawrenceville was Edward Albee, destined to become a famous playwright. In *SAAS,* Thompson recalled how he received a much higher grade than Albee in English, "which should tell you something about the correlation between grades in school and success in later life." Thompson entered Princeton University in 1945 on another scholarship, but did not consider himself a great student. He continued coaching during his college years, and he also volunteered at a juvenile institution in New Jersey where he came face to face with offenders for the first time in his life and learned what forces come to play in leading kids to commit criminal acts. These activities, as well as his social life, sometimes came into conflict with Thompson's study schedule. By his senior year he had lost his scholarship but continued on to graduate in 1949.

JULIAN F. THOMPSON

Upon graduation, Thompson took a teaching position back at his alma mater, Lawrenceville, though he had a tough time at first, teaching Greek and Roman history, two subjects he was ill-prepared to teach. Coaching, however, again saved him, and with success in that field, he soon developed an academic curriculum that suited his style. His third year at Lawrenceville, he was put in charge of a Lower School House, and for the next ten years built a fine career as teacher, coach, and house-master. But there was always in the back of his mind the question of whether or not he could become a writer like his father. So, in 1962, at age thirty-five, Thompson quit his job at Lawrenceville. "Then I loaded up my white '57 T-bird ... and took off into New England, deciding I would write the Great American Novel," Thompson recalled in *SAAS*.

It was not as easy as all that, however. Accepted as a participant at the prestigious Bread Loaf Writers' Conference in Vermont, he was initially discouraged in his goal by the editor who worked personally with him. Leaving Bread Loaf, he continued work on his novel in progress, and when it was finished, his New York agent had further discouraging words, advising against sending it out to publishers. Thompson returned to Lawrenceville as a part-time teacher from 1965 to 1967, and then a small inheritance let him pursue writing full-time

again. He was able to purchase land in Vermont and traded in his beloved T-bird for a Jeep in the process. Living a simple life in Vermont, Thompson completed another novel, but again his agent advised against showing it. This time, Thompson did not follow the advice but sent it off to a publisher who gave him an encouraging rejection, but a rejection, nonetheless.

Then came more years of teaching, but in unexpected places, working in alternative schools in New Jersey through most of the 1970s. The second of these schools, CHANGES, Inc., changed Thompson's life, as well. It was there that he found his own voice as a writer, teaching creative writing classes and learning a new literary language as he went along—one that was closer to his own heart, and one that was not "literary" at all. It was there also that he met his wife, marrying for the first time at the age of fifty. After seven years of working as director, teacher, and janitor at CHANGES, Thompson and his wife went back to his home in Vermont, he to pursue his writing, and she initially to study medicine and work on her art.

It was then he began writing his third novel, and his first to be published, *Facing It*. Like many writers, Thompson did not realize he was writing a genre novel when he started. It was his agent who informed him that he had just written a young adult title. "I'd never heard the expression before," Thompson once told *SATA*. "To be honest, I didn't care what anybody called my books, so long as somebody published them and other people got to read them, and I still don't." While his agent hunted for a publisher, Thompson continued writing, finishing *The Grounding of Group 6,* and soon it transpired that Avon publishers wanted to publish both titles. "My twenty-year-old dream was going to come true," Thompson noted in *SAAS*. "I was going to be a published writer!"

With these first novels, Thompson mapped out a territory quintessentially his own, mining his storehouse of sports lore as well as his experiences at a private school. *Facing It* recreates some of Thompson's own experiences as a camp counselor and coach in the persona of a young man whose promising athletic career is ended by the loss of three fingers. Taking a job at a summer camp, he begins to heal and help others to heal, as well, forming a special bond with a dancer recovering from a hysterectomy and a young boy soprano. *Booklist*'s Stephanie Zvirin noted that Thompson "effectively maintains a difficult narrative device; his dialogue and situation display both freshness and realism; and he combines humor and poignancy in equal proportions." Thompson announced in this first novel an uncompromising approach to dealing with teen problems such as drugs, sex, venereal disease, and difficult relations with parents, and his text employed a full panoply of teen-speak, including the use of four-letter words. While some critics found this style too convoluted and hard-edged, others, such as Zena Sutherland in *Bulletin of the Center for Children's Books,* concluded that Thompson's writing "sparkles with intellectual sophistication, and the story is imbued with a persuasive warmth."

Parent-child disharmony is taken to a surreal extreme in *The Grounding of Group 6,* in which disgruntled parents make arrangements with a private school to permanently "ground" their children by killing them. But Nat, the hired killer, discovers he likes his supposed victims and takes their side, which sets the school authorities after him and his charges. A *Publishers Weekly* critic felt that Thompson displayed "a remarkable literary style and frightening inventiveness" in this suspense yarn, and concluded that "Everyone will be looking for more feats by the talented author." Nancy C. Hammond, writing in *Horn Book,* called the book a "satiric thriller" and one "not for squeamish teenagers," but also noted that the novel was "pure, page-turning entertainment." Thompson set his novel in Vermont, a territory, like his protagonists, with which he was very familiar.

An outback setting also informs *A Question of Survival,* Thompson's next book. But in this case, a teenage boy and girl, Toby and Zack, are sent off to the woods for survival training, and not to be "grounded." Kathy Fritts in *School Library Journal* took exception to Thompson's style, noting that "the book is drenched in sex, foul language, images of violence and sexual fantasy to an extent seldom encountered in young adult fiction." Other critics found honesty in the story, however,

and looked beyond the surface for inner depths. Dorothy M. Broderick noted in *Voice of Youth Advocates* that "Thompson has done a masterful job in creating two very interesting teenage characters while giving life to the adults as well. That makes this something special, and there isn't even room here to tell you about how funny it is, and how tender it is in describing the growing sexual attraction between Toby and Zack."

The nuclear threat was dealt with in *Discontinued* and *A Band of Angels,* both of which present typical attitudes and situations with just enough exaggeration to make them frighteningly possible and one step from the macabre. Both involve complex mysteries surrounding adult attitudes toward nuclear war, and both are uncompromising in their language and sexual expression. While many reviewers complained of these elements, Broderick, reviewing *A Band of Angels* in *Voice of Youth Advocates,* announced that Thompson was "a unique voice among the new male YA authors." She found that his female-male relations were "loving, caring without any of the phoniness found in the series romances," that his female characters were "strong, independent without being males-in-disguise," and that "his faith in the young to build a better world is unbounded." *A Band of Angels* was selected as a Best Book for Young Adults by the American Library Association.

A further award-winning title was Thompson's *Simon Pure,* set at a fictional Vermont university about to be secretly taken over by power-hungry business students. These plans are thwarted by fifteen-year-old Simon Storm and his ally, a psychology professor. Again, Thompson's lengthy, discursive style irritated some reviewers, but others, such as Pam Spencer in *Voice of Youth Advocates,* declared that "young adults will love it! *Simon Pure* is a pure delight to read—it's clever, inventive and funny. . . ." Further advocacy of teens came in *The Taking of Mariasburg,* the story of a young girl who buys a town for teens with inherited money, *Goofbang Value Daze,* a satire about a town where the rights of teenagers are threatened, and in *Herb Seasoning,* an off-beat comedy about a high school senior trying to decide what to do with his life after graduation. Reviewing that last title, *Booklist*'s Zvirin noted that Thompson was "one of the most original and humorous of today's YA writers. While his books will either enchant you or make you furious with their wholesale stereotyping, and smart-aleck characters, you shouldn't ignore them."

Thompson deals with environmental problems in *Gypsyworld,* in which he constructs an ecological utopia along with a twist of mystery in an "uneven though thought-provoking story," according to a reviewer in *Publishers Weekly*. A more typical novel of adolescent anxieties is *Shepherd,* about a high school senior who falls for a flirting freshman girl. Again set in Vermont, the book might appeal to young male readers, according to Jeanne Triner in *Booklist,* who "will identify with Shep, his raging hormones, false bravado, insecurities, and good heart. . . ." *The Fling* is also set in a high school, but here reality gives way to a sort of magic when Felicia Gordon's short stories start anticipating real events leading to a mystery which surrounds the brooding David Mycroft. While a *Kirkus Reviews* critic found the book to be an "ambiguous, rather dark comedy," Drue Wagner-Mees, writing in *Voice of Youth Advocates,* thought the work was "immediately engrossing, provocative, and titillating."

With *Philo Fortune's Awesome Journey to His Comfort Zone,* Thompson created something of a humorous departure from his big-issue books. Seventeen-year-old Philo is a virgin badly in need of adventures, which he gets with a solo drive west. He picks up a sexy hitchhiker, gets imprisoned by a band of burnt-out druggies, and finally comes to some basic conclusions about his life. Karen Simonetti, writing in *Booklist,* thought the book was "Classic laugh bait for teens. . . . Fast-paced and peppered with teenage slang and testosterone, this is an honest, humorous story. . . ." Vermont is once again the setting, though book-censorship is the theme, for *The Trials of Molly Sheldon,* while in *Ghost Story* Thompson turns to a ghost at a Vermont inn as one of his main characters; the others are a teenage girl and an aspiring pornographer.

If Thompson's books continue to earn him the label of "controversial," he is beyond worrying about that. Writing is his main concern, which he does in long-hand in a three-ring binder. He also happily admits to deciding on the theme of a book before beginning the plotting. Thompson feels he has led a charmed life. "I feel blessed to have had the life I've had so far," he concluded in *SAAS.* "I haven't ever made much money, or had a lot of *things,* but I've had enough that I haven't suffered want, or felt deprived. . . . Although I've never fathered any children, I've always had some great kids in my life, most recently the ones I've come to know because I've been a writer. I can't believe that anyone has gotten greater pleasure from the work he's done."

■ Works Cited

Broderick, Dorothy M., review of *A Question of Survival, Voice of Youth Advocates,* February, 1985, p. 333.

Broderick, Dorothy M., review of *A Band of Angels, Voice of Youth Advocates,* June, 1986, p. 84.

Review of *The Fling, Kirkus Reviews,* May 15, 1994, p. 708.

Fritts, Kathy, review of *A Question of Survival, School Library Journal,* October, 1984, p. 171.

Review of *The Grounding of Group 6, Publishers Weekly,* January 28, 1983, p. 86.

Review of *Gypsyworld, Publishers Weekly,* July 13, 1992, p. 56.

Hammond, Nancy C., review of *The Grounding of Group 6, Horn Book,* October, 1983, pp. 586-87.

Simonetti, Karen, review of *Philo Fortune's Awesome Journey to His Comfort Zone, Booklist,* May 1, 1995, p. 1564.

Spencer, Pam, review of *Simon Pure, Voice of Youth Advocates,* April, 1987, p. 34.

Sutherland, Zena, review of *Facing It, Bulletin of the Center for Children's Books,* February, 1984, p. 119.

Thompson, Julian F., essay in *Something about the Author Autobiography Series,* Volume 13, Gale, 1993, pp. 231-45.

Triner, Jeanne, review of *Shepherd, Booklist,* December 15, 1993, p. 748.

Wagner-Mees, Drue, review of *The Fling, Voice of Youth Advocates,* August, 1994, p. 151.

Zvirin, Stephanie, review of *Facing It, Booklist,* September, 1983, p. 76.

Zvirin, Stephanie, review of *Herb Seasoning, Booklist,* May 15, 1990, p. 1792.

■ For More Information See

BOOKS

Children's Literature Review, Volume 24, Gale, 1991, pp. 226-33.

PERIODICALS

Bulletin of the Center for Children's Books, January, 1986, pp. 97-98; October, 1986, p. 39; May, 1988, p. 190; August, 1989, p. 285; September, 1992, pp. 24-25; June, 1995, pp. 361-62; January, 1996, p. 172; March, 1997, p. 260.

Emergency Librarian, March-April, 1985, pp. 47-48; November-December, 1988, pp. 60-64.

Kirkus Reviews, October 1, 1995, p. 1437; February 1, 1997, p. 229.

Publishers Weekly, December 9, 1983, p. 51; August 16, 1985, p. 70; March 13, 1987, pp. 86-87; February 17, 1997, p. 220.

School Library Journal, August, 1983, p. 81; October, 1985, p. 188; March, 1987, p. 177; May, 1988, p. 113; February, 1989, p. 103; March, 1990, p. 240; September, 1992, p. 280; November, 1993, p. 126; May, 1995, p. 123.

Voice of Youth Advocates, February, 1994, pp. 374-75; February, 1996, p. 377.

—Sketch by J. Sydney Jones

*   *   *

TOTEN, Teresa 1955-

■ Personal

Born October 13, 1955, in Zagreb, Croatia; immigrated to Canada, 1955, Canadian citizen; daughter of Adam (a real estate agent) and Jan (a cook) Vukovic; married Ken Toten (a banker), September 22, 1979; children: Sasha, Nikki. *Education:* University of Toronto, B.A., 1978, M.A. (political economy), 1979; attended writing workshops at George Brown College, Toronto, 1986-1995. *Politics:* "Left of center." *Religion:* Roman Catholic. *Hobbies and other interests:* Working with children's groups to promote all aspects of children's literature and book production; travel; sports, especially tennis, basketball, and walking.

■ Addresses

Home—26 Sunny Brae Pl., Bronxville, NY 10708.

■ Career

Writer. Radio Canada, Montreal, Quebec, freelance writer and broadcaster, 1980; Royal Commission on Conditions of Foreign Service, Ottawa, Ontario, senior analyst, 1982; Canada Museum Construction Corporation, Ottawa, assistant to the chairman, 1982-1984; Canadian Institute for International Peace and Security, Ottawa, corporate secretary, 1984-1985; freelance book reviewer, 1996—. *Member:* Canadian Society of Children's Authors, Illustrators and Performers (CANSCAIP), Canadian Children's Book Centre, Writers' Union of Canada, National Writers' Union, Society of Children's Book Writers and Illustrators.

■ Awards, Honors

Imperial Order of Daughters of the Empire (IODE) Book Award finalist, Municipal Chapter of Toronto IODE, 1995, Violet Downey Book Award finalist, National Chapter of Canada IODE, 1995, Ruth Schwartz Children's Book Award finalist, Ontario Arts Council, 1995, Canadian Library Association Notable Book, 1996, and Our Choice selection, Canadian Children's Book Centre, 1996-97, all for *The Onlyhouse.*

■ Writings

The Onlyhouse (Northern Lights Young Novels), Red Deer College Press, 1995.

■ Work in Progress

The Game (working title), a young adult novel.

■ Sidelights

The positive critical response to Teresa Toten's first novel speaks volumes about her arrival on the Canadian children's literature scene. Selected for the short lists of several important literary awards and included on the "best books" lists of both the Canadian Children's Book Centre and the Canadian Library Association, *The Onlyhouse* is a story about roots, identity, and belonging. Presented from the perspective of eleven-year-old protagonist Lucy, it tells about an immigrant child's experiences in Toronto in the 1960s.

Quill & Quire reviewer Kenneth Oppel described Toten's narrative as "so authentic and compelling it draws us with instant enthusiasm into the story." On the book's back cover, Toten's publisher compares *The Onlyhouse* with the popular, humor-tinged realistic fiction Brian Doyle writes for pre-teens. "The laugh-alouds are a delight," said Sarah Ellis in a review of *The Onlyhouse* in *Resource Links.* "Even better are the rueful smiles with sadness at their edges."

Toten's parents married in Croatia. Her father, a Canadian citizen with Croatian roots, met Toten's mother on one of his visits "home." After their marriage, he returned to Canada to tackle the red tape that would allow her to leave Croatia and join him. By the time the immigration process untangled two years later, Toten had arrived on the Croatian scene. She was an

TERESA TOTEN

infant in 1955 when her parents finally reunited in Toronto.

Shortly after the family's reunion, however, Toten's father died. Her mother was suddenly a single parent in a new country. Like Lucy's mother in *The Onlyhouse,* Toten's mother worked hard to achieve the immigrant dream of buying a home in a well-established, middle-class neighborhood. As a child, Toten called that Toronto home an "only house." There were two reasons for her description: the house was detached and it was the first and, therefore, the only house she and her mother had ever lived in. The "only house" image was important to Toten as a child and its impact remained with her as an adult. When Red Deer College Press accepted her autobiographical novel for publication, Toten knew its title had to be *The Onlyhouse.*

Toten grew up and went to school in a neighborhood much like the one in her book. She completed high school and earned two academic degrees at the University of Toronto. In 1979, she married Ken Toten, moved to Montreal, and worked as a writer and broadcaster. A year later, the couple moved to Ottawa. During their five years in Canada's capital, Toten worked for a variety of government-affiliated organizations.

In 1985, the Totens returned to Toronto. After the birth of their first child in 1986, Toten began to pursue her lifelong interest in writing. She attended a series of writing workshops at George Brown College. An exer-

The Onlyhouse
Teresa Toten

Her very own Onlyhouse,
a new neighborhood of
"real Canadians."

It's everything Lucy Vakovik could
ask for. And a whole lot more!

Lucy Vakovik endeavors to fit into her new Canadian neighborhood and maintain her dignity in the face of taunts about being Croatian. (Cover illustration by Jeff Hitch.)

cise in one of the workshops required her to write a scene about being ten-years-old. *The Onlyhouse,* based on Toten's own childhood, grew out of that assignment.

The Onlyhouse relives much of Toten's experience of moving from Toronto's lively, mixed Kensington Market district to the quiet, homogeneous Davisville neighborhood. As she wrote *The Onlyhouse,* she worked hard at portraying the diverse and distinctive communities that characterized Toronto in the 1960s and continue to characterize it today.

"Most of all, I wanted to tell the story of a child who feels quite different from the norm and wants very much to belong, to be part of the inside group," Toten remarked in comments to *Junior DISCovering Authors* (*JrDA*). "Lucy, the main character, and I have a lot in common and the other characters are a combination of real people I've known." Toten's Lucy impressed author Sarah Ellis. In a *Quill & Quire* article on great books for girls, Ellis included Lucy in a discussion of characters "who show passion, imagination, and humor in the face of oppression." She described Lucy specifically as "gregarious, optimistic, articulate and a bit of a goof."

Toten is a passionate reader and admires the work of Canadian authors for children such as Brian Doyle, Sarah Ellis, and Tim Wynne-Jones. During Canadian Children's Book Week in 1996, she had the opportunity to revisit the greater Toronto area as one of the Canadian Children's Book Centre's touring authors. She is an energetic advocate for children's literature and particularly enjoys working with groups of children. She is involved, as a volunteer, in a lunch-hour book program at a school in Bronxville, New York, where she lives with her husband and two daughters.

Toten is working on a second book, a novel for young adults. She told *JrDA,* "I want to continue to write about the theme of belonging, what it is that motivates our need for this very human desire, and how we go about achieving it. I hope my writing will reach children who will feel less alone when they read it."

■ Works Cited

Ellis, Sarah, review of *The Onlyhouse, Resource Links,* February, 1996, p. 118.
Ellis, Sarah, "Great Canadian Books for Girls," *Quill & Quire,* July, 1997, p. 51.
Oppel, Kenneth, review of *The Onlyhouse, Quill & Quire,* December, 1995, p. 12.
Toten, Teresa, comments in *Junior DISCovering Authors,* Gale, 1998.

■ For More Information See

PERIODICALS

Children's Book News, Spring, 1996, pp. 13-14; Winter, 1997, pp. 7-12.
School Library Journal, July, 1996, pp. 86-87.*

V–W

VAN HOOK, Beverly H. 1941-

■ Personal

Born February 2, 1941, in Huntington, WV; daughter of John C. (a banker) and Arretta (Gwinn) Hennen; married Donald W. Van Hook (an advertising executive), October 26, 1963; children: Andrea, James, Alison. *Education:* Ohio University, B.S. (cum laude, journalism), 1962. *Politics:* Democrat. *Religion:* Presbyterian. *Hobbies and other interests:* Reading, travel, tennis, swimming.

BEVERLY H. VAN HOOK

■ Addresses

Home—180 Walnut Lane, Charlottesville, VA 22911. *Electronic mail*—LizanDutch@aol.com. *Agent*—Evva Pryor, McIntosh and Otis, Inc., 310 Madison Ave., New York, NY 10017.

■ Career

Writer. Conducts "Teaching with Mysteries," a volunteer reading workshop in elementary schools. *Member:* Mystery Writers of America, Sisters in Crime, Society of Midland Authors (Chicago), Virginia Writers Club.

■ Awards, Honors

Cornelia Meigs Award for Children's Literature, *Quad City Times* (Davenport, IA); Author Achievement Award, Davenport Public Library; Isabel Bloom Award for the Arts, Quad-Cities Women's Coalition.

■ Writings

"SUPERGRANNY" SERIES

Supergranny 1: The Mystery of the Shrunken Heads, Holderby & Bierce, 1985.
Supergranny 2: The Case of the Riverboat Riverbelle, Holderby & Bierce, 1986.
Supergranny 3: The Ghost of Heidelberg Castle, Holderby & Bierce, 1987.
Supergranny 4: The Secret of Devil Mountain, Holderby & Bierce, 1988.
Supergranny 5: The Character Who Came to Life, Holderby & Bierce, 1989.
Supergranny 6: The Great College Caper, Holderby & Bierce, 1991.
Supergranny 7: The Villainous Vicar, Holderby & Bierce, 1996.

FOR ADULTS

Fiction, Fact, & Murder, Holderby & Bierce, 1995.

■ Work in Progress

Juliet's Ghost (working title), a follow-up to *Fiction, Fact, & Murder.*

■ Sidelights

Beverly H. Van Hook told *SATA:* "After working as a journalist for twenty-two years, I resigned from the newspaper to write the 'Supergranny' children's mysteries about a gray-haired detective who drives a red Ferrari and fights crime. My former agent took Supergranny to New York and showed her around. An editor at Little, Brown said, 'Hilarious characters, good idea for a series, we can't use it.'

"Merger mania was just hitting publishing and my agent was discouraged. 'They don't know what they want,' she said. So several friends and I decided to publish Supergranny ourselves. The first book, *Supergranny 1: The Mystery of the Shrunken Heads,* sold out in ten months. It's now in its fifth printing. *Supergranny 2: The Case of the Riverboat Riverbelle,* received our first national review in *School Library Journal,* and we began getting orders from all over the country through Baker & Taylor and other wholesalers. Seven titles are now in print.

"I was fortunate enough that after Supergranny did so well, investors who are avid readers became interested in my work. In 1995, Dave and Lanni Stowe (Dave, recently retired, was then president of Deere & Company) financed my first adult mystery, *Fiction, Fact, & Murder.* It introduced amateur sleuths Liza Randolph, who writes a children's mystery series called 'Supergramps,' and her husband, Dutch. I'm now working on their second case."

*　　*　　*

WALLACE, Daisy
See CUYLER, Margery (Stuyvesant)

*　　*　　*

WALSH, Ellen Stoll 1942-

■ Personal

Born September 2, 1942, in Baltimore, MD; daughter of Joseph Adolphus (a businessman) and Nell (Orum) Stoll; married David Albert Walsh (a professor), August 25, 1964; children: Benjamin Martin. *Education:* Maryland Institute of Art, B.F.A., 1964; attended University of Minnesota, 1966-69.

■ Addresses

Home—29 West St., Fairport, NY 14450.

ELLEN STOLL WALSH

■ Career

Writer and illustrator. Freelance illustrator for Houghton Mifflin, 1984—.

■ Awards, Honors

Merit Award, Art Director's Club 59th Annual Exhibition, and Award of Excellence, American Institute of Graphic Arts, both 1980, both for *Brunus and the New Bear;* one of International Reading Association's Children's Choices, 1982, for *Theodore All Grown Up;* Ezra Jack Keats Fellow at the Kerlan Collection, University of Minnesota, 1986; Reading Magic Award, *Parenting Magazine,* 1989, for *Mouse Paint.*

■ Writings

SELF-ILLUSTRATED

Brunus and the New Bear, Doubleday, 1979.
Theodore All Grown Up, Doubleday, 1981.
Mouse Paint, Harcourt Brace, 1989.
Mouse Count, Harcourt Brace, 1991.
You Silly· Goose, Harcourt Brace, 1992.
Hop Jump, Harcourt Brace, 1993.
Pip's Magic, Harcourt Brace, 1994.
Samantha, Harcourt Brace, 1996.
Jack's Tale, Harcourt Brace, 1997.
For Pete's Sake, Harcourt Brace, 1998.

ILLUSTRATOR

Marian K. Towne, *A Midwest Gardner's Cookbook,* Indiana University Press (Bloomington, IN), 1996.

■ Adaptations

Brunus and the New Bear was made into a filmstrip by Imperial Educational Resources, 1980; *Theodore All Grown Up* was made into a filmstrip by Spoken Arts, narrated by Frances Sternhagen with music by Michael Barber, 1982.

■ Sidelights

"I was born in Baltimore and grew up in the midst of a very large family," Ellen Stoll Walsh once told *SATA*. "There were ten children in all, and those of us who were older shared the responsibility of looking after the younger ones. Life was often chaotic with so many people around, but there were many wonderful moments. We were all very close then, and though we are now scattered around the country, we feel closer than ever.

"As a child I loved to read and draw and was very fond of sports. I enjoyed being by myself and would spend hours alone in the woods, often practicing to be an Indian. One of my first great disappointments was learning that no matter how hard I practiced being an Indian, I could never grow up to be one. I loved summer camp, and when I was too old to be a camper, I worked as a counselor until I graduated from college . . . .

"It never occurred to me to write children's books until my son Ben was three years old. Ben was curled up in my arms and we were reading *Alexander and the Wind-Up Mouse* by Leo Leonni. And all of a sudden I realized that I wanted to write and illustrate children's books more than anything else. I started immediately and from scratch. Since *Alexander* was a cut paper book, my first attempt was with cut paper. I experimented with a number of media and finally decided on colored inks. I

was amazed to find out how difficult it is to write a good children's story. I quickly learned that no matter how nice the pictures are, if a story is not well thought out, an editor will not give it a second thought!"

Walsh's self-illustrated *Mouse Paint* and *Mouse Count*, published in 1989 and 1991, respectively, display the author's use of cut paper illustrations and her ability to write good children's stories. Both books provide creative ways to teach colors and counting to pre-schoolers. In *Mouse Paint*, three white mice camouflage themselves on a piece of white paper, remaining inconspicuous to a preying cat. When they decide to venture away from their safe haven, the mice stumble upon pots of red, blue, and yellow paint. Curiously, the mice dip their bodies into the paint, discovering that the original colors form new ones (green, orange, and purple) when blended. After bathing, the mice retreat to their white space to avoid contact with the cat. *School Library Journal* contributor Karen K. Radtke describes *Mouse Paint* as a "real charmer that's great fun as well as informative." Isabel Schon, a reviewer for *Horn Book*, also notes that the book is "strikingly illustrated with torn paper collage in bright primary colors."

The mice reappear with seven new friends in *Mouse Count*, this time trying to escape a multi-colored snake. The rodents find themselves trapped when the snake catches them during nap time and puts them in a jar, counting each mouse from one to ten. One of the mice deceives the snake by sending him away to find another mouse. While the snake is gone, the mice escape from the jar. Walsh's illustrations "display a naive charm and exuberance," writes a *Publishers Weekly* reviewer. *Horn Book* reviewer Elizabeth Watson contends that the book provides "counting fun for two-year-olds."

Pip the salamander thinks he can overcome his fear of the dark with the help of Old Abra but instead finds the necessary inner strength on his journey in search of the wizard. (From *Pip's Magic*, written and illustrated by Walsh.)

"The first step in making a picture book is finding a good idea for a story," Stoll continued. "This is probably the most difficult time for me. During this 'waiting period' I read a lot of other people's stories, talk and listen to children to find out what is important to them, and probe my childhood and my son's for interesting material. I always try out lots of ideas before settling down to one that I think is not only important to write about, but will be visually exciting as well.

"Once I have a good idea for a story it grows so fast and in so many directions that I often have to remind myself to stop and remember what the original idea was all about. I find it almost impossible to confine myself to an outline, but write pages and pages trying to find the best way to tell my story."

Relaying a message of tolerance and diversity proves evident in Walsh's well-received children's book *Hop Jump*. Betsy's boredom with hopping and jumping like other frogs stimulates her need to experiment with different movements. The motion of leaves captivates Betsy, so she decides to pattern her own bodily rhythms after them. Betsy calls her new style "dance," but the other frogs proclaim that there is "no room for dancing." Betsy ignores them and continues to enjoy her newfound leaps and twirls. The frogs, however, gradually begin to join in on the fun. One frog still protests dancing and is quickly shunned by the converts who now oppose hopping. Betsy tries to unify the lone frog and the rest of the group by promoting dancing and hopping, thus eradicating the underlying discrimination. *School Library Journal* contributor Nancy Seiner praises *Hop Jump*'s "large, clearly seen figures and flowing language." Seiner continues by saying Walsh's book is "a popular and useful story time choice." According to a *Kirkus Reviews* contributor, *Hop Jump* is a "beautifully designed book that ... yields new subtleties and visual delights with each reading."

Pip's Magic, published in 1994, touches on another subject that affects many children—the fear of the dark. Pip, an eager salamander, wants to combat his fear of darkness. A trio of frogs suggests he visit Old Abra, an omniscient wizard turtle, to help with his anxiety of the dark. Pip follows an obscure and lightless path to reach Old Abra, urged on by the frogs, a bird, and a mouse. Once the salamander reaches Old Abra, the turtle praises Pip and tells him that he has already conquered his fear by following the dark trail, in addition to gaining a little extra courage. Elated over his new sense of confidence, Pip retreats to a safe resting place. The book's "imaginative, boldly colored treatment of a common anxiety is [Walsh's] best work yet," declares a contributor in *Kirkus Reviews*. Elizabeth Bush, writing in *Bulletin of the Center for Children's Books*, praises Walsh's picture book, claiming the tale is "brief, simple, and direct, enlivened by neatly turned similes in Pip's soliloquies."

Walsh explores another common childhood occurrence in *Samantha*, published in 1996. Samantha, a young mouse, wishes her siblings would not play roughly with her. Samantha's thoughts are acknowledged when a fairy godmother appears and acts as her guardian. The fairy godmother takes her task very seriously and becomes overly protective of Samantha, thus eliminating the little one's fun. The unhappy mouse drives her protector away so that she can regain her normal lifestyle. Although Samantha begins to enjoy her siblings, she is once again susceptible to harm. The young mouse ends up falling in a snowdrift, but is rescued by her fairy godmother who never ventured far away from her tiny friend. Samantha and her guardian reconcile their relationship by making a new rule: the fairy godmother promises to assist the mouse only in emergencies. Eunice Weech, a reviewer in *School Library Journal*, regards *Samantha* as a "pleasing combination of a short, well-told story and simple but expressive illustrations." Deborah Stevenson asserts in *Bulletin of the Center for Children's Books* that the story will make a "cozy but not suffocating readaloud."

"While I'm writing my stories," Walsh added, "I begin to imagine what the characters who move through them look like, and I want to see them on paper. Drawing my characters helps establish their personalities and makes them and my stories come alive for me. It is unwise but often difficult to resist beginning to illustrate a story before it is finished, especially since the story is still undergoing change and a favorite illustration may no longer be appropriate when the story is finished. If you have ever tried to work around a well-turned sentence or paragraph in order to save it, even though it no longer fits in with what you are writing, then you can imagine how difficult it is to edit out a favorite illustration.

"It takes weeks of writing before a story will feel right to me, and after so much writing the story is invariably too long. I must always keep in mind what the real point of my story is as I cut and chop my favorite paragraphs and sentences. After weeks of work I hope to end up with a story that is no more than eight hundred words long and appears to have been written effortlessly.

"After my story is finished it will take me about nine months to complete the illustrations. The medium that I like best is colored inks which I apply with pen and brush after carefully drawing the design first in pencil. I will often use black-and-white photographs to establish the way a person stands or sits in my illustrations. Once the basic proportions of a figure are set down I put the photographs aside and work from nature and my imagination . . . . "

■ Works Cited

Bush, Elizabeth, review of *Pip's Magic*, *Bulletin of the Center for Children's Books*, September, 1994, pp. 27-28.

Review of *Hop Jump*, *Kirkus Reviews*, October 15, 1993, p. 1339.

Review of *Mouse Count*, *Publishers Weekly*, January 25, 1991, p. 56.

Review of *Pip's Magic*, *Kirkus Reviews*, September 15, 1994, p. 1285.

Radtke, Karen K., review of *Mouse Paint, School Library Journal,* June, 1989, p. 96.

Schon, Isabel, review of *Mouse Paint, Horn Book,* November-December, 1993, p. 769.

Seiner, Nancy, review of *Hop Jump, School Library Journal,* October, 1993, p. 113.

Stevenson, Deborah, review of *Samantha, Bulletin of the Center for Children's Books,* June, 1996, p. 355.

Watson, Elizabeth, review of *Mouse Count, Horn Book,* May-June, 1991, p. 325.

Weech, Eunice, review of *Samantha, School Library Journal,* May, 1996, p. 101.

■ For More Information See

PERIODICALS

Booklist, November 15, 1981, p. 444; November 1, 1993, p. 532; February 15, 1996, p. 1027.

Horn Book, July-August, 1989, p. 479; January, 1993, p. 104; November-December, 1993, p. 739; June, 1995, p. 56.

Junior Bookshelf, December, 1983, p. 238; December, 1985, p. 271; February, 1990, p. 19.

Kirkus Reviews, August 1, 1992, p. 995.

New York Times Book Review, January 26, 1992, p. 21.

Publishers Weekly, December 24, 1979, p. 59; August 3, 1992, p. 70; September 20, 1993, p. 70; August 22, 1994, p. 54.

School Library Journal, October, 1979, p. 146; February, 1982, p. 71; November, 1994, pp. 92-93.

*   *   *

WALTERS, Eric (Robert) 1957-

■ Personal

Born March 3, 1957, in Toronto, Ontario, Canada; son of Eric (a woodworker) and Christina (a homemaker) Walters; married Anita (a social worker), December 26, 1984; children: Christina, Nicholas, Julia. *Education:* York University, B.A., 1979, B.S.W., 1983, M.S.W., 1985; University of Toronto, B.Ed., 1989. *Politics:* Liberal. *Religion:* United Church of Canada. *Hobbies and other interests:* Playing and coaching basketball and soccer.

■ Addresses

Home—Mississauga, Ontario, Canada. *Electronic mail*—ewalters@interlog.com.

■ Career

Writer, 1991—. Affiliated with Children's Aid Society, Simcoe County, Ontario, 1979-81, Region of Peel, 1981-85; Strothers Treatment Centre, social worker, 1986-89; Emergency Department, Credit Valley Hospital, Mississauga, Ontario, crisis social worker, 1989—; Peel Region Board of Education, teacher, 1989—. *Member:* Canadian Society of Children's Authors, Illustrators, and Performers (CANSCAIP), Writers' Union, Ontario Public School Teachers' Federation.

■ Awards, Honors

Silver Birch Award, Ontario Library Association, 1997, Blue Heron Book Award, Blue Heron Books, 1997, and Children's Choice Award, Canadian Children's Book Centre, all for *STARS;* Children's Choice Award, Canadian Children's Book Centre, and Ruth Schwartz Award nomination, both for *Trapped in Ice.*

■ Writings

(With Norm Rippon) *Improve Your Child's Spelling 1,* Momentum Publishing, 1991.

(With Norm Rippon) *Improve Your Child's Spelling 2,* Momentum Publishing, 1993.

Stand Your Ground, Stoddart (Toronto, ON, Canada), 1994.

STARS, Stoddart, 1996.

Trapped in Ice, Viking, 1997.

Diamonds in the Rough, Stoddart, 1998.

War of the Eagles, Orca, 1998.

The Stranding, HarperCollins, 1998.

The Hydrofoil Mystery, Penguin, in press.

■ Work in Progress

Old McCurdy Had a Farm, a novel for young adults about two youths in Eastern Canada who join forces to save a barn full of circus animals; *Visions,* a novel for young adults set in the Canadian Arctic which features Inuit legends and stories woven into an eerie mystery.

ERIC WALTERS

■ Sidelights

Eric Walters's novels, which present the world through the eyes of young adults who are struggling to overcome obstacles, have been enthusiastically received. His first, *Stand Your Ground,* sold out instantly and is now in its third printing. Both *Stand Your Ground* and *STARS,* his second novel, won both the Silver Birch Award and the Blue Heron Book Award. The books nominated for both awards are selected by juries of young adults, a testament to Walters's success at writing stories with which his audience can identify.

It wasn't until 1991 that Walters, who had pursued a career as a social worker before becoming a teacher, decided to try his hand at writing books for children. As he read aloud novels to the young students in his classes and taught them the rudiments of writing, he became intrigued by the idea of writing books himself. After this, creative writing classes became a sharing process for Walters—and the students. They took turns reading one another's writing, and he expected the students to give his work the same critical appraisal that he gave theirs. In fact, it was his students' enthusiasm after hearing the first draft of *Stand Your Ground* that sparked him to send the completed work to a publisher. Though it was rejected by the first seven that he approached, he persisted until Stoddart Publishing finally accepted his manuscript.

"The underlying theme of many of my books is about a sense of belonging," Walters comments, "and about how you sometimes have to work to get to that place." Walters's protagonists are frequently gifted individuals whom life has dealt severe blows. He builds his stories around the challenges they experience when they are suddenly offered the opportunity they have always lacked. Will they recognize and accept it—or turn their backs?

In both *Stand Your Ground* and *STARS,* seizing the opportunity involves rejecting the thrill of living outside the law, and recognizing the potential of the ordinary. In *Stand Your Ground,* for example, it takes a while for Jonathan to realize that he prefers living with his old-fashioned Dutch grandparents to wheeling deals with his con-artist father. In *STARS,* Joseph, a city boy, spends much of his time planning his escape from a Northern Ontario camp for young offenders before he realizes how much he has come to love the wilderness. Though Walters's protagonists profess to love flouting the law, it soon becomes clear that they simply haven't had an opportunity to explore the more positive side of their characters and to enjoy a sense of belonging.

Walters identifies with street-smart but sensitive youths like Jonathan and Joseph because they remind him of children he grew up with. He was born in the same "ramshackle shack" where his father had been raised in west-end Toronto. His mother died when he was four, and he and his older sister ended up raising themselves. For much of his youth, he ran wild, playing in the stockyards that formed part of his neighborhood, run-

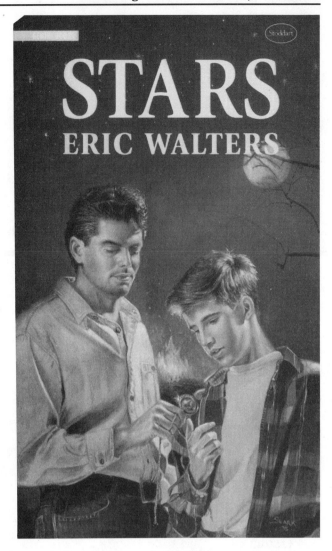

Joseph, in trouble with the law, vacillates when faced with the opportunity to better his life in Walters's novel for young adults. (Cover illustration by Albert Slark.)

ning through sewers, and fleeing the police. His world was populated by "smart people pushed in the wrong directions," and these are the people who provide the dramatic backdrop to his stories. When Joseph says in *STARS* that "the only criminals who get caught are stupid," he is echoing what Walters believed as a youth. Like his protagonists, however, Walters managed to escape this world, a cultural move he compares to immigrating to a new country: "You leave things behind and there's a sense of loss."

Walters's own experiences as a youth, combined with things he has seen in his career as a social worker, family therapist, and teacher, tell him that many good people caught in a dead end "don't get out alive." As a result, he finds that writing about characters who *do* manage to escape is a form of catharsis. He identifies so closely with his characters that he worries about them even after a book is finished. He notes, for instance, that he worries about Joseph because he grew very attached to this character while writing *STARS* and, when the book ends, a better future is not a sure thing. "I don't know if

Joseph will win," Walters says, "because in reality he probably wouldn't. But I pray he does."

Recalling what people said of him when he was a youth, Walters acknowledges, "A lot of my life has been dedicated to proving people wrong." Even now, this impulse remains strong. One of the rejection letters he received when he was sending *Stand Your Ground* to publishers was particularly nasty. Rather than burying it in a file or throwing it out, Walters placed it over his desk and uses it to keep himself motivated.

This motivation to prove people wrong also shines through in the characters Walters creates. They invariably succeed, despite the hurdles they face. The opportunity to spread the message that obstacles can be overcome is what attracts Walters to writing for young adults. "I prefer writing children's novels because they are like morality plays," he asserts. "There is much more right and wrong in them. In adult novels, it's almost as if you have to emphasize the bad or wrong, and I don't want the wrong people to win. I like happy endings."

The key to helping people like Joseph win, Walters believes, is benevolent authority figures who recognize potential and lend a helping hand. Gord, the social worker in *STARS,* says, "To make it in life, the most important thing is to have somebody, even just one person, believe in you." For Walters, it was his teachers who filled this role—like Mr. Roberts, the exacting math teacher in *Stand Your Ground.* "As a teacher, I try to remember how much influence you have to motivate, and move, and change students," he notes. Other role models in Walters's writing are Jonathan's energetic grandfather in *Stand Your Ground* and Gord, the firm but understanding social worker in *STARS,* who patiently show Jonathan and Joseph and other youths like them how to believe in themselves.

Like these role models, Walters devotes much of his own life to helping people. When he is not teaching or coaching his children's soccer teams, he works at a nearby hospital, counselling people whose lives have crumbled around them. "I've become a better writer, and I'm a good teacher, but my first love is social work," he maintains. "Gord in *STARS* is the person I try to be like, and the grandfather in *Stand Your Ground* is who I want to be one day."

■ For More Information See

PERIODICALS

Journal of Adolescent & Adult Literacy, October, 1996, p. 158.
Quill & Quire, February, 1995, p. 39; May, 1996, p. 35.

WATERTON, Betty (Marie) 1923-

■ Personal

Born August 31, 1923, in Oshawa, Ontario, Canada; daughter of Eric Williams Wrightmeyer and Mary Irene (Hewson) Wrightmeyer; married Claude Waterton (a Royal Canadian Air Force pilot), April 7, 1942; children: Eric, Julia, Karen Maxwell. *Education:* Attended Vancouver School of Art. *Religion:* Evangelical.

■ Addresses

Home—10135 Tsaykum Rd., R. R. 1, Sidney, British Columbia, Canada V8L 5T6.

■ Career

Writer. *Vancouver Sun,* Vancouver, British Columbia, retoucher, 1957; freelance caricaturist during the early 1960s; KVOS-TV, Vancouver, animator during the mid-1960s; adult education teacher of art, School District 63, Sidney, British Columbia, c. 1971. *Member:* CWILL (British Columbia).

■ Awards, Honors

Co-winner, Children's Literature Prize, Canada Council, and runner-up, Children's Book of the Year Award, Canadian Library Association, both 1978, and Amelia Frances Howard-Gibbon Award for illustration, 1979, all for *A Salmon for Simon,* illustrated by Ann Blades; finalist for Book of the Year for Children, Canadian Library Association, 1981, for *Pettranella.*

■ Writings

FOR CHILDREN

A Salmon for Simon, illustrated by Ann Blades, Douglas & McIntyre, 1978, Atheneum, 1978.
Pettranella, illustrated by Ann Blades, Vanguard Press (New York City), 1980.
Mustard, illustrated by Barbara Spurll, Scholastic-TAB Publications, 1983.
The Cat of Quinty, Thomas Nelson (Nashville, TN), 1984.
The White Moose, Ginn (Lexington, MA), 1984.
Orff, 27 Dragons (and a Snarkel!), illustrated by Karen Kulyk, Annick Press, 1984.
Quincy Rumpel, Douglas & McIntyre, 1984.
The Dog Who Stopped the War (adapted from the film *The Dog Who Stopped the War,* directed by Andre Melancon, Les Productions La Fete, 1984), Douglas & McIntyre, 1985.
Starring Quincy Rumpel, Douglas & McIntyre, 1986.
Quincy Rumpel, P.I., Douglas & McIntyre, 1988.
Baby Boat, illustrated by Joanne Fitzgerald, Knopf, 1989, published as *Plain Noodles,* Douglas & McIntyre, 1989.
Morris Rumpel and the Wings of Icarus, Groundwood/ Douglas & McIntyre, 1989.
Quincy Rumpel and the Sasquatch of Phantom Cove, Groundwood/Douglas & McIntyre, 1990.

BETTY WATERTON

Quincy Rumpel and the Woolly Chaps, Groundwood/
Douglas & McIntyre, 1992.
Quincy Rumpel and the Mystifying Experience, Ground-
wood/Douglas & McIntyre, 1994.
Quincy Rumpel and the All-Day Breakfast, Ground-
wood/Douglas & McIntyre, 1996.
The Lighthouse Dog, Orca, 1997.

Some of Waterton's works have been translated into
foreign languages, including French, Danish, Swedish,
German, and Norwegian. Some have also been published in Braille and large print editions.

■ **Work in Progress**

Quincy Rumpel and the Tower of London, Groundwood/
Douglas & McIntyre.

■ **Adaptations**

A Salmon for Simon was issued as a filmstrip by Weston
Woods, 1980, and as a sound recording by Library
Services Branch (Vancouver), 1991.

■ **Sidelights**

Canadian children's writer Betty Waterton is the author
of numerous lively and insightful picture books and
chapter books. She received several awards for her first

published work, the 1978 picture book *A Salmon for
Simon.* This simple story involves Simon, a Canadian-
Indian boy who has been trying unsuccessfully to catch a
salmon at the beach. Finally he gives up and digs a hole
for clams instead. When an eagle in flight accidentally
drops a live salmon into his hole, Simon finds the
silvery fish so beautiful that he decides to dig a channel
so it can swim back to sea.

Barbara Elleman commented in *Booklist* that Simon's
"recognition of nature in its own element" and his
resulting decision "are perceptively and warmly told in
spite of the contrived appearance of the fish." A
Publishers Weekly writer noted, "Waterton makes readers feel very close to her little hero." A *Bulletin of the
Center for Children's Books* reviewer commented that
"the story is static in tone" and "the writing style a bit
stiff." Overall, however, the critic appreciated the boy's
response to the salmon.

In a completely different vein, Waterton's next work
was *Pettranella,* a picture book based on historical fact.
Pettranella and her family are nineteenth-century European immigrants whose long voyage by ship is followed
by another journey, this time in an oxcart. The young
child is sad to have left her grandmother behind, but
looks forward to planting a garden with the bag of seeds
her grandmother gave her as a farewell gift. When she
loses the seeds, Pettranella fears she has lost her

connection to the past. Later, she is surprised to learn that the seeds have taken root and produced a garden where she dropped them along the homesteaders' trail.

A *Publishers Weekly* contributor felt that the "warm, simply-told story" is, like *A Salmon for Simon*, worthy of honors. According to a reviewer for *Quill & Quire*, "Waterton's prose is relaxed and direct, and the story is touching in its simplicity." *Booklist* critic Barbara Elleman noted the story's "old-fashioned warm flavor that provides, for young readers, an evocation of the westward movement."

Other Waterton titles published in the 1980s include *Mustard,* which concerns a big, clumsy yellow dog who performs a daring rescue; *Orff, 27 Dragons (and a Snarkel!),* a story about a dragon who doesn't fit in; and *Baby Boat* (also published as *Plain Noodles*), in which a lonely woman is happily surprised when a boatload of babies appears on the shore of her island home.

Beginning in 1984, Waterton published a series of chapter books for pre-teens about the unusual Rumpel family, who experience wacky mishaps as they move from one adventure to the next. The stories revolve around Quincy, an energetic girl with a knack for getting into trouble. In the series debut, *Quincy Rumpel,* the family endure a series of minor crises as they prepare to move. *Starring Quincy Rumpel* focuses on Mr. Rumpel's new job. Having failed at growing mushrooms in the garage, he has gone into business selling Rumpel Re-

Waterton's award-winning tale portrays a young boy whose elation over the salmon he has found is weighed against his desire to spare its life. (From *A Salmon for Simon,* written by Waterton and illustrated by Ann Blades.)

bounders. Yet another venture almost fails in *Quincy Rumpel and the Sasquatch of Phantom Cove,* in which the family purchases a vacation resort that turns out to be a dump. *Quincy Rumpel and the Mystifying Experience* is a mystery in which the entire Rumpel clan search Ontario for their ninety-one-year-old great-grandmother. The shrewd Quincy plays detective and finds Great-Grandma at Niagara Falls.

Reviewers praised the series for its humorous dialogue and realistic portrayal of childhood. In her assessment of *Quincy Rumpel, Canadian Children's Literature* contributor Frances Fraser remarked that "Waterton is ... good at defining and conveying small shivers in universal experience that are seldom recorded in children's fiction." However, Fraser also commented that "Waterton's frequently awkward narrative style, a contrast to her assured dialogue, prevents the reader from becoming immersed in the fiction."

In her *Quill & Quire* review of *Quincy Rumpel and the Mystifying Experience,* Kit Pearson commented that "the author has perfected her spare style, with its swift pacing and delicate characterization; her writing appears artless." *Canadian Children's Literature* critic Brenda M. Schmidt noted of *Starring Quincy Rumpel* that "one of the book's strengths—its appeal to today's ten-to-twelve-year-olds—may also be its weakness. It is so contemporary and trendy ... it may not survive

Mustard the dog is so accident prone, he's considered a menace until his swimming skills make him indispensable. (From *Mustard,* written by Waterton and illustrated by Barbara Spurll.)

beyond this generation of children." However, Schmidt added that Quincy's "return ... will delight her followers and increase her popularity."

Waterton commented: "All my books are juvenile fiction, and though I once thought I would illustrate one of them, this hasn't happened yet. *A Salmon for Simon, Pettranella, Mustard,* and *Plain Noodles* have been translated into foreign languages."

■ Works Cited

Elleman, Barbara, review of *A Salmon for Simon, Booklist,* May 1, 1980, p. 1300.

Elleman, Barbara, review of *Pettranella, Booklist,* April 1, 1981, p. 1109.

Fraser, Frances, review of *Quincy Rumpel, Canadian Children's Literature,* Number 42, 1986, pp. 95-96.

Pearson, Kit, review of *Quincy Rumpel and the Mystifying Experience, Quill & Quire,* April, 1994, p. 40.

Review of *Pettranella, Publishers Weekly,* February 27, 1981, p. 149.

Review of *Pettranella, Quill & Quire,* June, 1981.

Review of *A Salmon for Simon, Bulletin of the Center for Children's Books,* July-August, 1980, p. 225.

Review of *A Salmon for Simon, Publishers Weekly,* May 23, 1980, p. 76.

Schmidt, Brenda M., review of *Starring Quincy Rumpel, Canadian Children's Literature,* Number 46, 1987, pp. 81-82.

■ For More Information See

PERIODICALS

Canadian Author, Volume 71, number 4, 1996.

Canadian Children's Literature, Number 30, 1984, pp. 69-71; Numbers 39/40, 1985, pp. 158-63; Number 5, 1990, pp. 83-85; Number 76, 1994, pp. 66-69.

Canadian Materials, March, 1989, p. 69; September, 1994, pp. 125-26.

Quill & Quire, August, 1983; November, 1984, p. 12; December, 1989.

School Library Journal, August, 1981, p. 72.

*   *   *

WEGEN, Ronald 1946-1985

■ Personal

Born September 22, 1946, in New Jersey; died in 1985. *Education:* Pratt Institute, B.F.A., 1968. *Hobbies and other interests:* Reading ancient history, cooking, opera, ballet, museums, farming.

■ Career

Author and illustrator of children's books. Worked in interior design for an architectural firm and as a jewelry and fabric designer for companies including Givenchy and Anne Klein; worked as a sculptor; exhibited artwork including paintings, drawings, and collage in Bogota, Columbia.

■ Awards, Honors

American Library Association Honor book citation, for *Where Can the Animals Go?;* New Jersey Authors Award, for *The Halloween Costume Party.*

■ Writings

Sand Castle, Greenwillow, 1977.
Where Can the Animals Go?, Greenwillow, 1978.
Balloon Trip, Clarion, 1981.
Sky Dragon, Greenwillow, 1982.
Billy Gorilla, Lothrop, Lee & Shepard, 1983.
The Halloween Costume Party, Clarion, 1983.
What's Wrong, Ralph?, Lothrop, Lee & Shepard, 1984.
The Gingerbread Boy, illustrated by David Allender, Crown (New York City), 1990.

ILLUSTRATOR

Bach, Richard, *There's No Such Place as Far Away,* Delacorte Press, 1979.

■ Sidelights

Children's author Ronald Wegen described his own childhood as "great" and explained how his parents, who owned a bakery, always encouraged him to become an artist. After graduating from New York City's Pratt Institute, Wegen worked as an interior architect, jewelry designer, fabric designer, and sculptor. His work took him around the world; he lived in New York, London, Rome, Amsterdam, Rio de Janeiro and Bogota, Columbia, and traveled to Germany, Spain, Morocco, and the Caribbean. Wegen maintained that this nomadic lifestyle prevented him from marrying or having children of his own. However, his five nieces and nephews afforded him companionship and provided inspiration for his books.

Prior to his death in 1985, Wegen wrote eight children's books and created the illustrations for another. His artwork distinguished his books, which were often wordless or of sparse text. Wegen garnered his most favorable reception for *Balloon Trip* and *Sky Dragon.* The first book, which pictures a balloon voyage taken by a father and his two children, was described by a *Kirkus Reviews* contributor as "quite glorious," and by a *Publishers Weekly* critic as "an adventure exciting to share in boldly colored pictures displaying a remarkable talent for perspective." *Sky Dragon* features illustrations that show young readers how clouds can be seen as objects. *Booklist* reviewer Ilene Cooper asserted that Wegen "twirls the clouds into shapes that are wispy yet imaginative renderings." Wegen's vivid imagination has also elicited comments such as "wacky," "surreal," and "spacey" in reviews of his works. One such story is *The Halloween Costume Party,* in which the central character is a little girl who goes to a party that—as she discovers at the end—is otherwise solely attended by little green beings from another planet. *School Library Journal* contributor Craighton Hippenhammer said children would enjoy the "engaging, boldly colorful" Halloween story.

A more serious theme is explored in *Where Can the Animals Go?* Wegen warned of the impending extinction of African animals due to lax poaching laws and man's disregard for the environment. The sober theme is exemplified by stark images and spare text. "The unconventional perspectives and odd-angled views work to demonstrate the beauty of the creatures and reiterate their value, while the ominous tones of text and illustrations evoke the realization that the solution is not a simple one," stated *School Library Journal* critic Michele Woggon.

■ Works Cited

Review of *Balloon Trip, Kirkus Reviews,* December 1, 1981, p. 1464.
Review of *Balloon Trip, Publishers Weekly,* September 15, 1981, pp. 154-55.
Cooper, Ilene, review of *Sky Dragon, Booklist,* November 1, 1982, p. 374.
Hippenhammer, Craighton, review of *The Halloween Party, School Library Journal,* January, 1984, p. 69.
Woggon, Michele, review of *Where Can the Animals Go?, School Library Journal,* September, 1978, p. 127.

■ For More Information See

PERIODICALS

Bulletin of the Center for Children's Books, February, 1983, p. 120; October, 1983, p. 38.
Kirkus Reviews, March 15, 1977, p. 282; June 1, 1978, p. 593; March 1, 1983, p. 243; September 1, 1983, p. J-156.
Publishers Weekly, August 26, 1983, p. 386.
School Library Journal, December, 1981, p. 58; August, 1982, p. 103; October, 1982, p. 144; August, 1983, p. 59; October, 1984, p. 153.*

* * *

WEIR, Joan S(herman) 1928-

■ Personal

Born April 21, 1928, in Calgary, Alberta, Canada; daughter of Louis Ralph (an archbishop) and Carolyn (a musician; maiden name, Gillmor) Sherman; married Ormond Weir (a surgeon), May 14, 1955; children: Ian, Paul, Michael, Richard. *Education:* University of Manitoba, B.A., 1948. *Religion:* Anglican. *Hobbies and other interests:* Dogs, jogging, "keeping up with my four grown sons."

■ Addresses

Home—463 Greenstone Dr., Kamloops, British Columbia, Canada V2C 1N8.

■ Career

Writer and educator. T. Eaton Co. (retail chain), Winnipeg, Manitoba, director of radio programming for children, author and producer of weekly fantasy programs, 1948-55, assistant fashion coordinator, 1955-56; freelance writer, 1956-73; CFJC-TV, Kamloops, British Columbia, author, host, and producer of "Story Corner," a weekly half-hour series for children, 1973-77; University College of the Cariboo, Kamloops, lecturer in English and creative writing, 1978—. Conducts weekend workshops in creative writing throughout British Columbia, Alberta, and Manitoba; gives readings to schools and adult groups in Canadian cities, including Surrey, Vancouver, Winnipeg, and Kamloops. President of Kamloops Music Festival, 1968-70; member of Western Canada Theatre Co. board of directors, 1975-80. *Member:* Canadian Authors Association, Canadian Society of Children's Authors, Illustrators, and Performers, Writers' Union of Canada, British Columbia Federation of Writers.

■ Writings

FICTION; FOR YOUNG PEOPLE

Three-Day Challenge (novel), Scholastic/TAB (New York City), 1976.
Exile at the Rocking Seven (young adult novel), Macmillan (New York City), 1977, Macmillan (Toronto), 1977.
Career Girl (novel), Tree Frog Press (Edmonton, Alberta, British Columbia), 1979.
So I'm Different (novel), Douglas & McIntyre (Vancouver, British Columbia), 1981.
The Secret at Westwind (mystery), Scholastic/TAB (Richmond Hill, Ontario), 1981.

JOAN S. WEIR

Ski Lodge Mystery and Other Stories, Overlea House (Markham, Ontario), 1988, second edition, 1990.
Storm Rider (young adult novel), Scholastic/TAB, 1988.
Balloon Race Mystery and Other Stories, Overlea House, 1988.
Sixteen Is Spelled O-U-C-H (young adult novel), Stoddart, 1988, second edition, 1991, third edition, 1995.
Mystery at Lighthouse Rock (novel), Overlea House, 1989, published as *Mystery at the Lighthouse,* General Distribution Services, 1991.
Say Yes (young adult novel; "Northwood" series), Grecy de Pencier (Toronto), 1991.
Secret Ballot (young adult novel), Grecy de Pencier, 1991.
The Witcher (mystery), Polestar, 1998.
Brideship (young adult historical novel), Stoddart, 1998.

STAGE PLAYS FOR YOUNG PEOPLE

The Ladder of Golden Arrows (one-act), first produced in British Columbia, 1976.
Guardian Spirits (one-act), first produced in British Columbia, 1977.
Winnie-the-Pooh Stories (one-act; adapted from A. A. Milne's book *Winnie-the-Pooh*), first produced in Kamloops, British Columbia, at the Sagebrush Theatre, 1977.

Also author of *Christmas Fantasies* (five short plays), first broadcast by Canadian Broadcasting Corp. (CBC), 1948.

NONFICTION

(Compiler, as Joan Sherman Weir) *Sherman: Reflections, with Recollections by Those Who Knew Him Best* (biography), Anglican Book Centre (Toronto), 1976.
The Caledonians (history), Peerless Press (New Orleans, LA), 1977.
Walhachin: Catastrophe or Camelot (history), Hancock House (Blaine, WA), 1984, Hancock House (Surrey, British Columbia), 1984, second edition, 1995.
Canada's Gold Rush Church (history), Anglican Church, 1986.
Back Door to the Klondike (history), Boston Mills Press (Erin Mills, Ontario), 1988.
Catalysts & Watchdogs: B.C.'s Men of God (history), Sono Nis Press (Victoria, British Columbia), 1995.

OTHER

Contributor to *Canadian Children's Annual 1988* (anthology), to *Winds Through Time* (young adult anthology of historical fiction), and to numerous periodicals, including *Discovery, Friend, Trials,* and *Kamloops Sentinel.* Several of Weir's books have been published in Braille, and have been translated into foreign languages, including Swedish, Norwegian, Finnish, and German.

■ Adaptations

Career Girl was made into a sound recording by Alberta Education in 1986; *Sixteen Is Spelled O-U-C-H* was made into sound recordings by Winnipeg, Manitoba Education and Training in 1989 and by the Vancouver, British Columbia Library Services Branch in 1992.

■ Sidelights

Joan S. Weir is a Canadian author of fiction, nonfiction, and short stories for middle graders and young adults; a writer of informational books for adults; and a children's playwright for the stage and radio. In addition, she has been a university instructor of English and creative writing as well as a lecturer to children and adults. As a writer of books for young people, Weir has written realistic fiction and mysteries, several of which are set in and around her home of British Columbia. As a writer for adults, Weir addresses events in Canadian history such as the Canadian Gold Rush as well as topics related specifically to British Columbia, such as the contributions made by men in religious orders to the development of the province.

Born in Calgary, Alberta, Weir is the daughter of L. Ralph Sherman, a noted Anglican archbishop whose meditations she collected in a tribute volume published in 1976. After receiving her bachelor's degree from the University of Manitoba, Weir worked as the director of

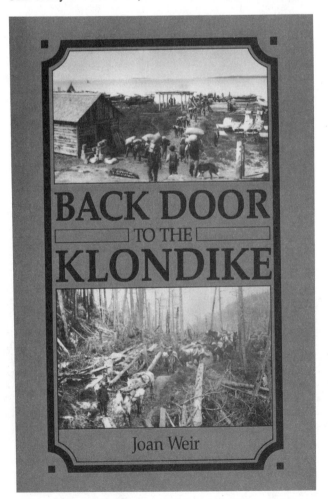

Weir's nonfiction title documents the Canadian route to the Klondike undertaken by an Irish nobleman in the late nineteenth century.

radio programming for Eaton department stores in Winnipeg; for seven years, she wrote, produced, and hosted weekly fantasy programs for children promoted by the store. After moving to British Columbia, she became the writer, producer, and host of "Story Corner," a television program for a station in Kamloops, British Columbia, with which she was associated for four years. In 1976, Weir began producing one-act plays, both original works and adaptations; in 1977, her version of A. A. Milne's *Winnie-the-Pooh* was produced in Kamloops. In 1978, Weir became a lecturer in English and creative writing at University College of the Cariboo in Kamloops. She has also traveled across Canada conducting writing workshops and giving readings to schools and adult groups.

With her background in the performing arts, it seemed natural for Weir to write about them for children. In *Career Girl,* a story for middle graders, the author focuses on Patti Maxwell, an ambitious young ballerina who is trying to secure a position with a prestigious Canadian ballet company. Patti becomes so involved with dancing that she ignores her family and friends; when she forgets to return a phone call to Sharon Boles, a friend with polio, she helps to cause Sharon's severe fall. Realizing that she has become too self-absorbed, Patti chooses to help Sharon at the hospital rather than rehearse. At the end of the story, Sharon is able to come to Patti's audition for the ballet company; although she is not chosen as a dancer, Patti is pleased that her efforts have contributed to Sharon's progress. *In Review* critic Judith McLean noted, "The author is obviously familiar with her subject" and praised Weir's descriptions of "the intense dedication required by traditional ballet training" as well as the "excellent glossary of terms" included in the book. However, McLean concluded, "characterization is ignored." Writing in *School Library Journal,* Shaaron Girty commented that the story line of *Career Girl* is "loose and the beginning and the glossary of ballet terms too technical, but the relationship between ballet student and handicapped friend is noteworthy."

In her next book, *So I'm Different,* Weir features Nicky, a young Native boy who has moved to a new neighborhood and a new school. Nicky is grieving over the death of his dog, who was run over when Nicky had to leave him behind, and is experiencing difficulties at home and in the classroom. At the end of the novel, Nicky's wise grandfather and a student teacher help the boy to adjust to his new situation.

In *The Secret at Westwind,* Weir combines the genres of mystery story, horse story, and problem novel in a book directed to readers in the upper elementary grades that also includes elements of Canadian art history. Fourteen-year-old Sandy Middleton, a girl who comes from Toronto to Langely, British Columbia, to spend the summer with her uncle and cousin, is coping with the loss of her grandmother, whom she used to avoid making friends her own age. Sandy is drawn into a mystery surrounding the disappearance of three paintings by noted Canadian artists Group of Seven. Through

Each chapter of Weir's book poses a mystery that draws upon the reader's knowledge of science or social studies to arrive at a solution. (Cover illustration by Janet Wilson.)

her relationship with the owner of the pieces, curmudgeonly Miss Rachel, Sandy is able to reach out to her cousin Jody, who is dealing with her mother's abandonment of the family.

Writing in *Canadian Children's Literature,* Laurence Steven claimed that *The Secret at Westwind* "has too many aspirations" that lead "to a lack of distinctive character for the book." Steven concluded that "the range of Weir's interests proves to be anathema to anything solid. Potential is there, but remains potential." *In Review* critic Barbara Hutcheson proposed that the novel resembles "the mythical side-hill gouger: its mystery leg is longer and better developed than its psychological leg. The suspense held up well although the solution to the mystery required two readings and I'm still not sure I understand all the details." Noting that the characters are "too thinly drawn for us to care ... about their emotional development," Hutcheson concluded that it is "a treat to see a girl taking the lead in solving a mystery, even if she needs the help of a horse and a parrot to do so," deeming the work "standard ... fare" for preteens. However, *Quill & Quire*'s Joan McGrath, reviewing the paperback edition of the book, called the novel, "which," she said, "combines art, horses, and teen-family problems into a potpourri calculated to intrigue readers about ages 10-14," a favorite mystery story.

With *Ski Lodge Mystery and Other Stories,* Weir premiered her popular series of tales featuring the members of the Canville Elementary School Mystery Club. In *Ski Lodge Mystery,* the author describes the creation of the club by Mike and Tony, a pair of fifth graders who recruit ten members. The volume contains eleven chapters that include a mystery either posed to or by the members of the club that are presented to young readers to solve. The mysteries, which feature a variety of Canadian settings, often include solutions that draw upon the audience's knowledge of science or social studies; Weir includes the detailed answers to her mysteries at the back of the book. In his review of *Ski Lodge Mystery* in *Canadian Materials,* Dave Jenkinson said that readers "who have enjoyed the Encyclopedia Brown books ... should appreciate [these] mysteries.... The book will find a ready audience in the upper elementary grades...." Critic Gisela Sherman concurred: "Fans of Encyclopedia Brown and other solve-your-own mysteries will enjoy [this book]," she wrote in *Canadian Children's Literature.*

In the next volume of the series, *Balloon Race Mystery and Other Stories,* Weir again features the Canville Mystery Club. In this book, the fifth graders try and stump other students at the school and end up involving moms and dads on Parents Night. Writing in *Canadian Materials,* Elizabeth Woodger predicted that the book "should appeal to youngsters who like mysteries in which they choose their own ending as well as to adults who buy educational toys for their children." Woodger noted that the most attractive feature of *Balloon Race Mystery* is that "solutions are not merely catchy but depend on good reasoning skills and the ability to detect a story carefully and detect fallacies." In *Mystery at Lighthouse Rock,* a book also published as *Mystery at the Lighthouse,* Weir joins several Mystery Club puzzles with the story of two school friends. Writing in *Quill & Quire,* Jane Cobb said that although the main plot is "weak, the dialogue is realistic, the mysteries are interesting, and the book has been designed in a way that invites reader participation.... A bonus for serious mystery buffs!"

In addition to her works for middle graders and junior high school students, Weir is also the author of works directed to older teenagers. For example, in *Sixteen Is Spelled O-U-C-H,* Weir outlines how Tim, a teenager who tries to adjust to life on a ranch, learns about the values of hard work, racial tolerance, and honesty as well as the pleasures of strong community life. While assisting on the ranch, Tim learns to examine his own actions and motivations; after much self-examination, he admits his responsibility for an accident involving the ranch's prize horse. "What makes this chivalric

Tim spends a difficult but fulfilling summer working on a ranch in British Columbia. (Cover illustration by Janet Wilson.)

rebuilding of character so disconcerting," wrote Marnie Parsons of *Canadian Children's Literature,* "is its objectification of Hilary," the sixteen-year-old daughter of the ranch owners and Tim's love interest. The critic noted that Hilary responds to Tim's "movement toward maturity, and she is merely its sexual monitor. Sex is the reward for virtue here, and Tim and the novel are the less for it." Weir is also the creator of *Say Yes,* a novelization of the popular "Northwood" television series on CBC. A program that targets adolescents as its core audience and explores issues relevant to them, "Northwood" features teenagers Jason Williams and Maria Giovanni. *Say Yes* outlines the couple's early relationship and describes Jason's attempts to make the hockey team and win Maria. Reviewing the novel for *Quill and Quire,* Ken Setterington concluded that it "suffers from very sketchy characters and subplots that are not resolved in the book—problems that may result from creating a book based on characters and stories from a television series." Writing in *Canadian Materials,* Anne Louise Mahoney called *Say Yes* "simply a quick read ... with very little substance." However, Mahoney concluded, there is a place for books of this type: "they may appeal to nonreaders as well as to fans of the series and to teens looking for a brief escape into other people's lives."

Weir once commented: "Talent, of course, is absolutely essential, but the successful writer needs other things too—one of them is a driving sense of self-motivation. Another is the ability to step over disappointment and start again.

"Aspiring writers seem to ask the same standard questions. The first is, 'What is it like to be a writer?' To this my answer is simple: 'It is exciting; it is demanding; it is often lonely; it is even more often frustrating; but it is the greatest craft in the world.' The second question, which invariably follows, is 'Where do you get your ideas?' I am often tempted to reply, 'At dollar-forty-nine-day,' but I curb the urge and answer instead that having more ideas than time to write about them is one sure proof that a person is indeed a 'writer.' And that leads to the third question, namely, 'How can I tell if my work is any good?' To this query I can reply with conviction and assurance. If your characters come to life as the story is unfolding and start to take the plot twists into their own hands, arguing back at you when you try to force them into a set mold or pattern, then you can be pretty sure that your story is going to be 'good.' It may still require seventeen rewrites, but there is life in it, and that is the vital ingredient."

■ Works Cited

Cobb, Jane, review of *Mystery at Lighthouse Rock, Quill & Quire,* March, 1992, p. 67.

Girty, Shaaron, review of *Career Girl, School Library Journal,* January, 1981, p. 66.

Hutcheson, Barbara, review of *The Secret at Westwind, In Review,* February, 1982, pp. 53-54.

Jenkinson, Dave, review of *Ski Lodge Mystery and Other Stories, Canadian Materials,* November, 1988, p. 219.

Mahoney, Anne Louise, review of *Say Yes, Canadian Materials,* March, 1992, p. 93.

McGrath, Joan, review of *The Secret at Westwind, Quill & Quire,* February, 1992, p. 16.

McLean, Judith, review of *Career Girl, In Review,* December, 1980, p. 58.

Parsons, Marnie, "Of Post Holes and Fences," *Canadian Children's Literature,* Number 61, 1991, pp. 87-88.

Setterington, Ken, review of *Say Yes, Quill & Quire,* November, 1991, p. 27.

Sherman, Gisela, "Welcome Adventures and Mysteries," *Canadian Children's Literature,* Number 53, 1989, p. 71.

Steven, Laurence, "Getting into Focus," *Canadian Children's Literature,* Number 41, 1986, pp. 76-77.

Woodger, Elizabeth, review of *Balloon Race Mystery and Other Stories, Canadian Materials,* March, 1989, p. 75.

■ For More Information See

PERIODICALS

Books for Young People, February, 1989, p. 8; October, 1987, p. 16.
Books in Canada, Summer, 1992, p. 38.
Canadian Materials, July, 1989, p. 182.
Emergency Librarian, May, 1982, p. 30.
In Review, October, 1981, pp. 57-58.
Maclean's, December 21, 1981, p. 44.

—*Sketch by Gerard J. Senick*

*   *   *

WELLINGTON, Monica 1957-

■ Personal

Born June 17, 1957, in London, England; daughter of Roger (a business executive) and Diana (Guerin) Wellington; children: Lydia. *Education:* University of Michigan, B.F.A., 1978; additional study at School of Visual Arts, New York, 1986. *Hobbies and other interests:* Travel, ballet, sewing, quilting.

■ Addresses

Home—905 West End Ave., New York, NY 10025.

■ Career

Artist; freelance writer and illustrator of children's books, 1987—. Teacher at School of Visual Arts, New York City, 1994—. Formerly worked in antique galleries and at the Victoria and Albert Museum, London, England.

MONICA WELLINGTON

■ Writings

SELF-ILLUSTRATED

Molly Chelsea and Her Calico Cat, Dutton, 1988.
All My Little Ducklings, Dutton, 1989.
Seasons of Swans, Dutton, 1990.
The Sheep Follow, Dutton, 1992.
Mr. Cookie Baker, Dutton, 1992.
Night Rabbits, Dutton, 1995.
Baby in a Buggy, Dutton, 1995.
Baby in a Car, Dutton, 1995.
Baby at Home, Dutton, 1997.
Baby Goes Shopping, Dutton, 1997.
Night House, Bright House, Dutton, 1997.
Night City, Dutton, 1998.

ILLUSTRATOR

Alhambra G. Deming, *Who Is Tapping at My Window?,* Dutton, 1988.
Virginia Griest, *In Between,* Dutton, 1989.
Arnold Shapiro, *Who Says That?,* Dutton, 1991.
Debra Leventhal, *What Is Your Language?,* Dutton, 1994.

■ Work in Progress

Bunny's Rainbow Day.

■ Sidelights

The work of author and illustrator Monica Wellington is heavily influenced by memories of her childhood. Born in London, England, she had lived in England, Germany and Switzerland before reaching the age of seven. As Wellington once told *Something about the Author* (*SATA*), "I think my early childhood has a big influence on my books. In Switzerland we lived close to a small town. We were surrounded by mountains, woods, lakes, orchards, fields, and farms. Again in my books, I find myself doing pictures of these kinds of places." In fact, the natural world plays a prominent role in each of Wellington's picture books for young children, which include *Night Rabbits, Seasons of Swans,* and *The Sheep Follow.*

Wellington fell in love with art early. "I always loved to draw as a child. I recently found some of the first pictures I did when we were living in Europe and they are not that different from what I am doing now! I still like to do pictures full of color, of the same things!" Despite her creative streak, however, Wellington did not decide to become a children's book illustrator until she was in her late twenties.

In the meantime, she and her family relocated to the United States—they still continued to travel, and Wellington lived in four states while going to junior high and high school. After high school graduation, she enrolled at the University of Michigan's School of Art, where she studied pottery, painting, and printmaking. After college, she moved back to England for several years, studying the decorative arts and working in a London antique gallery specializing in English porcelain as well

as in the ceramics department of the Victoria and Albert Museum. Despite her interest in the decorative arts, Wellington eventually realized that she needed to do something more creative. A move to New York City in 1981 marked her change to a career as a freelance artist.

"For about three years I worked in a pottery studio," Wellington recalled of her first years in New York City. "Then gradually I started to do more painting projects. The more pictures I did, because of the style and images that were developing, the more I thought of doing children's books. I kind of wandered into the field and then was struck by how much I absolutely loved doing this. I had finally found the perfect outlet for my creative energy."

In 1986 Wellington studied under noted illustrator Bruce Degen at the School of Visual Arts, which prompted her to bring her portfolio to publishers. One of the pictures in Wellington's portfolio—a proposed illustration for a poem by writer Alhambra G. Deming—had been a class assignment. That picture eventually was expanded into Wellington's first picture book, Deming's *Who Is Tapping at My Window?,* which a *Publishers Weekly* reviewer deemed the work of "a seasoned illustrator rather than a first-time artist."

Who Is Tapping at My Window was quickly followed by several more books, including *All My Little Ducklings,* which Wellington both wrote and illustrated. Tracing the typical day of an average duckling, Wellington's pictures show the little creatures engaged in such pursuits as visiting nearby farmyard animals, floating on the pond, and nosing around the local beehive, all accompanied by a simple text filled with words that elicit the sounds of the ducks' activities: "Scurry Hurry Plunk / Flipping Dipping Splatter Splash / Paddle in the Pond." The idea for *All My Little Ducklings* came from a German song that Wellington recalled from her childhood: "Alle Meine Entchen." "'All my little ducklings, swimming in the sea, heads are in the water, tails are to the sun,'—I took this image as a starting point and it grew into a book about a day in the life of this family of ducks," the author/illustrator explained. Ellen Fader of *Horn Book* praised the "graceful story," noting that Wellington's illustrations "are bright and clear, pruned of unnecessary detail," while Ilene Cooper described the ducklings as "winsome" in her review for *Booklist,* predicting that the author's choice of words "will help instill a love of language in young ears."

Seasons of Swans also features feathered protagonists; Wellington's story of the cycle of nature revolves around a family of swans as they nest, lay eggs, and hatch their young, called cygnets. By autumn, the young swans have learned to swim and fish, and are ready to leave their parents' nest and make their own home before winter falls. *School Library Journal* contributor Danita Nichols praised the book's colorful but "uncluttered" illustrations, as well as Wellington's "spare and precise prose," which Nichols deemed a match for the straightforward drawings.

As ten mice are chased by a cat, objects in the house come to life and offer rhyming comments. (From *Night House, Bright House*, written and illustrated by Wellington.)

In *The Sheep Follow,* youngsters witness what happens when a flock of sheep are left to their own devices while their shepherd takes a nap. Following first a butterfly, then a cat, pigs, rabbits, and a succession of other animals, the silly sheep eventually arrive back at the pasture in which the young shepherd is finally awakening. "The stylized graphic art and simple narration insure the book's success with the toddler set," maintained Nancy Seiner in *School Library Journal.* Deborah Abbott of *Booklist* commented on the "sprightly outdoor scenes" and "buoyant simplicity" of the book, concluding, "Be prepared to read this again and again." Traveling animals are also a feature of *Night Rabbits,* as frisky white bunnies come out to play when the sun sets and the countryside is quiet. While they have to watch for predators—an owl and fox are also out and about in the rabbit's vicinity—the pair find much to do and eat before returning to their cozy burrow for another nap until dusk. *Booklist* reviewer Lauren Peterson praised Wellington's simple, unadorned prose, calling it "rich" and "poetic" and hailing the inclusion of "sensory images, onomatopoeia, and rhyme." "Totally charming and uncynical," observed a *Kirkus Reviews* critic, adding, "Wellington's simplicity is a stand-out."

The world of the night is also the backdrop for *Night House, Bright House* and *Night City.* In the former, a group of ten mice hunting for something to nibble on meets up with the family tabby cat. Their chase is watched by household objects, which come to life at night and offer helpful, rhyming commentary. "Some of the rhymes are wildly funny to read aloud," noted a *Kirkus Reviews* critic, who maintained that many would be adopted by young listeners for use in their own homes. "The art," added a *Publishers Weekly* reviewer, "is inventive and diverting," while adults have the further pleasure of recognizing "playful knockoffs of well-known paintings." *Night City* highlights the bustle of activity occurring late at night in a large city while a little girl sleeps soundly at home. "The text imparts plenty of information, offering windows on new worlds for children," noted a *Kirkus Reviews* critic, who commented favorably on Wellington's "congenially depicted scenes."

In addition to picture books, Wellington has also created a series of board books for toddlers, including *Baby in a Buggy, Baby at Home,* and *Baby Goes Shopping,* that feature brightly colored, graphic illustrations which reviewers have compared to fellow author-illustrator Eric Carle's work. A *Publishers Weekly* critic lauded Wellington's illustrations as "pack[ing] a punch," while Darla Remple in *School Library Journal* noted how the simple shapes are "positioned jauntily" against colorful backgrounds in these "appealing" books for youngsters under two.

Wellington has served as author and illustrator for more than half of the books on which her name appears; on the remainder she has provided illustrations only. "My own books usually start with an idea of what I want to paint pictures about," she explained to *SATA.* "The pictures come before the words for me. I am usually still working on the words after I finish the pictures. My books so far are all picture books for very young children—perhaps because that was such a wonderful and idyllic time in my own childhood."

■ Works Cited

Abbott, Deborah, review of *The Sheep Follow, Booklist,* February 1, 1992, p. 1042.

Review of *Baby in a Buggy, Publishers Weekly,* July 3, 1995, p. 59.

Cooper, Ilene, review of *All My Little Ducklings, Booklist,* April 15, 1989, p. 1473.

Fader, Ellen, review of *All My Little Ducklings, Horn Book,* May, 1989, pp. 366-67.

Nichols, Danita, review of *Seasons of Swans, School Library Journal,* October 1990, p. 104.

Review of *Night City, Kirkus Reviews,* May 1, 1998, p. 666.

Review of *Night House, Bright House, Kirkus Reviews,* November 15, 1996, p. 1677.

Review of *Night House, Bright House, Publishers Weekly,* December 16, 1996, p. 58.

Review of *Night Rabbits, Kirkus Reviews,* February 15, 1995, p. 234.

Review of *Night Rabbits, Publishers Weekly,* February 13, 1995, p. 77.

Peterson, Lauren, review of *Night Rabbits, Booklist,* April 15, 1995, p. 8.

Remple, Darla, review of *Baby at Home, School Library Journal,* June, 1997, p. 102.

Seiner, Nancy, review of *The Sheep Follow, School Library Journal,* March, 1992, p. 225.

Review of *Who Is Tapping at My Window?, Publishers Weekly,* February 26, 1988, p. 194.

■ For More Information See

PERIODICALS

Booklist, October 15, 1992, p. 443.

Kirkus Reviews, April 1, 1989, p. 556; December 15, 1991, p. 1600; May 1, 1998, p. 666.

School Library Journal, January, 1993, p. 88; March, 1995, p. 189; September, 1995, p. 188.

*   *   *

WILLIAMS, Karen Lynn 1952-

■ Personal

Born March 22, 1952, in New Haven, CT; daughter of Russell Drake (an optometrist) and Lenora Mary (a homemaker; maiden name, Yohans) Howard; married Steven Cranston Williams (a physician), June 18, 1978; children: Peter, Christopher, Rachel, Jonathan. *Education:* University of Connecticut, B.S., 1974; Southern Connecticut State University, M.S., 1977. *Religion:* Unitarian-Universalist. *Hobbies and other interests:* Reading, quilting, jogging, flea markets.

Addresses

Home—6645 Northumberland St., Pittsburgh, PA 15217.

Career

Teacher of the deaf in North Haven, CT, 1977-80; U.S. Peace Corps, Washington, DC, teacher of English in Malawi, 1980-83; writer in Haiti, 1991-93.

Writings

PICTURE BOOKS

Galimoto, illustrated by Catherine Stock, Lothrop, 1990.
When Africa Was Home, illustrated by Floyd Cooper, Orchard Books, 1991.
Tap-Tap, illustrated by Catherine Stock, Clarion, 1994.
Painted Dreams, illustrated by Catherine Stock, Lothrop, 1998.

JUVENILE NOVELS

Baseball and Butterflies, illustrated by Linda Storm, Lothrop, 1990.
First Grade King, illustrated by Lena Shiffman, Clarion, 1992.
Applebaum's Garage, Clarion, 1993.
A Real Christmas This Year, Clarion, 1995.

Contributor of articles and stories to adult and children's magazines.

Sidelights

Author Karen Lynn Williams taught deaf children in North Haven, Connecticut, for years before becoming a teacher of English in Malawi with the U.S. Peace Corps. She also spent a few years in Haiti. With picture books set in Africa and Haiti, and novels for young readers based on her experiences and those of her children, Williams has won praise from critics.

Williams began her career as a children's writer with a picture book. *Galimoto* tells how seven-year-old Kondi creates a galimoto (a moving push toy) despite a lack of wire and his brother's warning that the project is too difficult. Determined to make the toy, Kondi seeks materials for it in his Malawi village. Kondi's uncle, the village miller, and a little girl all give him wire, and Kondi constructs the galimoto. According to Patricia C. McKissack in the *New York Times Book Review,* Williams's text is "smooth and lyrical—a joy to read aloud." In *Booklist* Julie Corsaro described the story as "enlightening," with "universal appeal."

When Africa Was Home, another picture book, is about Peter's return to America. Peter, a white child born to American parents, does not want to leave Africa because he loves life in his village. When Peter is in America, he feels homesick for the cool shade and the warm rain in Africa. Upon the family's return to the village, Peter is once again happy. Throughout the text, Williams intro-

Seven-year-old Kondi creates a moving push-toy, a galimoto, despite his brother's warning that the project is too difficult. (From *Galimoto,* written by Karen Lynn Williams and illustrated by Catherine Stock.)

duces words in Chichewa, a language used in Malawi. "Williams evokes Africa as . . . a place of warmth, belonging, and freedom," wrote Susan Giffard in *School Library Journal.* "Peter's viewpoint is refreshingly Afrocentric," commented Ruth Ann Smith in *Bulletin of the Center for Children's Books.*

Tap-Tap features eight-year-old Sasifi, a Haitian girl who is just old enough to help her mother at the market. Although Sasifi would rather ride in a tap-tap, or truck, Sasifi and her mother carry their oranges to market. Sasifi earns enough money at the market to buy them a ride on the colorful, crowded tap-tap for the trip home. (The truck is called a tap-tap because riders tap the side of the truck to let the driver know they want to get off.) When her new hat flies away, Sasifi must tap-tap the side of the truck so she can retrieve it. Julie Corsaro of *Booklist* concluded that *Tap-Tap* is a "satisfying journey." *Painted Dreams,* another picture book set in Haiti, was published in 1998; in this story, an eight-year-old girl joyfully expresses herself through art.

Baseball and Butterflies, the author's first novel, introduces Daniel. Daniel is not looking forward to baseball season; even his younger brother Joey is better at it than he is. Daniel really wants to spend the summer tending to his butterfly collection. "Williams provides enough information about Daniel's favorite insect to help us understand . . . his fascination," wrote Ruth Ann Smith in *Bulletin of the Center for Children's Books.* Pamela K.

Megan assists her family emotionally and financially when her disabled brother needs special help. (Cover illustration by Gail Owens.)

Bomboy remarked that the book would be useful for instructors in "discussions intended to develop a conservation ethic" in *School Library Journal. First Grade King,* a chapter book, features Joey, Daniel's little brother. Readers follow Joey as he makes his way through the first grade. He learns to read and deals with a bully. A *Publishers Weekly* critic found the book "[r]eminiscent of the classic Ramona series."

Applebaum's Garage, a novel for older children, is about a boy whose best friend becomes interested in a new group of playmates. Jeremy responds by visiting the handy man who lives next door. Mr. Applebaum is elderly, and his garage and yard are full of things that fascinate Jeremy. He works next to Mr. Applebaum creating things, and he even builds a fort on Mr. Applebaum's property. However, when a girl breaks her arm in the fort, her father demands a clean-up. Mr. Applebaum grows depressed, and Jeremy feels guilty. Meanwhile, Jeremy's friend Randy is in trouble for his delinquent activities. Jeremy finds a way to make things

right, and, as a *Kirkus Reviews* critic noted, Jeremy and Mr. Applebaum "demonstrate that a good friendship is based on loyalty and respect."

The novel *A Real Christmas This Year* features a female protagonist with a disabled brother. Twelve-year-old Megan is adjusting to seventh grade and new friends when Kevin destroys his glasses and hearing aid. Without them, Kevin acts in a destructive fashion, and the whole family is affected. To replace the expensive equipment, the family will have to do without a Christmas tree. Megan does what she can to help the family, from trying to earn money to making creative, meaningful gifts. According to Deborah Stevenson in *Bulletin of the Center for Children's Books,* the conclusion of the book is "a cozy Christmas finale that the characters have earned and readers will appreciate."

■ Works Cited

Review of *Applebaum's Garage, Kirkus Reviews,* October 15, 1993, p. 1340.

Bomboy, Pamela K., review of *Baseball and Butterflies, School Library Journal,* December, 1990, pp. 90-91.

Corsaro, Julie, review of *Galimoto, Booklist,* March 15, 1990, pp. 1460-62.

Corsaro, Julie, review of *Tap-Tap, Booklist,* April 15, 1994, p. 1541.

Review of *First Grade King, Publishers Weekly,* March 2, 1992, p. 66.

Giffard, Susan, review of *When Africa Was Home, School Library Journal,* April, 1991, p. 106.

McKissack, Patricia C., review of *Galimoto, New York Times Book Review,* May 20, 1990, p. 42.

Smith, Ruth Ann, review of *Baseball and Butterflies, Bulletin of the Center for Children's Books,* October, 1990, p. 49.

Smith, Ruth Ann, review of *When Africa Was Home, Bulletin of the Center for Children's Books,* February, 1991, pp. 155-56.

Stevenson, Deborah, review of *A Real Christmas This Year, Bulletin of the Center for Children's Books,* November, 1995, p. 110.

■ For More Information See

PERIODICALS

Booklist, September 15, 1990, p. 165; April 15, 1992, p. 1529; April 15, 1994, p. 154.

Bulletin of the Center for Children's Books, April, 1992, p. 225; March, 1994, p. 238.

Horn Book, July-August, 1994, pp. 445-46; November-December, 1995, p. 731.

Kirkus Reviews, March 1, 1994, p. 312.

Publishers Weekly, February 9, 1990, pp. 60-62.

School Library Journal, June, 1990, p. 106.

Voice of Youth Advocates, December, 1995, p. 311.*

Cumulative Indexes

Illustrations Index

(In the following index, the number of the volume in which an illustrator's work appears is given *before* the colon, and the page number on which it appears is given *after* the colon. For example, a drawing by Adams, Adrienne appears in Volume 2 on page 6, another drawing by her appears in Volume 3 on page 80, another drawing in Volume 8 on page 1, another drawing in Volume 15 on page 107, and so on and so on....)

YABC

Index citations including this abbreviation refer to listings appearing in *Yesterday's Authors of Books for Children,* also published by Gale Research, which covers authors who died prior to 1960.

A

Aas, Ulf *5:* 174
Abbé, S. van
 See van Abbé, S.
Abel, Raymond *6:* 122; *7:* 195; *12:* 3; *21:* 86; *25:* 119
Abelliera, Aldo *71:* 120
Abolafia, Yossi *60:* 2; *93:* 163
Abrahams, Hilary *26:* 205; *29:* 24-25; *53:* 61
Abrams, Kathie *36:* 170
Abrams, Lester *49:* 26
Accorsi, William *11:* 198
Acs, Laszlo *14:* 156; *42:* 22
Adams, Adrienne *2:* 6; *3:* 80; *8:* 1; *15:* 107; *16:* 180; *20:* 65; *22:* 134-135; *33:* 75; *36:* 103, 112; *39:* 74; *86:* 54; *90:* 2, 3
Adams, John Wolcott *17:* 162
Adams, Lynn *96:* 44
Adams, Norman *55:* 82
Adams, Sarah *98:* 126
Adamson, George *30:* 23, 24; *69:* 64
Addams, Charles *55:* 5
Ade, Rene *76:* 198
Adkins, Alta *22:* 250
Adkins, Jan *8:* 3; *69:* 4
Adler, Peggy *22:* 6; *29:* 31
Adler, Ruth *29:* 29
Adragna, Robert *47:* 145
Agard, Nadema *18:* 1
Agre, Patricia *47:* 195
Ahl, Anna Maria *32:* 24
Ahlberg, Allan *68:* 6-7, 9
Ahlberg, Janet *68:* 6-7, 9
Aicher-Scholl, Inge *63:* 127
Aichinger, Helga *4:* 5, 45
Aitken, Amy *31:* 34
Akaba, Suekichi *46:* 23; *53:* 127
Akasaka, Miyoshi *YABC 2:* 261
Akino, Fuku *6:* 144
Alain *40:* 41
Alajalov *2:* 226
Alborough, Jez *86:* 1, 2, 3
Albrecht, Jan *37:* 176
Albright, Donn *1:* 91
Alcala, Alfredo *91:* 128
Alcorn, John *3:* 159; *7:* 165; *31:* 22; *44:* 127; *46:* 23, 170
Alda, Arlene *44:* 24
Alden, Albert *11:* 103
Aldridge, Andy *27:* 131
Alex, Ben *45:* 25, 26
Alexander, Ellen *91:* 3
Alexander, Lloyd *49:* 34
Alexander, Martha *3:* 206; *11:* 103; *13:* 109; *25:* 100; *36:* 131; *70:* 6, 7
Alexander, Paul *85:* 57; *90:* 9
Alexeieff, Alexander *14:* 6; *26:* 199
Alfano, Wayne *80:* 69

Aliki
 See Brandenberg, Aliki
Allamand, Pascale *12:* 9
Allan, Judith *38:* 166
Alland, Alexandra *16:* 255
Allen, Gertrude *9:* 6
Allen, Graham *31:* 145
Allen, Pamela *50:* 25, 26-27, 28; *81:* 9, 10
Allen, Rowena *47:* 75
Allen, Thomas B. *81:* 101; *82:* 248; *89:* 37
Allen, Tom *85:* 176
Allender, David *73:* 223
Alley, R. W. *80:* 183; *95:* 187
Allison, Linda *43:* 27
Allport, Mike *71:* 55
Almquist, Don *11:* 8; *12:* 128; *17:* 46; *22:* 110
Aloise, Frank *5:* 38; *10:* 133; *30:* 92
Althea
 See Braithwaite, Althea
Altschuler, Franz *11:* 185; *23:* 141; *40:* 48; *45:* 29; *57:* 181
Ambrus, Victor G. *1:* 6-7, 194; *3:* 69; *5:* 15; *6:* 44; *7:* 36; *8:* 210; *12:* 227; *14:* 213; *15:* 213; *22:* 209; *24:* 36; *28:* 179; *30:* 178; *32:* 44, 46; *38:* 143; *41:* 25, 26, 27, 28, 29, 30, 31, 32; *42:* 87; *44:* 190; *55:* 172; *62:* 30, 144, 145, 148; *86:* 99, 100, 101; *87:* 66, 137; *89:* 162
Ames, Lee J. *3:* 12; *9:* 130; *10:* 69; *17:* 214; *22:* 124
Amon, Aline *9:* 9
Amoss, Berthe *5:* 5
Amundsen, Dick *7:* 77
Amundsen, Richard E. *5:* 10; *24:* 122
Ancona, George *12:* 11; *55:* 144
Anderson, Alasdair *18:* 122
Anderson, Brad *33:* 28
Anderson, C. W. *11:* 10
Anderson, Carl *7:* 4
Anderson, Catherine Corley *72:* 2
Anderson, Doug *40:* 111
Anderson, Erica *23:* 65
Anderson, Laurie *12:* 153, 155
Anderson, Lena *99:* 26
Anderson, Susan *90:* 12
Anderson, Wayne *23:* 119; *41:* 239; *56:* 7; *62:* 26
Andreasen, Daniel *86:* 157; *87:* 104
Andrew, John *22:* 4
Andrews, Benny *14:* 251; *31:* 24; *57:* 6, 7
Anelay, Henry *57:* 173
Angel, Marie *47:* 22
Angelo, Valenti *14:* 8; *18:* 100; *20:* 232; *32:* 70
Anglund, Joan Walsh *2:* 7, 250-251; *37:* 198, 199, 200
Anholt, Catherine *74:* 8
Anno, Mitsumasa *5:* 7; *38:* 25, 26-27, 28, 29, 30, 31, 32; *77:* 3, 4

Antal, Andrew *1:* 124; *30:* 145
Apple, Margot *33:* 25; *35:* 206; *46:* 81; *53:* 8; *61:* 109; *64:* 21, 22, 24, 25, 27; *71:* 176; *77:* 53; *82:* 245; *92:* 39; *94:* 180; *96:* 107
Appleyard, Dev *2:* 192
Aragonés, Sergio *48:* 23, 24, 25, 26, 27
Araneus *40:* 29
Archambault, Matthew *85:* 173
Archer, Janet *16:* 69
Ardizzone, Edward *1:* 11, 12; *2:* 105; *3:* 258; *4:* 78; *7:* 79; *10:* 100; *15:* 232; *20:* 69, 178; *23:* 223; *24:* 125; *28:* 25, 26, 27, 28, 29, 30, 31, 33, 34, 35, 36, 37; *31:* 192, 193; *34:* 215, 217; *60:* 173; *64:* 145; *87:* 176; *YABC 2:* 25
Arenella, Roy *14:* 9
Armer, Austin *13:* 3
Armer, Laura Adams *13:* 3
Armer, Sidney *13:* 3
Armitage, David *47:* 23; *99:* 5
Armitage, Eileen *4:* 16
Armstrong, George *10:* 6; *21:* 72
Arno, Enrico *1:* 217; *2:* 22, 210; *4:* 9; *5:* 43; *6:* 52; *29:* 217, 219; *33:* 152; *35:* 99; *43:* 31, 32, 33; *45:* 212, 213, 214; *72:* 72; *74:* 166
Arnold, Emily *76:* 7, 9, 10
Arnosky, Jim *22:* 20; *70:* 9, 10, 11
Arrowood, Clinton *12:* 193; *19:* 11; *65:* 210
Artell, Mike *89:* 8
Arting, Fred J. *41:* 63
Artzybasheff, Boris *13:* 143; *14:* 15; *40:* 152, 155
Aruego, Ariane *6:* 4
Aruego, Jose *4:* 140; *6:* 4; *7:* 64; *33:* 195; *35:* 208; *68:* 16, 17; *75:* 46; *93:* 91, 92; *94:* 197
Asare, Meshack *86:* 9
Asch, Frank *5:* 9; *66:* 2, 4, 6, 7, 9, 10
Ashby, Gail *11:* 135
Ashby, Gwynneth *44:* 26
Ashley, C. W. *19:* 197
Ashmead, Hal *8:* 70
Aska, Warabe *56:* 10
Assel, Steven *44:* 153; *77:* 22, 97
Astrop, John *32:* 56
Atene, Ann *12:* 18
Atherton, Lisa *38:* 198
Atkinson, Allen *60:* 5
Atkinson, J. Priestman *17:* 275
Atkinson, Janet *86:* 147
Atkinson, Wayne *40:* 46
Attebery, Charles *38:* 170
Atwood, Ann *7:* 9
Aubrey, Meg Kelleher *77:* 159
Augarde, Steve *25:* 22
Austerman, Miriam *23:* 107
Austin, Margot *11:* 16
Austin, Robert *3:* 44
Austin, Virginia *81:* 205

Auth, Tony *51:* 5
Avedon, Richard *57:* 140
Averill, Esther *1:* 17; *28:* 39, 40, 41
Axeman, Lois *2:* 32; *11:* 84; *13:* 165; *22:* 8; *23:* 49; *61:* 116
Ayer, Jacqueline *13:* 7
Ayer, Margaret *15:* 12; *50:* 120
Ayers, Alan *91:* 58
Ayliffe, Alex *95:* 164

B

B. T. B.
  See Blackwell, Basil T.
Babbitt, Bradford *33:* 158
Babbitt, Natalie *6:* 6; *8:* 220; *68:* 20; *70:* 242, 243
Bacchus, Andy *94:* 87
Bachem, Paul *48:* 180; *67:* 65
Back, Adam *63:* 125
Back, George *31:* 161
Backhouse, Colin *78:* 142
Bacon, Bruce *4:* 74
Bacon, Paul *7:* 155; *8:* 121; *31:* 55; *50:* 42; *56:* 175; *62:* 82, 84
Bacon, Peggy *2:* 11, 228; *46:* 44
Bailey, Peter *58:* 174; *87:* 221
Baker, Alan *22:* 22; *61:* 134; *93:* 11, 12
Baker, Charlotte *2:* 12
Baker, Garin *89:* 65
Baker, Jeannie *23:* 4; *88:* 18, 19, 20
Baker, Jim *22:* 24
Baker, Joe *82:* 188
Baldridge, Cyrus LeRoy *19:* 69; *44:* 50
Balet, Jan *11:* 22
Balian, Lorna *9:* 16; *91:* 16
Ballantyne, R. M. *24:* 34
Ballis, George *14:* 199
Baltzer, Hans *40:* 30
Banbery, Fred *58:* 15
Banfill, A. Scott *98:* 7
Bang, Molly Garrett *24:* 37, 38; *69:* 8, 9, 10
Banik, Yvette Santiago *21:* 136
Banner, Angela
  See Maddison, Angela Mary
Bannerman, Helen *19:* 13, 14
Bannon, Laura *6:* 10; *23:* 8
Bantock, Nick *74:* 229; *95:* 6
Baptist, Michael *37:* 208
Barbarin, Lucien C., Jr. *89:* 88
Barbour, Karen *96:* 5
Barbour, Karen *74:* 209
Bare, Arnold Edwin *16:* 31
Bare, Colleen Stanley *32:* 33
Bargery, Geoffrey *14:* 258
Barker, Carol *31:* 27
Barker, Cicely Mary *49:* 50, 51
Barkley, James *4:* 13; *6:* 11; *13:* 112
Barks, Carl *37:* 27, 28, 29, 30-31, 32, 33, 34
Barling, Joy *62:* 148
Barling, Tom *9:* 23
Barlow, Gillian *62:* 20
Barlow, Perry *35:* 28
Barlowe, Dot *30:* 223
Barlowe, Wayne *37:* 72; *84:* 43
Barnard, Bryn *88:* 53
Barner, Bob *29:* 37
Barnes, Hiram P. *20:* 28
Barnes-Murphy, Rowan *88:* 22
Barnett, Ivan *70:* 14
Barnett, Moneta *16:* 89; *19:* 142; *31:* 102; *33:* 30, 31, 32; *41:* 153; *61:* 94, 97
Barney, Maginel Wright *39:* 32, 33, 34; *YABC 2:* 306

Barnum, Jay Hyde *11:* 224; *20:* 5; *37:* 189, 190
Baron, Alan *80:* 3; *89:* 123
Barr, George *60:* 74; *69:* 64
Barrauds *33:* 114
Barrer-Russell, Gertrude *9:* 65; *27:* 31
Barret, Robert *85:* 134
Barrett, Angela *40:* 136, 137; *62:* 74; *75:* 10; *76:* 142
Barrett, Jennifer *58:* 149
Barrett, John E. *43:* 119
Barrett, Moneta *74:* 10
Barrett, Peter *55:* 169; *86:* 111
Barrett, Robert *62:* 145; *77:* 146; *82:* 35
Barrett, Ron *14:* 24; *26:* 35
Barron, John N. *3:* 261; *5:* 101; *14:* 220
Barrows, Walter *14:* 268
Barry, Ethelred B. *37:* 79; *YABC 1:* 229
Barry, James *14:* 25
Barry, Katharina *2:* 159; *4:* 22
Barry, Robert E. *6:* 12
Barry, Scott *32:* 35
Bartenbach, Jean *40:* 31
Barth, Ernest Kurt *2:* 172; *3:* 160; *8:* 26; *10:* 31
Barton, Byron *8:* 207; *9:* 18; *23:* 66; *80:* 181; *90:* 18, 19, 20, 21
Barton, Harriett *30:* 71
Bartram, Robert *10:* 42
Bartsch, Jochen *8:* 105; *39:* 38
Bascove, Barbara *45:* 73
Baskin, Leonard *30:* 42, 43, 46, 47; *49:* 125, 126, 128, 129, 133
Bass, Saul *49:* 192
Bassett, Jeni *40:* 99; *64:* 30
Basso, Bill *99:* 139
Batchelor, Joy *29:* 41, 47, 48
Bate, Norman *5:* 16
Bates, Leo *24:* 35
Batet, Carmen *39:* 134
Batherman, Muriel *31:* 79; *45:* 185
Battaglia, Aurelius *50:* 44
Batten, John D. *25:* 161, 162
Battles, Asa *32:* 94, 95
Bauernschmidt, Marjorie *15:* 15
Baum, Allyn *20:* 10
Baum, Willi *4:* 24-25; *7:* 173
Bauman, Leslie *61:* 121
Baumann, Jill *34:* 170
Baumhauer, Hans *11:* 218; *15:* 163, 165, 167
Baxter, Glen *57:* 100
Baxter, Leon *59:* 102
Baxter, Robert *87:* 129
Bayley, Dorothy *37:* 195
Bayley, Nicola *40:* 104; *41:* 34, 35; *69:* 15
Baynes, Pauline *2:* 244; *3:* 149; *13:* 133, 135, 137-141; *19:* 18, 19, 20; *32:* 208, 213, 214; *36:* 105, 108; *59:* 12, 13, 14, 16, 17, 18, 20
Beame, Rona *12:* 40
Bear's Heart *73:* 215
Beard, Dan *22:* 31, 32
Beard, J. H. *YABC 1:* 158
Bearden, Romare *9:* 7; *22:* 35
Beardsley, Aubrey *17:* 14; *23:* 181; *59:* 130, 131
Bearman, Jane *29:* 38
Beaton, Cecil *24:* 208
Beaucé, J. A. *18:* 103
Beaujard, Sophie *81:* 54
Beck, Charles *11:* 169; *51:* 173
Beck, Ruth *13:* 11
Becker, Harriet *12:* 211
Beckett, Sheilah *25:* 5; *33:* 37, 38
Beckhoff, Harry *1:* 78; *5:* 163
Beckman, Kaj *45:* 38, 39, 40, 41
Beckman, Per *45:* 42, 43
Beddows, Eric *72:* 70

Bedford, F. D. *20:* 118, 122; *33:* 170; *41:* 220, 221, 230, 233
Bee, Joyce *19:* 62
Beeby, Betty *25:* 36
Beech, Carol *9:* 149
Beek *25:* 51, 55, 59
Beerbohm, Max *24:* 208
Begin, Maryjane *82:* 13
Behr, Joyce *15:* 15; *21:* 132; *23:* 161
Behrens, Hans *5:* 97
Beinicke, Steve *69:* 18
Beisner, Monika *46:* 128, 131
Belden, Charles J. *12:* 182
Belina, Renate *39:* 132
Bell, Corydon *3:* 20
Bell, Graham *54:* 48
Bell, Thomas P. *76:* 182
Beltran, Alberto *43:* 37
Bemelmans, Ludwig *15:* 19, 21
Ben-Ami, Doron *75:* 96; *84:* 107
Benda, Wladyslaw T. *15:* 256; *30:* 76, 77; *44:* 182
Bender, Robert *77:* 162; *79:* 13
Bendick, Jeanne *2:* 24; *68:* 27, 28
Benner, Cheryl *80:* 11
Bennett, Charles H. *64:* 6
Bennett, F. I. *YABC 1:* 134
Bennett, Jill *26:* 61; *41:* 38, 39; *45:* 54
Bennett, Rainey *15:* 26; *23:* 53
Bennett, Richard *15:* 45; *21:* 11, 12, 13; *25:* 175
Bennett, Susan *5:* 55
Benoit, Elise *77:* 74
Benson, Linda *60:* 130; *62:* 91; *75:* 101; *79:* 156
Benson, Patrick *68:* 162
Bentley, Carolyn *46:* 153
Bentley, Roy *30:* 162
Benton, Thomas Hart *2:* 99
Berelson, Howard *5:* 20; *16:* 58; *31:* 50
Berenstain, Jan *12:* 47; *64:* 33, 34, 36, 37, 38, 40, 42, 44
Berenstain, Stan *12:* 47; *64:* 33, 34, 36, 37, 38, 40, 42, 44
Berenzy, Alix *65:* 13; *73:* 6; *78:* 115
Berg, Joan *1:* 115; *3:* 156; *6:* 26, 58
Berg, Ron *36:* 48, 49; *48:* 37, 38; *67:* 72
Berger, Barbara *77:* 14
Berger, William M. *14:* 143; *YABC 1:* 204
Bergherr, Mary *74:* 170
Bergstreser, Douglas *69:* 76
Bering, Claus *13:* 14
Berkowitz, Jeanette *3:* 249
Berman, Paul *66:* 14
Bernadette
  See Watts, Bernadette
Bernath, Stefen *32:* 76
Bernhard, Durga *80:* 13
Bernstein, Michel J. *51:* 71
Bernstein, Ted *38:* 183; *50:* 131
Bernstein, Zena *23:* 46
Berridge, Celia *86:* 63
Berrill, Jacquelyn *12:* 50
Berry, Erick
  See Best, Allena
Berry, William D. *14:* 29; *19:* 48·
Berry, William A. *6:* 219
Berson, Harold *2:* 17-18; *4:* 28-29, 220; *9:* 10; *12:* 19; *17:* 45; *18:* 193; *22:* 85; *34:* 172; *44:* 120; *46:* 42; *80:* 240
Berton, Patsy *99:* 16
Bertschmann, Harry *16:* 1
Besco, Don *70:* 99
Beskow, Elsa *20:* 13, 14, 15
Bess, Clayton *63:* 94
Best, Allena *2:* 26; *34:* 76
Betera, Carol *74:* 68
Bethell, Thomas N. *61:* 169
Bethers, Ray *6:* 22
Bettina

See Ehrlich, Bettina
Betts, Ethel Franklin *17:* 161, 164-165; *YABC 2:* 47
Betz, Rudolf *59:* 161
Bewick, Thomas *16:* 40-41, 43-45, 47; *54:* 150; *YABC 1:* 107
Beyer, Paul J. III *74:* 24
Bezencon, Jacqueline *48:* 40
Biamonte, Daniel *40:* 90
Bianchi, John *91:* 19
Bianco, Pamela *15:* 31; *28:* 44, 45, 46
Bible, Charles *13:* 15
Bice, Clare *22:* 40
Bierman, Don *57:* 184
Biggers, John *2:* 123
Bileck, Marvin *3:* 102; *40:* 36-37
Bilibin, Ivan *61:* 8, 9, 12, 13, 14, 15, 151, 152, 154, 162
Billington, Patrick *98:* 71
Bimen, Levent *5:* 179
Binch, Caroline *81:* 18
Binks, Robert *25:* 150
Binzen, Bill *24:* 47
Birch, Reginald *15:* 150; *19:* 33, 34, 35, 36; *37:* 196, 197; *44:* 182; *46:* 176; *YABC 1:* 84; *2:* 34, 39
Bird, Esther Brock *1:* 36; *25:* 66
Birkett, Rachel *78:* 206
Birmingham, Lloyd P. *12:* 51; *83:* 13
Biro, Val *1:* 26; *41:* 42; *60:* 178; *67:* 23, 24; *84:* 242, 243
Bischoff, Ilse *44:* 51
Bishop, Gavin *97:* 17, 18
Bishop, Rich *56:* 43
Bite, I. *60:* 14
Bittinger, Ned *93:* 117
Bjorklund, Lorence *3:* 188, 252; *7:* 100; *9:* 113; *10:* 66; *19:* 178; *33:* 122, 123; *35:* 36, 37, 38, 39, 41, 42, 43; *36:* 185; *38:* 93; *47:* 106; *66:* 194; *YABC 1:* 242
Bjorkman, Steve *91:* 199
Blackburn, Loren H. *63:* 10
Blackwell, Basil T. *YABC 1:* 68, 69
Blades, Ann *16:* 52; *37:* 213; *50:* 41; *69:* 21; *99:* 215
Blair, Jay *45:* 46; *46:* 155
Blaisdell, Elinore *1:* 121; *3:* 134; *35:* 63
Blake, Quentin *3:* 170; *10:* 48; *13:* 38; *21:* 180; *26:* 60; *28:* 228; *30:* 29, 31; *40:* 108; *45:* 219; *46:* 165, 168; *48:* 196; *52:* 10, 11, 12, 13, 14, 15, 16, 17; *73:* 41, 43; *78:* 84, 86; *80:* 250, 251; *84:* 210, 211, 212; *87:* 177; *96:* 24, 26, 28
Blake, Robert J. *37:* 90; *53:* 67; *54:* 23
Blake, William *30:* 54, 56, 57, 58, 59, 60
Blanchard, N. Taylor *82:* 140
Blass, Jacqueline *8:* 215
Blazek, Scott R. *91:* 71
Blegvad, Erik *2:* 59; *3:* 98; *5:* 117; *7:* 131; *11:* 149; *14:* 34, 35; *18:* 237; *32:* 219; *60:* 106; *66:* 16, 17, 18, 19; *70:* 233; *76:* 18; *82:* 106; *87:* 45; *YABC 1:* 201
Blessen, Karen *93:* 126
Bliss, Corinne Demas *37:* 38
Bloch, Lucienne *10:* 12
Bloom, Lloyd *35:* 180; *36:* 149; *47:* 99; *62:* 117; *68:* 231; *72:* 136; *75:* 185; *83:* 99
Blossom, Dave *34:* 29
Blumenschein, E. L. *YABC 1:* 113, 115
Blumer, Patt *29:* 214
Blundell, Kim *29:* 36
Bluthenthal, Diana Cain *93:* 32
Boardman, Gwenn *12:* 60
Bobri *30:* 138; *47:* 27
Bock, Vera *1:* 187; *21:* 41
Bock, William Sauts *8:* 7; *14:* 37; *16:* 120; *21:* 141; *36:* 177; *62:* 203
Bodecker, N(iels) M(ogens) *8:* 13; *14:* 2; *17:* 55-57; *73:* 22, 23, 24

Boehm, Linda *40:* 31
Bohdal, Susi *22:* 44
Bohlen, Nina *58:* 13
Boies, Alex *96:* 53
Bolian, Polly *3:* 270; *4:* 30; *13:* 77; *29:* 197
Bolle, Frank *87:* 100
Bollen, Roger *79:* 186; *83:* 16
Bolognese, Don *2:* 147, 231; *4:* 176; *7:* 146; *17:* 43; *23:* 192; *24:* 50; *34:* 108; *36:* 133; *71:* 24, 25
Bolton, A. T. *57:* 158
Bond, Arnold *18:* 116
Bond, Barbara Higgins *21:* 102
Bond, Bruce *52:* 97
Bond, Felicia *38:* 197; *49:* 55, 56; *89:* 170; *90:* 171
Bonn, Pat *43:* 40
Bonners, Susan *41:* 40; *85:* 36; *94:* 99, 100
Bonsall, Crosby *23:* 6
Boon, Emilie *86:* 23, 24
Boore, Sara *60:* 73
Booth, Franklin *YABC 2:* 76
Booth, Graham *32:* 193; *37:* 41, 42
Bordier, Georgette *16:* 54
Boren, Tinka *27:* 128
Borja, Robert *22:* 48
Born, Adolf *49:* 63
Bornstein, Ruth *14:* 44; *88:* 45, 46
Borten, Helen *3:* 54; *5:* 24
Bosin, Blackbear *69:* 104
Bossom, Naomi *35:* 48
Bostock, Mike *83:* 221
Boston, Peter *19:* 42
Bosustow, Stephen *34:* 202
Boszko, Ron *75:* 47
Bottner, Barbara *14:* 46
Boucher, Joelle *41:* 138
Boulat, Pierre *44:* 40
Boulet, Susan Seddon *50:* 47
Bour, Daniele *66:* 145
Bourke-White, Margaret *15:* 286-287; *57:* 102
Boutet de Monvel, M. *30:* 61, 62, 63, 65
Bowen, Richard *42:* 134
Bowen, Ruth *31:* 188
Bower, Ron *29:* 33
Bowers, David *95:* 38
Bowman, Leslie *85:* 203
Bowser, Carolyn Ewing *22:* 253
Boyd, Patti *45:* 31
Boyle, Eleanor Vere *28:* 50, 51
Boynton, Sandra *57:* 13, 14, 15
Bozzo, Frank *4:* 154
Brabbs, Derry *55:* 170
Bradford, Ron *7:* 157
Bradley, David P. *69:* 105
Bradley, Richard D. *26:* 182
Bradley, William *5:* 164
Brady, Irene *4:* 31; *42:* 37; *68:* 191
Bragg, Michael *32:* 78; *46:* 31
Bragg, Ruth Gembicki *77:* 18
Brainerd, John W. *65:* 19
Braithwaite, Althea *23:* 12-13
Bralds, Braldt *90:* 28; *91:* 151
Bram, Elizabeth *30:* 67
Bramley, Peter *4:* 3
Brandenberg, Aliki *2:* 36-37; *24:* 222; *35:* 49, 50, 51, 52, 53, 54, 56, 57; *75:* 15, 17; *92:* 205
Brandenburg, Alexa *75:* 19
Brandenburg, Jim *47:* 58
Brandi, Lillian *31:* 158
Brandon, Brumsic, Jr. *9:* 25
Bransom, Paul *17:* 121; *43:* 44
Braren, Loretta Trezzo *87:* 193
Braun, Wendy *80:* 17, 18
Brazell, Derek *75:* 105; *79:* 9
Breathed, Berkeley *86:* 27, 28, 29
Brennan, Steve *83:* 230

Brenner, Fred *22:* 85; *36:* 34; *42:* 34
Brett, Bernard *22:* 54
Brett, Harold M. *26:* 98, 99, 100
Brett, Jan *30:* 135; *42:* 39; *71:* 31, 32
Brewer, Sally King *33:* 44
Brewster, Patience *40:* 68; *45:* 22, 183; *51:* 20; *66:* 144; *89:* 4; *97:* 30, 31
Brick, John *10:* 15
Bridge, David R. *45:* 28
Bridgman, L. J. *37:* 77
Bridwell, Norman *4:* 37
Brierley, Louise *91:* 22; *96:* 165
Briggs, Raymond *10:* 168; *23:* 20, 21; *66:* 29, 31, 32
Brigham, Grace A. *37:* 148
Bright, Robert *24:* 55
Brinckloe, Julie *13:* 18; *24:* 79, 115; *29:* 35; *63:* 140; *81:* 131
Brion *47:* 116
Brisley, Joyce L. *22:* 57
Brittingham, Geoffrey *88:* 37
Brix-Henker, Silke *81:* 194
Brock, Charles E. *15:* 97; *19:* 247, 249; *23:* 224, 225; *36:* 88; *42:* 41, 42, 43, 44, 45; *YABC 1:* 194, 196, 203
Brock, Emma *7:* 21
Brock, Henry Matthew *15:* 81; *16:* 141; *19:* 71; *34:* 115; *40:* 164; *42:* 47, 48, 49; *49:* 66
Brocksopp, Arthur *57:* 157
Brodkin, Gwen *34:* 135
Brodovitch, Alexi *52:* 22
Bromhall, Winifred *5:* 11; *26:* 38
Brooke, L. Leslie *16:* 181-183, 186; *17:* 15-17; *18:* 194
Brooker, Christopher *15:* 251
Brooks, Maya Itzna *92:* 153
Brooks, Ron *94:* 15
Broomfield, Maurice *40:* 141
Brotman, Adolph E. *5:* 21
Brown, Buck *45:* 48
Brown, Christopher *62:* 124, 125, 127, 128
Brown, Craig McFarland *73:* 28; *84:* 65
Brown, Dan *61:* 167
Brown, David *7:* 47; *48:* 52
Brown, Denise *11:* 213
Brown, Ford Madox *48:* 74
Brown, Judith Gwyn *1:* 45; *7:* 5; *8:* 167; *9:* 182, 190; *20:* 16, 17, 18; *23:* 142; *29:* 117; *33:* 97; *36:* 23, 26; *43:* 184; *48:* 201, 223; *49:* 69; *86:* 227
Brown, Kathryn *98:* 26
Brown, Laurie Krasny *99:* 30
Brown, Marc (Tolon) *10:* 17, 197; *14:* 263; *51:* 18; *53:* 11, 12, 13, 15, 16-17; *75:* 58; *80:* 24, 25, 26; *82:* 261; *99:* 29
Brown, Marcia *7:* 30; *25:* 203; *47:* 31, 32, 33, 34, 35, 36-37, 38, 39, 40, 42, 43, 44; *YABC 1:* 27
Brown, Margery W. *5:* 32-33; *10:* 3
Brown, Mary Barrett *97:* 74
Brown, Palmer *36:* 40
Brown, Paul *25:* 26; *26:* 107
Brown, Richard *61:* 18; *67:* 30
Brown, Rick *78:* 71
Brown, Robert S. *85:* 33
Brown, Ruth *55:* 165; *86:* 112, 113
Brown, Trevor *99:* 160
Browne, Anthony *45:* 50, 51, 52; *61:* 21, 22, 23, 24, 25
Browne, Dik *8:* 212; *67:* 32, 33, 35, 37, 39
Browne, Gordon *16:* 97; *64:* 114, 116, 117, 119, 121
Browne, Hablot K. *15:* 65, 80; *21:* 14, 15, 16, 17, 18, 19, 20; *24:* 25
Browning, Coleen *4:* 132
Browning, Mary Eleanor *24:* 84
Bruce, Robert *23:* 23
Brude, Dick *48:* 215

Brule, Al *3:* 135
Bruna, Dick *43:* 48, 49, 50; *76:* 27, 28
Brundage, Frances *19:* 244
Brunhoff, Jean de *24:* 57, 58
Brunhoff, Laurent de *24:* 60; *71:* 35, 36, 37
Brunkus, Denise *84:* 50
Brunson, Bob *43:* 135
Bryan, Ashley F. *31:* 44; *72:* 27, 28, 29
Bryant, Michael *93:* 74
Brychta, Alex *21:* 21
Bryson, Bernarda *3:* 88, 146; *39:* 26; *44:* 185
Buba, Joy *12:* 83; *30:* 226; *44:* 56
Buchanan, Lilian *13:* 16
Bucholtz-Ross, Linda *44:* 137
Buchs, Thomas *40:* 38
Buck, Margaret Waring *3:* 30
Buehr, Walter *3:* 31
Buff, Conrad *19:* 52, 53, 54
Buff, Mary *19:* 52, 53
Bull, Charles Livingston *18:* 207; *88:* 175, 176
Bullen, Anne *3:* 166, 167
Bullock, Kathleen *77:* 24
Bumgarner-Kirby, Claudia *77:* 194
Burbank, Addison *37:* 43
Burchard, Peter *3:* 197; *5:* 35; *6:* 158, 218
Burckhardt, Marc *94:* 48
Burger, Carl *3:* 33; *45:* 160, 162
Burgeson, Marjorie *19:* 31
Burgess, Anne *76:* 252
Burgess, Gelett *32:* 39, 42
Burke, Phillip *95:* 117
Burkert, Nancy Ekholm *18:* 186; *22:* 140; *24:* 62, 63, 64, 65; *26:* 53; *29:* 60, 61; *46:* 171; *YABC 1:* 46
Burn, Doris *6:* 172
Burn, Jeffrey *89:* 125
Burnett, Virgil *44:* 42
Burningham, John *9:* 68; *16:* 60-61; *59:* 28, 29, 30, 31, 32, 33, 35
Burns, Howard M. *12:* 173
Burns, Jim *47:* 70; *86:* 32; *91:* 197
Burns, M. F. *26:* 69
Burns, Raymond *9:* 29
Burns, Robert *24:* 106
Burr, Dan *65:* 28
Burr, Dane *12:* 2
Burra, Edward *YABC 2:* 68
Burrell, Galen *56:* 76
Burri, René *41:* 143; *54:* 166
Burridge, Marge Opitz *14:* 42
Burris, Burmah *4:* 81
Burroughs, John Coleman *41:* 64
Burroughs, Studley O. *41:* 65
Burton, Marilee Robin *46:* 33
Burton, Virginia Lee *2:* 43; *44:* 49, 51; *YABC 1:* 24
Busoni, Rafaello *1:* 186; *3:* 224; *6:* 126; *14:* 5; *16:* 62-63
Butchkes, Sidney *50:* 58
Butler, Geoff *94:* 20
Butterfield, Ned *1:* 153; *27:* 128; *79:* 63
Buzonas, Gail *29:* 88
Buzzell, Russ W. *12:* 177
Byard, Carole *39:* 44; *57:* 18, 19, 20; *60:* 60; *61:* 93, 96; *69:* 210; *78:* 246; *79:* 227
Byars, Betsy *46:* 35
Byfield, Barbara Ninde *8:* 18
Byfield, Graham *32:* 29
Byrd, Robert *13:* 218; *33:* 46

C

Cabat, Erni *74:* 38

Caddy, Alice *6:* 41
Cady, Harrison *17:* 21, 23; *19:* 57, 58
Caffrey, Aileen *72:* 223
Caldecott, Randolph *16:* 98, 103; *17:* 32-33, 36, 38-39; *26:* 90; *YABC 2:* 172
Calder, Alexander *18:* 168
Calderon, W. Frank *25:* 160
Caldwell, Clyde *98:* 100
Caldwell, Doreen *23:* 77; *71:* 41
Caldwell, John *46:* 225
Callahan, Kevin *22:* 42
Callahan, Philip S. *25:* 77
Callan, Jamie *59:* 37
Calvin, James *61:* 92
Cameron, Julia Margaret *19:* 203
Cameron, Scott *99:* 18
Campbell, Ann *11:* 43
Campbell, Bill *89:* 39
Campbell, Robert *55:* 120
Campbell, Rod *51:* 27; *98:* 34
Campbell, Walter M. *YABC 2:* 158
Camps, Luis *28:* 120-121; *66:* 35
Cannon, Janell *78:* 25
Canright, David *36:* 162
Canty, Thomas *85:* 161; *92:* 47
Caporale, Wende *70:* 42
Capp, Al *61:* 28, 30, 31, 40, 41, 43, 44
Caras, Peter *36:* 64
Caraway, Caren *57:* 22
Caraway, James *3:* 200-201
Carbe, Nino *29:* 183
Cares, Linda *67:* 176
Carigiet, Alois *24:* 67
Carle, Eric *4:* 42; *11:* 121; *12:* 29; *65:* 32, 33, 34, 36; *73:* 63, 65
Carlson, Nancy L. *41:* 116; *56:* 25; *90:* 45
Carmi, Giora *79:* 35
Carpenter, Nancy *76:* 128; *86:* 173; *89:* 171
Carr, Archie *37:* 225
Carrick, Donald *5:* 194; *39:* 97; *49:* 70; *53:* 156; *63:* 15, 16, 17, 18, 19, 21; *80:* 131; *86:* 151
Carrick, Malcolm *28:* 59, 60
Carrick, Valery *21:* 47
Carrier, Lark *71:* 43
Carroll, Jim *88:* 211
Carroll, Lewis
    See Dodgson, Charles L.
Carroll, Michael *72:* 5
Carroll, Pamela *84:* 68
Carroll, Ruth *7:* 41; *10:* 68
Carter, Abby *81:* 32; *97:* 121
Carter, Barbara *47:* 167, 169
Carter, Harry *22:* 179
Carter, Helene *15:* 38; *22:* 202, 203; *YABC 2:* 220-221
Cartlidge, Michelle *49:* 65; *96:* 50, 51
Cartwright, Reg *63:* 61, 62; *78:* 26
Carty, Leo *4:* 196; *7:* 163; *58:* 131
Cary *4:* 133; *9:* 32; *20:* 2; *21:* 143
Cary, Page *12:* 41
Casale, Paul *71:* 63
Case, Sandra E. *16:* 2
Caseley, Judith *87:* 36
Casilla, Robert *78:* 7
Casino, Steve *85:* 193
Cassel, Lili
    See Wronker, Lili Cassel
Cassel-Wronker, Lili
    See Wronker, Lili Cassel
Cassels, Jean *8:* 50
Cassler, Carl *75:* 137, 138; *82:* 162
Casson, Hugh *65:* 38, 40, 42, 43
Castellon, Federico *48:* 45, 46, 47, 48
Castle, Jane *4:* 80
Castro, Antonio *84:* 71
Catalano, Dominic *94:* 79

Catalanotto, Peter *63:* 170; *70:* 23; *71:* 182; *72:* 96; *74:* 114; *76:* 194, 195; *77:* 7; *79:* 157; *80:* 28, 67; *83:* 157; *85:* 27
Catania, Tom *68:* 82
Cather, Carolyn *3:* 83; *15:* 203; *34:* 216
Cauley, Lorinda Bryan *44:* 135; *46:* 49
Cayard, Bruce *38:* 67
Cazet, Denys *52:* 27; *99:* 39, 40
Cellini, Joseph *2:* 73; *3:* 35; *16:* 116; *47:* 103
Cepeda, Joe *90:* 62
Chabrian, Debbi *45:* 55
Chabrian, Deborah *51:* 182; *53:* 124; *63:* 107; *75:* 84; *79:* 85; *82:* 247; *89:* 93
Chagnon, Mary *37:* 158
Chalmers, Mary *3:* 145; *13:* 148; *33:* 125; *66:* 214
Chamberlain, Christopher *45:* 57
Chamberlain, Margaret *46:* 51
Chamberlain, Nigel *78:* 140
Chambers, C. E. *17:* 230
Chambers, Dave *12:* 151
Chambers, Mary *4:* 188
Chambliss, Maxie *42:* 186; *56:* 159; *93:* 163, 164
Chan, Harvey *96:* 236; *99:* 153
Chandler, David P. *28:* 62
Chapel, Jody *68:* 20
Chapman, C. H. *13:* 83, 85, 87
Chapman, Frederick T. *6:* 27; *44:* 28
Chapman, Gaynor *32:* 52, 53
Chappell, Warren *3:* 172; *21:* 56; *27:* 125
Charles, Donald *30:* 154, 155
Charlip, Remy *4:* 48; *34:* 138; *68:* 53, 54
Charlot, Jean *1:* 137, 138; *8:* 23; *14:* 31; *48:* 151; *56:* 21
Charlot, Martin *64:* 72
Charlton, Michael *34:* 50; *37:* 39
Charmatz, Bill *7:* 45
Chartier, Normand *9:* 36; *52:* 49; *66:* 40; *74:* 220
Chase, Lynwood M. *14:* 4
Chast, Roz *97:* 39, 40
Chastain, Madye Lee *4:* 50
Chatterton, Martin *68:* 102
Chauncy, Francis *24:* 158
Chee, Cheng-Khee *79:* 42; *81:* 224
Chen, Chih-sien *90:* 226
Chen, Tony *6:* 45; *19:* 131; *29:* 126; *34:* 160
Cheney, T. A. *11:* 47
Cheng, Judith *36:* 45; *51:* 16
Chermayeff, Ivan *47:* 53
Cherry, David *93:* 40
Cherry, Lynne *34:* 52; *65:* 184; *87:* 111; *99:* 46, 47
Chess, Victoria *12:* 6; *33:* 42, 48, 49; *40:* 194; *41:* 145; *69:* 80; *72:* 100; *92:* 33, 34
Chessare, Michele *41:* 50; *56:* 48; *69:* 145
Chesterton, G. K. *27:* 43, 44, 45, 47
Chestnutt, David *47:* 217
Chesworth, Michael *75:* 24, 152; *88:* 136; *94:* 25; *98:* 155
Chetwin, Grace *86:* 40
Chevalier, Christa *35:* 66
Chew, Ruth *7:* 46
Chewning, Randy *92:* 206
Chichester Clark, Emma *72:* 121; *77:* 212; *78:* 209; *87:* 143
Chifflart *47:* 113, 127
Chin, Alex *28:* 54
Cho, Shinta *8:* 126
Chodos, Margaret *52:* 102, 103, 107
Chollick, Jay *25:* 175
Choma, Christina *99:* 169
Chorao, Kay *7:* 200-201; *8:* 25; *11:* 234; *33:* 187; *35:* 239; *69:* 35; *70:* 235
Chowdhury, Subrata *62:* 130
Christelow, Eileen *38:* 44; *83:* 198, 199; *90:* 57, 58
Christensen, Bonnie *93:* 100

Christensen, Gardell Dano *1:* 57
Christiana, David *90:* 64
Christiansen, Per *40:* 24
Christy, Howard Chandler *17:* 163-165, 168-169; *19:* 186, 187; *21:* 22, 23, 24, 25
Chronister, Robert *23:* 138; *63:* 27; *69:* 167
Church, Frederick *YABC 1:* 155
Chute, Marchette *1:* 59
Chwast, Jacqueline *1:* 63; *2:* 275; *6:* 46-47; *11:* 125; *12:* 202; *14:* 235
Chwast, Seymour *3:* 128-129; *18:* 43; *27:* 152; *92:* 79; *96:* 56, 57, 58
Cirlin, Edgard *2:* 168
Clairin, Georges *53:* 109
Clark, David *77:* 164
Clark, Emma Chichester
  See Chichester Clark, Emma
Clark, Victoria *35:* 159
Clarke, Gus *72:* 226
Clarke, Harry *23:* 172, 173
Clarke, Peter *75:* 102
Claverie, Jean *38:* 46; *88:* 29
Clayton, Robert *9:* 181
Cleaver, Elizabeth *8:* 204; *23:* 36
Cleland, T. M. *26:* 92
Clemens, Peter *61:* 125
Clement, Charles *20:* 38
Clement, Rod *97:* 42
Clement, Stephen *88:* 3
Clementson, John *84:* 213
Clevin, Jörgen *7:* 50
Clifford, Judy *34:* 163; *45:* 198
Clokey, Art *59:* 44
Clouse, James *84:* 15
Clouse, Nancy L. *78:* 31
Coalson, Glo *9:* 72, 85; *25:* 155; *26:* 42; *35:* 212; *53:* 31; *56:* 154; *94:* 37, 38, 193
Cober, Alan E. *17:* 158; *32:* 77; *49:* 127
Cober-Gentry, Leslie *92:* 111
Cocca-Leffler, Maryann *80:* 46
Cochran, Bobbye *11:* 52
CoConis, Ted *4:* 41; *46:* 41; *51:* 104
Cocozza, Cris *87:* 18
Coerr, Eleanor *1:* 64; *67:* 52
Coes, Peter *35:* 172
Cogancherry, Helen *52:* 143; *69:* 131; *77:* 93; *78:* 220
Coggins, Jack *2:* 69
Cohen, Alix *7:* 53
Cohen, Vincent O. *19:* 243
Cohen, Vivien *11:* 112
Coker, Paul *51:* 172
Colbert, Anthony *15:* 41; *20:* 193
Colby, C. B. *3:* 47
Cole, Babette *58:* 172; *96:* 63, 64
Cole, Brock *68:* 223; *72:* 36, 37, 38, 192
Cole, Gwen *87:* 185
Cole, Herbert *28:* 104
Cole, Michael *59:* 46
Cole, Olivia H. H. *1:* 134; *3:* 223; *9:* 111; *38:* 104
Collicott, Sharleen *98:* 39
Collier, David *13:* 127
Collier, John *27:* 179
Collier, Steven *50:* 52
Collins, Heather *66:* 84; *67:* 68; *81:* 40; *98:* 192, 193
Colonna, Bernard *21:* 50; *28:* 103; *34:* 140; *43:* 180; *78:* 150
Condon, Grattan *54:* 85
Cone, Ferne Geller *39:* 49
Cone, J. Morton *39:* 49
Conklin, Paul *43:* 62
Connolly, Howard *67:* 88
Connolly, Jerome P. *4:* 128; *28:* 52
Connolly, Peter *47:* 60
Conover, Chris *31:* 52; *40:* 184; *41:* 51; *44:* 79
Contreras, Gerry *72:* 9
Converse, James *38:* 70

Conway *62:* 62
Conway, Michael *69:* 12; *81:* 3; *92:* 108
Cook, G. R. *29:* 165
Cookburn, W. V. *29:* 204
Cooke, Donald E. *2:* 77
Cooke, Tom *52:* 118
Coomaraswamy, A. K. *50:* 100
Coombs, Charles *43:* 65
Coombs, Patricia *2:* 82; *3:* 52; *22:* 119; *51:* 32, 33, 34, 35, 36-37, 38, 39, 40, 42, 43
Cooney, Barbara *6:* 16-17, 50; *12:* 42; *13:* 92; *15:* 145; *16:* 74, 111; *18:* 189; *23:* 38, 89, 93; *32:* 138; *38:* 105; *59:* 48, 49, 51, 52, 53; *74:* 222; *81:* 100; *91:* 25; *96:* 71, 72, 74; *YABC 2:* 10
Cooper, Floyd *79:* 95; *81:* 45; *84:* 82; *85:* 74; *91:* 118; *96:* 77, 78
Cooper, Heather *50:* 39
Cooper, Mario *24:* 107
Cooper, Marjorie *7:* 112
Cope, Jane *61:* 201
Copelman, Evelyn *8:* 61; *18:* 25
Copley, Heather *30:* 86; *45:* 57
Corbett, Grahame *30:* 114; *43:* 67
Corbino, John *19:* 248
Corcos, Lucille *2:* 223; *10:* 27; *34:* 66
Corey, Robert *9:* 34
Corlass, Heather *10:* 7
Cornell, James *27:* 60
Cornell, Jeff *11:* 58
Cornell, Laura *94:* 179; *95:* 25
Corrigan, Barbara *8:* 37
Corwin, Judith Hoffman *10:* 28
Cory, Fanny Y. *20:* 113; *48:* 29
Cosgrove, Margaret *3:* 100; *47:* 63; *82:* 133
Costabel, Eva Deutsch *45:* 66, 67
Costanza, John *58:* 7, 8, 9
Costello, Chris *86:* 78
Costello, David F. *23:* 55
Couch, Greg *94:* 124
Councell, Ruth Tietjen *79:* 29
Courtney, Cathy *58:* 69, 144; *59:* 15; *61:* 20, 87
Courtney, R. *35:* 110
Cousineau, Normand *89:* 180
Couture, Christin *41:* 209
Covarrubias, Miguel *35:* 118, 119, 123, 124, 125
Coville, Katherine *32:* 57; *36:* 167; *92:* 38
Cowell, Lucinda *77:* 54
Cox *43:* 93
Cox, Charles *8:* 20
Cox, David *56:* 37; *90:* 63
Cox, Palmer *24:* 76, 77
Coxe, Molly *69:* 44
Crabb, Gordon *70:* 39
Crabtree, Judith *98:* 42
Craft, Kinuko *22:* 182; *36:* 220; *53:* 122, 123, 148, 149; *74:* 12; *81:* 129; *86:* 31; *89:* 139
Craig, Helen *49:* 76; *62:* 70, 71, 72; *69:* 141; *94:* 42, 43, 44
Crane, Alan H. *1:* 217
Crane, H. M. *13:* 111
Crane, Jack *43:* 183
Crane, Walter *18:* 46-49, 53-54, 56-57, 59-61; *22:* 128; *24:* 210, 217
Cravath, Lynne W. *98:* 45
Crawford, Will *43:* 77
Credle, Ellis *1:* 69
Crespi, Francesca *87:* 90
Crews, Donald *32:* 59, 60; *76:* 42, 43, 44
Crews, Nina *97:* 49
Crichlow, Ernest *74:* 88; *83:* 203
Crofut, Bob *80:* 87; *81:* 47
Crofut, Susan *23:* 61
Croll, Carolyn *80:* 137
Cross, Peter *56:* 78; *63:* 60, 65
Crowe, Elizabeth *88:* 144
Crowell, Pers *3:* 125

Cruikshank, George *15:* 76, 83; *22:* 74, 75, 76, 77, 78, 79, 80, 81, 82, 84, 137; *24:* 22, 23
Crump, Fred H. *11:* 62
Cruz, Ray *6:* 55; *70:* 234
Csatari, Joe *44:* 82; *55:* 152; *63:* 25, 28
Cuffari, Richard *4:* 75; *5:* 98; *6:* 56; *7:* 13, 84, 153; *8:* 148, 155; *9:* 89; *11:* 19; *12:* 55, 96, 114; *15:* 51, 202; *18:* 5; *20:* 139; *21:* 197; *22:* 14, 192; *23:* 15, 106; *25:* 97; *27:* 133; *28:* 196; *29:* 54; *30:* 85; *31:* 35; *36:* 101; *38:* 171; *42:* 97; *44:* 92, 192; *45:* 212, 213; *46:* 36, 198; *50:* 164; *54:* 80, 136, 137, 145; *56:* 17; *60:* 63; *66:* 49, 50; *70:* 41; *71:* 132; *77:* 157; *78:* 58, 149; *79:* 120; *85:* 2, 152
Cugat, Xavier *19:* 120
Cumings, Art *35:* 160
Cummings, Chris *29:* 167
Cummings, Pat *42:* 61; *61:* 99; *69:* 205; *71:* 57, 58; *78:* 24, 25; *93:* 75
Cummings, Richard *24:* 119
Cunette, Lou *20:* 93; *22:* 125
Cunningham, Aline *25:* 180
Cunningham, David *11:* 13
Cunningham, Imogene *16:* 122, 127
Curlee, Lynn *98:* 48
Curry, John Steuart *2:* 5; *19:* 84; *34:* 36
Curtis, Bruce *23:* 96; *30:* 88; *36:* 22
Cusack, Margaret *58:* 49, 50, 51
Cushman, Doug *65:* 57
Czechowski, Alicia *95:* 21

D

Dabcovich, Lydia *25:* 105; *40:* 114; *99:* 75, 76
Dacey, Bob *82:* 175
Dailey, Don *78:* 197
Dain, Martin J. *35:* 75
Dale, Rae *72:* 197
Daley, Joann *50:* 22
Dalton, Anne *40:* 62; *63:* 119
Daly, Deborah M. *74:* 213
Daly, Nicholas *37:* 53; *76:* 48, 49
Daly, Paul *97:* 205
Dalziel, Brothers *33:* 113
D'Amato, Alex *9:* 48; *20:* 25
D'Amato, Janet *9:* 48; *20:* 25; *26:* 118
Daniel, Alan *23:* 59; *29:* 110; *76:* 50, 53, 55, 56
Daniel, Lea *76:* 53, 55
Daniel, Lewis C. *20:* 216
Daniels, Beau *73:* 4
Daniels, Steve *22:* 16
Daniels, Stewart *56:* 12
Dann, Bonnie *31:* 83
Dann, Penny *82:* 128
Danska, Herbert *24:* 219
Danyell, Alice *20:* 27
Darley, F.O.C. *16:* 145; *19:* 79, 86, 88, 185; *21:* 28, 36; *35:* 76, 77, 78, 79, 80-81; *YABC 2:* 175
Darling, Lois *3:* 59; *23:* 30, 31
Darling, Louis *1:* 40-41; *2:* 63; *3:* 59; *23:* 30, 31; *43:* 54, 57, 59
Darrow, David R. *84:* 101
Darrow, Whitney, Jr. *13:* 25; *38:* 220, 221
Darwin, Beatrice *43:* 54
Darwin, Len *24:* 82
Dastolfo, Frank *33:* 179
Dauber, Liz *1:* 22; *3:* 266; *30:* 49
Daugherty, James *3:* 66; *8:* 178; *13:* 27-28, 161; *18:* 101; *19:* 72; *29:* 108; *32:* 156; *42:* 84; *YABC 1:* 256; *2:* 174
d'Aulaire, Edgar Parin *5:* 51; *66:* 53

d'Aulaire, Ingri Parin *5:* 51; *66:* 53
Davalos, Felipe *99:* 197
David, Jonathan *19:* 37
Davidson, Kevin *28:* 154
Davidson, Raymond *32:* 61
Davie, Helen K. *77:* 48, 49
Davis, Allen *20:* 11; *22:* 45; *27:* 222; *29:* 157; *41:* 99; *47:* 99; *50:* 84; *52:* 105
Davis, Bette J. *15:* 53; *23:* 95
Davis, Dimitris *45:* 95
Davis, Jim *32:* 63, 64
Davis, Marguerite *31:* 38; *34:* 69, 70; *YABC 1:* 126, 230
Davis, Nelle *69:* 191
Davis, Paul *78:* 214
Davis, Yvonne LeBrun *94:* 144
Davisson, Virginia H. *44:* 178
DaVolls, Andy *85:* 53
Dawson, Diane *24:* 127; *42:* 126; *52:* 130; *68:* 104
Day, Alexandra *67:* 59; *97:* 54
Day, Rob *94:* 110
Dean, Bob *19:* 211
de Angeli, Marguerite *1:* 77; *27:* 62, 65, 66, 67, 69, 70, 72; *YABC 1:* 166
DeArmond, Dale *70:* 47
Deas, Michael *27:* 219, 221; *30:* 156; *67:* 134; *72:* 24; *75:* 155; *84:* 206; *88:* 124
de Bosschère, Jean *19:* 252; *21:* 4
De Bruyn, M(onica) G. *13:* 30-31
De Cuir, John F. *1:* 28-29
Deeter, Cathy *74:* 110
Degen, Bruce *40:* 227, 229; *57:* 28, 29; *56:* 156; *75:* 229; *76:* 19; *81:* 36, 37; *92:* 26; *93:* 199; *97:* 56, 58, 59
De Grazia *14:* 59; *39:* 56, 57
DeGrazio, George *88:* 40
de Groat, Diane *9:* 39; *18:* 7; *23:* 123; *28:* 200-201; *31:* 58, 59; *34:* 151; *41:* 152; *43:* 88; *46:* 40, 200; *49:* 163; *50:* 89; *52:* 30, 34; *54:* 43; *63:* 5; *70:* 136; *71:* 99; *73:* 117, 156; *77:* 34; *85:* 48; *86:* 201; *87:* 142; *90:* 72, 73, 143; *95:* 182
de Groot, Lee *6:* 21
DeJohn, Marie *89:* 78
Dekhteryov, B. *61:* 158
de Kiefte, Kees *94:* 107
Delacre, Lulu *36:* 66
Delaney, A. *21:* 78
Delaney, Molly *80:* 43
Delaney, Ned *28:* 68; *56:* 80
DeLapine, Jim *79:* 21
De La Roche Saint Andre, Anne *75:* 37
de Larrea, Victoria *6:* 119, 204; *29:* 103; *72:* 203; *87:* 199
Delessert, Etienne *7:* 140; *46:* 61, 62, 63, 65, 67, 68; *YABC 2:* 209
Delulio, John *15:* 54
DeLuna, Tony *88:* 95
Demarest, Chris L. *45:* 68-69, 70; *73:* 172, 173, 176; *78:* 106; *82:* 48, 49; *89:* 212; *92:* 86
De Mejo, Oscar *40:* 67
Demi *89:* 216
Denetsosie, Hoke *13:* 126; *82:* 34
Dennis, Morgan *18:* 68-69; *64:* 89
Dennis, Wesley *2:* 87; *3:* 111; *11:* 132; *18:* 71-74; *22:* 9; *24:* 196, 200; *46:* 178; *69:* 94, 96
Denslow, W. W. *16:* 84-87; *18:* 19-20, 24; *29:* 211
Denton, Terry *72:* 163
de Paola, Tomie *8:* 95; *9:* 93; *11:* 69; *25:* 103; *28:* 157; *29:* 80; *39:* 52-53; *40:* 226; *46:* 187; *59:* 61, 62, 63, 64, 65, 66, 67, 68, 69, 71, 72, 74; *62:* 19
Deraney, Michael J. *77:* 35; *78:* 148
deRosa, Dee *70:* 48; *71:* 210; *91:* 78
Deshaprabhu, Meera Dayal *86:* 192
Desimini, Lisa *86:* 68; *94:* 47; *96:* 7

de St. Menin, Charles *70:* 17
Detmold, Edward J. *22:* 104, 105, 106, 107; *35:* 120; *64:* 5; *YABC 2:* 203
Detrich, Susan *20:* 133
Deutermann, Diana *77:* 175
DeVelasco, Joseph E. *21:* 51
de Veyrac, Robert *YABC 2:* 19
DeVille, Edward A. *4:* 235
de Visser, John *55:* 119
Devito, Bert *12:* 164
Devlin, Harry *11:* 74; *74:* 63, 65
Dewey, Ariane *7:* 64; *33:* 195; *35:* 208; *68:* 16, 17; *75:* 46; *93:* 91; *94:* 197
Dewey, Jennifer (Owings) *58:* 54; *64:* 214; *65:* 207; *88:* 169
Dewey, Kenneth *39:* 62; *51:* 23; *56:* 163
de Zanger, Arie *30:* 40
Diamond, Donna *21:* 200; *23:* 63; *26:* 142; *35:* 83, 84, 85, 86-87, 88, 89; *38:* 78; *40:* 147; *44:* 152; *50:* 144; *53:* 126; *69:* 46, 47, 48, 201; *71:* 133
Dias, Ron *71:* 67
Diaz, David *80:* 213; *96:* 83, 84
DiCesare, Joe *70:* 38; *71:* 63, 106; *79:* 214; *93:* 147
Dick, John Henry *8:* 181
Dickens, Frank *34:* 131
Dickey, Robert L. *15:* 279
Dickson, Mora *84:* 21
Di Fate, Vincent *37:* 70; *90:* 11; *93:* 60
Di Fiori, Lawrence *10:* 51; *12:* 190; *27:* 97; *40:* 219; *93:* 57
Digby, Desmond *97:* 180
Di Grazia, Thomas *32:* 66; *35:* 241
Dillard, Annie *10:* 32
Dillon, Corinne B. *1:* 139
Dillon, Diane *4:* 104, 167; *6:* 23; *13:* 29; *15:* 99; *26:* 148; *27:* 136, 201; *51:* 29, 48, 51, 52, 53, 54, 55, 56-57, 58, 59, 60, 61, 62; *54:* 155; *56:* 69; *58:* 127, 128; *61:* 95; *62:* 27; *64:* 46; *68:* 3; *69:* 209; *74:* 89; *79:* 92; *86:* 89; *92:* 28, 177; *93:* 7, 210; *94:* 239, 240; *97:* 167
Dillon, Leo *4:* 104, 167; *6:* 23; *13:* 29; *15:* 99; *26:* 148; *27:* 136, 201; *51:* 29, 48, 51, 52, 53, 54, 55, 56-57, 58, 59, 60, 61, 62; *54:* 155; *56:* 69; *58:* 127, 128; *61:* 95; *62:* 27; *64:* 46; *68:* 3; *69:* 209; *74:* 89; *79:* 92; *86:* 89; *92:* 28, 177; *93:* 7, 210; *94:* 239, 240; *97:* 167
Dillon, Sharon Saseen *59:* 179, 188
DiMaggio, Joe *36:* 22
Dinan, Carol *25:* 169; *59:* 75
Dines, Glen *7:* 66-67
Dinesen, Thomas *44:* 37
Dinnerstein, Harvey *42:* 63, 64, 65, 66, 67, 68; *50:* 146
Dinsdale, Mary *10:* 65; *11:* 171
Dinyer, Eric *86:* 148
DiSalvo-Ryan, DyAnne *59:* 77; *62:* 185
Disney, Walt *28:* 71, 72, 73, 76, 77, 78, 79, 80, 81, 87, 88, 89, 90, 91, 94
Divito, Anna *83:* 159
Dixon, Don *74:* 17
Dixon, Maynard *20:* 165
Doares, Robert G. *20:* 39
Dobias, Frank *22:* 162
Dobrin, Arnold *4:* 68
Docktor, Irv *43:* 70
Dodd, Ed *4:* 69
Dodd, Julie *74:* 73
Dodd, Lynley *35:* 92; *86:* 71
Dodge, Bill *96:* 36
Dodgson, Charles L. *20:* 148; *33:* 146; *YABC 2:* 98
Dodson, Bert *9:* 138; *14:* 195; *42:* 55; *54:* 8; *60:* 49
Dohanos, Stevan *16:* 10
Dolce, J. Ellen *74:* 147; *75:* 41
Dolch, Marguerite P. *50:* 64

Dolesch, Susanne *34:* 49
Dollar, Diane *57:* 32
Dolobowsky, Mena *81:* 54
Dolson, Hildegarde *5:* 57
Domanska, Janina *6:* 66-67; *YABC 1:* 166
Dominguez, El *53:* 94
Domjan, Joseph *25:* 93
Domm, Jeffrey C. *84:* 69
Donahey, William *68:* 209
Donahue, Dorothy *76:* 170
Donahue, Vic *2:* 93; *3:* 190; *9:* 44
Donald, Elizabeth *4:* 18
Donato *85:* 59
Doney, Todd L. W. *87:* 12; *93:* 112; *98:* 135
Donna, Natalie *9:* 52
Donohue, Dorothy *95:* 2
Dooling, Michael *82:* 19
Doré, Gustave *18:* 169, 172, 175; *19:* 93, 94, 95, 96, 97, 98, 99, 100, 101, 102, 103, 104, 105; *23:* 188; *25:* 197, 199
Doremus, Robert *6:* 62; *13:* 90; *30:* 95, 96, 97; *38:* 97
Dorfman, Ronald *11:* 128
Doriau *86:* 59; *91:* 152
Dorros, Arthur *78:* 42, 43; *91:* 28
dos Santos, Joyce Audy *57:* 187, 189
Doty, Roy *28:* 98; *31:* 32; *32:* 224; *46:* 157; *82:* 71
Dougherty, Charles *16:* 204; *18:* 74
Douglas, Aaron *31:* 103
Douglas, Carole Nelson *73:* 48
Douglas, Goray *13:* 151
Dowd, Vic *3:* 244; *10:* 97
Dowden, Anne Ophelia *7:* 70-71; *13:* 120
Dowdy, Mrs. Regera *29:* 100
Downing, Julie *60:* 140; *81:* 50; *86:* 200; *99:* 129
Doyle, Janet *56:* 31
Doyle, Richard *21:* 31, 32, 33; *23:* 231; *24:* 177; *31:* 87
Draper, Angie *43:* 84
Drath, Bill *26:* 34
Drawson, Blair *17:* 53
Drescher, Joan *30:* 100, 101; *35:* 245; *52:* 168
Drew, Patricia *15:* 100
Drummond, V. H. *6:* 70
Dubanevich, Arlene *56:* 44
Ducak, Danilo *99:* 130
Duchesne, Janet *6:* 162; *79:* 8
Dudash, Michael *32:* 122; *77:* 134; *82:* 149
Duer, Douglas *34:* 177
Duffy, Daniel Mark *76:* 37
Duffy, Joseph *38:* 203
Duffy, Pat *28:* 153
Dugin, Andrej *77:* 60
Dugina, Olga *77:* 60
Duke, Chris *8:* 195
Duke, Kate *87:* 186; *90:* 78, 79, 80, 81
Dulac, Edmund *19:* 108, 109, 110, 111, 112, 113, 114, 115, 117; *23:* 187; *25:* 152; *YABC 1:* 37; *2:* 147
Dulac, Jean *13:* 64
Dumas, Philippe *52:* 36, 37, 38, 39, 40-41, 42, 43, 45
Dunbar, James *76:* 63
Duncan, Beverly *72:* 92
Dunn, H. T. *62:* 196
Dunn, Harvey *34:* 78, 79, 80, 81
Dunn, Iris *5:* 175
Dunn, Phoebe *5:* 175
Dunne, Jeanette *72:* 57, 173, 222
Dunnington, Tom *3:* 36; *18:* 281; *25:* 61; *31:* 159; *35:* 168; *48:* 195; *79:* 144; *82:* 230
Dunrea, Olivier *59:* 81
Duntze, Dorothee *88:* 28
Dupasquier, Philippe *86:* 75

DuQuette, Keith *90:* 83
Durrell, Julie *82:* 62; *94:* 62
Dutz *6:* 59
Duvoisin, Roger *2:* 95; *6:* 76-77; *7:* 197; *28:* 125; *30:* 101, 102, 103, 104, 105, 107; *47:* 205; *84:* 254
Dyer, Jane *75:* 219
Dypold, Pat *15:* 37

E

E. V. B.
  See Boyle, Eleanor Vere (Gordon)
Eachus, Jennifer *29:* 74; *82:* 201
Eadie, Bob *63:* 36
Eagle, Bruce *95:* 119
Eagle, Ellen *82:* 121; *89:* 3
Eagle, Michael *11:* 86; *20:* 9; *23:* 18; *27:* 122; *28:* 57; *34:* 201; *44:* 189; *73:* 9; *78:* 235; *85:* 43
Earle, Edwin *56:* 27
Earle, Olive L. *7:* 75
Earle, Vana *27:* 99
Early, Margaret *72:* 59
Eastman, P. D. *33:* 57
Easton, Reginald *29:* 181
Eaton, Tom *4:* 62; *6:* 64; *22:* 99; *24:* 124
Ebel, Alex *11:* 89
Ebert, Len *9:* 191; *44:* 47
Echevarria, Abe *37:* 69
Eckersley, Maureen *48:* 62
Eckert, Horst *72:* 62
Ede, Janina *33:* 59
Edens, Cooper *49:* 81, 82, 83, 84, 85
Edgar, Sarah E. *41:* 97
Edrien *11:* 53
Edwards, Freya *45:* 102
Edwards, George Wharton *31:* 155
Edwards, Gunvor *2:* 71; *25:* 47; *32:* 71; *54:* 106
Edwards, Jeanne *29:* 257
Edwards, Linda Strauss *21:* 134; *39:* 123; *49:* 88-89
Eggenhofer, Nicholas *2:* 81
Eggleton, Bob *74:* 40; *81:* 190, 191
Egielski, Richard *11:* 90; *16:* 208; *33:* 236; *38:* 35; *49:* 91, 92, 93, 95, 212, 213, 214, 216; *79:* 122
Ehlert, Lois *35:* 97; *69:* 51
Ehrlich, Bettina *1:* 83
Eichenberg, Fritz *1:* 79; *9:* 54; *19:* 248; *23:* 170; *24:* 200; *26:* 208; *50:* 67, 68, 69, 70, 71, 72, 73, 74, 75, 77, 79, 80, 81; *60:* 165; *YABC 1:* 104-105; *2:* 213
Einsel, Naiad *10:* 35; *29:* 136
Einsel, Walter *10:* 37
Einzig, Susan *3:* 77; *43:* 78; *67:* 155
Eitzen, Allan *9:* 56; *12:* 212; *14:* 226; *21:* 194; *38:* 162; *76:* 218
Eldridge, H. *54:* 109
Eldridge, Harold *43:* 83
Elgaard, Greta *19:* 241
Elgin, Kathleen *9:* 188; *39:* 69
Ellacott, S. E. *19:* 118
Elliott, Mark *93:* 69
Elliott, Sarah M. *14:* 58
Ellis, Jan Davey *88:* 50
Ellison, Pauline *55:* 21
Elmer, Richard *78:* 5
Elmore, Larry *90:* 8
Elzbieta *88:* 80, 81
Emberley, Ed *8:* 53; *70:* 53, 54
Emberley, Michael *34:* 83; *80:* 72
Emery, Leslie *49:* 187
Emmett, Bruce *49:* 147; *80:* 175
Emry-Perrott, Jennifer *61:* 57

Engel, Diana *70:* 57
Engle, Mort *38:* 64
Englebert, Victor *8:* 54
Enos, Randall *20:* 183
Enright, Maginel Wright *19:* 240, 243; *39:* 31, 35, 36
Enrique, Romeo *34:* 135
Epstein, Stephen *50:* 142, 148
Erhard, Walter *1:* 152
Erickson, Phoebe *11:* 83; *59:* 85
Erikson, Mel *31:* 69
Eriksson, Eva *63:* 88, 90, 92, 93
Ernst, Lisa Campbell *47:* 147; *95:* 47
Esco, Jo *61:* 103
Escourido, Joseph *4:* 81
Esté, Kirk *33:* 111
Estep, David *73:* 57
Estes, Eleanor *91:* 66
Estoril, Jean *32:* 27
Estrada, Pau *74:* 76
Estrada, Ric *5:* 52, 146; *13:* 174
Etchemendy, Teje *38:* 68
Etheredges, the *73:* 12
Ets, Marie Hall *2:* 102
Eulalie *YABC 2:* 315
Evans, Greg *73:* 54, 55, 56
Evans, Katherine *5:* 64
Ewart, Claire *76:* 69
Ewing, Carolyn *66:* 143; *79:* 52
Ewing, Juliana Horatia *16:* 92
Eyolfson, Norman *98:* 154

F

Falconer, Pearl *34:* 23
Falkenstern, Lisa *70:* 34; *76:* 133; *78:* 171
Falls, C. B. *1:* 19; *38:* 71, 72, 73, 74
Falter, John *40:* 169, 170
Fanelli, Sara *89:* 63
Farmer, Andrew *49:* 102
Farmer, Peter *24:* 108; *38:* 75
Farnsworth, Bill *93:* 189
Farquharson, Alexander *46:* 75
Farrell, David *40:* 135
Farris, David *74:* 42
Fatigati, Evelyn *24:* 112
Faul-Jansen, Regina *22:* 117
Faulkner, Jack *6:* 169
Fava, Rita *2:* 29
Fax, Elton C. *1:* 101; *4:* 2; *12:* 77; *25:* 107
Fay *43:* 93
Federspiel, Marian *33:* 51
Feelings, Tom *5:* 22; *8:* 56; *12:* 153; *16:* 105; *30:* 196; *49:* 37; *61:* 101; *69:* 56, 57; *93:* 74
Fehr, Terrence *21:* 87
Feiffer, Jules *3:* 91; *8:* 58; *61:* 66, 67, 70, 74, 76, 77, 78
Feigeles, Neil *41:* 242
Feldman, Elyse *86:* 7
Feller, Gene *33:* 130
Fellows, Muriel H. *10:* 42
Felts, Shirley *33:* 71; *48:* 59
Fennelli, Maureen *38:* 181
Fenton, Carroll Lane *5:* 66; *21:* 39
Fenton, Mildred Adams *5:* 66; *21:* 39
Ferguson, Walter W. *34:* 86
Fernandes, Eugenie *77:* 67
Fernandes, Stanislaw *70:* 28
Fernandez, Fernando *77:* 57
Fernandez, Laura *77:* 153
Fetz, Ingrid *11:* 67; *12:* 52; *16:* 205; *17:* 59; *29:* 105; *30:* 108, 109; *32:* 149; *43:* 142; *56:* 29; *60:* 34; *85:* 48; *87:* 146

Fiammenghi, Gioia *9:* 66; *11:* 44; *12:* 206; *13:* 57, 59; *52:* 126, 129; *66:* 64; *85:* 83; *91:* 161
Fiedler, Joseph Daniel *96:* 42
Field, Rachel *15:* 113
Fielding, David *70:* 124
Fine, Peter K. *43:* 210
Finger, Helen *42:* 81
Fink, Sam *18:* 119
Finlay, Winifred *23:* 72
Finney, Pat *79:* 215
Fiore, Peter *99:* 196
Fiorentino, Al *3:* 240
Firmin, Charlotte *29:* 75; *48:* 70
Firmin, Peter *58:* 63, 64, 65, 67, 68, 70, 71
Firth, Barbara *81:* 208
Fischel, Lillian *40:* 204
Fischer, Hans *25:* 202
Fischer-Nagel, Andreas *56:* 50
Fischer-Nagel, Heiderose *56:* 50
Fisher, Chris *79:* 62
Fisher, Leonard Everett *3:* 6; *4:* 72, 86; *6:* 197; *9:* 59; *16:* 151, 153; *23:* 44; *27:* 134; *29:* 26; *34:* 87, 89, 90, 91, 93, 94, 95, 96; *40:* 206; *50:* 158; *60:* 158; *73:* 68, 70, 71, 72, 73; *YABC 2:* 169
Fisher, Lois *20:* 62; *21:* 7
Fisk, Nicholas *25:* 112
Fitschen, Marilyn *2:* 20-21; *20:* 48
Fitzgerald, F. A. *15:* 116; *25:* 86-87
Fitzhugh, Louise *1:* 94; *9:* 163; *45:* 75, 78
Fitzhugh, Susie *11:* 117
Fitzsimmons, Arthur *14:* 128
Fix, Philippe *26:* 102
Flack, Marjorie *21:* 67; *YABC 2:* 122
Flagg, James Montgomery *17:* 227
Flax, Zeona *2:* 245
Fleishman, Seymour *14:* 232; *24:* 87
Fleming, Denise *71:* 179; *81:* 58
Fleming, Guy *18:* 41
Flesher, Vivienne *85:* 55
Fletcher, Claire *80:* 106
Flint, Russ *74:* 80
Floethe, Richard *3:* 131; *4:* 90
Floherty, John J., Jr. *5:* 68
Flora, James *1:* 96; *30:* 111, 112
Florian, Douglas *19:* 122; *83:* 64, 65
Flory, Jane *22:* 111
Floyd, Gareth *1:* 74; *17:* 245; *48:* 63; *62:* 35, 36, 37, 39, 40, 41; *74:* 245; *79:* 56
Fluchère, Henri A. *40:* 79
Flynn, Barbara *7:* 31; *9:* 70
Fogarty, Thomas *15:* 89
Folger, Joseph *9:* 100
Folkard, Charles *22:* 132; *29:* 128, 257-258
Foott, Jeff *42:* 202
Forberg, Ati *12:* 71, 205; *14:* 1; *22:* 113; *26:* 22; *48:* 64, 65
Ford, George *24:* 120; *31:* 70, 177; *58:* 126; *81:* 103
Ford, H. J. *16:* 185-186
Ford, Pamela Baldwin *27:* 104
Foreman, Michael *2:* 110-111; *67:* 99; *73:* 78, 79, 80, 81, 82; *93:* 146
Forrester, Victoria *40:* 83
Fortnum, Peggy *6:* 29; *20:* 179; *24:* 211; *26:* 76, 77, 78; *39:* 78; *58:* 19, 21, 23, 27; *YABC 1:* 148
Foster, Brad W. *34:* 99
Foster, Genevieve *2:* 112
Foster, Gerald *7:* 78
Foster, Laura Louise *6:* 79
Foster, Marian Curtis *23:* 74; *40:* 42
Foster, Sally *58:* 73, 74
Foucher, Adèle *47:* 118
Fowler, Mel *36:* 127
Fowler, Richard *87:* 219
Fox, Charles Phillip *12:* 84
Fox, Jim *6:* 187
Fox-Davies, Sarah *76:* 150

Fracé, Charles *15:* 118
Frailey, Joy *72:* 108
Frame, Paul *2:* 45, 145; *9:* 153; *10:* 124; *21:* 71; *23:* 62; *24:* 123; *27:* 106; *31:* 48; *32:* 159; *34:* 195; *38:* 136; *42:* 55; *44:* 139; *60:* 39, 40, 41, 42, 43, 44, 46; *73:* 183
Frampton, David *85:* 72
Francois, André *25:* 117
Francoise
    See Seignobosc, Francoise
Frank, Lola Edick *2:* 199
Frank, Mary *4:* 54; *34:* 100
Franké, Phil *45:* 91
Frankel, Alona *66:* 70
Frankel, Julie *40:* 84, 85, 202
Frankenberg, Robert *22:* 116; *30:* 50; *38:* 92, 94, 95; *68:* 111
Frankfeldt, Gwen *84:* 223
Franklin, John *24:* 22
Frascino, Edward *9:* 133; *29:* 229; *33:* 190; *48:* 80, 81, 82, 83, 84-85, 86
Frasconi, Antonio *6:* 80; *27:* 208; *53:* 41, 43, 45, 47, 48; *68:* 145; *73:* 226
Fraser, Betty *2:* 212; *6:* 185; *8:* 103; *31:* 72, 73; *43:* 136
Fraser, Eric *38:* 78; *41:* 149, 151
Fraser, F. A. *22:* 234
Frasier, Debra *69:* 60
Frazee, Marla *72:* 98
Frazetta, Frank *41:* 72; *58:* 77, 78, 79, 80, 81, 82, 83
Freas, John *25:* 207
Freeman, Don *2:* 15; *13:* 249; *17:* 62-63, 65, 67-68; *18:* 243; *20:* 195; *23:* 213, 217; *32:* 155; *55:* 129
Freeman, Irving *67:* 150
Fregosi, Claudia *24:* 117
French, Fiona *6:* 82-83; *75:* 61
Freynet, Gilbert *72:* 221
Friedman, Judith *43:* 197
Friedman, Marvin *19:* 59; *42:* 86
Frinta, Dagmar *36:* 42
Frith, Michael K. *15:* 138; *18:* 120
Fritz, Ronald *46:* 73; *82:* 124
Fromm, Lilo *29:* 85; *40:* 197
Frost, A. B. *17:* 6-7; *19:* 123, 124, 125, 126, 127, 128, 129, 130; *YABC 1:* 156-157, 160; *2:* 107
Fry, Guy *2:* 224
Fry, Rosalie *3:* 72; *YABC 2:* 180-181
Fry, Rosalind *21:* 153, 168
Fryer, Elmer *34:* 115
Fuchs, Erich *6:* 84
Fuchshuber, Annegert *43:* 96
Fufuka, Mahiri *32:* 146
Fujikawa, Gyo *39:* 75, 76; *76:* 72, 73, 74
Fulford, Deborah *23:* 159
Fuller, Margaret *25:* 189
Fulweiler, John *93:* 99
Funai, Mamoru *38:* 105
Funk, Tom *7:* 17, 99
Furchgott, Terry *29:* 86
Furness, William Henry, Jr. *94:* 18
Furukawa, Mel *25:* 42

G

Gaadt, David *78:* 212
Gaadt, George *71:* 9
Gaber, Susan *99:* 33
Gaberell, J. *19:* 236
Gabler, Mirko *99:* 71
Gackenbach, Dick *19:* 168; *41:* 81; *48:* 89, 90, 91, 92, 93, 94; *54:* 105; *79:* 75, 76, 77
GAD, VictoR *87:* 161
Gaetano, Nicholas *23:* 209
Gaffney-Kessell, Walter *94:* 219

Gag, Flavia *17:* 49, 52
Gág, Wanda *YABC 1:* 135, 137-138, 141, 143
Gagnon, Cécile *11:* 77; *58:* 87
Gal, Laszlo *14:* 127; *52:* 54, 55, 56; *65:* 142; *68:* 150; *81:* 185; *96:* 104, 105
Galazinski, Tom *55:* 13
Galdone, Paul *1:* 156, 181, 206; *2:* 40, 241; *3:* 42, 144; *4:* 141; *10:* 109, 158; *11:* 21; *12:* 118, 210; *14:* 12; *16:* 36-37; *17:* 70-74; *18:* 111, 230; *19:* 183; *21:* 154; *22:* 150, 245; *33:* 126; *39:* 136, 137; *42:* 57; *51:* 169; *55:* 110; *66:* 80, 82, 139; *72:* 73
Gallagher, Sears *20:* 112
Galloway, Ewing *51:* 154
Galouchko, Annouchka Gravel *95:* 55
Galster, Robert *1:* 66
Galsworthy, Gay John *35:* 232
Gammell, Stephen *7:* 48; *13:* 149; *29:* 82; *33:* 209; *41:* 88; *50:* 185, 186-187; *53:* 51, 52-53, 54, 55, 56, 57, 58; *54:* 24, 25; *56:* 147, 148, 150; *57:* 27, 66; *81:* 62, 63; *87:* 88; *89:* 10
Gamper, Ruth *84:* 198
Gampert, John *58:* 94
Ganly, Helen *56:* 56
Gannett, Ruth Chrisman *3:* 74; *18:* 254; *33:* 77, 78
Gantschev, Ivan *45:* 32
Garafano, Marie *73:* 33
Garbutt, Bernard *23:* 68
Garcia *37:* 71
Garcia, Manuel *74:* 145
Gardner, Earle *45:* 167
Gardner, Joan *40:* 87
Gardner, Joel *40:* 87, 92
Gardner, John *40:* 87
Gardner, Lucy *40:* 87
Gardner, Richard
    See Cummings, Richard
Gargiulo, Frank *84:* 158
Garland, Michael *36:* 29; *38:* 83; *44:* 168; *48:* 78, 221, 222; *49:* 161; *60:* 139; *71:* 6, 11; *72:* 229; *74:* 142; *89:* 187; *93:* 183
Garland, Peggy *60:* 139
Garland, Sarah *62:* 45
Garn, Aimee *75:* 47
Garneray, Ambroise Louis *59:* 140
Garnett, Eve *3:* 75
Garnett, Gary *39:* 184
Garns, Allen *80:* 125; *84:* 39
Garraty, Gail *4:* 142; *52:* 106
Garrett, Agnes *46:* 110; *47:* 157
Garrett, Edmund H. *20:* 29
Garrick, Jacqueline *67:* 42, 43; *77:* 94
Garrison, Barbara *19:* 133
Garvey, Robert *98:* 222
Garza, Carmen Lomas *80:* 211
Gates, Frieda *26:* 80
Gaughan, Jack *26:* 79; *43:* 185
Gaver, Becky *20:* 61
Gawing, Toby *72:* 52
Gay, Marie-Louise *68:* 76-77, 78
Gay, Zhenya *19:* 135, 136
Gaydos, Tim *62:* 201
Gazsi, Ed *80:* 48
Gazso, Gabriel *73:* 85
Geary, Clifford N. *1:* 122; *9:* 104; *51:* 74
Gee, Frank *33:* 26
Geer, Charles *1:* 91; *3:* 179; *4:* 201; *6:* 168; *7:* 96; *9:* 58; *10:* 72; *12:* 127; *39:* 156, 157, 158, 159, 160; *42:* 88, 89, 90, 91; *55:* 111, 116
Gehm, Charlie *36:* 65; *57:* 117; *62:* 60, 138
Geisel, Theodor Seuss *1:* 104-105, 106; *28:* 108, 109, 110, 111, 112, 113; *75:* 67, 68, 69, 70, 71; *89:* 127, 128
Geisert, Arthur *92:* 67, 68
Geldart, William *15:* 121; *21:* 202
Genia *4:* 84

Gentry, Cyrille R. *12:* 66
George, Jean *2:* 113
George, Lindsay Barrett *95:* 57
Gérard, Jean Ignace *45:* 80
Gérard, Rolf *27:* 147, 150
Gerber, Mark *61:* 105
Gerber, Stephanie *71:* 195
Gergely, Tibor *54:* 15, 16
Geritz, Franz *17:* 135
Gerlach, Geff *42:* 58
Gerrard, Roy *47:* 78; *90:* 96, 97, 98, 99
Gershinowitz, George *36:* 27
Gerstein, Mordicai *31:* 117; *47:* 80, 81, 82, 83, 84, 85, 86; *51:* 173; *69:* 134
Gervase *12:* 27
Getz, Arthur *32:* 148
Gewirtz, Bina *61:* 81
Giancola, Donato *95:* 146
Gibbons, Gail *23:* 78; *72:* 77, 78, 79; *82:* 182
Gibbs, Tony *40:* 95
Gibran, Kahlil *32:* 116
Gider, Iskender *81:* 193
Giesen, Rosemary *34:* 192-193
Giffard, Hannah *83:* 70
Giguère, George *20:* 111
Gilbert, John *19:* 184; *54:* 115; *YABC 2:* 287
Gilbert, W. S. *36:* 83, 85, 96
Gilchrist, Jan Spivey *72:* 82, 83, 84-85, 87; *77:* 90
Giles, Will *41:* 218
Gili, Phillida *70:* 73
Gill, Margery *4:* 57; *7:* 7; *22:* 122; *25:* 166; *26:* 146, 147
Gillen, Denver *28:* 216
Gillette, Henry J. *23:* 237
Gilliam, Stan *39:* 64, 81
Gillies, Chuck *62:* 31
Gilliland, Jillian *87:* 58
Gillman, Alec *98:* 105
Gilman, Esther *15:* 124
Ginsburg, Max *62:* 59; *68:* 194
Giovanopoulos, Paul *7:* 104; *60:* 36
Giovine, Sergio *79:* 12; *93:* 118
Githens, Elizabeth M. *5:* 47
Gladden, Scott *99:* 108
Gladstone, Gary *12:* 89; *13:* 190
Gladstone, Lise *15:* 273
Glanzman, Louis S. *2:* 177; *3:* 182; *36:* 97, 98; *38:* 120, 122; *52:* 141, 144; *71:* 191; *91:* 54, 56
Glaser, Milton *3:* 5; *5:* 156; *11:* 107; *30:* 26; *36:* 112; *54:* 141
Glass, Andrew *36:* 38; *44:* 133; *48:* 205; *65:* 3; *68:* 43, 45; *90:* 104, 105
Glass, Marvin *9:* 174
Glasser, Judy *41:* 156; *56:* 140; *69:* 79; *72:* 101
Glattauer, Ned *5:* 84; *13:* 224; *14:* 26
Glauber, Uta *17:* 76
Gleeson, J. M. *YABC 2:* 207
Glegg, Creina *36:* 100
Glienke, Amelie *63:* 150
Gliewe, Unada *3:* 78-79; *21:* 73; *30:* 220
Gliori, Debi *72:* 91
Glovach, Linda *7:* 105
Gobbato, Imero *3:* 180-181; *6:* 213; *7:* 58; *9:* 150; *18:* 39; *21:* 167; *39:* 82, 83; *41:* 137, 251; *59:* 177
Goble, Paul *25:* 121; *26:* 86; *33:* 65; *69:* 68-69
Goble, Warwick *46:* 78, 79
Godal, Eric *36:* 93
Godfrey, Michael *17:* 279
Goembel, Ponder *42:* 124
Goffe, Toni *61:* 83, 84, 85; *89:* 11; *90:* 124
Goffstein, M. B. *8:* 71; *70:* 75, 76, 77
Golbin, Andrée *15:* 125

Goldfeder, Cheryl *11:* 191
Goldsborough, June *5:* 154-155; *8:* 92, *14:* 226; *19:* 139; *54:* 165
Goldstein, Leslie *5:* 8; *6:* 60; *10:* 106
Goldstein, Nathan *1:* 175; *2:* 79; *11:* 41, 232; *16:* 55
Goldstrom, Robert *98:* 36
Golembe, Carla *79:* 80, 81
Golin, Carlo *74:* 112
Gomi, Taro *64:* 102
Goodall, John S. *4:* 92-93; *10:* 132; *66:* 92, 93; *YABC 1:* 198
Goode, Diane *15:* 126; *50:* 183; *52:* 114-115; *76:* 195; *84:* 94; *99:* 141
Goodelman, Aaron *40:* 203
Goodenow, Earle *40:* 97
Goodfellow, Peter *62:* 95; *94:* 202
Goodman, Joan Elizabeth *50:* 86
Goodman, Vivian *82:* 251
Goodwin, Harold *13:* 74
Goodwin, Philip R. *18:* 206
Goor, Nancy *39:* 85, 86
Goor, Ron *39:* 85, 86
Gorbachev, Valeri *89:* 96
Gordon, Gwen *12:* 151
Gordon, Margaret *4:* 147; *5:* 48-49; *9:* 79
Gore, Leonid *89:* 51; *94:* 74
Gorecka-Egan, Erica *18:* 35
Gorey, Edward *85:* 136
Gorey, Edward *1:* 60-61; *13:* 169; *18:* 192; *20:* 201; *29:* 90, 91, 92-93, 94, 95, 96, 97, 98, 99, 100; *30:* 129; *32:* 90; *34:* 200, 65: 48; *68:* 24, 25; *69:* 79; *70:* 80, 82, 83, 84
Gorsline, Douglas *1:* 98; *6:* 13; *11:* 113; *13:* 104; *15:* 14; *28:* 117, 118; *YABC 1:* 15
Gosner, Kenneth *5:* 135
Gotlieb, Jules *6:* 127
Gottlieb, Dale *67:* 162
Goudey, Ray *97:* 86
Gough, Alan *91:* 57
Gough, Philip *23:* 47; *45:* 90
Gould, Chester *49:* 112, 113, 114, 116, 117, 118
Govern, Elaine R. *26:* 94
Gowing, Toby *60:* 25; *63:* 33; *78:* 70, 252; *83:* 228; *86:* 187; *93:* 145
Grabianski *20:* 144
Grabia ski, Janusz *39:* 92, 93, 94, 95
Graboff, Abner *35:* 103, 104
Graef, Renee *61:* 188; *72:* 207
Graham, A. B. *11:* 61
Graham, L. *7:* 108
Graham, Margaret Bloy *11:* 120; *18:* 305, 307
Graham, Mark *88:* 208
Grahame-Johnstone, Janet *13:* 61
Grahame-Johnstone, Anne *13:* 61
Grainger, Sam *42:* 95
Gramatky, Hardie *1:* 107; *30:* 116, 119, 120, 122, 123
Granahan, Julie *84:* 84
GrandPre, Mary *84:* 131
Grandville, J. J. *45:* 81, 82, 83, 84, 85, 86, 87, 88, *47:* 125; *64:* 10
Granger, Paul *39:* 153
Grant, (Alice) Leigh *10:* 52; *15:* 131; *20:* 20; *26:* 119; *48:* 202
Grant, Gordon *17:* 230, 234; *25:* 123, 124, 125, 126; *52:* 69; *YABC 1:* 164
Grant, Renee *77:* 40
Graves, Elizabeth *45:* 101
Gray, Harold *33:* 87, 88
Gray, Les *82:* 76; *83:* 232
Gray, Reginald *6:* 69
Greder, Armin *76:* 235
Green, Ann Canevari *62:* 48
Green, Eileen *6:* 97
Green, Jonathan *86:* 135

Green, Michael *32:* 216
Green, Robina *87:* 138
Greenaway, Kate *17:* 275; *24:* 180; *26:* 107; *41:* 222, 232; *YABC 1:* 88-89; *2:* 131, 133, 136, 138-139, 141
Greenberg, Melanie Hope *72:* 93; *80:* 125
Greenwald, Sheila *1:* 34; *3:* 99; *8:* 72
Greger, Carol *76:* 86
Gregorian, Joyce Ballou *30:* 125
Gregory, Frank M. *29:* 107
Greiffenhagen, Maurice *16:* 137; *27:* 57; *YABC 2:* 288
Greiner, Robert *6:* 86
Gretter, J. Clemens *31:* 134
Gretz, Susanna *7:* 114
Gretzer, John *1:* 54; *3:* 26; *4:* 162; *7:* 125; *16:* 247; *18:* 117; *28:* 66; *30:* 85, 211; *33:* 235; *56:* 16
Grey Owl *24:* 41
Gri *25:* 90
Grieder, Walter *9:* 84
Griesbach/Martucci *59:* 3
Grifalconi, Ann *2:* 126; *3:* 248; *11:* 18; *13:* 182; *46:* 38; *50:* 145; *66:* 99, 100, 101, 104, 106; *69:* 38; *70:* 64; *87:* 128; *90:* 53; *93:* 49
Griffin, Gillett Good *26:* 96
Griffin, James *30:* 166
Griffin, John Howard *59:* 186
Griffith, Gershom *94:* 214
Griffiths, Dave *29:* 76
Grimsdell, Jeremy *83:* 75
Grimwood, Brian *82:* 89
Gringhuis, Dirk *6:* 98; *9:* 196
Gripe, Harald *2:* 127; *74:* 98
Grisha *3:* 71
Grohmann, Susan *84:* 97
Gropper, William *27:* 93; *37:* 193
Gros *60:* 199
Grose, Helen Mason *YABC 1:* 260; *2:* 150
Grossman, Nancy *24:* 130; *29:* 101
Grossman, Robert *11:* 124; *46:* 39
Groth, John *15:* 79; *21:* 53, 54; *83:* 230
Gruelle, Johnny *35:* 107
Gschwind, William *11:* 72
Guback, Georgia *88:* 102
Guevara, Susan *97:* 87
Guggenheim, Hans *2:* 10; *3:* 37; *8:* 136
Guilbeau, Honoré *22:* 69
Guisewite, Cathy *57:* 52, 53, 54, 56, 57
Gukova, Julia *95:* 104
Gundersheimer, Karen *35:* 240; *82:* 100
Gunderson, Nick *57:* 120
Gurney, James *76:* 97; *86:* 32
Gurney, John *75:* 39, 82
Gusman, Annie *38:* 62
Gustafson, Scott *34:* 111; *43:* 40
Guthrie, R. Dale *64:* 143
Guthrie, Robin *20:* 122
Gutierrez, Rudy *97:* 162
Gutmann, Bessie Pease *73:* 93, 94
Gwynne, Fred *41:* 94, 95
Gyberg, Bo-Erik *38:* 131

H

Haas, Irene *17:* 77; *87:* 46; *96:* 117
Hack, Konrad *51:* 127
Hader, Berta H. *16:* 126
Hader, Elmer S. *16:* 126
Haeffele, Deborah *76:* 99
Haemer, Alan *62:* 109
Hafner, Marylin *22:* 196, 216; *24:* 44; *30:* 51; *35:* 95; *51:* 25, 160, 164; *86:* 16
Hagerty, Sean *62:* 181
Hague, Michael *32:* 128; *48:* 98, 99, 100-101, 103, 105, 106-107, 108, 109, 110;

49: 121; *51:* 105; *64:* 14, 15; *79:* 134; *80:* 91, 92; *83:* 135
Halas, John *29:* 41, 47, 48
Haldane, Roger *13:* 76; *14:* 202
Hale, Christy *79:* 124; *84:* 200
Hale, Irina *26:* 97
Hale, James Graham *88:* 207
Hale, Kathleen *17:* 79; *66:* 114, 116, 118
Haley, Gail E. *43:* 102, 103, 104, 105; *78:* 65, 67
Hall, Amanda *96:* 110
Hall, Chuck *30:* 189
Hall, Douglas *15:* 184; *43:* 106, 107; *86:* 100; *87:* 82
Hall, H. Tom *1:* 227; *30:* 210
Hall, Sydney P. *31:* 89
Hall, Vicki *20:* 24
Hallinan, P. K. *39:* 98
Hallman, Tom *98:* 166
Halperin, Wendy Anderson *96:* 151
Halpern, Joan *10:* 25
Halsey, Megan *96:* 172
Halverson, Janet *49:* 38, 42, 44
Hamanaka, Sheila *71:* 100
Hamann, Brad *78:* 151
Hamberger, John *6:* 8; *8:* 32; *14:* 79; *34:* 136; *88:* 78
Hamil, Tom *14:* 80; *43:* 163
Hamilton, Bill and Associates *26:* 215
Hamilton, Helen S. *2:* 238
Hamilton, J. *19:* 83, 85, 87
Hamilton, Todd Cameron *84:* 15
Hamlin, Janet *97:* 136
Hamlin, Louise *71:* 135
Hammond, Chris *21:* 37
Hammond, Elizabeth *5:* 36, 203
Hampshire, Michael *5:* 187; *7:* 110-111; *48:* 150; *51:* 129
Hampson, Denman *10:* 155; *15:* 130
Hampton, Blake *41:* 244
Handford, Martin *64:* 105, 106-07, 109
Handforth, Thomas *42:* 100, 101, 102, 103, 104, 105, 107
Handville, Robert *1:* 89; *38:* 76; *45:* 108, 109
Hane, Roger *17:* 239; *44:* 54
Haney, Elizabeth Mathieu *34:* 84
Hanke, Ted *71:* 10
Hanley, Catherine *8:* 161
Hann, Jacquie *19:* 144
Hanna, Cheryl *91:* 133
Hanna, Wayne A. *67:* 145
Hannon, Mark *38:* 37
Hanson, Joan *8:* 76; *11:* 139
Hanson, Peter E. *52:* 47; *54:* 99, 100; *73:* 21; *84:* 79
Hansson, Gunilla *64:* 111, 112
Hardy, David A. *9:* 96
Hardy, Paul *YABC 2:* 245
Harlan, Jerry *3:* 96
Harlin, Greg *89:* 194
Harnischfeger *18:* 121
Harper, Arthur *YABC 2:* 121
Harper, Piers *79:* 27
Harrington, Glenn *82:* 18; *94:* 66, 68
Harrington, Jack *83:* 162
Harrington, Richard *5:* 81
Harris, John *83:* 25
Harris, Nick *86:* 177
Harris, Susan Yard *42:* 121
Harrison, Florence *20:* 150, 152
Harrison, Harry *4:* 103
Harrison, Jack *28:* 149
Harrison, Ted *56:* 73
Harsh, Fred *72:* 107
Hart, Lewis *98:* 115
Hart, William *13:* 72
Hartelius, Margaret *10:* 24
Hartshorn, Ruth *5:* 115; *11:* 129
Harvey, Bob *48:* 219

Harvey, Gerry *7:* 180
Harvey, Lisa *97:* 21
Harvey, Paul *88:* 74
Harvey, Roland *71:* 88
Hassall, Joan *43:* 108, 109
Hassell, Hilton *YABC 1:* 187
Hasselriis, Else *18:* 87; *YABC 1:* 96
Hastings, Glenn *89:* 183
Hastings, Ian *62:* 67
Hauman, Doris *2:* 184; *29:* 58, 59; *32:* 85, 86, 87
Hauman, George *2:* 184; *29:* 58, 59; *32:* 85, 86, 87
Hausherr, Rosmarie *15:* 29
Hawkes, Kevin *78:* 72
Hawkinson, John *4:* 109; *7:* 83; *21:* 64
Hawkinson, Lucy *21:* 64
Haxton, Elaine *28:* 131
Haydock, Robert *4:* 95
Hayes, Geoffrey *26:* 111; *44:* 133; *91:* 85
Haynes, Max *72:* 107
Hays, Michael *73:* 207; *83:* 93
Haywood, Carolyn *1:* 112; *29:* 104
Healy, Daty *12:* 143
Healy, Deborah *58:* 181, 182
Hearn, Diane Dawson *79:* 99
Hearon, Dorothy *34:* 69
Heaslip, William *57:* 24, 25
Hechtkopf, H. *11:* 110
Hedderwick, Mairi *30:* 127; *32:* 47; *36:* 104; *77:* 86
Hefter, Richard *28:* 170; *31:* 81, 82; *33:* 183
Heigh, James *22:* 98
Heighway, Richard *25:* 160; *64:* 4
Heine, Helme *67:* 86
Heinly, John *45:* 113
Hellard, Susan *81:* 21
Hellebrand, Nancy *26:* 57
Heller, Linda *46:* 86
Heller, Ruth M. *66:* 125; *77:* 30, 32
Hellmuth, Jim *38:* 164
Helms, Georgeann *33:* 62
Helweg, Hans *41:* 118; *50:* 93; *58:* 22, 26
Henba, Bobbie *90:* 195
Henderson, Dave *73:* 76; *75:* 191, 192, 193, 194; *82:* 4
Henderson, Kathy *55:* 32
Henderson, Keith *35:* 122
Hendry, Linda *80:* 104; *83:* 83
Henkes, Kevin *43:* 111
Henneberger, Robert *1:* 42; *2:* 237; *25:* 83
Henriksen, Harold *35:* 26; *48:* 68
Henriquez, Elsa *82:* 260
Henriquez, Emile F. *89:* 88
Henry, Everett *29:* 191
Henry, Paul *93:* 121
Henry, Thomas *5:* 102
Hensel *27:* 119
Henstra, Friso *8:* 80; *36:* 70; *40:* 222; *41:* 250; *73:* 100, 101
Henterly, Jamichael *93:* 4
Heo, Yumi *89:* 85, 86; *94:* 89, 90
Hepple, Norman *28:* 198
Herbert, Helen *57:* 70
Herbert, Wally *23:* 101
Herbster, Mary Lee *9:* 33
Hergé
    See Rémi, Georges
Hermanson, Dennis *10:* 55
Hermes, Gertrude *54:* 161
Herr, Margo *57:* 191
Herr, Susan *83:* 163
Herriman, Lisa *87:* 190
Herrington, Roger *3:* 161
Hescox, Richard *85:* 86; *90:* 30
Heslop, Mike *38:* 60; *40:* 130
Hess, Lydia J. *85:* 17
Hess, Richard *42:* 31
Hester, Ronnie *37:* 85

Heustis, Louise L. *20:* 28
Hewitson, Jennifer *74:* 119
Hewitt, Kathryn *80:* 126
Hewitt, Margaret *84:* 112
Heyduck-Huth, Hilde *8:* 82
Heyer, Carol *74:* 122
Heyer, Hermann *20:* 114, 115
Heyman, Ken *8:* 33; *34:* 113
Heywood, Karen *48:* 114
Hickling, P. B. *40:* 165
Hickman, Steve *85:* 58
Hierstein, Judy *56:* 40
Higginbottom, J. Winslow *8:* 170; *29:* 105, 106
Higham, David *50:* 104
Hildebrandt, Greg *8:* 191; *55:* 35, 36, 38, 39, 40, 42, 46
Hildebrandt, Tim *8:* 191; *55:* 44, 45, 46
Hilder, Rowland *19:* 207
Hill, Eric *66:* 127, 128
Hill, Gregory *35:* 190
Hill, Pat *49:* 120
Hillenbrand, Will *84:* 115; *92:* 76, 80; *93:* 131
Hillier, Matthew *45:* 205
Hillman, Priscilla *48:* 115
Himler, Ronald *6:* 114; *7:* 162; *8:* 17, 84, 125; *14:* 76; *19:* 145; *26:* 160; *31:* 43; *38:* 116; *41:* 44, 79; *43:* 52; *45:* 120; *46:* 43; *54:* 44, 83; *58:* 180; *59:* 38; *68:* 146; *69:* 231; *70:* 98; *71:* 177, 178; *77:* 219; *79:* 212; *83:* 62; *89:* 5; *91:* 160; *92:* 91, 92, 93; *94:* 93; *95:* 69, 174, 194; *99:* 99, 112
Himmelman, John C. *47:* 109; *65:* 87; *94:* 96, 97
Hinds, Bill *37:* 127, 130
Hines, Anna Grossnickle *51:* 90; *74:* 124; *95:* 78, 79, 80, 81
Hiroko *99:* 61
Hiroshige *25:* 71
Hirsh, Marilyn *7:* 126
Hitch, Jeff *99:* 206
Hitz, Demi *11:* 135; *15:* 245; *66:* 129, 130
Hnizdovsky, Jacques *32:* 96; *76:* 187
Ho, Kwoncjan *15:* 132
Hoban, Lillian *1:* 114; *22:* 157; *26:* 72; *29:* 53; *40:* 105, 107, 195; *41:* 80; *69:* 107, 108; *71:* 98; *77:* 168
Hoban, Tana *22:* 159
Hoberman, Norman *5:* 82
Hobson, Sally *77:* 185
Hockerman, Dennis *39:* 22; *56:* 23
Hodgell, P. C. *42:* 114
Hodges, C. Walter *2:* 139; *11:* 15; *12:* 25; *23:* 34; *25:* 96; *38:* 165; *44:* 197; *45:* 95; *YABC 2:* 62-63
Hodges, David *9:* 98
Hodgetts, Victoria *43:* 132
Hofbauer, Imre *2:* 162
Hoff, Syd *9:* 107; *10:* 128; *33:* 94; *72:* 115, 116, 117, 118
Hoffman, Rosekrans *15:* 133; *50:* 219; *63:* 97
Hoffman, Sanford *38:* 208; *76:* 174; *88:* 160, 161
Hoffmann, Felix *9:* 109
Hoffnung, Gerard *66:* 76, 77
Hofsinde, Robert *21:* 70
Hogan, Inez *2:* 141
Hogarth, Burne *41:* 58; *63:* 46, 48, 49, 50, 52, 53, 54, 55, 56
Hogarth, Paul *41:* 102, 103, 104; *YABC 1:* 16
Hogarth, William *42:* 33
Hogenbyl, Jan *1:* 35
Hogner, Nils *4:* 122; *25:* 144
Hogrogian, Nonny *3:* 221; *4:* 106-107; *5:* 166; *7:* 129; *15:* 2; *16:* 176; *20:* 154;

22: 146; *25:* 217; *27:* 206; *74:* 127, 128, 129, 149, 152; *YABC 2:* 84, 94
Hokanson, Lars *93:* 111
Hokusai *25:* 71
Holberg, Richard *2:* 51
Holdcroft, Tina *38:* 109
Holden, Caroline *55:* 159
Holder, Heidi *36:* 99; *64:* 9
Holiday, Henry *YABC 2:* 107
Holl, F. *36:* 91
Holland, Brad *45:* 59, 159
Holland, Janice *18:* 118
Holland, Marion *6:* 116
Holldobler, Turid *26:* 120
Holling, Holling C. *15:* 136-137
Hollinger, Deanne *12:* 116
Holmes, B. *3:* 82
Holmes, Bea *7:* 74; *24:* 156; *31:* 93
Holmes, Dave *54:* 22
Holmgren, George Ellen *45:* 112
Holt, Norma *44:* 106
Holtan, Gene *32:* 192
Holz, Loretta *17:* 81
Hom, Nancy *79:* 195
Homar, Lorenzo *6:* 2
Homer, Winslow *YABC 2:* 87
Hong, Lily Toy *76:* 104
Honigman, Marian *3:* 2
Honoré, Paul *42:* 77, 79, 81, 82
Hood, Alun *69:* 145, 218; *72:* 41; *80:* 226; *87:* 4; *95:* 139
Hood, Susan *12:* 43
Hook, Frances *26:* 188; *27:* 127
Hook, Jeff *14:* 137
Hook, Richard *26:* 188
Hooks *63:* 30
Hoover, Carol A. *21:* 77
Hoover, Russell *12:* 95; *17:* 2; *34:* 156
Hopkins, Chris *99:* 127
Hoppin, Augustus *34:* 66
Horder, Margaret *2:* 108; *73:* 75
Horen, Michael *45:* 121
Horne, Daniel *73:* 106; *91:* 153
Horvat, Laurel *12:* 201
Horvath, Ferdinand Kusati *24:* 176
Horvath, Maria *57:* 171
Horwitz, Richard *57:* 174
Hotchkiss, De Wolfe *20:* 49
Hough, Charlotte *9:* 112; *13:* 98; *17:* 83; *24:* 195
Houlihan, Ray *11:* 214
Housman, Laurence *25:* 146, 147
Houston, James *13:* 107; *74:* 132, 134, 135
Hovland, Gary *88:* 172
How, W. E. *20:* 47
Howard, Alan *16:* 80; *34:* 58; *45:* 114
Howard, J. N. *15:* 234
Howard, John *33:* 179
Howard, Rob *40:* 161
Howe, John F. *79:* 101; *80:* 150
Howe, Phillip *79:* 117
Howe, Stephen *1:* 232
Howell, Pat *15:* 139
Howell, Troy *23:* 24; *31:* 61; *36:* 158; *37:* 184; *41:* 76, 235; *48:* 112; *56:* 13; *57:* 3; *59:* 174; *63:* 5; *74:* 46; *89:* 188; *90:* 231; *95:* 97; *98:* 130; *99:* 189
Howes, Charles *22:* 17
Hubbard, Woodleigh Marx *98:* 67
Hubley, Faith *48:* 120-121, 125, 130, 131, 132, 134
Hubley, John *48:* 125, 130, 131, 132, 134
Hudnut, Robin *14:* 62
Huerta, Catherine *76:* 178; *77:* 44, 45; *90:* 182
Huffaker, Sandy *10:* 56
Huffman, Joan *13:* 33
Huffman, Tom *13:* 180; *17:* 212; *21:* 116; *24:* 132; *33:* 154; *38:* 59; *42:* 147

Hughes, Arthur *20:* 148, 149, 150; *33:* 114, 148, 149
Hughes, Darren *95:* 44
Hughes, David *36:* 197
Hughes, Shirley *1:* 20, 21; *7:* 3; *12:* 217; *16:* 163; *29:* 154; *63:* 118; *70:* 102, 103, 104; *73:* 169; *88:* 70
Hugo, Victor *47:* 112
Hull, Cathy *78:* 29
Hull, Richard *95:* 120
Hülsmann, Eva *16:* 166
Hummel, Berta *43:* 137, 138, 139
Hummel, Lisl *29:* 109; *YABC 2:* 333-334
Humphrey, Henry *16:* 167
Humphreys, Graham *25:* 168
Humphries, Tudor *76:* 66; *80:* 4
Hunt, James *2:* 143
Hunt, Jonathan *84:* 120
Hurd, Clement *2:* 148, 149; *64:* 127, 128, 129, 131, 133, 134, 135, 136
Hurd, Peter; *24:* 30, 31,; *YABC 2:* 56
Hurd, Thacher *46:* 88-89; *94:* 114, 115, 116
Hürlimann, Ruth *32:* 99
Hustler, Tom *6:* 105
Hutchins, Laurence *55:* 22
Hutchins, Pat *15:* 142; *70:* 106-107, 108
Hutchinson, Sascha *95:* 211
Hutchinson, William M. *6:* 3, 138; *46:* 70
Hutchison, Paula *23:* 10
Hutton, Clarke *YABC 2:* 335
Hutton, Kathryn *35:* 155; *89:* 91
Hutton, Warwick *20:* 91
Huyette, Marcia *29:* 188
Hyatt, John *54:* 7
Hyde, Maureen *82:* 17
Hyman, Trina Schart *1:* 204; *2:* 194; *5:* 153; *6:* 106; *7:* 138, 145; *8:* 22; *10:* 196; *13:* 96; *14:* 114; *15:* 204; *16:* 234; *20:* 82; *22:* 133; *24:* 151; *25:* 79, 82; *26:* 82; *29:* 83; *31:* 37, 39; *34:* 104; *38:* 84, 100, 128; *41:* 49; *43:* 146; *46:* 91, 92, 93, 95, 96, 97, 98, 99, 100, 101, 102, 103, 104-105, 108, 109, 111, 197; *48:* 60, 61; *52:* 32; *60:* 168; *66:* 38; *67:* 214; *72:* 74; *75:* 92; *79:* 57; *82:* 95, 238; *89:* 46; *95:* 91, 92, 93

I

Ichikawa, Satomi *29:* 152; *41:* 52; *47:* 133, 134, 135, 136; *78:* 93, 94; *80:* 81
Ide, Jacqueline *YABC 1:* 39
Ilsley, Velma *3:* 1; *7:* 55; *12:* 109; *37:* 62; *38:* 184
Inga *1:* 142
Ingraham, Erick *21:* 177; *84:* 256
Inkpen, Mick *99:* 104, 105
Innocenti, Roberto *21:* 123; *96:* 122
Inoue, Yosuke *24:* 118
Iofin, Michael *97:* 157
Iosa, Ann *63:* 189
Ipcar, Dahlov *1:* 124-125; *49:* 137, 138, 139, 140-141, 142, 143, 144, 145
Irvin, Fred *13:* 166; *15:* 143-144; *27:* 175
Irving, Jay *45:* 72
Irving, Laurence *27:* 50
Isaac, Joanne *21:* 76
Isadora, Rachel *43:* 159, 160; *54:* 31; *79:* 106-107, 108
Ishmael, Woodi *24:* 111; *31:* 99
Ives, Ruth *15:* 257

J

Jackness, Andrew *94:* 237
Jackson, Julian *91:* 104, 106
Jackson, Michael *43:* 42
Jackson, Shelley *79:* 71; *99:* 109
Jacob, Murv *89:* 30
Jacobi, Kathy *62:* 118
Jacobs, Barbara *9:* 136
Jacobs, Lou, Jr. *9:* 136; *15:* 128
Jacobus, Tim *79:* 140
Jacques, Robin *1:* 70; *2:* 1; *8:* 46; *9:* 20; *15:* 187; *19:* 253; *32:* 102, 103, 104; *43:* 184; *73:* 135; *YABC 1:* 42
Jaffee, Al *66:* 131, 132
Jagr, Miloslav *13:* 197
Jahn-Clough, Lisa *88:* 114
Jahnke, Robert *84:* 24
Jainschigg, Nicholas *80:* 64; *91:* 138; *95:* 63; *99:* 25
Jakesavic, Nenad *85:* 102
Jakubowski, Charles *14:* 192
Jambor, Louis *YABC 1:* 11
James, Ann *73:* 50; *82:* 113
James, Derek *35:* 187; *44:* 91; *61:* 133; *74:* 2; *80:* 57; *86:* 88
James, Gilbert *YABC 1:* 43
James, Harold *2:* 151; *3:* 62; *8:* 79; *29:* 113; *51:* 195; *74:* 90
James, Robin *50:* 106; *53:* 32, 34, 35
James, Will *19:* 150, 152, 153, 155, 163
Janosch
    See Eckert, Horst
Janovitch, Marilyn *68:* 168
Janovitz, Marilyn *87:* 187
Jansons, Inese *48:* 117
Jansson, Tove *3:* 90; *41:* 106, 108, 109, 110, 111, 113, 114
Jaques, Faith *7:* 11, 132-33; *21:* 83, 84; *69:* 114, 116; *73:* 170
Jaques, Frances Lee *29:* 224
Jauss, Anne Marie *1:* 139; *3:* 34; *10:* 57, 119; *11:* 205; *23:* 194
Jeffers, Susan *17:* 86-87; *25:* 164-165; *26:* 112; *50:* 132, 134-135; *70:* 111, 112-113
Jefferson, Louise E. *4:* 160
Jenkin-Pearce, Susie *78:* 16
Jenkins, Debra Reid *85:* 202
Jenkins, Jean *98:* 79, 102
Jenkins, Patrick *72:* 126
Jenks, Aleta *73:* 117
Jenkyns, Chris *51:* 97
Jensen, Bruce *95:* 39
Jensinius, Kirsten *56:* 58
Jeram, Anita *89:* 135
Jernigan, E. Wesley *85:* 92
Jerome, Karen A. *72:* 194
Jeruchim, Simon *6:* 173; *15:* 250
Jeschke, Susan *20:* 89; *39:* 161; *41:* 84; *42:* 120
Jessel, Camilla *29:* 115
Jimenez, Maria *77:* 158; *93:* 127
Joerns, Consuelo *38:* 36; *44:* 94
John, Diana *12:* 209
John, Helen *1:* 215; *28:* 204
Johns, Jasper *61:* 172
Johns, Jeanne *24:* 114
Johnson, Bruce *9:* 47
Johnson, Cathy *92:* 136
Johnson, Crockett
    See Leisk, David
Johnson, D. William *23:* 104
Johnson, Harper *1:* 27; *2:* 33; *18:* 302; *19:* 61; *31:* 181; *44:* 46, 50, 95
Johnson, Ingrid *37:* 118
Johnson, James Ralph *1:* 23, 127
Johnson, James David *12:* 195
Johnson, Jane *48:* 136
Johnson, Joel Peter *98:* 18

Johnson, John E. *34:* 133
Johnson, Kevin *72:* 44
Johnson, Larry *47:* 56
Johnson, Margaret S. *35:* 131
Johnson, Meredith *71:* 181; *83:* 158; *89:* 103
Johnson, Milton *1:* 67; *2:* 71; *26:* 45; *31:* 107; *60:* 112; *68:* 96
Johnson, Pamela *16:* 174; *52:* 145; *62:* 140; *73:* 116; *85:* 64
Johnson, Paul Brett *83:* 95
Johnson, Stephen *80:* 15
Johnson, William R. *38:* 91
Johnston, David McCall *50:* 131, 133
Johnstone, Anne *8:* 120; *36:* 89
Johnstone, Janet Grahame *8:* 120; *36:* 89
Jonas, Ann *50:* 107, 108, 109
Jones, Bob *71:* 5; *77:* 199
Jones, Carol *5:* 131; *72:* 185, 186
Jones, Chuck *53:* 70, 71
Jones, Davy *89:* 176
Jones, Elizabeth Orton *18:* 124, 126, 128-129
Jones, Harold *14:* 88; *52:* 50
Jones, Jeff *41:* 64
Jones, Laurian *25:* 24, 27
Jones, Margaret *74:* 57
Jones, Robert *25:* 67
Jones, Wilfred *35:* 115; *YABC 1:* 163
Jordan, Charles *89:* 58
Jordan, Martin George *84:* 127
Jordan, Richard *84:* 36
Jorgenson, Andrea *91:* 111
Joseph, James *53:* 88
Joudrey, Ken *64:* 145; *78:* 6
Joyce, William *72:* 131, 132, 133, 134; *73:* 227
Joyner, Jerry *34:* 138
Jucker, Sita *5:* 93
Judkis, Jim *37:* 38
Juhasz, Victor *31:* 67
Jullian, Philippe *24:* 206; *25:* 203
Jung, Tom *91:* 217
Junge, Walter *67:* 150
Jupo, Frank *7:* 148-149
Justice, Martin *34:* 72

K

Kahl, David *74:* 95; *97:* 35
Kahl, M. P. *37:* 83
Kahl, Virginia *48:* 138
Kahn, Katherine Janus *90:* 135
Kakimoo, Kozo *11:* 148
Kalett, Jim *48:* 159, 160, 161
Kalin, Victor *39:* 186
Kalman, Maira *96:* 131, 132
Kalmenoff, Matthew *22:* 191
Kalow, Gisela *32:* 105
Kamen, Gloria *1:* 41; *9:* 119; *10:* 178; *35:* 157; *78:* 236; *98:* 82
Kandell, Alice *35:* 133
Kane, Henry B. *14:* 90; *18:* 219-220
Kane, Robert *18:* 131
Kanfer, Larry *66:* 141
Kappes, Alfred *28:* 104
Karalus, Bob *41:* 157
Karas, G. Brian *80:* 60; *99:* 179
Karlin, Eugene *10:* 63; *20:* 131
Karlin, Nurit *63:* 78
Kassian, Olena *64:* 94
Kastner, Jill *79:* 135
Kasuya, Masahiro *41:* 206-207; *51:* 100
Katona, Robert *21:* 85; *24:* 126
Kauffer, E. McKnight *33:* 103; *35:* 127; *63:* 67
Kaufman, Angelika *15:* 156
Kaufman, Joe *33:* 119
Kaufman, John *13:* 158

Kaufman, Stuart *62:* 64; *68:* 226
Kaufmann, John *1:* 174; *4:* 159; *8:* 43, 1;
   10: 102; *18:* 133-134; *22:* 251
Kaye, Graham *1:* 9; *67:* 7, 8
Kaye, M. M. *62:* 95
Kazalovski, Nata *40:* 205
Keane, Bil *4:* 135
Kearney, David *72:* 47
Keating, Pamel T. *77:* 37
Keats, Ezra Jack *3:* 18, 105, 257; *14:* 101,
   102; *33:* 129; *57:* 79, 80, 82, 83, 84, 87
Keegan, Marcia *9:* 122; *32:* 93
Keeler, Patricia A. *81:* 56
Keely, John *26:* 104; *48:* 214
Keen, Eliot *25:* 213
Keeping, Charles *9:* 124, 185; *15:* 28,
   134; *18:* 115; *44:* 194, 196; *47:* 25; *52:*
   3; *54:* 156; *69:* 123, 124; *74:* 56
Keith, Eros *4:* 98; *5:* 138; *31:* 29; *43:*
   220; *52:* 91, 92, 93, 94; *56:* 64, 66; *60:*
   37; *79:* 93
Keleinikov, Andrei *65:* 101, 102
Kelen, Emery *13:* 115
Keller, A. J. *62:* 198
Keller, Arthur I. *26:* 106
Keller, Dick *36:* 123, 125
Keller, Holly *45:* 79; *76:* 118, 119, 120, 121
Keller, Katie *79:* 222; *93:* 108
Keller, Ronald *45:* 208
Kelley, True *41:* 114, 115; *42:* 137; *75:*
   35; *92:* 104, 105
Kellogg, Steven *8:* 96; *11:* 207; *14:* 130;
   20: 58; *29:* 140-141; *30:* 35; *41:* 141;
   57: 89, 90, 92, 93, 94, 96; *59:* 182; *73:*
   141; *77:* 129; *YABC 1:* 65, 73
Kelly, Geoff *97:* 196
Kelly, Kathleen M. *71:* 109
Kelly, Laura *89:* 217
Kelly, Walt *18:* 136-141, 144-146, 148-
   149
Kemble, E. W. *34:* 75; *44:* 178; *YABC 2:*
   54, 59
Kemp-Welsh, Lucy *24:* 197
Kendrick, Dennis *79:* 213
Kennaway, Adrienne *60:* 55, 56
Kennedy, Paul Edward *6:* 190; *8:* 132; *33:*
   120
Kennedy, Richard *3:* 93; *12:* 179; *44:* 193;
   YABC 1: 57
Kent, Jack *24:* 136; *37:* 37; *40:* 81; *84:*
   89; *86:* 150; *88:* 77
Kent, Rockwell *5:* 166; *6:* 129; *20:* 225,
   226, 227, 229; *59:* 144
Kenyon, Tony *81:* 201
Kepes, Juliet *13:* 119
Kerins, Anthony *76:* 84
Kerr, Judity *24:* 137
Kerr, Phyllis Forbes *72:* 141
Kessler, Leonard *1:* 108; *7:* 139; *14:*
   107, 227; *22:* 101; *44:* 96; *67:* 79;
   82: 123
Kesteven, Peter *35:* 189
Ketcham, Hank *28:* 140, 141, 142
Kettelkamp, Larry *2:* 164
Key, Alexander *8:* 99
Khalsa, Dayal Kaur *62:* 99
Kiakshuk *8:* 59
Kidd, Chip *94:* 23
Kidd, Tom *64:* 199; *81:* 189
Kiddell-Monroe, Joan *19:* 201; *55:* 59, 60;
   87: 174
Kidder, Harvey *9:* 105; *80:* 41
Kidwell, Carl *43:* 145
Kieffer, Christa *41:* 89
Kiff, Ken *40:* 45
Kilbride, Robert *37:* 100
Kim, Glenn *99:* 82
Kimball, Anton *78:* 114
Kimball, Yeffe *23:* 116; *37:* 88
Kincade, Orin *34:* 116

Kindersley, Barnabas *96:* 110
Kindred, Wendy *7:* 151
King, Colin *53:* 3
King, Robin *10:* 164-165
King, Tony *39:* 121
Kingman, Dong *16:* 287; *44:* 100, 102,
   104
Kingsley, Charles *YABC 2:* 182
Kingston, Maxine Hong *53:* 92
Kipling, John Lockwood *YABC 2:* 198
Kipling, Rudyard *YABC 2:* 196
Kipniss, Robert *29:* 59
Kirchherr, Astrid *55:* 23
Kirchhoff, Art *28:* 136
Kirk, Ruth *5:* 96
Kirk, Tim *32:* 209, 211; *72:* 89; *83:* 49
Kirmse, Marguerite *15:* 283; *18:* 153
Kirschner, Ruth *22:* 154
Kish, Ely *73:* 119; *79:* 2
Kitamura, Satoshi *62:* 102; *98:* 91
Kitchen, Herbert Thomas *70:* 126
Kittelsen, Theodor *62:* 14
Klapholz, Mel *13:* 35
Klein, Bill *89:* 105
Klein, Robert *55:* 77
Klein, Suzanna *63:* 104
Kleinman, Zalman *28:* 143
Kliban, B. *35:* 137, 138
Knabel, Lonnie *73:* 103; *75:* 187, 228
Knight, Ann *34:* 143
Knight, Christopher *13:* 125
Knight, Hilary *1:* 233; *3:* 21; *15:* 92, 158-
   159; *16:* 258-260; *18:* 235; *19:* 169;
   35: 242; *46:* 167; *52:* 116; *69:* 126,
   127; *YABC 1:* 168-169, 172
Knotts, Howard *20:* 4; *25:* 170; *36:* 163
Kobayashi, Ann *39:* 58
Kocsis, J. C.
   See Paul, James
Koehn, Ilse *34:* 198; *79:* 123
Koelsch, Michael *99:* 182
Koering, Ursula *85:* 46
Koering, Ursula *3:* 28; *4:* 14; *44:* 5; *64:*
   140, 141
Koerner, Henry
   See Koerner, W.H.D.
Koerner, W.H.D. *14:* 216; *21:* 88, 89, 90,
   91; *23:* 211
Koffler, Camilla *36:* 113
Koide, Yasuko *50:* 114
Komoda, Kiyo *9:* 128; *13:* 214
Konashevich, Vladimir *61:* 160
Konashevicha, V. *YABC 1:* 26
Konigsburg, E. L. *4:* 138; *48:* 141, 142,
   144, 145; *94:* 129, 130
Kooiker, Leonie *48:* 148
Koonook, Simon *65:* 157
Kopper, Lisa *72:* 152, 153
Korach, Mimi *1:* 128-129; *2:* 52; *4:* 39;
   5: 159; *9:* 129; *10:* 21; *24:* 69
Koren, Edward *5:* 100; *65:* 65, 67
Koscielniak, Bruce *99:* 122
Koshkin, Alexander *92:* 180
Kossin, Sandy *10:* 71; *23:* 105
Kostin, Andrej *26:* 204
Kotzky, Brian *68:* 184
Kovacevi , Zivojin *13:* 247
Kovalski, Maryann *58:* 120; *84:* 88; *97:*
   124, 125, 126
Krahn, Fernando *2:* 257; *34:* 206; *49:*
   152
Kramer, Anthony *33:* 81
Kramer, David *96:* 162
Kramer, Frank *6:* 121
Krantz, Kathy *35:* 83
Kraus, Robert *13:* 217; *65:* 113; *93:* 93,
   94
Kredel, Fritz *6:* 35; *17:* 93-96; *22:* 147;
   24: 175; *29:* 130; *35:* 77; *YABC 2:* 166,
   300

Krementz, Jill *17:* 98; *49:* 41
Kresin, Robert *23:* 19
Krieger, Salem *54:* 164
Kriegler, Lyn *73:* 29
Kruck, Gerald *88:* 181
Krupinski, Loretta *67:* 104
Krupp, Robin Rector *53:* 96, 98
Krush, Beth *1:* 51, 85; *2:* 233; *4:* 115; *9:*
   61; *10:* 191; *11:* 196; *18:* 164-165; *32:*
   72; *37:* 203; *43:* 57; *60:* 102, 103, 107,
   108, 109
Krush, Joe *2:* 233; *4:* 115; *9:* 61; *10:* 191;
   11: 196; *18:* 164-165; *32:* 72, 91; *37:*
   203; *43:* 57; *60:* 102, 103, 107, 108,
   109
Krych, Duane *91:* 43
Krykorka, Vladyana *96:* 147
Kubinyi, Laszlo *4:* 116; *6:* 113; *16:* 118;
   17: 100; *28:* 227; *30:* 172; *49:* 24, 28;
   54: 23
Kubricht, Mary *73:* 118
Kuchera, Kathleen *84:* 5
Kuhn, Bob *17:* 91; *35:* 235
Kukalis, Romas *90:* 27
Kuklin, Susan *63:* 82, 83, 84
Kunhardt, Dorothy *53:* 101
Kunhardt, Edith *67:* 105, 106
Künstler, Mort *10:* 73; *32:* 143
Kurchevsky, V. *34:* 61
Kurelek, William *8:* 107
Kuriloff, Ron *13:* 19
Kuskin, Karla *2:* 170; *68:* 115, 116
Kutzer, Ernst *19:* 249
Kuzma, Steve *57:* 8; *62:* 93
Kuznetsova, Berta *74:* 45
Kvasnosky, Laura McGee *93:* 103

L

LaBlanc, André *24:* 146
Laboccetta, Mario *27:* 120
Labrosse, Darcia *58:* 88
LaCava, Vince *95:* 118
Laceky, Adam *32:* 121
Lacis, Astra *85:* 117
La Croix *YABC 2:* 4
Ladwig, Tim *98:* 212
La Farge, Margaret *47:* 141
LaFave, Kim *64:* 177; *72:* 39; *97:* 146;
   99: 172
Laimgruber, Monika *11:* 153
Laite, Gordon *1:* 130-131; *8:* 209; *31:*
   113; *40:* 63; *46:* 117
LaMarche, Jim *46:* 204; *61:* 56; *94:* 69
Lamb, Jim *10:* 117
Lambert, J. K. *38:* 129; *39:* 24
Lambert, Saul *23:* 112; *33:* 107; *54:*
   136
Lambo, Don *6:* 156; *35:* 115; *36:* 146
Lamut, Sonja *57:* 193
Lamut, Sonya *85:* 102
Landa, Peter *11:* 95; *13:* 177; *53:* 119
Landau, Jacob *38:* 111
Landon, Lucinda *79:* 31
Landshoff, Ursula *13:* 124
Lane, John R. *8:* 145
Lane, John *15:* 176-177; *30:* 146
Lang, G. D. *48:* 56
Lang, Gary *73:* 75
Lang, Jerry *18:* 295
Lange, Dorothea *50:* 141
Langner, Nola *8:* 110; *42:* 36
Lantz, Paul *1:* 82, 102; *27:* 88; *34:* 102;
   45: 123
Larkin, Bob *84:* 225
Larrecq, John *44:* 108; *68:* 56
Larsen, Suzanne *1:* 13

Larson, Gary *57:* 121, 122, 123, 124, 125, 126, 127
Larsson, Carl *35:* 144, 145, 146, 147, 148-149, 150, 152, 153, 154
Larsson, Karl *19:* 177
La Rue, Michael D. *13:* 215
Lasker, Joe *7:* 186-187; *14:* 55; *38:* 115; *39:* 47; *83:* 113, 114, 115
Latham, Barbara *16:* 188-189; *43:* 71
Lathrop, Dorothy *14:* 117, 118-119; *15:* 109; *16:* 78-79, 81; *32:* 201, 203; *33:* 112; *YABC 2:* 301
Lattimore, Eleanor Frances *7:* 156
Lauden, Claire *16:* 173
Lauden, George, Jr. *16:* 173
Laune, Paul *2:* 235; *34:* 31
Lauré, Jason *49:* 53; *50:* 122
Lauter, Richard *63:* 29; *67:* 111; *77:* 198
Lavallee, Barbara *74:* 157; *92:* 154; *96:* 126
Lave, Fitz Hugh *59:* 139
Lavis, Stephen *43:* 143; *87:* 137, 164, 165
Lawrence, John *25:* 131; *30:* 141; *44:* 198, 200
Lawrence, Stephen *20:* 195
Lawson, Carol *6:* 38; *42:* 93, 131
Lawson, George *17:* 280
Lawson, Robert *5:* 26; *6:* 94; *13:* 39; *16:* 11; *20:* 100, 102, 103; *54:* 3; *66:* 12; *YABC 2:* 222, 224-225, 227-235, 237-241
Layfield, Kathie *60:* 194
Lazare, Jerry *44:* 109; *74:* 28
Lazarevich, Mila *17:* 118
Lazarus, Keo Felker *21:* 94
Lazzaro, Victor *11:* 126
Lea, Tom *43:* 72, 74
Leacroft, Richard *6:* 140
Leaf, Munro *20:* 99
Leake, Donald *70:* 41
Leander, Patricia *23:* 27
Lear, Edward *18:* 183-185
Lebenson, Richard *6:* 209; *7:* 76; *23:* 145; *44:* 191; *87:* 153
Le Cain, Errol *6:* 141; *9:* 3; *22:* 142; *25:* 198; *28:* 173; *68:* 128, 129; *86:* 49
Lee, Alan *62:* 25, 28
Lee, Bryce *99:* 60
Lee, Dom *83:* 118, 120; *93:* 123
Lee, Doris *13:* 246; *32:* 183; *44:* 111
Lee, Jared *93:* 200
Lee, Jody *81:* 121; *82:* 225; *91:* 155
Lee, Manning de V. *2:* 200; *17:* 12; *27:* 87; *37:* 102, 103, 104; *YABC 2:* 304
Lee, Paul *97:* 100
Lee, Robert J. *3:* 97; *67:* 124
Lee, Victor *96:* 228
Leech, Dorothy *98:* 76
Leech, John *15:* 59
Leedy, Loreen *84:* 142
Leeman, Michael *44:* 157
Leeming, Catherine *87:* 39
Lees, Harry *6:* 112
LeFever, Bill *88:* 220, 221
Legènisel *47:* 111
Legrand, Edy *18:* 89, 93
Lehman, Barbara *73:* 123
Lehrman, Rosalie *2:* 180
Leichman, Seymour *5:* 107
Leighton, Clare *25:* 130; *33:* 168; *37:* 105, 106, 108, 109
Leisk, David *1:* 140-141; *11:* 54; *30:* 137, 142, 143, 144
Leister, Bryan *89:* 45
Leloir, Maurice *18:* 77, 80, 83, 99
Lemke, Horst *14:* 98; *38:* 117, 118, 119
Lemke, R. W. *42:* 162
Lemon, David Gwynne *9:* 1
LeMoult, Adolph *82:* 116

Lennox, Elsie *95:* 163
Lenski, Lois *1:* 144; *26:* 135, 137, 139, 141
Lent, Blair *1:* 116-117; *2:* 174; *3:* 206-207; *7:* 168-169; *34:* 62; *68:* 217
Leonard, Richard *91:* 128
Leone, Leonard *49:* 190
Lerner, Carol *86:* 140, 141, 142
Lerner, Sharon *11:* 157; *22:* 56
Leslie, Cecil *19:* 244
Lessac, Frane *80:* 182, 207; *96:* 182
Lester, Alison *50:* 124; *90:* 147, 148
Le Tord, Bijou *49:* 156; *95:* 112
Levai, Blaise *39:* 130
Levin, Ted *12:* 148
Levine, David *43:* 147, 149, 150, 151, 152; *64:* 11
Levine, Joe *71:* 88
Levine, Marge *81:* 127
Levit, Herschel *24:* 223
Levy, Jessica Ann *19:* 225; *39:* 191
Lewin, Betsy *32:* 114; *48:* 177; *90:* 151; *91:* 125; *92:* 85
Lewin, Ted *4:* 77; *8:* 168; *20:* 110; *21:* 99, 100; *27:* 110; *28:* 96, 97; *31:* 49; *45:* 55; *48:* 223; *60:* 20, 119, 120; *62:* 139; *66:* 108; *71:* 12; *72:* 21; *74:* 226; *76:* 139, 140; *77:* 82; *79:* 87; *85:* 49, 177; *86:* 55; *88:* 182; *93:* 28, 29; *94:* 34, 182, 194; *99:* 156
Lewis, Allen *15:* 112
Lewis, E. B. *88:* 143; *93:* 109
Lewis, Jan *81:* 22
Lewis, Richard W. *52:* 25
Lewis, Robin Baird *98:* 193
Leydon, Rita Flodén *21:* 101
Lieblich, Irene *22:* 173; *27:* 209, 214
Lies, Brian *92:* 40
Liese, Charles *4:* 222
Life, Kay *79:* 49
Lifton, Robert Jay *66:* 154
Lightburn, Ron *86:* 153; *91:* 122
Lightfoot, Norman R. *45:* 47
Lignell, Lois *37:* 114
Lilly, Charles *8:* 73; *20:* 127; *48:* 53; *72:* 9, 16; *77:* 98
Lilly, Ken *37:* 224
Lim, John *43:* 153
Limona, Mercedes *51:* 183
Lincoln, Patricia Henderson *27:* 27; *78:* 127
Lindahn, Ron *84:* 17
Lindahn, Val *84:* 17
Lindberg, Howard *10:* 123; *16:* 190
Lindberg, Jeffrey *64:* 77; *77:* 71; *79:* 54; *80:* 149
Linden, Seymour *18:* 200-201; *43:* 140
Linder, Richard *27:* 119
Lindman, Maj *43:* 154
Lindsay, Norman *67:* 114
Lindsay, Vachel *40:* 118
Line, Les *27:* 143
Linell
    See Smith, Linell
Lionni, Leo *8:* 115; *72:* 159, 160, 161
Lipinsky, Lino *2:* 156; *22:* 175
Lippincott, Gary A. *70:* 35
Lippman, Peter *8:* 31; *31:* 119, 120, 160
Lisi, Victoria *89:* 145
Lisker, Sonia O. *16:* 274; *31:* 31; *44:* 113, 114
Lisowski, Gabriel *47:* 144; *49:* 157
Lissim, Simon *17:* 138
Little, Ed *89:* 145
Little, Harold *16:* 72
Little, Mary E. *28:* 146
Livesly, Lorna *19:* 216
Livingston, Susan *95:* 22
Llerena, Carlos Antonio *19:* 181
Lloyd, Errol *11:* 39; *22:* 178

Lloyd, Megan *77:* 118; *80:* 113; *97:* 75
Lo, Koon-chiu *7:* 134
Loates, Glen *63:* 76
Lobel, Anita *6:* 87; *9:* 141; *18:* 248; *55:* 85, 86, 87, 88, 93, 104; *60:* 67; *78:* 263; *82:* 110; *96:* 157, 159
Lobel, Arnold *1:* 188-189; *5:* 12; *6:* 147; *7:* 167, 209; *18:* 190-191; *25:* 39, 43; *27:* 40; *29:* 174; *52:* 127; *55:* 89, 91, 94, 95, 97, 98, 99, 100, 101, 102, 103, 105, 106; *60:* 18, 31; *66:* 181, 183; *75:* 57; *82:* 246
Loefgren, Ulf *3:* 108
Loescher, Ann *20:* 108
Loescher, Gil *20:* 108
Loew, David *93:* 184
Lofting, Hugh *15:* 182-183
Lofts, Pamela *60:* 188
Loh, George *38:* 88
Lomberg, Jon *58:* 160
Lonette, Reisie *11:* 211; *12:* 168; *13:* 56; *36:* 122; *43:* 155
Long, Loren *99:* 176
Long, Sally *42:* 184
Long, Sylvia *74:* 168
Longoni, Eduardo *73:* 85
Longtemps, Ken *17:* 123; *29:* 221; *69:* 82
Looser, Heinz *YABC 2:* 208
Lopshire, Robert *6:* 149; *21:* 117; *34:* 166; *73:* 13
Lord, John Vernon *21:* 104; *23:* 25; *51:* 22
Lorenz, Al *40:* 146
Loretta, Sister Mary *33:* 73
Lorraine, Walter H. *3:* 110; *4:* 123; *16:* 192
Loss, Joan *11:* 163
Louderback, Walt *YABC 1:* 164
Lousada, Sandra *40:* 138
Low, Joseph *14:* 124, 125; *18:* 68; *19:* 194; *31:* 166; *80:* 239
Low, William *62:* 175; *80:* 147
Lowenheim, Alfred *13:* 65-66
Lowitz, Anson *17:* 124; *18:* 215
Lowrey, Jo *8:* 133
Lubell, Winifred *1:* 207; *3:* 15; *6:* 151
Lubin, Leonard B. *19:* 224; *36:* 79, 80; *45:* 128, 129, 131, 132, 133, 134, 135, 136, 137, 139, 140, 141; *70:* 95; *YABC 2:* 96
Lucht, Irmgard *82:* 145
Ludwig, Helen *33:* 144, 145
Lufkin, Raymond *38:* 138; *44:* 48
Luhrs, Henry *7:* 123; *11:* 120
Lujan, Tonita *82:* 33
Lupo, Dom *4:* 204
Lustig, Loretta *30:* 186; *46:* 134, 135, 136, 137
Luzak, Dennis *52:* 121; *99:* 142
Lydbury, Jane *82:* 98
Lydecker, Laura *21:* 113; *42:* 53
Lynch, Charles *16:* 33
Lynch, Marietta *29:* 137; *30:* 171
Lyon, Elinor *6:* 154
Lyon, Fred *14:* 16
Lyons, Oren *8:* 193
Lyster, Michael *26:* 41

M

Maas, Dorothy *6:* 175
Maas, Julie *47:* 61
Macaulay, David *46:* 139, 140-141, 142, 143, 144-145, 147, 149, 150; *72:* 167, 168, 169

MacCarthy, Patricia *69:* 141
Macdonald, Alister *21:* 55
Macdonald, Roberta *19:* 237; *52:* 164
MacDonald, Norman *13:* 99
MacDonald, Suse *54:* 41
Mace, Varian *49:* 159
Macguire, Robert Reid *18:* 67
Machetanz, Fredrick *34:* 147, 148
MacInnes, Ian *35:* 59
MacIntyre, Elisabeth *17:* 127-128
Mack, Stan *17:* 129; *96:* 33
Mackay, Donald *17:* 60
MacKaye, Arvia *32:* 119
Mackenzie, Stuart *73:* 213
MacKenzie, Garry *33:* 159
Mackie, Clare *87:* 134
Mackinlay, Miguel *27:* 22
MacKinstry, Elizabeth *15:* 110; *42:* 139,
    140, 141, 142, 143, 144, 145
MacLeod, Lee *91:* 167
Maclise, Daniel *YABC 2:* 257
Madden, Don *3:* 112-113; *4:* 33, 108,
    155; *7:* 193; *78:* 12; *YABC 2:* 211
Maddison, Angela Mary *10:* 83
Maestro, Giulio *8:* 124; *12:* 17; *13:* 108;
    25: 182; *54:* 147; *59:* 114, 115, 116,
    117, 118, 121, 123, 124, 125, 126,
    127; *68:* 37, 38
Maffia, Daniel *60:* 200
Maggio, Viqui *58:* 136, 181; *74:* 150; *75:*
    90; *85:* 159; *90:* 158
Magnus, Erica *77:* 123
Magnuson, Diana *28:* 102; *34:* 190; *41:*
    175
Maguire, Sheila *41:* 100
Magurn, Susan *91:* 30
Mahony, Will *37:* 120
Mahony, Will *85:* 116
Mahood, Kenneth *24:* 141
Maik, Henri *9:* 102
Maisto, Carol *29:* 87
Maitland, Antony *1:* 100, 176; *8:* 41; *17:*
    246; *24:* 46; *25:* 177, 178; *32:* 74; *60:*
    65, 195; *67:* 156; *87:* 131
Mak, Kam *72:* 25; *75:* 43; *87:* 186; *97:*
    24
Makie, Pam *37:* 117
Maland, Nick *99:* 77
Malone, James Hiram *84:* 161
Malone, Nola Langner *82:* 239
Malsberg, Edward *51:* 175
Malvern, Corinne *2:* 13; *34:* 148, 149
Mancusi, Stephen *63:* 198, 199
Mandelbaum, Ira *31:* 115
Manet, Edouard *23:* 170
Mangurian, David *14:* 133
Manham, Allan *42:* 109; *77:* 180; *80:* 227
Manniche, Lise *31:* 121
Manning, Jane *96:* 203
Manning, Jo *63:* 154
Manning, Samuel F. *5:* 75
Mantel, Richard *57:* 73; *63:* 106; *82:* 255
Maraja *15:* 86; *YABC 1:* 28; *2:* 115
Marcellino, Fred *20:* 125; *34:* 222; *53:*
    125; *58:* 205; *61:* 64, 121, 122; *68:*
    154, 156-157, 158, 159; *72:* 25; *86:*
    184; *98:* 181
Marchesi, Stephen *34:* 140; *46:* 72; *50:*
    147; *66:* 239; *70:* 33; *73:* 18, 114, 163;
    77: 47, 76, 147; *78:* 79; *80:* 30; *81:* 6;
    89: 66; *93:* 21, 130; *94:* 94; *97:* 66;
    98: 96
Marchiori, Carlos *14:* 60
Margules, Gabriele *21:* 120
Mariana
    See Foster, Marian Curtis
Mariano, Michael *52:* 108
Marino, Dorothy *6:* 37; *14:* 135
Maris, Ron *71:* 123
Maritz, Nicolaas *85:* 123

Mark, Mona *65:* 105; *68:* 205
Markham, R. L. *17:* 240
Marks, Cara *54:* 9
Marokvia, Artur *31:* 122
Marrella, Maria Pia *62:* 116
Marriott, Pat *30:* 30; *34:* 39; *35:* 164,
    165, 166; *44:* 170; *48:* 186, 187, 188,
    189, 191, 192, 193; *91:* 92
Mars, W. T. *1:* 161; *3:* 115; *4:* 208, 225;
    5: 92, 105, 186; *8:* 214; *9:* 12; *13:* 121;
    27: 151; *31:* 180; *38:* 102; *48:* 66; *62:*
    164, 165; *64:* 62; *68:* 229; *79:* 55
Marschall, Ken *85:* 29
Marsh, Christine *3:* 164
Marsh, James *73:* 137
Marsh, Reginald *17:* 5; *19:* 89; *22:* 90, 96
Marshall, Anthony D. *18:* 216
Marshall, James *6:* 160; *40:* 221; *42:* 24,
    25, 29; *51:* 111, 112, 113, 114, 115,
    116, 117, 118, 119, 120, 121; *64:* 13;
    75: 126, 127, 128, 129
Marshall, Janet *97:* 154
Marstall, Bob *55:* 145; *84:* 153, 170
Martchenko, Michael *50:* 129, 153, 155,
    156, 157; *83:* 144, 145
Martin, Charles E. *70:* 144
Martin, David Stone *24:* 232; *62:* 4
Martin, Fletcher *18:* 213; *23:* 151
Martin, René *7:* 144; *42:* 148, 149, 150
Martin, Richard E. *51:* 157
Martin, Ron *32:* 81
Martin, Stefan *8:* 68; *32:* 124, 126; *56:*
    33
Martinez, Ed *58:* 192; *72:* 231; *77:* 33;
    80: 214
Martinez, John *6:* 113
Marton, Jirina *95:* 127, 128
Martorell, Antonio *84:* 6; *97:* 161
Martucci, Griesbach *52:* 106
Marvin, Frederic *83:* 86
Marx, Robert F. *24:* 143
Masefield, Judith *19:* 208, 209
Masheris, Robert *78:* 51
Mason, George F. *14:* 139
Mason, Robert *84:* 96
Massey, Barbara *68:* 142
Massie, Diane Redfield *16:* 194
Massie, Kim *31:* 43
Mathewuse, James *51:* 143
Mathieu, Joseph *14:* 33; *39:* 206; *43:* 167;
    56: 180; *79:* 126; *94:* 147
Matsubara, Naoko *12:* 121
Matsuda, Shizu *13:* 167
Matte, L'Enc *22:* 183
Mattelson, Marvin *36:* 50, 51
Matthews, F. Leslie *4:* 216
Mattingly, David *71:* 76, 77; *82:* 64; *91:*
    216, 217
Matulay, Laszlo *5:* 18; *43:* 168
Matus, Greta *12:* 142
Mauldin, Bill *27:* 23
Mawicke, Tran *9:* 137; *15:* 191; *47:*
    100
Mawson, Matt *74:* 115
Max, Peter *45:* 146, 147, 148-149,
    150
Maxie, Betty *40:* 135
Maxwell, John Alan *1:* 148
Mayan, Earl *7:* 193
Mayer, Marianna *32:* 132
Mayer, Mercer *11:* 192; *16:* 195-196; *20:*
    55, 57; *32:* 129, 130, 132, 133, 134;
    41: 144, 248, 252; *58:* 186; *73:* 140,
    142, 143
Mayhew, James *85:* 121
Mayhew, Richard *3:* 106
Mayo, Gretchen Will *38:* 81; *84:* 166
Mays, Victor *5:* 127; *8:* 45, 153; *14:* 245;
    23: 50; *34:* 155; *40:* 79; *45:* 158; *54:*
    91; *66:* 240

Mazal, Chanan *49:* 104
Maze, Deborah *71:* 83
Mazellan, Ron *75:* 97, 98
Mazille, Capucine *96:* 168
Mazza, Adriana Saviozzi *19:* 215
Mazzella, Mary Jo *82:* 165
Mazzetti, Alan *45:* 210
McBride, Angus *28:* 49
McBride, Will *30:* 110
McCaffery, Janet *38:* 145
McCallum, Graham *78:* 78
McCann, Gerald *3:* 50; *4:* 94; *7:* 54; *41:*
    121
McCay, Winsor *41:* 124, 126, 128-129,
    130-131
McClary, Nelson *1:* 111
McClintock, Barbara *57:* 135; *95:* 130
McClintock, Theodore *14:* 141
McCloskey, Robert *85:* 150, 151
McCloskey, Robert *1:* 184-185; *2:* 186-
    187; *17:* 209; *39:* 139, 140, 141, 142,
    143, 146, 147, 148
McClung, Robert *2:* 189; *68:* 166, 167
McClure, Gillian *31:* 132
McConnel, Jerry *31:* 75, 187
McCord, Kathleen Garry *78:* 236
McCormack, John *66:* 193
McCormick, A. D. *35:* 119
McCormick, Dell J. *19:* 216
McCrady, Lady *16:* 198; *39:* 127
McCrea, James *3:* 122; *33:* 216
McCrea, Ruth *3:* 122; *27:* 102; *33:* 216
McCue, Lisa *65:* 148, 149; *77:* 54; *80:*
    132
McCully, Emily Arnold *2:* 89; *4:* 120-121,
    146, 197; *5:* 2, 129; *7:* 191; *11:* 122;
    15: 210; *33:* 23; *35:* 244; *37:* 122; *39:*
    88; *40:* 103; *50:* 30, 31, 32, 33, 34, 35,
    36-37; *52:* 89, 90; *57:* 6; *62:* 3; *70:*
    195; *86:* 82; *96:* 192; *97:* 93
McCurdy, Michael *13:* 153; *24:* 85; *81:*
    160; *82:* 157, 158; *86:* 125; *97:* 92
McCusker, Paul *99:* 19
McDermott, Beverly Brodsky *11:* 180
McDermott, Gerald *16:* 201; *74:* 174-175
McDermott, Mike *96:* 187
McDonald, Jill *13:* 155; *26:* 128
McDonald, Ralph J. *5:* 123, 195
McDonough, Don *10:* 163
McEntee, Dorothy *37:* 124
McEwan, Keith *88:* 116
McFall, Christie *12:* 144
McGee, Barbara *6:* 165
McGovern, Tara *98:* 171
McGraw, Sheila *83:* 146
McGregor, Malcolm *23:* 27
McHugh, Tom *23:* 64
McIntosh, Jon *42:* 56
McKay, Donald *2:* 118; *32:* 157; *45:* 151,
    152
McKeating, Eileen *44:* 58
McKee, David *10:* 48; *21:* 9; *70:* 154,
    155
McKie, Roy *7:* 44
McKillip, Kathy *30:* 153
McKinney, Ena *26:* 39
McLachlan, Edward *5:* 89
McLean, Meg *94:* 196
McLean, Sammis *32:* 197
McLean, Wilson *90:* 29
McLoughlin, John C. *47:* 149
McMahon, Robert *36:* 155; *69:* 169
McManus, Shawn *85:* 71
McMillan, Bruce *22:* 184
McMullan, James *40:* 33; *67:* 172; *87:*
    142; *99:* 63, 64
McNaught, Harry *12:* 80; *32:* 136
McNaughton, Colin *39:* 149; *40:* 108; *92:*
    144, 145, 146
McNicholas, Maureen *38:* 148

McPhail, David *14:* 105; *23:* 135; *37:* 217, 218, 220, 221; *47:* 151, 152, 153, 154, 155, 156, 158-159, 160, 162-163, 164; *71:* 211; *81:* 139, 140, 142; *86:* 123

McPhee, Richard B. *41:* 133

McPheeters, Neal *78:* 132; *86:* 90; *99:* 162

McQueen, Lucinda *28:* 149; *41:* 249; *46:* 206; *53:* 103

McVay, Tracy *11:* 68

McVicker, Charles *39:* 150

Mead, Ben Carlton *43:* 75

Meade, Holly *90:* 102; *94:* 101

Mecray, John *33:* 62

Meddaugh, Susan *20:* 42; *29:* 143; *41:* 241; *77:* 50; *84:* 173, 174, 175, 176-77, 178

Meehan, Dennis B. *56:* 144

Meents, Len W. *73:* 147, 150

Meers, Tony *99:* 113

Meisel, Paul *98:* 137

Melendez, Francisco *72:* 180

Melo, John *16:* 285; *58:* 203

Meloni, Maria Teresa *98:* 62

Menasco, Milton *43:* 85

Mendelson, Steven T. *86:* 154

Mendelssohn, Felix *19:* 170

Mendola, Christopher *88:* 223

Meng, Heinz *13:* 158

Mero, Lee *34:* 68

Merrill, Frank T. *16:* 147; *19:* 71; *YABC 1:* 226, 229, 273

Merriman, Rachel *98:* 108

Meryman, Hope *27:* 41

Meryweather, Jack *10:* 179

Messick, Dale *64:* 150, 151, 152

Meth, Harold *24:* 203

Meyer, Herbert *19:* 189

Meyer, Renate *6:* 170

Meyers, Bob *11:* 136

Meynell, Louis *37:* 76

Micale, Albert *2:* 65; *22:* 185

Miccuci, Charles *82:* 163

Middleton-Sandford, Betty *2:* 125

Mieke, Anne *45:* 74

Mighell, Patricia *43:* 134

Mikolaycak, Charles *9:* 144; *12:* 101; *13:* 212; *21:* 121; *22:* 168; *30:* 187; *34:* 103, 150; *37:* 183; *43:* 179; *44:* 90; *46:* 115, 118-119; *49:* 25; *78:* 121, 122, 205, 207; *81:* 4

Miles, Jennifer *17:* 278

Milhous, Katherine *15:* 193; *17:* 51

Millais, John E. *22:* 230, 231

Millar, H. R. *YABC 1:* 194-195, 203

Millard, C. E. *28:* 186

Miller, Don *15:* 195; *16:* 71; *20:* 106; *31:* 178

Miller, Edna *29:* 148

Miller, Frank J. *25:* 94

Miller, Grambs *18:* 38; *23:* 16

Miller, Ian *99:* 128

Miller, Jane *15:* 196

Miller, Marcia *13:* 233

Miller, Marilyn *1:* 87; *31:* 69; *33:* 157

Miller, Mitchell *28:* 183; *34:* 207

Miller, Shane *5:* 140

Miller, Virginia *81:* 206

Mills, Elaine *72:* 181

Mills, Lauren *92:* 170

Mills, Yaroslava Surmach *35:* 169, 170; *46:* 114

Millsap, Darrel *51:* 102

Milone, Karen *89:* 169

Miner, Julia *98:* 69

Minor, Wendell *39:* 188; *52:* 87; *56:* 171; *58:* 116; *62:* 56; *66:* 109; *74:* 93; *78:* 129; *94:* 67

Mirocha, Paul *81:* 133

Mitchell, Mark *91:* 208

Mitgutsch, Ali *76:* 161

Mitsuhashi, Yoko *45:* 153

Miyake, Yoshi *38:* 141

Mizumura, Kazue *10:* 143; *18:* 223; *36:* 159

Mochi, Ugo *8:* 122; *38:* 150

Mock, Paul *55:* 83

Modarressi, Mitra *90:* 236

Modell, Frank *39:* 152

Mogenson, Jan *74:* 183

Mohn, Susan *89:* 224

Mohr, Nicholasa *8:* 139

Molan, Christine *60:* 177; *84:* 183

Moldon, Peter L. *49:* 168

Molk, Laurel *92:* 150

Momaday, N. Scott *48:* 159

Montiel, David *69:* 106; *84:* 145

Montresor, Beni *2:* 91; *3:* 138; *38:* 152, 153, 154, 155, 156-157, 158, 159, 160; *68:* 63

Moon, Carl *25:* 183, 184, 185

Moon, Eliza *14:* 40

Moon, Ivan *22:* 39; *38:* 140

Moore, Adrienne *67:* 147

Moore, Agnes Kay Randall *43:* 187

Moore, Janet *63:* 153

Moore, Mary *29:* 160

Mora, Raul Mina *20:* 41

Moran, Tom *60:* 100

Mordvinoff, Nicolas *15:* 179

Morgan, Jacqui *58:* 57

Morgan, Tom *42:* 157

Morice, Dave *93:* 142

Morin, Paul *73:* 132; *79:* 130; *88:* 140

Morrill, Leslie *18:* 218; *29:* 177; *33:* 84; *38:* 147; *42:* 127; *44:* 93; *48:* 164, 165, 167, 168, 169, 170, 171; *49:* 162; *63:* 136, 180; *70:* 72; *71:* 70, 91, 92; *72:* 228; *80:* 163, 164, 165; *90:* 121

Morrill, Rowena A. *84:* 16; *98:* 163

Morris *47:* 91

Morris, Frank *55:* 133; *60:* 28; *76:* 2

Morris, Tony *62:* 146; *70:* 97

Morrison, Bill *42:* 116; *66:* 170; *69:* 40

Morrison, Gordon *87:* 150

Morrow, Gray *2:* 64; *5:* 200; *10:* 103, 114; *14:* 175

Morton, Lee Jack *32:* 140

Morton, Marian *3:* 185

Moser, Barry *56:* 68, 117, 118, 119, 120, 121, 122, 123, 124; *59:* 141; *60:* 160; *79:* 91, 147, 149, 151, 152; *82:* 81; *90:* 118; *91:* 35; *95:* 210; *97:* 91, 93

Moser, Cara *90:* 118

Moses, Grandma *18:* 228

Moskof, Martin Stephen *27:* 152

Mosley, Francis *57:* 144

Moss, Donald *11:* 184

Moss, Geoffrey *32:* 198

Moss, Marissa *71:* 130

Most, Bernard *48:* 173; *91:* 142, 143

Mowry, Carmen *50:* 62

Moxley, Sheila *96:* 174

Moyers, William *21:* 65

Moyler, Alan *36:* 142

Mozley, Charles *9:* 87; *20:* 176, 192, 193; *22:* 228; *25:* 205; *33:* 150; *43:* 170, 171, 172, 173, 174; *YABC 2:* 89

Mueller, Hans Alexander *26:* 64; *27:* 52, 53

Mugnaini, Joseph *11:* 35; *27:* 52, 53; *35:* 62

Mujica, Rick *72:* 67; *88:* 95

Muller, Robin *86:* 161

Muller, Steven *32:* 167

Müller, Jörg *35:* 215; *67:* 138, 139

Mullins, Edward S. *10:* 101

Mullins, Patricia *51:* 68

Multer, Scott *80:* 108

Munari, Bruno *15:* 200

Munowitz, Ken *14:* 148; *72:* 178, 179

Munro, Roxie *58:* 134

Munsinger, Lynn *33:* 161; *46:* 126; *71:* 92; *82:* 80; *89:* 218; *92:* 125; *94:* 157, 158, 159, 160; *98:* 196

Munson, Russell *13:* 9

Muñoz, William *42:* 160

Murdocca, Sal *73:* 212; *98:* 132

Murphy, Bill *5:* 138

Murphy, Jill *37:* 142; *70:* 166

Murr, Karl *20:* 62

Murray, Ossie *43:* 176

Mussino, Attilio *29:* 131

Mutchler, Dwight *1:* 25

Myers, Bernice *9:* 147; *36:* 75; *81:* 146, 147, 148

Myers, Duane O. *99:* 145

Myers, Lou *11:* 2

N

Nachreiner, Tom *29:* 182

Nacht, Merle *65:* 49

Nadler, Ellis *88:* 91

Najaka, Marlies *62:* 101

Nakai, Michael *30:* 217; *54:* 29

Nakatani, Chiyoko *12:* 124

Narahashi, Keiko *77:* 188; *82:* 213

Nash, Lesa *87:* 135

Nash, Linell *46:* 175

Naso, John *33:* 183

Nason, Thomas W. *14:* 68

Nasser, Muriel *48:* 74

Nast, Thomas *21:* 29; *28:* 23; *51:* 132, 133, 134, 135, 136, 137, 138, 139, 141

Nasta, Vincent *78:* 185

Natale, Vincent *76:* 3; *78:* 125

Natchev, Alexi *96:* 177

Natti, Susanna *20:* 146; *32:* 141, 142; *35:* 178; *37:* 143; *71:* 49; *93:* 98

Navarra, Celeste Scala *8:* 142

Naylor, Penelope *10:* 104

Nazz, James *72:* 8

Nebel, M. *45:* 154

Neebe, William *7:* 93

Needler, Jerry *12:* 93

Neel, Alice *31:* 23

Neely, Keith R. *46:* 124

Neff, Leland *78:* 74

Negri, Rocco *3:* 213; *5:* 67; *6:* 91, 108; *12:* 159

Neill, John R. *18:* 8, 10-11, 21, 30

Nelson, Craig *62:* 151; *153*

Nelson, Gail White *68:* 140

Ness, Evaline *1:* 164-165; *2:* 39; *3:* 8; *10:* 147; *12:* 53; *26:* 150, 151, 152, 153; *49:* 30, 31, 32; *56:* 30; *60:* 113

Neville, Vera *2:* 182

Nevwirth, Allan *79:* 168

Newberry, Clare Turlay *1:* 170

Newfeld, Frank *14:* 121; *26:* 154

Newman, Ann *43:* 90

Newsom, Carol *40:* 159; *44:* 60; *47:* 189; *65:* 29; *70:* 192; *80:* 36; *85:* 137, 138; *92:* 167

Newsom, Tom *49:* 149; *71:* 13, 62; *75:* 156; *91:* 113

Newton, Jill *83:* 105

Ng, Michael *29:* 171

Nicholson, William *15:* 33-34; *16:* 48

Nicklaus, Carol *45:* 194; *62:* 132, 133

Nickless, Will *16:* 139

Nicolas *17:* 130, 132-133; *YABC 2:* 215

Niebrugge, Jane *6:* 118

Nielsen, Cliff *95:* 207, 208

Nielsen, Jon *6:* 100; *24:* 202
Nielsen, Kay *15:* 7; *16:* 211-213, 215, 217; *22:* 143; *YABC 1:* 32-33
Niland, Deborah *25:* 191; *27:* 156
Niland, Kilmeny *25:* 191; *75:* 143
Nino, Alex *59:* 145
Ninon *1:* 5; *38:* 101, 103, 108
Nissen, Rie *44:* 35
Nivola, Claire A. *78:* 126
Nixon, K. *14:* 152
Noble, Louise *61:* 170
Noble, Marty *97:* 168
Noble, Trinka Hakes *39:* 162; *84:* 157
Noguchi, Yoshie *30:* 99
Nolan, Dennis *42:* 163; *67:* 163; *78:* 189; *82:* 225; *83:* 26; *92:* 169, 170
Noll, Sally *82:* 171
Nones, Eric Jon *61:* 111; *76:* 38; *77:* 177
Noonan, Julia *4:* 163; *7:* 207; *25:* 151; *91:* 29; *95:* 149
Nordenskjold, Birgitta *2:* 208
Norman, Elaine *77:* 72, 176; *94:* 35
Norman, Mary *36:* 138, 147
Norman, Michael *12:* 117; *27:* 168
Northway, Jennifer *85:* 96
Novelli, Luca *61:* 137
Numeroff, Laura Joffe *28:* 161; *30:* 177
Nussbaumer, Paul *16:* 219; *39:* 117
Nutt, Ken *72:* 69; *97:* 170
Nyce, Helene *19:* 219
Nygren, Tord *30:* 148

O

Oakley, Graham *8:* 112; *30:* 164, 165; *84:* 188, 189, 190, 191, 192
Oakley, Thornton *YABC 2:* 189
Obligado, Lilian *2:* 28, 66-67; *6:* 30; *14:* 179; *15:* 103; *25:* 84; *61:* 138, 139, 140, 141, 143
Obrant, Susan *11:* 186
O'Brien, Anne Sibley *53:* 116, 117
O'Brien, John *41:* 253; *72:* 12; *89:* 59, 60; *98:* 16
O'Brien, Teresa *87:* 89
O'Brien, Tim *93:* 25
Odell, Carole *35:* 47
Odom, Mel *99:* 164
O'Donohue, Thomas *40:* 89
Oechsli, Kelly *5:* 144-145; *7:* 115; *8:* 83, 183; *13:* 117; *20:* 94; *81:* 199
Offen, Hilda *42:* 207
Ogden, Bill *42:* 59; *47:* 55
Ogg, Oscar *33:* 34
Ohi, Ruth *90:* 175, 177
Ohlsson, Ib *4:* 152; *7:* 57; *10:* 20; *11:* 90; *19:* 217; *41:* 246; *82:* 106; *92:* 213
Ohtomo, Yasuo *37:* 146; *39:* 212, 213
O'Kelley, Mattie Lou *36:* 150
Oliver, Jenni *23:* 121; *35:* 112
Olschewski, Alfred *7:* 172
Olsen, Ib Spang *6:* 178-179; *81:* 164
Olson, Alan *77:* 229
Olugebefola, Ademola *15:* 205
O'Malley, Kevin *94:* 180
O'Neil, Dan IV *7:* 176
O'Neill, Catharine *72:* 113
O'Neill, Catherine *84:* 78
O'Neill, Jean *22:* 146
O'Neill, Michael J. *54:* 172
O'Neill, Rose *48:* 30, 31
O'Neill, Steve *21:* 118
Ono, Chiyo *7:* 97
Orbaan, Albert *2:* 31; *5:* 65, 171; *9:* 8; *14:* 241; *20:* 109
Orbach, Ruth *21:* 112

Orfe, Joan *20:* 81
Ormai, Stella *72:* 129
Ormerod, Jan *55:* 124; *70:* 170, 171; *90:* 39
Ormsby, Virginia H. *11:* 187
Orozco, José Clemente *9:* 177
Orr, Forrest W. *23:* 9
Orr, N. *19:* 70
Ortiz, Vilma *88:* 158
Osborn, Robert *65:* 49
Osborne, Billie Jean *35:* 209
Osmond, Edward *10:* 111
O'Sullivan, Tom *3:* 176; *4:* 55; *78:* 195
Otto, Svend *22:* 130, 141; *67:* 188, 189
Oudry, J. B. *18:* 167
Oughton, Taylor *5:* 23
Övereng, Johannes *44:* 36
Overlie, George *11:* 156
Owens, Carl *2:* 35; *23:* 521
Owens, Gail *10:* 170; *12:* 157; *19:* 16; *22:* 70; *25:* 81; *28:* 203, 205; *32:* 221, 222; *36:* 132; *46:* 40; *47:* 57; *54:* 66, 67, 68, 69, 70, 71, 72, 73; *71:* 100; *73:* 64; *77:* 157; *80:* 32; *82:* 3; *99:* 226
Owens, Nubia *84:* 74
Oxenbury, Helen *3:* 150-151; *24:* 81; *68:* 174, 175, 176; *81:* 209; *84:* 213, 245
Oz, Robin *88:* 167

P

Padgett, Jim *12:* 165
Page, Homer *14:* 145
Paget, Sidney *24:* 90, 91, 93, 95, 97
Paget, Walter *64:* 122
Pak *12:* 76
Pak, Yu Cha *86:* 174
Palazzo, Tony *3:* 152-153
Palecek, Josef *56:* 136; *89:* 158
Palencar, John Jude *84:* 12, 45; *85:* 87; *92:* 187; *99:* 128
Palin, Nicki *81:* 201; *89:* 161
Palladini, David *4:* 113; *40:* 176, 177, 178-179, 181, 224-225; *50:* 138; *78:* 186
Pallarito, Don *43:* 36
Palmer, Heidi *15:* 207; *29:* 102
Palmer, Jan *42:* 153; *82:* 161
Palmer, Juliette *6:* 89; *15:* 208
Palmer, Lemuel *17:* 25, 29
Palmquist, Eric *38:* 133
Panesis, Nicholas *3:* 127
Panton, Doug *52:* 99
Papas, William *11:* 223; *50:* 160
Papin, Joseph *26:* 113
Papish, Robin Lloyd *10:* 80
Paradis, Susan *40:* 216
Paraquin, Charles H. *18:* 166
Paris, Peter *31:* 127
Park, Seho *39:* 110
Park, W. B. *22:* 189
Parker, Ant *82:* 87, 88
Parker, Lewis *2:* 179
Parker, Nancy Winslow *10:* 113; *22:* 164; *28:* 47, 144; *52:* 7; *69:* 153; *91:* 171, 174
Parker, Robert *4:* 161; *5:* 74; *9:* 136; *29:* 39
Parker, Robert Andrew *11:* 81; *29:* 186; *39:* 165; *40:* 25; *41:* 78; *42:* 123; *43:* 144; *48:* 182; *54:* 140; *74:* 141; *91:* 24
Parkinson, Kathy *71:* 143
Parkinson, Keith *70:* 66
Parks, Gordon, Jr. *33:* 228
Parnall, Peter *5:* 137; *16:* 221; *24:* 70; *40:* 78; *51:* 130; *69:* 17, 155
Parnall, Virginia *40:* 78

Parrish, Anne *27:* 159, 160
Parrish, Dillwyn *27:* 159
Parrish, Maxfield *14:* 160, 161, 164, 165; *16:* 109; *18:* 12-13; *YABC 1:* 149, 152, 267; *2:* 146, 149
Parry, David *26:* 156
Parry, Marian *13:* 176; *19:* 179
Partch, Virgil *45:* 163, 165
Pascal, David *14:* 174
Pasquier, J. A. *16:* 91
Paterson, Diane *13:* 116; *39:* 163; *59:* 164, 165, 166, 167; *72:* 51, 53
Paterson, Helen *16:* 93
Paton, Jane *15:* 271; *35:* 176
Patrick, Pamela *90:* 160; *93:* 211
Patterson, Geoffrey *54:* 75
Patterson, Robert *25:* 118
Paul, James *4:* 130; *23:* 161
Paull, Grace *24:* 157; *87:* 127
Paulsen, Ruth Wright *79:* 160, 164
Pavlov, Elena *80:* 49
Payne, Joan Balfour *1:* 118
Payson, Dale *7:* 34; *9:* 151; *20:* 140; *37:* 22
Payzant, Charles *21:* 147
Peacock, Ralph *64:* 118
Peake, Mervyn *22:* 136, 149; *23:* 162, 163, 164; *YABC 2:* 307
Pearson, Larry *38:* 225
Pearson, Tracey Campbell *64:* 163, 164, 167, 168, 169
Peat, Fern B. *16:* 115
Peck, Anne Merriman *18:* 241; *24:* 155
Peck, Beth *66:* 242; *79:* 166; *80:* 136; *91:* 34; *95:* 9
Pedersen, Judy *66:* 217
Pedersen, Vilhelm *YABC 1:* 40
Pederson, Sharleen *12:* 92
Peek, Merle *39:* 168
Peet, Bill *2:* 203; *41:* 159, 160, 161, 162, 163; *78:* 158, 159, 160, 161
Pels, Winslow Pinney *55:* 126
Peltier, Leslie C. *13:* 178
Pendle, Alexy *7:* 159; *13:* 34; *29:* 161; *33:* 215; *86:* 62
Pendola, Joanne *76:* 203; *81:* 125
Pene du Bois, William *4:* 70; *10:* 122; *26:* 61; *27:* 145, 211; *35:* 243; *41:* 216; *68:* 180, 181; *73:* 45
Pennington, Eunice *27:* 162
Peppé, Mark *28:* 142
Peppé, Rodney *4:* 164-165; *74:* 187, 188, 189
Pepper, Hubert *64:* 143
Percy, Graham *63:* 2
Perkins, David *60:* 68
Perkins, Lucy Fitch *72:* 199
Perl, Susan *2:* 98; *4:* 231; *5:* 44-45, 118; *6:* 199; *8:* 137; *12:* 88; *22:* 193; *34:* 54-55; *52:* 128; *YABC 1:* 176
Perrone, Donna *78:* 166
Perry, Patricia *29:* 137; *30:* 171
Perry, Roger *27:* 163
Perske, Martha *46:* 83; *51:* 108, 147
Pesek, Ludek *15:* 237
Peters, David *72:* 205
Petersham, Maud *17:* 108, 147-153
Petersham, Miska *17:* 108, 147-153
Peterson, Nisse *99:* 27
Peterson, R. F. *7:* 101
Peterson, Russell *7:* 130
Petie, Haris *2:* 3; *10:* 41, 118; *11:* 227; *12:* 70
Petrides, Heidrun *19:* 223
Petruccio, Steven James *67:* 159
Pettingill, Ondre *64:* 181; *70:* 64
Peyo *40:* 56, 57
Peyton, K. M. *15:* 212

Pfeifer, Herman *15:* 262
Pfister, Marcus *83:* 165, 166, 167
Phillips, Craig *70:* 151
Phillips, Douglas *1:* 19
Phillips, F. D. *6:* 202
Phillips, Thomas *30:* 55
Philpot, Glyn *54:* 46
Phiz
    See Browne, Hablot K.
Piatti, Celestino *16:* 223
Picarella, Joseph *13:* 147
Pickard, Charles *12:* 38; *18:* 203; *36:* 152
Picken, George A. *23:* 150
Pickens, David *22:* 156
Pienkowski, Jan *6:* 183; *30:* 32; *58:* 140, 141, 142, 143, 146, 147; *73:* 3; *87:* 156, 157
Pilkey, Dav *68:* 186
Pimlott, John *10:* 205
Pincus, Harriet *4:* 186; *8:* 179; *22:* 148; *27:* 164, 165; *66:* 202
Pini, Wendy *89:* 166
Pinkett, Neil *60:* 8
Pinkney, Brian *81:* 184, 185; *94:* 107
Pinkney, Jerry *8:* 218; *10:* 40; *15:* 276; *20:* 66; *24:* 121; *33:* 109; *36:* 222; *38:* 200; *41:* 165, 166, 167, 168, 169, 170, 171, 173, 174; *44:* 198; *48:* 51; *53:* 20; *56:* 61, 68; *58:* 184; *60:* 59; *61:* 91; *71:* 146, 148, 149; *72:* 17; *73:* 149; *74:* 159, 192; *75:* 45; *80:* 206; *81:* 44; *85:* 144; *95:* 50
Pinkwater, Daniel Manus *46:* 180, 181, 182, 185, 188, 189, 190; *76:* 178, 179, 180
Pinkwater, Manus *8:* 156; *46:* 180
    See also Pinkwater, Daniel Manus
Pinto, Ralph *10:* 131; *45:* 93
Piñón, Mark *74:* 22
Pistolesi *73:* 211
Pittman, Helena Clare *71:* 151
Pitz, Henry C. *4:* 168; *19:* 165; *35:* 128; *42:* 80; *YABC 2:* 95, 176
Pitzenberger, Lawrence J. *26:* 94
Player, Stephen *82:* 190
Plecas, Jennifer *84:* 201
Plowden, David *52:* 135, 136
Plummer, William *32:* 31
Podwal, Mark *56:* 170, 173
Pogány, Willy *15:* 46, 49; *19:* 222, 256; *25:* 214; *44:* 142, 143, 144, 145, 146, 147, 148
Pohrt, Tom *67:* 116
Poirson, V. A. *26:* 89
Polacco, Patricia *74:* 195, 196-197, 198
Polgreen, John *21:* 44
Politi, Leo *1:* 178; *4:* 53; *21:* 48; *47:* 173, 174, 176, 178, 179, 180, 181
Pollen, Samson *64:* 80
Polonsky, Arthur *34:* 168
Polseno, Jo *1:* 53; *3:* 117; *5:* 114; *17:* 154; *20:* 87; *32:* 49; *41:* 245
Ponter, James *5:* 204
Poortvliet, Rien *6:* 212; *65:* 165, 166-67
Popp, Wendy *72:* 122
Poppel, Hans *71:* 154, 155
Porfirio, Guy *76:* 134
Portal, Colette *6:* 186; *11:* 203
Porter, George *7:* 181
Porter, Pat Grant *84:* 112
Postma, Lidia *79:* 17
Potter, Beatrix *YABC 1:* 208-210, 212, 213
Potter, Miriam Clark *3:* 162
Poulin, Stephane *98:* 140, 141
Powell, Ivan *67:* 219

Powers, Richard M. *1:* 230; *3:* 218; *7:* 194; *26:* 186
Powledge, Fred *37:* 154
Powzyk, Joyce *74:* 214
Poydar, Nancy *96:* 149
Pracher, Richard *91:* 166
Pratt, Charles *23:* 29
Prebenna, David *73:* 174
Pretro, Korinna *91:* 126
Price, Christine *2:* 247; *3:* 163, 253; *8:* 166
Price, Edward *33:* 34
Price, Garrett *1:* 76; *2:* 42
Price, Hattie Longstreet *17:* 13
Price, Norman *YABC 1:* 129
Price, Willard *48:* 184
Priceman, Marjorie *81:* 171
Primavera, Elise *26:* 95; *58:* 151; *73:* 37; *80:* 79; *86:* 156
Primrose, Jean *36:* 109
Prince, Alison *86:* 188, 189
Prince, Leonora E. *7:* 170
Prittie, Edwin J. *YABC 1:* 120
Provensen, Alice *37:* 204, 215, 222; *70:* 176, 177, 178, 180, *71:* 213
Provensen, Martin *37:* 204, 215, 222; *70:* 176, 177, 178, 180; *71:* 213
Pucci, Albert John *44:* 154
Pudlo *8:* 59
Punchatz, Don *99:* 57
Purdy, Susan *8:* 162
Pursell, Weimer *55:* 18
Purtscher, Alfons *97:* 6
Puskas, James *5:* 141
Pyk, Jan *7:* 26; *38:* 123
Pyle, Chuck *99:* 149
Pyle, Howard *16:* 225-228, 230-232, 235; *24:* 27; *34:* 124, 125, 127, 128; *59:* 132

Q

Quackenbush, Robert *4:* 190; *6:* 166; *7:* 175, 178; *9:* 86; *11:* 65, 221; *41:* 154; *43:* 157; *70:* 185, 186; *71:* 137; *85:* 47; *92:* 148
Quennell, Marjorie (Courtney) *29:* 163, 164
Quidor, John *19:* 82
Quirk, John *62:* 170
Quirk, Thomas *12:* 81

R

Rackham, Arthur *15:* 32, 78, 214-227; *17:* 105, 115; *18:* 233; *19:* 254; *20:* 151; *22:* 129, 131, 132, 133; *23:* 175; *24:* 161, 181; *26:* 91; *32:* 118; *64:* 18; *YABC 1:* 25, 45, 55, 147; *2:* 103, 142, 173, 210
Racz, Michael *56:* 134
Radcliffe, Andrew *82:* 215
Rafilson, Sidney *11:* 172
Raible, Alton *1:* 202-203; *28:* 193; *35:* 181
Raine, Patricia *82:* 74; *88:* 154
Ramsey, James *16:* 41
Ramsey, Marcy Dunn *82:* 11
Ramus, Michael *51:* 171
Rand, Paul *6:* 188
Rand, Ted *67:* 9, 10, 121, 123; *74:* 190; *84:* 170

Randazzo, Tony *81:* 98
Randell, William *55:* 54
Rane, Walter *93:* 144
Ransome, Arthur *22:* 201
Ransome, James E. *74:* 137; *75:* 80; *84:* 181; *94:* 108
Rao, Anthony *28:* 126
Raphael, Elaine *23:* 192; *71:* 24, 25
Rappaport, Eva *6:* 190
Raschka, Christopher *80:* 187, 189, 190; *97:* 211
Raskin, Ellen *2:* 208-209; *4:* 142; *13:* 183; *22:* 68; *29:* 139; *36:* 134; *38:* 173, 174, 175, 176, 177, 178, 179, 180, 181; *60:* 163; *86:* 81
Rathmann, Peggy *93:* 32; *94:* 168
Ratkus, Tony *77:* 133
Ratzkin, Lawrence *40:* 143
Rau, Margaret *9:* 157
Raverat, Gwen *YABC 1:* 152
Ravid, Joyce *61:* 73
Ravielli, Anthony *1:* 198; *3:* 168; *11:* 143
Ravilious, Robin *77:* 169
Rawlins, Donna *72:* 198; *73:* 15, 129
Rawlins, Janet *76:* 79
Rawlinson, Debbie *75:* 132
Ray, Deborah Kogan *8:* 164; *29:* 238; *50:* 112, 113; *62:* 119; *78:* 191
Ray, Jane *96:* 166; *97:* 104
Ray, Ralph *2:* 239; *5:* 73
Rayevsky, Robert *64:* 17; *70:* 173; *80:* 204
Raymond, Larry *31:* 108; *97:* 109
Rayner, Mary *22:* 207; *47:* 140; *72:* 191; *87:* 171, 172
Raynes, John *71:* 19
Raynor, Dorka *28:* 168
Raynor, Paul *24:* 73
Razzi, James *10:* 127
Read, Alexander D. *20:* 45
Reader, Dennis *71:* 157
Reasoner, Charles *53:* 33, 36, 37
Reed, Tom *34:* 171
Reeder, Colin *74:* 202; *77:* 113
Reese, Bob *60:* 135
Reid, Barbara *82:* 178; *92:* 17; *93:* 169, 170
Reid, Stephen *19:* 213; *22:* 89
Reinert, Kirk *89:* 138
Reinertson, Barbara *44:* 150; *62:* 103
Reiniger, Lotte *40:* 185
Reiser, Lynn *81:* 175
Reiss, John J. *23:* 193
Relf, Douglas *3:* 63
Relyea, C. M. *16:* 29; *31:* 153
Rémi, Georges *13:* 184
Remington, Frederic *19:* 188; *41:* 178, 179, 180, 181, 183, 184, 185, 186, 187, 188; *62:* 197
Remkiewicz, Frank *67:* 102; *77:* 171; *80:* 130
Renfro, Ed *79:* 176
Renlie, Frank *11:* 200
Reschofsky, Jean *7:* 118
Rethi *60:* 181
Réthi, Lili *2:* 153; *36:* 156
Reusswig, William *3:* 267
Rey, H. A. *1:* 182; *26:* 163, 164, 166, 167, 169; *69:* 172, 173, 174, 175; *86:* 195, 196, 197; *YABC 2:* 17
Reynolds, Doris *5:* 71; *31:* 77
Rhead, Louis *31:* 91
Rhodes, Andrew *38:* 204; *50:* 163; *54:* 76; *61:* 123, 124; *87:* 200
Ribbons, Ian *3:* 10; *37:* 161; *40:* 76
Ricci, Regolo *93:* 22
Rice, Elizabeth *2:* 53, 214
Rice, Eve *34:* 174, 175; *91:* 172
Rice, James *22:* 210; *93:* 173
Richards, George *40:* 116, 119, 121; *44:* 179
Richards, Henry *YABC 1:* 228, 231
Richardson, Ernest *2:* 144

Richardson, Frederick *18:* 27, 31
Richman, Hilda *26:* 132
Richmond, George *24:* 179
Riddle, Tohby *74:* 204
Riding, Peter *63:* 195
Rieniets, Judy King *14:* 28
Riger, Bob *2:* 166
Riggio, Anita *73:* 191; *85:* 63
Riley, Jon *74:* 70
Riley, Kenneth *22:* 230
Ringgold, Faith *71:* 162
Ringi, Kjell *12:* 171
Rios, Tere
    See Versace, Marie
Ripper, Charles L. *3:* 175
Ritchie, William *74:* 183
Ritz, Karen *41:* 117; *72:* 239; *87:* 125
Rivkin, Jay *15:* 230
Rivoche, Paul *45:* 125
Roach, Marilynne *9:* 158
Robbin, Jodi *44:* 156, 159
Robbins, Frank *42:* 167
Robbins, Ruth *52:* 102
Roberts, Cliff *4:* 126
Roberts, Doreen *4:* 230; *28:* 105
Roberts, Jim *22:* 166; *23:* 69; *31:* 110
Roberts, W. *22:* 2, 3
Robinson, Aminah Brenda Lynn *86:* 205
Robinson, Charles [1870-1937] *17:* 157, 171, 172, 173, 175, 176; *24:* 207; *25:* 204; *YABC 2:* 308, 309, 310, 331
Robinson, Charles *3:* 53; *5:* 14; *6:* 193; *7:* 150; *7:* 183; *8:* 38; *9:* 81; *13:* 188; *14:* 248-249; *23:* 149; *26:* 115; *27:* 48; *28:* 191; *32:* 28; *35:* 210; *36:* 37; *48:* 96; *52:* 33; *53:* 157; *56:* 15; *62:* 142; *77:* 41
Robinson, Jerry *3:* 262
Robinson, Joan G. *7:* 184
Robinson, Lolly *90:* 227
Robinson, T. H. *17:* 179, 181-183; *29:* 254
Robinson, W. Heath *17:* 185, 187, 189, 191, 193, 195, 197, 199, 202; *23:* 167; *25:* 194; *29:* 150; *YABC 1:* 44; *2:* 183
Roche, Christine *41:* 98
Roche, Denis *99:* 184
Roche, P. K. *57:* 151, 152
Rocker, Fermin *7:* 34; *13:* 21; *31:* 40; *40:* 190, 191
Rockwell, Anne *5:* 147; *33:* 171, 173; *71:* 166, 167, 168
Rockwell, Gail *7:* 186
Rockwell, Harlow *33:* 171, 173, 175
Rockwell, Norman *23:* 39, 196, 197, 199, 200, 203, 204, 207; *41:* 140, 143; *YABC 2:* 60
Rodegast, Roland *43:* 100
Rodgers, Frank *69:* 177
Rodriguez, Joel *16:* 65
Roennfeldt, Robert *66:* 243
Roever, J. M. *4:* 119; *26:* 170
Roffey, Maureen *33:* 142, 176, 177
Rogasky, Barbara *46:* 90
Rogers, Carol *2:* 262; *6:* 164; *26:* 129
Rogers, Forest *87:* 160
Rogers, Frances *10:* 130
Rogers, Jacqueline *78:* 249; *80:* 34; *86:* 54
Rogers, Walter S. *31:* 135, 138; *67:* 65, 168
Rogers, William A. *15:* 151, 153-154; *33:* 35
Rogoff, Barbara *95:* 20
Rojankovsky, Feodor *6:* 134, 136; *10:* 183; *21:* 128, 129, 130; *25:* 110; *28:* 42; *68:* 120
Rolfsen, Alf *62:* 15
Romano, Robert *64:* 68
Root, Barry *80:* 212; *90:* 196

Root, Kimberly Bulcken *86:* 72; *98:* 21
Roper, Bob *65:* 153
Rorer, Abigail *43:* 222; *85:* 155
Rosales, Melodye *80:* 35
Rosamilia, Patricia *36:* 120
Rose, Carl *5:* 62
Rose, David S. *29:* 109; *70:* 120
Rose, Gerald *68:* 200, 201; *86:* 48
Rose, Ted *93:* 178
Rosenbaum, Jonathan *50:* 46
Rosenberg, Amye *74:* 207, 208
Rosenberry, Vera *87:* 22, 26
Rosenblum, Richard *11:* 202; *18:* 18
Rosier, Lydia *16:* 236; *20:* 104; *21:* 109; *22:* 125; *30:* 151, 158; *42:* 128; *45:* 214; *77:* 227, 228
Rosing, Jens *85:* 142
Ross, Christine *83:* 172-173
Ross, Clare Romano *3:* 123; *21:* 45; *48:* 199
Ross, Dave *32:* 152; *57:* 108
Ross, Herbert *37:* 78
Ross, John *3:* 123; *21:* 45
Ross, Johnny *32:* 190
Ross, Larry *47:* 168; *60:* 62
Ross
    See Thomson, Ross
Ross, Tony *17:* 204; *56:* 132; *65:* 176, 177, 179; *90:* 123
Rossetti, Dante Gabriel *20:* 151, 153
Roth, Arnold *4:* 238; *21:* 133
Roth, Roger *61:* 128
Roth, Susan L. *80:* 38; *93:* 78
Rotondo, Pat *32:* 158
Roughsey, Dick *35:* 186
Rouille, M. *11:* 96
Rounds, Glen *8:* 173; *9:* 171; *12:* 56; *32:* 194; *40:* 230; *51:* 161, 162, 166; *56:* 149; *70:* 198, 199; *YABC 1:* 1-3
Rowan, Evadne *52:* 51
Rowe, Gavin *27:* 144; *72:* 47; *88:* 201
Rowell, Kenneth *40:* 72
Rowen, Amy *52:* 143
Rowland, Jada *83:* 73
Rowles, Daphne *58:* 24
Roy, Jeroo *27:* 229; *36:* 110
Rubel, Nicole *18:* 255; *20:* 59; *81:* 66, 67; *95:* 169, 170
Rubel, Reina *33:* 217
Rud, Borghild *6:* 15
Rudolph, Norman Guthrie *17:* 13
Rue, Leonard Lee III *37:* 164
Ruff, Donna *50:* 173; *72:* 203; *78:* 49; *80:* 120, 121; *93:* 162
Ruffins, Reynold *10:* 134-135; *41:* 191, 192-193, 194-195, 196
Ruhlin, Roger *34:* 44
Ruiz, Art *95:* 154
Runnerstroem, Bengt Arne *75:* 161
Ruse, Margaret *24:* 155
Rush, Ken *98:* 74
Rush, Peter *42:* 75
Russell, E. B. *18:* 177, 182
Russell, Jim *53:* 134
Russell, P. Craig *80:* 196
Russo, Marisabina *84:* 51
Russo, Susan *30:* 182; *36:* 144
Russon, Mary *87:* 145
Ruth, Rod *9:* 161
Rutherford, Jenny *78:* 5
Rutherford, Meg *25:* 174; *34:* 178, 179; *69:* 73; *72:* 31
Rutland, Jonathan *31:* 126
Ryan, Will *86:* 134
Ryden, Hope *8:* 176
Rymer, Alta M. *34:* 181
Rystedt, Rex *49:* 80

S

Saaf, Chuck *49:* 179
Sabaka, Donna R. *21:* 172
Sabin, Robert *45:* 35; *60:* 30; *99:* 161
Sacker, Amy *16:* 100
Saffioti, Lino *36:* 176, *48:* 60
Saflund, Birgitta *94:* 2
Sagsoorian, Paul *12:* 183; *22:* 154; *33:* 106; *87:* 152
Sahlberg, Myron *57:* 165
Saint Exupéry, Antoine de *20:* 157
Saldutti, Denise *39:* 186; *57:* 178
Sale, Morton *YABC 2:* 31
Salter, George *72:* 128, 130
Saltzman, David *86:* 209
Salwowski, Mark *71:* 54
Salzman, Yuri *86:* 12
Sambourne, Linley *YABC 2:* 181
Sampson, Katherine *9:* 197
Samson, Anne S. *2:* 216
San Souci, Daniel *40:* 200; *96:* 199, 200
Sancha, Sheila *38:* 185
Sand, George X. *45:* 182
Sandberg, Lasse *15:* 239, 241
Sanders, Beryl *39:* 173
Sanderson, Ruth *21:* 126; *24:* 53; *28:* 63; *33:* 67; *41:* 48, 198, 199, 200, 201, 202, 203; *43:* 79; *46:* 36, 44; *47:* 102; *49:* 58; *62:* 121, 122; *85:* 3
Sandin, Joan *4:* 36; *6:* 194; *7:* 177; *12:* 145, 185; *20:* 43; *21:* 74; *26:* 144; *27:* 142; *28:* 224, 225; *38:* 86; *41:* 46; *42:* 35; *59:* 6; *80:* 136; *94:* 188
Sandland, Reg *39:* 215
Sandoz, Edouard *26:* 45, 47
Sanford, John *66:* 96, 97
Sankey, Tom *72:* 103
Santore, Charles *54:* 139
Santoro, Christopher *74:* 215
Santos, Jesse J. *99:* 24
Sapieha, Christine *1:* 180
Sara
    See De La Roche Saint Andre, Anne
Sarg, Tony *YABC 2:* 236
Sargent, Claudia *64:* 181
Sargent, Robert *2:* 217
Saris *1:* 33
Sarony *YABC 2:* 170
Sasek, Miroslav *16:* 239-242
Sassman, David *9:* 79
Sätty *29:* 203, 205
Sauber, Robert *40:* 183; *76:* 256; *78:* 154; *87:* 92
Saunders, Dave *85:* 163, 164, 165
Savadier, Elivia *84:* 50
Savage, Naomi *56:* 172
Savage, Steele *10:* 203; *20:* 77; *35:* 28
Savio *76:* 4
Savitt, Sam *8:* 66, 182; *15:* 278; *20:* 96; *24:* 192; *28:* 98
Sawyer, Kem Knapp *84:* 228, 229
Say, Allen *28:* 178; *69:* 182, 183, 232
Sayles, Elizabeth *82:* 93
Scabrini, Janet *13:* 191; *44:* 128
Scanlan, Peter *83:* 27
Scanlon, Paul *83:* 87
Scarry, Huck *35:* 204-205
Scarry, Richard *2:* 220-221; *18:* 20; *35:* 193, 194-195, 196, 197, 198, 199, 200-201, 202; *75:* 165, 167, 168
Schachner, Judith Byron *88:* 180; *92:* 163; *93:* 102
Schaeffer, Mead *18:* 81, 94; *21:* 137, 138, 139; *47:* 128
Schaffer, Amanda *90:* 206
Scharl, Josef *20:* 132; *22:* 128
Scheel, Lita *11:* 230
Scheib, Ida *29:* 28

Schermer, Judith *30:* 184
Schick, Eleanor *82:* 210, 211
Schick, Joel *16:* 160; *17:* 167; *22:* 12; *27:* 176; *31:* 147, 148; *36:* 23; *38:* 64; *45:* 116, 117; *52:* 5, 85
Schields, Gretchen *75:* 171, 203
Schindelman, Joseph *1:* 74; *4:* 101; *12:* 49; *26:* 51; *40:* 146; *56:* 158; *73:* 40
Schindler, Edith *7:* 22
Schindler, S. D. *38:* 107; *46:* 196; *74:* 162; *75:* 172, 173; *99:* 133
Schlesinger, Bret *7:* 77
Schmid, Eleanore *12:* 188
Schmiderer, Dorothy *19:* 224
Schmidt, Bill *73:* 34; *76:* 220, 222, 224
Schmidt, Elizabeth *15:* 242
Schmidt, Karen *54:* 12; *71:* 174; *92:* 56; *94:* 190, 191
Schmidt, Lynette *76:* 205
Schneider, Rex *29:* 64; *44:* 171
Schoberle, Cecile *80:* 200; *92:* 134
Schoenherr, Ian *32:* 83
Schoenherr, John *1:* 146-147, 173; *3:* 39, 139; *17:* 75; *29:* 72; *32:* 83; *37:* 168, 169, 170; *43:* 164, 165; *45:* 160, 162; *51:* 127; 66; 196, 197, 198; *68:* 83; *72:* 240; *75:* 225; *88:* 176
Scholder, Fritz *69:* 103
Schomburg, Alex *13:* 23
Schongut, Emanuel *4:* 102; *15:* 186; *47:* 218, 219; *52:* 147, 148, 149, 150
Schoonover, Frank *17:* 107; *19:* 81, 190, 233; *22:* 88, 129; *24:* 189; *31:* 88; *41:* 69; *YABC 2:* 282, 316
Schottland, Miriam *22:* 172
Schramm, Ulrik *2:* 16; *14:* 112
Schreiber, Elizabeth Anne *13:* 193
Schreiber, Ralph W. *13:* 193
Schreiter, Rick *14:* 97; *23:* 171; *41:* 247; *49:* 131
Schroeder, Binette *56:* 128, 129
Schroeder, E. Peter *12:* 112
Schroeder, Ted *11:* 160; *15:* 189; *30:* 91; *34:* 43
Schrotter, Gustav *22:* 212; *30:* 225
Schucker, James *31:* 163
Schuett, Stacey *72:* 137
Schulke, Debra *57:* 167
Schulke, Flip *57:* 167
Schulz, Charles M. *10:* 137-142
Schwark, Mary Beth *51:* 155; *72:* 175
Schwartz, Amy *47:* 191; *82:* 100; *83:* 178, 179, 180, 181
Schwartz, Charles *8:* 184
Schwartz, Daniel *46:* 37
Schwartzberg, Joan *3:* 208
Schweitzer, Iris *2:* 137; *6:* 207
Schweninger, Ann *29:* 172; *82:* 246
Schwinger, Laurence *84:* 44; *91:* 61
Scofield, Penrod *61:* 107; *62:* 160
Scott, Anita Walker *7:* 38
Scott, Art *39:* 41
Scott, Frances Gruse *38:* 43
Scott, Julian *34:* 126
Scott, Roszel *33:* 238
Scott, Sally *87:* 27
Scott, Trudy *27:* 172
Scribner, Joanne *14:* 236; *29:* 78; *33:* 185; *34:* 208; *78:* 75
Scrofani, Joseph *31:* 65; *74:* 225
Seaman, Mary Lott *34:* 64
Searle, Ronald *24:* 98; *42:* 172, 173, 174, 176, 177, 179; *66:* 73, 74; *70:* 205, 206, 207
Searle, Townley *36:* 85
Sebree, Charles *18:* 65
Sedacca, Joseph M. *11:* 25; *22:* 36
Seeley, Laura L. *97:* 105
Segar, E. C. *61:* 179, 181
Ségur, Adrienne *27:* 121

Seibold, J. Otto *83:* 188, 190, 191
Seignobosc, Francoise *21:* 145, 146
Sejima, Yoshimasa *8:* 187
Selig, Sylvie *13:* 199
Seltzer, Isadore *6:* 18
Seltzer, Meyer *17:* 214
Selznick, Brian *79:* 192
Sempé, Jean-Jacques *47:* 92; *YABC 2:* 109
Sendak, Maurice *1:* 135, 190; *3:* 204; *7:* 142; *15:* 199; *17:* 210; *27:* 181, 182, 183, 185, 186, 187, 189, 190-191, 192, 193, 194, 195, 197, 198, 199, 203; *28:* 181, 182; *32:* 108; *33:* 148, 149; *35:* 238; *44:* 180, 181; *45:* 97, 99; *46:* 174; *73:* 225; *91:* 10, 11 *YABC 1:* 167
Sengler, Johanna *18:* 256
Senn, Steve *60:* 145
Seredy, Kate *1:* 192; *14:* 20-21; *17:* 210
Sergeant, John *6:* 74
Servello, Joe *10:* 144; *24:* 139; *40:* 91; *70:* 130, 131
Seton, Ernest Thompson *18:* 260-269, 271
Seuss, Dr.
    See Geisel, Theodor
Severin, John Powers *7:* 62
Sewall, Marcia *15:* 8; *22:* 170; *37:* 171, 172, 173; *39:* 73; *45:* 209; *62:* 117; *69:* 185, 186; *71:* 212; *90:* 232; *96:* 127
Seward, James *70:* 35
Seward, Prudence *16:* 243
Sewell, Helen *3:* 186; *15:* 308; *33:* 102; *38:* 189, 190, 191, 192
Seymour, Stephen *54:* 21
Shachat, Andrew *82:* 179
Shahn, Ben *39:* 178; *46:* 193
Shalansky, Len *38:* 167
Shanks, Anne Zane *10:* 149
Shannon, David *57:* 137
Sharp, Paul *52:* 60
Sharp, William *6:* 131; *19:* 241; *20:* 112; *25:* 141
Shaw, Barclay *74:* 14, 16
Shaw, Charles *21:* 135; *38:* 187; *47:* 124
Shaw, Charles G. *13:* 200
Shea, Edmund *56:* 19
Shearer, Ted *43:* 193, 194, 195, 196
Shecter, Ben *16:* 244; *25:* 109; *33:* 188, 191; *41:* 77
Shed, Greg *74:* 94; *84:* 204
Shefcik, James *48:* 221, 222; *60:* 141
Shefelman, Karl *58:* 168
Shefts, Joelle *48:* 210
Shekerjian, Haig *16:* 245
Shekerjian, Regina *16:* 245; *25:* 73
Shemie, Bonnie *96:* 207
Shenton, Edward *45:* 187, 188, 189; *YABC 1:* 218-219, 221
Shepard, Ernest H. *3:* 193; *4:* 74; *16:* 101; *17:* 109; *25:* 148; *33:* 152, 199, 200, 201, 202, 203, 204, 205, 206, 207; *46:* 194; *YABC 1:* 148, 153, 174, 176, 180-181; *98:* 114
Shepard, Mary *4:* 210; *22:* 205; *30:* 132, 133; *54:* 150, 152, 153, 157, 158; *59:* 108, 109, 111
Shepperson, Rob *96:* 153
Sherman, Theresa *27:* 167
Sherwan, Earl *3:* 196
Shields, Charles *10:* 150; *36:* 63
Shields, Leonard *13:* 83, 85, 87
Shigley, Neil K. *66:* 219
Shillabeer, Mary *35:* 74
Shilston, Arthur *49:* 61; *62:* 58
Shimin, Symeon *1:* 93; *2:* 128-129; *3:* 202; *7:* 85; *11:* 177; *12:* 139; *13:* 202-203; *27:* 138; *28:* 65; *35:* 129; *36:* 130; *48:* 151; *49:* 59; *56:* 63, 65, 153
Shinn, Everett *16:* 148; *18:* 229; *21:* 149, 150, 151; *24:* 218

Shinn, Florence Scovel *63:* 133, 135
Shore, Robert *27:* 54; *39:* 192, 193; *YABC 2:* 200
Shortall, Leonard *4:* 144; *8:* 196; *10:* 166; *19:* 227, 228-229, 230; *25:* 78; *28:* 66, 167; *33:* 127; *52:* 125; *73:* 12, 212
Shortt, T. M. *27:* 36
Shpitalnik, Vladimir *83:* 194
Shtainments, Leon *32:* 161
Shulevitz, Uri *3:* 198-199; *17:* 85; *22:* 204; *27:* 212; *28:* 184; *50:* 190, 191, 192, 193, 194-195, 196, 197, 198, 199, 201
Shute, A. B. *67:* 196
Shute, Linda *46:* 59; *74:* 118
Siberell, Anne *29:* 193
Sibley, Don *1:* 39; *12:* 196; *31:* 47
Sibthorp, Fletcher *94:* 111, 112
Sidjakov, Nicolas *18:* 274
Siebel, Fritz *3:* 120; *17:* 145
Siegel, Hal *74:* 246
Siegl, Helen *12:* 166; *23:* 216; *34:* 185, 186
Sills, Joyce *5:* 199
Silver, Maggie *85:* 210
Silveria, Gordon *96:* 44
Silverstein, Alvin *8:* 189
Silverstein, Shel *33:* 211; *92:* 209, 210
Silverstein, Virginia *8:* 189
Simard, Remy *95:* 156
Simon, Eric M. *7:* 82
Simon, Hilda *28:* 189
Simon, Howard *2:* 175; *5:* 132; *19:* 199; *32:* 163, 164, 165
Simont, Marc *2:* 119; *4:* 213; *9:* 168; *13:* 238, 240; *14:* 262; *16:* 179; *18:* 221; *26:* 210; *33:* 189, 194; *44:* 132; *58:* 122; *68:* 117; *73:* 204, 205, 206; *74:* 221
Sims, Agnes *54:* 152
Sims, Blanche *44:* 116; *57:* 129; *75:* 179, 180; *77:* 92
Singer, Edith G. *2:* 30
Singer, Gloria *34:* 56; *36:* 43
Singer, Julia *28:* 190
Siracusa, Catherine *68:* 135; *82:* 218
Sis, Peter *67:* 179, 181, 183, 184, 185; *96:* 96, 98
Sivard, Robert *26:* 124
Skardinski, Stanley *23:* 144; *32:* 84; *66:* 122; *84:* 108
Slackman, Charles B. *12:* 201
Slade, Paul *61:* 170
Slark, Albert *99:* 212
Slater, Rod *25:* 167
Sloan, Joseph *16:* 68
Sloane, Eric *21:* 3; *52:* 153, 154, 155, 156, 157, 158, 160
Slobodkin, Louis *1:* 200; *3:* 232; *5:* 168; *13:* 251; *15:* 13, 88; *26:* 173, 174, 175, 176, 178, 179; *60:* 180
Slobodkina, Esphyr *1:* 201
Small, David *50:* 204-205; *79:* 44; *95:* 189, 190, 191
Small, W. *33:* 113
Smalley, Janet *1:* 154
Smedley, William T. *34:* 129
Smee, David *14:* 78; *62:* 30
Smith, A. G., Jr. *35:* 182
Smith, Alvin *1:* 31, 229; *13:* 187; *27:* 216; *28:* 226; *48:* 149; *49:* 60
Smith, Anne Warren *41:* 212
Smith, Barry *75:* 183
Smith, Carl *36:* 41
Smith, Craig *97:* 197
Smith, Doris Susan *41:* 139
Smith, E. Boyd *19:* 70; *22:* 89; *26:* 63; *YABC 1:* 4-5, 240, 248-249
Smith, Edward J. *4:* 224
Smith, Eunice Young *5:* 170

Smith, Howard *19:* 196
Smith, J. Gerard *95:* 42
Smith, Jacqueline Bardner *27:* 108; *39:* 197
Smith, Jay J. *61:* 119
Smith, Jeff *93:* 191
Smith, Jessie Willcox *15:* 91; *16:* 95; *18:* 231; *19:* 57, 242; *21:* 29, 156, 157, 158, 159, 160, 161; *34:* 65; *YABC 1:* 6; *2:* 180, 185, 191, 311, 325
Smith, Jos. A. *52:* 131; *72:* 120; *74:* 151; *84:* 147, 148; *85:* 146; *87:* 96; *94:* 219; *96:* 97
Smith, Kenneth R. *47:* 182
Smith, Kevin Warren *89:* 112
Smith, L. H. *35:* 174
Smith, Lane *76:* 211, 213; *88:* 115
Smith, Lee *29:* 32
Smith, Linell Nash *2:* 195
Smith, Maggie Kaufman *13:* 205; *35:* 191
Smith, Moishe *33:* 155
Smith, Philip *44:* 134; *46:* 203
Smith, Ralph Crosby *2:* 267; *49:* 203
Smith, Robert D. *5:* 63
Smith, Sally J. *84:* 55
Smith, Susan Carlton *12:* 208
Smith, Terry *12:* 106; *33:* 158
Smith, Virginia *3:* 157; *33:* 72
Smith, William A. *1:* 36; *10:* 154; *25:* 65
Smith-Moore, J. J. *98:* 147
Smolinski, Dick *84:* 217
Smollin, Mike *39:* 203
Smyth, M. Jane *12:* 15
Snyder, Andrew A. *30:* 212
Snyder, Jerome *13:* 207; *30:* 173
Snyder, Joel *28:* 163
Soentpiet, Chris K. *97:* 208
Sofia *1:* 62; *5:* 90; *32:* 166; *86:* 43
Sofilas, Mark *93:* 157
Sokol, Bill *37:* 178; *49:* 23
Sokolov, Kirill *34:* 188
Solbert, Ronni *1:* 159; *2:* 232; *5:* 121; *6:* 34; *17:* 249
Solonevich, George *15:* 246; *17:* 47
Soma, Liana *81:* 118
Soman, David *90:* 122
Sommer, Robert *12:* 211
Sorel, Edward *4:* 61; *36:* 82; *65:* 191, 193
Sorensen, Henrik *62:* 16
Sorensen, Svend Otto *22:* 130, 141; *67:* 188, 189
Sotomayor, Antonio *11:* 215
Souza, Diana *71:* 139
Soyer, Moses *20:* 177
Spaenkuch, August *16:* 28
Spanfeller, James *1:* 72, 149; *2:* 183; *19:* 230, 231, 232; *22:* 66; *36:* 160, 161; *40:* 75; *52:* 166; *76:* 37
Sparks, Mary Walker *15:* 247
Speidel, Sandra *78:* 233; *94:* 178
Speirs, John *67:* 178
Spence, Geraldine *21:* 163; *47:* 196
Spence, Jim *38:* 89; *50:* 102
Spencer, Mark *57:* 170
Spiegel, Doris *29:* 111
Spier, Jo *10:* 30
Spier, Peter *3:* 155; *4:* 200; *7:* 61; *11:* 78; *38:* 106; *54:* 120, 121, 122-123, 124-125, 126, 127, 128-129, 130, 131, 132-133, 134
Spilka, Arnold *5:* 120; *6:* 204; *8:* 131
Spirin, Gennady *95:* 196, 197
Spivak, I. Howard *8:* 10
Spohn, David *72:* 233
Spohn, Kate *87:* 195
Spollen, Christopher J. *12:* 214
Spooner, Malcolm *40:* 142
Spowart, Robin *82:* 228; *92:* 149
Sprattler, Rob *12:* 176
Spring, Bob *5:* 60

Spring, Ira *5:* 60
Springer, Harriet *31:* 92
Spurll, Barbara *78:* 199; *88:* 141, 142; *99:* 215
Spurrier, Steven *28:* 198
Spuvilas, Anne *85:* 114
Spy
   See Ward, Leslie
St. John, J. Allen *41:* 62
Stadler, John *62:* 33
Staffan, Alvin E. *11:* 56; *12:* 187
Stahl, Ben *5:* 181; *12:* 91; *49:* 122; *71:* 128; *87:* 206
Stair, Gobin *35:* 214
Stallwood, Karen *73:* 126
Stamaty, Mark Alan *12:* 215
Stampnick, Ken *51:* 142
Stanley, Diane *3:* 45; *37:* 180; *80:* 217, 219
Starcke, Helmut *86:* 217
Starr, Branka *73:* 25
Stasiak, Krystyna *49:* 181; *64:* 194
Stead, L. *55:* 51, 56
Steadman, Broeck *97:* 185, 186; *99:* 56
Steadman, Ralph *32:* 180
Steckler, June *90:* 178
Steichen, Edward *30:* 79
Steig, William *18:* 275-276; *70:* 215, 216, 217, 218
Stein, Harve *1:* 109
Steinberg, Saul *47:* 193
Steinel, William *23:* 146
Steiner, Charlotte *45:* 196
Steirnagel, Michael *80:* 56
Stemp, Eric *60:* 184
Stephens, Alice Barber *66:* 208, 209
Stephens, Charles H. *YABC 2:* 279
Stephens, William M. *21:* 165
Steptoe, John *8:* 197; *57:* 9; *63:* 158, 159, 160, 161, 163, 164, 165, 166, 167; *96:* 4
Stern, Simon *15:* 249-250; *17:* 58; *34:* 192-193
Sterret, Jane *53:* 27
Stevens, David *62:* 44
Stevens, Janet *40:* 126; *57:* 10, 11; *80:* 112; *90:* 221, 222
Stevens, Mary *11:* 193; *13:* 129; *43:* 95
Stevenson, Harvey *66:* 143; *80:* 201, 221
Stevenson, James *42:* 182, 183; *51:* 163; *66:* 184; *71:* 185, 187, 188; *78:* 262; *87:* 97
Stevenson, Sucie *92:* 27
Stewart, April Blair *75:* 210
Stewart, Arvis *33:* 98; *36:* 69; *60:* 118; *75:* 91
Stewart, Charles *2:* 205
Stiles, Fran *26:* 85; *78:* 56; *82:* 150
Stillman, Susan *44:* 130; *76:* 83
Stimpson, Tom *49:* 171
Stinemetz, Morgan *40:* 151
Stirnweis, Shannon *10:* 164
Stites, Joe *86:* 96
Stobbs, William *1:* 48, 49; *3:* 68; *6:* 20; *17:* 117, 121; *24:* 150; *29:* 250; *60:* 179; *87:* 204, 205, 206
Stock, Catherine *37:* 55; *65:* 198; *72:* 7; *99:* 225
Stoeke, Janet Morgan *90:* 225
Stoerrle, Tom *55:* 147
Stolp, Jaap *49:* 98
Stolp, Todd *89:* 195
Stone, David L. *87:* 154
Stone, David *9:* 173
Stone, David K. *4:* 38; *6:* 124; *9:* 180; *43:* 182; *60:* 70
Stone, Helen V. *6:* 209
Stone, Helen *44:* 121, 122, 126
Stone, Phoebe *86:* 212
Stoud, Virginia A. *89:* 31

Stover, Jill *82:* 234
Stratton, Helen *33:* 151
Stratton-Porter, Gene *15:* 254, 259, 263-264, 268-269
Streano, Vince *20:* 173
Street, Janet Travell *84:* 235
Strodl, Daniel *47:* 95
Strogart, Alexander *63:* 139
Strong, Joseph D., Jr. *YABC 2:* 330
Ströyer, Poul *13:* 221
Strugnell, Ann *27:* 38
Stubbs, William *73:* 196
Stubis, Talivaldis *5:* 182, 183; *10:* 45; *11:* 9; *18:* 304; *20:* 127
Stubley, Trevor *14:* 43; *22:* 219; *23:* 37; *28:* 61; *87:* 26
Stuecklen, Karl W. *8:* 34, 65; *23:* 103
Stull, Betty *11:* 46
Stutzmann, Laura *73:* 185
Suba, Susanne *4:* 202-203; *14:* 261; *23:* 134; *29:* 222; *32:* 30
Sueling, Barbara *98:* 185
Sueling, Gwenn *98:* 186
Sugarman, Tracy *3:* 76; *8:* 199; *37:* 181, 182
Sugita, Yutaka *36:* 180-181
Suh, John *80:* 157
Sullivan, Dorothy *89:* 113
Sullivan, Edmund J. *31:* 86
Sullivan, James F. *19:* 280; *20:* 192
Sumichrast, Jözef *14:* 253; *29:* 168, 213
Sumiko *46:* 57
Summers, Leo *1:* 177; *2:* 273; *13:* 22
Sutton, Judith *94:* 164
Svarez, Juan *56:* 113
Svolinsky, Karel *17:* 104
Swain, Su Zan Noguchi *21:* 170
Swan, Susan *22:* 220-221; *37:* 66; *60:* 146
Swann, Susan *86:* 55
Swanson, Karl *79:* 65; *89:* 186
Swayne, Sam *53:* 143, 145
Swayne, Zoa *53:* 143, 145
Sweat, Lynn *25:* 206; *57:* 176; *73:* 184
Sweet, Darrell K. *60:* 9; *69:* 86; *74:* 15; *75:* 215; *76:* 130, 131; *81:* 96, 122; *82:* 253; *83:* 11; *84:* 14; *85:* 37; *89:* 140; *90:* 6; *91:* 137, 139; *95:* 160, 161
Sweet, Darryl *1:* 163; *4:* 136
Sweet, Melissa *71:* 94; *72:* 172
Sweet, Ozzie *31:* 149, 151, 152
Sweetland, Robert *12:* 194
Swope, Martha *43:* 160; *56:* 86, 87, 89
Sylvester, Natalie G. *22:* 222
Szafran, Gene *24:* 144
Szasz, Susanne *13:* 55, 226; *14:* 48
Szekeres, Cyndy *2:* 218; *5:* 185; *8:* 85; *11:* 166; *14:* 19; *16:* 57, 159; *26:* 49, 214; *34:* 205; *60:* 150, 151, 152, 153, 154; *73:* 224; *74:* 218
Szpura, Beata *81:* 68

T

Taback, Simms *40:* 207; *52:* 120; *57:* 34; *80:* 241
Taber, Patricia *75:* 124
Tabor, Nancy Maria Grande *89:* 210
Tafuri, Nancy *39:* 210; *75:* 199, 200; *92:* 75
Tailfeathers, Gerald *86:* 85
Tait, Douglas *12:* 220; *74:* 105, 106
Takakjian, Portia *15:* 274
Takashima, Shizuye *13:* 228
Talarczyk, June *4:* 173
Talbott, Hudson *84:* 240
Tallon, Robert *2:* 228; *43:* 200, 201, 202, 203, 204, 205, 206, 207, 209

Tamas, Szecskó *29:* 135
Tamburine, Jean *12:* 222
Tandy, H. R. *13:* 69
Tandy, Russell H. *65:* 9
Tang, Charles *81:* 202; *90:* 192
Tang, Susan *80:* 174
Tang, You-shan *63:* 100
Tankersley, Paul *69:* 206
Tannenbaum, Robert *48:* 181
Tanner, Jane *87:* 13; *97:* 37
Tanner, Tim *72:* 192; *84:* 35
Tanobe, Miyuki *23:* 221
Tarkington, Booth *17:* 224-225
Tarlow, Phyllis *61:* 198
Tauss, Herbert *95:* 179
Taylor, Ann *41:* 226
Taylor, Geoff *93:* 156
Taylor, Isaac *41:* 228
Teague, Mark *83:* 6
Teale, Edwin Way *7:* 196
Teason, James *1:* 14
Teeple, Lyn *33:* 147
Tee-Van, Helen Damrosch *10:* 176; *11:* 182
Teicher, Dick *50:* 211
Teichman, Mary *77:* 220
Temertey, Ludmilla *96:* 232
Tempest, Margaret *3:* 237, 238; *88:* 200
Temple, Frances *85:* 185, 186, 187
Temple, Herbert *45:* 201
Templeton, Owen *11:* 77
Tenggren, Gustaf *18:* 277-279; *19:* 15; *28:* 86; *YABC 2:* 145
Tennent, Julie *81:* 105
Tenney, Gordon *24:* 204
Tenniel, John *74:* 234, 235; *YABC 2:* 99
Teskey, Donald *71:* 51
Thacher, Mary M. *30:* 72
Thackeray, William Makepeace *23:* 224, 228
Thamer, Katie *42:* 187
Thelwell, Norman *14:* 201
Theobalds, Prue *40:* 23
Theurer, Marilyn Churchill *39:* 195
Thiesing, Lisa *89:* 134; *95:* 202
Thistlethwaite, Miles *12:* 224
Thollander, Earl *11:* 47; *18:* 112; *22:* 224
Thomas, Allan *22:* 13
Thomas, Art *48:* 217
Thomas, Eric *28:* 49
Thomas, Harold *20:* 98
Thomas, Mark *42:* 136
Thomas, Martin *14:* 255
Thompson, Arthur *47:* 107
Thompson, Carol *85:* 189; *95:* 75
Thompson, Colin *95:* 204
Thompson, Ellen *51:* 88, 151; *60:* 33; *67:* 42; *77:* 148; *78:* 75, 219; *79:* 122, 170; *84:* 219; *85:* 97; *87:* 37; *88:* 192, 194; *89:* 80; *93:* 37; *98:* 59
Thompson, George W. *22:* 18; *28:* 150; *33:* 135
Thompson, John *58:* 201
Thompson, Julie *44:* 158
Thompson, K. Dyble *84:* 6
Thompson, Sharon *74:* 113
Thomson, Arline K. *3:* 264
Thomson, Hugh *26:* 88
Thomson, Ross *36:* 179
Thorkelson, Gregg *95:* 183, 184; *98:* 58
Thorne, Diana *25:* 212
Thornhill, Jan *77:* 213
Thorpe, Peter *58:* 109
Thorvall, Kerstin *13:* 235
Threadgall, Colin *77:* 215
Thurber, James *13:* 239, 242-245, 248-249
Thurman, Mark *63:* 173
Tibbles, Paul *45:* 23
Tibo, Gilles *67:* 207

Tichenor, Tom *14:* 207
Tichnor, Richard *90:* 218
Tiegreen, Alan *36:* 143; *43:* 55, 56, 58; *77:* 200; *94:* 216, 217
Tilney, F. C. *22:* 231
Timbs, Gloria *36:* 90
Timmins, Harry *2:* 171
Tinkelman, Murray *12:* 225; *35:* 44
Titherington, Jean *58:* 138
Titherington, Jeanne *39:* 90; *75:* 79
Tolford, Joshua *1:* 221
Tolkien, J. R. R. *2:* 243; *32:* 215
Tolmie, Ken *15:* 292
Tomei, Lorna *47:* 168, 171
Tomes, Jacqueline *2:* 117; *12:* 139
Tomes, Margot *1:* 224; *2:* 120-121; *16:* 207; *18:* 250; *20:* 7; *25:* 62; *27:* 78, 79; *29:* 81, 199; *33:* 82; *36:* 186, 187, 188, 189, 190; *46:* 129; *56:* 71; *58:* 183; *70:* 228; *75:* 73, 75; *80:* 80; *83:* 97; *90:* 205
Toner, Raymond John *10:* 179
Tong, Gary *66:* 215
Tongier, Stephen *82:* 32
Toothill, Harry *6:* 54; *7:* 49; *25:* 219; *42:* 192
Toothill, Ilse *6:* 54
Topolski, Feliks *44:* 48
Torbert, Floyd James *22:* 226
Torgersen, Don *55:* 157
Tormey, Bertram M. *75:* 3, 4
Torrey, Helen *87:* 41
Torrey, Marjorie *34:* 105
Toschik, Larry *6:* 102
Totten, Bob *13:* 93
Tracy, Libba *82:* 24
Trail, Lee *55:* 157
Trang, Winson *89:* 151
Travers, Bob *49:* 100; *63:* 145
Treatner, Meryl *95:* 180
Tremain, Ruthven *17:* 238
Tresilian, Stuart *25:* 53; *40:* 212
Trez, Alain *17:* 236
Trezzo, Loretta *86:* 45
Trier, Walter *14:* 96
Trimby, Elisa *47:* 199
Trinkle, Sally *53:* 27
Tripp, F. J. *24:* 167
Tripp, Wallace *2:* 48; *7:* 28; *8:* 94; *10:* 54, 76; *11:* 92; *31:* 170, 171; *34:* 203; *42:* 57; *60:* 157; *73:* 182
Trivas, Irene *53:* 4; *54:* 168; *82:* 46, 101
Trnka, Jiri *22:* 151; *43:* 212, 213, 214, 215; *YABC 1:* 30-31
Troughton, Joanna *37:* 186; *48:* 72
Troyer, Johannes *3:* 16; *7:* 18
Trudeau, G. B. *35:* 220, 221, 222; *48:* 119, 123, 126, 127, 128-129, 133
Truesdell, Sue *55:* 142
Tryon, Leslie *84:* 7
Tseng, Jean *72:* 195; *94:* 102
Tseng, Mou-sien *72:* 195; *94:* 102
Tsinajinie, Andy *2:* 62
Tsugami, Kyuzo *18:* 198-199
Tuckwell, Jennifer *17:* 205
Tudor, Bethany *7:* 103
Tudor, Tasha *18:* 227; *20:* 185, 186, 187; *36:* 111; *69:* 196, 198; *YABC 2:* 46, 314
Tuerk, Hanne *71:* 201
Tulloch, Maurice *24:* 79
Tunis, Edwin *1:* 218-219; *28:* 209, 210, 211, 212
Tunnicliffe, C. F. *62:* 176; 177; 178, 179; 181
Turkle, Brinton *1:* 211, 213; *2:* 249; *3:* 226; *11:* 3; *16:* 209; *20:* 22; *50:* 23; *67:* 50; *68:* 65; *79:* 205, 206, 207; *YABC 1:* 79
Turner, Gwenda *59:* 195

Turska, Krystyna *12:* 103; *31:* 173, 174-175; *56:* 32, 34
Tusa, Tricia *72:* 242
Tusan, Stan *6:* 58; *22:* 236-237
Tworkov, Jack *47:* 207
Tyers, Jenny *89:* 220
Tzimoulis, Paul *12:* 104

U

Uchida, Yoshiko *1:* 220
Uderzo *47:* 88
Ueno, Noriko *59:* 155
Ulm, Robert *17:* 238
Ulrich, George *73:* 15; *75:* 136, 139; *99:* 150
Unada *84:* 67
　See Gliewe, Unada
Underhill, Liz *53:* 159
Underwood, Clarence *40:* 166
Unger, Jim *67:* 208
Ungerer, Tomi *5:* 188; *9:* 40; *18:* 188; *29:* 175; *33:* 221, 222-223, 225; *71:* 48
Unwin, Nora S. *3:* 65, 234-235; *4:* 237; *44:* 173, 174; *YABC 1:* 59; *2:* 301
Urbanovic, Jackie *86:* 86
Uris, Jill *49:* 188, 197
Ursell, Martin *50:* 51
Utpatel, Frank *18:* 114
Utz, Lois *5:* 190

V

Vagin, Vladimir *66:* 10
Vallejo, Boris *62:* 130; *72:* 212; *91:* 38; *93:* 61
Van Abbé, S. *16:* 142; *18:* 282; *31:* 90; *YABC 2:* 157, 161
Van Allsburg, Chris *37:* 205, 206; *53:* 161, 162, 163, 165, 166, 167, 168, 169, 170-171
Vance, James *65:* 28
Van Der Linde, Henry *99:* 17
van der Meer, Ron *98:* 204, 205
van der Meer, Atie *98:* 204, 205
Vandivert, William *21:* 175
Van Dongen, H. R. *81:* 97
Van Everen, Jay *13:* 160; *YABC 1:* 121
Van Horn, William *43:* 218
van Lawick, Hugo *62:* 76, 79
Van Loon, Hendrik Willem *18:* 285, 289, 291
Van Munching, Paul *83:* 85
Van Sciver, Ruth *37:* 162
VanSeveren, Joe *63:* 182
Van Stockum, Hilda *5:* 193
Van Wely, Babs *16:* 50; *79:* 16
Van Wright, Cornelius *72:* 18
Vardzigulyants, Ruben *90:* 54
Varga, Judy *29:* 196
Vargo, Kurt *79:* 224
Varley, Susan *61:* 199; *63:* 176, 177
Vasconcellos, Daniel *80:* 42
Vasiliu, Mircea *2:* 166, 253; *9:* 166; *13:* 58; *68:* 42
Vaughn, Frank *34:* 157
Vavra, Robert *8:* 206
Vawter, Will *17:* 163
Vayas, Diana *71:* 61
Veeder, Larry *18:* 4
Velasquez, Eric *45:* 217; *61:* 45; *63:* 110, 111; *88:* 162; *90:* 34, 144; *94:* 213
Velasquez, Jose A. *63:* 73

Velez, Walter *71:* 75; *91:* 154
Vendrell, Carme Solé *42:* 205
Venezia, Mike *54:* 17
Venturo, Piero *61:* 194, 195
Ver Beck, Frank *18:* 16-17
Verling, John *71:* 27
Verney, John *14:* 225; *75:* 8
Verrier, Suzanne *5:* 20; *23:* 212
Versace, Marie *2:* 255
Vestal, H. B. *9:* 134; *11:* 101; *27:* 25; *34:* 158
Vicatan *59:* 146
Vickrey, Robert *45:* 59, 64
Victor, Joan Berg *30:* 193
Viereck, Ellen *3:* 242; *14:* 229
Vigna, Judith *15:* 293
Vilato, Gaspar E. *5:* 41
Villiard, Paul *51:* 178
Vimnèra, A. *23:* 154
Vincent, Eric *34:* 98
Vincent, Félix *41:* 237
Vip *45:* 164
Viskupic, Gary *83:* 48
Vivas, Julie *51:* 67, 69; *96:* 225
Vo-Dinh, Mai *16:* 272; *60:* 191
Vogel, Ilse-Margret *14:* 230
Voigt, Erna *35:* 228
Vojnar, Kamil *95:* 31
Vojtech, Anna *42:* 190
von Schmidt, Eric *8:* 62; *50:* 209, 210
von Schmidt, Harold *30:* 80
Vosburgh, Leonard *1:* 161; *7:* 32; *15:* 295-296; *23:* 110; *30:* 214; *43:* 181
Voter, Thomas W. *19:* 3, 9
Vroman, Tom *10:* 29
Vulliamy, Clara *72:* 65

W

Waber, Bernard *47:* 209, 210, 211, 212, 213, 214; *95:* 215, 216, 217
Wack, Jeff *95:* 140
Wagner, John *8:* 200; *52:* 104
Wagner, Ken *2:* 59
Waide, Jan *29:* 225; *36:* 139
Wainwright, Jerry *14:* 85
Wakeen, Sandra *47:* 97
Waldherr, Kris *81:* 186
Waldman, Bruce *15:* 297; *43:* 178
Waldman, Neil *35:* 141; *50:* 163; *51:* 180; *54:* 78; *77:* 112; *79:* 162; *82:* 174; *84:* 5, 56, 106; *94:* 232, 233, 234; *96:* 41
Walker, Charles *1:* 46; *4:* 59; *5:* 177; *11:* 115; *19:* 45; *34:* 74; *62:* 168; *72:* 218
Walker, Dugald Stewart *15:* 47; *32:* 202; *33:* 112
Walker, Gil *8:* 49; *23:* 132; *34:* 42
Walker, Jeff *55:* 154
Walker, Jim *10:* 94
Walker, Mort *8:* 213
Walker, Norman *41:* 37; *45:* 58
Walker, Stephen *12:* 229; *21:* 174
Wallace, Beverly Dobrin *19:* 259
Wallace, Cly *87:* 93
Wallace, Ian *53:* 176, 177; *56:* 165, 166; *58:* 4; *98:* 4
Waller, S. E. *24:* 36
Wallner, Alexandra *15:* 120
Wallner, John C. *9:* 77; *10:* 188; *11:* 28; *14:* 209; *31:* 56, 118; *37:* 64; *51:* 186, 187, 188-189, 190-191, 192-193, 194, 195; *52:* 96; *53:* 23, 26; *71:* 99; *73:* 158; *89:* 215
Wallower, Lucille *11:* 226
Walotsky, Ron *93:* 87
Walsh, Ellen Stoll *99:* 209
Walters, Audrey *18:* 294
Walther, Tom *31:* 179

Walton, Garry *69:* 149
Walton, Tony *11:* 164; *24:* 209
Waltrip, Lela *9:* 195
Waltrip, Mildred *3:* 209; *37:* 211
Waltrip, Rufus *9:* 195
Wan *12:* 76
Ward, Fred *52:* 19
Ward, Helen *72:* 244
Ward, John *42:* 191; *96:* 54; *97:* 110
Ward, Keith *2:* 107
Ward, Leslie *34:* 126; *36:* 87
Ward, Lynd *1:* 99, 132, 133, 150; *2:* 108, 158, 196, 259; *18:* 86; *27:* 56; *29:* 79, 187, 253, 255; *36:* 199, 200, 201, 202, 203, 204, 205, 206, 207, 209; *43:* 34; *56:* 28; *60:* 116
Ward, Peter *37:* 116
Warhola, James *92:* 5
Warner, Peter *14:* 87
Warren, Betsy *2:* 101
Warren, Jim *85:* 81
Warren, Marion Cray *14:* 215
Warshaw, Jerry *30:* 197, 198; *42:* 165
Washington, Nevin *20:* 123
Washington, Phyllis *20:* 123
Wasserman, Amy L. *92:* 110
Waterman, Stan *11:* 76
Watkins-Pitchford, D. J. *6:* 215, 217
Watling, James *67:* 210; *78:* 112
Watson, Aldren A. *2:* 267; *5:* 94; *13:* 71; *19:* 253; *32:* 220; *42:* 193, 194, 195, 196, 197, 198, 199, 200, 201; *YABC 2:* 202
Watson, G. *83:* 162
Watson, Gary *19:* 147; *36:* 68; *41:* 122; *47:* 139
Watson, J. D. *22:* 86
Watson, Karen *11:* 26
Watson, Richard Jesse *62:* 188, 189
Watson, Wendy *5:* 197; *13:* 101; *33:* 116; *46:* 163; *64:* 12; *74:* 242, 243; *91:* 21
Watterson, Bill *66:* 223, 225, 226
Watts, Bernadette *4:* 227
Watts, James *59:* 197; *74:* 145; *86:* 124
Watts, John *37:* 149
Weatherby, Mark Alan *77:* 141
Webber, Helen *3:* 141
Webber, Irma E. *14:* 238
Weber, Erik *56:* 19, 20
Weber, Florence *40:* 153
Weber, Roland *61:* 204
Weber, William J. *14:* 239
Webster, Jean *17:* 241
Wegman, William *78:* 243
Wegner, Fritz *14:* 250; *20:* 189; *44:* 165; *86:* 62
Weidenear, Reynold H. *21:* 122
Weihs, Erika *4:* 21; *15:* 299; *72:* 201
Weil, Lisl *7:* 203; *10:* 58; *21:* 95; *22:* 188, 217; *33:* 193
Weiman, Jon *50:* 162, 165; *52:* 103; *54:* 78, 79, 81; *78:* 80; *82:* 107; *93:* 82; *97:* 69
Weiner, Sandra *14:* 240
Weiner, Scott *55:* 27
Weinhaus, Karen Ann *53:* 90; *71:* 50; *86:* 124
Weisgard, Leonard *1:* 65; *2:* 191, 197, 204, 264-265; *5:* 108; *21:* 42; *30:* 200, 201, 203, 204; *41:* 47; *44:* 125; *53:* 25; *85:* 196, 198, 200, 201; *YABC 2:* 13
Weiss, Ellen *44:* 202
Weiss, Emil *1:* 168; *7:* 60
Weiss, Harvey *1:* 145, 223; *27:* 224, 227; *68:* 214; *76:* 245, 246, 247
Weiss, Nicki *33:* 229
Weissman, Bari *49:* 72; *90:* 125
Welkes, Allen *68:* 218
Wellington, Monica *99:* 223
Welliver, Norma *76:* 94
Wells, Frances *1:* 183
Wells, H. G. *20:* 194, 200

Wells, Haru *53:* 120, 121
Wells, Rosemary *6:* 49; *18:* 297; *60:* 32; *66:* 203; *69:* 215, 216
Wells, Rufus III *56:* 111, 113
Wells, Susan *22:* 43
Wendelin, Rudolph *23:* 234
Wengenroth, Stow *37:* 47
Werenskiold, Erik *15:* 6; *62:* 17
Werner, Honi *24:* 110; *33:* 41; *88:* 122
Werth, Kurt *7:* 122; *14:* 157; *20:* 214; *39:* 128
Westcott, Nadine Bernard *68:* 46; *84:* 49; *86:* 133
Westerberg, Christine *29:* 226
Weston, Martha *29:* 116; *30:* 213; *33:* 85, 100; *53:* 181, 182, 183, 184; *77:* 95; *80:* 152
Wetherbee, Margaret *5:* 3
Wexler, Jerome *49:* 73
Whalley, Peter *50:* 49
Wheatley, Arabelle *11:* 231; *16:* 276
Wheeler, Cindy *49:* 205
Wheeler, Dora *44:* 179
Wheelright, Rowland *15:* 81; *YABC 2:* 286
Whelan, Michael *56:* 108; *70:* 27, 29, 67, 68, 148; *74:* 18; *84:* 14; *91:* 195, 196; *95:* 147; *98:* 150, 151
Whistler, Rex *16:* 75; *30:* 207, 208
White, David Omar *5:* 56; *18:* 6
White, Joan *83:* 225
White, Martin *51:* 197; *85:* 127
Whitear *32:* 26
Whitehead, Beck *86:* 171
Whithorne, H. S. *7:* 49
Whitney, George Gillett *3:* 24
Whitney, Jean *99:* 53
Whittam, Geoffrey *30:* 191
Whyte, Mary *96:* 127
Wiberg, Harald *38:* 127; *93:* 215
Wick, Walter *77:* 128
Wiese, Kurt *3:* 255; *4:* 206; *14:* 17; *17:* 18-19; *19:* 47; *24:* 152; *25:* 212; *32:* 184; *36:* 211, 213, 214, 215, 216, 217, 218; *45:* 161
Wiesner, David *33:* 47; *51:* 106; *57:* 67; *58:* 55; *64:* 78, 79, 81; *69:* 233; *72:* 247, 248-49, 251, 252-53, 254; *83:* 134
Wiesner, William *4:* 100; *5:* 200, 201; *14:* 262
Wiggins, George *6:* 133
Wikkelsoe, Otto *45:* 25, 26
Wikland, Ilon *5:* 113; *8:* 150; *38:* 124, 125, 130
Wilbur, C. Keith, M.D. *27:* 228
Wilburn, Kathy *53:* 102; *68:* 234
Wilcox, J.A.J. *34:* 122
Wilcox, R. Turner *36:* 219
Wild, Jocelyn *46:* 220-221, 222; *80:* 117
Wilde, George *7:* 139
Wildsmith, Brian *16:* 281-282; *18:* 170-171; *66:* 25; *69:* 224-225, 227; *77:* 103; *83:* 218
Wilhelm, Hans *58:* 189, 191; *73:* 157; *77:* 127
Wilkin, Eloise *36:* 173; *49:* 208, 209, 210
Wilkinson, Barry *50:* 213
Wilkinson, Gerald *3:* 40
Wilkon, Jozef *31:* 183, 184; *71:* 206, 207, 209
Wilks, Mike *34:* 24; *44:* 203
Willhoite, Michael A. *71:* 214
Williams, Berkeley, Jr. *64:* 75
Williams, Ferelith Eccles *22:* 238
Williams, Garth *1:* 197; *2:* 49, 270; *4:* 205; *15:* 198, 302-304, 307; *16:* 34; *18:* 283, 298-301; *29:* 177, 178, 179, 232-233, 241-245, 248; *40:* 106; *66:*

229, 230, 231, 233, 234; *71:* 192; *73:* 218, 219, 220; *78:* 261; *YABC 2:* 15-16, 19
Williams, J. Scott *48:* 28
Williams, Jenny *60:* 202; *81:* 21; *88:* 71
Williams, Kit *44:* 206-207, 208, 209, 211, 212
Williams, Marcia *97:* 214
Williams, Maureen *12:* 238
Williams, Patrick *14:* 218
Williams, Richard *44:* 93; *72:* 229; *74:* 133; *78:* 155, 237; *91:* 178
Williams, Vera B. *53:* 186, 187, 188, 189
Williamson, Mel *60:* 9
Willmore, J. T. *54:* 113, 114
Wilson, Charles Banks *17:* 92; *43:* 73
Wilson, Dagmar *10:* 47
Wilson, Dawn *67:* 161; *81:* 120
Wilson, Edward A. *6:* 24; *16:* 149; *20:* 220-221; *22:* 87; *26:* 67; *38:* 212, 214, 215, 216, 217
Wilson, Forrest *27:* 231
Wilson, Gahan *35:* 234; *41:* 136
Wilson, George *76:* 87
Wilson, Jack *17:* 139
Wilson, Janet *77:* 154; *96:* 114; *99:* 219, 220
Wilson, John *22:* 240
Wilson, Maurice *46:* 224
Wilson, Patten *35:* 61
Wilson, Peggy *15:* 4; *84:* 20
Wilson, Rowland B. *30:* 170
Wilson, Sarah *50:* 215
Wilson, Tom *33:* 232
Wilson, W. N. *22:* 26
Wilwerding, Walter J. *9:* 202
Wimmer, Mike *63:* 6; *70:* 121; *75:* 186; *76:* 21, 22, 23; *91:* 114; *97:* 45, 68; *98:* 28
Winborn, Marsha *78:* 34; *99:* 70
Winchester, Linda *13:* 231
Wind, Betty *28:* 158
Windham, Kathryn Tucker *14:* 260
Winfield, Wayne *72:* 23
Wing, Gary *64:* 147
Wing, Ron *50:* 85
Winslow, Will *21:* 124
Winsten, Melanie Willa *41:* 41
Winter, Milo *15:* 97; *19:* 221; *21:* 181, 203, 204, 205; *64:* 19; *YABC 2:* 144
Winter, Paula *48:* 227
Winters, Greg *70:* 117
Winters, Nina *62:* 194
Wise, Louis *13:* 68
Wiseman, Ann *31:* 187
Wiseman, B. *4:* 233
Wishnefsky, Phillip *3:* 14
Wiskur, Darrell *5:* 72; *10:* 50; *18:* 246
Wisniewski, David *95:* 220, 221
Wisniewski, Robert *95:* 10
Witt, Dick *80:* 244
Wittman, Sally *30:* 219
Wittner, Dale *99:* 43

Woehr, Lois *12:* 5
Wohlberg, Meg *12:* 100; *14:* 197; *41:* 255
Woldin, Beth Weiner *34:* 211
Wolf, J. *16:* 91
Wolf, Janet *78:* 254
Wolf, Linda *33:* 163
Wolfe, Corey *72:* 213
Wolff, Ashley *50:* 217; *81:* 216
Wondriska, William *6:* 220
Wong, Janet S. *98:* 225
Wonsetler, John C. *5:* 168
Wood, Audrey *50:* 221, 222, 223; *81:* 219, 221
Wood, Don *50:* 220, 225, 226, 228-229; *81:* 218, 220
Wood, Grant *19:* 198
Wood, Ivor *58:* 17
Wood, Muriel *36:* 119; *77:* 167
Wood, Myron *6:* 220
Wood, Owen *18:* 187; *64:* 202, 204-05, 206, 208, 210
Wood, Ruth *8:* 11
Wooding, Sharon L. *66:* 237
Woodson, Jack *10:* 201
Woodson, Jacqueline *94:* 242
Woodward, Alice *26:* 89; *36:* 81
Wool, David *26:* 27
Wooten, Vernon *23:* 70; *51:* 170
Worboys, Evelyn *1:* 166-167
Worth, Jo *34:* 143
Worth, Wendy *4:* 133
Wosmek, Frances *29:* 251
Wrenn, Charles L. *38:* 96; *YABC 1:* 20, 21
Wright, Barbara Mullarney *98:* 161
Wright, Dare *21:* 206
Wright-Frierson, Virginia *58:* 194
Wright, George *YABC 1:* 268
Wright, Joseph *30:* 160
Wronker, Lili Cassel *3:* 247; *10:* 204; *21:* 10
Wyatt, David *97:* 9
Wyatt, Stanley *46:* 210
Wyeth, Andrew *13:* 40; *YABC 1:* 133-134
Wyeth, Jamie *41:* 257
Wyeth, N. C. *13:* 41; *17:* 252-259, 264-268; *18:* 181; *19:* 80, 191, 200; *21:* 57, 183; *22:* 91; *23:* 152; *24:* 28, 99; *35:* 61; *41:* 65; *YABC 1:* 133, 223; *2:* 53, 75, 171, 187, 317
Wyman, Cherie R. *91:* 42

Y

Yakovetic, Joe *59:* 202; *75:* 85
Yalowitz, Paul *93:* 33
Yamaguchi, Marianne *85:* 118
Yang, Jay *1:* 8; *12:* 239
Yap, Weda *6:* 176

Yaroslava
See Mills, Yaroslava Surmach
Yashima, Taro *14:* 84
Yates, John *74:* 249, 250
Ylla
See Koffler, Camilla
Yohn, F. C. *23:* 128; *YABC 1:* 269
Yorke, David *80:* 178
Yoshida, Toshi *77:* 231
Youll, Paul *91:* 218
Youll, Stephen *92:* 227
Young, Ed *7:* 205; *10:* 206; *40:* 124; *63:* 142; *74:* 250, 251, 252, 253; *75:* 227; *81:* 159; *83:* 98; *94:* 154; *YABC 2:* 242
Young, Mary O'Keefe *77:* 95; *80:* 247
Young, Noela *8:* 221; *89:* 231; *97:* 195
Yun, Cheng Mung *60:* 143

Z

Zacharow, Christopher *88:* 98
Zacks, Lewis *10:* 161
Zadig *50:* 58
Zaffo, George *42:* 208
Zaid, Barry *50:* 127; *51:* 201
Zaidenberg, Arthur *34:* 218, 219, 220
Zalben, Jane Breskin *7:* 211; *79:* 230, 231, 233
Zallinger, Jean *4:* 192; *8:* 8, 129; *14:* 273; *68:* 36; *80:* 254
Zallinger, Rudolph F. *3:* 245
Zebot, George *83:* 214
Zeck, Gerry *40:* 232
Zeiring, Bob *42:* 130
Zeldich, Arieh *49:* 124; *62:* 120
Zeldis, Malcah *86:* 239; *94:* 198
Zelinsky, Paul O. *14:* 269; *43:* 56; *49:* 218, 219, 220, 221, 222-223; *53:* 111; *68:* 195
Zelvin, Diana *72:* 190; *76:* 101; *93:* 207
Zemach, Margot *3:* 270; *8:* 201; *21:* 210-211; *27:* 204, 205, 210; *28:* 185; *49:* 22, 183, 224; *53:* 151; *56:* 146; *70:* 245, 246; *92:* 74
Zemsky, Jessica *10:* 62
Zepelinsky, Paul *35:* 93
Ziegler, Jack *84:* 134
Zimic, Tricia *72:* 95
Zimmer, Dirk *38:* 195; *49:* 71; *56:* 151; *65:* 214; *84:* 159; *89:* 26
Zimnik, Reiner *36:* 224
Zinkeisen, Anna *13:* 106
Zinn, David *97:* 97
Zoellick, Scott *33:* 231
Zonia, Dhimitri *20:* 234-235
Zudeck, Darryl *58:* 129; *63:* 98; *80:* 52
Zug, Mark *88:* 131
Zuma *99:* 36
Zvorykin, Boris *61:* 155
Zweifel, Francis *14:* 274; *28:* 187
Zwerger, Lisbeth *54:* 176, 178; *66:* 246, 247, 248
Zwinger, Herman H. *46:* 227
Zwolak, Paul *67:* 69, 71, 73, 74

Illustrations Index

Author Index

The following index gives the number of the volume in which an author's biographical sketch, Brief Entry, or Obituary appears.

This index includes references to all entries in the following series, which are also published by Gale Research:

YABC—*Yesterday's Authors of Books for Children: Facts and Pictures about Authors and Illustrators of Books for Young People from Early Times to 1960*
CLR—*Children's Literature Review: Excerpts from Reviews, Criticism, and Commentary on Books for Children*
SAAS—*Something about the Author Autobiography Series*

A

Aardema, Verna 1911- 68
  Earlier sketch in SATA *4*
  See also CLR *17*
  See also SAAS *8*
Aaron, Anna
  See Selden, Neil R(oy)
Aaron, Chester 1923- 74
  Earlier sketch in SATA *9*
  See also SAAS *12*
Aaseng, Nate
  See Aaseng, Nathan
Aaseng, Nathan 1953- 88
  Brief entry 38
  Earlier sketch in SATA *51*
  See also SAAS *12*
Abbas, Jailan 1952- 91
Abbott, Alice
  See Speicher, Helen Ross (Smith)
Abbott, Alice
  See Borland, Kathryn Kilby
Abbott, Jacob 1803-1879 22
Abbott, Manager Henry
  See Stratemeyer, Edward L.
Abbott, R(obert) Tucker 1919-1995 61
  Obituary 87
Abbott, Sarah
  See Zolotow, Charlotte S(hapiro)
Abdul, Raoul 1929- 12
Abel, Raymond 1911- 12
Abell, Kathleen 1938- 9
Abels, Harriette S(heffer) 1926- 50
Abelson, Ann
  See Cavallaro, Ann (Abelson)
Abercrombie, Barbara (Mattes) 1939- 16
Abernethy, Robert G. 1935- 5
Abisch, Roslyn Kroop 1927- 9
Abisch, Roz
  See Abisch, Roslyn Kroop
Abodaher, David J. (Naiph) 1919- 17
Abolafia, Yossi 60
  Brief entry 46
Abrahall, C. H.
  See Hoskyns-Abrahall, Clare
Abrahall, Clare Hoskyns
  See Hoskyns-Abrahall, Clare
Abrahams, Hilary (Ruth) 1938- 29
Abrahams, Robert D(avid) 1905- 4
Abrams, Joy 1941- 16
Abrams, Lawrence F. 1944- 58
  Brief entry 47
Abrashkin, Raymond 1911-1960 50
Achebe, (Albert) Chinua(lumagu) 1930- 40
  Brief entry 38
  See also CLR *20*
Ackerman, Eugene 1888-1974 10
Ackerman, Susan Yoder 1945- 92
Ackley, Peggy Jo 1955- 58
Acorn, John (Harrison) 1958- 79
Acs, Laszlo (Bela) 1931- 42
  Brief entry 32
Acuff, Selma Boyd 1924- 45

Ada, Alma Flor 1938- 84
  Earlier sketch in SATA *43*
Adair, Gilbert 98
Adair, Ian 1942- 53
Adair, Margaret Weeks (?)-1971 10
Adam, Cornel
  See Lengyel, Cornel Adam
Adam, Robert 1948- 93
Adams, Adrienne 1906- 90
  Earlier sketch in SATA *8*
Adams, Andy 1859-1935
  See YABC *1*
Adams, Barbara Johnston 1943- 60
Adams, Christopher
  See Hopkins, (Hector) Kenneth
Adams, Dale
  See Quinn, Elisabeth
Adams, Debra
  See Speregen, Devra Newberger
Adams, Edith
  See Shine, Deborah
Adams, Florence 1932- 61
Adams, Harriet S(tratemeyer) 1893(?)-1982 1
  Obituary 29
Adams, Harrison
  See Stratemeyer, Edward L.
Adams, Hazard 1926- 6
Adams, John Anthony 1944- 67
Adams, Laurie 1941- 33
Adams, Lowell
  See Joseph, James (Herz)
Adams, Nicholas
  See Peel, John
Adams, Nicholas
  See Macdonald, James D.
Adams, Nicholas
  See Smith, Sherwood
Adams, Nicholas
  See Pine, Nicholas
Adams, Richard 1920- 69
  Earlier sketch in SATA *7*
  See also CLR *20*
Adams, Ruth Joyce 14
Adams, Tricia
  See Kite, (L.) Patricia
Adams, William Taylor 1822-1897 28
Adam Smith, Janet (Buchanan) 1905- 63
Adamson, Gareth 1925-1982 46
  Obituary 30
Adamson, George 1906-1989
  Obituary 63
Adamson, George Worsley 1913- 30
Adamson, Graham
  See Groom, Arthur William
Adamson, Joy 1910-1980 11
  Obituary 22
Adamson, Wendy Wriston 1942- 22
Addams, Charles (Samuel) 1912-1988 55
Addona, Angelo F. 1925- 14
Addy, Ted
  See Winterbotham, R(ussell) R(obert)
Adelberg, Doris
  See Orgel, Doris

Adelson, Leone 1908- 11
Adkins, Jan 1944- 69
  Earlier sketch in SATA *8*
  See also CLR *7*
  See also SAAS *19*
Adler, C(arole) S(chwerdtfeger) 1932- 63
  Earlier sketch in SATA *26*
  See also SAAS *15*
Adler, David A. 1947- 70
  Earlier sketch in SATA *14*
Adler, Irene
  See Storr, Catherine (Cole)
Adler, Irving 1913- 29
  Earlier sketch in SATA *1*
  See also CLR *27*
  See also SAAS *15*
Adler, Larry 1939- 36
Adler, Peggy 22
Adler, Ruth 1915-1968 1
Adlerman, Daniel 1963- 96
Adlerman, Kimberly M. 1964- 96
Adoff, Arnold 1935- 96
  Earlier sketches in SATA *5, 57*
  See also CLR *7*
  See also SAAS *15*
Adorjan, Carol 1934- 71
  Earlier sketch in SATA *10*
Adrian, Frances
  See Polland, Madeleine A(ngela Cahill)
Adrian, Mary
  See Jorgensen, Mary Venn
Adshead, Gladys L. 1896- 3
Aesop 620(?)B.C.-560(?)B.C. 64
  See also CLR *14*
Aesop, Abraham
  See Newbery, John
Affabee, Eric
  See Stine, R(obert) L(awrence)
Agapida, Fray Antonio
  See Irving, Washington
Agard, Nadema 1948- 18
Agell, Charlotte 1959- 99
Agle, Nan Hayden 1905- 3
  See also SAAS *10*
Agnew, Edith J(osephine) 1897- 11
Ahern, Margaret McCrohan 1921- 10
Ahl, Anna Maria 1926- 32
Ahlberg, Allan 1938- 68
  Brief entry 35
  See also CLR *18*
Ahlberg, Janet 1944-1994 68
  Brief entry 32
  Obituary 83
  See also CLR *18*
Aichinger, Helga 1937- 4
Aiken, Clarissa (Lorenz) 1899- 12
Aiken, Conrad (Potter) 1889-1973 30
  Earlier sketch in SATA *3*
Aiken, Joan (Delano) 1924- 73
  Earlier sketches in SATA *2, 30*
  See also CLR *19*
  See also SAAS *1*
Ainsley, Alix
  See Steiner, Barbara A(nnette)
Ainsworth, Catherine Harris 1910- 56

Ainsworth, Norma 9
Ainsworth, Ruth (Gallard) 1908- 73
  Earlier sketch in SATA 7
Ainsworth, William Harrison
  1805-1882 24
Aistrop, Jack 1916- 14
Aitken, Amy 1952- 54
  Brief entry 40
Aitken, Dorothy 1916- 10
Aitmatov, Chinghiz 1928- 56
Akaba, Suekichi 1910- 46
Akers, Floyd
  See Baum, L(yman) Frank
Aks, Patricia 1926- 68
Alain
  See Brustlein, Daniel
Alajalov, Constantin 1900-1987
  Obituary 53
Albert, Burton, Jr. 1936- 22
Albert, Richard E. 1909- 82
Alberts, Frances Jacobs 1907- 14
Albertson, Susan
  See Wojciechowski, Susan
Albion, Lee Smith 29
Alborough, Jez 1959- 86
Albrecht, Lillie (Vanderveer) 1894- 12
Albyn, Carole Lisa 1955- 83
Alcock, Gudrun 1908- 56
  Brief entry 33
Alcock, Vivien 1924- 76
  Brief entry 38
  Earlier sketch in SATA 45
  See also CLR 26
Alcorn, John 1935- 31
  Brief entry 30
Alcott, Louisa May 1832-1888
  See YABC 1
  See also CLR 38
Alda, Arlene 1933- 44
  Brief entry 36
Alden, Isabella (Macdonald) 1841-1930
  See YABC 2
Alderman, Clifford Lindsey 1902- 3
Alderson, Sue Ann 1940- 59
  Brief entry 48
Aldis, Dorothy (Keeley) 1896-1966 2
Aldiss, Brian W(ilson) 1925- 34
Aldon, Adair
  See Meigs, Cornelia Lynde
Aldous, Allan (Charles) 1911- 27
Aldrich, Ann
  See Meaker, Marijane (Agnes)
Aldrich, Thomas Bailey 1836-1907 17
Aldridge, Alan 1943(?)-
  Brief entry 33
Aldridge, (Harold Edward) James
  1918- 87
Aldridge, Josephine Haskell 14
Alegria, Ricardo E. 1921- 6
Aleksin, Anatolii (Georgievich)
  1924- 36
Alenov, Lydia 1948- 61
Alex, Ben [a pseudonym] 1946- 45
Alex, Marlee [a pseudonym] 1948- 45
Alexander, Anna Cooke 1913- 1
Alexander, Ellen 1938- 91
Alexander, Frances 1888- 4
Alexander, Janet
  See McNeill, Janet
Alexander, Jocelyn (Anne) Arundel
  1930- 22
Alexander, Linda 1935- 2
Alexander, Lloyd (Chudley) 1924- 81
  Earlier sketches in SATA 3, 49
  See also CLR 48
  See also SAAS 19
Alexander, Martha G. 1920- 70
  Earlier sketch in SATA 11
Alexander, Rae Pace
  See Alexander, Raymond Pace
Alexander, Raymond Pace
  1898-1974 22
Alexander, Rod
  See Pellowski, Michael (Joseph)
Alexander, Sally Hobart 1943- 84

Alexander, Sue 1933- 89
  Earlier sketch in SATA 12
  See also SAAS 15
Alexander, Vincent Arthur 1925-1980
  Obituary 23
Alexeieff, Alexandre A. 1901- 14
Alger, Horatio, Jr.
  See Stratemeyer, Edward L.
Alger, Horatio, Jr. 1832-1899 16
Alger, Leclaire (Gowans)
  1898-1969 15
Aliki
  See CLR 9
  See Brandenberg, Aliki (Liacouras)
Alkema, Chester Jay 1932- 12
Allamand, Pascale 1942- 12
Allan, Mabel Esther 1915- 75
  Earlier sketches in SATA 5, 32
  See also CLR 43
  See also SAAS 11
Allan, Nicholas 1956- 79
Allard, Harry
  See Allard, Harry G(rover), Jr.
Allard, Harry G(rover), Jr. 1928- 42
Allee, Marjorie Hill 1890-1945 17
Allen, Adam [Joint pseudonym]
  See Epstein, Beryl (M. Williams)
  and Epstein, Samuel
Allen, Alex B.
  See Heide, Florence Parry
Allen, Allyn
  See Eberle, Irmengarde
Allen, Betsy
  See Cavanna, Betty
Allen, Bob 1961- 76
Allen, Gertrude E(lizabeth) 1888- 9
Allen, Grace
  See Hogarth, Grace (Weston) Allen
Allen, Jack 1899-
  Brief entry 29
Allen, Jeffrey (Yale) 1948- 42
Allen, Judy (Christina) 1941- 80
Allen, Kenneth S(ydney) 1913- 56
Allen, Laura Jean
  Brief entry 53
Allen, Leroy 1912- 11
Allen, Linda 1925- 33
Allen, Marjorie 1931- 22
Allen, Maury 1932- 26
Allen, Merritt Parmelee 1892-1954 22
Allen, Nina (Stroemgren) 1935- 22
Allen, Pamela 1934- 81
  Earlier sketch in SATA 50
  See also CLR 44
Allen, Rodney F. 1938- 27
Allen, Ruth
  See Peterson, Esther (Allen)
Allen, Samuel (Washington) 1917- 9
Allen, T. D. [Joint pseudonym]
  See Allen, Terril Diener
Allen, Terril Diener 1908- 35
Allen, Terry D.
  See Allen, Terril Diener
Allen, Thomas B(enton) 1929- 45
Allen, Tom
  See Allen, Thomas B(enton)
Allerton, Mary
  See Govan, Christine Noble
Alleyn, Ellen
  See Rossetti, Christina (Georgina)
Allington, Richard L(loyd) 1947- 39
  Brief entry 35
Allison, Bob 14
Allison, Diane Worfolk 78
Allison, Linda 1948- 43
Allmendinger, David F(rederick), Jr.
  1938- 35
Allred, Gordon T. 1930- 10
Allsop, Kenneth 1920-1973 17
Almedingen, E. M. 1898-1971 3
Almedingen, Martha Edith von
  See Almedingen, E. M.
Almon, Russell
  See Clevenger, William R(ussell)
  and Downing, David A(lmon)
Almond, Linda Stevens 1881(?)-1987
  Obituary 50

Almquist, Don 1929- 11
Alphin, Elaine Marie 1955- 80
Alsop, Mary O'Hara 1885-1980 34
  Obituary 24
  Earlier sketch in SATA 2
Alter, Judith (MacBain) 1938- 52
Alter, Judy
  See Alter, Judith (MacBain)
Alter, Robert Edmond 1925-1965 9
Althea
  See Braithwaite, Althea
Altman, Suzanne
  See Orgel, Doris
  and Schecter, Ellen
Altschuler, Franz 1923- 45
Altsheler, Joseph A(lexander) 1862-1919
  See YABC 1
Alvarez, John
  See del Rey, Lester
Alvarez, Joseph A. 1930- 18
Alzada, Juan Sanchez
  See Joseph, James (Herz)
Amann, Janet 1951- 79
Amato, Carol A. 1942- 92
Ambler, C(hristopher) Gifford 1886-
  Brief entry 29
Ambrose, Stephen E(dward) 1936- 40
Ambrus, Gyozo (Laszlo) 1935- 41
  Earlier sketch in SATA 1
Ambrus, Victor G.
  See SAAS 4
  See Ambrus, Gyozo (Laszlo)
Amerman, Lockhart 1911-1969 3
Ames, Evelyn 1908-1990 13
  Obituary 64
Ames, Gerald 1906-1993 11
  Obituary 74
Ames, Lee J. 1921- 3
Ames, Mildred 1919-1994 85
  Obituary 81
  Earlier sketch in SATA 22
Amon, Aline 1928- 9
Amoss, Berthe 1925- 5
Anastasio, Dina 1941- 94
  Brief entry 30
  Earlier sketch in SATA 37
Anckarsvard, Karin 1915-1969 6
Ancona, George 1929- 85
  Earlier sketch in SATA 12
  See also SAAS 18
Andersdatter, Karla M(argaret)
  1938- 34
Andersen, Hans Christian 1805-1875
  See YABC 1
  See also CLR 6
Andersen, Ted
  See Boyd, Waldo T.
Andersen, Yvonne 1932- 27
Anderson, Bernice G(oudy) 1894- 33
Anderson, Brad(ley Jay) 1924- 33
  Brief entry 31
Anderson, C. C.
  See Anderson, Catherine Corley
Anderson, C(larence) W(illiam)
  1891-1971 11
Anderson, Catherine C.
  See Anderson, Catherine Corley
Anderson, Catherine Corley 1909- 72
Anderson, Clifford [Joint pseudonym]
  See Gardner, Richard
Anderson, Daryl Shon 1963- 93
Anderson, Dave
  See Anderson, David Poole
Anderson, David Poole 1929- 60
Anderson, Ella
  See MacLeod, Ellen Jane (Anderson)
Anderson, Eloise Adell 1927- 9
Anderson, George
  See Groom, Arthur William
Anderson, Grace Fox 1932- 43
Anderson, J(ohn) R(ichard) L(ane)
  1911-1981 15
  Obituary 27
Anderson, Joy 1928- 1
Anderson, Kevin J(ames) 1962- 74
Anderson, Laurie Halse 1961- 95

Anderson, LaVere (Francis Shoenfelt)
　1907- 27
Anderson, Leone Castell 1923- 53
　Brief entry 49
Anderson, (John) Lonzo 1905- 2
Anderson, Lucia (Lewis) 1922- 10
Anderson, M. T(obin) 1968- 97
Anderson, Madelyn Klein 28
Anderson, Margaret J(ean) 1931- 27
　See also SAAS 8
Anderson, Mary 1939- 82
　Earlier sketch in SATA 7
　See also SAAS 23
Anderson, Mona 1910- 40
Anderson, Mrs. Melvin
　See Anderson, Catherine Corley
Anderson, Norman D(ean) 1928- 22
Anderson, Peggy Perry 1953- 84
Anderson, Poul (William) 1926- 90
　Brief entry 39
Anderson, Rachel 1943- 86
　Earlier sketch in SATA 34
　See also SAAS 18
Anderson, Susan 1952- 90
Anderson, Wayne 1946- 56
Andre, Evelyn M(arie) 1924- 27
Andree, Louise
　See Coury, Louise Andree
Andrew, Prudence (Hastings) 1924- 87
Andrews, Benny 1930- 31
Andrews, F(rank) Emerson
　1902-1978 22
Andrews, J(ames) S(ydney) 1934- 4
Andrews, Jan 1942- 98
　Brief entry 49
　Earlier sketch in SATA 58
Andrews, Julie 1935- 7
Andrews, Laura
　See Coury, Louise Andree
Andrews, Roy Chapman 1884-1960 19
Andrews, V(irginia) C(leo) (?)-1986
　Obituary 50
Andrews, Wendy
　See Sharmat, Marjorie Weinman
Andrews, William G. 1930- 74
Andrezel, Pierre
　See Blixen, Karen (Christentze Dinesen)
Andriani, Renee
　See Williams-Andriani, Renee
Andriola, Alfred J. 1912-1983
　Obituary 34
Andrist, Ralph K. 1914- 45
Andryszewski, Tricia 1956- 88
Anfousse, Ginette 1944-
　Brief entry 48
Angel, Marie (Felicity) 1923- 47
Angeles, Peter A. 1931- 40
Angell, Judie 1937- 78
　Earlier sketch in SATA 22
　See also CLR 33
Angell, Madeline 1919- 18
Angelo, Valenti 1897- 14
Angelou, Maya 1928- 49
Angier, Bradford 12
Angle, Paul M(cClelland) 1900-1975
　Obituary 20
Anglund, Joan Walsh 1926- 2
　See also CLR 1
Angrist, Stanley W(olff) 1933- 4
Anholt, Catherine 1958- 74
Anholt, Laurence 1959- 74
Anita
　See Daniel, Anita
Annett, Cora
　See Scott, Cora Annett (Pipitone)
Annixter, Jane
　See Sturtzel, Jane Levington
Annixter, Paul
　See Sturtzel, Howard A(llison)
Anno, Mitsumasa 1926- 77
　Earlier sketches in SATA 5, 38
　See also CLR 14
Anrooy, Frans van
　See Van Anrooy, Francine
Anstey, Caroline 1958- 81
Antell, Will D. 1935- 31
Anthony, Barbara 1932- 29

Anthony, C. L.
　See Smith, Dorothy Gladys
Anthony, Edward 1895-1971 21
Anthony, John
　See Ciardi, John (Anthony)
Anthony, Piers 1934- 84
　See also SAAS 22
Anthony, Susan C(arol) 1953- 87
Anticaglia, Elizabeth 1939- 12
Antolini, Margaret Fishback 1904-1985
　Obituary 45
Anton, Michael (James) 1940- 12
Antonacci, Robert J(oseph) 1916- 45
　Brief entry 37
Aoki, Hisako 1942- 45
Apfel, Necia H(alpern) 1930- 51
　Brief entry 41
Aphrodite, J.
　See Livingston, Carole
Apostolou, Christine Hale 1955- 82
Appel, Benjamin 1907-1977 39
　Obituary 21
Appel, Martin E(liot) 1948- 45
Appel, Marty
　See Appel, Martin E(liot)
Appelt, Kathi 1954- 83
Appiah, Peggy 1921- 84
　Earlier sketch in SATA 15
　See also SAAS 19
Apple, Margot 64
　Brief entry 42
Applebaum, Stan 1929- 45
Appleton, Victor
　See Macdonald, James D.
Appleton, Victor [Collective
　pseudonym] 67
　Earlier sketch in SATA 1
Appleton, Victor II [Collective
　pseudonym] 67
　Earlier sketch in SATA 1
Apsler, Alfred 1907- 10
Aquillo, Don
　See Prince, J(ack) H(arvey)
Aragones, Sergio 1937- 48
　Brief entry 39
Araujo, Frank P. 1937- 86
Arbuckle, Dorothy Fry 1910-1982
　Obituary 33
Arbuthnot, May Hill 1884-1969 2
Archambault, John 67
Archbold, Rick 1950- 97
Archer, Frank
　See O'Connor, Richard
Archer, Jules 1915- 85
　Earlier sketch in SATA 4
　See also SAAS 5
Archer, Marion Fuller 1917- 11
Archibald, Joe
　See Archibald, Joseph S(topford)
Archibald, Joseph S(topford)
　1898-1986 3
　Obituary 47
Ardai, Charles 1969- 85
Arden, Barbie
　See Stoutenburg, Adrien
Arden, William
　See Lynds, Dennis
Ardizzone, Edward 1900-1979 28
　Obituary 21
　Earlier sketch in SATA 1
　See also CLR 3
Ardley, Neil (Richard) 1937- 43
Arehart-Treichel, Joan 1942- 22
Arenella, Roy 1939- 14
Arkin, Alan (Wolf) 1934- 59
　Brief entry 32
Arley, Robert
　See Jackson, Mike
Armer, Alberta (Roller) 1904- 9
Armer, Laura Adams 1874-1963 13
Armitage, David 1943- 99
　Brief entry 38
Armitage, Ronda (Jacqueline)
　1943- 99
　Brief entry 38
　Earlier sketch in SATA 47

Armour, Richard (Willard)
　1906-1989 14
　Obituary 61
Armstrong, George D. 1927- 10
Armstrong, Gerry (Breen) 1929- 10
Armstrong, Jennifer 1961- 77
　See also SAAS 24
Armstrong, Louise 43
　Brief entry 33
Armstrong, Richard 1903- 11
Armstrong, William H. 1914- 4
　See also CLR 1
　See also SAAS 7
Arndt, Ursula (Martha H.) 56
　Brief entry 39
Arneson, D(on) J(on) 1935- 37
Arnett, Carolyn
　See Cole, Lois Dwight
Arno, Enrico 1913-1981 43
　Obituary 28
Arnold, Caroline 1944- 85
　Brief entry 34
　Earlier sketch in SATA 36
　See also SAAS 23
Arnold, Elliott 1912-1980 5
　Obituary 22
Arnold, Emily 1939- 76
　Earlier sketch in SATA 50
Arnold, Katya 1947- 82
Arnold, Marsha Diane 1948- 93
Arnold, Oren 1900- 4
Arnold, Susan (Riser) 1951- 58
Arnold, Tedd 1949- 69
Arnoldy, Julie
　See Bischoff, Julia Bristol
Arnosky, Jim 1946- 70
　Earlier sketch in SATA 22
　See also CLR 15
Arnott, Kathleen 1914- 20
Arnov, Boris, Jr. 1926- 12
Arnow, Harriette (Louisa) Simpson
　1908-1986 42
　Obituary 47
Arnsteen, Katy Keck 1934- 68
Arnstein, Helene S(olomon) 1915- 12
Arntson, Herbert E(dward) 1911- 12
Aroner, Miriam 82
Aronin, Ben 1904-1980
　Obituary 25
Arora, Shirley (Lease) 1930- 2
Arquette, Lois S(teinmetz) 1934- 1
　See Duncan, Lois S(teinmetz)
Arrick, Fran
　See Angell, Judie
Arrington, Stephen L(ee) 1948- 97
Arrowood, (McKendrick Lee) Clinton
　1939- 19
Arrowsmith, Pat
　See Barton, Pat
Artell, Mike 1948- 89
Arthur, Robert
　See Feder, Robert Arthur
Arthur, Ruth M(abel) 1905-1979 7
　Obituary 26
Artis, Vicki Kimmel 1945- 12
Artzybasheff, Boris (Miklailovich)
　1899-1965 14
Aruego, Ariane
　See Dewey, Ariane
Aruego, Jose 1932- 68
　Earlier sketch in SATA 6
　See also CLR 5
Arundel, Honor (Morfydd)
　1919-1973 4
　Obituary 24
　See also CLR 35
Arundel, Jocelyn
　See Alexander, Jocelyn (Anne) Arundel
Arvey, Michael 1948- 79
Asare, Meshack (Yaw) 1945- 86
Asbjoernsen, Peter Christen
　1812-1885 15
Asch, Frank 1946- 66
　Earlier sketch in SATA 5
Ash, Jutta 1942- 38

Ashabranner, Brent (Kenneth)
1921- 67
Earlier sketch in SATA *1*
See also CLR 28
See also SAAS 14
Ashby, Gwynneth 1922- *44*
Ashe, Arthur (Robert, Jr.), Jr.
1943-1993 ....*65*
Obituary *87*
Ashe, Geoffrey (Thomas) 1923- *17*
Ashe, Mary Ann
See Lewis, Mary (Christianna)
Asher, Sandy (Fenichel) 1942- *71*
Brief entry *34*
Earlier sketch in SATA *36*
See also SAAS 13
Ashey, Bella
See Breinburg, Petronella
Ashford, Daisy
See Ashford, Margaret Mary
Ashford, Margaret Mary 1881-1972 ......*10*
Ashley, Bernard 1935- *79*
Brief entry *39*
Earlier sketch in SATA *47*
See also CLR 4
Ashley, Elizabeth
See Salmon, Annie Elizabeth
Ashley, Ray
See Abrashkin, Raymond
Ashton, Lorayne
See Gottfried, Theodore Mark
Ashton, Warren T.
See Adams, William Taylor
Asimov, Isaac 1920-1992 ....*74*
Earlier sketches in SATA *1, 26*
See also CLR 12
Asimov, Janet (Jeppson) 1926- *54*
Asinof, Eliot 1919- *6*
Aska, Warabe 1944- *56*
Asprin, Robert L(ynn) 1946- *92*
Astley, Juliet
See Lofts, Norah (Robinson)
Aston, James
See White, T(erence) H(anbury)
Atene, Ann
See Atene, (Rita) Anna
Atene, (Rita) Anna 1922- *12*
Atheling, William, Jr.
See Blish, James (Benjamin)
Atkinson, Allen 1953(?)-1987 ....*60*
Brief entry *46*
Obituary *55*
Atkinson, M. E.
See Frankau, Mary Evelyn
Atkinson, Margaret Fleming *14*
Attema, Martha 1949- *94*
Atticus
See Fleming, Ian (Lancaster)
Atwater, Florence (Hasseltine Carroll)
1896-1979 ....*66*
Earlier sketch in SATA *16*
See also CLR 19
Atwater, Montgomery Meigs 1904- *15*
Atwater, Richard (Tupper)
1892-1948 ....*66*
Brief entry *27*
Earlier sketch in SATA *54*
See also CLR 19
Atwell, Debby 1953- *87*
Atwood, Ann 1913- *7*
Atwood, Margaret (Eleanor) 1939- *50*
Aubrey, Meg Kelleher 1963- *83*
Aubry, Claude B. 1914-1984 ....*29*
Obituary *40*
Auclair, Joan 1960- *68*
Auel, Jean M(arie) 1936- *91*
Auer, Martin 1951- *77*
Augarde, Steve 1950- *25*
Augelli, John P(at) 1921- *46*
Augustine, Mildred
See Benson, Mildred (Augustine Wirt)
Ault, Phillip H. 1914- *23*
Ault, Rosalie Sain 1942- *38*
Ault, Roz
See Ault, Rosalie Sain
Aung, (Maung) Htin 1910- *21*

Aung, U. Htin
See Aung, (Maung) Htin
Auntie Deb
See Coury, Louise Andree
Auntie Louise
See Coury, Louise Andree
Austin, Carrie
See Seuling, Barbara
Austin, Elizabeth S. 1907- *5*
Austin, Harry
See McInerny, Ralph
Austin, Margot 1909(?)-1990 ....*11*
Obituary *66*
Austin, Oliver L., Jr. 1903-1988 ....*7*
Obituary *59*
Austin, R. G.
See Lamb, Nancy
Austin, R. G.
See Gelman, Rita Golden
Austin, Tom
See Jacobs, Linda C.
Austin, Virginia *80*
Auth, Tony
See Auth, William Anthony, Jr.
Auth, William Anthony, Jr. 1942- *51*
Averill, Esther (Holden) 1902-1992 ......*28*
Obituary *72*
Earlier sketch in SATA *1*
Avery, Al
See Montgomery, Rutherford George
Avery, Gillian (Elise) 1926- *75*
Earlier sketch in SATA *7*
See also SAAS 6
Avery, Kay 1908- *5*
Avery, Lynn
See Cole, Lois Dwight
Avi 1937- *71*
Earlier sketch in SATA *14*
See also CLR 24
Avishai, Susan 1949- *82*
Awdry, Christopher Vere 1940- *67*
Awdry, Wilbert Vere 1911-1997 ....*67*
Obituary *94*
See also CLR 23
Axton, David
See Koontz, Dean R(ay)
Ayars, James S(terling) 1898- *4*
Ayer, Eleanor H. 1947- *78*
Ayer, Jacqueline 1930- *13*
Ayer, Margaret *15*
Aylesworth, Jim 1943- *89*
Earlier sketch in SATA *38*
Aylesworth, Thomas G(ibbons)
1927-1995 ....*88*
Earlier sketch in SATA *4*
See also CLR 6
See also SAAS 17
Aymar, Brandt 1911- *22*
Ayme, Marcel 1902-1967
See CLR 25
Ayme, Marcel (Andre) 1902-1967 ....*91*
Ayres, Carole Briggs
See Briggs, Carole S(uzanne)
Ayres, Pam 1947- *90*
Ayres, Patricia Miller 1923-1985
Obituary *46*
Azaid
See Zaidenberg, Arthur

B

B
See Gilbert, W(illiam) S(chwenk)
B., Tania
See Blixen, Karen (Christentze Dinesen)
Baastad, Babbis Friis
See Friis-Baastad, Babbis
Bab
See Gilbert, W(illiam) S(chwenk)
Babbis, Eleanor
See Friis-Baastad, Babbis
Babbitt, Lucy Cullyford 1960- *85*

Babbitt, Natalie (Zane Moore)
1932- *68*
Earlier sketch in SATA *6*
See also CLR 2
See also SAAS 5
Babcock, Chris 1963- *83*
Babcock, Dennis Arthur 1948- *22*
Baber, Carolyn Stonnell 1936- *96*
Bach, Alice (Hendricks) 1942- *93*
Brief entry *27*
Earlier sketch in SATA *30*
Bach, Richard David 1936- *13*
Bachman, Fred 1949- *12*
Bachman, Richard
See King, Stephen (Edwin)
Bachrach, Deborah *80*
Backus, James Gilmore 1913-1989
Obituary *63*
Backus, Jim
See Backus, James Gilmore
Bacmeister, Rhoda W(arner) 1893- *11*
Bacon, Elizabeth 1914- *3*
Bacon, Joan Chase
See Bowden, Joan Chase
Bacon, Josephine Dodge (Daskam)
1876-1961 ....*48*
Bacon, Margaret Frances 1895-1987
Obituary *50*
Bacon, Margaret Hope 1921- *6*
Bacon, Martha Sherman 1917-1981 ......*18*
Obituary *27*
See also CLR 3
Bacon, Melvin (L.) 1950- *93*
Bacon, Peggy 1895- *2*
See Bacon, Margaret Frances
Bacon, R(onald) L(eonard) 1924- *84*
Earlier sketch in SATA *26*
Baden, Robert 1936- *70*
Baden-Powell, Robert (Stephenson Smyth)
1857-1941 ....*16*
Badt, Karin L(uisa) 1963- *91*
Baehr, Kingsley M. 1937- *89*
Baehr, Patricia (Goehner) 1952- *65*
Baer, Judy 1951- *71*
Baerg, Harry J(ohn) 1909- *12*
Baeten, Lieve 1954- *83*
Bagert, Brod 1947- *80*
Bagnold, Enid 1889-1981 ....*25*
Earlier sketch in SATA *1*
Bahlke, Valerie Worth 1933-1994
Obituary *81*
See Worth, Valerie
Bahous, Sally 1939- *86*
Bahr, Mary M(adelyn) 1946- *95*
Bahr, Robert 1940- *38*
Bahti, Tom 1926-1972 ....*57*
Brief entry *31*
Bailey, Alice Cooper 1890- *12*
Bailey, Anne 1958- *71*
Bailey, Bernadine Freeman *14*
Bailey, Carolyn Sherwin 1875-1961 ......*14*
Bailey, Donna (Veronica Anne)
1938- *68*
Bailey, Jane H(orton) 1916- *12*
Bailey, John (Robert) 1940- *52*
Bailey, Maralyn Collins (Harrison)
1941- *12*
Bailey, Matilda
See Radford, Ruby L(orraine)
Bailey, Maurice Charles 1932- *12*
Bailey, Pearl (Mae) 1918-1990 ....*81*
Bailey, Ralph Edgar 1893- *11*
Baillie, Allan (Stuart) 1943- *87*
See also CLR 49
See also SAAS 21
Baines, John (David) 1943- *71*
Baird, Bil 1904-1987 ....*30*
Obituary *52*
Baird, Thomas (P.) 1923-1990 ....*45*
Brief entry *39*
Obituary *64*
Baity, Elizabeth Chesley 1907- *1*
Bakeless, John (Edwin) 1894- *9*
Bakeless, Katherine Little 1895- *9*
Baker, Alan 1951- *93*
Earlier sketch in SATA *22*
Baker, Augusta 1911- *3*

Baker, Betty Lou 1928-1987 73
  Obituary 54
  Earlier sketch in SATA 5
Baker, C. G.
  See Baker, Carin Greenberg
Baker, Carin Greenberg 1959- 79
Baker, Charlotte 1910- 2
Baker, Elizabeth 1923- 7
Baker, Eugene H.
  Brief entry 50
Baker, Gayle C(unningham) 1950- 39
Baker, James W. 1924- 22
Baker, James W. 1926- 65
Baker, Janice E(dla) 1941- 22
Baker, Jeannie 1950- 88
  Earlier sketch in SATA 23
  See also CLR 28
Baker, Jeffrey J(ohn) W(heeler)
  1931- 5
Baker, Jim
  See Baker, James W.
Baker, Laura Nelson 1911- 3
Baker, Margaret 1890- 4
Baker, Margaret J(oyce) 1918- 12
Baker, Mary Gladys Steel
  1892-1974 12
Baker, (Robert) Michael 1938- 4
Baker, Nina (Brown) 1888-1957 15
Baker, Pamela J. 1947- 66
Baker, Rachel 1904-1978 2
  Obituary 26
Baker, Samm Sinclair 1909-1997 12
  Obituary 96
Baker, Susan (Catherine) 1942- 29
Balaam
  See Lamb, G(eoffrey) F(rederick)
Balch, Glenn 1902-1989 83
  Earlier sketch in SATA 3
  See also SAAS 11
Balderose, Nancy Ward 1952- 93
Baldridge, Cyrus LeRoy 1889-
  Brief entry 29
Baldry, Cherith 1947- 72
Balducci, Carolyn Feleppa 1946- 5
Baldwin, Anne Norris 1938- 5
Baldwin, Clara 11
Baldwin, Gordo
  See Baldwin, Gordon C.
Baldwin, Gordon C. 1908- 12
Baldwin, James 1841-1925 24
Baldwin, James (Arthur) 1924-1987 9
  Obituary 54
Baldwin, Margaret
  See Weis, Margaret (Edith)
Baldwin, Stan(ley C.) 1929- 62
  Brief entry 28
Bales, Carol Ann 1940- 57
  Brief entry 29
Balet, Jan (Bernard) 1913- 11
Balian, Lorna 1929- 91
  Earlier sketch in SATA 9
Ball, Duncan 1941- 73
Ball, Zachary
  See Masters, Kelly R.
Ballantine, Lesley Frost
  See Frost, Lesley
Ballantyne, R(obert) M(ichael)
  1825-1894 24
Ballard, J(ames) G(raham) 1930- 93
Ballard, Lowell Clyne 1904-1986 12
  Obituary 49
Ballard, (Charles) Martin 1929- 1
Ballard, Mignon Franklin 1934- 64
  Brief entry 49
Ballard, Robert D(uane) 1942- 85
Ballouhey, Pierre 1944- 90
Balogh, Penelope 1916-1975 1
  Obituary 34
Balow, Tom 1931- 12
Baltazzi, Evan S(erge) 1921- 90
Baltimore, J.
  See Catherall, Arthur
Baltzer, Hans (Adolf) 1900- 40
Bamfylde, Walter
  See Bevan, Tom
Bamman, Henry A. 1918- 12
Bancroft, Griffing 1907- 6

Bancroft, Laura
  See Baum, L(yman) Frank
Bandel, Betty 1912- 47
Baner, Skulda V(anadis) 1897-1964 10
Banfill, A. Scott 1956- 98
Bang, Betsy (Garrett) 1912- 48
  Brief entry 37
Bang, Molly 1943- 69
  Earlier sketch in SATA 24
  See also CLR 8
Banjo, The
  See Paterson, A(ndrew) B(arton)
Banks, Laura Stockton Voorhees 1908(?)-
  1980
  Obituary 23
Banks, Sara (Jeanne Gordon Harrell)
  1937- 26
Banner, Angela
  See Maddison, Angela Mary
Banner, Rachel
  See Roddy, Lee
Bannerman, Helen (Brodie Cowan Watson)
  1863(?)-1946 19
  See also CLR 21
Banning, Evelyn I. 1903- 36
Bannon, Laura (?)-1963 6
Bantock, Nick 1949- 95
Barasch, Lynne 1939- 74
Barbalet, Margaret 1949- 77
Barbary, James
  See Baumann, Amy (Brown)
Barbary, James
  See Beeching, Jack
Barbash, Shepard 1957- 84
Barbe, Walter Burke 1926- 45
Barber, Antonia
  See Anthony, Barbara
Barber, Linda
  See Graham-Barber, Lynda
Barber, Richard (William) 1941- 35
Barbera, Joe
  See Barbera, Joseph Roland
Barbera, Joseph Roland 1911- 51
Barberis, Juan C(arlos) 1920- 61
Barbour, Karen 1956- 63
Barbour, Ralph Henry 1870-1944 16
Barclay, Bill
  See Moorcock, Michael (John)
Barclay, Isabel
  See Dobell, I(sabel) M(arian) B(arclay)
Barclay, William Ewert
  See Moorcock, Michael (John)
Bardell, Graham 92
Bare, Arnold Edwin 1920- 16
Bare, Colleen Stanley 32
Barenholtz, Bernard 1914-1989
  Obituary 64
Bargar, Gary W. 1947-1985 63
Barish, Matthew 1907- 12
Barkan, Joanne 77
Barker, Albert W. 1900- 8
Barker, Carol (Minturn) 1938- 31
Barker, Cicely Mary 1895-1973 49
  Brief entry 39
Barker, Melvern 1907- 11
Barker, S. Omar 1894- 10
Barker, Will 1908- 8
Barkhouse, Joyce 1913-
  Brief entry 48
Barkin, Carol 1944- 52
Barklem, Jill 1951- 96
  See also CLR 31
Barkley, James Edward 1941- 6
Barks, Carl 1901- 37
Barley, Janet Crane 1934- 95
Barnaby, Ralph S(tanton) 1893- 9
Barne, Kitty
  See Barne, Marion Catherine
Barne, Marion Catherine
  1883-1957 97
Barner, Bob 1947- 29
Barnes, (Frank) Eric Wollencott
  1907-1962 22
Barnes, Joyce Annette 1958- 85
Barnes, Malcolm 1909(?)-1984
  Obituary 41
Barnes, Michael 1934- 55

Barnes-Murphy, Frances 1951- 88
Barnes-Murphy, Rowan 1952- 88
Barnes-Svarney, Patricia L(ou)
  1953- 67
Barnet, Nancy 1954- 84
Barnett, Ivan 1947- 70
Barnett, Lincoln (Kinnear)
  1909-1979 36
Barnett, Moneta 1922-1976 33
Barnett, Naomi 1927- 40
Barney, Maginel Wright 1881-1966 39
  Brief entry 32
Barnhart, Clarence L(ewis)
  1900-1993 48
  Obituary 78
Barnouw, Adriaan Jacob 1877-1968
  Obituary 27
Barnouw, Victor 1915- 43
  Brief entry 28
Barnstone, Willis 1927- 20
Barnum, Jay Hyde 1888(?)-1962 20
Barnum, Richard [Collective
  pseudonym] 67
  Earlier sketch in SATA 1
Baron, Kathy 1954- 90
Baron, Virginia Olsen 1931- 46
  Brief entry 28
Barr, Donald 1921- 20
Barr, George 1907- 2
Barr, Jene 1900-1985 16
  Obituary 42
Barrer, Gertrude
  See Barrer-Russell, Gertrude
Barrer-Russell, Gertrude 1921- 27
Barrett, Angela (Jane) 1955- 75
Barrett, Ethel 87
  Brief entry 44
Barrett, Jennifer
  See Plecas, Jennifer
Barrett, Judith 1941- 26
Barrett, Robert T(heodore) 1949- 92
Barrett, Ron 1937- 14
Barrett, Tracy 1955- 84
Barrett, William E(dmund) 1900-1986
  Obituary 49
Barrie, J(ames) M(atthew) 1860-1937
  See YABC 1
  See also CLR 16
Barrington, Michael
  See Moorcock, Michael (John)
Barris, George 1925- 47
Barrol, Grady
  See Bograd, Larry
Barron, Rex 1951- 84
Barron, T(om) A. 1952- 83
Barrow, Lloyd H. 1942- 73
Barry, James P(otvin) 1918- 14
Barry, Katharina (Watjen) 1936- 4
Barry, Robert 1931- 6
Barry, Scott 1952- 32
Barry, Sheila Anne 91
Bartenbach, Jean 1918- 40
Barth, Edna 1914-1980 7
  Obituary 24
Barthelme, Donald 1931-1989 7
  Obituary 62
Bartholomew, Barbara 1941- 86
  Brief entry 42
Bartholomew, Jean
  See Beatty, Patricia (Robbins)
Bartlett, Philip A. [Collective
  pseudonym] 1
Bartlett, Robert Merill 1899- 12
Bartoletti, Susan Campbell 1958- 88
Barton, Byron 1930- 90
  Earlier sketch in SATA 9
Barton, Harriett
  Brief entry 43
Barton, Jill(ian) 1940- 75
Barton, May Hollis [Collective
  pseudonym] 67
  Earlier sketch in SATA 1
Barton, Pat 1928- 59
Bartos-Hoeppner, Barbara 1923- 5
Bartsch, Jochen 1906- 39
Baruch, Dorothy W(alter)
  1899-1962 21

Bas, Rutger
  See Rutgers van der Loeff, An(na)
    Basenau
Base, Graeme (Rowland) 1958- *67*
  See also CLR *22*
Bashevis, Isaac
  See Singer, Isaac Bashevis
Baskin, Leonard 1922- *30*
  Brief entry *27*
Bason, Lillian 1913- *20*
Bassett, Jeni 1959- *64*
  Brief entry *43*
Bassett, John Keith
  See Keating, Lawrence A.
Bassett, Lisa 1958- *61*
Bassil, Andrea 1948- *96*
Bat-Ami, Miriam 1950- *82*
Batchelor, Joy 1914-
  Brief entry *29*
Bate, Lucy 1939- *18*
Bate, Norman 1916- *5*
Bates, Barbara S(nedeker) 1919- *12*
Bates, Betty 1921- *19*
Batey, Tom 1946- *52*
  Brief entry *41*
Batherman, Muriel
  See Sheldon, Muriel
Batiuk, Thomas M(artin) 1947-
  Brief entry *40*
Batson, Larry 1930- *35*
Battaglia, Aurelius 1910- *50*
  Brief entry *33*
Batten, H(arry) Mortimer
    1888-1958 ....*25*
Batten, Mary 1937- *5*
Batterberry, Ariane Ruskin 1935- *13*
Batterberry, Michael (Carver)
    1932- *32*
Battle-Lavert, Gwendolyn 1951- *85*
Battles, Edith 1921- *7*
Baudouy, Michel-Aime 1909- *7*
Bauer, Caroline Feller 1935- *98*
  Brief entry *46*
  Earlier sketch in SATA *52*
  See also SAAS *24*
Bauer, Fred 1934- *36*
Bauer, Helen 1900- *2*
Bauer, Marion Dane 1938- *69*
  Earlier sketch in SATA *20*
  See also SAAS *9*
Bauernschmidt, Marjorie 1926- *15*
Baughman, Dorothy 1940- *61*
Baum, Allyn Z(elton) 1924-1997 ....*20*
  Obituary *98*
Baum, L. Frank
  See Thompson, Ruth Plumly
Baum, L(yman) Frank 1856-1919 ....*18*
  See also CLR *15*
Baum, Louis 1948- *64*
  Brief entry *52*
Baum, Willi 1931- *4*
Baumann, Amy (Brown) 1922- *10*
Baumann, Elwood D.
  Brief entry *33*
Baumann, Hans 1914- *2*
  See also CLR *35*
Baumann, Kurt 1935- *21*
Baumgartner, Barbara 1939- *86*
Bawden, Nina (Mary Mabey)
    1925- *72*
  Earlier sketch in SATA *4*
  See also CLR *2*
  See also SAAS *16*
Baxter, Valerie
  See Meynell, Laurence Walter
Bay, Jeanette Graham 1928- *88*
Bayer, Harold
  See Gregg, Andy
Bayer, Jane E. (?)-1985
  Obituary *44*
Bayley, Nicola 1949- *69*
  Earlier sketch in SATA *41*
Baylor, Byrd 1924- *69*
  Earlier sketch in SATA *16*
  See also CLR *3*
Baynes, Pauline (Diana) 1922- *59*
  Earlier sketch in SATA *19*

BB
  See Watkins-Pitchford, Denys James
Beach, Charles
  See Reid, (Thomas) Mayne
Beach, Charles Amory [Collective
    pseudonym] *1*
Beach, Edward L(atimer) 1918- *12*
Beach, Lynn
  See Lance, Kathryn
Beach, Stewart Taft 1899- *23*
Beachcroft, Nina 1931- *18*
Beagle, Peter S. 1939- *60*
Bealer, Alex W(inkler III)
    1921-1980 ....*8*
  Obituary *22*
Beales, Valerie 1915- *74*
Beals, Carleton 1893- *12*
Beals, Frank Lee 1881-1972
  Obituary *26*
Beame, Rona 1934- *12*
Beamer, (G.) Charles, (Jr.) 1942- *43*
Beaney, Jan
  See Udall, Jan Beaney
Bear, Greg(ory Dale) 1951- *65*
Beard, Charles Austin 1874-1948 ....*18*
Beard, Dan(iel Carter) 1850-1941 ....*22*
Beard, Darleen Bailey 1961- *96*
Bearden, Romare (Howard)
    1914-1988 ....*22*
  Obituary *56*
Beardmore, Cedric
  See Beardmore, George
Beardmore, George 1908-1979 ....*20*
Bearman, Jane (Ruth) 1917- *29*
Beatty, Elizabeth
  See Holloway, Teresa (Bragunier)
Beatty, Hetty Burlingame 1907-1971 ......*5*
Beatty, Jerome, Jr. 1918- *5*
Beatty, John (Louis) 1922-1975 ....*6*
  Obituary *25*
Beatty, Patricia (Robbins)
    1922-1991 ....*73*
  Obituary *68*
  Earlier sketches in SATA *1, 30*
  See also SAAS *4*
Bechard, Margaret 1953- *85*
Bechtel, Louise Seaman 1894-1985 ....*4*
  Obituary *43*
Beck, Barbara L. 1927- *12*
Becker, Beril 1901- *11*
Becker, John (Leonard) 1901- *12*
Becker, Joyce 1936- *39*
Becker, May Lamberton 1873-1958 ......*33*
Beckett, Sheilah 1913- *33*
Beckman, Delores 1914- *51*
Beckman, Gunnel 1910- *6*
  See also CLR *25*
  See also SAAS *9*
Beckman, Kaj
  See Beckman, Karin
Beckman, Karin 1913- *45*
Beckman, Per (Frithiof) 1913- *45*
Bedard, Michael 1949- *93*
  See also CLR *35*
Beddows, Eric
  See Nutt, Ken
Bedford, A. N.
  See Watson, Jane Werner
Bedford, Annie North
  See Watson, Jane Werner
Bedoukian, Kerop 1907-1981 ....*53*
Bee, Jay
  See Brainerd, John W(hiting)
Beebe, B(urdetta) F(aye) 1920- *1*
Beebe, (Charles) William
    1877-1962 ....*19*
Beeby, Betty 1923- *25*
Beech, Webb
  See Butterworth, W(illiam) E(dmund III)
Beeching, Jack 1922- *14*
Beeler, Janet
  See Shaw, Janet
Beeler, Nelson F(rederick) 1910- *13*
Beere, Peter 1951- *97*
Beers, Dorothy Sands 1917- *9*
Beers, Lorna 1897- *14*
Beers, V(ictor) Gilbert 1928- *9*

Begin, Maryjane 1963- *82*
Begin-Callanan, Maryjane
  See Begin, Maryjane
Begley, Kathleen A(nne) 1948- *21*
Behn, Harry 1898-1973 ....*2*
  Obituary *34*
Behnke, Frances L. *8*
Behr, Joyce 1929- *15*
Behrens, June York 1925- *19*
Behrman, Carol H(elen) 1925- *14*
Beifuss, John (Jr.) 1959- *92*
Beiler, Edna 1923- *61*
Beinicke, Steve 1956- *69*
Beirne, Barbara 1933- *71*
Beiser, Arthur 1931- *22*
Beiser, Germaine 1931- *11*
Belair, Richard L. 1934- *45*
Belaney, Archibald Stansfeld
    1888-1938 ....*24*
Belden, Wilanne Schneider 1925- *56*
Belfrage, Sally 1936-1994 ....*65*
  Obituary *79*
Belknap, B. H.
  See Ellis, Edward S(ylvester)
Bell, Anthea 1936- *88*
Bell, Clare (Louise) 1952- *99*
Bell, Corydon 1894- *3*
Bell, David Owen 1949- *99*
Bell, Emily Mary
  See Cason, Mabel Earp
Bell, Frank
  See Benson, Mildred (Augustine Wirt)
Bell, Gertrude (Wood) 1911- *12*
Bell, Gina
  See Iannone, Jeanne
Bell, Janet
  See Clymer, Eleanor
Bell, Margaret E(lizabeth) 1898- *2*
Bell, Mary Reeves 1946- *88*
Bell, Neill 1946-
  Brief entry *50*
Bell, Norman (Edward) 1899- *11*
Bell, Raymond Martin 1907- *13*
Bell, Robert S(tanley) W(arren) 1871-1921
  Brief entry *27*
Bell, Thelma Harrington 1896- *3*
Bell, William 1945- *90*
Bellairs, John 1938-1991 ....*68*
  Obituary *66*
  Earlier sketch in SATA *2*
  See also CLR *37*
Beller, Susan Provost 1949- *84*
Bellingham, Brenda 1931- *99*
  Brief entry *51*
Belloc, (Joseph) Hilaire (Pierre) 1870-1953
  See YABC *1*
Belloli, Andrea P. A. 1947- *86*
Bellville, Cheryl Walsh 1944- *54*
  Brief entry *49*
  See also SAAS *25*
Bell-Zano, Gina
  See Iannone, Jeanne
Belpre, Pura 1899-1982 ....*16*
  Obituary *30*
Belting, Natalie Maree 1915- *6*
Belton, John Raynor 1931- *22*
Belton, Sandra (Yvonne) 1939- *85*
Beltran, Alberto 1923- *43*
Beltran-Hernandez, Irene 1945- *74*
Belvedere, Lee
  See Grayland, Valerie
Bemelmans, Ludwig 1898-1962 ....*15*
  See also CLR *6*
Benander, Carl D. 1941- *74*
Benary, Margot
  See Benary-Isbert, Margot
Benary-Isbert, Margot 1889-1979 ....*2*
  Obituary *21*
  See also CLR *12*
Benasutti, Marion 1908- *6*
Benchley, Nathaniel (Goddard)
    1915-1981 ....*25*
  Obituary *28*
  Earlier sketch in SATA *3*
Benchley, Peter (Bradford) 1940- *89*
  Earlier sketch in SATA *3*
Bender, Edna 1941- *92*

Bender, Esther 1942- 88
Bender, Lucy Ellen 1942- 22
Bender, Robert 1962- 79
Bendick, Jeanne 1919- 68
  Earlier sketch in SATA 2
  See also CLR 5
  See also SAAS 4
Bendick, Robert L(ouis) 1917- 11
Benedict, Dorothy Potter
  1889-1979 11
  Obituary 23
Benedict, Lois Trimble 1902-1967 12
Benedict, Rex 1920- 8
Benedict, Stewart H(urd) 1924- 26
Benet, Laura 1884-1979 3
  Obituary 23
Benet, Stephen Vincent 1898-1943
  See YABC 1
Benet, Sula 1903(?)-1982 21
  Obituary 33
Benezra, Barbara 1921- 10
Benham, Leslie 1922- 48
Benham, Lois (Dakin) 1924- 48
Benham, Mary Lile 1914- 55
Benjamin, Nora
  See Kubie, Nora (Gottheil) Benjamin
Benjamin, Saragail Katzman 1953- 86
Benner, Cheryl 1962- 80
Benner, J(udith) A(nn) 1942- 94
Bennett, Cherie 1960- 97
Bennett, Dorothea
  See Young, Dorothea Bennett
Bennett, James (W.) 1942- 93
Bennett, Jay 1912- 87
  Brief entry 27
  Earlier sketch in SATA 41
  See also SAAS 4
Bennett, Jill (Crawford) 1934- 41
Bennett, John 1865-1956
  See YABC 1
Bennett, Penelope 1938- 94
Bennett, Rachel
  See Hill, Margaret (Ohler)
Bennett, Rainey 1907- 15
Bennett, Richard 1899- 21
Bennett, Russell H(oradley) 1896- 25
Benning, Elizabeth
  See Rice, Bebe Faas
Benson, Elizabeth P(olk) 1924- 65
Benson, Kathleen 1947- 62
Benson, Linda M(aria) 1959- 84
Benson, Mildred (Augustine Wirt)
  1905- 65
Benson, Mildred Wirt
  See Benson, Mildred (Augustine Wirt)
Benson, Sally 1900-1972 35
  Obituary 27
  Earlier sketch in SATA 1
Bentley, Bill
  See Bentley, William (George)
Bentley, Judith (McBride) 1945- 89
  Earlier sketch in SATA 40
Bentley, Nancy 1946- 78
Bentley, Nicolas Clerihew 1907-1978
  Obituary 24
Bentley, Phyllis (Eleanor) 1894-1977 6
  Obituary 25
Bentley, Roy 1947- 46
Bentley, William (George) 1916- 84
Berck, Judith 1960- 75
Berelson, Howard 1940- 5
Berends, Polly B(errien) 1939- 50
  Brief entry 38
Berenstain, Jan(ice) 1923- 64
  Earlier sketch in SATA 12
  See also CLR 19
  See also SAAS 20
Berenstain, Michael 1951-
  Brief entry 45
Berenstain, Stan(ley) 1923- 64
  Earlier sketch in SATA 12
  See also CLR 19
  See also SAAS 20
Berenzy, Alix 1957- 65
Beresford, Elisabeth 86
  Earlier sketch in SATA 25
  See also SAAS 20

Berg, Bjoern 1923-
  Brief entry 47
Berg, Dave
  See Berg, David
Berg, David 1920- 27
Berg, Jean Horton 1913- 6
Berg, Joan
  See Victor, Joan Berg
Berg, Ron 1952- 48
Bergaust, Erik 1925-1978 20
Bergen, Joyce 1949- 95
Berger, Barbara (Helen) 1945- 77
Berger, Gilda 1935- 88
  Brief entry 42
Berger, Josef 1903-1971 36
Berger, Melvin H. 1927- 88
  Earlier sketch in SATA 5
  See also CLR 32
  See also SAAS 2
Berger, Phil 1942- 62
Berger, Terry 1933- 8
Bergey, Alyce (Mae) 1934- 45
Bergman, Donna 1934- 73
Bergman, Tamar 1939- 95
Berkebile, Fred D(onovan) 1900-1978
  Obituary 26
Berkey, Barry Robert 1935- 24
Berkowitz, Freda Pastor 1910- 12
Berkus, Clara Widess 1909- 78
Berlan, Kathryn Hook 1946- 78
Berlfein, Judy Reiss 1958- 79
Berliner, Don 1930- 33
Berliner, Franz 1930- 13
Berlitz, Charles L. (Frambach)
  1913- 32
Berman, Linda 1948- 38
Berman, Paul (Lawrence) 1949- 66
Berman, Ruth 1958- 92
Berna, Paul 1910-1994 15
  Obituary 78
  See also CLR 19
Bernadette
  See Watts, Bernadette
Bernard, Bruce 78
Bernard, George I. 1949- 39
Bernard, Jacqueline (de Sieyes)
  1921-1983 8
  Obituary 45
Bernards, Neal 1963- 71
Bernays, Anne
  See Kaplan, Anne Bernays
Bernhard, Durga T. 1961- 80
Bernhard, Emery 1950- 80
Bernstein, Daryl (Evan) 1976- 81
Bernstein, Joanne E(ckstein) 1943- 15
Bernstein, Theodore M(enline)
  1904-1979 12
  Obituary 27
Berrien, Edith Heal
  See Heal, Edith
Berrill, Jacquelyn (Batsel) 1905- 12
Berrington, John
  See Brownjohn, Alan
Berry, B. J.
  See Berry, Barbara J.
Berry, Barbara J. 1937- 7
Berry, Erick
  See Best, (Evangel) Allena Champlin
Berry, James 1925- 67
  See also CLR 22
Berry, Jane Cobb 1915(?)-1979
  Obituary 22
Berry, Joy Wilt 1944- 58
  Brief entry 46
Berry, William D(avid) 1926- 14
Berson, Harold 1926- 4
Bert, Norman A(llen) 1942- 82
Bertolet, Paul
  See McLaughlin, Frank
Berton, Pierre (Francis DeMarigny)
  1920- 99
Bertrand, Cecile 1953- 76
Bertrand, Lynne 1963- 81
Berwick, Jean
  See Meyer, Jean Shepherd

Beskow, Elsa (Maartman)
  1874-1953 20
  See also CLR 17
Bess, Clayton
  See Locke, Robert
Best, (Evangel) Allena Champlin
  1892-1974 2
  Obituary 25
Best, (Oswald) Herbert 1894- 2
Bestall, A(lfred) E(dmeades)
  1892-1986 97
  Obituary 48
Betancourt, Jeanne 1941- 96
  Brief entry 43
  Earlier sketch in SATA 55
Beth, Mary
  See Miller, Mary Beth
Bethancourt, T. Ernesto
  See CLR 3
  See Paisley, Tom
Bethel, Dell 1929- 52
Bethell, Jean (Frankenberry) 1922- 8
Bethers, Ray 1902- 6
Bethune, J. G.
  See Ellis, Edward S(ylvester)
Betteridge, Anne
  See Potter, Margaret (Newman)
Bettina
  See Ehrlich, Bettina Bauer
Bettmann, Otto Ludwig 1903- 46
Betts, James
  See Haynes, Betsy
Betts, James [Joint pseudonym]
  See Haynes, Betsy
Betz, Eva Kelly 1897-1968 10
Bevan, Tom 1868(?)-
  See YABC 2
Bewick, Thomas 1753-1828 16
Beyer, Audrey White 1916- 9
Beyer, Paul J. III 1950- 74
Bezencon, Jacqueline (Buxcel)
  1924- 48
Bhatia, June
  See Forrester, Helen
Bial, Morrison David 1917- 62
Bial, Raymond 1948- 76
Biale, Rachel 1952- 99
Bialk, Elisa
  See Krautter, Elisa (Bialk)
Bianchi, John 1947- 91
Bianchi, Robert Steven 1943- 92
Bianco, Margery (Williams)
  1881-1944 15
  See also CLR 19
Bianco, Pamela 1906- 28
Bibby, Violet 1908- 24
Bible, Charles 1937- 13
Bice, Clare 1909-1976 22
Bickerstaff, Isaac
  See Swift, Jonathan
Biegel, Paul 1925- 79
  Earlier sketch in SATA 16
  See also CLR 27
  See also SAAS 18
Biemiller, Carl L(udwig) 1912-1979 40
  Obituary 21
Bienenfeld, Florence L(ucille)
  1929- 39
Bierhorst, John (William) 1936- 91
  Earlier sketch in SATA 6
  See also SAAS 10
Biggle, Lloyd, Jr. 1923- 65
Bilal, Abdel W(ahab) 1970- 92
Bileck, Marvin 1920- 40
Bilibin, Ivan (Iakolevich)
  1876-1942 61
Bill, Alfred Hoyt 1879-1964 44
Billiam, Rosemary 1952- 61
Billings, Charlene W(interer) 1941- 41
Billington, Elizabeth T(hain) 50
  Brief entry 43
Billout, Guy Rene 1941- 10
  See also CLR 33
Bilson, Geoffrey 1938-1987 99
Binch, Caroline 1947- 81
Bingham, Sam(uel) (A.) 1944- 96
Bingley, Margaret (Jane) 1947- 72

Binkley, Anne
  See Rand, Ann (Binkley)
Binzen, Bill *24*
Binzen, William
  See Binzen, Bill
Birch, David (W.) 1913- *89*
Birch, Reginald B(athurst)
  1856-1943 ....*19*
Birchman, David 1949- *72*
Birchmore, Daniel A. 1951- *92*
Bird, E(lzy) J(ay) 1911- *58*
Birdseye, Tom 1951- *98*
  Earlier sketch in SATA *66*
Birenbaum, Barbara 1941- *65*
Birmingham, Lloyd P(aul) 1924- *83*
  Earlier sketch in SATA *12*
Birney, Betty G. 1947- *98*
Biro, B.
  See Biro, B(alint) S(tephen)
Biro, B(alint) S(tephen) 1921- *67*
  Earlier sketch in SATA *1*
  See also CLR *28*
  See also SAAS *13*
Biro, Val
  See Biro, B(alint) S(tephen)
Bischoff, Julia Bristol 1909-1970 ....*12*
Bishop, Bonnie 1943- *37*
Bishop, Claire Huchet
  1899(?)-1993 ....*14*
  Obituary *74*
Bishop, Courtney
  See Ruemmler, John D(avid)
Bishop, Curtis 1912-1967 ....*6*
Bishop, Elizabeth 1911-1979
  Obituary *24*
Bishop, Gavin 1946- *97*
Bisset, Donald 1910-1995 ....*86*
  Earlier sketch in SATA *7*
Bisson, Terry (Ballantine) 1942- *99*
Bitter, Gary G(len) 1940- *22*
Bixby, William (Courtney)
  1920-1986 ....*6*
  Obituary *47*
Bjerregaard-Jensen, Vilhelm Hans
  See Hillcourt, William
Bjoerk, Christina 1938- *99*
  Earlier sketch in SATA *67*
  See also CLR *22*
Bjorklund, Lorence F. 1913-1978 ....*35*
  Brief entry *32*
Black, Algernon David 1900-1993 ....*12*
  Obituary *76*
Black, Irma S(imonton) 1906-1972 ....*2*
  Obituary *25*
Black, Mansell
  See Trevor, Elleston
Black, MaryAnn
  See Easley, MaryAnn
Black, Susan Adams 1953- *40*
Blackburn, Claire
  See Jacobs, Linda C.
Blackburn, John(ny) Brewton 1952- *15*
Blackburn, Joyce Knight 1920- *29*
Blackett, Veronica Heath 1927- *12*
Blackie, Jean Cutler 1943- *79*
Blacklin, Malcolm
  See Chambers, Aidan
Blackman, Malorie 1962- *83*
Blackton, Peter
  See Wilson, Lionel
Blackwood, Alan 1932- *70*
Blackwood, Gary L. 1945- *72*
Blades, Ann 1947- *69*
  Earlier sketch in SATA *16*
  See also CLR *15*
Bladow, Suzanne Wilson 1937- *14*
Blaine, John
  See Harkins, Philip
Blaine, John
  See Goodwin, Harold L(eland)
Blaine, Margery Kay 1937- *11*
Blair, Anne Denton 1914- *46*
Blair, David Nelson 1954- *80*
Blair, Eric Arthur 1903-1950 ....*29*
Blair, Helen 1910-
  Brief entry *29*
Blair, Jay 1953- *45*

Blair, L. E.
  See Calhoun, B. B.
Blair, Ruth Van Ness 1912- *12*
Blair, Shannon
  See Kaye, Marilyn
Blair, Walter 1900-1992 ....*12*
  Obituary *72*
Blake, Jon 1954- *78*
Blake, Olive
  See Supraner, Robyn
Blake, Quentin 1932- *96*
  Earlier sketch in SATA *52*
  See also CLR *31*
Blake, Robert 1949- *42*
Blake, Walker E.
  See Butterworth, W(illiam) E(dmund III)
Blake, William 1757-1827 ....*30*
Blakely, Roger K. 1922- *82*
Blakeney, Jay D.
  See Chester, Deborah
Blakey, Nancy 1955- *94*
Blanc, Esther Silverstein 1913- *66*
Blanc, Mel 1908-1989
  Obituary *64*
Blanco, Richard L(idio) 1926- *63*
Bland, Edith Nesbit
  See Nesbit, E(dith)
Bland, Fabian [Joint pseudonym]
  See Nesbit, E(dith)
Blane, Gertrude
  See Blumenthal, Gertrude
Blank, Clair
  See Blank, Clarissa Mabel
Blank, Clarissa Mabel 1915-1965 ....*62*
Blassingame, Wyatt Rainey
  1909-1985 ....*34*
  Obituary *41*
  Earlier sketch in SATA *1*
Blatchford, Claire H. 1944- *94*
Blauer, Ettagale 1940- *49*
Bledsoe, Lucy Jane 1957- *97*
Bleeker, Sonia 1909-1971 ....*2*
  Obituary *26*
Blegen, Daniel M. 1950- *92*
Blegvad, Erik 1923- *66*
  Earlier sketch in SATA *14*
Blegvad, Lenore 1926- *66*
  Earlier sketch in SATA *14*
Blish, James (Benjamin) 1921-1975 ......*66*
Blishen, Edward 1920-1996 ....*66*
  Obituary *93*
  Earlier sketch in SATA *8*
Bliss, Corinne D(emas) 1947- *37*
Bliss, Reginald
  See Wells, H(erbert) G(eorge)
Bliss, Ronald G(ene) 1942- *12*
Bliven, Bruce, Jr. 1916- *2*
Blixen, Karen (Christentze Dinesen)
  1885-1962 ....*44*
Blizzard, Gladys S. -1992 ....*79*
Bloch, Lucienne 1909- *10*
Bloch, Marie Halun 1910- *6*
  See also SAAS *9*
Bloch, Robert (Albert) 1917-1994 ....*82*
  Earlier sketch in SATA *12*
Blochman, Lawrence G(oldtree)
  1900-1975 ....*22*
Block, Francesca Lia 1962- *80*
  See also CLR *33*
  See also SAAS *21*
Block, Irvin 1917- *12*
Blocksma, Mary
  Brief entry *44*
Blood, Charles Lewis 1929- *28*
Bloom, Freddy 1914- *37*
Bloom, Lloyd
  Brief entry *43*
Bloomfield, Michaela 1966- *70*
Bloor, Edward (William) 1950- *98*
Blos, Joan W. 1928- *69*
  Brief entry *27*
  Earlier sketch in SATA *33*
  See also CLR *18*
  See also SAAS *11*
Blough, Glenn O(rlando) 1907- *1*

Blue, Rose *93*
  Earlier sketch in SATA *5*
  See also SAAS *24*
Blue, Zachary
  See Stine, R(obert) L(awrence)
Blumberg, Leda 1956- *59*
Blumberg, Rhoda 1917- *70*
  Earlier sketch in SATA *35*
  See also CLR *21*
Blume, Judy (Sussman) 1938- *79*
  Earlier sketches in SATA *2, 31*
  See also CLR *15*
Blumenthal, Gertrude 1907-1971
  Obituary *27*
Blumenthal, Shirley 1943- *46*
Blutig, Eduard
  See Gorey, Edward (St. John)
Bly, Janet Chester 1945- *43*
Bly, Robert W(ayne) 1957-
  Brief entry *48*
Bly, Stephen A(rthur) 1944- *43*
Blyler, Allison Lee 1966- *74*
Blyton, Carey 1932- *9*
Blyton, Enid (Mary) 1897-1968 ....*25*
  See also CLR *31*
Boardman, Fon Wyman, Jr. 1911- *6*
Boardman, Gwenn R.
  See Petersen, Gwenn Boardman
Boardman, Gwenn R. 1924- *12*
Boase, Wendy 1944- *28*
Boatner, Mark Mayo III 1921- *29*
Bobbe, Dorothie 1905-1975 ....*1*
  Obituary *25*
Bober, Natalie S. 1930- *87*
  See also SAAS *23*
Bobri
  See Bobritsky, Vladimir
Bobri, Vladimir
  See Bobritsky, Vladimir
Bobritsky, Vladimir 1898- *47*
  Brief entry *32*
Bochak, Grayce 1956- *76*
Bock, Hal
  See Bock, Harold I.
Bock, Harold I. 1939- *10*
Bock, William Sauts Netamux'we *14*
Bode, Janet 1943- *96*
  Earlier sketch in SATA *60*
Bodecker, N(iels) M(ogens)
  1922-1988 ....*73*
  Obituary *54*
  Earlier sketch in SATA *8*
Boden, Hilda
  See Bodenham, Hilda Esther
Bodenham, Hilda Esther 1901- *13*
Bodett, Tom 1955- *70*
Bodie, Idella F(allaw) 1925- *89*
  Earlier sketch in SATA *12*
Bodker, Cecil 1927- *14*
  See also CLR *23*
Bodsworth, (Charles) Fred(erick)
  1918- *27*
Boeckman, Charles 1920- *12*
Boegehold, Betty (Doyle) 1913-1985
  Obituary *42*
Boelts, Maribeth 1964- *78*
Boesch, Mark J(oseph) 1917- *12*
Boesen, Victor 1908- *16*
Bogaerts, Gert 1965- *80*
Bogart, Jo Ellen 1945- *92*
Boggs, Ralph Steele 1901- *7*
Bograd, Larry 1953- *89*
  Earlier sketch in SATA *33*
  See also SAAS *21*
Bohdal, Susi 1951- *22*
Bohlen, Nina 1931- *58*
Bohlmeijer, Arno 1956- *94*
Bohner, Charles (Henry) 1927- *62*
Bohnhoff, Maya Kaathryn 1954- *88*
Boissard, Janine 1932- *59*
Boland, Janice *98*
Bolden, Tonya (Wilyce) 1959- *79*
Boles, Paul Darcy 1916-1984 ....*9*
  Obituary *38*
Bolian, Polly 1925- *4*
Bollen, Roger 1941(?)- *83*
  Brief entry *29*

Bolliger, Max 1929- 7
Bolognese, Don(ald Alan) 1934- 71
  Earlier sketch in SATA 24
Bolotin, Norman (Phillip) 1951- 93
Bolton, Carole 1926- 6
Bolton, Elizabeth
  See St. John, Nicole
Bolton, Evelyn
  See Bunting, Eve
Bonar, Veronica
  See Bailey, Donna (Veronica Anne)
Bond, B. J.
  See Heneghan, James
Bond, Bruce 1939- 61
Bond, Felicia 1954- 49
Bond, Gladys Baker 1912- 14
Bond, Higgins 1951- 83
Bond, J. Harvey
  See Winterbotham, R(ussell) R(obert)
Bond, Michael 1926- 58
  Earlier sketch in SATA 6
  See also CLR 1
  See also SAAS 3
Bond, Nancy (Barbara) 1945- 82
  Earlier sketch in SATA 22
  See also CLR 11
  See also SAAS 13
Bond, Ruskin 1934- 87
  Earlier sketch in SATA 14
Bonehill, Captain Ralph
  See Stratemeyer, Edward L.
Bonestell, Chesley 1888-1986
  Obituary 48
Bonham, Barbara 1926- 7
Bonham, Frank 1914-1989 49
  Obituary 62
  Earlier sketch in SATA 1
  See also SAAS 3
Bonn, Pat
  See Bonn, Patricia Carolyn
Bonn, Patricia Carolyn 1948- 43
Bonner, Mary Graham 1890-1974 19
Bonners, Susan 1947- 85
  Brief entry 48
Bonsall, Crosby Barbara (Newell)
  1921-1995 23
  Obituary 84
Bontemps, Arna 1902-1973 44
  Obituary 24
  Earlier sketch in SATA 2
  See also CLR 6
Bonzon, Paul-Jacques 1908- 22
Booher, Dianna Daniels 1948- 33
Bookman, Charlotte
  See Zolotow, Charlotte S(hapiro)
Boon, Emilie (Laetitia) 1958- 86
Boone, Pat 1934- 7
Boorman, Linda (Kay) 1940- 46
Boorstin, Daniel J(oseph) 1914- 52
Booth, Ernest Sheldon 1915-1984 43
Booth, Graham (Charles) 1935- 37
Borden, Louise (Walker) 1949- 68
Bordier, Georgette 1924- 16
Boring, Mel 1939- 35
Borja, Corinne 1929- 22
Borja, Robert 1923- 22
Borland, Hal 1900-1978 5
  Obituary 24
Borland, Harold Glen
  See Borland, Hal
Borland, Kathryn Kilby 1916- 16
Borlenghi, Patricia 1951- 79
Born, Adolf 1930- 49
Bornstein, Ruth 1927- 14
Bornstein, Ruth Lercher 1927- 88
Borski, Lucia Merecka 18
Borten, Helen Jacobson 1930- 5
Borton, Elizabeth
  See Trevino, Elizabeth B(orton) de
Borton, Lady 1942- 98
Bortstein, Larry 1942- 16
Bortz, Fred 1944- 74
Bosco, Jack
  See Holliday, Joseph
Boshell, Gordon 1908- 15
Boshinski, Blanche 1922- 10

Bosse, Malcolm J(oseph) 1933- 84
  Earlier sketch in SATA 35
Bossom, Naomi 1933- 35
Boston, Lucy Maria (Wood)
  1892-1990 19
  Obituary 64
  See also CLR 3
Bosworth, J. Allan 1925- 19
Bothwell, Jean 2
Botkin, B(enjamin) A(lbert)
  1901-1975 40
Botsford, Ward 1927- 66
Botting, Douglas (Scott) 1934- 43
Bottner, Barbara 1943- 93
  Earlier sketch in SATA 14
  See also SAAS 26
Boughton, Richard 1954- 75
Boulet, Susan Seddon 1941- 50
Boulle, Pierre (Francois Marie-Louis)
  1912-1994 22
  Obituary 78
Boulton, Jane 1921- 91
Bour, Daniele 1939- 62
Bourdon, David 1934- 46
Bourne, Leslie
  See Marshall, Evelyn
Bourne, Miriam Anne 1931-1989 16
  Obituary 63
Boutet De Monvel, (Louis) M(aurice)
  1850(?)-1913 30
  See also CLR 32
Bova, Ben(jamin William) 1932- 68
  Earlier sketch in SATA 6
  See also CLR 3
Bovaird, Anne E(lizabeth) 1960- 90
Bowden, Joan Chase 1925- 51
  Brief entry 38
Bowen, Alexandria Russell 97
Bowen, Andy Russell
  See Bowen, Alexandria Russell
Bowen, Betty Morgan
  See West, Betty
Bowen, Catherine Drinker
  1897-1973 7
Bowen, David
  See Bowen, Joshua David
Bowen, Joshua David 1930- 22
Bowen, Robert Sydney
  1900(?)-1977 52
  Obituary 21
Bowermaster, Jon 1954- 77
Bowie, Jim
  See Stratemeyer, Edward L.
Bowkett, Stephen 1953- 67
Bowler, Jan Brett
  See Brett, Jan (Churchill)
Bowman, James Cloyd 1880-1961 23
Bowman, John S(tewart) 1931- 16
Bowman, Kathleen (Gill) 1942- 52
  Brief entry 40
Boyce, George A(rthur) 1898- 19
Boyd, Candy Dawson 1946- 72
Boyd, Pauline
  See Schock, Pauline
Boyd, Selma
  See Acuff, Selma Boyd
Boyd, Waldo T. 1918- 18
Boyer, Robert E(rnst) 1929- 22
Boyle, Ann (Peters) 1916- 10
Boyle, Eleanor Vere (Gordon)
  1825-1916 28
Boyle, Robert H. 1928- 65
Boylston, Helen (Dore) 1895-1984 23
  Obituary 39
Boynton, Sandra (Keith) 1953- 57
  Brief entry 38
Boz
  See Dickens, Charles
Bracken, Charles
  See Pellowski, Michael (Joseph)
Bradbury, Bianca 1908-1982 56
  Earlier sketch in SATA 3
Bradbury, Edward P.
  See Moorcock, Michael (John)
Bradbury, Ray (Douglas) 1920- 64
  Earlier sketch in SATA 11
Bradfield, Carl 1942- 91

Bradford, Ann (Liddell) 1917- 56
  Brief entry 38
Bradford, Barbara Taylor 1933- 66
Bradford, Karleen 1936- 96
  Earlier sketch in SATA 48
Bradford, Lois J(ean) 1936- 36
Bradford, Richard (Roark) 1932- 59
Bradley, Duane
  See Sanborn, Duane
Bradley, Marion Zimmer 1930- 90
Bradley, Virginia 1912- 23
Bradley, Will
  See Strickland, (William) Brad(ley)
Bradman, Tony 1954- 81
Brady, Esther Wood 1905-1987 31
  Obituary 53
Brady, Irene 1943- 4
Brady, Lillian 1902- 28
Bragdon, Elspeth 1897- 6
Bragdon, Lillian (Jacot) 24
Bragg, Mabel Caroline 1870-1945 24
Bragg, Michael 1948- 46
Bragg, Ruth Gembicki 1943- 77
Brahm, Sumishta 1954- 58
Brainerd, John W(hiting) 1918- 65
Braithwaite, Althea 1940- 23
  See also SAAS 24
Bram, Elizabeth 1948- 30
Brancato, Robin F(idler) 1936- 23
  See also CLR 32
  See also SAAS 9
Brancato, Robin F. 1936- 97
Branch, Muriel Miller 1943- 94
Brand, Christianna
  See Lewis, Mary (Christianna)
Brandel, Marc 1919- 71
Brandenberg, Alexa (Demetria)
  1966- 97
Brandenberg, Aliki (Liacouras)
  1929- 75
  Earlier sketches in SATA 2, 35
Brandenberg, Franz 1932- 75
  Earlier sketches in SATA 8, 35
Brandenburg, Jim 1945- 87
Brandhorst, Carl T(heodore) 1898- 23
Brandis, Marianne 1938- 96
  Earlier sketch in SATA 59
Brandon, Brumsic, Jr. 1927- 9
Brandon, Curt
  See Bishop, Curtis
Brandreth, Gyles 1948- 28
Brandt, Catharine 1905- 40
Brandt, Keith
  See Sabin, Louis
Brandt, Sue R(eading) 1916- 59
Branfield, John (Charles) 1931- 11
Branley, Franklyn M(ansfield)
  1915- 68
  Earlier sketch in SATA 4
  See also CLR 13
  See also SAAS 16
Branscum, Robbie 1937-1997 72
  Obituary 96
  Earlier sketch in SATA 23
  See also SAAS 17
Bransom, (John) Paul 1885-1979 43
Bratton, Helen 1899- 4
Bratun, Katy 1950- 83
Braude, Michael 1936- 23
Brautigan, Richard (Gary)
  1935-1984 56
Braymer, Marjorie 1911- 6
Breathed, Berke
  See Breathed, (Guy) Berkeley
Breathed, (Guy) Berkeley 1957- 86
Brecht, Edith 1895-1975 6
  Obituary 25
Breck, Vivian
  See Breckenfeld, Vivian Gurney
Breckenfeld, Vivian Gurney 1895- 1
Breda, Tjalmar
  See DeJong, David C(ornel)
Bredeson, Carmen 1944- 98
Breinburg, Petronella 1927- 11
  See also CLR 31
Breisky, William J(ohn) 1928- 22

Brennan, Gale (Patrick) 1927- *64*
  Brief entry *53*
Brennan, Joseph L. 1903- *6*
Brennan, Tim
  See Conroy, John Wesley
Brenner, Anita 1905-1974 ....*56*
Brenner, Barbara (Johnes) 1925- *76*
  Earlier sketches in SATA *4, 42*
  See also SAAS *14*
Brenner, Fred 1920- *36*
  Brief entry *34*
Brent, Hope 1935(?)-1984
  Obituary *39*
Brent, Stuart *14*
Breslin, Theresa *70*
Breslow, Maurice Allen 1935- *72*
Breslow, Susan 1951- *69*
Brett, Bernard 1925- *22*
Brett, Grace N(eff) 1900-1975 ....*23*
Brett, Hawksley
  See Bell, Robert S(tanley) W(arren)
Brett, Jan (Churchill) 1949- *71*
  Earlier sketch in SATA *42*
  See also CLR *27*
Brewer, Sally King 1947- *33*
Brewster, Benjamin
  See Folsom, Franklin (Brewster)
Brewster, Hugh 1950- *95*
Brewster, Patience 1952- *97*
  Earlier sketch in SATA *51*
Brewton, John E(dmund) 1898- *5*
Brick, John 1922-1973 ....*10*
Bride, Nadja
  See Nobisso, Josephine
Bridgers, Sue Ellen 1942- *90*
  Earlier sketch in SATA *22*
  See also CLR *18*
  See also SAAS *1*
Bridges, Laurie
  See Bruck, Lorraine
Bridges, William (Andrew) 1901- *5*
Bridwell, Norman (Ray) 1928- *68*
  Earlier sketch in SATA *4*
Brier, Howard M(axwell) 1903-1969 .....*8*
Brierley, (Louise) 1958- *59*
Briggs, Carole S(uzanne) 1950-
  Brief entry *47*
Briggs, Katharine Mary 1898-1980
  Obituary *25*
Briggs, Peter 1921-1975 ....*39*
  Obituary *31*
Briggs, Raymond (Redvers) 1934- *66*
  Earlier sketch in SATA *23*
  See also CLR *10*
Bright, Robert (Douglas Sr.)
  1902-1988 ....*63*
  Obituary *60*
  Earlier sketch in SATA *24*
Bright, Sarah
  See Shine, Deborah
Brightfield, Richard 1927- *65*
  Brief entry *53*
Brightfield, Rick
  See Brightfield, Richard
Brighton, Catherine 1943- *65*
Brightwell, L(eonard) R(obert) 1889-
  Brief entry *29*
Brill, Marlene Targ 1945- *77*
Brimberg, Stanlee 1947- *9*
Brimner, Larry Dane 1949- *79*
Brin, David 1950- *65*
Brin, Ruth F(irestone) 1921- *22*
Brinckloe, Julie (Lorraine) 1950- *13*
Brindel, June (Rachuy) 1919- *7*
Brindze, Ruth 1903- *23*
Brink, Carol Ryrie 1895-1981 ....*31*
  Obituary *27*
  Earlier sketch in SATA *1*
  See also CLR *30*
Brinsmead, H(esba) F(ay) 1922- *78*
  Earlier sketch in SATA *18*
  See also CLR *47*
  See also SAAS *5*
Briquebec, John
  See Rowland-Entwistle, (Arthur)
    Theodore (Henry)

Brisco, Pat A.
  See Matthews, Patricia
Brisco, Patty
  See Matthews, Patricia
Briscoe, Jill (Pauline) 1935- *56*
  Brief entry *47*
Brisley, Joyce Lankester 1896-1978 .....*22*
  Obituary *84*
Brisson, Pat 1951- *67*
Britt, Albert 1874-1969
  Obituary *28*
Britt, Dell 1934- *1*
Brittain, Bill
  See SAAS *7*
  See Brittain, William (E.)
Brittain, C. Dale 1948- *82*
Brittain, William (E.) 1930- *76*
  Earlier sketch in SATA *36*
Brittingham, Geoffrey (Hugh)
  1959- *76*
Britton, Kate
  See Stegeman, Janet Allais
Britton, Louisa
  See McGuire, Leslie (Sarah)
Britton, Rick 1952- *82*
Bro, Margueritte (Harmon)
  1894-1977 ....*19*
  Obituary *27*
Broadhead, Helen Cross 1913- *25*
Brochmann, Elizabeth (Anne)
  1938- *41*
Brock, Betty 1923- *7*
Brock, C(harles) E(dmund)
  1870-1938 ....*42*
  Brief entry *32*
Brock, Delia
  See Ephron, Delia
Brock, Emma L(illian) 1886-1974 ....*8*
Brock, H(enry) M(atthew)
  1875-1960 ....*42*
Brockett, Eleanor Hall 1913-1967 ....*10*
Brockman, C(hristian) Frank 1902- *26*
Broderick, Dorothy M. 1929- *5*
Brodie, Sally
  See Cavin, Ruth (Brodie)
Broeger, Achim 1944- *31*
Broekel, Rainer Lothar 1923- *38*
Broekel, Ray
  See Broekel, Rainer Lothar
Brokamp, Marilyn 1920- *10*
Bromhall, Winifred *26*
Bromley, Dudley 1948-
  Brief entry *51*
Brommer, Gerald F(rederick) 1927- *28*
Brondfield, Jerome 1913- *22*
Brondfield, Jerry
  See Brondfield, Jerome
Bronowski, Jacob 1908-1974 ....*55*
Bronson, Lynn
  See Lampman, Evelyn Sibley
Bronson, Wilfrid Swancourt 1894-1985
  Obituary *43*
Brook, Judith Penelope 1926- *59*
  Brief entry *51*
Brook, Judy
  See Brook, Judith Penelope
Brooke, L(eonard) Leslie
  1862-1940 ....*17*
  See also CLR *20*
Brooke-Haven, P.
  See Wodehouse, P(elham) G(renville)
Brookins, Dana 1931- *28*
Brooks, Anita 1914- *5*
Brooks, Barbara
  See Simons, Barbara B(rooks)
Brooks, Bill 1939- *59*
Brooks, Bruce 1950- *72*
  Brief entry *53*
  See also CLR *25*
Brooks, Caryl 1924- *84*
Brooks, Charlotte K. *24*
Brooks, Gwendolyn 1917- *6*
  See also CLR *27*
Brooks, Jerome 1931- *23*
Brooks, Lester 1924- *7*
Brooks, Martha *68*
Brooks, Maurice (Graham) 1900- *45*

Brooks, Polly Schoyer 1912- *12*
Brooks, Ron(ald George) 1948- *94*
  Brief entry *33*
Brooks, Terry 1944- *60*
Brooks, Walter R(ollin) 1886-1958 ......*17*
Brooks-Hill, Helen (Mason) 1908- *59*
Brophy, Nannette 1963- *73*
Brosnan, James Patrick 1929- *14*
Brosnan, Jim
  See Brosnan, James Patrick
Brothers Hildebrandt, The
  See Hildebrandt, Tim(othy)
Broun, Emily
  See Sterne, Emma Gelders
Brow, Thea 1934- *60*
Brower, Millicent *8*
Brower, Pauline (York) 1929- *22*
Browin, Frances Williams 1898- *5*
Brown, Alexis
  See Baumann, Amy (Brown)
Brown, Anne Ensign 1937- *61*
Brown, Beverly Swerdlow *97*
Brown, Bill
  See Brown, William L(ouis)
Brown, Billye Walker
  See Cutchen, Billye Walker
Brown, Bob
  See Brown, Robert Joseph
Brown, Buck 1936- *45*
Brown, Cassie 1919-1986 ....*55*
Brown, Conrad 1922- *31*
Brown, Craig McFarland 1947- *73*
Brown, David
  See Myller, Rolf
Brown, Dee (Alexander) 1908- *5*
Brown, Drew T. III 1955- *83*
Brown, Drollene P. 1939- *53*
Brown, Eleanor Frances 1908- *3*
Brown, Elizabeth M(yers) 1915- *43*
Brown, Fern G. 1918- *34*
Brown, (Robert) Fletch 1923- *42*
Brown, Fornan 1901-1996 ....*71*
  Obituary *88*
Brown, George Earl 1883-1964 ....*11*
Brown, George Mackay 1921- *35*
Brown, Irene Bennett 1932- *3*
Brown, Irving
  See Adams, William Taylor
Brown, Ivor (John Carnegie)
  1891-1974 ....*5*
  Obituary *26*
Brown, Jane Clark 1930- *81*
Brown, Janet Mitsui *87*
Brown, Joe David 1915-1976 ....*44*
Brown, Joseph E(dward) 1929- *59*
  Brief entry *51*
Brown, Judith Gwyn 1933- *20*
Brown, Kathryn 1955- *98*
Brown, Laurene Krasny
  See Brown, Laurie Krasny
Brown, Laurie Krasny 1945- *99*
  Earlier sketch in SATA *54*
Brown, Lloyd Arnold 1907-1966 ....*36*
Brown, Marc (Tolon) 1946- *80*
  Earlier sketches in SATA *10, 53*
  See also CLR *29*
Brown, Marcia 1918- *47*
  Earlier sketch in SATA *7*
  See also CLR *12*
Brown, Margaret Wise 1910-1952
  See YABC *2*
  See also CLR *10*
Brown, Margery (Wheeler) *78*
  Earlier sketch in SATA *5*
Brown, Marion Marsh 1908- *6*
Brown, Myra Berry 1918- *6*
Brown, Palmer 1919- *36*
Brown, Pamela (Beatrice) 1924-1989 .....*5*
  Obituary *61*
Brown, Richard (Eric) 1946- *61*
Brown, Robert Joseph 1907- *14*
Brown, Rosalie (Gertrude) Moore
  1910- *9*
Brown, Roswell
  See Webb, Jean Francis (III)
Brown, Roy (Frederick) 1921-1982 ......*51*
  Obituary *39*

Brown, Sue Ellen 1954- *81*
Brown, Vinson 1912- *19*
Brown, Walter R(eed) 1929- *19*
Brown, Will
  See Ainsworth, William Harrison
Brown, William L(ouis) 1910-1964 ....*5*
Browne, Anthony (Edward Tudor)
  1946- *61*
  Brief entry *44*
  Earlier sketch in SATA 45
  See also CLR 19
Browne, Dik
  See Browne, Richard Arthur Allan
Browne, Hablot Knight 1815-1882 ....*21*
Browne, Matthew
  See Rands, William Brighty
Browne, Richard Arthur Allan
  1917-1989 ....*67*
  Brief entry *38*
Browne, Vee F(rances) 1956- *90*
Browning, Robert 1812-1889
  See YABC 1
Brownjohn, Alan 1931- *6*
Brownlee, Walter D. 1930- *62*
Brownlow, Kevin 1938- *65*
Brownridge, William R(oy) 1932- *94*
Bruce, Dorita Fairlie 1885-1970
  Obituary *27*
Bruce, (William) Harry 1934- *77*
Bruce, Mary 1927- *1*
Bruchac, Joseph III 1942- *89*
  Earlier sketch in SATA 42
  See also CLR 46
Bruck, Lorraine 1921- *55*
  Brief entry *46*
Bruemmer, Fred 1929- *47*
Bruna, Dick 1927- *76*
  Brief entry *30*
  Earlier sketch in SATA 43
  See also CLR 7
Brunhoff, Jean de 1899-1937 ....*24*
  See also CLR 4
Brunhoff, Laurent de 1925- *71*
  Earlier sketch in SATA 24
  See also CLR 4
Brunskill, Elizabeth Ann Flatt
  1966- *88*
Brush, Karen A(lexandra) 1960- *85*
Brussel-Smith, Bernard 1914- *58*
Brust, Steven K. (Zoltan) 1955- *86*
Brustlein, Daniel 1904- *40*
Brustlein, Janice Tworkov *40*
Brutschy, Jennifer 1960- *84*
Bryan, Ashley F. 1923- *72*
  Earlier sketch in SATA 31
  See also CLR 18
Bryan, Dorothy (Marie) 1896(?)-1984
  Obituary *39*
Bryant, Bernice (Morgan) 1908- *11*
Bryant, Jennifer (Fisher) 1960- *94*
Brychta, Alex 1956- *21*
Bryson, Bernarda 1905- *9*
Buba, Joy Flinsch 1904- *44*
Buchan, Bryan 1945- *36*
Buchan, John 1875-1940
  See YABC 2
Buchan, Stuart 1942-1987
  Obituary *54*
Buchanan, Debby 1952- *82*
Buchanan, Ken 1952- *82*
Buchheimer, Naomi Barnett
  See Barnett, Naomi
Buchignani, Walter 1965- *84*
Buchwald, Art(hur) 1925- *10*
Buchwald, Emilie 1935- *7*
Buck, Lewis 1925- *18*
Buck, Margaret Waring 1910- *3*
Buck, Pearl S(ydenstricker)
  1892-1973 ....*25*
  Earlier sketch in SATA 1
Buckeridge, Anthony (Malcolm)
  1912- *85*
  Earlier sketch in SATA 6
Buckholtz, Eileen (Garber) 1949- *54*
  Brief entry *47*
Buckler, Ernest 1908-1984 ....*47*

Buckley, Helen E(lizabeth) 1918- *90*
  Earlier sketch in SATA 2
Buckmaster, Henrietta *6*
Budd, Lillian 1897- *7*
Buehler, Stephanie Jona 1956- *83*
Buehr, Walter 1897-1971 ....*3*
Buergel, Paul-Hermann H. 1949- *83*
Buettner, Dan 1960- *95*
Buff, Conrad 1886-1975 ....*19*
Buff, Mary Marsh 1890-1970 ....*19*
Buffett, Jimmy 1946- *76*
Buffie, Margaret 1945- *71*
  See also CLR 39
Bugbee, Emma 1888(?)-1981
  Obituary *29*
Bulfinch, Thomas 1796-1867 ....*35*
Bull, Angela (Mary) 1936- *45*
Bull, Emma 1954- *99*
Bull, Norman John 1916- *41*
Bull, Peter (Cecil) 1912-1984
  Obituary *39*
Bulla, Clyde Robert 1914- *91*
  Earlier sketches in SATA 2, 41
  See also SAAS 6
Bullock, Kathleen (Mary) 1946- *77*
Bullock, Robert (D.) 1947- *92*
Bulpin, (Barbara) Vicki *92*
Bumstead, Kathleen (Mary)
  1918-1987 ....*53*
Bundles, A'Lelia Perry 1952- *76*
Bunin, Catherine 1967- *30*
Bunin, Sherry 1925- *30*
Bunting, A. E.
  See Bunting, Eve
Bunting, Eve 1928- *64*
  Earlier sketch in SATA 18
  See also CLR 28
Bunting, Glenn (Davison) 1957- *22*
Burack, Sylvia K. 1916- *35*
Burbank, Addison (Buswell)
  1895-1961 ....*37*
Burch, Joann J(ohansen) *75*
Burch, Robert J(oseph) 1925- *74*
  Earlier sketch in SATA 1
Burchard, Peter Duncan 1921- *74*
  Earlier sketch in SATA 5
  See also SAAS 13
Burchard, Sue 1937- *22*
Burchardt, Nellie 1921- *7*
Burdick, Eugene (Leonard)
  1918-1965 ....*22*
Burford, Eleanor
  See Hibbert, Eleanor Alice Burford
Burger, Carl 1888-1967 ....*9*
Burgess, Anne Marie
  See Gerson, Noel B(ertram)
Burgess, Barbara Hood 1926- *69*
Burgess, Em
  See Burgess, Mary Wyche
Burgess, (Frank) Gelett 1866-1951 ....*32*
  Brief entry *30*
Burgess, Mary Wyche 1916- *18*
Burgess, Melvin 1954- *96*
Burgess, Michael
  See Gerson, Noel B(ertram)
Burgess, Robert F(orrest) 1927- *4*
Burgess, Thornton Waldo
  1874-1965 ....*17*
Burgess, Trevor
  See Trevor, Elleston
Burgwyn, Mebane H. 1914- *7*
Burke, David 1927- *46*
Burke, Dianne O'Quinn 1940- *89*
Burke, John
  See O'Connor, Richard
Burkert, Nancy Ekholm 1933- *24*
  See also SAAS 14
Burke-Weiner, Kimberly 1962- *95*
Burks, Brian 1955- *95*
Burland, Brian (Berkeley) 1931- *34*
Burland, C. A.
  See Burland, Cottie A.
Burland, Cottie A. 1905- *5*
Burleigh, Robert 1936- *98*
  Earlier sketch in SATA 55
Burlingame, (William) Roger
  1889-1967 ....*2*

Burman, Alice Caddy 1896(?)-1977
  Obituary *24*
Burman, Ben Lucien 1896-1984 ....*6*
  Obituary *40*
Burn, Doris 1923- *1*
Burnett, Constance Buel 1893-1975 .....*36*
Burnett, Frances (Eliza) Hodgson 1849-
  1924
  See YABC 2
  See also CLR 24
Burney, Anton
  See Hopkins, (Hector) Kenneth
Burnford, S. D.
  See Burnford, Sheila
Burnford, Sheila 1918-1984 ....*3*
  Obituary *38*
  See also CLR 2
Burnham, Sophy 1936- *65*
Burningham, John (Mackintosh)
  1936- *59*
  Earlier sketch in SATA 16
  See also CLR 9
Burns, Diane L. 1950- *81*
  See also SAAS 24
Burns, Florence M. 1905-1988 ....*61*
Burns, Khephra 1950- *92*
Burns, Marilyn *96*
  Brief entry *33*
Burns, Olive Ann 1924-1990 ....*65*
Burns, Paul C. *5*
Burns, Raymond (Howard) 1924- *9*
Burns, Theresa 1961- *84*
Burns, William A. 1909- *5*
Burr, Dan 1951- *65*
Burr, Lonnie 1943- *47*
Burrell, R(oy) E(ric) C(harles)
  1923- *72*
Burroughs, Edgar Rice 1875-1950 ......*41*
Burroughs, Jean Mitchell 1908- *28*
Burroughs, Polly 1925- *2*
Burroway, Janet (Gay) 1936- *23*
Burstein, Chaya M(alamud) 1923- *64*
Burstein, Fred 1950- *83*
Burstein, John 1949- *54*
  Brief entry *40*
Burt, Jesse Clifton 1921-1976 ....*46*
  Obituary *20*
Burt, Olive Woolley 1894- *4*
Burton, Gennett 1945- *95*
Burton, Hester (Wood-Hill) 1913- *74*
  Earlier sketch in SATA 7
  See also CLR 1
  See also SAAS 8
Burton, Leslie
  See McGuire, Leslie (Sarah)
Burton, Marilee Robin 1950- *82*
  Earlier sketch in SATA 46
Burton, Maurice 1898- *23*
Burton, Robert (Wellesley) 1941- *22*
Burton, Virginia Lee 1909-1968 ....*2*
  See also CLR 11
Burton, William H(enry)
  1890-1964 ....*11*
Busby, Edith (?)-1964
  Obituary *29*
Buscaglia, (Felice) Leo(nardo)
  1924- *65*
Buscaglia, Leo F.
  See Buscaglia, (Felice) Leo(nardo)
Busch, Phyllis S. 1909- *30*
Bush, Anne Kelleher 1959- *97*
Bushmiller, Ernie 1905-1982
  Obituary *31*
Bushnell, Jack 1952- *86*
Busoni, Rafaello 1900-1962 ....*16*
Busselle, Rebecca 1941- *80*
Butenko, Bohdan 1931- *90*
Butler, Beverly 1932- *7*
Butler, Bill
  See Butler, William (Arthur) Vivian
Butler, Dorothy 1925- *73*
Butler, Geoff 1945- *94*
Butler, M. Christina 1934- *72*
Butler, Octavia E(stelle) 1947- *84*
Butler, Suzanne
  See Perreard, Suzanne Louise Butler

Butler, Vivian
  See Butler, William (Arthur) Vivian
Butler, William
  See Butler, William (Arthur) Vivian
Butler, William (Arthur) Vivian
  1927- 79
Butters, Dorothy Gilman 1923- 5
Butterworth, Emma Macalik 1928- 43
Butterworth, Oliver 1915-1990 1
  Obituary 66
Butterworth, W(illiam) E(dmund III)
  1929- 5
Butts, Ellen R(ubinstein) 1942- 93
Buxton, Ralph
  See Silverstein, Alvin
Byalick, Marcia 1947- 97
Byard, Carole (Marie) 1941- 57
Byars, Betsy (Cromer) 1928- 80
  Earlier sketches in SATA 4, 46
  See also CLR 16
  See also SAAS 1
Byfield, Barbara Ninde 1930- 8
Byrd, Elizabeth 1912- 34
Byrd, Robert (John) 1942- 33

C

C.3.3.
  See Wilde, Oscar (Fingal O'Flahertie
  Wills)
Cabat, Erni 1914- 74
Cable, Mary 1920- 9
Cabral, O. M.
  See Cabral, Olga
Cabral, Olga 1909- 46
Cabrera, Marcela 1966- 90
Caddy, Alice
  See Burman, Alice Caddy
Cadnum, Michael 1949- 87
Cadwallader, Sharon 1936- 7
Cady, (Walter) Harrison 1877-1970 19
Cagle, Malcolm W(infield) 1918- 32
Cahn, Rhoda 1922- 37
Cahn, William 1912-1976 37
Cain, Arthur H. 1913- 3
Cain, Christopher
  See Fleming, Thomas J(ames)
Caine, Geoffrey
  See Walker, Robert W(ayne)
Caines, Jeannette (Franklin) 1938- 78
  Brief entry 43
  See also CLR 24
Cairns, Trevor 1922- 14
Calabro, Marian 1954- 79
Caldecott, Moyra 1927- 22
Caldecott, Randolph (J.)
  1846-1886 17
  See also CLR 14
Calder, Lyn
  See Calmenson, Stephanie
Calder, Marie D(onais) 1948- 96
Caldwell, Doreen (Mary) 1942- 71
Caldwell, John C(ope) 1913- 7
Calhoun, B. B. 1961- 98
Calhoun, Mary 1926- 2
  See also CLR 42
  See Wilkins, Mary Huiskamp
Calhoun, T. B.
  See Bisson, Terry (Ballantine)
Calif, Ruth 1922- 67
Calkins, Franklin
  See Stratemeyer, Edward L.
Call, Hughie Florence 1890-1969 1
Callahan, Dorothy M. 1934- 39
  Brief entry 35
Callahan, Philip S(erna) 1923- 25
Callan, Jamie 1954- 59
Callaway, Bernice (Anne) 1923- 48
Callaway, Kathy 1943- 36
Callen, Larry
  See Callen, Lawrence Willard, Jr.
Callen, Lawrence Willard, Jr.
  1927- 19
Calley, Karin 1965- 92

Calmenson, Stephanie 1952- 84
  Brief entry 37
  Earlier sketch in SATA 51
Calvert, John
  See Leaf, (Wilbur) Munro
Calvert, Patricia 1931- 69
  Earlier sketch in SATA 45
  See also SAAS 17
Cameron, Ann 1943- 89
  Earlier sketch in SATA 27
  See also SAAS 20
Cameron, Edna M. 1905- 3
Cameron, Eleanor (Butler)
  1912-1996 25
  Obituary 93
  Earlier sketch in SATA 1
  See also CLR 1
  See also SAAS 10
Cameron, Elizabeth
  See Nowell, Elizabeth Cameron
Cameron, Elizabeth Jane
  1910-1976 32
  Obituary 30
Cameron, Ian
  See Payne, Donald Gordon
Cameron, Polly 1928- 2
Cameron, Scott 1962- 84
Camp, Charles Lewis 1893-1975
  Obituary 31
Camp, Walter (Chauncey) 1859-1925
  See YABC 1
Campbell, (Elizabeth) Andrea
  1963- 50
Campbell, Ann R. 1925- 11
Campbell, Bill 1960- 89
Campbell, Bruce
  See Epstein, Samuel
Campbell, Camilla 1905- 26
Campbell, Hope 1925- 20
Campbell, Hugh 1930- 90
Campbell, Jane
  See Edwards, Jane Campbell
Campbell, Julie
  See Tatham, Julie Campbell
Campbell, Patricia J(ean) 1930- 45
Campbell, Patty
  See Campbell, Patricia J(ean)
Campbell, Peter A. 1948- 99
Campbell, R. W.
  See Campbell, Rosemae Wells
Campbell, Robin
  See Strachan, Ian
Campbell, Rod 1945- 98
  Brief entry 44
  Earlier sketch in SATA 51
Campbell, Rosemae Wells 1909- 1
Campion, Nardi Reeder 1917- 22
Campling, Elizabeth 1948- 53
Camps, Luis 1928- 66
Candell, Victor 1903-1977
  Obituary 24
Canfield, Dorothy
  See Fisher, Dorothy Canfield
Canfield, Jane White 1897-1984 32
  Obituary 38
Canfield, Muriel
  See Kanoza, Muriel Canfield
Caniff, Milton (Arthur) 1907-1988
  Obituary 58
Cannan, Joanna (Maxwell)
  1896-1961 82
Cannon, A(nn) E(dwards) 93
Cannon, Bettie (Waddell) 1922- 59
Cannon, Cornelia (James) 1876-1969
  Brief entry 28
Cannon, Janell 1957- 78
Cannon, Marian G. 1923- 85
Cannon, Ravenna
  See Mayhar, Ardath
Canusi, Jose
  See Barker, S. Omar
Capek, Michael 1947- 96
Caplin, Alfred Gerald 1909-1979 61
  Obituary 21
Caponigro, John Paul 1965- 84
Capote, Truman 1924-1984 91

Capp, Al
  See Caplin, Alfred Gerald
Cappel, Constance 1936- 22
Capps, Benjamin (Franklin) 1922- 9
Captain, W. E. Johns
  See Johns, W(illiam) E(arl)
Captain Kangaroo
  See Keeshan, Robert J.
Capucin
  See Mazille, Capucine
Carafoli, Marci
  See Ridlon, Marci
Caraker, Mary 1929- 74
Caras, Roger A(ndrew) 1928- 12
Caraway, Caren 1939- 57
Carbone, Elisa Lynn 1954- 81
Carbonnier, Jeanne 1894-1974 3
  Obituary 34
Card, Orson Scott 1951- 83
Care, Felicity
  See Coury, Louise Andree
Carew, Jan (Rynveld) 1925- 51
  Brief entry 40
Carey, Bonnie 1941- 18
Carey, Ernestine Gilbreth 1908- 2
Carey, M. V.
  See Carey, Mary (Virginia)
Carey, Mary (Virginia) 1925- 44
  Brief entry 39
Carey, Peter 1943- 94
Carey, Valerie Scho 1949- 60
Carigiet, Alois 1902-1985 24
  Obituary 47
  See also CLR 38
Carini, Edward 1923- 9
Carkeet, David 1946- 75
Carle, Eric 1929- 65
  Earlier sketch in SATA 4
  See also CLR 10
  See also SAAS 6
Carleton, Captain L. C.
  See Ellis, Edward S(ylvester)
Carley, V(an Ness) Royal 1906-1976
  Obituary 20
Carlisle, Clark, Jr.
  See Holding, James
Carlisle, Olga A(ndreyev) 1930- 35
Carlsen, G(eorge) Robert 1917- 30
Carlsen, Ruth C(hristoffer) 2
Carlson, Bernice Wells 1910- 8
Carlson, Dale Bick 1935- 1
Carlson, Daniel 1960- 27
Carlson, Nancy L(ee) 1953- 90
  Brief entry 45
  Earlier sketch in SATA 56
Carlson, Natalie Savage 1906- 68
  Earlier sketch in SATA 2
  See also SAAS 4
Carlson, Susan Johnston 1953- 88
Carlson, Vada F. 1897- 16
Carlstrom, Nancy White 1948- 92
  Brief entry 48
  Earlier sketch in SATA 53
Carlyon, Richard 55
Carmer, Carl (Lamson) 1893-1976 37
  Obituary 30
Carmer, Elizabeth Black 1904- 24
Carmi, Giora 1944- 79
Carmichael, Carrie 40
Carmichael, Harriet
  See Carmichael, Carrie
Carol, Bill J.
  See Knott, William Cecil, Jr.
Caron, Romi
  See Caron-Kyselkova', Romana
Caron-Kyselkova' Romana 1967- 94
Caroselli, Remus F(rancis) 1916- 36
Carpelan, Bo (Gustaf Bertelsson)
  1926- 8
Carpenter, (John) Allan 1917- 81
  Earlier sketch in SATA 3
Carpenter, Angelica Shirley 1945- 71
Carpenter, Frances 1890-1972 3
  Obituary 27
Carpenter, John 1948- 58
Carpenter, Patricia (Healy Evans)
  1920- 11

Carr, Glyn
  See Styles, Frank Showell
Carr, Harriett Helen 1899- *3*
Carr, Jan 1953- *89*
Carr, M. J.
  See Carr, Jan
Carr, Mary Jane 1899-1988 ....*2*
  Obituary *55*
Carr, Philippa
  See Hibbert, Eleanor Alice Burford
Carr, Roger Vaughan 1937- *95*
Carrel, Annette Felder 1929- *90*
Carrick, Carol (Hatfield) 1935- *63*
  Earlier sketch in SATA *7*
  See also SAAS *18*
Carrick, Donald 1929-1989 ....*63*
  Earlier sketch in SATA *7*
Carrick, Malcolm 1945- *28*
Carrier, Lark 1947- *71*
  Brief entry *50*
Carrighar, Sally *24*
Carris, Joan Davenport 1938- *44*
  Brief entry *42*
Carroll, Curt
  See Bishop, Curtis
Carroll, Elizabeth
  See James, Elizabeth
Carroll, Latrobe *7*
Carroll, Laura
  See Parr, Lucy
Carroll, Lewis
  See CLR *18*
  See Dodgson, Charles Lutwidge
Carroll, Raymond 1924- *86*
  Brief entry *47*
Carruth, Hayden 1921- *47*
Carse, Robert 1902-1971 ....*5*
Carson, Captain James
  See Stratemeyer, Edward L.
Carson, John F. 1920- *1*
Carson, Rachel (Louise) 1907-1964 ....*23*
Carson, Robert
  See Somerlott, Robert
Carson, Rosalind
  See Chittenden, Margaret
Carson, S. M.
  See Gorsline, (Sally) Marie
Carter, Alden R(ichardson) 1947- *67*
  See also CLR *22*
  See also SAAS *18*
Carter, Angela (Olive) 1940-1992 ......*66*
  Obituary *70*
Carter, Avis Murton
  See Allen, Kenneth S(ydney)
Carter, Bruce
  See Hough, Richard (Alexander)
Carter, Dorothy Sharp 1921- *8*
Carter, Forrest 1927(?)-1979 ....*32*
Carter, Helene 1887-1960 ....*15*
Carter, (William) Hodding
  1907-1972 ....*2*
  Obituary *27*
Carter, James Earl, Jr. 1924- *79*
Carter, Jimmy
  See Carter, James Earl, Jr.
Carter, Katharine J(ones) 1905- *2*
Carter, Lin(wood Vrooman)
  1930-1988 ....*91*
Carter, Nick
  See Crider, (Allen) Bill(y)
Carter, Nick
  See Lynds, Dennis
  and Stratemeyer, Edward L.
Carter, Peter 1929- *57*
Carter, Phyllis Ann
  See Eberle, Irmengarde
Carter, Samuel III 1904-1988 ....*37*
  Obituary *60*
Carter, William E. 1926-1983 ....*1*
  Obituary *35*
Cartlidge, Michelle 1950- *96*
  Brief entry *37*
  Earlier sketch in SATA *49*
Cartner, William Carruthers 1910- *11*
Cartwright, Ann 1940- *78*
Cartwright, Reg(inald Ainsley)
  1938- *64*

Cartwright, Sally 1923- *9*
Carusone, Al 1949- *89*
Carver, John
  See Gardner, Richard
Carwell, L'Ann
  See McKissack, Patricia C.
Cary
  See Cary, Louis F(avreau)
Cary, Barbara Knapp 1912(?)-1975
  Obituary *31*
Cary, Louis F(avreau) 1915- *9*
Caryl, Jean
  See Kaplan, Jean Caryl Korn
Casanova, Mary 1957- *94*
Case, Marshal T(aylor) 1941- *9*
Case, Michael
  See Howard, Robert West
Caseley, Judith 1951- *87*
  Brief entry *53*
  See also SAAS *25*
Casewit, Curtis 1922- *4*
Casey, Barbara 1944- *79*
Casey, Brigid 1950- *9*
Casey, Winifred Rosen
  See Rosen, Winifred
Cash, Ellen Lewis Buell 1905-1989
  Obituary *64*
Casilla, Robert 1959- *75*
Cason, Mabel Earp 1892-1965 ....*10*
Cass, Joan E(velyn) *1*
Cass-Beggs, Barbara 1904- *62*
Cassedy, Sylvia 1930-1989 ....*77*
  Obituary *61*
  Earlier sketch in SATA *27*
  See also CLR *26*
Cassel, Lili
  See Wronker, Lili Cassel
Cassel-Wronker, Lili
  See Wronker, Lili Cassel
Casson, Hugh Maxwell 1910- *65*
Cassutt, Michael (Joseph) 1954- *78*
Castaldo, Nancy Fusco 1962- *93*
Castaneda, Omar S. 1954- *71*
Castellanos, Jane Mollie (Robinson)
  1913- *9*
Castellon, Federico 1914-1971 ....*48*
Castillo, Edmund L. 1924- *1*
Castle, Lee [Joint pseudonym]
  See Ogan, George F.
  and Ogan, Margaret E. (Nettles)
Castle, Paul
  See Howard, Vernon (Linwood)
Caswell, Brian 1954- *97*
Caswell, Helen (Rayburn) 1923- *12*
Catalano, Dominic 1956- *76*
Catalano, Grace (A.) 1961- *99*
Catalanotto, Peter 1959- *70*
  See also SAAS *25*
Cate, Dick
  See Cate, Richard (Edward Nelson)
Cate, Richard (Edward Nelson)
  1932- *28*
Cather, Willa (Sibert) 1873-1947 ......*30*
Catherall, Arthur 1906-1980 ....*74*
  Earlier sketch in SATA *3*
Cathon, Laura E(lizabeth) 1908- *27*
Catlett, Elizabeth 1919(?)- *82*
Catlin, Wynelle 1930- *13*
Catton, (Charles) Bruce 1899-1978 .....*2*
  Obituary *24*
Catz, Max
  See Glaser, Milton
Caudell, Marian 1930- *52*
Caudill, Rebecca 1899-1985 ....*1*
  Obituary *44*
Cauley, Lorinda Bryan 1951- *46*
  Brief entry *43*
Caulfield, Peggy F. 1926-1987
  Obituary *53*
Cauman, Samuel 1910-1971 ....*48*
Causley, Charles (Stanley) 1917- *66*
  Earlier sketch in SATA *3*
  See also CLR *30*
Cavallaro, Ann (Abelson) 1918- *62*
Cavallo, Diana 1931- *7*

Cavanagh, Helen (Carol) 1939- *98*
  Brief entry *37*
  Earlier sketch in SATA *48*
Cavanah, Frances 1899-1982 ....*31*
  Earlier sketch in SATA *1*
Cavanna, Betty 1909- *30*
  Earlier sketch in SATA *1*
  See also SAAS *4*
Cave, Kathryn 1948- *76*
Cavin, Ruth (Brodie) 1918- *38*
Cavoukian, Raffi 1948- *68*
Cawley, Winifred 1915- *13*
Caxton, Pisistratus
  See Lytton, Edward G(eorge) E(arle)
    L(ytton) Bulwer-Lytton Baron
Cazeau, Charles J(ay) 1931- *65*
Cazet, Denys 1938- *99*
  Brief entry *41*
  Earlier sketch in SATA *52*
Cazzola, Gus 1934- *73*
Cebulash, Mel 1937- *91*
  Earlier sketch in SATA *10*
Ceder, Georgiana Dorcas *10*
Celestino, Martha Laing 1951- *39*
CEM
  See Martin, Charles E.
Cerf, Bennett 1898-1971 ....*7*
Cerf, Christopher (Bennett) 1941- *2*
Cermak, Martin
  See Duchacek, Ivo D(uka)
Cerullo, Mary M. 1949- *86*
Cervon, Jacqueline
  See Moussard, Jacqueline
Cetin, Frank (Stanley) 1921- *2*
Chadwick, Lester [Collective
  pseudonym] *67*
  Earlier sketch in SATA *1*
Chaffee, Allen *3*
Chaffin, Lillie D(orton) 1925- *4*
Chaikin, Miriam 1928- *24*
Challand, Helen J(ean) 1921- *64*
Challans, Mary 1905-1983 ....*23*
  Obituary *36*
Chalmers, Mary 1927- *6*
  See also SAAS *14*
Chamberlain, Margaret 1954- *46*
Chambers, Aidan 1934- *69*
  Earlier sketch in SATA *1*
  See also SAAS *12*
Chambers, Bradford 1922-1984
  Obituary *39*
Chambers, Catherine E.
  See St. John, Nicole
Chambers, John W. 1933- *57*
  Brief entry *46*
Chambers, Kate
  See St. John, Nicole
Chambers, Margaret Ada Eastwood
  1911- *2*
Chambers, Peggy
  See Chambers, Margaret Ada Eastwood
Chance, Stephen
  See Turner, Philip (William)
Chance, Stephen
  See Turner, Philip (William)
Chandler, Caroline A(ugusta)
  1906-1979 ....*22*
  Obituary *24*
Chandler, David Porter 1933- *28*
Chandler, Edna Walker 1908-1982 .....*11*
  Obituary *31*
Chandler, Linda S(mith) 1929- *39*
Chandler, Robert 1953- *40*
Chandler, Ruth Forbes 1894-1978 .....*2*
  Obituary *26*
Chandonnet, Ann 1943- *92*
Chaney, Jill 1932- *87*
Chang, Cindy 1968- *90*
Chang, Margaret (Scrogin) 1941- *71*
Chang, Raymond *71*
Chanin, Michael 1952- *84*
Channel, A. R.
  See Catherall, Arthur
Chapian, Marie 1938- *29*
Chapin, Alene Olsen Dalton 1915(?)-1986
  Obituary *47*
Chapin, Tom 1945- *83*

Chapman, Allen [Collective
    pseudonym] 67
    Earlier sketch in SATA 1
Chapman, Cheryl O(rth) 1948- 80
Chapman, (Constance) Elizabeth (Mann)
    1919- 10
Chapman, Gaynor 1935- 32
Chapman, Jean 34
Chapman, John Stanton Higham 1891-
    1972
    Obituary 27
Chapman, Lee
    See Bradley, Marion Zimmer
Chapman, Lynne F(erguson) 1963- 94
Chapman, Maristan [Joint pseudonym]
    See Chapman, John Stanton Higham
Chapman, Vera 1898- 33
Chapman, Walker
    See Silverberg, Robert
Chappell, Audrey 1954- 72
Chappell, Warren 1904-1991 68
    Obituary 67
    Earlier sketch in SATA 6
    See also SAAS 10
Charbonneau, Eileen 1951- 84
Charbonnet, Gabrielle 1961- 81
Chardiet, Bernice (Kroll) 27
Charles, Donald
    See Meighan, Donald Charles
Charles, Louis
    See Stratemeyer, Edward L.
Charles, Nicholas J.
    See Kuskin, Karla
Charlip, Remy 1929- 68
    Earlier sketch in SATA 4
    See also CLR 8
Charlot, Jean 1898-1979 8
    Obituary 31
Charlot, Martin (Day) 1944- 64
Charlton, Michael (Alan) 1923- 34
Charmatz, Bill 1925- 7
Charnas, Suzy M(cKee) 1939- 61
Charosh, Mannis 1906- 5
Chartier, Normand L. 1945- 66
Chase, Alice
    See McHargue, Georgess
Chase, Alyssa 1965- 92
Chase, Andra 1942- 91
Chase, Emily
    See Aks, Patricia
    and Sachs, Judith
Chase, Mary (Coyle) 1907-1981 17
    Obituary 29
Chase, Mary Ellen 1887-1973 10
Chase, Richard 1904-1988 64
    Obituary 56
Chase, Samantha
    See Buckholtz, Eileen (Garber)
Chast, Roz 1954- 97
Chastain, Madye Lee 1908- 4
Chatterjee, Debjani 1952- 83
Chauncy, Nan 1900-1970 6
    See also CLR 6
Chaundler, Christine 1887-1972 1
    Obituary 25
Chee, Cheng-Khee 1934- 79
Chekhonte, Antosha
    See Chekhov, Anton (Pavlovich)
Chekhov, Anton (Pavlovich)
    1860-1904 90
Chen, Ju-Hong 1941- 78
Chen, Tony 1929- 6
Chen, Yuan-tsung 1932- 65
Chenault, Nell
    See Smith, Linell Nash
Chenery, Janet (Dai) 1923- 25
Cheney, Cora 1916- 3
Cheney, Glenn (Alan) 1951- 99
Cheney, Ted
    See Cheney, Theodore Albert
Cheney, Theodore Albert 1928- 11
Cheng, Judith 1955- 36
Cheripko, Jan 1951- 83
Chermayeff, Ivan 1932- 47
Chernoff, Dorothy A.
    See Ernst, (Lyman) John
Chernoff, Goldie Taub 1909- 10

Cherry, Carolyn Janice
    See Cherryh, C. J.
Cherry, Lynne 1952- 99
    Earlier sketch in SATA 34
Cherryh, C. J. 1942- 93
Cherryholmes, Anne
    See Price, Olive
Chesler, Bernice 1932- 59
Chess, Victoria (Dickerson) 1939- 92
    Earlier sketch in SATA 33
Chessare, Michele
    Brief entry 42
Chester, Deborah 1957- 85
Chesterton, G(ilbert) K(eith)
    1874-1936 27
Chetin, Helen 1922- 6
Chetwin, Grace 86
    Brief entry 50
Chevalier, Christa 1937- 35
Chew, Ruth 7
Chidsey, Donald Barr 1902-1981 3
    Obituary 27
Chiefari, Janet D. 1942- 58
Child, L. Maria
    See Child, Lydia Maria
Child, Lydia Maria 1802-1880 67
Child, Mrs.
    See Child, Lydia Maria
Child, Philip 1898-1978 47
Children's Shepherd, The
    See Westphal, Arnold Carl
Childress, Alice 1920-1994 48
    Obituary 81
    Earlier sketch in SATA 7
    See also CLR 14
Childs, (Halla) Fay (Cochrane)
    1890-1971 1
    Obituary 25
Chimaera
    See Farjeon, Eleanor
Chin, Richard (M.) 1946- 52
Chinery, Michael 1938- 26
Chipperfield, Joseph E(ugene)
    1912-1976 87
    Earlier sketch in SATA 2
Chislett, Gail (Elaine) 1948- 58
Chittenden, Elizabeth F. 1903- 9
Chittenden, Margaret 1933- 28
Chittum, Ida 1918- 7
Chmielarz, Sharon 1940- 72
Choate, Judith (Newkirk) 1940- 30
Chocolate, Debbi 1954- 96
Chocolate, Deborah M. Newton
    See Chocolate, Debbi
Choi, Sook Nyul 73
Chorao, Kay 1936- 69
    Earlier sketch in SATA 8
Chorpenning, Charlotte (Lee Barrows)
    1872-1955
    Brief entry 37
Choyce, Lesley 1951- 94
Chrisman, Arthur Bowie 1889-1953
    See YABC 1
Christelow, Eileen 1943- 90
    Brief entry 35
    Earlier sketch in SATA 38
    See also SAAS 25
Christensen, Bonnie 1951- 82
Christensen, Gardell Dano 1907- 1
Christesen, Barbara 1940- 40
Christgau, Alice Erickson 1902- 13
Christian, Mary Blount 1933- 9
Christie, Agatha (Mary Clarissa)
    1890-1976 36
Christie, Marie
    See Marie, Geraldine
Christopher, John
    See CLR 2
    See Youd, (Christopher) Samuel
Christopher, Louise
    See Hale, Arlene
Christopher, Matt(hew Frederick)
    1917-1997 80
    Obituary 99
    Earlier sketches in SATA 2, 47
    See also CLR 33
    See also SAAS 9

Christopher, Milbourne
    1914(?)-1984 46
Christy, Howard Chandler
    1873-1952 21
Chrystie, Frances N(icholson)
    1904-1986 60
Chu, Daniel 1933- 11
Chukovsky, Kornei (Ivanovich)
    1882-1969 34
    Earlier sketch in SATA 5
Church, Kristine
    See Jensen, Kristine Mary
Church, Richard 1893-1972 3
Churchill, E. Richard 1937- 11
Chute, B(eatrice) J(oy) 1913-1987 2
    Obituary 53
Chute, Marchette (Gaylord) 1909- 1
Chwast, Jacqueline 1932- 6
Chwast, Seymour 1931- 96
    Earlier sketch in SATA 18
Ciardi, John (Anthony) 1916-1986 65
    Obituary 46
    Earlier sketch in SATA 1
    See also CLR 19
    See also SAAS 26
Clair, Andree 19
Clampett, Bob
    Obituary 38
    See Clampett, Robert
Clampett, Robert 1914(?)-1984 44
Clapp, Patricia 1912- 74
    Earlier sketch in SATA 4
    See also SAAS 4
Clare, Helen
    See Hunter Blair, Pauline
Claremont, Chris(topher Simon)
    1950- 87
Clark, Ann Nolan 1896-1995 82
    Obituary 87
    Earlier sketch in SATA 4
    See also CLR 16
    See also SAAS 16
Clark, Champ 1923- 47
Clark, Clara Gillow 1951- 84
Clark, David
    See Hardcastle, Michael
Clark, David Allen
    See Ernst, (Lyman) John
Clark, Emma Chichester 1955- 69
Clark, Frank J(ames) 1922- 18
Clark, Garel [Joint pseudonym]
    See Garelick, May
Clark, Joan
    See Benson, Mildred (Augustine Wirt)
Clark, Joan 1934- 96
    Earlier sketch in SATA 59
Clark, Leonard 1905-1981 30
    Obituary 29
Clark, M. R.
    See Clark, Mavis Thorpe
Clark, Margaret Goff 1913- 82
    Earlier sketch in SATA 8
Clark, Mary Higgins 46
Clark, Mavis Thorpe 1909- 74
    Earlier sketch in SATA 8
    See also CLR 30
    See also SAAS 5
Clark, Merle
    See Gessner, Lynne
Clark, Patricia (Finrow) 1929- 11
Clark, Ronald William 1916-1987 2
    Obituary 52
Clark, Van D(eusen) 1909- 2
Clark, Virginia
    See Gray, Patricia
Clark, Walter Van Tilburg
    1909-1971 8
Clarke, Arthur C(harles) 1917- 70
    Earlier sketch in SATA 13
Clarke, Clorinda 1917- 7
Clarke, J.
    See Clarke, Judith
Clarke, Joan 1921- 42
    Brief entry 27
Clarke, John
    See Laklan, Carli
Clarke, Judith 1943- 75

Clarke, Mary Stetson 1911- 5
Clarke, Michael
  See Newlon, (Frank) Clarke
Clarke, Pauline
  See Hunter Blair, Pauline
Clarkson, E(dith) Margaret 1915- 37
Clarkson, Ewan 1929- 9
Claverie, Jean 1946- 38
Clay, Patrice 1947- 47
Claypool, Jane
  See Miner, Jane Claypool
Clayton, Elaine 1961- 94
Clayton, Lawrence (Otto, Jr.)
  1945- 75
Cleary, Beverly (Atlee Bunn) 1916- 79
  Earlier sketches in SATA *2, 43*
  See also CLR *8*
  See also SAAS *20*
Cleary, Brian P. 1959- 93
Cleaver, Bill 1920-1981 22
  Obituary 27
  See also CLR *6*
Cleaver, Carole 1934- 6
Cleaver, Elizabeth (Mrazik)
  1939-1985 23
  Obituary 43
  See also CLR *13*
Cleaver, Hylton (Reginald)
  1891-1961 49
Cleaver, Vera 1919-1992 76
  Earlier sketch in SATA *22*
  See also CLR *6*
Cleishbotham, Jebediah
  See Scott, Sir Walter
Cleland, Mabel
  See Widdemer, Mabel Cleland
Clem, Margaret H(ollingsworth)
  1923- 90
Clemens, Samuel Langhorne 1835-1910
  See YABC *2*
Clemens, Virginia Phelps 1941- 35
Clement, Rod 97
Clements, Bruce 1931- 94
  Earlier sketch in SATA *27*
Clemons, Elizabeth
  See Nowell, Elizabeth Cameron
Clerk, N. W.
  See Lewis, C(live) S(taples)
Cleveland, Bob
  See Cleveland, George
Cleveland, George 1903(?)-1985
  Obituary 43
Cleveland-Peck, Patricia 80
Cleven, Cathrine
  See Cleven, Kathryn Seward
Cleven, Kathryn Seward 2
Clevenger, William R(ussell) 1954- 84
Clevin, Joergen 1920- 7
Clewes, Dorothy (Mary) 1907- 86
  Earlier sketch in SATA *1*
Clifford, David
  See Clifford, Eth
  and Rosenberg, Ethel
Clifford, Eth 1915- 92
  See also SAAS *22*
  See Rosenberg, Ethel
Clifford, Harold B. 1893- 10
Clifford, Margaret Cort 1929- 1
Clifford, Martin
  See Hamilton, Charles (Harold St. John)
Clifford, Mary Louise (Beneway)
  1926- 23
Clifford, Peggy
  See Clifford, Margaret Cort
Clifford, Rachel Mark
  See Lewis, Brenda Ralph
Clifton, Harry
  See Hamilton, Charles (Harold St. John)
Clifton, Lucille 1936- 69
  Earlier sketch in SATA *20*
  See also CLR *5*
Clifton, Martin
  See Hamilton, Charles (Harold St. John)
Climo, Shirley 1928- 77
  Brief entry 35
  Earlier sketch in SATA *39*

Clinton, Jon
  See Prince, J(ack) H(arvey)
Clish, (Lee) Marian 1946- 43
Clive, Clifford
  See Hamilton, Charles (Harold St. John)
Clokey, Art 1921- 59
Cloudsley-Thompson, J(ohn) L(eonard)
  1921- 19
Clouse, Nancy L. 1938- 78
Clymer, Eleanor 1906- 85
  Earlier sketch in SATA *9*
  See also SAAS *17*
Clyne, Patricia Edwards 31
Coalson, Glo 1946- 94
  Earlier sketch in SATA *26*
Coates, Anna 1958- 73
Coates, Belle 1896- 2
Coates, Ruth Allison 1915- 11
Coats, Alice M(argaret) 1905- 11
Coatsworth, Elizabeth (Jane)
  1893-1986 56
  Obituary 49
  Earlier sketch in SATA *2*
  See also CLR *2*
Cobalt, Martin
  See Mayne, William (James Carter)
Cobb, Jane
  See Berry, Jane Cobb
Cobb, Mary 1931- 88
Cobb, Vicki 1938- 69
  Earlier sketch in SATA *8*
  See also CLR *2*
  See also SAAS *6*
Cobbett, Richard
  See Pluckrose, Henry (Arthur)
Cober, Alan E. 1935- 7
Cobham, Sir Alan
  See Hamilton, Charles (Harold St. John)
Cocagnac, Augustin Maurice(-Jean)
  1924- 7
Cocca-Leffler, Maryann 1958- 80
Cochran, Bobbye A. 1949- 11
Cockett, Mary 3
Coe, Anne (E.) 1949- 95
Coe, Douglas [Joint pseudonym]
  See Epstein, Beryl (M. Williams)
  and Epstein, Samuel
Coe, Lloyd 1899-1976
  Obituary 30
Coen, Rena Neumann 1925- 20
Coerr, Eleanor (Beatrice) 1922- 67
  Earlier sketch in SATA *1*
Coffin, Geoffrey
  See Mason, F. van Wyck
Coffman, Ramon Peyton 1896- 4
Coggins, Jack (Banham) 1911- 2
Cohen, Barbara 1932-1992 77
  Obituary 74
  Earlier sketch in SATA *10*
  See also SAAS *7*
Cohen, Daniel (E.) 1936- 70
  Earlier sketch in SATA *8*
  See also CLR *43*
  See also SAAS *4*
Cohen, Jene Barr
  See Barr, Jene
Cohen, Joan Lebold 1932- 4
Cohen, Judith Love 1933- 78
Cohen, Miriam 1926- 29
  See also SAAS *11*
Cohen, Nora 75
Cohen, Paul S. 1945- 58
Cohen, Peter Zachary 1931- 4
Cohen, Robert Carl 1930- 8
Cohen, Sholom 1951- 94
Cohn, Angelo 1914- 19
Coit, Margaret L(ouise) 2
Colbert, Anthony 1934- 15
Colby, C(arroll) B(urleigh)
  1904-1977 35
  Earlier sketch in SATA *3*
Colby, Jean Poindexter 1909- 23
Cole, Alison 79
Cole, Annette
  See Steiner, Barbara A(nnette)
Cole, Babette 1949- 96
  Earlier sketch in SATA *61*

Cole, Betsy 1940- 83
Cole, Brock 1938- 72
  See also CLR *18*
Cole, Davis
  See Elting, Mary
Cole, Hannah 1954- 74
Cole, Jack
  See Stewart, John (William)
Cole, Jackson
  See Schisgall, Oscar
Cole, Jennifer
  See Stevens, Serita (Deborah)
  and Zach, Cheryl (Byrd)
Cole, Joanna 1944- 81
  Brief entry 37
  Earlier sketch in SATA *49*
  See also CLR *40*
Cole, Lois Dwight 1903(?)-1979 10
  Obituary 26
Cole, Michael 1947- 59
Cole, Sheila R(otenberg) 1939- 95
  Earlier sketch in SATA *24*
Cole, William (Rossa) 1919- 71
  Earlier sketch in SATA *9*
  See also SAAS *9*
Coleman, Andrew
  See Pine, Nicholas
Coleman, Clare
  See Bell, Clare (Louise)
Coleman, Mary Ann 1928- 83
Coleman, William L(eRoy) 1938- 49
  Brief entry 34
Coles, Robert (Martin) 1929- 23
Colin, Ann
  See Ure, Jean
Collard, Sneed B. III 1959- 84
Collicott, Sharleen 1937- 98
Collier, Christopher 1930- 70
  Earlier sketch in SATA *16*
Collier, Ethel 1903- 22
Collier, James Lincoln 1928- 70
  Earlier sketch in SATA *8*
  See also CLR *3*
  See also SAAS *21*
Collier, Jane
  See Collier, Zena
Collier, Steven 1942- 61
Collier, Zena 1926- 23
Collington, Peter 1948- 99
  Earlier sketch in SATA *59*
Collins, Ace 1953- 82
Collins, Andrew J.
  See Collins, Ace
Collins, David 1940- 7
Collins, Heather 1946- 81
Collins, Hunt
  See Hunter, Evan
Collins, Michael
  See Lynds, Dennis
Collins, Michael 1930- 58
Collins, Pat Lowery 1932- 31
Collins, Ruth Philpott 1890-1975
  Obituary 30
Collinson, A. S.
  See Collinson, Alan S.
Collinson, Alan S. 1934- 80
Collodi, Carlo
  See CLR *5*
  See Lorenzini, Carlo
Colloms, Brenda 1919- 40
Colman, Hila 53
  Earlier sketch in SATA *1*
  See also SAAS *14*
Colman, Morris 1899(?)-1981
  Obituary 25
Colman, Penny (Morgan) 1944- 77
Colman, Warren (David) 1944- 67
Colombo, John Robert 1936- 50
Colonius, Lillian 1911- 3
Colorado (Capella), Antonio J(ulio)
  1903-1994 23
  Obituary 79
Colt, Martin [Joint pseudonym]
  See Epstein, Beryl (M. Williams)
  and Epstein, Samuel
Colum, Padraic 1881-1972 15
  See also CLR *36*

Columbus, Chris(topher) 1959- 97
Columella
   See Moore, Clement Clarke
Colver, Anne 1908- 7
Colvin, James
   See Moorcock, Michael (John)
Colwell, Eileen (Hilda) 1904- 2
Colwyn, Stewart
   See Pepper, Frank S.
Combs, Robert
   See Murray, John
Comfort, Jane Levington
   See Sturtzel, Jane Levington
Comfort, Mildred Houghton 1886- 3
Comins, Ethel M(ae) 11
Comins, Jeremy 1933- 28
Commager, Henry Steele 1902- 23
Compton, Patricia A. 1936- 75
Comus
   See Ballantyne, R(obert) M(ichael)
Comyns, Nantz
   See Comyns-Toohey, Nantz
Comyns-Toohey, Nantz 1956- 86
Conan Doyle, Arthur
   See Doyle, Arthur Conan
Condit, Martha Olson 1913- 28
Condon, Judith 83
Condy, Roy 1942- 96
Cone, Ferne Geller 1921- 39
Cone, Molly Lamken 1918- 28
   Earlier sketch in SATA *1*
   See also SAAS *11*
Cone, Patrick 1954- 89
Coney, Michael (Greatrex) 1932- 61
Conford, Ellen 1942- 68
   Earlier sketch in SATA *6*
   See also CLR *10*
Conger, Lesley
   See Suttles, Shirley (Smith)
Conklin, Gladys (Plemon) 1903- 2
Conklin, Paul S. 43
   Brief entry 33
Conkling, Hilda 1910- 23
Conlon-McKenna, Marita 1956- 71
Conly, Jane Leslie 1948- 80
Conly, Robert Leslie 1918(?)-1973 23
Connell, Kirk [Joint pseudonym]
   See Chapman, John Stanton Higham
Connelly, Marc(us Cook) 1890-1980
   Obituary 25
Connolly, Jerome P(atrick) 1931- 8
Connolly, Pat 1943- 74
Connolly, Peter 1935- 47
Conover, Chris 1950- 31
Conquest, Owen
   See Hamilton, Charles (Harold St. John)
Conrad, Joseph 1857-1924 27
Conrad, Pam 1947-1996 80
   Brief entry 49
   Obituary 90
   Earlier sketch in SATA *52*
   See also CLR *18*
   See also SAAS *19*
Conroy, Jack
   See Conroy, John Wesley
Conroy, John Wesley 1899-1990 19
   Obituary 65
Constant, Alberta Wilson
   1908-1981 22
   Obituary 28
Conway, Diana C(ohen) 1943- 91
Conway, Gordon
   See Hamilton, Charles (Harold St. John)
Cook, Bernadine 1924- 11
Cook, Fred J(ames) 1911- 2
Cook, Hugh (Walter Gilbert) 1956- 85
Cook, Jean Thor 1930- 94
Cook, Joel 1934- 79
Cook, Joseph J(ay) 1924- 8
Cook, Lyn
   See Waddell, Evelyn Margaret
Cook, Roy
   See Silverberg, Robert
Cooke, Ann
   See Cole, Joanna
Cooke, David Coxe 1917- 2

Cooke, Donald Ewin 1916-1985 2
   Obituary 45
Cooke, Frank E. 1920- 87
Cooke, Jean (Isobel Esther) 1929- 74
Cookson, Catherine (McMullen) 1906- 9
Coolidge, Olivia E(nsor) 1908- 26
   Earlier sketch in SATA *1*
Coombs, Charles I(ra) 1914- 43
   Earlier sketch in SATA *3*
   See also SAAS *15*
Coombs, Chick
   See Coombs, Charles I(ra)
Coombs, Patricia 1926- 51
   Earlier sketch in SATA *3*
   See also SAAS *22*
Cooney, Barbara 1917- 96
   Earlier sketches in SATA *6, 59*
   See also CLR *23*
Cooney, Caroline B. 1947- 80
   Brief entry 41
   Earlier sketch in SATA *48*
Cooney, Nancy Evans 1932- 42
Coontz, Otto 1946- 33
Cooper, Elisha 1971- 99
Cooper, Elizabeth Keyser 47
Cooper, Floyd 96
Cooper, Gordon 1932- 23
Cooper, Henry S. F., Jr.
   See Cooper, Henry Spotswood Fenimore, Jr.
Cooper, Henry Spotswood Fenimore, Jr.
   1933- 65
Cooper, Ilene 1948- 97
   Earlier sketch in SATA *66*
Cooper, James Fenimore
   1789-1851 19
Cooper, James R.
   See Stratemeyer, Edward L.
Cooper, John R. [Collective
   pseudonym] 1
Cooper, Kay 1941- 11
Cooper, Lee (Pelham) 5
Cooper, Lester (Irving) 1919-1985 32
   Obituary 43
Cooper, Lettice (Ulpha) 1897-1994 35
   Obituary 82
Cooper, M. E.
   See Davis, Maggie S.
Cooper, Melrose
   See Kroll, Virginia L(ouise)
Cooper, Michael L. 1950- 79
Cooper, Susan (Mary) 1935- 64
   Earlier sketch in SATA *4*
   See also CLR *4*
   See also SAAS *6*
Copeland, Helen 1920- 4
Copeland, Paul W. 23
Coplans, Peta 1951- 84
Copley, (Diana) Heather Pickering
   1918- 45
Coppard, A(lfred) E(dgar) 1878-1957
   See YABC *1*
Cora Lee
   See Anderson, Catherine Corley
Coralie
   See Anderson, Catherine Corley
Corbett, Grahame 43
   Brief entry 36
Corbett, Scott 1913- 42
   Earlier sketch in SATA *2*
   See also CLR *1*
   See also SAAS *2*
Corbett, W(illiam) J(esse) 1938- 50
   Brief entry 44
   See also CLR *19*
Corbin, Sabra Lee
   See Malvern, Gladys
Corbin, William
   See McGraw, William Corbin
Corby, Dan
   See Catherall, Arthur
Corcoran, Barbara 1911- 77
   Earlier sketch in SATA *3*
   See also SAAS *20*
Corcos, Lucille 1908-1973 10
Cordell, Alexander
   See Graber, (George) Alexander

Coren, Alan 1938- 32
Corey, Dorothy 23
Corfe, Thomas Howell 1928- 27
Corfe, Tom
   See Corfe, Thomas Howell
Corfield, Robin Bell 1952- 74
Corlett, William 1938- 46
   Brief entry 39
Cormack, M(argaret) Grant 1913- 11
Cormack, Maribelle B. 1902-1984 39
Cormier, Robert (Edmund) 1925- 83
   Earlier sketches in SATA *10, 45*
   See also CLR *12*
Cornelius, Carol 1942- 40
Cornell, J.
   See Cornell, Jeffrey
Cornell, James (Clayton, Jr.) 1938- 27
Cornell, Jean Gay 1920- 23
Cornell, Jeffrey 1945- 11
Cornish, Samuel James 1935- 23
Cornwall, Nellie
   See Sloggett, Nellie
Correy, Lee
   See Stine, G(eorge) Harry
Corrick, James A. 1945- 76
Corrigan, (Helen) Adeline 1909- 23
Corrigan, Barbara 1922- 8
Corrin, Sara 1918- 86
   Brief entry 48
Corrin, Stephen 86
   Brief entry 48
Cort, M. C.
   See Clifford, Margaret Cort
Corwin, Judith Hoffman 1946- 10
Cory, Rowena
   See Lindquist, Rowena Cory
Cosby, Bill
   See Cosby, William Henry, Jr.
Cosby, William Henry, Jr. 1937- 66
Cosgrave, John O'Hara II 1908-1968
   Obituary 21
Cosgrove, Margaret (Leota) 1926- 47
Cosgrove, Stephen E(dward) 1945- 53
   Brief entry 40
Coskey, Evelyn 1932- 7
Cosner, Shaaron 1940- 43
Cossi, Olga 67
Costabel, Eva Deutsch 1924- 45
Costello, David F(rancis) 1904- 23
Cott, Jonathan 1942- 23
Cottam, Clarence 1899-1974 25
Cottler, Joseph 1899- 22
Cottonwood, Joe 1947- 92
Cottrell, Leonard 1913-1974 24
Cottringer, Anne 1952- 97
Counsel, June 1926- 70
Courlander, Harold 1908-1996 6
   Obituary 88
Courtis, Stuart Appleton 1874-1969
   Obituary 29
Coury, Louise Andree 1895(?)-1983
   Obituary 34
Cousins, Linda 1946- 90
Cousins, Margaret 1905-1996 2
   Obituary 92
Cousteau, Jacques-Yves 1910-1997 38
   Obituary 98
Couture, Christin 1951- 73
Coville, Bruce 1950- 77
   Earlier sketch in SATA *32*
Cowen, Eve
   See Werner, Herma
Cowen, Ida 1898- 64
Cowie, Leonard W(allace) 1919- 4
Cowles, Kathleen
   See Krull, Kathleen
Cowley, (Cassia) Joy 1936- 90
   Earlier sketch in SATA *4*
   See also SAAS *26*
Cox, (Christopher) Barry 1931- 62
Cox, Clinton 74
Cox, David (Dundas) 1933- 56
Cox, Donald William 1921- 23
Cox, Jack
   See Cox, John Roberts
Cox, John Roberts 1915- 9

Cox, Palmer 1840-1924 24
  See also CLR 24
Cox, Vic 1942- 88
Cox, Victoria
  See Garretson, Victoria Diane
Cox, Wally 1924-1973 25
Cox, William R(obert) 1901-1988 46
  Brief entry 31
  Obituary 57
Coxe, Molly 1959- 69
Coxon, Michele 1950- 76
Coy, Harold 1902- 3
Crabtree, Judith 1928- 98
  Earlier sketch in SATA 63
Craft, K. Y.
  See Craft, Kinuko Y(amabe)
Craft, Kinuko
  See Craft, Kinuko Y(amabe)
Craft, Kinuko Y(amabe) 1940- 65
Craft, Ruth 87
  Brief entry 31
Craig, A. A.
  See Anderson, Poul (William)
Craig, Alisa
  See MacLeod, Charlotte (Matilda
  Hughes)
Craig, Helen 1934- 94
  Brief entry 46
  Earlier sketch in SATA 49
Craig, John Eland
  See Chipperfield, Joseph E(ugene)
Craig, John Ernest 1921- 23
Craig, M. F.
  See Craig, Mary (Francis) Shura
Craig, M. Jean 17
Craig, M. S.
  See Craig, Mary (Francis) Shura
Craig, Margaret Maze 1911-1964 9
Craig, Mary
  See Craig, Mary (Francis) Shura
Craig, Mary S.
  See Craig, Mary (Francis) Shura
Craig, Mary (Francis) Shura
  1923-1991 86
  Obituary 65
  Earlier sketch in SATA 6
  See also SAAS 7
Craig, Ruth 1922- 95
Craik, Dinah Maria (Mulock)
  1826-1887 34
Crane, Barbara J. 1934- 31
Crane, Caroline 1930- 11
Crane, M. A.
  See Wartski, Maureen (Ann Crane)
Crane, Roy
  See Crane, Royston Campbell
Crane, Royston Campbell 1901-1977
  Obituary 22
Crane, Stephen (Townley) 1871-1900
  See YABC 2
Crane, Walter 1845-1915 18
Crane, William D(wight) 1892- 1
Cranfield, Ingrid 1945- 74
Crary, Elizabeth (Ann) 1942- 99
  Brief entry 43
Crary, Margaret (Coleman) 1906- 9
Cravath, Lynne W. 1951- 98
Craven, Thomas 1889-1969 22
Crawford, Charles P. 1945- 28
Crawford, Deborah 1922- 6
Crawford, John E. 1904-1971 3
Crawford, Mel 1925- 44
  Brief entry 33
Crawford, Phyllis 1899- 3
Crayder, Dorothy 1906- 7
Crayder, Teresa
  See Colman, Hila
Crayon, Geoffrey
  See Irving, Washington
Craz, Albert G. 1926- 24
Crebbin, June 1938- 80
Crecy, Jeanne
  See Williams, Jeanne
Credle, Ellis 1902- 1
Creech, Sharon 1945- 94
  See also CLR 42
Creeden, Sharon 1938- 91

Creighton, (Mary) Helen 1899-1989
  Obituary 64
Creighton, Jill 1949- 96
Crenson, Victoria 1952- 88
Crespo, George 1962- 82
Cresswell, Helen 1934- 79
  Earlier sketches in SATA 1, 48
  See also CLR 18
  See also SAAS 20
Cretan, Gladys (Yessayan) 1921- 2
Crew, Gary 1947- 75
  See also CLR 42
Crew, Helen (Cecilia) Coale 1866-1941
  See YABC 2
Crew, Linda 1951- 71
Crews, Donald 1938- 76
  Brief entry 30
  Earlier sketch in SATA 32
  See also CLR 7
Crews, Nina 1963- 97
Crichton, (John) Michael 1942- 88
  Earlier sketch in SATA 9
Crider, (Allen) Bill(y) 1941- 99
Crisman, Ruth 1914- 73
Crispin, A(nn) C(arol) 1950- 86
Cristall, Barbara 79
Crofford, Emily 1927- 61
Crofut, Bill
  See Crofut, William E. III
Crofut, William E. III 1934- 23
Croll, Carolyn 1945- 56
  Brief entry 52
Croman, Dorothy Young
  See Rosenberg, Dorothy
Cromie, Alice Hamilton 1914- 24
Cromie, William J(oseph) 1930- 4
Crompton, Anne Eliot 1930- 73
  Earlier sketch in SATA 23
Crompton, Richmal
  See Lamburn, Richmal Crompton
Cronbach, Abraham 1882-1965 11
Crone, Ruth 1919- 4
Cronin, A(rchibald) J(oseph)
  1896-1981 47
  Obituary 25
Crook, Beverly Courtney 38
  Brief entry 35
Crook, Connie Brummel
  See Crook, Constance
Crook, Constance 98
Cros, Earl
  See Rose, Carl
Crosby, Alexander L. 1906-1980 2
  Obituary 23
Crosher, G(eoffry) R(obins) 1911- 14
Cross, Gilbert B. 1939- 60
  Brief entry 51
Cross, Gillian (Clare) 1945- 71
  Earlier sketch in SATA 38
  See also CLR 28
Cross, Helen Reeder
  See Broadhead, Helen Cross
Cross, Peter 1951- 95
Cross, Verda 1914- 75
Cross, Wilbur Lucius III 1918- 2
Crossland, Caroline 1964- 83
Crossley-Holland, Kevin (John William)
  1941- 74
  Earlier sketch in SATA 5
  See also CLR 47
  See also SAAS 20
Crouch, Marcus 1913- 4
Crout, George C(lement) 1917- 11
Crow, Donna Fletcher 1941- 40
Crowe, Bettina Lum 1911- 6
Crowe, John
  See Lynds, Dennis
Crowell, Grace Noll 1877-1969 34
Crowell, Pers 1910- 2
Crowell, Robert L(eland) 1909- 63
Crowfield, Christopher
  See Stowe, Harriet (Elizabeth) Beecher
Crowley, Arthur M(cBlair) 1945- 38
Crowley, John 1942- 65
Crownfield, Gertrude 1867-1945
  See YABC 1
Crowther, James Gerald 1899- 14

Cruikshank, George 1792-1878 22
Crump, Fred H., Jr. 1931- 76
  Earlier sketch in SATA 11
Crump, J(ames) Irving 1887-1979 57
  Obituary 21
Crunden, Reginald
  See Cleaver, Hylton (Reginald)
Crutcher, Chris(topher C.) 1946- 99
  Earlier sketch in SATA 52
  See also CLR 28
Cruz, Ray 1933- 6
Cruz Martinez, Alejandro (?)-1987 74
Ctvrtek, Vaclav 1911-1976
  Obituary 27
Cuffari, Richard 1925-1978 66
  Obituary 25
  Earlier sketch in SATA 6
Cullen, Countee 1903-1946 18
Culliford, Pierre 1928-1992 40
  Obituary 74
Culp, Louanna McNary 1901-1965 2
Cumbaa, Stephen 1947- 72
Cumming, Primrose (Amy) 1915- 24
Cumming, Robert 1945- 65
Cummings, Betty Sue 1918- 15
  See also SAAS 9
Cummings, Parke 1902-1987 2
  Obituary 53
Cummings, Pat (Marie) 1950- 71
  Earlier sketch in SATA 42
  See also CLR 48
  See also SAAS 13
Cummings, Phil 1957- 74
Cummings, Richard
  See Gardner, Richard
Cummins, Maria Susanna 1827-1866
  See YABC 1
Cuneo, Mary Louise 1924- 85
Cunliffe, John Arthur 1933- 86
  Earlier sketch in SATA 11
Cunliffe, Marcus (Falkner)
  1922-1990 37
  Obituary 66
Cunningham, Captain Frank
  See Glick, Carl (Cannon)
Cunningham, Cathy
  See Cunningham, Chet
Cunningham, Chet 1928- 23
Cunningham, Dale S(peers) 1932- 11
Cunningham, Dru 91
Cunningham, E.V.
  See Fast, Howard
Cunningham, Julia W(oolfolk)
  1916- 26
  Earlier sketch in SATA 1
  See also SAAS 2
Cunningham, Virginia
  See Holmgren, Virginia C(unningham)
Curiae, Amicus
  See Fuller, Edmund (Maybank)
Curie, Eve 1904- 1
Curlee, Lynn 1947- 98
Curley, Daniel 1918-1988 23
  Obituary 61
Currie, Stephen 1960- 82
Curry, Ann (Gabrielle) 1934- 72
Curry, Jane L(ouise) 1932- 90
  Earlier sketches in SATA 1, 52
  See also CLR 31
  See also SAAS 6
Curry, Peggy Simson 1911-1987 8
  Obituary 50
Curtis, Bruce (Richard) 1944- 30
Curtis, Chara M(ahar) 1950- 78
Curtis, Christopher Paul 1954(?)- 93
Curtis, Jamie Lee 1958- 95
Curtis, Patricia 1921- 23
Curtis, Peter
  See Lofts, Norah (Robinson)
Curtis, Philip (Delacourt) 1920- 62
Curtis, Richard (Alan) 1937- 29
Curtis, Wade
  See Pournelle, Jerry (Eugene)
Curtiss, A(rlene) B. 1934- 90
Cusack, Margaret 1945- 58
Cushman, Doug 1953- 65
Cushman, Jerome 2

Cushman, Karen 1941- *89*
Cusick, Richie Tankersley 1952- *67*
Cutchen, Billye Walker 1930- *15*
Cutchins, Judy 1947- *59*
Cutler, Daniel S(olomon) 1951- *78*
Cutler, (May) Ebbitt 1923- *9*
Cutler, Ivor 1923- *24*
Cutler, Jane 1936- *75*
Cutler, Samuel
  See Folsom, Franklin (Brewster)
Cutt, W(illiam) Towrie 1898-1981 ....*16*
  Obituary *85*
Cuyler, Margery (Stuyvesant) 1948- *99*
  Earlier sketch in SATA *39*
Cuyler, Stephen
  See Bates, Barbara S(nedeker)

D

Dabcovich, Lydia *99*
  Brief entry *47*
  Earlier sketch in SATA *58*
Dace, Dolores B(oelens) 1929- *89*
Dadey, Debbie 1959- *73*
Dahl, Borghild 1890-1984 ....*7*
  Obituary *37*
Dahl, Roald 1916-1990 ....*73*
  Obituary *65*
  Earlier sketches in SATA *1, 26*
  See also CLR *41*
Dahlstedt, Marden 1921- *8*
Dain, Martin J. 1924- *35*
Dakos, Kalli 1950- *80*
Dale, George E.
  See Asimov, Isaac
Dale, Jack
  See Holliday, Joseph
Dale, Margaret J(essy) Miller
  1911- *39*
Dale, Norman
  See Denny, Norman (George)
Dale, Penny 1954- *70*
Dalgliesh, Alice 1893-1979 ....*17*
  Obituary *21*
Dallas, Ruth
  See Mumford, Ruth
Dalmas, John
  See Jones, John R(obert)
Dalton, Alene
  See Chapin, Alene Olsen Dalton
Dalton, Anne 1948- *40*
Dalton, Sean
  See Chester, Deborah
Daly, Jim
  See Stratemeyer, Edward L.
Daly, Kathleen N(orah)
  Brief entry *37*
Daly, Maureen *2*
  See also SAAS *1*
Daly, Nicholas 1946- *76*
  Earlier sketch in SATA *37*
  See also CLR *41*
  See also SAAS *21*
Daly, Niki
  See Daly, Nicholas
D'Amato, Alex 1919- *20*
D'Amato, Janet 1925- *9*
Damerow, Gail (Jane) 1944- *83*
Damrell, Liz 1956- *77*
Damrosch, Helen Therese
  See Tee-Van, Helen Damrosch
Dana, Barbara 1940- *22*
Dana, Richard Henry, Jr.
  1815-1882 ....*26*
Danachair, Caoimhin O.
  See Danaher, Kevin
Danaher, Kevin 1913- *22*
Danakas, John 1963- *94*
D'Andrea, Kate
  See Steiner, Barbara A(nnette)
Dangerfield, Balfour
  See McCloskey, (John) Robert
Daniel, Alan 1939- *76*
  Brief entry *53*
Daniel, Anita 1893(?)-1978 ....*23*
  Obituary *24*

Daniel, Anne
  See Steiner, Barbara A(nnette)
Daniel, Becky 1947- *56*
Daniel, Colin
  See Windsor, Patricia
Daniel, Hawthorne 1890- *8*
Daniel, (Donna) Lea 1944- *76*
Daniel, Rebecca
  See Daniel, Becky
Daniels, Guy 1919-1989 ....*11*
  Obituary *62*
Daniels, Patricia 1955- *93*
Daniels, Zoe
  See Laux, Constance
Dank, Gloria Rand 1955- *56*
  Brief entry *46*
Dank, Leonard D(ewey) 1929- *44*
Dank, Milton 1920- *31*
Dann, Max 1955- *62*
Danziger, Paula 1944- *63*
  Brief entry *30*
  Earlier sketch in SATA *36*
  See also CLR *20*
Darby, J. N.
  See Govan, Christine Noble
Darby, Jean 1921- *68*
Darby, Patricia (Paulsen) *14*
Darby, Ray K. 1912- *7*
d'Arcy, Willard
  See Cox, William R(obert)
Darian, Shea 1959- *97*
Daringer, Helen Fern 1892- *1*
Darke, Marjorie Sheila 1929- *87*
  Earlier sketch in SATA *16*
Darley, F(elix) O(ctavius) C(arr)
  1822-1888 ....*35*
Darling, David J. 1953- *60*
  Brief entry *44*
Darling, Kathy
  See Darling, Mary Kathleen
Darling, Lois MacIntyre 1917-1989 ....*3*
  Obituary *64*
Darling, Louis, Jr. 1916-1970 ....*3*
  Obituary *23*
Darling, Mary Kathleen 1943- *79*
  Earlier sketch in SATA *9*
Darling, Sandra
  See Day, Alexandra
Darroll, Sally
  See Odgers, Sally Farrell
Darrow, Whitney, Jr. 1909- *13*
Darwin, Len
  See Darwin, Leonard
Darwin, Leonard 1916- *24*
Dasent, George Webbe 1817-1896 ....*62*
  Brief entry *29*
Daskam, Josephine Dodge
  See Bacon, Josephine Dodge (Daskam)
Dauer, Rosamond 1934- *23*
Daugherty, Charles Michael 1914- *16*
Daugherty, James (Henry)
  1889-1974 ....*13*
Daugherty, Richard D(eo) 1922- *35*
Daugherty, Sonia Medwedeff (?)-1971
  Obituary *27*
d'Aulaire, Edgar Parin 1898-1986 ....*66*
  Obituary *47*
  Earlier sketch in SATA *5*
  See also CLR *21*
d'Aulaire, Ingri (Mortenson Parin)
  1904-1980 ....*66*
  Obituary *24*
  Earlier sketch in SATA *5*
  See also CLR *21*
Daveluy, Paule Cloutier 1919- *11*
Davenport, Spencer
  See Stratemeyer, Edward L.
Daves, Michael 1938- *40*
David, Jonathan
  See Ames, Lee J.
Davidson, Alice Joyce 1932- *54*
  Brief entry *45*
Davidson, Basil 1914- *13*
Davidson, (Marie) Diane 1924- *91*
Davidson, Jessica 1915- *5*
Davidson, Judith 1953- *40*
Davidson, Lionel 1922- *87*

Davidson, Margaret 1936- *5*
Davidson, Marion
  See Garis, Howard R(oger)
Davidson, Mary R. 1885-1973 ....*9*
Davidson, Mary S. 1940- *61*
Davidson, Nicole
  See Jensen, Kathryn
Davidson, R.
  See Davidson, Raymond
Davidson, Raymond 1926- *32*
Davidson, Rosalie 1921- *23*
Davie, Helen K(ay) 1952- *77*
Davies, Andrew (Wynford) 1936- *27*
Davies, Bettilu D(onna) 1942- *33*
Davies, (Edward) Hunter 1936- *55*
  Brief entry *45*
Davies, Joan 1934- *50*
  Brief entry *47*
Davies, Nicola 1958- *99*
Davies, Peter 1937- *52*
Davies, Sumiko 1942- *46*
Davis, Barbara Steincrohn
  See Davis, Maggie S.
Davis, Bette J. 1923- *15*
Davis, Burke 1913- *4*
Davis, Christopher 1928- *6*
Davis, D(elbert) Dwight 1908-1965 ......*33*
Davis, Daniel S(heldon) 1936- *12*
Davis, Donald 1944- *93*
Davis, Emma
  See Davis, Maggie S.
Davis, Gibbs 1953- *46*
  Brief entry *41*
Davis, Grania 1943- *88*
  Brief entry *50*
Davis, Hubert J(ackson) 1904- *31*
Davis, James Robert 1945- *32*
Davis, Jenny 1953- *74*
Davis, Jim
  See Davis, James Robert
Davis, Julia 1900-1993 ....*6*
  Obituary *75*
Davis, Leslie
  See Guccione, Leslie Davis
Davis, Louise Littleton 1921- *25*
Davis, Maggie S. 1943- *57*
Davis, Marguerite 1889- *34*
Davis, Mary L(ee) 1935- *9*
Davis, Mary Octavia 1901- *6*
Davis, Nelle 1958- *73*
Davis, Ossie 1917- *81*
Davis, Paxton 1925- *16*
Davis, Robert 1881-1949
  See YABC *1*
Davis, Robin W(orks) 1962- *87*
Davis, Russell G. 1922- *3*
Davis, Tim(othy N.) 1957- *94*
Davis, Verne T. 1889-1973 ....*6*
Davol, Marguerite W. 1928- *82*
DaVolls, Andy (P.) 1967- *85*
DaVolls, Linda 1966- *85*
Dawson, Elmer A. [Collective
  pseudonym] *67*
  Earlier sketch in SATA *1*
Dawson, Imogen (Zoe) 1948- *90*
Dawson, Mary 1919- *11*
Day, A(rthur) Grove 1904- *59*
Day, Alexandra 1941- *97*
  Earlier sketch in SATA *67*
  See also CLR *22*
  See also SAAS *19*
Day, Beth (Feagles) 1924- *33*
Day, Edward C. 1932- *72*
Day, Jon 1936(?)- *79*
Day, Maurice 1892-
  Brief entry *30*
Day, Nancy Raines 1951- *93*
Day, Shirley 1962- *94*
Day, Thomas 1748-1789
  See YABC *1*
Dazey, Agnes J(ohnston) *2*
Dazey, Frank M. *2*
Deacon, Eileen
  See Geipel, Eileen
Deacon, Richard
  See McCormick, (George) Donald (King)

Deadman, Ronald 1919-1988(?)
 Obituary *56*
Dean, Anabel 1915- *12*
Dean, Elinor
 See McCann, Helen
Dean, Karen Strickler 1923- *49*
de Angeli, Marguerite 1889-1987 ......*27*
 Obituary *51*
 Earlier sketch in SATA *1*
 See also CLR *1*
Deans, Sis Boulos 1955- *78*
DeArmand, Frances Ullmann
 1904(?)-1984 ....*10*
 Obituary *38*
DeArmond, Dale 1914- *70*
DeArmond, Dale Burlison
 See DeArmond, Dale
Deary, Terry 1946- *51*
 Brief entry *41*
Deaver, Julie Reece 1953- *68*
deBanke, Cecile 1889-1965 ....*11*
De Bello, Rosario 1923- *89*
de Bono, Edward 1933- *66*
De Bruyn, Monica 1952- *13*
DeBry, Roger K. 1942- *91*
de Camp, Catherine Crook 1907- *83*
 Earlier sketch in SATA *12*
de Camp, L(yon) Sprague 1907- *83*
 Earlier sketch in SATA *9*
Dechausay, Sonia E. *94*
Decker, Duane 1910-1964 ....*5*
DeClements, Barthe 1920- *71*
 Earlier sketch in SATA *35*
 See also CLR *23*
Dee, Ruby 1923(?)- *77*
Deedy, John 1923- *24*
Deegan, Paul Joseph 1937- *48*
 Brief entry *38*
Deem, James M(organ) 1950- *75*
DeFelice, Cynthia 1951- *79*
Defoe, Daniel 1660(?)-1731 ....*22*
deFrance, Anthony
 See Di Franco, Anthony (Mario)
Degen, Bruce 1945- *97*
 Brief entry *47*
 Earlier sketch in SATA *57*
DeGering, Etta 1898- *7*
De Grazia
 See De Grazia, Ted
De Grazia, Ettore
 See De Grazia, Ted
De Grazia, Ted 1909-1982 ....*39*
de Groat, Diane 1947- *90*
 Earlier sketch in SATA *31*
deGros, J. H.
 See Villiard, Paul
de Grummond, Lena Young *62*
 Earlier sketch in SATA *1*
de Hamel, Joan Littledale 1924- *86*
De Haven, Tom 1949- *72*
Deiss, Joseph J. 1915- *12*
DeJong, David C(ornel) 1905-1967 ...*10*
de Jong, Dola *7*
DeJong, Meindert 1906-1991 ....*2*
 Obituary *68*
 See also CLR *1*
DeJonge, Joanne E. 1943- *56*
Deka, Connie
 See Laux, Constance
de Kay, Ormonde, Jr. 1923- *7*
de Kiriline, Louise
 See Lawrence, Louise de Kiriline
Dekker, Carl
 See Lynds, Dennis
Dekker, Carl
 See Laffin, John (Alfred Charles)
deKruif, Paul (Henry) 1890-1971 ......*50*
 Earlier sketch in SATA *5*
Delacre, Lulu 1957- *36*
DeLaCroix, Alice 1940- *75*
De Lage, Ida 1918- *11*
de la Mare, Walter 1873-1956 ....*16*
 See also CLR *23*
Delaney, Harry 1932- *3*
Delaney, Michael 1955- *96*
Delaney, Ned 1951- *28*
Delano, Hugh 1933- *20*

Delany, Samuel R(ay), (Jr.) 1942- *92*
De La Ramee, (Marie) Louise
 1839-1908 ....*20*
De La Roche, Mazo 1879-1961 ....*64*
De La Roche Saint Andre, Anne
 1950- *75*
Delaune, Lynne *7*
DeLaurentis, Louise Budde 1920- *12*
del Barco, Lucy Salamanca -1989
 Obituary *64*
Delderfield, Eric R(aymond) 1909- *14*
Delderfield, R(onald) F(rederick)
 1912-1972 ....*20*
De Leeuw, Adele Louise
 1899-1988 ....*30*
 Obituary *56*
 Earlier sketch in SATA *1*
De Leon, Nephtali 1945- *97*
Delessert, Etienne 1941- *46*
 Brief entry *27*
Delmar, Roy
 See Wexler, Jerome (LeRoy)
Deloria, Vine (Victor), Jr. 1933- *21*
del Rey, Lester 1915-1993 ....*22*
 Obituary *76*
Delton, Judy 1931- *77*
 Earlier sketch in SATA *14*
 See also SAAS *9*
Delulio, John 1938- *15*
Delving, Michael
 See Williams, Jay
Demarest, Chris(topher) L(ynn)
 1951- *82*
 Brief entry *44*
 Earlier sketch in SATA *45*
Demarest, Doug
 See Barker, Will
Demas, Vida 1927- *9*
De Mejo, Oscar 1911- *40*
de Messieres, Nicole 1930- *39*
Demi
 See Hitz, Demi
Demijohn, Thom
 See Disch, Thomas M(ichael)
Deming, Richard 1915- *24*
Demuth, Patricia Brennan 1948- *84*
 Brief entry *51*
Dengler, Sandy 1939- *54*
 Brief entry *40*
Denmark, Harrison
 See Zelazny, Roger
Dennard, Deborah 1953- *78*
Denney, Diana 1910- *25*
Dennis, Morgan 1891(?)-1960 ....*18*
Dennis, Wesley 1903-1966 ....*18*
Denniston, Elinore 1900-1978
 Obituary *24*
Denny, Norman (George)
 1901-1982 ....*43*
Denslow, Sharon Phillips 1947- *68*
Denslow, W(illiam) W(allace)
 1856-1915 ....*16*
 See also CLR *15*
Denton, Kady MacDonald *66*
Denzel, Justin F(rancis) 1917- *46*
 Brief entry *38*
Denzer, Ann Wiseman
 See Wiseman, Ann (Sayre)
de Paola, Thomas Anthony 1934- *59*
 Earlier sketch in SATA *11*
 See also CLR *24*
 See also SAAS *15*
de Paola, Tomie
 See CLR *4*
 See de Paola, Thomas Anthony
deParrie, Paul 1949- *74*
DePauw, Linda Grant 1940- *24*
DeRan, David 1946- *76*
Derby, Sally 1934- *89*
de Regniers, Beatrice Schenk (Freedman)
 1914- *68*
 Earlier sketch in SATA *2*
 See also SAAS *6*
Dereske, Jo 1947- *72*
Derleth, August (William)
 1909-1971 ....*5*
Derman, Martha (Winn) *74*

Derman, Sarah Audrey 1915- *11*
de Roo, Anne Louise 1931- *84*
 Earlier sketch in SATA *25*
deRosa, Dee *70*
De Roussan, Jacques 1929-
 Brief entry *31*
Derry Down Derry
 See Lear, Edward
Derwent, Lavinia *14*
Desai, Anita 1937- *63*
Desbarats, Peter 1933- *39*
De Selincourt, Aubrey 1894-1962 ......*14*
Deshpande, Chris 1950- *69*
Desimini, Lisa 1964- *86*
Desjarlais, John 1953- *71*
Desmond, Adrian J(ohn) 1947- *51*
Desmond, Alice Curtis 1897- *8*
DeSpain, Pleasant 1943- *87*
Desputeaux, Helene 1959- *95*
Detine, Padre
 See Olsen, Ib Spang
Detwiler, Susan Dill 1956- *58*
Deuker, Carl 1950- *82*
Deutsch, Babette 1895-1982 ....*1*
 Obituary *33*
Deutsch, Helen 1906-1992 ....*76*
De Valera, Sinead 1870(?)-1975
 Obituary *30*
Devaney, John 1926- *12*
de Varona, Frank J. 1943- *83*
Devereux, Frederick L(eonard), Jr.
 1914- *9*
deVinck, Christopher 1951- *85*
DeVito, Cara 1956- *80*
Devlin, Harry 1918- *74*
 Earlier sketch in SATA *11*
Devlin, (Dorothy) Wende 1918- *74*
 Earlier sketch in SATA *11*
Devon, Paddie 1953- *92*
Devons, Sonia 1974- *72*
DeWaard, E. John 1935- *7*
Dewdney, Selwyn (Hanington)
 1909-1979 ....*64*
DeWeese, Gene
 See DeWeese, Thomas Eugene
DeWeese, Jean
 See DeWeese, Thomas Eugene
DeWeese, Thomas Eugene 1934- *46*
 Brief entry *45*
Dewey, Ariane 1937- *7*
Dewey, Jennifer (Owings) 1941- *58*
 Brief entry *48*
Dewey, Ken(neth Francis) 1940- *39*
DeWit, Dorothy (May Knowles)
 1916-1980 ....*39*
 Obituary *28*
Dexter, John
 See Bradley, Marion Zimmer
Deyneka, Anita 1943- *24*
Deyrup, Astrith Johnson 1923- *24*
Dhondy, Farrukh 1944- *65*
 See also CLR *41*
Diamond, Arthur 1957- *76*
Diamond, Donna 1950- *69*
 Brief entry *30*
 Earlier sketch in SATA *35*
Diamond, Petra
 See Sachs, Judith
Diamond, Rebecca
 See Sachs, Judith
Dias, Earl Joseph 1916- *41*
Dias, Ron 1937- *71*
Diaz, David 1958- *96*
Di Certo, Joseph J(ohn) 1933- *60*
Dick, Cappy
 See Cleveland, George
Dick, Trella Lamson 1889-1974 ....*9*
Dickens, Charles 1812-1870 ....*15*
Dickens, Frank
 See Huline-Dickens, Frank William
Dickens, Monica (Enid) 1915-1992 ....*4*
 Obituary *74*
Dickerson, Roy Ernest 1886-1965
 Obituary *26*
Dickinson, Emily (Elizabeth)
 1830-1886 ....*29*

Dickinson, Mary 1949- 48
  Brief entry 41
Dickinson, Peter (Malcolm) 1927- 95
  Earlier sketches in SATA 5, 62
  See also CLR 29
Dickinson, Susan 1931- 8
Dickinson, William Croft
  1897-1973 13
Dickmeyer, Lowell A. 1939-
  Brief entry 51
Dickson, Gordon R(upert) 1923- 77
Dickson, Helen
  See Reynolds, Helen Mary Greenwood
  Campbell
Dickson, Naida 1916- 8
Diehn, Gwen 1943- 80
Dieterich, Michele M. 1962- 78
Dietz, David H(enry) 1897-1984 10
  Obituary 41
Dietz, Lew 1907-1997 11
  Obituary 95
Di Franco, Anthony (Mario) 1945- 42
Digby, Anne 1935- 72
Digges, Jeremiah
  See Berger, Josef
D'Ignazio, Fred 1949- 39
  Brief entry 35
Di Grazia, Thomas (?)-1983 32
Dillard, Annie 1945- 10
Dillard, Polly (Hargis) 1916- 24
Diller, Harriett 1953- 78
Dillon, Barbara 1927- 44
  Brief entry 39
Dillon, Diane 1933- 51
  Earlier sketch in SATA 15
  See also CLR 44
Dillon, Eilis 1920-1994 74
  Obituary 83
  Earlier sketch in SATA 2
  See also CLR 26
Dillon, Leo 1933- 51
  Earlier sketch in SATA 15
  See also CLR 44
Dillon, Sharon Saseen
  See Saseen, Sharon (Dillon)
Dils, Tracey E. 1958- 83
Dilson, Jesse 1914- 24
Dinan, Carolyn 59
  Brief entry 47
Dines, Glen 1925- 7
Dinesen, Isak
  See Blixen, Karen (Christentze Dinesen)
Dinneen, Betty 1929- 61
Dinnerstein, Harvey 1928- 42
Dinsdale, Tim 1924- 11
Diop, Birago (Ismael) 1906-1989
  Obituary 64
Dirks, Rudolph 1877-1968
  Brief entry 31
Dirks, Wilhelmina 1916- 59
Dirks, Willy
  See Dirks, Wilhelmina
DiSalvo-Ryan, DyAnne 1954- 59
Disch, Thomas M(ichael) 1940- 92
  Earlier sketch in SATA 54
  See also CLR 18
  See also SAAS 15
Disch, Tom
  See Disch, Thomas M(ichael)
Disher, Garry 1949- 81
Disney, Walt(er Elias) 1901-1966 28
  Brief entry 27
DiValentin, Maria 1911- 7
Divine, Arthur Durham 1904-1987
  Obituary 52
Divine, David
  See Divine, Arthur Durham
Dixon, Ann R. 1954- 77
Dixon, Dougal 1947- 45
Dixon, Franklin W. [Collective
  pseudonym] 67
  Earlier sketch in SATA 1
Dixon, Jeanne 1936- 31
Dixon, Paige
  See Corcoran, Barbara
Dixon, Peter L. 1931- 6
Dixon, Rachel 1952- 74

Djoleto, (Solomon Alexander) Amu
  1929- 80
Doane, Pelagie 1906-1966 7
Dobell, I(sabel) M(arian) B(arclay)
  1909- 11
Dobie, J(ames) Frank 1888-1964 43
Dobkin, Alexander 1908-1975
  Obituary 30
Dobler, Lavinia G. 1910- 6
Dobrin, Arnold 1928- 4
Dobson, Julia 1941- 48
Dockery, Wallene T. 1941- 27
Doctor, Bernard
  See Doctor, Bernard Aquina
Doctor, Bernard Aquina 1950- 81
Dodd, Ed(ward Benton) 1902-1991 4
  Obituary 68
Dodd, Lynley (Stuart) 1941- 86
  Earlier sketch in SATA 35
Dodds, Bill 1952- 78
Dodds, Dayle Ann 1952- 75
Dodge, Bertha S(anford) 1902- 8
Dodge, Fremont
  See Grimes, Lee
Dodge, Mary (Elizabeth) Mapes
  1831-1905 21
Dodgson, Charles Lutwidge 1832-1898
  See YABC 2
Dodson, Kenneth M(acKenzie)
  1907- 11
Dodson, Susan 1941- 50
  Brief entry 40
Doerksen, Nan 1934-
  Brief entry 50
Doherty, Berlie 1943- 72
  See also CLR 21
  See also SAAS 16
Doherty, C. H. 1913- 6
Doherty, Craig A. 1951- 83
Doherty, Katherine M(ann) 1951- 83
Dokey, Cameron 1956- 97
Dolan, Edward F(rancis), Jr. 1924- 94
  Brief entry 31
  Earlier sketch in SATA 45
Dolan, Ellen M(eara) 1929- 88
Dolan, Sean J. 1958- 74
Dolce, J. Ellen 1948- 75
Dolch, Edward William 1889-1961 50
Dolch, Marguerite Pierce
  1891-1978 50
Dollar, Diane (Hills) 1933- 57
Dolson, Hildegarde 1908- 5
Domanska, Janina 1913(?)-1995 68
  Obituary 84
  Earlier sketch in SATA 6
  See also CLR 40
  See also SAAS 18
Dominguez, Angel 1953- 76
Domino, John
  See Averill, Esther (Holden)
Domjan, Joseph 1907- 25
Domm, Jeffrey C. 1958- 84
Donalds, Gordon
  See Shirreffs, Gordon D(onald)
Donaldson, Bryna
  See Stevens, Bryna
Donaldson, Gordon 1913-1993 64
  Obituary 76
Donaldson, Joan 1953- 78
Donaldson, Julia 1948- 82
Doner, Kim 1955- 91
Donkin, Nance (Clare) 1915- 95
Donna, Natalie 1934- 9
Donovan, Frank (Robert) 1906-1975
  Obituary 30
Donovan, John 1928-1992 72
  Brief entry 29
  See also CLR 3
Donovan, Mary Lee 1961- 86
Donovan, William
  See Berkebile, Fred D(onovan)
Donze, Mary Terese 1911- 89
Doob, Leonard W(illiam) 1909- 8
Dooley, Norah 1953- 74
Dor, Ana
  See Ceder, Georgiana Dorcas

Dore, (Louis Christophe Paul) Gustave
  1832-1883 19
Doremus, Robert 1913- 30
Doren, Marion (Walker) 1928- 57
Dorenkamp, Michelle 1957- 89
Dorflinger, Carolyn 1953- 91
Dorian, Edith M(cEwen) 1900- 5
Dorian, Harry
  See Hamilton, Charles (Harold St. John)
Dorian, Marguerite 7
Dorin, Patrick C(arberry) 1939- 59
  Brief entry 52
Dorman, Michael 1932- 7
Dorman, N. B. 1927- 39
Dorris, Michael (Anthony)
  1945-1997 75
  Obituary 94
Dorris, Michael A.
  See Dorris, Michael (Anthony)
Dorritt, Susan
  See Schlein, Miriam
Dorros, Arthur (M.) 1950- 78
  See also CLR 42
  See also SAAS 20
Dorson, Richard M(ercer)
  1916-1981 30
Doss, Helen (Grigsby) 1918- 20
Doss, Margot Patterson 6
dos Santos, Joyce Audy 1949- 57
  Brief entry 42
Dothers, Anne
  See Chess, Victoria (Dickerson)
Dottig
  See Grider, Dorothy
Dotts, Maryann J. 1933- 35
Doty, Jean Slaughter 1929- 28
Doty, Roy 1922- 28
Doubtfire, Dianne (Abrams) 1918- 29
Dougherty, Charles 1922- 18
Douglas, Carole Nelson 1944- 73
Douglas, Garry
  See Kilworth, Garry (D.)
Douglas, James McM.
  See Butterworth, W(illiam) E(dmund III)
Douglas, Kathryn
  See Ewing, Kathryn
Douglas, Marjory Stoneman 1890- 10
Douglas, Michael
  See Bright, Robert (Douglas Sr.)
Douglas, Michael
  See Crichton, (John) Michael
Douglass, Barbara 1930- 40
Douglass, Frederick 1817(?)-1895 29
Douty, Esther M(orris) 1911-1978 8
  Obituary 23
Dow, Emily R. 1904- 10
Dow, Vicki
  See McVey, Vicki
Dowd, John David 1945- 78
Dowdell, Dorothy (Florence) Karns
  1910- 12
Dowden, Anne Ophelia 1907- 7
  See also SAAS 10
Dowdey, Landon Gerald 1923- 11
Dowdy, Mrs. Regera
  See Gorey, Edward (St. John)
Downer, Marion 1892(?)-1971 25
Downey, Fairfax D(avis) 1893-1990 3
  Obituary 66
Downie, John 1931- 87
Downie, Mary Alice (Dawe) 1934- 87
  Earlier sketch in SATA 13
Downing, David A(lmon) 1958- 84
Downing, Julie 1956- 81
Downing, Paula E. 1951- 80
Doyle, Arthur Conan 1859-1930 24
Doyle, Brian 1935- 67
  See also CLR 22
  See also SAAS 16
Doyle, Charlotte (Lackner) 1937- 94
Doyle, Donovan
  See Boegehold, Betty (Doyle)
Doyle, Richard 1824-1883 21
Dr. A
  See Asimov, Isaac

Dr. A
See Silverstein, Alvin
and Silverstein, Virginia B(arbara
Opshelor)
Dr. Alphabet
See Morice, Dave
Dr. Seuss
See Geisel, Theodor Seuss
Dr. X
See Nourse, Alan E(dward)
Dr. Zed
See Penrose, Gordon
Drabble, Margaret 1939- 48
Drackett, Phil(ip Arthur) 1922- 53
Draco, F.
See Davis, Julia
Dracup, Angela 1943- 74
Drager, Gary
See Edens, Cooper
Dragonwagon, Crescent 1952- 75
Earlier sketches in SATA *11, 41*
See also SAAS *14*
Drake, David (Allen) 1945- 85
Drake, Frank
See Hamilton, Charles (Harold St. John)
Drake, Jane 1954- 82
Draper, Sharon M(ills) 98
Drapier, M. B.
See Swift, Jonathan
Drawson, Blair 1943- 17
Dresang, Eliza (Carolyn Timberlake)
1941- 19
Drescher, Henrik 1955- 67
See also CLR *20*
Drescher, Joan E(lizabeth) 1939- 30
Dreves, Veronica R. 1927-1986
Obituary 50
Drew, Patricia (Mary) 1938- 15
Drewery, Mary 1918- 6
Drial, J. E.
See Laird, Jean E(louise)
Drimmer, Frederick 60
Driskill, J. Lawrence 1920- 90
Driving Hawk, Virginia
See Sneve, Virginia Driving Hawk
Drucker, Malka 1945- 39
Brief entry 29
Drucker, Olga Levy 1927- 79
Drummond, V(iolet) H. 1911- 6
Drummond, Walter
See Silverberg, Robert
Drury, Roger W(olcott) 1914- 15
Dryden, Pamela
See St. John, Nicole
Duane, Diane (Elizabeth) 1952- 95
Brief entry 46
Earlier sketch in SATA *58*
Duane-Smyth, Diane (Elizabeth)
See Duane, Diane (Elizabeth)
Dubanevich, Arlene 1950- 56
Dubelaar, Thea 1947- 60
du Blanc, Daphne
See Groom, Arthur William
DuBois, Rochelle Holt
See Holt, Rochelle Lynn
Du Bois, Shirley Graham
1907-1977 24
Du Bois, W(illiam) E(dward) B(urghardt)
1868-1963 42
du Bois, William Pene
Obituary 74
See Pene du Bois, William (Sherman)
Duboise, Novella 1911- 88
DuBose, LaRocque (Russ) 1926- 2
Dubrovin, Vivian 1931- 65
See also SAAS *25*
Ducey, Jean Sparks 1915- 93
Duchacek, Ivo D(uka) 1913-1988
Obituary 55
Du Chaillu, Paul (Belloni)
1831(?)-1903 26
Duchesne, Janet 1930-
Brief entry 32
Ducornet, Erica 1943- 7
Duder, Tessa 1940- 80
See also CLR *43*
See also SAAS *23*

Dudley, Martha Ward 1909(?)-1985
Obituary 45
Dudley, Nancy
See Cole, Lois Dwight
Dudley, Robert
See Baldwin, James
Dudley, Ruth H(ubbell) 1905- 11
Due, Linnea A. 1948- 64
Dueck, Adele 1955- 97
Dueland, Joy V(ivian) 27
Duerr, Gisela 1968- 89
Duff, Annis (James) 1904(?)-1986
Obituary 49
Duff, Maggie
See Duff, Margaret K.
Duff, Margaret K. 37
Duffey, Betsy (Byars) 1953- 80
Duffy, Carol Ann 1955- 95
Dugan, Michael (Gray) 1947- 15
Duggan, Alfred Leo 1903-1964 25
Duggan, Maurice (Noel) 1922-1974 40
Obituary 30
Duggleby, John 1952- 94
Dugin, Andrej 1955- 77
Dugina, Olga 1964- 77
du Jardin, Rosamond (Neal)
1902-1963 2
Duka, Ivo
See Duchacek, Ivo D(uka)
Duke, Kate 1956- 90
Dulac, Edmund 1882-1953 19
Dumas, Alexandre (the elder)
1802-1870 18
Dumas, Jacqueline (Claudia) 1946- 55
Dumas, Philippe 1940- 52
du Maurier, Daphne 1907-1989 27
Obituary 60
Dumbleton, Mike 1948- 73
Dunbar, Joyce 1944- 76
Dunbar, Paul Laurence 1872-1906 34
Dunbar, Robert E(verett) 1926- 32
Duncan, Alice Faye 1967- 95
Duncan, Frances (Mary) 1942-
Brief entry 48
Duncan, Gregory
See McClintock, Marshall
Duncan, Jane
See Cameron, Elizabeth Jane
Duncan, Julia K. [Collective
pseudonym] 1
See Benson, Mildred (Augustine Wirt)
Duncan, Lois S(teinmetz) 1934- 75
Earlier sketches in SATA *1, 36*
See also CLR *29*
See also SAAS *2*
Duncan, Norman 1871-1916
See YABC *1*
Duncombe, Frances (Riker)
1900-1994 25
Obituary 82
Dunlap, Julie 1958- 84
Dunlop, Agnes M(ary) R(obertson)
(?)-1982 87
Earlier sketch in SATA *3*
Dunlop, Eileen (Rhona) 1938- 76
Earlier sketch in SATA *24*
See also SAAS *12*
Dunn, Harvey T(homas)
1884-1952 34
Dunn, John M. (III) 1949- 93
Dunn, Judy
See Spangenberg, Judith Dunn
Dunn, Mary Lois 1930- 6
Dunnahoo, Terry 1927- 7
Dunne, Jeanette 1952- 72
Dunne, Marie
See Clark, Ann Nolan
Dunne, Mary Collins 1914- 11
Dunnett, Margaret (Rosalind)
1909-1977 42
Dunrea, Olivier 1953- 59
Brief entry 46
Dunton, Dorothy 1912- 92
Dupasquier, Philippe 1955- 86
Dupuy, T(revor) N(evitt) 1916-1995 4
Obituary 86
DuQuette, Keith 1960- 90

Durant, John 1902- 27
Durell, Ann 1930- 66
Durrant, Lynda 1954- 96
Durrell, Gerald (Malcolm)
1925-1995 8
Obituary 84
Durrell, Julie 1955- 94
Durrett, Deanne 1940- 92
Du Soe, Robert C. 1892-1958
See YABC *2*
Dussling, Jennifer 1970- 96
Dutz
See Davis, Mary Octavia
Duval, Katherine
See James, Elizabeth
Duvall, Evelyn Millis 1906- 9
Duvoisin, Roger (Antoine)
1904-1980 30
Obituary 23
Earlier sketch in SATA *2*
See also CLR *23*
Dwiggins, Don 1913-1988 4
Obituary 60
Dwight, Allan
See Cole, Lois Dwight
Dwyer, Deanna
See Koontz, Dean R(ay)
Dwyer, K. R.
See Koontz, Dean R(ay)
Dyck, Peter J. 1914- 75
Dyer, James (Frederick) 1934- 37
Dyess, John (Foster) 1939- 76
Dygard, Thomas J. 1931-1996 97
Obituary 92
Earlier sketch in SATA *24*
See also SAAS *15*
Dyke, John 1935- 35

E

Eager, Frances (Elisabeth Stuart)
1940-1978 11
Obituary 55
Eager, Edward (McMaken)
1911-1964 17
See also CLR *43*
Eager, George B. 1921- 56
Eagle, Ellen 1953- 61
Eagle, Kin
See Adlerman, Daniel
and Adlerman, Kimberly M.
Eagle, Mike 1942- 11
Earle, Olive L. 7
Earle, William
See Johns, W(illiam) E(arl)
Earls, Nick 1963- 95
Early, Jack
See Scoppettone, Sandra
Early, Jon
See Johns, W(illiam) E(arl)
Early, Margaret 1951- 72
Earnshaw, Brian 1929- 17
Earnshaw, Micky
See Earnshaw, Spencer Wright
Earnshaw, Spencer Wright 1939- 88
Easley, MaryAnn 94
Eastman, Charles A(lexander) 1858-1939
See YABC *1*
Eastman, P(hilip) D(ey) 1909-1986 33
Obituary 46
Eastwick, Ivy O. 3
Eaton, Anne T(haxter) 1881-1971 32
Eaton, George L.
See Verral, Charles Spain
Eaton, Janet
See Givens, Janet E(aton)
Eaton, Jeanette 1886-1968 24
Eaton, Tom 1940- 22
Ebel, Alex 1927- 11
Eber, Dorothy (Margaret) Harley
1930- 27
Eberle, Irmengarde 1898-1979 2
Obituary 23
Eble, Diane 1956- 74
Eccles
See Williams, Ferelith Eccles

Eckblad, Edith Berven 1923- 23
Ecke, Wolfgang 1927-1983
    Obituary 37
Eckert, Allan W. 1931- 91
    Brief entry 27
    Earlier sketch in SATA 29
    See also SAAS 21
Eckert, Horst 1931- 72
    Earlier sketch in SATA 8
Eddings, David (Carroll) 1931- 91
Ede, Janina 1937- 33
Edell, Celeste 12
Edelman, Elaine
    Brief entry 50
Edelman, Lily (Judith) 1915- 22
Edelson, Edward 1932- 51
Edens, Cooper 1945- 49
Edens, (Bishop) David 1926- 39
Edey, Maitland A(rmstrong)
    1910-1992 25
    Obituary 71
Edgeworth, Maria 1767-1849 21
Edler, Tim(othy) 1948- 56
Edmiston, Jim 1948- 80
Edmonds, I(vy) G(ordon) 1917- 8
Edmonds, Walter D(umaux)
    1903-1998 27
    Obituary 99
    Earlier sketch in SATA 1
    See also SAAS 4
Edmund, Sean
    See Pringle, Laurence P(atrick)
Edsall, Marian S(tickney) 1920- 8
Edwards, Al
    See Nourse, Alan E(dward)
Edwards, Alexander
    See Fleischer, Leonore
Edwards, Anne 1927- 35
Edwards, Audrey 1947- 52
    Brief entry 31
Edwards, Bertram
    See Edwards, Herbert Charles
Edwards, Bronwen Elizabeth
    See Rose, Wendy
Edwards, Cecile (Pepin) 1916- 25
Edwards, Dorothy 1914-1982 88
    Obituary 31
    Earlier sketch in SATA 4
Edwards, Frank B. 1952- 93
Edwards, Gunvor 32
Edwards, Harvey 1929- 5
Edwards, Herbert Charles 1912- 12
Edwards, Jane Campbell 1932- 10
Edwards, Julia
    See Stratemeyer, Edward L.
Edwards, Julie
    See Andrews, Julie
Edwards, June
    See Forrester, Helen
Edwards, Linda Strauss 1948- 49
    Brief entry 42
Edwards, Margaret (Alexander) 1902-1988
    Obituary 56
Edwards, Michelle 1955- 70
Edwards, Monica le' Doux Newton
    1912- 12
Edwards, Olwen
    See Gater, Dilys
Edwards, Page L., Jr. 1941- 59
Edwards, Sally 1929- 7
Edwards, Samuel
    See Gerson, Noel B(ertram)
Egan, E(dward) W(elstead) 1922- 35
Egan, Lorraine Hopping 1960- 91
Egan, Tim 1957- 89
Egermeier, Elsie E(milie)
    1890-1986 65
Eggenberger, David 1918- 6
Eggleston, Edward 1837-1902 27
Egielski, Richard 1952- 49
    Earlier sketch in SATA 11
Egypt, Ophelia Settle 1903-1984 16
    Obituary 38
Ehlert, Lois 1934- 69
    Earlier sketch in SATA 35
    See also CLR 28
Ehling, Katalin Olah 1941- 93

Ehrenfreund, Norbert 1921- 86
Ehrlich, Amy 1942- 96
    Earlier sketches in SATA 25, 65
Ehrlich, Bettina Bauer 1903- 1
Eichberg, James Bandman
    See Garfield, James B.
Eichenberg, Fritz 1901- 50
    Earlier sketch in SATA 9
Eichler, Margrit 1942- 35
Eichner, James A. 1927- 4
Eifert, Virginia S(nider) 1911-1966 2
Eige, (Elizabeth) Lillian 1915- 65
Einsel, Naiad 10
Einsel, Walter 1926- 10
Einzig, Susan 1922- 43
Eiseman, Alberta 1925- 15
Eisenberg, Azriel 1903- 12
Eisenberg, Lisa 1949- 57
    Brief entry 50
Eisenberg, Phyllis Rose 1924- 41
Eisner, Vivienne
    See Margolis, Vivienne
Eisner, Will(iam Erwin) 1917- 31
Eitzen, Allan 1928- 9
Eitzen, Ruth (Carper) 1924- 9
Ekwensi, C. O. D.
    See Ekwensi, Cyprian (Odiatu Duaka)
Ekwensi, Cyprian (Odiatu Duaka)
    1921- 66
Elam, Richard M(ace, Jr.) 1920- 9
Elfman, Blossom 1925- 8
Elgin, Kathleen 1923- 39
Elia
    See Lamb, Charles
Eliot, Anne
    See Cole, Lois Dwight
Eliot, Dan
    See Silverberg, Robert
Elish, Dan 1960- 68
Elisofon, Eliot 1911-1973
    Obituary 21
Elkin, Benjamin 1911- 3
Elkins, Dov Peretz 1937- 5
Ellacott, S(amuel) E(rnest) 1911- 19
Ellen, Jaye
    See Nixon, Joan Lowery
Eller, Scott
    See Holinger, William (Jacques)
    and Shepard, Jim
Elliott, Don
    See Silverberg, Robert
Elliott, Joey
    See Houk, Randy
Elliott, Odette 1939- 75
Elliott, Sarah M(cCarn) 1930- 14
Ellis, Anyon
    See Rowland-Entwistle, (Arthur)
    Theodore (Henry)
Ellis, Edward S(ylvester) 1840-1916
    See YABC 1
Ellis, Ella Thorp 1928- 7
    See also SAAS 9
Ellis, Harry Bearse 1921- 9
Ellis, Herbert
    See Wilson, Lionel
Ellis, Mel 1912-1984 7
    Obituary 39
Ellis, Sarah 1952- 68
    See also CLR 42
Ellison, Lucile Watkins
    1907(?)-1979 50
    Obituary 22
Ellison, Virginia Howell 1910- 4
Ellsberg, Edward 1891- 7
Elmer, Robert 1958- 99
Elmore, (Carolyn) Patricia 1933- 38
    Brief entry 35
El-Moslimany, Ann P(axton) 1937- 90
Elspeth
    See Bragdon, Elspeth
Elting, Mary 1906- 88
    Earlier sketch in SATA 2
    See also SAAS 20
Elwart, Joan Potter 1927- 2
Elwood, Ann 1931- 55
    Brief entry 52
Elwood, Roger 1943- 58

Elzbieta 88
Emberley, Barbara A(nne) 8
    See also CLR 5
Emberley, Barbara A(nne) 1932- 70
Emberley, Ed(ward Randolph)
    1931- 70
    Earlier sketch in SATA 8
    See also CLR 5
Emberley, Michael 1960- 80
    Earlier sketch in SATA 34
Embry, Margaret (Jacob) 1919- 5
Emecheta, (Florence Onye) Buchi
    1944- 66
Emerson, Alice B. [Collective
    pseudonym] 67
    Earlier sketch in SATA 1
Emerson, Kathy Lynn 1947- 63
Emerson, Ru 1944- 70
Emerson, William K(eith) 1925- 25
Emert, Phyllis R(aybin) 1947- 93
Emery, Anne (McGuigan) 1907- 33
    Earlier sketch in SATA 1
Emmens, Carol Ann 1944- 39
Emmons, Della (Florence) Gould 1890-
    1983
    Obituary 39
Emory, Jerry 1957- 96
Emrich, Duncan (Black Macdonald)
    1908- 11
Emslie, M. L.
    See Simpson, Myrtle L(illias)
Ende, Michael (Andreas Helmuth)
    1929-1995 61
    Brief entry 42
    Obituary 86
    See also CLR 14
Enderle, Judith (Ann) Ross 1941- 89
    Earlier sketch in SATA 38
    See also SAAS 26
Enell, Trinka (Gochenour) 1951- 79
Enfield, Carrie
    See Smith, Susan Vernon
Engdahl, Sylvia Louise 1933- 4
    See also CLR 2
    See also SAAS 5
Engel, Diana 1947- 70
Engelhart, Margaret S(tevens)
    1924- 59
Engelmann, Kim (V.) 1959- 87
Engle, Eloise Katherine 1923- 9
Engle, Marion
    See Ladd, Louise
Englebert, Victor 1933- 8
English, James W(ilson) 1915- 37
Enright, D(ennis) J(oseph) 1920- 25
Enright, Elizabeth 1909-1968 9
    See also CLR 4
Enright, Maginel Wright
    See Barney, Maginel Wright
Ensor, Robert 1922- 93
Enys, Sarah L.
    See Sloggett, Nellie
Epanya, Christian A(rthur Kingue)
    1956- 91
Ephraim, Shelly S(chonebaum)
    1952- 97
Ephron, Delia 1944- 65
    Brief entry 50
Epler, Doris M. 1928- 73
Epp, Margaret A(gnes) 20
Eppenstein, Louise (Kohn) 1892-1987
    Obituary 54
Epple, Anne Orth 1927- 20
Epstein, Anne Merrick 1931- 20
Epstein, Beryl (M. Williams) 1910- 31
    Earlier sketch in SATA 1
    See also CLR 26
    See also SAAS 17
Epstein, Perle S(herry) 1938- 27
Epstein, Samuel 1909- 31
    Earlier sketch in SATA 1
    See also CLR 26
    See also SAAS 17
Erdman, Loula Grace 1
Erdoes, Richard 1912- 33
    Brief entry 28
Erdrich, Louise 1954- 94

Erhard, Walter 1920-
  Brief entry 30
Erickson, Betty J(ean) 1923- 97
Erickson, John R. 1943- 70
Erickson, Phoebe 59
Erickson, Russell E(verett) 1932- 27
Erickson, Sabra R(ollins) 1912- 35
Ericson, Walter
  See Fast, Howard
Erikson, Mel 1937- 31
Erlanger, Baba
  See Trahey, Jane
Erlanger, Ellen (Louise) 1950-
  Brief entry 52
Erlbach, Arlene 1948- 78
Erlich, Lillian (Feldman) 1910- 10
Ernest, William
  See Berkebile, Fred D(onovan)
Ernst, (Lyman) John 1940- 39
Ernst, Kathryn (Fitzgerald) 1942- 25
Ernst, Lisa Campbell 1957- 95
  Brief entry 44
  Earlier sketch in SATA 55
Ervin, Janet Halliday 1923- 4
Erwin, Will
  See Eisner, Will(iam Erwin)
Esbensen, Barbara J(uster)
  1925-1996 97
  Brief entry 53
  Earlier sketch in SATA 62
Eshmeyer, R(einhart) E(rnst) 1898- 29
Eskridge, Ann E. 1949- 84
Espeland, Pamela (Lee) 1951- 52
  Brief entry 38
Espriella, Don Manuel Alvarez
  See Southey, Robert
Espy, Willard R(ichardson) 1910- 38
Essrig, Harry 1912- 66
Estep, Irene (Compton) 5
Esterl, Arnica 1933- 77
Estes, Eleanor 1906-1988 91
  Obituary 56
  Earlier sketch in SATA 7
  See also CLR 2
Estoril, Jean
  See Allan, Mabel Esther
Estrada, Pau 1961- 74
Etchemendy, Nancy 1952- 38
Etchison, Birdie L(ee) 1937- 38
Etherington, Frank 1945- 58
Eton, Robert
  See Meynell, Laurence Walter
Ets, Marie Hall 2
  See also CLR 33
Eunson, Dale 1904- 5
Evanoff, Vlad 1916- 59
Evans, Douglas 1953- 93
Evans, Eva Knox 1905- 27
Evans, Greg 1947- 73
Evans, Hubert Reginald 1892-1986
  Obituary 48
Evans, Katherine (Floyd) 1901-1964 5
Evans, Larry
  See Evans, Laurence Chubb
Evans, Laurence Chubb 1939- 88
Evans, Mari 10
Evans, Mark 19
Evans, Nancy 1950- 65
Evans, Patricia Healy
  See Carpenter, Patricia (Healy Evans)
Evans, (Alice) Pearl 1927- 83
Evans, Shirlee 1931- 58
Evarts, Esther
  See Benson, Sally
Evarts, Hal G. (Jr.) 1915- 6
E.V.B.
  See Boyle, Eleanor Vere (Gordon)
Everett, Gail
  See Hale, Arlene
Evernden, Margery 1916- 5
Eversole, Robyn Harbert 1971- 74
Evslin, Bernard 1916-1993 83
  Brief entry 28
  Obituary 77
  Earlier sketch in SATA 45
Ewart, Claire 1958- 76

Ewen, David 1907-1985 4
  Obituary 47
Ewing, Juliana (Horatia Gatty)
  1841-1885 16
Ewing, Kathryn 1921- 20
Eyerly, Jeannette 1908- 86
  Earlier sketch in SATA 4
  See also SAAS 10
Eyre, Dorothy
  See McGuire, Leslie (Sarah)
Eyre, Frank 1910-1988
  Obituary 62
Eyre, Katherine Wigmore
  1901-1970 26
Eyvindson, Peter (Knowles) 1946-
  Brief entry 52
Ezzell, Marilyn 1937- 42
  Brief entry 38

F

Fabe, Maxene 1943- 15
Faber, Doris (Greenberg) 1924- 78
  Earlier sketch in SATA 3
Faber, Harold 1919- 5
Fabre, Jean Henri (Casimir)
  1823-1915 22
Facklam, Margery (Metz) 1927- 85
  Earlier sketch in SATA 20
Fadiman, Clifton (Paul) 1904- 11
Fair, David 1952- 96
Fair, Sylvia 1933- 13
Fairfax-Lucy, Brian (Fulke Cameron-
  Ramsay) 1898-1974 6
  Obituary 26
Fairlie, Gerard 1899-1983
  Obituary 34
Fairman, Joan A(lexandra) 1935- 10
Fairstar, Mrs.
  See Horne, Richard Henry
Faithfull, Gail 1936- 8
Falconer, James
  See Kirkup, James
Falkner, Leonard 1900- 12
Fall, Thomas
  See Snow, Donald Clifford
Falls, C(harles) B(uckles)
  1874-1960 38
  Brief entry 27
Falstein, Louis 1909- 37
Fanelli, Sara 1969- 89
Fanning, Leonard M(ulliken)
  1888-1967 5
Faralla, Dana 1909- 9
Faralla, Dorothy W.
  See Faralla, Dana
Farb, Peter 1929-1980 12
  Obituary 22
Farber, Norma 1909-1984 75
  Obituary 38
  Earlier sketch in SATA 25
Farge, Monique
  See Gree, Alain
Farish, Terry 1947- 82
Farjeon, (Eve) Annabel 1919- 11
Farjeon, Eleanor 1881-1965 2
  See also CLR 34
Farley, Carol 1936- 4
Farley, Walter 1920- 43
  Earlier sketch in SATA 2
Farlow, James O(rville, Jr.) 1951- 75
Farmer, Nancy 1941- 79
Farmer, Patti 1948- 79
Farmer, Penelope (Jane) 1939- 40
  Brief entry 39
  See also CLR 8
  See also SAAS 22
Farmer, Peter 1950- 38
Farmer, Philip Jose 1918- 93
Farnham, Burt
  See Clifford, Harold B.
Farnsworth, Bill 1958- 84
Farquhar, Margaret C(utting) 1905- 13
Farquharson, Alexander 1944- 46
Farquharson, Martha
  See Finley, Martha

Farr, Diana 1930- 82
  See Pullein-Thompson, Diana
Farr, Finis (King) 1904- 10
Farrar, Susan Clement 1917- 33
Farrell, Ben
  See Cebulash, Mel
Farrell, Sally
  See Odgers, Sally Farrell
Farrington, Benjamin 1891-1974
  Obituary 20
Farrington, Selwyn Kip, Jr. 1904- 20
Farthing, Alison 1936- 45
  Brief entry 36
Farthing-Knight, Catherine 1933- 92
Fassler, Joan (Grace) 1931- 11
Fast, Howard 1914- 7
Fasulo, Michael 1963- 83
Fatchen, Max 1920- 84
  Earlier sketch in SATA 20
  See also SAAS 20
Father Xavier
  See Hurwood, Bernhardt J.
Fatigati, (Frances) Evelyn de Buhr
  1948- 24
Fatio, Louise 6
Faulhaber, Martha 1926- 7
Faulkner, Anne Irvin 1906- 23
Faulkner, Nancy
  See Faulkner, Anne Irvin
Faulknor, Cliff(ord Vernon) 1913- 86
Fax, Elton Clay 1909- 25
Faxon, Lavinia
  See Russ, Lavinia
Feagles, Anita MacRae 9
Feagles, Elizabeth
  See Day, Beth (Feagles)
Feague, Mildred H. 1915- 14
Fecher, Constance 1911- 7
Feder, Chris Welles 1938- 81
Feder, Harriet K. 1928- 73
Feder, Paula (Kurzband) 1935- 26
Feder, Robert Arthur 1909-1969
  Brief entry 35
Feelings, Muriel (Grey) 1938- 16
  See also CLR 5
  See also SAAS 8
Feelings, Tom 1933- 69
  Earlier sketch in SATA 8
  See also SAAS 19
Fehler, Gene 1940- 74
Fehrenbach, T(heodore) R(eed, Jr.)
  1925- 33
Feiffer, Jules 1929- 61
  Earlier sketch in SATA 8
Feig, Barbara Krane 1937- 34
Feikema, Feike
  See Manfred, Frederick F(eikema)
Feil, Hila 1942- 12
Feilen, John
  See May, Julian
Feinberg, Barbara Jane 1938- 58
Feinberg, Barbara Silberdick
  See Feinberg, Barbara Jane
Feldman, Anne (Rodgers) 1939- 19
Feldman, Elane 79
Felix
  See Vincent, Felix
Fellows, Muriel H. 10
Felsen, Henry Gregor 1916- 1
  See also SAAS 2
Felton, Harold William 1902- 1
Felton, Ronald Oliver 1909- 3
Felts, Shirley 1934- 33
Fenderson, Lewis H. 1907-1983 47
  Obituary 37
Fenner, Carol (Elizabeth) 1929- 89
  Earlier sketch in SATA 7
  See also SAAS 24
Fenner, Phyllis R(eid) 1899-1982 1
  Obituary 29
Fenten, Barbara D(oris) 1935- 26
Fenten, D. X. 1932- 4
Fenton, Carroll Lane 1900-1969 5
Fenton, Edward 1917-1995 7
  Obituary 89
Fenton, Mildred Adams 1899- 21

Fenwick, Patti
  See Grider, Dorothy
Feravolo, Rocco Vincent 1922- *10*
Ferber, Edna 1887-1968 ....*7*
Ferguson, Alane 1957- *85*
Ferguson, Bob
  See Ferguson, Robert Bruce
Ferguson, Cecil 1931- *45*
Ferguson, Robert Bruce 1927- *13*
Ferguson, Sarah (Margaret) 1959- *66*
Ferguson, Walter (W.) 1930- *34*
Fergusson, Erna 1888-1964 ....*5*
Fermi, Laura (Capon) 1907-1977 ....*6*
  Obituary *28*
Fern, Eugene A. 1919-1987 ....*10*
  Obituary *54*
Fernandes, Eugenie 1943- *77*
Ferrell, Nancy Warren 1932- *70*
Ferrier, Lucy
  See Penzler, Otto
Ferris, Helen Josephine 1890-1969 ....*21*
Ferris, James Cody [Collective
    pseudonym] *1*
  See McFarlane, Leslie
  and Stratemeyer, Edward L.
Ferris, Jean 1939- *56*
  Brief entry *50*
Ferris, Jeri Chase 1937- *84*
Ferry, Charles 1927- *92*
  Earlier sketch in SATA *43*
  See also CLR *34*
  See also SAAS *20*
Fetz, Ingrid 1915- *30*
Feydy, Anne Lindbergh
  Brief entry *32*
  See Lindbergh, Anne (Spencer)
Fiammenghi, Gioia 1929- *66*
  Earlier sketch in SATA *9*
Fiarotta, Noel 1944- *15*
Fiarotta, Phyllis 1942- *15*
Fichter, George S. 1922- *7*
Fidler, Kathleen (Annie) 1899-1980 .....*87*
  Obituary *45*
  Earlier sketch in SATA *3*
Fiedler, Jean *4*
Field, Dorothy 1944- *97*
Field, Edward 1924- *8*
Field, Elinor Whitney 1889-1980
  Obituary *28*
Field, Eugene 1850-1895 ....*16*
Field, Gans T.
  See Wellman, Manly Wade
Field, Peter
  See Hobson, Laura Z(ametkin)
Field, Rachel (Lyman) 1894-1942 ....*15*
  See also CLR *21*
Fife, Dale (Odile) 1901- *18*
Fighter Pilot, A
  See Johnston, H(ugh) A(nthony)
    S(tephen)
Figley, Marty Rhodes 1948- *88*
Figueroa, Pablo 1938- *9*
Fijan, Carol 1918- *12*
Filderman, Diane E(lizabeth) 1959- *87*
Filipovic, Zlata 1980- *82*
Fillmore, Parker H(oysted) 1878-1944
  See YABC *1*
Filstrup, Chris
  See Filstrup, E(dward) Christian
Filstrup, E(dward) Christian 1942- *43*
Filstrup, Jane Merrill
  See Merrill, Jane
Filstrup, Janie
  See Merrill, Jane
Finchler, Judy 1943- *93*
Finder, Martin
  See Salzmann, Siegmund
Fine, Anne 1947- *72*
  Earlier sketch in SATA *29*
  See also CLR *25*
  See also SAAS *15*
Finger, Charles J(oseph)
    1869(?)-1941 ....*42*
Fink, William B(ertrand) 1916- *22*
Finke, Blythe F(oote) 1922- *26*
Finkel, George (Irvine) 1909-1975 ....*8*
Finkelstein, Norman H. 1941- *73*

Finlay, Alice Sullivan 1946- *82*
Finlay, Winifred 1910- *23*
Finlayson, Ann 1925- *8*
Finley, Martha 1828-1909 ....*43*
Finley, Mary Peace 1942- *83*
Finney, Shan 1944- *65*
Firer, Benzion 1914- *64*
Fireside, Bryna J. 1932- *73*
Firmin, Charlotte 1954- *29*
Firmin, Peter 1928- *58*
  Earlier sketch in SATA *15*
Fischbach, Julius 1894- *10*
Fischer-Nagel, Andreas 1951- *56*
Fischer-Nagel, Heiderose 1956- *56*
Fischler, Shirley (Walton) *66*
Fischler, Stan(ley I.) *66*
  Brief entry *36*
Fishback, Margaret
  See Antolini, Margaret Fishback
Fisher, Aileen (Lucia) 1906- *73*
  Earlier sketches in SATA *1, 25*
  See also CLR *49*
Fisher, Barbara 1940- *44*
  Brief entry *34*
Fisher, Chris 1958- *80*
Fisher, Clavin C(argill) 1912- *24*
Fisher, Dorothy Canfield 1879-1958
  See YABC *1*
Fisher, Gary L. 1949- *86*
Fisher, John (Oswald Hamilton)
    1909- *15*
Fisher, Laura Harrison 1934- *5*
Fisher, Leonard Everett 1924- *73*
  Earlier sketches in SATA *4, 34*
  See also CLR *18*
  See also SAAS *1*
Fisher, Lois I. 1948- *38*
  Brief entry *35*
Fisher, Margery (Turner)
    1913-1992 ....*20*
  Obituary *74*
Fisher, Nikki
  See Strachan, Ian
Fisher, Robert (Tempest) 1943- *47*
Fisher, Suzanne
  See Staples, Suzanne Fisher
Fisk, Nicholas 1923- *25*
  See Higginbottom, David
Fisk, Pauline 1948- *66*
Fitch, Clarke
  See Sinclair, Upton (Beall)
Fitch, John IV
  See Cormier, Robert (Edmund)
Fitschen, Dale 1937- *20*
Fitzalan, Roger
  See Trevor, Elleston
Fitzgerald, Captain Hugh
  See Baum, L(yman) Frank
FitzGerald, Cathleen 1932-1987
  Obituary *50*
Fitzgerald, Edward Earl 1919- *20*
Fitzgerald, F(rancis) A(nthony)
    1940- *15*
Fitzgerald, John D(ennis)
    1907-1988 ....*20*
  Obituary *56*
  See also CLR *1*
Fitzgerald, Merni I(ngrassia) 1955- *53*
Fitzhardinge, Joan Margaret 1912- *73*
  Earlier sketch in SATA *2*
Fitzhugh, Louise (Perkins)
    1928-1974 ....*45*
  Obituary *24*
  Earlier sketch in SATA *1*
  See also CLR *1*
Fitzhugh, Percy Keese 1876-1950 ....*65*
FitzRalph, Matthew
  See McInerny, Ralph
Fitz-Randolph, Jane (Currens)
    1915- *51*
Fitzsimons, Cecilia (A. L.) 1952- *97*
Flack, Marjorie 1899-1958
  See YABC *2*
  See also CLR *28*
Flack, Naomi John (White) *40*
  Brief entry *35*

Flash Flood
  See Robinson, Jan M.
Flatt, Lizann
  See Brunskill, Elizabeth Ann Flatt
Fleetwood, Jenni 1947- *80*
Fleischer, Jane
  See Oppenheim, Joanne
Fleischer, Leonore 1934(?)-
  Brief entry *47*
Fleischer, Max 1889-1972
  Brief entry *30*
Fleischhauer-Hardt, Helga 1936- *30*
Fleischman, Paul 1952- *72*
  Brief entry *32*
  Earlier sketch in SATA *39*
  See also CLR *20*
  See also SAAS *20*
Fleischman, (Albert) Sid(ney) 1920- *96*
  Earlier sketches in SATA *8, 59*
  See also CLR *15*
Fleischner, Jennifer 1956- *93*
Fleisher, Paul 1948- *81*
Fleisher, Robbin 1951-1977 ....*52*
  Brief entry *49*
Fleishman, Seymour 1918- *66*
  Brief entry *32*
Fleming, Alice Mulcahey 1928- *9*
Fleming, Candace 1962- *94*
Fleming, Denise 1950- *81*
Fleming, Elizabeth P. 1888-1985
  Obituary *48*
Fleming, Ian (Lancaster) 1908-1964 ......*9*
Fleming, Susan 1932- *32*
Fleming, Thomas J(ames) 1927- *8*
Fleming, Virginia (Edwards) 1923- *84*
Flemming, Ronald Lee 1941- *56*
Flesch, Yolande (Catarina) 1950- *55*
Fletcher, Charlie May 1897- *3*
Fletcher, Colin 1922- *28*
Fletcher, Helen Jill 1911- *13*
Fletcher, Richard E. 1917(?)-1983
  Obituary *34*
Fletcher, Rick
  See Fletcher, Richard E.
Fletcher, Susan (Clemens) 1951- *70*
  See also SAAS *25*
Fleur, Anne 1901-
  Brief entry *31*
Flexner, James Thomas 1908- *9*
Flint, Russ 1944- *74*
Flitner, David P. 1949- *7*
Floethe, Louise Lee 1913- *4*
Floethe, Richard 1901- *4*
Floherty, John Joseph 1882-1964 ....*25*
Flood, Flash
  See Robinson, Jan M.
Flora, James (Royer) 1914- *30*
  Earlier sketch in SATA *1*
  See also SAAS *6*
Florian, Douglas 1950- *83*
  Earlier sketch in SATA *19*
Flory, Jane Trescott 1917- *22*
Flournoy, Valerie (Rose) 1952- *95*
Flowerdew, Phyllis *33*
Flowers, Sarah 1952- *98*
Floyd, Gareth 1940- *62*
  Brief entry *31*
Fluchere, Henri A(ndre) 1914- *40*
Fluke, Joanne
  See Gibson, Jo
Flynn, Barbara 1928- *9*
Flynn, Jackson
  See Shirreffs, Gordon D(onald)
Flynn, Mary
  See Welsh, Mary Flynn
Fodor, Ronald V(ictor) 1944- *25*
Foley, (Anna) Bernice Williams
    1902- *28*
Foley, June 1944- *44*
Foley, (Mary) Louise Munro 1933- *54*
  Brief entry *40*
Foley, Rae
  See Denniston, Elinore
Folkard, Charles James 1878-1963
  Brief entry *28*
Follett, Helen (Thomas) 1884(?)-1970
  Obituary *27*

Folsom, Franklin (Brewster) 1907-1995 ...5
  Obituary 88
Folsom, Michael (Brewster)
  1938-1990 40
  Obituary 88
Fontenot, Mary Alice 1910- 91
  Earlier sketch in SATA 34
Fooner, Michael 22
Foote, Timothy (Gilson) 1926- 52
Forberg, Ati 1925- 22
Forbes, Bryan 1926- 37
Forbes, Cabot L.
  See Hoyt, Edwin P(almer), Jr.
Forbes, Esther 1891-1967 2
  See also CLR 27
Forbes, Graham B. [Collective
  pseudonym] 1
Forbes, Kathryn
  See McLean, Kathryn (Anderson)
Ford, Albert Lee
  See Stratemeyer, Edward L.
Ford, Barbara 56
  Brief entry 34
Ford, Brian J(ohn) 1939- 49
Ford, Carolyn (Mott) 1938- 98
Ford, Elbur
  See Hibbert, Eleanor Alice Burford
Ford, Ellen 1949- 89
Ford, George (Jr.) 31
Ford, Hilary
  See Youd, (Christopher) Samuel
Ford, Hildegarde
  See Morrison, Velma Ford
Ford, Jerome W. 1949- 78
Ford, Jerry
  See Ford, Jerome W.
Ford, Marcia
  See Radford, Ruby L(orraine)
Ford, Nancy K(effer) 1906-1961
  Obituary 29
Ford, Peter 1936- 59
Foreman, Michael 1938- 73
  Earlier sketch in SATA 2
  See also CLR 32
  See also SAAS 21
Forest, Antonia 29
Forester, C(ecil) S(cott) 1899-1966 13
Forman, Brenda 1936- 4
Forman, James Douglas 1932- 70
  Earlier sketch in SATA 8
Forrest, Sybil
  See Markun, Patricia M(aloney)
Forrester, Frank H. 1919(?)-1986
  Obituary 52
Forrester, Helen 1919- 48
Forrester, Marian
  See Schachtel, Roger (Bernard)
Forrester, Sandra 1949- 90
Forrester, Victoria 1940- 40
  Brief entry 35
Forsee, (Frances) Aylesa 1
Forsey, Chris 1950- 59
Forshay-Lunsford, Cin 1965- 60
Forster, E(dward) M(organ)
  1879-1970 57
Fort, Paul
  See Stockton, Francis Richard
Forth, Melissa D(eal) 96
Fortnum, Peggy 1919- 26
Forward, Robert L(ull) 1932- 82
Foster, Alan Dean 1946- 70
Foster, Brad W. 1955- 34
Foster, Doris Van Liew 1899- 10
Foster, E(lizabeth) C(onnell) 1902- 9
Foster, Elizabeth 1905-1963 10
Foster, Elizabeth Vincent 1902- 12
Foster, F. Blanche 1919- 11
Foster, G(eorge) Allen 1907-1969 26
Foster, Genevieve (Stump)
  1893-1979 2
  Obituary 23
  See also CLR 7
Foster, Hal
  See Foster, Harold Rudolf
Foster, Harold Rudolf 1892-1982
  Obituary 31
Foster, John T(homas) 1925- 8

Foster, Laura Louise 1918- 6
Foster, Leila Merrell 1929- 73
Foster, Lynne 1937- 74
Foster, Margaret Lesser 1899-1979
  Obituary 21
Foster, Marian Curtis 1909-1978 23
Foster, Sally 58
Foulds, Elfrida Vipont 1902- 52
Fourie, Corlia 1944- 91
Fourth Brother, The
  See Aung, (Maung) Htin
Fowke, Edith (Margaret) 1913- 14
Fowles, John 1926- 22
Fox, Aileen 1907- 58
Fox, Charles Philip 1913- 12
Fox, Eleanor
  See St. John, Wylly Folk
Fox, Fontaine Talbot, Jr. 1884-1964
  Obituary 23
Fox, Fred 1903(?)-1981
  Obituary 27
Fox, Freeman
  See Hamilton, Charles (Harold St. John)
Fox, Geoffrey 1941- 73
Fox, Grace
  See Anderson, Grace Fox
Fox, Larry 30
Fox, Lorraine 1922-1975 11
  Obituary 27
Fox, Mary Virginia 1919- 88
  Brief entry 39
  Earlier sketch in SATA 44
Fox, Mem
  See Fox, Merrion Frances
Fox, Merrion Frances 1946- 51
  See also CLR 23
Fox, Michael Wilson 1937- 15
Fox, Paula 1923- 60
  Earlier sketch in SATA 17
  See also CLR 44
Fox, Petronella
  See Balogh, Penelope
Fox, Robert J. 1927- 33
Fradin, Dennis Brindell 1945- 90
  Earlier sketch in SATA 29
Fradin, Judith (Bernette) Bloom
  1945- 90
Frailey, Paige (Menefee) 1965- 82
Frame, Paul 1913-1994 60
  Brief entry 33
  Obituary 83
Franchere, Ruth 18
Francis, Charles
  See Holme, Bryan
Francis, Dee
  See Haas, Dorothy F.
Francis, Dorothy Brenner 1926- 10
Francis, Pamela (Mary) 1926- 11
Franck, Eddie
  See Cooke, Frank E.
Franco, Eloise (Bauder) 1910- 62
Franco, Johan (Henri Gustave)
  1908-1988 62
Franco, Marjorie 38
Francois, Andre 1915- 25
Francoise
  See Seignobosc, Francoise
Frank, Anne(lies Marie) 1929-1945 87
  Brief entry 42
Frank, Daniel B. 1956- 55
Frank, Helene
  See Vautier, Ghislaine
Frank, Josette 1893-1989 10
  Obituary 63
Frank, Lucy 1947- 94
Frank, Mary 1933- 34
Frank, R., Jr.
  See Ross, Frank (Xavier), Jr.
Frankau, Mary Evelyn 1899- 4
Frankel, Alona 1937- 66
Frankel, Bernice 9
Frankel, Edward 1910- 44
Frankel, Ellen 1951- 78
Frankel, Julie 1947- 40
  Brief entry 34
Frankenberg, Robert 1911- 22
Franklin, Cheryl J. 1955- 70

Franklin, Harold 1920- 13
Franklin, Kristine L. 1958- 80
Franklin, Lance
  See Lantz, Francess L(in)
Franklin, Max
  See Deming, Richard
Franklin, Steve
  See Stevens, Franklin
Franzen, Nils-Olof 1916- 10
Frascino, Edward 1938- 48
  Brief entry 33
  See also SAAS 9
Frasconi, Antonio 1919- 53
  Earlier sketch in SATA 6
  See also SAAS 11
Fraser, Antonia (Pakenham) 1932-
  Brief entry 32
Fraser, Betty
  See Fraser, Elizabeth Marr
Fraser, Elizabeth Marr 1928- 31
Fraser, Eric (George) 1902-1983 38
Fraser, Mary Ann 1959- 76
  See also SAAS 23
Fraser, Wynnette (McFaddin)
  1925- 90
Frasier, Debra 1953- 69
Fraustino, Lisa Rowe 1961- 84
Frazetta, Frank 1928- 58
Frazier, Neta Lohnes 7
Frederic, Mike
  See Cox, William R(obert)
Freed, Alvyn M. 1913- 22
Freedman, Benedict 1919- 27
Freedman, Jeff 1953- 90
Freedman, Nancy 1920- 27
Freedman, Russell 1929- 71
  Earlier sketch in SATA 16
  See also CLR 20
Freeman, Barbara C(onstance)
  1906- 28
Freeman, Bill
  See Freeman, William Bradford
Freeman, Don 1908-1978 17
  See also CLR 30
Freeman, Ira M(aximilian) 1905- 21
Freeman, Lucy (Greenbaum) 1916- 24
Freeman, Mae (Blacker) 1907- 25
Freeman, Nancy 1932- 61
Freeman, Peter J.
  See Calvert, Patricia
Freeman, Sarah (Caroline) 1940- 66
Freeman, Tony
  Brief entry 44
Freeman, William Bradford 1938- 58
  Brief entry 48
Fregosi, Claudia (Anne Marie)
  1946- 24
French, Allen 1870-1946
  See YABC 1
French, Dorothy Kayser 1926- 5
French, Fiona 1944- 75
  Earlier sketch in SATA 6
  See also CLR 37
  See also SAAS 21
French, Kathryn
  See Mosesson, Gloria R(ubin)
French, Michael 1944- 49
  Brief entry 38
French, Paul
  See Asimov, Isaac
French, Simon 1957- 86
Freund, Rudolf 1915-1969
  Brief entry 28
Frewer, Glyn 1931- 11
Frey, Darcy 98
Frick, C. H.
  See Irwin, Constance Frick
Frick, Constance
  See Irwin, Constance Frick
Fricke, Aaron 1962- 89
Friedlander, Joanne K(ohn) 1930- 9
Friedman, Estelle 1920- 7
Friedman, Frieda 1905- 43
Friedman, Ina R(osen) 1926- 49
  Brief entry 41
Friedman, Judi 1935- 59

Friedman, Marvin 1930- ...._42_
  Brief entry ...._33_
Friedmann, Stan 1953- ...._80_
Friedrich, Otto (Alva) 1929- ...._33_
Friedrich, Priscilla 1927- ...._39_
Friendlich, Dick
  See Friendlich, Richard J.
Friendlich, Richard J. 1909- ...._11_
Friermood, Elisabeth Hamilton
  1903- ...._5_
Friesner, Esther M. 1951- ...._71_
Friis, Babbis
  See Friis-Baastad, Babbis
Friis-Baastad, Babbis 1921-1970 ...._7_
Frimmer, Steven 1928- ...._31_
Friskey, Margaret Richards 1901- ...._5_
Fritts, Mary Bahr
  See Bahr, Mary M(adelyn)
Fritz
  See Frazetta, Frank
Fritz, Jean (Guttery) 1915- ...._72_
  Earlier sketches in SATA _1, 29_
  See also CLR _14_
  See also SAAS _2_
Froehlich, Margaret Walden 1930- ...._56_
Frois, Jeanne 1953- ...._73_
Froissart, Jean 1338(?)-1410(?) ...._28_
Froman, Elizabeth Hull 1920-1975 ...._10_
Froman, Robert (Winslow) 1917- ...._8_
Fromm, Lilo 1928- ...._29_
Frommer, Harvey 1937- ...._41_
Frost, A(rthur) B(urdett) 1851-1928 ...._19_
Frost, Erica
  See Supraner, Robyn
Frost, Lesley 1899(?)-1983 ...._14_
  Obituary ...._34_
Frost, Robert (Lee) 1874-1963 ...._14_
Fry, Annette R(iley) ...._89_
Fry, Christopher 1907- ...._66_
Fry, Edward Bernard 1925- ...._35_
Fry, Rosalie Kingsmill 1911- ...._3_
  See also SAAS _11_
Fry, Virginia Lynn 1952- ...._95_
Frye, Sally
  See Moore, Elaine
Fuchs, Bernie 1932- ...._95_
Fuchs, Erich 1916- ...._6_
Fuchs, Lucy 1935-
  Brief entry ...._52_
Fuchshuber, Annegert 1940- ...._43_
Fuge, Charles 1966- ...._74_
Fujikawa, Gyo 1908- ...._76_
  Brief entry ...._30_
  Earlier sketch in SATA _39_
  See also CLR _25_
  See also SAAS _16_
Fujita, Tamao 1905- ...._7_
Fujiwara, Kim 1957- ...._81_
Fujiwara, Michiko 1946- ...._15_
Fuka, Vladimir 1926-1977
  Obituary ...._27_
Fuller, Catherine L(euthold) 1916- ...._9_
Fuller, Edmund (Maybank) 1914- ...._21_
Fuller, Iola
  See McCoy, Iola Fuller
Fuller, John G(rant, Jr.) 1913-1990 ...._65_
Fuller, Kathleen
  See Gottfried, Theodore Mark
Fuller, Lois Hamilton 1915- ...._11_
Fuller, Margaret
  See Ossoli, Sarah Margaret (Fuller)
  marchesa d'
Fuller, Roy (Broadbent) 1912-1991 ...._87_
Fults, John Lee 1932- ...._33_
Funai, Mamoru (Rolland) 1932-
  Brief entry ...._46_
Funk, Thompson
  See Funk, Tom
Funk, Tom 1911- ...._7_
Funke, Lewis 1912- ...._11_
Furchgott, Terry 1948- ...._29_
Furlong, Monica (Mavis) 1930- ...._86_
Furniss, Tim 1948- ...._49_
Furukawa, Toshi 1924- ...._24_
Futcher, Jane P. 1947- ...._76_
Fyleman, Rose 1877-1957 ...._21_
Fyson, J(enny) G(race) 1904- ...._42_

G

Gaan, Margaret 1914- ...._65_
Gabhart, Ann 1947- ...._75_
Gabler, Mirko 1951- ...._77_
Gabriel, Adriana
  See Rojany, Lisa
Gackenbach, Dick ...._48_
  Brief entry ...._30_
Gackenbach, Dick 1927- ...._79_
  Brief entry ...._30_
  Earlier sketch in SATA _48_
Gaddis, Vincent H. 1913- ...._35_
Gadler, Steve J. 1905- ...._36_
Gaeddert, Lou Ann (Bigge) 1931- ...._20_
Gaffney, Timothy R. 1951- ...._69_
Gaffron, Norma (Bondeson) 1931- ...._97_
Gag, Flavia 1907-1979
  Obituary ...._24_
Gag, Wanda (Hazel) 1893-1946
  See YABC _1_
  See also CLR _4_
Gage, Wilson
  See Steele, Mary Q(uintard Govan)
Gagliardo, Ruth Garver 1895(?)-1980
  Obituary ...._22_
Gagnon, Cecile 1936- ...._58_
Gaiman, Neil (Richard) 1960- ...._85_
Gainer, Cindy 1962- ...._74_
Gaines, Ernest J(ames) 1933- ...._86_
Gal, Laszlo 1933- ...._96_
  Brief entry ...._32_
  Earlier sketch in SATA _52_
Galbraith, Kathryn O(sebold)
  1945- ...._85_
Galdone, Paul 1907(?)-1986 ...._66_
  Obituary ...._49_
  Earlier sketch in SATA _17_
  See also CLR _16_
Galinsky, Ellen 1942- ...._23_
Gallant, Roy A(rthur) 1924- ...._68_
  Earlier sketch in SATA _4_
  See also CLR _30_
Gallardo, Evelyn 1948- ...._78_
Gallico, Paul 1897-1976 ...._13_
Galloway, Priscilla 1930- ...._66_
Galouchko, Annouchka Gravel
  1960- ...._95_
Galt, Thomas Franklin, Jr. 1908- ...._5_
Galt, Tom
  See Galt, Thomas Franklin, Jr.
Galvin, Matthew R(eppert) 1950- ...._93_
Gamble, Kim 1952- ...._81_
Gambrell, Jamey ...._82_
Gamerman, Martha 1941- ...._15_
Gammell, Stephen 1943- ...._81_
  Earlier sketch in SATA _53_
Ganly, Helen (Mary) 1940- ...._56_
Gannett, Ruth Chrisman (Arens)
  1896-1979 ...._33_
Gannett, Ruth Stiles 1923- ...._3_
Gannon, Robert (Haines) 1931- ...._8_
Gano, Lila 1949- ...._76_
Gans, Roma 1894-1996 ...._45_
  Obituary ...._93_
Gantner, Susan (Verble) 1939- ...._63_
Gantos, Jack
  See CLR _18_
  See Gantos, John (Byran), Jr.
Gantos, John (Byran), Jr. 1951- ...._81_
  Earlier sketch in SATA _20_
Ganz, Yaffa 1938- ...._61_
  Brief entry ...._52_
Garafano, Marie 1942- ...._84_
Garbutt, Bernard 1900-
  Brief entry ...._31_
Gard, Janice
  See Latham, Jean Lee
Gard, Joyce
  See Reeves, Joyce
Gard, Robert Edward 1910-1992 ...._18_
  Obituary ...._74_
Gard, (Sanford) Wayne 1899-1986
  Obituary ...._49_

Gardam, Jane 1928- ...._76_
  Brief entry ...._28_
  Earlier sketch in SATA _39_
  See also CLR _12_
  See also SAAS _9_
Gardella, Tricia 1944- ...._96_
Garden, Nancy 1938- ...._77_
  Earlier sketch in SATA _12_
  See also SAAS _8_
Gardiner, John Reynolds 1944- ...._64_
Gardner, Beau
  Brief entry ...._50_
Gardner, Craig Shaw 1949- ...._99_
Gardner, Dic
  See Gardner, Richard
Gardner, Hugh 1910-1986
  Obituary ...._49_
Gardner, Jane Mylum 1946- ...._83_
Gardner, Jeanne LeMonnier ...._5_
Gardner, John (Champlin, Jr.)
  1933-1982 ...._40_
  Obituary ...._31_
Gardner, Martin 1914- ...._16_
Gardner, Miriam
  See Bradley, Marion Zimmer
Gardner, Richard 1931- ...._24_
Gardner, Richard A. 1931- ...._13_
Gardner, Robert 1929-
  Brief entry ...._43_
Gardner, Sandra 1940- ...._70_
Gardner, Sheldon 1934- 101 33
Gardner, Theodore Roosevelt II
  1934- ...._84_
Garelick, May ...._19_
Garfield, James B. 1881-1984 ...._6_
  Obituary ...._38_
Garfield, Leon 1921-1996 ...._76_
  Obituary ...._90_
  Earlier sketches in SATA _1, 32_
  See also CLR _21_
Garis, Howard R(oger) 1873-1962 ...._13_
Garland, Mark (A.) 1953- ...._79_
Garland, Sarah 1944- ...._62_
Garland, Sherry 1948- ...._73_
Garner, Alan 1934- ...._69_
  Earlier sketch in SATA _18_
  See also CLR _20_
Garner, David 1958- ...._78_
Garner, James Finn 1960(?)- ...._92_
Garnet, A. H.
  See Slote, Alfred
Garnett, Eve C. R. 1900-1991 ...._3_
  Obituary ...._70_
Garou, Louis P.
  See Bowkett, Stephen
Garraty, John A. 1920- ...._23_
Garret, Maxwell R. 1917- ...._39_
Garretson, Victoria Diane 1945- ...._44_
Garrett, Helen 1895- ...._21_
Garrett, Richard 1920- ...._82_
Garrigue, Sheila 1931- ...._21_
Garrison, Barbara 1931- 19
Garrison, Frederick
  See Sinclair, Upton (Beall)
Garrison, Webb B(lack) 1919- ...._25_
Garst, Doris Shannon 1894- ...._1_
Garst, Shannon
  See Garst, Doris Shannon
Garthwaite, Marion H. 1893- ...._7_
Garton, Malinda D(ean) (?)-1976
  Obituary ...._26_
Gascoigne, Bamber 1935- ...._62_
Gasperini, Jim 1952- ...._54_
  Brief entry ...._49_
Gater, Dilys 1944- ...._41_
Gates, Doris 1901-1987 ...._34_
  Obituary ...._54_
  Earlier sketch in SATA _1_
  See also SAAS _1_
Gates, Frieda 1933- ...._26_
Gathorne-Hardy, Jonathan G.
  1933- ...._26_
Gatty, Juliana Horatia
  See Ewing, Juliana (Horatia Gatty)
Gatty, Margaret Scott 1809-1873
  Brief entry ...._27_

Gauch, Patricia Lee 1934- *80*
  Earlier sketch in SATA *26*
  See also SAAS *21*
Gaul, Randy 1959- *63*
Gault, Clare S. 1925- *36*
Gault, Frank 1926-1982 ....*36*
  Brief entry *30*
Gault, William Campbell 1910- *8*
Gaver, Becky
  See Gaver, Rebecca
Gaver, Rebecca 1952- *20*
Gavin, Jamila 1941- *96*
Gay, Amelia
  See Hogarth, Grace (Weston) Allen
Gay, Francis
  See Gee, H(erbert) L(eslie)
Gay, Kathlyn 1930- *9*
Gay, Marie-Louise 1952- *68*
  See also CLR *27*
  See also SAAS *21*
Gay, Zhenya 1906-1978 ....*19*
Gaze, Gillian
  See Barklem, Jill
Gear, Kathleen M. O'Neal
  See Gear, Kathleen O'Neal
Gear, Kathleen O'Neal 1954- *71*
Gear, W. Michael 1955- *71*
Gee, H(erbert) L(eslie) 1901-1977
  Obituary *26*
Gee, Maurice (Gough) 1931- *46*
Geer, Charles 1922- *42*
  Brief entry *32*
Gehman, Mary W. 1923- *86*
Gehr, Mary -1997 ....*32*
  Obituary *99*
Geipel, Eileen 1932- *30*
Geis, Darlene *7*
Geisel, Helen 1898-1967 ....*26*
Geisel, Theodor Seuss 1904-1991 ....*75*
  Obituary *67*
  Earlier sketches in SATA *1, 28*
  See also CLR *1*
Geisert, Arthur (Frederick) 1941- *92*
  Brief entry *52*
  Earlier sketch in SATA *56*
  See also SAAS *23*
Geisert, Bonnie 1942- *92*
Geldart, William 1936- *15*
Gelinas, Paul J. 1911- *10*
Gelman, Amy 1961- *72*
Gelman, Jan 1963- *58*
Gelman, Rita Golden 1937- *84*
  Brief entry *51*
Gelman, Steve 1934- *3*
Gemming, Elizabeth 1932- *11*
Gendel, Evelyn W. 1916(?)-1977
  Obituary *27*
Gennaro, Joseph F(rancis), Jr.
  1924- *53*
Gentile, Petrina 1969- *91*
Gentle, Mary 1956- *48*
Gentleman, David 1930- *7*
George, Jean Craighead 1919- *68*
  Earlier sketch in SATA *2*
  See also CLR *1*
George, John L(othar) 1916- *2*
George, Lindsay Barrett 1952- *95*
George, S(idney) C(harles) 1898- *11*
George, W(illiam) Lloyd 1900(?)-1975
  Obituary *30*
Georgiou, Constantine 1927- *7*
Gerard, Jean Ignace Isidore
  1803-1847 ....*45*
Geras, Adele (Daphne) 1944- *87*
  Earlier sketch in SATA *23*
  See also SAAS *21*
Gerber, Merrill Joan 1938- *64*
Gerberg, Mort 1931- *64*
Gergely, Tibor 1900-1978 ....*54*
  Obituary *20*
Geringer, Laura 1948- *94*
  Earlier sketch in SATA *29*
Gerler, William R(obert) 1917- *47*
Gerrard, Jean 1933- *51*

Gerrard, Roy 1935-1997 ....*90*
  Brief entry *45*
  Obituary *99*
  Earlier sketch in SATA *47*
  See also CLR *23*
Gerrold, David 1944- *66*
Gershator, Phillis 1942- *90*
Gerson, Corinne *37*
Gerson, Mary-Joan *79*
Gerson, Noel B(ertram) 1914-1988 ......*22*
  Obituary *60*
Gerstein, Mordicai 1935- *81*
  Brief entry *36*
  Earlier sketch in SATA *47*
Gervais, Bernadette 1959- *80*
Gesner, Clark 1938- *40*
Gessner, Lynne 1919- *16*
Getz, David 1957- *91*
Gevirtz, Eliezer 1950- *49*
Gewe, Raddory
  See Gorey, Edward (St. John)
Ghan, Linda (R.) 1947- *77*
Gherman, Beverly 1934- *68*
Giannini, Enzo 1946- *68*
Gibbons, Faye 1938- *65*
Gibbons, Gail (Gretchen) 1944- *72*
  Earlier sketch in SATA *23*
  See also CLR *8*
  See also SAAS *12*
Gibbs, Alonzo (Lawrence) 1915- *5*
Gibbs, (Cecilia) May 1877-1969
  Obituary *27*
Gibbs, Tony
  See Gibbs, Wolcott, Jr.
Gibbs, Wolcott, Jr. 1935- *40*
Giblin, James Cross 1933- *75*
  Earlier sketch in SATA *33*
  See also CLR *29*
  See also SAAS *12*
Gibson, Andrew (William) 1949- *72*
Gibson, Betty 1911- *75*
Gibson, Jo *88*
Gibson, Josephine
  See Joslin, Sesyle
Gibson, William 1914- *66*
Gidal, Sonia 1922- *2*
Gidal, Tim N(ahum) 1909- *2*
Giegling, John A(llan) 1935- *17*
Gifaldi, David 1950- *76*
Giff, Patricia Reilly 1935- *70*
  Earlier sketch in SATA *33*
Giffard, Hannah 1962- *83*
Gifford, Griselda 1931- *42*
Gifford, Kerri 1961- *91*
Gilbert, Ann
  See Taylor, Ann
Gilbert, Barbara Snow 1954- *97*
Gilbert, Harriett 1948- *30*
Gilbert, (Agnes) Joan (Sewell)
  1931- *10*
Gilbert, John (Raphael) 1926- *36*
Gilbert, Miriam
  See Presberg, Miriam Goldstein
Gilbert, Nan
  See Gilbertson, Mildred Geiger
Gilbert, Roby Goodale 1966- *90*
Gilbert, Sara (Dulaney) 1943- *82*
  Earlier sketch in SATA *11*
Gilbert, Suzie 1956- *97*
Gilbert, W(illiam) S(chwenk)
  1836-1911 ....*36*
Gilbertson, Mildred Geiger 1908- *2*
Gilbreath, Alice (Thompson) 1921- *12*
Gilbreth, Frank B., Jr. 1911- *2*
Gilchrist, Jan Spivey 1949- *72*
Gilden, Mel 1947- *97*
Gilfond, Henry *2*
Gilge, Jeanette 1924- *22*
Gili, Phillida 1944- *70*
Gill, Derek L(ewis) T(heodore)
  1919- *9*
Gill, Margery Jean 1925- *22*
Gill, Stephen 1932- *63*
Gillett, Mary *7*
Gillette, Henry Sampson 1915- *14*
Gillham, Bill
  See Gillham, William Edwin Charles

Gillham, William Edwin Charles
  1936- *42*
Gilliam, Stan 1946- *39*
  Brief entry *35*
Gilliland, Alexis A. 1931- *72*
Gilliland, (Cleburne) Hap 1918- *92*
Gilman, Dorothy
  See Butters, Dorothy Gilman
Gilman, Esther 1925- *15*
Gilman, Phoebe 1940- *58*
Gilmore, Iris 1900- *22*
Gilmore, Kate 1931- *87*
Gilmore, Mary (Jean Cameron)
  1865-1962 ....*49*
Gilmore, Susan 1954- *59*
Gilroy, Beryl 1924- *80*
Gilson, Barbara
  See Gilson, Charles James Louis
Gilson, Charles James Louis 1878-1943
  See YABC *2*
Gilson, Jamie 1933- *91*
  Brief entry *34*
  Earlier sketch in SATA *37*
Ginsburg, Mirra *92*
  Earlier sketch in SATA *6*
  See also CLR *45*
Giovanni, Nikki 1943- *24*
  See also CLR *6*
Giovanopoulos, Paul 1939- *7*
Gipson, Frederick B. 1908-1973 ....*2*
  Obituary *24*
Girard, Linda Walvoord 1942- *41*
Girion, Barbara 1937- *78*
  Earlier sketch in SATA *26*
  See also SAAS *14*
Girzone, Joseph F(rancis) 1930- *76*
Gittings, Jo Manton 1919- *3*
Gittings, Robert (William Victor)
  1911-1992 ....*6*
  Obituary *70*
Givens, Janet E(aton) 1932- *60*
Gladstone, Eve
  See Werner, Herma
Gladstone, Gary 1935- *12*
Gladstone, M(yron) J. 1923- *37*
Gladwin, William Zachary
  See Zollinger, Gulielma
Glanville, Brian (Lester) 1931- *42*
Glanzman, Louis S. 1922- *36*
Glaser, Dianne E(lizabeth) 1937- *50*
  Brief entry *31*
Glaser, Isabel Joshlin 1929- *94*
Glaser, Milton 1929- *11*
Glaspell, Susan 1882-1948
  See YABC *2*
Glass, Andrew *90*
  Brief entry *46*
Glassman, Bruce 1961- *76*
Glauber, Uta (Heil) 1936- *17*
Glazer, Tom 1914- *9*
Gleasner, Diana (Cottle) 1936- *29*
Gleason, Judith 1929- *24*
Gleeson, Libby 1950- *82*
Gleitzman, Morris 1953- *88*
Glen, Maggie 1944- *88*
Glendinning, Richard 1917- *24*
Glendinning, Sally
  See Glendinning, Sara W(ilson)
Glendinning, Sara W(ilson) 1913- *24*
Glenn, Mel 1943- *93*
  Brief entry *45*
  Earlier sketch in SATA *51*
Glenn, Patricia Brown 1953- *86*
Glennon, Karen M. 1946- *85*
Gles, Margaret Breitmaier 1940- *22*
Glick, Carl (Cannon) 1890-1971 ....*14*
Glick, Virginia Kirkus 1893-1980
  Obituary *23*
Gliewe, Unada 1927- *3*
Glimmerveen, Ulco 1958- *85*
Glines, Carroll V(ane), Jr. 1920- *19*
Gliori, Debi 1959- *72*
Globe, Leah Ain 1900- *41*
Glovach, Linda 1947- *7*

Glubok, Shirley (Astor) 1933- *68*
  Earlier sketch in SATA 6
  See also CLR *1*
  See also SAAS *7*
Gluck, Felix 1924(?)-1981
  Obituary *25*
Glynne-Jones, William 1907- *11*
Gobbato, Imero 1923- *39*
Goble, Dorothy *26*
Goble, Paul 1933- *69*
  Earlier sketch in SATA 25
  See also CLR *21*
Goble, Warwick (?)-1943 ....*46*
Godden, (Margaret) Rumer 1907- *36*
  Earlier sketch in SATA 3
  See also CLR *20*
  See also SAAS *12*
Gode, Alexander
  See Gode von Aesch, Alexander
  (Gottfried Friedrich)
Gode von Aesch, Alexander (Gottfried
  Friedrich) 1906-1970 ....*14*
Godfrey, Jane
  See Bowden, Joan Chase
Godfrey, Martyn N. 1949- *95*
Godfrey, William
  See Youd, (Christopher) Samuel
Godkin, Celia (Marilyn) 1948- *66*
Goedecke, Christopher (John)
  1951- *81*
Goettel, Elinor 1930- *12*
Goetz, Delia 1898-1996 ....*22*
  Obituary *91*
Goffe, Toni 1936- *61*
Goffstein, Brooke
  See Goffstein, M. B.
Goffstein, M. B. 1940- *70*
  Earlier sketch in SATA 8
  See also CLR *3*
Gogol, Sara 1948- *80*
Golann, Cecil Paige 1921- *11*
Golbin, Andree 1923- *15*
Gold, Phyllis 1941- *21*
Gold, Robert S(tanley) 1924- *63*
Gold, Sharlya *9*
Goldberg, Grace 1956- *78*
Goldberg, Herbert S. 1926- *25*
Goldberg, Jacob 1943- *94*
Goldberg, Jake
  See Goldberg, Jacob
Goldberg, Stan J. 1939- *26*
Goldberg, Susan 1948- *71*
Goldberger, Judith M.
  See Mathews, Judith
Goldentyer, Debra 1960- *84*
Goldfeder, Cheryl
  See Pahz, (Anne) Cheryl Suzanne
Goldfeder, Jim
  See Pahz, James Alon
Goldfrank, Helen Colodny 1912- *6*
Goldin, Augusta 1906- *13*
Goldin, Barbara Diamond 1946- *92*
  See also SAAS 26
Goldman, Alex J. 1917- *65*
Goldman, Elizabeth 1949- *90*
Goldsborough, June 1923- *19*
Goldsmith, Howard 1943- *24*
Goldsmith, John Herman Thorburn 1903-
  1987
  Obituary *52*
Goldsmith, Oliver 1728-1774 ....*26*
Goldsmith, Ruth M. 1919- *62*
Goldstein, Ernest A. 1933-
  Brief entry *52*
Goldstein, Nathan 1927- *47*
Goldstein, Philip 1910- *23*
Goldston, Robert (Conroy) 1927- *6*
Goldszmit, Henryk
  See Korczak, Janusz
Golembe, Carla 1951- *79*
Golenbock, Peter 1946- *99*
Goll, Reinhold W(eimar) 1897- *26*
Gollub, Matthew 1960- *83*
Gomi, Taro 1945- *64*
Gondosch, Linda 1944- *58*
Gonzalez, Catherine Troxell 1917- *87*
Gonzalez, Gloria 1940- *23*

Good, Alice 1950- *73*
Goodall, John S(trickland)
  1908-1996 ....*66*
  Obituary *91*
  Earlier sketch in SATA 4
  See also CLR 25
Goodbody, Slim
  See Burstein, John
Goode, Diane (Capuozzo) 1949- *84*
  Earlier sketch in SATA 15
Goode, Stephen 1943- *55*
  Brief entry *40*
Goodenow, Earle 1913- *40*
Goodin, Sallie (Brown) 1953- *74*
Goodman, Deborah Lerme 1956- *50*
  Brief entry *49*
Goodman, Elaine 1930- *9*
Goodman, Joan Elizabeth 1950- *94*
  Earlier sketch in SATA 50
Goodman, Walter 1927- *9*
Goodrich, Samuel Griswold
  1793-1860 ....*23*
Goodsell, Jane Neuberger 1921(?)-1988
  Obituary *56*
Goodwin, Hal
  See Goodwin, Harold L(eland)
Goodwin, Harold L(eland)
  1914-1990 ....*51*
  Obituary *65*
  Earlier sketch in SATA 13
Goor, Nancy (Ruth Miller) 1944- *39*
  Brief entry *34*
Goor, Ron(ald Stephen) 1940- *39*
  Brief entry *34*
Goossen, Agnes
  See Epp, Margaret A(gnes)
Gorbachev, Valeri 1944- *98*
Gordon, Bernard Ludwig 1931- *27*
Gordon, Colonel H. R.
  See Ellis, Edward S(ylvester)
Gordon, Donald
  See Payne, Donald Gordon
Gordon, Dorothy 1893-1970 ....*20*
Gordon, Esther S(aranga) 1935- *10*
Gordon, Frederick [Collective
  pseudonym] *1*
Gordon, Hal
  See Goodwin, Harold L(eland)
Gordon, Jeffie Ross
  See Enderle, Judith (Ann) Ross
  and Tessler, Stephanie Gordon
Gordon, John
  See Gesner, Clark
Gordon, John (William) 1925- *84*
  Earlier sketch in SATA 6
Gordon, Lew
  See Baldwin, Gordon C.
Gordon, Margaret (Anna) 1939- *9*
Gordon, Mildred 1912-1979
  Obituary *24*
Gordon, Selma
  See Lanes, Selma G.
Gordon, Sheila 1927- *88*
  See also CLR 27
Gordon, Shirley 1921- *48*
  Brief entry *41*
Gordon, Sol 1923- *11*
Gordon, Stewart
  See Shirreffs, Gordon D(onald)
Gordons, The [Joint pseudonym]
  See Gordon, Mildred
Gorelick, Molly C. 1920- *9*
Gorey, Edward (St. John) 1925- *70*
  Brief entry *27*
  Earlier sketch in SATA 29
  See also CLR 36
Gorham, Charles Orson 1911-1975 ......*36*
Gorham, Michael
  See Folsom, Franklin (Brewster)
Gormley, Beatrice 1942- *39*
  Brief entry *35*
Gorog, Judith (Katharine Allen)
  1938- *75*
  Earlier sketch in SATA 39
Gorsline, Douglas (Warner)
  1913-1985 ....*11*
  Obituary *43*

Gorsline, (Sally) Marie 1928- *28*
Gorsline, S. M.
  See Gorsline, (Sally) Marie
Gorton, Kaitlyn
  See Emerson, Kathy Lynn
Goryan, Sirak
  See Saroyan, William
Goscinny, Rene 1926-1977 ....*47*
  Brief entry *39*
  See also CLR 37
Goss, Clay(ton E.) 1946- *82*
Gottfried, Ted
  See Gottfried, Theodore Mark
Gottfried, Theodore Mark 1928- *85*
Gottlieb, Bill
  See Gottlieb, William P(aul)
Gottlieb, Gerald 1923- *7*
Gottlieb, William P(aul) *24*
Goudey, Alice E. 1898- *20*
Goudge, Eileen 1950- *88*
Goudge, Elizabeth 1900-1984 ....*2*
  Obituary *38*
Gough, Catherine 1931- *24*
Gough, Philip 1908- *45*
Goulart, Ron 1933- *6*
Gould, Alberta 1945- *96*
Gould, Chester 1900-1985 ....*49*
  Obituary *43*
Gould, Jean R(osalind)
  1909(?)-1993 ....*11*
  Obituary *77*
Gould, Lilian 1920- *6*
Gould, Marilyn 1928- *76*
  Earlier sketch in SATA 15
Gould, Steven (Charles) 1955- *95*
Gourley, Catherine 1950- *95*
Gourse, Leslie 1939- *89*
Govan, Christine Noble 1898- *9*
Gove, Doris 1944- *72*
Govern, Elaine 1939- *26*
Graaf, Peter
  See Youd, (Christopher) Samuel
Graber, (George) Alexander 1914-1997 ...*7*
  Obituary *98*
Graber, Richard (Fredrick) 1927- *26*
Grabianski, Janusz 1929-1976 ....*39*
  Obituary *30*
Graboff, Abner 1919- *35*
Grace, F(rances Jane) *45*
Gracza, Margaret Young 1928- *56*
Graeber, Charlotte Towner *56*
  Brief entry *44*
Graff, Polly Anne
  See Colver, Anne
Graff, (S.) Stewart 1908- *9*
Graham, Ada 1931- *11*
Graham, Alastair 1945- *74*
Graham, Arthur Kennon
  See Harrison, David L(ee)
Graham, Bob 1942- *63*
  See also CLR 31
Graham, Brenda Knight 1942- *32*
Graham, Charlotte
  See Bowden, Joan Chase
Graham, Eleanor 1896-1984 ....*18*
  Obituary *38*
Graham, Ennis
  See Molesworth, Mary Louisa
Graham, Frank, Jr. 1925- *11*
Graham, John 1926- *11*
Graham, Kennon
  See Harrison, David L(ee)
Graham, Larry
  See Graham, Lawrence (Otis)
Graham, Lawrence (Otis) 1962- *63*
Graham, Lorenz (Bell) 1902-1989 ....*74*
  Obituary *63*
  Earlier sketch in SATA 2
  See also CLR 10
  See also SAAS 5
Graham, Margaret Bloy 1920- *11*
Graham, Robin Lee 1949- *7*
Graham, Shirley
  See Du Bois, Shirley Graham
Graham-Barber, Lynda 1944- *42*

Graham-Cameron, M.
  See Graham-Cameron, M(alcolm)
  G(ordon)
Graham-Cameron, M(alcolm) G(ordon)
  1931- 53
  Brief entry 45
Graham-Cameron, Mike
  See Graham-Cameron, M(alcolm)
  G(ordon)
Grahame, Kenneth 1859-1932
  See YABC *1*
  See also CLR *5*
Gramatky, Hardie 1907-1979 30
  Obituary 23
  Earlier sketch in SATA *1*
  See also CLR *22*
Grambling, Lois G. 1927- 71
Grammer, June Amos 1927- 58
Grand, Samuel 1912- 42
Grandville, J. J.
  See Gerard, Jean Ignace Isidore
Grandville, Jean Ignace Isidore Gerard
  See Gerard, Jean Ignace Isidore
Granfield, Linda 1950- 96
Grange, Peter
  See Nicole, Christopher Robin
Granger, Margaret Jane 1925(?)-1977
  Obituary 27
Granger, Michele 1949- 88
Granger, Peggy
  See Granger, Margaret Jane
Granstaff, Bill 1925- 10
Grant, Bruce 1893-1977 5
  Obituary 25
Grant, Cynthia D. 1950- 77
  Earlier sketch in SATA *33*
Grant, Eva 1907- 7
Grant, Evva H. 1913-1977
  Obituary 27
Grant, Gordon 1875-1962 25
Grant, Gwen(doline Ellen) 1940- 47
Grant, (Alice) Leigh 1947- 10
Grant, Matthew C.
  See May, Julian
Grant, Maxwell
  See Lynds, Dennis
Grant, Myrna (Lois) 1934- 21
Grant, Neil 1938- 14
Grant, Richard 1948- 80
Grater, Michael 1923- 57
Gravel, Fern
  See Hall, James Norman
Gravelle, Karen 1942- 78
Graves, Charles Parlin 1911-1972 4
Graves, Robert (von Ranke)
  1895-1985 45
Graves, Valerie
  See Bradley, Marion Zimmer
Gray, Elizabeth Janet 1902- 6
Gray, Genevieve S. 1920- 4
Gray, Harold (Lincoln) 1894-1968 33
  Brief entry 32
Gray, Jenny
  See Gray, Genevieve S.
Gray, Judith A(nne) 1949- 93
Gray, Les 1929- 82
Gray, Libba Moore 1937- 83
Gray, Luli 1945- 90
Gray, Marian
  See Pierce, Edith Gray
Gray, Nicholas Stuart 1922-1981 4
  Obituary 27
Gray, Nigel 1941- 33
Gray, (Lucy) Noel (Clervaux)
  1898-1983 47
Gray, Patricia 7
Gray, Patsey
  See Gray, Patricia
Grayland, V. Merle
  See Grayland, Valerie
Grayland, Valerie 7
Grayson, Paul 1946- 79
Great Comte, The
  See Hawkesworth, Eric
Greaves, Margaret 1914-1995 87
  Earlier sketch in SATA *7*
Greaves, Nick 1955- 77

Gree, Alain 1936- 28
Green, Adam
  See Weisgard, Leonard (Joseph)
Green, Anne Canevari 1943- 62
Green, Brian
  See Card, Orson Scott
Green, Connie Jordan 1938- 80
Green, D.
  See Casewit, Curtis
Green, Hannah
  See Greenberg, Joanne (Goldenberg)
Green, Jane 1937- 9
Green, Mary Moore 1906- 11
Green, Morton 1937- 8
Green, Norma B(erger) 1925- 11
Green, Phyllis 1932- 20
Green, Roger James 1944-
  Brief entry 52
Green, Roger (Gilbert) Lancelyn
  1918-1987 2
  Obituary 53
Green, (James Le)Roy 1948- 89
Green, Sheila Ellen 1934- 87
  Earlier sketch in SATA *8*
Green, Timothy 1953- 91
Greenaway, Kate 1846-1901
  See YABC *2*
  See also CLR *6*
Greenbank, Anthony Hunt 1933- 39
Greenberg, Harvey R. 1935- 5
Greenberg, Jan 1942- 61
Greenberg, Joanne (Goldenberg)
  1932- 25
Greenberg, Melanie Hope 1954- 72
Greenberg, Polly 1932- 52
  Brief entry 43
Greene, Bette 1934- 8
  See also CLR *2*
  See also SAAS *16*
Greene, Carla 1916- 67
  Earlier sketch in SATA *1*
Greene, Carol 66
  Brief entry 44
Greene, Constance C(larke) 1924- 72
  Earlier sketch in SATA *11*
  See also SAAS *11*
Greene, Ellin 1927- 23
Greene, Graham 1904- 20
Greene, Jacqueline Dembar 1946- 76
Greene, Laura 1935- 38
Greene, Wade 1933- 11
Greene, Yvonne
  See Flesch, Yolande (Catarina)
Greenfeld, Howard 19
Greenfeld, Josh 1928- 62
Greenfield, Eloise 1929- 61
  Earlier sketch in SATA *19*
  See also CLR *38*
  See also SAAS *16*
Greenhaus, Thelma Nurenberg
  1903-1984 45
Greening, Hamilton
  See Hamilton, Charles (Harold St. John)
Greenleaf, Barbara Kaye 1942- 6
Greenleaf, Peter 1910- 33
Greenlee, Sharon 1935- 77
Greeno, Gayle 1949- 81
Greenseid, Diane 1948- 93
Greenspun, Adele Aron 1938- 76
Greenstein, Elaine 1959- 82
Greenwald, Sheila
  See Green, Sheila Ellen
Greenwood, Barbara 1940- 90
Gregg, Andy 1929- 81
Gregg, Charles T(hornton) 1927- 65
Gregg, Walter H(arold) 1919- 20
Gregor, Arthur 1923- 36
Gregori, Leon 1919- 15
Gregorian, Joyce Ballou 1946-1991 30
  Obituary 83
Gregorich, Barbara 1943- 66
Gregorowski, Christopher 1940- 30
Gregory, Diana (Jean) 1933- 49
  Brief entry 42
Gregory, Jean
  See Ure, Jean
Gregory, Kristiana 1951- 74

Gregory, Stephen
  See Penzler, Otto
Gregory, Valiska 1940- 82
Greisman, Joan Ruth 1937- 31
Grendon, Stephen
  See Derleth, August (William)
Grenville, Pelham
  See Wodehouse, P(elham) G(renville)
Gretz, Susanna 1937- 7
Gretzer, John 18
Grey, Jerry 1926- 11
Greybeard the Pirate
  See Macintosh, Brownie
Grey Owl
  See CLR *32*
  See Belaney, Archibald Stansfeld
Gri
  See Denney, Diana
Grice, Frederick 1910- 6
Grider, Dorothy 1915- 31
Gridley, Marion E(leanor)
  1906-1974 35
  Obituary 26
Grieder, Walter 1924- 9
Griego, Tony A. 1955- 77
Griese, Arnold A(lfred) 1921- 9
Grifalconi, Ann 1929- 66
  Earlier sketch in SATA *2*
  See also CLR *35*
  See also SAAS *16*
Griffin, Elizabeth May 1985- 89
Griffin, Gillett Good 1928- 26
Griffin, Judith Berry 34
Griffin, Peni R(ae Robinson)
  1961- 99
  Earlier sketch in SATA *67*
Griffin, Steven A(rthur) 1953- 89
Griffith, Connie 1946- 89
Griffith, Gershom 1960- 85
Griffith, Helen V(irginia) 1934- 87
  Earlier sketch in SATA *39*
Griffith, Jeannette [Joint pseudonym]
  See Eyerly, Jeannette
Griffiths, G(ordon) D(ouglas) 1910-1973
  Obituary 20
Griffiths, Helen 1939- 86
  Earlier sketch in SATA *5*
  See also SAAS *5*
Grigson, Jane 1928- 63
Grimes, Lee 1920- 68
Grimes, Nikki 1950- 93
  See also CLR *42*
Grimm, Cherry Barbara Lockett 1930-
  Brief entry 43
Grimm, Jacob Ludwig Karl
  1785-1863 22
Grimm, Wilhelm Karl 1786-1859 22
Grimm, William C(arey) 1907- 14
Grimsdell, Jeremy 1942- 83
Grimshaw, Nigel (Gilroy) 1925- 23
Grimsley, Gordon
  See Groom, Arthur William
Gringhuis, Dirk
  See Gringhuis, Richard H.
Gringhuis, Richard H. 1918-1974 6
  Obituary 25
Grinnell, David
  See Wollheim, Donald A(llen)
Grinnell, George Bird 1849-1938 16
Gripe, Maria (Kristina) 1923- 74
  Earlier sketch in SATA *2*
  See also CLR *5*
Groch, Judith (Goldstein) 1929- 25
Grode, Redway
  See Gorey, Edward (St. John)
Groening, Matt 1954- 81
Grohmann, Susan 1948- 84
Grohskopf, Bernice 7
Grol, Lini Richards 1913- 9
Grollman, Earl A. 1925- 22
Groom, Arthur William 1898-1964 10
Gross, Alan 1947- 54
  Brief entry 43
Gross, Ernie 1913- 67
Gross, Philip (John) 1952- 84
Gross, Ruth Belov 1929- 33

Gross, Sarah Chokla 1906-1976 9
    Obituary 26
Grosser, Morton 1931- 74
Grosser, Vicky 1958- 83
Grossman, Bill 1948- 72
Grossman, Nancy 1940- 29
Grossman, Patricia 1951- 73
Grossman, Robert 1940- 11
Groten, Dallas 1951- 64
Groth, John 1908-1988 21
    Obituary 56
Grover, Wayne 1934- 69
Groves, Georgina
    See Symons, (Dorothy) Geraldine
Groves, Seli 77
Gruber, Terry (deRoy) 1953- 66
Gruelle, John (Barton) 1880-1938 35
    Brief entry 32
Gruelle, Johnny
    See CLR 34
    See Gruelle, John (Barton)
Gruenberg, Sidonie M(atsner)
    1881-1974 2
    Obituary 27
Grummer, Arnold E(dward) 1923- 49
Grunewalt, Pine
    See Kunhardt, Edith
Gryski, Camilla 1948- 72
Guarino, Dagmar
    See Guarino, Deborah
Guarino, Deborah 1954- 68
Guay, Georgette (Marie Jeanne)
    1952- 54
Guback, Georgia 88
Guccione, Leslie Davis 1946- 72
Guck, Dorothy 1913- 27
Guevara, Susan 97
Gugler, Laurel Dee 95
Gugliotta, Bobette 1918- 7
Guiberson, Brenda Z. 1946- 71
Guillaume, Jeanette G. (Flierl)
    1899- 8
Guillot, Rene 1900-1969 7
    See also CLR 22
Guisewite, Cathy 1950- 57
Gulley, Judie 1942- 58
Gundersheimer, Karen
    Brief entry 44
Gundrey, Elizabeth 1924- 23
Gunn, James E(dwin) 1923- 35
Gunn, Robin Jones 1955- 84
Gunston, Bill
    See Gunston, William Tudor
Gunston, William Tudor 1927- 9
Gunterman, Bertha Lisette 1886(?)-1975
    Obituary 27
Gunther, John 1901-1970 2
Guravich, Dan 1918- 74
Gurko, Leo 1914- 9
Gurko, Miriam 1910(?)-1988 9
    Obituary 58
Gurney, Gene 1924- 65
Gurney, James 1958- 76
Gurney, John Steven 1962- 75
Gustafson, Anita 1942-
    Brief entry 45
    See Larsen, Anita
Gustafson, Sarah R.
    See Riedman, Sarah R(egal)
Gustafson, Scott 1956- 34
Guthrie, A(lfred) B(ertram), Jr.
    1901-1991 62
    Obituary 67
Guthrie, Anne 1890-1979 28
Guthrie, Donna W. 1946- 63
Gutman, Bill 67
    Brief entry 43
Gutman, Dan 1955- 77
Gutman, Naham 1899(?)-1981
    Obituary 25
Gutmann, Bessie Pease 1876-1960 73
Guy, Rosa (Cuthbert) 1928- 62
    Earlier sketch in SATA *14*
    See also CLR *13*
Guymer, (Wilhelmina) Mary 1909- 50

Gwynne, Fred(erick Hubbard)
    1926-1993 41
    Brief entry 27
    Obituary 75

H

Haab, Sherri 1964- 91
Haar, Jaap ter 1922-
    See CLR 15
Haas, Carolyn Buhai 1926- 43
Haas, Dorothy F. 46
    Brief entry 43
    See also SAAS 17
Haas, Irene 1929- 96
    Earlier sketch in SATA *17*
Haas, James E(dward) 1943- 40
Haas, (Katherine) Jessie 1959- 98
Haas, Merle S. 1896(?)-1985
    Obituary 41
Habenstreit, Barbara 1937- 5
Haber, Karen 1955- 78
Haber, Louis 1910- 12
Hackett, John Winthrop 1910- 65
Haddix, Margaret Peterson 1964- 94
Hader, Berta (Hoerner)
    1891(?)-1976 16
Hader, Elmer (Stanley) 1889-1973 16
Hadithi, Mwenye
    See Hobson, Bruce
Hadley, Franklin
    See Winterbotham, R(ussell) R(obert)
Hadley, Lee 1934-1995 89
    Brief entry 38
    Obituary 86
    Earlier sketch in SATA *47*
    See also SAAS *14*
    See Irwin, Hadley Joint pseudonym
Haeffele, Deborah 1954- 76
Haenel, Wolfram 1956- 89
Haertling, Peter 1933- 66
    See also CLR 29
Hafner, Marylin 1925- 7
Hager, Alice Rogers 1894-1969
    Obituary 26
Hager, Betty 1923- 89
Haggard, H(enry) Rider 1856-1925 16
Haggerty, James J(oseph) 1920- 5
Hagon, Priscilla
    See Allan, Mabel Esther
Hague, (Susan) Kathleen 1949- 49
    Brief entry 45
Hague, Michael R(iley) 1948- 80
    Brief entry 32
    Earlier sketch in SATA *48*
Hahn, Emily 1905-1997 3
    Obituary 96
Hahn, Hannelore 1926- 8
Hahn, James (Sage) 1947- 9
Hahn, (Mona) Lynn 1949- 9
Hahn, Mary Downing 1937- 81
    Brief entry 44
    Earlier sketch in SATA *50*
    See also SAAS *12*
Hahn, Michael T. 1953- 92
Haig-Brown, Roderick (Langmere)
    1909-1976 12
    See also CLR *31*
Haight, Anne Lyon 1895-1977
    Obituary 30
Haight, Sandy 1949- 79
Haines, Gail Kay 1943- 11
Haining, Peter 1940- 14
Hains, Harriet
    See Watson, Carol
Hakim, Joy 1931- 83
Halacy, D(aniel) S(tephen), Jr.
    1919- 36
    See also SAAS 8
Haldane, Roger John 1945- 13
Hale, Arlene 1924-1982 49
Hale, Christy
    See Apostolou, Christine Hale
Hale, Edward Everett 1822-1909 16
Hale, Glenn
    See Walker, Robert W(ayne)

Hale, Helen
    See Mulcahy, Lucille Burnett
Hale, Irina 1932- 26
Hale, Kathleen 1898- 66
    Earlier sketch in SATA *17*
Hale, Linda 1929- 6
Hale, Lucretia Peabody 1820-1900 26
Hale, Nancy 1908-1988 31
    Obituary 57
Haley, Gail E(inhart) 1939- 78
    Brief entry 28
    Earlier sketch in SATA *43*
    See also CLR *21*
    See also SAAS *13*
Haley, Neale 52
Hall, Adam
    See Trevor, Elleston
Hall, Adele 1910- 7
Hall, Anna Gertrude 1882-1967 8
Hall, Barbara 1960- 68
Hall, Beverly B. 1918- 95
Hall, Borden
    See Yates, Raymond F(rancis)
Hall, Brian P(atrick) 1935- 31
Hall, Cameron
    See del Rey, Lester
Hall, Caryl
    See Hansen, Caryl (Hall)
Hall, Donald (Andrew, Jr.) 1928- 97
    Earlier sketch in SATA *23*
Hall, Douglas 1931- 43
Hall, Elizabeth 1929- 77
Hall, Elvajean 6
Hall, James Norman 1887-1951 21
Hall, Jesse
    See Boesen, Victor
Hall, Katy
    See McMullan, Kate (Hall)
Hall, Kirsten Marie 1974- 67
Hall, Lynn 1937- 79
    Earlier sketches in SATA *2, 47*
    See also SAAS *4*
Hall, Malcolm 1945- 7
Hall, Marjory
    See Yeakley, Marjory Hall
Hall, Melanie 1949- 78
Hall, Rosalys Haskell 1914- 7
Hall, Willis 1929- 66
Hallard, Peter
    See Catherall, Arthur
Hallas, Richard
    See Knight, Eric (Mowbray)
Hall-Clarke, James
    See Rowland-Entwistle, (Arthur)
    Theodore (Henry)
Haller, Dorcas Woodbury 1946- 46
Hallett, Mark 1947- 83
Halliburton, Richard 1900-1939(?) 81
Halliburton, Warren J. 1924- 19
Halliday, William R(oss) 1926- 52
Hallin, Emily Watson 1919- 6
Hallinan, P(atrick) K(enneth) 1944- 39
    Brief entry 37
Hallman, Ruth 1929- 43
    Brief entry 28
Hallowell, Tommy
    See Hill, Thomas (Hallowell)
Hall-Quest, (Edna) Olga W(ilbourne)
    1899-1986 11
    Obituary 47
Hallstead, William F(inn) III 1924- 11
Hallward, Michael 1889- 12
Halperin, Wendy Anderson 1952- 80
Halpin, Marlene 1927- 88
Halsell, Grace 1923- 13
Halsted, Anna Roosevelt 1906-1975
    Obituary 30
Halter, Jon C(harles) 1941- 22
Hamalian, Leo 1920- 41
Hamberger, John 1934- 14
Hamblin, Dora Jane 1920- 36
Hamerstrom, Frances 1907- 24
Hamil, Thomas Arthur 1928- 14
Hamil, Tom
    See Hamil, Thomas Arthur
Hamill, Ethel
    See Webb, Jean Francis (III)

Hamilton, (John) Alan 1943- 66
Hamilton, Alice
  See Cromie, Alice Hamilton
Hamilton, Anita 1919- 92
Hamilton, Buzz
  See Hemming, Roy (G.)
Hamilton, Carol (Jean Barber)
  1935- 94
Hamilton, Charles (Harold St. John)
  1875-1961 13
Hamilton, Charles 1913-1996 65
  Obituary 93
Hamilton, Clive
  See Lewis, C(live) S(taples)
Hamilton, Dorothy 1906-1983 12
  Obituary 35
Hamilton, Edith 1867-1963 20
Hamilton, Elizabeth 1906- 23
Hamilton, Franklin
  See Silverberg, Robert
Hamilton, Gail
  See Corcoran, Barbara
Hamilton, Mary (E.) 1927- 55
Hamilton, Mollie
  See Kaye, M(ary) M(argaret)
Hamilton, Morse 1943- 35
Hamilton, Robert W.
  See Stratemeyer, Edward L.
Hamilton, Virginia (Esther) 1936- 79
  Earlier sketches in SATA 4, 56
  See also CLR 40
Hamilton-Paterson, James 1941- 82
Hamlet, Ova
  See Lupoff, Richard A(llen)
Hamley, Dennis 1935- 69
  Earlier sketch in SATA 39
  See also CLR 47
  See also SAAS 22
Hamlin, Peter J. 1970- 84
Hamm, Diane Johnston 1949- 78
Hammer, Charles 1934- 58
Hammer, Richard 1928- 6
Hammerman, Gay M(orenus) 1926- 9
Hammond, Winifred G(raham)
  1899- 29
Hammontree, Marie (Gertrude)
  1913- 13
Hampshire, Joyce Gregorian
  See Gregorian, Joyce Ballou
Hampshire, Susan 1942- 98
Hampson, (Richard) Denman
  1929- 15
Hampson, Frank 1918(?)-1985
  Obituary 46
Hamre, Leif 1914- 5
Hamsa, Bobbie 1944- 52
  Brief entry 38
Han, Suzanne Crowder 1953- 89
Hancock, Mary A. 1923- 31
Hancock, Sibyl 1940- 9
Handford, Martin (John) 1956- 64
Handforth, Thomas (Schofield)
  1897-1948 42
Handville, Robert (Tompkins)
  1924- 45
Hane, Roger 1940-1974
  Obituary 20
Haney, Lynn 1941- 23
Hanff, Helene 1916-1997 11
  Obituary 97
Hanley, Boniface (Francis) 1924- 65
Hanlon, Emily 1945- 15
Hann, Jacquie 1951- 19
Hann, Judith 1942- 77
Hanna, Bill
  See Hanna, William
Hanna, Cheryl 1951- 84
Hanna, Jack (Bushnell) 1947- 74
Hanna, Nell(ie L.) 1908- 55
Hanna, Paul R(obert) 1902- 9
Hanna, William 1910- 51
Hannam, Charles 1925- 50
Hannele, Pirkko
  See Vainio, Pirkko
Hano, Arnold 1922- 12
Hansen, Ann Larkin 1958- 96
Hansen, Caryl (Hall) 1929- 39

Hansen, Joyce 1942- 46
  Brief entry 39
  See also CLR 21
  See also SAAS 15
Hansen, Ron 1947- 56
Hanser, Richard (Frederick) 1909- 13
Hanson, Joan 1938- 8
Hanson, Joseph E. 1894(?)-1971
  Obituary 27
Hansson, Gunilla 1939- 64
Harald, Eric
  See Boesen, Victor
Harcourt, Ellen Knowles 1890(?)-1984
  Obituary 36
Hard, Charlotte (Ann) 1969- 98
Hardcastle, Michael 1933- 47
  Brief entry 38
Harding, Lee 1937- 32
  Brief entry 31
Hardwick, Richard Holmes, Jr.
  1923- 12
Hardy, Alice Dale [Collective
  pseudonym] 67
  Earlier sketch in SATA 1
Hardy, David A(ndrews) 1936- 9
Hardy, Jon 1958- 53
Hardy, Stuart
  See Schisgall, Oscar
Hardy, Thomas 1840-1928 25
Hare, Norma Q(uarles) 1924- 46
  Brief entry 41
Harford, Henry
  See Hudson, W(illiam) H(enry)
Hargrave, Leonie
  See Disch, Thomas M(ichael)
Hargreaves, Roger 1935(?)-1988
  Obituary 56
Hargrove, James 1947- 57
  Brief entry 50
Hargrove, Jim
  See Hargrove, James
Hariton, Anca I. 1955- 79
Hark, Mildred
  See McQueen, Mildred Hark
Harkaway, Hal
  See Stratemeyer, Edward L.
Harkins, Philip 1912- 6
Harlan, Elizabeth 1945- 41
  Brief entry 35
Harlan, Glen
  See Cebulash, Mel
Harlan, Judith 1949- 74
Harler, Anne
  See Van Steenwyk, Elizabeth (Ann)
Harley, Bill 1954- 87
Harlow, Rosie 1961- 82
Harman, Fred 1902(?)-1982
  Obituary 30
Harman, Hugh 1903-1982
  Obituary 33
Harmelink, Barbara (Mary) 9
Harmer, Mabel 1894- 45
Harmon, Margaret 1906- 20
Harmon, William (Ruth) 1938- 65
Harnan, Terry 1920- 12
Harnett, Cynthia (Mary) 1893-1981 5
  Obituary 32
Harper, Anita 1943- 41
Harper, Jo 1932- 97
Harper, Mary Wood
  See Dixon, Jeanne
Harper, Wilhelmina 1884-1973 4
  Obituary 26
Harrah, Michael 1940- 41
Harrell, Beatrice Orcutt 1943- 93
Harrell, Janice 1945- 70
Harrell, Sara Gordon
  See Banks, Sara (Jeanne Gordon Harrell)
Harries, Joan 1922- 39
Harrill, Ronald 1950- 90
Harrington, Denis J(ames) 1932- 88
Harrington, Lyn 1911- 5
Harris, Alan 1944- 71
Harris, Aurand 1915-1996 37
  Obituary 91
Harris, Catherine
  See Ainsworth, Catherine Harris

Harris, Christie (Lucy) Irwin 1907- 74
  Earlier sketch in SATA 6
  See also CLR 47
  See also SAAS 10
Harris, Colver
  See Colver, Anne
Harris, Dorothy Joan 1931- 13
Harris, Geraldine (Rachel) 1951- 54
Harris, Jacqueline L. 1929- 62
Harris, Janet 1932-1979 4
  Obituary 23
Harris, Jesse
  See Standiford, Natalie
Harris, Joel Chandler 1848-1908
  See YABC 1
  See also CLR 49
Harris, Jonathan 1921- 52
Harris, Larry Vincent 1939- 59
Harris, Lavinia
  See St. John, Nicole
Harris, Leon A., Jr. 1926- 4
Harris, Lorle K(empe) 1912- 22
Harris, Marilyn
  See Springer, Marilyn Harris
Harris, Mark Jonathan 1941- 84
  Earlier sketch in SATA 32
Harris, Robie H. 1940- 90
  Brief entry 53
Harris, Robin
  See Shine, Deborah
Harris, Rosemary (Jeanne) 1923- 82
  Earlier sketch in SATA 4
  See also CLR 30
  See also SAAS 7
Harris, Sherwood 1932- 25
Harris, Steven Michael 1957- 55
Harris-Filderman, Diane
  See Filderman, Diane E(lizabeth)
Harrison, C. William 1913- 35
Harrison, David L(ee) 1937- 92
  Earlier sketch in SATA 26
Harrison, Deloris 1938- 9
Harrison, Edward Hardy 1926- 56
Harrison, Harry 1925- 4
Harrison, Molly 1909- 41
Harrison, Sarah 1946- 63
Harrison, Ted
  See Harrison, Edward Hardy
Harsh, Fred (T.) 1925- 72
Harshaw, Ruth H(etzel) 1890-1968 27
Harshman, Marc 1950- 71
Hart, Bruce 1938- 57
  Brief entry 39
Hart, Carole 1943- 57
  Brief entry 39
Hart, Carolyn G(impel) 1936- 74
Hart, Jan Siegel 1940- 79
Hart, Virginia 1949- 83
Harte, (Francis) Bret(t) 1836-1902 26
Hartley, Ellen (Raphael) 1915- 23
Hartley, Fred Allan III 1953- 41
Hartley, William B(rown) 1913- 23
Hartman, Evert 1937- 38
  Brief entry 35
Hartman, Jane E(vangeline) 1928- 47
Hartman, Louis F(rancis)
  1901-1970 22
Hartman, Victoria 1942- 91
Hartnett, Sonya 1968- 93
Hartshorn, Ruth M. 1928- 11
Hartwig, Manfred 1950- 81
Harvey, Brett 1936- 61
Harvey, Edith 1908(?)-1972
  Obituary 27
Harvey, Karen D. 1935- 88
Harvey, Roland 1945- 71
Harwick, B. L.
  See Keller, Beverly L(ou)
Harwin, Brian
  See Henderson, LeGrand
Harwood, Pearl Augusta (Bragdon)
  1903- 9
Haseley, Dennis 1950- 57
  Brief entry 44
Haskell, Arnold 1903- 6

Haskins, James 1941- 69
  Earlier sketch in SATA 9
  See also CLR 39
Haskins, Jim
  See SAAS 4
  See Haskins, James
Hasler, Joan 1931- 28
Hass, Robert 1941- 94
Hassall, Joan 1906-1988 43
  Obituary 56
Hassler, Jon (Francis) 1933- 19
Hastings, Beverly
  See James, Elizabeth
Hastings, Ian 1912- 62
Haszard, Patricia Moyes
  See Moyes, Patricia
Hatch, Lynda S. 1950- 90
Hatch, Mary Cottam 1912-1970
  Brief entry 28
Hathorn, Libby 1943- 74
Hatlo, Jimmy 1898-1963
  Obituary 23
Haugaard, Erik Christian 1923- 68
  Earlier sketch in SATA 4
  See also CLR 11
  See also SAAS 12
Haugen, Tormod 1945- 66
Hauman, Doris 1898- 32
Hauman, George 1890-1961 32
Hauptly, Denis J(ames) 1945- 57
Hauser, Margaret L(ouise) 1909- 10
Hauserr, Rosmarie 1943- 86
Hausman, Gerald 1945- 90
  Earlier sketch in SATA 13
Hausman, Gerry
  See Hausman, Gerald
Hauth, Katherine B. 1940- 99
Hautman, Pete(r Murray) 1952- 82
Hautzig, Deborah 1956- 31
Hautzig, Esther Rudomin 1930- 68
  Earlier sketch in SATA 4
  See also CLR 22
  See also SAAS 15
Havel, Jennifer
  See Havill, Juanita
Havenhand, John
  See Cox, John Roberts
Havighurst, Walter (Edwin) 1901-1994 ...1
  Obituary 79
Haviland, Virginia 1911-1988 6
  Obituary 54
Havill, Juanita 1949- 74
Hawes, Judy 1913- 4
Hawes, Louise 1943- 60
Hawk, Virginia Driving
  See Sneve, Virginia Driving Hawk
Hawkes, Kevin 1959- 78
Hawkesworth, Eric 1921- 13
Hawkins, Arthur 1903- 19
Hawkins, Laura 1951- 74
Hawkins, Quail 1905- 6
Hawkinson, John 1912- 4
Hawkinson, Lucy (Ozone)
  1924-1971 21
Hawks, Robert 1961- 85
Hawley, Mabel C. [Collective
  pseudonym] 67
  Earlier sketch in SATA 1
Hawthorne, Captain R. M.
  See Ellis, Edward S(ylvester)
Hawthorne, Nathaniel 1804-1864
  See YABC 2
Hay, John 1915- 13
Hay, Timothy
  See Brown, Margaret Wise
Hayashi, Nancy 1939- 80
Haycock, Kate 1962- 77
Haycraft, Howard 1905-1991 6
  Obituary 70
Haycraft, Molly Costain 1911- 6
Hayden, Gwendolen Lampshire
  1904- 35
Hayden, Robert C(arter), Jr. 1937- 47
  Brief entry 28
Hayden, Robert E(arl) 1913-1980 19
  Obituary 26
Hayden, Torey L(ynn) 1951- 65

Hayes, Carlton J. H. 1882-1964 11
Hayes, Daniel 1952- 73
Hayes, Geoffrey 1947- 91
  Earlier sketch in SATA 26
Hayes, Joe 1945- 88
Hayes, John F. 1904- 11
Hayes, Sheila 1937- 51
  Brief entry 50
Hayes, Will 7
Hayes, William D(imitt) 1913- 8
Haynes, Betsy 1937- 94
  Brief entry 37
  Earlier sketch in SATA 48
Haynes, David 1955- 97
Haynes, Linda
  See Swinford, Betty (June Wells)
Haynes, Mary 1938- 65
Haynes, Max 1956- 72
Hays, H(offman) R(eynolds)
  1904-1980 26
Hays, Thomas Anthony 1957- 84
Hays, Tony
  See Hays, Thomas Anthony
Hays, Wilma Pitchford 1909- 28
  Earlier sketch in SATA 1
  See also SAAS 3
Hayward, Linda 1943-
  Brief entry 39
Haywood, Carolyn 1898-1990 75
  Obituary 64
  Earlier sketches in SATA 1, 29
  See also CLR 22
Hazen, Barbara Shook 1930- 90
  Earlier sketch in SATA 27
Head, Gay
  See Hauser, Margaret L(ouise)
Headley, Elizabeth
  See Cavanna, Betty
Headstrom, Richard 1902- 8
Heady, Eleanor B(utler) 1917- 8
Heagy, William D. 1964- 76
Heal, Edith 1903- 7
Heal, Gillian 1934- 89
Heale, Jay (Jeremy Peter Wingfield)
  1937- 84
Healey, Brooks
  See Albert, Burton, Jr.
Healey, Larry 1927- 44
  Brief entry 42
Heaps, Willard (Allison) 1909- 26
Hearn, Diane Dawson 1952- 79
Hearn, Emily
  See Valleau, Emily
Hearn, Sneed
  See Gregg, Andy
Hearne, Betsy Gould 1942- 95
  Earlier sketch in SATA 38
Heath, Charles D(ickinson) 1941- 46
Heath, Veronica
  See Blackett, Veronica Heath
Heaven, Constance
  See Fecher, Constance
Hecht, George J(oseph) 1895-1980
  Obituary 22
Hecht, Henri Joseph 1922- 9
Hechtkopf, Henryk 1910- 17
Heck, Bessie Holland 1911- 26
Heckert, Connie K(aye Delp)
  1948- 82
Hedderwick, Mairi 1939- 77
  Earlier sketch in SATA 30
Hedges, Sid(ney) G(eorge)
  1897-1974 28
Heerboth, Sharon
  See Leon, Sharon
Heffron, Dorris 1944- 68
Hefter, Richard 1942- 31
Hegan, Alice Caldwell
  See Rice, Alice (Caldwell) Hegan
Hegarty, Reginald Beaton
  1906-1973 10
Heide, Florence Parry 1919- 69
  Earlier sketch in SATA 32
  See also SAAS 6
Heiderstadt, Dorothy 1907- 6
Heilbroner, Joan (Knapp) 1922- 63

Heilbrun, Lois Hussey 1922(?)-1987
  Obituary 54
Heiligman, Deborah 1958- 90
Heilman, Joan Rattner 50
Hein, Lucille Eleanor 1915- 20
Heine, Helme 1941- 67
  See also CLR 18
Heinemann, George Alfred 1918-
  Brief entry 31
Heinlein, Robert A. 1907-1988 69
  Obituary 56
  Earlier sketch in SATA 9
Heins, Paul 1909- 13
Heintze, Carl 1922- 26
Heinz, Brian J(ames) 1946- 95
Heinz, W(ilfred) C(harles) 1915- 26
Heinzen, Mildred
  See Masters, Mildred
Heisel, Sharon E(laine) 1941- 84
Heitzmann, William Ray 1948- 73
Heitzmann, Wm. Ray
  See Heitzmann, William Ray
Helfman, Elizabeth S(eaver) 1911- 3
Helfman, Harry 1910- 3
Hellberg, Hans-Eric 1927- 38
Heller, Linda 1944- 46
  Brief entry 40
Heller, Ruth M. 1924- 66
Hellman, Hal
  See Hellman, Harold
Hellman, Harold 1927- 4
Helmer, Diana Star 1962- 86
Helps, Racey 1913-1971 2
  Obituary 25
Helweg, Hans H. 1917- 50
  Brief entry 33
Helyar, Jane Penelope Josephine
  1933- 82
  See also SAAS 2
  See Poole, Josephine
Hemmant, Lynette 1938- 69
Hemming, Roy (G.) 1928-1995 86
  Earlier sketch in SATA 11
Hemphill, Martha Locke
  1904-1973 37
Henba, Bobbie 1926- 87
Henbest, Nigel 1951- 55
  Brief entry 52
Henderley, Brooks [Collective
  pseudonym] 1
Henderson, Gordon 1950- 53
Henderson, Kathy 1949- 95
  Brief entry 53
  Earlier sketch in SATA 55
Henderson, LeGrand 1901-1965 9
Henderson, Nancy Wallace 1916- 22
Henderson, Zenna (Chlarson) 1917- 5
Hendrickson, Walter Brookfield, Jr.
  1936- 9
Hendry, Diana 1941- 68
Hendry, Linda (Gail) 1961- 83
Heneghan, James 1930- 97
  Earlier sketch in SATA 53
Henkes, Kevin 1960- 76
  Earlier sketch in SATA 43
  See also CLR 23
Hennefrund, Bet
  See Ring, Elizabeth
Hennefrund, Elizabeth
  See Ring, Elizabeth
Henning, Ann 1948- 92
Henriod, Lorraine 1925- 26
Henriquez, Emile F. 1937- 89
Henry, Joanne Landers 1927- 6
Henry, Maeve 1960- 75
Henry, Marguerite 1902-1997 69
  Obituary 99
  Earlier sketch in SATA 11
  See also CLR 4
  See also SAAS 7
Henry, Marie H. 1935- 65
Henry, Marion
  See del Rey, Lester
Henry, O.
  See Porter, William Sydney
Henry, Oliver
  See Porter, William Sydney

Henry, T. E.
　　See Rowland-Entwistle, (Arthur)
　　Theodore (Henry)
Henschel, (Elizabeth) Georgie 56
Henson, James Maury 1936-1990 43
　　Obituary 65
Henson, Jim
　　See Henson, James Maury
Henstra, Friso 1928- 73
　　Earlier sketch in SATA 8
　　See also SAAS 14
Hentoff, Nat 1925- 69
　　Brief entry 27
　　Earlier sketch in SATA 42
　　See also CLR 1
Henty, G(eorge) A(lfred)
　　1832-1902 64
Heo, Yumi 94
Herald, Kathleen
　　See Peyton, Kathleen (Wendy)
Herb, Angela M. 1970- 92
Herbert, Cecil
　　See Hamilton, Charles (Harold St. John)
Herbert, Don 1917- 2
Herbert, Frank (Patrick) 1920-1986 37
　　Obituary 47
　　Earlier sketch in SATA 9
Herbert, Helen (Jean) 1947- 57
Herbert, Wally
　　See Herbert, Walter William
Herbert, Walter William 1934- 23
Herbst, Judith 1947- 74
Herda, D. J. 1948- 80
Herge
　　See CLR 6
　　See Remi, Georges
Herkimer, L(awrence) R(ussell)
　　1925- 42
Herlihy, Dirlie Anne 1935- 73
Herman, Charlotte 1937- 99
　　Earlier sketch in SATA 20
Hermanson, Dennis (Everett)
　　1947- 10
Hermes, Jules 1962- 92
Hermes, Patricia 1936- 78
　　Earlier sketch in SATA 31
Herndon, Ernest 91
Herold, Ann Bixby 1937- 72
Herriot, James 1916-1995 86
　　See Wight, James Alfred
Herrmanns, Ralph 1933- 11
Herrold, Tracey
　　See Dils, Tracey E.
Herron, Edward A(lbert) 1912- 4
Hersey, John (Richard) 1914-1993 25
　　Obituary 76
Hershberger, Priscilla (Gorman)
　　1951- 81
Hershey, Kathleen M. 1934- 80
Hersom, Kathleen 1911- 73
Hertz, Grete Janus 1915- 23
Herzig, Alison Cragin 1935- 87
Heslewood, Juliet 1951- 82
Hess, Lilo 1916- 4
Hesse, Hermann 1877-1962 50
Hesse, Karen 1952- 74
　　See also SAAS 25
Hest, Amy 1950- 82
　　Earlier sketch in SATA 55
Heuer, Kenneth John 1927- 44
Heuman, William 1912-1971 21
Hewes, Agnes Danforth 1874-1963 35
Hewett, Anita 1918- 13
Hewett, Joan 1930- 81
Hewett, Richard 1929- 81
Hewitson, Jennifer 1961- 97
Hewitt, Margaret 1961- 84
Hext, Harrington
　　See Phillpotts, Eden
Hey, Nigel S(tewart) 1936- 20
Heyduck-Huth, Hilde 1929- 8
Heyer, Carol 1950- 74
Heyer, Marilee 1942- 64
Heyerdahl, Thor 1914- 52
　　Earlier sketch in SATA 2
Heyes, (Nancy) Eileen 1956- 80

Heyliger, William 1884-1955
　　See YABC 1
Heyman, Ken(neth Louis) 1930- 34
Heyward, Du Bose 1885-1940 21
Heywood, Karen 1946- 48
Hezlep, William (Earl) 1936- 88
Hibbert, Christopher 1924- 4
Hibbert, Eleanor Alice Burford
　　1906-1993 2
　　Obituary 74
Hickman, Janet 1940- 12
Hickman, Martha Whitmore 1925- 26
Hickok, Lorena A. 1892(?)-1968 20
Hickok, Will
　　See Harrison, C. William
Hicks, Clifford B. 1920- 50
Hicks, Eleanor B.
　　See Coerr, Eleanor (Beatrice)
Hicks, Harvey
　　See Stratemeyer, Edward L.
Hicyilmaz, Gay 1947- 77
Hieatt, Constance B(artlett) 1928- 4
Hiebert, Ray Eldon 1932- 13
Higdon, Hal 1931- 4
Higginbottom, David 1923- 87
　　See Fisk, Nicholas
Higginbottom, J(effrey) Winslow
　　1945- 29
Higginsen, Vy 79
High, Linda Oatman 1958- 94
Higham, David (Michael) 1949- 50
Higham, Jon Atlas
　　See Higham, Jonathan Huw
Higham, Jonathan Huw 1960- 59
Highet, Helen
　　See MacInnes, Helen
Hightower, Florence Cole 1916-1981 4
　　Obituary 27
Highwater, Jamake 1942(?)- 69
　　Brief entry 30
　　Earlier sketch in SATA 32
　　See also CLR 17
Hildebrandt, Greg 1939- 55
　　Brief entry 33
Hildebrandt, The Brothers
　　See Hildebrandt, Tim(othy)
Hildebrandt, Tim(othy) 1939- 55
　　Brief entry 33
Hildebrandts, The
　　See Hildebrandt, Tim(othy)
Hilder, Rowland 1905-1993 36
　　Obituary 77
Hildick, E. W.
　　See Hildick, (Edmund) Wallace
Hildick, (Edmund) Wallace 1925- 68
　　Earlier sketch in SATA 2
　　See also SAAS 6
Hilgartner, Beth 1957- 58
Hill, Alexis
　　See Craig, Mary (Francis) Shura
Hill, Anthony R(obert) 1942- 91
Hill, Donna (Marie) 24
Hill, Douglas (Arthur) 1935- 78
　　Earlier sketch in SATA 39
Hill, Elizabeth Starr 1925- 24
Hill, Eric 1927- 66
　　Brief entry 53
　　See also CLR 13
Hill, Grace Brooks [Collective
　　pseudonym] 67
　　Earlier sketch in SATA 1
Hill, Grace Livingston 1865-1947
　　See YABC 2
Hill, Helen M(orey) 1915- 27
Hill, John
　　See Koontz, Dean R(ay)
Hill, Johnson
　　See Kunhardt, Edith
Hill, Judy I. R.
　　See Roberts, Judy I.
Hill, Kathleen Louise 1917- 4
Hill, Kay
　　See Hill, Kathleen Louise
Hill, Kirkpatrick 1938- 72
Hill, Lee Sullivan 1958- 96
Hill, Lorna 1902- 12
Hill, Margaret (Ohler) 1915- 36

Hill, Meg
　　See Hill, Margaret (Ohler)
Hill, Meredith
　　See Craig, Mary (Francis) Shura
Hill, Monica
　　See Watson, Jane Werner
Hill, Ralph Nading 1917-1987 65
Hill, Robert W(hite) 1919-1982 12
　　Obituary 31
Hill, Ruth A.
　　See Viguers, Ruth Hill
Hill, Ruth Livingston
　　See Munce, Ruth Hill
Hill, Thomas (Hallowell) 1960- 82
Hillcourt, William 1900- 27
Hillenbrand, Will 1960- 84
Hiller, Ilo (Ann) 1938- 59
Hillerman, Tony 1925- 6
Hillert, Margaret 1920- 91
　　Earlier sketch in SATA 8
Hillman, Elizabeth 1942- 75
Hillman, Martin
　　See Hill, Douglas (Arthur)
Hillman, Priscilla 1940- 48
　　Brief entry 39
Hills, C(harles) A(lbert) R(eis)
　　1955- 39
Hilton, Irene (P.) 1912- 7
Hilton, James 1900-1954 34
Hilton, Margaret Lynette 1946- 68
　　See also CLR 25
　　See also SAAS 21
Hilton, Nette
　　See Hilton, Margaret Lynette
Hilton, Ralph 1907- 8
Hilton, Suzanne 1922- 4
Him, George 1900-1982
　　Obituary 30
Himelstein, Shmuel 1940- 83
Himler, Ann 1946- 8
Himler, Ronald (Norbert) 1937- 92
　　Earlier sketch in SATA 6
Himmelman, John C(arl) 1959- 94
　　Earlier sketch in SATA 47
Hinckley, Helen
　　See Jones, Helen Hinckley
Hind, Dolores (Ellen) 1931- 53
　　Brief entry 49
Hinds, P(atricia) Mignon 98
Hines, Anna Grossnickle 1946- 95
　　Brief entry 45
　　Earlier sketch in SATA 51
　　See also SAAS 16
Hines, Gary (Roger) 1944- 74
Hinojosa, Maria (de Lourdes)
　　1961- 88
Hinton, S(usan) E(loise) 1950- 58
　　Earlier sketch in SATA 19
　　See also CLR 23
Hinton, Sam 1917- 43
Hintz, (Loren) Martin 1945- 47
　　Brief entry 39
Hippopotamus, Eugene H.
　　See Kraus, (Herman) Robert
Hirano, Cathy 1957- 68
Hirsch, Karen 1941- 61
Hirsch, Phil 1926- 35
Hirsch, S. Carl 1913- 2
　　See also SAAS 7
Hirschfelder, Arlene B. 1943- 80
Hirschi, Ron 1948- 95
　　Earlier sketch in SATA 56
Hirschmann, Linda (Ann) 1941- 40
Hirsh, Marilyn 1944-1988 7
　　Obituary 58
Hirshberg, Al(bert Simon)
　　1909-1973 38
Hiscock, Bruce 1940- 57
Hiser, Constance 1950- 71
Hiser, Iona Seibert 1901- 4
Hislop, Julia Rose Catherine 1962- 74
Hissey, Jane (Elizabeth) 1952- 58
Hitchcock, Alfred (Joseph)
　　1899-1980 27
　　Obituary 24
Hite, Sid 1954- 75
Hitte, Kathryn 1919- 16

Hitz, Demi 1942- 66
  Earlier sketch in SATA *11*
Hitzeroth, Deborah L. 1961- 78
Hnizdovsky, Jacques 1915- 32
Ho, Minfong 1951- 94
  Earlier sketch in SATA *15*
  See also CLR *28*
Hoagland, Edward 1932- 51
Hoare, Robert J(ohn) 1921-1975 38
Hoban, Lillian 69
  Earlier sketch in SATA *22*
Hoban, Russell (Conwell) 1925- 78
  Earlier sketches in SATA *1, 40*
  See also CLR *3*
Hoban, Tana 70
  Earlier sketch in SATA *22*
  See also CLR *13*
  See also SAAS *12*
Hobart, Lois 7
Hobbs, Valerie 1941- 93
Hobbs, Will 1947- 72
Hoberman, Mary Ann 1930- 72
  Earlier sketch in SATA *5*
  See also CLR *22*
  See also SAAS *18*
Hobson, Bruce 1950- 62
Hobson, Burton (Harold) 1933- 28
Hobson, Laura Z(ametkin)
  1900-1986 52
Hobson, Sally 1967- 84
Hochschild, Arlie Russell 1940- 11
Hockaby, Stephen
  See Mitchell, Gladys (Maude Winifred)
Hockenberry, Hope
  See Newell, Hope (Hockenberry)
Hodge, P(aul) W(illiam) 1934- 12
Hodgell, P(atricia) C(hristine)
  1951- 42
Hodges, C(yril) Walter 1909- 2
Hodges, Carl G. 1902-1964 10
Hodges, Elizabeth Jamison 1
Hodges, Margaret Moore 1911- 75
  Earlier sketches in SATA *1, 33*
  See also SAAS *9*
Hodgetts, Blake Christopher 1967- 43
Hodgson, Harriet 1935- 84
Hoehne, Marcia 1951- 89
Hoestlandt, Jo(celyne) 1948- 94
Hoexter, Corinne K. 1927- 6
Hoff, Carol 1900- 11
Hoff, Mary (King) 1956- 74
Hoff, Syd(ney) 1912- 72
  Earlier sketch in SATA *9*
  See also SAAS *4*
Hoffman, Edwin D. 49
Hoffman, Mary (Margaret) 1945- 97
  Earlier sketch in SATA *59*
  See also SAAS *24*
Hoffman, Phyllis M. 1944- 4
Hoffman, Rosekrans 1926- 15
Hoffmann, E(rnst) T(heodor) A(madeus)
  1776-1822 27
Hoffmann, Felix 1911-1975 9
Hoffmann, Margaret Jones 1910- 48
Hoffmann, Peggy
  See Hoffmann, Margaret Jones
Hofsepian, Sylvia A. 1932- 74
Hofsinde, Robert 1902-1973 21
Hogan, Bernice Harris 1929- 12
Hogan, Inez 1895- 2
Hogan, James P(atrick) 1941- 81
Hogarth, Burne 1911-1996 63
  Obituary 89
Hogarth, Grace (Weston) Allen
  1905-1995 91
Hogarth, Jr.
  See Kent, Rockwell
Hogarth, Paul 1917- 41
Hogg, Garry 1902- 2
Hogner, Dorothy Childs 4
Hogner, Nils 1893-1970 25
Hogrogian, Nonny 1932- 74
  Earlier sketch in SATA *7*
  See also CLR *2*
  See also SAAS *1*
Hoh, Diane 1937- 52
  Brief entry 48

Hoke, Helen (L.) 1903-1990 15
  Obituary 65
Hoke, John 1925- 7
Holabird, Katharine 1948- 62
Holbeach, Henry
  See Rands, William Brighty
Holberg, Ruth Langland 1889- 1
Holbrook, Peter
  See Glick, Carl (Cannon)
Holbrook, Sabra
  See Erickson, Sabra R(ollins)
Holbrook, Stewart Hall 1893-1964 2
Holcomb, Nan
  See McPhee, Norma H.
Holding, James 1907- 3
Holinger, William (Jacques) 1944- 90
Holisher, Desider 1901-1972 6
Holl, Adelaide (Hinkle) 8
Holl, Kristi D(iane) 1951- 51
Holland, Isabelle 1920- 70
  Earlier sketch in SATA *8*
Holland, Janice 1913-1962 18
Holland, John L(ewis) 1919- 20
Holland, Joyce
  See Morice, Dave
Holland, Lynda (H.) 1959- 77
Holland, Lys
  See Gater, Dilys
Holland, Marion 1908-1989 6
  Obituary 61
Hollander, John 1929- 13
Hollander, Paul
  See Silverberg, Robert
Hollander, Phyllis 1928- 39
Hollander, Zander 1923- 63
Holldobler, Turid 1939- 26
Holliday, Joe
  See Holliday, Joseph
Holliday, Joseph 1910- 11
Holling, Holling C(lancy)
  1900-1973 15
  Obituary 26
Hollingsworth, Alvin C(arl) 1930- 39
Hollingsworth, Mary 1947- 91
Holloway, Teresa (Bragunier) 1906- 26
Holm, (Else) Anne (Lise) 1922- 1
  See also SAAS *7*
Holm, Sharon Lane 1955- 78
Holman, Felice 1919- 82
  Earlier sketch in SATA *7*
  See also SAAS *17*
Holme, Bryan 1913-1990 26
  Obituary 66
Holmes, Barbara Ware 1945- 65
Holmes, John
  See Souster, (Holmes) Raymond
Holmes, Marjorie 1910- 43
Holmes, Martha 1961- 72
Holmes, Mary Z(astrow) 1943- 80
Holmes, Oliver Wendell 1809-1894 34
Holmes, Peggy 1898- 60
Holmes, Raymond
  See Souster, (Holmes) Raymond
Holmes, Rick
  See Hardwick, Richard Holmes, Jr.
Holmgren, George Ellen
  See Holmgren, Helen Jean
Holmgren, Helen Jean 1930- 45
Holmgren, Virginia C(unningham)
  1909- 26
Holmquist, Eve 1921- 11
Holt, Margaret 1937- 4
Holt, Margaret Van Vechten (Saunders)
  1899-1963 32
Holt, Michael (Paul) 1929- 13
Holt, Rackham
  See Holt, Margaret Van Vechten
  (Saunders)
Holt, Rochelle Lynn 1946- 41
Holt, Stephen
  See Thompson, Harlan H.
Holt, Victoria
  See Hibbert, Eleanor Alice Burford
Holton, Leonard
  See Wibberley, Leonard (Patrick
  O'Connor)
Holtze, Sally Holmes 1952- 64

Holtzman, Jerome 1926- 57
Holub, Joan 1956- 99
Holyer, Erna Maria 1925- 22
Holyer, Ernie
  See Holyer, Erna Maria
Holz, Loretta (Marie) 1943- 17
Homel, David 1952- 97
Homze, Alma C. 1932- 17
Honeycutt, Natalie 1945- 97
Hong, Lily Toy 1958- 76
Honig, Donald 1931- 18
Honness, Elizabeth H. 1904- 2
Hoobler, Dorothy 28
Hoobler, Thomas 28
Hood, Joseph F. 1925- 4
Hood, Robert E. 1926- 21
Hook, Frances 1912- 27
Hook, Martha 1936- 27
Hooker, Ruth 1920- 21
Hooks, William H(arris) 1921- 94
  Earlier sketch in SATA *16*
Hoon, Patricia Easterly 1954- 90
Hooper, Byrd
  See St. Clair, Byrd Hooper
Hooper, Maureen Brett 1927- 76
Hooper, Meredith (Jean) 1939- 28
Hooper, Patricia 1941- 95
Hoopes, Lyn L(ittlefield) 1953- 49
  Brief entry 44
Hoopes, Ned E(dward) 1932- 21
Hoopes, Roy 1922- 11
Hoople, Cheryl G.
  Brief entry 32
Hoover, H(elen) M(ary) 1935- 83
  Brief entry 33
  Earlier sketch in SATA *44*
  See also SAAS *8*
Hoover, Helen (Drusilla Blackburn)
  1910-1984 12
  Obituary 39
Hope, Christopher (David Tully)
  1944- 62
Hope, Laura Lee [Collective
  pseudonym] 67
  Earlier sketch in SATA *1*
Hope Simpson, Jacynth 1930- 12
Hopf, Alice
  See Hopf, Alice (Martha) L(ightner)
Hopf, Alice (Martha) L(ightner)
  1904-1988 5
  Obituary 55
Hopkins, A. T.
  See Turngren, Annette
Hopkins, Clark 1895-1976
  Obituary 34
Hopkins, Jackie (Mims) 1952- 92
Hopkins, Joseph G(erard) E(dward)
  1909- 11
Hopkins, (Hector) Kenneth 1914-1988
  Obituary 58
Hopkins, Lee Bennett 1938- 68
  Earlier sketch in SATA *3*
  See also CLR *44*
  See also SAAS *4*
Hopkins, Lyman
  See Folsom, Franklin (Brewster)
Hopkins, Marjorie 1911- 9
Hopkins, Mary R(ice) 1956- 97
Hopkinson, Amanda 1948- 84
Hopkinson, Deborah 1952- 76
Hoppe, Joanne 1932- 42
Hoppe, Matthias 1952- 76
Hopper, Nancy J. 1937- 38
  Brief entry 35
Horgan, Paul (George Vincent
  O'Shaughnessy) 1903-1995 13
  Obituary 84
Hornblow, Arthur (Jr.) 1893-1976 15
Hornblow, Leonora (Schinasi)
  1920- 18
Horne, Richard Henry 1803-1884 29
Horner, Althea (Jane) 1926- 36
Horner, Dave 1934- 12
Horniman, Joanne 1951- 98
Hornos, Axel 1907- 20
Hornstein, Reuben Aaron 1912- 64
Horton, Madelyn (Stacey) 1962- 77

Horvath, Betty 1927- 4
Horvath, Polly 1957- 85
Horwich, Frances R(appaport)
  1908- 11
Horwitz, Elinor Lander 45
  Brief entry 33
Horwood, William 1944- 85
Hosford, Dorothy (Grant)
  1900-1952 22
Hosford, Jessie 1892- 5
Hoskyns-Abrahall, Clare 13
Hossack, Sylvia 1939- 83
Hossack, Sylvie Adams
  See Hossack, Sylvia
Hostetler, Marian 1932- 91
Houck, Carter 1924- 22
Hough, (Helen) Charlotte 1924- 9
Hough, Judy Taylor 1932- 63
  Brief entry 51
  Earlier sketch in SATA 56
Hough, Richard (Alexander) 1922- 17
Houghton, Eric 1930- 7
Houk, Randy 1944- 97
Houlehen, Robert J. 1918- 18
Household, Geoffrey (Edward West)
  1900-1988 14
  Obituary 59
Houselander, (Frances) Caryll 1900-1954
  Brief entry 31
Housman, Laurence 1865-1959 25
Houston, Dick 1943- 74
Houston, Gloria 81
Houston, James A(rchibald) 1921- 74
  Earlier sketch in SATA 13
  See also CLR 3
  See also SAAS 17
Houston, James D. 1933- 78
Houston, Jeanne (Toyo) Wakatsuki
  1934- 78
Houton, Kathleen
  See Kilgore, Kathleen
Howard, Alan 1922- 45
Howard, Alyssa
  See Buckholtz, Eileen (Garber)
Howard, Elizabeth
  See Mizner, Elizabeth Howard
Howard, Elizabeth Fitzgerald 1927- ...74
Howard, Ellen 1943- 99
  Earlier sketch in SATA 67
Howard, Jane R(uble) 1924- 87
Howard, John
  See Stidworthy, John
Howard, Norman Barry 1949- 90
Howard, Prosper
  See Hamilton, Charles (Harold St. John)
Howard, Robert West 1908- 5
Howard, Vernon (Linwood)
  1918-1992 40
  Obituary 73
Howarth, David (Armine)
  1912-1991 6
  Obituary 68
Howarth, Lesley 1952- 94
Howat, Jean
  See Herbert, Helen (Jean)
Howe, Deborah 1946-1978 29
Howe, Fanny 1940-
  Brief entry 52
Howe, James 1946- 71
  Earlier sketch in SATA 29
  See also CLR 9
Howe, John F. 1957- 79
Howell, Pat 1947- 15
Howell, S.
  See Styles, Frank Showell
Howell, Virginia Tier
  See Ellison, Virginia Howell
Howes, Barbara 1914- 5
Howker, Janni 1957- 72
  Brief entry 46
  See also CLR 14
  See also SAAS 13
Hoy, Linda 1946- 65
Hoy, Nina
  See Roth, Arthur J(oseph)
Hoyle, Geoffrey 1942- 18
Hoyt, Edwin P(almer), Jr. 1923- 28

Hoyt, Erich 1950- 65
Hoyt, Olga (Gruhzit) 1922- 16
Huang, Benrei 1959- 86
Hubbard, Woodleigh Marx 98
Hubbell, Patricia 1928- 8
Hubley, Faith (Elliot) 1924- 48
Hubley, John 1914-1977 48
  Obituary 24
Huck, Charlotte 1922- 82
Hudson, Cheryl Willis 1948- 81
Hudson, Jan 1954-1990 77
  See also CLR 40
Hudson, Jeffrey
  See Crichton, (John) Michael
Hudson, (Margaret) Kirsty 1947- 32
Hudson, Margaret
  See Shuter, Jane Margaret
Hudson, W(illiam) H(enry)
  1841-1922 35
Hudson, Wade 1946- 74
Huelsmann, Eva 1928- 16
Huerlimann, Bettina 1909-1983 39
  Obituary 34
Huerlimann, Ruth 1939- 32
  Brief entry 31
Huff, Barbara A. 1929- 67
Huff, T. S.
  See Huff, Tanya (Sue)
Huff, Tanya (Sue) 1957- 85
Huff, Vivian 1948- 59
Huffaker, Sandy 1943- 10
Huffman, Tom 24
Huggins, Nathan I(rvin) 1927- 63
Hughes, D. T.
  See Hughes, Dean
Hughes, Dean 1943- 77
  Earlier sketch in SATA 33
Hughes, (James) Langston
  1902-1967 33
  Earlier sketch in SATA 4
  See also CLR 17
Hughes, Libby 71
Hughes, Matilda
  See MacLeod, Charlotte (Matilda Hughes)
Hughes, Monica (Ince) 1925- 70
  Earlier sketch in SATA 15
  See also CLR 9
  See also SAAS 11
Hughes, Richard (Arthur Warren)
  1900-1976 8
  Obituary 25
Hughes, Sara
  See Saunders, Susan
Hughes, Shirley 1927- 70
  Earlier sketch in SATA 16
  See also CLR 15
Hughes, Ted 1930- 49
  Brief entry 27
  See also CLR 3
Hughes, Thomas 1822-1896 31
Hughes, Walter (Llewellyn) 1910- 26
Hughey, Roberta 1942- 61
Hugo, Victor (Marie) 1802-1885 47
Huline-Dickens, Frank William
  1931- 34
Hull, Eleanor (Means) 1913- 21
Hull, Eric Traviss
  See Harnan, Terry
Hull, H. Braxton
  See Jacobs, Helen Hull
Hull, Jesse Redding
  See Hull, Jessie Redding
Hull, Jessie Redding 1932- 51
Hull, Katharine 1921-1977 23
Hulme, Joy N. 1922- 74
Hults, Dorothy Niebrugge 1898- 6
Humble, Richard 1945- 60
Hume, Lotta Carswell 7
Hume, Ruth (Fox) 1922-1980 26
  Obituary 22
Hummel, Berta 1909-1946 43
Hummel, Sister Maria Innocentia
  See Hummel, Berta
Humphrey, Henry (III) 1930- 16
Humphrey, Sandra McLeod 1936- 95

Humphreys, Graham 1945-
  Brief entry 32
Humphreys, Martha 1943- 71
Hungerford, Pixie
  See Brinsmead, H(esba) F(ay)
Hunkin, Tim(othy Mark Trelawney)
  1950- 53
Hunt, Angela Elwell 1957- 75
Hunt, Francis
  See Stratemeyer, Edward L.
Hunt, Irene 1907- 91
  Earlier sketch in SATA 2
  See also CLR 1
Hunt, Jonathan 1966- 84
Hunt, Joyce 1927- 31
Hunt, Linda Lawrence 1940- 39
Hunt, Lisa B(ehnke) 1967- 84
Hunt, Mabel Leigh 1892-1971 1
  Obituary 26
Hunt, Morton 1920- 22
Hunt, Nigel
  See Greenbank, Anthony Hunt
Hunt, Peter 1945- 76
Hunter, Bernice Thurman 1922- 85
  Brief entry 45
Hunter, Bobbi Dooley 1945- 89
Hunter, Chris
  See Gibson, Jo
Hunter, Clingham M.D.
  See Adams, William Taylor
Hunter, Dawe
  See Downie, Mary Alice (Dawe)
Hunter, Edith Fisher 1919- 31
Hunter, Evan 1926- 25
Hunter, Hilda 1921- 7
Hunter, Jim 1939- 65
Hunter, Kristin (Eggleston) 1931- 12
  See also CLR 3
  See also SAAS 10
Hunter, Leigh
  See Etchison, Birdie L(ee)
Hunter, Mel 1927- 39
Hunter, Mollie 1922- 54
  See also CLR 25
  See also SAAS 7
Hunter, Norman (George Lorimer)
  1899-1995 26
  Obituary 84
Hunter, Sara Hoagland 1954- 98
Hunter Blair, Pauline 1921- 3
  See also CLR 28
Huntington, Harriet E(lizabeth)
  1909- 1
Huntsberry, William E(mery) 1916- 5
Hurd, Clement (G.) 1908-1988 64
  Obituary 54
  Earlier sketch in SATA 2
  See also CLR 49
Hurd, Edith Thacher 1910-1997 64
  Obituary 95
  Earlier sketch in SATA 2
  See also CLR 49
  See also SAAS 13
Hurd, (John) Thacher 1949- 94
  Brief entry 45
Hurmence, Belinda 1921- 77
  See also CLR 25
  See also SAAS 20
Hurt-Newton, Tania 1968- 84
Hurwitz, Johanna 1937- 71
  Earlier sketch in SATA 20
  See also SAAS 18
Hurwood, Bernhardt J. 1926-1987 12
  Obituary 50
Hutchens, Paul 1902-1977 31
Hutchins, Carleen Maley 1911- 9
Hutchins, Hazel J. 1952- 81
  Brief entry 51
  See also SAAS 24
Hutchins, Pat 1942- 70
  Earlier sketch in SATA 15
  See also CLR 20
  See also SAAS 16
Hutchins, Ross E(lliott) 1906- 4
Hutchmacher, J. Joseph 1929- 5
Hutto, Nelson (Allen) 1904- 20
Hutton, Kathryn 1915- 89

Hutton, Warwick 1939-1994 ....*20*
  Obituary *83*
  See also SAAS *17*
Huxley, Aldous (Leonard)
  1894-1963 ....*63*
Huxley, Elspeth (Josceline Grant)
  1907-1997 ....*62*
  Obituary *95*
Hyde, Dayton O(gden) *9*
Hyde, Hawk
  See Hyde, Dayton O(gden)
Hyde, Margaret O(ldroyd) 1917- *76*
  Earlier sketches in SATA *1, 42*
  See also CLR *23*
  See also SAAS *8*
Hyde, Shelley
  See Reed, Kit
Hyde, Wayne F. 1922- *7*
Hylander, Clarence J. 1897-1964 ....*7*
Hyman, Robin P(hilip) 1931- *12*
Hyman, Trina Schart 1939- *95*
  Earlier sketches in SATA *7, 46*
Hymes, Lucia M. 1907- *7*
Hyndman, Jane Andrews
  1912-1978 ....*46*
  Obituary *23*
  Earlier sketch in SATA *1*
Hyndman, Robert Utley
  1906(?)-1973 ....*18*
Hynes, Pat *98*

I

Iannone, Jeanne *7*
Ibbotson, Eva 1925- *13*
Ibbotson, M. C(hristine) 1930- *5*
Ichikawa, Satomi 1949- *78*
  Brief entry *36*
  Earlier sketch in SATA *47*
Ignoffo, Matthew 1945- *92*
Igus, Toyomi 1953- *76*
Ikeda, Daisaku 1928- *77*
Ilowite, Sheldon A. 1931- *27*
Ilsley, Dent [Joint pseudonym]
  See Chapman, John Stanton Higham
Ilsley, Velma (Elizabeth) 1918- *12*
Imai, Miko 1963- *90*
Imershein, Betsy 1953- *62*
Immel, Mary Blair 1930- *28*
Immell, Myra H. 1941- *92*
Impey, Rose *69*
Ingelow, Jean 1820-1897 ....*33*
Ingersoll, Norman 1928- *79*
Ingham, Colonel Frederic
  See Hale, Edward Everett
Ingman, Nicholas 1948- *52*
Ingraham, Leonard W(illiam) 1913- *4*
Ingram, Scott 1948- *92*
Ingrams, Doreen 1906-1997 ....*20*
  Obituary *97*
Inkpen, Mick 1952- *99*
Innocenti, Roberto 1940- *96*
Inyart, Gene 1927- *6*
Ionesco, Eugene 1912-1994 ....*7*
  Obituary *79*
Ipcar, Dahlov (Zorach) 1917- *49*
  Earlier sketch in SATA *1*
  See also SAAS *8*
Ironside, Jetske 1940- *60*
Irvin, Fred 1914- *15*
Irvine, Georgeanne 1955- *72*
Irvine, Joan 1951- *80*
Irving, Alexander
  See Hume, Ruth (Fox)
Irving, Robert
  See Adler, Irving
Irving, Washington 1783-1859
  See YABC *2*
Irwin, Ann(abelle Bowen) 1915- *89*
  Brief entry *38*
  Earlier sketch in SATA *44*
  See also SAAS *14*
  See Irwin, Hadley Joint pseudonym
Irwin, Constance Frick 1913- *6*

Irwin, Hadley [Joint pseudonym]
  See CLR *40*
  See Hadley, Lee
  and Irwin, Ann(abelle Bowen)
Irwin, Keith Gordon 1885-1964 ....*11*
Isaac, Joanne 1934- *21*
Isaacs, Anne 1949- *90*
Isaacs, Jacob
  See Kranzler, George G(ershon)
Isaacson, Philip M(arshal) 1924- *87*
Isadora, Rachel 1953(?)- *79*
  Brief entry *32*
  Earlier sketch in SATA *54*
  See also CLR *7*
Isham, Charlotte H(ickox) 1912- *21*
Ish-Kishor, Judith 1892-1972 ....*11*
Ish-Kishor, Sulamith 1896-1977 ....*17*
Ishmael, Woodi 1914- *31*
Israel, Elaine 1945- *12*
Israel, Marion Louise 1882-1973
  Obituary *26*
Iverson, Genie 1942-
  Brief entry *52*
Ives, Morgan
  See Bradley, Marion Zimmer
I.W.
  See Watts, Isaac
Iwamatsu, Jun Atsushi 1908-1994 ....*14*
  Obituary *81*
Iwasaki, Chihiro 1918-1974
  See CLR *18*

J

Jac, Lee
  See Morton, Lee Jack, Jr.
Jacka, Martin 1943- *72*
Jackson, Alison 1953- *73*
Jackson, Anne 1896(?)-1984
  Obituary *37*
Jackson, C. Paul 1902- *6*
Jackson, Caary
  See Jackson, C. Paul
Jackson, Charlotte E. (Cobden) 1903(?)-
  1989
  Obituary *62*
Jackson, Dave 1944- *91*
Jackson, Ellen B. 1943- *75*
Jackson, Garnet Nelson 1944- *87*
Jackson, Geoffrey (Holt Seymour) 1915-
  1987
  Obituary *53*
Jackson, Guida M. 1930- *71*
Jackson, Jacqueline 1928- *65*
Jackson, Jesse 1908-1983 ....*29*
  Obituary *48*
  Earlier sketch in SATA *2*
  See also CLR *28*
Jackson, Mike 1946- *91*
Jackson, Neta 1944- *91*
Jackson, O. B.
  See Jackson, C. Paul
Jackson, Robert B(lake) 1926- *8*
Jackson, Sally
  See Kellogg, Jean
Jackson, Shirley 1919-1965 ....*2*
Jackson, Woody 1948- *92*
Jacob, Helen Pierce 1927- *21*
Jacobi, Kathy
  Brief entry *42*
Jacobs, Flora Gill 1918- *5*
Jacobs, Francine 1935- *43*
  Brief entry *42*
Jacobs, Frank 1929- *30*
Jacobs, Helen Hull 1908- *12*
Jacobs, Joseph 1854-1916 ....*25*
Jacobs, Judy 1952- *69*
Jacobs, Laurie A. 1956- *89*
Jacobs, Leland Blair 1907-1992 ....*20*
  Obituary *71*
Jacobs, Linda C. 1943- *21*
Jacobs, Lou(is), Jr. 1921- *2*
Jacobs, Shannon K. 1947- *77*
Jacobs, Susan 1940- *30*
Jacobs, William Jay 1933- *89*
  Earlier sketch in SATA *28*

Jacobson, Daniel 1923- *12*
Jacobson, Morris K(arl) 1906- *21*
Jacopetti, Alexandra 1939- *14*
Jacques, Brian 1939- *95*
  Earlier sketch in SATA *62*
  See also CLR *21*
Jacques, Robin 1920-1995 ....*32*
  Brief entry *30*
  Obituary *86*
  See also SAAS *5*
Jaekel, Susan M. 1948- *89*
Jaffee, Al(lan) 1921- *66*
  Brief entry *37*
Jagendorf, Moritz (Adolf) 1888-1981 ......*2*
  Obituary *24*
Jahn, (Joseph) Michael 1943- *28*
Jahn, Mike
  See Jahn, (Joseph) Michael
Jahn-Clough, Lisa 1967- *88*
Jahsmann, Allan Hart 1916- *28*
Jakes, John (William) 1932- *62*
James, Andrew
  See Kirkup, James
James, Ann 1952- *82*
James, Bronte
  See Nash, Renea Denise
James, Dynely
  See Mayne, William (James Carter)
James, Edwin
  See Gunn, James E(dwin)
James, Elizabeth 1942- *97*
  Earlier sketch in SATA *52*
James, Emily
  See Standiford, Natalie
James, Harry Clebourne 1896- *11*
James, J. Alison 1962- *83*
James, Josephine
  See Sterne, Emma Gelders
James, Mary
  See Meaker, Marijane (Agnes)
James, Philip
  See del Rey, Lester
James, Robin (Irene) 1953- *50*
James, T. F.
  See Fleming, Thomas J(ames)
James, Will(iam Roderick)
  1892-1942 ....*19*
Jameson, W. C. 1942- *93*
Jamiolkowski, Raymond M. 1953- *81*
Jance, J. A.
  See Jance, Judith A(nn)
Jance, Judith A(nn) 1944-
  Brief entry *50*
Jane, Mary Childs 1909- *6*
Janeczko, Paul B(ryan) 1945- *98*
  Earlier sketch in SATA *53*
  See also CLR *47*
  See also SAAS *18*
Janes, Edward C. 1908- *25*
Janes, J(oseph) Robert 1935-
  Brief entry *50*
Janeway, Elizabeth (Hall) 1913- *19*
Janger, Kathleen N. 1940- *66*
Janice
  See Brustlein, Janice Tworkov
Janosch
  See CLR *26*
  See Eckert, Horst
Janover, Caroline (Davis) 1943- *89*
Jansen, Jared
  See Cebulash, Mel
Janson, Dora Jane 1916- *31*
Janson, H(orst) W(oldemar) 1913- *9*
Jansson, Tove (Marika) 1914- *41*
  Earlier sketch in SATA *3*
  See also CLR *2*
Janus, Grete
  See Hertz, Grete Janus
Jaques, Faith 1923-1997 ....*69*
  Obituary *97*
  Earlier sketch in SATA *21*
Jaques, Francis Lee 1887-1969
  Brief entry *28*
Jaquith, Priscilla 1908- *51*
Jarman, Rosemary Hawley 1935- *7*
Jarrell, Mary von Schrader 1914- *35*

Jarrell, Randall 1914-1965 7
  See also CLR *6*
Jarrett, Roxanne
  See Werner, Herma
Jarrow, Gail 1952- 84
Jasner, W. K.
  See Watson, Jane Werner
Jassem, Kate
  See Oppenheim, Joanne
Jauss, Anne Marie 1902(?)-1991 10
  Obituary 69
Javernick, Ellen 1938- 89
Jayne, Lieutenant R. H.
  See Ellis, Edward S(ylvester)
Jaynes, Clare [Joint pseudonym]
  See Mayer, Jane Rothschild
Jeake, Samuel, Jr.
  See Aiken, Conrad (Potter)
Jefferds, Vincent H(arris) 1916- 59
  Brief entry 49
Jefferies, (John) Richard
  1848-1887 16
Jeffers, Susan 1942- 70
  Earlier sketch in SATA *17*
  See also CLR *30*
Jefferson, Sarah
  See Farjeon, (Eve) Annabel
Jeffries, Roderic 1926- 4
Jenkin-Pearce, Susie 1943- 80
Jenkins, Debra Reid
  See Reid Jenkins, Debra
Jenkins, Jean 98
Jenkins, Marie M. 1909- 7
Jenkins, Patrick 1955- 72
Jenkins, William A(twell) 1922- 9
Jenkyns, Chris 1924- 51
Jennings, Coleman A(lonzo) 1933- 64
Jennings, Dana Andrew 1957- 93
Jennings, Elizabeth (Joan) 1926- 66
Jennings, Gary (Gayne) 1928- 9
Jennings, Patrick 1962- 96
Jennings, Paul 1943- 88
  See also CLR *40*
Jennings, Robert
  See Hamilton, Charles (Harold St. John)
Jennings, S. M.
  See Meyer, Jerome Sydney
Jennings, Sharon (Elizabeth) 1954- 95
Jennison, C. S.
  See Starbird, Kaye
Jennison, Keith Warren 1911- 14
Jensen, Kathryn 1949- 81
Jensen, Kristine Mary 1961- 78
Jensen, Niels 1927- 25
Jensen, Vickie (Dee) 1946- 81
Jensen, Virginia Allen 1927- 8
Jeppson, J. O.
  See Asimov, Janet (Jeppson)
Jeram, Anita 1965- 71
Jerman, Jerry 1949- 89
Jernigan, E. Wesley 1940- 85
Jernigan, Gisela (Evelyn) 1948- 85
Jeschke, Susan 42
  Brief entry 27
Jessel, Camilla (Ruth) 1937- 29
Jessey, Cornelia
  See Sussman, Cornelia (Silver)
Jewell, Nancy 1940-
  Brief entry 41
Jewett, Eleanore Myers 1890-1967 5
Jewett, Sarah Orne 1849-1909 15
Jezard, Alison 1919- 57
  Brief entry 34
Jiler, John 1946- 42
  Brief entry 35
Jinks, Catherine 1963- 94
Jobb, Jamie 1945- 29
Joerns, Consuelo 44
  Brief entry 33
Joey D.
  See Macaulay, Teresa (E.)
John, Joyce 59
John, Naomi
  See Flack, Naomi John (White)
Johns, Avery
  See Cousins, Margaret
Johns, Elizabeth 1943- 88

Johns, Janetta
  See Quin-Harkin, Janet
Johns, W(illiam) E(arl) 1893-1968 55
Johnson, A.
  See Johnson, Annabell (Jones)
Johnson, A. E. [Joint pseudonym]
  See Johnson, Annabell (Jones)
  and Johnson, Edgar (Raymond)
Johnson, Angela 1961- 69
  See also CLR *33*
Johnson, Annabel
  See Johnson, Annabell (Jones)
Johnson, Annabell (Jones) 1921- 72
  Earlier sketch in SATA *2*
Johnson, Benj. F. of Boo
  See Riley, James Whitcomb
Johnson, Charles R. 1925- 11
Johnson, Charlotte Buel 1918-1982 46
Johnson, Chuck
  See Johnson, Charles R.
Johnson, Crockett
  See Leisk, David (Johnson)
Johnson, D(ana) William 1945- 23
Johnson, Daniel Shahid 1954- 73
Johnson, Dolores 1949- 69
Johnson, Dorothy M(arie)
  1905-1984 6
  Obituary 40
Johnson, E(ugene) Harper 44
Johnson, Edgar (Raymond)
  1912-1990 72
  Earlier sketch in SATA *2*
Johnson, Eleanor (Murdock) 1892-1987
  Obituary 54
Johnson, Elizabeth 1911-1984 7
  Obituary 39
Johnson, Eric W(arner) 1918-1994 8
  Obituary 82
Johnson, Evelyne 1932- 20
Johnson, Fred 19th cent. (?)-1982 63
Johnson, Gaylord 1884- 7
Johnson, Gerald White 1890-1980 19
  Obituary 28
Johnson, Harper
  See Johnson, E(ugene) Harper
Johnson, Harriett 1908-1987
  Obituary 53
Johnson, James Ralph 1922- 1
Johnson, James Weldon
  See CLR *32*
  See Johnson, James William
Johnson, James William 1871-1938 31
Johnson, Jane 1951- 48
Johnson, Joan J. 1942- 59
Johnson, John E(mil) 1929- 34
Johnson, LaVerne B(ravo) 1925- 13
Johnson, Lee Kaiser 1962- 78
Johnson, Lissa H(alls) 1955- 65
Johnson, Lois S(mith) 6
Johnson, Lois Walfrid 1936- 91
  Earlier sketch in SATA *22*
Johnson, Margaret S(weet)
  1893-1964 35
Johnson, Mary Frances K. 1929(?)-1979
  Obituary 27
Johnson, Maud Battle 1918(?)-1985
  Obituary 46
Johnson, Milton 1932- 31
Johnson, Natalie
  See Robison, Nancy L(ouise)
Johnson, Neil 1954- 73
Johnson, Pamela 1949- 71
Johnson, Patricia Polin 1956- 84
Johnson, Paul Brett 1947- 83
Johnson, Rebecca L. 1956- 67
Johnson, Rick L. 1954- 79
Johnson, (Walter) Ryerson 1901- 10
Johnson, Scott 1952- 76
Johnson, Sherrie 1948- 87
Johnson, Shirley K(ing) 1927- 10
Johnson, Siddie Joe 1905-1977
  Obituary 20
Johnson, Spencer 1938-
  Brief entry 38
Johnson, Stephen T. 1964- 84
Johnson, Sue Kaiser 1963- 78

Johnson, Sylvia A.
  Brief entry 52
Johnson, William R. 38
Johnson, William Weber 1909- 7
Johnston, Agnes Christine
  See Dazey, Agnes J(ohnston)
Johnston, Annie Fellows
  1863-1931 37
Johnston, Dorothy Grunbock
  1915-1979 54
Johnston, Ginny 1946- 60
Johnston, H(ugh) A(nthony) S(tephen)
  1913-1967 14
Johnston, Janet 1944- 71
Johnston, Johanna 1914(?)-1982 12
  Obituary 33
Johnston, Julie 1941- 78
  See also CLR *41*
  See also SAAS *24*
Johnston, Norma 29
  See St. John, Nicole
Johnston, Portia
  See Takakjian, Portia
Johnston, Susan Taylor 1942- 83
  Earlier sketch in SATA *8*
Johnston, Tony
  See Johnston, Susan Taylor
Jonas, Ann 1932- 50
  Brief entry 42
  See also CLR *12*
Jones, Adrienne 1915- 82
  Earlier sketch in SATA *7*
  See also SAAS *10*
Jones, Annabel
  See Lewis, Mary (Christianna)
Jones, Betty Millsaps 1940- 54
Jones, Carol 1942- 79
Jones, Charles M(artin) 1912- 53
Jones, Charlotte Foltz 1945- 77
Jones, Chuck
  See Jones, Charles M(artin)
Jones, Diana Wynne 1934- 70
  Earlier sketch in SATA *9*
  See also CLR *23*
  See also SAAS *7*
Jones, Douglas C(lyde) 1924- 52
Jones, Elizabeth Orton 1910- 18
Jones, Evan 1915- 3
Jones, Geraldine 1951- 43
  See McCaughrean, Geraldine
Jones, Gillingham
  See Hamilton, Charles (Harold St. John)
Jones, Harold 1904-1992 14
  Obituary 72
Jones, Helen Hinckley 1903- 26
Jones, Helen L. 1904(?)-1973
  Obituary 22
Jones, Hettie 1934- 42
  Brief entry 27
Jones, Hortense P. 1918- 9
Jones, Jennifer (Berry) 1947- 90
Jones, Jessie Mae Orton 1887(?)-1983
  Obituary 37
Jones, John R(obert) 1926- 76
Jones, Marcia Thornton 1958- 73
Jones, Margaret Boone
  See Zarif, Margaret Min'imah
Jones, Mary Alice 6
Jones, McClure 34
Jones, Penelope 1938- 31
Jones, Rebecca C(astaldi) 1947- 99
  Earlier sketch in SATA *33*
Jones, Robin D(orothy) 1959- 80
Jones, Sanford W.
  See Thorn, John
Jones, Terry 1942- 67
  Brief entry 51
Jones, Weyman (B.) 1928- 4
  See also SAAS *11*
Jonk, Clarence 1906- 10
Joos, Francoise 1956- 78
Joos, Frederic 1953- 78
Joosse, Barbara M(onnot) 1949- 96
  Earlier sketch in SATA *52*
Jordan, Anne Devereaux 1943- 80
Jordan, Don
  See Howard, Vernon (Linwood)

Jordan, E(mil) L(eopold) 1900-
  Brief entry *31*
Jordan, Hope (Dahle) 1905- *15*
Jordan, Jael (Michal) 1949- *30*
Jordan, June 1936- *4*
  See also CLR *10*
Jordan, Lee
  See Scholefield, Alan
Jordan, Martin George 1944- *84*
Jordan, Mildred 1901- *5*
Jordan, Robert
  See Rigney, James Oliver, Jr.
Jordan, Sherryl 1949- *71*
  See also SAAS *23*
Jordan, Tanis 1946- *84*
Jorgensen, Mary Venn *36*
Jorgenson, Ivar
  See Silverberg, Robert
Joseph, Anne
  See Coates, Anna
Joseph, James (Herz) 1924- *53*
Joseph, Joan 1939- *34*
Joseph, Joseph M(aron) 1903-1979 .....*22*
Joslin, Sesyle 1929- *2*
Joyce, Bill
  See Joyce, William
Joyce, J(ames) Avery 1902-1987 ....*11*
  Obituary *50*
Joyce, William 1957- *72*
  Brief entry *46*
  See also CLR *26*
Joyner, Jerry 1938- *34*
Jucker, Sita 1921- *5*
Judd, Denis (O'Nan) 1938- *33*
Judd, Frances K. [Collective
  pseudonym] *1*
  See Benson, Mildred (Augustine Wirt)
Jude, Conny *81*
Judson, Clara Ingram 1879-1960 ....*38*
  Brief entry *27*
Judy, Stephen
  See Tchudi, Stephen N.
Judy, Stephen N.
  See Tchudi, Stephen N.
Jukes, Mavis 1947- *72*
  Brief entry *43*
  See also SAAS *12*
Jumpp, Hugo
  See MacPeek, Walter G.
Jupo, Frank J. 1904- *7*
Jurmain, Suzanne 1945- *72*
Juster, Norton 1929- *3*
Justus, May 1898- *1*
Juvenilia
  See Taylor, Ann

K

Kabdebo, Tamas
  See Kabdebo, Thomas
Kabdebo, Thomas 1934- *10*
Kabibble, Osh
  See Jobb, Jamie
Kadesch, Robert R(udstone) 1922- *31*
Kaempfert, Wade
  See del Rey, Lester
Kaestner, Erich 1899-1974 ....*14*
  See also CLR *4*
Kahl, Jonathan (D.) 1959- *77*
Kahl, M(arvin) P(hilip) 1934- *37*
Kahl, Virginia (Caroline) 1919- *48*
  Brief entry *38*
Kahn, Joan 1914-1994 ....*48*
  Obituary *82*
Kahn, Katherine Janus 1942- *90*
Kahn, Roger 1927- *37*
Kaizuki, Kiyonori 1950- *72*
Kakimoto, Kozo 1915- *11*
Kalashnikoff, Nicholas 1888-1961 ....*16*
Kalb, Jonah 1926- *23*
Kalbacken, Joan 1925- *96*
Kalechofsky, Roberta 1931- *92*
Kaler, James Otis 1848-1912 ....*15*
Kalish, Claire M. 1947- *92*
Kallen, Stuart A(rnold) 1955- *86*
Kalman, Bobbie 1947- *63*

Kalman, Maira *96*
  See also CLR *32*
Kalnay, Francis 1899- *7*
Kaloustian, Rosanne 1955- *93*
Kalow, Gisela 1946- *32*
Kamen, Gloria 1923- *98*
  Earlier sketch in SATA *9*
Kamerman, Sylvia E.
  See Burack, Sylvia K.
Kamm, Josephine (Hart) 1905- *24*
Kandel, Michael 1941- *93*
Kandell, Alice S. 1938- *35*
Kane, Henry Bugbee 1902-1971 ....*14*
Kane, L. A.
  See Mannetti, Lisa
Kane, Robert W. 1910- *18*
Kanetzke, Howard W(illiam) 1932- *38*
Kanoza, Muriel Canfield 1935- *94*
Kanzawa, Toshiko
  See Furukawa, Toshi
Kaplan, Andrew 1960- *78*
Kaplan, Anne Bernays 1930- *32*
Kaplan, Bess 1927- *22*
Kaplan, Boche 1926- *24*
Kaplan, Elizabeth (A.) 1956- *83*
Kaplan, Irma 1900- *10*
Kaplan, Jean Caryl Korn 1926- *10*
Kaplow, Robert 1954- *70*
Karageorge, Michael
  See Anderson, Poul (William)
Karasz, Ilonka 1896-1981
  Obituary *29*
Karen, Ruth 1922-1987 ....*9*
  Obituary *54*
Kark, Nina Mary
  See Bawden, Nina (Mary Mabey)
Karl, Herb 1938- *73*
Karl, Jean E(dna) 1927- *34*
  See also SAAS *10*
Karlin, Bernie 1927- *68*
Karlin, Eugene 1918- *10*
Karlin, Nurit *63*
Karp, Naomi J. 1926- *16*
Karpinski, J. Rick
  See Karpinski, John Eric
Karpinski, John Eric 1952- *81*
Karpinski, Rick
  See Karpinski, John Eric
Karr, Kathleen 1946- *82*
Kashiwagi, Isami 1925- *10*
Kassem, Lou(ise Morrell) *62*
  Brief entry *51*
Kastner, Jill (Marie) 1964- *70*
Kasuya, Masahiro 1937- *51*
Katchen, Carole 1944- *9*
Kathryn
  See Searle, Kathryn Adrienne
Katona, Robert 1949- *21*
Katsarakis, Joan Harries
  See Harries, Joan
Katz, Bobbi 1933- *12*
Katz, Fred 1938- *6*
Katz, Jane 1934- *33*
Katz, Marjorie P.
  See Weiser, Marjorie P(hillis) K(atz)
Katz, Welwyn Wilton 1948- *96*
  Earlier sketch in SATA *62*
  See also CLR *45*
  See also SAAS *25*
Katz, William Loren 1927- *98*
  Earlier sketch in SATA *13*
Kaufman, Bel *57*
Kaufman, Jeff 1955- *84*
Kaufman, Joe 1911- *33*
Kaufman, Mervyn D. 1932- *4*
Kaufmann, Angelika 1935- *15*
Kaufmann, John 1931- *18*
Kaula, Edna Mason 1906- *13*
Kavaler, Lucy 1930- *23*
Kavanagh, Jack 1920- *85*
Kay, Helen
  See Goldfrank, Helen Colodny
Kay, Jackie
  See Kay, Jacqueline Margaret
Kay, Jacqueline Margaret 1961- *97*
Kay, Mara *13*

Kaye, Danny 1913-1987
  Obituary *50*
Kaye, Geraldine (Hughesdon)
  1925- *85*
  Earlier sketch in SATA *10*
Kaye, Judy
  See Baer, Judy
Kaye, M(ary) M(argaret) 1908- *62*
Kaye, Marilyn 1949- *56*
Kaye, Mollie
  See Kaye, M(ary) M(argaret)
Keane, Bil 1922- *4*
Keating, Bern
  See Keating, Leo Bernard
Keating, Lawrence A. 1903-1966 ....*23*
Keating, Leo Bernard 1915- *10*
Keats, Emma 1899(?)-1979(?) *68*
Keats, Ezra Jack 1916-1983 ....*57*
  Obituary *34*
  Earlier sketch in SATA *14*
  See also CLR *35*
Keegan, Marcia 1943- *9*
Keehn, Sally M. 1947- *87*
Keel, Frank
  See Keeler, Ronald F(ranklin)
Keeler, Ronald F(ranklin)
  1913-1983 ....*47*
Keen, Martin L. 1913- *4*
Keenan, Sheila 1953- *95*
Keene, Ann T(odd) 1940- *86*
Keene, Carolyn [Collective
  pseudonym] *65*
Keens-Douglas, Richardo 1953- *95*
Keeping, Charles 1924-1988 ....*69*
  Obituary *56*
  Earlier sketch in SATA *9*
  See also CLR *34*
Keeshan, Robert J. 1927- *32*
Kehret, Peg 1936- *73*
Keillor, Garrison 1942- *58*
Keir, Christine
  See Popescu, Christine
Keister, Douglas 1948- *88*
Keith, Carlton
  See Robertson, Keith (Carlton)
Keith, Doug 1952- *81*
Keith, Eros 1942- *52*
Keith, Hal 1934- *36*
Keith, Harold (Verne) 1903- *74*
  Earlier sketch in SATA *2*
Keith, Robert
  See Applebaum, Stan
Keleinikov, Andrei 1924- *65*
Kelemen, Julie 1959- *78*
Kelen, Emery 1896-1978 ....*13*
  Obituary *26*
Kelleam, Joseph E(veridge)
  1913-1975 ....*31*
Kelleher, Daria Valerian 1955- *79*
Kelleher, Victor (Michael Kitchener)
  1939- *75*
  Brief entry *52*
  See also CLR *36*
Keller, Beverly L(ou) *91*
  Earlier sketch in SATA *13*
Keller, Charles 1942- *82*
  Earlier sketch in SATA *8*
Keller, Debra 1958- *94*
Keller, Dick 1923- *36*
Keller, Emily *96*
Keller, Gail Faithfull
  See Faithfull, Gail
Keller, Holly 1942- *76*
  Brief entry *42*
  See also CLR *45*
Keller, Irene (Barron) 1927- *36*
Keller, Mollie
  Brief entry *50*
Kelley, Leo P(atrick) 1928- *32*
  Brief entry *31*
Kelley, Patte 1947- *93*
Kelley, True (Adelaide) 1946- *92*
  Brief entry *39*
  Earlier sketch in SATA *41*
Kellin, Sally Moffet 1932- *9*
Kelling, Furn L. 1914- *37*

Kellogg, Gene
  See Kellogg, Jean
Kellogg, Jean 1916- ...._10_
Kellogg, Steven (Castle) 1941- ...._57_
  Earlier sketch in SATA _8_
  See also CLR _16_
Kellow, Kathleen
  See Hibbert, Eleanor Alice Burford
Kelly, Eric P(hilbrook) 1884-1960
  See YABC _1_
Kelly, Fiona
  See Welford, Sue
Kelly, Jeff
  See Kelly, Jeffrey
Kelly, Jeffrey 1946- ...._65_
Kelly, Joanne (W.) 1934- ...._87_
Kelly, Kate 1958- ...._91_
Kelly, Kathleen M. 1964- ...._71_
Kelly, Martha Rose 1914-1983 ...._37_
Kelly, Marty
  See Kelly, Martha Rose
Kelly, Ralph
  See Geis, Darlene
Kelly, Regina Z. ...._5_
Kelly, Rosalie (Ruth) ...._43_
Kelly, Walt(er Crawford)
  1913-1973 ...._18_
Kelsey, Alice Geer 1896- ...._1_
Kemp, Gene 1926- ...._75_
  Earlier sketch in SATA _25_
  See also CLR _29_
Kempner, Mary Jean 1913-1969 ...._10_
Kempton, Jean Welch 1914- ...._10_
Kenda, Margaret 1942- ...._71_
Kendall, Carol (Seeger) 1917- ...._74_
  Earlier sketch in SATA _11_
  See also SAAS _7_
Kendall, Gordon
  See Shwartz, Susan (Martha)
Kendall, Lace
  See Stoutenburg, Adrien
Kendall, Martha E. ...._87_
Kendall, Russ 1957- ...._83_
Kenealy, James P. 1927- ...._52_
  Brief entry ...._29_
Kenealy, Jim
  See Kenealy, James P.
Kennaway, Adrienne 1945- ...._60_
Kennedy, Brendan 1970- ...._57_
Kennedy, Dana Forrest 1917- ...._74_
Kennedy, Dorothy M(intzlaff)
  1931- ...._53_
Kennedy, John Fitzgerald
  1917-1963 ...._11_
Kennedy, Joseph Charles 1929- ...._86_
  Earlier sketch in SATA _14_
  See also CLR _27_
Kennedy, Pamela 1946- ...._87_
Kennedy, Paul E(dward) 1929- ...._33_
Kennedy, Richard (Pitt) 1910-1989
  Obituary ...._60_
Kennedy, (Jerome) Richard 1932- ...._22_
Kennedy, Robert 1938- ...._63_
Kennedy, T(eresa) A. 1953- ...._42_
  Brief entry ...._35_
Kennedy, William 1928- ...._57_
Kennedy, X. J.
  See SAAS _22_
  See Kennedy, Joseph Charles
Kennell, Ruth E(pperson) 1893-1977 ......_6_
  Obituary ...._25_
Kenny, Ellsworth Newcomb 1909-1971
  Obituary ...._26_
Kenny, Herbert A(ndrew) 1912- ...._13_
Kenny, Kathryn
  See Krull, Kathleen
Kenny, Kevin
  See Krull, Kathleen
Kent, Alexander
  See Reeman, Douglas Edward
Kent, David
  See Lambert, David (Compton)
Kent, Deborah Ann 1948- ...._47_
  Brief entry ...._41_
Kent, Jack
  See Kent, John Wellington

Kent, John Wellington 1920-1985 ...._24_
  Obituary ...._45_
Kent, Lisa 1942- ...._90_
Kent, Margaret 1894- ...._2_
Kent, Rockwell 1882-1971 ...._6_
Kent, Sherman 1903-1986 ...._20_
  Obituary ...._47_
Kenward, Jean 1920- ...._42_
Kenworthy, Leonard S. 1912- ...._6_
Kenyon, Kate
  See Ransom, Candice F.
Kenyon, Ley 1913- ...._6_
Keown, Elizabeth 1913- ...._78_
Kepes, Juliet A(ppleby) 1919- ...._13_
Kerby, Mona 1951- ...._75_
Kerigan, Florence 1896- ...._12_
Kerman, Gertrude Lerner 1909- ...._21_
Kerr, Jessica 1901- ...._13_
Kerr, (Anne) Judith 1923- ...._24_
Kerr, M. E.
  See CLR _29_
  See also SAAS _1_
  See Meaker, Marijane (Agnes)
Kerr, Phyllis Forbes 1942- ...._72_
Kerr, Tom 1950- ...._77_
Kerry, Frances
  See Kerigan, Florence
Kerry, Lois
  See Duncan, Lois S(teinmetz)
Kershen, (L.) Michael 1982- ...._82_
Kerven, Rosalind 1954- ...._83_
Ker Wilson, Barbara 1929- ...._70_
  Earlier sketch in SATA _20_
  See also SAAS _18_
Kesey, Ken (Elton) 1935- ...._66_
Kesler, Jay (L.) 1935- ...._65_
Kessel, Joyce Karen 1937- ...._41_
Kessler, Ethel 1922- ...._44_
  Brief entry ...._37_
Kessler, Leonard P. 1921- ...._14_
Kesteven, G. R.
  See Crosher, G(eoffry) R(obins)
Ketcham, Hank
  See Ketcham, Henry King
Ketcham, Henry King 1920- ...._28_
  Brief entry ...._27_
Ketner, Mary Grace 1946- ...._75_
Kettelkamp, Larry 1933- ...._2_
  See also SAAS _3_
Ketteman, Helen 1945- ...._73_
Kevles, Bettyann 1938- ...._23_
Key, Alexander (Hill) 1904-1979 ...._8_
  Obituary ...._23_
Keyes, Daniel 1927- ...._37_
Keyes, Fenton 1915- ...._34_
Keyser, Marcia 1933- ...._42_
Keyser, Sarah
  See McGuire, Leslie (Sarah)
Khalsa, Dayal Kaur 1943-1989 ...._62_
  See also CLR _30_
Khanshendel, Chiron
  See Rose, Wendy
Khemir, Sabiha ...._87_
Kherdian, David 1931- ...._74_
  Earlier sketch in SATA _16_
  See also CLR _24_
Kibbe, Pat (Hosley) ...._60_
Kidd, Ronald 1948- ...._92_
  Earlier sketch in SATA _42_
Kiddell, John 1922- ...._3_
Kiddell-Monroe, Joan 1908- ...._55_
Kidwell, Carl 1910- ...._43_
Kiefer, Irene 1926- ...._21_
Kiesel, Stanley 1925- ...._35_
Kiesler, Kate (A.) 1971- ...._90_
Kikukawa, Cecily H. 1919- ...._44_
  Brief entry ...._35_
Kile, Joan 1940- ...._78_
Kilgore, Kathleen 1946- ...._42_
Kilian, Crawford 1941- ...._35_
Killien, Christi 1956- ...._73_
Killilea, Marie (Lyons) 1913- ...._2_
Killingback, Julia 1944- ...._63_
Killough, (Karen) Lee 1942- ...._64_
Kilreon, Beth
  See Walker, Barbara (Jeanne) K(erlin)

Kilreon, Beth
  See Walker, Barbara (Jeanne) K(erlin)
Kilworth, Garry (D.) 1941- ...._94_
Kim, Helen 1959- ...._98_
Kimball, Captain Kim
  See Scribner, Kimball
Kimball, Gayle 1943- ...._90_
Kimball, Yeffe 1914-1978 ...._37_
Kimbrough, Emily 1899-1989 ...._2_
  Obituary ...._59_
Kimmel, Eric A. 1946- ...._80_
  Earlier sketch in SATA _13_
Kimmel, Margaret Mary 1938- ...._43_
  Brief entry ...._33_
Kimmelman, Leslie (Grodinsky)
  1958- ...._85_
Kincher, Jonni 1949- ...._79_
Kindl, Patrice 1951- ...._82_
Kindred, Wendy 1937- ...._7_
Kines, Pat Decker 1937- ...._12_
King, Adam
  See Hoare, Robert J(ohn)
King, (Maria) Anna 1964- ...._72_
King, Arthur
  See Cain, Arthur H.
King, Billie Jean 1943- ...._12_
King, Christopher (L.) 1945- ...._84_
King, (David) Clive 1924- ...._28_
King, Colin 1943- ...._76_
King, Cynthia 1925- ...._7_
King, Elizabeth 1953- ...._83_
King, Frank O. 1883-1969
  Obituary ...._22_
King, Larry L. 1929- ...._66_
King, Laurie R. 1952- ...._88_
King, Marian 1900(?)-1986 ...._23_
  Obituary ...._47_
King, Martin
  See Marks, Stan(ley)
King, Martin Luther, Jr.
  1929-1968 ...._14_
King, Mary Ellen 1958- ...._93_
King, Paul
  See Drackett, Phil(ip Arthur)
King, Paula
  See Downing, Paula E.
King, Reefe
  See Barker, Albert W.
King, Stephen (Edwin) 1947- ...._55_
  Earlier sketch in SATA _9_
King, Thomas 1943- ...._96_
King, Tony 1947- ...._39_
Kingman, Dong (Moy Shu) 1911- ...._44_
Kingman, (Mary) Lee 1919- ...._67_
  Earlier sketch in SATA _1_
  See also SAAS _3_
Kingsland, Leslie William 1912- ...._13_
Kingsley, Charles 1819-1875
  See YABC _2_
Kingsley, Emily Perl 1940- ...._33_
King-Smith, Dick 1922- ...._80_
  Brief entry ...._38_
  Earlier sketch in SATA _47_
  See also CLR _40_
Kingston, Maxine (Ting Ting) Hong
  1940- ...._53_
Kinney, C. Cle 1915- ...._6_
Kinney, Harrison 1921- ...._13_
Kinney, Jean Stout 1912- ...._12_
Kinsey, Elizabeth
  See Clymer, Eleanor
Kinsey, Helen 1948- ...._82_
Kinsey-Warnock, Natalie 1956- ...._71_
Kinzel, Dorothy 1950- ...._57_
Kinzel, Dottie
  See Kinzel, Dorothy
Kipling, (Joseph) Rudyard 1865-1936
  See YABC _2_
  See also CLR _39_
Kippax, Frank
  See Needle, Jan
Kirby, David K(irk) 1944- ...._78_
Kirby, Margaret
  See Bingley, Margaret (Jane)
Kirby, Susan E. 1949- ...._62_
Kirk, Ruth (Kratz) 1925- ...._5_

Kirkland, Will
  See Hale, Arlene
Kirkup, James 1927- *12*
Kirkus, Virginia
  See Glick, Virginia Kirkus
Kirshenbaum, Binnie *79*
Kirtland, G. B.
  See Joslin, Sesyle
Kish, Eleanor M(ary) 1924- *73*
Kish, Ely
  See Kish, Eleanor M(ary)
Kishida, Eriko 1929- *12*
Kisinger, Grace Gelvin 1913-1965 ....*10*
Kissin, Eva H. 1923- *10*
Kitamura, Satoshi 1956- *98*
  Earlier sketch in SATA *62*
Kitchen, Bert
  See Kitchen, Herbert Thomas
Kitchen, Herbert Thomas 1940- *70*
Kite, (L.) Patricia 1940- *78*
Kitt, Tamara
  See de Regniers, Beatrice Schenk
    (Freedman)
Kittinger, Jo S(usenbach) 1955- *96*
Kituomba
  See Odaga, Asenath (Bole)
Kitzinger, Sheila 1929- *57*
Kjelgaard, James Arthur 1910-1959 ......*17*
Kjelgaard, Jim
  See Kjelgaard, James Arthur
Klagsbrun, Francine (Lifton) *36*
Klaits, Barrie 1944- *52*
Klaperman, Gilbert 1921- *33*
Klaperman, Libby Mindlin
  1921-1982 ....*33*
  Obituary *31*
Klass, David 1960- *88*
Klass, Morton 1927- *11*
Klass, Sheila Solomon 1927- *99*
  Earlier sketch in SATA *45*
  See also SAAS *26*
Klause, Annette Curtis 1953- *79*
Klaveness, Jan O'Donnell 1939- *86*
Kleberger, Ilse 1921- *5*
Kleeberg, Irene (Flitner) Cumming
  1932- *65*
Klein, Aaron E. 1930- *45*
  Brief entry *28*
Klein, Bill 1945- *89*
Klein, David 1919- *59*
Klein, Gerda Weissmann 1924- *44*
Klein, H. Arthur *8*
Klein, Leonore 1916- *6*
Klein, Mina C(ooper) *8*
Klein, Norma 1938-1989 ....*57*
  Earlier sketch in SATA *7*
  See also CLR *19*
  See also SAAS *1*
Klein, Robin 1936- *80*
  Brief entry *45*
  Earlier sketch in SATA *55*
  See also CLR *21*
Klemin, Diana *65*
Klemm, Edward G., Jr. 1910- *30*
Klemm, Roberta K(ohnhorst)
  1884- *30*
Kleven, Elisa 1958- *76*
Klevin, Jill Ross 1935- *39*
  Brief entry *38*
Kliban, B(ernard) 1935-1990 ....*35*
  Obituary *66*
Klimowicz, Barbara 1927- *10*
Kline, Suzy 1943- *99*
  Brief entry *48*
  Earlier sketch in SATA *67*
Klots, Alexander Barrett 1903-1989
  Obituary *62*
Klug, Ron(ald) 1939- *31*
Knaak, Richard A. 1961- *86*
Knapp, Edward
  See Kunhardt, Edith
Knapp, Ron 1952- *34*
Knebel, Fletcher 1911-1993 ....*36*
  Obituary *75*
Kneeland, Linda Clarke 1947- *94*
Knickerbocker, Diedrich
  See Irving, Washington

Knifesmith
  See Cutler, Ivor
Knigge, Robert (R.) 1921(?)-1987
  Obituary *50*
Knight, Anne (Katherine) 1946- *34*
Knight, Christopher G. 1943- *96*
Knight, Damon 1922- *9*
Knight, David C(arpenter) *14*
  See also CLR *38*
Knight, Eric (Mowbray) 1897-1943 .....*18*
Knight, Francis Edgar *14*
Knight, Frank
  See Knight, Francis Edgar
Knight, Hilary 1926- *69*
  Earlier sketch in SATA *15*
Knight, Joan (M.) *82*
Knight, Kathryn Lasky
  See Lasky, Kathryn
Knight, Mallory T.
  See Hurwood, Bernhardt J.
Knight, Ruth Adams 1898-1974
  Obituary *20*
Knight, Theodore O. 1946- *77*
Knobloch, Dorothea 1951- *88*
Knoepfle, John (Ignatius) 1923- *66*
Knott, Bill
  See Knott, William Cecil, Jr.
Knott, William Cecil, Jr. 1927- *3*
Knotts, Howard (Clayton, Jr.)
  1922- *25*
Knowles, Anne 1933- *37*
Knowles, John 1926- *89*
  Earlier sketch in SATA *8*
Knox, Calvin
  See Silverberg, Robert
Knox, Calvin M.
  See Silverberg, Robert
Knox, (Mary) Eleanor Jessie 1909- *59*
  Earlier sketch in SATA *30*
Knox, James
  See Brittain, William (E.)
Knox, Jolyne 1937- *76*
Knudsen, James 1950- *42*
Knudson, R. R.
  See SAAS *18*
  See Knudson, (Ruth) Rozanne
Knudson, Richard L(ewis) 1930- *34*
Knudson, (Ruth) Rozanne 1932- *79*
  Earlier sketch in SATA *7*
Knye, Cassandra
  See Disch, Thomas M(ichael)
Koch, Dorothy Clarke 1924- *6*
Koch, Kenneth 1925- *65*
Kocsis, J. C.
  See Paul, James
Koda-Callan, Elizabeth 1944- *67*
Koehler, Phoebe 1955- *85*
Koehler-Pentacoff, Elizabeth 1957- *96*
Koehn, Ilse
  See Van Zwienen, Ilse Charlotte Koehn
Koenig, Viviane 1950- *80*
Koering, Ursula 1921-1976 ....*64*
Koerner, W(illiam) H(enry) D(avid)
  1878-1938 ....*21*
Koertge, Ron(ald) 1940- *92*
  Earlier sketch in SATA *53*
Koff, Richard M(yram) 1926- *62*
Koffinke, Carol 1949- *82*
Kogan, Deborah 1940- *50*
Kogawa, Joy (Nozomi) 1935- *99*
Kohl, Herbert 1937- *47*
Kohl, MaryAnn F. 1947- *74*
Kohler, Julilly H(ouse) 1908-1976
  Obituary *20*
Kohn, Bernice (Herstein) 1920- *4*
Kohn, Rita (T.) 1933- *89*
Kohner, Frederick 1905-1986 ....*10*
  Obituary *48*
Koide, Tan 1938-1986 ....*50*
Koike, Kay 1940- *72*
Kolba, Tamara *22*
Koller, Jackie French 1948- *72*
Kolodny, Nancy J. 1946- *76*
Komaiko, Leah 1954- *97*
Komisar, Lucy 1942- *9*
Komoda, Beverly 1939- *25*
Komoda, Kiyo 1937- *9*

Komroff, Manuel 1890-1974 ....*2*
  Obituary *20*
Konigsburg, E(laine) L(obl) 1930- *94*
  Earlier sketches in SATA *4, 48*
  See also CLR *47*
Koning, Hans
  See Koningsberger, Hans
Koningsberger, Hans 1921- *5*
Konkle, Janet Everest 1917- *12*
Koob, Theodora (Johanna Foth)
  1918- *23*
Kooiker, Leonie
  See Kooyker-Romijn, Johanna Maria
Koons, James
  See Pernu, Dennis
Koontz, Dean R(ay) 1945- *92*
Koontz, Robin Michal 1954- *70*
Kooyker-Romijn, Johanna Maria
  1927- *48*
Kopper, Lisa (Esther) 1950-
  Brief entry *51*
Korach, Mimi 1922- *9*
Koralek, Jenny 1934- *71*
Korczak, Janusz 1878-1942 ....*65*
Koren, Edward 1935- *5*
Korinetz, Yuri (Iosifovich) 1923- *9*
  See also CLR *4*
Korman, Bernice 1937- *78*
Korman, Gordon (Richard) 1963- *81*
  Brief entry *41*
  Earlier sketch in SATA *49*
  See also CLR *25*
Korman, Justine 1958- *70*
Kornblatt, Marc 1954- *84*
Korte, Gene J. 1950- *74*
Korty, Carol 1937- *15*
Koscielniak, Bruce 1947- *99*
  Earlier sketch in SATA *67*
Koshkin, Alexander (A.) 1952- *86*
Kossin, Sandy (Sanford) 1926- *10*
Kossman, Nina 1959- *84*
Kotzwinkle, William 1938- *70*
  Earlier sketch in SATA *24*
  See also CLR *6*
Kouhi, Elizabeth 1917- *54*
  Brief entry *49*
Koutoukas, H. M.
  See Rivoli, Mario
Kouts, Anne 1945- *8*
Kovacs, Deborah 1954- *79*
Kovalski, Maryann 1951- *97*
  Earlier sketch in SATA *58*
  See also CLR *34*
  See also SAAS *21*
Kowalski, Kathiann M. 1955- *96*
Krahn, Fernando 1935- *49*
  Brief entry *31*
  See also CLR *3*
Krakauer, Hoong Yee Lee 1955- *86*
Kramer, Anthony
  Brief entry *42*
Kramer, George
  See Heuman, William
Kramer, Nora 1896(?)-1984 ....*26*
  Obituary *39*
Kramer, Remi (Thomas) 1935- *90*
Krantz, Hazel (Newman) 1920- *12*
Kranzler, George G(ershon) 1916- *28*
Kranzler, Gershon
  See Kranzler, George G(ershon)
Krasilovsky, Phyllis 1926- *38*
  Earlier sketch in SATA *1*
  See also SAAS *5*
Kraske, Robert
  Brief entry *36*
Krasne, Betty
  See Levine, Betty K(rasne)
Kraus, Joanna Halpert 1937- *87*
Kraus, (Herman) Robert 1925- *93*
  Earlier sketches in SATA *4, 65*
  See also SAAS *11*
Krauss, Ruth (Ida) 1911-1993 ....*30*
  Obituary *75*
  Earlier sketch in SATA *1*
  See also CLR *42*
Krautter, Elisa (Bialk) 1912(?)-1990 .....*1*
  Obituary *65*

Krautwurst, Terry 1946- 79
Krauze, Andrzej 1947-
    Brief entry 46
Kray, Robert Clement 1930- 82
Kredel, Fritz 1900-1973 17
Kreikemeier, Gregory Scott 1965- 85
Krementz, Jill 1940- 71
    Earlier sketch in SATA 17
    See also CLR 5
    See also SAAS 8
Kremer, Marcie
    See Sorenson, Margo
Krensky, Stephen (Alan) 1953- 93
    Brief entry 41
    Earlier sketch in SATA 47
Kresh, Paul 1919-1997 61
    Obituary 94
Kress, Nancy 1948- 85
Krieger, Melanie 96
Kripke, Dorothy Karp 30
Krisher, Trudy (B.) 1946- 86
Kristof, Jane 1932- 8
Kroeber, Theodora (Kracaw) 1897- 1
Kroeger, Mary Kay 1950- 92
Krohn, Katherine E(lizabeth) 1961- 84
Kroll, Francis Lynde 1904-1973 10
Kroll, Steven 1941- 66
    Earlier sketch in SATA 19
    See also SAAS 7
Kroll, Virginia L(ouise) 1948- 76
Kronenwetter, Michael 1943- 62
Kroniuk, Lisa
    See Berton, Pierre (Francis DeMarigny)
Kropp, Paul (Stephen) 1948- 38
    Brief entry 34
Kruess, James 1926- 8
    See also CLR 9
Krull, Kathleen 1952- 80
    Brief entry 39
    Earlier sketch in SATA 52
    See also CLR 44
Krumgold, Joseph 1908-1980 48
    Obituary 23
    Earlier sketch in SATA 1
Krupinski, Loretta 1940- 67
Krupnick, Karen 1947- 89
Krupp, E(dwin) C(harles) 1944- 53
Krupp, Robin Rector 1946- 53
Krush, Beth 1918- 18
Krush, Joe 1918- 18
Krykorka, Vladyana 1945- 96
Kubie, Nora (Gottheil) Benjamin
    1899-1988 39
    Obituary 59
Kubinyi, Laszlo 1937- 94
    Earlier sketch in SATA 17
Kuenstler, Morton 1927- 10
Kuh, Charlotte 1892(?)-1985
    Obituary 43
Kujoth, Jean Spealman 1935-1975
    Obituary 30
Kuklin, Susan 1941- 95
    Earlier sketch in SATA 63
Kulling, Monica 1952- 89
Kullman, Harry 1919-1982 35
Kumin, Maxine (Winokur) 1925- 12
Kumpa
    See Barberis, Juan C(arlos)
Kunhardt, Dorothy (Meserve)
    1901-1979 53
    Obituary 22
Kunhardt, Edith 1937- 67
Kunjufu, Jawanza 1953- 73
Kuntz, J(ohn) L. 1947- 91
Kunz, Roxane (Brown) 1932-
    Brief entry 53
Kupferberg, Herbert 1918- 19
Kuratomi, Chizuko 1939- 12
    See also CLR 32
Kurelek, William 1927-1977 8
    Obituary 27
    See also CLR 2
Kurian, George 1928- 65
Kurland, Gerald 1942- 13
Kurland, Michael (Joseph) 1938- 48
Kurokawa, Mitsuhiro 1954- 88
Kurten, Bjoern (Olof) 1924-1988 64

Kurtz, Jane 1952- 91
Kurtz, Katherine (Irene) 1944- 76
Kurz, Rudolf 1952- 95
Kushner, Donn 1927- 52
Kushner, Ellen (Ruth) 1955- 98
Kushner, Jill Menkes 1951- 62
Kushner, Lawrence 1943- 83
Kuskin, Karla 1932- 68
    Earlier sketch in SATA 2
    See also CLR 4
    See also SAAS 3
Kuttner, Paul 1931- 18
Kuzma, Kay 1941- 39
Kvale, Velma R(uth) 1898- 8
Kvasnosky, Laura McGee 1951- 93
Kyle, Benjamin
    See Gottfried, Theodore Mark
Kyle, Elisabeth
    See Dunlop, Agnes M(ary) R(obertson)
Kyte, Kathy S. 1946- 50
    Brief entry 44

L

L., Tommy
    See Lorkowski, Thomas V(incent)
Lachner, Dorothea
    See Knobloch, Dorothea
Lackey, Mercedes (R.) 1950- 81
Lacoe, Addie 78
Lacome, Julie 1961- 80
Lacy, Leslie Alexander 1937- 6
Ladd, Louise 1943- 97
Ladd, Veronica
    See Miner, Jane Claypool
Laden, Nina 1962- 85
Lader, Lawrence 1919- 6
LaDoux, Rita C. 1951- 74
Lady, A
    See Taylor, Ann
Lady Mears
    See Tempest, Margaret Mary
Lady of Quality, A
    See Bagnold, Enid
La Farge, Oliver (Hazard Perry)
    1901-1963 19
La Farge, Phyllis 14
Laffin, John (Alfred Charles) 1922- 31
La Fontaine, Jean de 1621-1695 18
Lager, Claude
    See Lapp, Christiane (Germain)
Lager, Marilyn 1939- 52
Lagercrantz, Rose (Elsa) 1947- 39
Lagerloef, Selma (Ottiliana Lovisa)
    1858-1940 15
    See also CLR 7
Laiken, Deirdre S(usan) 1948- 48
    Brief entry 40
Laimgruber, Monika 1946- 11
Lain, Anna
    See Lamb, Nancy
Laing, Martha
    See Celestino, Martha Laing
Laird, Christa 1944-
    See SAAS 26
Laird, Elizabeth 1943- 77
Laird, Jean E(louise) 1930- 38
Laite, Gordon 1925- 31
Lake, Harriet
    See Taylor, Paula (Wright)
Laklan, Carli 1907- 5
Lalicki, Barbara 61
la Mare, Walter de
    See de la Mare, Walter
Lamb, Beatrice Pitney 1904- 21
Lamb, Charles 1775-1834 17
Lamb, Elizabeth Searle 1917- 31
Lamb, G(eoffrey) F(rederick) 10
Lamb, Harold (Albert) 1892-1962 53
Lamb, Lynton 1907- 10
Lamb, Mary Ann 1764-1847 17
Lamb, Nancy 1939- 80
Lamb, Robert (Boyden) 1941- 13
Lambert, David (Compton) 1932- 84
    Brief entry 49
Lambert, Janet (Snyder) 1894-1973 25

Lambert, Saul 1928- 23
Lamburn, Richmal Crompton
    1890-1969 5
Lamorisse, Albert (Emmanuel)
    1922-1970 23
Lampert, Emily 1951- 52
    Brief entry 49
Lamplugh, Lois 1921- 17
Lampman, Evelyn Sibley
    1907-1980 87
    Obituary 23
    Earlier sketch in SATA 4
Lamprey, Louise 1869-1951
    See YABC 2
Lampton, Christopher (F.) 67
    Brief entry 47
Lancaster, Bruce 1896-1963 9
Lancaster, Matthew 1973(?)-1983
    Obituary 45
Lance, Kathryn 1943- 76
Land, Barbara (Neblett) 1923- 16
Land, Jane [Joint pseudonym]
    See Borland, Kathryn Kilby
    and Speicher, Helen Ross (Smith)
Land, Myrick (Ebben) 1922- 15
Land, Ross [Joint pseudonym]
    See Borland, Kathryn Kilby
    and Speicher, Helen Ross (Smith)
Landau, Elaine 1948- 94
    Earlier sketch in SATA 10
Landau, Jacob 1917- 38
Landeck, Beatrice 1904- 15
Landin, Les(lie) 1923- 2
Landis, J(ames) D(avid) 1942- 60
    Brief entry 52
Landon, Lucinda 1950- 56
    Brief entry 51
Landon, Margaret (Dorothea Mortenson)
    1903- 50
Landshoff, Ursula 1908- 13
Lane, Carolyn 1926- 10
Lane, Jerry
    See Martin, Patricia Miles
Lane, John 1932- 15
Lane, Margaret 1907-1994 65
    Brief entry 38
    Obituary 79
Lane, Rose Wilder 1886-1968 29
    Brief entry 28
Lanes, Selma G. 1929- 3
Lanfredi, Judy 1964- 83
Lang, Andrew 1844-1912 16
Lang, Paul 1948- 83
Lang, Susan S. 1950- 68
Lang, T. T.
    See Taylor, Theodore
Lange, John
    See Crichton, (John) Michael
Lange, Suzanne 1945- 5
Langley, Noel 1911-1980
    Obituary 25
Langner, Nola 1930- 8
Langone, John (Michael) 1929- 46
    Brief entry 38
Langsen, Richard C. 1953- 95
Langstaff, John Meredith 1920- 68
    Earlier sketch in SATA 6
    See also CLR 3
Langstaff, Launcelot
    See Irving, Washington
Langton, Jane (Gillson) 1922- 68
    Earlier sketch in SATA 3
    See also CLR 33
    See also SAAS 5
Lanier, Sidney 1842-1881 18
Lankford, Mary D. 1932- 77
Lansing, Alfred 1921-1975 35
Lansing, Karen E. 1954- 71
Lantier-Sampon, Patricia 1952- 92
Lantz, Fran
    See Lantz, Francess L(in)
Lantz, Francess L(in) 1952- 63
Lantz, Paul 1908- 45
Lantz, Walter 1900-1994 37
    Obituary 79
Lapp, Christiane (Germain) 1948- 74
Lapp, Eleanor J. 1936- 61

Lappin, Peter 1911- 32
Larkin, Amy
  See Burns, Olive Ann
Laroche, Giles 1956- 71
Larom, Henry V. 1903(?)-1975
  Obituary 30
Larrabee, Lisa 1947- 84
Larrecq, John M(aurice) 1926-1980 44
  Obituary 25
Larrick, Nancy G. 1910- 4
Larsen, Anita 1942- 78
Larsen, Egon 1904- 14
Larsen, Rebecca 1944- 54
Larson, Eve
  See St. John, Wylly Folk
Larson, Gary 1950- 57
Larson, Ingrid D(ana) 1965- 92
Larson, Kirby 1954- 96
Larson, Norita D. 1944- 29
Larson, William H. 1938- 10
Larsson, Carl (Olof) 1853-1919 35
Lasell, Elinor H. 1929- 19
Lasell, Fen H.
  See Lasell, Elinor H.
Lasenby, Jack 1931- 65
Lash, Joseph P. 1909- 43
Lasher, Faith B. 1921- 12
Lasker, David 1950- 38
Lasker, Joe 1919- 83
  Earlier sketch in SATA 9
  See also SAAS 17
Laski, Marghanita 1915-1988 55
Laskin, Pamela L. 1954- 75
Lasky, Kathryn 1944- 69
  Earlier sketch in SATA 13
  See also CLR 11
Lassalle, C. E.
  See Ellis, Edward S(ylvester)
Lassiter, Mary
  See Hoffman, Mary (Margaret)
Latham, Barbara 1896- 16
Latham, Frank B. 1910- 6
Latham, Jean Lee 1902- 68
  Earlier sketch in SATA 2
Latham, Mavis
  See Clark, Mavis Thorpe
Latham, Philip
  See Richardson, Robert S(hirley)
Lathrop, Dorothy P(ulis)
  1891-1980 14
  Obituary 24
Lathrop, Francis
  See Leiber, Fritz (Reuter, Jr.)
Latimer, Jim 1943- 80
Lattimore, Eleanor Frances 1904-1986 7
  Obituary 48
Lauber, Patricia (Grace) 1924- 75
  Earlier sketches in SATA 1, 33
  See also CLR 16
Laugesen, Mary E(akin) 1906- 5
Laughbaum, Steve 1945- 12
Laughlin, Florence 1910- 3
Laure, Ettagale
  See Blauer, Ettagale
Laure, Jason 1940- 50
  Brief entry 44
Laurence, Ester Hauser 1935- 7
Laurence, (Jean) Margaret (Wemyss) 1926-1987
  Obituary 50
Laurie, Rona 1916- 55
Laurin, Anne
  See McLaurin, Anne
Lauritzen, Jonreed 1902- 13
Lauscher, Hermann
  See Hesse, Hermann
Lauture, Denize 1946- 86
Laux, Connie
  See Laux, Constance
Laux, Constance 1952- 97
Laux, Dorothy 1920- 49
Lavallee, Barbara 1941- 74
Lavender, David (Sievert) 1910- 97
  Earlier sketch in SATA 64
Laverty, Donald
  See Blish, James (Benjamin)
Lavine, David 1928- 31

Lavine, Sigmund A(rnold) 1908- 82
  Earlier sketch in SATA 3
  See also CLR 35
Laviolette, Emily A. 1923(?)-1975
  Brief entry 49
Lawford, Paula Jane 1960-
  Brief entry 53
  See Martyr, Paula (Jane)
Lawlor, Laurie 1953- 80
Lawrence, Ann (Margaret)
  1942-1987 41
  Obituary 54
Lawrence, Isabelle (Wentworth)
  Brief entry 29
Lawrence, J. T.
  See Rowland-Entwistle, (Arthur)
    Theodore (Henry)
Lawrence, Jerome 1915- 65
Lawrence, John 1933- 30
Lawrence, Josephine 1890(?)-1978
  Obituary 24
Lawrence, Linda
  See Hunt, Linda Lawrence
Lawrence, Louise 1943- 78
  Earlier sketch in SATA 38
Lawrence, Louise de Kiriline 1894- 13
Lawrence, Lynn
  See Garland, Sherry
Lawrence, Mildred 1907- 3
Lawrence, R(onald) D(ouglas)
  1921- 55
Lawson, Carol (Antell) 1946- 42
Lawson, Don(ald Elmer) 1917- 9
Lawson, Joan 1906- 55
Lawson, Julie 1947- 79
Lawson, Marion Tubbs 1896- 22
Lawson, Robert 1892-1957
  See YABC 2
  See also CLR 2
Laycock, George (Edwin) 1921- 5
Lazare, Gerald John 1927- 44
Lazare, Jerry
  See Lazare, Gerald John
Lazarevich, Mila 1942- 17
Lazarus, Keo Felker 1913- 21
Lea, Alec 1907- 19
Lea, Joan
  See Neufeld, John (Arthur)
Lea, Richard
  See Lea, Alec
Leach, Maria 1892-1977 39
  Brief entry 28
Leacroft, Helen 1919- 6
Leacroft, Richard 1914- 6
Leaf, Margaret P. 1909(?)-1988
  Obituary 55
Leaf, (Wilbur) Munro 1905-1976 20
  See also CLR 25
Leaf, VaDonna Jean 1929- 26
Leakey, Richard E(rskine Frere)
  1944- 42
Leander, Ed
  See Richelson, Geraldine
Lear, Edward 1812-1888 18
  See also CLR 1
Leasor, (Thomas) James 1923- 54
Leavitt, Jerome E(dward) 1916- 23
LeBar, Mary E(velyn) 1910-1982 35
LeBlanc, Annette M. 1965- 68
LeBlanc, L(ee) 1913- 54
Lebrun, Claude 1929- 66
Le Cain, Errol (John) 1941-1989 68
  Obituary 60
Lecourt, Nancy (Hoyt) 1951- 73
Leder, Jane M(ersky) 1945- 61
  Brief entry 51
Lederer, Muriel 1929- 48
Lederer, William J(ulius) 1912- 62
Lee, Amanda
  See Buckholtz, Eileen (Garber)
Lee, Benjamin 1921- 27
Lee, Betsy 1949- 37
Lee, Carol
  See Fletcher, Helen Jill
Lee, Dennis (Beynon) 1939- 14
  See also CLR 3

Lee, Dom 1959- 83
  See also SAAS 26
Lee, Doris (Emrick) 1905-1983 44
  Obituary 35
Lee, Elizabeth Rogers 1940- 90
Lee, (Nelle) Harper 1926- 11
Lee, John R(obert) 1923-1976 27
Lee, Julian
  See Latham, Jean Lee
Lee, Liz
  See Lee, Elizabeth Rogers
Lee, Manning de V(illeneuve)
  1894-1980 37
  Obituary 22
Lee, Marian
  See Clish, (Lee) Marian
Lee, Marie G. 1964- 81
Lee, Mary Price 1934- 82
  Earlier sketch in SATA 8
Lee, Mildred 1908- 6
  See also SAAS 12
Lee, Richard S. 1927- 82
Lee, Robert C. 1931- 20
Lee, Robert E(dwin) 1918-1994 65
  Obituary 82
Lee, Robert J. 1921- 10
Lee, Roy
  See Hopkins, Clark
Lee, Sally 1943- 67
Lee, Tammie
  See Townsend, Thomas L.
Lee, Tanith 1947- 88
  Earlier sketch in SATA 8
Leedy, Loreen (Janelle) 1959- 84
  Brief entry 50
  Earlier sketch in SATA 54
Lee-Hostetler, Jeri 1940- 63
Leekley, Thomas B(riggs) 1910- 23
Leeming, Jo Ann
  See Leeming, Joseph
Leeming, Joseph 1897-1968 26
Leemis, Ralph B. 1954- 72
Leeson, Muriel 1920- 54
Leeson, R. A.
  See Leeson, Robert (Arthur)
Leeson, Robert (Arthur) 1928- 76
  Earlier sketch in SATA 42
Leffland, Ella 1931- 65
Lefler, Irene (Whitney) 1917- 12
Le Gallienne, Eva 1899-1991 9
  Obituary 68
Legg, Sarah Martha Ross Bruggeman (?)-1982
  Obituary 40
LeGrand
  See Henderson, LeGrand
Le Guin, Ursula K(roeber) 1929- 99
  Earlier sketches in SATA 4, 52
  See also CLR 28
Legum, Colin 1919- 10
Lehman, Bob 91
Lehman, Elaine 91
Lehn, Cornelia 1920- 46
Lehne, Judith Logan 1947- 93
Lehr, Delores 1920- 10
Lehr, Norma 1930- 71
Leiber, Fritz (Reuter, Jr.)
  1910-1992 45
  Obituary 73
Leibold, Jay 1957- 57
  Brief entry 52
Leichman, Seymour 1933- 5
Leigh, Nila K. 1981- 81
Leigh, Tom 1947- 46
Leigh-Pemberton, John 1911- 35
Leighton, Clare (Veronica Hope)
  1900(?)- 37
Leighton, Margaret 1896-1987 1
  Obituary 52
Leiner, Al(an) 1938- 83
Leiner, Katherine 1949- 93
Leipold, L. Edmond 1902- 16
Leisk, David (Johnson) 1906-1975 30
  Obituary 26
  Earlier sketch in SATA 1
Leister, Mary 1917- 29

Leitch, Patricia 1933- *98*
  Earlier sketch in SATA *11*
Leitner, Isabella 1924- *86*
Leland, Bob 1956- *92*
Leland, Robert E.
  See Leland, Bob
LeMair, H(enriette) Willebeek 1889-1966
  Brief entry *29*
Lember, Barbara Hirsch 1941- *92*
LeMieux, A(nne) C(onnelly) 1954- *90*
Lemke, Horst 1922- *38*
Lenanton, C.
  See Oman, Carola (Mary Anima)
Lenard, Alexander 1910-1972
  Obituary *21*
L'Engle, Madeleine (Camp Franklin)
  1918- *75*
  Earlier sketches in SATA *1, 27*
  See also CLR *14*
  See also SAAS *15*
Lengyel, Cornel Adam 1915- *27*
Lengyel, Emil 1895-1985 ....*3*
  Obituary *42*
LeNoir, Janice 1941- *89*
Lens, Sidney 1912-1986 ....*13*
  Obituary *48*
Lenski, Lois 1893-1974 ....*26*
  Earlier sketch in SATA *1*
  See also CLR *26*
Lent, Blair 1930- *2*
Lent, Henry Bolles 1901-1973 ....*17*
Leodhas, Sorche Nic
  See Alger, Leclaire (Gowans)
Leokum, Arkady 1916(?)- *45*
Leon, Sharon 1959- *79*
Leonard, Alison 1944- *70*
Leonard, Constance (Brink) 1923- *42*
  Brief entry *40*
Leonard, Jonathan N(orton)
  1903-1975 ....*36*
Leonard, Laura 1923- *75*
Leong Gor Yun
  See Ellison, Virginia Howell
Lerangis, Peter 1955- *72*
Lerner, Aaron B(unsen) 1920- *35*
Lerner, Carol 1927- *86*
  Earlier sketch in SATA *33*
  See also CLR *34*
  See also SAAS *12*
Lerner, Gerda 1920- *65*
Lerner, Marguerite Rush
  1924-1987 ....*11*
  Obituary *51*
Lerner, Sharon (Ruth) 1938-1982 ....*11*
  Obituary *29*
Leroe, Ellen W(hitney) 1949- *99*
  Brief entry *51*
  Earlier sketch in SATA *61*
Leroux, Gaston 1868-1927 ....*65*
LeRoy, Gen *52*
  Brief entry *36*
Lerrigo, Marion Olive 1898-1968
  Obituary *29*
LeShan, Eda J(oan) 1922- *21*
  See also CLR *6*
LeSieg, Theo.
  See Geisel, Theodor Seuss
Leslie, Robert Franklin 1911- *7*
Leslie, Sarah
  See McGuire, Leslie (Sarah)
Lessac, Frane 1954- *61*
Lessem, Don 1951- *97*
Lesser, Margaret 1899(?)-1979
  Obituary *22*
Lesser, Rika 1953- *53*
Lester, Alison 1952- *90*
  Earlier sketch in SATA *50*
Lester, Helen 1936- *92*
  Earlier sketch in SATA *46*
Lester, Julius (Bernard) 1939- *74*
  Earlier sketch in SATA *12*
  See also CLR *41*
Le Sueur, Meridel 1900- *6*
Le Tord, Bijou 1945- *95*
  Earlier sketch in SATA *49*
Leuck, Laura 1962- *85*
Leutscher, Alfred (George) 1913- *23*

Levai, Blaise 1919- *39*
Levenkron, Steven 1941- *86*
LeVert (William) John 1946- *55*
Levin, Betty 1927- *84*
  Earlier sketch in SATA *19*
  See also SAAS *11*
Levin, Ira 1929- *66*
Levin, Marcia Obrasky 1918- *13*
Levin, Meyer 1905-1981 ....*21*
  Obituary *27*
Levin, Miriam (Ramsfelder) 1962- *97*
Levine, Abby 1943- *54*
  Brief entry *52*
Levine, Betty K(rasne) 1933- *66*
Levine, David 1926- *43*
  Brief entry *35*
Levine, Edna S(imon) *35*
Levine, Evan 1962- *77*
Levine, Gail Carson 1947- *98*
Levine, I(srael) E. 1923- *12*
Levine, Joan Goldman *11*
Levine, Joseph 1910- *33*
Levine, Marge 1934- *81*
Levine, Rhoda *14*
Levine, Sarah 1970- *57*
Levine-Freidus, Gail
  See Provost, Gail Levine
Levinson, Nancy Smiler 1938- *80*
  Earlier sketch in SATA *33*
Levinson, Riki *99*
  Brief entry *49*
  Earlier sketch in SATA *52*
Levitin, Sonia (Wolff) 1934- *68*
  Earlier sketch in SATA *4*
  See also SAAS *2*
Levitt, Sidney (Mark) 1947- *68*
Levoy, Myron *49*
  Brief entry *37*
Levy, Constance 1931- *73*
  See also SAAS *22*
Levy, Elizabeth 1942- *69*
  Earlier sketch in SATA *31*
  See also SAAS *18*
Levy, Marilyn 1937- *67*
Levy, Nathan 1945- *63*
Levy, Robert 1945- *82*
Lewees, John
  See Stockton, Francis Richard
Lewin, Betsy 1937- *90*
  Earlier sketch in SATA *32*
  See also SAAS *25*
Lewin, Hugh 1939- *72*
  Brief entry *40*
  See also CLR *9*
Lewin, Ted 1935- *76*
  Earlier sketch in SATA *21*
  See also SAAS *25*
Lewis, Alfred E. 1912-1968
  Brief entry *32*
Lewis, Alice C. 1936- *46*
Lewis, Alice Hudson 1895(?)-1971
  Obituary *29*
Lewis, Amanda 1955- *80*
Lewis, (Joseph) Anthony 1927- *27*
Lewis, Barbara A. 1943- *73*
Lewis, Beverly 1949- *80*
Lewis, Brenda Ralph 1932- *72*
Lewis, C(live) S(taples) 1898-1963 .....*13*
  See also CLR *27*
Lewis, Claudia (Louise) 1907- *5*
Lewis, E(arl) B(radley) 1956- *93*
Lewis, E. M. *20*
Lewis, Elizabeth Foreman 1892-1958
  See YABC *2*
Lewis, Francine
  See Wells, Helen
Lewis, Hilda (Winifred) 1896-1974
  Obituary *20*
Lewis, J. Patrick 1942- *69*
Lewis, Jack P(earl) 1919- *65*
Lewis, Jean 1924- *61*
Lewis, Julinda
  See Lewis-Ferguson, Julinda
Lewis, Kim 1951- *84*
Lewis, Linda (Joy) 1946- *67*
Lewis, Lucia Z.
  See Anderson, Lucia (Lewis)

Lewis, Marjorie 1929- *40*
  Brief entry *35*
Lewis, Mary (Christianna)
  1907(?)-1988 ....*64*
  Obituary *56*
Lewis, Naomi *76*
Lewis, Paul
  See Gerson, Noel B(ertram)
Lewis, Richard 1935- *3*
Lewis, Rob 1962- *72*
Lewis, Roger
  See Zarchy, Harry
Lewis, Shari 1934- *35*
  Brief entry *30*
Lewis, Thomas P(arker) 1936- *27*
Lewis-Ferguson, Julinda 1955- *85*
Lewiton, Mina 1904-1970 ....*2*
Lexau, Joan M. *36*
  Earlier sketch in SATA *1*
Ley, Willy 1906-1969 ....*2*
Leydon, Rita (Floden) 1949- *21*
Leyland, Eric (Arthur) 1911- *37*
L'Hommedieu, Dorothy K(easley) 1885-
  1961
  Obituary *29*
Li, Xiao Jun 1952- *86*
Libby, Bill
  See Libby, William M.
Libby, William M. 1927-1984 ....*5*
  Obituary *39*
Liberty, Gene 1924- *3*
Liddell, Kenneth 1912-1975 ....*63*
Lieberman, E(dwin) James 1934- *62*
Liebers, Arthur 1913- *12*
Lieblich, Irene 1923- *22*
Liers, Emil E(rnest) 1890-1975 ....*37*
Liestman, Vicki 1961- *72*
Lietz, Gerald S. 1918- *11*
Life, Kay (Guinn) 1930- *83*
Lifton, Betty Jean *6*
Lifton, Robert Jay 1926- *66*
Lightburn, Ron 1954- *91*
Lightburn, Sandra 1955- *91*
Lightner, A. M.
  See Hopf, Alice (Martha) L(ightner)
Lightner, Alice
  See Hopf, Alice (Martha) L(ightner)
Lignell, Lois 1911- *37*
Liles, Maurine Walpole 1935- *81*
Lilley, Stephen R(ay) 1950- *97*
Lillington, Kenneth (James) 1916- *39*
Lilly, Charles
  Brief entry *33*
Lilly, Ray
  See Curtis, Richard (Alan)
Lim, John 1932- *43*
Liman, Ellen (Fogelson) 1936- *22*
Limburg, Peter R(ichard) 1929- *13*
Lincoln, C(harles) Eric 1924- *5*
Lindbergh, Anne (Spencer)
  1940-1993 ....*81*
  See Sapieyevski, Anne Lindbergh
Lindbergh, Anne Morrow (Spencer)
  1906- *33*
Lindbergh, Charles A(ugustus, Jr.)
  1902-1974 ....*33*
Lindblom, Steven (Winther) 1946- *94*
  Brief entry *39*
  Earlier sketch in SATA *42*
Linde, Gunnel 1924- *5*
Lindenbaum, Pija 1955- *77*
Lindgren, Astrid 1907- *38*
  Earlier sketch in SATA *2*
  See also CLR *39*
Lindgren, Barbro 1937- *63*
  Brief entry *46*
  See also CLR *20*
Lindman, Maj (Jan) 1886-1972 ....*43*
Lindop, Edmund 1925- *5*
Lindquist, Jennie Dorothea
  1899-1977 ....*13*
Lindquist, Rowena Cory 1958- *98*
Lindquist, Willis 1908- *20*
Lindsay, Norman (Alfred William)
  1879-1969 ....*67*
  See also CLR *8*

Lindsay, (Nicholas) Vachel
1879-1931 ....*40*
Line, David
See Davidson, Lionel
Line, Les 1935- *27*
Lines, Kathleen Mary 1902-1988
Obituary *61*
Linfield, Esther *40*
Lingard, Joan 1932- *74*
Earlier sketch in SATA *8*
See also SAAS *5*
Link, Martin 1934- *28*
Linnea, Sharon 1956- *82*
Lionni, Leo(nard) 1910- *72*
Earlier sketch in SATA *8*
See also CLR *7*
Lipinsky de Orlov, Lino S. 1908- *22*
Lipkind, William 1904-1974 ....*15*
Lipman, David 1931- *21*
Lipman, Matthew 1923- *14*
Lippincott, Bertram 1898(?)-1985
Obituary *42*
Lippincott, Gary A. 1953- *73*
Lippincott, Joseph Wharton
1887-1976 ....*17*
Lippincott, Sarah Lee 1920- *22*
Lippman, Peter J. 1936- *31*
Lipsyte, Robert (Michael) 1938- *68*
Earlier sketch in SATA *5*
See also CLR *23*
Lisandrelli, Elaine Slivinski 1951- *94*
Lisker, Sonia O. 1933- *44*
Lisle, Holly 1960- *98*
Lisle, Janet Taylor 1947- *96*
Brief entry *47*
Earlier sketch in SATA *59*
See also SAAS *14*
Lisle, Seward D.
See Ellis, Edward S(ylvester)
Lisowski, Gabriel 1946- *47*
Brief entry *31*
Liss, Howard 1922-1995 ....*4*
Obituary *84*
Lissim, Simon 1900-1981
Brief entry *28*
Lisson, Deborah 1941- *71*
List, Ilka Katherine 1935- *6*
Liston, Robert A. 1927- *5*
Litchfield, Ada B(assett) 1916- *5*
Litowinsky, Olga (Jean) 1936- *26*
Littke, Lael J. 1929- *83*
Earlier sketch in SATA *51*
Little, A. Edward
See Klein, Aaron E.
Little, Douglas 1942- *96*
Little, (Flora) Jean 1932- *68*
Earlier sketch in SATA *2*
See also CLR *4*
See also SAAS *17*
Little, Lessie Jones 1906-1986 ....*60*
Obituary *50*
Little, Mary E. 1912- *28*
Littlechild, George 1958- *85*
Littledale, Freya (Lota Brown)
1929-1992 ....*74*
Earlier sketch in SATA *2*
Littlefield, Bill 1948- *83*
Littlefield, Holly 1963- *97*
Littleton, Mark (R.) 1950- *89*
Lively, Penelope 1933- *60*
Earlier sketch in SATA *7*
See also CLR *7*
Liversidge, (Henry) Douglas 1913- *8*
Livingston, Carole 1941- *42*
Livingston, Myra Cohn 1926-1996 ....*68*
Obituary *92*
Earlier sketch in SATA *5*
See also CLR *7*
See also SAAS *1*
Livingston, Richard R(oland) 1922- *8*
Livo, Norma J. 1929- *76*
Llerena-Aguirre, Carlos Antonio
1952- *19*
Llewellyn, Claire 1954- *77*
Llewellyn, Richard
See Llewellyn Lloyd, Richard Dafydd
Vyvyan

Llewellyn, Sam 1948- *95*
Llewellyn, T. Harcourt
See Hamilton, Charles (Harold St. John)
Llewellyn Lloyd, Richard Dafydd Vyvyan
1906-1983 ....*11*
Obituary *37*
Lloyd, A(lan) R(ichard) 1927- *97*
Lloyd, Alan
See Lloyd, A(lan) R(ichard)
Lloyd, E. James
See James, Elizabeth
Lloyd, Errol 1943- *22*
Lloyd, Hugh
See Fitzhugh, Percy Keese
Lloyd, James
See James, Elizabeth
Lloyd, Megan 1958- *77*
Lloyd, Norman 1909-1980
Obituary *23*
Lloyd, (Mary) Norris 1908-1993 ....*10*
Obituary *75*
Lloyd Webber, Andrew 1948- *56*
Lobel, Anita (Kempler) 1934- *96*
Earlier sketches in SATA *6, 55*
Lobel, Arnold (Stark) 1933-1987 ....*55*
Obituary *54*
Earlier sketch in SATA *6*
See also CLR *5*
Lobsenz, Amelia *12*
Lobsenz, Norman M. 1919- *6*
Lochak, Michele 1936- *39*
Lochlons, Colin
See Jackson, C. Paul
Locke, Clinton W. [Collective
pseudonym] *1*
Locke, Elsie (Violet) 1912- *87*
Locke, Lucie 1904- *10*
Locke, Robert 1944- *63*
See also CLR *39*
Locker, Thomas 1937- *59*
See also CLR *14*
Lockwood, Mary
See Spelman, Mary
Lodge, Bernard 1933- *33*
Lodge, Maureen Roffey
See Roffey, Maureen
Loeb, Jeffrey 1946- *57*
Loeb, Robert H., Jr. 1917- *21*
Loefgren, Ulf 1931- *3*
Loeper, John J(oseph) 1929- *10*
Loescher, Ann Dull 1942- *20*
Loescher, Gil(burt Damian) 1945- *20*
Loewenstein, Bernice
Brief entry *40*
Loewer, Jean
See Jenkins, Jean
Loewer, Peter 1934- *98*
LoFaro, Jerry 1959- *77*
Lofting, Hugh 1886-1947 ....*15*
See also CLR *19*
Lofts, Norah (Robinson) 1904-1983 ....*8*
Obituary *36*
Logue, Christopher 1926- *23*
Loh, Morag 1935- *73*
Loken, Newton (Clayton) 1919- *26*
Lomas, Steve
See Brennan, Joseph L.
Lomask, Milton 1909- *20*
London, Jack 1876-1916 ....*18*
London, Jane
See Geis, Darlene
London, John Griffith
See London, Jack
London, Jonathan (Paul) 1947- *74*
Lonergan, (Pauline) Joy (Maclean)
1909- *10*
Lonette, Reisie (Dominee) 1924- *43*
Long, Cathryn J. 1946- *89*
Long, Earlene (Roberta) 1938- *50*
Long, Helen Beecher [Collective
pseudonym] *1*
Long, Judith Elaine 1953- *20*
Long, Judy
See Long, Judith Elaine
Long, Kim 1949- *69*
Long, Laura Mooney 1892-1967
Obituary *29*

Longfellow, Henry Wadsworth
1807-1882 ....*19*
Longman, Harold S. 1919- *5*
Longsworth, Polly 1933- *28*
Longtemps, Kenneth 1933- *17*
Longway, A. Hugh
See Lang, Andrew
Loomans, Diane 1955- *90*
Loomis, Robert D. *5*
Lopez, Angelo (Cayas) 1967- *83*
Lopez, Barry (Holstun) 1945- *67*
Lopshire, Robert 1927- *6*
Lord, Athena V. 1932- *39*
Lord, Beman 1924-1991 ....*5*
Obituary *69*
Lord, Bette Bao 1938- *58*
Lord, (Doreen Mildred) Douglas
1904- *12*
Lord, John Vernon 1939- *21*
Lord, Nancy
See Titus, Eve
Lord, Patricia C. 1927-1988
Obituary *58*
Lord, Walter 1917- *3*
Lorenz, Lee (Sharp) 1932(?)-
Brief entry *39*
Lorenzini, Carlo 1826-1890 ....*29*
Lorimer, Janet 1941- *60*
Loring, Emilie (Baker)
1864(?)-1951 ....*51*
Lorkowski, Thomas V(incent)
1950- *92*
Lorkowski, Tom
See Lorkowski, Thomas V(incent)
Lorraine, Walter (Henry) 1929- *16*
Loss, Joan 1933- *11*
Lot, Parson
See Kingsley, Charles
Lothrop, Harriet Mulford Stone
1844-1924 ....*20*
LoTurco, Laura 1963- *84*
Lotz, Wolfgang 1912-1981 ....*65*
Louie, Ai-Ling 1949- *40*
Brief entry *34*
Louisburgh, Sheila Burnford
See Burnford, Sheila
Lourie, Helen
See Storr, Catherine (Cole)
Lourie, Peter (King) 1952- *82*
Love, (Kathleen) Ann 1947- *79*
Love, D. Anne 1949- *96*
Love, Douglas 1967- *92*
Love, Katherine 1907- *3*
Love, Sandra (Weller) 1940- *26*
Lovelace, Delos Wheeler 1894-1967 ....*7*
Lovelace, Maud Hart 1892-1980 ....*2*
Obituary *23*
Lovell, Ingraham
See Bacon, Josephine Dodge (Daskam)
Loverseed, Amanda (Jane) 1965- *75*
Lovett, Margaret (Rose) 1915- *22*
Low, Alice 1926- *76*
Earlier sketch in SATA *11*
Low, Elizabeth Hammond 1898- *5*
Low, Joseph 1911- *14*
Lowe, Jay, Jr.
See Loeper, John J(oseph)
Lowell, Susan 1950- *81*
Lowenstein, Dyno 1914- *6*
Lowery, Linda 1949- *74*
Lowitz, Anson C. 1901(?)-1978 ....*18*
Lowitz, Sadyebeth (Heath)
1901-1969 ....*17*
Lowrey, Janette Sebring 1892- *43*
Lowry, Lois 1937- *70*
Earlier sketch in SATA *23*
See also CLR *46*
See also SAAS *3*
Lowry, Peter 1953- *7*
Lowther, George F. 1913-1975
Obituary *30*
Lozansky, Edward D. 1941- *62*
Lozier, Herbert 1915- *26*
Lubell, Cecil 1912- *6*
Lubell, Winifred 1914- *6*
Lubin, Leonard B. 1943- *45*
Brief entry *37*

Lucas, E(dward) V(errall)
   1868-1938 20
Lucas, Eileen 1956- 76
Lucas, George (Walton) 1944- 56
Lucas, Jerry 1940- 33
Lucas, Victoria
   See Plath, Sylvia
Luccarelli, Vincent 1923- 90
Luce, Celia (Geneva Larsen) 1914- 38
Luce, Willard (Ray) 1914- 38
Lucht, Irmgard 1937- 82
Luckhardt, Mildred Corell 1898- 5
Ludden, Allen (Ellsworth) 1918(?)-1981
   Obituary 27
Ludel, Jacqueline 1945- 64
Ludlam, Mabel Cleland
   See Widdemer, Mabel Cleland
Ludlow, Geoffrey
   See Meynell, Laurence Walter
Ludwig, Helen 33
Ludwig, Lyndell 1923- 63
Lueders, Edward (George) 1923- 14
Luenn, Nancy 1954- 79
   Earlier sketch in SATA *51*
Lufkin, Raymond H. 1897- 38
Lugard, Flora Louisa Shaw
   1852-1929 21
Luger, Harriett M(andelay) 1914- 23
Luhrmann, Winifred B(ruce) 1934- 11
Luis, Earlene W. 1929- 11
Lum, Peter
   See Crowe, Bettina Lum
Lund, Doris (Herold) 1919- 12
Lung, Chang
   See Rigney, James Oliver, Jr.
Lunn, Carolyn (Kowalczyk) 1960- 67
Lunn, Janet (Louise Swoboda)
   1928- 68
   Earlier sketch in SATA *4*
   See also CLR *18*
   See also SAAS *12*
Lupoff, Dick
   See Lupoff, Richard A(llen)
Lupoff, Richard A(llen) 1935- 60
Lurie, Alison 1926- 46
Lurie, Morris 1938- 72
Lustig, Arnost 1926- 56
Lustig, Loretta 1944- 46
Luther, Frank 1905-1980
   Obituary 25
Luther, Rebekah (Lyn) S(tiles)
   1960- 90
Luttmann, Gail
   See Damerow, Gail (Jane)
Luttrell, Guy L. 1938- 22
Luttrell, Ida (Alleene) 1934- 91
   Brief entry 35
   Earlier sketch in SATA *40*
Lutzeier, Elizabeth 1952- 72
Lutzker, Edythe 1904- 5
Luzadder, Patrick 1954- 89
Luzzati, Emanuele 1912- 7
Luzzatto, Paola (Caboara) 1938- 38
Lybbert, Tyler 1970- 88
Lydon, Michael 1942- 11
Luttmann, Warren
Lyfick, Warren
   See Reeves, Lawrence F.
Lyle, Katie Letcher 1938- 8
Lynch, Chris 1962- 95
Lynch, Lorenzo 1932- 7
Lynch, Marietta 1947- 29
Lynch, P. J. 1962- 79
Lynch, Patricia (Nora) 1898-1972 9
Lynds, Dennis 1924- 47
   Brief entry 37
Lyngseth, Joan
   See Davies, Joan
Lynn, Elizabeth A(nne) 1946- 99
Lynn, Mary
   See Brokamp, Marilyn
Lynn, Patricia
   See Watts, Mabel Pizzey
Lyon, Elinor 1921- 6
Lyon, George Ella 1949- 68
Lyons, Dorothy 1907- 3
Lyons, Grant 1941- 30

Lyons, Marcus
   See Blish, James (Benjamin)
Lyons, Mary E(velyn) 1947- 93
Lystad, Mary (Hanemann) 1928- 11
Lytle, Elizabeth Stewart 1949- 79
Lyttle, Richard B(ard) 1927- 23
Lytton, Edward G(eorge) E(arle) L(ytton)
   Bulwer-Lytton Baron 1803-1873 23

M

Ma, Wenhai 1954- 84
Maar, Leonard (F., Jr.) 1927- 30
Maartens, Maretha 1945- 73
Maas, Selve 14
Mabery, D. L. 1953-
   Brief entry 53
Mac
   See MacManus, Seumas
MacAodhagain, Eamon
   See Egan, E(dward) W(elstead)
MacArthur-Onslow, Annette (Rosemary)
   1933- 26
Macaulay, David (Alexander)
   1946- 72
   Brief entry 27
   Earlier sketch in SATA *46*
   See also CLR *14*
Macaulay, Teresa (E.) 1947- 95
MacBeth, George 1932- 4
MacBeth, George (Mann) 1932-1992
   Obituary 70
MacBride, Roger Lea 1929-1995 85
MacCarter, Don 1944- 91
MacClintock, Dorcas 1932- 8
MacDonald, Amy 1951- 76
MacDonald, Anson
   See Heinlein, Robert A.
MacDonald, Betty (Campbell Bard) 1908-
   1958
   See YABC *1*
Macdonald, Blackie
   See Emrich, Duncan (Black Macdonald)
Macdonald, Caroline 1948- 86
Macdonald, Dwight 1906-1982 29
   Obituary 33
MacDonald, George 1824-1905 33
Mac Donald, Golden
   See Brown, Margaret Wise
Macdonald, James D. 1954- 81
Macdonald, Marcia
   See Hill, Grace Livingston
MacDonald, Margaret Read 1940- 94
Macdonald, Mary
   See Gifford, Griselda
MacDonald, Maryann 1947- 72
Macdonald, Shelagh 1937- 25
MacDonald, Suse 1940- 54
   Brief entry 52
Macdonald, Zillah K(atherine)
   1885- 11
MacDonnell, Megan
   See Stevens, Serita (Deborah)
MacDougal, John
   See Blish, James (Benjamin)
Mace, Elisabeth 1933- 27
Mace, Varian 1938- 49
MacEwen, Gwendolyn (Margaret)
   1941-1987 50
   Obituary 55
MacFarlan, Allan A. 1892-1982 35
MacFarlane, Iris 1922- 11
MacGill-Callahan, Sheila 1926- 78
MacGregor, Ellen 1906-1954 39
   Brief entry 27
MacGregor-Hastie, Roy 1929- 3
Machetanz, Frederick 1908- 34
Machin Goodall, Daphne (Edith) 37
MacInnes, Helen 1907-1985 22
   Obituary 44
Macintosh, Brownie 1950- 98
MacIntyre, Elisabeth 1916- 17
Mack, Stan(ley) 17

Mackay, Claire 1930- 97
   Earlier sketch in SATA *40*
   See also CLR *43*
   See also SAAS *25*
Mackay, Donald A(lexander) 1914- 81
MacKaye, Percy (Wallace)
   1875-1956 32
MacKellar, William 1914- 4
Macken, Walter 1915-1967 36
Mackenzie, Dr. Willard
   See Stratemeyer, Edward L.
MacKenzie, Garry 1921-
   Brief entry 31
MacKenzie, Jill (Kelly) 1947- 75
Mackey, Ernan
   See McInerny, Ralph
Mackin, Edward
   See McInerny, Ralph
MacKinnon, Bernie 1957- 69
MacKinnon Groomer, Vera 1915- 57
MacKinstry, Elizabeth 1879-1956 42
MacLachlan, Patricia 1938- 62
   Brief entry 42
   See also CLR *14*
MacLane, Jack
   See Crider, (Allen) Bill(y)
MacLean, Alistair (Stuart)
   1923-1987 23
   Obituary 50
MacLeod, Beatrice (Beach) 1910- 10
MacLeod, Charlotte (Matilda Hughes)
   1922- 28
MacLeod, Doug 1959- 60
MacLeod, Ellen Jane (Anderson)
   1916- 14
MacManus, James
   See MacManus, Seumas
MacManus, Seumas 1869-1960 25
MacMaster, Eve (Ruth) B(owers)
   1942- 46
MacMillan, Annabelle
   See Quick, Annabelle
MacMillan, Dianne M(arie) 1943- 84
MacPeek, Walter G. 1902-1973 4
   Obituary 25
MacPherson, Margaret 1908- 9
   See also SAAS *4*
MacPherson, Thomas George 1915-1976
   Obituary 30
Macrae, Hawk
   See Barker, Albert W.
MacRae, Travis
   See Feagles, Anita MacRae
MacRaois, Cormac 1944- 72
Macumber, Mari
   See Sandoz, Mari(e Susette)
Macy, Sue 1954- 88
Madden, Don 1927- 3
Maddison, Angela Mary 1923- 10
   See also CLR *24*
Maddock, Reginald 1912- 15
Madenski, Melissa (Ann) 1949- 77
Madian, Jon 1941- 9
Madison, Arnold 1937- 6
Madison, Winifred 5
Madsen, Ross Martin 1946- 82
Madsen, Susan A(rrington) 1954- 90
Maehlqvist, (Karl) Stefan 1943- 30
Maestro, Betsy 1944- 59
   Brief entry 30
   See also CLR *45*
Maestro, Giulio 1942- 59
   Earlier sketch in SATA *8*
   See also CLR *45*
Maeterlinck, Maurice 1862-1949 66
Magee, Doug 1947- 78
Magee, Wes 1939- 64
Maggio, Rosalie 1943- 69
Magid, Ken(neth Marshall) 65
Magnus, Erica 1946- 77
Magorian, James 1942- 92
   Earlier sketch in SATA *32*
Magorian, Michelle 1947- 67
Maguire, Anne
   See Nearing, Penny

Maguire, Gregory 1954- *84*
  Earlier sketch in SATA *28*
  See also SAAS *22*
Maguire, Jack 1945- *74*
Maguire, Jesse
  See Smith, Sherwood
Maher, Ramona 1934- *13*
Mahon, Julia C(unha) 1916- *11*
Mahony, Elizabeth Winthrop 1948- *8*
  See Winthrop, Elizabeth
Mahood, Kenneth 1930- *24*
Mahy, Margaret 1936- *69*
  Earlier sketch in SATA *14*
  See also CLR *7*
Maiden, Cecil (Edward) 1902-1981 ......*52*
Maidoff, Ilka List
  See List, Ilka Katherine
Maifair, Linda Lee 1947- *83*
Maik, Henri
  See Hecht, Henri Joseph
Maine, Trevor
  See Catherall, Arthur
Mains, Randolph P. 1946- *80*
Maiorano, Robert 1946- *43*
Maisner, Heather 1947- *89*
Maitland, Antony (Jasper) 1935- *25*
Major, Kevin (Gerald) 1949- *82*
  Earlier sketch in SATA *32*
  See also CLR *11*
Majure, Janet 1954- *96*
Makie, Pam 1943- *37*
Malam, John 1957- *89*
Malcolmson, Anne
  See Storch, Anne B. von
Malcolmson, David 1899- *6*
Mali, Jane Lawrence 1937-1995 ....*51*
  Brief entry *44*
  Obituary *86*
Mallett, Jerry J. 1939- *76*
Mallowan, Agatha Christie
  See Christie, Agatha (Mary Clarissa)
Malmberg, Carl 1904- *9*
Malmgren, Dallin 1949- *65*
Malo, John 1911- *4*
Malone, James Hiram 1930- *84*
Malory, (Sir) Thomas
  1410(?)-1471(?) *59*
  Brief entry *33*
Maltese, Michael 1908(?)-1981
  Obituary *24*
Malvern, Corinne 1905-1956 ....*34*
Malvern, Gladys (?)-1962 ....*23*
Mama G.
  See Davis, Grania
Mamonova, Tatyana V. *93*
Manchel, Frank 1935- *10*
Manchester, William (Raymond)
  1922- *65*
Mandel, Peter (Bevan) 1957- *87*
Mandel, Sally (Elizabeth) 1944- *64*
Mandell, Muriel (Hortense Levin)
  1921- *63*
Manes, Stephen 1949- *99*
  Brief entry *40*
  Earlier sketch in SATA *42*
Manfred, Frederick F(eikema)
  1912- *30*
Mangin, Marie France 1940- *59*
Mangione, Jerre 1909- *6*
Mango, Karin N. 1936- *52*
Mangurian, David 1938- *14*
Maniatty, Taramesha 1978- *92*
Maniscalco, Joseph 1926- *10*
Manley, Deborah 1932- *28*
Manley, Seon *15*
  See also CLR *3*
  See also SAAS *2*
Mann, Josephine
  See Pullein-Thompson, Josephine
Mann, Kenny 1946- *91*
Mann, Pamela 1946- *91*
Mann, Peggy *6*
Mannetti, Lisa 1953- *57*
  Brief entry *51*
Mannheim, Grete (Salomon) 1909- *10*
Manniche, Lise 1943- *31*
Manning, Rosemary 1911- *10*

Manning-Sanders, Ruth
  1895(?)-1988 ....*73*
  Obituary *57*
  Earlier sketch in SATA *15*
Mannon, Warwick
  See Hopkins, (Hector) Kenneth
Manson, Beverlie 1945- *57*
  Brief entry *44*
Mantinband, Gerda (B.) 1917- *74*
Manton, Jo
  See Gittings, Jo Manton
Manuel, Lynn 1948- *99*
Manushkin, Fran(ces) 1942- *93*
  Earlier sketches in SATA *7, 54*
Mapes, Mary A.
  See Ellison, Virginia Howell
Maple, Marilyn 1931- *80*
Mara, Barney
  See Roth, Arthur J(oseph)
Mara, Jeanette
  See Cebulash, Mel
Marais, Josef 1905-1978
  Obituary *24*
Marasmus, Seymour
  See Rivoli, Mario
Marbach, Ethel
  See Pochocki, Ethel (Frances)
Marcellino
  See Agnew, Edith J(osephine)
Marcellino, Fred 1939- *68*
March, Carl
  See Fleischman, (Albert) Sid(ney)
Marchant, Bessie 1862-1941
  See YABC *2*
Marchant, Catherine
  See Cookson, Catherine (McMullen)
Marcher, Marion Walden 1890- *10*
Marcus, Paul 1953- *82*
Marcus, Rebecca B(rian) 1907- *9*
Marcuse, Aida E. 1934- *89*
Marek, Margot L. 1934(?)-1987
  Obituary *54*
Margaret, Karla
  See Andersdatter, Karla M(argaret)
Margolis, Richard J(ules)
  1929-1991 ....*86*
  Obituary *67*
  Earlier sketch in SATA *4*
Margolis, Vivienne 1922- *46*
Mariana
  See Foster, Marian Curtis
Marie, Geraldine 1949- *61*
Marino, Dorothy Bronson 1912- *14*
Marion, Henry
  See del Rey, Lester
Maris, Ron *71*
  Brief entry *45*
Mark, Jan 1943- *69*
  Earlier sketch in SATA *22*
  See also CLR *11*
Mark, Pauline (Dahlin) 1913- *14*
Mark, Polly
  See Mark, Pauline (Dahlin)
Marker, Sherry 1941- *76*
Markert, Jennifer 1965- *83*
Markert, Jenny
  See Markert, Jennifer
Markham, Marion M. 1929- *60*
Markins, W. S.
  See Jenkins, Marie M.
Markle, Sandra L(ee) 1946- *92*
  Brief entry *41*
  Earlier sketch in SATA *57*
Marko, Katherine D(olores) *28*
Markoosie 1942-
  See CLR *23*
Marks, Alan 1957- *77*
Marks, Burton 1930- *47*
  Brief entry *43*
Marks, Hannah K.
  See Trivelpiece, Laurel
Marks, J
  See Highwater, Jamake
Marks, J(ames) M(acdonald) 1921- *13*
Marks, Laurie J. 1957- *68*
Marks, Margaret L. 1911(?)-1980
  Obituary *23*

Marks, Mickey Klar *12*
Marks, Peter
  See Smith, Robert Kimmel
Marks, Rita 1938- *47*
Marks, Stan(ley) 1929- *14*
Marks-Highwater, J
  See Highwater, Jamake
Markun, Patricia M(aloney) 1924- *15*
Marlowe, Amy Bell [Collective
  pseudonym] *67*
  Earlier sketch in SATA *1*
Marney, Dean 1952- *90*
Marokvia, Artur 1909- *31*
Marokvia, Mireille (Journet) 1918- *5*
Marr, John S(tuart) 1940- *48*
Marric, J. J.
  See Butler, William (Arthur) Vivian
Marrin, Albert 1936- *90*
  Brief entry *43*
  Earlier sketch in SATA *53*
Marriott, Alice Lee 1910-1992 ....*31*
  Obituary *71*
Marriott, Pat(ricia) 1920- *35*
Mars, W. T.
  See Mars, Witold Tadeusz J.
Mars, Witold Tadeusz J. 1912- *3*
Marsden, John 1950- *97*
  Earlier sketch in SATA *66*
  See also CLR *34*
  See also SAAS *22*
Marsh, Dave 1950- *66*
Marsh, J. E.
  See Marshall, Evelyn
Marsh, James 1946- *73*
Marsh, Jean
  See Marshall, Evelyn
Marsh, Jeri
  See Lee-Hostetler, Jeri
Marsh, Joan F. 1923- *83*
Marsh, Paul
  See Hopkins, (Hector) Kenneth
Marsh, Valerie 1954- *89*
Marshall, Anthony D(ryden) 1924- *18*
Marshall, (Sarah) Catherine 1914-1983 ...*2*
  Obituary *34*
Marshall, Douglas
  See McClintock, Marshall
Marshall, Edmund
  See Hopkins, (Hector) Kenneth
Marshall, Edward
  See Marshall, James (Edward)
Marshall, Evelyn 1897- *11*
Marshall, Garry 1934- *60*
Marshall, James (Edward)
  1942-1992 ....*75*
  Earlier sketches in SATA *6, 51*
  See also CLR *21*
Marshall, James Vance
  See Payne, Donald Gordon
Marshall, Janet (Perry) 1938- *97*
Marshall, Kim
  See Marshall, Michael (Kimbrough)
Marshall, Michael (Kimbrough)
  1948- *37*
Marshall, Percy
  See Young, Percy M(arshall)
Marshall, S(amuel) L(yman) A(twood)
  1900-1977 ....*21*
Marsoli, Lisa Ann 1958-
  Brief entry *53*
Marsten, Richard
  See Hunter, Evan
Marston, Hope Irvin 1935- *31*
Martchenko, Michael 1942- *95*
  Earlier sketch in SATA *50*
Martel, Suzanne 1924- *99*
Martignoni, Margaret E. 1908(?)-1974
  Obituary *27*
Martin, Ann M(atthews) 1955- *70*
  Brief entry *41*
  Earlier sketch in SATA *44*
  See also CLR *32*
Martin, Bill
  See Martin, Bill, Jr.
Martin, Bill, Jr. 1916- *67*
  Brief entry *40*
  See also CLR *31*

Martin, Charles E. 1910- 70
Martin, Claire 1933- 76
Martin, David Stone 1913- 39
Martin, Dorothy 1921- 47
Martin, Eugene [Collective
    pseudonym] 1
Martin, Eva M. 1939- 65
Martin, Frances M(cEntee) 1906- 36
Martin, Fredric
    See Christopher, Matt(hew Frederick)
Martin, J(ohn) P(ercival)
    1880(?)-1966 15
Martin, Jacqueline Briggs 1945- 98
Martin, Jane Read 1957- 84
Martin, Jeremy
    See Levin, Marcia Obrasky
Martin, Linda 1961- 82
Martin, Lynne 1923- 21
Martin, Marcia
    See Levin, Marcia Obrasky
Martin, Melanie
    See Pellowski, Michael (Joseph)
Martin, Nancy
    See Salmon, Annie Elizabeth
Martin, Patricia Miles 1899-1986 43
    Obituary 48
    Earlier sketch in SATA 1
Martin, Peter
    See Chaundler, Christine
Martin, Rene 1891-1977 42
    Obituary 20
Martin, Rupert (Claude) 1905- 31
Martin, Stefan 1936- 32
Martin, Vicky
    See Storey, Victoria Carolyn
Martineau, Harriet 1802-1876
    See YABC 2
Martinet, Jeanne 1958- 80
Martinez, Ed(ward) 1954- 98
Martinez, Elizabeth Coonrod 1954- 85
Martinez, Victor 95
Martini, Teri 1930- 3
Marton, Jirina 1946- 95
Martyr, Paula (Jane) 1960- 57
Maruki, Toshi
    See CLR 19
Marvin, Isabel R(idout) 1924- 84
Marx, Robert F(rank) 1936- 24
Marzani, Carl (Aldo) 1912- 12
Marzollo, Jean 1942- 77
    Earlier sketch in SATA 29
    See also SAAS 15
Masefield, John 1878-1967 19
Mason, Edwin A. 1905-1979
    Obituary 32
Mason, F. van Wyck 1901-1978 3
    Obituary 26
Mason, Frank W.
    See Mason, F. van Wyck
Mason, George Frederick 1904- 14
Mason, Miriam (Evangeline)
    1900-1973 2
    Obituary 26
Mason, Tally
    See Derleth, August (William)
Mason, Van Wyck
    See Mason, F. van Wyck
Masselman, George 1897-1971 19
Massie, Diane Redfield 16
Masters, Kelly R. 1897- 3
Masters, Mildred 1932- 42
Masters, William
    See Cousins, Margaret
Masuda, Takeshi
    See Aska, Warabe
Matas, Carol 1949- 93
Matchette, Katharine E. 1941- 38
Math, Irwin 1940- 42
Mather, Kirtley F(letcher)
    1888-1978 65
Mathews, Janet 1914- 41
Mathews, Judith 1948- 80
Mathews, Louise
    See Tooke, Louise Mathews
Mathiesen, Egon 1907-1976
    Obituary 28

Mathieu, Joe
    See Mathieu, Joseph P.
Mathieu, Joseph P. 1949- 94
    Brief entry 36
    Earlier sketch in SATA 43
Mathis, Sharon Bell 1937- 58
    Earlier sketch in SATA 7
    See also CLR 3
    See also SAAS 3
Matloff, Gregory 1945- 73
Matranga, Frances Carfi 1922- 78
Matson, Emerson N(els) 1926- 12
Matsui, Tadashi 1926- 8
Matsuno, Masako 1935- 6
Matte, (Encarnacion) L'Enc 1936- 22
Matthews, Ann
    See Martin, Ann M(atthews)
Matthews, Downs 1925- 71
Matthews, Ellen 1950- 28
Matthews, Jacklyn Meek
    See Meek, Jacklyn O'Hanlon
Matthews, Liz
    See Pellowski, Michael (Joseph)
Matthews, Morgan
    See Pellowski, Michael (Joseph)
Matthews, Patricia 1927- 28
Matthews, William Henry III
    1919- 45
    Brief entry 28
Matthias, Catherine 1945-
    Brief entry 41
Matthiessen, Peter 1927- 27
Mattingley, Christobel (Rosemary)
    1931- 85
    Earlier sketch in SATA 37
    See also CLR 24
    See also SAAS 18
Matulay, Laszlo 1912- 43
Matulka, Jan 1890-1972
    Brief entry 28
Matus, Greta 1938- 12
Maugham, W(illiam) Somerset
    1874-1965 54
Maurer, Diane Philippoff
    See Maurer-Mathison, Diane V(ogel)
Maurer, Diane Vogel
    See Maurer-Mathison, Diane V(ogel)
Maurer-Mathison, Diane V(ogel)
    1944- 89
Mauser, Patricia Rhoads 1943- 37
Maves, Mary Carolyn 1916- 10
Maves, Paul B(enjamin) 1913- 10
Mawicke, Tran 1911- 15
Max, Peter 1939- 45
Maxon, Anne
    See Best, (Evangel) Allena Champlin
Maxwell, Arthur S. 1896-1970 11
Maxwell, Edith 1923- 7
Maxwell, Gavin 1914-1969 65
May, Charles Paul 1920- 4
May, Julian 1931- 11
May, Robert Lewis 1905-1976
    Obituary 27
May, Robert Stephen 1929- 46
May, Robin
    See May, Robert Stephen
Mayberry, Florence V(irginia Wilson) ......
    10
Maybury, Richard J. 1946- 72
Mayer, Albert Ignatius, Jr. 1906-1960
    Obituary 29
Mayer, Ann M(argaret) 1938- 14
Mayer, Barbara 1939- 77
Mayer, Jane Rothschild 1903- 38
Mayer, Marianna 1945- 83
    Earlier sketch in SATA 32
Mayer, Mercer 1943- 73
    Earlier sketches in SATA 16, 32
    See also CLR 11
Mayerson, Charlotte Leon 36
Mayerson, Evelyn Wilde 1935- 55
Mayfield, Sue 1963- 72
Mayhar, Ardath 1930- 38
Mayhew, James (John) 1964- 85
Maynard, Chris
    See Maynard, Christopher

Maynard, Christopher 1949-
    Brief entry 43
Maynard, Olga 1920- 40
Mayne, William (James Carter)
    1928- 68
    Earlier sketch in SATA 6
    See also SAAS 11
Maynes, Dr. J. O. Rocky
    See Maynes, J. Oscar, Jr.
Maynes, J. O. Rocky, Jr.
    See Maynes, J. Oscar, Jr.
Maynes, J. Oscar, Jr. 1929- 38
Mayo, Gretchen Will 1936- 84
Mayo, Margaret (Mary) 1935- 96
    Earlier sketch in SATA 38
Mays, Lucinda L(a Bella) 1924- 49
Mays, (Lewis) Victor, (Jr.) 1927- 5
Mazer, Anne 1953- 67
Mazer, Harry 1925- 67
    Earlier sketch in SATA 31
    See also CLR 16
    See also SAAS 11
Mazer, Norma Fox 1931- 67
    Earlier sketch in SATA 24
    See also CLR 23
    See also SAAS 1
Mazille, Capucine 1953- 96
Mazza, Adriana 1928- 19
Mazzio, Joann 1926- 74
Mbugua, Kioi Wa 1962- 83
McAfee, Carol 1955- 81
McAllister, P. K.
    See Downing, Paula E.
McArthur, Nancy 96
McBain, Ed
    See Hunter, Evan
McBratney, Sam 1943- 89
    See also CLR 44
McCafferty, Jim 1954- 84
McCaffery, Janet 1936- 38
McCaffrey, Anne 1926- 70
    Earlier sketch in SATA 8
    See also CLR 49
McCaffrey, Mary
    See Szudek, Agnes S(usan) P(hilomena)
McCain, Murray (David, Jr.)
    1926-1981 7
    Obituary 29
McCall, Edith S. 1911- 6
McCall, Virginia Nielsen 1909- 13
McCall Smith, Alexander 1948- 73
McCallum, Phyllis 1911- 10
McCallum, Stephen 1960- 91
McCampbell, Darlene Z. 1942- 83
McCann, Edson
    See del Rey, Lester
McCann, Gerald 1916- 41
McCann, Helen 1948- 75
McCannon, Dindga Fatima 1947- 41
McCants, William D. 1961- 82
McCarter, Neely Dixon 1929- 47
McCarthy, Agnes 1933- 4
McCarthy, Colin (John) 1951- 77
McCarthy-Tucker, Sherri N. 1958- 83
McCarty, Rega Kramer 1904- 10
McCaslin, Nellie 1914- 12
McCaughrean, Geraldine 1951- 87
    See also CLR 38
    See Jones, Geraldine
McCaughren, Tom 1936- 75
McCay, Winsor 1869-1934 41
McClary, Jane Stevenson 1919-1990
    Obituary 64
McCleery, Patsy R. 1925- 88
McClintock, Barbara 1955- 95
    Earlier sketch in SATA 57
McClintock, Marshall 1906-1967 3
McClintock, Mike
    See McClintock, Marshall
McClintock, Theodore 1902-1971 14
McClinton, Leon 1933- 11
McCloskey, Kevin 1951- 79
McCloskey, (John) Robert 1914- 39
    Earlier sketch in SATA 2
    See also CLR 7
McCloy, James F(loyd) 1941- 59

McClung, Robert M(arshall) 1916- 68
  Earlier sketch in SATA 2
  See also CLR 11
  See also SAAS 15
McClure, Gillian Mary 1948- 31
McColley, Kevin 1961- 80
  See also SAAS 23
McConduit, Denise Walter 1950- 89
McConnell, James Douglas (Rutherford)
  1915-1988 40
  Obituary 56
McCord, Anne 1942- 41
McCord, David (Thompson Watson)
  1897-1997 18
  Obituary 96
  See also CLR 9
McCord, Jean 1924- 34
McCormick, Brooks
  See Adams, William Taylor
McCormick, Dell J. 1892-1949 19
McCormick, (George) Donald (King)
  1911- 14
McCormick, Edith (Joan) 1934- 30
McCourt, Edward (Alexander) 1907-1972
  Obituary 28
McCoy, Iola Fuller 3
McCoy, J(oseph) J(erome) 1917- 8
McCoy, Karen Kawamoto 1953- 82
McCoy, Lois (Rich) 1941- 38
McCrady, Lady 1951- 16
McCraffrey, Anne 1926- 8
  See also SAAS 11
McCrea, James 1920- 3
McCrea, Ruth 1921- 3
McCue, Lisa (Emiline) 1959- 65
McCullers, (Lula) Carson
  1917-1967 27
McCulloch, Derek (Ivor Breashur) 1897-
  1967
  Obituary 29
McCulloch, Sarah
  See Ure, Jean
McCullough, David (Gaub) 1933- 62
McCullough, Frances Monson 1938- 8
McCully, Emily Arnold 1939- 5
  See also CLR 46
  See also SAAS 7
  See Arnold, Emily
McCunn, Ruthanne Lum 1946- 63
McCurdy, Michael (Charles) 1942- 82
  Earlier sketch in SATA 13
McCutcheon, Elsie 1937- 60
McCutcheon, John 1952- 97
McDaniel, Becky B(ring) 1953- 61
McDaniel, Lurlene 1944- 71
McDearmon, Kay 20
McDermott, Beverly Brodsky
  1941- 11
McDermott, Gerald (Edward)
  1941- 74
  Earlier sketch in SATA 16
  See also CLR 9
McDermott, Michael 1962- 76
McDevitt, Jack
  See McDevitt, John Charles
McDevitt, John Charles 1935- 94
McDole, Carol
  See Farley, Carol
McDonald, Collin 1943- 79
McDonald, Gerald D. 1905-1970 3
McDonald, Jamie
  See Heide, Florence Parry
McDonald, Jill (Masefield)
  1927-1982 13
  Obituary 29
McDonald, Lucile Saunders 1898- 10
McDonald, Mary Ann 1956- 84
McDonald, Megan 1959- 99
  Earlier sketch in SATA 67
McDonald, Mercedes 1956- 97
McDonnell, Christine 1949- 34
McDonnell, Flora (Mary) 1963- 90
McDonnell, Lois Eddy 1914- 10
McDonough, Yona Zeldis 1957- 73
McElrath, William N. 1932- 65
McElrath-Eslick, Lori 1960- 96
McEntee, Dorothy (Layng) 1902- 37

McEwen, Robert (Lindley) 1926-1980
  Obituary 23
McFall, Christie 1918- 12
McFarlan, Donald M(aitland)
  1915- 59
McFarland, Kenton D(ean) 1920- 11
McFarlane, Leslie 1902-1977 31
McFarlane, Peter (William) 1940- 95
McFarlane, Sheryl P. 1954- 86
McGaw, Jessie Brewer 1913- 10
McGee, Barbara 1943- 6
McGiffin, (Lewis) Lee (Shaffer)
  1908- 1
McGill, Marci
  See Ridlon, Marci
McGill, Ormond 1913- 92
McGinley, Phyllis 1905-1978 44
  Obituary 24
  Earlier sketch in SATA 2
McGinnis, Lila S(prague) 1924- 44
McGough, Elizabeth (Hemmes)
  1934- 33
McGovern, Ann 1930- 70
  Earlier sketch in SATA 8
  See also SAAS 17
McGowen, Thomas E. 1927- 2
McGowen, Tom
  See McGowen, Thomas E.
McGrady, Mike 1933- 6
McGrath, Thomas (Matthew)
  1916-1990 41
  Obituary 66
McGraw, Eloise Jarvis 1915- 67
  Earlier sketch in SATA 1
  See also SAAS 6
McGraw, William Corbin 1916- 3
McGregor, Barbara 1959- 82
McGregor, Craig 1933- 8
McGregor, Iona 1929- 25
McGuffey, Alexander Hamilton
  1816-1896 60
McGuffey, William Holmes
  1800-1873 60
McGuire, Edna 1899- 13
McGuire, Leslie (Sarah) 1945- 94
  Brief entry 45
  Earlier sketch in SATA 52
McGurk, Slater
  See Roth, Arthur J(oseph)
McHargue, Georgess 1941- 77
  Earlier sketch in SATA 4
  See also CLR 2
  See also SAAS 5
McHugh, (Berit) Elisabet 1941- 55
  Brief entry 44
McIlwraith, Maureen 1922- 2
McIlwraith, Maureen Mollie Hunter
  See Hunter, Mollie
McInerney, Judith Whitelock 1945- 49
  Brief entry 46
McInerny, Ralph 1929- 93
McKaughan, Larry (Scott) 1941- 75
McKay, Donald 1895- 45
McKay, Hilary 1959- 92
  See also SAAS 23
McKay, Robert W. 1921- 15
McKeating, Eileen 1957- 81
McKee, David 1935- 70
  See also CLR 38
McKeever, Marcia
  See Laird, Jean E(louise)
McKelvey, Carole A. 1942- 78
McKendrick, Melveena (Christine)
  1941- 55
McKenna, Colleen O'Shaughnessy
  1948- 76
McKenzie, Dorothy Clayton 1910-1981
  Obituary 28
McKenzie, Ellen Kindt 1928- 80
McKillip, Patricia A(nne) 1948- 80
  Earlier sketch in SATA 30
McKim, Audrey Margaret 1909- 47
McKinley, (Jennifer Carolyn) Robin
  1952- 89
  Brief entry 32
  Earlier sketch in SATA 50
  See also CLR 10

McKinney, Nadine 1938- 91
McKissack, Fredrick L(emuel)
  1939- 73
  Brief entry 53
McKissack, Patricia C. 1944- 73
  Earlier sketch in SATA 51
  See also CLR 23
McKown, Robin 6
McLaughlin, Frank 1934- 73
McLaurin, Anne 1953- 27
McLean, Kathryn (Anderson)
  1909-1966 9
McLean, Virginia Overton 1946- 90
McLeish, Kenneth 1940- 35
McLenighan, Valjean 1947- 46
  Brief entry 40
McLeod, Chum 1955- 95
McLeod, Emilie Warren 1926-1982 23
  Obituary 31
McLeod, Kirsty
  See Hudson, (Margaret) Kirsty
McLeod, Margaret Vail
  See Holloway, Teresa (Bragunier)
McLerran, Alice 1933- 68
McLoughlin, John C. 1949- 47
McMahan, Ian
  Brief entry 45
McManus, Patrick (Francis) 1933- 46
McMeekin, Clark
  See McMeekin, Isabel McLennan
McMeekin, Isabel McLennan 1895- 3
McMillan, Bruce 70
  Earlier sketch in SATA 22
  See also CLR 47
McMillan, Naomi
  See Grimes, Nikki
McMorey, James L.
  See Moyer, Terry J.
McMullan, Jim 1934- 87
McMullan, Kate (Hall) 1947- 87
  Brief entry 48
  Earlier sketch in SATA 52
McMullan, Katy Hall
  See McMullan, Kate (Hall)
McMullen, Catherine
  See Cookson, Catherine (McMullen)
McMurtrey, Martin A(loysius)
  1921- 21
McNair, Kate 3
McNair, Sylvia 1924- 74
McNamara, Margaret C(raig) 1915-1981
  Obituary 24
McNaught, Harry 32
McNaughton, Colin 1951- 92
  Earlier sketch in SATA 39
McNeely, Jeannette 1918- 25
McNeer, May (Yonge) 1902-1994 1
  Obituary 81
McNeill, Janet 1907-1994 87
  Earlier sketch in SATA 1
McNickle, (William) D'Arcy 1904-1977
  Obituary 22
McNulty, Faith 1918- 84
  Earlier sketch in SATA 12
McPhail, David M(ichael) 1940- 81
  Brief entry 32
  Earlier sketch in SATA 47
McPharlin, Paul 1903-1948
  Brief entry 31
McPhee, Norma H. 1928- 95
McPhee, Richard B(yron) 1934- 41
McPherson, James M. 1936- 16
McQueen, Lucinda 1950- 58
  Brief entry 48
McQueen, Mildred Hark 1908- 12
McRae, Russell (William) 1934- 63
McShean, Gordon 1936- 41
McSwigan, Marie 1907-1962 24
McVey, Vicki 1946- 80
McVicker, Charles (Taggart) 1930- 39
McVicker, Chuck
  See McVicker, Charles (Taggart)
McWhirter, Norris (Dewar) 1925- 37
McWhirter, (Alan) Ross 1925-1975 37
  Obituary 31
McWilliams, Karen 1943- 65
Mdurvwa, Hajara E. 1962- 92

Meacham, Margaret 1952- *95*
Meachum, Virginia 1918- *87*
Mead, Alice 1952- *94*
Mead, Margaret 1901-1978
  Obituary *20*
Mead, Russell (M., Jr.) 1935- *10*
Mead, Stella (?)-1981
  Obituary *27*
Meade, Ellen (Roddick) 1936- *5*
Meade, Marion 1934- *23*
Meader, Stephen W(arren) 1892- *1*
Meadmore, Susan
  See Sallis, Susan (Diana)
Meadow, Charles T(roub) 1929- *23*
Meadowcroft, Enid LaMonte
  See Wright, Enid Meadowcroft
Meaker, M. J.
  See Meaker, Marijane (Agnes)
Meaker, Marijane (Agnes) 1927- *99*
  Earlier sketches in SATA *20, 61*
Means, Florence Crannell 1891-1980 ......*1*
  Obituary *25*
Mearian, Judy Frank 1936- *49*
Medary, Marjorie 1890- *14*
Meddaugh, Susan 1944- *84*
  Earlier sketch in SATA *29*
Medearis, Angela Shelf 1956- *72*
Medearis, Mary 1915- *5*
Medlicott, Mary 1946- *88*
Mee, Charles L., Jr. 1938- *72*
  Earlier sketch in SATA *8*
Meek, Jacklyn O'Hanlon 1933- *51*
  Brief entry *34*
Meek, S(terner St.) P(aul) 1894-1972
  Obituary *28*
Meeker, Clare Hodgson 1952- *96*
Meeker, Oden 1918(?)-1976 ....*14*
Meeker, Richard
  See Brown, Fornan
Meeks, Esther MacBain *1*
Meggendorfer, Lothar 1847-1925
  Brief entry *36*
Mehdevi, Alexander 1947- *7*
Mehdevi, Anne (Marie) Sinclair *8*
Meidell, Sherry 1951- *73*
Meier, Minta 1906- *55*
Meighan, Donald Charles 1929- *30*
Meigs, Cornelia Lynde 1884-1973 ....*6*
Meilach, Dona Z(weigoron) 1926- *34*
Meilman, Philip W(arren) 1951- *79*
Melady, John 1938-
  Brief entry *49*
Melcher, Daniel 1912-1985
  Obituary *43*
Melcher, Frederic Gershom 1879-1963
  Obituary *22*
Melcher, Marguerite Fellows
  1879-1969 ....*10*
Melendez, Francisco 1964- *72*
Melin, Grace Hathaway 1892-1973 ....*10*
Mellersh, H(arold) E(dward) L(eslie)
  1897- *10*
Melnikoff, Pamela (Rita) *97*
Meltzer, Milton 1915- *80*
  Earlier sketches in SATA *1, 50*
  See also CLR *13*
  See also SAAS *1*
Melville, Anne
  See Potter, Margaret (Newman)
Melville, Herman 1819-1891 ....*59*
Melwood, Mary
  See Lewis, E. M.
Melzack, Ronald 1929- *5*
Memling, Carl 1918-1969 ....*6*
Mendel, Jo [House pseudonym]
  See Bond, Gladys Baker
Mendelson, Steven T. 1958-1995 ....*86*
Mendez, Raymond A. 1947- *66*
Mendonca, Susan
  Brief entry *49*
  See Smith, Susan Vernon
Mendoza, George 1934- *41*
  Brief entry *39*
  See also SAAS *7*
Meng, Heinz (Karl) 1924- *13*
Mennen, Ingrid 1954- *85*
Menotti, Gian Carlo 1911- *29*

Menuhin, Yehudi 1916- *40*
Menville, Douglas 1935- *64*
Menzel, Barbara J(ean) 1946- *63*
Mercer, Charles (Edward)
  1917-1988 ....*16*
  Obituary *61*
Meredith, Arnold
  See Hopkins, (Hector) Kenneth
Meredith, David William
  See Miers, Earl Schenck
Meringoff, Laurene Krasny
  See Brown, Laurie Krasny
Meriwether, Louise 1923- *52*
  Brief entry *31*
Merlin, Arthur
  See Blish, James (Benjamin)
Merriam, Eve 1916-1992 ....*73*
  Earlier sketches in SATA *3, 40*
  See also CLR *14*
Merrill, Jane 1946- *42*
Merrill, Jean (Fairbanks) 1923- *82*
  Earlier sketch in SATA *1*
Merrill, Phil
  See Merrill, Jane
Merriman, Rachel 1971- *98*
Merrit, Elizabeth
  See Goudge, Eileen
Mertz, Barbara (Gross) 1927- *49*
Merwin, Decie 1894-1961
  Brief entry *32*
Meschel, Susan V. 1936- *83*
Messenger, Charles (Rynd Milles)
  1941- *59*
Messick, Dale 1906- *64*
  Brief entry *48*
Messmer, Otto 1892(?)-1983 ....*37*
Metcalf, Doris H(unter) *91*
Metcalf, Suzanne
  See Baum, L(yman) Frank
Metos, Thomas H(arry) 1932- *37*
Metter, Bert(ram Milton) 1927- *56*
Meyer, Carolyn (Mae) 1935- *70*
  Earlier sketch in SATA *9*
  See also SAAS *9*
Meyer, Edith Patterson 1895- *5*
Meyer, F(ranklyn) E(dward) 1932- *9*
Meyer, Jean Shepherd 1929- *11*
Meyer, Jerome Sydney 1895-1975 ....*3*
  Obituary *25*
Meyer, June
  See Jordan, June
Meyer, Kathleen Allan 1918- *51*
  Brief entry *46*
Meyer, Louis A(lbert) 1942- *12*
Meyer, Renate 1930- *6*
Meyer, Susan E. 1940- *64*
Meyers, Susan 1942- *19*
Meynell, Laurence Walter 1899-1989
  Obituary *61*
Meynier, Yvonne (Pollet) 1908- *14*
Mezey, Robert 1935- *33*
Mian, Mary (Lawrence Shipman) 1902-
  Brief entry *47*
Micale, Albert 1913- *22*
Michael, Manfred
  See Winterfeld, Henry
Michaels, Barbara
  See Mertz, Barbara (Gross)
Michaels, Joanne Louise
  See Teitelbaum, Michael
Michaels, Neal
  See Teitelbaum, Michael
Michaels, Ski
  See Pellowski, Michael (Joseph)
Michaels, Steve 1955- *71*
Michaels, William M. 1917- *77*
Michel, Anna 1943- *49*
  Brief entry *40*
Michel, Francois 1948- *82*
Micich, Paul *74*
Micklish, Rita 1931- *12*
Micucci, Charles (Patrick, Jr.)
  1959- *82*
Middleton, Haydn 1955- *85*
Miers, Earl Schenck 1910-1972 ....*1*
  Obituary *26*
Migdale, Lawrence 1951- *89*

Mikaelsen, Ben(jamin John) 1952- *73*
Miklowitz, Gloria D. 1927- *68*
  Earlier sketch in SATA *4*
  See also SAAS *17*
Mikolaycak, Charles 1937-1993 ....*78*
  Obituary *75*
  Earlier sketch in SATA *9*
  See also SAAS *4*
Mild, Warren (Paul) 1922- *41*
Miles, Betty 1928- *78*
  Earlier sketch in SATA *8*
  See also SAAS *9*
Miles, Miska
  See Martin, Patricia Miles
Miles, (Mary) Patricia 1930- *29*
Miles, Patricia A.
  See Martin, Patricia Miles
Milgrom, Harry 1912- *25*
Milhous, Katherine 1894-1977 ....*15*
Milios, Rita 1949- *79*
Militant
  See Sandburg, Carl (August)
Millais, Raoul 1901- *77*
Millar, Barbara F. 1924- *12*
Millar, Margaret (Ellis Sturm)
  1915-1994 ....*61*
  Obituary *79*
Miller, Albert G(riffith) 1905-1982 ....*12*
  Obituary *31*
Miller, Alice P(atricia McCarthy) *22*
Miller, Deborah Uchill 1944- *61*
Miller, Don 1923- *15*
Miller, Doris R.
  See Mosesson, Gloria R(ubin)
Miller, Eddie
  See Miller, Edward
Miller, Edna (Anita) 1920- *29*
Miller, Edward 1905-1974 ....*8*
Miller, Elizabeth 1933- *41*
Miller, Ellanita 1957- *87*
Miller, Eugene 1925- *33*
Miller, Frances A. 1937- *52*
  Brief entry *46*
Miller, Helen M(arkley) *5*
Miller, Helen Topping 1884-1960
  Obituary *29*
Miller, Jane (Judith) 1925- *15*
Miller, Jewel 1956- *73*
Miller, John
  See Samachson, Joseph
Miller, Louise (Rolfe) 1940- *76*
Miller, M. L. *85*
Miller, Madge 1918- *63*
Miller, Margaret J.
  See Dale, Margaret J(essy) Miller
Miller, Marilyn (Jean) 1925- *33*
Miller, Marvin *65*
Miller, Mary
  See Northcott, (William) Cecil
Miller, Mary Beth 1942- *9*
Miller, Maryann 1943- *73*
Miller, Natalie 1917-1976 ....*35*
Miller, Robert H. 1944- *91*
Miller, Ruth White
  See White, Ruth C.
Miller, Sandy (Peden) 1948- *41*
  Brief entry *35*
Miller, Virginia
  See Austin, Virginia
Milligan, Spike
  See Milligan, Terence Alan
Milligan, Terence Alan 1918- *29*
Mills, Claudia 1954- *89*
  Brief entry *41*
  Earlier sketch in SATA *44*
Mills, Elaine (Rosemary) 1941- *72*
Mills, Yaroslava Surmach 1925- *35*
Millspaugh, Ben P. 1936- *77*
Millstead, Thomas Edward *30*
Milne, A(lan) A(lexander) 1882-1956
  See YABC *1*
  See also CLR *26*
Milne, Lorus J. *5*
  See also CLR *22*
  See also SAAS *18*

Milne, Margery 5
    See also CLR *22*
    See also SAAS *18*
Milne, Terry
    See Milne, Theresa Ann
Milne, Theresa Ann 1964- *84*
Milonas, Rolf
    See Myller, Rolf
Milord, Susan 1954- *74*
Milotte, Alfred G(eorge) 1904-1989 ......*11*
    Obituary *62*
Milstein, Linda 1954- *80*
Milton, Hilary (Herbert) 1920- *23*
Milton, John R(onald) 1924- *24*
Milton, Joyce 1946- *52*
    Brief entry *41*
Milverton, Charles A.
    See Penzler, Otto
Minahan, John A. 1956- *92*
Minar, Barbra (Goodyear) 1940- *79*
Minard, Rosemary 1939- *63*
Minarik, Else Holmelund 1920- *15*
    See also CLR *33*
Miner, Jane Claypool 1933- *38*
    Brief entry *37*
Miner, Lewis S. 1909- *11*
Mines, Jeanette (Marie) 1948- *61*
Minier, Nelson
    See Stoutenburg, Adrien
Minor, Wendell G. 1944- *78*
Mintonye, Grace *4*
Miranda, Anne 1954- *71*
Mirsky, Jeannette 1903-1987 ....*8*
    Obituary *51*
Mirsky, Reba Paeff 1902-1966 ....*1*
Mishica, Clare 1960- *91*
Miskovits, Christine 1939- *10*
Miss Francis
    See Horwich, Frances R(appaport)
Miss Read
    See Saint, Dora Jessie
Mister Rogers
    See Rogers, Fred (McFeely)
Mitchard, Jacquelyn 1952- *98*
Mitchell, Cynthia 1922- *29*
Mitchell, (Sibyl) Elyne (Keith)
    1913- *10*
Mitchell, Gladys (Maude Winifred)
    1901-1983 ....*46*
    Obituary *35*
Mitchell, Jay
    See Roberson, Jennifer
Mitchell, Joyce Slayton 1933- *46*
    Brief entry *43*
Mitchell, Kathy 1948- *59*
Mitchell, Margaree King 1953- *84*
Mitchell, Rhonda 1954- *89*
Mitchell, Yvonne 1925-1979
    Obituary *24*
Mitchison, Naomi Margaret (Haldane)
    1897- *24*
Mitchnik, Helen 1901- *41*
    Brief entry *35*
Mitgutsch, Ali 1935- *76*
Mitsuhashi, Yoko *45*
    Brief entry *33*
Mitton, Jacqueline 1948- *66*
Mitton, Simon 1946- *66*
Mizner, Elizabeth Howard 1907- *27*
Mizumura, Kazue *18*
Mobley, Joe A. 1945- *91*
Moche, Dinah (Rachel) L(evine)
    1936- *44*
    Brief entry *40*
Mochi, Ugo (A.) 1889-1977 ....*38*
Mochizuki, Ken 1954- *81*
    See also SAAS *22*
Modell, Frank B. 1917- *39*
    Brief entry *36*
Modesitt, Jeanne 1953- *92*
Modesitt, L(eland) E(xton), Jr.
    1943- *91*
Modrell, Dolores 1933- *72*
Moe, Barbara 1937- *20*
Moerbeek, Kees 1955- *98*

Moeri, Louise 1924- *93*
    Earlier sketch in SATA *24*
    See also SAAS *10*
Moffett, Jami 1952- *84*
Moffett, Martha (Leatherwood)
    1934- *8*
Mofsie, Louis B. 1936-
    Brief entry *33*
Mohn, Peter B(urnet) 1934- *28*
Mohn, Viola Kohl 1914- *8*
Mohr, Nicholasa 1938- *97*
    Earlier sketch in SATA *8*
    See also CLR *22*
    See also SAAS *8*
Mok, Esther 1953- *93*
Molan, Christine 1943- *84*
Molarsky, Osmond 1909- *16*
Moldon, Peter L(eonard) 1937- *49*
Mole, John 1941- *36*
Molesworth, Mary Louisa
    1839-1921 ....*98*
Molin, Charles
    See Mayne, William (James Carter)
Molina, Silvia 1946- *97*
Molk, Laurel 1957- *92*
Mollel, Tololwa M. 1952- *88*
Molloy, Anne Baker 1907- *32*
Molloy, Paul 1920- *5*
Moloney, James 1954- *94*
Momaday, N(avarre) Scott 1934- *48*
    Brief entry *30*
Moncure, Jane Belk *23*
Monjo, F(erdinand) N. 1924-1978 ....*16*
    See also CLR *2*
Monroe, Lyle
    See Heinlein, Robert A.
Monroe, Marion 1898-1983
    Obituary *34*
Monsell, Helen (Albee) 1895-1971 ....*24*
Montana, Bob 1920-1975
    Obituary *21*
Montenegro, Laura Nyman 1953- *95*
Montgomerie, Norah Mary 1913- *26*
Montgomery, Constance
    See Cappel, Constance
Montgomery, Elizabeth Rider
    1902-1985 ....*34*
    Obituary *41*
    Earlier sketch in SATA *3*
Montgomery, L(ucy) M(aud) 1874-1942
    See YABC *1*
    See also CLR *8*
Montgomery, R(aymond) A., (Jr.)
    1936- *39*
Montgomery, Rutherford George
    1894- *3*
Montgomery, Vivian *36*
Montresor, Beni 1926- *38*
    Earlier sketch in SATA *3*
    See also SAAS *4*
Monty Python
    See Jones, Terry
    and Palin, Michael (Edward)
Moody, Ralph Owen 1898- *1*
Moon, Carl 1879-1948 ....*25*
Moon, Grace 1877(?)-1947 ....*25*
Moon, Nicola 1952- *96*
Moon, Sheila (Elizabeth) 1910- *5*
Mooney, Bel 1946- *95*
Mooney, Elizabeth C(omstock) 1918-1986
    Obituary *48*
Moor, Emily
    See Deming, Richard
Moorcock, Michael (John) 1939- *93*
Moore, Anne Carroll 1871-1961 ....*13*
Moore, Clement Clarke 1779-1863 ....*18*
Moore, Cyd 1957- *83*
Moore, Don W. 1905(?)-1986
    Obituary *48*
Moore, Elaine 1944- *86*
Moore, Eva 1942- *20*
Moore, Fenworth
    See Stratemeyer, Edward L.
Moore, Jack (William) 1941- *46*
    Brief entry *32*
Moore, Janet Gaylord 1905- *18*
Moore, Jim 1946- *42*

Moore, John Travers 1908- *12*
Moore, Lamont 1909-
    Brief entry *29*
Moore, Lilian 1909- *52*
    See also CLR *15*
Moore, Margaret Rumberger 1903- *12*
Moore, Marianne (Craig)
    1887-1972 ....*20*
Moore, Patrick (Alfred) 1923- *49*
    Brief entry *39*
    See also SAAS *8*
Moore, Ray (S.) 1905(?)-1984
    Obituary *37*
Moore, Regina
    See Dunne, Mary Collins
Moore, Rosalie
    See Brown, Rosalie (Gertrude) Moore
Moore, Ruth *23*
Moore, Ruth Nulton 1923- *38*
Moore, S. E. *23*
Moore, Tara 1950- *61*
Moore, Yvette 1958- *70*
Moores, Dick
    See Moores, Richard (Arnold)
Moores, Richard (Arnold) 1909-1986
    Obituary *48*
Mooser, Stephen 1941- *75*
    Earlier sketch in SATA *28*
Mora, Francisco X(avier) 1952- *90*
Mora, Pat(ricia) 1942- *92*
Moran, Tom 1943- *60*
Moray Williams, Ursula 1911- *73*
    Earlier sketch in SATA *3*
    See also SAAS *9*
Mordvinoff, Nicolas 1911-1973 ....*17*
More, Caroline [Joint pseudonym]
    See Cone, Molly Lamken
    and Strachan, Margaret Pitcairn
Morey, Charles
    See Fletcher, Helen Jill
Morey, Walt(er Nelson) 1907-1992 ....*51*
    Obituary *70*
    Earlier sketch in SATA *3*
    See also SAAS *9*
Morgan, Alfred P(owell) 1889-1972 ....*33*
Morgan, Alison (Mary) 1930- *85*
    Earlier sketch in SATA *30*
Morgan, Ellen
    See Bumstead, Kathleen (Mary)
Morgan, Geoffrey 1916- *46*
Morgan, Helen (Gertrude Louise)
    1921- *29*
Morgan, Helen Tudor
    See Morgan, Helen (Gertrude Louise)
Morgan, Jane
    See Cooper, James Fenimore
Morgan, Lenore 1908- *8*
Morgan, Louise
    See Morgan, Helen (Gertrude Louise)
Morgan, Mary 1957- *81*
Morgan, Pierr 1952- *77*
Morgan, Robin (Evonne) 1941- *80*
Morgan, Sarah (Nicola) 1959- *68*
Morgan, Shirley 1933- *10*
Morgan, Stevie
    See Davies, Nicola
Morgan, Tom 1942- *42*
Morgenroth, Barbara
    Brief entry *36*
Mori, Hana 1909-1990(?) *88*
Mori, Kyoko 1957- *82*
    See also SAAS *26*
Morice, Dave 1946- *93*
Morine, Hoder
    See Conroy, John Wesley
Morninghouse, Sundaira
    See Wilson, Carletta
Morningstar, Mildred 1912- *61*
Morpurgo, Michael 1943- *93*
Morrah, Dave
    See Morrah, David Wardlaw, Jr.
Morrah, David Wardlaw, Jr. 1914- *10*
Morressy, John 1930- *23*
Morrill, Leslie H(olt) 1934- *80*
    Brief entry *33*
    Earlier sketch in SATA *48*
    See also SAAS *22*

Morris, Chris(topher Crosby) 1946- 66
Morris, Deborah 1956- 91
Morris, Desmond (John) 1928- 14
Morris, Don 1954- 83
Morris, Janet (Ellen) 1946- 66
Morris, Jay
   See Tatham, Julie Campbell
Morris, (Margaret) Jean 1924- 98
Morris, Jeffrey B(randon) 1941- 92
Morris, Juddi 85
Morris, Judy K. 1936- 61
Morris, Robert A. 1933- 7
Morris, William 1913- 29
Morrison, Bill 1935- 66
   Brief entry 37
Morrison, Dorothy Nafus 29
Morrison, Gert W.
   See Stratemeyer, Edward L.
Morrison, Gordon 1944- 87
Morrison, Joan 1922- 65
Morrison, Lillian 1917- 3
Morrison, Lucile Phillips 1896- 17
Morrison, Martha A. 1948- 77
Morrison, Meighan 1966- 90
Morrison, Roberta
   See Webb, Jean Francis (III)
Morrison, Taylor 1971- 95
Morrison, Toni 1931- 57
Morrison, Velma Ford 1909- 21
Morrison, Wilbur Howard 1915- 64
Morrison, William
   See Samachson, Joseph
Morriss, James E(dward) 1932- 8
Morrow, Betty
   See Bacon, Elizabeth
Morse, Carol
   See Yeakley, Marjory Hall
Morse, Dorothy B(ayley) 1906-1979
   Obituary 24
Morse, Flo 1921- 30
Mort, Vivian
   See Cromie, Alice Hamilton
Mortimer, Mary H.
   See Coury, Louise Andree
Morton, (Eva) Jane 1931- 50
Morton, Lee Jack, Jr. 1928- 32
Morton, Miriam 1918(?)-1985 9
   Obituary 46
Moscow, Alvin 1925- 3
Mosel, Arlene 1921- 7
Moseng, Elisabeth 1967- 90
Moser, Barry 1940- 79
   Earlier sketch in SATA 56
   See also CLR 49
   See also SAAS 15
Moser, Don
   See Moser, Donald Bruce
Moser, Donald Bruce 1932- 31
Mosesson, Gloria R(ubin) 24
Moskin, Marietta D(unston) 1928- 23
Moskof, Martin Stephen 1930- 27
Mosley, Francis 1957- 57
Moss, Don(ald) 1920- 11
Moss, Elaine (Dora) 1924- 57
   Brief entry 31
Moss, Jeff(rey) 73
Moss, Marissa 1959- 71
Moss, Miriam 1955- 76
Most, Bernard 1937- 91
   Brief entry 40
   Earlier sketch in SATA 48
Mott, Evelyn Clarke 1962- 75
   See also SAAS 25
Motz, Lloyd 20
Mountain, Robert
   See Montgomery, R(aymond) A., (Jr.)
Mountfield, David
   See Grant, Neil
Moussard, Jacqueline 1924- 24
Mowat, Farley (McGill) 1921- 55
   Earlier sketch in SATA 3
   See also CLR 20
Moxley, Sheila 1966- 96
Moyer, Terry J. 1937- 94
Moyes, Patricia 1923- 63
Moyler, Alan (Frank Powell) 1926- 36

Mozley, Charles 1915- 43
   Brief entry 32
Mrs. Fairstar
   See Horne, Richard Henry
Mueller, Joerg 1942- 67
   See also CLR 43
Mueller, Virginia 1924- 28
Muggs
   See Watkins, Lois
Muir, Frank 1920- 30
Muir, Helen 1937- 65
Mukerji, Dhan Gopal 1890-1936 40
   See also CLR 10
Mulcahy, Lucille Burnett 12
Mulford, Philippa Greene 1948- 43
Mulgan, Catherine
   See Gough, Catherine
Muller, Billex
   See Ellis, Edward S(ylvester)
Muller, Jorg
   See Mueller, Joerg
Muller, (Lester) Robin 1953- 86
Mullins, Edward S(wift) 1922- 10
Mullins, Hilary 1962- 84
Mulock, Dinah Maria
   See Craik, Dinah Maria (Mulock)
Mulvihill, William Patrick 1923- 8
Mumford, Ruth 1919- 86
Mun
   See Leaf, (Wilbur) Munro
Munari, Bruno 1907- 15
   See also CLR 9
Munce, Ruth Hill 1898- 12
Mundy, Simon (Andrew James Hainault)
   1954- 64
Munowitz, Ken 1935-1977 14
Munoz, William 1949- 92
   Earlier sketch in SATA 42
Munro, Alice 1931- 29
Munro, Eleanor 1928- 37
Munro, Roxie 1945- 58
Munsch, Robert (Norman) 1945- 83
   Brief entry 48
   Earlier sketch in SATA 50
   See also CLR 19
Munsinger, Lynn 1951- 94
   Earlier sketch in SATA 33
Munson(-Benson), Tunie 1946- 15
Munthe, Nelly 1947- 53
Munves, James (Albert) 1922- 30
Munzer, Martha E. 1899- 4
Murch, Mel
   See Manes, Stephen
Murdoch, David H. 1937- 96
Murphy, Barbara Beasley 1933- 5
Murphy, Claire Rudolf 1951- 76
Murphy, E(mmett) Jefferson 1926- 4
Murphy, Jill 1949- 70
   Earlier sketch in SATA 37
   See also CLR 39
Murphy, Jim 1947- 77
   Brief entry 32
   Earlier sketch in SATA 37
Murphy, Joseph E., Jr. 1930- 65
Murphy, Pat
   See Murphy, E(mmett) Jefferson
Murphy, Robert (William)
   1902-1971 10
Murphy, Shirley Rousseau 1928- 71
   Earlier sketch in SATA 36
   See also SAAS 18
Murray, John 1923- 39
Murray, Marguerite 1917- 63
Murray, Marian 5
Murray, Michele 1933-1974 7
Murray, Ossie 1938- 43
Murray, Peter
   See Hautman, Pete(r Murray)
Murrow, Liza Ketchum 1946- 78
Musgrave, Florence 1902- 3
Musgrove, Margaret W(ynkoop)
   1943- 26
Mussey, Virginia T. H.
   See Ellison, Virginia Howell
Mutel, Cornelia F. 1947- 74
Mutz
   See Kuenstler, Morton

My
   See Barberis, Juan C(arlos)
My Brother's Brother
   See Chekhov, Anton (Pavlovich)
Myers, Arthur 1917- 91
   Earlier sketch in SATA 35
Myers, Bernice 81
   Earlier sketch in SATA 9
Myers, Caroline Elizabeth (Clark)
   1887-1980 28
Myers, Edward 1950- 96
Myers, Elisabeth P(erkins) 1918- 36
Myers, Hortense (Powner) 1913- 10
Myers, Jack 1913- 83
Myers, Lou(is) 1915- 81
Myers, Walter Dean 1937- 71
   Brief entry 27
   Earlier sketch in SATA 41
   See also CLR 35
   See also SAAS 2
Myers, Walter M.
   See Myers, Walter Dean
Myller, Rolf 1926- 27
Myra, Harold L(awrence) 1939- 46
   Brief entry 42
Myrus, Donald (Richard) 1927- 23

N

Nadel, Laurie 1948- 74
Naden, Corinne J. 1930- 79
Naidoo, Beverley 1943- 63
   See also CLR 29
Nakae, Noriko 1940- 59
Nakatani, Chiyoko 1930-1981 55
   Brief entry 40
   See also CLR 30
Nally, Susan W. 1947- 90
Namioka, Lensey 1929- 89
   Earlier sketch in SATA 27
   See also CLR 48
   See also SAAS 24
Nanogak, Agnes 1925- 61
Napier, Mark
   See Laffin, John (Alfred Charles)
Napoli, Donna Jo 1948- 92
   See also SAAS 23
Narahashi, Keiko 1959- 79
Narayan, R(asipuram) K(rishnaswami)
   1906- 62
Nash, Bruce M(itchell) 1947- 34
Nash, Linell
   See Smith, Linell Nash
Nash, Mary (Hughes) 1925- 41
Nash, (Frederic) Ogden 1902-1971 46
   Earlier sketch in SATA 2
Nash, Renea Denise 1963- 81
Nast, Elsa Ruth
   See Watson, Jane Werner
Nast, Thomas 1840-1902 51
   Brief entry 33
Nastick, Sharon 1954- 41
Nathan, Adele (Gutman) 1900(?)-1986
   Obituary 48
Nathan, Dorothy (Goldeen)
   (?)-1966 15
Nathan, Robert (Gruntal) 1894-1985 6
   Obituary 43
Nathanson, Laura Walther 1941- 57
Natti, Susanna 1948- 32
Naughton, Bill
   See Naughton, William John (Francis)
Naughton, James Franklin 1957- 85
Naughton, Jim
   See Naughton, James Franklin
Naughton, William John (Francis)
   1910-1992 86
Navarra, John Gabriel 1927- 8
Naylor, Penelope 1941- 10
Naylor, Phyllis
   See Naylor, Phyllis Reynolds
Naylor, Phyllis Reynolds 1933- 66
   Earlier sketch in SATA 12
   See also CLR 17
   See also SAAS 10
Nazaroff, Alexander I. 1898- 4

Neal, Harry Edward 1906-1993 ....*5*
  Obituary *76*
Neal, Michael
  See Teitelbaum, Michael
Nearing, Penny 1916- *47*
  Brief entry *42*
Nebel, Gustave E. *45*
  Brief entry *33*
Nebel, Mimouca
  See Nebel, Gustave E.
Nee, Kay Bonner *10*
Needham, Kate 1962- *95*
Needle, Jan 1943- *98*
  Earlier sketch in SATA *30*
  See also CLR *43*
  See also SAAS *23*
Needleman, Jacob 1934- *6*
Neel, David 1960- *82*
Neel, Preston 1959- *93*
Negri, Rocco 1932- *12*
Neier, Aryeh 1937- *59*
Neigoff, Anne *13*
Neigoff, Mike 1920- *13*
Neilson, Frances Fullerton (Jones)
  1910- *14*
Neimark, Anne E. 1935- *4*
Neimark, Paul G. 1934- *80*
  Brief entry *37*
Neitzel, Shirley 1941- *77*
Nell
  See Hanna, Nell(ie L.)
Nelson, Catherine Chadwick 1926- *87*
Nelson, Cordner (Bruce) 1918- *54*
  Brief entry *29*
Nelson, Drew 1952- *77*
Nelson, Esther L. 1928- *13*
Nelson, Lawrence E(rnest) 1928-1977
  Obituary *28*
Nelson, Mary Carroll 1929- *23*
Nelson, O. Terry 1941- *62*
Nelson, Peter N. 1953- *73*
Nelson, Richard K(ing) 1941- *65*
Nelson, Roy Paul 1923- *59*
Nelson, Sharlene (P.) 1933- *96*
Nelson, Ted (W.) 1931- *96*
Nelson, Theresa 1948- *79*
Nerlove, Miriam 1959- *53*
  Brief entry *49*
Nesbit, E(dith) 1858-1924
  See YABC *1*
  See also CLR *3*
Nesbit, Troy
  See Folsom, Franklin (Brewster)
Nespojohn, Katherine V. 1912- *7*
Ness, Evaline (Michelow)
  1911-1986 ....*26*
  Obituary *49*
  Earlier sketch in SATA *1*
  See also CLR *6*
  See also SAAS *1*
Nestor, William P(rodromos) 1947- *49*
Nethery, Mary *93*
Neuberger, Julia 1950- *78*
Neufeld, John (Arthur) 1938- *81*
  Earlier sketch in SATA *6*
  See also SAAS *3*
Neuhaus, David 1958- *83*
Neumeyer, Peter F(lorian) 1929- *13*
Neurath, Marie (Reidemeister)
  1898- *1*
Neusner, Jacob 1932- *38*
Neville, Emily Cheney 1919- *1*
  See also SAAS *2*
Neville, Mary
  See Woodrich, Mary Neville
Nevins, Albert J. 1915- *20*
Newark, Elizabeth
  See Dinneen, Betty
Newberger, Devra
  See Speregen, Devra Newberger
Newberry, Clare Turlay 1903-1970 ....*1*
  Obituary *26*
Newbery, John 1713-1767 ....*20*
Newcomb, Ellsworth
  See Kenny, Ellsworth Newcomb
Newcombe, Jack *45*
  Brief entry *33*

Newcome, Robert 1955- *91*
Newcome, Zita 1959- *88*
Newell, Crosby
  See Bonsall, Crosby Barbara (Newell)
Newell, Edythe W. 1910- *11*
Newell, Hope (Hockenberry)
  1896-1965 ....*24*
Newfeld, Frank 1928- *26*
Newlon, (Frank) Clarke
  1905(?)-1982 ....*6*
  Obituary *33*
Newman, Daisy 1904-1994 ....*27*
  Obituary *78*
Newman, Gerald 1939- *46*
  Brief entry *42*
Newman, Jerry 1935- *82*
Newman, Leslea 1955- *71*
Newman, Matthew (Harrison)
  1955- *56*
Newman, Robert (Howard)
  1909-1988 ....*87*
  Obituary *60*
  Earlier sketch in SATA *4*
Newman, Shirlee P(etkin) 1924- *90*
  Earlier sketch in SATA *10*
Newsom, Carol 1948- *92*
  Earlier sketch in SATA *40*
Newsom, Tom 1944- *80*
Newton, David E(dward) 1933- *67*
Newton, James R(obert) 1935- *23*
Newton, Suzanne 1936- *77*
  Earlier sketch in SATA *5*
Ney, John 1923- *43*
  Brief entry *33*
Ng, Franklin *82*
Nichol, B(arrie) P(hillip)
  1944-1988 ....*66*
Nicholls, Judith (Ann) 1941- *61*
Nichols, Cecilia Fawn 1906- *12*
Nichols, Grace 1950- *98*
Nichols, Janet (Louise) 1952- *67*
Nichols, Leigh
  See Koontz, Dean R(ay)
Nichols, Paul
  See Hawks, Robert
Nichols, Peter
  See Youd, (Christopher) Samuel
Nichols, (Joanna) Ruth 1948- *15*
Nicholson, Joyce Thorpe 1919- *35*
Nicholson, Lois P. 1949- *88*
Nickell, Joe 1944- *73*
Nickelsburg, Janet 1893- *11*
Nickerson, Betty
  See Nickerson, Elizabeth
Nickerson, Elizabeth 1922- *14*
Nickl, Barbara (Elisabeth) 1939- *56*
Nicklaus, Carol *62*
  Brief entry *33*
Nickless, Will 1902-1979(?) *66*
Nic Leodhas, Sorche
  See Alger, Leclaire (Gowans)
Nicol, Ann
  See Turnbull, Ann (Christine)
Nicolas
  See Mordvinoff, Nicolas
Nicolay, Helen 1866-1954
  See YABC *1*
Nicole, Christopher Robin 1930- *5*
Nicoll, Helen 1937- *87*
Ni Dhuibhne, Eilis 1954- *91*
Nielsen, Kay (Rasmus) 1886-1957 ....*16*
Nielsen, Laura F(arnsworth) 1960- *93*
Nielsen, Nancy J. 1951- *77*
Nielsen, Virginia
  See McCall, Virginia Nielsen
Nightingale, Sandy 1953- *76*
Nikola-Lisa, W. 1951- *71*
Niland, Deborah 1951- *27*
Niland, Kilmeny *75*
Nilsen, Anna
  See Bassil, Andrea
Nilsson, Eleanor 1939- *81*
  See also SAAS *23*
Nimmo, Jenny 1942- *87*
  See also CLR *44*
Niven, Larry
  See Niven, Laurence Van Cott

Niven, Laurence Van Cott 1938- *95*
Nivola, Claire A. 1947- *84*
Nix, Garth 1963- *97*
Nixon, Hershell Howard 1923- *42*
Nixon, Joan Lowery 1927- *78*
  Earlier sketches in SATA *8, 44*
  See also CLR *24*
  See also SAAS *9*
Nixon, K.
  See Nixon, Kathleen Irene (Blundell)
Nixon, Kathleen Irene (Blundell)
  1894-1988(?) *14*
  Obituary *59*
Nobisso, Josephine 1953- *78*
Noble, Iris 1922-1986 ....*5*
  Obituary *49*
Noble, Marty 1947- *97*
Noble, Trinka Hakes
  Brief entry *37*
Nodset, Joan L.
  See Lexau, Joan M.
Noel Hume, Ivor 1927- *65*
Noestlinger, Christine
  See Noestlinger, Christine
Noestlinger, Christine 1936- *64*
  Brief entry *37*
  See also CLR *12*
Noguere, Suzanne 1947- *34*
Nolan, Dennis 1945- *92*
  Brief entry *34*
  Earlier sketch in SATA *42*
Nolan, Jeannette Covert 1897-1974 .....*2*
  Obituary *27*
Nolan, Paul T(homas) 1919- *48*
Nolan, William F(rancis) 1928- *88*
  Brief entry *28*
Noll, Sally 1946- *82*
Noonan, Julia 1946- *95*
  Earlier sketch in SATA *4*
Norcross, John
  See Conroy, John Wesley
Nordhoff, Charles (Bernard)
  1887-1947 ....*23*
Nordlicht, Lillian *29*
Nordstrom, Ursula 1910-1988 ....*3*
  Obituary *57*
Nordtvedt, Matilda 1926- *67*
Norman, Charles 1904-1996 ....*38*
  Obituary *92*
Norman, Howard A. 1949- *81*
Norman, James
  See Schmidt, James Norman
Norman, Lilith 1927- *86*
Norman, Mary 1931- *36*
Norman, Steve
  See Pashko, Stanley
Norment, Lisa 1966- *91*
Norris, Gunilla B(rodde) 1939- *20*
North, Andrew
  See Norton, Andre
North, Anthony
  See Koontz, Dean R(ay)
North, Captain George
  See Stevenson, Robert Louis
North, Joan 1920- *16*
North, Rick
  See Peel, John
North, Robert
  See Withers, Carl A.
North, Sterling 1906-1974 ....*45*
  Obituary *26*
  Earlier sketch in SATA *1*
Northcott, (William) Cecil 1902-1987
  Obituary *55*
Norton, Alice Mary 1912-
  See Norton, Andre
Norton, Andre 1912- *91*
  Earlier sketches in SATA *1, 43*
  See Norton, Alice Mary
Norton, Browning
  See Norton, Frank R(owland) B(rowning)
Norton, Frank R(owland) B(rowning)
  1909- *10*
Norton, Mary 1903-1992 ....*60*
  Obituary *72*
  Earlier sketch in SATA *18*
  See also CLR *6*

Nourse, Alan E(dward) 1928- *48*
  See also CLR *33*
Novak, Matt 1962- *60*
  Brief entry *52*
Novelli, Luca 1947- *61*
Nowell, Elizabeth Cameron *12*
Nugent, Nicholas 1949- *73*
Numeroff, Laura Joffe 1953- *90*
  Earlier sketch in SATA *28*
Nunes, Lygia Bojunga 1932- *75*
Nurenberg, Thelma
  See Greenhaus, Thelma Nurenberg
Nurnberg, Maxwell 1897-1984 ....*27*
  Obituary *41*
Nussbaumer, Paul (Edmond) 1934- ...*16*
Nutt, Ken 1951- *97*
Nuygen, Mathieu 1967- *80*
Nyberg, (Everett Wayne) Morgan
  1944- *87*
Nyce, (Nellie) Helene von Strecker
  1885-1969 ....*19*
Nyce, Vera 1862-1925 ....*19*
Nye, Harold G.
  See Harding, Lee
Nye, Naomi Shihab 1952- *86*
Nye, Robert 1939- *6*
Nystrom, Carolyn 1940- *67*

O

Oakes, Vanya 1909-1983 ....*6*
  Obituary *37*
Oakley, Don(ald G.) 1927- *8*
Oakley, Graham 1929- *84*
  Earlier sketch in SATA *30*
  See also CLR *7*
Oakley, Helen 1906- *10*
Oana, Katherine D. 1929- *53*
  Brief entry *37*
Oana, Kay D.
  See Oana, Katherine D.
Oates, Eddie H. 1943- *88*
Oates, Stephen B. 1936- *59*
Obed, Ellen Bryan 1944- *74*
Oberle, Joseph 1958- *69*
Oberman, Sheldon 1949- *85*
  See also SAAS *26*
Obligado, Lilian (Isabel) 1931- *61*
  Brief entry *45*
Obrant, Susan 1946- *11*
O'Brien, Anne Sibley 1952- *80*
  Brief entry *48*
  Earlier sketch in SATA *53*
O'Brien, E. G.
  See Clarke, Arthur C(harles)
O'Brien, Esse Forrester 1895(?)-1975
  Obituary *30*
O'Brien, Robert C.
  See CLR *2*
  See Conly, Robert Leslie
O'Brien, Thomas C(lement) 1938- *29*
O'Callahan, Jay 1938- *88*
O'Carroll, Ryan
  See Markun, Patricia M(aloney)
O'Connell, Margaret F(orster)
  1935-1977 ....*49*
  Obituary *30*
O'Connell, Peg
  See Ahern, Margaret McCrohan
O'Connor, Francine M(arie) 1930- *90*
O'Connor, Genevieve A. 1914- *75*
O'Connor, Jane 1947- *59*
  Brief entry *47*
O'Connor, Karen 1938- *89*
  Earlier sketch in SATA *34*
O'Connor, Patrick
  See Wibberley, Leonard (Patrick
  O'Connor)
O'Connor, Richard 1915-1975
  Obituary *21*
O'Conor, Jane 1958- *78*
Odaga, Asenath (Bole) 1938- *67*
  See also SAAS *19*
O'Daniel, Janet 1921- *24*

O'Dell, Scott 1898-1989 ....*60*
  Earlier sketch in SATA *12*
  See also CLR *16*
Odenwald, Robert P(aul)
  1899-1965 ....*11*
Odgers, Sally Farrell 1957- *72*
O'Donnell, Dick
  See Lupoff, Richard A(llen)
Odor, Ruth Shannon 1926-
  Brief entry *44*
Oechsli, Kelly 1918- *5*
Ofek, Uriel 1926- *36*
  See also CLR *28*
Offenbacher, Ami 1958- *91*
Offit, Sidney 1928- *10*
Ofosu-Appiah, L(awrence) H(enry)
  1920- *13*
Ogan, George F. 1912- *13*
Ogan, M. G. [Joint pseudonym]
  See Ogan, George F.
  and Ogan, Margaret E. (Nettles)
Ogan, Margaret E. (Nettles) 1923- *13*
Ogburn, Charlton, Jr. 1911- *3*
Ogilvie, Elisabeth May 1917- *40*
  Brief entry *29*
Ogle, Lucille Edith 1904-1988
  Obituary *59*
O'Green, Jennifer
  See Roberson, Jennifer
O'Green, Jennifer Roberson
  See Roberson, Jennifer
O'Hagan, Caroline 1946- *38*
O'Hanlon, Jacklyn
  See Meek, Jacklyn O'Hanlon
O'Hara, Elizabeth
  See Ni Dhuibhne, Eilis
O'Hara, Kenneth
  See Morris, (Margaret) Jean
O'Hara, Mary
  See Alsop, Mary O'Hara
Ohi, Ruth 1964- *95*
Ohlsson, Ib 1935- *7*
Ohtomo, Yasuo 1946- *37*
Oke, Janette 1935- *97*
O'Keeffe, Frank 1938- *99*
O'Kelley, Mattie Lou 1908-1997 ....*36*
  Obituary *97*
Okimoto, Jean Davies 1942- *34*
Okomfo, Amasewa
  See Cousins, Linda
Olaleye, Isaac O. 1941- *96*
  See also SAAS *23*
Olcott, Frances Jenkins
  1872(?)-1963 ....*19*
Old Boy
  See Hughes, Thomas
Oldenburg, E(gbert) William
  1936-1974 ....*35*
Old Fag
  See Bell, Robert S(tanley) W(arren)
Oldfield, Margaret J(ean) 1932- *56*
Oldfield, Pamela 1931- *86*
Oldham, June *70*
Oldham, Mary 1944- *65*
Olds, Elizabeth 1896-1991 ....*3*
  Obituary *66*
Olds, Helen Diehl 1895-1981 ....*9*
  Obituary *25*
Oldstyle, Jonathan
  See Irving, Washington
O'Leary, Brian 1940- *6*
O'Leary, Patsy B(aker) 1937- *97*
Oleksy, Walter 1930- *33*
Olesky, Walter
  See Oleksy, Walter
Oliver, John Edward 1933- *21*
Oliver, Marilyn Tower 1935- *89*
Oliver, Shirley (Louise Dawkins)
  1958- *74*
Oliviero, Jamie 1950- *84*
Olmstead, Lorena Ann 1890- *13*
Olney, Ross R. 1929- *13*
Olschewski, Alfred 1920- *7*
Olsen, Carol 1945- *89*
Olsen, Ib Spang 1921- *81*
  Earlier sketch in SATA *6*
Olsen, Violet (Mae) 1922- *58*

Olson, Arielle North 1932- *67*
Olson, Gene 1922- *32*
Olson, Helen Kronberg *48*
Olugebefola, Ademole 1941- *15*
Om
  See Gorey, Edward (St. John)
Oman, Carola (Mary Anima)
  1897-1978 ....*35*
O'Meara, Walter A(ndrew)
  1897-1989 ....*65*
Ommanney, F(rancis) D(ownes)
  1903-1980 ....*23*
O Mude
  See Gorey, Edward (St. John)
Oneal, Elizabeth 1934- *82*
  Earlier sketch in SATA *30*
O'Neal, Reagan
  See Rigney, James Oliver, Jr.
Oneal, Zibby
  See CLR *13*
  See Oneal, Elizabeth
O'Neill, Gerard K(itchen) 1927- *65*
O'Neill, Judith (Beatrice) 1930- *34*
O'Neill, Mary L(e Duc)
  1908(?)-1990 ....*2*
  Obituary *64*
Onslow, John 1906-1985
  Obituary *47*
Onyefulu, Ifeoma 1959- *81*
Opgenoorth, Winfried 1939-
  Brief entry *50*
Opie, Iona 1923- *63*
  Earlier sketch in SATA *3*
  See also SAAS *6*
Opie, Peter 1918-1982 ....*63*
  Obituary *28*
  Earlier sketch in SATA *3*
Oppel, Kenneth 1967- *99*
Oppenheim, Joanne 1934- *82*
  Earlier sketch in SATA *5*
Oppenheimer, Joan L(etson) 1925- *28*
Optic, Oliver
  See Adams, William Taylor
  and Stratemeyer, Edward L.
Oram, Hiawyn 1946- *56*
Orbach, Ruth Gary 1941- *21*
Orczy, Emmuska Barone
  1865-1947 ....*40*
O'Reilly, Jackson
  See Rigney, James Oliver, Jr.
O'Reilly, Sean
  See Deegan, Paul Joseph
Orgel, Doris 1929- *85*
  Earlier sketch in SATA *7*
  See also CLR *48*
  See also SAAS *19*
Oriolo, Joe
  See Oriolo, Joseph
Oriolo, Joseph 1913-1985
  Obituary *46*
Orleans, Ilo 1897-1962 ....*10*
Orlev, Uri 1931- *58*
  See also CLR *30*
  See also SAAS *19*
Ormai, Stella *57*
  Brief entry *48*
Ormerod, Jan(ette Louise) 1946- *70*
  Brief entry *44*
  Earlier sketch in SATA *55*
  See also CLR *20*
Ormes, Jackie
  See Ormes, Zelda J.
Ormes, Zelda J. 1914-1986
  Obituary *47*
Ormondroyd, Edward 1925- *14*
Ormsby, Virginia H(aire) *11*
Orr, Katherine S(helley) 1950- *72*
Orr, Wendy 1953- *90*
Orris
  See Ingelow, Jean
Orth, Richard
  See Gardner, Richard
Orwell, George
  See Blair, Eric Arthur
Osborn, Lois D(orothy) 1915- *61*
Osborne, Charles 1927- *59*
Osborne, Chester G. 1915- *11*

Osborne, David
  See Silverberg, Robert
Osborne, Leone Neal 1914- 2
Osborne, Mary Pope 1949- 98
  Brief entry 41
  Earlier sketch in SATA 55
Osceola
  See Blixen, Karen (Christentze Dinesen)
Osgood, William E(dward) 1926- 37
O'Shaughnessy, Ellen Cassels 1937- 78
O'Shea, (Catherine) Pat(ricia Shiels)
  1931- 87
  See also CLR 18
Osmond, Edward 1900- 10
Ossoli, Sarah Margaret (Fuller) marchesa d'
  1810-1850 25
Ostendorf, (Arthur) Lloyd (Jr.)
  1921- 65
Otfinoski, Steven 1949- 56
Otis, James
  See Kaler, James Otis
O'Toole, Thomas 1941- 71
O'Trigger, Sir Lucius
  See Horne, Richard Henry
Otten, Charlotte F. 1926- 98
Ottley, Reginald (Leslie) 26
  See also CLR 16
Otto, Margaret Glover 1909-1976
  Obituary 30
Otto, Svend
  See Soerensen, Svend Otto
Oughton, Jerrie 1937- 76
Ouida
  See De La Ramee, (Marie) Louise
Ousley, Odille 1896- 10
Overmyer, James E. 1946- 88
Overton, Jenny (Margaret Mary)
  1942- 52
  Brief entry 36
Owen, Annie 1949- 75
Owen, Caroline Dale
  See Snedeker, Caroline Dale (Parke)
Owen, Clifford
  See Hamilton, Charles (Harold St. John)
Owen, Dilys
  See Gater, Dilys
Owen, (Benjamin) Evan 1918-1984 38
Owen, Gareth 1936- 83
  See also CLR 31
  See also SAAS 14
Owens, Gail 1939- 54
Owens, Thomas S(heldon) 1960- 86
Owens, Tom
  See Owens, Thomas S(heldon)
Oxenbury, Helen 1938- 68
  Earlier sketch in SATA 3
  See also CLR 22
Oxendine, Bess Holland 1933- 90
Oz, Frank (Richard) 1944- 60
Ozer, Jerome S. 1927- 59

P

Pace, Mildred Mastin 1907- 46
  Brief entry 29
Pachter, Hedwig
  19th cent. (?)-1988 63
Pack, Janet 1952- 77
Packard, Edward 1931- 90
  Earlier sketch in SATA 47
Packer, Vin
  See Meaker, Marijane (Agnes)
Page, Eileen
  See Heal, Edith
Page, Eleanor
  See Coerr, Eleanor (Beatrice)
Page, Jake
  See Page, James K(eena), Jr.
Page, James K(eena), Jr. 1936- 81
Page, Lou Williams 1912- 38
Paget-Fredericks, Joseph E. P. Rous-
  Marten 1903-1963
  Brief entry 30
Pagnucci, Susan 1944- 90
Pahz, (Anne) Cheryl Suzanne
  1949- 11

Pahz, James Alon 1943- 11
Paice, Margaret 1920- 10
Paige, Harry W. 1922- 41
  Brief entry 35
Paige, Richard
  See Koontz, Dean R(ay)
Paine, Penelope Colville 1946- 87
Paine, Roberta M. 1925- 13
Paisley, Tom 1932- 78
  Earlier sketch in SATA 11
Palazzo, Anthony D. 1905-1970 3
Palazzo, Tony
  See Palazzo, Anthony D.
Palder, Edward L. 1922- 5
Palecek, Josef 1932- 56
Palecek, Libuse 1937- 89
Palin, Michael (Edward) 1943- 67
Palladini, David (Mario) 1946- 40
  Brief entry 32
Pallas, Norvin 1918- 23
Pallister, John C(lare) 1891-1980
  Obituary 26
Palmer, Bernard 1914- 26
Palmer, C(yril) Everard 1930- 14
Palmer, (Ruth) Candida 1926- 11
Palmer, Don
  See Benson, Mildred (Augustine Wirt)
Palmer, Hap 1942- 68
Palmer, Heidi 1948- 15
Palmer, Helen Marion
  See Geisel, Helen
Palmer, Juliette 1930- 15
Palmer, Kate Salley 1946- 97
Palmer, Maria
  See Strachan, Ian
Palmer, Robin 1911- 43
Paltrowitz, Donna (Milman) 1950- 61
  Brief entry 50
Paltrowitz, Stuart 1946- 61
  Brief entry 50
Panati, Charles 1943- 65
Panetta, George 1915-1969 15
Panetta, Joseph N. 1953- 96
Panik, Sharon 1952- 82
Panowski, Eileen Thompson 1920- 49
Pansy
  See Alden, Isabella (Macdonald)
Pantell, Dora (Fuchs) 1915- 39
Panter, Carol 1936- 9
Papas, William 1927- 50
Papashvily, George 1898-1978 17
Papashvily, Helen (Waite) 1906- 17
Pape, Donna (Lugg) 1930- 82
  Earlier sketch in SATA 2
Paperny, Myra (Green) 1932- 51
  Brief entry 33
Paradis, Adrian A(lexis) 1912- 67
  Earlier sketch in SATA 1
  See also SAAS 8
Paradis, Marjorie (Bartholomew)
  1886(?)-1970 17
Parenteau, Shirley (Laurolyn)
  1935- 47
  Brief entry 40
Parish, Margaret Cecile 1927-1988 73
  Obituary 59
  Earlier sketch in SATA 17
Parish, Peggy
  See CLR 22
  See Parish, Margaret Cecile
Park, Barbara 1947- 78
  Brief entry 35
  Earlier sketch in SATA 40
  See also CLR 34
Park, Bill
  See Park, W(illiam) B(ryan)
Park, Ruth 25
Park, (Rosina) Ruth (Lucia) 93
Park, W(illiam) B(ryan) 1936- 22
Parke, Marilyn 1928- 82
Parker, Elinor 1906- 3
Parker, Julie F. 1961- 92
Parker, Kristy (Kettelkamp) 1957- 59
Parker, Lois M(ay) 1912- 30
Parker, Margot M. 1937- 52
Parker, Mary Jessie 1948- 71

Parker, Nancy Winslow 1930- 69
  Earlier sketch in SATA 10
  See also SAAS 20
Parker, Richard 1915- 14
Parker, Robert
  See Boyd, Waldo T.
Parkhill, John
  See Cox, William R(obert)
Parkinson, Ethelyn M(inerva)
  1906- 11
Parkinson, Kathy 1954- 71
Parks, Deborah A. 1948- 91
Parks, Edd Winfield 1906-1968 10
Parks, Gordon (Alexander Buchanan)
  1912- 8
Parks, Rosa (Louise Lee) 1913- 83
Parks, Van Dyke 1943- 62
Parley, Peter
  See Goodrich, Samuel Griswold
Parlin, John
  See Graves, Charles Parlin
Parnall, Peter 1936- 69
  Earlier sketch in SATA 16
  See also SAAS 11
Parr, Letitia (Evelyn) 1906- 37
Parr, Lucy 1924- 10
Parrish, Anne 1888-1957 27
Parrish, Mary
  See Cousins, Margaret
Parrish, (Frederick) Maxfield
  1870-1966 14
Parry, Marian 1924- 13
Parsons, Alexandra 1947- 92
Parsons, Ellen
  See Dragonwagon, Crescent
Parsons, Tom
  See MacPherson, Thomas George
Partch, Virgil Franklin II
  1916-1984 45
  Obituary 39
Parton, Dolly (Rebecca) 1946- 94
Partridge, Benjamin W(aring), Jr.
  1915- 28
Partridge, Jenny (Lilian) 1947- 52
  Brief entry 37
Pascal, David 1918- 14
Pascal, Francine 1938- 80
  Brief entry 37
  Earlier sketch in SATA 51
  See also CLR 25
Paschal, Nancy
  See Trotter, Grace V(iolet)
Pascudniak, Pascal
  See Lupoff, Richard A(llen)
Pashko, Stanley 1913- 29
Pateman, Robert 1954- 84
Patent, Dorothy Hinshaw 1940- 69
  Earlier sketch in SATA 22
  See also CLR 19
  See also SAAS 13
Paterson, A(ndrew) B(arton)
  1864-1941 97
Paterson, Diane (R. Cole) 1946- 59
  Brief entry 33
Paterson, Katherine (Womeldorf)
  1932- 92
  Earlier sketches in SATA 13, 53
  See also CLR 7
Patience, John 1949- 90
Patneaude, David 1944- 85
Paton, Alan (Stewart) 1903-1988 11
  Obituary 56
Paton, Jane (Elizabeth) 1934- 35
Paton, Priscilla 1952- 98
Paton Walsh, Gillian 1937- 72
  Earlier sketch in SATA 4
  See also SAAS 3
Paton Walsh, Jill
  See Paton Walsh, Gillian
Patron, Susan 1948- 76
Patten, Brian 1946- 29
Patterson, Charles 1935- 59
Patterson, Geoffrey 1943- 54
  Brief entry 44
Patterson, Lillie G. 88
  Earlier sketch in SATA 14
Patterson, Nancy Ruth 1944- 72

Pattison, Darcy (S.) 1954- 72
Paul, Aileen 1917- 12
Paul, Ann Whitford 1941- 76
Paul, David (Tyler) 1934-1988
    Obituary 56
Paul, Elizabeth
    See Crow, Donna Fletcher
Paul, James 1936- 23
Paul, Robert
    See Roberts, John G(aither)
Pauli, Hertha (Ernestine) 1909-1973 3
    Obituary 26
Paull, Grace A. 1898- 24
Paulsen, Gary 1939- 79
    Earlier sketches in SATA 22, 54
    See also CLR 19
Paulson, Jack
    See Jackson, C. Paul
Pausacker, Jenny 1948- 72
    See also SAAS 23
Pavel, Frances 1907- 10
Paxton, Tom 1937- 70
Payne, Alan
    See Jakes, John (William)
Payne, Bernal C., Jr. 1941- 60
Payne, Donald Gordon 1924- 37
Payne, Emmy
    See West, Emily G(ovan)
Payne, Rachel Ann
    See Jakes, John (William)
Payson, Dale 1943- 9
Payzant, Charles 18
Payzant, Jessie Mercer Knechtel
    See Shannon, Terry
Paz, A.
    See Pahz, James Alon
Paz, Zan
    See Pahz, (Anne) Cheryl Suzanne
Peace, Mary
    See Finley, Mary Peace
Peake, Mervyn 1911-1968 23
Peale, Norman Vincent 1898-1993 20
    Obituary 78
Pearce, Ann Philippa
    See Pearce, Philippa
Pearce, Philippa 1920- 67
    Earlier sketch in SATA 1
    See also CLR 9
Peare, Catherine Owens 1911- 9
Pears, Charles 1873-1958
    Brief entry 30
Pearson, Gayle 1947- 53
Pearson, Kit 1947- 77
    See also CLR 26
    See also SAAS 25
Pearson, Susan 1946- 91
    Brief entry 27
    Earlier sketch in SATA 39
Pearson, Tracey Campbell 1956- 64
Pease, Howard 1894-1974 2
    Obituary 25
Peavy, Linda 1943- 54
Peck, Anne Merriman 1884- 18
Peck, Beth 1957- 79
Peck, Marshall III 1951- 92
Peck, Richard 1934- 97
    Earlier sketches in SATA 18, 55
    See also CLR 15
    See also SAAS 2
Peck, Robert Newton 1928- 62
    Earlier sketch in SATA 21
    See also CLR 45
    See also SAAS 1
Pederson, Sharleen
    See Collicott, Sharleen
Peebles, Anne
    See Galloway, Priscilla
Peek, Merle 1938- 39
Peel, John 1954- 79
Peel, Norman Lemon
    See Hirsch, Phil
Peeples, Edwin A. 1915- 6
Peet, Bill
    See CLR 12
    See Peet, William Bartlett
Peet, Creighton B. 1899-1977 30

Peet, William Bartlett 1915- 78
    Earlier sketches in SATA 2, 41
Peirce, Waldo 1884-1970
    Brief entry 28
Pelaez, Jill 1924- 12
Pelham, David 1938- 70
Pellowski, Anne 1933- 20
Pellowski, Michael (Joseph) 1949- 88
    Brief entry 48
Pellowski, Michael Morgan
    See Pellowski, Michael (Joseph)
Pelta, Kathy 1928- 18
Peltier, Leslie C(opus) 1900- 13
Pembury, Bill
    See Groom, Arthur William
Pemsteen, Hans
    See Manes, Stephen
Pendennis, Arthur Esquir
    See Thackeray, William Makepeace
Pender, Lydia (Podger) 1907- 61
    Earlier sketch in SATA 3
Pendery, Rosemary 7
Pendle, Alexy 1943- 29
Pendle, George 1906-1977
    Obituary 28
Pene du Bois, William (Sherman)
    1916-1993 68
    Obituary 74
    Earlier sketch in SATA 4
    See also CLR 1
Penn, Ruth Bonn
    See Clifford, Eth
    and Rosenberg, Ethel
Pennage, E. M.
    See Finkel, George (Irvine)
Penner, Fred (Ralph Cornelius)
    1946- 67
Penney, Grace Jackson 1904- 35
Penney, Ian 1960- 76
Pennington, Eunice 1923- 27
Pennington, Lillian Boyer 1904- 45
Penrose, Gordon 1925- 66
Penrose, Margaret
    See Stratemeyer, Edward L.
Penson, Mary E. 1917- 78
Penzler, Otto 1942- 38
Pepe, Phil(ip) 1935- 20
Peppe, Rodney (Darrell) 1934- 74
    Earlier sketch in SATA 4
    See also SAAS 10
Pepper, Frank S. 1910-1988
    Obituary 61
Percy, Charles Henry
    See Smith, Dorothy Gladys
Percy, Rachel 1930- 63
Perdrizet, Marie-Pierre 1952- 79
Perenyi, Constance (Marie) 1954- 93
Perera, Thomas Biddle 1938- 13
Peretti, Frank E. 1951- 80
Perez, Walter
    See Joseph, James (Herz)
Perkins, Al(bert Rogers) 1904-1975 30
Perkins, Lucy Fitch 1865-1937 72
Perkins, Marlin 1905-1986 21
    Obituary 48
Perkins, Mitali 1963- 88
Perl, Lila 72
    Earlier sketch in SATA 6
Perl, Susan 1922-1983 22
    Obituary 34
Perlmutter, O(scar) William 1920-1975 ...8
Pernu, Dennis 1970- 87
Perrault, Charles 1628-1703 25
Perreard, Suzanne Louise Butler 1919-
    Brief entry 29
Perret, Gene 1937- 76
Perrine, Mary 1913- 2
Perrins, Lesley 1953- 56
Perry, Barbara Fisher
    See Fisher, Barbara
Perry, Patricia 1949- 30
Perry, Phyllis J. 1933- 60
Perry, Roger 1933- 27
Perry, Steve 1947- 76
Pershall, Mary K. 1951- 70
Pershing, Marie
    See Schultz, Pearle Henriksen

Perske, Robert 1927- 57
Peters, Alexander
    See Hollander, Zander
Peters, Caroline
    See Betz, Eva Kelly
Peters, David 1954- 72
Peters, Elizabeth
    See Mertz, Barbara (Gross)
Peters, Julie Anne 1952- 82
Peters, Linda
    See Catherall, Arthur
Peters, Lisa Westberg 1951- 74
Peters, Patricia 1953- 84
Peters, Russell M. 1929- 78
Peters, S. H.
    See Porter, William Sydney
Petersen, David 1946- 62
Petersen, Gwenn Boardman 1924- 61
Petersen, P(eter) J(ames) 1941- 83
    Brief entry 43
    Earlier sketch in SATA 48
Petersen, Palle 1943- 85
Petersham, Maud (Fuller)
    1890-1971 17
    See also CLR 24
Petersham, Miska 1888-1960 17
    See also CLR 24
Peterson, Cris 1952- 84
Peterson, Dawn 1934- 86
Peterson, Esther (Allen) 1934- 35
Peterson, Hans 1922- 8
Peterson, Harold L(eslie) 1922- 8
Peterson, Helen Stone 1910- 8
Peterson, Jeanne Whitehouse
    See Whitehouse, Jeanne
Peterson, Lorraine 1940- 56
    Brief entry 44
Petie, Haris 1915- 10
Petrides, Heidrun 1944- 19
Petrie, Catherine 1947- 52
    Brief entry 41
Petroski, Catherine (Ann Groom)
    1939- 48
Petrovich, Michael B(oro) 1922- 40
Petrovskaya, Kyra
    See Wayne, Kyra Petrovskaya
Petruccio, Steven James 1961- 67
Petry, Ann (Lane) 1908-1997 5
    Obituary 94
    See also CLR 12
Pevsner, Stella 77
    Earlier sketch in SATA 8
    See also SAAS 14
Peyo
    See Culliford, Pierre
Peyton, K. M.
    See CLR 3
    See Peyton, Kathleen (Wendy)
Peyton, Kathleen (Wendy) 1929- 62
    Earlier sketch in SATA 15
    See also SAAS 17
Pfanner, (Anne) Louise 1955- 68
Pfeffer, Susan Beth 1948- 83
    Earlier sketch in SATA 4
    See also CLR 11
    See also SAAS 17
Pfeffer, Wendy 1929- 78
Pfeiffer, Janet (B.) 1949- 96
Pfister, Marcus 83
    See also CLR 42
Pflieger, Pat 1955- 84
Phelan, Josephine 1905-
    Brief entry 30
Phelan, Mary Kay 1914- 3
Phelan, Terry Wolfe 1941- 56
Phelps, Ethel Johnston 1914- 35
Philbrook, Clem(ent E.) 1917- 24
Phillips, Betty Lou
    See Phillips, Elizabeth Louise
Phillips, Bob 1940- 95
Phillips, Elizabeth Louise 58
    Brief entry 48
Phillips, Irv
    See Phillips, Irving W.
Phillips, Irving W. 1908- 11
Phillips, Jack
    See Sandburg, Carl (August)

Phillips, Leon
　See Gerson, Noel B(ertram)
Phillips, Loretta (Hosey) 1893- *10*
Phillips, Louis 1942- *8*
Phillips, Mary Geisler 1881-1964 ....*10*
Phillips, Prentice 1894- *10*
Phillpotts, Eden 1862-1960 ....*24*
Phin
　See Thayer, Ernest Lawrence
Phipson, Joan
　See CLR 5
　See also SAAS 3
　See Fitzhardinge, Joan Margaret
Phiz
　See Browne, Hablot Knight
Phleger, Fred B. 1909- *34*
Phleger, Marjorie Temple 1908(?)-1986 ...*1*
　Obituary *47*
Phypps, Hyacinthe
　See Gorey, Edward (St. John)
Piaget, Jean 1896-1980
　Obituary *23*
Piatti, Celestino 1922- *16*
Picard, Barbara Leonie 1917- *89*
　Earlier sketch in SATA 2
　See also SAAS 10
Pickard, Charles 1932- *36*
Pickering, James Sayre 1897-1969 ....*36*
　Obituary *28*
Pickering, Robert B. 1950- *93*
Pienkowski, Jan 1936- *58*
　Earlier sketch in SATA 6
　See also CLR 6
Pierce, Edith Gray 1893-1977 ....*45*
Pierce, Katherine
　See St. John, Wylly Folk
Pierce, Meredith Ann 1958- *67*
　Brief entry *48*
　See also CLR 20
Pierce, Ruth (Ireland) 1936- *5*
Pierce, Tamora 1954- *96*
　Brief entry *49*
　Earlier sketch in SATA 51
Pierik, Robert 1921- *13*
Piers, Robert
　See Anthony, Piers
Pig, Edward
　See Gorey, Edward (St. John)
Pike, Christopher *68*
　See also CLR 29
Pike, Deborah 1951- *89*
Pike, E(dgar) Royston 1896-1980 ....*22*
　Obituary *56*
Pike, R. William 1956- *92*
Pilarski, Laura 1926- *13*
Pilgrim, Anne
　See Allan, Mabel Esther
Pilkey, Dav 1966- *68*
　See also CLR 48
Pilkington, Francis Meredyth 1907- *4*
Pilkington, Roger (Windle) 1915- *10*
Pinchot, David 1914(?)-1983
　Obituary *34*
Pincus, Harriet 1938- *27*
Pinczes, Elinor J(ane) 1940- *81*
Pine, Nicholas 1951- *91*
Pine, Tillie S(chloss) 1897- *13*
Pini, Richard (Alan) 1950- *89*
Pini, Wendy 1951- *89*
Pinkerton, Kathrene Sutherland (Gedney)
　1887-1967
　Obituary *26*
Pinkney, (Jerry) Brian 1961- *74*
Pinkney, Gloria Jean 1941- *85*
Pinkney, J. Brian
　See Pinkney, (Jerry) Brian
Pinkney, Jerry 1939- *71*
　Brief entry *32*
　Earlier sketch in SATA 41
　See also CLR 43
　See also SAAS 12
Pinkney, John *97*
Pinkwater, Daniel Manus 1941- *76*
　Earlier sketches in SATA 8, 46
　See also CLR 4
　See also SAAS 3

Pinkwater, Manus
　See Pinkwater, Daniel Manus
Pinner, Joma
　See Werner, Herma
Pioneer
　See Yates, Raymond F(rancis)
Piowaty, Kim Kennelly 1957- *49*
Piper, Roger
　See Fisher, John (Oswald Hamilton)
Piper, Watty
　See Bragg, Mabel Caroline
Pirner, Connie White 1955- *72*
Piro, Richard 1934- *7*
Pirsig, Robert M(aynard) 1928- *39*
Pitman, (Isaac) James 1901-1985
　Obituary *46*
Pitre, Felix 1949- *84*
Pitrone, Jean Maddern 1920- *4*
Pittman, Helena Clare 1945- *71*
Pitz, Henry C(larence) 1895-1976 ....*4*
　Obituary *24*
Pizer, Vernon 1918- *21*
Place, Marian T. 1910- *3*
Place, Robin (Mary) 1926- *71*
Plaidy, Jean
　See Hibbert, Eleanor Alice Burford
Plain, Belva 1919- *62*
Plaine, Alfred R. 1898(?)-1981
　Obituary *29*
Plath, Sylvia 1932-1963 ....*96*
Platt, Kin 1911- *86*
　Earlier sketch in SATA 21
　See also SAAS 17
Platt, Randall (Beth) 1948- *95*
Plecas, Jennifer 1966- *84*
Plimpton, George (Ames) 1927- *10*
Plomer, William (Charles Franklin)
　1903-1973 ....*24*
Plotz, Helen (Ratnoff) 1913- *38*
Plowden, David 1932- *52*
Plowden, Martha Ward 1948- *98*
Plowhead, Ruth Gipson 1877-1967 ......*43*
Plowman, Stephanie 1922- *6*
Pluckrose, Henry (Arthur) 1931- *13*
Plum, J.
　See Wodehouse, P(elham) G(renville)
Plum, Jennifer
　See Kurland, Michael (Joseph)
Plumb, Charles P. 1900(?)-1982
　Obituary *29*
Plume, Ilse
　Brief entry *43*
Plummer, Margaret 1911- *2*
Pochocki, Ethel (Frances) 1925- *76*
Podendorf, Illa E. 1903(?)-1983 ....*18*
　Obituary *35*
Poe, Edgar Allan 1809-1849 ....*23*
Poe, Ty (Christopher) 1975- *94*
Pogany, William Andrew
　1882-1955 ....*44*
Pogany, Willy
　Brief entry *30*
　See Pogany, William Andrew
Pohl, Frederik 1919- *24*
Pohlmann, Lillian (Grenfell) 1902- *11*
Pohrt, Tom *67*
Pointon, Robert
　See Rooke, Daphne (Marie)
Pola
　See Watson, Pauline
Polacco, Patricia 1944- *74*
　See also CLR 40
Polatnick, Florence T. 1923- *5*
Polder, Markus
　See Kruess, James
Polese, Carolyn 1947- *58*
Polese, James 1914- *87*
Polette, Nancy (Jane) 1930- *42*
Polhamus, Jean Burt 1928- *21*
Policoff, Stephen Phillip 1948- *77*
Polikoff, Barbara G(arland) 1929- *77*
Polisar, Barry Louis 1954- *77*
Politi, Leo 1908-1996 ....*47*
　Obituary *88*
　Earlier sketch in SATA 1
　See also CLR 29
Polking, Kirk 1925- *5*

Pollack, Jill S. 1963- *88*
Pollack, Merrill S. 1924-1988
　Obituary *55*
Pollack, Rachel (Grace) 1945- *99*
Polland, Barbara K(ay) 1939- *44*
Polland, Madeleine A(ngela Cahill)
　1918- *68*
　Earlier sketch in SATA 6
　See also SAAS 8
Pollock, Bruce 1945- *46*
Pollock, Mary
　See Blyton, Enid (Mary)
Pollock, Penny 1935- *44*
　Brief entry *42*
Pollowitz, Melinda (Kilborn) 1944- *26*
Polner, Murray 1928- *64*
Polonsky, Arthur 1925- *34*
Polseno, Jo *17*
Pomerantz, Charlotte 1930- *80*
　Earlier sketch in SATA 20
Pomeroy, Pete
　See Roth, Arthur J(oseph)
Pond, Alonzo W(illiam) 1894- *5*
Pontiflet, Ted 1932- *32*
Poole, Gray Johnson 1906- *1*
Poole, Josephine 1933- *5*
　See Helyar, Jane Penelope Josephine
Poole, Lynn 1910-1969 ....*1*
Poole, Peggy 1925- *39*
Poortvliet, Marien
　See Poortvliet, Rien
Poortvliet, Rien 1932- *65*
　Brief entry *37*
Pope, Elizabeth Marie 1917- *38*
　Brief entry *36*
Popescu, Christine 1930- *82*
　See Pullein-Thompson, Christine
Poploff, Michelle 1956- *67*
Popp, K. Wendy *91*
Poppel, Hans 1942- *71*
Portal, Colette 1936- *6*
Porte, Barbara Ann *93*
　Brief entry *45*
　Earlier sketch in SATA 57
Porter, A(nthony) P(eyton) 1945- *68*
Porter, Connie (Rose) 1959(?)- *81*
Porter, Donald Clayton
　See Gerson, Noel B(ertram)
Porter, Janice Lee 1953- *68*
Porter, Katherine Anne 1890-1980 ....*39*
　Obituary *23*
Porter, Kathryn
　See Swinford, Betty (June Wells)
Porter, Sheena 1935- *24*
　See also SAAS 10
Porter, Sue 1951- *76*
Porter, William Sydney 1862-1910
　See YABC 2
Porte-Thomas, Barbara Ann
　See Porte, Barbara Ann
Portteus, Eleanora Marie Manthei (?)-1983
　Obituary *36*
Posell, Elsa Z. *3*
Posten, Margaret L(ois) 1915- *10*
Potok, Chaim 1929- *33*
Potter, (Helen) Beatrix 1866-1943
　See YABC 1
　See also CLR 19
Potter, Margaret (Newman) 1926- *21*
Potter, Marian 1915- *9*
Potter, Miriam Clark 1886-1965 ....*3*
Poulin, Stephane 1961- *98*
　See also CLR 28
Pournelle, Jerry (Eugene) 1933- *91*
　Earlier sketch in SATA 26
Powell, A. M.
　See Morgan, Alfred P(owell)
Powell, Ann 1951-
　Brief entry *51*
Powell, E. Sandy 1947- *72*
Powell, Pamela 1960- *78*
Powell, Richard Stillman
　See Barbour, Ralph Henry
Powell, Stephanie 1953- *93*
Power, Margaret (M.) *75*
Powers, Anne
　See Schwartz, Anne Powers

Powers, Bill 1931- *52*
  Brief entry *31*
Powers, Margaret
  See Heal, Edith
Powledge, Fred 1935- *37*
Poynter, Margaret 1927- *27*
Prager, Arthur *44*
Pratchett, Terry 1948- *82*
Prater, John 1947- *72*
Pratt, Kristin Joy 1976- *87*
Pratt, Pierre 1962- *95*
Preiss, Byron (Cary) *47*
  Brief entry *42*
Preller, James 1961- *88*
Prelutsky, Jack 1940- *66*
  Earlier sketch in SATA *22*
  See also CLR *13*
Presberg, Miriam Goldstein 1919-1978
  Brief entry *38*
Prescott, Casey
  See Morris, Chris(topher Crosby)
Presnall, Judith (Ann) Janda 1943- *96*
Preston, Edna Mitchell *40*
Preston, Lillian Elvira 1918- *47*
Preussler, Otfried 1923- *24*
Prevert, Jacques (Henri Marie) 1900-1977
  Obituary *30*
Price, Beverley Joan 1931- *98*
Price, Christine 1928-1980 ....*3*
  Obituary *23*
Price, Garrett 1896-1979
  Obituary *22*
Price, Jennifer
  See Hoover, Helen (Drusilla Blackburn)
Price, Jonathan (Reeve) 1941- *46*
Price, Lucie Locke
  See Locke, Lucie
Price, Margaret (Evans) 1888-1973
  Brief entry *28*
Price, Olive 1903- *8*
Price, Susan 1955- *85*
  Earlier sketch in SATA *25*
Price, Willard 1887-1983 ....*48*
  Brief entry *38*
Priceman, Marjorie *81*
Prichard, Katharine Susannah
  1883-1969 ....*66*
Prideaux, Tom 1908-1993 ....*37*
  Obituary *76*
Priestley, Alice 1962- *95*
Priestley, Lee (Shore) 1904- *27*
Prieto, Mariana B(eeching) 1912- *8*
Primavera, Elise 1954- *58*
  Brief entry *48*
Prime, Derek (James) 1931- *34*
Prince, Alison (Mary) 1931- *86*
  Earlier sketch in SATA *28*
Prince, J(ack) H(arvey) 1908- *17*
Pringle, Laurence P(atrick) 1935- *68*
  Earlier sketch in SATA *4*
  See also CLR *4*
  See also SAAS *6*
Pritchett, Elaine H(illyer) 1920- *36*
Pritts, Kim Derek 1953- *83*
Prochazkova, Iva 1953- *68*
Proctor, Everitt
  See Montgomery, Rutherford George
Professor Scribbler
  See Hollingsworth, Mary
Professor Zingara
  See Leeming, Joseph
Provensen, Alice 1918- *70*
  Earlier sketch in SATA *9*
  See also CLR *11*
Provensen, Martin (Elias)
  1916-1987 ....*70*
  Obituary *51*
  Earlier sketch in SATA *9*
  See also CLR *11*
Provenzo, Eugene (F., Jr.) 1949- *78*
Provost, Gail Levine 1944- *65*
Provost, Gary (Richard) 1944- *66*
Proysen, Alf 1914-1970 ....*67*
  See also CLR *24*
Pryor, Bonnie 1942- *69*
Pryor, Helen Brenton 1897-1972 ....*4*
Pucci, Albert John 1920- *44*

Pudney, John (Sleigh) 1909-1977 ....*24*
Pugh, Ellen T. 1920- *7*
Pullein-Thompson, Christine 1930- *3*
  See Popescu, Christine
Pullein-Thompson, Diana 1930- *3*
  See Farr, Diana
Pullein-Thompson, Josephine *82*
  Earlier sketch in SATA *3*
Pullman, Philip (N.) 1946- *65*
  See also CLR *20*
  See also SAAS *17*
Pulver, Robin 1945- *76*
Puner, Helen W(alker) 1915-1989 ....*37*
  Obituary *63*
Purdy, Carol 1943- *66*
Purdy, Susan Gold 1939- *8*
Purscell, Phyllis 1934- *7*
Purtill, Richard L. 1931- *53*
Pushker, Gloria (Teles) 1927- *75*
Pushkin, Alexander (Sergeyevich)
  1799-1837 ....*61*
Putnam, Alice (Marie) 1916- *61*
Putnam, Arthur Lee
  See Alger, Horatio, Jr.
Putnam, Peter B(rock) 1920- *30*
Pyle, Howard 1853-1911 ....*16*
  See also CLR *22*
Pyle, Katharine 1863-1938 ....*66*
Pyne, Mable Mandeville 1903-1969 ....*9*

Q

Quackenbush, Robert M(ead)
  1929- *70*
  Earlier sketch in SATA *7*
  See also SAAS *7*
Qualey, Marsha 1953- *79*
Quammen, David 1948- *7*
Quarles, Benjamin 1904- *12*
Quattlebaum, Mary 1958- *88*
Queen, Ellery, Jr.
  See Holding, James
Quennell, Marjorie (Courtney)
  1884-1972 ....*29*
Quentin, Brad
  See Bisson, Terry (Ballantine)
Quick, Annabelle 1922- *2*
Quigg, Jane (Hulda) (?)-1986
  Obituary *49*
Quill, Monica
  See McInerny, Ralph
Quin-Harkin, Janet 1941- *90*
  Earlier sketch in SATA *18*
Quinlan, Susan E(lizabeth) 1954- *88*
Quinn, Elisabeth 1881-1962 ....*22*
Quinn, Patrick 1950- *73*
Quinn, Susan
  See Jacobs, Susan
Quinn, Vernon
  See Quinn, Elisabeth
Quirk, Anne (E.) 1956- *99*
Quixley, Jim 1931- *56*

R

Ra, Carol F. 1939- *76*
Rabe, Berniece (Louise) 1928- *77*
  Earlier sketch in SATA *7*
  See also SAAS *10*
Rabe, Olive H(anson) 1887-1968 ....*13*
Rabin, Staton 1958- *84*
Rabinowich, Ellen 1946- *29*
Rabinowitz, Sandy 1954- *52*
  Brief entry *39*
Raboff, Ernest Lloyd
  Brief entry *37*
Rachlin, Carol K(ing) 1919- *64*
Rachlin, Harvey (Brant) 1951- *47*
Rachlin, Nahid *64*
Rachlis, Eugene (Jacob) 1920-1986
  Obituary *50*
Rackham, Arthur 1867-1939 ....*15*
Radencich, Marguerite C. 1952- *79*

Radford, Ruby L(orraine)
  1891-1971 ....*6*
Radin, Ruth Yaffe 1938- *56*
  Brief entry *52*
Radlauer, David 1952- *28*
Radlauer, Edward 1921- *15*
Radlauer, Ruth (Shaw) 1926- *98*
  Earlier sketch in SATA *15*
Radley, Gail 1951- *25*
Rae, Gwynedd 1892-1977 ....*37*
Raebeck, Lois 1921- *5*
Raffi
  See Cavoukian, Raffi
Raftery, Gerald (Bransfield) 1905- *11*
Ragan-Reid, Gale 1956- *90*
Rahaman, Vashanti 1953- *98*
Rahn, Joan Elma 1929- *27*
Raible, Alton (Robert) 1918- *35*
Raiff, Stan 1930- *11*
Rainey, W. B.
  See Blassingame, Wyatt Rainey
Ralston, Jan
  See Dunlop, Agnes M(ary) R(obertson)
Ramal, Walter
  See de la Mare, Walter
Ramanujan, A(ttipat) K(rishnaswami)
  1929-1993 ....*86*
Rame, David
  See Divine, Arthur Durham
Rana, Indi
  See Rana, Indira Higham
Rana, Indira Higham 1944- *82*
Rana, J.
  See Forrester, Helen
Ranadive, Gail 1944- *10*
Rand, Ann (Binkley) *30*
Rand, Paul 1914- *6*
Randall, Carrie
  See Ransom, Candice F.
Randall, Florence Engel 1917- *5*
Randall, Janet [Joint pseudonym]
  See Young, Janet Randall
  and Young, Robert W(illiam)
Randall, Robert
  See Silverberg, Robert
Randall, Ruth Painter 1892-1971 ....*3*
Randell, Beverley
  See Price, Beverley Joan
Randle, Kristen D(owney) 1952- *92*
  See also SAAS *24*
Randolph, Lieutenant J. H.
  See Ellis, Edward S(ylvester)
Rands, William Brighty 1823-1882 ......*17*
Raney, Ken 1953- *74*
Rankin, Joan 1940- *88*
Ranney, Agnes V. 1916- *6*
Ransom, Candice F. 1952- *89*
  Brief entry *49*
  Earlier sketch in SATA *52*
Ransome, Arthur (Michell)
  1884-1967 ....*22*
  See also CLR *8*
Ransome, James E. 1961- *76*
Rapaport, Stella F(read) *10*
Raphael, Elaine (Chionchio) 1933- *23*
Raposo, Joseph Guilherme 1938-1989
  Obituary *61*
Rappaport, Eva 1924- *6*
Rappoport, Ken 1935- *89*
Rarick, Carrie 1911- *41*
Raschka, Chris
  See Raschka, Christopher
Raschka, Christopher 1959- *80*
Raskin, Edith (Lefkowitz) 1908- *9*
Raskin, Ellen 1928-1984 ....*38*
  Earlier sketch in SATA *2*
  See also CLR *12*
Raskin, Joseph 1897-1982 ....*12*
  Obituary *29*
Rasmussen, Knud Johan Victor 1879-1933
  Brief entry *34*
Rathjen, Carl H(enry) 1909- *11*
Rathmann, Peggy (Margaret Crosby)
  1953- *94*
Rattigan, Jama Kim 1951- *99*
Ratto, Linda Lee 1952- *79*

Rattray, Simon
    See Trevor, Elleston
Ratz de Tagyos, Paul 1958- 76
Rau, Dana Meachen 1971- 94
Rau, Margaret 1913- 9
    See also CLR 8
Rauch, Mabel Thompson 1888-1972
    Obituary 26
Raucher, Herman 1928- 8
Ravielli, Anthony 1916-1997 3
    Obituary 95
Ravilious, Robin 1944- 77
Rawding, F(rederick) W(illiam)
    1930- 55
Rawlings, Marjorie Kinnan 1896-1953
    See YABC 1
Rawls, (Woodrow) Wilson 1913- 22
Rawlyk, George Alexander 1935- 64
Rawn, Melanie (Robin) 1954- 98
Ray, Carl 1943-1978 63
Ray, Deborah
    See Kogan, Deborah
Ray, Deborah Kogan
    See Kogan, Deborah
Ray, Delia 1963- 70
Ray, Irene
    See Sutton, Margaret Beebe
Ray, Jane 1960- 72
Ray, JoAnne 1935- 9
Ray, Mary (Eva Pedder) 1932- 2
Ray, Mary Lyn 1946- 90
Rayevsky, Robert 1955- 81
Raymond, James Crossley 1917-1981
    Obituary 29
Raymond, Robert
    See Alter, Robert Edmond
Rayner, Mary 1933- 87
    Earlier sketch in SATA 22
    See also CLR 41
Rayner, William 1929- 55
    Brief entry 36
Raynor, Dorka 28
Rayson, Steven 1932- 30
Razzell, Arthur (George) 1925- 11
Razzi, James 1931- 10
Read, Elfreida 1920- 2
Read, Piers Paul 1941- 21
Reade, Deborah 1949- 69
Reader, Dennis 1929- 71
Readman, Jo 1958- 89
Ready, Kirk L. 1943- 39
Reaney, James 1926- 43
Reaver, Chap 1935-1993 69
    Obituary 77
Reaves, J. Michael
    See Reaves, (James) Michael
Reaves, (James) Michael 1950- 99
Reck, Franklin Mering 1896-1965
    Brief entry 30
Redding, Robert Hull 1919- 2
Redekopp, Elsa 61
Redway, Ralph
    See Hamilton, Charles (Harold St. John)
Redway, Ridley
    See Hamilton, Charles (Harold St. John)
Reed, Betty Jane 1921- 4
Reed, Gwendolyn E(lizabeth) 1932- 21
Reed, Kit 1932- 34
Reed, Neil 1961- 99
Reed, Philip G. 1908-
    Brief entry 29
Reed, Thomas (James) 1947- 34
Reed, William Maxwell 1871-1962 15
Reeder, Carolyn 1937- 97
    Earlier sketch in SATA 66
Reeder, Colin (Dawson) 1938- 74
Reeder, Colonel Red
    See Reeder, Russell P., Jr.
Reeder, Russell P., Jr. 1902- 4
Reef, Catherine 1951- 73
Reeman, Douglas Edward 1924- 63
    Brief entry 28
Rees, David Bartlett 1936-1993 69
    Obituary 76
    Earlier sketch in SATA 36
    See also SAAS 5
Rees, Ennis 1925- 3

Reese, Bob
    See Reese, Robert A.
Reese, (Caro)lyn (Johnson) 1938- 64
Reese, Robert A. 1938- 60
    Brief entry 53
Reese, (John) Terence 1913- 59
Reeve, Joel
    See Cox, William R(obert)
Reeves, Faye Couch 1953- 76
Reeves, James 1909- 15
    See Reeves, John Morris
Reeves, John Morris 1909-1978 87
    See Reeves, James
Reeves, Joyce 1911- 17
Reeves, Lawrence F. 1926- 29
Reeves, Ruth Ellen
    See Ranney, Agnes V.
Regan, Dian Curtis 1950- 75
Regehr, Lydia 1903- 37
Reggiani, Renee 18
Rehm, Karl M. 1935- 72
Reichert, Edwin C(lark) 1909-1988
    Obituary 57
Reichert, Mickey Zucker
    See Zucker, Miriam S.
Reid, Alastair 1926- 46
Reid, Barbara 1922- 21
Reid, Barbara 1957- 93
Reid, Desmond
    See Moorcock, Michael (John)
Reid, Dorothy M(arion) (?)-1974
    Brief entry 29
Reid, Eugenie Chazal 1924- 12
Reid, John Calvin 21
Reid, (Thomas) Mayne 1818-1883 24
Reid, Meta Mayne 1905- 58
    Brief entry 36
Reid Banks, Lynne 1929- 75
    Earlier sketch in SATA 22
    See also CLR 24
Reid Jenkins, Debra 1955- 87
Reiff, Stephanie Ann 1948- 47
    Brief entry 28
Reig, June 1933- 30
Reigot, Betty Polisar 1924- 55
    Brief entry 41
Reinach, Jacquelyn (Krasne) 1930- 28
Reiner, William B(uck) 1910-1976 46
    Obituary 30
Reinfeld, Fred 1910-1964 3
Reiniger, Lotte 1899-1981 40
    Obituary 33
Reinsma, Carol 1949- 91
Reisberg, Mira 1955- 82
Reisberg, Veg
    See Reisberg, Mira
Reiser, Lynn (Whisnant) 1944- 81
Reisgies, Teresa (Maria) 1966- 74
Reiss, Johanna de Leeuw 1932- 18
    See also CLR 19
Reiss, John J. 23
Reiss, Kathryn 1957- 76
Reit, Seymour 21
Reit, Sy
    See Reit, Seymour
Relf, Patricia 1954- 71
Remi, Georges 1907-1983 13
    Obituary 32
Remington, Frederic (Sackrider)
    1861-1909 41
Remkiewicz, Frank 1939- 77
Renaud, Bernadette 1945- 66
Renault, Mary
    See Challans, Mary
Rendell, Joan 28
Rendina, Laura Cooper 1902- 10
Rendon, Marcie R. 1952- 97
Renfro, Ed 1924- 79
Renick, Marion (Lewis) 1905- 1
Renken, Aleda 1907- 27
Renlie, Frank H. 1936- 11
Rennert, Richard Scott 1956- 67
Rensie, Willis
    See Eisner, Will(iam Erwin)
Renvoize, Jean 1930- 5
Resciniti, Angelo G. 1952- 75
Resnick, Michael D(iamond) 1942- 38

Resnick, Mike
    See Resnick, Michael D(iamond)
Resnick, Seymour 1920- 23
Retla, Robert
    See Alter, Robert Edmond
Reuter, Bjarne (B.) 1950- 68
Reuter, Carol (Joan) 1931- 2
Revena
    See Wright, Betty Ren
Revsbech, Vicki
    See Liestman, Vicki
Rey, H. A. 1898-1977 69
    Earlier sketches in SATA 1, 26
    See also CLR 5
Rey, Margret (Elisabeth)
    1906-1996 86
    Obituary 93
    Earlier sketch in SATA 26
    See also CLR 5
Reyher, Becky
    See Reyher, Rebecca Hourwich
Reyher, Rebecca Hourwich
    1897-1987 18
    Obituary 50
Reynolds, Dickson
    See Reynolds, Helen Mary Greenwood
    Campbell
Reynolds, Helen Mary Greenwood
    Campbell 1884-1969
    Obituary 26
Reynolds, John
    See Whitlock, Ralph
Reynolds, Madge
    See Whitlock, Ralph
Reynolds, Malvina 1900-1978 44
    Obituary 24
Reynolds, Marilyn 1935-
    See SAAS 23
Reynolds, Marilynn 1940- 80
Reynolds, Pamela 1923- 34
Rhine, Richard
    See Silverstein, Alvin
Rhoades, Diane 1952- 90
Rhodes, Bennie (Loran) 1927- 35
Rhodes, Donna McKee 1962- 87
Rhodes, Frank H(arold Trevor)
    1926- 37
Rhue, Morton
    See Strasser, Todd
Rhyne, Nancy 1926- 66
Rhys, Megan
    See Williams, Jeanne
Ribbons, Ian 1924- 37
    Brief entry 30
    See also SAAS 3
Ricciuti, Edward R(aphael) 1938- 10
Rice, Alice (Caldwell) Hegan
    1870-1942 63
Rice, Bebe Faas 1932- 89
Rice, Charles D(uane) 1910-1971
    Obituary 27
Rice, Dale R(ichard) 1948- 42
Rice, Earle, Jr. 1928- 92
Rice, Edward 1918- 47
    Brief entry 42
Rice, Elizabeth 1913- 2
Rice, Eve (Hart) 1951- 91
    Earlier sketch in SATA 34
Rice, Inez 1907- 13
Rice, James 1934- 93
    Earlier sketch in SATA 22
Rice, John F. 1958- 82
Rich, Elaine Sommers 1926- 6
Rich, Josephine 1912- 10
Rich, Louise Dickinson 1903-1991 54
    Obituary 67
Rich, Mark J. 1948-
    Brief entry 53
Richard, Adrienne 1921- 5
    See also SAAS 9
Richard, James Robert
    See Bowen, Robert Sydney
Richards, Curtis
    See Curtis, Richard (Alan)
Richards, Frank
    See Hamilton, Charles (Harold St. John)

Richards, Hilda
  See Hamilton, Charles (Harold St. John)
Richards, Kay
  See Baker, Susan (Catherine)
Richards, Laura E(lizabeth Howe) 1850-1943
  See YABC *1*
Richards, Norman 1932- 48
Richards, R(onald) C(harles) W(illiam) 1923- 59
  Brief entry 43
Richards, Walter (Jr.) 1907-1988
  Obituary 56
Richardson, Carol 1932- 58
Richardson, Frank Howard 1882-1970
  Obituary 27
Richardson, Grace Lee
  See Dickson, Naida
Richardson, Jean (Mary) 59
Richardson, Judith Benet 1941- 77
Richardson, Robert S(hirley) 1902- 8
Richardson, Willis 1889-1977 60
Richelson, Geraldine 1922- 29
Richemont, Enid 1940- 82
Richler, Mordecai 1931- 98
  Brief entry 27
  Earlier sketch in SATA *44*
  See also CLR *17*
Richmond, Robin 1951- 75
Richoux, Pat 1927- 7
Richter, Alice 1941- 30
Richter, Conrad 1890-1968 3
Richter, Hans Peter 1925- 6
  See also CLR *21*
  See also SAAS *11*
Rickard, Graham 1949- 71
Rico, Don(ato) 1917-1985
  Obituary 43
Riddell, Edwina 1955- 82
Riddle, Tohby 1965- 74
Ridge, Antonia (Florence) (?)-1981 7
  Obituary 27
Ridge, Martin 1923- 43
Ridley, Nat, Jr.
  See Stratemeyer, Edward L.
Ridley, Philip 88
Ridlon, Marci 1942- 22
Riedman, Sarah R(egal) 1902- 1
Riesenberg, Felix, Jr. 1913-1962 23
Rieu, E(mile) V(ictor) 1887-1972 46
  Obituary 26
Riggio, Anita 1952- 73
Riggs, Sidney Noyes 1892-1975
  Obituary 28
Rigney, James Oliver, Jr. 1948- 95
Rikhoff, Jean 1928- 9
Riley, James A. 1939- 97
Riley, James Whitcomb 1849-1916 17
Riley, Jocelyn (Carol) 1949- 60
  Brief entry 50
Riley, Linda Capus 1950- 85
Riley, Martin 1948- 81
Rinaldi, Ann 1934- 78
  Brief entry 50
  Earlier sketch in SATA *51*
  See also CLR *46*
Rinard, Judith E(llen) 1947- 44
Rinder, Lenore 1949- 92
Ring, Elizabeth 1920- 79
Ring, Paul H.
  See Ring, Elizabeth
Ringgold, Faith 1930- 71
  See also CLR *30*
Ringi, Kjell (Arne Soerensen) 1939- 12
Rinkoff, Barbara (Jean) 1923-1975 4
  Obituary 27
Riordan, James 1936- 95
  Earlier sketch in SATA *28*
Rios, Tere
  See Versace, Marie Teresa Rios
Ripley, Catherine 1957- 82
Ripley, Elizabeth Blake 1906-1969 5
Ripper, Charles L. 1929- 3
Riq
  See Atwater, Richard (Tupper)

Riskind, Mary (Julia Longenberger) 1944- 60
Rissinger, Matt 1956- 93
Rissman, Art
  See Sussman, Susan
Rissman, Susan
  See Sussman, Susan
Ritchie, Barbara (Gibbons) 14
Ritter, Lawrence S(tanley) 1922- 58
Ritthaler, Shelly 1955- 91
Ritts, Paul 1920(?)-1980
  Obituary 25
Ritz, Karen 1957- 80
Rivera, Geraldo (Miguel) 1943- 54
  Brief entry 28
Rivers, Elfrida
  See Bradley, Marion Zimmer
Riverside, John
  See Heinlein, Robert A.
Rivkin, Ann 1920- 41
Rivoli, Mario 1943- 10
Roach, Marilynne K(athleen) 1946- 9
Roach, Portia
  See Takakjian, Portia
Robb, Laura 1937- 95
Robbins, Frank 1917- 42
  Brief entry 32
Robbins, Ken 94
  Brief entry 53
Robbins, Raleigh
  See Hamilton, Charles (Harold St. John)
Robbins, Ruth 1917(?)- 14
Robbins, Tony
  See Pashko, Stanley
Robbins, Wayne
  See Cox, William R(obert)
Robel, S. L.
  See Fraustino, Lisa Rowe
Roberson, Jennifer 1953- 72
Roberson, John R(oyster) 1930- 53
Robert, Adrian
  See St. John, Nicole
Roberts, Bruce (Stuart) 1930- 47
  Brief entry 39
Roberts, Charles G(eorge) D(ouglas) 1860-1943 88
  Brief entry 29
  See also CLR *33*
Roberts, David
  See Cox, John Roberts
Roberts, Elizabeth 1944- 80
Roberts, Elizabeth Madox 1886-1941 33
  Brief entry 27
Roberts, Jim
  See Bates, Barbara S(nedeker)
Roberts, John G(aither) 1913- 27
Roberts, Judy I. 1957- 93
Roberts, Nancy Correll 1924- 52
  Brief entry 28
Roberts, Terence
  See Sanderson, Ivan T.
Roberts, Willo Davis 1928- 70
  Earlier sketch in SATA *21*
  See also SAAS *8*
Robertson, Barbara (Anne) 1931- 12
Robertson, Don 1929- 8
Robertson, Dorothy Lewis 1912- 12
Robertson, Janet (E.) 1935- 68
Robertson, Jennifer (Sinclair) 1942- 12
Robertson, Keith (Carlton) 1914-1991 85
  Obituary 69
  Earlier sketch in SATA *1*
  See also SAAS *15*
Robertson, Stephen
  See Walker, Robert W(ayne)
Robertus, Polly M. 1948- 73
Robinet, Harriette Gillem 1931- 27
Robins, Seelin
  See Ellis, Edward S(ylvester)
Robinson, Adjai 1932- 8
Robinson, Aminah Brenda Lynn 1940- 77
Robinson, Barbara (Webb) 1927- 84
  Earlier sketch in SATA *8*

Robinson, C(harles) A(lexander), Jr. 1900-1965 36
Robinson, Charles 1870-1937 17
Robinson, Charles 1931- 6
Robinson, Dorothy W. 1929- 54
Robinson, Glen(dal P.) 1953- 92
Robinson, Jan M. 1933- 6
Robinson, Jean O. 1934- 7
Robinson, Jerry 1922-
  Brief entry 34
Robinson, Joan (Mary) G(ale Thomas) 1910- 7
Robinson, Lloyd
  See Silverberg, Robert
Robinson, Marileta 1942- 32
Robinson, Maudie (Millian Oller) 1914- 11
Robinson, Maurice R. 1895-1982
  Obituary 29
Robinson, Nancy K(onheim) 1942-1994 91
  Brief entry 31
  Obituary 79
  Earlier sketch in SATA *32*
Robinson, Ray(mond Kenneth) 1920- 23
Robinson, Shari
  See McGuire, Leslie (Sarah)
Robinson, T(homas) H(eath) 1869-1950 17
Robinson, (Wanda) Veronica 1926- 30
Robinson, W(illiam) Heath 1872-1944 17
Robison, Bonnie 1924- 12
Robison, Nancy L(ouise) 1934- 32
Robles, Harold E. 1948- 87
Robottom, John 1934- 7
Robson, Eric 1939- 82
Roche, A. K. [Joint pseudonym]
  See Abisch, Roslyn Kroop
  and Kaplan, Boche
Roche, Denis (Mary) 1967- 99
Roche, P(atricia) K. 57
  Brief entry 34
Roche, Terry
  See Poole, Peggy
Rock, Gail
  Brief entry 32
Rocker, Fermin 1907- 40
Rocklin, Joanne 1946- 86
Rockwell, Anne F. 1934- 71
  Earlier sketch in SATA *33*
  See also SAAS *19*
Rockwell, Bart
  See Pellowski, Michael (Joseph)
Rockwell, Gail
  Brief entry 36
Rockwell, Harlow 1910-1988 33
  Obituary 56
Rockwell, Norman (Percevel) 1894-1978 23
Rockwell, Thomas 1933- 70
  Earlier sketch in SATA *7*
  See also CLR *6*
Rockwood, Joyce 1947- 39
Rockwood, Roy [Collective pseudonym] 67
  Earlier sketch in SATA *1*
Rodari, Gianni 1920-1980
  See CLR *24*
Rodd, Kathleen Tennant 1912-1988 57
  Obituary 55
  Earlier sketch in SATA *6*
Rodda, Emily 1948- 97
  See also CLR *32*
Roddenberry, Eugene Wesley 1921-1991 45
  Obituary 69
Roddenberry, Gene
  See Roddenberry, Eugene Wesley
Roddy, Lee 1921- 57
Rodenas, Paula 73
Rodgers, Frank 1944- 69
Rodgers, Mary 1931- 8
  See also CLR *20*

Rodman, Emerson
See Ellis, Edward S(ylvester)
Rodman, Maia
See Wojciechowska, Maia (Teresa)
Rodman, Selden 1909- 9
Rodowsky, Colby 1932- 77
Earlier sketch in SATA 21
See also SAAS 22
Rodriguez, Alejo 1941- 83
Roe, Harry Mason
See Stratemeyer, Edward L.
Roeder, Virginia Marsh 1926- 98
Roehrig, Catharine H. 1949- 67
Roennfeldt, Robert 1953- 78
Roessel-Waugh, C. C. [Joint pseudonym]
See Waugh, Carol-Lynn Roessel
Roets, Lois F. 1937- 91
Roever, J(oan) M(arilyn) 1935- 26
Rofes, Eric Edward 1954- 52
Roffey, Maureen 1936- 33
Rogak, Lisa Angowski 1962- 80
Rogasky, Barbara 1933- 86
Rogers, (Thomas) Alan (Stinchcombe)
1937- 81
Earlier sketch in SATA 2
Rogers, Cindy 1950- 89
Rogers, Emma 1951- 74
Rogers, Frances 1888-1974 10
Rogers, Fred (McFeely) 1928- 33
Rogers, Jean 1919- 55
Brief entry 47
Rogers, Matilda 1894-1976 5
Obituary 34
Rogers, Pamela 1927- 9
Rogers, Paul 1950- 98
Earlier sketch in SATA 54
Rogers, Robert
See Hamilton, Charles (Harold St. John)
Rogers, W(illiam) G(arland)
1896-1978 23
Rohan, Michael Scott 1951- 98
Rohan, Mike Scott
See Rohan, Michael Scott
Rohmer, Harriet 1938- 56
Rohrer, Doug 1962- 89
Rojan
See Rojankovsky, Feodor (Stepanovich)
Rojankovsky, Feodor (Stepanovich)
1891-1970 21
Rojany, Lisa 94
Rokeby-Thomas, Anna E(lma)
1911- 15
Roland, Albert 1925- 11
Roland, Mary
See Lewis, Mary (Christianna)
Rolerson, Darrell A(llen) 1946- 8
Roll, Winifred 1909- 6
Rollins, Charlemae Hill 1897-1979 3
Obituary 26
Rollock, Barbara T(herese) 1924- 64
Romack, Janice Reed
See LeNoir, Janice
Romano, Clare
See Ross, Clare (Romano)
Romano, Louis 1921- 35
Rongen, Bjoern 1906- 10
Rood, Ronald (N.) 1920- 12
Rooke, Daphne (Marie) 1914- 12
Roop, Connie
See Roop, Constance Betzer
Roop, Constance Betzer 1951- 54
Brief entry 49
Roop, Peter (G.) 1951- 54
Brief entry 49
Roos, Stephen 1945- 77
Brief entry 41
Earlier sketch in SATA 47
Roose-Evans, James 1927- 65
Roosevelt, (Anna) Eleanor
1884-1962 50
Root, Betty 84
Root, Phyllis 1949- 94
Brief entry 48
Earlier sketch in SATA 55
Root, Shelton L., Jr. 1923-1986
Obituary 51

Roote, Mike
See Fleischer, Leonore
Roper, Laura Wood 1911- 34
Roper, Robert 1946- 78
Rorby, Ginny 1944- 94
Rorer, Abigail 1949- 85
Roscoe, D(onald) T(homas) 1934- 42
Rose, Anna Perrot
See Wright, Anna (Maria Louisa Perrot)
Rose
Rose, Anne 8
Rose, Carl 1903-1971
Brief entry 31
Rose, Deborah Lee 1955- 71
Rose, Elizabeth (Jane Pretty) 1933- ...68
Brief entry 28
Rose, Florella
See Carlson, Vada F.
Rose, Gerald (Hembdon Seymour)
1935- 68
Brief entry 30
Rose, Nancy A.
See Sweetland, Nancy A(nn)
Rose, Ted 1940- 93
Rose, Wendy 1948- 12
Roseman, Kenneth David 1939-
Brief entry 52
Rosen, Lillian (Diamond) 1928- 63
Rosen, Michael (Wayne) 1946- 84
Brief entry 40
Earlier sketch in SATA 48
See also CLR 45
Rosen, Michael J(oel) 1954- 86
Rosen, Sidney 1916- 1
Rosen, Winifred 1943- 8
Rosenbaum, Maurice 1907- 6
Rosenberg, Amye 1950- 74
Rosenberg, Dorothy 1906- 40
Rosenberg, Ethel 3
See Clifford, Eth
Rosenberg, Ethel (Clifford)
See Clifford, Eth
and Rosenberg, Ethel
Rosenberg, Jane 1949- 58
Rosenberg, Liz 1958- 75
Rosenberg, Maxine B(erta) 1939- 93
Brief entry 47
Earlier sketch in SATA 55
Rosenberg, Nancy Sherman 1931- 4
Rosenberg, Sharon 1942- 8
Rosenberry, Vera 1948- 83
Rosenblatt, Arthur S. 1938- 68
Brief entry 45
Rosenblatt, Lily 1956- 90
Rosenbloom, Joseph 1928- 21
Rosenblum, Richard 1928- 11
Rosenburg, John M. 1918- 6
Rosenfeld, Dina 1962- 99
Rosenthal, Harold 1914- 35
Rosenthal, M(acha) L(ouis) 1917- 59
Rosenthal, Mark A(lan) 1946- 64
Rosman, Steven M(ichael) 1956- 81
Ross, Alan
See Warwick, Alan R(oss)
Ross, Alex(ander) 1909-
Brief entry 29
Ross, Christine 1950- 83
Ross, Clare (Romano) 1922- 48
Ross, Dana Fuller
See Gerson, Noel B(ertram)
Ross, Dave 1949- 32
Ross, David 1896-1975 49
Obituary 20
Ross, Diana
See Denney, Diana
Ross, Edward S(hearman) 1915- 85
Ross, Frank (Xavier), Jr. 1914- 28
Ross, Jane 1961- 79
Ross, John 1921- 45
Ross, Judy 1942- 54
Ross, Katharine (Reynolds) 1948- 89
Ross, Kent 1956- 91
Ross, Lillian Hammer 1925- 72
Ross, Michael Elsohn 1952- 80
Ross, Pat(ricia Kienzle) 1943- 53
Brief entry 48
Ross, Ramon R(oyal) 1930- 62

Ross, Stewart 92
See also SAAS 23
Ross, Tom 1958- 84
Ross, Tony 1938- 65
Earlier sketch in SATA 17
Ross, Wilda 1915- 51
Brief entry 39
Rossel, Seymour 1945- 28
Rossetti, Christina (Georgina)
1830-1894 20
Rossotti, Hazel Swaine 1930- 95
Rostkowski, Margaret I. 1945- 59
Roth, Arnold 1929- 21
Roth, Arthur J(oseph) 1925-1993 43
Brief entry 28
Obituary 75
See also SAAS 11
Roth, David 1940- 36
Roth, Harold
Brief entry 49
Rothberg, Abraham 1922- 59
Roth-Hano, Renee 1931- 85
Rothkopf, Carol Z. 1929- 4
Rothman, Joel 1938- 7
Rotner, Shelley 1951- 76
Roueche, Berton 1911- 28
Roughsey, Dick 1921(?)- 35
See also CLR 41
Rounds, Glen (Harold) 1906- 70
Earlier sketch in SATA 8
Rourke, Constance (Mayfield) 1885-1941
See YABC 1
Rowe, Jennifer
See Rodda, Emily
Rowe, Viola Carson 1903-1969
Obituary 26
Rowh, Mark 1952- 90
Rowland, Florence Wightman 1900- 8
Rowland-Entwistle, (Arthur) Theodore
(Henry) 1925- 94
Earlier sketch in SATA 31
Rowsome, Frank (Howard), Jr.
1914-1983 36
Roy, Jacqueline 1954- 74
Roy, Jessie Hailstalk 1895-1986
Obituary 51
Roy, Liam
See Scarry, Patricia (Murphy)
Roy, Ron(ald) 1940- 40
Brief entry 35
Roybal, Laura (Husby) 1956- 85
Royds, Caroline 1953- 55
Rozakis, Laurie E. 1952- 84
Rubel, Nicole 1953- 95
Earlier sketch in SATA 18
Rubin, Eva Johanna 1925- 38
Rubin, Susan Goldman 1939- 84
Rubinetti, Donald 1947- 92
Rubinstein, Gillian (Margaret)
1942- 68
See also CLR 35
See also SAAS 25
Rubinstein, Robert E(dward) 1943- 49
Rublowsky, John M(artin) 1928- 62
Ruby, Lois (F.) 1942- 95
Brief entry 34
Earlier sketch in SATA 35
Ruchlis, Hy(man) 1913-1992 3
Obituary 72
Rucker, Mike 1940- 91
Ruckman, Ivy 1931- 93
Earlier sketch in SATA 37
Ruck-Pauquet, Gina 1931- 40
Brief entry 37
Rudeen, Kenneth
Brief entry 36
Rudley, Stephen 1946- 30
Rudolph, Marguerita 1908- 21
Rudomin, Esther
See Hautzig, Esther Rudomin
Rue, Leonard Lee III 1926- 37
Ruedi, Norma Paul
See Ainsworth, Norma
Ruelle, Karen Gray 1957- 84
Ruemmler, John D(avid) 1948- 78
Ruffell, Ann 1941- 30
Ruffins, Reynold 1930- 41

Rugoff, Milton 1913- 30
Ruhen, Olaf 1911- 17
Rukeyser, Muriel 1913-1980
　Obituary 22
Rumbaut, Hendle 1949- 84
Rumsey, Marian (Barritt) 1928- 16
Runnerstroem, Bengt Arne 1944- 75
Runyan, John
　See Palmer, Bernard
Runyon, Catherine 1947- 62
Ruoff, A. LaVonne Brown 1930- 76
Rush, Alison 1951- 41
Rush, Peter 1937- 32
Rushmore, Helen 1898- 3
Rushmore, Robert (William)
　1926-1986 8
　Obituary 49
Ruskin, Ariane
　See Batterberry, Ariane Ruskin
Ruskin, John 1819-1900 24
Russ, Lavinia 1904-1992 74
Russell, Charlotte
　See Rathjen, Carl H(enry)
Russell, Don(ald Bert) 1899-1986
　Obituary 47
Russell, Franklin 1926- 11
Russell, Helen Ross 1915- 8
Russell, James 1933- 53
Russell, Jim
　See Russell, James
Russell, P. Craig 1951- 80
Russell, Patrick
　See Sammis, John
Russell, Paul (Gary) 1942- 57
Russell, Sarah
　See Laski, Marghanita
Russell, Solveig Paulson 1904- 3
Russo, Monica J. 1950- 83
Russo, Susan 1947- 30
Rutgers van der Loeff, An(na) Basenau
　1910- 22
Ruth, Rod 1912- 9
Rutherford, Douglas
　See McConnell, James Douglas
　(Rutherford)
Rutherford, Meg 1932- 34
Ruthin, Margaret 4
　See Catherall, Arthur
Rutz, Viola Larkin 1932- 12
Ruurs, Margriet 1952- 97
Ruzicka, Rudolph 1883-1978
　Obituary 24
Ryan, Betsy
　See Ryan, Elizabeth (Anne)
Ryan, Cheli Duran 20
Ryan, Elizabeth (Anne) 1943- 30
Ryan, Jeanette Mines
　See Mines, Jeanette (Marie)
Ryan, John (Gerald Christopher)
　1921- 22
Ryan, Margaret 1950- 78
Ryan, Mary E(lizabeth) 1953- 61
Ryan, Peter (Charles) 1939- 15
Ryan-Lush, Geraldine 1949- 89
Rybakov, Anatoli (Naumovich)
　1911- 79
Rybolt, Thomas R(oy) 1954- 62
Rydberg, Ernest E(mil) 1901- 21
Rydberg, Lou(isa Hampton) 1908- 27
Rydell, Katy 1942- 91
Rydell, Wendell
　See Rydell, Wendy
Rydell, Wendy 4
Ryden, Hope 91
　Earlier sketch in SATA 8
Ryder, Joanne (Rose) 1946- 65
　Brief entry 34
　See also CLR 37
Ryder, Pamela
　See Lamb, Nancy
Rye, Anthony
　See Youd, (Christopher) Samuel
Rylant, Cynthia 1954- 76
　Brief entry 44
　Earlier sketch in SATA 50
　See also CLR 15
　See also SAAS 13

Rymer, Alta May 1925- 34

S

S., Svend Otto
　See Soerensen, Svend Otto
Saal, Jocelyn
　See Sachs, Judith
Saberhagen, Fred (Thomas) 1930- 89
　Earlier sketch in SATA 37
Sabin, Edwin Legrand 1870-1952
　See YABC 2
Sabin, Francene 27
Sabin, Louis 1930- 27
Sabre, Dirk
　See Laffin, John (Alfred Charles)
Sabuda, Robert (James) 1965- 81
Sabuso
　See Phillips, Irving W.
Sachar, Louis 1954- 63
　Brief entry 50
　See also CLR 28
Sachs, Elizabeth-Ann 1946- 48
Sachs, Judith 1947- 52
　Brief entry 51
Sachs, Marilyn (Stickle) 1927- 68
　Earlier sketches in SATA 3,52
　See also CLR 2
　See also SAAS 2
Sackett, S(amuel) J(ohn) 1928- 12
Sackson, Sid 1920- 16
Saddler, Allen
　See Richards, R(onald) C(harles)
　W(illiam)
Saddler, K. Allen
　See Richards, R(onald) C(harles)
　W(illiam)
Sadie, Stanley (John) 1930- 14
Sadler, Catherine Edwards 1952- 60
　Brief entry 45
Sadler, Marilyn 1950- 79
Sadler, Mark
　See Lynds, Dennis
Sagan, Carl 1934-1996 58
　Obituary 94
Sage, Juniper [Joint pseudonym]
　See Brown, Margaret Wise
　and Hurd, Edith Thacher
Sagsoorian, Paul 1923- 12
Saida
　See LeMair, H(enriette) Willebeek
Saidman, Anne 1952- 75
Saint, Dora Jessie 1913- 10
St. Antoine, Sara L. 1966- 84
St. Briavels, James
　See Wood, James Playsted
St. Clair, Byrd Hooper 1905-1976
　Obituary 28
Saint Exupery, Antoine de
　1900-1944 20
　See also CLR 10
St. George, Judith 1931- 99
　Earlier sketch in SATA 13
　See also SAAS 12
Saint James, Synthia 1949- 84
St. John, Nicole 89
　See also CLR 46
　See also SAAS 7
　See Johnston, Norma
St. John, Patricia Mary 1919-1993
　Obituary 79
St. John, Philip
　See del Rey, Lester
St. John, Wylly Folk 1908-1985 10
　Obituary 45
St. Meyer, Ned
　See Stratemeyer, Edward L.
St. Tamara
　See Kolba, Tamara
Saito, Michiko
　See Fujiwara, Michiko
Sakers, Don 1958- 72
Sakharnov, S.
　See Sakharnov, Svyatoslav
　(Vladimirovich)

Sakharnov, Svyatoslav (Vladimirovich)
　1923- 65
Sakurai, Gail 1952- 87
Salassi, Otto R(ussell) 1939-1993 38
　Obituary 77
Salat, Cristina 82
Saldutti, Denise 1953- 39
Salem, Kay 1952- 92
Salinger, J(erome) D(avid) 1919- 67
　See also CLR 18
Salisbury, Graham 1944- 76
Salkey, (Felix) Andrew (Alexander)
　1928- 35
Sallis, Susan (Diana) 1929- 55
Salmon, Annie Elizabeth 1899- 13
Salten, Felix
　See Salzmann, Siegmund
Salter, Cedric
　See Knight, Francis Edgar
Saltman, Judith 1947- 64
Saltzman, David (Charles Laertes)
　1967-1990 86
Salvadori, Mario (George)
　1907-1997 40
　Obituary 97
Salwood, F. K.
　See Kilworth, Garry (D.)
Salzer, L. E.
　See Wilson, Lionel
Salzman, Marian 1959- 77
Salzman, Yuri
　Brief entry 42
Salzmann, Siegmund 1869-1945 25
Samachson, Dorothy 1914- 3
Samachson, Joseph 1906-1980 3
　Obituary 52
Sammis, John 1942- 4
Sampson, Emma (Keats) Speed
　1868-1947 68
Sampson, Fay (Elizabeth) 1935- 42
　Brief entry 40
Sampson, Michael 1952- 95
Samson, Anne S(tringer) 1933- 2
Samson, Joan 1937-1976 13
Samson, Suzanne M. 1959- 91
Samuels, Charles 1902- 12
Samuels, Cynthia K(alish) 1946- 79
Samuels, Gertrude 17
Sanborn, Duane 1914- 38
Sancha, Sheila 1924- 38
Sanchez, Sonia 1934- 22
　See also CLR 18
Sanchez Alzada, Juan
　See Joseph, James (Herz)
Sanchez-Silva, Jose Maria 1911- 16
　See also CLR 12
Sand, George X. 45
Sandak, Cass R(obert) 1950- 51
　Brief entry 37
Sandberg, (Karin) Inger 1930- 15
Sandberg, Karl C. 1931- 35
Sandberg, Lasse (E. M.) 1924- 15
Sandburg, Carl (August) 1878-1967 8
Sandburg, Charles A.
　See Sandburg, Carl (August)
Sandburg, Helga 1918- 3
　See also SAAS 10
Sanderlin, George 1915- 4
Sanderlin, Owenita (Harrah) 1916- 11
Sanders, Nancy I. 1952- 90
Sanders, Scott R(ussell) 1945- 56
Sanders, Winston P.
　See Anderson, Poul (William)
Sanderson, Irma 1912- 66
Sanderson, Ivan T. 1911-1973 6
Sanderson, Margaret Love
　See Sampson, Emma (Keats) Speed
Sanderson, Ruth (L.) 1951- 41
Sandin, Joan 1942- 94
　Earlier sketch in SATA 12
Sandison, Janet
　See Cameron, Elizabeth Jane
Sandoz, Mari(e Susette) 1901-1966 5
Sanford, Agnes (White) 1897-1976 61
Sanford, Doris 1937- 69
Sanger, Marjory Bartlett 1920- 8
Sankey, Alice (Ann-Susan) 1910- 27

San Souci, Daniel 96
San Souci, Robert D. 1946- 81
  Earlier sketch in SATA 40
  See also CLR 43
Santesson, Hans Stefan 1914(?)-1975
  Obituary 30
Santos, Helen
  See Griffiths, Helen
Sapieyevski, Anne Lindbergh 1940-1993
  See Lindbergh, Anne (Spencer)
Sara
  See De La Roche Saint Andre, Anne
Sarac, Roger
  See Caras, Roger A(ndrew)
Sarah, Duchess of York
  See Ferguson, Sarah (Margaret)
Sarasin, Jennifer
  See Sachs, Judith
Sarg, Anthony Fredrick
  See Sarg, Tony
Sarg, Tony 1880-1942
  See YABC 1
Sargent, Pamela 1948- 78
  Earlier sketch in SATA 29
Sargent, Robert 1933- 2
Sargent, Sarah 1937- 44
  Brief entry 41
Sargent, Shirley 1927- 11
Sari
  See Fleur, Anne
Sarnoff, Jane 1937- 10
Saroyan, William 1908-1981 23
  Obituary 24
Sarton, Eleanore Marie
  See Sarton, (Eleanor) May
Sarton, (Eleanor) May 1912-1995 36
  Obituary 86
Saseen, Sharon (Dillon) 1949- 59
Sasek, Miroslav 1916-1980 16
  Obituary 23
  See also CLR 4
Sasso, Sandy Eisenberg 1947- 86
Satchwell, John
  Brief entry 49
Sathre, Vivian 1952- 79
Satterfield, Charles
  See del Rey, Lester
Sattgast, L. J.
  See Sattgast, Linda J.
Sattgast, Linda J. 1953- 91
Sattler, Helen Roney 1921-1992 74
  Earlier sketch in SATA 4
  See also CLR 24
Sauer, Julia (Lina) 1891-1983 32
  Obituary 36
Saul, Carol P. 1947- 78
Saul, John 1942- 98
Saul, (E.) Wendy 1946- 42
Saulnier, Karen Luczak 1940- 80
Saunders, Caleb
  See Heinlein, Robert A.
Saunders, Dave 1939- 85
Saunders, Julie 1939- 85
Saunders, Keith 1910- 12
Saunders, Rubie (Agnes) 1929- 21
Saunders, Susan 1945- 96
  Brief entry 41
  Earlier sketch in SATA 46
Savadier, Elivia 1950- 79
Savage, Blake
  See Goodwin, Harold L(eland)
Savage, Deborah 1955- 76
Savage, Jeff 1961- 97
Savage, Katharine James 1905-1989
  Obituary 61
Savageau, Cheryl 1950- 96
Savery, Constance (Winifred) 1897- 1
Saville, (Leonard) Malcolm
  1901-1982 23
  Obituary 31
Saviozzi, Adriana
  See Mazza, Adriana
Savitt, Sam 8
Savitz, Harriet May 1933- 72
  Earlier sketch in SATA 5
  See also SAAS 26
Sawicki, Mary 1950- 90

Sawyer, (Frederick) Don(ald) 1947- 72
Sawyer, Kem Knapp 1953- 84
Sawyer, Robert J(ames) 1960- 81
Sawyer, Ruth 1880-1970 17
  See also CLR 36
Saxby, H. M.
  See Saxby, (Henry) Maurice
Saxby, (Henry) Maurice 1924- 71
Saxon, Antonia
  See Sachs, Judith
Say, Allen 1937- 69
  Earlier sketch in SATA 28
  See also CLR 22
Sayers, Frances Clarke 1897-1989 3
  Obituary 62
Saylor-Marchant, Linda 1963- 82
Sayre, April Pulley 1966- 88
Sazer, Nina 1949- 13
Scabrini, Janet 1953- 13
Scagnetti, Jack 1924- 7
Scamell, Ragnhild 1940- 77
Scanlon, Marion Stephany 11
Scannell, Vernon 1922- 59
Scarborough, Elizabeth Ann 1947- 98
Scarf, Maggi
  See Scarf, Maggie
Scarf, Maggie 1932- 5
Scariano, Margaret M. 1924- 86
Scarlett, Susan
  See Streatfeild, (Mary) Noel
Scarry, Huck
  See Scarry, Richard, Jr.
Scarry, Patricia (Murphy) 1924- 2
Scarry, Patsy
  See Scarry, Patricia (Murphy)
Scarry, Richard, Jr. 1953- 35
Scarry, Richard (McClure)
  1919-1994 75
  Obituary 90
  Earlier sketches in SATA 2, 35
  See also CLR 41
Schachner, Judith Byron 1951- 88
Schachtel, Roger (Bernard) 1949- 38
Schaefer, Jack (Warner) 1907-1991 66
  Obituary 65
  Earlier sketch in SATA 3
Schaefer, Lola M. 1950- 91
Schaeffer, Mead 1898- 21
Schaller, George B(eals) 1933- 30
Schanzer, Ros
  See Schanzer, Rosalyn
Schanzer, Rosalyn 1942- 77
Schanzer, Roz
  See Schanzer, Rosalyn
Schatell, Brian 66
  Brief entry 47
Schatzki, Walter 1899-
  Brief entry 31
Schechter, Betty (Goodstein) 1921- 5
Schecter, Ellen 1944- 85
Scheer, Julian (Weisel) 1926- 8
Scheffer, Victor B. 1906- 6
Scheffler, Ursel 1938- 81
Scheffrin-Falk, Gladys 1928- 76
Scheidl, Gerda Marie 1913- 85
Scheier, Michael 1943- 40
  Brief entry 36
Schell, Mildred 1922- 41
Schell, Orville H. 1940- 10
Scheller, Melanie 1953- 77
Schellie, Don 1932- 29
Schemm, Mildred Walker 1905- 21
Schenker, Dona 1947- 68
Scher, Paula 1948- 47
Scherf, Margaret 1908- 10
Schermer, Judith (Denise) 1941- 30
Schertle, Alice 1941- 90
  Earlier sketch in SATA 36
Schick, Alice 1946- 27
Schick, Eleanor 1942- 82
  Earlier sketch in SATA 9
Schick, Joel 1945- 31
  Brief entry 30
Schields, Gretchen 1948- 75
Schiff, Ken 1942- 7
Schiller, Andrew 1919- 21
Schiller, Barbara (Heyman) 1928- 21

Schiller, Justin G. 1943-
  Brief entry 31
Schindel, John 1955- 77
Schindelman, Joseph 1923- 67
  Brief entry 32
Schindler, S(teven) D. 1952- 75
  Brief entry 50
Schinto, Jeanne 1951- 93
Schisgall, Oscar 1901-1984 12
  Obituary 38
Schlee, Ann 1934- 44
  Brief entry 36
Schleichert, Elizabeth 1945- 77
Schlein, Miriam 1926- 87
  Earlier sketch in SATA 2
  See also CLR 41
Schlesinger, Arthur M(eier), Jr.
  1917- 61
Schloat, G. Warren, Jr. 1914- 4
Schmid, Eleonore 1939- 84
  Earlier sketch in SATA 12
Schmiderer, Dorothy 1940- 19
Schmidt, Annie M. G. 1911-1995 67
  Obituary 91
  See also CLR 22
Schmidt, Diane 1953- 70
Schmidt, Elizabeth 1915- 15
Schmidt, Gary D. 1957- 93
Schmidt, James Norman 1912- 21
Schmidt, Karen Lee 1953- 94
Schmidt, Lynette 1952- 76
Schneider, Antonie 1954- 89
Schneider, Elisa
  See Kleven, Elisa
Schneider, Herman 1905- 7
Schneider, Laurie
  See Adams, Laurie
Schneider, Nina 1913- 2
Schneider, Rex 1937- 44
Schnirel, James R(einhold) 1931- 14
Schnitter, Jane T. 1958- 88
Schnur, Steven 1952- 95
Schnurre, Wolfdietrich 1920-1989
  Obituary 63
Schoberle, Cecile 1949- 80
Schock, Pauline 1928- 45
Schoen, Barbara 1924- 13
Schoenherr, John (Carl) 1935- 66
  Earlier sketch in SATA 37
  See also SAAS 13
Scholastica, Sister Mary
  See Jenkins, Marie M.
Scholefield, A. T.
  See Scholefield, Alan
Scholefield, Alan 1931- 66
Scholefield, Edmund O.
  See Butterworth, W(illiam) E(dmund III)
Scholey, Arthur 1932- 28
Scholz, Jackson (Volney) 1897-1986
  Obituary 49
Schone, Virginia 22
Schongut, Emanuel 52
  Brief entry 36
Schoonover, Frank (Earle)
  1877-1972 24
Schoor, Gene 1921- 3
Schorsch, Laurence 1960- 81
Schraff, Anne E(laine) 1939- 92
  Earlier sketch in SATA 27
Schrank, Joseph 1900-1984
  Obituary 38
Schrecker, Judie 1954- 90
Schreiber, Elizabeth Anne (Ferguson)
  1947- 13
Schreiber, Georges 1904-1977
  Brief entry 29
Schreiber, Ralph W(alter) 1942- 13
Schreiner, Samuel A(gnew), Jr.
  1921- 70
Schroder, Walter K. 1928- 82
Schroeder, Alan 1961- 98
  Earlier sketch in SATA 66
Schroeder, Binette
  See Nickl, Barbara (Elisabeth)
Schroeder, Ted 1931(?)-1973
  Obituary 20
Schubert, Dieter 1947- 62

Schubert-Gabrys, Ingrid 1953- *62*
Schuett, Stacey 1960- *75*
Schulke, Flip (Phelps Graeme)
  1930- *57*
Schulman, Janet 1933- *22*
Schulman, L(ester) M(artin) 1934- *13*
Schulte, Elaine L(ouise) 1934- *36*
Schultz, Gwendolyn *21*
Schultz, James Willard 1859-1947
  See YABC *1*
Schultz, Pearle Henriksen 1918- *21*
Schulz, Charles M(onroe) 1922- *10*
Schumaker, Ward 1943- *96*
Schuman, Michael A. 1953- *85*
Schur, Maxine Rose 1948- *98*
  Brief entry *49*
  Earlier sketch in SATA *53*
Schurfranz, Vivian 1925- *13*
Schutzer, A. I. 1922- *13*
Schuyler, Pamela R(icka) 1948- *30*
Schwandt, Stephen (William) 1947- *61*
Schwark, Mary Beth 1954- *51*
Schwartz, Alvin 1927-1992 ....*56*
  Obituary *71*
  Earlier sketch in SATA *4*
  See also CLR *3*
Schwartz, Amy 1954- *83*
  Brief entry *41*
  Earlier sketch in SATA *47*
  See also CLR *25*
  See also SAAS *18*
Schwartz, Anne Powers 1913- *10*
Schwartz, Carol 1954- *77*
Schwartz, Charles W(alsh) 1914- *8*
Schwartz, Daniel (Bennet) 1929-
  Brief entry *29*
Schwartz, David M(artin) 1951- *59*
Schwartz, Elizabeth Reeder 1912- *8*
Schwartz, Joel L. 1940- *54*
  Brief entry *51*
Schwartz, Joyce R. 1950- *93*
Schwartz, Julius 1907- *45*
Schwartz, Perry 1942- *75*
Schwartz, Sheila (Ruth) 1929- *27*
Schwartz, Stephen (Lawrence)
  1948- *19*
Schwarz, Adele Aron
  See Greenspun, Adele Aron
Schweitzer, Byrd Baylor
  See Baylor, Byrd
Schweitzer, Iris *59*
  Brief entry *36*
Schweninger, Ann 1951- *98*
  Earlier sketch in SATA *29*
Schwerin, Doris (Halpern) 1922- *64*
Scieszka, Jon 1954- *68*
  See also CLR *27*
Scioscia, Mary (Hershey) 1926- *63*
Scofield, Penrod 1933-1993 ....*62*
  Obituary *78*
Scoggin, Margaret C. 1905-1968 ....*47*
  Brief entry *28*
Scoltock, Jack 1942- *72*
Scoppettone, Sandra 1936- *92*
  Earlier sketch in SATA *9*
Scot, Michael
  See Rohan, Michael Scott
Scotland, Jay
  See Jakes, John (William)
Scott, Alastair
  See Allen, Kenneth S(ydney)
Scott, Ann Herbert 1926- *94*
  Brief entry *29*
  Earlier sketch in SATA *56*
Scott, Bill
  See Scott, William N(eville)
Scott, Bill 1902(?)-
  Obituary *46*
Scott, Cora Annett (Pipitone)
  1931- *11*
Scott, Dan [House pseudonym]
  See Barker, S. Omar
  and Stratemeyer, Edward L.
Scott, Elaine 1940- *90*
  Earlier sketch in SATA *36*

Scott, Jack Denton 1915-1995 ....*83*
  Earlier sketch in SATA *31*
  See also CLR *20*
  See also SAAS *14*
Scott, Jane (Harrington) 1931- *55*
Scott, John 1912-1976 ....*14*
Scott, John Anthony 1916- *23*
Scott, John M(artin) 1913- *12*
Scott, Richard
  See Rennert, Richard Scott
Scott, Sally (Elisabeth) 1948- *44*
Scott, Sally Fisher 1909-1978 ....*43*
Scott, Sir Walter 1771-1832
  See YABC *2*
Scott, Tony
  See Scott, John Anthony
Scott, W. N.
  See Scott, William N(eville)
Scott, Warwick
  See Trevor, Elleston
Scott, William N(eville) 1923- *87*
Scotti, Anna
  See Coates, Anna
Scribner, Charles, Jr. 1921-1995 ....*13*
  Obituary *87*
Scribner, Joanne L. 1949- *33*
Scribner, Kimball 1917- *63*
Scrimsher, Lila Gravatt 1897-1974
  Obituary *28*
Scruggs, Sandy 1961- *89*
Scull, Marie-Louise 1943-1993 ....*77*
Scuro, Vincent 1951- *21*
Seabrooke, Brenda 1941- *88*
  Earlier sketch in SATA *30*
Seaman, Augusta Huiell 1879-1950 .....*31*
Seamands, Ruth (Childers) 1916- *9*
Searcy, Margaret Z(ehmer) 1926- *54*
  Brief entry *39*
Searight, Mary W(illiams) 1918- *17*
Searle, Kathryn Adrienne 1942- *10*
Searle, Ronald (William Fordham)
  1920- *70*
  Earlier sketch in SATA *42*
Sears, Stephen W. 1932- *4*
Sebastian, Lee
  See Silverberg, Robert
Sebestyen, Igen
  See Sebestyen, Ouida
Sebestyen, Ouida 1924- *39*
  See also CLR *17*
  See also SAAS *10*
Sechrist, Elizabeth Hough 1903- *2*
Sedges, John
  See Buck, Pearl S(ydenstricker)
Seed, Cecile Eugenie 1930- *86*
  See Seed, Jenny
Seed, Jenny 1930- *8*
  See Seed, Cecile Eugenie
Seed, Sheila Turner 1937(?)-1979
  Obituary *23*
Seeger, Elizabeth 1889-1973
  Obituary *20*
Seeger, Pete(r) 1919- *13*
Seeley, Laura L. 1958- *71*
Seever, R.
  See Reeves, Lawrence F.
Sefton, Catherine
  See Waddell, Martin
Segal, Joyce 1940- *35*
Segal, Lore (Groszmann) 1928- *66*
  Earlier sketch in SATA *4*
  See also SAAS *11*
Segar, E(lzie) C(risler) 1894-1938 ....*61*
Segovia, Andres 1893(?)-1987
  Obituary *52*
Seguin, Marilyn W(eymouth) 1951- *91*
Seibold, J. Otto 1960- *83*
  See also SAAS *22*
Seidel, Ross *95*
Seidelman, James Edward 1926- *6*
Seiden, Art(hur)
  Brief entry *42*
Seidler, Tor 1952- *98*
  Brief entry *46*
  Earlier sketch in SATA *52*
Seidman, Laurence (Ivan) 1925- *15*
Seigel, Kalman 1917- *12*

Seignobosc, Francoise 1897-1961 ....*21*
Seitz, Jacqueline 1931- *50*
Seixas, Judith S. 1922- *17*
Sejima, Yoshimasa 1913- *8*
Selberg, Ingrid (Maria) 1950- *68*
Selden, George
  See CLR *8*
  See Thompson, George Selden
Selden, Neil R(oy) 1931- *61*
Self, Margaret Cabell 1902- *24*
Selig, Sylvie 1942- *13*
Selkirk, Jane [Joint pseudonym]
  See Chapman, John Stanton Higham
Sellers, Naomi John
  See Flack, Naomi John (White)
Selman, LaRue W. 1927- *55*
Selsam, Millicent E(llis) 1912-1996 ......*29*
  Obituary *92*
  Earlier sketch in SATA *1*
  See also CLR *1*
Seltzer, Meyer 1932- *17*
Seltzer, Richard (Warren, Jr.)
  1946- *41*
Selway, Martina 1940- *74*
Selznick, Brian 1966- *79*
Semloh
  See Holmes, Peggy
Sendak, Jack *28*
Sendak, Maurice (Bernard) 1928- *27*
  Earlier sketch in SATA *1*
  See also CLR *17*
Sender, Ruth M(insky) 1926- *62*
Sengler, Johanna 1924- *18*
Senn, Steve 1950- *60*
  Brief entry *48*
Serage, Nancy 1924- *10*
Seredy, Kate 1899-1975 ....*1*
  Obituary *24*
  See also CLR *10*
Serfozo, Mary 1925- *82*
Seroff, Victor I(lyitch) 1902-1979 ....*12*
  Obituary *26*
Serraillier, Ian (Lucien) 1912-1994 ......*73*
  Obituary *83*
  Earlier sketch in SATA *1*
  See also CLR *2*
  See also SAAS *3*
Servello, Joe 1932- *10*
Service, Pamela F. 1945- *64*
Service, Robert W(illiam)
  1874(?)-1958 ....*20*
Serwadda, William Moses 1931- *27*
Serwer, Blanche L. 1910- *10*
Seth, Marie
  See Lexau, Joan M.
Seton, Anya 1904(?)-1990 ....*3*
  Obituary *66*
Seton, Ernest Thompson
  1860-1946 ....*18*
Seuling, Barbara 1937- *98*
  Earlier sketch in SATA *10*
  See also SAAS *24*
Seuss, Dr.
  See CLR *9*
  See Geisel, Theodor Seuss
Severn, Bill
  See Severn, William Irving
Severn, David
  See Unwin, David S(torr)
Severn, William Irving 1914- *1*
Sewall, Marcia 1935- *69*
  Earlier sketch in SATA *37*
Seward, Prudence 1926- *16*
Sewell, Anna 1820-1878 ....*24*
  See also CLR *17*
Sewell, Helen (Moore) 1896-1957 ....*38*
Sexton, Anne (Harvey) 1928-1974 ....*10*
Seymour, Alta Halverson *10*
Seymour, Tres 1966- *82*
Shachtman, Tom 1942- *49*
Shackleton, C. C.
  See Aldiss, Brian W(ilson)
Shafer, Robert E(ugene) 1925- *9*
Shaffer, Terea 1968- *79*
Shahan, Sherry 1949- *92*
Shahn, Ben(jamin) 1898-1969
  Obituary *21*

Shahn, Bernarda Bryson
See Bryson, Bernarda
Shane, Harold Gray 1914-1993 ....*36*
Obituary *76*
Shanks, Ann Zane (Kushner) *10*
Shannon, George (William Bones)
1952- *94*
Earlier sketch in SATA *35*
Shannon, Jacqueline *63*
Shannon, Margaret
See Silverwood, Margaret Shannon
Shannon, Monica (?)-1965 ....*28*
Shannon, Terry *21*
Shapiro, Irwin 1911-1981 ....*32*
Shapiro, Milton J. 1926- *32*
Shapp, Charles M(orris) 1906-1989
Obituary *61*
Shapp, Martha 1910- *3*
Sharfman, Amalie *14*
Sharma, Partap 1939- *15*
Sharma, Rashmi
See Singh, Rashmi Sharma
Sharman, Alison
See Leonard, Alison
Sharmat, Marjorie Weinman 1928- *74*
Earlier sketches in SATA *4, 33*
Sharmat, Mitchell 1927- *33*
Sharp, Margery 1905-1991 ....*29*
Obituary *67*
Earlier sketch in SATA *1*
See also CLR *27*
Sharp, Zerna A. 1889-1981
Obituary *27*
Sharpe, Mitchell R(aymond) 1924- *12*
Sharpe, Susan 1946- *71*
Shasha, Mark 1961- *80*
Shattuck, Roger (Whitney) 1923- *64*
Shaw, Arnold 1909-1989 ....*4*
Obituary *63*
Shaw, Carolyn V. 1934- *91*
Shaw, Charles (Green) 1892-1974 ....*13*
Shaw, Evelyn 1927- *28*
Shaw, Flora Louisa
See Lugard, Flora Louisa Shaw
Shaw, Janet 1937- *61*
Shaw, Janet Beeler
See Shaw, Janet
Shaw, Margret 1940- *68*
Shaw, Nancy 1946- *71*
Shaw, Ray *7*
Shaw, Richard 1923- *12*
Shay, Arthur 1922- *4*
Shay, Lacey
See Shebar, Sharon Sigmond
Shea, George 1940- *54*
Brief entry *42*
Shea, Pegi Deitz 1960- *77*
Shearer, John 1947- *43*
Brief entry *27*
See also CLR *34*
Shearer, Ted 1919- *43*
Shebar, Sharon Sigmond 1945- *36*
Shecter, Ben 1935- *16*
Shedd, Warner 1934- *87*
Sheedy, Alexandra (Elizabeth)
1962- *39*
Earlier sketch in SATA *19*
Sheedy, Ally
See Sheedy, Alexandra (Elizabeth)
Sheehan, Ethna 1908- *9*
Sheehan, Patty 1945- *77*
Sheehan, Sean 1951- *86*
Shefelman, Janice (Jordan) 1930- *58*
Shefelman, Tom (Whitehead)
1927- *58*
Sheffer, H. R.
See Abels, Harriette S(heffer)
Sheffield, Janet N. 1926- *26*
Shefts, Joelle
Brief entry *49*
Shekerjian, Regina Tor *16*
Shelby, Anne 1948- *85*
See also SAAS *26*
Sheldon, Ann [Collective
pseudonym] *67*
Earlier sketch in SATA *1*
Sheldon, Aure 1917-1976 ....*12*

Sheldon, Muriel 1926- *45*
Brief entry *39*
Shelley, Frances
See Wees, Frances Shelley
Shelley, Mary Wollstonecraft (Godwin)
1797-1851 ....*29*
Shelton, William Roy 1919- *5*
Shemie, Bonnie (Jean Brenner)
1949- *96*
Shemin, Margaretha 1928- *4*
Shenton, Edward 1895-1977 ....*45*
Shepard, Aaron 1950- *75*
Shepard, Ernest Howard
1879-1976 ....*33*
Obituary *24*
Earlier sketch in SATA *3*
See also CLR *27*
Shepard, Jim 1956- *90*
Shepard, Mary
See Knox, (Mary) Eleanor Jessie
Shephard, Esther 1891-1975 ....*5*
Obituary *26*
Shepherd, Donna Walsh
See Walsh Shepherd, Donna
Shepherd, Elizabeth *4*
Sherburne, Zoa 1912- *3*
See also SAAS *18*
Sherlock, Patti *71*
Sherman, D(enis) R(onald) 1934- *48*
Brief entry *29*
Sherman, Diane (Finn) 1928- *12*
Sherman, Elizabeth
See Friskey, Margaret Richards
Sherman, Harold (Morrow) 1898- *37*
Sherman, Josepha *75*
Sherman, Nancy
See Rosenberg, Nancy Sherman
Sherrod, Jane
See Singer, Jane Sherrod
Sherry, Clifford J. 1943- *84*
Sherry, (Dulcie) Sylvia 1932- *8*
Sherwan, Earl 1917- *3*
Sherwood, Jonathan
See London, Jonathan (Paul)
Shetterly, Will(iam Howard) 1955- *78*
Shiefman, Vicky *22*
Shields, Brenda Desmond (Armstrong)
1914- *37*
Shields, Charles 1944- *10*
Shiels, Barbara
See Adams, Barbara Johnston
Shiina, Makoto 1944- *83*
Shimin, Symeon 1902- *13*
Shine, Deborah 1932- *71*
Shinn, Everett 1876-1953 ....*21*
Shippen, Katherine B(inney)
1892-1980 ....*1*
Obituary *23*
See also CLR *36*
Shipton, Eric 1907- *10*
Shirer, William L(awrence)
1904-1993 ....*45*
Obituary *78*
Shirley, Gayle C(orbett) 1955- *96*
Shirley, Jean 1919- *70*
Shirreffs, Gordon D(onald) 1914- *11*
Shirts, Morris A(lpine) 1922- *63*
Shlichta, Joe 1968- *84*
Sholokhov, Mikhail A. 1905-1984
Obituary *36*
Shore, June Lewis *30*
Shore, Robert 1924- *39*
Short, Michael 1937- *65*
Short, Roger
See Arkin, Alan (Wolf)
Shortall, Leonard W. *19*
Shortt, Tim(othy Donald) 1961- *96*
Shotwell, Louisa R. 1902- *3*
Shoup, Barbara 1947- *86*
See also SAAS *24*
Showalter, Jean B(reckinridge) *12*
Showell, Ellen Harvey 1934- *33*
Showers, Paul C. 1910- *92*
Earlier sketch in SATA *21*
See also CLR *6*
See also SAAS *7*
Shpakow, Tanya 1959(?)- *94*

Shpitalnik, Vladimir 1964- *83*
Shreve, Susan Richards 1939- *95*
Brief entry *41*
Earlier sketch in SATA *46*
Shriver, Jean Adair 1932- *75*
Shrode, Mary
See Hollingsworth, Mary
Shtainmets, Leon *32*
Shub, Elizabeth *5*
Shuken, Julia 1948- *84*
Shulevitz, Uri 1935- *50*
Earlier sketch in SATA *3*
See also CLR *5*
Shulman, Alix Kates 1932- *7*
Shulman, Irving 1913- *13*
Shulman, Max 1919-1988
Obituary *59*
Shulman, Neil B(arnett) 1945- *89*
Shumsky, Zena
See Collier, Zena
Shura, Mary Francis
See Craig, Mary (Francis) Shura
Shusterman, Neal 1962- *85*
Shuter, Jane Margaret 1955- *90*
Shuttlesworth, Dorothy *3*
Shwartz, Susan (Martha) 1949- *94*
Shyer, Christopher 1961- *98*
Shyer, Marlene Fanta *13*
Siberell, Anne *29*
Sibley, Don 1922- *12*
Sibson, Caroline
See Dracup, Angela
Siculan, Daniel 1922- *12*
Sidjakov, Nicolas 1924- *18*
Sidney, Frank [Joint pseudonym]
See Warwick, Alan R(oss)
Sidney, Margaret
See Lothrop, Harriet Mulford Stone
Siebel, Fritz (Frederick) 1913-
Brief entry *44*
Siegal, Aranka 1930- *88*
Brief entry *37*
Siegel, Beatrice *36*
Siegel, Helen
See Siegl, Helen
Siegel, Robert (Harold) 1939- *39*
Siegl, Helen 1924- *34*
Silas
See McCay, Winsor
Silcock, Sara Lesley 1947- *12*
Sill, Cathryn 1953- *74*
Sill, John 1947- *74*
Sillitoe, Alan 1928- *61*
Silly, E. S.
See Kraus, (Herman) Robert
Silsbe, Brenda 1953- *73*
Silver, Ruth
See Chew, Ruth
Silverberg, Robert 1935- *91*
Earlier sketch in SATA *13*
Silverman, Erica 1955- *78*
Silverman, Mel(vin Frank)
1931-1966 ....*9*
Silverman, Robin L(andew) 1954- *96*
Silverstein, Alvin 1933- *69*
Earlier sketch in SATA *8*
See also CLR *25*
Silverstein, Robert Alan 1959- *77*
Silverstein, Shel(by) 1932- *92*
Brief entry *27*
Earlier sketch in SATA *33*
See also CLR *5*
Silverstein, Virginia B(arbara Opshelor)
1937- *69*
Earlier sketch in SATA *8*
See also CLR *25*
Silverthorne, Elizabeth 1930- *35*
Silverwood, Margaret Shannon
1966- *83*
Sim, Dorrith M. 1931- *96*
Simak, Clifford D(onald) 1904-1988
Obituary *56*
Simmonds, Posy 19 ?(?)-
See CLR *23*
Simon, Charlie May
See Fletcher, Charlie May

Simon, Hilda (Rita) 1921- *28*
  See also CLR *39*
Simon, Howard 1903-1979 ....*32*
  Obituary *21*
Simon, Joe
  See Simon, Joseph H.
Simon, Joseph H. 1913- *7*
Simon, Martin P(aul William)
  1903-1969 ....*12*
Simon, Mina Lewiton
  See Lewiton, Mina
Simon, Norma (Feldstein) 1927- *68*
  Earlier sketch in SATA *3*
Simon, Seymour 1931- *73*
  Earlier sketch in SATA *4*
  See also CLR *9*
Simon, Shirley (Schwartz) 1921- *11*
Simon, Solomon 1895-1970 ....*40*
Simonetta, Linda 1948- *14*
Simonetta, Sam 1936- *14*
Simons, Barbara B(rooks) 1934- *41*
Simont, Marc 1915- *73*
  Earlier sketch in SATA *9*
Simpson, Colin 1908- *14*
Simpson, Harriette
  See Arnow, Harriette (Louisa) Simpson
Simpson, Myrtle L(illias) 1931- *14*
Sims, Blanche (L.) *75*
Simundsson, Elva 1950- *63*
Sinclair, Clover
  See Gater, Dilys
Sinclair, Emil
  See Hesse, Hermann
Sinclair, Jeff 1958- *77*
Sinclair, Upton (Beall) 1878-1968 ....*9*
Singer, A. L.
  See Lerangis, Peter
Singer, Arthur 1917-1990 ....*64*
Singer, Isaac
  See Singer, Isaac Bashevis
Singer, Isaac Bashevis 1904-1991 ....*27*
  Obituary *68*
  Earlier sketch in SATA *3*
  See also CLR *1*
Singer, Jane Sherrod 1917-1985 ....*4*
  Obituary *42*
Singer, Julia 1917- *28*
Singer, Kurt D(eutsch) 1911- *38*
Singer, Marilyn 1948- *80*
  Brief entry *38*
  Earlier sketch in SATA *48*
  See also CLR *48*
  See also SAAS *13*
Singer, Susan (Mahler) 1941- *9*
Singh, Rashmi Sharma 1952- *90*
Singleton, Linda Joy 1957- *88*
Sinykin, Sheri Cooper 1950- *72*
Sipiera, Paul P. (Jr.) 1948- *89*
Siracusa, Catherine (Jane) 1947- *82*
Sirett, Dawn (Karen) 1966- *88*
Sirof, Harriet 1930- *94*
  Earlier sketch in SATA *37*
Sirois, Allen L. 1950- *76*
Sirvaitis (Chernyaev), Karen (Ann)
  1961- *79*
Sis, Peter 1949- *67*
  See also CLR *45*
Sisson, Rosemary Anne 1923- *11*
Sister Mary Terese
  See Donze, Mary Terese
Sister Rosario De Bello
  See De Bello, Rosario
Sita, Lisa 1962- *87*
Sitomer, Harry 1903- *31*
Sitomer, Mindel 1903- *31*
Sive, Helen R. 1951- *30*
Sivulich, Sandra (Jeanne) Stroner
  1941- *9*
Skarmeta, Antonio 1940- *57*
Skelly, James R(ichard) 1927- *17*
Skinner, Constance Lindsay 1882-1939
  See YABC *1*
Skinner, Cornelia Otis 1901- *2*
Skipper, G. C. 1939- *46*
  Brief entry *38*
Skofield, James *95*
  Brief entry *44*

Skold, Betty Westrom 1923- *41*
Skorpen, Liesel Moak 1935- *3*
Skurzynski, Gloria (Joan) 1930- *74*
  Earlier sketch in SATA *8*
  See also SAAS *9*
Skutch, Robert 1925- *89*
Slackman, Charles B. 1934- *12*
Slade, Richard 1910-1971 ....*9*
Slate, Joseph (Frank) 1928- *38*
Slater, James (Derrick) 1929- *58*
Slater, Jim 1929-
  Brief entry *34*
  See Slater, James (Derrick)
Slaughter, Hope 1940- *84*
Slaughter, Jean
  See Doty, Jean Slaughter
Slavin, Bill 1959- *76*
Sleator, William (Warner III)
  1945- *68*
  Earlier sketch in SATA *3*
  See also CLR *29*
Sleigh, Barbara 1906-1982 ....*86*
  Obituary *30*
  Earlier sketch in SATA *3*
Slepian, Jan(ice B.) 1921- *85*
  Brief entry *45*
  Earlier sketch in SATA *51*
  See also SAAS *8*
Slicer, Margaret O. 1920- *4*
Slier, Debby
  See Shine, Deborah
Sloan, Carolyn 1937- *58*
Sloane, Eric 1910(?)-1985 ....*52*
  Obituary *42*
Sloane, Todd 1955- *88*
Sloat, Teri 1948- *70*
Slobodkin, Florence (Gersh) 1905- *5*
Slobodkin, Louis 1903-1975 ....*26*
  Earlier sketch in SATA *1*
Slobodkina, Esphyr 1909- *1*
  See also SAAS *8*
Sloggett, Nellie 1851-1923 ....*44*
Sloss, Lesley Lord 1965- *72*
Slote, Alfred 1926- *72*
  Earlier sketch in SATA *8*
  See also CLR *4*
  See also SAAS *21*
Slote, Elizabeth 1956- *80*
Small, David 1945- *95*
  Brief entry *46*
  Earlier sketch in SATA *50*
Small, Ernest
  See Lent, Blair
Small, Terry 1942- *75*
Smalls-Hector, Irene 1950- *73*
Smallwood, Norah (Evelyn) 1910(?)-1984
  Obituary *41*
Smaridge, Norah 1903- *6*
Smee, Nicola 1948- *76*
Smiley, Virginia Kester 1923- *2*
Smith, Anne Warren 1938- *41*
  Brief entry *34*
Smith, Barry (Edward Jervis)
  1943- *75*
Smith, Beatrice S(chillinger) *12*
Smith, Betsy Covington 1937- *55*
  Brief entry *43*
Smith, Betty 1896-1972 ....*6*
Smith, Betty Sharon
  See Smith, Sharon
Smith, Bradford 1909-1964 ....*5*
Smith, Brenda 1946- *82*
Smith, Caesar
  See Trevor, Elleston
Smith, Craig 1955- *81*
Smith, Datus C(lifford), Jr. 1907- *13*
Smith, Debra 1955- *89*
Smith, Dodie
  See Smith, Dorothy Gladys
Smith, Doris Buchanan 1934- *75*
  Earlier sketch in SATA *28*
  See also SAAS *10*
Smith, Dorothy Gladys 1896-1990 ....*82*
  Obituary *65*
  Earlier sketch in SATA *4*
Smith, Dorothy Stafford 1905- *6*

Smith, E(lmer) Boyd 1860-1943
  See YABC *1*
Smith, E(dric) Brooks 1917- *40*
Smith, Elva S(ophronia) 1871-1965
  Brief entry *31*
Smith, Emma 1923- *52*
  Brief entry *36*
Smith, Eunice Young 1902- *5*
Smith, Frances C. 1904- *3*
Smith, Fredrika Shumway 1877-1968
  Brief entry *30*
Smith, Gary R(ichard) 1932- *14*
Smith, George Harmon 1920- *5*
Smith, H(arry) Allen 1907-1976
  Obituary *20*
Smith, Howard Everett, Jr. 1927- *12*
Smith, Hugh L(etcher) 1921-1968 ....*5*
Smith, Imogene Henderson 1922- *12*
Smith, Jacqueline B. 1937- *39*
Smith, Janice Lee 1949- *54*
Smith, Jean
  See Smith, Frances C.
Smith, Jean Pajot 1945- *10*
Smith, Jeff(rey A.) 1960- *93*
Smith, Jenny 1963- *90*
Smith, Jessie
  See Kunhardt, Edith
Smith, Jessie Willcox 1863-1935 ....*21*
Smith, Jim 1920- *61*
  Brief entry *36*
Smith, Joan (Mary) 1933- *54*
  Brief entry *46*
Smith, Johnston
  See Crane, Stephen (Townley)
Smith, Jos(eph) A. 1936- *73*
Smith, Judie R. 1936- *80*
Smith, Lafayette
  See Higdon, Hal
Smith, Lane 1959- *76*
  See also CLR *47*
Smith, Lee
  See Albion, Lee Smith
Smith, Lendon (Howard) 1921- *64*
Smith, Lillian H(elena) 1887-1983
  Obituary *32*
Smith, Linell Nash 1932- *2*
Smith, Lucia B. 1943- *30*
Smith, Marion Hagens 1913- *12*
Smith, Marion Jaques 1899- *13*
Smith, Mary Ellen *10*
Smith, Marya 1945- *78*
Smith, Mike
  See Smith, Mary Ellen
Smith, Nancy Covert 1935- *12*
Smith, Norman F. 1920- *70*
  Earlier sketch in SATA *5*
Smith, Patricia Clark 1943- *96*
Smith, Pauline C(oggeshall) 1908- *27*
Smith, Philip Warren 1936- *46*
Smith, Robert Kimmel 1930- *77*
  Earlier sketch in SATA *12*
Smith, Robert Paul 1915-1977 ....*52*
  Obituary *30*
Smith, Ruth Leslie 1902- *2*
Smith, Samantha 1972-1985
  Obituary *45*
Smith, Sandra Lee 1945- *75*
Smith, Sarah Stafford
  See Smith, Dorothy Stafford
Smith, Sharon 1943- *82*
Smith, Sherwood 1951- *82*
Smith, Susan Carlton 1923- *12*
Smith, Susan Mathias 1950- *43*
  Brief entry *35*
Smith, Susan Vernon 1950- *48*
Smith, Ursula 1934- *54*
Smith, Vian (Crocker) 1919-1969 ....*11*
Smith, Wanda VanHoy 1926- *65*
Smith, Ward
  See Goldsmith, Howard
Smith, William A. *10*
Smith, William Jay 1918- *68*
  Earlier sketch in SATA *2*
  See also SAAS *22*
Smith, Winsome 1935- *45*
Smith, Z. Z.
  See Westheimer, David

Author Index

Smith-Griswold, Wendy 1955- *88*
Smith-Rex, Susan J. 1950- *94*
Smithsen, Richard
  See Pellowski, Michael (Joseph)
Smits, Teo
  See Smits, Theodore R(ichard)
Smits, Theodore R(ichard) 1905- *45*
  Brief entry *28*
Smolinski, Dick 1932- *86*
Smothers, Ethel Footman 1944- *76*
Smucker, Barbara (Claassen) 1915- *76*
  Earlier sketch in SATA *29*
  See also CLR *10*
  See also SAAS *11*
Snedeker, Caroline Dale (Parke) 1871-1956
  See YABC *2*
Snell, Nigel (Edward Creagh)
  1936- *57*
  Brief entry *40*
Snellgrove, L(aurence) E(rnest)
  1928- *53*
Snelling, Dennis (Wayne) 1958- *84*
Sneve, Virginia Driving Hawk
  1933- *95*
  Earlier sketch in SATA *8*
  See also CLR *2*
Sniff, Mr.
  See Abisch, Roslyn Kroop
Snodgrass, Mary Ellen 1944- *75*
Snodgrass, Thomas Jefferson
  See Clemens, Samuel Langhorne
Snook, Barbara (Lillian) 1913-1976 ......*34*
Snow, Donald Clifford 1917- *16*
Snow, Dorothea J(ohnston) 1909- *9*
Snow, Richard F(olger) 1947- *52*
  Brief entry *37*
Snyder, Anne 1922- *4*
Snyder, Bernadette McCarver
  1930- *97*
Snyder, Carol 1941- *35*
Snyder, Gerald S(eymour) 1933- *48*
  Brief entry *34*
Snyder, Jerome 1916-1976
  Obituary *20*
Snyder, Zilpha Keatley 1927- *75*
  Earlier sketches in SATA *1, 28*
  See also CLR *31*
  See also SAAS *2*
Snyderman, Reuven K. 1922- *5*
Soble, Jennie
  See Cavin, Ruth (Brodie)
Sobol, Donald J. 1924- *73*
  Earlier sketches in SATA *1, 31*
  See also CLR *4*
Sobol, Harriet Langsam 1936- *47*
  Brief entry *34*
Sobol, Rose 1931- *76*
Sobott-Mogwe, Gaele 1956- *97*
Soderlind, Arthur E(dwin) 1920- *14*
Soentpiet, Chris K. 1970- *97*
Soerensen, Svend Otto 1916- *67*
Softly, Barbara (Frewin) 1924- *12*
Soglow, Otto 1900-1975
  Obituary *30*
Sohl, Frederic J(ohn) 1916- *10*
Sokol, Bill
  See Sokol, William
Sokol, William 1923- *37*
Sokolov, Kirill 1930- *34*
Solbert, Romaine G. 1925- *2*
Solbert, Ronni
  See Solbert, Romaine G.
Solomon, Joan 1930(?)- *51*
  Brief entry *40*
Solomons, Ikey Esquir
  See Thackeray, William Makepeace
Solonevich, George 1915- *15*
Solot, Mary Lynn 1939- *12*
Somerlott, Robert 1928- *62*
Sommer, Elyse 1929- *7*
Sommer, Robert 1929- *12*
Sommer-Bodenburg, Angela 1948- *63*
Sommerfelt, Aimee 1892- *5*
Sonneborn, Ruth (Cantor) A.
  1899-1974 ....*4*
  Obituary *27*
Sonnenmark, Laura A. 1958- *73*

Sopko, Eugen 1949- *58*
Sorche, Nic Leodhas
  See Alger, Leclaire (Gowans)
Sorel, Edward 1929- *65*
  Brief entry *37*
Sorensen, Henri 1950- *77*
Sorensen, Svend Otto
  See Soerensen, Svend Otto
Sorensen, Virginia 1912-1991 ....*2*
  Obituary *72*
  See also SAAS *15*
Sorenson, Jane 1926- *63*
Sorenson, Margo 1946- *96*
Sorley Walker, Kathrine *41*
Sorrentino, Joseph N. *6*
Sortor, June Elizabeth 1939- *12*
Sortor, Toni
  See Sortor, June Elizabeth
Soskin, V. H.
  See Ellison, Virginia Howell
Soto, Gary 1952- *80*
  See also CLR *38*
Sotomayor, Antonio 1902- *11*
Soudley, Henry
  See Wood, James Playsted
Soule, Gardner (Bosworth) 1913- *14*
Soule, Jean Conder 1919- *10*
Souster, (Holmes) Raymond 1921- *63*
South, Sheri Cobb 1959- *82*
Southall, Ivan (Francis) 1921- *68*
  Earlier sketch in SATA *3*
  See also CLR *2*
  See also SAAS *3*
Southey, Robert 1774-1843 ....*54*
Southgate, Vera *54*
Sowter, Nita *69*
Spagnoli, Cathy 1950- *79*
Spanfeller, James J(ohn) 1930- *19*
  See also SAAS *8*
Spangenberg, Judith Dunn 1942- *5*
Spar, Jerome 1918- *10*
Sparks, Barbara 1942- *78*
Sparks, Beatrice Mathews 1918- *44*
  Brief entry *28*
Sparks, Mary W. 1920- *15*
Spaulding, Leonard
  See Bradbury, Ray (Douglas)
Speare, Elizabeth George
  1908-1994 ....*62*
  Obituary *83*
  Earlier sketch in SATA *5*
  See also CLR *8*
Spearing, Judith (Mary Harlow) 1922- *9*
Specking, Inez 1890-196(?) *11*
Speed, Nell (Ewing) 1878-1913 ....*68*
Speer, Tammie L.
  See Speer-Lyon, Tammie L.
Speer-Lyon, Tammie L. 1965- *89*
Speicher, Helen Ross (Smith) 1915- *8*
Speir, Nancy 1958- *81*
Spellman, John W(illard) 1934- *14*
Spellman, Roger G.
  See Cox, William R(obert)
Spelman, Cornelia 1946- *96*
Spelman, Mary 1934- *28*
Spence, Cynthia
  See Eble, Diane
Spence, Eleanor (Rachel) 1927- *21*
  See also CLR *26*
Spence, Geraldine 1931- *47*
Spencer, Ann 1918- *10*
Spencer, Cornelia
  See Yaukey, Grace S(ydenstricker)
Spencer, Cornelia
  See Yaukey, Grace S(ydenstricker)
Spencer, Donald D(ean) 1931- *41*
Spencer, Elizabeth 1921- *14*
Spencer, William 1922- *9*
Spencer, Zane A(nn) 1935- *35*
Speregen, Devra Newberger 1964- *84*
Sperling, Dan(iel Lee) 1949- *65*
Sperry, Armstrong W. 1897-1976 ....*1*
  Obituary *27*
Sperry, Raymond, Jr. [Collective
  pseudonym] *1*
Spicer, Dorothy (Gladys) (?)-1975 ....*32*
Spiegelman, Judith M. *5*

Spielberg, Steven 1947- *32*
Spier, Peter (Edward) 1927- *54*
  Earlier sketch in SATA *4*
  See also CLR *5*
Spilhaus, Athelstan 1911- *13*
Spilka, Arnold 1917- *6*
Spillane, Frank Morrison 1918- *66*
Spillane, Mickey
  See Spillane, Frank Morrison
Spinelli, Eileen 1942- *38*
Spinelli, Jerry 1941- *71*
  Earlier sketch in SATA *39*
  See also CLR *26*
Spink, Reginald (William) 1905- *11*
Spinka, Penina Keen 1945- *72*
Spinner, Stephanie 1943- *91*
  Earlier sketch in SATA *38*
Spinossimus
  See White, William, Jr.
Spires, Elizabeth 1952- *71*
Spirin, Gennady 1948- *95*
Splaver, Sarah 1921-
  Brief entry *28*
Spohn, David 1948- *72*
Spohn, Kate 1962- *87*
Spollen, Christopher 1952- *12*
Spooner, Michael (Tim) 1954- *92*
Spowart, Robin 1947- *82*
Sprague, Gretchen (Burnham)
  1926- *27*
Sprigge, Elizabeth 1900-1974 ....*10*
Spring, (Robert) Howard
  1889-1965 ....*28*
Springer, Margaret 1941- *78*
Springer, Marilyn Harris 1931- *47*
Springer, Nancy 1948- *65*
Springstubb, Tricia 1950- *78*
  Brief entry *40*
  Earlier sketch in SATA *46*
Spudvilas, Anne 1951- *94*
Spurll, Barbara 1952- *78*
Spykman, E(lizabeth) C. 1896-1965 ......*10*
  See also CLR *35*
Spyri, Johanna (Heusser)
  1827-1901 ....*19*
  See also CLR *13*
Squire, Miriam
  See Sprigge, Elizabeth
Squires, Phil
  See Barker, S. Omar
Srba, Lynne *98*
S-Ringi, Kjell
  See Ringi, Kjell (Arne Soerensen)
Srivastava, Jane Jonas
  Brief entry *37*
Stacey, Cherylyn 1945- *96*
Stadtler, Bea 1921- *17*
Stafford, Jean 1915-1979
  Obituary *22*
Stahl, Ben(jamin Albert) 1910-1987 ....*5*
  Obituary *54*
Stahl, Hilda 1938-1993 ....*48*
  Obituary *77*
Stair, Gobin (John) 1912- *35*
Stalder, Valerie *27*
Stamaty, Mark Alan 1947- *12*
Stambler, Irwin 1924- *5*
Standiford, Natalie 1961- *81*
Stanek, Lou Willett 1931- *63*
Stanek, Muriel (Novella) 1915-
  Brief entry *34*
Stang, Judit 1921-1977 ....*29*
Stang, Judy
  See Stang, Judit
Stangl, (Mary) Jean 1928- *67*
Stanhope, Eric
  See Hamilton, Charles (Harold St. John)
Stankevich, Boris 1928- *2*
Stanley, Diana 1909-
  Brief entry *30*
Stanley, Diane 1943- *80*
  Brief entry *32*
  Earlier sketch in SATA *37*
  See also CLR *46*
  See also SAAS *15*
Stanley, George Edward 1942- *53*
Stanley, Jerry 1941- *79*

Stanley, Robert
  See Hamilton, Charles (Harold St. John)
Stanli, Sue
  See Meilach, Dona Z(weigoron)
Stanovich, Betty Jo 1954-
  Brief entry *51*
Stanstead, John
  See Groom, Arthur William
Staples, Suzanne Fisher 1945- *70*
Stapleton, Marjorie (Winifred)
  1932- *28*
Stapp, Arthur D(onald) 1906-1972 ....*4*
Starbird, Kaye 1916- *6*
Stark, Evan 1942- *78*
Stark, James
  See Goldston, Robert (Conroy)
Starkey, Marion L. 1901- *13*
Starr, Ward
  See Manes, Stephen
Starr, Ward and Murch Mel [J
  See Manes, Stephen
Starret, William
  See McClintock, Marshall
Starr Taylor, Bridget 1959- *99*
Stasiak, Krystyna *49*
Stauffer, Don
  See Berkebile, Fred D(onovan)
Staunton, Schuyler
  See Baum, L(yman) Frank
Steadman, Ralph (Idris) 1936- *32*
Stearns, Monroe (Mather)
  1913-1987 ....*5*
  Obituary *55*
Steckler, Arthur 1921-1985 ....*65*
Steel, Danielle (Fernande) 1947- *66*
Steele, Addison II
  See Lupoff, Richard A(llen)
Steele, Chester K.
  See Stratemeyer, Edward L.
Steele, Mary 1930- *94*
Steele, Mary Q(uintard Govan)
  1922-1992 ....*51*
  Obituary *72*
  Earlier sketch in SATA *3*
Steele, (Henry) Max(well) 1922- *10*
Steele, Philip 1948- *81*
Steele, William O(wen) 1917-1979 ....*51*
  Obituary *27*
  Earlier sketch in SATA *1*
Steelhammer, Ilona 1952- *98*
Steelsmith, Shari 1962- *72*
Stefanik, Alfred T. 1939- *55*
Steffens, Bradley 1955- *77*
Stegeman, Janet Allais 1923- *53*
  Brief entry *49*
Steig, William H. 1907- *70*
  Earlier sketch in SATA *18*
  See also CLR *15*
Stein, Harve 1904-
  Brief entry *30*
Stein, M(eyer) L(ewis) *6*
Stein, Mini *2*
Stein, R(ichard) Conrad 1937- *31*
Stein, R. Conrad 1937- *82*
Stein, Sara Bonnett
  Brief entry *34*
Stein, Wendy 1951- *77*
Steinbeck, John (Ernst) 1902-1968 ....*9*
Steinberg, Alfred 1917- *9*
Steinberg, Fannie 1899- *43*
Steinberg, Fred J. 1933- *4*
Steinberg, Phillip Orso 1921- *34*
Steinberg, Rafael (Mark) 1927- *45*
Steinberg, Saul 1914- *67*
Steiner, Barbara A(nnette) 1934- *83*
  Earlier sketch in SATA *13*
  See also SAAS *13*
Steiner, Charlotte 1900-1981 ....*45*
Steiner, George 1929- *62*
Steiner, Joerg 1930- *35*
Steiner, K. Leslie
  See Delany, Samuel R(ay), (Jr.)
Steiner, Stan(ley) 1925-1987 ....*14*
  Obituary *50*
Steiner-Prag, Hugo 1880-1945
  Brief entry *32*
Steins, Richard 1942- *79*

Stephens, Alice Barber 1858-1932 ....*66*
Stephens, Mary Jo 1935- *8*
Stephens, Suzanne
  See Kirby, Susan E.
Stephens, William M(cLain) 1925- *21*
Stephensen, A. M.
  See Manes, Stephen
Stepp, Ann 1935- *29*
Stepto, Michele 1946- *61*
Steptoe, John (Lewis) 1950-1989 ....*63*
  Earlier sketch in SATA *8*
  See also CLR *12*
Sterling, Brett
  See Samachson, Joseph
Sterling, Dorothy 1913- *83*
  Earlier sketch in SATA *1*
  See also CLR *1*
  See also SAAS *2*
Sterling, Helen
  See Hoke, Helen (L.)
Sterling, Philip 1907-1989 ....*8*
  Obituary *63*
Stern, Ellen N(orman) 1927- *26*
Stern, Judith M. 1951- *75*
Stern, Madeleine B(ettina) 1912- *14*
Stern, Philip Van Doren
  1900-1984 ....*13*
  Obituary *39*
Stern, Simon 1943- *15*
Sterne, Emma Gelders 1894-1971 ....*6*
Steurt, Marjorie Rankin 1888- *10*
Stevens, Bryna 1924- *65*
Stevens, Carla M(cBride) 1928- *13*
Stevens, Diane 1939- *94*
Stevens, Franklin 1933- *6*
Stevens, Gwendolyn 1944- *33*
Stevens, Jan Romero 1953- *95*
Stevens, Janet 1953- *90*
Stevens, Kathleen 1936- *49*
Stevens, Leonard A. 1920- *67*
Stevens, Lucile V(ernon) 1899- *59*
Stevens, Patricia Bunning 1931- *27*
Stevens, Peter
  See Geis, Darlene
Stevens, Serita (Deborah) 1949- *70*
Stevens, Shira
  See Stevens, Serita (Deborah)
Stevenson, Anna (M.) 1905- *12*
Stevenson, Augusta 1869(?)-1976 ....*2*
  Obituary *26*
Stevenson, Burton E(gbert)
  1872-1962 ....*25*
Stevenson, Drew 1947- *60*
Stevenson, Harvey 1960- *80*
Stevenson, James 1929- *71*
  Brief entry *34*
  Earlier sketch in SATA *42*
  See also CLR *17*
Stevenson, Janet 1913- *8*
Stevenson, Robert Louis 1850-1894
  See YABC *2*
  See also CLR *11*
Stewart, A(gnes) C(harlotte) *15*
Stewart, Charles
  See Zurhorst, Charles (Stewart, Jr.)
Stewart, Elisabeth J(ane) 1927- *93*
Stewart, Elizabeth Laing 1907- *6*
Stewart, George Rippey 1895-1980 ....*3*
  Obituary *23*
Stewart, John (William) 1920- *14*
Stewart, Mary (Florence Elinor)
  1916- *12*
Stewart, Robert Neil 1891-1972 ....*7*
Stewart, Scott
  See Zaffo, George J.
Stewart, W(alter) P. 1924- *53*
Stewart, Whitney 1959- *92*
Stewig, John Warren 1937- *26*
Stidworthy, John 1943- *63*
Stiles, Martha Bennett *6*
Stiles, Norman B. 1942-
  Brief entry *36*
Still, James 1906- *29*
Stillerman, Robbie 1947- *12*
Stilley, Frank 1918- *29*
Stine, G(eorge) Harry 1928- *10*

Stine, Jovial Bob
  See Stine, R(obert) L(awrence)
Stine, R(obert) L(awrence) 1943- *76*
  Earlier sketch in SATA *31*
  See also CLR *37*
Stinetorf, Louise 1900- *10*
Stinson, Kathy 1952- *98*
Stirling, Arthur
  See Sinclair, Upton (Beall)
Stirling, Ian 1941- *77*
Stirling, Nora B. *3*
Stirnweis, Shannon 1931- *10*
Stobbs, William 1914- *17*
Stock, Carolmarie 1951- *75*
Stock, Catherine 1952- *65*
Stockdale, Susan 1954- *98*
Stockham, Peter (Alan) 1928- *57*
Stockton, Francis Richard
  1834-1902 ....*44*
Stockton, Frank R(ichard)
  Brief entry *32*
  See Stockton, Francis Richard
Stoddard, Edward G. 1923- *10*
Stoddard, Hope 1900- *6*
Stoddard, Sandol 1927- *98*
  See Warburg, Sandol Stoddard
Stoeke, Janet Morgan 1957- *90*
Stoiko, Michael 1919- *14*
Stoker, Abraham 1847-1912 ....*29*
Stoker, Bram
  See Stoker, Abraham
Stokes, Cedric
  See Beardmore, George
Stokes, Jack (Tilden) 1923- *13*
Stokes, Olivia Pearl 1916- *32*
Stolz, Mary (Slattery) 1920- *71*
  Earlier sketch in SATA *10*
  See also SAAS *3*
Stone, Alan [Collective pseudonym] *1*
  See Svenson, Andrew E.
Stone, D(avid) K(arl) 1922- *9*
Stone, Eugenia 1879-1971 ....*7*
Stone, Gene
  See Stone, Eugenia
Stone, Helen V. *6*
Stone, Irving 1903-1989 ....*3*
  Obituary *64*
Stone, Jon 1931-1997 ....*39*
  Obituary *95*
Stone, Josephine Rector
  See Dixon, Jeanne
Stone, Peter 1930- *65*
Stone, Raymond [Collective
  pseudonym] *1*
Stone, Richard A.
  See Stratemeyer, Edward L.
Stone, Rosetta
  See Geisel, Theodor Seuss
Stonehouse, Bernard 1926- *80*
  Earlier sketch in SATA *13*
Stones, (Cyril) Anthony 1934- *72*
Stong, Phil(ip Duffield) 1899-1957 ....*32*
Stoops, Erik D. 1966- *78*
Stops, Sue 1936- *86*
Storch, Anne B. von
  See von Storch, Anne B.
Storey, (Elizabeth) Margaret (Carlton)
  1926- *9*
Storey, Victoria Carolyn 1945- *16*
Stormcrow
  See Talifero, Gerald
Storme, Peter
  See Stern, Philip Van Doren
Storr, Catherine (Cole) 1913- *87*
  Earlier sketch in SATA *9*
Story, Josephine
  See Loring, Emilie (Baker)
Stott, Dorothy (M.) 1958- *99*
  Earlier sketch in SATA *67*
Stott, Dot
  See Stott, Dorothy (M.)
Stoutenburg, Adrien 1916- *3*
Stover, Allan C(arl) 1938- *14*
Stover, Jill (Griffin) 1958- *82*
Stover, Marjorie Filley 1914- *9*
Stow, Jenny 1948- *82*
Stowe, Cynthia 1944- *78*

8

Stowe, Harriet (Elizabeth) Beecher 1811-1896
See YABC 1
Stowe, Leland 1899-1994 60
Obituary 78
Strachan, Ian 1938- 85
Strachan, Margaret Pitcairn 1908- 14
Strahinich, H. C.
See Strahinich, Helen C.
Strahinich, Helen C. 1949- 78
Strait, Treva Adams 1909- 35
Strand, Mark 1934- 41
Strange, Philippa
See Coury, Louise Andree
Stranger, Joyce
See SAAS 24
See Wilson, Joyce M(uriel Judson)
Strannigan, Shawn (Alyne) 1956- 93
Strasser, Todd 1950- 71
Earlier sketch in SATA 45
See also CLR 11
Stratemeyer, Edward L. 1862-1930 67
Earlier sketch in SATA 1
Stratford, Philip 1927- 47
Stratton, Thomas [Joint pseudonym]
See DeWeese, Thomas Eugene
Stratton-Porter, Gene 1863-1924 15
Strauss, Gwen 1963- 77
Strauss, Joyce 1936- 53
Strauss, Susan (Elizabeth) 1954- 75
Strayer, E. Ward
See Stratemeyer, Edward L.
Streano, Vince(nt Catello) 1945- 20
Streatfeild, (Mary) Noel 1897-1985 20
Obituary 48
See also CLR 17
Street, Janet Travell 1959- 84
Street, Julia Montgomery 1898- 11
Strelkoff, Tatiana 1957- 89
Stren, Patti 1949- 88
Brief entry 41
See also CLR 5
Strete, Craig Kee 1950- 96
Earlier sketch in SATA 44
Stretton, Barbara (Humphrey) 1936- 43
Brief entry 35
Strickland, (William) Brad(ley) 1947- ...83
Strickland, Dorothy S(alley) 1933- 89
Strickland, Michael R. 1965- 83
Striker, Susan 1942- 63
Stroeyer, Poul 1923- 13
Strong, Charles [Joint pseudonym]
See Epstein, Beryl (M. Williams)
and Epstein, Samuel
Strong, David
See McGuire, Leslie (Sarah)
Strong, J. J.
See Strong, Jeremy
Strong, Jeremy 1949- 36
Strong, Stacie 1965- 74
Stroud, Bettye 1939- 96
Stryker, Daniel
See Morris, Chris(topher Crosby)
Stuart, David
See Hoyt, Edwin P(almer), Jr.
Stuart, Forbes 1924- 13
Stuart, Ian
See MacLean, Alistair (Stuart)
Stuart, (Hilton) Jesse 1907-1984 2
Obituary 36
Stuart, Sheila
See Baker, Mary Gladys Steel
Stuart-Clark, Christopher 1940- 32
Stubbs, Joanna 1940-
Brief entry 53
Stubis, Talivaldis 1926- 5
Stubley, Trevor (Hugh) 1932- 22
Stucky, Naomi R. 1922- 72
Stultifer, Morton
See Curtis, Richard (Alan)
Sture-Vasa, Mary
See Alsop, Mary O'Hara
Sturton, Hugh
See Johnston, H(ugh) A(nthony) S(tephen)

Sturtzel, Howard A(llison) 1894- 1
Sturtzel, Jane Levington 1903- 1
Styles, Frank Showell 1908- 10
Suba, Susanne 4
Subond, Valerie
See Grayland, Valerie
Sudbery, Rodie 1943- 42
Sufrin, Mark 1925- 76
Sugarman, Joan G. 1917- 64
Sugarman, Tracy 1921- 37
Sugita, Yutaka 1930- 36
Suhl, Yuri 1908-1986 8
Obituary 50
See also CLR 2
See also SAAS 1
Suid, Murray 1942- 27
Sullivan, George (Edward) 1927- 89
Earlier sketch in SATA 4
Sullivan, Mary Ann 1954- 63
Sullivan, Mary W(ilson) 1907- 13
Sullivan, Thomas Joseph, Jr. 1947- 16
Sullivan, Tom
See Sullivan, Thomas Joseph, Jr.
Sumichrast, Joezef 1948- 29
Sumiko
See Davies, Sumiko
Summers, James L(evingston) 1910-1973 ...57
Brief entry 28
Sun, Chyng Feng 1959- 90
Sunderlin, Sylvia (S.) 1911-1997 28
Obituary 99
Sung, Betty Lee 26
Supraner, Robyn 1930- 20
Supree, Burt(on) 1941-1992 73
Surge, Frank 1931- 13
Susac, Andrew 1929- 5
Susi, Geraldine Lee 1942- 98
Sussman, Cornelia (Silver) 1914- 59
Sussman, Irving 1908- 59
Sussman, Susan 1942- 48
Sutcliff, Rosemary 1920-1992 78
Obituary 73
Earlier sketches in SATA 6, 44
See also CLR 37
Sutherland, Colleen 1944- 79
Sutherland, Efua (Theodora Morgue) 1924- ...25
Sutherland, Margaret 1941- 15
Sutherland, Zena B(ailey) 1915- 37
Suttles, Shirley (Smith) 1922- 21
Sutton, Ann (Livesay) 1923- 31
Sutton, Eve(lyn Mary) 1906- 26
Sutton, Felix 1910(?)- 31
Sutton, Jane 1950- 52
Brief entry 43
Sutton, Larry M(atthew) 1931- 29
Sutton, Margaret Beebe 1903- 1
Sutton, Myron Daniel 1925- 31
Sutton, Roger 1956- 93
Suzanne, Jamie
See Zach, Cheryl (Byrd)
Suzanne, Jamie
See Singleton, Linda Joy
Suzanne, Jamie
See Lantz, Francess L(in)
Suzanne, Jamie
See Hawes, Louise
Svenson, Andrew E. 1910-1975 2
Obituary 26
Swain, Gwenyth 1961- 84
Swain, Su Zan (Noguchi) 1916- 21
Swamp, Jake 1941- 98
Swan, Susan 1944- 22
Swann, Ruth Rice 1920- 84
Swanson, Helen M(cKendry) 1919- 94
Swanson, June 1931- 76
Swarthout, Glendon (Fred) 1918- 26
Swarthout, Kathryn 1919- 7
Swayne, Sam(uel F.) 1907- 53
Swayne, Zoa (Lourana) 1905- 53
Sweat, Lynn 1934- 57
Swede, George 1940- 67
Sweeney, James B(artholomew) 1910- 21
Sweeney, Joyce (Kay) 1955- 68
Earlier sketch in SATA 65

Sweeney, Karen O'Connor
See O'Connor, Karen
Sweetland, Nancy A(nn) 1934- 48
Swenson, Allan A(rmstrong) 1933- 21
Swenson, May 1919- 15
Swentzell, Rina 1939- 79
Swift, David
See Kaufmann, John
Swift, Hildegarde Hoyt 1890(?)-1977
Obituary 20
Swift, Jonathan 1667-1745 19
Swift, Merlin
See Leeming, Joseph
Swiger, Elinor Porter 1927- 8
Swinburne, Laurence 1924- 9
Swindells, Robert (Edward) 1939- 80
Brief entry 34
Earlier sketch in SATA 50
See also SAAS 14
Swinford, Betty (June Wells) 1927- 58
Swinford, Bob
See Swinford, Betty (June Wells)
Switzer, Ellen 1923- 48
Sybesma, Jetske
See Ironside, Jetske
Sydney, Frank [Joint pseudonym]
See Warwick, Alan R(oss)
Sylvester, Natalie G(abry) 1922- 22
Syme, (Neville) Ronald 1913-1992 87
Earlier sketch in SATA 2
Symes, R. F. 77
Symons, (Dorothy) Geraldine 1909- 33
Symons, Stuart
See Stanley, George Edward
Symynkywicz, Jeffrey B(ruce) 1954- 87
Synge, (Phyllis) Ursula 1930- 9
Sypher, Lucy Johnston 1907- 7
Szasz, Suzanne (Shorr) 1915-1997 13
Obituary 99
Szekeres, Cyndy 1933- 60
Earlier sketch in SATA 5
See also SAAS 13
Szekessy, Tanja 98
Szpura, Beata 1961- 93
Szudek, Agnes S(usan) P(hilomena) 57
Brief entry 49
Szulc, Tad 1926- 26
Szydlow, Jarl
See Szydlowski, Mary Vigliante
Szydlowski, Mary Vigliante 1946- 94
Szymanski, Lois 1957- 91

T

Taback, Simms 1932- 40
Brief entry 36
Taber, Gladys (Bagg) 1899-1980
Obituary 22
Tabor, Nancy Maria Grande 1949- 89
Tabrah, Ruth Milander 1921- 14
Tafuri, Nancy 1946- 75
Earlier sketch in SATA 39
See also SAAS 14
Taha, Karen T(erry) 1942- 71
Tait, Douglas 1944- 12
Takakjian, Portia 1930- 15
Takashima, Shizuye 1928- 13
Talbert, Marc 1953- 99
Earlier sketch in SATA 68
Talbot, Charlene Joy 1928- 10
Talbot, Toby 1928- 14
Talbott, Hudson 1949- 84
Talifero, Gerald 1950- 75
Talker, T.
See Rands, William Brighty
Tallcott, Emogene 10
Tallis, Robyn
See Macdonald, James D.
Tallis, Robyn
See Zambreno, Mary Frances
Tallis, Robyn
See Smith, Sherwood
Tallon, Robert 1939- 43
Brief entry 28

Talmadge, Marian *14*
Tamar, Erika 1934- *62*
Tamarin, Alfred *13*
Tamburine, Jean 1930- *12*
Tames, Richard (Lawrence) 1946- *67*
Tamminga, Frederick William
  1934- *66*
Tammuz, Benjamin 1919-1989
  Obituary *63*
Tan, Amy 1952- *75*
Tanaka, Beatrice 1932- *76*
Tang, Charles 1948- *81*
Tang, You-Shan 1946- *53*
Tannen, Mary 1943- *37*
Tannenbaum, Beulah 1916- *3*
Tannenbaum, D(onald) Leb 1948- *42*
Tanner, Jane 1946- *74*
Tanner, Louise S(tickney) 1922- *9*
Tanobe, Miyuki 1937- *23*
Tapio, Pat Decker
  See Kines, Pat Decker
Tapp, Kathy Kennedy 1949- *88*
  Brief entry *50*
Targ Brill, Marlene
  See Brill, Marlene Targ
Tarkington, (Newton) Booth
  1869-1946 ....*17*
Tarlow, Nora
  See Cohen, Nora
Tarr, Judith 1955- *64*
Tarry, Ellen 1906- *16*
  See also CLR *26*
  See also SAAS *16*
Tarshis, Jerome 1936- *9*
Tarsky, Sue 1946- *41*
Tashjian, Virginia A. 1921- *3*
Tasker, James *9*
Tate, Eleanora E(laine) 1948- *94*
  Earlier sketch in SATA *38*
  See also CLR *37*
Tate, Ellalice
  See Hibbert, Eleanor Alice Burford
Tate, Joan 1922- *86*
  Earlier sketch in SATA *9*
  See also SAAS *20*
Tate, Mary Anne
  See Hale, Arlene
Tate, Suzanne 1930- *91*
Tatham, Campbell
  See Elting, Mary
Tatham, Julie
  See Tatham, Julie Campbell
Tatham, Julie Campbell 1908- *80*
Taves, Isabella 1915- *27*
Taylor, Andrew (John Robert)
  1951- *70*
Taylor, Ann 1782-1866 ....*41*
  Brief entry *35*
Taylor, Audilee Boyd 1931- *59*
Taylor, Barbara J. 1927- *10*
Taylor, Ben
  See Strachan, Ian
Taylor, Carl 1937- *14*
Taylor, Cheryl Munro 1957- *96*
Taylor, Cora (Lorraine) 1936- *64*
Taylor, Dave 1948- *78*
Taylor, David
  See Taylor, Dave
Taylor, David 1900-1965 ....*10*
Taylor, Elizabeth 1912-1975 ....*13*
Taylor, Florence M(arion Tompkins)
  1892- *9*
Taylor, Florence Walton *9*
Taylor, Gage 1942- *87*
Taylor, Herb(ert Norman, Jr.)
  1942-1987 ....*22*
  Obituary *54*
Taylor, J. David
  See Taylor, Dave
Taylor, Jane 1783-1824 ....*41*
  Brief entry *35*
Taylor, Jerry Duncan 1938- *47*
Taylor, John Robert
  See Taylor, Andrew (John Robert)
Taylor, Judy
  See Hough, Judy Taylor
Taylor, Kenneth N(athaniel) 1917- *26*

Taylor, L(ester) B(arbour), Jr.
  1932- *27*
Taylor, Louise Todd 1939- *47*
Taylor, Mark 1927- *32*
  Brief entry *28*
Taylor, Mildred D. 1943- *70*
  Earlier sketch in SATA *15*
  See also CLR *9*
  See also SAAS *5*
Taylor, Paula (Wright) 1942- *48*
  Brief entry *33*
Taylor, Robert Lewis 1912- *10*
Taylor, Sydney (Brenner)
  1904(?)-1978 ....*28*
  Obituary *26*
  Earlier sketch in SATA *1*
Taylor, Theodore 1921- *83*
  Earlier sketches in SATA *5, 54*
  See also CLR *30*
  See also SAAS *4*
Taylor, William 1938- *78*
Tazewell, Charles 1900-1972 ....*74*
Tchudi, Stephen N. 1942- *55*
Teague, Bob
  See Teague, Robert
Teague, Mark (Christopher) 1963- *99*
  Earlier sketch in SATA *68*
Teague, Robert 1929- *32*
  Brief entry *31*
Teal, Val 1903- *10*
Teale, Edwin Way 1899-1980 ....*7*
  Obituary *25*
Teasdale, Sara 1884-1933 ....*32*
Tebbel, John (William) 1912- *26*
Tee-Van, Helen Damrosch
  1893-1976 ....*10*
  Obituary *27*
Tegner, Bruce 1928-1985 ....*62*
Teitelbaum, Michael 1953- *59*
Tejima 1931-
  See CLR *20*
Telander, Todd (G.) 1967- *88*
Teleki, Geza 1943- *45*
Telemaque, Eleanor Wong 1934- *43*
Telescope, Tom
  See Newbery, John
Temkin, Sara Anne (Schlossberg)
  1913- *26*
Temko, Florence *13*
Tempest, Margaret Mary 1892-1982
  Obituary *33*
Templar, Maurice
  See Groom, Arthur William
Temple, Arthur
  See Northcott, (William) Cecil
Temple, Charles 1947- *79*
Temple, Frances (Nolting)
  1945-1995 ....*85*
Temple, Herbert 1919- *45*
Temple, Paul [Joint pseudonym]
  See McConnell, James Douglas
  (Rutherford)
Tenggren, Gustaf 1896-1970 ....*18*
  Obituary *26*
Tennant, Kylie
  See Rodd, Kathleen Tennant
Tennant, Veronica 1946- *36*
Tenniel, John 1820-1914 ....*74*
  Brief entry *27*
  See also CLR *18*
Terada, Alice M. 1928- *90*
Terban, Marvin 1940- *54*
  Brief entry *45*
ter Haar, Jaap 1922- *6*
Terhune, Albert Payson 1872-1942 ......*15*
Terkel, Susan N(eiburg) 1948- *59*
Terlouw, Jan (Cornelis) 1931- *30*
Terrell, John Upton 1900-1988
  Obituary *60*
Terris, Susan 1937- *77*
  Earlier sketch in SATA *3*
Terry, Luther L(eonidas)
  1911-1985 ....*11*
  Obituary *42*
Terry, Walter 1913- *14*
Terzian, James P. 1915- *14*

Tessendorf, K(enneth) C(harles)
  1925- *75*
Tessler, Stephanie Gordon 1940- *89*
  Earlier sketch in SATA *64*
  See also SAAS *26*
Tester, Sylvia Root 1939- *64*
  Brief entry *37*
Tether, (Cynthia) Graham 1950- *46*
  Brief entry *36*
Thacher, Mary McGrath 1933- *9*
Thackeray, William Makepeace
  1811-1863 ....*23*
Thaler, Michael C. 1936- *93*
  Brief entry *47*
  Earlier sketch in SATA *56*
Thaler, Mike
  See Thaler, Michael C.
Thaler, Shmuel 1958- *72*
Thamer, Katie 1955- *42*
  See Treherne, Katie Thamer
Thane, Elswyth 1900- *32*
Tharp, Louise Hall 1898- *3*
Thayer, Ernest Lawrence
  1863-1940 ....*60*
Thayer, Jane
  See Woolley, Catherine
Thayer, Marjorie 1908-1992 ....*74*
  Brief entry *37*
Thayer, Peter
  See Wyler, Rose
The Countryman
  See Whitlock, Ralph
Thelwell, Norman 1923- *14*
Themerson, Stefan 1910-1988 ....*65*
Theroux, Paul 1941- *44*
Thesman, Jean *74*
The Tjong Khing 1933- *76*
Thieda, Shirley Ann 1943- *13*
Thiele, Colin (Milton) 1920- *72*
  Earlier sketch in SATA *14*
  See also CLR *27*
  See also SAAS *2*
Thiesing, Lisa 1958- *95*
Thiry, Joan (Marie) 1926- *45*
Thistlethwaite, Miles 1945- *12*
Thollander, Earl 1922- *22*
Thomas, Allison
  See Fleischer, Leonore
Thomas, Andrea
  See Hill, Margaret (Ohler)
Thomas, Art(hur Lawrence) 1952- *48*
  Brief entry *38*
Thomas, Dylan (Marlais)
  1914-1953 ....*60*
Thomas, Estelle Webb 1899- *26*
Thomas, Frances 1943- *92*
Thomas, H. C.
  See Keating, Lawrence A.
Thomas, Ianthe 1951-
  Brief entry *42*
  See also CLR *8*
Thomas, J. F.
  See Fleming, Thomas J(ames)
Thomas, Jane Resh 1936- *90*
  Earlier sketch in SATA *38*
Thomas, Jerry D. 1959- *91*
Thomas, Joan Gale
  See Robinson, Joan (Mary) G(ale
  Thomas)
Thomas, Joyce Carol 1938- *78*
  Earlier sketch in SATA *40*
  See also CLR *19*
  See also SAAS *7*
Thomas, Lowell (Jackson), Jr.
  1923- *15*
Thomas, Patricia J. 1934- *51*
Thomas, Rob *97*
Thomas, Vernon (Arthur) 1934- *56*
Thomas, Victoria [Joint pseudonym]
  See DeWeese, Thomas Eugene
Thomasma, Kenneth R. 1930- *90*
Thomassie, Tynia 1959- *92*
Thompson, Brenda 1935- *34*
Thompson, Carol 1951- *85*
Thompson, China
  See Lewis, Mary (Christianna)

Thompson, Christine Pullein
  See Pullein-Thompson, Christine
Thompson, Colin (Edward) 1942- *95*
Thompson, David H(ugh) 1941- *17*
Thompson, Diana Pullein
  See Pullein-Thompson, Diana
Thompson, Eileen
  See Panowski, Eileen Thompson
Thompson, George Selden
  1929-1989 ....*73*
  Obituary *63*
  Earlier sketch in SATA *4*
Thompson, Harlan H. 1894-1987 ....*10*
  Obituary *53*
Thompson, Hilary 1945- *56*
  Brief entry *49*
Thompson, Josephine
  See Pullein-Thompson, Josephine
Thompson, Julian F(rancis) 1927- *99*
  Brief entry *40*
  Earlier sketch in SATA *55*
  See also CLR *24*
  See also SAAS *13*
Thompson, K(athryn Carolyn) Dyble
  1952- *82*
Thompson, Kay 1912- *16*
  See also CLR *22*
Thompson, Ruth Plumly
  1891-1976 ....*66*
Thompson, Stith 1885-1976 ....*57*
  Obituary *20*
Thompson, Vivian L. 1911- *3*
Thomson, David (Robert Alexander)
  1914-1988 ....*40*
  Obituary *55*
Thomson, Pat 1939- *77*
Thomson, Peggy 1922- *31*
Thorburn, John
  See Goldsmith, John Herman Thorburn
Thorn, John 1947- *59*
Thorndyke, Helen Louise [Collective
  pseudonym] *67*
  Earlier sketch in SATA *1*
Thorne, Ian
  See May, Julian
Thornhill, Jan 1955- *77*
Thornton, W. B.
  See Burgess, Thornton Waldo
Thornton, Yvonne S(hirley) 1947- *96*
Thorpe, E(ustace) G(eorge) 1916- *21*
Thorpe, J. K.
  See Nathanson, Laura Walther
Thorvall, Kerstin 1925- *13*
Thrasher, Crystal (Faye) 1921- *27*
Threadgall, Colin 1941- *77*
Thum, Gladys 1920- *26*
Thum, Marcella *28*
  Earlier sketch in SATA *3*
Thundercloud, Katherine
  See Witt, Shirley Hill
Thurber, James (Grover)
  1894-1961 ....*13*
Thurman, Judith 1946- *33*
Thurman, Mark (Gordon Ian)
  1948- *63*
Thwaite, Ann (Barbara Harrop)
  1932- *14*
Tibo, Gilles 1951- *67*
Tiburzi, Bonnie 1948- *65*
Ticheburn, Cheviot
  See Ainsworth, William Harrison
Tichenor, Tom 1923- *14*
Tichnor, Richard 1959- *90*
Tichy, William 1924- *31*
Tiegreen, Alan (F.) 1935- *94*
  Brief entry *36*
Tierney, Frank M. 1930- *54*
Tiffault, Benette W. 1955- *77*
Tiller, Ruth L. 1949- *83*
Tilly, Nancy 1935- *62*
Tilton, Madonna Elaine 1929- *41*
Tilton, Rafael
  See Tilton, Madonna Elaine
Timmins, William F. *10*
Tinbergen, Niko(laas) 1907-1988
  Obituary *60*
Tiner, John Hudson 1944- *32*

Tingum, Janice 1958- *91*
Tinkelman, Murray 1933- *12*
Tinkle, (Julien) Lon 1906-1980 ....*36*
Tippett, James S(terling)
  1885-1958 ....*66*
Titler, Dale M(ilton) 1926- *35*
  Brief entry *28*
Titmarsh, Michael Angelo
  See Thackeray, William Makepeace
Titus, Eve 1922- *2*
Tivil, Mr.
  See Lorkowski, Thomas V(incent)
Tobias, Tobi 1938- *82*
  Earlier sketch in SATA *5*
  See also CLR *4*
Todd, Anne Ophelia
  See Dowden, Anne Ophelia
Todd, Barbara K. 1917- *10*
Todd, H. E.
  See Todd, Herbert Eatton
Todd, Herbert Eatton 1908-1988 ....*84*
  Earlier sketch in SATA *11*
Todd, Loreto 1942- *30*
Tolan, Stephanie S. 1942- *78*
  Earlier sketch in SATA *38*
Toland, John (Willard) 1912- *38*
Tolkien, J(ohn) R(onald) R(euel)
  1892-1973 ....*32*
  Obituary *24*
  Earlier sketch in SATA *2*
Toll, Nelly S. 1935- *78*
Tolland, W. R.
  See Heitzmann, William Ray
Tolles, Martha 1921- *76*
  Earlier sketch in SATA *8*
Tolliver, Ruby C(hangos) 1922- *55*
  Brief entry *41*
Tolmie, Ken(neth Donald) 1941- *15*
Tolstoi, Leo (Nikolaevich)
  1828-1910 ....*26*
Tomalin, Ruth *29*
Tomes, Margot (Ladd) 1917-1991 ....*70*
  Brief entry *27*
  Obituary *69*
  Earlier sketch in SATA *36*
Tomey, Ingrid 1943- *77*
Tomfool
  See Farjeon, Eleanor
Tomkins, Jasper
  See Batey, Tom
Tomline, F. Latour
  See Gilbert, W(illiam) S(chwenk)
Tomlinson, Jill 1931-1976 ....*3*
  Obituary *24*
Tomlinson, Reginald R(obert) 1885-1979(?)
  Obituary *27*
Tompert, Ann 1918- *89*
  Earlier sketch in SATA *14*
Toner, Raymond John 1908- *10*
Tong, Gary S. 1942- *66*
Took, Belladonna
  See Chapman, Vera
Tooke, Louise Mathews 1950- *38*
Toonder, Martin
  See Groom, Arthur William
Toothaker, Roy Eugene 1928- *18*
Tooze, Ruth 1892-1972 ....*4*
Topek, Susan Remick 1955- *78*
Topping, Audrey R(onning) 1928- *14*
Tor, Regina
  See Shekerjian, Regina Tor
Torbert, Floyd James 1922- *22*
Torgersen, Don Arthur 1934- *55*
  Brief entry *41*
Torley, Luke
  See Blish, James (Benjamin)
Torres, John A(lbert) 1965- *94*
Torres, Laura 1967- *87*
Torrie, Malcolm
  See Mitchell, Gladys (Maude Winifred)
Toten, Teresa 1955- *99*
Totham, Mary
  See Breinburg, Petronella
Tournier, Michel 1924- *23*
Towle, Wendy 1963- *79*
Towne, Mary
  See Spelman, Mary

Townsend, Brad W. 1962- *91*
Townsend, John Rowe 1922- *68*
  Earlier sketch in SATA *4*
  See also CLR *2*
  See also SAAS *2*
Townsend, Sue 1946- *93*
  Brief entry *48*
  Earlier sketch in SATA *55*
Townsend, Thomas L. 1944- *59*
Townsend, Tom
  See Townsend, Thomas L.
Toye, Clive 1933(?)-
  Brief entry *30*
Toye, William E(ldred) 1926- *8*
Traherne, Michael
  See Watkins-Pitchford, Denys James
Trahey, Jane 1923- *36*
Trapani, Iza 1954- *80*
Trapp, Maria (Augusta) von 1905- *16*
Travers, P(amela) L(yndon)
  1899-1996 ....*54*
  Obituary *90*
  Earlier sketch in SATA *4*
  See also CLR *2*
  See also SAAS *2*
Travis, Lucille *88*
Treadgold, Mary 1910- *49*
Trease, (Robert) Geoffrey 1909- *60*
  Earlier sketch in SATA *2*
  See also CLR *42*
  See also SAAS *6*
Treat, Lawrence 1903- *59*
Tredez, Alain 1926- *17*
Tredez, Denise (Laugier) 1930- *50*
Treece, Henry 1911-1966 ....*2*
  See also CLR *2*
Tregarthen, Enys
  See Sloggett, Nellie
Tregaskis, Richard 1916-1973 ....*3*
  Obituary *26*
Treherne, Katie Thamer 1955- *76*
Trell, Max 1900- *14*
Tremain, Ruthven 1922- *17*
Trembath, Don 1963- *96*
Tremens, Del
  See MacDonald, Amy
Trent, Robbie 1894- *26*
Trent, Timothy
  See Malmberg, Carl
Treseder, Terry Walton 1956- *68*
Tresilian, (Cecil) Stuart 1891(?)- *40*
Tresselt, Alvin 1916- *7*
  See also CLR *30*
Trevino, Elizabeth B(orton) de
  1904- *29*
  Earlier sketch in SATA *1*
  See also SAAS *5*
Trevor, Elleston 1920- *28*
Trevor, Glen
  See Hilton, James
Trevor, (Lucy) Meriol 1919- *10*
Trez, Alain
  See Tredez, Alain
Trez, Denise
  See Tredez, Denise (Laugier)
Trezise, Percy (James) 1923-
  See CLR *41*
Triggs, Tony D. 1946- *70*
Trimble, Marshall 1939- *93*
Trimby, Elisa 1948- *47*
  Brief entry *40*
Tring, A. Stephen
  See Meynell, Laurence Walter
Tripp, Eleanor B. 1936- *4*
Tripp, Paul *8*
Tripp, Valerie 1951- *78*
Tripp, Wallace (Whitney) 1940- *31*
Trivelpiece, Laurel 1926- *56*
  Brief entry *46*
Trivett, Daphne (Harwood) 1940- *22*
Trivizas, Eugene 1946- *84*
Trnka, Jiri 1912-1969 ....*43*
  Brief entry *32*
Trollope, Anthony 1815-1882 ....*22*
Trost, Lucille Wood 1938- *12*
Trott, Betty 1933- *91*
Trotter, Grace V(iolet) 1900- *10*

Troughton, Joanna (Margaret)
  1947- *37*
Trout, Kilgore
  See Farmer, Philip Jose
Troyer, Johannes 1902-1969
  Brief entry *40*
Trudeau, G(arretson) B(eekman)
  1948- *35*
Trudeau, Garry B.
  See Trudeau, G(arretson) B(eekman)
Truesdell, Sue
  See Truesdell, Susan G.
Truesdell, Susan G.
  Brief entry *45*
Truss, Jan 1925- *35*
Tubb, Jonathan N. 1951- *78*
Tubby, I. M.
  See Kraus, (Herman) Robert
Tucker, Caroline
  See Nolan, Jeannette Covert
Tudor, Tasha 1915- *69*
  Earlier sketch in SATA *20*
  See also CLR *13*
Tuerk, Hanne 1951- *71*
Tulloch, Richard (George) 1949- *76*
Tully, John (Kimberley) 1923- *14*
Tunis, Edwin (Burdett) 1897-1973 ....*28*
  Obituary *24*
  Earlier sketch in SATA *1*
  See also CLR *2*
Tunis, John R(oberts) 1889-1975 ....*37*
  Brief entry *30*
Tunnicliffe, C(harles) F(rederick)
  1901-1979 ....*62*
Turk, Ruth 1917- *82*
Turkle, Brinton 1915- *79*
  Earlier sketch in SATA *2*
Turlington, Bayly 1919-1977 ....*5*
  Obituary *52*
Turnbull, Agnes Sligh *14*
Turnbull, Ann (Christine) 1943- *18*
Turner, Alice K. 1940- *10*
Turner, Ann (Warren) 1945- *77*
  Earlier sketch in SATA *14*
Turner, Bonnie 1932- *75*
Turner, Elizabeth 1774-1846
  See YABC *2*
Turner, Glennette Tilley 1933- *71*
Turner, Gwenda 1947- *59*
Turner, Josie
  See Crawford, Phyllis
Turner, Megan Whalen 1965- *94*
Turner, Philip (William) 1925- *83*
  Earlier sketch in SATA *11*
  See also SAAS *6*
Turner, Robyn 1947- *77*
Turner, Sheila R.
  See Seed, Sheila Turner
Turngren, Annette 1902(?)-1980
  Obituary *23*
Turngren, Ellen (?)-1964 ....*3*
Turska, Krystyna Zofia 1933- *31*
  Brief entry *27*
Tusa, Tricia 1960- *72*
Tusan, Stan 1936- *22*
Tusiani, Joseph 1924- *45*
Twain, Mark
  See Clemens, Samuel Langhorne
Tweedsmuir, Baron
  See Buchan, John
Tweit, Susan J(oan) 1956- *94*
Tweton, D. Jerome 1933- *48*
Twinem, Neecy 1958- *92*
Twohill, Maggie
  See Angell, Judie
Tworkov, Jack 1900-1982 ....*47*
  Obituary *31*
Tyers, Jenny 1969- *89*
Tyers, Kathy 1952- *82*
Tyler, Anne 1941- *90*
  Earlier sketch in SATA *7*
Tyler, Linda
  See Tyler, Linda W(agner)
Tyler, Linda W(agner) 1952- *65*
Tyler, Vicki 1952- *64*

U

Ubell, Earl 1926- *4*
Uchida, Yoshiko 1921-1992 ....*53*
  Obituary *72*
  Earlier sketch in SATA *1*
  See also CLR *6*
  See also SAAS *1*
Udall, Jan Beaney 1938- *10*
Uden, (Bernard Gilbert) Grant
  1910- *26*
Uderzo, Albert 1927-
  See CLR *37*
Udry, Janice May 1928- *4*
Ueno, Noriko
  See Nakae, Noriko
Ulam, S(tanislaw) M(arcin)
  1909-1984 ....*51*
Ullman, James Ramsey 1907-1971 ....*7*
Ulm, Robert 1934-1977 ....*17*
Ulmer, Louise 1943- *53*
Ulyatt, Kenneth 1920- *14*
Unada
  See Gliewe, Unada
Uncle Gus
  See Rey, H. A.
Uncle Mac
  See McCulloch, Derek (Ivor Breashur)
Uncle Ray
  See Coffman, Ramon Peyton
Uncle Shelby
  See Silverstein, Shel(by)
Underhill, Liz 1948- *53*
  Brief entry *49*
Unger, Harlow G. 1931- *75*
Unger, Jim 1937- *67*
Ungerer, (Jean) Thomas 1931- *33*
  Earlier sketch in SATA *5*
Ungerer, Tomi
  See CLR *3*
  See Ungerer, (Jean) Thomas
Unkelbach, Kurt 1913- *4*
Unnerstad, Edith 1900- *3*
  See also CLR *36*
Unrau, Ruth 1922- *9*
Unstead, R(obert) J(ohn)
  1915-1988 ....*12*
  Obituary *56*
Unsworth, Walt 1928- *4*
Untermeyer, Bryna Ivens
  1909-1985 ....*61*
Untermeyer, Louis 1885-1977 ....*37*
  Obituary *26*
  Earlier sketch in SATA *2*
Unwin, David S(torr) 1918- *14*
Unwin, Nora S. 1907-1982 ....*3*
  Obituary *49*
Unzner, Christa 1958- *80*
Unzner-Fischer, Christa
  See Unzner, Christa
Ure, Jean 1943- *78*
  Earlier sketch in SATA *48*
  See also CLR *34*
  See also SAAS *14*
Uris, Leon (Marcus) 1924- *49*
Ury, Allen B. 1954- *98*
Usher, Margo Scegge
  See McHargue, Georgess
Uston, Ken(neth Senzo) 1935-1987 ......*65*
Uttley, Alice Jane (Taylor)
  1884-1976 ....*88*
  Obituary *26*
  Earlier sketch in SATA *3*
Uttley, Alison
  See Uttley, Alice Jane (Taylor)
Utz, Lois 1932-1986 ....*5*
  Obituary *50*
Uzair, Salem ben
  See Horne, Richard Henry

V

Vaeth, J(oseph) Gordon 1921- *17*
Vail, Rachel 1966- *94*
Vainio, Pirkko 1957- *76*

Valen, Nanine 1950- *21*
Valencak, Hannelore 1929- *42*
Valens, Amy 1946- *70*
Valens, Evans G., Jr. 1920- *1*
Valentine, Johnny *72*
Valleau, Emily 1925- *51*
Van Abbe, Salaman 1883-1955 ....*18*
Van Allsburg, Chris 1949- *53*
  Earlier sketch in SATA *37*
  See also CLR *13*
Van Anrooy, Francine 1924- *2*
Van Anrooy, Frans
  See Van Anrooy, Francine
Vance, Eleanor Graham 1908- *11*
Vance, Marguerite 1889-1965 ....*29*
VanCleave, Janice 1942- *75*
Vandenburg, Mary Lou 1943- *17*
Vander Boom, Mae M. *14*
Vander-Els, Betty 1936- *63*
van der Linde, Laurel 1952- *78*
van der Meer, Ron 1945- *98*
Van der Veer, Judy 1912-1982 ....*4*
  Obituary *33*
Vande Velde, Vivian 1951- *95*
  Earlier sketch in SATA *62*
Vandivert, Rita (Andre) 1905- *21*
Van Duyn, Janet 1910- *18*
Van Dyne, Edith
  See Baum, L(yman) Frank
  and Sampson, Emma (Keats) Speed
Van Hook, Beverly H. 1941- *99*
Van Horn, William 1939- *43*
Van Iterson, S(iny) R(ose) *26*
Van Kampen, Vlasta 1943- *54*
Van Leeuwen, Jean 1937- *82*
  Earlier sketch in SATA *6*
  See also SAAS *8*
van Lhin, Erik
  See del Rey, Lester
Van Loon, Hendrik Willem
  1882-1944 ....*18*
Van Orden, M(erton) D(ick) 1921- *4*
Van Raven, Pieter 1923- *93*
Van Rensselaer, Alexander (Taylor Mason)
  1892-1962 ....*14*
Van Riper, Guernsey, Jr. 1909- *3*
Vansant, Rhonda Joy Edwards
  1950- *92*
Van Steenwyk, Elizabeth (Ann)
  1928- *89*
  Earlier sketch in SATA *34*
Van Stockum, Hilda 1908- *5*
Van Tuyl, Barbara 1940- *11*
Van Vogt, A(lfred) E(lton) 1912- *14*
Van Woerkom, Dorothy (O'Brien)
  1924- *21*
Van Wormer, Joe
  See Van Wormer, Joseph Edward
Van Wormer, Joseph Edward
  1913- *35*
Van-Wyck Mason, F.
  See Mason, F. van Wyck
Van Zwienen, Ilse Charlotte Koehn
  1929-1991 ....*34*
  Brief entry *28*
  Obituary *67*
Van Zyle, Jon 1942- *84*
Varga, Judy
  See Stang, Judit
Varley, Dimitry V. 1906- *10*
Varley, Susan 1961- *63*
Vasiliev, Valery 1949- *80*
Vasiliu, Mircea 1920- *2*
Vass, George 1927- *57*
  Brief entry *31*
Vaughan, Carter A.
  See Gerson, Noel B(ertram)
Vaughan, Harold Cecil 1923- *14*
Vaughan, Marcia (K.) 1951- *95*
  Earlier sketch in SATA *60*
Vaughan, Richard 1947- *87*
Vaughan, Sam(uel) S. 1928- *14*
Vaughn, Ruth 1935- *14*
Vautier, Ghislaine 1932- *53*
Vavra, Robert James 1944- *8*
Vecsey, George 1939- *9*
Vedral, Joyce L(auretta) 1943- *65*

Veglahn, Nancy (Crary) 1937- 5
Velthuijs, Max 1923- 53
Venable, Alan (Hudson) 1944- 8
Venn, Cecilia
  See Keenan, Sheila
Venn, Mary Eleanor
  See Jorgensen, Mary Venn
Ventura, Piero (Luigi) 1937- 61
  Brief entry 43
  See also CLR 16
Vequin, Capini
  See Quinn, Elisabeth
Verba, Joan Marie 1953- 78
verDorn, Bethea (Stewart) 1952- 76
Verne, Jules 1828-1905 21
Verner, Gerald 1897(?)-1980
  Obituary 25
Verney, John 1913-1993 14
  Obituary 75
Vernon, (Elda) Louise A(nderson)
  1914- 14
Vernon, Rosemary
  See Smith, Susan Vernon
Vernor, D.
  See Casewit, Curtis
Verr, Harry Coe
  See Kunhardt, Edith
Verral, Charles Spain 1904-1990 11
  Obituary 65
Verrone, Robert J. 1935(?)-1984
  Obituary 39
Versace, Marie Teresa Rios 1917- 2
Vertreace, Martha M. 1945- 78
Vesey, A(manda) 1939- 62
Vesey, Paul
  See Allen, Samuel (Washington)
Vestly, Anne-Cath(arina) 1920- 14
Vevers, (Henry) Gwynne
  1916-1988 45
  Obituary 57
Viator, Vacuus
  See Hughes, Thomas
Vicarion, Count Palmiro
  See Logue, Christopher
Vick, Helen Hughes 1950- 88
Vicker, Angus
  See Felsen, Henry Gregor
Vickers, Sheena 1960- 94
Vickery, Kate
  See Kennedy, T(eresa) A.
Victor, Edward 1914- 3
Victor, Joan Berg 1937- 30
Viereck, Ellen K. 1928- 14
Viereck, Phillip 1925- 3
Viertel, Janet 1915- 10
Vigliante, Mary
  See Szydlowski, Mary Vigliante
Vigna, Judith 1936- 15
Viguers, Ruth Hill 1903-1971 6
Villiard, Paul 1910-1974 51
  Obituary 20
Villiers, Alan (John) 1903- 10
Vincent, Eric Douglas 1953- 40
Vincent, Felix 1946- 41
Vincent, Gabrielle 61
  See also CLR 13
Vincent, John
  See Peel, John
Vincent, Mary Keith
  See St. John, Wylly Folk
Vincent, W. R.
  See Heitzmann, William Ray
Vinge, Joan D(ennison) 1948- 36
Vining, Elizabeth Gray
  See Gray, Elizabeth Janet
Vinson, Kathryn 1911- 21
Vinton, Iris 1906(?)-1988 24
  Obituary 55
Viorst, Judith 1931- 70
  Earlier sketch in SATA 7
  See also CLR 3
Vip
  See Partch, Virgil Franklin II
Vipont, Charles
  See Foulds, Elfrida Vipont
Vipont, Elfrida
  See Foulds, Elfrida Vipont

Viscott, David S(teven) 1938- 65
Visser, W(illiam) F(rederick) H(endrik)
  1900-1968 10
Vivas, Julie 1947- 96
Vivelo, Jackie
  See Vivelo, Jacqueline J.
Vivelo, Jacqueline J. 1943- 63
Vlahos, Olivia 1924- 31
Vlasic, Bob
  See Hirsch, Phil
Vo-Dinh, Mai 1933- 16
Vogel, Carole Garbuny 1951- 70
Vogel, Ilse-Margret 1914- 14
Vogel, John H(ollister), Jr. 1950- 18
Vogt, Esther Loewen 1915- 14
Vogt, Gregory L. 94
  Brief entry 45
Vogt, Marie Bollinger 1921- 45
Voight, Virginia Frances 1909- 8
Voigt, Cynthia 1942- 79
  Brief entry 33
  Earlier sketch in SATA 48
  See also CLR 48
Voigt, Erna 1925- 35
Voigt-Rother, Erna
  See Voigt, Erna
Vojtech, Anna 1946- 42
Von Ahnen, Katherine 1922- 93
von Almedingen, Martha Edith
  See Almedingen, E. M.
Von Hagen, Victor Wolfgang
  1908- 29
von Klopp, Vahrah
  See Malvern, Gladys
von Schmidt, Eric 1931- 50
  Brief entry 36
von Storch, Anne B. 1910- 1
Vos, Ida 1931- 69
Vosburgh, Leonard (W.) 1912- 15
Voyle, Mary
  See Manning, Rosemary
Vulture, Elizabeth T.
  See Gilbert, Suzie
Vuong, Lynette (Dyer) 1938- 60

W

Waas, Uli
  See Waas-Pommer, Ulrike
Waas-Pommer, Ulrike 1949- 85
Waber, Bernard 1924- 95
  Brief entry 40
  Earlier sketch in SATA 47
Wachtel, Shirley Russak 1951- 88
Wachter, Oralee (Roberts) 1935- 61
  Brief entry 51
Waddell, Evelyn Margaret 1918- 10
Waddell, Martin 1941- 81
  Earlier sketch in SATA 43
  See also CLR 31
  See also SAAS 15
Waddy, Lawrence (Heber) 1914- 91
Wade, Mary Dodson 1930- 79
Wade, Theodore E., Jr. 1936- 37
Wagenheim, Kal 1935- 21
Wagner, Jane 33
Wagner, Sharon B. 1936- 4
Wagoner, David (Russell) 1926- 14
Wahl, Jan (Boyer) 1933- 73
  Earlier sketches in SATA 2, 34
  See also SAAS 3
Waide, Jan 1952- 29
Wainscott, John Milton 1910-1981 53
Wainwright, Richard M. 1935- 91
Waite, P(eter) B(usby) 1922- 64
Waitley, Douglas 1927- 30
Wakefield, Jean L.
  See Laird, Jean E(louise)
Wakin, Daniel (Joseph) 1961- 84
Wakin, Edward 1927- 37
Walck, Henry Z(eigler) 1908-1984
  Obituary 40
Walden, Amelia Elizabeth 3
Waldherr, Kris 1963- 76
Waldman, Bruce 1949- 15

Waldman, Neil 1947- 94
  Earlier sketch in SATA 51
Waldron, Ann Wood 1924- 16
Walker, Alice 1944- 31
Walker, Barbara (Jeanne) K(erlin)
  1921- 80
  Earlier sketch in SATA 4
Walker, Barbara M(uhs) 1928- 57
Walker, (James) Braz(elton)
  1934-1983 45
Walker, David G(ordon) 1926- 60
Walker, David Harry 1911-1992 8
  Obituary 71
Walker, Diana 1925- 9
Walker, Dianne Marie Catherine
  1950- 82
Walker, Dick
  See Pellowski, Michael (Joseph)
Walker, Frank 1930- 36
Walker, Holly Beth
  See Bond, Gladys Baker
Walker, Kate
  See Walker, Dianne Marie Catherine
Walker, Lou Ann 1952- 66
  Brief entry 53
Walker, Louise Jean 1891-1976
  Obituary 35
Walker, Mary Alexander 1927- 61
Walker, Mildred
  See Schemm, Mildred Walker
Walker, (Addison) Mort 1923- 8
Walker, Pamela 1948- 24
Walker, Robert W(ayne) 1948- 66
Walker, Stephen J. 1951- 12
Walker-Blondell, Becky 1951- 89
Wallace, Barbara Brooks 1922- 78
  Earlier sketch in SATA 4
  See also SAAS 17
Wallace, Beverly Dobrin 1921- 19
Wallace, Bill 1947-
  Brief entry 47
  See Wallace, William Keith
Wallace, Daisy
  See Cuyler, Margery (Stuyvesant)
Wallace, Ian 1950- 56
  See also CLR 37
Wallace, John A. 1915- 3
Wallace, Karen 1951- 83
Wallace, Nigel
  See Hamilton, Charles (Harold St. John)
Wallace, Robert 1932- 47
  Brief entry 37
Wallace, William Keith 1947- 53
Wallace-Brodeur, Ruth 1941- 88
  Brief entry 41
  Earlier sketch in SATA 51
Waller, Leslie 1923- 20
Walley, Byron
  See Card, Orson Scott
Wallis, Diz 1949- 77
Wallis, G. McDonald
  See Campbell, Hope
Wallner, Alexandra 1946- 98
  Brief entry 41
  Earlier sketch in SATA 51
Wallner, John C. 1945- 51
  Earlier sketch in SATA 10
Wallower, Lucille 11
Walsh, Ann 1942- 62
Walsh, Ellen Stoll 1942- 99
  Earlier sketch in SATA 49
Walsh, George Johnston 1889-1981 53
Walsh, Jill Paton
  See CLR 2
  See Paton Walsh, Gillian
Walsh Shepherd, Donna 1948- 78
Walter, Francis V. 1923- 71
Walter, Mildred Pitts 1922- 69
  Brief entry 45
  See also CLR 15
  See also SAAS 12
Walter, Villiam Christian
  See Andersen, Hans Christian
Walters, Audrey 1929- 18
Walters, Eric (Robert) 1957- 99
Walters, Helen B. (?)-1987
  Obituary 50

Walters, Hugh
  See Hughes, Walter (Llewellyn)
Walther, Thomas A. 1950- *31*
Walther, Tom
  See Walther, Thomas A.
Waltner, Elma 1912- *40*
Waltner, Willard H. 1909- *40*
Walton, Fiona L. M. 1959- *89*
Walton, Richard J. 1928- *4*
Waltrip, Lela (Kingston) 1904- *9*
Waltrip, Mildred 1911- *37*
Waltrip, Rufus (Charles) 1898- *9*
Walworth, Nancy Zinsser 1917- *14*
Wangerin, Walter, Jr. 1944- *98*
  Brief entry *37*
  Earlier sketch in SATA *45*
Waniek, Marilyn (Nelson) 1946- *60*
Wannamaker, Bruce
  See Moncure, Jane Belk
Warbler, J. M.
  See Cocagnac, Augustin Maurice(-Jean)
Warburg, Sandol Stoddard 1927- *14*
  See Stoddard, Sandol
Ward, E. D.
  See Gorey, Edward (St. John)
Ward, Helen 1962- *72*
Ward, Jay 1920-1989
  Obituary *63*
Ward, John (Stanton) 1917- *42*
Ward, Jonas
  See Cox, William R(obert)
Ward, Lynd (Kendall) 1905-1985 ....*36*
  Obituary *42*
  Earlier sketch in SATA *2*
Ward, Martha (Eads) 1921- *5*
Ward, Melanie
  See Curtis, Richard (Alan)
Wardell, Dean
  See Prince, J(ack) H(arvey)
Wardlaw, Lee 1955- *79*
Ware, Leon (Vernon) 1909- *4*
Warner, Frank A. [Collective
  pseudonym] *67*
  Earlier sketch in SATA *1*
Warner, Gertrude Chandler 1890-1979 ...*9*
  Obituary *73*
Warner, J(ohn) F. 1929- *75*
Warner, Lucille Schulberg *30*
Warner, Oliver 1903-1976 ....*29*
Warren, Andrea 1946- *98*
Warren, Betsy
  See Warren, Elizabeth Avery
Warren, Billy
  See Warren, William Stephen
Warren, Cathy *62*
  Brief entry *46*
Warren, Elizabeth
  See Supraner, Robyn
Warren, Elizabeth Avery 1916- *46*
  Brief entry *38*
Warren, Joyce W(illiams) 1935- *18*
Warren, Mary Phraner 1929- *10*
Warren, Robert Penn 1905-1989 ....*46*
  Obituary *63*
Warren, Scott S. 1957- *79*
Warren, William Stephen 1882-1968 ......*9*
Warrick, Patricia Scott 1925- *35*
Warriner, John 1907(?)-1987
  Obituary *53*
Warsh
  See Warshaw, Jerry
Warshaw, Jerry 1929- *30*
Warshaw, Mary 1931- *89*
Warshofsky, Fred 1931- *24*
Warshofsky, Isaac
  See Singer, Isaac Bashevis
Wartski, Maureen (Ann Crane)
  1940- *50*
  Brief entry *37*
Warwick, Alan R(oss) 1900-1973 ....*42*
Wa-sha-quon-asin
  See Belaney, Archibald Stansfeld
Washburn, (Henry) Bradford (Jr.)
  1910- *38*
Washburn, Jan(ice) 1926- *63*
Washburne, Carolyn Kott 1944- *86*

Washburne, Heluiz Chandler
  1892-1970 ....*10*
  Obituary *26*
Washington, Booker T(aliaferro)
  1858(?)-1915 ....*28*
Washington, Donna L. 1967- *98*
Wasserstein, Wendy 1950- *94*
Watanabe, Shigeo 1928- *39*
  Brief entry *32*
  See also CLR *8*
Waters, John F(rederick) 1930- *4*
Waters, Tony 1958- *75*
Waterton, Betty (Marie) 1923- *99*
  Brief entry *34*
  Earlier sketch in SATA *37*
Watkins, Lois 1930- *88*
Watkins, Peter 1934- *66*
Watkins, Yoko Kawashima 1933- *93*
Watkins-Pitchford, Denys James
  1905-1990 ....*87*
  Obituary *66*
  Earlier sketch in SATA *6*
  See also SAAS *4*
Watling, James 1933- *67*
Watson, Aldren A(uld) 1917- *42*
  Brief entry *36*
Watson, Amy Zakrzewski 1965- *76*
Watson, B.S.
  See Teitelbaum, Michael
Watson, Carol 1949- *78*
Watson, Clyde 1947- *68*
  Earlier sketch in SATA *5*
  See also CLR *3*
Watson, Helen Orr 1892-1978
  Obituary *24*
Watson, James 1936- *10*
Watson, Jane Werner 1915- *54*
  Earlier sketch in SATA *3*
Watson, John H.
  See Farmer, Philip Jose
Watson, N. Cameron 1955- *81*
Watson, Nancy Dingman *32*
Watson, Pauline 1925- *14*
Watson, Richard Jesse 1951- *62*
Watson, Sally 1924- *3*
Watson, Wendy (McLeod) 1942- *74*
  Earlier sketch in SATA *5*
Watson Taylor, Elizabeth 1915- *41*
Watt, Thomas 1935- *4*
Watterson, Bill 1958- *66*
Watts, Bernadette 1942- *4*
Watts, Ephraim
  See Horne, Richard Henry
Watts, Franklin (Mowry)
  1904-1978 ....*46*
  Obituary *21*
Watts, Helen L. Hoke
  See Hoke, Helen (L.)
Watts, Irene N(aemi) 1931- *56*
Watts, Isaac 1674-1748 ....*52*
Watts, James K(ennedy) M(offitt)
  1955- *59*
Watts, Mabel Pizzey 1906- *11*
Waugh, Carol-Lynn Roessel 1947- *41*
Waugh, Dorothy *11*
Wax, Wendy A. 1963- *73*
Wayland, April Halprin 1954- *78*
  See also SAAS *26*
Wayland, Patrick
  See O'Connor, Richard
Wayne, (Anne) Jenifer 1917-1982 ....*32*
Wayne, Kyra Petrovskaya 1918- *8*
Wayne, Richard
  See Decker, Duane
Waystaff, Simon
  See Swift, Jonathan
Weales, Gerald (Clifford) 1925- *11*
Weary, Ogdred
  See Gorey, Edward (St. John)
Weaver, Harriett E. 1908- *65*
Weaver, John L. 1949- *42*
Weaver, Ward
  See Mason, F. van Wyck
Weaver, Will(iam Weller) 1950- *88*
Weaver-Gelzer, Charlotte 1950- *79*

Webb, Christopher
  See Wibberley, Leonard (Patrick
  O'Connor)
Webb, Jean Francis (III) 1910- *35*
Webb, Kaye 1914- *60*
Webb, Lois Sinaiko 1922- *82*
Webb, Margot 1934- *67*
Webb, Sharon 1936- *41*
Webber, Irma E(leanor Schmidt)
  1904- *14*
Weber, Alfons 1921- *8*
Weber, Bruce 1942- *73*
Weber, Debora 1955- *58*
Weber, Judith E(ichler) 1938- *64*
Weber, Ken(neth J.) 1940- *90*
Weber, Lenora Mattingly 1895-1971 ......*2*
  Obituary *26*
Weber, Michael 1945- *87*
Weber, William John 1927- *14*
Webster, Alice (Jane Chandler)
  1876-1916 ....*17*
Webster, David 1930- *11*
Webster, Frank V. [Collective
  pseudonym] *67*
  Earlier sketch in SATA *1*
Webster, Gary
  See Garrison, Webb B(lack)
Webster, James 1925-1981 ....*17*
  Obituary *27*
Webster, Jean
  See Webster, Alice (Jane Chandler)
Wechsler, Herman 1904-1976
  Obituary *20*
Wechter, Nell Wise 1913- *60*
Weck, Thomas L. 1942- *62*
Weddle, Ethel H(arshbarger) 1897- *11*
Weems, David B(urnola) 1922- *80*
Wees, Frances Shelley 1902-1982 ....*58*
Weevers, Peter 1944- *59*
Wegen, Ronald 1946-1985 ....*99*
  Brief entry *44*
Wegman, William 1943- *78*
Wegner, Fritz 1924- *20*
Weidhorn, Manfred 1931- *60*
Weidt, Maryann N. 1944- *85*
Weihs, Erika 1917- *15*
Weik, Mary Hays 1898(?)-1979 ....*3*
  Obituary *23*
Weil, Ann Yezner 1908-1969 ....*9*
Weil, Lisl *7*
Weilerstein, Sadie Rose 1894-1993 ....*3*
  Obituary *75*
Wein, Elizabeth E(ve) 1964- *82*
Weinberg, Larry
  See Weinberg, Lawrence (E.)
Weinberg, Lawrence (E.) *92*
  Brief entry *48*
Weinberger, Tanya 1939- *84*
Weiner, Sandra 1922- *14*
Weingarten, Violet (Brown) 1915-1976 ...*3*
  Obituary *27*
Weingartner, Charles 1922- *5*
Weinstein, Nina 1951- *73*
Weir, Bob 1947- *76*
Weir, Joan S(herman) 1928- *99*
Weir, LaVada *2*
Weir, Rosemary (Green) 1905- *21*
Weir, Wendy 1949- *76*
Weis, Margaret (Edith) 1948- *92*
  Earlier sketch in SATA *38*
Weisberger, Bernard A(llen) 1922- *21*
Weiser, Marjorie P(hillis) K(atz)
  1934- *33*
Weisgard, Leonard (Joseph) 1916- *85*
  Earlier sketches in SATA *2, 30*
  See also SAAS *19*
Weiss, Adelle 1920- *18*
Weiss, Ann E. 1943- *69*
  Earlier sketch in SATA *30*
  See also SAAS *13*
Weiss, Ellen 1953- *44*
Weiss, Harvey 1922- *76*
  Earlier sketches in SATA *1, 27*
  See also CLR *4*
  See also SAAS *19*
Weiss, Jacqueline Shachter 1926- *65*

Weiss, Leatie 1928-
  Brief entry *50*
Weiss, Malcolm E. 1928- *3*
Weiss, Miriam
  See Schlein, Miriam
Weiss, Nicki 1954- *86*
  Earlier sketch in SATA *33*
Weiss, Renee Karol 1923- *5*
Weissenborn, Hellmuth 1898-1982
  Obituary *31*
Wekesser, Carol A. 1963- *76*
Welber, Robert *26*
Welch, Amanda (Jane) 1945- *75*
Welch, D'Alte Aldridge 1907-1970
  Obituary *27*
Welch, Jean-Louise
  See Kempton, Jean Welch
Welch, Martha McKeen 1914-
  Brief entry *45*
Welch, Pauline
  See Bodenham, Hilda Esther
Welch, Ronald
  See Felton, Ronald Oliver
Welch, Willy 1952- *93*
Welford, Sue 1942- *75*
Weller, George (Anthony) 1907- *31*
Welles, Winifred 1893-1939
  Brief entry *27*
Wellington, Monica 1957- *99*
  Earlier sketch in SATA *67*
Wellman, Alice 1900-1984 ....*51*
  Brief entry *36*
Wellman, Manly Wade 1903-1986 ....*6*
  Obituary *47*
Wellman, Paul I. 1898-1966 ....*3*
Wells, H(erbert) G(eorge)
  1866-1946 ....*20*
Wells, Helen 1910-1986 ....*49*
  Earlier sketch in SATA *2*
Wells, June
  See Swinford, Betty (June Wells)
Wells, Rosemary 1943- *69*
  Earlier sketch in SATA *18*
  See also CLR *16*
  See also SAAS *1*
Wells, Susan (Mary) 1951- *78*
Wels, Byron G(erald) 1924- *9*
Welsbacher, Anne 1955- *89*
Welsch, Roger L(ee) 1936- *82*
Welsh, Mary Flynn 1910(?)-1984
  Obituary *38*
Weltner, Linda R(iverly) 1938- *38*
Welton, Jude 1955- *79*
Welty, S. F.
  See Welty, Susan F.
Welty, Susan F. 1905- *9*
Wendelin, Rudolph 1910- *23*
Werlin, Nancy 1961- *87*
Werner, Elsa Jane
  See Watson, Jane Werner
Werner, Herma 1926- *47*
  Brief entry *41*
Werner, Jane
  See Watson, Jane Werner
Werner, K.
  See Casewit, Curtis
Wersba, Barbara 1932- *58*
  Earlier sketch in SATA *1*
  See also CLR *3*
  See also SAAS *2*
Werstein, Irving 1914-1971 ....*14*
Werth, Kurt 1896- *20*
Wesley, Alison
  See Barnes, Michael
Wesley, Mary 1912- *66*
West, Anna 1938- *40*
West, Barbara
  See Price, Olive
West, Betty 1921- *11*
West, Bruce 1951- *63*
West, C. P.
  See Wodehouse, P(elham) G(renville)
West, Dorothy
  See Benson, Mildred (Augustine Wirt)
West, Emily G(ovan) 1919- *38*
West, Emmy
  See West, Emily G(ovan)

West, James
  See Withers, Carl A.
West, Jerry
  See Stratemeyer, Edward L.
West, Jerry
  See Svenson, Andrew E.
West, (Mary) Jessamyn 1902(?)-1984
  Obituary *37*
West, Owen
  See Koontz, Dean R(ay)
West, Ward
  See Borland, Hal
Westall, Robert (Atkinson)
  1929-1993 ....*69*
  Obituary *75*
  Earlier sketch in SATA *23*
  See also CLR *13*
  See also SAAS *2*
Westerberg, Christine 1950- *29*
Westervelt, Virginia (Veeder) 1914- *10*
Westheimer, David 1917- *14*
Westmacott, Mary
  See Christie, Agatha (Mary Clarissa)
Westman, Barbara *70*
Westman, Paul (Wendell) 1956- *39*
Westmoreland, William C(hilds)
  1914- *63*
Weston, Allen
  See Hogarth, Grace (Weston) Allen
  and Norton, Andre
Weston, Allen [Joint pseudonym]
  See Norton, Alice Mary
Weston, John (Harrison) 1932- *21*
Weston, Martha 1947- *53*
Westphal, Arnold Carl 1987- *57*
Westwood, Jennifer 1940- *10*
Wexler, Jerome (LeRoy) 1923- *14*
Weyland, Jack 1940- *81*
Weyn, Suzanne 1955- *63*
Wezyk, Joanna 1966- *82*
Whalin, W. Terry 1953- *93*
Whalley, Joyce Irene 1923- *61*
Wharf, Michael
  See Weller, George (Anthony)
Wharmby, Margot (Alison Winn) *63*
Wheatley, Arabelle 1921- *16*
Wheeler, Captain
  See Ellis, Edward S(ylvester)
Wheeler, Cindy 1955- *49*
  Brief entry *40*
Wheeler, Deborah (Jean Ross)
  1947- *83*
Wheeler, Janet D. [Collective
  pseudonym] *1*
Wheeler, Jill 1964- *86*
Wheeler, Jody 1952- *84*
Wheeler, Opal 1898- *23*
Whelan, Elizabeth M(urphy) 1943- *14*
Whelan, Gloria (Ann) 1923- *85*
Whipple, A(ddison) B(eecher) C(olvin)
  1918- *64*
Whistler, Reginald John 1905-1944 ......*30*
Whistler, Rex
  See Whistler, Reginald John
Whitcher, Susan (Godsil) 1952- *96*
Whitcomb, Jon 1906-1988 ....*10*
  Obituary *56*
White, Anne Hitchcock 1902-1970
  Brief entry *33*
White, Anne Terry 1896- *2*
White, Bessie (Felstiner) 1892(?)-1986
  Obituary *50*
White, Dale
  See Place, Marian T.
White, Dana
  See Larsen, Anita
White, Dori 1919- *10*
White, E(lwyn) B(rooks) 1899-1985 ....*29*
  Obituary *44*
  Earlier sketch in SATA *2*
  See also CLR *21*
White, Eliza Orne 1856-1947
  See YABC *2*
White, Florence M(eiman) 1910- *14*
White, Laurence B., Jr. 1935- *10*
White, Martin 1943- *51*

White, Ramy Allison [Collective
  pseudonym] *67*
  Earlier sketch in SATA *1*
White, Robb 1909- *83*
  Earlier sketch in SATA *1*
  See also CLR *3*
  See also SAAS *1*
White, Ruth C. 1942- *39*
White, T(erence) H(anbury)
  1906-1964 ....*12*
White, Timothy (Thomas Anthony)
  1952- *60*
White, William, Jr. 1934- *16*
Whitehead, Don(ald) F. 1908- *4*
Whitehouse, Arch
  See Whitehouse, Arthur George
Whitehouse, Arthur George
  1895-1979 ....*14*
  Obituary *23*
Whitehouse, Elizabeth S(cott)
  1893-1968 ....*35*
Whitehouse, Jeanne 1939- *29*
Whitelaw, Nancy 1933- *76*
Whitinger, R. D.
  See Place, Marian T.
Whitley, Mary A(nn) 1951- *62*
Whitlock, Pamela 1921(?)-1982
  Obituary *31*
Whitlock, Ralph 1914- *35*
Whitman, Alice
  See Marker, Sherry
Whitman, Sylvia (Choate) 1961- *85*
Whitman, Walt(er) 1819-1892 ....*20*
Whitney, Alex(andra) 1922- *14*
Whitney, David C(harles) 1921- *48*
  Brief entry *29*
Whitney, Phyllis A(yame) 1903- *30*
  Earlier sketch in SATA *1*
Whitney, Sharon 1937- *63*
Whitney, Thomas P(orter) 1917- *25*
Whittington, Mary K(athrine)
  1941- *75*
  See also SAAS *25*
Whyte, Mal(colm Kenneth, Jr.)
  1933- *62*
Whyte, Mary 1953- *94*
Whyte, Ron 1942(?)-1989
  Obituary *63*
Wiater, Stanley 1953- *84*
Wibbelsman, Charles J(oseph)
  1945- *59*
Wibberley, Leonard (Patrick O'Connor)
  1915-1983 ....*45*
  Obituary *36*
  Earlier sketch in SATA *2*
  See also CLR *3*
Wiberg, Harald (Albin) 1908- *93*
  Brief entry *40*
Wickens, Elaine *86*
Wicker, Ireene 1905(?)-1987
  Obituary *55*
Widdemer, Mabel Cleland
  1902-1964 ....*5*
Widenberg, Siv 1931- *10*
Wiener, Lori 1956- *84*
Wier, Ester 1910- *3*
Wiese, Kurt 1887-1974 ....*36*
  Obituary *24*
  Earlier sketch in SATA *3*
Wiesel, Elie(zer) 1928- *56*
Wiesner, David 1956- *72*
  See also CLR *43*
Wiesner, Portia
  See Takakjian, Portia
Wiesner, William 1899- *5*
Wiggers, Raymond 1952- *82*
Wiggin, Eric E(llsworth) 1939- *88*
Wiggin, Kate Douglas (Smith) 1856-1923
  See YABC *1*
Wiggins, VeraLee (Chesnut)
  1928-1995 ....*89*
Wight, James Alfred 1916-1995 ....*55*
  Brief entry *44*
  See Herriot, James
Wignell, Edel 1936- *69*
Wijnberg, Ellen *85*

Wikland, Ilon 1930- *93*
  Brief entry *32*
Wilber, Donald N(ewton) 1907- *35*
Wilbur, C. Keith 1923- *27*
Wilbur, Richard (Purdy) 1921- *9*
Wilburn, Kathy 1948- *68*
Wilcox, Charlotte 1948- *72*
Wilcox, R(uth) Turner 1888-1970 ....*36*
Wild, Jocelyn 1941- *46*
Wild, Robin (Evans) 1936- *46*
Wilde, D. Gunther
  See Hurwood, Bernhardt J.
Wilde, Oscar (Fingal O'Flahertie Wills)
  1854-1900 ....*24*
Wilder, Cherry
  See Grimm, Cherry Barbara Lockett
Wilder, Laura Ingalls 1867-1957 ....*29*
  See also CLR *2*
Wildsmith, Brian 1930- *69*
  Earlier sketch in SATA *16*
  See also CLR *2*
  See also SAAS *5*
Wilhelm, Hans 1945- *58*
  See also CLR *46*
  See also SAAS *21*
Wilkie, Katharine E(lliott)
  1904-1980 ....*31*
Wilkin, Eloise (Burns) 1904-1987 ....*49*
  Obituary *54*
Wilkins, Frances 1923- *14*
Wilkins, Marilyn (Ruth) 1926- *30*
Wilkins, Marne
  See Wilkins, Marilyn (Ruth)
Wilkins, Mary Huiskamp 1926- *84*
Wilkinson, (Thomas) Barry 1923- *50*
  Brief entry *32*
Wilkinson, Beth 1925- *80*
Wilkinson, Brenda 1946- *91*
  Earlier sketch in SATA *14*
  See also CLR *20*
Wilkinson, Burke 1913- *4*
Wilkinson, Sylvia J. 1940- *56*
  Brief entry *39*
Wilkon, Jozef 1930- *71*
  Earlier sketch in SATA *31*
Wilks, Michael Thomas 1947- *44*
Wilks, Mike
  See Wilks, Michael Thomas
Will
  See Lipkind, William
Willard, Barbara (Mary) 1909- *74*
  Earlier sketch in SATA *17*
  See also CLR *2*
  See also SAAS *5*
Willard, Mildred Wilds 1911- *14*
Willard, Nancy 1936- *71*
  Brief entry *30*
  Earlier sketch in SATA *37*
  See also CLR *5*
Willcox, Isobel 1907- *42*
Willey, Margaret 1950- *86*
Willey, Robert
  See Ley, Willy
Willhoite, Michael A. 1946- *71*
William, Earle
  See Johns, W(illiam) E(arl)
Williams, Barbara 1925- *11*
  See also CLR *48*
  See also SAAS *16*
Williams, Barbara 1937- *62*
Williams, Beryl
  See Epstein, Beryl (M. Williams)
Williams, Brian (Peter) 1943- *54*
Williams, Charles
  See Collier, James Lincoln
Williams, Clyde C. 1881-1974 ....*8*
  Obituary *27*
Williams, Coe
  See Harrison, C. William
Williams, Donna Reilly 1945- *83*
Williams, Dorothy
  See Williams, Marcia (Dorothy)
Williams, (Marcia) Dorothy 1945- *71*
Williams, Eric (Ernest) 1911-1983 ......*14*
  Obituary *38*
Williams, Ferelith Eccles 1920- *22*

Williams, Frances B.
  See Browin, Frances Williams
Williams, Garth (Montgomery)
  1912-1996 ....*66*
  Obituary *90*
  Earlier sketch in SATA *18*
  See also SAAS *7*
Williams, Guy R. 1920- *11*
Williams, Hawley
  See Heyliger, William
Williams, Helen 1948- *77*
Williams, J. R.
  See Williams, Jeanne
Williams, J. Walker
  See Wodehouse, P(elham) G(renville)
Williams, Jay 1914-1978 ....*41*
  Obituary *24*
  Earlier sketch in SATA *3*
  See also CLR *8*
Williams, Jeanne 1930- *5*
Williams, Jenny 1939- *60*
Williams, Karen Lynn 1952- *99*
  Earlier sketch in SATA *66*
Williams, Kit 1946(?)- *44*
  See also CLR *4*
Williams, Leslie 1941- *42*
Williams, Linda 1948- *59*
Williams, Louise Bonino 1904(?)-1984
  Obituary *39*
Williams, Lynn
  See Hale, Arlene
Williams, Marcia (Dorothy) 1945- *97*
Williams, Maureen 1951- *12*
Williams, Michael
  See St. John, Wylly Folk
Williams, Patrick J.
  See Butterworth, W(illiam) E(dmund III)
Williams, Pete
  See Faulknor, Cliff(ord Vernon)
Williams, S. P.
  See Hart, Virginia
Williams, Selma R(uth) 1925- *14*
Williams, Sherley Anne 1944- *78*
Williams, Sheron 1955- *77*
Williams, Shirley
  See Williams, Sherley Anne
Williams, Slim
  See Williams, Clyde C.
Williams, Suzanne (Bullock) 1953- *71*
Williams, Ursula Moray
  See Moray Williams, Ursula
Williams, Vera B. 1927- *53*
  Brief entry *33*
  See also CLR *9*
Williams-Andriani, Renee 1963- *98*
Williams-Ellis, (Mary) Amabel (Nassau)
  1894-1984 ....*29*
  Obituary *41*
Williams-Garcia, Rita *98*
  See also CLR *36*
Williamson, Henry 1895-1977 ....*37*
  Obituary *30*
Williamson, Joanne Small 1926- *3*
Willis, Charles
  See Clarke, Arthur C(harles)
Willis, Jeanne (Mary) 1959- *61*
Willis, Nancy Carol 1952- *93*
Willius, T. F.
  See Tamminga, Frederick William
Willms, Russ *95*
Willson, Robina Beckles (Ballard)
  1930- *27*
Wilma, Dana
  See Faralla, Dana
Wilson, April *80*
Wilson, Barbara
  See Williams, Barbara
Wilson, Barbara Ker
  See Ker Wilson, Barbara
Wilson, Beth P(ierre) *8*
Wilson, Budge 1927- *55*
Wilson, Carletta 1951- *81*
Wilson, Carter 1941- *6*
Wilson, Charles Morrow
  1905-1977 ....*30*
Wilson, Christopher B. 1910(?)-1985
  Obituary *46*

Wilson, Dagmar 1916-
  Brief entry *31*
Wilson, Darryl B(abe) 1939- *90*
Wilson, Dorothy Clarke 1904- *16*
Wilson, Edward A(rthur)
  1886-1970 ....*38*
Wilson, Ellen (Janet Cameron)
  (?)-1976 ....*9*
  Obituary *26*
Wilson, Eric H. 1940- *34*
  Brief entry *32*
Wilson, Erica *51*
Wilson, Forrest 1918- *27*
Wilson, Gahan 1930- *35*
  Brief entry *27*
Wilson, Gina 1943- *85*
  Brief entry *34*
  Earlier sketch in SATA *36*
Wilson, (Leslie) Granville 1912- *14*
Wilson, Hazel (Hutchins) 1898-1992 ......*3*
  Obituary *73*
Wilson, Jacqueline 1945- *61*
  Brief entry *52*
Wilson, John 1922- *22*
Wilson, Johnniece Marshall 1944- *75*
Wilson, Joyce M(uriel Judson) *84*
  Earlier sketch in SATA *21*
Wilson, Lionel 1924- *33*
  Brief entry *31*
Wilson, Marjorie
  See Wilson, Budge
Wilson, Marjorie 1927-
  Brief entry *51*
Wilson, Maurice (Charles John)
  1914- *46*
Wilson, Nancy Hope 1947- *81*
Wilson, Ron(ald William) *38*
Wilson, Sarah 1934- *50*
Wilson, Tom 1931- *33*
  Brief entry *30*
Wilson, Walt(er N.) 1939- *14*
Wilson-Max, Ken 1965- *93*
Wilton, Elizabeth 1937- *14*
Wilton, Hal
  See Pepper, Frank S.
Wilwerding, Walter Joseph 1891-1966 ....*9*
Wimmer, Mike 1961- *70*
Winborn, Marsha (Lynn) 1947- *75*
Winchester, James H(ugh)
  1917-1985 ....*30*
  Obituary *45*
Winders, Gertrude Hecker *3*
Windham, Basil
  See Wodehouse, P(elham) G(renville)
Windham, Kathryn T(ucker) 1918- *14*
Windrow, Martin (Clive) 1944- *68*
Windsor, Claire
  See Hamerstrom, Frances
Windsor, Patricia 1938- *78*
  Earlier sketch in SATA *30*
  See also SAAS *19*
Wineman-Marcus, Irene 1952- *81*
Winfield, Arthur M.
  See Stratemeyer, Edward L.
Winfield, Edna
  See Stratemeyer, Edward L.
Winfield, Julia
  See Armstrong, Jennifer
Wing, Natasha (Lazutin) 1960- *82*
Winks, Robin W(illiam) 1930- *61*
Winn, Bob
  See Seuling, Barbara
Winn, Chris 1952- *42*
Winn, Janet Bruce 1928- *43*
Winn, Marie 1936- *38*
Winnick, Karen B(eth) B(inkoff)
  1946- *51*
Winslow, Barbara 1947- *91*
Winston, Clara 1921-1983 ....*54*
  Obituary *39*
Winston, Richard 1917-1979 ....*54*
Winter, Milo (Kendall) 1888-1956 ....*21*
Winter, Paula Cecelia 1929- *48*
Winter, R. R.
  See Winterbotham, R(ussell) R(obert)
Winterbotham, R(ussell) R(obert)
  1904-1971 ....*10*

Winterfeld, Henry 55
Winters, J.C.
    See Cross, Gilbert B.
Winters, Jon
    See Cross, Gilbert B.
Winters, Nina 1944- 62
Winterton, Gayle
    See Adams, William Taylor
Winthrop, Elizabeth 1948- 76
Winton, Ian (Kenneth) 1960- 76
Winton, Tim 1960- 98
Wirt, Ann
    See Benson, Mildred (Augustine Wirt)
Wirt, Mildred A.
    See Benson, Mildred (Augustine Wirt)
Wirtenberg, Patricia Z. 1932- 10
Wirth, Beverly 1938- 63
Wirths, Claudine (Turner) G(ibson)
    1926- 64
Wise, William 1923- 4
Wise, Winifred E. 2
Wiseman, Ann (Sayre) 1926- 31
Wiseman, B(ernard) 1922- 4
Wiseman, David 1916- 43
    Brief entry 40
Wishinsky, Frieda 1948- 70
Wisler, G(ary) Clifton 1950- 58
    Brief entry 46
Wismer, Donald (Richard) 1946- 59
Wisner, Bill
    See Wisner, William L.
Wisner, William L. 1914(?)-1983 42
Wisniewski, David 1953- 95
Wister, Owen 1860-1938 62
Witham, (Phillip) Ross 1917- 37
Withers, Carl A. 1900-1970 14
Witt, Dick 1948- 80
Witt, Shirley Hill 1934- 17
Wittanen, Etolin 1907- 55
Wittels, Harriet Joan 1938- 31
Wittlinger, Ellen 1948- 83
    See also SAAS 25
Wittman, Sally (Anne Christensen)
    1941- 30
Witty, Paul A(ndrew) 1898-1976 50
    Obituary 30
Wizard, Mr.
    See Herbert, Don
Wodehouse, P(elham) G(renville)
    1881-1975 22
Wodge, Dreary
    See Gorey, Edward (St. John)
Wohlberg, Meg 1905-1990 41
    Obituary 66
Wohlrabe, Raymond A. 1900- 4
Wojciechowska, Maia (Teresa)
    1927- 83
    Earlier sketches in SATA 1, 28
    See also CLR 1
    See also SAAS 1
Wojciechowski, Susan 78
Wolcott, Patty 1929- 14
Wold, Allen L. 1943- 64
Wold, Jo Anne 1938- 30
Woldin, Beth Weiner 1955- 34
Wolf, Bernard 1930-
    Brief entry 37
Wolf, Janet 1957- 78
Wolf, Sallie 1950- 80
Wolfe, Art 1952- 76
Wolfe, Burton H. 1932- 5
Wolfe, Louis 1905- 8
Wolfe, Rinna (Evelyn) 1925- 38
Wolfenden, George
    See Beardmore, George
Wolff, Alexander 1957- 63
Wolff, (Jenifer) Ashley 1956- 81
    Earlier sketch in SATA 50
Wolff, Diane 1945- 27
Wolff, Ferida 1946- 79
Wolff, Robert Jay 1905- 10
Wolff, Sonia
    See Levitin, Sonia (Wolff)
Wolff, Virginia Euwer 1937- 78
Wolfson, Evelyn 1937- 62
Wolitzer, Hilma 1930- 31

Wolkoff, Judie (Edwards) 93
    Brief entry 37
Wolkstein, Diane 1942- 82
    Earlier sketch in SATA 7
Wollheim, Donald A(llen) 1914-1990
    Obituary 69
Wolny, P.
    See Janeczko, Paul B(ryan)
Wolters, Richard A. 1920- 35
Wondriska, William 1931- 6
Wong, Janet S. 1962- 98
Wood, Anne (Savage) 1937- 64
Wood, Audrey 81
    Brief entry 44
    Earlier sketch in SATA 50
    See also CLR 26
Wood, Catherine
    See Etchison, Birdie L(ee)
Wood, David 1944- 87
Wood, Don 1945- 50
    Brief entry 44
    See also CLR 26
Wood, Douglas (Eric) 1951- 81
Wood, Edgar A(llardyce) 1907- 14
Wood, Esther
    See Brady, Esther Wood
Wood, Frances Elizabeth 34
Wood, Frances M. 1951- 97
Wood, James Playsted 1905- 1
Wood, Jenny 1955- 88
Wood, John Norris 1930- 85
Wood, June Rae 1946- 79
Wood, Kerry
    See Wood, Edgar A(llardyce)
Wood, Laura N.
    See Roper, Laura Wood
Wood, Linda C(arol) 1945- 59
Wood, Marcia (Mae) 1956- 80
Wood, Nancy 1936- 6
Wood, Nuria
    See Nobisso, Josephine
Wood, Owen 1929- 64
Wood, Phyllis Anderson 1923- 33
    Brief entry 30
Wood, Tim(othy William Russell)
    1946- 88
Wood, Wallace 1927-1981
    Obituary 33
Woodard, Carol 1929- 14
Woodburn, John Henry 1914- 11
Woodbury, David Oakes
    1896-1981 62
Woodford, Peggy 1937- 25
Woodhouse, Barbara (Blackburn)
    1910-1988 63
Wooding, Sharon
    See Wooding, Sharon L(ouise)
Wooding, Sharon L(ouise) 1943- 66
Woodman, Allen 1954- 76
Woodrich, Mary Neville 1915- 2
Woodruff, Elvira 1951- 70
Woodruff, Marian
    See Goudge, Eileen
Woodruff, Noah 1977- 86
Woods, George A(llen) 1926-1988 ...30
    Obituary 57
Woods, Geraldine 1948- 56
    Brief entry 42
Woods, Harold 1945- 56
    Brief entry 42
Woods, Margaret 1921- 2
Woods, Nat
    See Stratemeyer, Edward L.
Woodson, Jack
    See Woodson, John Waddie, Jr.
Woodson, Jacqueline 1964- 94
    See also CLR 49
Woodson, John Waddie, Jr. 10
Woodtor, Dee Parmer 93
Woodward, Cleveland 1900-1986 10
    Obituary 48
Woody, Regina Jones 1894- 3
Woog, Adam 1953- 84
Wooldridge, Connie Nordhielm
    1950- 92
Wooldridge, Rhoda 1906- 22
Woolley, Catherine 1904- 3

Woolman, Steven 1969- 90
Woolsey, Janette 1904- 3
Worcester, Donald Emmet 1915- 18
Work, Virginia 1946- 57
    Brief entry 45
Worline, Bonnie Bess 1914- 14
Wormell, Mary 1959- 96
Wormser, Richard 1933-
    See SAAS 26
Wormser, Sophie 1896- 22
Worth, Richard 1945- 59
    Brief entry 46
Worth, Valerie 1933-1994 70
    Earlier sketch in SATA 8
    See also CLR 21
    See Bahlke, Valerie Worth
Worthington, Phoebe 1910-
    Brief entry 52
Wortis, Avi
    See Avi
Wosmek, Frances 1917- 29
Woychuk, Denis 1953- 71
Wrede, Patricia C(ollins) 1953- 67
Wriggins, Sally Hovey 1922- 17
Wright, Anna (Maria Louisa Perrot) Rose
    1890-1968
    Brief entry 35
Wright, Betty Ren 1927- 63
    Brief entry 48
Wright, Cliff 1963- 76
Wright, Courtni C(rump) 1950- 84
Wright, Dare 1926(?)- 21
Wright, David K. 1943- 73
Wright, Enid Meadowcroft
    1898-1966 3
Wright, Esmond 1915- 10
Wright, Frances Fitzpatrick 1897- ...10
Wright, J. B.
    See Barkan, Joanne
Wright, Judith 1915- 14
Wright, Katrina
    See Gater, Dilys
Wright, Kenneth
    See del Rey, Lester
Wright, Kit 1944- 87
Wright, Leslie B(ailey) 1959- 91
Wright, Nancy Means 38
Wright, R(obert) H. 1906- 6
Wright, Susan Kimmel 1950- 97
Wrightfrierson
    See Wright-Frierson, Virginia
Wright-Frierson, Virginia 1949- 58
Wrightson, (Alice) Patricia 1921- 66
    Earlier sketch in SATA 8
    See also CLR 14
    See also SAAS 4
Wronker, Lili Cassel 1924- 10
Wryde, Dogear
    See Gorey, Edward (St. John)
Wulffson, Don L. 1943- 88
    Earlier sketch in SATA 32
Wunderli, Stephen 1958- 79
Wunsch, Josephine (McLean)
    1914- 64
Wunsch, Marjory 1942- 82
Wuorio, Eva-Lis 1918- 34
    Brief entry 28
Wurts, Janny 1953- 98
Wyatt, Jane
    See Bradbury, Bianca
Wyatt, Molly
    See Bradbury, Bianca
Wyeth, Betsy James 1921- 41
Wyeth, N(ewell) C(onvers)
    1882-1945 17
Wyler, Rose 1909- 18
Wylie, Betty Jane 48
Wylie, Laura
    See Matthews, Patricia
Wyllie, Stephen 86
Wyman, Andrea 75
Wyman, Carolyn 1956- 83
Wymer, Norman George 1911- 25
Wynants, Miche 1934-
    Brief entry 31
Wyndham, Lee
    See Hyndman, Jane Andrews

Author Index

Wyndham, Robert
  See Hyndman, Robert Utley
Wynne-Jones, Tim(othy) 1948- *96*
  Earlier sketch in SATA *67*
  See also CLR *21*
Wynter, Edward (John) 1914- *14*
Wynyard, Talbot
  See Hamilton, Charles (Harold St. John)
Wyss, Johann David Von
  1743-1818 ....*29*
  Brief entry *27*
Wyss, Thelma Hatch 1934- *10*

Y

Yadin, Yigael 1917-1984 ....*55*
Yaffe, Alan
  See Yorinks, Arthur
Yakovetic, (Joseph Sandy) 1952- *59*
Yakovetic, Joe
  See Yakovetic, (Joseph Sandy)
Yamaguchi, Marianne 1936- *7*
Yamaka, Sara 1978- *92*
Yancey, Diane 1951- *81*
Yang, Jay 1941- *12*
Yang, Mingyi 1943- *72*
Yarbrough, Camille 1938- *79*
  See also CLR *29*
Yarbrough, Ira 1910(?)-1983
  Obituary *35*
Yaroslava
  See Mills, Yaroslava Surmach
Yashima, Taro
  See CLR *4*
  See Iwamatsu, Jun Atsushi
Yates, Elizabeth 1905- *68*
  Earlier sketch in SATA *4*
  See also SAAS *6*
Yates, Janelle K(aye) 1957- *77*
Yates, John 1939- *74*
Yates, Philip 1956- *92*
Yates, Raymond F(rancis)
  1895-1966 ....*31*
Yaukey, Grace S(ydenstricker)
  1899-1994 ....*5*
  Obituary *80*
Yeakley, Marjory Hall 1908- *21*
Yeatman, Linda 1938- *42*
Yee, Paul (R.) 1956- *96*
  Earlier sketch in SATA *67*
  See also CLR *44*
Yee, Wong Herbert 1953- *78*
Yeh, Chun-Chan 1914- *79*
Yenawine, Philip 1942- *85*
Yensid, Retlaw
  See Disney, Walt(er Elias)
Yeo, Wilma (Lethem) 1918-1994 ....*24*
  Obituary *81*
Yeoman, John (Brian) 1934- *80*
  Earlier sketch in SATA *28*
  See also CLR *46*
Yep, Laurence Michael 1948- *69*
  Earlier sketch in SATA *7*
  See also CLR *17*
Yepsen, Roger B(ennet), Jr. 1947- *59*
Yerian, Cameron John *21*
Yerian, Margaret A. *21*
Yetska
  See Ironside, Jetske
Yoder, Dorothy Meenen 1921- *96*
Yoder, Dot
  See Yoder, Dorothy Meenen
Yoder, Walter D. 1933- *88*
Yolen, Jane (Hyatt) 1939- *75*
  Earlier sketches in SATA *4, 40*
  See also CLR *44*
  See also SAAS *1*
Yonge, Charlotte Mary 1823-1901 ....*17*
Yorinks, Arthur 1953- *85*
  Earlier sketches in SATA *33, 49*
  See also CLR *20*
York, Andrew
  See Nicole, Christopher Robin
York, Carol Beach 1928- *77*
  Earlier sketch in SATA *6*

York, Rebecca
  See Buckholtz, Eileen (Garber)
York, Simon
  See Heinlein, Robert A.
Yoshida, Toshi 1911- *77*
Yost, Edna 1889-1971
  Obituary *26*
Youd, C. S. 1922-
  See SAAS *6*
Youd, (Christopher) Samuel 1922- *47*
  Brief entry *30*
  See also SAAS *6*
Young, Bob
  See Young, Robert W(illiam)
Young, Clarence [Collective
  pseudonym] *67*
  Earlier sketch in SATA *1*
Young, Dianne 1959- *88*
Young, Dorothea Bennett 1924- *31*
Young, Ed (Tse-chun) 1931- *74*
  Earlier sketch in SATA *10*
  See also CLR *27*
Young, Edward
  See Reinfeld, Fred
Young, Elaine L.
  See Schulte, Elaine L(ouise)
Young, Jan
  See Young, Janet Randall
Young, Janet Randall 1919- *3*
Young, John
  See Macintosh, Brownie
Young, Judy (Elaine) Dockrey
  1949- *72*
Young, Ken 1956- *86*
Young, Lois Horton 1911-1981 ....*26*
Young, Louise B. 1919- *64*
Young, Margaret B(uckner) 1922- *2*
Young, Mary 1940- *89*
Young, Miriam 1913-1974 ....*7*
Young, Noela 1930- *89*
Young, (Rodney Lee) Patrick (Jr.)
  1937- *22*
Young, Percy M(arshall) 1912- *31*
Young, Richard Alan 1946- *72*
Young, Robert W(illiam) 1916-1969 ......*3*
Young, Ruth 1946- *67*
Young, Scott A(lexander) 1918- *5*
Young, Vivien
  See Gater, Dilys
Youngs, Betty 1934-1985 ....*53*
  Obituary *42*
Younkin, Paula 1942- *77*
Yount, Lisa 1944- *74*
Yuditskaya, Tatyana 1964- *75*

Z

Zach, Cheryl (Byrd) 1947- *98*
  Brief entry *51*
  Earlier sketch in SATA *58*
  See also SAAS *24*
Zaffo, George J. (?)-1984 ....*42*
Zagwyn, Deborah Turney 1953- *78*
Zahn, Timothy 1951- *91*
Zaid, Barry 1938- *51*
Zaidenberg, Arthur 1908(?)-1990 ....*34*
  Obituary *66*
Zalben, Jane Breskin 1950- *79*
  Earlier sketch in SATA *7*
Zallinger, Jean (Day) 1918- *80*
  Earlier sketch in SATA *14*
Zallinger, Peter Franz 1943- *49*
Zambreno, Mary Frances 1954- *75*
Zappler, Lisbeth 1930- *10*
Zarchy, Harry 1912- *34*
Zarif, Margaret Min'imah (?)-1983 ....*33*
Zaring, Jane (Thomas) 1936- *51*
  Brief entry *40*
Zarins, Joyce Audy
  See dos Santos, Joyce Audy
Zaslavsky, Claudia 1917- *36*
Zawadzki, Marek 1958- *97*
Zebra, A.
  See Scoltock, Jack
Zebrowski, George 1945- *67*

Zeck, Gerald Anthony 1939- *40*
Zeck, Gerry
  See Zeck, Gerald Anthony
Zed, Dr.
  See Penrose, Gordon
Zei, Alki *24*
  See also CLR *6*
Zeier, Joan T(heresa) 1931- *81*
Zeinert, Karen 1942- *79*
Zelazny, Roger 1937- *57*
  Brief entry *39*
Zeldis, Malcah 1931- *86*
Zelinsky, Paul O. 1953- *49*
  Brief entry *33*
Zellan, Audrey Penn 1950- *22*
Zemach, Harve 1933- *3*
Zemach, Kaethe 1958- *49*
  Brief entry *39*
Zemach, Margot 1931-1989 ....*70*
  Obituary *59*
  Earlier sketch in SATA *21*
Zens, Patricia Martin 1926-1972
  Brief entry *50*
Zephaniah, Benjamin (Obadiah Iqbal)
  1958- *86*
Zerman, Melvyn Bernard 1930- *46*
Zettner, Pat 1940- *70*
Zhang, Christopher Zhong-Yuan
  1954- *91*
Zhang, Song Nan 1942- *85*
Ziegler, Jack (Denmore) 1942- *60*
Ziemienski, Dennis 1947- *10*
Zillah
  See Macdonald, Zillah K(atherine)
Zim, Herbert S(pencer) 1909-1994 ....*30*
  Obituary *85*
  Earlier sketch in SATA *1*
  See also CLR *2*
  See also SAAS *2*
Zim, Sonia Bleeker
  See Bleeker, Sonia
Zima, Gordon 1920- *90*
Zimelman, Nathan 1921- *65*
  Brief entry *37*
Zimmer, Dirk 1943- *65*
Zimmerman, Naoma 1914- *10*
Zimmermann, Arnold E(rnst Alfred)
  1909- *58*
Zimnik, Reiner 1930- *36*
  See also CLR *3*
Zindel, Bonnie 1943- *34*
Zindel, Paul 1936- *58*
  Earlier sketch in SATA *16*
  See also CLR *45*
Ziner, (Florence) Feenie 1921- *5*
Zion, (Eu)Gene 1913-1975 ....*18*
Zollinger, Gulielma 1856-1917
  Brief entry *27*
Zolotow, Charlotte S(hapiro) 1915- *78*
  Earlier sketches in SATA *1, 35*
  See also CLR *2*
Zonderman, Jon 1957- *92*
Zonia, Dhimitri 1921- *20*
Zubrowski, Bernard 1939- *90*
  Earlier sketch in SATA *35*
Zubrowski, Bernie
  See Zubrowski, Bernard
Zucker, Miriam S. 1962- *85*
Zudeck, Darryl 1961- *61*
Zupa, G. Anthony
  See Zeck, Gerald Anthony
Zurbo, Matt(hew) 1967- *98*
Zurhorst, Charles (Stewart, Jr.)
  1913- *12*
Zuromskis, Diane
  See Stanley, Diane
Zuromskis, Diane Stanley
  See Stanley, Diane
Zwahlen, Diana 1947- *88*
Zweifel, Frances 1931- *14*
Zwerger, Lisbeth 1954- *66*
  See also CLR *46*
  See also SAAS *13*
Zwinger, Ann 1925- *46*